"大学堂" 开放给所有向往知识、崇尚科学，对宇宙和人生有所追问的人。

"大学堂" 中展开一本本书，阐明各种传统和新兴的学科，导向真理和智慧。既有接引之台阶，又具深化之门径。无论何时，无论何地，请你把它翻开……

后浪出版公司
大学堂043-02

主 编：李 峰
副主编：张跃明 郭力　执行主编：吴兴元

影印第7版

ELLIOT ARONSON
TIMOTHY D. WILSON
ROBIN M. AKERT

Social Psychology, 7e

社会心理学

（美）埃略特·阿伦森 提摩太·D·威尔逊 罗宾·M·埃克特 著

世界图书出版公司
北京·广州·上海·西安

Why Do You Need this New Edition?

If you're wondering why you should buy this new edition of *Social Psychology*, here are 6 good reasons!

1. A brand new section at the end of each chapter called, "Critical Thinking: How Could You Use This?" We pose questions to students about their everyday lives—ones that they should find interesting and intriguing—and ask them to address the questions using one or more of the major concepts from the chapter. The purpose of this feature is to encourage students to think critically about the material and apply it to their own lives.

2. Also new to this edition are end of chapter sample test questions that are designed to communicate how to study and learn the material. These questions, which are mostly from our own test files, are critical-thinking type questions that are designed to encourage students to understand social psychological concepts and apply them to new situations, rather than viewing the material as a set of facts to be memorized.

3. Chapter 2, "Methodology: How Social Psychologists Do Research" includes a new section entitled, "New Frontiers in Social Psychological Research." This section discusses new methods and approaches that social psychologists have adopted in recent years, including cross-cultural research, evolutionary psychology, and social neuroscience.

4. Chapter 5 has been reorganized and renamed, "The Self: Understanding Ourselves in a Social Context," to reflect the fact that it is includes a broad coverage of research on the self and not just self-knowledge. Reflecting the broader coverage of research on the self, there is a new major heading called, "Self-Control: The Executive Function Of The Self" that discusses recent research on self-regulation. There is also increased coverage of cultural differences in the self.

5. Chapter 9, "Group Processes: Influence in Social Groups" has a new opening vignette that discusses President George W. Bush's decision to initiate the Iraq War. Later in the chapter we return to this example (in a "Connections" feature) that discusses whether the decision to invade Iraq was the result of groupthink, based on recent books by Bob Woodward, Scott McClelland, and others. The section on "Why People Join Groups" has been revised to include research on social rejection and social identity, and the section on gender and leadership is updated with a discussion of recent research on the "glass cliff."

6. Chapter 11, "Prosocial Behavior: Why Do People Help?" features two new Try It! exercises. This popular feature makes concepts from social psychology concrete and helps you see how they can be applied to your own life. Also, discussions of group selection, what causes people to feel empathy, and research on religion and prosocial behavior have been added.

PEARSON

To my grandchildren: Jacob, Jason, Ruth, Eliana, Natalie, Rachel and Leo Aronson. My hope is that your wonderful capacity for empathy and compassion will help make the world a better place.

—E.A.

To my family, Deirdre Smith, Christopher and Leigh Wilson

—T.D.W.

To my mentor, colleague, and friend, Dane Archer

—R.M.A.

出版前言

社会心理学是一方万象纷呈、引人入胜的领土。顾名思义，社会心理学这一学科意在实现群体与个人两种向度的交汇，由此探询世界与自我之间的微妙关系。它既不单纯是对气质各异的个体的纵深钻研，也不完全是通过社会、历史等视角对人的行为进行宏观的考察；它恰恰结合了两者，从整体层次出发挖掘个体，追问人在特定社会情境的影响下做出某行为的心理动因。借助社会心理学，我们可以看到身边人在种种社会现象中的具体表现，剖析生活的真实本质。我们为什么会这样看待某个人？我们又是怎样认识自己的？在一个团体中，我们是如何受到影响甚至控制的？我们为什么喜欢上某个人？为什么人们有时给予帮助，有时又会伤害别人？生活难免遇到这些问题，我们自然会对答案感到好奇；而社会心理学与所有这些问题联系得如此紧密，它给我们提供了一种求解的途径。

《社会心理学》无疑是这方领土上的一部重磅之作。三位作者都是该研究领域的佼佼者，包括《社会动物》的作者阿伦森教授。他们通力合作，希望为读者讲述他们所理解的答案。不难看出，本书的章节经过用心安排，易于由浅入深。有理有据，重点突出，实例生动，语言流畅，学术性与生活化并行不悖，寓教于乐又不失严谨，这些特点都使本书跻身社会心理学最佳教科书之列。

作者十分注重与日常生活的关联、与读者的互动，特意编排了三章"实践中的社会心理学"，运用社会心理学的理论来研究环境、健康和法律的现实问题。每章开篇都用某个生活实例或具体情境引出主题，"链接"也为读者提供了真实事件的心理学解读。每章贯穿了"试一试！""如何学以致用？"等特别栏目，引导读者积极思考相关话题。随文还配有很多鲜明的图表，以使所述内容更为直观；重要概念都会标注于正文旁，以示强调。每章章末均设置总结、习题和答案，有助于读者梳理和复习该章的知识。最关键的是，作者将他们的生活感悟和人文关怀融进写作本书的过程。在本书开始，三位作者的自述无不传达出这一点。相信读者阅读时既能享受思考的种种乐趣，又能强烈地体会到书中流露出的对生活的热忱、对我们所处世界的关注。通过思考、研究来解决人的精神世界的问题，乃至促进我们的生活，正是社会心理学等人文社会科学的意义。

因此，我们若要起步探索人与社会这片瑰丽的疆域，这本书是颇好的向导。《社会心理学》是三位作者的心血结晶，经过不断增删变化，迄今已更新至第7版，内容愈趋成熟，理论要点和实例也坚持贴近当下。为使读者接触到这本广受欢迎的著作的原文，以最直接的方式深入理解社会心理学，我们影印出版了第7版。影印本在章节标题处加上了相应中文，以供参考。我们也已出版了第7版的中文版，读者可以对照阅读。

希望本书的出版，能满足广大读者阅读原文以掌握社会心理学精髓的需要，帮助读者加深对社会心理学的理解。

服务热线：133-6631-2326　139-1140-1220
服务信箱：reader@hinabook.com

后浪出版咨询（北京）有限责任公司
2012年10月

Preface 前言

When we began writing this book, our overriding goal was to capture the excitement of social psychology. We have been pleased to hear, in many kind letters and e-mail messages from professors and students, that we succeeded. One of our favorites was from a student who said that the book was so interesting that she always saved it for last, to reward herself for finishing her other work. With that one student, at least, we succeeded in making our book an enjoyable, fascinating story, not a dry report of facts and figures.

There is always room for improvement, however, and our goal in this, the seventh edition, is to make the field of social psychology an even better read. When we teach the course, there is nothing more gratifying than seeing the sleepy students in the back row sit up with interest and say, "Wow, I didn't know that! Now *that's* interesting." We hope that students who read our book will have that very same reaction.

What's New in This Edition?

We are pleased to add two new features to this edition that we believe will appeal greatly to students. The first being the, "Critical Thinking: How Could You Use This?" feature. In Chapter 9, for example, we point out to students that sooner or later they will be part of a group that needs to make an important decision, and invite them to think about how they might use concepts from the chapter to ensure that the group makes the best decision it can. The purpose of this feature is to encourage students to think critically about the material and apply it to their own lives.

In addition, we added sample test questions at the end of each chapter. Both of these new features, we believe, will be of substantial help in teaching students how to approach the material presented in the book.

In addition to adding these new features we have updated the seventh edition substantially with numerous references to new research. Here is a sampling of the new research that is covered:

- A brand new section at the end of each chapter called, "Critical Thinking: How Could You Use This?" We pose questions to students about their everyday lives—ones that they should find interesting and intriguing—and ask them to address the questions using one or more of the major concepts from the chapter. The purpose of this feature is to encourage students to think critically about the material and apply it to their own lives.

- Also new to this edition are end of chapter sample test questions that are designed to communicate how to study and learn the material. These questions, which are mostly from our own test files, are critical-thinking type questions that are designed to encourage students to understand social psychological concepts and apply them to new situations, rather than viewing the material as a set of facts to be memorized.

- Chapter 2, "Methodology: How Social Psychologists Do Research" includes a new section entitled, "New Frontiers in Social Psychological Research." This section discusses new methods and approaches that social psychologists have adopted in recent years, including cross-cultural research, evolutionary psychology, and social neuroscience.

- Chapter 3, "Social Cognition: How We Think about the Social World," has been updated with over 40 references to recent research. We added a major new section entitled "Cultural Differences in Social Cognition" that discusses cultural influences on schemas and recent research on holistic versus analytic thinking in different cultures.

- In Chapter 4, "Social Perception: How We Come to Understand Other People," we have updated the section on nonverbal communication, discussing several recent studies that address the evolutionary significance of facial expressions of emotion (for example, the work on pride and shame by Tracy & Matsumoto, 2008). We have revised and updated the section on attribution and culture. We begin this section with holistic versus analytic thinking, discussing the research of Masuda and colleagues (2008). We continue with studies that have used a social neuroscience methodology to study cultural differences in attribution, discussing the work of Hedden and colleagues (2008) and Lewis and colleagues (2008). In the area of attributional biases, we include new research on how perceptual saliency affects the correspondence bias in police interrogations and new research on cultural differences in the self-serving bias.

- Chapter 5 has been reorganized and renamed, "The Self: Understanding Ourselves in a Social Context," to reflect the fact that it is includes a broad coverage of research on the self and not just self-knowledge. Reflecting the broader coverage of research on the self, there is a new major heading called, "Self-Control: The Executive Function Of The Self" that discusses recent research on self-regulation. There is also increased coverage of cultural differences in the self.

- In Chapter 6, "The Need to Justify Our Actions," we have sharpened and updated our coverage of self-justification and included some new research on cultural differences. We have also included some recent research showing cognitive dissonance in monkeys. We have also expanded our coverage of research by Harmon-Jones showing differences in brain activity during the experience of dissonance and dissonance reduction.

- Chapter 7, "Attitudes and Attitude Change: Influencing Thoughts and Feelings," includes over 50 references to recent research. There is an expanded discussion of implicit attitudes, including recent research on the origins of implicit attitudes. We added a new section with the heading "Confidence in One's Thoughts and Attitude Change" that discusses recent research by Petty and Briñol and colleagues. Finally, we revised substantially the section on subliminal advertising, with new research examples, and added a section on the effects of the media on attitudes toward weight in men and women.

- Chapter 8, "Conformity: Influencing Behavior," includes over 45 new references to recent research. The opening vignette (the McDonald's hoax) has been updated to reflect the recent conclusion of the suspect's criminal trial. We have substantially revised the section on injunctive and descriptive norms, including discussion of the "boomerang effect." We discuss new research on the use of informational conformity to change people's behavior. The section on body image and conformity has also been updated with recent research. A major new section has been added, "The Obedience Studies, Then and Now," which discusses the startling results of Jerry Burger's (2009) research, the first replication of the Milgram obedience study in the United States in 30 years. This section has also been expanded to include a discussion of the ethical issues surrounding the obedience studies.

- Chapter 9, "Group Processes: Influence in Social Groups" has a new opening vignette that discusses President George W. Bush's decision to initiate the Iraq War. Later in the chapter we return to this example (in a "Connections" feature) that discusses whether the decision to invade Iraq was the result of groupthink, based on recent books by Bob Woodward, Scott McClelland, and others. The section on "Why People Join Groups" has been revised to include research on social rejection and social identity, and the section on gender and leadership is updated with a discussion of recent research on the "glass cliff."

- Chapter 10, "Interpersonal Attraction: From First Impressions to Close Relationships," includes over 50 new references to recent research. The section on evolution and love has been substantially revised. For example, recent research by Johnston and colleagues (2001) and Gangestad and colleagues (2007) is presented, which focuses on how the menstrual/ovulatory cycle affects women's perceptions of male attractiveness. A second major addition is to the attachment styles section, which focuses on the genetic contribution to attachment styles, and discusses the recent work of Gillath and colleagues (2008) and Donnellan and colleagues (2008). Additional new material and revisions occur throughout the chapter, for example, in the sections on propinquity, similarity, facial attractiveness, assumptions about attractive people, and cultural definitions of love.

- Chapter 11, "Prosocial Behavior: Why Do People Help?" features two new Try It! exercises. This popular feature makes concepts from social psychology concrete and helps you see how they can be applied to your own life. Also, discussions of group selection, what causes people to feel empathy, and research on religion and prosocial behavior have been added.

- In Chapter 12, "Aggression: Why We Hurt Other People," we have added comments on Craig Anderson's recent study (2009) on the possible effects of global warming on aggression. We have also discussed Bushman's (2007) research on scriptural violence and aggressive behavior. We have also included some recent research on building empathy as a way of curbing aggression.

- In Chapter 13, "Prejudice: Causes and Cures," one of the major additions is on the election of an African American to the presidency. It has produced what one social psychologist has dubbed the Obama effect. Shortly after the election of Barack Obama, researchers were able to show two consequences of that election. Plant and colleagues (2009) showed a decrease in prejudice against African Americans; Dillon (2009) showed an apparent decrease in stereotype threat among African American test takers.

- Social Psychology in Action 1, "Making a Difference with Social Psychology: Attaining a Sustainable Future," was new to the previous edition. We believe it was a timely addition, given current interest in global warming and other environmental issues, as well as the more general question of how social psychology can be used to address important social problems. We updated the chapter in this edition with a discussion of recent research, including studies by Goldstein, Cialdini, and Griskevicius (2008) on getting hotel guests to reuse their towels, research by Graham, Koo, and Wilson (in press) on how to get college students to conserve energy by driving less, and a study by Holland, Aarts, and Langendam (2006) on getting people to recycle more. Finally, in the section, "What Makes People Happy?" we added a description of a study by Dunn, Aknin, and Norton (2008) showing that helping others makes people happy.

- Social Psychology in Action 2: "Social Psychology and Health" includes a new opening vignette, namely a true story about a woman who showed remarkable resilence after losing 12 family members in a four-year period. The section on social support is completely revised, including the addition of recent reseach by Shelley Taylor and colleagues on cultural differences in social support and research by Niall Bolger and colleagues on visible versus invisible social support.

- Social Psychology in Action 3: "Social Psychology and the Law" has been updated considerably. For example, the section on line-ups and how to improve them is updated with an example of recent research by Gary Wells, research on individual differences in detecting lies by Bond and DePaulo (2008), and a study on recovered memories by Geraerts and colleagues (2007).

Social psychology comes alive for students when they understand the whole context of the field: how theories inspire research, why research is performed as it is, how further research triggers yet new avenues of study. We have tried to convey our own fascination with the research process in a down-to-earth, meaningful way and have presented the results of the scientific process in terms of the everyday experience of the reader; however, we did not want to "water down" our presentation of the field. In a world where human behavior can be endlessly surprising and where research results can be quite counterintuitive, students need a firm foundation on which to build their understanding of this challenging discipline.

The main way we try to engage students is with a storytelling approach. Social psychology is full of good stories, such as how the Holocaust inspired investigations into obedience to authority and how reactions to the marriage of the crown prince of Japan to Masako Owada, a career diplomat, illustrates cultural differences in the self-concept. By placing research in a real-world context, we make the material more familiar, understandable, and memorable. Each chapter begins with a real-life vignette that illustrates the concepts to come. We refer to this event at several points in the chapter, clarifying to students the relevance of the material they are learning. Examples of the opening vignettes include the tragic death of Amadou Diallo, who was shot 41 times by four white police officers, as he reached for his wallet in the vestibule of his New York apartment building (Chapter 3, "Social Cognition: How We Think about the Social World"), and some amazing acts of altruism at the sites of the terrorist attacks on September 11, 2001 (Chapter 11, "Prosocial Behavior: Why do People Help?").

We also weave "mini-stories" into each chapter that both illustrate specific concepts and bring the material to life. For each one, we first describe an example of a real-life phenomenon that is designed to pique students' interest. These stories are taken from current events, literature, and our own lives. Next, we describe an experiment that attempts to explain the phenomenon. This experiment is typically described in some detail because we believe that students should not only learn the major theories in social psychology, but also understand and appreciate the methods used to test those theories. For example, in Chapter 4 on social perception, we introduce the correspondence bias by discussing public reaction to an event celebrating Rosa Parks's courageous refusal in 1955 to move to the back of the bus in segregationist Montgomery, Alabama. In 2005, at the time of her death, transit companies across America posted signs in their city buses, asking people to leave the seat behind the driver empty for the day, in tribute to her. Despite the sign, some people sat in the seat anyway. A journalist, traveling on New York City buses, asked other riders what they thought of these "sitters." Very negative internal attributions were made about them (e.g., that they were disrespectful, contemptuous or even racist). In fact, the explanation for their behavior was typically situational, that is, something external to them as a person. They hadn't seen the sign, which was small in size and lost in the visual clutter of other signs in the bus, and therefore didn't know that they weren't supposed to sit in that seat. We invite you to thumb through the book to find examples of these mini-stories.

Last but not least, we discuss the methods used by social psychologists in some detail. How can "boring" details about methodology be part of a storytelling approach, you might ask? We believe that part of what makes the story of social psycyhology so interesting is explaining to students how to test hypotheses scientifically. In recent years, the trend has been for textbooks to include only short sections on research methodology and provide only brief descriptions of the findings of individual studies. In this book, we integrate the science and methodology of the field into our story in several ways. First, we devote an entire chapter to methodology (Chapter 2). We use our storytelling approach by presenting two compelling real-world problems related to violence and aggression: Does pornography promote violence against women? Why don't bystanders intervene more to help victims of violence? We then use actual research studies on these questions to illustrate the three major scientific methods (observational research, correlational research, and experimental research). Rather than a dry recitation of methodological principles, the scientific method unfolds like a story with a "hook" (what are the causes of real-world aggression and apathy toward violence?) and a moral (such interesting, real-world questions can be addressed scientifically). We have been pleased by the positive reactions to this chapter in the previous editions.

Second, we describe prototypical studies in more detail than most texts. We discuss how a study was set up, what the research participants perceived and did, how the research design derives from theoretical issues, and the ways in which the findings support the initial hypotheses. We often ask readers to pretend that they were participants so they can better understand the study from the participants' point of view. Whenever pertinent, we've also included anecdotal information about how a study was done or came to be; these brief stories allow readers insights into the heretofore hidden world of creating research. See, for example, the description of how Nisbett and Wilson (1977) designed one of their experiments on the accuracy of people's causal inferences in Chapter 5 and the description of the origins of Aronson's jigsaw puzzle technique in Chapter 13.

Finally, we include a balanced coverage of classic and modern research. The field of social psychology is expanding rapidly, and exciting new work is being done in all areas of the discipline. In this seventh edition, we have added a great deal of new material, describing dozens of major studies done within the past few years. We have added hundreds of references from the past few years. Thus the book provides thorough coverage of up-to-date, cutting-edge research. But by emphasizing what is new, some texts have a tendency to ignore what is old. We have tried to strike a balance between the latest research findings and classic research in social psychology. Some older studies (e.g., early work in dissonance, conformity, and attribution) deserve their status as classics and are important cornerstones of the discipline. For example, unlike several other current texts, we present detailed descriptions of the Schachter and Singer (1962) study on misattribution of emotion (Chapter 5), the Festinger and Carlsmith (1959) dissonance study (Chapter 6), and the Asch (1956), and Sherif (1936) conformity studies (Chapter 8). We then bring up the older theories to date, following our discussions of the classics with modern approaches to the same topics. This allows students to experience the continuity and depth of the field, rather than regarding it as a collection of studies published in the past few years.

Ancillary Package

A really good textbook should become part of the classroom experience, supporting and augmenting the professor's vision for the class. *Social Psychology* offers a number of supplements that enrich both the professor's presentation of social psychology and the students' understanding of it.

Pearson/Prentice Hall is pleased to announce the **Association for Psychological Science (APS)** reader series, *Current Directions in Social Psychology*, 2e (ISBN: 0136062806) edited by Janet Ruscher and Elizabeth Yost Hammer.

This reader contains selected articles from APS's journal ***Current Directions in Psychological Science***. *Current Directions* was created for scientists to quickly and easily learn about new and significant research developments outside their major field of study. The journal's concise reviews span all of scientific psychology, and because of the journal's accessibility to audiences outside specialty areas, it is a natural fit for use in college courses. These readers offer a rich resource that connects students and scholars directly to leading scientists working in psychology today.

The APS is the only association dedicated solely to advancing psychology as a science-based discipline. APS members include the field's most respected researchers and educators representing the full range of topics within psychological science. The APS is widely recognized as a leading voice for the science of psychology in Washington, and is focused on increasing public understanding and use of the knowledge generated by psychological research.

Instructor Supplements

- **MyPsychLab** (www.mypsychlab.com) This robust course management platform enables instructors to assign tests, quizzes, and projects online, and view the results of those assignments as a class aggregate, or as focused as on a student-by-student, text section-by-text section basis. A series of self-diagnostic tests serves as the foundation of this exciting new platform, which also includes and integrates assignments, remediation content, and study activities that feed results into the platform's gradebook. The diversified collection of study content and activities encompasses videos, quizzes, the American Psychological Society (APS) reader *Current Directions in Social Psychology*, author-recommended websites, and more. All supplementary resources are also housed on the MyPsychLab platform.

- **Contemporary Videos in Social Psychology** (0132398060) Contemporary Videos in Social Psychology is now available on DVD, and contains a series of segments illustrating key social psychological concepts. Through filmed experiments, interviews, documentary and more, we've provided a visual component that will enhance class lectures and discussions. Please contact your local Pearson sales representative to obtain a copy.

ABC Social Psychology DVD: Through Pearson Education's partnership with ABC, we are pleased to produce a DVD product featuring over 30 clips from various ABC news programs. These clips are a great way of showing the relevance of social psychology theory and research to everyday life.

- **PowerPoints** (0138144834) The PowerPoints provide an active format for presenting concepts from each chapter and incorporating relevant figures and tables. The PowerPoint files can be downloaded from the www.pearsonhighered.com

- **Classroom Response System** (0138144893) The Classroom Response System (CRS) facilitates class participation in lectures as well as a method of measurement of student comprehension. CRS also enables student polling and in-class quizzes. CRS is highly effective in engaging students with class lectures, in addition to adding an element of excitement to the classroom. Simply, CRS is a technology that allows professors to ask questions to their students through text-specific PowerPoint slides provided by Pearson. Students reply using handheld transmitters called "clickers," which capture and immediately display student responses. These responses are saved in the system gradebook and/or can later be downloaded to either a Blackboard or WebCT gradebook for assessment purposes.

NEW! Social Psychology Community (SPC). Pearson is excited to announce the launch of the SPC. The SPC is the ultimate instructor's tool offering two unique features:

1. A collection of our best instructor resources from all of our Social Psychology products organized by topic and by teaching resource type, for use in lecture, classroom activities, homework assignments, and assessment.
2. Dynamic environment that enables you to share lecture ideas and resources with your colleagues around the world.

- **Instructor's Resource Manual** (0138144796) The Instructor's Manual includes key terms, lecture ideas, teaching tips, suggested readings, chapter outlines, student projects and research assignments, *Try It!* exercises, critical thinking topics and discussion questions, and a media resource guide.
- **Test Bank** (013814480X) Each of the over 2,000 questions in this test bank is page-referenced to the text and categorized by topic and skill level. Each question in the test bank was reviewed by several instructors to ensure that we are providing you with the best and most accurate content in the industry. We thank the following professors for their contribution and suggestions: Jesse Rude (University of California, Davis), Christopher Leone (University of North Florida), Vincent Fortunato (Boise State University), Steve Kilianski (Rutgers University), Paul Silvia (University of North Carolina, Greensboro), Mary Johannesen-Schmidt (Oakton Community College), William Rick Fry (Youngstown State University), Esther Jenkins (Chicago State University), Jackie White (University of North Carolina, Greensboro). The test bank is available to adopters in both Windows and Macintosh computerized format.
- **MyTest Testing Software** (0138144850) This web, based test generating software provides instructors "best in class" features in an easy to use program. Create tests and easily select questions with drag-and-drop or point-and-click functionality. Add or modify test questions using the built-in Question Editor and print tests in a variety of formats. The program comes with full technical support.

Student Supplements

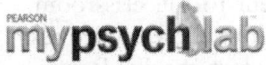

- **MyPsychLab** (www.mypsychlab.com) This robust learning management platform contains chapter learning objectives to help students focus on key concepts, online quizzes that include instant scoring and coaching responses, videos, flashcards, writing resources and activities designed to promote critical thinking, and built-in routing that gives students the ability to forward essay responses and graded quizzes to their instructors. Students are provided with a customized study plan to help them prepare for tests and quizzes based upon the results of their pre- and posttests.
- **Student Study Guide** (0138144826) The Student Study Guide contains chapter overviews, learning objectives and outlines, a guided review section, study activities, key terms, and practice tests.

Other Titles of Interest

- **Thinking Critically about Research on Sex and Gender (Harper Collins Publishing, 2009)** (020564645X) Now in its third edition, this supplement, written by Paula J. Caplan of Brown University and Jeremy B. Caplan of Brandeis University, encourages students to evaluate the massive and diverse research that has appeared on this subject of sex and gender in recent decades. After demonstrating that much of the existing research is not as well established as one would think, the book provides readers with the critical tools necessary to assess the huge body of literature and to draw realistic and constructive conclusions.
- **Influence: Science and Practice (Allyn and Bacon Publishing, 2000)** (0321011473) This fascinating bestseller by Robert B. Cialdini of Arizona State University, now in its fourth edition, draws on evidence from research and the working world of influence professionals to examine the psychology of compliance. Focus is on the six basic psychological principles directing human behavior—reciprocation, consistency, social validation, liking, authority, and scarcity. This is must reading!

Acknowledgments

Elliot Aronson is delighted to acknowledge the collaboration of his son, Hal Aronson, an environmental sociologist. Hal's insights and creativity were of enormous value in bringing the current edition up-to-date. He would also like to acknowledge the general contributions of his best friend (who also happens to be his wife of 55 years), Vera Aronson. Vera, as usual, provided a great deal of inspiration for his ideas and acted as the sounding board for and supportive critic of many of his semi-formed notions, helping to mold them into more sensible analyses.

Tim Wilson would like to thank his graduate mentor, Richard E. Nisbett, who nurtured his interest in the field and showed him the continuity between social psychological research and everyday life. He thanks his parents, Elizabeth and Geoffrey Wilson, for their overall support. Most of all, he thanks his wife, Deirdre Smith, and his children, Christopher and Leigh, for their love, patience, and understanding, even when the hour was late and the computer was still on.

Robin Akert is beholden to Prof. Jonathan Cheek, Prof. Julie Donnelly, Nan Vaida, Melody Tortosa, and Lila McCain for their interest in her work, their feedback and advice, their unconditional support, and their wonderful senses of humor. She also wishes to thank her students in social psychology. Their intelligence, perspicacity, dedication, and joie de vivre are her continuing sources of energy and motivation for this book. She is deeply grateful to her family, Michaela and Wayne Akert, and Linda and Jerry Wuichet; their enthusiasm and boundless support have sustained her on this project as on all the ones before it. Finally, no words can express her gratitude and indebtedness to Dane Archer, mentor, colleague, and friend, who opened the world of social psychology to her and who has been her guide ever since.

No book can be written and published without the help of a great many people working with the authors behind the scenes, and our book is no exception. We would like to thank the many colleagues who read one or more chapters of this edition and of previous editions of the book.

Reviewers of the Seventh Edition

Amber Bush Amspoker, *University of Houston*
David M. Tom, *Columbus State Community College*
Michael G. Dudley, *Southern Illinois University Edwardsville*
Florette Cohen, *Rutgers University*
Gina Hoover, *Ohio State University*
H. Anna Han, *Ohio State University*
Lisa Harrison, *California State University, Sacramento*
Jessica Gonzalez, *Ohio State University*
John Lu, *Concordia University*
JoNell Strough, *West Virginia University*
Megan Clegg-Kraynok, *West Virginia University*
Kosha Bramesfeld, *Pennsylvania State University*
Melissa Burkley, *Oklahoma State University*
Nathan Arbuckle, *Ohio State University*
Paul Rose, *Southern Illinois University Edwardsville*
Fred Sanborn, *North Carolina Wesleyan College*
Sara Gorchoff, *University of California, Berkeley*
Stephen Kilianski, *Rutgers University*
Traci Craig, *University of Idaho*
Matylda Osika, *University of Houston*
Jackie White, *University of North Carolina at Greensboro*

Reviewers of Past Editions

Jeffrey B. Adams, *Saint Michael's College*
Bill Adler, *Collin County Community College*
John R. Aiello, *Rutgers University*
Charles A. Alexander, *Rock Valley College*
Sowmya Anand, *Ohio State University*
Art Aron, *State University of New York, Stony Brook*
Danny Axsom, *Virginia Polytechnic Institute and State University*
Joan W. Baily, *Jersey City State College*
Norma Baker, *Belmont University*
Austin Baldwin, *University of Iowa*
John Bargh, *New York University*
William A. Barnard, *University of Northern Colorado*
Doris G. Bazzini, *Appalachian State University*
Gordon Bear, *Ramapo College*
Susan E. Beers, *Sweet Briar College*
Kathy L. Bell, *University of North Carolina at Greensboro*
Leonard Berkowitz, *University of Wisconsin—Madison*
Ellen S. Berscheid, *University of Minnesota*
John Bickford, *University of Massachusetts, Amherst*
Thomas Blass, *University of Maryland*
C. George Boeree, *Shippensburg University*
Lisa M. Bohon, *California State University, Sacramento*
Jennifer Bosson, *The University of Oklahoma*
Chante C. Boyd, *Carnegie Mellon University*
Peter J. Brady, *Clark State Community College*
Kelly A. Brennan, *University of Texas, Austin*
Richard W. Brislin, *East-West Center of the University of Hawaii*
Jeff Bryson, *San Diego State University*
Amy Bush, *University of Houston*
Brad Bushman, *Iowa State University*
Thomas P. Cafferty, *University of South Carolina, Columbia*
Melissa A. Cahoon, *Wright State University*
Frank Calabrese, *Community College of Philadelphia*
Michael Caruso, *University of Toledo*
Nicholas Christenfeld, *University of California, San Diego*
Margaret S. Clark, *Carnegie Mellon University*
Russell D. Clark, III, *University of North Texas*
Susan D. Clayton, *Allegheny College*
Brian M. Cohen, *University of Texas, San Antonio*
Jack Cohen, *Camden County College*
Eric Cooley, *Western Oregon State University*
Steven G. Cole, *Texas Christian University*
Eric J. Cooley, *Western Oregon State College*
Diana Cordova, *Yale University*
Jack Croxton, *State University of New York, Fredonia*
Keith E. Davis, *University of South Carolina, Columbia*
Mary Ellen Dello Stritto, *Ball State University*
Dorothee Dietrich, *Hamline University*
Kate Dockery, *University of Florida*
Susann Doyle, *Gainesville College*
Steve Duck, *University of Iowa*
Karen G. Duffy, *State University of New York, Geneseo*
Valerie Eastman, *Drury College*
Tami Eggleston, *McKendree College*
Timothy Elliot, *University of Alabama—Birmingham*
Steve L. Ellyson, *Youngstown State University*
Cindy Elrod, *Georgia State University*
Rebecca S. Fahrlander, *University of Nebraska at Omaha*
Alan Feingold, *Yale University*
Edward Fernandes, *East Carolina University*

Phil Finney, *Southeast Missouri State University*
Susan Fiske, *University of Massachusetts*
Robin Franck, *Southwestern College*
Denise Frank, *Ramapo College of New Jersey*
Timothy M. Franz, *St. John Fisher College*
William Rick Fry, *Youngstown State University*
Russell Geen, *University of Missouri*
Glenn Geher, *State University of New York at New Paltz*
David Gersh, *Houston Community College*
Frederick X. Gibbons, *Iowa State University*
Cynthia Gilliland, *Louisiana State University*
Genaro Gonzalez, *University of Texas*
Beverly Gray, *Youngstown State University*
Gordon Hammerle, *Adrian College*
Judith Harackiewicz, *University of Wisconsin—Madison*
Elaine Hatfield, *University of Hawaii, Manoa*
Vicki S. Helgeson, *Carnegie Mellon University*
Joyce Hemphill, *Cazenovia College*
Tracy B. Henley, *Mississippi State University*
Ed Hirt, *Indiana University*
David E. Hyatt, *University of Wisconsin—Oshkosh*
Marita Inglehart, *University of Michigan*
Carl Kallgren, *Behrend College, Pennsylvania State University, Erie*
Suzanne Kieffer, *University of Houston*
Stephen Kilianski, *Rutgers University*
Bill Klein, *Colby College*
James D. Johnson, *University of North Carolina, Wilmington*
Lee Jussim, *Rutgers University*
Fredrick Koenig, *Tulane University*
Alan Lambert, *Washington University, St. Louis*
Emmett Lampkin, *Kirkwook Community College*
Elizabeth C. Lanthier, *Northern Virginia Community College*
Patricia Laser, *Bucks County Community College*
G. Daniel Lassiter, *Ohio University*
Dianne Leader, *Georgia Institute of Technology*
Stephanie Madon, *Iowa State University*
John Malarkey, *Wilmington College*
Andrew Manion, *St. Mary's University of Minnesota*
Allen R. McConnell, *Michigan State University*
Joann M. Montepare, *Tufts University*
Richard Moreland, *University of Pittsburgh*
Carrie Nance, *Stetson University*
Todd D. Nelson, *Michigan State University*
Elaine Nocks, *Furman University*
Cheri Parks, *Colorado Christian University*
David Peterson, *Mount Senario College*
W. Gerrod Parrott, *Georgetown University*
Mary Pritchard, *Boise State University*
Cynthia K.S. Reed, *Tarrant County College*
Dan Richard, *University of North Florida*
Neal Roese, *University of Illinios*

Darrin L. Rogers, *Ohio State University*
Joan Rollins, *Rhode Island College*
Lee D. Ross, *Stanford University*
Alex Rothman, *University of Minnesota*
M. Susan Rowley, *Champlain College*
Delia Saenz, *Arizona State University*
Brad Sagarin, *Northern Illinois University*
Connie Schick, *Bloomsburg University*
Norbert Schwartz, *University of Michigan*
Gretchen Sechrist, *University at Buffalo*
Richard C. Sherman, *Miami University of Ohio*
Paul Silvia, *University of North Carolina at Greensboro*
Randolph A. Smith, *Ouachita Baptist University*
Linda Solomon, *Marymount Manhattan College*
Janice Steil, *Adelphi University*
Jakob Steinberg, *Fairleigh Dickinson University*
Mark Stewart, *American River College*
Lori Stone, *The University of Texas at Austin*
JoNell Strough, *West Virginia University*
T. Gale Thompson, *Bethany College*
Scott Tindale, *Loyola University of Chicago*
David Trafimow, *New Mexico State University*
Anne Weiher, *Metropolitan State College of Denver*
Gary L. Wells, *Iowa State University*
Paul L. Wienir, *Western Michigan University*
Kipling D. Williams, *University of Toledo*
Paul Windschitl, *University of Iowa*
Mike Witmer, *Skagit Valley College*
Gwen Wittenbaum, *Michigan State University*
William Douglas Woody, *University of Northern Colorado*
Clare Zaborowski, *San Jacinto College*
William H. Zachry, *University of Tennessee, Martin*
Leah Zinner, *University of Wisconsin—Madison*

We also thank the wonderful editorial staff of Prentice Hall for their expertise and professionalism, including Leah Jewell (Editorial Director), Nicole Kunzmann (Marketing Manager), Amy Trudell (Editorial Assistant), Paul Deluca (Media Editor), LeeAnn Doherty (Associate Editor), and Annemarie Franklin (Production Editor). Most of all, we thank Jeff Marshall (Executive Editor), whose tireless belief in our book, and vision for it, have truly made a difference. Finally, we thank Mary Falcon, but for whom we never would have begun this project.

Thank you for inviting us into your classroom. We welcome your suggestions, and we would be delighted to hear your comments about this book.

Elliot Aronson
elliot@cats.ucsc.edu

Tim Wilson
tdw@virginia.edu

Robin Akert
rakert@wellesley.edu

About the Authors 关于作者

Elliot Aronson

When I was a kid, we were the only Jewish family in a virulently anti-Semitic neighborhood. I had to go to Hebrew school every day, late in the afternoon. Being the only youngster in my neighborhood going to Hebrew school made me an easy target for some of the older neighborhood toughs. On my way home from Hebrew school, after dark, I was frequently waylaid and roughed up by roving gangs shouting anti-Semitic epithets.

I have a vivid memory of sitting on a curb after one of these beatings, nursing a bloody nose or a split lip, feeling very sorry for myself and wondering how these kids could hate me so much when they didn't even know me. I thought about whether those kids were taught to hate Jews or whether, somehow, they were born that way. I wondered if their hatred could be changed—if they got to know me better, would they hate me less? I speculated about my own character. What would I have done if the shoe were on the other foot—that is, if I were bigger and stronger than they—would I be capable of beating them up for no good reason?

I didn't realize it at the time, of course, but eventually I discovered that these were profound questions. And some thirty years later, as an experimental social psychologist, I had the great good fortune to be in a position to answer some of those questions and to invent techniques to reduce the kind of prejudice that had claimed me as a victim.

Elliot Aronson is one of the most renowned social psychologists in the world. In 2002 he was chosen as one of the 100 most eminent psychologists of the twentieth century. He is currently Professor Emeritus at the University of California at Santa Cruz and Distinguished Visiting Professor at Stanford University.

Dr. Aronson is the only person in the 110-year history of the American Psychological Association to have received all three of its major awards: for distinguished writing, distinguished teaching, and distinguished research. Many other professional societies have honored his research and teaching as well. These include the American Association for the Advancement of Science, which gave him its highest honor, the Distinguished Scientific Research award; the American Council for the Advancement and Support of Education, which named him Professor of the Year of 1989; and the Society for the Psychological Study of Social Issues, which awarded him the Gordon Allport prize for his contributions to the reduction of prejudice among racial and ethnic groups. In 1992, he was named a Fellow of the American Academy of Arts and Sciences. He has served as president of the Western Psychological Association as well as president of the Society of Personality and Social Psychology.

Tim Wilson

One day, when I was 8, a couple of older kids rode up on their bikes to share some big news: They had discovered an abandoned house down a country road. "It's really neat," they said. "We broke a window and nobody cared!" My friend and I hopped onto our bikes to investigate. We had no trouble finding the house—there it was, sitting off by itself, with a big, jagged hole in a first-floor window. We got off of our bikes and looked around. My friend found a baseball-sized rock lying on the ground and threw a perfect strike through another first-floor window. There was something exhilarating about the smash-and-tingle of shattering glass, especially when we knew there was nothing wrong with what we were doing. After all, the house was abandoned, wasn't it? We broke nearly every window in the house and then climbed through one of the first-floor windows to look around.

It was then that we realized something was terribly wrong. The house certainly did not look abandoned. There were pictures on the wall, nice furniture, books in shelves. We went home feeling frightened and confused. We soon learned that the house was the residence of an elderly couple who were away on vacation. Eventually my parents discovered what we had done and paid a substantial sum to repair the windows. For years, I pondered this incident: Why did I do such a terrible thing? Was I a bad kid? I didn't think so, and neither did my parents. How, then, could a good kid do such a bad thing? Even though the neighborhood kids said the house was abandoned, why couldn't my friend and I see the clear signs that someone lived there? How crucial was it that my friend was there and threw the first rock? Although I didn't know it at the time, these reflections touched on several classic social psychological issues, such as whether only bad people do bad things, whether the social situation can be powerful enough to make good people do bad things, and the way in which our expectations about an event can make it difficult to see it as it really is. Fortunately, my career as a vandal ended with this one incident. It did, however, mark the beginning of my fascination with basic questions about how people understand themselves and the social world—questions I continue to investigate to this day.

Tim Wilson did his undergraduate work at Williams College and Hampshire College and received his Ph.D. from the University of Michigan. Currently Sherrell J. Aston Professor of Psychology at the University of Virginia, he has published numerous articles in the areas of introspection, attitude change, self-knowledge, and affective forecasting, as well as the recent book, Strangers to Ourselves: Discovering the Adaptive Unconscious. *His research has received the support of the National*

Science Foundation and the National Institute for Mental Health. He has been associate editor of the Journal of Personality and Social Psychology *and a member of the Social and Groups Processes Review Committee at the National Institute of Mental Health. He has been elected twice to the Executive Board of the Society for Experimental Social Psychology and is a Fellow in the American Psychological Society and the Society for Personality and Social Psychology. In 2009, he was named a Fellow of the American Academy of Arts and Sciences. Wilson has taught the Introduction to Social Psychology course at the University of Virginia for more than twenty years. In 2001 he was awarded an All University Outstanding Teaching Award.*

Robin Akert

One fall day, when I was about 16, I was walking with a friend along the shore of the San Francisco Bay. Deep in conversation, I glanced over my shoulder and saw a sailboat capsize. I pointed it out to my friend, who took only a perfunctory interest and went on talking. However, I kept watching as we walked, and I realized that the two sailors were in the water, clinging to the capsized boat. Again I said something to my friend, who replied, "Oh, they'll get it upright, don't worry."

But I was worried. Was this an emergency? My friend didn't think so. And I was no sailor; I knew nothing about boats. But I kept thinking, "That water is really cold. They can't stay in that water too long." I remember feeling very confused and unsure. What should I do? Should I do anything? Did they really need help?

We were near a restaurant with a big window overlooking the bay, and I decided to go in and see if anyone had done anything about the boat. Lots of people were watching but not doing anything. This confused me too. Very meekly, I asked the bartender to call for some kind of help. He just shrugged. I went back to the window and watched the two small figures in the water. Why was everyone so unconcerned? Was I crazy?

Years later, I reflected on how hard it was for me to do what I did next: I demanded that the bartender let me use his phone. In those days before "911," it was lucky that I knew there was a Coast Guard station on the bay, and I asked the operator for the number. I was relieved to hear the Guardsman take my message very seriously.

It had been an emergency. I watched as the Coast Guard cutter sped across the bay and pulled the two sailors out of the water. Maybe I saved their lives that day. What really stuck with me over the years was how other people behaved and how it made me feel. The other bystanders seemed unconcerned and did nothing to help. Their reactions made me doubt myself and made it harder for me to decide to take action. When I later studied social psychology in college, I realized that on the shore of the San Francisco Bay that day, I had experienced the "bystander effect" fully: The presence of other, apparently unconcerned bystanders had made it difficult for me to decide if the situation was an emergency and whether it was my responsibility to help.

Robin Akert graduated summa cum laude from the University of California at Santa Cruz, where she majored in psychology and sociology. She received her Ph.D. in experimental social psychology from Princeton University. She is currently a Professor of psychology at Wellesley College, where she was awarded the Pinanski Prize for Excellence in Teaching early in her career. She publishes primarily in the area of nonverbal communication and recently received the AAUW American Fellowship in support of her research. She has taught the Social Psychology course at Wellesley College for nearly thirty years.

Special Tips for Students 给学生们的特别提示

The two quotes in the margin below, taken together, sum up everything you need to know to be a proficient student: Be an active, creative consumer of information, and make sure it sticks! How do you accomplish these two feats? Actually, it's not difficult at all. Like everything else in life, it just takes some work—some clever, well-planned, purposeful work. Here are some suggestions about how to do it.

Get to Know the Textbook

There is then creative reading as well as creative writing.
—Ralph Waldo Emerson, 1837

Believe it or not, in writing this book, we thought very carefully about the organization and structure of each chapter. Things are the way they appear for a reason, and that reason is to help you learn the material in the best way possible. Here are some tips on what to look for in each chapter.

Key terms are in boldface type in the text so that you'll notice them. We define the terms in the text, and that definition appears again in the margin. These marginal definitions are there to help you out if later in the chapter you forget what something means. The marginal definitions are quick and easy to find. You can also look up key terms in the alphabetical Glossary at the end of this textbook.

Make sure you notice the headings and subheadings. The headings are the skeleton that holds a chapter together. They link together like vertebrae. If you ever feel lost, look back to the last heading and the headings before that one—this will give you the "big picture" of where the chapter is going. It should also help you see the connections between sections.

The summary at the end of each chapter is a succinct shorthand presentation of the chapter information. You should read it and make sure there are no surprises when you do so. If anything in the summary doesn't ring a bell, go back to the chapter and reread that section. Most important, remember that the summary is intentionally brief, whereas your understanding of the material should be full and complete. Use the summary as a study aid before your exams. When you read it over, everything should be familiar and you should have that wonderful feeling of knowing more than is in the summary (in which case you are ready to take the exam).

I am a kind of burr, I shall stick.
—William Shakespeare, 1604

Be sure to do the *Try It!* exercises. They will make concepts from social psychology concrete and help you see how they can be applied to your own life. Some of the *Try It!* exercises replicate social psychology experiments. Other *Try It!* exercises reproduce self-report scales so you can see where you stand in relation to other people. Still other *Try It!* exercises are short quizzes that illustrate social psychological concepts.

Visit our Website at www.prenhall.com/aronson. You will be able to do more *Try It!* exercises, take interactive practice tests, and link to other sites.

Just Say No to the Couch Potato Within

Because social psychology is about everyday life, you might lull yourself into believing that the material is all common sense. Don't be fooled. The material is more complicated than it might seem. Therefore, we want to emphasize that the best way to learn it is to work with it in an active, not passive, fashion. You can't just read a chapter once and expect it to stick with you. You have to go over the material, wrestle with it, make your own connections to it, question it, think about it, interact with it. Actively working with material makes it memorable and makes it your own. Because it's a safe bet that someone is going to ask you about this material later and you're going to have to pull it out of memory, do what you can to get it into memory now. Here are some techniques to use:

- Go ahead and be bold—use a highlighter! Go crazy—write in the margins! If you underline, highlight, circle, or draw little hieroglyphics next to important points, you will remember them better. We recall taking exams in college where we not only remembered the material but could actually see in our minds the textbook page it was written on and the little squiggles and stars we'd drawn in the margin.

- Read the textbook chapter before the applicable class lecture, not afterward. This way, you'll get more out of the lecture, which will introduce new material. The chapter will give you the big picture, as well as a lot of detail. The lecture will enhance that information and help you put it all together. If you don't read the chapter first, you may not understand some of the points made in the lecture or realize that they are important.

- Here's a good way to study material: Write out a difficult concept or a study (or say it out loud to yourself) in your own words, without looking at the book or your notes. Can you do it? How good was your version? Did you omit anything important? Did you get stuck at some point, unable to remember what comes next? If so, you now know that you need to go over that information in more detail. You can also study with someone else, describing theories and studies to each other and seeing if you're making sense.

- If you have trouble remembering the results of an important study, try drawing your own version of a graph of the findings (you can use our data graphs for an idea of how to proceed). If all the various points in a theory are confusing you, try drawing your own flowchart of how it works. You will probably find that you remember the research results much better in pictorial form than in words and that the theory isn't so confusing (or missing a critical part) if you've outlined it. Draw information a few times and it will stay with you.

- Remember, the more you work with the material, the better you will learn and remember it. Write it in your own words, talk about it, explain it to others, or draw visual representations of it.

- Last but not least, remember that this material is a lot of fun. You haven't even started reading the book yet, but we think you're going to like it. In particular, you'll see how much social psychology has to tell you about your real, everyday life. As this course progresses, you might want to remind yourself to observe the events of your daily life with new eyes, the eyes of a social psychologist, and try to apply what you are learning to the behavior of your friends, acquaintances, strangers, and, yes, even yourself. Make sure you use the *Try It!* exercises and visit the Website. You will find out how much social psychology can help us understand our lives. When you read newspapers or magazines or watch the nightly news, think about what social psychology has to say about such events and behaviors—we believe you will find that your understanding of daily life is richer. If you notice a newspaper or magazine article that you think is an especially good example of "social psychology in action," please send it to us, with a full reference to where you found it and on what page. If we decide to use it in the next edition of this book, we'll list your name in the Acknowledgments.

We suspect that ten years from now you may not remember all the facts, theories, and names you learn now. Although we hope you will remember some of them, our main goal is for you to take with you into your future a great many of the broad social psychological concepts presented herein. If you open yourself to social psychology's magic, we believe it will enrich the way you look at the world and the way you live in it.

Brief Contents 简目

CHAPTER 1   Introducing Social Psychology   社会心理学导论   1

CHAPTER 2   Methodology: How Social Psychologists Do Research
方法论：社会心理学家如何进行研究   22

CHAPTER 3   Social Cognition: How We Think about the Social World
社会认知：我们如何思考社会性世界   50

CHAPTER 4   Social Perception: How We Come to Understand Other People
社会知觉：我们如何理解他人   82

CHAPTER 5   The Self: Understanding Ourselves in a Social Context
自我：在社会情境中理解我们自己   116

CHAPTER 6   The Need to Justify Our Actions: The Costs and Benefits of Dissonance Reduction   合理化行为的需要：减少失调的代价和收益   148

CHAPTER 7   Attitudes and Attitude Change: Influencing Thoughts and Feelings
态度与态度改变：影响思维和情绪   176

CHAPTER 8   Conformity: Influencing Behavior   从众：影响行为   210

CHAPTER 9   Group Processes: Influence in Social Groups
团体过程：社会团体的影响   252

CHAPTER 10   Interpersonal Attraction: From First Impressions to Close Relationships   人际吸引：从第一印象到亲密关系   286

CHAPTER 11   Prosocial Behavior: Why Do People Help?
亲社会行为：为什么人们助人？   322

CHAPTER 12   Aggression: Why Do We Hurt Other People? Can We Prevent It?
侵犯：我们为什么伤害他人？能防止吗？   350

CHAPTER 13   Prejudice: Causes and Cures   偏见：原因与消除   386

SOCIAL PSYCHOLOGY IN ACTION 1   Making a Difference with Social Psychology: Attaining a Sustainable Future

实践中的社会心理学之一：获得可持续的未来 426

SOCIAL PSYCHOLOGY IN ACTION 2　Social Psychology and Health

实践中的社会心理学之二：社会心理学与健康 446

SOCIAL PSYCHOLOGY IN ACTION 3　Social Psychology and the Law

实践中的社会心理学之三：社会心理学与法律 472

Contents 目录

出版前言　iii

前言　iv

关于作者　xi

给学生们的特别提示　xiii

CHAPTER 1

Introducing Social Psychology　社会心理学导论　1

What Is Social Psychology?　什么是社会心理学?　3

TRY IT! How Do Values Change?　试一试! 价值观是如何改变的?　3

The Power of Social Interpretation　社会性解读的力量　4

How Else Can We Understand Social Influence?　了解社会影响的其他方法　6

Social Psychology Compared with Personality Psychology　社会心理学与人格心理学的比较　8

TRY IT! Social Situations and Behavior　试一试! 社会情境与行为　9

Social Psychology Compared with Sociology　社会心理学与社会学的比较　9

The Power of Social Influence　社会影响的威力　11

Underestimating the Power of Social Influence　低估社会影响的力量　11

The Subjectivity of the Social Situation　社会情境的主观性　12

Where Construals Come From: Basic Human Motives　解读从何而来: 人性的基本动机　14

The Self-Esteem Approach: The Need to Feel Good about Ourselves

自尊取向: 保持良好自我感觉的需要　15

The Social Cognition Approach: The Need to Be Accurate　社会认知取向: 对准确性的需求　16

Additional Motives　其他动机　18

Social Psychology and Social Problems　社会心理学与社会问题　18

CHAPTER 2

Methodology: How Social Psychologists Do Research

方法论: 社会心理学家如何进行研究　22

Social Psychology: An Empirical Science　社会心理学: 一门实证科学　24

TRY IT! Social Psychology Quiz: What's Your Prediction?

试一试! 社会心理学小测试: 你的预期是什么?　25

Formulating Hypotheses and Theories　假说和理论的形成　25

Inspiration from Earlier Theories and Research　从过去的理论和研究成果中获得灵感　25

Hypotheses Based on Personal Observations　以个人观察为依据建立假说　26

The Observational Method: Describing Social Behavior　观察法: 描述社会行为　27

Archival Analysis　档案分析法　27

TRY IT! Archival Analysis: Women, Men, and the Media

试一试！档案分析：女性、男性和媒体 28

Limits of the Observational Method 观察法的局限性 29

The Correlational Method: Predicting Social Behavior 相关法：预测社会行为 29

Surveys 调查法 30

CONNECTIONS Random Selection in Political Polls 链接 政治民意调查中的随机抽样 31

Limits of the Correlational Method: Correlation Does Not Equal Causation
相关法的局限性：相关分析不等于因果分析 32

TRY IT! Correlation and Causation: Knowing the Difference
试一试！相关和因果：了解它们的差异 33

The Experimental Method: Answering Causal Questions 实验法：解释因果关系 33

Independent and Dependent Variables 自变量与因变量 35

Internal Validity in Experiments 实验的内部效度 36

External Validity in Experiments 实验的外部效度 37

Basic Versus Applied Research 基础研究与应用研究 40

New Frontiers in Social Psychological Research 社会心理学研究的新思路 41

Culture and Social Psychology 文化与社会心理学 41

The Evolutionary Approach 进化心理学 42

Social Neuroscience 社会神经科学 42

Ethical Issues in Social Psychology 社会心理学的伦理问题 43

Guidelines for Ethical Research 伦理研究的指导方针 44

CHAPTER 3

Social Cognition: How We Think about the Social World
社会认知： 我们如何思考社会性世界 50

On Automatic Pilot: Low-Effort Thinking 自动化：低努力水平思维 52

People as Everyday Theorists: Automatic Thinking with Schemas
作为日常理论家的人们：运用图式进行自动化思考 53

TRY IT! Avoiding Self-Fulfilling Prophecies 试一试！避免自证预言 62

Mental Strategies and Shortcuts 心理策略与心理捷径 62

CONNECTIONS Personality Tests and the Representativeness Heuristic
链接 人格测验与代表性法则 66

TRY IT! Reasoning Quiz 试一试！推理小测验 67

The Power of Unconscious Thinking 无意识思维的力量 67

Cultural Differences in Social Cognition 社会认知的文化差异 68

Controlled Social Cognition: High-Effort Thinking 控制性社会认知：高努力水平思维 72

Mentally Undoing the Past: Counterfactual Reasoning 在心理上改变历史：反事实推理 73

Thought Suppression and Ironic Processing 思考抑制和反向加工 74

Improving Human Thinking 改进人类思维 75

TRY IT! How Well Do You Reason? 试一试！你的推理能力如何？ 76

The Amadou Diallo Case Revisited 阿马登·戴尔罗案例反思 77

CHAPTER 4

Social Perception: How We Come to Understand Other People
社会知觉：我们如何理解他人 **82**

Nonverbal Behavior 非语言行为 84

TRY IT! Using Your Voice as a Nonverbal Cue 试一试！用你的声音作为非语言线索 85

Facial Expressions of Emotion 表达情绪的面部表情 86

Culture and the Channels of Nonverbal Communication 文化与非语言交流的渠道 88

Multichannel Nonverbal Communication 多渠道的非语言交流 89

CONNECTIONS The E-Mail Dilemma: Communicating Without Nonverbal Cues
链接 e-mail 的两难：没有非语言线索的交流 91

Implicit Personality Theories: Filling In the Blanks 内隐人格理论：填补空白 92

Culture and Implicit Personality Theories 文化与内隐人格理论 93

Causal Attribution: Answering the "Why" Question 因果归因：回答"为什么"的问题 95

The Nature of the Attribution Process 归因过程的本质 95

The Covariation Model: Internal versus External Attributions 共变模式：内部归因与外部归因 96

TRY IT! Listen as People Make Attributions 试一试！听听别人如何进行归因 97

The Correspondence Bias: People as Personality Psychologists
一致性偏见：人人都是人格心理学家 98

CONECTIONS Police Interrogations and the Correspondence Bias
链接 警察审问和一致性偏见 102

Culture and the Correspondence Bias 文化与一致性偏见 103

The Actor/Observer Difference 当事人与旁观者差异 107

Self-Serving Attributions 自利归因 109

TRY IT! Self-Serving Attributions in the Sports Pages 试一试！体育专栏中的自利归因 110

Culture and Other Attributional Biases 文化与其他归因偏见 111

CHAPTER 5

The Self: Understanding Ourselves in a Social Context
自我：在社会情境中理解我们自己 **116**

Self-Knowledge 自我认知 119

Cultural Differences in Defining the Self 自我定义的文化差异 119

TRY IT! A Measure of Independence and Interdependence
试一试！独立性与相互依存性量表 120

Gender Differences in Defining the Self 自我定义的性别差异 121

TRY IT! A Measure of Relational Interdependence
试一试！对关系的相互依存性的量表 122

Knowing Ourselves Through Introspection 通过内省来认识自己 122

TRY IT! Measure Your Private Self-Consciousness 试一试！测量你的内在自我意识 126

Knowing Ourselves by Observing Our Own Behavior 通过观察自己的行为来认识自己 129

CONNECTIONS How Should Parents Praise Their Children?
链接 父母应怎样赞扬孩子？ 132

xix

Mindsets: Understanding Our Own Abilities　心态：理解我们的能力　136

Using Other People to Know Ourselves　通过他人来认识自己　137

Self-Control: The Executive Function of the Self　自我控制：自我的执行功能　140

Impression Management: All the World's a Stage　印象管理：世界是个大舞台　141

Culture, Impression Management, and Self-Enhancement　文化、印象管理和自我提升　144

CHAPTER 6

The Need to Justify Our Actions: The Costs and Benefits of Dissonance Reduction
合理化行为的需要：减少失调的代价和收益　148

Maintaining a Stable, Positive Self-Image　保持稳定、积极的自我形象　150

The Theory of Cognitive Dissonance　认知失调理论　150

Rational Behavior versus Rationalizing Behavior　理性行为与合理化行为　152

Decisions, Decisions, Decisions　决策，决策，还是决策　153

TRY IT! The Advantage of Finality　试一试！一锤子买卖的好处　155

Dissonance, the Brain, and Evolution　认知失调、大脑和进化　157

Justifying Your Effort　合理化你的努力　158

TRY IT! Justifying Actions　试一试！合理化你的行为　159

The Psychology of Insufficient Justification　非充分合理化的心理学　159

Advocacy and Hypocrisy Applied to Social Problems　社会问题中的拥护和伪善　161

Good and Bad Deeds　善行与恶行　166

TRY IT! Good Deeds　试一试！善 行　167

Culture and Dissonance　文化与失调　170

CONNECTIONS　Dissonance Theory Used by Mainstream Journalist to Explain the Actions of Suicide Bombers　链接　主流记者基于认知失调理论对自杀性爆炸事件的解释　170

Some Final Thoughts on Dissonance: Learning from Our Mistakes
关于失调的最后几点思考：从我们所犯的错误中学习　171

Heaven's Gate Revisited　再探天门教事件　172

CHAPTER 7

Attitudes and Attitude Change: Influencing Thoughts and Feelings
态度与态度改变：影响思维和情绪　176

The Nature and Origin of Attitudes　态度的本质与根源　178

Where Do Attitudes Come From?　态度从何而来？　179

TRY IT! Affective and Cognitive Bases of Attitudes　试一试！态度的情感和认知基础　181

Explicit versus Implicit Attitudes　外显态度与内隐态度　182

How Do Attitudes Change?　态度是如何改变的？　183

Changing Attitudes by Changing Behavior: Cognitive Dissonance Theory Revisited
通过改变行为来改变态度：重返认知失调理论　183

Persuasive Communications and Attitude Change　说服性沟通与态度改变　184

TRY IT! The Need for Cognition　试一试！认知需求　189

Emotion and Attitude Change　情绪与态度改变　189

Confidence in One's Thoughts and Attitude Change　对个人想法的信心与态度改变　193
Resisting Persuasive Messages　抗拒说服信息　194
Attitude Inoculation　态度的预防免疫　194
Be Alert to Product Placement　警惕产品内置　195
Resisting Peer Pressure　拒绝同伴压力　195
When Persuasion Attempts Boomerang: Reactance Theory　当说服产生反作用：抗拒理论　196
When Will Attitudes Predict Behavior?　态度何时能预测行为？　197
Predicting Spontaneous Behaviors　预测自发行为　197
Predicting Deliberative Behaviors　预测有意行为　198
The Power of Advertising　广告的威力　200
How Advertising Works　广告如何发挥作用　200
CONNECTIONS　Do Media Campaigns to Reduce Drug Use Work?
链接　减少药物使用的媒体宣传有用吗？　201
Subliminal Advertising: A Form of Mind Control?　阈下广告：一种精神控制方式？　202
Advertising, Cultural Stereotypes, and Social Behavior　广告、文化的刻板印象与社会行为　204
TRY IT! Advertising and Mind Control　试一试！广告与思想控制　204

CHAPTER 8

Conformity: Influencing Behavior　**从众：影响行为　210**
Conformity: When and Why　从众行为：发生的时机与原因　213
Informational Social Influence: The Need to Know What's "Right"
信息性社会影响：想知道"正确"情况的需要　214
The Importance of Being Accurate　保持正确的重要性　216
When Informational Conformity Backfires　当信息性社会影响导致相反的效果时　218
When Will People Conform to Informational Social Influence?　何时人们会顺从信息性社会影响？　219
TRY IT! Informational Social Influence and Emergencies
试一试！信息性社会影响与突发事件　220
Normative Social Influence: The Need to Be Accepted
规范性社会影响：希望被接受的需要　221
Conformity and Social Approval: The Asch Line Judgment Studies
从众与社会认同：阿希线段判断研究　222
The Importance of Being Accurate, Revisited　回顾：保持正确的重要性　225
The Consequences of Resisting Normative Social Influence　拒绝规范性社会影响的后果　226
TRY IT! Unveiling Normative Social Influence by Breaking the Rules
试一试！违规：揭开规范性社会影响的面纱　227
Normative Social Influence in Everyday Life　日常生活中的规范性社会影响　227
When Will People Conform to Normative Social Influence?　何时人们会顺从规范性社会影响？　232
TRY IT! Fashion: Normative Social Influence in Action
试一试！时装：现实中的规范性社会影响　234
Minority Influence: When the Few Influence the Many

少数人的影响：少数人何时能影响多数人　235
CONNECTIONS The Power of Propaganda　链接　宣传的威力　236
Using Social Influence to Promote Beneficial Behavior　利用社会影响以促进有益行为　237
The Role of Injunctive and Descriptive Norms　命令性规范与描述性规范的作用　238
Obedience to Authority 服从权威　240
The Role of Normative Social Influence　规范性社会影响的作用　243
The Role of Informational Social Influence　信息性社会影响的作用　244
Other Reasons Why We Obey　服从的其他原因　245
The Obedience Studies, Then and Now　过去和现在的服从研究　247

CHAPTER 9

Group Processes: Influence in Social Groups　团体过程：社会团体的影响　252
What Is a Group? 什么是团体？　254
Why Do People Join Groups?　人们为什么要加入团体？　254
The Composition and Functions of Groups　团体的组成与功能　254
TRY IT! What Happens When You Violate a Role?　试一试！当你违背角色时会怎样？　258
Groups and Individuals' Behavior 团体与个人行为　258
Social Facilitation: When the Presence of Others Energizes Us
社会促进：他人在场为我们增添活力　259
Social Loafing: When the Presence of Others Relaxes Us　社会懈怠：他人在场使我们放松　262
Gender and Cultural Differences in Social Loafing: Who Slacks Off the Most?
社会懈怠的性别和文化差异：谁最偷懒？　263
Deindividuation: Getting Lost in the Crowd　去个体化：迷失在人群中　263
Group Decisions: Are Two (or More) Heads Better Than One?
团体决策：两人（或者更多人）的决策一定优于单独决策吗？　265
Process Loss: When Group Interactions Inhibit Good Problem Solving
过程损失：团体互动抑制了良好的解决办法　265
CONNECTIONS Was the Decision to Invade Iraq a Result of Groupthink?
链接　出兵伊拉克的决定是团体思维的结果吗？　270
Group Polarization: Going to Extremes　团体极化：走向极端　271
TRY IT! Choice Dilemmas Questionnaire　试一试！选择困境问卷　272
Leadership in Groups　团体中的领导　273
Conflict and Cooperation 冲突与合作　276
Social Dilemmas　社会困境　277
TRY IT! The Prisoner's Dilemma　试一试！囚徒困境　278
Using Threats to Resolve Conflict　用威胁解决冲突　279
Effects of Communication　沟通的作用　280
Negotiation and Bargaining　协商与讨价还价　281

CHAPTER 10

Interpersonal Attraction: From First Impressions to Close Relationships
人际吸引：从第一印象到亲密关系 286

What Causes Attraction? 产生吸引的原因 288

The Person Next Door: The Propinquity Effect 住在隔壁的人：时空接近效应 289

TRY IT! Mapping the Effect of Propinquity in Your Life
试一试！在生活中体验时空接近效应 290

Similarity 相似性 291

Reciprocal Liking 互惠式的好感 292

Physical Attractiveness and Liking 外表的吸引力与好感 293

Theories of Interpersonal Attraction: Social Exchange and Equity
人际吸引理论：社会交换理论和公平理论 299

Close Relationships 亲密关系 301

Defining Love 爱的定义 301

TRY IT! Passionate Love Scale 试一试！激情之爱量表 302

Culture and Love 文化和爱 303

Love and Relationships 爱情和人际关系 304

Evolution and Love: Choosing a Mate 进化和爱：选择配偶 304

CONNECTIONS Does Ovulation Affect Perceptions of Male Attractiveness?
链接 排卵是否会影响对男性吸引力的知觉 306

Attachment Styles in Intimate Relationships 亲密关系中的依恋类型 307

CONNECTIONS This Is Your Brain ... In Love 链接 恋爱中的大脑 309

Social Exchange in Long-Term Relationships 长期人际关系中的社会交换 312

Equity in Long-Term Relationships 长期人际关系中的公平性 314

Ending Intimate Relationships 亲密关系的结束 316

The Process of Breaking Up 分手的过程 316

The Experience of Breaking Up 分手的体验 317

CHAPTER 11

Prosocial Behavior: Why Do People Help? 亲社会行为：为什么人们助人？ 322

Basic Motives Underlying Prosocial Behavior: Why Do People Help?
亲社会行为的基本动机：为什么人们助人？ 324

Evolutionary Psychology: Instincts and Genes 进化心理学：本能与基因 324

TRY IT! Does the Reciprocity Norm Increase Helping?
试一试！互惠规范能促进帮助行为吗？ 326

Social Exchange: The Costs and Rewards of Helping 社会交换：助人的成本与报酬 327

Empathy and Altruism: The Pure Motive for Helping 移情与利他主义：助人的纯粹动机 328

Personal Qualities and Prosocial Behavior: Why Do Some People Help More Than Others?
个人品质与亲社会行为：为什么一些人比其他人更多助人？ 332

Individual Differences: The Altruistic Personality 个体差异：利他人格 332

Gender Differences in Prosocial Behavior 亲社会行为中的性别差异 332

Cultural Differences in Prosocial Behavior 亲社会行为中的文化差异 332

Religion and Prosocial Behavior 宗教和亲社会行为 333

The Effects of Mood on Prosocial Behavior 心境对亲社会行为的影响 334

TRY IT! Do Good, Feel Good? 试一试！心情好，做好事？ 335

Situational Determinants of Prosocial Behavior: When Will People Help?
亲社会行为的情境决定因素：什么时候人们会助人？ 336

Environment: Rural versus Urban 环境：乡村与城市 336

Residential Mobility 居民流动性 337

The Number of Bystanders: The Bystander Effect 旁观者数目：旁观者效应 337

The Nature of the Relationship: Communal versus Exchange Relationships
关系的性质：共有关系与交换关系 342

TRY IT! The Lost Letter Technique 试一试！遗失信件技术 343

How Can Helping Be Increased? 怎样增加助人行为？ 344

Increasing the Likelihood That Bystanders Will Intervene 增加旁观者干预的可能性 344

Positive Psychology and Prosocial Behavior 积极心理学与亲社会行为 345

CONNECTIONS Increasing Volunteerism 链接 增加志愿主义 346

CHAPTER 12

Aggression: Why Do We Hurt Other People? Can We Prevent It?
侵犯：我们为什么伤害他人？能防止吗？ **350**

What Is Aggression? 什么是侵犯？ 352

Is Aggression Inborn or Learned? 侵犯是天生的还是后天习得的？ 353

Is Aggression Instinctual? Situational? Optional?
侵犯行为是本能的、情境性的还是选择性的？ 353

TRY IT! Fighting and Its Attractiveness 试一试！打架及其吸引力 354

Aggression and Culture 侵犯与文化 355

Neural and Chemical Influences on Aggression 神经生化因素对侵犯的影响 356

Gender and Aggression 性别与侵犯 357

Alcohol and Aggression 酒精与侵犯 359

Pain, Discomfort, and Aggression 疼痛、不适与侵犯 359

TRY IT! Heat, Humidity, and Aggression 试一试！炎热、潮湿与侵犯 361

Social Situations and Aggression 社会情境与侵犯 361

Frustration and Aggression 挫折感与侵犯 361

Being Provoked and Reciprocating 被激怒和报复 363

Aggressive Objects as Cues 攻击性物体的提示作用 363

TRY IT! Insults and Aggression 试一试！侮辱和侵犯 364

Endorsement, Imitation, and Aggression 社会赞许、模仿和侵犯 364

Violence in the Media: TV, Movies, and Video Games
媒体中的暴力：电视、电影和电子游戏 365

Does Violence Sell? 暴力能提高销售吗？ 370

Violent Pornography and Violence against Women 暴力色情与对女性的暴力 370
How to Reduce Aggression 如何减少侵犯 372
Does Punishing Aggression Reduce Aggressive Behavior? 惩罚能减少侵犯行为吗？ 372
CONNECTIONS Curbing Bullying: A Case Study in Reducing Agression at School
链接 阻止恃强凌弱：一项减少学校中侵犯行为的个案研究 373
Catharsis and Aggression 宣泄与侵犯 374
The Effect of War on General Aggression 战争对总体侵犯性的影响 377
What Are We Supposed to Do with Our Anger? 我们应该怎么处理愤怒？ 377
Dehumanization: The Opposite of Empathy 去人性化：同情心的反面 380
CONNECTIONS Teaching Empathy in School 链接 学校里的同情心教育 381
Could the Columbine Massacre Have Been Prevented?
哥伦比亚屠杀本来可以避免吗？ 381

CHAPTER 13

Prejudice: Causes and Cures 偏见：原因与消除 386
Prejudice: The Ubiquitous Social Phenomenon 偏见：普遍的社会现象 388
Prejudice and Self-Esteem 偏见和自尊 389
A Progress Report 发展的报告 390
Prejudice Defined 偏见的定义 390
Stereotypes: The Cognitive Component "刻板印象"：认知要素 391
TRY IT! Stereotype and Aggression 试一试！刻板印象和攻击 392
Discrimination: The Behavioral Component "歧视"：行为要素 394
What Causes Prejudice? 偏见的起因 396
The Way We Think: Social Cognition 我们的思维方式：社会认知 397
How We Assign Meaning: Attributional Biases 如何赋予意义：归因偏差 406
Blaming the Victim 责怪受害者 409
Prejudice and Economic Competition: Realistic Conflict Theory
偏见和经济竞争："现实冲突理论" 411
The Way We Conform: Normative Rules 从众行为：规范性标准 414
Subtle Sexism 内隐性别歧视 416
How Can Prejudice be Reduced? 如何消除偏见？ 417
The Contact Hypothesis 接触假说 417
When Contact Reduces Prejudice: Six Conditions 接触减少偏见的六个条件 418
Why Early Desegregation Failed 早期种族混合教育为什么会失败 419
CONNECTIONS Cooperation and Interdependence: The Jigsaw Classroom
链接 合作与互倚：拼图教室 420
Why Does Jigsaw Work? 拼图教室法为什么有效 421
TRY IT! Jigsaw-Type Group Study 试一试！拼图式的学习小组 422
CONNECTIONS A Letter from "Carlos" 链接 来自"卡洛斯"的一封信 423

xxv

SPA 1

SOCIAL PSYCHOLOGY IN ACTION 1
Making a Difference with Social Psychology: Attaining a Sustainable Future
实践中的社会心理学之一：获得可持续的未来 426

Applied Research in Social Psychology 社会心理学的应用性研究 429
Capitalizing on the Experimental Method 利用实验法 430
Social Psychology to the Rescue 社会心理救援 432

Using Social Psychology to Achieve a Sustainable Future
利用社会心理学实现可持续发展 432
Resolving Social Dilemmas 解决社会困境 432
Conveying and Changing Social Norms 传递并改变社会规范 433
TRY IT! Reducing Littering with Descriptive Norms
试一试！ 通过描述性规范减少乱丢垃圾的行为 435
Keeping Track of Consumption 追踪消费 436
Introducing a Little Competitiveness 适当引入竞争 436
Inducing Hypocrisy 诱导伪善 437
Removing Small Barriers to Achieve Big Changes 消除小障碍，实现大变化 438
TRY IT! Changing Environmentally Damaging Behaviors **试一试！** 改变破坏环境的行为 439

Happiness and a Sustainable Lifestyle 幸福和可持续的生活方式 440
What Makes People Happy? 让人们幸福的是什么？ 440
Money, Materialism, and Happiness 金钱，物质主义和幸福 441
Do People Know What Makes Them Happy? 人们知道让他们幸福的是什么吗？ 442

SPA 2

SOCIAL PSYCHOLOGY IN ACTION 2
Social Psychology and Health
实践中的社会心理学之二：社会心理学与健康 446

Stress and Human Health 压力与人类健康 448
Resilience 恢复力 448
TRY IT! The College Life Stress Inventory **试一试！** 大学生生活压力量表 451
Perceived Stress and Health 知觉压力与健康 452
Feeling in Charge: The Importance of Perceived Control 自主感：知觉控制感的重要性 453
Knowing You Can Do It: Self-Efficacy 知道自己能做得到：自我效能 456
Explaining Negative Events: Learned Helplessness 解释负性事件：习得性无助 457
Optimism: Looking on the Bright Side 乐观：从光明面看 460
TRY IT! The Life Orientation Test **试一试！** 生活定向测验 460

Coping with Stress 压力的应对 461
Gender Differences in Coping with Stress 应对压力的性别差异 461
Social Support: Getting Help from Others 社会支持：获得他人的帮助 462
TRY IT! Social Support **试一试！** 社会支持 463
Opening Up: Making Sense of Traumatic Events 敞开心扉：弄清创伤性事件的意义 464

Prevention: Promoting Healthier Behavior 预防之道：改善健康习惯 **465**

Preventable Health Problems 可预防的健康问题 465

Social Psychological Interventions: Targeting Safer Sex 社会心理学干预：更安全的性行为 466

TRY IT! Changing Your Health Habits 试一试！改变你的健康习惯 468

SPA 3

SOCIAL PSYCHOLOGY IN ACTION 3
Social Psychology and the Law
实践中的社会心理学之三：社会心理学与法律 **472**

Eyewitness Testimony 目击者证词 **474**

Why Are Eyewitnesses Often Wrong? 为何目击者经常指认错误？ 475

Judging Whether Eyewitnesses Are Mistaken 判断目击证人是否犯错 482

TRY IT! The Accuracy of Eyewitness Testimony 试一试！目击者证词的准确性 484

Judging Whether Witnesses Are Lying 判断证人是否撒谎 484

TRY IT! Lie Detection 试一试！测谎 486

Can Eyewitness Testimony Be Improved? 目击者的证词能够得到改进吗？ 486

The Recovered Memory Debate 关于恢复性记忆的争论 487

Juries: Group Processes in Action 陪审团：团体判决过程 **488**

How Jurors Process Information During the Trial 审判过程中陪审员对信息的处理 489

Confessions: Are They Always What They Seem? 认罪：它们总是像看起来那样吗？ 489

Deliberations in the Jury Room 陪审室内的商议 491

Why Do People Obey the Law? 公民为何守法？ **492**

Do Severe Penalties Deter Crime? 严惩能够阻止犯罪吗？ 492

TRY IT! Are You Aware of the Penalties for Federal Crimes? 试一试！你了解各种联邦罪名的量刑吗？ 494

Procedural Justice: People's Sense of Fairness 程序公平：人们对公平的理解 495

Glossary 重要词汇 499

References 参考文献 507

Credits 鸣谢 567

Name Index 人名索引 569

Subject Index 主题索引 579

1

Introducing Social Psychology
社会心理学导论

T HE TASK OF THE PSYCHOLOGIST IS TO TRY TO UNDERSTAND and predict human behavior. Different kinds of psychologists go about this in different ways, and in this book we attempt to show you how social psychologists do it. Let's begin with a few examples of human behavior. Some of these might seem important; others might seem trivial; one or two might seem frightening. To a social psychologist, all of them are interesting. Our hope is that by the time you finish reading this book, you will find all these examples as fascinating as we do. As you read these examples, try to think about how you would explain why what happened, happened.

- Just before dawn, the residents of a trendy neighborhood in Los Angeles heard desperate cries for help coming from a yellow house. "Please don't kill me!" screamed one woman. Other neighbors reported hearing tortured screams and cries for mercy, yet not one neighbor bothered to investigate or help in any way. No one even called the police. One woman, who lived two houses away, went out onto her balcony when she heard the screams but went back into her house without doing anything. Twelve hours later, an acquaintance arrived at the yellow house and discovered that four people had been brutally murdered. A fifth person was critically wounded and had spent those twelve hours lying in a bedroom, bleeding from her wounds, waiting in vain for just one neighbor to lift a finger and dial 911 (*New York Times*, July 3, 1981).

  Why do you think the neighbors failed to do anything after hearing the cries for help? Stop and think for a moment: What kinds of people are these neighbors? Would you like to have them as friends? If you had a small child, would you hire one of these neighbors as a babysitter?

- You're on campus after listening to a lecture on homeland security. The speaker addressed an important issue: whether or not the government should have the right to eavesdrop on phone calls. You are about to express your belief that, given that we are in the midst of a war on terrorism, the president's major responsibility is to protect the American people from attack; therefore, he should have unlimited power to monitor our phone calls. Compared to the events of September 11, it is a small price to pay. Just as you are about to open your mouth to speak, your friend Maria says, "I can't even believe this is happening! Our privacy is being invaded for no good reason. It is like living in a totalitarian country." Steve chimes in, "You are absolutely right. The government's behavior is unconstitutional. They should not be allowed to listen to our conversations without getting a warrant from the courts—that's what checks and balances are all about." "I agree," says Emily. "Besides, the so-called war on terror isn't really a war." All eyes turn to you. What do you say? Do you state your own opinion, or do you conform to the unanimous opinion of your friends?

OUTLINE 提纲

- What Is Social Psychology?
  - The Power of Social Interpretation
  - Connections
  - How Else Can We Understand Social Influence?
  - Social Psychology Compared with Personality Psychology
  - Social Psychology Compared with Sociology
- The Power of Social Influence
  - Underestimating the Power of Social Influence
  - The Subjectivity of the Social Situation
- Where Construals Come From: Basic Human Motives
  - The Self-Esteem Approach: The Need to Feel Good About Ourselves
  - The Social Cognition Approach: The Need to Be Accurate
  - Additional Motives
- Social Psychology and Social Problems
- Summary

Would it surprise you to learn that when placed in a similar situation, most college students would go along with the majority opinion rather than appear to be out of step?

- We have a friend whom we will call Oscar. Oscar is a middle-aged executive with a computer software company. As a student, Oscar had attended a large state university in the Midwest, where he was a member of a fraternity we will call Delta Nu. He remembers having gone through a severe and scary hazing ritual to become a member but believes it was worthwhile. Although he had been terribly frightened by the hazing, he loved his fraternity brothers and was proud to be a member of Delta Nu—easily the best of all fraternities. A few years ago, his son, Sam, was about to enroll in the same university; naturally, Oscar urged Sam to pledge Delta Nu: "It's a great fraternity—always attracts a wonderful bunch of fellows. You'll really love it." Sam did in fact pledge Delta Nu and was accepted. Oscar was relieved to learn that Sam was not required to undergo a severe initiation in order to become a member; times had changed, and hazing was now forbidden. When Sam came home for Christmas break, Oscar asked him how he liked the fraternity. "It's all right, I guess," he said, "but most of my friends are outside the fraternity." Oscar was astonished.

  How is it that Oscar had been so enamored of his fraternity brothers and Sam wasn't? Had the standards of old Delta Nu slipped? Was the fraternity now admitting a less desirable group of young men than in Oscar's day? What do you think might be going on?

- In the mid-1970s, several hundred members of the Peoples Temple, a California-based religious cult, emigrated to Guyana under the guidance of their leader the Reverend Jim Jones. Their aim was to found a model interracial community, called Jonestown, based on "love, hard work, and spiritual enlightenment." In November 1978, Congressman Leo Ryan of California flew to Jonestown to investigate reports that some of the members were being held against their will. He visited the commune and found that several residents wanted to return with him to the United States. Jones agreed they could leave, but as Ryan was boarding a plane, he and several other members of his party were shot and killed by a member of the Peoples Temple on Jones's orders. On hearing that several members of Ryan's party had escaped, Jones grew despondent and began to speak over the public address system about the beauty of dying and the certainty that everyone would meet again in another place. The residents lined up in a pavilion in front of a vat containing a mixture of Kool-Aid and cyanide. According to a survivor, almost all the residents drank willingly of the deadly solution. At least eighty babies and infants were given the poison by their parents, who then drank it themselves. Nine hundred and fourteen people died, including the Reverend Jones.

  How is it that people can agree to kill themselves and their own children? Were they crazy? Were they under some kind of hypnotic spell? How would you explain their behavior?

We now have several questions about human social behavior—questions we find fascinating: Why did the Los Angeles residents ignore the screams coming from the yellow house when by dialing 911 they might have averted a tragedy? In the situation of the college students discussing domestic surveillance, what are the factors that cause most people to conform to the opinion of others? Why did Oscar like his frat brothers so much more than his son Sam did? And how could large numbers of people be induced to kill their own children and commit suicide in Jonestown? In this chapter, we will consider what these examples have in common and why they are of interest to us. We will also suggest reasonable explanations based on social psychological research.

What Is Social Psychology? 什么是社会心理学?

At the very heart of social psychology is the phenomenon of **social influence**: We are all influenced by other people. When we think of social influence, the kinds of examples that readily come to mind are direct attempts at persuasion, whereby one person deliberately tries to change another person's behavior. This is what happens in an advertising campaign when creative people use sophisticated techniques to persuade us to buy a particular brand of toothpaste, or during an election campaign when similar techniques are used to get us to vote for a particular political candidate. Direct attempts at persuasion also occur when our friends try to get us to do something we don't really want to do ("Come on, have another beer—everyone is doing it"), or when the schoolyard bully uses force or threats to get smaller kids to part with their lunch money or homework.

These direct attempts at social influence form a major part of social psychology and will be discussed in our chapters on conformity, attitudes, and group processes. To the social psychologist, however, social influence is broader than attempts by one person to change another person's behavior. Social influence extends beyond behavior— it includes our thoughts and feelings as well as our overt acts. In addition, social influence takes on many forms other than deliberate attempts at persuasion. We are often influenced merely by the presence of other people. Moreover, even when we are not in the physical presence of others, we are still influenced by them. Thus in a sense we carry our mothers, fathers, friends, and teachers around with us as we attempt to make decisions that would make them proud of us.

On a still subtler level, each of us is immersed in a social and cultural context. Social psychologists are interested in studying how and why our thoughts, feelings, and behaviors are shaped by the entire social environment. Taking all these factors into account, we can define **social psychology** as the scientific study of the way in which people's thoughts, feelings, and behaviors are influenced by the real or imagined presence of other people (Allport, 1985). Of particular interest to social psychologists is what happens in the mind of an individual when various influences come into conflict with one another. This is frequently the case when young people (like many of our readers) go off to college and find themselves torn between the beliefs and values they learned at home and the beliefs and values their professors or peers are expressing. (See the following Try It! exercise.)

Social Influence
The effect that the words, actions, or mere presence of other people have on our thoughts, feelings, attitudes, or behavior

Social Psychology
The scientific study of the way in which people's thoughts, feelings, and behaviors are influenced by the real or imagined presence of other people

How Do Values Change? 试一试！价值观是如何改变的？

Make a list of the explicit and implicit beliefs and values of your parents and close relatives; then make such a list for your favorite professors and closest college friends. Note the similarities and differences in your lists. How do these differences affect you? Do you find yourself rejecting one set of values in favor of the other? Are you trying to make a compromise between the two? Are you attempting to form a whole new set of values that are your own?

Our thoughts, feelings, behaviors are influenced by our immediate surroundings as well as by our cultural and family background.

The Power of Social Interpretation
社会性解读的力量

Other disciplines, like anthropology and sociology, are also interested in how people are influenced by their social environment. Social psychology is distinct, however, primarily because it is concerned not so much with social situations in any objective sense, but rather with how people are influenced by their interpretation, or **construal,** of their social environment. To understand how people are influenced by their social world, social psychologists believe it is more important to understand how people perceive, comprehend, and interpret the social world than it is to understand the objective properties of the social world itself (Lewin, 1943).

An example will clarify. Imagine that Jason is a shy high school student who admires Debbie from afar. Suppose that as a budding social psychologist, you have the job of predicting whether or not Jason will ask Debbie to the senior prom. One way you might do this is to observe Debbie's objective behavior toward Jason. Does she pay attention to him and smile a lot? If so, the casual observer might decide that Jason will ask her out. As a social psychologist, however, you are more interested in viewing Debbie's behavior through Jason's eyes—that is, in seeing how Jason interprets Debbie's behavior. If she smiles at him, does Jason construe her behavior as mere politeness, the kind of politeness she would extend to any of the dozens of nerds and losers in the senior class? Or does he view her smile as an encouraging sign, one that inspires him to gather the courage to ask her out? If she ignores him, does Jason figure that she's playing hard to get? Or does he take it as a sign that she's not interested in dating him? To predict Jason's behavior, it is not enough to know the details of Debbie's behavior; it is imperative to know how Jason *interprets* Debbie's behavior.

Given the importance placed on the way people interpret the social world, social psychologists pay special attention to the origins of these interpretations. For example, when construing their environment, are most people concerned with making an interpretation that places them in the most positive light (e.g., Jason believing "Debbie is going to the prom with Eric because she is just trying to make me jealous") or with making the most accurate interpretation, even if it is unflattering (e.g., "Painful as it may be, I must admit that Debbie would rather go to the prom with a sea slug than with me")?

As you can see from Ross's research as discussed in Connections on the following page, construal is important and has wide ramifications. Consider a murder trial. Even when the prosecution presents compelling evidence it believes will prove the defen-

Construal

The way in which people perceive, comprehend, and interpret the social world

CONNECTIONS 链接

A special kind of construal is what Lee Ross calls "naïve realism." Ross is a social psychologist who has been working closely with Israeli and Palestinian negotiators. These negotiations frequently run aground because of naïve realism—the conviction all of us have that we perceive things "as they really are" (Ross, 2004; Ehrlinger, Gilovich, & Ross, 2005). We assume that other reasonable people see things the same way that we do.

> [E]ven when each side recognizes that the other side perceives the issues differently, each thinks that the other side is biased while they themselves are objective and that their own perceptions of reality should provide the basis for settlement.

Although both the Israelis and the Palestinians understand intellectually that the other side perceives the issues differently, both sides resist compromise, fearing that their "biased" opponent will benefit more than they. In a simple experiment, Ross took peace proposals created by Israeli negotiators, labeled them as Palestinian proposals, and asked Israeli citizens to judge them. The Israelis liked the Palestinian proposal attributed to Israel more than they liked the Israeli proposal attributed to the Palestinians. Ross concludes, "If your own proposal isn't going to be attractive to you when it comes from the other side, what chance is there that the *other* side's proposal is going to be attractive when it comes from the other side?" The hope is that once negotiators on both sides become fully aware of this phenomenon, and how it impedes conflict resolution, a reasonable compromise will be more likely.

Is this an example of political protest or of prejudice? How would you interpret this photo?

dant guilty, the verdict always hinges on precisely how each jury member construes that evidence. These construals rest on a variety of events and perceptions that often bear no objective relevance to the case. For instance, during cross-examination, did a key witness hesitate for a moment before answering, suggesting to some jurors that she might not be certain of her data? Or did some jurors consider the witness too remote, too arrogant, too certain of herself? Did the prosecutor appear to be smug and too sure of himself?

Another distinctive feature of social psychology is that it is an experimentally based science. As experimental scientists, we test our assumptions, guesses, and ideas about human social behavior empirically and systematically rather than by relying on folk wisdom, common sense, or the opinions and insights of philosophers, novelists, political pundits, our grandmothers, and others wise in the ways of human beings. As you will see, doing systematic experiments in social psychology presents a great many challenges—primarily because we are attempting to predict the behavior of highly sophisticated organisms in a variety of complex situations.

As scientists, our goal is to find objective answers to a wide array of important questions: What are the factors that cause aggression? How might we reduce prejudice? What variables cause two people to like or love each other? Why do certain kinds of political advertisements work better than others? The specific ways in which experimental social psychologists meet these challenges will be illustrated throughout this book.

We will spend most of this introductory chapter expanding on the issues raised in the preceding paragraphs—of what social psychology is and how it is distinct from other, related disciplines. A good place to begin is with what social psychology is not.

Construal and negotiation. Research by social psychologists can shed light on why negotiation between nations can be so difficult.

How Else Can We Understand Social Influence?
了解社会影响的其他方法

Let's take another look at the examples at the beginning of this chapter. Why did people behave the way they did? One way to answer this question might be simply to ask them. For example, we could question the residents in Los Angeles about why they didn't call the police. We could ask Sam why he wasn't especially excited about his fraternity brothers. The problem with this approach is that people are not always aware of the origins of their own responses and feelings (Gilbert, 2008; Nisbett & Wilson, 1977; Wilson, 2002). It is unlikely that the neighbors know exactly why they went back to sleep without calling the police. It is unlikely that Sam could pinpoint why he liked his Delta Nu fraternity brothers less than his father had liked his.

Journalists, Instant Experts, and Social Critics After the mass suicide at Jonestown, it was impossible to pick up a newspaper or turn on the TV without finding an explanation. These ranged from the (unfounded) assumption that the Reverend Jones employed hypnotism and drugs to weaken the resistance of his followers to suspicion that the people who were attracted to his cult must have been emotionally disturbed in the first place. Such speculations, because they underestimate the power of the situation, are almost always wrong—or, at the very least, oversimplified.

If we rely on commonsense explanations, we learn little from previous incidents. Jonestown was probably the first mass suicide involving Americans, but it wasn't the last. Near Waco, Texas, in 1993, the followers of cult leader David Koresh barricaded themselves into a fortresslike compound to avoid arrest for the possession of illegal firearms; under seige by the FBI, they apparently set fire to their own buildings. Eighty-six people died, including several children. Four years later, 39 members of an obscure cult called Heaven's Gate committed group suicide at a luxury estate in Rancho Santa Fe, California. The existing evidence makes it clear that the cult members died willingly and peacefully, believing that a huge alien spaceship, following closely behind the Hale-Bopp Comet, would pick up their souls and carry them into space (Purdham, 1997).

In the aftermath of both the Waco conflagration and the Heaven's Gate tragedy, the general population was just as confused as it had been following the Jonestown suicides. It is difficult for most people to grasp just how powerful a cult can be in affecting the hearts and minds of relatively normal people. Finding someone to blame became a national obsession. After the Heaven's Gate tragedy, many people blamed the victims themselves, accusing them of stupidity or derangement. But the evidence indicated that they were mentally healthy and, for the most part, uncommonly bright and well educated. After Waco, many pointed to the impatience of the FBI, the poor judgment of Attorney General Janet Reno, or the inadequate leadership of President Bill Clinton. Fixing blame may make us feel better by resolving our confusion, but it is no substitute for understanding the complexities of the situations that produced those events.

Don't get us wrong. We are not opposed to folk wisdom—far from it. We are convinced that a great deal can be learned about social behavior from journalists, social critics, and novelists—and in this book we quote from all these sources. There is, however, at least one problem with relying entirely on such sources: More often than not, they disagree with one another, and there is no easy way of determining which of them is correct.

Why did people obey Jim Jones's suicide order?

Consider what folk wisdom has to say about the factors that influence how much we like other people. On the one hand, we know that "birds of a feather flock together." With a little effort, each of us could come up with lots of examples where indeed we liked and hung around with people who shared our backgrounds and interests. But then again, folk wisdom also tells us that "opposites attract." If we tried, we could also come up with examples where people with different backgrounds and interests did attract us. Which is it?

Similarly, are we to believe that "out of sight is out of mind" or that "absence makes the heart grow fonder," that "haste makes waste" or that "he who hesitates is lost"? And who is to say whether the Jonestown massacre occurred because

- The Reverend Jones succeeded in attracting the kinds of people who were already psychologically depressed
- Only mentally ill people join cults
- Jones was such a powerful, charismatic figure that virtually anyone—even strong, nondepressed individuals like you or us—would have succumbed to his influence
- People cut off from society are particularly vulnerable to social influence
- All of the above
- None of the above

Philosophy Throughout history, philosophy has been a major source of insight about human nature. Indeed, the work of philosophers is part of the foundation of contemporary psychology. This has more than mere historical significance. In recent decades, psychologists have looked to philosophers for insights into the nature of consciousness (e.g., Dennett, 1991) and how people form beliefs about the social world (e.g., Gilbert, 1991). Sometimes, however, even great thinkers find themselves in disagreement with one another. When this occurs, how is one to know who is right? Are there some situations where philosopher A might be right, and other conditions where philosopher B might be right? How would you determine this?

We social psychologists address many of the same questions that philosophers address, but we attempt to look at these questions scientifically—even concerning that great human mystery, love. In 1663, the great Dutch philosopher Benedict Spinoza offered a highly original insight. He proposed that if we love someone whom we formerly hated, that love will be greater than if hatred had not preceded it. Spinoza's proposition is beautifully worked out. His logic is impeccable. But how can we be sure that it holds up? Does it always hold? What are the conditions under which it does or doesn't hold? These are empirical questions for the social psychologist (Aronson, 1999; Aronson & Linder, 1965).

One of the tasks of the social psychologist is to make educated guesses (called *hypotheses*) about the specific situations under which one outcome or the other would occur. Just as a physicist performs experiments to test hypotheses about the nature of the physical world, the social psychologist performs experiments to test hypotheses about the nature of the social world. The next task is to design well-controlled experiments sophisticated enough to tease out the situations that would result in one or another outcome. This enriches our understanding of human nature and allows us to make accurate predictions once we know the key aspects of the prevailing situation. We will discuss the scientific methods social psychologists use in more detail in Chapter 2.

The major reason we have conflicting philosophical positions (just as we have conflicting folk aphorisms) is that the world is a complicated place. Small differences in the situation might not be easily discernible, yet these small differences might produce very different effects.

To elaborate on this point, let's return to our earlier discussion about the kinds of people we like and the relationship between absence and liking. We would suggest that there are some conditions under which birds of a feather do flock together, and other conditions under which opposites do attract. Similarly, there are some conditions under which absence does make the heart grow fonder, and others under which out of sight does mean out of mind. So both can be true. That statement helps—but is it good enough? Not really, for if you really want to understand human behavior, knowing that both can be true is not sufficient.

Social Psychology Compared with Personality Psychology
社会心理学与人格心理学的比较

If you are like most people, when you read the examples that opened this chapter and started thinking about how those events might have come about, you probably wondered about the strengths, weaknesses, flaws, and personality traits that led the individuals involved to respond as they did. Why did the Los Angeles residents fail to call the police when they heard the cries for help? Most of us tend to assume that they possessed some personality flaw or quirk that made them reluctant to respond.

What character traits might these be? Some people are leaders and others are followers; some people are bold and others are timid; some people are public-spirited and others are selfish. Think back: How did you answer the question about whether you would want any of these people as a friend or a babysitter?

Asking—and trying to answer—questions like these is the work of personality psychologists. When trying to explain social behavior, personality psychologists generally focus on **individual differences**—the aspects of people's personalities that make them different from others. For example, to explain why the people at Jonestown ended their own lives and their children's by drinking poison, it seems natural to point to their personalities. Perhaps they were all "conformist types" or weak-willed; maybe they were even psychotic. The insights of personality psychologists increase our understanding of human behavior, but social psychologists are convinced that explaining behavior primarily through personality factors ignores a critical part of the story: the powerful role played by social influence. Remember that it was not just a handful of people who committed suicide at Jonestown, but almost 100 percent of the people in the village. Although it is conceivable that they were all psychotic, it is highly improbable. If we want a deeper, richer, more thorough explanation of this tragic event, we need to understand what kind of power and influence a charismatic figure like Jim Jones possesses, the nature of the impact of living in a closed society cut off from other points of view, and a myriad of other factors that might have contributed to that tragic outcome.

These two different approaches can be illustrated by focusing on a couple of mundane examples. Consider my friend Rosa. She is the wife of one of my colleagues, and I see her frequently at faculty cocktail parties. At these cocktail parties, she generally looks rather uncomfortable. She usually stands off by herself and when approached has very little to say. Some people regard her as shy; others regard her as aloof, standoffish, even arrogant. It is easy to see why. But I have been a dinner guest at Rosa's

Individual Differences
The aspects of people's personalities that make them different from other people

home, and in that situation she is charming, gracious, and vivacious, a good listener and an interesting conversationalist. So which is it? Is Rosa a shy person, an arrogant person, or a charming and gracious person? Will the real Rosa please stand up? It's the wrong question; the real Rosa is both and neither. All of us are capable of both shy and gracious behavior. A much more interesting question is, what factors are different in these two social situations that have such a profound effect on her (our) behavior? That is a social psychological question. (See the following Try It! exercise.)

TRY IT! Social Situations and Behavior 试一试！社会情境与行为

1. Think about one of your friends or acquaintances whom you regard as a shy person. For a moment, try not to think about him or her as "a shy person," but rather as someone who has difficulty relating to people in some situations but not in others.

2. Make a list of the social situations you think are most likely to bring out your friend's shy behavior.

3. Make a list of the social situations that might bring forth more outgoing behaviors on your friend's part. (For example, if someone showed a real interest in one of your friend's favorite hobbies or topics of conversation, it might bring out behaviors that could be classified as charming or vivacious.)

4. Set up a social environment in which this could be accomplished. Pay close attention to the effect that it has on your friend's behavior.

This is an important issue, so we'll give you one more example. Suppose you stop at a roadside restaurant for a cup of coffee and a piece of pie. The waitress comes over to take your order, but you are having a hard time deciding which kind of pie to order. While you are hesitating, the waitress impatiently taps her pen against her order book, rolls her eyes toward the ceiling, scowls at you, and finally snaps, "Hey, I haven't got all day, you know!" Like most people, you would probably think that the waitress is a nasty or unpleasant person; you might even complain about her to the manager.

But suppose you knew that the waitress is a single parent and was kept awake all night by the moaning of her youngest child, who has a painful terminal illness; that her car broke down on her way to work and she has no idea where she will find the money to have it repaired; that when she finally arrived at the restaurant, she learned that her co-worker was too drunk to work, requiring her to cover twice the usual number of tables; and that the short-order cook keeps screaming at her because she is not picking up the orders fast enough to please him. Given all that information, you might conclude that she is not necessarily a nasty person, just an ordinary person under enormous stress.

The key fact remains that without important information about a situation, when we are trying to understand someone's behavior in a complex situation, most people will find the reason for that behavior in the personality of the individual involved. And this fact—that we often fail to take the situation into account—is important to social psychologists because it has a profound impact on how human beings relate to one another.

Social Psychology Compared with Sociology
社会心理学与社会学的比较

Social psychology's focus on social behavior is shared by several other disciplines in the social sciences, including sociology, economics, and political science. Each of these examines the influence of social factors on human behavior, but important differences set social psychology apart, most notably in their level of analysis. Social psychology is a branch of psychology, rooted in the study of *individuals*, with an emphasis on internal psychological processes. *For the social psychologist, the level of analysis*

The people in this photo can be studied from a variety of perspectives: as individuals, as members of a family, a social class, an occupation, a culture, a region, and on and on.

is the individual in the context of a social situation. For example, to understand why people intentionally hurt one another, the social psychologist focuses on the specific psychological processes that trigger aggression in specific situations. To what extent is aggression preceded by frustration? Does frustration always precede aggression? If people are feeling frustrated, under what conditions will they vent their frustration with an overt, aggressive act? What factors might preclude an aggressive response by a frustrated individual? Besides frustration, what other factors might cause aggression? We will address these questions in Chapter 12.

Other social sciences are more concerned with broad social, economic, political, and historical factors that influence events in a given society. Sociology, for example, is concerned with such topics as social class, social structure, and social institutions. Of course, because society is made up of collections of people, some overlap is bound to exist between the domains of sociology and those of social psychology. The major difference is that sociology, rather than focusing on the psychology of the individual, looks toward society at large. So while sociologists are also interested in aggression, sociologists are more likely to be concerned with why a particular *society* (or *group* within a society) produces different levels of aggression in its members. Why, for example, is the murder rate in the United States so much higher than in Canada? Within the United States, why is the murder rate higher in some social classes than in others? How do changes in society relate to changes in aggressive behavior?

The difference between social psychology and other social sciences in level of analysis reflects another difference between the disciplines: what they are trying to explain. *The goal of social psychology is to identify universal properties of human nature that make everyone susceptible to social influence, regardless of social class or culture.* The laws governing the relationship between frustration and aggression, for example, are hypothesized to be true of most people in most places, not just members of one social class, age group, or race.

Social psychology is a young science that developed mostly in the United States; many of its findings have not yet been tested in other cultures to see if they are universal. Nonetheless, our goal as social psychologists is to discover such laws. And increasingly, as methods and theories developed by American social psychologists are adopted by European, Asian, African, Middle Eastern, and South American social psychologists, we are learning more about the extent to which these laws are universal. This type of cultural expansion is extremely valuable because it sharpens theories, either by demonstrating their universality or by leading us to discover additional variables whose incorporation will ultimately help us make more accurate predictions of human social behavior. We will encounter several examples of such cross-cultural research in subsequent chapters.

In sum, social psychology is located between its closest cousins, sociology and personality psychology (see Table 1.1). Social psychology and sociology share an interest in the way the situation and the larger society influence behavior. But social psychologists focus more on the psychological makeup of individuals *that renders people suscepti-*

TABLE 1.1	Social Psychology Compared to Related Disciplines	
Sociology	**Social Psychology**	**Personality Psychology**
Provides general laws and theories about societies, not individuals.	Studies the psychological processes people have in common with one another that make them susceptible to social influence.	Studies the characteristics that make individuals unique and different from one another.

ble to social influence. And although social psychology and personality psychology both emphasize the psychology of the individual rather than focusing on what makes people different from one another, social psychology emphasizes the *psychological processes* shared by most people that make them susceptible to social influence.

The Power of Social Influence 社会影响的威力

When trying to convince people that their behavior is greatly influenced by the social environment, the social psychologist is up against a formidable barrier: All of us tend to explain people's behavior in terms of their personalities. This barrier is known as the **fundamental attribution error**—the tendency to explain our own and other people's behavior entirely in terms of personality traits, thereby underestimating the power of social influence.

Underestimating the Power of Social Influence
低估社会影响的力量

When we underestimate the power of social influence, we gain a feeling of false security. For example, when trying to explain repugnant or bizarre behavior, such as the people of Jonestown, Waco, or Heaven's Gate taking their own lives or killing their own children, it is tempting and, in a strange way, comforting to write off the victims as flawed human beings. Doing so gives the rest of us the feeling that it could never happen to us. Ironically, this in turn increases our personal vulnerability to possibly destructive social influences by making us less aware of our own susceptibility to social psychological processes. Moreover, by failing to fully appreciate the power of the situation, we tend to oversimplify complex situations; oversimplification decreases our understanding of the causes of a great deal of human behavior. Among other things, this oversimplification can lead us to blame the victim in situations where the individual was overpowered by social forces too difficult for most of us to resist, as in the Jonestown tragedy.

To take a more mundane example, imagine a situation in which people are playing a two-person game wherein each player must choose one of two strategies: They can play competitively and try to win as much money as possible and make sure their partner loses as much as possible, or they can play cooperatively and try to make sure both they and their partner win some money. We will discuss the details of this game in Chapter 9. For now, just consider that there are only two basic strategies to use when playing the game—competition or cooperation. How do you think each of your friends would play this game?

Few people find this question hard to answer; we all have a feeling for the relative competitiveness of our friends. "Well," you might say, "I am certain that my friend Jennifer, who is a hardnosed business major, would play this game more competitively than my friend Anna, who is a really caring, loving person." That is, we think of our friends' personalities and answer accordingly. We usually do not think much about the nature of the social situation when making our predictions.

But how accurate are such predictions? Should we think about the social situation? To find out, Lee Ross and his students conducted the following experiment. They chose a group of students at Stanford University who were considered by the resident assistants in their dorm to be either especially cooperative or especially competitive. The researchers did this by describing the game to the resident assistants and asking them to think of students in their dormitories who would be most likely to adopt the competitive or cooperative strategy. As expected, the resident assistants easily identified students who fit each category.

Next, Ross invited these students to play the game in a psychology experiment. There was one added twist: The researchers varied a seemingly minor aspect of the social situation—what the game was called. They told half the participants that the name was the Wall Street Game and half that it was the Community Game. Everything else about the game was identical. Thus people who were judged as either

Fundamental Attribution Error
The tendency to overestimate the extent to which people's behavior is due to internal, dispositional factors, and to underestimate the role of situational factors

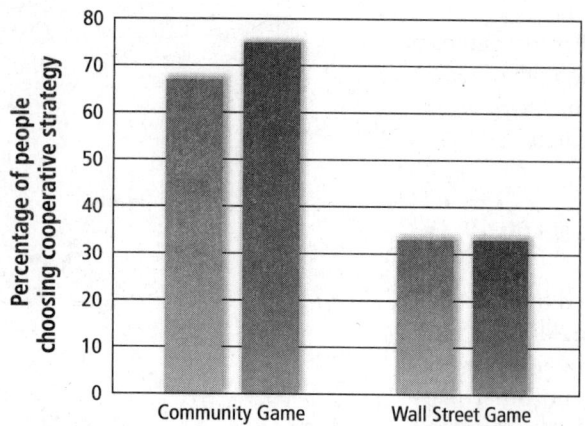

FIGURE 1.1
What influences how cooperative people will be—their personalities or the nature of the social situation?

(Adapted from Liberman, Samuels, & Ross, 2004)

competitive or cooperative played a game that was called either the Wall Street Game or the Community Game, resulting in four conditions.

Again, most of us go through life assuming that what really counts is an individual's personality, not something so trivial as what a game is called. Some people seem competitive by nature and would thus relish the opportunity to go head to head with a fellow student. Others seem much more cooperative and would thus achieve the most satisfaction by making sure no one lost too much money and no one's feelings were hurt. Right? Not so fast! As seen in Figure 1.1, even so trivial an aspect of the situation as the name of the game made a tremendous difference in how people behaved. When it was called the Wall Street Game, approximately two-thirds of the people responded competitively, whereas when it was called the Community Game, only a third of the people responded competitively. The name of the game sent a powerful message about how the players should behave. It alone conveyed strong social norms about what kind of behavior was appropriate in this situation. In Chapter 7, we will see that social norms can shape people's behaviors in powerful ways.

In this situation, a student's personality made no measurable difference in the student's behavior. The students labeled "competitive" were no more likely to adopt the competitive strategy than those who were labeled "cooperative." This pattern of results is one we will see throughout this book: Aspects of the social situation that may seem minor can have powerful effects, overwhelming the differences in people's personalities (Ross & Ward, 1996). This is not to say that personality differences do not exist or are unimportant; they do exist and frequently are of great importance. But we have learned that social and environmental situations are so powerful that they have dramatic effects on almost everyone. This is the domain of the social psychologist.

The Subjectivity of the Social Situation
社会情境的主观性

We have argued that the social situation often has profound effects on human behavior. But what exactly do we mean by the social situation? One strategy for defining it would be to specify the objective properties of the situation, such as how rewarding it is to people, and then document the behaviors that follow from these objective properties.

This was the approach taken by **behaviorism,** a school of psychology maintaining that to understand human behavior, one need only consider the reinforcing properties of the environment—that is, how positive and negative events in the environment are associated with specific behaviors. For example, dogs come when they are called because they have learned that compliance is followed by positive reinforcement (e.g., food or petting); children memorize their multiplication tables more quickly if you praise them, smile at them, and paste a gold star on their forehead following correct answers. Psychologists in this tradition, such as John Watson (1924) and B. F. Skinner (1938), suggested that all behavior could be understood by examining the rewards and punishments in the organism's environment and that there was no need to study such subjective states as thinking and feeling. Thus to understand the behavior of the Los Angeles residents who ignored their neighbor's predawn cries for help, a behaviorist would analyze the situation to see what specific, objective factors were inhibiting any attempts to help. What were the objective rewards and punishments implicit in taking a specific course of action? What were the rewards and punishments implicit in doing nothing?

Behaviorists chose not to deal with issues like cognition, thinking, and feeling because they considered these concepts too vague and mentalistic and not sufficiently anchored to observable behavior. Elegant in its simplicity, the behavioristic approach can account for a great deal of behavior. But because behaviorism does not deal with cognition, thinking, and feeling—phenomena vital to the human social experience—this approach has proved inadequate for a complete understanding of the social world. We

Behaviorism
A school of psychology maintaining that to understand human behavior, one need only consider the reinforcing properties of the environment—that is, how positive and negative events in the environment are associated with specific behaviors

have learned that social behavior cannot be fully understood by confining our observations to the physical properties of a situation. We need to look at the situation from the viewpoint of the people in it, to see how they construe the world around them (Griffin & Ross, 1991; Ross & Nisbett, 1991). For example, if a person approaches us, slaps us on the back, and asks us how we are feeling, is that rewarding or not? On the surface, it might seem like a reward. After all, isn't that person's interest in us a desirable thing? But in actuality, it is a complex situation that depends on our thoughts and feelings. We might construe the meaning differently, depending on whether the question is asked by a close friend who is deeply concerned about our health, a casual acquaintance simply passing the time of day, or an automobile salesperson attempting to ingratiate himself so that he might sell us a used car. This would be the case even if the question were worded the same and asked in the same tone of voice. For example, in responding to the salesperson's question, we would be unlikely to describe the pains we've been having in our kidney—something we might do in response to our closest friend's inquiry.

The head monkey at Paris puts on a traveller's cap, and all the monkeys in America do the same.

—Henry David Thoreau

This emphasis on construal, the way people interpret the social situation, has its roots in an approach called **Gestalt psychology**. First proposed as a theory of how people perceive the physical world, Gestalt psychology holds that we should study the subjective way in which an object appears in people's minds (the gestalt, or whole) rather than the way in which the objective, physical attributes of the object combine. For example, one way to try to understand how people perceive a painting would be to break it down into its individual elements, such as the exact amounts of primary colors applied to the different parts of the canvas, the types of brush strokes used to apply the colors, and the different geometric shapes they form. We might then attempt to determine how these elements are combined by the perceiver to form an overall image of the painting. According to Gestalt psychologists, however, it is impossible to understand the way in which an object is perceived simply by studying these building blocks of perception. The whole is different from the sum of its parts. One must focus on the phenomenology of the perceiver—on how an object appears to people—instead of on the individual elements of the objective stimulus.

One of the early steps toward the Holocaust. In the 1930s a woman reads a government-sponsored storefront sign urging the German people to boycott Jewish businesses.

The Gestalt approach was formulated in Germany in the first part of the twentieth century by Kurt Koffka, Wolfgang Kohler, Max Wertheimer, and their students and colleagues. In the late 1930s, several of these psychologists emigrated to the United States to escape the Nazi regime and subsequently had such a major influence on American psychology that one astute observer remarked, "If I were required to name the one person who has had the greatest impact on the field, it would have to be Adolf Hitler" (Cartwright, 1979, p. 84).

Among the émigrés was Kurt Lewin, generally considered the founding father of modern experimental social psychology. As a young German-Jewish professor in the 1930s, Lewin experienced the anti-Semitism rampant in Nazi Germany. The experience profoundly affected his thinking, and once in the United States, Lewin's ideas helped shape American social psychology, directing it toward a deep interest in exploring the causes and cures of prejudice and ethnic stereotyping.

As a theorist, Lewin took the bold step of applying Gestalt principles beyond the perception of objects to social perception—how people perceive other people and their motives, intentions, and behaviors. Lewin was the first scientist to fully realize the importance of taking the perspective of the people in a social situation to see how they perceive the situation. Social psychologists soon began to focus on the importance of considering subjective situations (how they are construed by people). These early social psychologists and their key statements are presented on the following pages.

Such construals can be rather simple, as in the example of the question "How are you feeling?" discussed earlier. Other construals might appear simple but are in reality

Gestalt Psychology

A school of psychology stressing the importance of studying the subjective way in which an object appears in people's minds rather than the objective, physical attributes of the object

remarkably complex. For example, suppose Maria gives Shawn a kiss on the cheek at the end of their first date. How will Shawn respond to the kiss? We would say that it depends on how he construes the situation: Does he interpret it as a first step—a sign of awakening romantic interest on Maria's part? Or does he see it as an aloof, sisterly expression—a signal that Maria wants to be friends but nothing more? Or does he see it as a sign that Maria is interested in him but wants to proceed slowly in their developing relationship?

Were Shawn to misinterpret the situation, he might commit a serious blunder; he might turn his back on what could have been the love of his life—or he might express passion inappropriately. In either case, we believe that the best strategy for understanding Shawn's reaction would be to find a way to determine Shawn's construal of Maria's behavior rather than to dissect the objective nature of the kiss itself (its length, degree of pressure, etc.). But how are these construals formed? Stay tuned.

Where Construals Come From: Basic Human Motives 解读从何而来：人性的基本动机

Kurt Lewin: "If an individual sits in a room trusting that the ceiling will not come down, should only his 'subjective probability' be taken into account for predicting behavior or should we also consider the 'objective probability' of the ceiling's coming down as determined by engineers? To my mind, only the first has to be taken into account."

Archives of the History of American Psychology—The University of Akron

How will Shawn determine why Maria kissed him? If it is true that subjective and not objective situations influence people, we need to understand how people arrive at their subjective impressions of the world. What are people trying to accomplish when they interpret the social world? Again, we could address this question from the perspective of people's personalities. What is it about Shawn, including his upbringing, family background, and unique experiences, that makes him perceive the world the way he does? As we have seen, such a focus on individual differences in people's personalities, though valuable, misses what is usually of far greater importance: the effects of the social situation on people. To understand these effects, we need to understand the fundamental laws of human nature, common to all, that explain why we construe the social world the way we do.

We human beings are complex organisms; at any given moment, various intersecting motives underlie our thoughts and behaviors. Over the years, social psychologists have found that two of these motives are of primary importance: *the need to feel good about ourselves* and *the need to be accurate*. There are times when each of these motives pulls us in the same direction. Often, though, these motives tug us in opposite directions—where to perceive the world accurately requires us to face up to the fact that we have behaved foolishly or immorally.

Leon Festinger, one of social psychology's most innovative theorists, was quick to realize that it is precisely when these two motives tug in opposite directions that we can gain our most valuable insights into the workings of the human heart and mind. An example will clarify. Imagine you are the president of the United States and your country is engaged in a difficult and costly war in Southeast Asia. You have poured hundreds of billions of dollars into that war, and it has consumed tens of thousands of American lives as well as a great many more lives of innocent Vietnamese civilians. The war seems to be at a stalemate; no end is in sight. You frequently wake up in the middle of the night bathed in the cold sweat of conflict: On the one hand, you deplore all the carnage that is going on; on the other hand, you don't want to go down in history as the first American president to lose a war.

Some of your advisers tell you that they can see the light at the end of the tunnel—that if you intensify the bombing, the enemy will soon capitulate and the war will be over. This would be a great outcome for you: Not only will you have succeeded in achieving your military and political aims, but history will consider you to have been a great leader as well. Other advisers, however, believe that intensifying the bombing will only strengthen the enemy's resolve; they advise you to sue for peace (McNamara, 1995).

Which advisers are you likely to believe? As we shall see in Chapter 6, President Lyndon Johnson faced this exact dilemma. Not surprisingly, he chose to believe the advisers who suggested that he escalate the war, because if he could succeed in winning the war, he would justify his prior behavior as commander in chief; however, if he withdrew from Vietnam, he not only would go down in history as the first president to lose a war but also would have to justify the fact that all those lives and all that money had been spent in vain. This advice proved erroneous. Increasing the bombing did strengthen the enemy's resolve, thereby prolonging the war. As this example illustrates, the need for self-justification can fly in the face of the need to be accurate—and can have catastrophic consequences. Some might find it expedient to view the Vietnam war as irrelevant; others may find it instructive in understanding challenges facing the nation in the twenty-first century (see, for example, Draper, 2008; McClellan, 2008; Woodward, 2008).

The Self-Esteem Approach: The Need to Feel Good About Ourselves
自尊取向：保持良好自我感觉的需要

Fritz Heider: "Generally, a person reacts to what he thinks the other person is perceiving, feeling, and thinking, in addition to what the other person may be doing."
Archives of the History of American Psychology—The University of Akron

Most people have a strong need to maintain reasonably high **self-esteem**—that is, to see themselves as good, competent, and decent (Aronson, 1998, 2007; Baumeister, 1993; Tavris & Aronson, 2007). The reason people view the world the way they do can often be traced to this underlying need to maintain a favorable image of themselves. Given the choice between distorting the world to feel good about themselves and representing the world accurately, people often take the first option.

Justifying Past Behavior Suppose that a couple gets divorced after ten years of a marriage made difficult by the husband's irrational jealousy. Rather than admitting the truth—that his jealousy and possessiveness drove her away—the husband blames the breakup of his marriage on the fact that his ex-wife was not responsive enough to his needs. His interpretation serves some purpose: It makes him feel better about himself. Acknowledging major deficiencies in ourselves is very difficult, even when the cost is seeing the world inaccurately. The consequence of this distortion, of course, is that learning from experience becomes very unlikely. In his next marriage, the husband is likely to run into the same problems.

We do not mean to imply that people totally distort reality, denying the existence of all information that reflects badly on them; such extreme behavior is rare outside of mental institutions. Yet it is often possible for normal people to put a slightly different spin on the existing facts, one that puts them in the best possible light. Consider Roger; everybody knows someone like Roger. He's the guy whose shoes are almost always untied and who frequently has coffee stains on the front of his shirt or mustard stains around his lips. Most observers might consider Roger a slob, but Roger might see himself as casual and noncompulsive.

The fact that people distort their interpretation of reality so that they feel better about themselves is not surprising, even to the most casual observer of human behavior. But the ways in which this motive operates are often startling. More important, an understanding of this phenomenon can shed a great deal of light on some otherwise mystifying thoughts and actions.

Leon Festinger: "The way I have always thought about it is that if the empirical world looks complicated, if people seem to react in bewilderingly different ways to similar forces, and if I cannot see the operation of universal underlying dynamics, then that is my fault. I have asked the wrong questions; I have, at a theoretical level, sliced up the world incorrectly. The underlying dynamics are there, and I have to find the theoretical apparatus that will enable me to reveal these uniformities."

Suffering and Self-Justification Let's go back to one of our early scenarios: the case of Oscar and his son, Sam. Why was Sam less enamored of his fraternity brothers than Oscar had been when he was in college? Recall that Oscar quickly formed the hypothesis that perhaps his fraternity was not attracting the kinds of wonderful people who were there when he was in college. This might be true. But we would assert that a far more compelling explanation involves the hazing itself. Specifically, we would contend that a major factor that increased Oscar's liking for his fraternity brothers was the degrading hazing ritual he underwent, a ritual Sam was able to avoid. That sounds a little strange. Why would something so negative cause Oscar to like his fraternity? Didn't behavioristic psychology teach us that rewards, not punishments, make us like things associated with them? Quite so. But as we indicated earlier, in recent years social psychologists have discovered that this formulation is far too simple to account for human thinking and motivation. Unlike rats and pigeons, human beings have a need to justify their past behavior, and this need leads them to thoughts, feelings, and behaviors that don't always fit into the simple categories of the behaviorist.

Self-Esteem

People's evaluations of their own self-worth—that is, the extent to which they view themselves as good, competent, and decent

Doing silly or dangerous things as part of fraternity hazing may be, well, silly or dangerous. At the same time, it does build cohesiveness.

Here's how it works. If Oscar goes through a severe hazing to become a member of the fraternity but later discovers unpleasant things about his fraternity brothers, he will feel like a fool: "Why did I go through all that pain and embarrassment to live in a house with a bunch of jerks? Only a moron would do a thing like that." To avoid feeling like a fool, he will try to justify his decision to undergo the hazing by distorting his interpretation of his fraternity experience. In other words, he will try to put a positive spin on his experiences.

Suppose that having gone through all that hazing, Oscar moves into the fraternity house and begins to experience things that to an outside observer are not very positive: The fraternity dues make a significant dent in Oscar's budget; the frequent parties seem frivolous and take a toll on the amount of studying he can do, and consequently his grades begin to suffer; most of the meals served in the house are only a small step up from dog chow. Whereas an unmotivated observer—someone who didn't go through the hazing—might consider these experiences rather negative, Oscar is motivated to see them differently; indeed, he considers them a small price to pay for the sense of brotherhood he feels toward his fraternity mates. He focuses on the good parts of living in the fraternity, and he distorts or dismisses the bad parts as inconsequential. The result of all this self-justification is bound to make Oscar more kindly disposed toward the fraternity and its members than Sam was, because Sam, not having gone through the hazing, had no need to justify his behavior and thus no need to see his fraternity experiences in a positive light. The end result? Oscar loved his fraternity; Sam did not.

Does this sound far-fetched? How do we know that the people in the fraternity were not objectively nicer when Oscar was a member than when Sam was a member? In a series of well-controlled laboratory experiments, social psychologists have investigated the phenomenon of hazing, holding constant everything in the situation, including the precise behavior of the fraternity members—except for the severity of the hazing students underwent in order to become members. These experiments demonstrated conclusively that the more unpleasant the procedure the participants underwent to get into a group, the better they liked the group—even though, objectively, the group members were the same people behaving in the same manner (Aronson & Mills, 1959; Gerard & Mathewson, 1966). We discuss this phenomenon more thoroughly in Chapter 6. The important points to remember here are that human beings are motivated to maintain a positive picture of themselves, in part by justifying their past behavior, and that under certain specifiable conditions, this leads them to do things that at first glance might seem surprising or paradoxical. For example, they might prefer people and things for whom they have suffered to people and things they associate with ease and pleasure.

Again, we want to emphasize that the results of this research tradition should not be taken to mean that behaviorist theories are dead wrong; those theories explain some behavior very well (see our discussion in Chapter 10 of the research on social exchange theory). In our view, however, behavioristic approaches are inadequate to account for a huge subset of important attitudes and behaviors. This will become much clearer as you read on. In future chapters, we will try to specify the precise conditions under which one or the other set of principles is more likely to apply.

The Social Cognition Approach: The Need to Be Accurate
社会认知取向：对准确性的需求

As we've seen, even when people are bending the facts to see themselves in as favorable a way as they can, they do not completely distort reality. It would not be very adaptive to live in a fantasy world, believing that the car speeding toward us as we step off the curb is really a mirage or that our future spouse will be Keira Knightley or Kanye West, who will soon give up performing and arrive at our doorstep. In fact, human beings are quite skilled at thinking, contemplating, and deducing. One of the major hallmarks of being human is the ability to reason. As a species, we have highly developed logical and computational abilities that are truly amazing. In our lifetime alone, we have witnessed such extraordinary cognitive achievements as the invention and development of computers, the exploration of outer space, and the conquering of many human diseases.

Moreover, on a more common (but perhaps more important) level, it is impossible to observe the cognitive development of a child without being awestruck. Just think of the vast gains in knowledge and reasoning that occur in the first few years of life. In a relatively short time, we see our child transform from a squirming, helpless newborn who can do little but eat, cry, and sleep into a sophisticated, garrulous 4-year-old who can utter complex sentences, hatch diabolical plots to frustrate a younger sibling, and evoke both consternation and pride in parents.

Social Cognition Given the amazing cognitive abilities of our species, it makes sense that social psychologists, when formulating theories of social behavior, would take into consideration the way in which human beings think about the world. We call this the cognitive approach to social psychology, or **social cognition** (Fiske & Taylor, 1991; Markus & Zajonc, 1985; Nisbett & Ross, 1980). Researchers who attempt to understand social behavior from the perspective of social cognition begin with the assumption that all people try to view the world as accurately as possible. Accordingly, human beings are viewed by researchers as amateur sleuths who are doing their best to understand and predict their social world.

But this is by no means easy, because we almost never know all the facts we need to accurately judge a given situation. Whether it is a relatively simple decision, such as which breakfast cereal offers the best combination of healthfulness and tastiness, or a slightly more complex decision, such as our desire to buy the best car we can for under $18,000, or a much more complex decision, such as choosing a marriage partner who will make us deliriously happy for the rest of our lives, it is almost never easy to gather all the relevant facts in advance. Moreover, we make countless decisions every day. Even if there were a way to gather all the facts for each decision, we simply lack the time or the stamina to do so.

Does this sound a bit overblown? Aren't most decisions fairly easy? Let's take a closer look. We will begin by asking you a simple question: Which breakfast cereal is better for you, Lucky Charms or 100% Natural from Quaker? If you are like most of our students, you answered "100% Natural from Quaker." After all, everybody knows that Lucky Charms is a kids' cereal, full of sugar and cute little marshmallows, with a picture of a leprechaun on the box. Quaker's 100% Natural has a picture of raw wheat on the box, the box is the color of natural wheat (light tan), and doesn't *natural* mean "good for you"? If that's the way you reasoned, you have fallen into a common cognitive trap—you have generalized from the cover to the product. A careful reading of the ingredients (in small print on the package) will reveal that although Lucky Charms has a bit more sugar in it than 100% Natural, the latter contains far more fat—so much so that *Consumer Reports* magazine ranked it a less healthful choice than Lucky Charms. Even in the simple world of cereals, things are not always what they seem.

Expectations about the Social World To add to the difficulty, sometimes our expectations about the social world interfere with perceiving it accurately. Our expectations can even change the *nature* of the social world. Imagine, for example, that you are an elementary school teacher dedicated to improving the lives of your students. At the beginning of the academic year, you review each student's standardized intelligence test scores. Early in your career, you were pretty sure, but not entirely sure, that these tests could gauge each child's true potential. But after several years of teaching, you have gradually become certain that these tests are accurate. Why the change? You have come to see that almost invariably, the kids who got high scores on these tests are the ones who did the best in your classroom, and the kids who got low scores performed poorly in class.

This scenario doesn't sound all that surprising, except for one key fact: You might be very wrong about the validity of the intelligence tests. It might be that the tests weren't very accurate but that you unintentionally treated the kids with high scores and the kids with low scores differently, making it look as if the tests were accurate. This is exactly what Robert Rosenthal and Lenore Jacobson (1968) found in their

Social Cognition
How people think about themselves and the social world; more specifically, how people select, interpret, remember, and use social information to make judgments and decisions

investigation of a phenomenon called the *self-fulfilling prophecy*. They entered elementary school classrooms and administered a test. They then informed each teacher that according to the test, a few specific students were "bloomers" who were about to take off and perform extremely well. In actuality, the test showed no such thing. The children labeled as bloomers were chosen at random by drawing names out of a hat and thus were no different, on average, from any of the other kids. Lo and behold, on returning to the classroom at the end of the school year, Rosenthal and Jacobson found that the bloomers were performing extremely well. The mere fact that the teachers were led to expect these students to do well caused an improvement in their performance. This striking phenomenon is no fluke; it has been replicated a number of times in a wide variety of schools (Rosenthal, 1995).

How did it come about? Although this outcome seems almost magical, it is embedded in an important aspect of human nature. If you were one of those teachers and were led to expect two or three specific students to perform well, you would be more likely to treat those students in special ways—paying more attention to them, listening to them with more respect, calling on them more frequently, encouraging them, and trying to teach them more challenging material. This, in turn, would almost certainly make these students feel happier, more respected, more motivated, and smarter, and—*voilà*—the prophecy is fulfilled. Thus even when we are trying to perceive the social world as accurately as we can, there are many ways in which we can go wrong, ending up with the wrong impressions. We will see why—and the conditions under which social perception is accurate—in Chapters 3 and 4.

Additional Motives 其他动机

We want to reiterate what we stated earlier: The two major sources of construals we have emphasized here—the need to maintain a positive view of ourselves (the self-esteem approach) and the need to view the world accurately (the social cognition approach)—are the most important of our social motives, but they are certainly not the only motives influencing people's thoughts and behaviors. Under various conditions, a variety of motives influence what we think, feel, and do. Biological drives such as hunger and thirst, of course, can be powerful motivators, especially under circumstances of extreme deprivation. At a more psychological level, we can be motivated by fear or by the promise of love, favors, and other rewards involving social exchange. These motives will be discussed at length in Chapters 10 and 11.

Still another significant motive is the need for control. Research has shown that people need to feel they exert some control over their environment (Langer, 1975; Taylor, 1989; Thompson, 1981). When people experience a loss of control, such that they believe they have little or no influence over whether good or bad things happen to them, there are a number of important consequences, which we will discuss further along in this book.

Social Psychology and Social Problems
社会心理学与社会问题

To recapitulate, social psychology can be defined as the scientific study of social influence. Social influence can best be understood by focusing on the major causes of human social behavior. It might have occurred to you to ask why we want to understand social influence in the first place. Who cares? And what difference does it make whether a behavior has its roots in the desire to be accurate or in the desire to bolster our self-esteem?

There are several answers to these questions. The most basic answer is simple: We are curious. Social psychologists are fascinated by human social behavior and want to understand it on the deepest possible level. In a sense, all of us are social psychologists. We all live in a social environment, and we are all more than mildly curious about such issues as how we become influenced, how we influence others, and why we fall in love with some people, dislike others, and are indifferent to still others.

Many social psychologists have another reason for studying the causes of social behavior: to contribute to the solution of social problems. From the very beginning of our young science, social psychologists have been keenly interested in such social challenges as reducing violence and prejudice and increasing altruism and tolerance. Contemporary social psychologists have continued this tradition and have broadened the issues of concern to include such endeavors as inducing people to conserve natural resources like water and energy (Dickerson, Thibodeau, Aronson, & Miller, 1992), educating people to practice safer sex in order to reduce the spread of AIDS (Aronson, 1997, 1998; Stone, 1994), understanding the relationship between viewing violence on television and the violent behavior of television watchers (Eron, 1996), developing effective negotiation strategies for the reduction of international conflict (Kelman, 1997; Ross, 2004), finding ways to reduce racial prejudice (Aronson & Patnoe, 1997), and reducing the high school dropout rate of minority students (Aronson, in press).

Social psychology can help us study, and potentially solve, social problems, such as whether watching violent television shows produces aggressive and violent behavior in children and the means by which this may happen.

The ability to understand and explain complex and dysfunctional social behavior brings with it the challenge to change it. For example, when our government began to take the AIDS epidemic seriously, it mounted an advertising campaign that seemed intent on frightening people into practicing safer sex. This seems consistent with common sense: If you want people to do something they wouldn't ordinarily do, why not scare the daylights out of them?

This is not a stupid idea. As we shall see in subsequent chapters, there are many dysfunctional acts (e.g., cigarette smoking, drunk driving) for which the induction of fear can and does motivate people to take rational, appropriate action to preserve their health (Aronson, 2009; Levy-Leboyer, 1988; Wilson, Purdon, & Wallston, 1988). But based on years of systematic research on persuasion, social psychologists were quick to realize that in the specific situation of AIDS, arousing fear would almost certainly not produce the desired effect for most people. The weight of the research evidence suggests that where sexual behavior is involved, the situation becomes murky. Specifically, most people do not want to be thinking about dying or contracting a horrible illness while they are getting ready to have sex. Such thoughts can, to say the least, interfere with the romantic aspect of the situation. Moreover, most people do not enjoy using condoms, because they feel that interrupting the sexual act to put on a condom tends to diminsh the mood. Given these considerations, when people have been exposed to frightening messages, instead of engaging in rational problem-solving behavior, most tend to reduce that fear by engaging in denial ("It can't happen to me," "Surely none of my friends have AIDS," etc.).

You may have figured out that the process of denial stems not from the desire to be accurate, but from the need to maintain one's self-esteem. If people can succeed in convincing themselves that their sexual partners do not have AIDS, they can continue to enjoy unprotected sex while maintaining a reasonably favorable picture of themselves as rational beings. By understanding how this process works, social psychologists have been able to contribute important insights to AIDS education and prevention, as we shall see (Aronson, 1997; Aronson, Fried, & Stone, 1991; Stone et al., 1994).

Throughout this book, we will examine many similar examples of the applications of social psychology. Likewise, throughout this book, we will also discuss some of the underlying human motives and the qualities of the social situation that produce significant social behaviors, with the assumption that if we are interested in changing our own or other people's behavior, we must first know something about these fundamental causes. Although most of the studies discussed in these chapters are concerned with such fundamental causes, they also address critical social problems, including the effects of the mass media on attitudes and behavior (Chapter 7), violence and aggression (Chapter 12), and prejudice (Chapter 13). For the benefit of interested readers, we have also included three separate "modules" centering on the application of social psychology to contemporary issues involving health, the environment, and law. Your instructor may assign them at any time during the semester or may decide not to assign them at all, leaving that decision to your own curiosity.

HOW WOULD YOU USE THIS? 如何学以致用？
像一个社会心理学家一样思考

Thinking Like a Social Psychologist

You're consulting for the Department of Defense. During a brainstorming session General Smith presents an idea for attracting new recruits to the Army. His notion is to make boot camp more appealing: While keeping the training rigorous, the idea is to make the living conditions more comfortable (air conditioning, gourmet food, comfortable beds). You realize that although on the surface this sounds like a good idea, there may be some unintended consequences regarding the cohesiveness and comradery within each platoon. What might these unintended consequences be? Hint: Consider the example of Oscar, Sam, and Delta Nu.

Summary 总 结

- **What Is Social Psychology?** The scientific study of the way in which people's thoughts, feelings, and behaviors are influenced by the real or imagined presence of other people. Social psychologists are interested in understanding how and why the social environment shapes the thoughts, feelings, and behaviors of the individual.
  - **The Power of Social Interpretation.** To understand social influence it is more important to understand how people *perceive and interpret* the social world than it is to understand that world objectively. The term *construal* refers to the world as it is interpreted by the individual.
  - **How Else Can We Understand Social Influence?** Social psychologists approach the understanding of social influence differently than philosophers, journalists, or the layperson. Social psychologists develop explanations of social influence through experiments in which the variables being studied are carefully controlled.
  - **Social Psychology Compared with Personality Psychology.** When trying to explain social behavior—how an individual acts within a social context (in relation to others)—personality psychologists explain the behavior in terms of the person's individual character traits. Although social psychologists would agree that personalities do vary, they explain social behavior in terms of the *power of the social situation* (as it is construed by the individual) to shape how one acts.
  - **Social Psychology Compared with Sociology.** A fundamental way in which the two disciplines vary is in their *level of analysis*. Social psychology is rooted in the study of the individual's internal psychological processes; *the level of analysis for social psychology is the individual in the context of a social situation.* In contrast, sociologists focus their analysis on groupings of people organized in social categories such as family, race, religion, and economic class. While sociologists aim to study larger social processes like historical and political changes or how larger social structures (race, class, gender, sexual orientation) shape an individual's life chances, the orientation of the social psychologist is on the internal processes that take place within individuals. Social psychologists seek to identify universal *properties of human nature* that make everyone susceptible to social influence regardless of social class or culture. Sociologists seek to explain *properties of societies*.

- **The Power of Social Influence.** Social psychologists have discovered, through rigorous empirical research, that individual behavior is powerfully influenced by the social environment.
  - **Underestimating the Power of Social Influence.** People tend to explain behavior in terms of individual personality traits and underestimate the power of social influence in shaping individual behavior. Social psychological researchers have shown time and again that social and environmental situations are usually more powerful than personality differences in determining an individual's behavior.
  - **The Subjectivity of the Social Situation.** Human beings are sense-making creatures; they are constantly interpreting things. How humans will behave in a given situation is not determined by the objective conditions of a situation but rather, how they perceive it (construal).

- **Where Construals Come From: Basic Human Motives.** The way in which an individual construes (perceives, comprehends, and interprets) a situation is largely shaped by the two basic *human motives: the need to be accurate* and *the need to feel good about ourselves*. At times these two motives tug in opposite directions; for example, when an accurate view of how we acted in a situation would reveal that we behaved selfishly.
  - **The Self-Esteem Approach: The Need to Feel Good about Ourselves.** Most people have a strong need to see themselves as good, competent, and decent. People often distort their perception of the world to preserve their self-esteem.

- **The Social Cognition Approach: The Need to Be Accurate.** The social cognition perspective is an approach to social psychology that takes into account the way in which human beings think about the world: Individuals are viewed as trying to gain accurate understandings so that they can make effective judgments and decisions that range from which cereal to eat to whom they will marry. In actuality, individuals typically act on the basis of incomplete and inaccurately interpreted information.
- **Additional Motives.** In addition to the two primary motives—the need to be accurate and the need to maintain a positive view of ourselves—there are several others that influence people. Among these additional motives are biological drives, the desire for rewards, and the need for control.
- **Social Psychology and Social Problems.** Social psychological theories about human behavior have been applied effectively to deal with a range of contemporary problems that include prejudice, energy shortages, the spread of AIDS, unhealthy habits, and violence in the schools. When recommending interventions to deal with serious social problems, it is imperative to act on the basis of scientifically grounded theories about human construal and behavior.

CHAPTER 1 TEST 第1章习题

1. The topic that would most interest a social psychologist is
   a. whether people who commit crimes tend to have more aggressive personalities than people who do not.
   b. whether people who commit crimes have different genes from people who do not.
   c. how the level of extroversion of different presidents affected their political decisions.
   d. whether people's decision about whether to cheat on a test is influenced by how they imagine their friends would react if they found out.
   e. the extent to which a person's social class predicts their income.

2. How does social psychology differ from personality psychology?
   a. Social psychology focuses on individual differences, whereas personality psychology focuses on how people behave in different situations.
   b. Social psychology focuses on the processes that people have in common with one another that make them susceptible to social influence, whereas personality psychology focuses on individual differences.
   c. Social psychology provides general laws and theories about societies, not individuals, whereas personality psychology studies the characteristics that make people unique and different from each other.
   d. Social psychology focuses on individual differences, whereas personality psychology provides general laws and theories about societies, not individuals

3. A stranger approaches Emily on campus and says he is a professional photographer. He asks if she will spend 15 minutes posing for pictures next to the student union. According to a social psychologist, Emily's decision will depend on which of the following?
   a. How well-dressed the man is.
   b. Whether the man offers to pay her.
   c. How Emily construes the situation.
   d. Whether the man has a criminal record.

4. Researchers who try to understand human behavior from the perspective of *social cognition* assume that
   a. people try to view the world as accurately as possible.
   b. people almost always view the world accurately.
   c. people almost always make mistakes in how they view the world.
   d. people distort reality in order to view themselves favorably.
   e. the need for control is the most important motive behind a person's behavior.

5. The *fundamental attribution error* is best defined as the tendency to
   a. explain our own and other people's behavior entirely in terms of personality traits, thereby underestimating the power of social influence.
   b. explain our own and other people's behavior in terms of the social situation, thereby underestimating the power of personality factors.
   c. believe that people's group memberships influence their behavior more than their personalities.
   d. believe that people's personalities influence their behavior more than their group memberships.

6. Which of the following is least consistent with the *self-esteem approach* to how people view themselves and the social world?
   a. After Sarah leaves Bob for someone else, Bob decides that he never really liked her very much and that she had several annoying habits.
   b. Students who want to take Prof. Lopez's seminar have to apply by writing a 10-page essay. Everyone who is selected ends up loving the class.
   c. Janetta did poorly on the first test in her psychology class. She admits to herself that she didn't study very much and vows to study harder for the next test.
   d. Sam has been involved in several minor traffic accidents since getting his driver's license. "There sure are a lot of terrible drivers out there," he says to himself. "People should learn to be good drivers like me."

Answer Key
1-d, 2-b, 3-c, 4-a, 5-a, 6-c

For more review plus practice tests, videos, flashcards, writing help and more, log on to MyPsychLab.

2

Methodology
How Social Psychologists Do Research
方法论：
社会心理学家如何进行研究

IN THIS INFORMATION AGE, WHEN PRETTY MUCH ANYTHING can be found on the Internet, pornography is more available than ever before. And not just on-line: One industry insider, Paul Fishbein, estimates that people rent 800 million adult movies from video stores each year. "And I don't think that it's 800 guys renting a million tapes each," he said ("Porn in the USA," 2004). It is thus important to ask whether exposure to pornography has harmful effects. Is it possible, for example, that looking at graphic sex increases the likelihood that men will become sexually violent?

There has been plenty of debate on both sides of this question. Legal scholar Catharine MacKinnon (1993) argued that "Pornography is the perfect preparation—motivator and instruction manual in one—for . . . sexual atrocities" (p. 28). In 1985 a group of experts, appointed by the attorney general of the United States, voiced a similar opinion, concluding that pornography is a cause of rape and other violent crimes. But in 1970 another commission reviewed much of the same evidence and concluded that pornography does *not* contribute significantly to sexual violence. Whom are we to believe? One national newsmagazine polls its readers about various psychological questions, such as the effects of pornography. But is this a case where majority opinion rules, or is there a more scientific way to determine the answer? We believe there is, and in this chapter we will discuss the kinds of research methods social psychologists use, using research on pornography as an example.

We will also use another example, this one having to do not with the causes of violence, but how people react to it when they see it. If you happen to witness someone being attacked by another person, you might not intervene directly out of fear for your own safety. Most of us assume that we would help in some way, though, such as by calling the police. It is because of this very assumption that people were shocked by an incident that occurred in the early 1960s. A woman named Kitty Genovese was brutally murdered in the alley of an apartment complex in Queens, New York. The attack lasted 45 minutes. No fewer than 38 of the apartment residents admitted later that they had rushed to their windows after hearing Genovese's screams for help. Not one attempted to help her—no one even bothered to telephone the police. For weeks after the crime, reporters, commentators, and critics of all kinds expressed their personal theories about why the bystanders had done nothing. Most agreed that living in a metropolis dehumanizes us and leads inevitably to apathy, indifference to human suffering, and lack of caring. New York and New Yorkers were to blame, concluded the observers; this kind of thing would not have happened in a small town, where people care more about each

OUTLINE 提 纲

- Social Psychology: An Empirical Science
- Formulating Hypotheses and Theories
  - Inspiration from Earlier Theories and Research
  - Hypotheses Based on Personal Observations
- The Observational Method: Describing Social Behavior
  - Archival Analysis
  - Limits of the Observational Method
- The Correlational Method: Predicting Social Behavior
  - Surveys
  - CONNECTIONS: Random Selection in Political Polls
  - Limits of the Correlational Method: Correlation Does Not Equal Causation
- The Experimental Method: Answering Causal Questions
  - Independent and Dependent Variables
  - Internal Validity in Experiments
  - External Validity in Experiments
  - Basic Versus Applied Research
- New Frontiers in Social Psychological Research
  - Culture and Social Psychology
  - The Evolutionary Approach
  - Social Neuroscience
- Ethical Issues in Social Psychology
  - Guidelines for Ethical Research
- Summary

other (Rosenthal, 1964). Is this true? Did big-city life cause the bystanders to ignore Kitty Genovese's screams for help, or was there some other explanation? How can we find out?

Social Psychology: An Empirical Science
社会心理学：一门实证科学

A fundamental principle of social psychology is that many social problems, like the causes of and reactions to violence, can be studied scientifically (Wilson, Aronson, & Carlsmith, in press; Reis & Judd, 2000). Before we discuss how social psychological research is done, we begin with a warning: The results of some of the experiments you encounter will seem obvious because social psychology concerns topics with which we are all intimately familiar—social behavior and social influence (Richard, Bond, & Stokes-Zoota, 2001). This familiarity sets social psychology apart from other sciences. When you read about an experiment in particle physics, it is unlikely that the results will connect with your personal experiences. We don't know about you, but we have never thought, "Wow! That experiment on quarks was just like what happened to me while I was waiting for the bus yesterday," or "My grandmother always told me to watch out for positrons and antimatter." When reading about the results of a study on helping behavior or aggression, however, it is quite common to think, "Come on. I could have predicted that. That's the same thing that happened to me last Friday."

> *I love games. I think I could be very happy being a chess player or dealing with some other kinds of games. But I grew up in the Depression. It didn't seem one could survive on chess, and science is also a game. You have very strict ground rules in science, and your ideas have to check out with the empirical world. That's very tough and also very fascinating.*
>
> —Leon Festinger, 1977

The thing to remember is that when we study human behavior, the results may appear to have been predictable—in retrospect. Indeed, there is a well-known human tendency called the **hindsight bias,** whereby people exaggerate how much they could have predicted an outcome *after* knowing that it occurred (Blank, Musch, & Pohl, 2007; Bradfield & Wells, 2005; Fischhoff, 2007; Sanna & Schwarz, 2007). After we know the winner of a political election, for example, we begin to look for reasons why that candidate won. After the fact, the outcome seems inevitable and easily predictable, even if we were quite unsure who would win before the election. The same is true of findings in psychology experiments; it seems like we could have easily predicted the outcomes—after we know them. The trick is to predict what will happen in an experiment before you know how it turned out. To illustrate what we mean when we say that not all obvious findings are easy to predict, take the quiz in the following Try It! exercise.

Social psychology is a scientific discipline with a well-developed set of methods to answer questions about social behavior, such as the ones about violence with which we began this chapter. These methods are of three types: the *observational method*, the *correlational method*, and the *experimental method*. Any of these methods could be used to explore a specific research question; each is a powerful tool in some ways and a weak tool in others. Part of the creativity in conducting social psychological research involves choosing the right method, maximizing its strengths, and minimizing its weaknesses.

In this chapter, we will discuss these methods in detail. We, the authors of this book, are social psychologists who have done a great deal of research. We will therefore try to provide you with a firsthand look at both the joy and the difficulty of conducting social psychological studies. The joy comes in unraveling the clues about the causes of interesting and important social behaviors, just as a sleuth gradually unmasks the culprit in a murder mystery. Each of us finds it exhilarating that we have the tools to provide definitive answers to questions philosophers have debated for centuries. At the same time, as seasoned researchers, we have learned to temper this exhilaration with a heavy dose of humility because the practical and ethical constraints involved in creating and conducting social psychological research are formidable.

Hindsight Bias
The tendency for people to exaggerate how much they could have predicted an outcome after knowing that it occurred

试一试！社会心理学小测试：你的预期是什么？
Social Psychology Quiz: What's Your Prediction?

Answer the following questions, each of which is based on social psychological research.

1. Suppose an authority figure asks college students to administer near-lethal electric shocks to another student who has not harmed them in any way. What percentage of these students will agree to do it?

2. If you give children a reward for doing something they already enjoy doing, they will subsequently like that activity (a) more, (b) the same, or (c) less.

3. Who do you think would be happiest with their choice of a consumer product, such as an art poster: (a) people who spend several minutes thinking about why they like or dislike each poster or (b) people who choose a poster without analyzing the reasons for their feelings?

4. Repeated exposure to a stimulus, such as a person, a song, or a painting, will make you like it (a) more, (b) the same, or (c) less.

5. You ask an acquaintance to do you a favor—for example, to lend you $10—and he or she agrees. As a result of doing you this favor, the person will probably like you (a) more, (b) the same, or (c) less.

6. When making a complex decision, is it best to (a) decide right away without any further thought, (b) think carefully about the different options, or (c) find something unrelated to distract you for awhile, then make up your mind.

7. In the United States, female college students tend not to do as well on math tests as males do. Under which of the following circumstances will women do as well as men: (a) when they are told that there are no gender differences on the test, (b) when they are told that women tend to do better on a difficult math test (because under these circumstances, they rise to the challenge), or (c) when they are told that men outperform women under almost all circumstances?

8. Which statement about the effects of advertising is most true? (a) Subliminal messages implanted in advertisements are more effective than normal, everyday advertising, (b) normal TV ads for painkillers or laundry detergents are more effective than subliminal messages implanted in ads, (c) both types of advertising are equally effective, or (d) neither type of advertising is effective.

9. In public settings in the United States, (a) women touch men more, (b) men touch women more, or (c) there is no difference—men and women touch each other equally.

10. Which things in their past do people regret the most: (a) things they did that they wish they hadn't done, (b) things they didn't do that they wish they had done, or (c) it depends on how long ago the events occurred?

See page 48 for the answers.

Formulating Hypotheses and Theories
假说和理论的形成

Research begins with a hunch, or hypothesis, that the researcher wants to test. There is a lore in science that brilliant insights come all of a sudden, as when Archimedes shouted, "Eureka! I have found it!" when the solution to a problem flashed into his mind. Although such insights do sometimes occur suddenly, science is a cumulative process, and people often generate hypotheses from previous theories and research.

Inspiration from Earlier Theories and Research
从过去的理论和研究成果中获得灵感

Many studies stem from a researcher's dissatisfaction with existing theories and explanations. After reading other people's work, a researcher might believe that he or she has a better way of explaining people's behavior (e.g., why they fail to help in an emergency). In the 1950s, for example, Leon Festinger was dissatisfied with the ability of a major theory of the day, behaviorism, to explain why people change their attitudes. He formulated a new approach—dissonance theory—that made specific predictions about when and how people would change their attitudes. As we will see in Chapter 6, other researchers were dissatisfied with Festinger's explanation of the results he obtained,

This is the area where Kitty Genovese was attacked, in full view of her neighbors. Why didn't anyone call the police?

and so they conducted further research to test other possible explanations. Social psychologists, like scientists in other disciplines, engage in a continual process of theory refinement: A theory is developed; specific hypotheses derived from that theory are tested; based on the results obtained, the theory is revised and new hypotheses are formulated.

Hypotheses Based on Personal Observations
以个人观察为依据建立假说

Social psychology deals with phenomena we encounter in everyday life. Researchers often observe something in their lives or the lives of others that they find curious and interesting, stimulating them to construct a theory about why this phenomenon occurred—and to design a study to see if they are right.

Consider the murder of Kitty Genovese that we described earlier. As we noted, most people blamed her neighbors' failure to intervene on the apathy, indifference, and callousness that big-city life breeds. Two social psychologists who taught at universities in New York, however, had a different idea. Bibb Latané and John Darley got to talking one day about the Genovese murder. Here is how Latané describes it: "One evening after [a] downtown cocktail party, John Darley . . . came back with me to my 12th Street apartment for a drink. Our common complaint was the distressing tendency of acquaintances, on finding that we called ourselves social psychologists, to ask why New Yorkers were so apathetic" (Latané, 1987, p. 78). Instead of focusing on "what was wrong with New Yorkers," Latané and Darley thought it would be more interesting and more important to examine the social situation in which Genovese's neighbors found themselves: "We came up with the insight that perhaps what made the Genovese case so fascinating was itself what made it happen—namely, that not just one or two, but 38 people had watched and done nothing" (Latané, 1987, p. 78).

The researchers had the hunch that, paradoxically, the more people who witness an emergency, the less likely it is that any given individual will intervene. Genovese's neighbors might have assumed that someone else had called the police, a phenomenon Latané and Darley (1968) referred to as the *diffusion of responsibility*. Perhaps the bystanders would have been more likely to help had each thought he or she alone was witnessing the murder.

After a researcher has a hypothesis, whether it comes from a theory, previous research, or an observation of everyday life, how can he or she tell if it is true? In science, idle speculation will not do; the researcher must collect data to test a hypothesis. Let's look at how the observational method, the correlational method, and the experimental method are used to explore research hypotheses such as Latané and Darley's (see Table 2.1).

TABLE 2.1	A Summary of Research Methods	
Method	Focus	Question Answered
Observational	Description	What is the nature of the phenomenon?
Correlational	Prediction	From knowing X, can we predict Y?
Experimental	Causality	Is variable X a cause of variable Y?

The Observational Method: Describing Social Behavior
观察法：描述社会行为

There is a lot to be learned by being an astute observer of human behavior. If the goal is to describe what a particular group of people or type of behavior is like, the **observational method** is very helpful. This is the technique whereby a researcher observes people and records measurements or impressions of their behavior. The observational method may take many forms, depending on what the researchers are looking for, how involved or detached they are from the people they are observing, and how much they want to quantify what they observe. One example is **ethnography**, the method by which researchers attempt to understand a group or culture by observing it from the inside, without imposing any preconceived notions they might have. The goal is to understand the richness and complexity of the group by observing it in action. Ethnography is the chief method of cultural anthropology, the study of human cultures and societies. As social psychology broadens its focus by studying social behavior in different cultures, ethnography is increasingly being used to describe different cultures and generate hypotheses about psychological principles (Fine & Elsbach, 2000; Hodson, 2004; Uzzel, 2000).

Consider this example from the early years of social psychological research. In the early 1950s, a group of people in the Midwest predicted that the world would come to an end in a violent cataclysm on a specific date. They also announced that they would be rescued in time by a spaceship that would land in their leader's backyard. Assuming that the end of the world was not imminent, Leon Festinger and his colleagues thought it would be interesting to observe this group closely and chronicle how they reacted when their beliefs and prophecy were disconfirmed (Festinger, Riecken, & Schachter, 1956). To monitor the hour-to-hour conversations of this group, the social psychologists found it necessary to join the group and pretend that they too believed the world was about to end.

The key to ethnography is to avoid as much as possible imposing one's preconceived notions in order to understand the point of view of the people being studied. Sometimes, however, researchers have a specific hypothesis that they want to test using the observational method. An investigator might be interested, for example, in how much aggression children exhibit during school recesses. In this case, the observer would be systematically looking for particular behaviors that are concretely defined before the observation begins. For example, aggression might be defined as hitting or shoving another child, taking a toy from another child without asking, and so on. The observer might stand at the edge of the playground and systematically record how often these behaviors occur. If the researcher were interested in exploring possible sex and age differences in social behavior, he or she would also note the child's gender and age. How do we know how accurate the observer is? In such studies, it is important to establish **interjudge reliability**, which is the level of agreement between two or more people who independently observe and code a set of data. By showing that two or more judges independently come up with the same observations, researchers ensure that the observations are not the subjective, distorted impressions of one individual.

Archival Analysis 档案分析法

The observational method is not limited to observations of real-life behavior. The researcher can also examine the accumulated documents, or archives, of a culture, a technique known as an **archival analysis** (Mullen, Rozell, & Johnson, 2001). For example, diaries, novels, suicide notes, popular music lyrics, television shows, movies, magazine and newspaper articles, and advertising all tell us a great deal about how a society views itself. Much like our example of aggression, specific, well-defined categories are created and then applied to the archival source. (See the following Try It! exercise.) Think back to the question of the relationship between pornography and

Observational Method
The technique whereby a researcher observes people and systematically records measurements or impressions of their behavior

Ethnography
The method by which researchers attempt to understand a group or culture by observing it from the inside, without imposing any preconceived notions they might have

Interjudge Reliability
The level of agreement between two or more people who independently observe and code a set of data; by showing that two or more judges independently come up with the same observations, researchers ensure that the observations are not the subjective, distorted impressions of one individual

Archival Analysis
A form of the observational method in which the researcher examines the accumulated documents, or archives, of a culture (e.g., diaries, novels, magazines, and newspapers)

试一试！档案分析：女性、男性和媒体
Archival Analysis: Women, Men, and the Media

Try doing your own archival analysis to see how women and men are portrayed in the media. Choose three or four magazines that focus on different topics and audiences, for example, a newsmagazine, a "women's" magazine such as *Cosmopolitan*, a "men's" magazine such as *GQ*, and a literary magazine such as the *New Yorker*. In each magazine, open the pages randomly until you find an advertisement that has at least one picture of a person in it. Repeat so that you look at two or three such ads in each magazine.

Make a note of how much of the image is devoted to the person's face and whether the person in the ad is a woman or a man. Specifically, place the picture of each person into one of these categories, depending on what part of the person you can see: (a) the entire body; (b) from the waist up, or (c) primarily the head and face. Were there differences in the way women and men are portrayed? If so, why do you think this is? Now turn to pages 48–49 to see how actual research of this sort turned out.

violence. One problem with addressing this question is in defining what pornography is. As Supreme Court Justice Potter Stewart put it, "I know it when I see it," but describing its exact content is not easy.

Archival analysis is a good tool for answering this question because it enables researchers to describe the content of documents present in the culture—in this case, the photographs and fictional stories that represent currently available pornography in the marketplace. One researcher, for example, studied the content of pornography in adults-only fiction paperback books sold at newsstands and regular bookstores (Smith, 1976). Another analyzed photographs posted on Internet Web sites (Mehta, 2001). One disturbing finding was that a lot of pornography involves the use of force (physical, mental, or blackmail) by a male to make a female engage in unwanted sex. Aggression against women is a major theme in some (though not all) pornography.

Observational research, in the form of archival analysis, can tell us a great deal about society's values and beliefs. The fact that sexual violence against women is common in pornography suggests that these images and stories appeal to many readers (Dietz & Evans, 1982; Gossett & Byrne, 2002) and leads to some disturbing questions: Is pornography associated with sexually violent crimes against women that occur in our society? Do reading and looking at pornography cause some men to commit violent sexual acts? To answer these questions, research methods other than archival analysis must be used. Later in this chapter, we will see how researchers have used the correlational method and the experimental method to address important questions about sexual violence against women.

Limits of the Observational Method 观察法的局限性

There are drawbacks to the observational method. Certain kinds of behavior are difficult to observe because they occur only rarely or only in private. For example, had Latané and Darley chosen the observational method to study the effects of the number of bystanders on people's willingness to help a victim, we might still be waiting for an answer, given the infrequency of emergencies and the difficulty of predicting when they will occur.

Instead, Latané and Darley might have used an archival analysis—for example, by examining newspaper accounts of violent crimes and noting the number of bystanders and how many offered assistance to the victim. Yet here too, the researchers would have quickly run into problems: Did each journalist mention how many bystanders were present? Was the number accurate? Were all forms of assistance noted in the newspaper article? Clearly, these are messy data. As is always the case with archival analysis, the researcher is at the mercy of the original compiler of the material; the journalists had different aims when they wrote their articles and may not have included all the information researchers would later need.

Perhaps most importantly, social psychologists want to do more than just describe behavior; they want to predict and explain it. To do so other methods are more appropriate.

The Correlational Method: Predicting Social Behavior
相关法：预测社会行为

A goal of social science is to understand relationships between variables and to be able to predict when different kinds of social behavior will occur. What is the relationship between the amount of pornography people see and their likelihood of engaging in sexually violent acts? Is there a relationship between the amount of violence children see on television and their aggressiveness? To answer such questions, researchers frequently use a different approach—the correlational method.

With the **correlational method**, two variables are systematically measured, and the relationship between them—how much you can predict one from the other—is assessed. People's behavior and attitudes can be measured in a variety of ways. Just as with the observational method, researchers sometimes make direct observations of people's behavior. For example, researchers might be interested in testing the relationship between children's aggressive behavior and how much violent television they watch. They too might observe children on the playground, but here the goal is to assess the relationship, or correlation, between the children's aggressiveness and other factors, like TV viewing habits, that the researchers also measure.

Correlational Method
The technique whereby two or more variables are systematically measured and the relationship between them (i.e., how much one can be predicted from the other) is assessed

30 Social Psychology

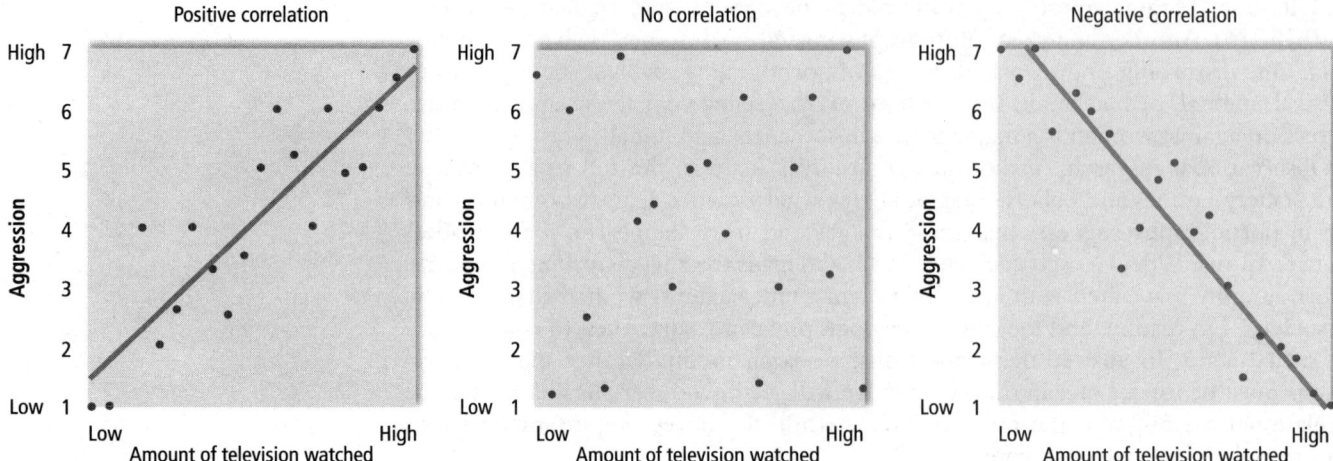

FIGURE 2.1
The correlation coefficient.

The diagrams show three possible correlations in a hypothetical study of watching violence on television and aggressive behavior in children. The diagram at the left shows a strong positive correlation: The more television children watched, the more aggressive they were. The diagram in the middle shows no correlation: The amount of television children watched is not related to how aggressive they were. The diagram at the right shows a strong negative correlation: The more television children watched, the less aggressive they were.

Correlation Coefficient

A statistical technique that assesses how well you can predict one variable from another—for example, how well you can predict people's weight from their height

Surveys

Research in which a representative sample of people are asked (often anonymously) questions about their attitudes or behavior

Random Selection

A way of ensuring that a sample of people is representative of a population by giving everyone in the population an equal chance of being selected for the sample

Researchers look at such relationships by calculating the **correlation coefficient,** a statistic that assesses how well you can predict one variable from another—for example, how well you can predict people's weight from their height. A positive correlation means that increases in the value of one variable are associated with increases in the value of the other variable. Height and weight are positively correlated; the taller people are, the more they tend to weigh. A negative correlation means that increases in the value of one variable are associated with decreases in the value of the other. If height and weight were negatively correlated in human beings, we would look very peculiar—short people, such as children, would look like penguins, whereas tall people, like NBA basketball players, would be all skin and bones! It is also possible, of course, for two variables to be completely unrelated, so that a researcher cannot predict one variable from the other (see Figure 2.1).

Surveys 调查法

The correlational method is often used in **surveys,** research in which a representative sample of people are asked questions about their attitudes or behavior. Surveys are a convenient way to measure people's attitudes; for example, people can be telephoned and asked which candidate they will support in an upcoming election or how they feel about a variety of social issues. Researchers often apply the correlational method to survey results to predict how people's responses to one question predict their other responses. Psychologists often use surveys to help understand social behavior and attitudes—for example, by seeing whether the amount of pornography men say they read is correlated with their attitudes toward women.

Surveys have a number of advantages, one of which is allowing researchers to judge the relationship between variables that are difficult to observe, such as how often people engage in safer sex. When the variables of interest cannot easily be observed, researchers rely on surveys, on which people are questioned about their beliefs, attitudes, and behaviors. The researcher looks at the relationship between the questions asked on the survey, such as whether people who know a lot about how AIDS is transmitted are more likely than other people to engage in safer sex.

Another advantage of surveys is the capability to sample representative segments of the population. Answers to a survey are useful only if they reflect the responses of people in general—not just the people actually tested (called the *sample*). Survey researchers go to great lengths to ensure that the people they test are typical. They select samples that are representative of the population on a number of characteristics important to a given research question (e.g., age, educational background, religion, gender, income level). They also make sure to use a **random selection** of people from the population at large, which is a way of ensuring that a sample of people is representative of a population by giving everyone in the population an equal chance of being selected for the sample. As long as the sample is selected randomly, we can assume that the responses are a reasonable match to those of the population as a whole.

A potential problem with survey data is the accuracy of the responses. Straightforward questions—regarding what people think about an issue or what they typically do—are relatively easy to answer. But asking survey participants to predict how they might behave in some hypothetical situation or to explain why they behaved as they did in the past is an invitation to inaccuracy (Schuman & Kalton, 1985; Schwarz, Groves, & Schuman, 1998). Often people simply don't know the answer—but they think they do. Richard Nisbett and Tim Wilson (1977) demonstrated this "telling more than you can know" phenomenon in a number of studies in which people often made inaccurate reports about why they responded the way they did. Their reports about the causes of their responses pertained more to their theories and beliefs about what should have influenced them than to what actually influenced them. (We discuss these studies at greater length in Chapter 5.)

CONNECTIONS 链 接

Random Selection in Political Polls
政治民意调查中的随机抽样

In the fall of 1936, a weekly magazine called *The Literary Digest* conducted a large survey asking people which candidate they planned to vote for in the upcoming presidential election. The magazine obtained the names and addresses of its sample from telephone directories and automobile registration lists. The results of its survey of 2 million people indicated that the Republican candidate, Alf Landon, would win by a landslide. Of course, you know that there never was a President Landon; instead, Franklin Delano Roosevelt won every state in the Union but two. What went wrong with *The Literary Digest* poll? In the depths of the Great Depression, many people could not afford telephones or cars. Those who had them were doing well financially; most well-to-do voters were Republican and overwhelmingly favored Alf Landon. However, the majority of the voters were not well off—and overwhelmingly supported the Democratic candidate, Roosevelt. By using a list of names that excluded the less affluent members of the population, *The Literary Digest* surveyed a nonrepresentative sample. (*The Literary Digest* never recovered from this methodological disaster and went out of business shortly after publishing its poll.)

Modern surveys and political polls are not immune from such sampling errors. During the 1984 presidential race, telephone polls conducted by Ronald Reagan's campaign staff found that Reagan had a comfortable lead over Walter Mondale—except when the polls were conducted on Friday nights. After an initial panic, they figured out that because Democrats are poorer, on average, than Republicans, they were less likely to be out at the movies or eating at restaurants on Friday nights and so were more likely to be at home when the pollsters called. Despite such notable glitches, or perhaps because of them, surveys have improved enormously over the years and can now accurately detect correlations between many interesting social variables (House et al., 2004; Visser, Krosnick, & Lavrakas, 2000).

Limits of the Correlational Method: Correlation Does Not Equal Causation
相关法的局限性：相关分析不等于因果分析

The major shortcoming of the correlational method is that it tells us only that two variables are related, whereas the goal of the social psychologist is to identify the *causes* of social behavior. We want to be able to say that A causes B, not just that A is correlated with B.

If a researcher finds that there is a correlation between two variables, it means that there are three possible causal relationships between these variables. For example, researchers have found a correlation between the amount of violent television children watch and how aggressive they are (similar to the pattern shown in the graph on the left side in Figure 2.1, though not quite as strong; see Eron, 1982). One explanation of this correlation is that watching TV violence causes kids to become more violent themselves. It is equally probable, however, that the reverse is true: that kids who are violent to begin with are more likely to watch violent TV. Or there might be no causal relationship between these two variables; instead, both TV watching and violent behavior could be caused by a third variable, such as having neglectful parents who do not pay much attention to their kids. (Experimental evidence does support one of these causal relationships; we will discuss which one in Chapter 12.) When using the correlational method, it is wrong to jump to the conclusion that one variable is causing the other to occur. *Correlation does not prove causation.*

A study conducted in the early 1990s found a correlation between the type of birth control women used and their likelihood of getting a sexually transmitted disease (STD). Surprisingly, women whose partners used condoms were more likely to have an STD than women who used diaphragms or contraceptive sponges. Does this mean the use of condoms caused the increase in STDs? Not necessarily—correlation does not imply causation. (See the text for some alternative explanations of this research finding.)

Unfortunately, forgetting this adage is one of the most common methodological errors in the social sciences, as occurred in a study of birth control methods and sexually transmitted diseases (STDs) in women (Rosenberg, Davidson, Chen, Judson, & Douglas, 1992). The researchers examined the records of women who had visited a clinic, noting which method of birth control they used and whether they had an STD. Surprisingly, the researchers found that women who relied on condoms had significantly more STDs than women who used diaphragms or contraceptive sponges. This result was widely reported in the popular press, with the conclusion that the use of diaphragms and sponges caused a lower incidence of disease. Some reporters urged women whose partners used condoms to switch to other methods.

Can you see the problem with this conclusion? The fact that the incidence of disease was correlated with the type of contraception women used is open to a number of causal interpretations. Perhaps the women who used sponges and diaphragms had sex with fewer partners. (In fact, condom users were more likely to have had sex with multiple partners in the previous month.) Perhaps the partners of women who relied on condoms were more likely to have STDs than the partners of women who used sponges and diaphragms. There is simply no way of knowing. Thus the conclusion that the birth control methods protected against STDs cannot be drawn from this correlational study.

As another example of the difficulty of inferring causality from correlational designs, let's return to the question of whether pornography causes aggressive sexual acts against women, such as rape. In one study, male college students at a large midwestern university completed an anonymous survey on which they indicated whether they had ever engaged in sexually coercive behavior as well as the frequency with which they viewed various forms of pornography (Carr & VanDeusen, 2004). The researchers found a small but statistically significant correlation, such that the more pornography the students reported using, the greater the likelihood that they had committed sexual violence.

As suggestive as this finding is, it does not establish that using pornography made the student more likely to commit sexual violence. Can you think of alternative explanations for the correlation? It is possible that men who are aggressive toward women are more interested in pornography; that is, it is their aggression causing their attraction to pornography, and not the pornography causing their aggression (Malamuth et al., 2000). Alternatively, there could be some third variable, such as something in a man's upbringing or subculture, that makes him more likely to commit sexual violence and use pornography. Other examples of the difficulty of inferring causality from correlational studies are shown in the following Try It! exercise.

试一试！相关和因果：了解它们的差异
TRY IT! Correlation and Causation: Knowing the Difference

It can be difficult to remember that when two variables are correlated, it doesn't necessarily mean that one caused the other; correlation does *not* allow us to make causal inferences. For each of the following examples, think about why the correlation was found. Even if it seems obvious which variable was causing the other, are there alternative explanations?

1. Recently, a politician extolled the virtues of the Boy Scouts and Girl Scouts. In his salute to the Scouts, the politician mentioned that few teenagers convicted of street crimes had been members of the Scouts. In other words, he was positing a negative correlation between activity in Scouting and frequency of criminal behavior. Why might this be?

2. A recent study found that college students who have "helicopter parents"—moms and dads who keep close track of their kids' academic life and intervene often—actually get lower grades than college students whose parents do not hover over them so closely. Does it follow that college students would do better in school if their parents backed off a little bit?

3. A recent study of soldiers stationed on army bases found that the number of tattoos a soldier had was correlated positively with becoming involved in a motorcycle accident. Why?

4. A recent study found that adolescents who are religious are less likely to commit crimes and more likely to wear seat belts than adolescents who are not religious. Does religion make people more likely to obey the law?

5. A correlation exists between people's tendency to eat breakfast and how long they live, such that people who skip breakfast die younger. Does eating Wheaties lead to a long life?

6. A recent study reported that the more milk children drank, the more weight they gained. One researcher concluded that children who need to control their weight should cut down on their milk consumption. Is this a valid conclusion?

7. A study found that the more people read newspapers and magazines, the less likely they were to believe in paranormal phenomena such as ghosts, astrology, and extrasensory perception (ESP). The researcher who conducted the study concluded that people who read newspapers and magazines are more exposed to "rational explanations for things" and thus become more skeptical of paranormal phenomena. Is this a valid conclusion?

8. A recent survey found that people who watch public television have more sex than people who do not. "Who would have thought," the researchers reported, "that National Geographic Specials or Ken Burns' history of baseball could get people in the mood?" How would you explain this correlation?

See page 49 for the answers.

The Experimental Method: Answering Causal Questions
实验法：解释因果关系

The only way to determine causal relationships is with the **experimental method.** Here, the researcher systematically orchestrates the event so that people experience it in one way (e.g., they witness an emergency along with other bystanders) or another way (e.g., they witness the same emergency but are the sole bystander). The experimental method is the method of choice in most social psychological research because it allows the experimenter to make causal inferences.

Experimental Method
The method in which the researcher randomly assigns participants to different conditions and ensures that these conditions are identical except for the independent variable (the one thought to have a causal effect on people's responses)

> *Theory is a good thing, but a good experiment lasts forever.*
> —Peter Leonidovich Kapista

The experimental method always involves a direct intervention on the part of the researcher. By carefully changing only one aspect of the situation (e.g., group size), the researcher can see whether this aspect is the cause of the behavior in question (e.g., whether people help in an emergency). Sound simple? Actually, it isn't. Staging an experiment to test Latané and Darley's hypothesis about the effects of group size involves severe practical and ethical difficulties. What kind of emergency should be used? Ideally (from a scientific perspective), it should be as true to the Genovese case as possible. Accordingly, you would want to stage a murder that passersby could witness. In one condition, you could stage the murder so that only a few onlookers were present; in another condition, you could stage it so that a great many onlookers were present.

Obviously, no scientist in his or her right mind would stage a murder for unsuspecting bystanders. But how can we arrange a realistic situation that is upsetting enough to be similar to the Genovese case without it being too upsetting? In addition, how can we ensure that each bystander experiences the same emergency except for the variable whose effect we want to test—in this case, the number of bystanders?

Let's see how Latané and Darley (1968) dealt with these problems. Imagine that you are a participant in their experiment. You arrive at the scheduled time and find yourself in a long corridor with doors to several small cubicles. An experimenter greets you and takes you into one of the cubicles, mentioning that five other students, seated in the other cubicles, will be participating with you. The experimenter leaves after giving you a pair of headphones with an attached microphone. You put on the headphones, and soon you hear the experimenter explaining to everyone that he is interested in learning about the kinds of personal problems college students experience.

To ensure that people will discuss their problems openly, he explains, each participant will remain anonymous; each will stay in his or her separate room and communicate with the others only via the intercom system. Further, the experimenter says, he will not be listening to the discussion so that people will feel freer to be open and honest. Finally, the experimenter asks that participants take turns presenting their problems, each speaking for 2 minutes, after which each person will comment on what the others said. To make sure this procedure is followed, he says, only one person's microphone will be turned on at a time.

The group discussion begins. You listen as the first participant admits that he has found it difficult to adjust to college. With some embarrassment, he mentions that he sometimes has seizures, especially when under stress. When his 2 minutes are up, you hear the other four participants discuss their problems; then it is your turn. When you have finished, the first person speaks again. To your astonishment, he soon begins to experience one of the seizures he mentioned earlier:

> I—er—um—I think I—I need—er—if—if could—er—er—somebody er—er—er—er—er—er—er—give me a little—er—give me a little help here because—er—I—er—I'm—er—er—h—h—having a—a—a real problem—er—right now and I—er—if somebody could help me out it would—it would—er—er s—s—sure be—sure be good . . . because—er—there—er—er—a cause I—er—I—uh—I've got a—a one of the—er—sei—er—er—things coming on and—and—and I could really—er—use some help so if somebody would—er—give me a little h—help—uh—er—er—er—er c—could somebody—er—er—help—er—uh—uh—uh (choking sounds) . . . I'm gonna die—er—er—I'm . . . gonna die—er—help—er—er—seizure—er (chokes, then quiet). (Darley & Latané, 1968, p. 379)

What would you have done in this situation? If you were like most of the participants in the actual study, you would have remained in your cubicle, listening to your fellow student having a seizure, and done nothing about it. Does this surprise you? Latané and Darley kept track of the number of people who left their cubicle to find the victim or the experimenter before the end of the victim's seizure. Only 31 percent of the participants sought help in this way. Fully 69 percent of the students remained in their cubicles and did nothing—just as Kitty Genovese's neighbors had failed to offer assistance in any way.

Does this finding prove that the failure to help was due to the number of people who witnessed the seizure? How do we know that it wasn't due to some other factor? We know because Latané and Darley included two other conditions in their experiment. In these conditions, the procedure was identical to the one we described, with one crucial difference: The size of the discussion group was smaller, meaning that fewer people witnessed the seizure. In one condition, the participants were told that there were three other people in the discussion group besides themselves (the victim plus two others). In another condition, participants were told that there was only one other person in their discussion group (the victim). In this latter condition, each participant believed he or she was the only one who could hear the seizure.

Independent and Dependent Variables 自变量与因变量

The number of people witnessing the emergency was the **independent variable** in the Latané and Darley (1968) study, which is the variable a researcher changes or varies to see if it has an effect on some other variable. The **dependent variable** is the variable a researcher measures to see if it is influenced by the independent variable; the researcher hypothesizes that the dependent variable will be influenced by the level of the independent variable. That is, the dependent variable is hypothesized to depend on the independent variable (see Figure 2.2). Latané and Darley found that their independent variable—the number of bystanders—did have an effect on the dependent variable—whether they tried to help. When the participants believed that four other people were witnesses to the seizure, only 31 percent offered assistance. When the participants believed that only two other people were aware of the seizure, helping behavior increased to 62 percent. When the participants believed that they were the only person listening to the seizure, nearly everyone helped (85 percent).

These results indicate that the number of bystanders strongly influences the rate of helping, but it does not mean that the size of the group is the only cause of people's decision to help. After all, when there were four bystanders, a third of the participants still helped; conversely, when participants thought they were the only witness, some of them failed to help. Obviously, other factors influence helping behavior—the bystanders' personalities, their prior experience with emergencies, and so on. Nonetheless, Latané and Darley succeeded in identifying one important determinant of whether people help—the number of bystanders that people think are present.

Independent Variable

The variable a researcher changes or varies to see if it has an effect on some other variable

Dependent Variable

The variable a researcher measures to see if it is influenced by the independent variable; the researcher hypothesizes that the dependent variable will depend on the level of the independent variable

Independent Variable	Dependent Variable
The variable that is hypothesized to influence the dependent variable. Participants are treated identically except for this variable.	The response that is hypothesized to depend on the independent variable. All participants are measured on this variable.
Example: Latané and Darley (1968)	
The number of bystanders	How many participants helped?
Participant + Victim	85%
Participant + Victim + Two others	62%
Participant + Victim + Four others	31%

FIGURE 2.2

Independent and dependent variables in experimental research.

Internal Validity in Experiments 实验的内部效度

How can we be sure that the differences in help across conditions in the Latané and Darley seizure study were due to the different numbers of bystanders who witnessed the emergency? Could this effect have been caused by some other aspect of the situation? This is the beauty of the experimental method: We can be sure of the causal connection between the number of bystanders and helping because Latané and Darley made sure that everything about the situation was the same in the different conditions except the independent variable, the number of bystanders. Keeping everything but the independent variable the same in an experiment is referred to as *internal validity*. Latané and Darley were careful to maintain high internal validity by making sure that everyone witnessed the same emergency. They prerecorded the supposed other participants and the victim and played their voices over the intercom system.

You may have noticed, however, that there was a key difference between the conditions of the Latané and Darley experiment other than the number of bystanders: Different people participated in the different conditions. Maybe the observed differences in helping were due to characteristics of the participants instead of the independent variable. The people in the sole witness condition might have differed in any number of ways from their counterparts in the other conditions, making them more likely to help. Maybe they were more likely to know something about epilepsy or to have experience helping in emergencies. If either of these possibilities is true, it would be difficult to conclude that it was the number of bystanders, rather than something about the participants' backgrounds, that led to differences in helping.

Fortunately, there is a technique that allows experimenters to minimize differences among participants as the cause of the results: **random assignment to condition**. This is the process whereby all participants have an equal chance of taking part in any condition of an experiment; through random assignment, researchers can be relatively certain that differences in the participants' personalities or backgrounds are distributed evenly across conditions. Because Latané and Darley's participants were randomly assigned to the conditions of their experiment, it is very unlikely that the ones who knew the most about epilepsy all ended up in one condition. Knowledge about epilepsy should be randomly (i.e., roughly evenly) dispersed across the three experimental conditions. This powerful technique is the most important part of the experimental method.

Even with random assignment, however, there is the (very small) possibility that different characteristics of people did not distribute themselves evenly across conditions. For example, if we randomly divide a group of 40 people into two groups, it is possible that those who know the most about epilepsy will by chance end up more in one group than the other—just as it is possible to get more heads than tails when you flip a coin 40 times. This is a possibility we take seriously in experimental science. The analyses of our data come with a **probability level (*p*-value)**, which is a number, calculated with statistical techniques, that tells researchers how likely it is that the results of their experiment occurred by chance and not because of the independent variable. The convention in science, including social psychology, is to consider results *significant* (trustworthy) if the probability level is less than 5 in 100 that the results might be due to chance factors rather than the independent variables studied. For example, if we flipped a coin 40 times and got 40 heads, we would probably assume that this was very unlikely to have occurred by chance and that there was something wrong with the coin (we might check the other side to make sure it wasn't one of those trick coins with heads on both sides!). Similarly, if the results in two conditions of an experiment differ significantly from what we would expect by chance, we assume that the difference was caused by the independent variable (e.g., the number of bystanders present during the emergency). The *p*-value tells us how confident we can be that the difference was due to chance rather than the independent variable.

To summarize, the key to a good experiment is to maintain high **internal validity**, which we can now define as making sure that the independent variable, and *only* the independent variable, influences the dependent variable; this is accomplished by

---

Random Assignment to Condition
A process ensuring that all participants have an equal chance of taking part in any condition of an experiment; through random assignment, researchers can be relatively certain that differences in the participants' personalities or backgrounds are distributed evenly across conditions

Probability Level (*p*-value)
A number calculated with statistical techniques that tells researchers how likely it is that the results of their experiment occurred by chance and not because of the independent variable or variables; the convention in science, including social psychology, is to consider results *significant* (trustworthy) if the probability level is less than 5 in 100 that the results might be due to chance factors and not the independent variables studied

Internal Validity
Making sure that nothing besides the independent variable can affect the dependent variable; this is accomplished by controlling all extraneous variables and by randomly assigning people to different experimental conditions

controlling all extraneous variables and by randomly assigning people to different experimental conditions (Campbell & Stanley, 1967). When internal validity is high, the experimenter is in a position to judge whether the independent variable causes the dependent variable. This is the hallmark of the experimental method that sets it apart from the observational and correlational methods: Only the experimental method can answer causal questions, such as whether exposure to pornography causes men to commit violent acts.

For example, researchers have tested whether pornography causes aggression by randomly assigning consenting participants to watch pornographic or nonpornographic films (the independent variable) and measuring the extent to which people acted aggressively toward women (the dependent variable). In a study by Donnerstein and Berkowitz (1981), males were angered by a female accomplice and then were randomly assigned to see one of three films: violent pornography (a rape scene), nonviolent pornography (sex without any violence), or a neutral film with no violence or sex (a talk show interview). The men were then given an opportunity to act aggressively toward the woman who had angered them by choosing the level of electric shock she would receive in an ostensibly unrelated learning experiment (the accomplice did not really receive shocks, but participants believed that she would). The men who had seen the violent pornography administered significantly more intense shocks to the woman than the men who had seen the nonviolent pornography or the neutral film, suggesting that it is not pornography per se that leads to aggressive behavior but the violence depicted in some pornography (Mussweiler & Förster, 2000). We review this area of research more generally in Chapter 12.

A good deal of social psychological research takes place in laboratory settings. How do social psychologists generalize from the findings of these studies to life outside the laboratory?

External Validity in Experiments 实验的外部效度

For all the advantages of the experimental method, there are some drawbacks. By virtue of gaining enough control over the situation so as to randomly assign people to conditions and rule out the effects of extraneous variables, the situation can become somewhat artificial and distant from real life. For example, one could argue that Latané and Darley strayed far from the original inspiration for their study, the Kitty Genovese murder. What does witnessing a seizure while participating in a laboratory experiment in a college building have to do with a brutal murder in a densely populated urban neighborhood? How often in everyday life do we have discussions with other people through an intercom system? Did the fact that the participants knew they were in a psychology experiment influence their behavior?

These are important questions that concern **external validity**, which is the extent to which the results of a study can be generalized to other situations and other people. Note that two kinds of generalizability are at issue: the extent to which we can generalize from the situation constructed by an experimenter to real-life situations (generalizability across *situations*), and the extent to which we can generalize from the people who participated in the experiment to people in general (generalizability across *people*).

Generalizability Across Situations Research in social psychology is sometimes criticized for being conducted in artificial settings, such as psychological experiments at a university, that cannot be generalized to real life. To address this problem, social psychologists attempt to increase the generalizability of their results by making their studies as realistic as possible. But this is hard to do in a laboratory setting in which people are placed in situations they would rarely, if ever, encounter in everyday life, such as occurred in Latané and Darley's group discussion of personal problems over an intercom system. Instead, psychologists attempt to maximize the study's **psychological realism**, which is the extent to which the psychological processes triggered in an

External Validity
The extent to which the results of a study can be generalized to other situations and to other people

Psychological Realism
The extent to which the psychological processes triggered in an experiment are similar to psychological processes that occur in everyday life

experiment are similar to psychological processes that occur in everyday life (Aronson, Wilson, & Brewer, 1998). Even though Latané and Darley staged an emergency that in significant ways was unlike ones encountered in everyday life, was it psychologically similar to real-life emergencies? Were the same psychological processes triggered? Did the participants have the same types of perceptions and thoughts, make the same types of decisions, and choose the same types of behaviors that they would in a real-life situation? If so, the study is high in psychological realism and we can generalize the results to everyday life.

Psychological realism is heightened if people feel involved in a real event. To accomplish this, experimenters often tell participants a **cover story**—a disguised version of the study's true purpose. Recall, for example, that Latané and Darley told people that they were studying the personal problems of college students and then staged an emergency. It would have been a lot easier to say to people, "Look, we are interested in how people react to emergencies, so at some point during this study we are going to stage an accident, and then we'll see how you respond." We think you'll agree that such a procedure would be very low in psychological realism. In real life, we never know when emergencies are going to occur, and we do not have time to plan our responses to them. If participants knew that an emergency was about to happen, the kinds of psychological processes triggered would have been quite different from those of a real emergency, reducing the psychological realism of the study.

Generalizability Across People Recall that social psychologists study the way in which people in general are susceptible to social influence. Latané and Darley's experiment documented an interesting, unexpected example of social influence, whereby the mere knowledge that others were present reduced the likelihood that people helped. But what have we learned about people in general? The participants in their study were 52 male and female students at New York University who received course credit for participating in the experiment. Would the study have turned out the same way if a different population had been used? Would the number of bystanders have influenced helping behavior had the participants been middle-aged blue-collar workers instead of college students? Midwesterners instead of New Yorkers? Japanese instead of American?

The only way to be certain that the results of an experiment represent the behavior of a particular population is to ensure that the participants are randomly selected from that population. Ideally, samples in experiments should be randomly selected, just as they are in surveys. Increasingly, social psychologists are conducting research with diverse populations and cultures, some of it over the Internet (e.g., Lane, Banaji, & Nosek, 2007). But unfortunately, it is impractical and expensive to select random samples for most social psychology experiments. It is difficult enough to convince a random sample of Americans to agree to answer a few questions over the telephone as part of a political poll, and such polls can cost thousands of dollars to conduct. Imagine the difficulty Latané and Darley would have had convincing a random sample of Americans to board a plane to New York to take part in their study, not to mention the cost of such an endeavor. Even trying to gather a random sample of students at New York University would not have been easy; each person contacted would have had to agree to spend an hour in Latané and Darley's laboratory.

Of course, concerns about practicality and expense are not good excuses for doing poor science. Many researchers address this problem by studying basic psychological processes that make people susceptible to social influence, assuming that these processes are so fundamental that they are universally shared. In that case, participants for social psychology experiments don't really have to come from many different cultures. Of course, some social psychological processes are likely to be quite dependent on cultural factors, and in those cases, we'd need diverse samples of people. The question then is, how can researchers tell whether the processes they are studying are universal?

Field Research One of the best ways to increase external validity is by conducting **field experiments.** In a field experiment, researchers study behavior outside of the laboratory, in its natural setting. As in a laboratory experiment, the researcher controls

Cover Story
A description of the purpose of a study, given to participants, that is different from its true purpose, used to maintain psychological realism

Field Experiments
Experiments conducted in natural settings rather than in the laboratory

the occurrence of an independent variable (e.g., group size) to see what effect it has on a dependent variable (e.g., helping behavior) and randomly assigns people to the different conditions. Thus a field experiment has the same design as a laboratory experiment except that it is conducted in a real-life setting, rather than in the relatively artificial setting of the laboratory. The participants in a field experiment are unaware that the events they experience are in fact an experiment. The external validity of such an experiment is high, since, after all, it is taking place in the real world, with real people who are more diverse than a typical college student sample.

Many such field studies have been conducted in social psychology. For example, Latané and Darley (1970) tested their hypothesis about group size and bystander intervention in a convenience store outside of New York City. Two "robbers" (with full knowledge and permission of the cashier and manager of the store) waited until there were either one or two other customers at the checkout counter. They then asked the cashier to name the most expensive beer the store carried. The cashier answered the question and then said he would have to check in the back to see how much of that brand was in stock. While the cashier was gone, the robbers picked up a case of beer in the front of the store, declared, "They'll never miss this," put the beer in their car, and drove off.

Because the robbers were rather burly fellows, no one attempted to intervene directly to stop the theft. The question was, when the cashier returned, how many people would help by telling him that a theft had just occurred? The number of bystanders had the same inhibiting effect on helping behavior as in the laboratory seizure study: Significantly fewer people reported the theft when there was another customer-witness in the store than when they were alone.

It might have occurred to you to ask why researchers conduct laboratory studies at all, given that external validity is so much better with field experiments. Indeed, it seems to us that the perfect experiment in social psychology would be one that was conducted in a field setting, with a sample randomly selected from a population of interest and with extremely high internal validity (all extraneous variables controlled; people randomly assigned to the conditions). Sounds good, doesn't it? The only problem is that it is very difficult to satisfy all these conditions in one study—making such studies virtually impossible to conduct.

There is almost always a trade-off between internal and external validity—that is, between being able to randomly assign people to conditions and having enough control over the situation to ensure that no extraneous variables are influencing the results, and making sure that the results can be generalized to everyday life. We have the most control in a laboratory setting, but the laboratory may be unlike real life. Real life can best be captured by doing a field experiment, but it is very difficult to control all extraneous variables in such studies. For example, the astute reader will have noticed that Latané and Darley's (1970) beer theft study differed from laboratory experiments in an important way: People could not be randomly assigned to the alone or in-pairs conditions. Were this the only study Latané and Darley had performed, we could not be sure whether the kinds of people who prefer to shop alone, as compared to the kinds of people who prefer to shop with a friend, differ in ways that might influence helping behavior. By randomly assigning people to conditions in their laboratory studies, Latané and Darley were able to rule out such alternative explanations.

Replications The trade-off between internal and external validity has been referred to as the *basic dilemma of the social psychologist* (Aronson & Carlsmith, 1968). The way to resolve this dilemma is not to try to do it all in a single experiment. Most social psychologists opt first for internal validity, conducting laboratory experiments in which people are randomly assigned to different conditions and all extraneous variables are controlled; here there is little ambiguity about what is causing what. Other social psychologists prefer to maximize external validity by conducting field studies. And many social psychologists do both. Taken together, both types of studies meet the requirements of our perfect experiment.

Replications are the ultimate test of an experiment's external validity. Only by conducting studies in different settings, with different populations, can we determine how

Replications
Repeating a study, often with different subject populations or in different settings

generalizable the results are. Often, though, when many studies on one problem are conducted, the results are somewhat variable. Several studies might find an effect of the number of bystanders on helping behavior, for example, while a few do not. How can we make sense of this? Does the number of bystanders make a difference or not? Fortunately, there is a statistical technique called **meta-analysis** that averages the results of two or more studies to see if the effect of an independent variable is reliable. Earlier we discussed p-values, which tell us the probability that the findings of one study are due to chance or to the independent variable. A meta-analysis essentially does the same thing, except that it averages the results of many different studies. If, say, an independent variable is found to have an effect in only 1 of 20 studies, the meta-analysis will tell us that that 1 study was probably an exception and that on average, the independent variable is not influencing the dependent variable. If an independent variable is having an effect in most of the studies, the meta-analysis is likely to tell us that on average, it does influence the dependent variable.

Most of the findings you will read about in this book have been replicated in several different settings, with different populations; we know then that they are reliable phenomena, not limited to the laboratory or to college sophomores. For example, Anderson and Bushman (1997) compared laboratory studies on the causes of aggression with studies conducted in the real world. In both types of studies, violence in the media caused aggressive behavior. Similarly, Latané and Darley's original findings have been replicated in numerous studies. Increasing the number of bystanders inhibited helping behavior with many kinds of people, including children, college students, and future ministers (Darley & Batson, 1973; Latané & Nida, 1981); in both small towns and large cities (Latané & Dabbs, 1975); in a variety of settings, such as psychology laboratories, city streets, and subway trains (Harrison & Wells, 1991; Latané & Darley, 1970; Piliavin, 1981; Piliavin & Piliavin, 1972); and with different kinds of emergencies, such as seizures, potential fires, fights, and accidents (Latané & Darley, 1968; Shotland & Straw, 1976; Staub, 1974), as well as with less serious events, such as having a flat tire (Hurley & Allen, 1974). Many of these replications took place in real-life settings (e.g., on a subway train) where people could not possibly have known that an experiment was being conducted. We will frequently point out similar replications of the major findings we discuss in this book.

Basic Versus Applied Research 基础研究与应用研究

You may have wondered how people decide which specific topic to study. Why would a social psychologist decide to study helping behavior, cognitive dissonance theory, or the effects of pornography on aggression? Is he or she simply curious? Or does the social psychologist have a specific purpose in mind, such as trying to reduce sexual violence?

The goal in **basic research** is to find the best answer to the question of why people behave as they do, purely for reasons of intellectual curiosity. The researchers aren't trying to solve a specific social or psychological problem. In contrast, **applied research** is geared toward solving a particular social problem. Building a theory of behavior is usually secondary to solving the specific problem, such as alleviating racism, reducing sexual violence, or stemming the spread of AIDS.

In social psychology, the distinction between basic and applied research is fuzzy. Even though many researchers label themselves as either basic or applied scientists, the endeavors of one group are not independent of those of the other group. There are countless examples of advances in basic science that at the time had no known applied value but later proved to be the key to solving a significant applied problem. As we will see later in this book, for example, basic research with dogs, rats, and fish on the effects of feeling in control of one's environment has led to the development of techniques to improve the health of elderly nursing home residents (Langer & Rodin, 1976; Richter, 1957; Schulz, 1976; Seligman, 1975).

Most social psychologists would agree that in order to solve a specific social problem, we must understand the psychological processes responsible for it. Indeed, Kurt

Meta-Analysis
A statistical technique that averages the results of two or more studies to see if the effect of an independent variable is reliable

Basic Research
Studies that are designed to find the best answer to the question of why people behave as they do and that are conducted purely for reasons of intellectual curiosity

Applied Research
Studies designed to solve a particular social problem

Lewin (1951), one of the founders of social psychology, coined a phrase that has become a motto for the field: "There is nothing so practical as a good theory." He meant that to solve such difficult social problems as urban violence or racial prejudice, one must first understand the underlying psychological dynamics of human nature and social interaction. Even when the goal is to discover the psychological processes underlying social behavior, the findings often have clear applied implications, as you'll see throughout this book.

> *There is nothing so practical as a good theory.*
>
> —Kurt Lewin, 1951

New Frontiers in Social Psychological Research 社会心理学研究的新思路

Social psychologists are always looking for new ways of investigating social behavior and in recent years some new approaches have received a good deal of attention.

Culture and Social Psychology 文化与社会心理学

Social psychology largely began as a Western science, conducted by Western social psychologists with Western participants. This raises the question of how universal the findings are. To study the effects of culture on social psychological process, social psychologists conduct **cross-cultural research** (Heine, 2008; Kitayama & Cohen, 2007; Nisbett, 2003; Smith & Bond, 1999). Some findings in social psychology are culture-dependent, as we will see throughout this book. In Chapter 3, for example, we will see that Westerners and East Asians rely on fundamentally different kinds of thought to perceive and understand the social world. In Chapter 5 we'll discuss cultural differences in the very way people define themselves. Whether we emphasize personal independence or social interdependence reflects our cultural values.

Conducting cross-cultural research is not simply a matter of traveling to another culture, translating materials into the local language, and replicating a study there (Heine, Lehman, Peng, & Greenholtz, 2002; van de Vijver & Leung, 1997). Researchers have to guard against imposing their own viewpoints and definitions, learned from their culture, onto another culture with which they are unfamiliar. They must also be sure that their independent and dependent variables are understood in the same way in different cultures (Bond, 1988; Lonner & Berry, 1986).

Suppose, for example, that you wanted to replicate the Latané and Darley (1968) seizure experiment in another culture. Clearly, you could not conduct the identical

Cross-Cultural Research
Research conducted with members of different cultures, to see whether the psychological processes of interest are present in both cultures or whether they are specific to the culture in which people were raised

Some basic psychological processes are universal, whereas others are shaped by the culture in which we live. For example, are people's self-concepts shaped by cultural rules of how people must present themselves, such as the requirement by the Taliban regime in Afghanistan that women cover themselves from head to toe? Are people's ideas about their relationships to their family and social groups influenced by cultural practices, such as cradling one's child while at work, as this woman from Indonesia is doing? Cross-cultural research is challenging but necessary to explore how culture influences the basic ways in which people think about and interact with others.

experiment somewhere else. The tape-recorded discussion of college life used by Latané and Darley was specific to the lives of New York University students in the 1960s and could not be used meaningfully elsewhere. What about more subtle aspects of the study, such as the way people viewed the person who had the seizure? Cultures vary considerably in how they define whether another person belongs to their social group; this factor figures significantly in how they behave toward that person (Gudykunst, 1988; Triandis, 1989). If people in one culture view the victim as a member of their social group, but people in another culture perceive the victim as a member of a rival social group, you might find very different results in the two cultures—not because the psychological processes of helping behavior are different, but because people interpreted the situation differently. It can be quite daunting to conduct a study that is interpreted and perceived similarly in dissimilar cultures. Cross-cultural researchers are sensitive to these issues, and as more and more cross-cultural research is conducted carefully, we will be able to determine which social psychological processes are universal and which are culture-bound (Heine, 2008).

The Evolutionary Approach 进化心理学

Evolutionary theory was developed by Charles Darwin (1859) to explain the ways in which animals adapt to their environments. Central to the theory is **natural selection**, which is the process by which heritable traits that promote survival in a particular environment are passed along to future generations, because organisms with that trait are more likely to produce offspring. A common example is how giraffes came to have long necks. In an environment where food is scarce, giraffes who happened to have long necks could feed on foliage that other animals couldn't reach. These giraffes were more likely to survive and produce offspring than other giraffes, the story goes, and the "long-neck" gene thus became common in subsequent generations.

In biology, evolutionary theory is used to explain how different species acquired physical traits like long necks. But what about social behaviors, such as the tendency to be aggressive toward a member of one's own species, or the tendency to be helpful toward others? Is it possible that social behaviors have genetic determinants that evolve through the process of natural selection, and if so, is this true in human beings as well as animals? These are the questions posed by **evolutionary psychology**, which attempts to explain social behavior in terms of genetic factors that evolved over time according to the principles of natural selection. The core idea is that evolution occurs very slowly, such that social behaviors that are prevalent today are due at least in part to adaptations to environments in our distant past (Buss, 2005; Schaller, Simpson, & Kenrick, 2006). We will discuss how evolutionary theory explains social behavior in upcoming chapters (e.g., Chapter 10 on interpersonal attraction, Chapter 11 on prosocial behavior, and Chapter 12 on aggression). Here we mention that a lively debate has arisen over the testability of evolutionary hypotheses. Because current behaviors are thought to be adaptations to environmental conditions that existed thousands of years ago, psychologists make their best guesses about what those conditions were and how specific kinds of behaviors gave people a reproductive advantage. But these hypotheses are obviously impossible to test with the experimental method. And just because hypotheses sound plausible does not mean they are true. For example, some scientists now believe that giraffes did not acquire a long neck in order to eat leaves in tall trees. Instead, they suggest, long necks first evolved in male giraffes to gain an advantage in fights with other males over access to females (Simmons & Scheepers, 1996). Which of these explanations is true? It's hard to tell. On the other hand, evolutionary approaches can generate novel hypotheses about social behavior that can be tested with the other methods described in this chapter.

Social Neuroscience 社会神经科学

As we have seen, social psychology is concerned with how people's thoughts, feelings, and behaviors are influenced by the real or imagined presence of other people. Most

Natural Selection
The process by which heritable traits that promote survival in a particular environment are passed along to future generations, because organisms with that trait are more likely to produce offspring

Evolutionary Psychology
The attempt to explain social behavior in terms of genetic factors that evolved over time according to the principles of natural selection

research studies in social psychology, then, study just that—thoughts, feelings, and behaviors. Human beings are biological organisms, however, and social psychologists have become increasingly interested in the connection between biological processes and social behavior. These include the study of hormones and behavior, the human immune system, and neurological processes in the human brain. To study the brain and its relation to behavior, psychologists use sophisticated technologies, including electroencephalography (EEG), in which electrodes are placed on the scalp to measure electrical activity in the brain, and functional magnetic resonance imaging (fMRI), in which people are placed in scanners that measure changes in blood flow in their brains. Social psychologists take these measurements while participants think about and process social information, allowing them to map the correlates of different kinds of brain activity to social information processing. This kind of research is in its infancy but promises to open up a whole new area of inquiry into the relationship of the brain to behavior (Harmon-Jones & Winkielman, 2007; Lieberman, 2008; Ochsner, 2007).

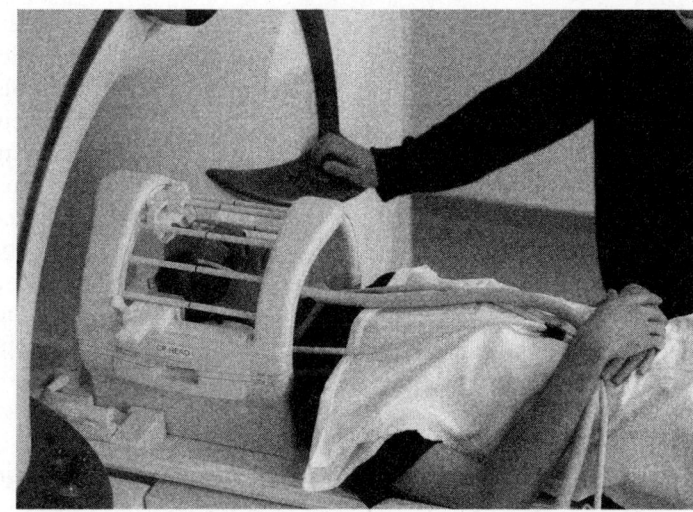

Social psychologists are studying the brain and its relation to behavior. They use technologies such as electroencephalography (EEG), in which electrodes are placed on the scalp to measure electrical activity in the brain, and functional magnetic resonance imaging (fMRI), in which people are placed in scanners that measure changes in blood flow in their brains. Social psychologists take these measurements while participants think about and process social information, allowing them to map the correlates of different kinds of brain activity to social information processing.

Ethical Issues in Social Psychology 社会心理学的伦理问题

As you read this chapter, did it bother you to learn that researchers sometimes mislead people about the true purpose of their study or that, in Latané and Darley's seizure study, people were put in a situation that might have been upsetting? This study illustrates that in their quest to create realistic, engaging situations, social psychologists frequently face an ethical dilemma. For scientific reasons, we want our experiments to resemble the real world as much as possible and to be as sound and well controlled as we can make them. But we also want to avoid causing our participants stress, discomfort, or unpleasantness. These two goals often conflict as the researcher goes about the business of creating and conducting experiments.

Researchers are concerned about the health and welfare of the individuals participating in their experiments. Researchers are also in the process of discovering important information about human social behavior—such as bystander intervention, prejudice, conformity, aggression, and obedience to authority. Many of these discoveries are bound to benefit society. Indeed, given the fact that social psychologists have developed powerful tools to investigate such issues scientifically, many scholars feel it would be immoral not to conduct these experiments. To gain insight into such critical issues, however, researchers must create vivid events that are involving for the participants. Some of these events might make the participants uncomfortable, such as witnessing someone having a seizure. We can't resolve the dilemma by making pious claims that participants never experience discomfort in an experiment or by insisting that all is fair in science and forging blindly ahead. Clearly, some middle ground is called for.

Informed Consent
Agreement to participate in an experiment, granted in full awareness of the nature of the experiment, which has been explained in advance

Deception
Misleading participants about the true purpose of a study or the events that will actually transpire

Institutional Review Board (IRB)
A group made up of at least one scientist, one nonscientist, and one member not affiliated with the institution that reviews all psychological research at that institution and decides whether it meets ethical guidelines; all research must be approved by the IRB before it is conducted

Debriefing
Explaining to participants, at the end of an experiment, the true purpose of the study and exactly what transpired

The dilemma would be less problematic if researchers could obtain **informed consent** from their participants before their participation. To obtain informed consent, the researcher explains the nature of the experiment to participants before it begins and asks for their agreement to participate. If participants are made fully aware of the kinds of experiences they are about to undergo and state that they are willing to participate, the ethical dilemma is resolved. In many social psychology experiments, this sort of description is feasible—and where it is feasible, it is done. But sometimes it is impossible. Suppose Latané and Darley had told their participants that a seizure was about to be staged, that it wouldn't be a real emergency, and that the hypothesis stated they should offer help. Such a procedure would be bad science. In this kind of experiment, it's essential that the participant experience contrived events as if they were real; this is called a deception experiment. **Deception** in social psychological research involves misleading participants about the true purpose of a study or the events that transpire. (Note that not all research in social psychology involves deception.)

Guidelines for Ethical Research 伦理研究的指导方针

To ensure that the dignity and safety of research participants are protected, the American Psychological Association has published a list of ethical principles that govern all research in psychology (see Figure 2.3). In addition, any institution (such as a university) that seeks federal funding for psychological research is required to have an **institutional review board (IRB)** that reviews research before it is conducted. The board, which must include at least one scientist, one nonscientist, and one person who is not affiliated with the institution, reviews all research proposals and decides whether the procedures meet ethical guidelines. Any aspect of the experimental procedure that this committee judges to be overly stressful or upsetting must be changed or deleted before the study can be conducted. (Note that some of the research described in later chapters was conducted before IRBs were required in the early 1970s. You will need to decide whether you would have approved these studies if you were on an IRB that judged them.)

When deception is used in a study, the postexperimental interview, called the debriefing session, is crucial and must occur. **Debriefing** is the process of explaining to the participants, at the end of an experiment, the true purpose of the study and exactly what transpired. If any participants experienced discomfort, the researchers attempt to undo and alleviate it. During debriefing, too, the participants learn about the goals

---

SELECTED ETHICAL PRINCIPLES OF PSYCHOLOGISTS IN THE CONDUCT OF RESEARCH

1. Psychologists seek to promote accuracy, honesty, and truthfulness in the science, teaching, and practice of psychology.
2. Psychologists respect the dignity and worth of all people, and the rights of individuals to privacy, confidentiality, and self-determination.
3. When psychologists conduct research . . . in person or via electronic transmission or other forms of communication, they obtain the informed consent of the individual.
4. When obtaining informed consent . . . psychologists inform participants about the purpose of the research, expected duration, and procedures, and their right to decline to participate and to withdraw from the research once participation has begun.
5. Psychologists have a primary obligation and take reasonable precautions to protect confidential information obtained through or stored in any medium.
6. Psychologists do not conduct a study involving deception unless they have determined that the use of deceptive techniques is justified by the study's significant prospective scientific, educational, or applied value and that effective nondeceptive alternative procedures are not feasible.
7. Psychologists explain any deception that is an integral feature of the design and conduct of an experiment to participants as early as is feasible.
8. Psychologists provide a prompt opportunity for participants to obtain appropriate information about the nature, results, and conclusions of the research, and they take reasonable steps to correct any misconceptions that participants may have.

FIGURE 2.3
Procedures for the protection of participants in psychological research.
Adapted from the American Psychological Association, 2003.

and purpose of the research. The best researchers question their participants carefully and listen to what they say, regardless of whether or not deception was used in the experiment. (For a detailed description of how debriefing interviews should be conducted, see Aronson, Ellsworth, Carlsmith, & Gonzales, 1990.)

In our experience, virtually all participants understand and appreciate the need for deception, as long as the time is taken in the postexperimental debriefing session to review the purpose of the research and to explain why alternative procedures could not be used. Several investigators have gone a step further and assessed the impact on people of participating in deception studies (e.g., Christensen, 1988; Epley & Huff, 1998; Finney, 1987; Gerdes, 1979; Sharpe, Adair, & Roese, 1992). These studies have consistently found that people do not object to the kinds of mild discomfort and deceptions typically used in social psychological research. In fact, some studies have found that most people who participated in deception experiments said they had learned more and enjoyed the experiments more than those who participated in nondeception experiments did (Smith & Richardson, 1983). For example, Latané and Darley (1970) reported that during their debriefing, the participants said that the deception was necessary and that they were willing to participate in similar studies in the future—even though they had experienced some stress and conflict during the study.

HOW WOULD YOU USE THIS? 如何学以致用?

As we have seen in this chapter, social psychologists use empirical methods to test hypotheses about social behavior. Now that you know something about these methods, you are in a good position to judge the quality of research findings you read about in newspapers and magazines. As we saw, for example, one of the most common mistakes is for people to assume that because two variables are correlated with each other, one caused the other. We hope that when you hear about correlational findings in the media, a little light will go off in your head that causes you to challenge any causal conclusions that are drawn. Suppose, for example, that you are browsing through a promotional brochure for the *Consumers Reports on Health* newsletter, as one of us recently was, and you came across this tidbit: "Need more motivation to exercise? Exercise leads to better sex. In one study, men who exercised were five times as likely to achieve normal sexual function as a less-active group." Did the little light go off? This is a correlational finding—men who exercised more functioned better sexually—and we cannot draw the conclusion that it is the exercise that "leads to" (e.g., causes) better sex. Can you think of alternative explanations of this finding? Better yet, can you design an experiment that would test the hypothesis that exercise helps people's sex lives?

Summary 总 结

- **Social Psychology: An Empirical Science** A fundamental principle of social psychology is that social influence can be studied scientifically.
- **Formulating Hypotheses and Theories** Social psychological research begins with a hypothesis about the effects of social influence.
    - **Inspiration from Earlier Theories and Research** Hypotheses often come from previous research findings; researchers conduct studies to test an alternative explanation of previous experiments.
- **Hypotheses Based on Personal Observations** Many other hypotheses come from observations of everyday life, such as Latané and Darley's hunches about why people failed to help Kitty Genovese.
- **The Observational Method: Describing Social Behavior** The observational method, whereby researchers observe people and systematically record their behavior, is useful for describing the nature of a phenomenon and generating hypotheses.

- **Archival Analysis** One form of the observational method is ethnography, the method by which researchers attempt to understand a group or culture by observing it from the inside, without imposing any preconceived notions they might have. Another is archival analysis, whereby researchers examine documents or archives, such as looking at photographs in magazines to see how men and women are portrayed.
- **Limits of the Observational Method** The observational method can be used only to study public behavior and records; it is not amenable to studying people's thoughts or private behaviors. Further, it can be difficult to generalize from observations of one particular group of people to people in general.

- **The Correlational Method: Predicting Social Behavior** The correlational method, whereby two or more variables are systematically measured and the relationship between them assessed, is very useful when the goal is to predict one variable from another. For example, researchers might be interested in whether there is a correlation between the amount of violent television children watch and how aggressive they are.
  - **Surveys** The correlational method is often applied to the results of surveys, in which a representative group of people are asked questions about their attitudes and behaviors. To make sure that the results are generalizable, researchers randomly select survey respondents from the population at large.
  - **Limits of the Correlational Method: Correlation Does Not Equal Causation** Social psychologists are usually interested in determining causality, such as whether watching violent television *causes* children to be more aggressive. The major limitation of the correlational method is that it cannot determine causality. If two variables, A and B, are correlated (such as television watching and aggression), it could be that A is causing B (e.g., television watching makes kids aggressive), B is causing A (e.g., aggressive kids like to watch violent television), or that some third variable, C, is causing both A and B (e.g., something about the way kids are raised makes them want to watch more violent television and makes them more aggressive).

- **The Experimental Method: Answering Causal Questions** The only way to determine causality is to use the experimental method, in which the researcher randomly assigns participants to different conditions and ensures that these conditions are identical except for the independent variable.
  - **Independent and Dependent Variables** The independent variable is the one researchers vary to see if it has a causal effect (e.g., how much TV children watch); the dependent variable is what researchers measure to see if it is affected (e.g., how aggressive children are).
  - **Internal Validity in Experiments** Experiments should be high in internal validity, which means that people in all conditions are treated identically, except for the independent variable (e.g., how much TV children watch).
  - **External Validity in Experiments** External validity—the extent to which researchers can generalize their results to other situations and people—is accomplished by increasing the realism of the experiment, particularly its psychological realism (the extent to which the psychological processes triggered in the experiment are similar to the psychological processes triggered in everyday life). It is also accomplished by replicating the study with different populations of participants.
  - **Basic Versus Applied Research** As in any other science, some social psychology studies are basic research experiments (designed to answer basic questions about why people do what they do), whereas others are applied studies (designed to find ways to solve specific social problems).

- **New Frontiers In Social Psychological Research** In recent years social psychologists have developed new ways of investigating social behavior.
  - **Culture and Social Psychology** To study the ways in which culture shapes people's thoughts, feelings, and behavior, social psychologists conduct cross-cultural research. Doing so is not simply a matter of replicating the same study in different cultures. Researchers have to guard against imposing their own viewpoints and definitions, learned from their culture, onto another culture with which they are unfamiliar.
  - **The Evolutionary Approach** Some social psychologists attempts to explain social behavior in terms of genetic factors that evolved over time according to the principles of natural selection. Such ideas are hard to test experimentally but can generate novel hypotheses about social behavior that can be tested with the experimental method.
  - **Social Neuroscience** Social psychologists have become increasingly interested in the connection between biological processes and social behavior. These include the study of hormones and behavior, the human immune system, and neurological processes in the human brain.

- **Ethical Issues in Social Psychology** Social psychologists are concerned with the welfare of their research participants.

- **Guidelines for Ethical Research** Social psychologists follow federal, state, and professional guidelines to ensure the welfare of their research participants. These include having an institutional review board approve their studies in advance, asking participants to sign informed consent forms, and debriefing participants afterwards about the purpose of the study and what transpired, especially if there was any deception involved.

CHAPTER 2 TEST 第2章习题

1. The basic dilemma of the social psychologist is that
   a. it is hard to teach social psychology to students because most people believe strongly in personality.
   b. there is a trade-off between internal and external validity in most experiments.
   c. it is nearly impossible to use a random selection of the population in laboratory experiments.
   d. almost all social behavior is influenced by the culture in which people grew up.
   e. it is difficult to teach social psychology at 3:30 in the afternoon when people are sleepy.

2. Suppose a researcher found a strong negative correlation between college students' grade point average (GPA) and the amount of alcohol they drink. Which of the following is the best conclusion from this study?
   a. Students with a high GPA study more and thus have less time to drink.
   b. Drinking a lot interferes with studying.
   c. If you know how much alcohol a student drinks, you can predict his or her GPA fairly well.
   d. The higher a student's GPA, the more he or she drinks.
   e. People who are intelligent get higher grades and drink less.

3. A team of researchers wants to test the hypothesis that drinking wine makes people like jazz more. They randomly assign college students who are 21 or over to one room in which they will drink wine and listen to jazz or to another room in which they will drink water and listen to jazz. It happens that the "wine" room has a big window with nice scenery outside while the "water" room is windowless, dark, and dingy. The most serious flaw in this experiment is that it
   a. is low in external validity.
   b. is low in internal validity.
   c. did not randomly select the participants from all college students in the country.
   d. is low in psychological realism.
   e. is low in mundane realism.

4. Mary wants to find out whether eating sugary snacks before an exam leads to better performance on the exam. Which of the following strategies would answer her question most conclusively?
   a. Identify a large number of students who perform exceptionally low and exceptionally high in exams, ask them whether they eat sugary snacks before exams, and see whether high performers eat more sugary snacks before exams than low performers.
   b. Wait for exam time in a big class, ask everyone whether they ate sugary snacks before the exam, and see whether those who ate sugary snacks before the exam do better compared to those who didn't.
   c. Wait for exam time in a big class, give a random half of the students M&Ms before the exam, and see whether the students who ate M&Ms perform better.
   d. Pick a big class, give all students sugary snacks before one exam and salty snacks before the next exam; then see whether students score on average lower in the second exam.
   e. Sit next to a snack machine, record whether students get sugary snacks or salty snacks, ask everyone for their GPA, and see whether students who get sugary snacks are more likely to have higher GPAs.

5. A researcher conducts a study with participants who are college students. The researcher then repeats the study using the same procedures but with members of the general population (i.e., adults) as participants. The results are similar for both samples. The research has established _____ through _____.
   a. external validity; replication
   b. internal validity; replication
   c. external validity; psychological realism
   d. internal validity; psychological realism
   e. psychological realism; internal validity

6. This chapter described an example of a laboratory experiment that was inspired by a real-life, tragic event: the Latané and Darley study in which people sat in their cubicles and heard someone have a seizure over an intercom system, inspired by the Kitty Genovese murder. All of the following reasons except one explain why social psychologists do laboratory studies that differ so much from the real-life events that inspired them. Which one?
   a. It is usually easier to randomly assign people to conditions in controlled laboratory studies.
   b. The participants in lab studies are often more representative of the general population than the people in the real life examples.
   c. A great advantage to laboratory studies is the ability to maintain high internal validity and know for sure what is causing what.
   d. To see how much you can generalize from a lab study, you can replicate the study with different populations and in different situations.
   e. It is often possible to capture the same psychological processes in the laboratory as those that occur in real-life settings, if psychological realism is high.

7. Professor X wants to make sure his study of gifted youngsters will get published, but he's worried that his findings could have been caused by something other than the independent variable of mutation. He is concerned with the _____ of his experiment.
   a. probability level   c. replication
   b. external validity   d. internal validity

8. Suppose a psychologist decides to join a local commune to understand and observe its members' social relationships. This is
   a. cross-cultural research.
   b. meta-analysis.
   c. applied research.
   d. an experiment.
   e. ethnography.

48 Social Psychology

9. Mary and Juan want to establish interjudge reliability in their study on child bullying and amount of time spent playing video games. To ensure interjudge reliability, they should
   a. observe and code the violent behavior together so they can obtain a reliable coding system.
   b. independently observe and code the data to see if they come up with the same observations.
   c. have one of them observe and code the data and then explain his or her system to the other.
   d. have one observe and code child bullying, whereas the other should observe and code the amount of time the kids play video games.

10. All of the following are part of the guidelines for ethical research except
    a. all research is reviewed by an IRB (institutional review board) that consists of at least one scientist, one nonscientist, and one person unaffiliated with the institution.
    b. a researcher receives informed consent from a participant unless deception is deemed necessary and the experiment meets ethical guidelines.
    c. when deception is used in a study, participants must be fully debriefed.
    d. there must be a cover story for every study, since all studies involve some type of deception.

Chapter 2 Answer Key
1-b, 2-c, 3-b, 4-c, 5-a, 6-b, 7-d, 8-e, 9-b, 10-d

For more review plus practice tests, videos, flashcards, writing help and more, log on to MyPsychLab.

Scoring the TRY IT! exercises "试一试！"答案

Page 25

1. In studies conducted by Stanley Milgram (1974), up to 65 percent of participants administered what they thought were near-lethal shocks to another subject. (In fact, no real shocks were administered.)

2. (c) Rewarding people for doing something they enjoy will typically make them like that activity less in the future (e.g., Lepper, 1995, 1996; Lepper, Greene, & Nisbett, 1973).

3. (b) Wilson and colleagues (1993) found that people who did not analyze their feelings were the most satisfied with their choice of posters when contacted a few weeks later.

4. (a) Under most circumstances, repeated exposure increases liking for a stimulus (Zajonc, 1968).

5. (a) More (Jecker & Landy, 1969).

6. (c) Research by Dijksterhuis and Nordgren (2006) found that people who were distracted made the best choices, possibly because distraction allowed them to consider the problem unconsciously but not consciously.

7. (a) Research by Spencer, Steele, and Quinn (1999) and Steele (1997) found that when women think there are sex differences on a test, they do worse. When women were told that there were no gender differences in performance on the test, they did as well as men.

8. (b) There is no evidence that subliminal messages in advertising have any effect; considerable evidence shows that normal advertising is quite effective (Abraham & Lodish, 1990; Chaiken, Wood, & Eagly, 1996; Liebert & Sprafkin, 1988; Moore, 1982; Weir, 1984; Wilson, Houston, & Meyers, 1998).

9. (b) Men touch women more than vice versa (Henley, 1977).

10. (c) In the short run, people regret things they did that they wish they hadn't done more than things they didn't do that they wish they had done. In the long run, however, the opposite is true (Gilovich & Medvec, 1995a; Gilovich, Medvec, & Chen, 1995).

Page 28

Two teams of researchers (Archer, 1983, and Akert, Chen, & Panter, 1991) performed an archival analysis of portrait art and news and advertising photographs in print and television media. They coded the photographs according to the number of images that were devoted to the person's face. Their results? Over 5 centuries, across cultures, and in different forms of media, men are visually presented in a more close-up style (focusing on the head and face), while women are shown in a more long-shot style (focusing on the body). These researchers interpret their findings as indicating a subtle form of sex-role stereotyping: Men are being portrayed in a stronger style that emphasizes their intellectual achievements, whereas women are being portrayed in a weaker style that emphasizes their total physical appearance.

Page 33

1. The politician ignored possible third variables that could cause both Scout membership and crime, such as socioeconomic class. Traditionally, Scouting has been most popular in small towns and suburbs among middle-class youngsters; it has never been very attractive or even available to youths growing up in densely populated, urban, high-crime areas.

2. Not necessarily. It might be the other way around, namely, that moms and dads are more likely to become helicopter parents if their kids are having academic problems. Or there could be a third variable that causes parents to hover and their kids to have academic problems.

3. Did tattoos cause motorcycle accidents? Or for that matter, did motorcycle accidents cause tattoos? The researchers suggested that a third (unmeasured) variable was in fact the cause of both: A tendency to take risks and to be involved in flamboyant personal displays led to tattooing one's body and to driving a motorcycle recklessly.

4. It is possible that religion makes people more likely to obey the law. It is equally possible, however, that some other variable increases the likelihood that people will be religious and follow the rules—such as having parents who are religious.

5. Not necessarily. People who do not eat breakfast might differ from people who do in any number of ways that influence longevity—for example, in how obese they are, in how hard-driving and high-strung they are, or even in how late they sleep in the morning.

6. Not necessarily because milk drinking may have little to do with weight gain. Children who drink a lot of milk might be more likely to eat cookies or other high-calorie foods.

7. It is not a valid conclusion. People who are skeptical of paranormal phenomena to begin with could be more likely to read newspapers and magazines. Or some third variable could cause both the skepticism and the desire to read newspapers and magazines (Spears, 2008).

8. It is possible that watching public television makes people want to have more sex. It is equally possible, however, that some third variable, such as health or education, influences both television preferences and sexual behavior. It is even possible that having sex makes people want to watch more public television. Based on the correlation the researchers reported, there is no way of telling which of these explanations is true.

3

Social Cognition
How We Think about the Social World
社会认知：
我们如何思考社会性世界

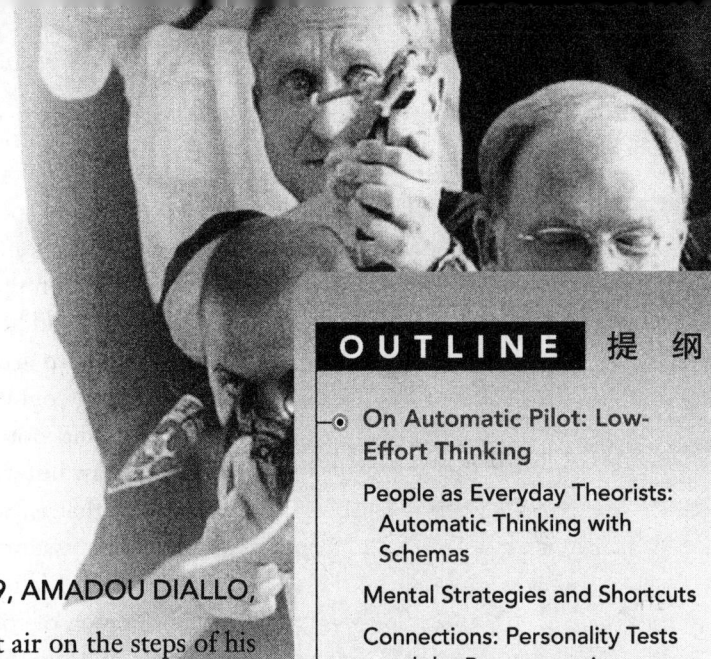

OUTLINE 提纲

- **On Automatic Pilot: Low-Effort Thinking**
  People as Everyday Theorists: Automatic Thinking with Schemas
  Mental Strategies and Shortcuts
  Connections: Personality Tests and the Representativeness Heuristic
  The Power of Unconscious Thinking
  Cultural Differences in Social Cognition
- **Controlled Social Cognition: High-Effort Thinking**
  Mentally Undoing the Past: Counterfactual Reasoning
  Thought Suppression and Ironic Processing
  Improving Human Thinking
- **The Amadou Diallo Case Revisited**
- **Summary**

LATE ON THE EVENING OF FEBRUARY 3, 1999, AMADOU DIALLO, an immigrant from West Africa, took in the night air on the steps of his apartment building in the South Bronx. In what was soon to become a fateful encounter, four undercover police officers on patrol, in an unmarked Ford Taurus, turned down Diallo's street. One of the officers noticed Diallo and thought that he looked like sketches of a man who had committed rapes in that area about a year earlier. The officers got out of their car and ordered Diallo to stop as he entered the vestibule of his apartment building. In fact, Diallo had no criminal record. He was working long hours as a street vendor and in his spare time was earning high school credits so that he could go to college. When the police approached Diallo, he reached for his wallet, probably so that he could show some identification. Alarmed by the sight of a black man reaching into his pocket, the four officers did not hesitate. They fired a total of 41 shots at Diallo, killing him instantly.

Unfortunately, incidents such as this one are not rare. On the night of April 7, 2001, a Cincinnati police officer chased 19-year-old Timothy Thomas into an alley and demanded that he show him his hands. Before Thomas had a chance to comply, the officer shot and killed him. On November 25, 2006, in Queens, New York, police officers fired 50 bullets at Sean Bell in the parking lot of a strip club, killing him instantly. Thomas and Bell were both African American, and both were unarmed. Bell was getting married later that day.

Police officers often have to make extremely quick decisions and have little time to stop and analyze whether someone poses a threat. In the Diallo, Thomas, and Bell cases, however, many people wondered whether the officers' decisions to open fire so quickly were influenced by the victims' race. Thomas was the 15th African American killed by the Cincinnati police in the preceding six years; no whites were killed by the police during this time period (Singer, 2002). Would the officers have acted any differently if the men had been white? More generally, how do people size up their social worlds and decide how to act, in life-and-death situations such as these or in everyday situations people face all the time? The ways in which people analyze and think about the social world are the topic of this chapter.

As we discussed in Chapter 1, a central topic in social psychology is the study of **social cognition**, or the ways in which people think about themselves and the social world, including how they select, interpret, remember, and use social information. The assumption is that people are generally trying to form accurate impressions of

Social Cognition
How people think about themselves and the social world, or more specifically, how people select, interpret, remember, and use social information to make judgments and decisions

Rodin's famous sculpture, *The Thinker*, mimics controlled thinking, where people sit down and consider something slowly and deliberately. Even when we do not know it, however, we are engaging in automatic thinking, which is nonconscious, unintentional, involuntary, and effortless.

the world and do so much of the time. Because of the nature of social thinking, however, people sometimes form erroneous impressions—such as the police officers' assumption that Amadou Diallo was reaching for a gun.

To understand how people think about their social worlds and how accurate their impressions are likely to be, we need to distinguish between two different kinds of social cognition. One kind of thought is quick and automatic. The police officers did not pause and think about what might be in Diallo's pocket; when they saw him reach for something, they opened fire. They acted "without thinking"—that is, without consciously deliberating about what they saw and whether their assumptions were correct (Bargh & Morsella, 2008; Lundqvist & Öhman, 2005; Richeson & Ambady, 2003; Shah, 2003; Wilson, 2002).

Sometimes, of course, people do pause and think about themselves and their environments and think carefully about the right course of action. You may have spent hours deliberating over important decisions in your life, such as where to go to college, which major to pursue, and whether to break up with your boyfriend or girlfriend. This is the second kind of social cognition—*controlled thinking*, which is more effortful and deliberate. Quite often the automatic and controlled modes of social cognition work very well together. Think of the automatic pilot that flies modern airplanes, monitoring hundreds of complex systems and adjusting instantly to changes in atmospheric conditions. The autopilot does just fine most of the time, although occasionally it is important for the human pilot to take over and fly the plane manually. Humans, too, have "automatic pilots" that monitor their environments, draw conclusions, and direct their behaviors. But we can also "override" this automatic type of thinking and analyze a situation slowly and deliberately. We will begin by examining the nature of automatic thinking.

> *It is the mind which creates the world about us, and even though we stand side by side in the same meadow, my eyes will never see what is beheld by yours.*
>
> —George Gissing, *The Private Papers of Henry Ryecroft*, 1903

On Automatic Pilot: Low-Effort Thinking 自动化：低努力水平思维

Despite our opening example of the shooting of Amadou Diallo, it is important to note that people often size up a new situation quickly and accurately. They figure out who is there, what is happening, and what might happen next. When you attended your first college class, for example, you probably made quick assumptions about who people were (the person standing at the lectern was the professor) and how to behave. We doubt that you confused the class with a fraternity party. And you probably reached these conclusions without even being aware that you were doing so.

Imagine a different approach: Every time you encounter a new situation you stop and think about it slowly and deliberately, like Rodin's statue *The Thinker*. When you are introduced to someone new, you have to excuse yourself for 15 minutes while you analyze what you have learned and how much you like the person. When you drive down an unfamiliar road, you have to pull over and analyze its twists and turns before knowing how to proceed. Sounds exhausting, doesn't it? Fortunately, we form impressions of people quickly and effortlessly and navigate new roads without much conscious analysis of what we are doing. We do these things by engaging in an automatic analysis of our environments, based on our past experiences and knowledge of the world. **Automatic thinking** is thought that is nonconscious, unintentional, involuntary, and effortless. Although different kinds of automatic thinking meet these criteria to varying degrees (Bargh & Ferguson, 2000; Moors & De Houwer, 2006; Wegner &

Automatic Thinking
Thinking that is nonconscious, unintentional, involuntary, and effortless

Bargh, 1998), for our purposes we can define automaticity as thinking that satisfies all or most of these criteria.

People as Everyday Theorists: Automatic Thinking with Schemas
作为日常理论家的人们：
运用图式进行自动化思考

Automatic thinking helps us understand new situations by relating them to our prior experiences. When we meet someone new, we don't start from scratch to figure out what he or she is like; we categorize the person as "an engineering student" or "like my cousin Helen." The same goes for places, objects, and situations. When we walk into a fast-food restaurant we've never visited, we know, without thinking, not to wait at a table for a waiter and a menu. We know that we have to go to the counter and order because our mental "script" automatically tells us that this is what we do in fast-food restaurants, and we assume that this one is no different.

More formally, people use **schemas**, which are mental structures that organize our knowledge about the social world. These mental structures influence the information we notice, think about, and remember (Bartlett, 1932; Heine, Proulx, & Vohs, 2006; Markus, 1977). The term *schema* is very general; it encompasses our knowledge about many things—other people, ourselves, social roles (e.g., what a librarian or an engineer is like), and specific events (e.g., what usually happens when people eat a meal in a restaurant). In each case, our schemas contain our basic knowledge and impressions that we use to organize what we know about the social world and interpret new situations. For example, our schema about the members of the Animal House fraternity might be that they're loud, obnoxious partygoers with a propensity for projectile vomiting.

In a study by Correll et al. (2002), people played a video game in which they saw photographs of men who were holding a handgun or nonthreatening objects such as cell phones, as in the picture shown here. Half of the men were African American and half were white. Participants were instructed to press a button labeled "shoot" if the man had a gun and a button labeled "don't shoot" if he did not. Like a real police officer they had very little time to make up their minds (just over half a second). The most common mistake people made was to "shoot" an African American man who was not holding a gun, such as the man in this picture.

Stereotypes about Race and Weapons When applied to members of a social group such as a fraternity or gender or race, schemas are commonly referred to as *stereotypes*, which we will discuss in detail in Chapter 13. For now, we point out that the stereotypes can be applied rapidly and automatically when we encounter other people. For example, recent experiments have tested whether people's stereotypes about African Americans influence their decision to "shoot" a suspect in a video game that simulates real-life situations faced by police officers (Correll, 2002; Payne, 2001, 2006). In one study, nonblack participants saw photographs of young men in realistic settings, such as in a park, at a train station, and on a city sidewalk. Half of the men were African American, and half were white. And half of the men in each group were holding a handgun and half were holding nonthreatening objects such as a cell phone, wallet, or camera. Participants were instructed to press a button labeled "shoot" if the man in the picture had a gun and a button labeled "don't shoot" if he did not. Like a real police officer, they had very little time to make up their minds (just over half a second). Participants won or lost points on each round of the game, modeled after the risks and benefits faced by officers in real life. Participants earned 5 points for not shooting someone who did not have a gun, and 10 points for shooting someone who did have a gun. They lost 20 points if they shot someone who was not holding a gun and lost 40 points if they failed to shoot someone who was holding a gun (which, in real life, would be the most life-threatening situation for a police officer).

The results? Participants were especially likely to pull the trigger when the people in the pictures were black, whether or not these people were holding a gun. This

Schemas
Mental structures people use to organize their knowledge about the social world around themes or subjects and that influence the information people notice, think about, and remember

FIGURE 3.1
Errors made in "shooting" people in video game.

Participants played a video game in which they were supposed to "shoot" a man if he was holding a gun and withhold fire if he was not. People were influenced by the race of the men in the pictures. As seen in the figure, people were prone to make mistakes by shooting black men who were unarmed.

(Adapted from Correll, Park, Judd, & Wittenbrink, 2002)

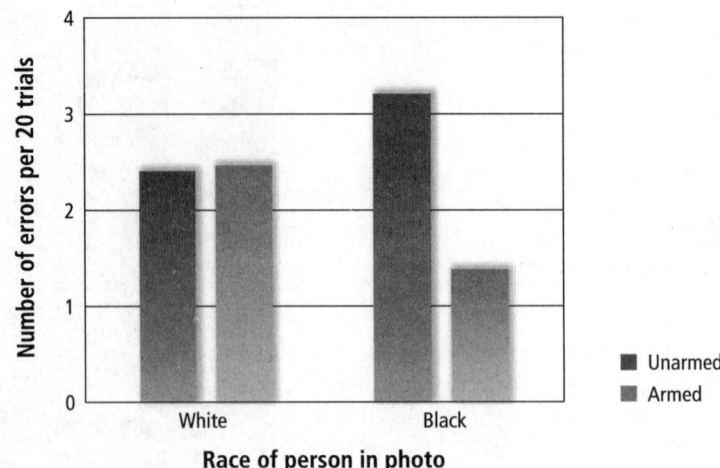

> It is a capital mistake to theorize before you have all the evidence. It biases the judgment.
>
> —Sherlock Holmes (Sir Arthur Conan Doyle), 1898

"shooter bias" meant that people made relatively few errors when a black person was in fact holding a gun but also that they made the most errors, shooting an unarmed person, when a black person was not holding a gun (see Figure 3.1). When the men in the picture were white, participants made about the same number of errors whether the men were armed or unarmed. (You can try a version of this test yourself at backhand.uchicago.edu/Center/ShooterEffect/.) Thus, here's a case in which people's schemas influenced a crucial decision, namely, whether to shoot someone. Of course, people were just playing a game and not *really* shooting anyone. And the participants were not trained police officers; perhaps the extensive training officers receive helps them overcome any biases they might have. Recent studies using video games have found that police officers show the same association between blacks and guns as do other people; for example, they take less time to shoot an armed black person than an armed white person (Correll et al., 2007; Eberhardt, Goff, Purdie, & Davies, 2004; Plant & Peruche, 2005). However, one study also found that officers were less likely than nonofficers to let racial stereotypes guide their ultimate decisions about whether to shoot (Correll et al., 2007). Thus, the jury is still out on the extent to which officers show the same "shooter bias" as nonofficers.

The Function of Schemas: Why Do We Have Them? We've just seen the negative consequences of schemas, cases in which people "fill in the blanks" in erroneous ways (e.g., assuming that a black person is holding a gun when he is not). We should keep in mind, though, that schemas are typically very useful for helping us organize and make sense of the world and to fill in the gaps of our knowledge. Think for a moment what it would be like to have no schemas at all. What if everything you encountered was inexplicable, confusing, and unlike anything else you've ever known? Tragically, this is what happens to people who suffer from a neurological disorder called Korsakov's syndrome. People with this disorder lose the ability to form new memories and must approach every situation as if they were encountering it for the first time, even if they have actually experienced it many times before. This can be so unsettling—even terrifying—that some people with Korsakov's syndrome go to great lengths to try to impose meaning on their experiences. The neurologist Oliver Sacks (1987) gives the following description of a Korsakov patient named Thompson:

> He remembered nothing for more than a few seconds. He was continually disoriented. Abysses of amnesia continually opened beneath him, but he would bridge them, nimbly, by fluent confabulations and fictions of all kinds. For him they were not fictions, but how he suddenly saw, or interpreted, the world. Its radical flux and incoherence could not be tolerated, acknowledged, for an instant—there was, instead, this strange, delirious, quasi-coherence, as Mr. Thompson, with his ceaseless, unconscious, quick-fire inventions, continually improvised a world around him . . . for such a patient must literally make himself (and his world) up every moment. *(pp. 109–110; emphasis in original)*

> *Theory helps us to bear our ignorance of facts.*
>
> —George Santayana, *The Sense of Beauty*, 1896

In short, having continuity, being able to relate new experiences to our past schemas, is so important that people who lose this ability invent schemas where none exist.

Schemas are particularly useful when we are in confusing situations because they help us figure out what is going on. Consider a classic study by Harold Kelley (1950) in which students in different sections of a college economics class were told that a guest lecturer would be filling in that day. To create a schema about what the guest lecturer would be like, Kelley told the students that the economics department was interested in how different classes reacted to different instructors and that the students would thus receive a brief biographical note about the instructor before he arrived. The note contained information about the instructor's age, background, teaching experience, and personality. One version said, "People who know him consider him to be a very warm person, industrious, critical, practical, and determined." The other version was identical, except that the phrase "a very warm person" was replaced with "a rather cold person." The students received one of these personality descriptions at random.

The guest lecturer then conducted a class discussion for 20 minutes, after which the students rated their impressions of him. How funny was he? How sociable? How considerate? Given that there was some ambiguity in this situation—after all, the students had seen the instructor for only a brief time—Kelley hypothesized that they would use the schema provided by the biographical note to fill in the blanks. This is exactly what happened. The students who expected the instructor to be warm gave him significantly higher ratings than the students who expected him to be cold, even though all the students had observed the exact same teacher behaving in the same way. The students who expected the instructor to be warm were also more likely to ask him questions and to participate in the class discussion. Has this happened to you? Have your expectations about a professor influenced your impressions of him or her? Did you find, oddly enough, that the professor acted just as you'd expected? Ask a classmate who had a different expectation about the professor what he or she thought. Do the two of you have different perceptions of the instructor based on the different schemas you were using?

Of course, people are not totally blind to what is actually out there in the world. Sometimes what we see is relatively unambiguous and we do not need to use our schemas to help us interpret it. For example, in one of the classes in which Kelley conducted his study, the guest instructor happened to be obviously self-confident, even a little arrogant. Given that arrogance is a relatively unambiguous trait, the students did not need to rely on their expectations to fill in the blanks. They rated the instructor as arrogant in both the warm and cold conditions. However, when they rated this instructor's sense of humor, which was less clear-cut, the students relied on their schemas: The students in the warm condition thought he was funnier than the

People who know him consider him a rather cold person, industrious, critical, practical, and determined.

People who know him consider him a very warm person, industrious, critical, practical, and determined.

Is this man an alcoholic or just down on his luck? Our judgments about other people can be influenced by schemas that are accessible in our memories. If you had just been talking to a friend about a relative who had an alcohol problem, you might be more likely to think that this man has an alcohol problem as well, because alcoholism is accessible in your memory.

> *I know that often I would not see a thing unless I thought of it first.*
> —Norman Maclean, *A River Runs through It*

Accessibility
The extent to which schemas and concepts are at the forefront of people's minds and are therefore likely to be used when making judgments about the social world

Priming
The process by which recent experiences increase the accessibility of a schema, trait, or concept

students in the cold condition did. The more ambiguous our information is, then, the more we use schemas to fill in the blanks.

It is important to note that there is nothing wrong with what the students in Kelley's study did. As long as people have reason to believe their schemas are accurate, it is perfectly reasonable to use them to resolve ambiguity. If a stranger comes up to you in a dark alley and says, "Take out your wallet," your schema about such encounters tells you that the person wants to steal your money, not admire pictures of your family. This schema helps you avert a serious and perhaps deadly misunderstanding. The danger comes when we automatically apply schemas that are *not* accurate, such as the police officers' assumption that Amadou Diallo was reaching for a gun.

Which Schemas Are Applied? Accessibility and Priming The social world is full of ambiguous information that is open to interpretation. Imagine, for example, that you are riding on a city bus and a man gets on and sits beside you. He mutters incoherently to himself and rocks back and forth in his seat. At one point he starts singing an old Beatles tune. How would you make sense of his behavior? You have several schemas you could use. Should you interpret his behavior with your "alcoholic" or "mentally ill person" schema? How will you decide?

The schema that comes to mind and guides your impressions of the man can be affected by **accessibility**, the extent to which schemas and concepts are at the forefront of the mind and are therefore likely to be used when making judgments about the social world (Higgins, 1996a; Sanna & Schwarz, 2004; Wyer & Srull, 1989). Something can become accessible for three reasons. Some schemas are chronically accessible due to past experience (Chen & Andersen, 1999; Dijksterhuis & van Knippenberg, 1996; Higgins & Brendl, 1995; Rudman & Borgida, 1995). This means that these schemas are constantly active and ready to use to interpret ambiguous situations. For example, if there is a history of alcoholism in your family, traits describing an alcoholic are likely to be chronically accessible to you, increasing the likelihood that you will assume that the man on the bus has had too much too drink. If someone you know suffers from mental illness, however, thoughts about how the mentally ill behave are more likely to be more accessible than thoughts about alcoholics, leading you to interpret the man's behavior very differently.

Second, something can become accessible because it is related to a current goal. The concept of mental illness might not be chronically accessible to you, but if you are studying for a test in your abnormal psychology class and need to learn about different kinds of mental disorders, this concept might be temporarily accessible. As a consequence, you might be more likely to notice the man on the bus and interpret his behavior as a sign of a mental disorder—at least until your test is over and you no longer have the goal to learn about mental illnesses (Forster, Liberman & Higgins, 2005; Kuhl, 1983; Martin & Tesser, 1996).

Finally, schemas can become temporarily accessible because of our recent experiences (Bargh, 1996; Higgins & Bargh, 1987; Oishi, Schimmack, & Colcombe, 2003; Stapel & Koomen, 2000). This means that a particular schema or trait is not always accessible but happens to be primed by something people have been thinking or doing before encountering an event. Suppose that right before the man on the bus sat down, you were reading *One Flew over the Cuckoo's Nest*, Ken Kesey's novel about patients in a mental hospital. Given that thoughts about mental patients were accessible in your mind, you would probably assume that the man was mentally ill. If, however, you had just looked out the window and seen an alcoholic leaning against a building drinking from a paper bag, you would probably assume that the man on the bus was drunk (see Figure 3.2). These are examples of **priming**, the process by which recent experiences increase the accessibility of a schema, trait, or concept. Reading Kesey's novel primes certain traits, such as those describing the mentally ill, making it more likely that these traits will be used to interpret a new event, such as the behavior of the man on the bus, even though this new event is completely unrelated to the one that originally primed the traits.

The following experiment illustrates the priming effect (Higgins, Rholes, & Jones, 1977). Research participants were told that they would take part in two unrelated studies. In the first, a perception study, they would have to identify different colors while at the same time memorizing a list of words. The second was a reading comprehension study in which they would be asked to read a paragraph about someone named Donald and then give their impressions of him. This paragraph is shown in Figure 3.3. Take a moment to read it. What do you think of Donald?

You might have noticed that many of Donald's actions are ambiguous, interpretable in either a positive or a negative manner, such as the fact that he piloted a boat without knowing much about it and that he wants to sail across the Atlantic. You might put a positive spin on these acts, deciding that Donald has an admirable sense of adventure. Or you could give the same behavior a negative spin, assuming that Donald is quite a reckless person.

How did the participants interpret Donald's behavior? As expected, it depended on whether positive or negative traits were primed and accessible. In the

FIGURE 3.2

How we interpret an ambiguous situation: The role of accessibility and priming.

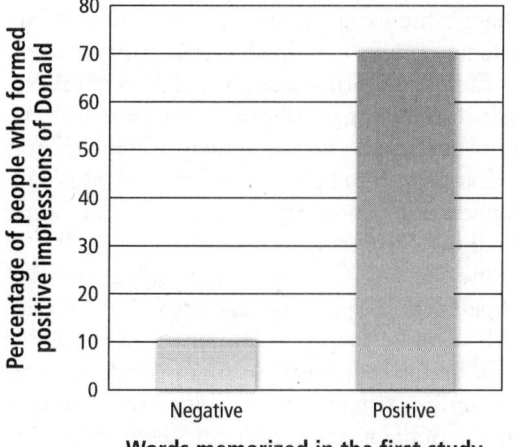

Description of Donald

Donald spent a great deal of time in his search of what he liked to call excitement. He had already climbed Mt. McKinley, shot the Colorado rapids in a kayak, driven in a demolition derby, and piloted a jet-powered boat—without knowing very much about boats. He had risked injury, and even death, a number of times. Now he was in search of new excitement. He was thinking perhaps he would do some skydiving or maybe cross the Atlantic in a sailboat. By the way he acted one could readily guess that Donald was well aware of his ability to do many things well. Other than business engagements, Donald's contacts with people were rather limited. He felt he didn't really need to rely on anyone. Once Donald made up his mind to do something it was as good as done no matter how long it might take or how difficult the going might be. Only rarely did he change his mind even when it might well have been better if he had.

FIGURE 3.3

Priming and accessibility.

In the second of a pair of studies, people were asked to read this paragraph about Donald and form an impression of him. In the first study, some of the participants had memorized words that could be used to interpret Donald in a negative way (e.g., reckless, conceited), while others had memorized words that could be used to interpret Donald in a positive way (e.g., adventurous, self-confident). As the graph shows, those who had memorized the negative words formed a much more negative impression of Donald than those who had memorized the positive words.

(Adapted from Higgins, Rholes, & Jones, 1977)

first study, the researchers divided people into two groups and gave them different words to memorize. People who had first memorized the words *adventurous, self-confident, independent,* and *persistent* later formed positive impressions of Donald, viewing him as a likable man who enjoyed new challenges. People who had first memorized *reckless, conceited, aloof,* and *stubborn* later formed negative impressions of Donald, viewing him as a stuck-up person who took needlessly dangerous chances.

But it was not just memorizing any positive or negative words that influenced people's impressions of Donald. In other conditions, research participants memorized words that were also positive or negative, such as *neat* or *disrespectful*. However, these traits didn't influence their impressions of Donald because the words did not apply to Donald's behavior. Thoughts, then, have to be both *accessible* and *applicable* before they will act as primes, exerting an influence on our impressions of the social world.

Priming is a good example of automatic thinking because it occurs quickly, unintentionally, and unconsciously. When judging others, people are usually not aware that they are applying concepts or schemas that they happened to be thinking about earlier. In fact, priming can occur even by flashing words at speeds that are too quick for people to recognize consciously. John Bargh and Paula Pietromonaco (1982) flashed words having to do with hostility (e.g., *hostile* and *unkind*) or neutral words (e.g., *water, between*) on a computer screen so quickly that people saw only a flash of light. People then read a paragraph describing a person who acted in ways that could or could not be interpreted as hostile (e.g., "A salesman knocked on the door, but Donald refused to let him enter"). Just as in the Higgins and colleagues' (1977) study, people interpreted Donald's behavior in terms of the traits that had been primed; in this case, the people who saw the hostile words rated Donald as more hostile than people who saw the neutral words. Remarkably, this occurred even though people did not know they had seen the words, which supports the idea that priming is an automatic, nonconscious process. The Bargh and Pietromonaco study raises the specter of subliminal influence—whether it is possible to influence people's beliefs and attitudes with messages that they do not perceive consciously. We address this question in Chapter 7.

> *Prophecy is the most gratuitous form of error.*
>
> —George Eliot
> (Mary Ann Evans Cross), 1871

Making Our Schemas Come True: The Self-Fulfilling Prophecy We've seen that when people encounter new evidence or have old evidence discredited, they tend not to revise their schemas as much as we might expect. People are not always passive recipients of information, however—they often act on their schemas in ways that change the extent to which these schemas are supported or contradicted. In fact, people can inadvertently make their schemas come true by the way they treat other people (Madon, Willard, Buller, & Scherr, in press). This **self-fulfilling prophecy** operates as follows: People have an expectation about what another person is like, which influences how they act toward that person, which causes that person to behave consistently with people's original expectations, making the expectations come true. Figure 3.4 illustrates the sad self-perpetuating cycle of a self-fulfilling prophecy.

Self-fulfilling prophecies can have some serious consequences. Consider these facts: In U.S. elementary schools, girls outperform boys on standardized tests of reading, writing, social studies, and math. By the middle school years, however, girls start to fall behind, and by high school, boys do better than girls on many kinds of standardized tests (Hedges & Nowell, 1995; Mendez, Mihalas, & Hardesty, 2006; Reis & Park, 2001; Stumpf & Stanley, 1998). On the Scholastic Assessment Test (SAT) used by many colleges to select students, males outscore females on the math and verbal sections (The College Board, 2007).

To be sure, this is a complicated issue, and we don't mean to imply that girls are always at a disadvantage. The gender gap in verbal SAT scores is narrowing; there was only a 2 point difference in favor of men in 2007. And, on the new SAT writing test, women have outperformed men. Boys are falling behind in other respects; whereas the majority of college students used to be male, today 56 percent are female (Tyre, 2006), and women are more likely to graduate from college than are men (Buchmann & DiPrete, 2006). But the fact remains that men get higher scores on math and sci-

Self-Fulfilling Prophecy

The case whereby people have an expectation about what another person is like, which influences how they act toward that person, which causes that person to behave consistently with people's original expectations, making the expectations come true

FIGURE 3.4
The self-fulfilling prophecy: A sad cycle in four acts.

ence tests on average, and it is highly unlikely that these differences can be fully explained by biological differences between men and women (Ghiselin, 1996; Halpern et al., 2007; Spelke, 2005; Spelke & Grace, 2007).

Consider these pieces of the puzzle: If you ask teachers which of their current students are most academically gifted or who their most outstanding students have been over the years, an embarrassing truth leaks out—most of the students they mention are male. Many teachers, even if they are women themselves, believe that males are brighter and more likely to succeed academically than females (Jussim & Eccles, 1992). Parents hold similar beliefs about the talents of their children, and so do adolescents about their own talents (Bhanot & Jovanovic, 2005; Yee & Eccles, 1988). These beliefs are particularly strong about boys' versus girls' abilities at math and science. One study found no difference between boys' and girls' interest in science or their grades in science classes. Nonetheless, their parents believed that their daughters were less interested in science than their sons, and that their daughters found science to be more difficult (Tenenbaum & Leaper, 2003).

Might girls do worse in math and science because of a self-fulfilling prophecy? Are teachers and parents treating boys and girls differently, in ways that make their expectations about gender and academic performance come true? Let's be very clear: No one is suggesting that teachers or parents deliberately treat girls in ways that impede their performance. There is evidence, however, that teachers and parents unintentionally behave in ways that make their expectations about girls' achievement come true.

Consider this example, described by researchers after years spent observing teachers' behavior toward boys versus girls (Sadker & Sadker, 1994). A fifth-grade teacher is explaining a difficult math problem and asks one of the girls to hold the book so that everyone can see the problem. She then does something interesting: She turns her

Teachers can unintentionally make their expectations about their students come true by treating some students differently from others.

back to the girls (who are seated on her right) and explains the problem to the boys (who are seated on her left). Although she occasionally turns to the girls to read an example from the book, she directs virtually all of her attention to the boys, such that the girls can see only the back of her head. "The girl holding the math book had become a prop," Sadker and Sadker note. "The teacher . . . had unwittingly transformed the girls into spectators, an audience for the boys" (p. 3). The Sadkers document many such cases of teachers treating boys more favorably than girls.

Such anecdotes, while interesting, certainly do not prove that self-fulfilling prophecies are at work in our schools. It is necessary to conduct studies in which teachers' expectations are controlled experimentally. Robert Rosenthal and Lenore Jacobson (1968) did so in an elementary school in what has become one of the most famous studies in social psychology. They administered a test to all the students in the school and told the teachers that some of the students had scored so well that they were sure to "bloom" academically in the upcoming year. In fact, this was not necessarily true: The students identified as "bloomers" were chosen at random by the researchers. As we discussed in Chapter 2, the use of random assignment means that on average, the students designated as bloomers were no smarter or more likely to bloom than any of the other kids. The only way in which these students differed from their peers was in the minds of the teachers (neither the students nor their parents were told anything about the results of the test).

After creating the expectation in the teachers that certain students would do especially well, Rosenthal and Jacobson waited to see what would happen. They observed the classroom dynamics periodically, and at the end of the school year, they gave all of the children an IQ test. Did the prophecy come true? Indeed it did—the students in each class who had been labeled as bloomers showed significantly greater gains in their IQ scores than the other students did (see Figure 3.5). The teachers' expectations had become reality. Rosenthal and Jacobson's findings have since been replicated in a number of both experimental and correlational studies (Babad, 1993; Blank, 1993; Jussim, 2005; Jussim & Harber, 2005; Madon, 2004).

Did the teachers in the Rosenthal and Jacobson (1968) study callously decide to give more attention and encouragement to the bloomers? Not at all. Most teachers are quite dedicated and would be upset to learn that they favored some students over others. Far from being a conscious, deliberate act, the self-fulfilling prophecy is instead an example of automatic thinking (Chen & Bargh, 1997). Interestingly, the teachers in the Rosenthal and Jacobson study reported that they spent slightly less time with the students who were labeled as bloomers. In subsequent studies, however, teachers have been found to treat bloomers (the students they expect to do better) differently in four general ways: They create a warmer emotional climate for bloomers, giving them more personal attention, encouragement, and support; they give

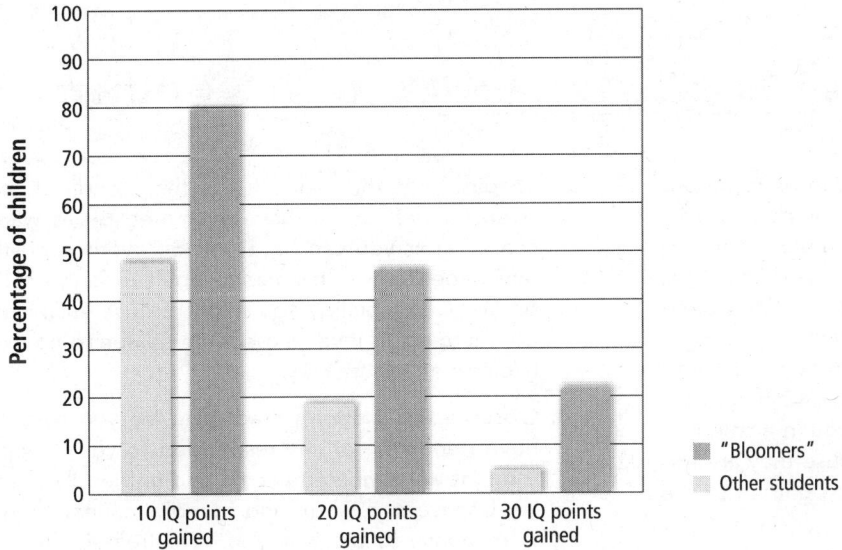

FIGURE 3.5

The self-fulfilling prophecy: Percentage of first and second graders who improved on an IQ test over the course of the school year.

Those whom the teachers expected to do well actually improved more than the other students.

(Adapted from Rosenthal & Jacobson, 1968)

bloomers more material to learn and material that is more difficult; they give bloomers more and better feedback on their work; and they give bloomers more opportunities to respond in class and give them longer to respond (Brophy, 1983; Rosenthal, 1994; Snyder, 1984).

Remember the teacher who taught math more to the boys than to the girls in her fifth-grade class? With her permission, she was being videotaped for a segment of the NBC television program *Dateline* on sexism in the schools. We can assume, then, that she was trying hard to treat the girls and the boys equally. Nonetheless, she favored the boys, which suggests how hard it can be to recognize that our expectations can strongly influence our behavior. A distressing implication of the fact that the self-fulfilling prophecy occurs automatically is that our schemas may be quite resistant to change. Suppose a teacher has the schema that boys are innately better at math than girls. "But Mr. Jones," we might reply, "how can you hold such a belief? There are plenty of girls who do very well in math." Mr. Jones would probably be unconvinced because he would have data to support his schema. "In my classes over the years," he might note, "nearly three times as many boys as girls have excelled at math." His error lies not with his characterization of the evidence but in his failure to realize his role in producing it. Robert Merton, an eminent sociologist, referred to this process as a "reign of error," whereby people can "cite the actual course of events as proof that [they were] right from the very beginning" (1948, p. 195).

Limits of Self-Fulfilling Prophecies Does all of this mean that we are like putty in the hands of powerful people who have incorrect expectations about us? Suppose that Sarah is about to be interviewed for a job at a law firm by someone who has negative expectations about her qualifications, based, perhaps, on her gender, race, previous place of employment, or college. Will she be able to overcome these expectations and show the interviewer that she really is highly qualified for the job? Or, consistent with research on the self-fulfilling prophecy, will the interviewer mold Sarah's behavior in such a way that Sarah finds herself giving halting, inadequate answers to the questions?

Recent research confirms that self-fulfilling prophecies often occur but also demonstrates some of the conditions under which people's true nature will win out in social interaction (Jussim & Harber, 2005; Madon et al., 2001; Madon et al., in press; Willard, in press).). For example, self-fulfilling prophecies are most likely to occur when interviewers are not paying careful attention to the person they are interviewing (Biesanz, 2001; Harris & Perkins, 1995). When interviewers are motivated to form an accurate impression and are paying attention, they are often able to put their expectations aside and see what the person is really like. Thus Sarah should hope that the lawyer interviewing her is not too busy or pressed for time. Otherwise, she might well fall prey to the interviewer's self-fulfilling prophecies. See the following Try It! exercise for a way to overcome your own self-fulfilling prophecies.

TRY IT! Avoiding Self-Fulfilling Prophecies 试一试！避免自证预言

1. Examine some of your own schemas and expectations about social groups, especially groups you don't particularly like. These might be members of a particular race or ethnic group, of a rival fraternity, of a political party, or people with a particular sexual orientation. Why don't you like members of this group? "Well," you might think, "one reason is that whenever I interact with these people, they seem cold and unfriendly." And you might be right. Perhaps they do respond to you in a cold and unfriendly fashion—not, however, because they are this way by nature but because they are responding to the way you have treated them.

2. Try this exercise to counteract the self-fulfilling prophecy: Find someone who is a member of a group you dislike and strike up a conversation with the person. For example, sit next to this person in one of your classes, or strike up a conversation at a party or gathering. Try to imagine that this individual is the friendliest, kindest, sweetest person you have ever met. Be as warm and charming as you can be. Don't go overboard—if, after never speaking to this person, you suddenly act like Mr. or Ms. Congeniality, you might arouse suspicion. The trick is to act as if you expect the person to be extremely pleasant and friendly.

3. Observe this person's reactions. Are you surprised by how friendly he or she responded to you? People you thought were inherently cold and unfriendly will probably behave in a warm and friendly manner themselves in response to the way you have treated them. If this doesn't work on your first encounter with the person, try it again on one or two later occasions. In all likelihood, you will find that friendliness really does breed friendliness (see Chapter 10).

To summarize, we have seen that the amount of information we face every day is so vast that we have to reduce it to a manageable size. In addition, much of this information is ambiguous or difficult to decipher. One way we deal with this "blooming, buzzing, confusion," in William James's words, is to rely on schemas, which help us reduce the amount of information we need to take in and help us interpret ambiguous information. These schemas are applied quickly, effortlessly, and unintentionally; in short, they are one form of automatic thinking. Another form of automatic thinking is to apply specific rules and shortcuts when thinking about the social world. These shortcuts are, for the most part, extremely useful, but as we will see, they can sometimes lead to erroneous inferences about the world.

Mental Strategies and Shortcuts 心理策略与心理捷径

Think back to your decision of where to apply to college. How did you narrow down your list from the schools you considered to the ones to which you actually applied? One strategy you might have taken would be to investigate thoroughly every one of the more than 3,000 colleges and universities in the United States. You could have read every catalog from cover to cover, visited every campus, and interviewed as many faculty members, deans, and students as you could find. Getting tired yet? Such a strategy would, of course, be prohibitively time-consuming and costly. Instead of considering every college and university, most high school students narrow down their choice to a small number of options and find out what they can about these schools.

This example is like many other decisions and judgments we make in everyday life. When deciding which job to accept, what car to buy, or whom to marry, we usually do not conduct a thorough search of every option ("OK, it's time for me to get married; I think I'll consult the Census Bureau's lists of unmarried adults in my town and begin my interviews tomorrow"). Instead, we use mental strategies and shortcuts that make the decisions easier, allowing us to get on with our lives without turning every decision into a major research project. These shortcuts do not always lead to the best decision. For example, if you had exhaustively studied every college and university in the United States, maybe you would have found one that you liked better than the one where you are now. Mental shortcuts are efficient, however, and usually lead to good decisions in a reasonable amount of time (Gigerenzer, 2008; Griffin & Kahneman, 2003; Gilovich & Griffin, 2002; Nisbett & Ross, 1980).

What shortcuts do people use? One, as we have already seen, is to use schemas to understand new situations. Rather than starting from scratch when examining our options, we often apply our previous knowledge and schemas. We have many such schemas, about everything from colleges and universities (e.g., what Ivy League colleges and big midwestern universities are like) to other people (e.g., teachers' beliefs about the abilities of boys versus girls). When making specific kinds of judgments and decisions, however, we do not always have a ready-made schema to apply. At other times, there are too many schemas that could apply, and it is not clear which one to use. What do we do?

At times like these, people often use mental shortcuts called **judgmental heuristics** (Gigerenzer, 2008; Shah & Oppenheimer, 2008; Tversky & Kahneman, 1974). The word *heuristic* comes from the Greek word meaning "discover"; in the field of social cognition, heuristics are the mental shortcuts people use to make judgments quickly and efficiently. Before discussing these heuristics, we should note that they do not guarantee that people will make accurate inferences about the world. Sometimes heuristics are inadequate for the job at hand or are misapplied, leading to faulty judgments. In fact, a good deal of research in social cognition has focused on just such mistakes in reasoning; we will document many such mental errors in this chapter, such as the case of teachers who mistakenly believed that boys were smarter than girls. As we discuss the mental strategies that sometimes lead to errors, however, keep in mind that people use heuristics for a reason: Most of the time, they are highly functional and serve us well.

How Easily Does It Come to Mind? The Availability Heuristic Suppose you are sitting in a restaurant with several friends one night when it becomes clear that the waiter made a mistake with one of the orders. Your friend Alphonse ordered the veggie burger with onion rings but instead got the veggie burger with fries. "Oh, well," he says, "I'll just eat the fries." This starts a discussion of whether he should have sent back his order, and some of the gang accuse Alphonse of not being assertive enough. Suppose he turns to you and asks, "Do you think I'm an unassertive person?" How would you answer?

One way, as we have seen, would be to call on a ready-made schema that provides the answer. If you know Alphonse well and have already formed a picture of how assertive he is, you can recite your answer easily and quickly: "Don't worry, Alphonse, if I had to deal with a used-car salesman, you'd be the first person I'd call." Suppose, though, that you've never really thought about how assertive Alphonse is and have to think about your answer. In these situations, we often rely on how easily different examples come to mind. If it is easy to think of times Alphonse acted assertively (e.g., the time he stopped someone from butting in line in front of him at the movies), you will conclude that Alphonse is a pretty assertive guy. If it is easier to think of times Alphonse acted unassertively (e.g., the time he let a salesperson talk him into an expensive cell phone plan), you will conclude that he is pretty unassertive.

This mental rule of thumb is called the **availability heuristic**, which is basing a judgment on the ease with which you can bring something to mind (Oppenheimer, 2004; Schwarz & Vaughn, 2002; Tversky & Kahneman, 1973). There are many situations in which the availability heuristic is a good strategy to use. If you can easily recall several instances when Alphonse stood up for himself, he probably is an assertive person; if you can easily recall several times when he was timid or meek, he probably is not. The trouble with the availability heuristic is that sometimes what is easiest to remember is not typical of the overall picture, leading to faulty conclusions.

When physicians are diagnosing diseases, for example, it might seem relatively straightforward for them to observe people's symptoms and figure out what disease, if any, they have. Sometimes, though, symptoms might be a sign of several different disorders. Do doctors use the availability heuristic, whereby they are more likely to consider diagnoses that come to mind easily? Several studies of medical diagnoses suggest that the answer is yes (Weber, 1993).

Judgmental Heuristics
Mental shortcuts people use to make judgments quickly and efficiently

Availability Heuristic
A mental rule of thumb whereby people base a judgment on the ease with which they can bring something to mind

Consider Dr. Robert Marion's diagnosis of Nicole, a bright, sweet, 9-year-old girl who came to his office one day. Nicole was normal in every way except that once or twice a year she had strange neurological attacks, characterized by disorientation, insomnia, slurred words, and strange mewing sounds. Nicole had been hospitalized three times, had seen over a dozen specialists, and had undergone many diagnostic tests, including CT scans, brain-wave tests, and virtually every blood test there is. Still, the doctors were stumped. Within minutes of seeing her, however, Dr. Marion correctly diagnosed her problem as a rare inherited blood disorder called acute intermittent porphyria (AIP). The blood chemistry of people with this disorder often gets out of sync, causing a variety of neurological symptoms. It can be controlled with a careful diet and by avoiding certain medications.

How did Dr. Marion diagnose Nicole's disorder so quickly when so many other doctors failed to do so? He had just finished writing a book on the genetic diseases of historical figures, including a chapter on King George III of England, who—you guessed it—suffered from AIP. "I didn't make the diagnosis because I'm a brilliant diagnostician or because I'm a sensitive listener," Dr. Marion admitted. "I succeeded where others failed because [Nicole] and I happened to run into each other in exactly the right place, at exactly the right time" (Marion, 1995, p. 40).

In other words, Dr. Marion used the availability heuristic. AIP happened to come to mind quickly because Dr. Marion had just read about it, making the diagnosis easy. Although this was a happy outcome of the use of the availability heuristic, it is easy to see how it can go wrong. As Dr. Marion says, "Doctors are just like everyone else. We go to the movies, watch TV, read newspapers and novels. If we happen to see a patient who has symptoms of a rare disease that was featured on the previous night's 'Movie of the Week,' we're more likely to consider that condition when making a diagnosis" (Marion, 1995, p. 40). That's fine if your disease happens to be the topic of last night's movie. It's not so good if your illness doesn't happen to be available in your doctor's memory, as was the case with the 12 doctors Nicole had seen previously.

Do people use the availability heuristic to make judgments about themselves? It might seem as if we have well-developed ideas about our own personalities, such as how assertive we are, but often we lack firm schemas about our own traits (Markus, 1977). We thus might make judgments about ourselves based on how easily we can recall examples of our own behavior. To see if this is true, researchers performed a clever experiment in which they altered how easy it was for people to remember examples of their own past behaviors (Schwarz et al., 1991). In one condition, they asked people to think of 6 times they had acted assertively. Most people readily thought of times they turned down persistent salespeople and stood up for themselves. In another condition, the researchers asked people to think of 12 times they had acted assertively. This group had to try very hard to think of this many examples. All participants were then asked to rate how assertive they thought they really were.

The question was, did people use the availability heuristic (the ease with which they could bring examples to mind) to infer how assertive they were? As seen on the left side of Figure 3.6, they did. People asked to think of six examples rated themselves as relatively assertive because it was easy to think of this many examples ("Hey, this is easy—I guess I'm a pretty assertive person"). People asked to think of 12 examples rated themselves as relatively unassertive because it was difficult to think of this many examples ("Hmm, this is hard—I must not be a very assertive person"). Other people were asked to think of 6 or 12 times they had acted unassertively, and similar results were found—those asked to think of six examples rated themselves as relatively unassertive (see the right side of Figure 3.6). In short, people use the availability heuristic—the ease with which they can bring examples to mind—when making judgments about themselves and other people (Caruso, 2008). Recently, a devious college professor used this technique to improve his course evaluations. He asked his students either to list 2 or 10 ways that the course could be improved

Physicians have been found to use the availability heuristic when making diagnoses. Their diagnoses are influenced by how easily they can bring different diseases to mind.

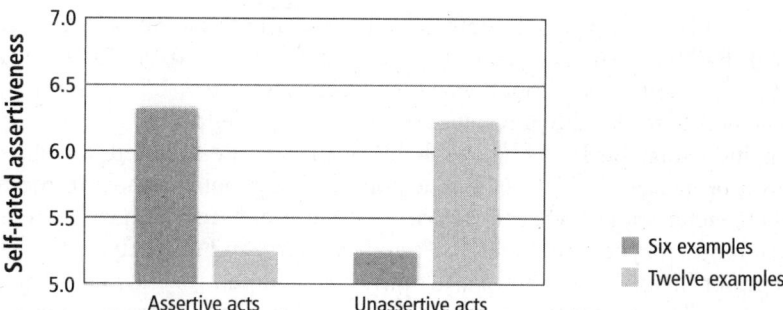

FIGURE 3.6
Availability and assertiveness.

People asked to think of six times they behaved assertively found it easy to do so and concluded that they were pretty assertive people. People asked to think of twelve times they behaved assertively found it difficult to think of so many examples and concluded they were not very assertive people (see the left-hand side of the graph). Similar results were found among people asked to think of six or twelve times they behaved unassertively (see the right-hand side of the graph). These results show that people often base their judgments on availability, or how easily they can bring information to mind.
(Adapted from Schwartz et al., 1991)

and then to rate their overall impression of the course. Who gave the course the highest ratings? Those asked to list 10 ways it could be improved, because they found it hard to think of that many ways in which the course was lacking and thought, "If I can't come up with that many criticisms it must be a great course!" (Fox, 2006).

How Similar Is A to B? The Representativeness Heuristic Suppose that you attend a state university in New York. At the student union one day, you meet a student named Brian. Brian has blond hair and a deep tan, seems to be very mellow, and likes to go to the beach. What state do you think Brian is from? Because Brian matches a common stereotype for Californians, you might guess that he was from there. If so, you would be using the **representativeness heuristic**, which is a mental shortcut we use to classify something according to how similar it is to a typical case, such as how similar Brian is to your conception of Californians (Gilovich & Savitsky, 2002; Kahneman & Tversky, 1973; Kahneman & Frederick, 2002).

Categorizing things according to representativeness is often a perfectly reasonable thing to do. If we did not use the representativeness heuristic, how else would we decide where Brian comes from? Should we just randomly choose a state, without making any attempt to judge his similarity to our conception of students from New York State versus out-of-state students? Actually, there is another source of information we might use. If we knew nothing about Brian, it would be wise to guess that he was from New York State because at state universities there are more in-state than out-of-state students. If we guessed New York State, we would be using what is called **base rate information**, information about the relative frequency of members of different categories in the population (e.g., the percentage of students at New York state universities who are from New York).

What do people do when they have both base rate information (e.g., knowing that there are more New Yorkers than Californians at a university) and contradictory information about the person in question (e.g., knowing that Brian is blond and mellow and likes to hang out at the beach)? Kahneman and Tversky (1973) found that people do not use base rate information sufficiently, paying most attention to how representative the information about the specific person is of the general category (e.g., Californians). Although this is not a bad strategy if the information about the person is very reliable, it can get us into trouble when the information is flimsy. Given that the base rate of Californians attending state universities in New York is low, you would need to have very good evidence that this person was a Californian before ignoring the base rate and guessing that he is one of the few exceptions. And given that it is not that unusual to find people from eastern states who have blond hair, are laid-back, and like to go to the beach, you would be wise to use the base rate in this instance.

Representativeness Heuristic

A mental shortcut whereby people classify something according to how similar it is to a typical case

Base Rate Information

Information about the frequency of members of different categories in the population

We don't mean to imply that people totally ignore base rate information (Koehler, 1993, 1996). Baseball managers consider the overall likelihood of left-handed batters getting a hit off of left-handed pitchers when deciding who to send up as a pinch hitter, and birdwatchers consider the prevalence of different species of birds in their area when identifying individual birds ("That probably wasn't a bay-breasted warbler because they've never been seen in this area"). The point is that people often focus too much on individual characteristics of what they observe ("But it did seem to have a chestnut-colored throat; hmm, maybe it was a bay-breasted warbler") and too little on the base rates.

Throughout history, for example, people have assumed that the cure for a disease must resemble—be representative of—the symptoms of the disease, even when this isn't the case. At one time, eating the lungs of a fox was thought to be a cure for asthma because foxes have a strong respiratory system (Mill, 1843). Such a reliance on representativeness may even impede the discovery of the actual cause of a disease. Around the turn of the twentieth century, an editorial in a Washington newspaper denounced the foolhardy use of federal funds to research far-fetched ideas about the causes of yellow fever, such as the absurd contention of one Walter Reed that yellow fever was caused by, of all things, a mosquito (Nisbett & Ross, 1980). How do heuristics influence your thinking? Take the quiz in the following Try It! exercise to find out.

CONNECTIONS 链接

Personality Tests and the Representativeness Heuristic
人格测验与代表性法则

Suppose you took a personality test, such as one of the many that are available online, and received the following feedback:

> You have a need for other people to like and admire you, and yet you tend to be critical of yourself. While you have some personality weaknesses you are generally able to compensate for them. You have considerable unused capacity that you have not turned to your advantage. Disciplined and self-controlled on the outside, you tend to be worrisome and insecure on the inside. At times you have serious doubts as to whether you have made the right decision or done the right thing. You prefer a certain amount of change and variety and become dissatisfied when hemmed in by restrictions and limitations. You also pride yourself as an independent thinker and do not accept others' statements without satisfactory proof. But you have found it unwise to be too frank in revealing yourself to others. At times you are extroverted, affable, and sociable, while at other times you are introverted, wary, and reserved. Some of your aspirations tend to be rather unrealistic.

"Wow," you might think. "This test is amazing; it is uncanny how well it captured who I am." If so, you are not alone. Bertram Forer (1949) gave this feedback to a group of students and asked them to rate how well it described them, on a scale from 0 = very poor to 5 = excellent. The average rating was 4.26—a phenomenon that has come to be known as the "Barnum effect" after the circus owner and showman P. T. Barnum.

Why do most people believe that this personality description describes them so well? One culprit is the representativeness heuristic: The statements are vague enough that virtually everyone can find a past behavior that is similar (representative of) to the feedback. Consider the statement, "At times you have serious doubts as to whether you have made the right decision or done the right thing." All of us can think of times this was true of us, that is, of examples that are representative of this statement. Who hasn't second-guessed themselves about an important decision, such as where to go to college or what major to choose? Similarly, all of us can think of times when we were independent thinkers and times when we revealed too much about ourselves. The reason the feedback seems to describe us so well is that we do not go beyond the representative examples that come to mind and think, "actually, there are just as many times when I didn't feel or act this way."

TRY IT! Reasoning Quiz 试一试！推理小测验

Answer each of the following questions.

1. Consider the letter *R* in the English language. Do you think that this letter occurs more often as the first letter of words (e.g., *rope*) or more often as the third letter of words (e.g., *park*)?

   more often as the first letter
   more often as the third letter
   about equally often as the first and as the third letter

2. Which of these do you think causes more fatalities in the United States?

   accidents
   strokes
   accidents and strokes in approximately equal numbers

3. Suppose you flipped a fair coin six times. Which sequence is more likely to occur, HTTHTH or HHHTTT? (H = heads, T = tails)

   HTTHTH is more likely
   HHHTTT is more likely
   both sequences are equally likely

4. After flipping a coin and observing the sequence TTTTT, what is the probability that the next flip will be heads?

   less than .5
   .5
   greater than .5

See page 81 for the answers.

The Power of Unconscious Thinking
无意识思维的力量

Part of the definition of automatic thinking is that it occurs unconsciously. Although it might seem magical that we can think without being aware that we are thinking, social psychologists are increasingly reaching the conclusion that we can do just that (Bargh & Morsella, 2008; Dijksterhuis, 2004; Dijksterhuis & Nordgren, 2006; Hassin, Uleman, & Bargh, 2005; Stapel & Koomen, 2006; Wilson, 2002). If we had to rely on slow, conscious thinking alone we would be in a pickle because we often need to make very fast decisions about what is happening around us, what to pay attention to, and which of our goals to pursue. We would be left scratching our heads while the world whizzed by. True enough, as we saw with the Amadou Diallo case, these fast, unconscious processes can sometimes lead to tragic errors. Most of the time, however, unconscious thinking is critical to navigating our way through the world.

Have you ever been chatting with someone at a party and suddenly realized that someone across the room had mentioned your name? The only way this could happen is if, while you were engrossed in conversation, you were unconsciously monitoring other conversations to see if something important came up (such as your name). This so-called "cocktail party" effect has been demonstrated under controlled experimental conditions (Moray, 1959; Harris & Pashler, 2004).

Another example of unconscious thinking is when we have competing goals and are not sure which one to act on. Suppose, for example, that you are taking a difficult math course in which the professor grades on a curve, guaranteeing that only a few people will get As. A classmate you don't know very well tells you he is having difficulty with some of the material and asks whether you can have coffee and go over your notes for the class. On the one hand you want to be helpful, satisfying your goal to be a caring, compassionate person. On the other hand you want to satisfy your goal of doing well in the class and are hesitant to hurt your chances by raising someone else's grade. Which goal do you act on? You could mull this over for awhile, consciously weighing your options. Often, however, it is our nonconscious minds that choose the goal for us, basing the decision in part on which goal has been recently activated or primed (Aarts, Custers, & Holland, 2007; Bargh et al., 2001; Förster, Liberman, & Friedman, 2007; Hassin, in press).

Social psychologists have tested this hypothesis by priming people's goals in a subtle way and then seeing if it influences their behavior. In a study by Azim Shariff and Ara Norenzayan (2007), for example, participants were asked to make sentences out of

Research has found that people's goals can be activated unconsciously by their recent experiences. For example, someone who walks by a church might have the "Golden Rule" activated, without knowing it, making them more likely to give money to a homeless person.

sets of provided words, such as "felt," "she," "eradicate," "spirit," and "the," from which they could make the sentence, "she felt the spirit." Next, as part of what was supposedly a different study, participants played an economic game in which they were given ten $1 coins and asked to divide them up between themselves and the next participant. Only the next participant would know what they decided, and that participant wouldn't know who they were. Think for a moment what you would do in this situation. Here's an opportunity to make a quick 10 bucks, and there is a definite temptation to pocket all the coins. But you might feel a little guilty hoarding all the money and leaving nothing for the next person. This is one of those situations in which there is a devil on one of our shoulders ("don't be a fool, take it all!") and an angel on the other ("do unto others as you would have them do unto you"). In short, people want the money but this conflicts with their goal to be nice to others. Which goal wins out?

It depends in part on which goal has been recently primed. Remember the sentence completion task people did first? For some participants, the words people were given had to do with God (spirit, divine, God, sacred, and prophet), which were designed to prime the goal of acting kindly to one's neighbor. In the control condition people got neutral words. An important detail is that participants did not make a connection between the sentence-making task and the economic game—they thought the two tasks were completely unrelated. Even so, the people who made sentences out of words having to do with God left significantly more money for the next participant ($4.56 on average) than did people who got the neutral words ($2.56 on average). And it turned out that it was not just words about God that primed the goal of being more altruistic. In a third condition, the sentence task contained nonreligious words that had to do with fairness to others, such as "civic" and "contract." People in this condition left nearly as much money for the next person as did people primed with God words ($4.44 on average). Studies such as this show that goals can be activated and influence people's behavior without their knowing it, because people didn't realize that the words they got in the first task had anything to do with their decision about how to divide the money in the second task. The moral? Your decision about whether to help your classmate in your math class might depend on which goals have recently been primed. If you had just walked by your place of worship, for example, or read a book in which people were kind to others, you might be especially likely to help your classmate.

> *Outside consciousness there rolls a vast tide of life which is perhaps more important to us than the little isle of our thoughts which lies within our ken.*
> —E. S. Dallas (1866)

Cultural Differences in Social Cognition 社会认知的文化差异

It may have occurred to you to wonder whether the kinds of automatic thinking we have been discussing are present in all people throughout the world, or whether they are more common in some cultures than others. If so, you are in good company; social psychologists have become increasingly interested in the influence of culture on **social cognition**.

Cultural Determinants of Schemas Although everyone uses schemas to understand the world, the *content* of our schemas is influenced by the culture in which we live. One researcher, for example, interviewed a Scottish settler and a local Bantu herdsman in Swaziland, a small country in southeastern Africa (Bartlett, 1932). Both men had been present at a complicated cattle transaction that had occurred a year earlier. The Scottish man needed to consult his records to recall how many cattle were bought and sold and for how much. The Bantu man promptly recited from memory every detail of the transaction, including from whom each ox and cow had been bought, the color of each animal, and the price of each transaction. The Bantu people's memory for cattle is so good that they do not bother to brand them; if a cow happens to wander away and get mixed up with a neighbor's herd, the owner simply goes over and takes it back, having no trouble distinguishing his cow from the dozens of others.

Clearly, an important source of our schemas is the culture in which we grow up. Cattle are a central part of the Bantu economy and culture, and therefore the Bantu have well-developed schemas about cattle. To an American, one cow might look like any other, though this person might have well-developed schemas and hence an excellent memory for transactions on the New York Stock Exchange or the lastest contestants on *American Idol*. Schemas are a very important way by which cultures exert their influence—namely, by instilling mental structures that influence the very way we understand and interpret the world. In Chapter 5, we will see that people in different cultures have fundamentally different schemas about themselves and the social world, with some interesting consequences (Wang & Ross, 2007). For now, we point out that the schemas that our culture teaches us strongly influence what we notice and remember about the world.

Take a quick look at these two photos and see if you notice any differences between them. As discussed in the text, the differences you notice may have to do with the culture in which you grew up.

Holistic Versus Analytic Thinking Culture influences social cognition in other fundamental ways. An analogy that is often used is that the human mind is like a toolbox, filled with specific tools to help people think about and act in the social world. All humans have access to the same tools, but the culture in which they grew up can influence the ones they use the most (Norenzayan & Heine, 2005). If you live in a house that has screws instead of nails, you will use your screwdriver more than a hammer, but if your house contains nails and not screws, the screwdriver won't get much use.

By the same token, culture can influence the kinds of thinking people automatically use to understand their worlds. Not *all* kinds of thinking, mind you—the kinds of automatic thinking we have discussed so far, such as unconscious thinking and the use of schemas, appear to be used by all humans. But some basic ways in which people typically perceive and think about the world *are* shaped by culture. To illustrate these differences, take a quick look at the picture at the very top of this page. Okay, now take a quick look at the picture right beneath it: Did you notice any differences between the two pictures? Your answer might depend on the culture in which you grew up. Richard Nisbett and his colleagues have found that people who grow up in Western cultures tend to have an **analytic thinking style**, a type of thinking in which people focus on the properties of objects without considering their surrounding context. For example, Westerners are most likely to focus on the planes because they are the main objects in the pictures. They thus are more likely to notice changes in these objects, such as the fact that the passenger plane has more windows in the second picture than in the first (Masuda & Nisbett, 2006). People who grow up in East Asian cultures (e.g., China, Japan, or Korea) tend to have a **holistic thinking style**, a type of thinking in which people focus on the overall context, particularly the ways in which objects relate to each other (Nisbett, 2003; Nisbett, 2001; Norenzayan & Nisbett, 2000).

For example, East Asians are more likely to notice changes in the background of the pictures, such as the fact that the shape of the control tower changes from one to the other. (Note that in the actual study people saw 20-second videos of these scenes and tried to find all the differences between them. The pictures on this page are the last scenes from these two videos.) In Chapter 4 we will see that these differences in thinking styles also influence how we perceive emotions in other people. Suppose, for

Analytic Thinking Style
A type of thinking in which people focus on the properties of objects without considering their surrounding context; this type of thinking is common in Western cultures

Holistic Thinking Style
A type of thinking in which people focus on the overall context, particularly the ways in which objects relate to each other; this type of thinking is common in East Asian cultures (e.g., China, Japan, and Korea)

example, that you ran into a classmate who was surrounded by a group of friends. If you grew up in the West, you would likely focus only on your classmate's face (the object of your attention) to judge how he or she is feeling. If you grew up in East Asia you would likely scan everyone's faces in the group (the overall context) and use this information to judge how your classmate is feeling (Masuda, Ellsworth, & Mesquita, 2008).

Where do these differences in holistic versus analytic thinking come from? Richard Nisbett (2003) suggests that they are rooted in the different philosophical traditions of the East versus West. Eastern thought has been shaped by the ideas of Confucianism, Taoism, and Buddhism, which emphasize the connectedness and relativity of all things. Western thought is rooted in the Greek philosophical tradition of Aristotle and Plato, which focuses on the laws governing objects independent of their context. Recent research suggests, however, that the different thinking styles might also stem from actual differences in the environments in the different cultures. Yuri Miyamoto, Richard Nisbett, and Takahiko Masuda took photographs in randomly chosen city scenes in Japan and the United States. They matched the scenes as best they could; for example, the sizes of the cities were equivalent, as were the buildings that were photographed in each city (e.g., hotels and public elementary schools). The researchers hypothesized that the scenes in the Japanese cities would be "busier", that is, they would contain more objects that competed for people's attention than the scenes in the American cities. As seen by the photos on page 71, they were right. The Japanese scenes contained significantly more information and objects than the American scenes.

Could this be one reason why Americans focus more on a foreground object whereas East Asians focus more on the overall context? To find out, Miyamoto and his colleagues did a second study in which they showed the pictures of American or Japanese cities to a sample of American and Japanese college students. The students were asked to imagine that they were in the scene depicted in the each picture, with the idea that the Japanese pictures would prime holistic thinking whereas the American pictures would prime analytic thinking. Then the students completed the same airplane picture task described above, in which they tried to detect the differences between two similar pictures. As predicted, the people who saw the photos of Japanese cities were more likely to detect changes in the *background* of the test pictures, whereas people who saw the pictures of the American cities were more likely to detect changes in the *main object* of the pictures. This finding suggests that people in all cultures are capable of thinking holistically or analytically (they have the same tools in their mental toolbox), but that the environment in which people live, or even which environment has been recently primed, triggers a reliance on one of the styles (Norenzayan, Choi, & Peng, 2007).

At this point, you might be wondering why we have spent so much time on the automatic, nonconscious type of social cognition. Didn't we say earlier that there are two modes of thinking, automatic and controlled? Isn't it possible to think about the social world slowly, carefully, and deliberately, such as when we take time to sit down and really think a problem through? Indeed it is. We've spent so much time on automatic thinking, however, because it is so pervasive and dominates much of our mental lives. Just as modern jetliners fly mostly on automatic pilot, so do people rely a great deal on automatic thinking to get through their days.

But how can this be when it seems as if so much of our lives is governed by our conscious deliberations? Many decisions, such as where to go to college or whom to date, are accompanied by deliberative, conscious thinking. Yet even big decisions like these can be influenced by automatic thinking, such as when we use judgmental heuristics when deciding where to apply to college. Obviously, conscious thinking is extremely important, though, especially when people try to correct or fix mistakes in their automatic thinking.

We cannot leave this topic, however, without pointing out that just because people think they are consciously controlling their actions does not necessarily mean they are. Daniel Wegner (2002, 2004; Preston & Wegner, 2007) argues that the sense that

Researchers took these photos of hotels and schools in randomly chosen locations in Japan and the United States. They hypothesized that the scenes in the Japanese cities would be "busier"; that is, that they would contain more objects that competed for people's attention than the scenes in the American cities. As seen in these photos they were correct; the ones taken in the United States depict scenes that are less "busy" than the ones taken in Japan. See the text for a discussion of how growing up in one of these environments might influence people's thinking styles.

people have of consciously willing an action can be an illusion, a feeling that we create when our actions were really controlled by either our automatic thinking or the external environment.

Have you ever seen children in a video arcade furiously working the controls, believing that they are playing the game, when in fact they never put money in the machine and are watching the demonstration program? Occasionally, when the children pushed the controls in one direction, the game did appear to respond to the commands, making it hard for the children to realize that in fact they had no control over what was happening (Wegner, 2002). Adults are not immune from such illusions of control. People who are able to choose their lottery numbers, for example, are more confident that they will win than people who are assigned numbers (Langer, 1975). And what sports fans haven't felt that they helped their favorite team by crossing their fingers or donning their lucky hat at a key moment in the game?

As these examples show, people sometimes believe that they are exerting more control over events than they really are. It can also work the other way—people can actually be controlling things more than they realize. A number of years ago a new technique called facilitated communication was developed to allow communication-impaired people, such as those suffering from autism and cerebral palsy, to express themselves. A trained facilitator held the fingers and arm of a communication-impaired client at a computer keyboard to make it easier for the client to type answers to questions. This technique caused great excitement. People who had been unable to communicate with the outside world suddenly became quite verbose, voicing all sorts of thoughts and feelings with the aide of the facilitator—or so it seemed. Parents were thrilled by the sudden opportunity to communicate with their previously silent autistic children.

Facilitated communication was soon discredited, however, when it became clear that it was not the communication-impaired person who was doing the typing but, unwittingly, the facilitator. In one well-designed study, researchers asked separate questions of the facilitator and the communication-impaired person over headphones. The facilitator might have heard "How do you feel about today's weather?" while the communication-impaired person heard "How did you like your lunch today?" The answers that were typed matched the questions the facilitator heard (e.g., "I wish it were sunnier"), not the ones posed to the communication-impaired client (Wegner, Fuller, & Sparrow, 2003; Wegner, Sparrow, & Winerman, 2004; Wheeler, Jacobson, Paglieri, & Schwartz, 1993). The facilitators were not deliberating faking it; they genuinely believed that it was the communication-impaired person who was choosing what to type and that they were simply helping them move their fingers on the keyboard.

These examples illustrate that there can be a disconnect between our conscious sense of how much we are causing our own actions and how much we really are causing them. Sometimes we overestimate the amount of control we have, as when we believe that wearing our lucky hat will help our favorite sports team score a goal. Sometimes we underestimate the amount of control we have, as with the facilitators who thought it was the client choosing what to type when they were unconsciously doing it themselves (Wegner, 2002).

Despite this disconnect, conscious, controlled thinking *does* sometimes take over and influence our behavior—sometimes for better, sometimes for worse.

Controlled Social Cognition: High-Effort Thinking
控制性社会认知：高努力水平思维

Richard Wilkins, a Washington, D.C., lawyer, was returning from his grandfather's funeral in Maryland when a state trooper pulled him over and asked to search his car. Wilkins refused, but the trooper let loose a drug-sniffing dog anyway. While Wilkins and his family sat in the car helplessly, the dog sniffed the entire exterior, including the windshield and taillights. The dog found nothing. "We were completely humiliated," Wilkins said ("Driving while Black," 1999). Wilkins, an African American, may have been a victim of racial profiling, whereby the police target and stop pedestrians, airline passengers, and motorists on the basis of their race.

Racial profiling has received a great deal of attention since the events of September 11, 2001. Because the terrorists who flew the planes into the World Trade Center towers were of Middle Eastern descent, some people feel that anyone who looks as if they might be of a similar background should receive special scrutiny when flying on commercial airlines. On the New Year's Eve after the attacks, for example, Michael Dasrath and Edgardo Cureg boarded a Continental Airlines flight from New Jersey to Tampa. Dasrath was a U.S. citizen who was born in South America, and Cureg was a U.S. resident from the Philippines. Both had successfully passed through extensive security checks. Dasrath, seated in first class, was removed from the plane when a woman with a dog complained that he made her uncomfortable. Dasrath was also removed from the flight, allegedly because he made other passengers nervous.

These alleged examples of racial profiling bear some similarities to the tragedy of Amadou Diallo, discussed at the beginning of the chapter. In both cases, innocent people were suspected of a crime because of the color of their skin. In other respects, however, the examples are quite different. In Diallo's case, the police had very little time to react—seconds or less—and could not think carefully about what Diallo was reaching for. More than likely, the police officers' automatic thinking took over. In Wilkins's case, the police officer had ample time to decide whether to pull him over. Presumably, the officer's decision was a more conscious and deliberative one. In fact, there is evidence that some police departments in the United States have encouraged their officers to stop black and Hispanic motorists in disproportionately high numbers, suggesting that racial profiling is a conscious policy decision in these departments and not the result of automatic thinking (Drummond, 1999). Similarly, in the case of the men removed from the airplane, the airline officials presumably had ample time to think about and consider their actions.

Racial prejudice can thus be the result of automatic thinking or conscious, deliberative thinking—an issue we will take up in detail in Chapter 13. For now, we use this example to illustrate the more conscious, controlled type of social cognition. **Controlled thinking** is defined as thinking that is conscious, intentional, voluntary, and effortful. People can usually turn on or turn off this type of thinking at will and are fully aware of what they are thinking. Further, this kind of thinking is effortful in the sense that it requires mental energy. People have the capacity to think in a conscious, controlled way about only one thing at a time; they cannot be thinking about what they will eat for lunch today at the same time they are thinking through a complex math problem. Automatic thinking, in contrast, can occur in the background with no conscious effort at all.

Mentally Undoing the Past: Counterfactual Reasoning
在心理上改变历史：反事实推理

Racial profiling is official action toward people based on their race, ethnicity, or national origin instead of their behavior. Some police departments in the United States have been accused of stopping motorists because they are African American or Hispanic and not because they were doing anything illegal.

When do people go off automatic pilot and think about things more slowly and consciously? One circumstance is when they experience a negative event that was a "close call," such as failing a test by just a point or two. Under these conditions, we engage in **counterfactual thinking**, mentally changing some aspect of the past as a way of imagining what might have been (Girotto, 2007; Kahneman & Miller, 1986; Markman, McMullen, & Elizaga, 2008; Roese, 1997; Tetlock, 2002). "If only I had answered that one question differently," you might think, "I would have passed the test."

Counterfactual thoughts can have a big influence on our emotional reactions to events. The easier it is to mentally undo an outcome, the stronger the emotional reaction to it (Camille et al., 2004; Miller & Taylor, 2002; Niedenthal, Tangney, & Gavanski, 1994). One group of researchers, for example, interviewed people who had suffered the loss of a spouse or child. As expected, the more people imagined ways in which the tragedy could have been averted, by mentally undoing the circumstances preceding it, the more distress they reported (Davis, Lehman, Wortman, Silver, & Thompson, 1995; see also Branscombe, Owen, Garstka, & Coleman, 1996).

Counterfactual reasoning can lead to some paradoxical effects on people's emotions. For example, who do you think would be happier, an Olympic athlete who won a silver medal (came in second) or an Olympic athlete who won a bronze medal (came in third)? Surely the one who got the silver, because they did better! Actually it might be the reverse, if the silver medal winner can more easily imagine having won the event and therefore engages in more counterfactual reasoning—especially if the silver medalist expected to do better than the bronze medalist (McGraw, Mellers, & Tetlock, 2005). To test these hypotheses, Medvec, Madey, and Gilovich (1995) analyzed videotapes of the 1992 Olympics. Both immediately after their event and while they received their medals, silver medal winners appeared less happy than bronze medal winners. And during interviews with reporters, silver medal winners engaged in more

Controlled Thinking
Thinking that is conscious, intentional, voluntary, and effortful

Counterfactual Thinking
Mentally changing some aspect of the past as a way of imagining what might have been

Who do you think would be happier, someone who won a silver medal at the Olympics (came in second) or someone who won a bronze medal (came in third)? Although silver medalists did better than bronze medalists, research shows that they are often less happy, because they can more easily imagine how they might have come in first and won a gold medal.

counterfactual reasoning by saying things like "I almost pulled it off; it's too bad." The moral seems to be that if you are going to lose, it is best not to lose by a slim margin.

Earlier we described controlled thinking as conscious, intentional, voluntary, and effortful; but like automatic thinking, different kinds of controlled thought meet these requirements to different degrees. Counterfactual reasoning is clearly conscious and effortful; we know we are obsessing about the past, and this kind of thinking often takes up so much mental energy that we cannot think about anything else. It is not, however, always intentional or voluntary. Even when we want to stop dwelling on the past and move on to something else, it can be difficult to turn off the kind of "if only" thinking that characterizes counterfactual reasoning (Goldionger, 2003).

This is not so good if counterfactual thinking results in rumination, whereby people repetitively focus on negative things in their lives. Rumination has been found to be a contributor to depression (Lyubomirsky, Caldwell, & Nolen-Hoeksema, 1993; Ward, 2003). Thus it is not advisable to ruminate constantly about a bad test grade to the point where you can't think about anything else. Counterfactual thinking can be useful, however, if it focuses people's attention on ways that they can cope better in the future. Thinking such thoughts as "If only I had studied a little harder, I would have passed the test" can be beneficial, to the extent that it gives people a heightened sense of control over their fate and motivates them to study harder for the next test (Nasco & Marsh, 1999; Roese & Olson, 1997).

Thought Suppression and Ironic Processing 思考抑制和反向加工

Instead of ruminating about something, we might simply do our best not to think about it. How successful will we be at such **thought suppression**, the attempt to avoid thinking about something we would just as soon forget, such as a lost love, an unpleasant encounter with one's boss, or a delectable piece of cheesecake in the refrigerator? That depends on the interaction of two processes, one relatively automatic and the other relatively controlled (Mitchell et al., 2007; Wegner, 1992, 1994; Wegner, Wenzlaff, & Kozak, 2004). The automatic part of the system, called the *monitoring process*, searches for evidence that the unwanted thought is about to intrude on consciousness. After the unwanted thought is detected, the more controlled part of the system, called the *operating process*, comes into play. This is the effortful, conscious attempt to distract oneself by finding something else to think about. These two processes

Thought Suppression
The attempt to avoid thinking about something we would prefer to forget

operate in tandem, like two parents conspiring to keep their kids away from junk food outlets at a mall. One parent's job, akin to the monitoring process, is to keep a watch out for the food joints and let the other one know when they are in the vicinity ("McDonald's alert!"). The other parent's job, akin to the operating process, is then to divert the kids' attention away from the food places ("Hey, kids, look at the giant picture of SpongeBob in that store window"). This system works pretty well as long as each process (parent) does its job, one ever alert for the topic we want to avoid and the other diverting our attention from this topic.

What happens, though, when the controlled operating process is unable to do its job because the person is tired or preoccupied? The monitoring process continues to find instances of the unwanted thought, which then intrudes on consciousness unchecked by the controlled system. A state of hyperaccessibility results in which the unwanted thought occurs with high frequency. If the parent whose job it is to distract the children falls down on the job, for example, the kids will become even more aware that fast-food joints are in the vicinity because they will keep hearing the other parent point them out (Renaud & McConnell, 2002; Wenzlaff & Bates, 2000).

The irony is that when people are trying their hardest not to think about something (e.g., you are on guard not to think about jokes about short people because your 4-foot-8-inch boss is standing next to you), if people are tired or preoccupied—that is, under *cognitive load*—these thoughts are especially likely to spill out unchecked. Further, there can be an emotional and physical cost to thought suppression. In one study, medical school students wrote about a personal topic once a day for three days (Petrie, Booth, & Pennebaker, 1998). After each writing episode, some participants were asked to suppress all thoughts about what they had just written for 5 minutes. Compared to people who did not suppress their thoughts, people in the suppress condition showed a significant decrease in immune system functioning. In another study, women who had had an abortion were asked how much they had tried to suppress thoughts about the abortion (Major & Gramzow, 1999). The more the women reported that they tried not to think about the abortion, the greater their reported psychological distress. As you will see in Chapter 15, "Social Psychology and Health," it is generally better to open up about one's problems by writing about or discussing them than to try to suppress thoughts about the problems.

Improving Human Thinking 改进人类思维

One purpose of controlled thinking is to provide checks and balances for automatic thinking. Just as an airline captain can turn off the automatic pilot and take control of the plane when trouble occurs, controlled thinking takes over when unusual events occur. How successful are people at correcting their mistakes? How can they be taught to do better?

One approach is to make people a little more humble about their reasoning abilities. Often we have greater confidence in our judgments than we should (Blanton, Pelham, DeHart, & Carvallo, 2001; Buehler, Griffin, & Ross, 2002; Juslin, Winman, & Hansson, 2007; Vallone, Griffin, Lin, & Ross, 1990). Teachers, for example, sometimes have greater confidence in their beliefs about the abilities of boys versus girls than is warranted. Anyone trying to improve human inference is thus up against an **overconfidence barrier** (Metcalfe, 1998). Many people seem to think that their reasoning processes are just fine the way they are and hence that there is no need for any remedial action. One approach, then, might be to address this overconfidence directly, getting people to consider the possibility that they might be wrong. This tack was taken by one team of researchers (Lord, Lepper, & Preston, 1984), who found that when asked to consider the opposite point of view to their own, people realized there were other ways to construe the world than their own way; consequently, they made fewer errors in judgment (Anderson, Lepper, & Ross, 1980; Hirt, Kardes, & Markman, 2004; Mussweiler, Strack, & Pfeiffer, 2000).

The greatest of all faults, I should say, is to become conscious of none.

—Thomas Carlyle

Overconfidence Barrier
The fact that people usually have too much confidence in the accuracy of their judgments

> *The sign of a first-rate intelligence is the ability to hold two opposed ideas at the same time.*
>
> —F. Scott Fitzgerald

Another approach is to teach people directly some basic statistical and methodological principles about how to reason correctly, with the hope they will apply these principles in their everyday lives. Many of these principles are already taught in courses in statistics and research design, such as the idea that if you want to generalize from a sample of information (e.g., a group of welfare mothers) to a population (e.g., all welfare mothers), you must have a large, unbiased sample. Do people who take such courses apply these principles in their everyday lives? Are they less likely to make the kinds of mistakes we have discussed in this chapter? A number of studies have provided encouraging answers to these questions, showing that people's reasoning processes can be improved by college statistics courses, graduate training in research design, and even brief one-time lessons (Crandall & Greenfield, 1986; Malloy, 2001; Nisbett, Fong, Lehman, & Cheng, 1987; Schaller, 1996).

TRY IT! How Well Do You Reason? 试一试！你的推理能力如何？

1. The city of Middleopolis has had an unpopular police chief for a year and a half. He is a political appointee who is a crony of the mayor and he had little previous experience in police administration when he was appointed. The mayor has recently defended the chief in public, announcing that in the time since he took office, crime rates have decreased by 12 percent. Which of the following pieces of evidence would most deflate the mayor's claim that his chief is competent?
   a. The crime rates of the two cities closest to Middleopolis in location and size have decreased by 18 percent in the same period.
   b. An independent survey of the citizens of Middleopolis shows that 40 percent more crime is reported by respondents in the survey than is reported in police records.
   c. Common sense indicates that there is little a police chief can do to lower crime rates. These are for the most part due to social and economic conditions beyond the control of officials.
   d. The police chief has been discovered to have business contacts with people who are known to be involved in organized crime.

2. After the first two weeks of the major league baseball season, newspapers begin to print the top ten batting averages. Typically, after 2 weeks, the leading batter has an average of about .450. Yet no batter in major league history has ever averaged .450 at the end of a season. Why do you think this is?
   a. A player's high average at the beginning of the season may be just a lucky fluke.
   b. A batter who has such a hot streak at the beginning of the season is under a lot of stress to maintain his performance record. Such stress adversely affects his playing.
   c. Pitchers tend to get better over the course of the season as they get more in shape. As pitchers improve, they are more likely to strike out batters, so batters' averages go down.
   d. When a batter is known to be hitting for a high average, pitchers bear down more when they pitch to him.
   e. When a batter is known to be hitting for a high average, he stops getting good pitches to hit. Instead, pitchers "play the corners" of the plate because they don't mind walking him.

See page 81 for the answers.

(Questions from Lehman, Lempert, & Nisbett, 1988, p. 442)

Richard Nisbett and his colleagues (1987), for example, examined how different kinds of graduate training influenced people's reasoning on everyday problems involving statistical and methodological reasoning—precisely the kind of reasoning we have considered in this chapter, such as people's understanding of how to generalize from small samples of information (see the Try It! Exercise on this page for sample questions). The researchers predicted that students in psychology and medicine would do better on the statistical reasoning problems than students in law and chemistry would because graduate programs in psychology and medicine include more training in statistics than programs in the other two disciplines do.

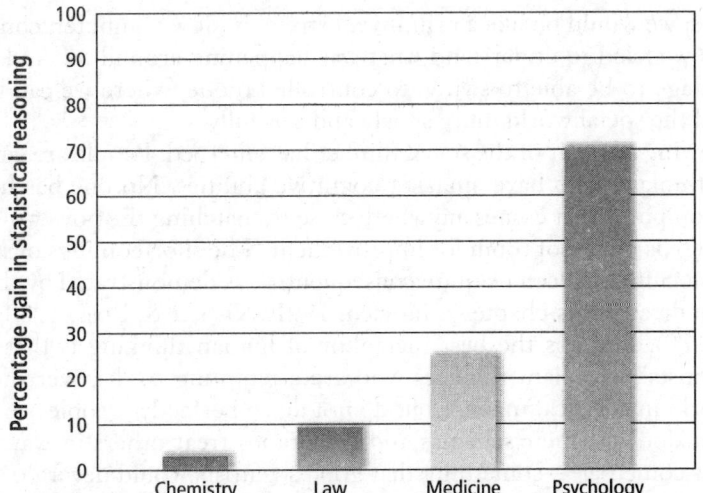

FIGURE 3.7
Performance on a test of statistical reasoning abilities by graduate students in different disciplines.

After two years of graduate study, students in psychology and medicine showed more improvement on statistical reasoning problems than students in law and chemistry did.

(Adapted from Nisbett, Fong, Lehman, & Cheng, 1987)

As Figure 3.7 shows, after two years of graduate work, students in psychology and medicine improved on the statistical reasoning problems more than students in law and chemistry did. The improvement among the psychology graduate students was particularly impressive. Interestingly, the students in the different disciplines performed equally well on sample items from the Graduate Record Exam, suggesting that they did not differ in overall intelligence. Instead, the different kinds of training they had received appeared to influence how accurately and logically they reasoned on everyday problems (Nisbett et al., 1987). Thus there are grounds for being optimistic about people's ability to overcome the kinds of mistakes we have documented in this chapter. And you don't have to go to graduate school to do it. Sometimes it helps simply to consider the opposite, as participants in the Lord and colleagues' (1984) study did. Beyond this, formal training in statistics helps, at both the graduate and undergraduate levels. So if you were dreading taking a college statistics course, take heart: It might not only satisfy a requirement for your major but improve your reasoning as well!

> *Modest doubt is called the beacon of the wise.*
>
> —William Shakespeare

The Amadou Diallo Case Revisited
阿马登·戴尔罗案例反思

By now we have seen two very different modes of social cognition, one that is effortless, involuntary, unintentional, and unconscious (automatic thinking) and another that is more effortful, voluntary, intentional, and conscious (controlled thinking). We have also seen that both kinds of thinking can lead to consequential errors. Amadou Diallo's death may have been the result of an automatic assumption made by the police officers who shot him, based on his race. Other kinds of racial prejudice may be the result of more controlled thinking, such as racial profiling. So how good a thinker is the typical human being anyway? How can we reconcile the fact that human beings have amazing cognitive abilities that have resulted in dazzling cultural and intellectual achievements but at the same time humans are prone to making consequential mental errors like the ones documented in this chapter? One way of addressing this question is to ask which kind of thinking—automatic or controlled—is more important in human functioning. The answer to this question has engendered a lively debate among social psychologists. Although the debate continues, it is fair to say that there has been an increasing appreciation of the role of automatic thinking in human thought; more and more research has shown that people operate on automatic pilot when thinking about the social world.

What is clear is that despite the troubles they can cause, both kinds of thinking are extremely useful. It would be difficult to live without the ability to process information about the social world automatically and make quick assumptions about our environments; we would be like a primitive, extremely slow computer, chugging away constantly as we tried to understand what was happening around us. And it is clearly to our advantage to be able to switch to controlled mode, where we can think about ourselves and the social world more slowly and carefully.

The following portrait of the social thinker has emerged: People are very sophisticated social thinkers who have amazing cognitive abilities. No one has been able to construct a computer that comes anywhere close to matching the power of the human brain. But there is plenty of room for improvement. The shortcomings of social thinking we have documented can be quite consequential, as demonstrated by the examples of racial prejudice in this chapter (Gilovich, 1991; Nisbett & Ross, 1980; Slusher & Anderson, 1989). Perhaps the best metaphor of human thinking is that people are "flawed scientists"—brilliant thinkers who are attempting to discover the nature of the social world in a logical manner but do not do so perfectly. People are often blind to truths that don't fit their schemas and sometimes treat others in ways that make their schemas come true—something that good scientists would never do.

HOW WOULD YOU USE THIS? 如何学以致用?

By definition it is hard to recognize our own automatic thinking, because it is nonconscious, unintentional, involuntary, and effortless. We don't have a special window through which we can watch our automatic minds at work, which makes it difficult to know the extent to which we are making quick assumptions about other people and the extent to which these assumptions are correct. Can you think of any indirect clues that people get suggesting that they have made automatic assumptions about other people that are incorrect? For example, think back to the section of the chapter on self-fulfilling prophecies. Is there some way a middle school teacher could tell whether he or she is making false assumptions about the math abilities of the boys and girls in his or her class? What about you in your everyday life: When you meet someone for the first time and get to know him or her, how can you tell whether your initial assumptions are correct? Would it help to compare notes with other people who know this person?

Summary 总 结

- **On Automatic Pilot: Low-Effort Thinking** A great deal of social cognition—how people think about themselves and the social world—involves automatic thinking, which is nonconscious, unintentional, involuntary, and effortless.
  - **People as Everyday Theorists: Automatic Thinking with Schemas** An important part of automatic thinking is using our past knowledge to organize and interpret new information. More specifically, people use schemas, which are mental structures that people use to organize their knowledge about the social world around themes or subjects and that influence what people notice, think about, and remember. Schemas are extremely useful tools to reduce ambiguity about the social world. They can cause problems, however, such as self-fulfilling prophecies, whereby a schema or expectation about another person influences how we act toward that person, which causes that person to behave consistently with our expectation.
  - **Mental Strategies and Shortcuts** Another form of automatic thinking is the use of judgmental heuristics, which are mental shortcuts people use to make judgments quickly and efficiently. Examples are the availability heuristic, whereby people base a judgment on the ease with which they can bring something to mind, and the representativeness heuristic, whereby people classify something according to how similar it is to a typical case. Heuristics are extremely useful and often produce accurate judgments but can be misused, producing faulty judgments.

- **The Power of Unconscious Thinking** Recent research suggests that a great deal of human thought occurs outside of conscious awareness. People unconsciously monitor what is going on around them, in case something important occurs that requires their conscious attention. Even people's goals can be unconsciously activated.

- **Cultural Differences in Social Cognition** The human mind is like a toolbox, filled with specific tools to help people think about and act in the social world. All humans have access to the same tools, but the culture in which they grew up can influence the ones they use the most. Western cultures tend to emphasize an **analytic thinking style**, a type of thinking in which people focus on the properties of objects without considering their surrounding context. People who grow up in East Asian cultures tend to have a **holistic thinking style**, a type of thinking in which people focus on the overall context, particularly the ways in which objects relate to each other.

◉ **Controlled Social Cognition: High-Effort Thinking** Not all social cognition is automatic; we also engage in controlled thinking, which is conscious, intentional, voluntary, and effortful.

- **Mentally Undoing the Past: Counterfactual Reasoning** One form of controlled thinking is counterfactual reasoning, whereby people mentally change some aspect of the past as a way of imagining what might have been.

- **Thought Suppression and Ironic Processing** Another kind of controlled thinking is thought suppression, which is the attempt to avoid thinking about something. Research shows that thought suppression often backfires, causing people to think more about the topic they are trying to forget—especially when people are tired or distracted.

- **Improving Human Thinking** In this chapter we documented several ways in which social cognition can go wrong, producing faulty judgments. Research shows that some kinds of thinking, such as statistical reasoning, can be improved dramatically with training—such as taking a course in statistics.

◉ **The Amadou Diallo Case Revisited** We used the death of Amadou Diallo to illustrate the tragic way in which social cognition can go wrong. We should keep in mind, however, that humans are very sophisticated social thinkers who have amazing cognitive abilities. People are like "flawed scientists"—brilliant thinkers who are attempting to discover the nature of the social world in a logical manner but do not do so perfectly.

CHAPTER 3 TEST 第3章习题

1. Over Thanksgiving break, your parents ask you if you can think of 12 reasons why your college is better than its arch rival. You find it hard to come up with so many reasons and so end up thinking, "Hm, maybe the schools aren't all that different." Which of the following mental strategies did you probably use to reach this conclusion?
   a. The representativeness heuristic
   b. Base rate information
   c. The anchoring and adjustment heuristic
   d. The availability heuristic
   e. Counterfactual thinking

2. Sam plays a carnival game in which he would have won a stuffed donkey if he had guessed the correct cup under which a ball was hidden. Unfortunately, from the line of 20 cups, he picked the cup directly to the left of the winning cup. According to social psychological research, he is *most likely* to
   a. experience cognitive dissonance
   b. engage in counterfactual thinking
   c. blame his mistake on the noise of the crowd
   d. subsequently avoid similar games

3. According to research on thought suppression, we
   a. are actually quite good at suppressing our thoughts
   b. have complete control over our thoughts
   c. are especially bad at suppressing thoughts when we are under cognitive load
   d. have no control over our thoughts
   e. are especially good at suppressing thoughts when we are under cognitive load

4. Suppose you're driving home from watching a scary movie about a hitchhiker who was a murderer when you see someone talking loudly with a friend. Because you saw the movie, you assume that you are witnessing an argument that will probably end up in a fight. This is an example of
   a. priming
   b. base rate information
   c. belief perseverance
   d. controlled thinking

5. Which of the following is LEAST true of the holistic thinking style discussed in this chapter?
   a. it is more common in East Asia than in the United States
   b. it involves a focus on the context and ways in which objects relate to each other
   c. people living in the West can think holistically if they are primed with pictures taken in Japan
   d. the holistic style of thinking probably has a genetic basis
   e. it may have its roots in the philosophic traditions of Confucianism, Taoism, and Buddhism

6. Rob is definitely not the most attractive guy in the dorms, but he is extremely confident about who he is and how he looks. He is convinced that most women find him to be very attractive, and he in fact usually gets dates with women who are much more attractive than he is. What is the best explanation of Rob's success?
   a. Self-affirmation theory
   b. the representativeness heuristic
   c. Self-fulfilling prophecy
   d. Self-esteem maintenance theory

7. Which of the following is the worst example of a self-fulfilling prophecy?
   a. A teacher believes that boys are better at math than girls, and boys in his class do better than girls in math.
   b. Bob thinks that members of the Alpha Beta Psi sorority are unfriendly and snobby. Whenever he meets members of this sorority, they are unfriendly toward him.
   c. Jill thinks her dog isn't very good at learning tricks. Her dog knows fewer tricks than most dogs.
   d. Sarah is worried that her son is not gifted in music, but he does better at his piano lessons than she expected.

8. According to this chapter, which is the best analogy to describe people's thinking abilities?
   a. People are cognitive misers.
   b. People are motivated tacticians.
   c. People are flawed scientists.
   d. People are skilled detectives.

9. Imagine you are trying to lose weight by reducing your consumption of desserts. To help you avoid the desserts that you love, you try not to think about them. According to the work done on thought suppression, if you are _____, you will actually be more likely to think about the desserts.
   a. unmotivated
   b. inattentive to your desires
   c. cognitively busy
   d. much higher than your target weight

10. Which of the following is the best summary of research on automatic thinking?
    a. Automatic thinking is a problem because it usually produces mistaken judgments
    b. Automatic thinking is amazingly accurate and rarely produces errors of any consequence
    c. Automatic thinking is vital to human survival, but it is not perfect and can produce mistaken judgments that have important consequences
    d. Automatic thinking works best when it occurs consciously

Chapter 3 Answer Key
1-d, 2-b, 3-c, 4-a, 5-d, 6-c, 7-d, 8-c, 9-c, 10-c

For more review plus practice tests, videos, flashcards, writing help and more, log on to MyPsychLab.

Scoring the TRY IT! exercises "试一试！" 答案

Page 67

1. The correct answer is (b), the third letter. Tversky and Kahneman (1974) found that most people thought that the answer was (a), the first letter. Why do people make this mistake? Because, say Tversky and Kahneman, they find it easier to think of examples of words that begin with *R*. By using the availability heuristic, they assumed that the ease with which they could bring examples to mind meant that such words were more common.

2. The correct answer is (b). Slovic, Fischhoff, and Lichtenstein (1976) found that most people think that (a) is correct (accidents). Why did people make this error? Again, it's the availability heuristic: Accidental deaths are more likely to be reported by the media, so people find it easier to bring to mind examples of such deaths than deaths from strokes.

3. The correct answer is (c). Both outcomes are equally likely, given that the outcomes of coin flips are random events. Tversky and Kahneman (1974) argue that due to the representativeness heuristic, people expect a sequence of random events to "look" random. That is, they expect events to be representative of their conception of randomness. Many people, therefore, choose HTTHTH because this sequence is more representative of people's idea of randomness than HHHTTT. In fact, the chance that either sequence will occur is 1 out of 2^6 times, or 1 in 64. As another illustration of this point, if you were to buy a lottery ticket with four numbers, would you rather have the number 6957 or 1111? Many people prefer the former number because it seems more "random" and thus more likely to be picked. In fact, both numbers have a 1 in 1,000 chance of being picked.

4. The correct answer is (b). Many people choose (c) because they think that after five tails in a row, heads is more likely "to even things out." This is called the gambler's fallacy, which is the belief that prior random events (e.g., five tails in a row) have an influence on subsequent random events. Assuming that the coin is fair, prior tosses have no influence on future ones. Tversky and Kahneman (1974) suggest that the gambler's fallacy is due in part to the representativeness heuristic: Five tails and one head seems more representative of a chance outcome than six tails in a row.

Page 76

1. (a) This question assesses methodological reasoning, the recognition that there are several reasons why crime has gone down other than actions taken by the police chief and that a better test of the mayor's claim is to compare the crime rate in Middleopolis with other, similar cities.

2. (a) This question assesses statistical reasoning, the recognition that large samples of information are more likely to reflect true scores and abilities than small samples of information. For example, if you flip a fair coin four times, it is not unusual to get all heads or all tails, but if you flip the coin a thousand times, it is extremely unlikely that you will get all heads or all tails. Applied to this example, this statistical principle says that when baseball players have a small number of at-bats, it is not unusual to see very high (or very low) averages just by chance. By the end of the season, however, when baseball players have hundreds of at-bats, it is highly unlikely that they will have a very high average just by luck.

4

Social Perception
How We Come to Understand Other People
社会知觉:
我们如何理解他人

OUTLINE 提纲

- **Nonverbal Behavior**
  - Facial Expressions of Emotion
  - Culture and the Channels of Nonverbal Communication
  - Multichannel Nonverbal Communication
  - CONNECTIONS: The E-Mail Dilemma: Communicating without Nonverbal Cues
- **Implicit Personality Theories: Filling in the Blanks**
  - Culture and Implicit Personality Theories
- **Causal Attribution: Answering the "Why" Question**
  - The Nature of the Attribution Process
  - The Covariation Model: Internal versus External Attributions
  - The Correspondence Bias: People as Personality Psychologists
  - CONNECTIONS: Police Interrogations and the Correspondence Bias
  - Culture and the Correspondence Bias
  - The Actor/Observer Difference
  - Self-Serving Attributions
- **Culture and Other Attributional Biases**
- **Summary**

OTHER PEOPLE ARE NOT EASY TO FIGURE OUT. WHY are they the way they are? Why do they do what they do? The frequency and urgency with which we pose these questions are clear in this touching story, sent in by a reader to the *New York Times*:

> After ending an office romance, a female friend of mine threw a bag full of her former paramour's love letters, cards, and poems into an outside dumpster. The following day he called and wanted to know why she would throw out his letters. She was stunned. He explained that a homeless person going through the garbage read the correspondence and called the number found on a piece of stationery. The homeless man was curious as to why two people who seemed so in love could now be apart. "I would have called you sooner," he told the former boyfriend, "but this was the first quarter I was given today." (De Marco, 1994)

The homeless man was down on his luck—no home, no money, reduced to rifling through garbage cans—and yet that endless fascination with the human condition still asserted itself. He needed to know why the couple broke up. He even spent his only quarter to find out.

We all have a fundamental fascination with explaining other people's behavior. But the reasons people behave as they do are usually hidden from us. All we have to go on is observable behavior: what people do, what they say, their facial expressions, gestures, tone of voice. Unfortunately, we can't read other people's minds; we can't know, truly and completely, who they are and what they mean. Instead, we rely on our impressions and personal theories, putting them together as well as we can, hoping they will lead to reasonably accurate and useful conclusions.

Our desire to understand other people is so fundamental that it carries over into our hobbies and recreational lives. We go to movies, read novels, watch soap operas, and "people watch" at airports because thinking about the behavior even of strangers and fictional characters fascinates us (Weiner, 1985). This basic aspect of human cognition has been exploited brilliantly by "reality TV" programmers, who cast television shows with real people, not actors, and place them in unusual or even difficult situations. This new genre of television show has proved a powerhouse. Since the original version of *Survivor*, shot in 2000, reality shows have crowded the top-10 list of most watched shows every year. Why are these shows so popular with the American public? Because we enjoy figuring people out.

We do it all day long as a necessary part of social survival, and then we go home, turn on the TV, and do it for fun and entertainment. For example, take two popular reality shows that are particularly interesting from a social psychological perspective: *Survivor* and *American Idol*. In the *Survivor* shows, the contestants scheme, lie, and form alliances as one by one they vote their fellow contestants off the show in the hope of being the last survivor, collecting the reward of $1 million. In a typical segment, we see one contestant form an alliance with another and then turn around and betray that person without blinking an eye (Gilbert, 2000; James, 2000). When are the contestants lying and when are they telling the truth? And what are they really like as people—are they deceitful, manipulative opportunists, or are they just playing the game?

In *American Idol*, we watch an array of contestants compete against each other to be named the best singer and winner of a lucrative recording contract. The compelling aspects of the show are threefold: The contestants are very much "real people," with a variety of backgrounds; their talent varies, so much so that the early weeks of the show present people who truly can't sing (but naively think they can); and the judges can be very critical and even cruel in their feedback. In short, an emotional trainwreck is put into motion, where some contestants will be embarrassed, maligned, and dissolve into tears on camera. Clearly, viewers enjoy watching this real-life emotional spectacle and competition (the show is currently rated number one in the country). And viewers play a critical role in the process—they vote someone off the show each week. Viewers so enjoy making these decisions that many Web sites (including online betting sites) have spontaneously arisen to allow them to communicate with each other about the show (Arthur, 2006).

Why do we spend so much time and energy thinking about other people and their behavior? Because doing so helps us understand and predict our social world (Heider, 1958; Kelley, 1967). In this chapter, we will discuss **social perception**—the study of how we form impressions of other people and how we make inferences about them. One important source of information that we use is people's nonverbal behavior, such as their facial expressions, body movements, and tone of voice.

Nonverbal Behavior 非语言行为

What do we know about people when we first meet them? We know what we can see and hear, and even though we know we should not judge a book by its cover, this kind of easily observable information is crucial to our first impression. For example, physical characteristics such as attractiveness influence the way we judge people (Hatfield & Sprecher, 1986). We also pay a great deal of attention to what people say. After all, our most noteworthy accomplishment as a species is the development of verbal language.

But our words tell only part of the story. With no words at all, we can communicate volumes (Ambady & Rosenthal, 1992, 1993; De Paulo & Friedman, 1998; Gifford, 1991, 1994). **Nonverbal communication** refers to how people communicate, intentionally or unintentionally, without words. Facial expressions, tone of voice, gestures, body positions and movement, the use of touch, and eye gaze are the most frequently used and most revealing channels of nonverbal communication (Henley, 1977; Knapp & Hall, 2006).

We do share our ability to read nonverbal cues with other species. For example, dogs are adept at reading not only "dog nonverbals" but human nonverbals as well, and even outperform chimpanzees when it comes to understanding human nonverbal cues (Hare & Tomasello, 2005). Nonetheless, we are a particularly eloquent and sophisticated nonverbal species. Recent research in neuroscience has found that humans (and our close relatives, primates) have a special kind of brain cell called *mirror neurons*. These neurons respond when we perform an action *and* when we see someone else perform the same action (Gallese, Fadiga, Fogassi, & Rizzolatti, 1996). Mirror neurons appear to be the basis of our ability to feel empathy. For example, when we see someone crying, these mirror neurons fire automatically and involuntarily, just as if we were crying

Social Perception
The study of how we form impressions of and make inferences about other people

Nonverbal Communication
The way in which people communicate, intentionally or unintentionally, without words; nonverbal cues include facial expressions, tone of voice, gestures, body position and movement, the use of touch, and gaze

ourselves. Bruno Wicker and his colleagues (2003) investigated the role of mirror neurons in the emotion of disgust. They used functional magnetic-resonating imaging (fMRI) to look at the pattern of brain cells' firing in research participants as they did two different tasks: smell really obnoxious, gross odors, and watch a film of an actor wrinkling his face in a disgusted look. The researchers found that feeling disgusted oneself (from smelling something gross) and observing someone else's facial expression of disgust activated the same region of participants' brains. Thus, one way that we are able to connect with each other emotionally is through the activation of these mirror neurons. At least some of the time, as researcher Vittorio Gallese put it, "We don't have to *think* about what other people are . . . feeling, we simply *know*"—in short, we feel it too (Winerman, 2005, p. 50). In addition, we understand others' emotions by spontaneously mimicking them on our own faces. The muscle movements of your face, created by empathy, help you understand how the other person is feeling (Stel & van Knippenberg, 2008).

Nonverbal cues serve many functions in communication. They help us express our emotions, our attitudes, and our personality. For example, you express "I'm angry" by narrowing your eyes, lowering your eyebrows, and setting your mouth in a thin, straight line. You communicate your personality traits, like being an extrovert, with broad gestures and frequent changes in voice pitch and inflection (Knapp & Hall, 2006). You can explore how you use one aspect of nonverbal communication—your voice—in the following Try It! Exercise.

Nonverbal cues are often considered more "honest" than words, reflecting what people really feel but will not say. And indeed, research indicates that suppressed emotions are often "leaked" via a facial expression or body movement (Ekman, 2003, 2006). However, it is difficult to notice or interpret these suppressed nonverbal cues; witness how often we don't know that someone is lying to us. Despite this difficulty, the U.S. Transportation Agency is currently training and deploying hundreds of security agents to read concealed emotions on the faces of passengers at airports, in hopes of stopping terrorist activity (Lipton, 2006; Wilber & Nakashima, 2007). (Note that a U.S. television drama, *Lie to Me*, which premiered in 2009, is based exactly on this premise!)

> *An eye can threaten like a loaded and leveled gun, or can insult like hissing or kicking; or, in its altered mood, by beams of kindness, it can make the heart dance with joy.*
>
> —Ralph Waldo Emerson, The Conduct of Life

试一试！用你的声音作为非语言线索
Using Your Voice as a Nonverbal Cue

Even though the words you say are full of information, the way you say them gives your listener even more of an idea of what you mean. You can take a perfectly straightforward sentence like "I don't know her" and give it many different meanings, depending on how you say it. Try saying that sentence out loud so that it communicates each of the emotions listed below. Experiment with the pitch of your voice (high or low), the speed with which you speak, the loudness or softness of your voice, and whether you stress some words and not others.

"I don't know her."

- You're angry.
- You're being sarcastic.
- You're scared.
- You're surprised.
- You're disgusted.
- You're very happy.

Now try this exercise with a friend. Turn your back to your friend as you say each sentence; you want your friend to have to rely on your voice as the only cue, without help from any facial expressions you might make. How well does he or she guess the emotions you are expressing? Have your friend try the exercise too—can you understand his or her nonverbal vocal cues? If you don't always correctly identify each other's voices, discuss what was missing or confusing about the voice. In this way, you'll be able to figure out, for example, what a "disgusted" voice sounds like as compared to an "angry" or "scared" voice.

Nonverbal forms of communication have typically been studied individually, in their separate "channels" (e.g., eye gaze or gestures), even though in everyday life nonverbal cues of many kinds occur all at the same time in a quite dazzling orchestration of information (Archer & Akert, 1980, 1984). Let's focus on a few of these channels and then turn to how we interpret the full symphony of nonverbal information as it occurs naturally.

Facial Expressions of Emotion 表达情绪的面部表情

The crown jewel of nonverbal communication is the facial expressions channel. This aspect of communication has the longest history of research, beginning with Charles Darwin's book *The Expression of the Emotions in Man and Animals* (1872). Its primacy is due to the exquisite communicativeness of the human face (Kappas, 1997; McHugo & Smith, 1996; Wehrle, Kaiser, Schmidt, & Scherer, 2000). Look at the photographs on the next page. We bet you can figure out the meaning of these expressions with very little effort.

Evolution and Facial Expressions Darwin's research on facial expressions has had a major impact on the field in many areas. We will focus on his belief that the primary emotions conveyed by the face are universal: All humans **encode** or express these emotions in the same way, and all humans can **decode** or interpret them with equal accuracy. Darwin's interest in evolution led him to believe that nonverbal forms of communication were "species-specific" and not "culture-specific." He stated that facial expressions were vestiges of once useful physiological reactions. For example, if early hominids ate something that tasted terrible, they would have wrinkled their noses in displeasure and expelled the food from their mouths. Recent research by Joshua Susskind and his colleagues (2008) offers support for Darwin's view. They studied the facial expressions of disgust and fear and found, first, that the muscle movements of each emotion were completely the opposite of the other. Second, they found that the fear face enhances perception, while the disgust face decreases it. For fear, the facial and eye muscle movements increase sensory input, such as widening the visual field, increasing the volume of air in the nose, and speeding up eye movements, all of which are useful responses to something that is frightening. In contrast, for disgust, the muscle movements decrease input from these senses: Eyes narrow, less air is breathed in, and eye movements slow down, all of which are useful reactions to something that smells or tastes disgusting (Susskind, Cusi, Feiman, Grabski, & Anderson, 2008).

Darwin (1872) argued further that facial expressions such as disgust and fear then acquired evolutionary significance. Being able to communicate emotional states (e.g., the feeling of disgust, not for food but for another person or a situation) had survival value for the developing species (Hansen & Hansen, 1988; Izard, 1994; McArthur & Baron, 1983). For example, being able to perceive that another person is angry (and therefore potentially dangerous) would have great evolutionary significance for early humans—it might have meant the difference between life and death. D. Vaughn Becker and his colleagues (2007) have intriguing results in this area. They found that research participants were faster and more accurate at decoding angry expressions on male faces and at detecting happy expressions on female faces. Furthermore, when they subtly manipulated (via computer-generated faces) how male or female the face looked, and the strength of the emotion shown, they again found a strong connection between anger and men's faces, and happiness and women's faces. The researchers suggest that from an evolutionary perspective, the costs and benefits of perceiving anger and happiness would vary depending on whether the encoder was male or female (Becker, Kenrick, Neuberg, Blackwell, & Smith, 2007).

Was Darwin right when he stated that facial expressions of emotion are universal? The answer is yes, for the six major emotional expressions: anger, happiness, surprise, fear, disgust, and sadness. For example, in a particularly well-designed study, Paul Ekman and Walter Friesen (1971) traveled to New Guinea, where they studied the decoding ability of the South Fore, a preliterate tribe that had had no contact with

> *When the eyes say one thing, and the tongue another, a practiced man relies on the language of the first.*
> —Ralph Waldo Emerson, The Conduct of Life

Encode
To express or emit nonverbal behavior, such as smiling or patting someone on the back

Decode
To interpret the meaning of the nonverbal behavior other people express, such as deciding that a pat on the back was an expression of condescension and not kindness

These photographs depict facial expressions of the six major emotions. Can you guess the emotion expressed on each face?

Answers (beginning in the upper left): Anger, fear, disgust, happiness, surprise, and sadness.

Western civilization. They told the Fore people brief stories with emotional content and then showed them photographs of American men and women expressing the six emotions; the Fores' job was to match the facial expressions of emotion to the stories. They were as accurate as Western subjects had been. The researchers then asked the Fore people to demonstrate, while being photographed, facial expressions that would match the stories they were told. These photographs, when later shown to American research participants, were also decoded accurately. Thus, there is considerable evidence that the ability to interpret at least the six major emotions is cross-cultural—part of being human and not a product of people's cultural experience (Biehl et al., 1997; Ekman, 1993, 1994; Ekman et al., 1987; Elfenbein & Ambady, 2002; Haidt & Keltner, 1999; Izard, 1994; Matsumoto & Wilingham, 2006).

These six major emotions are also the first to appear in human development. Children as young as six months to a year express these emotions with the facial expressions we associate with adults. This is true as well for young children who have been blind from birth; they are able to encode the basic emotions even though they have never seen them displayed by adults (Eibl-Eibesfeldt, 1975; Galati, Miceli, & Sini, 2001). Other emotions, such as guilt, shame, embarrassment, and pride, occur later in human development and presumably occurred later in evolution. These latter emotions are closely tied to social interaction. For example, you feel pride or shame only when you are old enough to have learned that other people have expectations for your behavior, and that there are consequences when you do or do not match those expectations (Adolphs, 2003).

Besides the six major emotions, are there other emotional states that are communicated with distinctive and readily identifiable facial expressions? Researchers are exploring just this question for emotions such as contempt, anxiety, shame, pride, and embarrassment (Ekman, O'Sullivan, & Matsumoto, 1991; Harrigan & O'Connell, 1996; Keltner & Shiota, 2003). For example, recent research on the facial expression

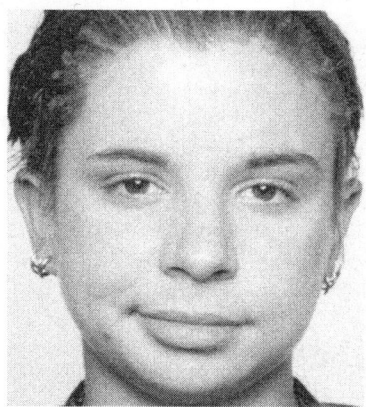

Recent research suggests that "contempt" may be a universally recognized expression.

of *contempt* suggests that it is recognized cross-culturally like the six major emotions discussed earlier. Research participants from countries as disparate culturally as Estonia, Japan, the United States, Sumatra, Italy, India, and Vietnam recognized the contempt expression: a tightening and raising of the lip on only one side of the face, as shown in the photograph on the left (e.g., Haidt & Keltner, 1999; Matsumoto & Ekman, 2004).

Similarly, research has indicated that the emotion of *pride* exists cross-culturally. Pride is a particularly interesting emotional display because it involves a facial expression as well as body posture and gesture cues. Specifically, the prototypical pride expression includes a small smile, the head tilted back slightly, a visibly expanded chest and posture, and the arms raised above the head or hands on hips (Tracy & Robins, 2004). Photographs of pride expressions were accurately decoded by research participants in the United States and Italy, and by individuals from a preliterate, isolated tribe in Burkina Faso, West Africa (Tracy & Robins, 2008). Jessica Tracy and David Matsumoto (2008) explored pride and its opposite, *shame*, by coding the spontaneous expressions of winning and losing athletes in judo matches at the 2004 Olympic and Paralympic Games. Sighted and blind athletes from 37 countries were coded on their nonverbal behavior just after they had won or lost their judo match. The pride expression was associated to a significant extent with winning for both sighted and blind athletes around the world. Shame, expressed by slumped shoulders and a sunken chest, was significantly associated with losing for all the athletes except one group: sighted athletes from highly individualistic cultures like the United States and Western Europe. In individualistic cultures, shame is a negative, stigmatized emotion that one hides rather than displays.

Why Is Decoding Sometimes Inaccurate? Decoding facial expressions accurately is more complicated than we have indicated, for two reasons. People frequently display **affect blends** (Ekman & Friesen, 1975): One part of their face registers one emotion while another part registers a different emotion. Take a look at the accompanying photographs and see if you can tell which two emotions are being expressed in each face. In the photograph on the left, we see a blend of anger (the eye and eyebrow region) and disgust (the nose and mouth region). (It may help to cover half of the photograph with your hand to see each emotional expression clearly.) This is the sort of expression you might display if a person told you something that was both horrible and inappropriate—you'd be disgusted with the content and angry that the person told you. A second reason why decoding facial expressions can be inaccurate has to do with culture.

Culture and the Channels of Nonverbal Communication
文化与非语言交流的渠道

For decades, Paul Ekman and his colleagues have studied the influence of culture on the facial display of emotions (Ekman & Davidson, 1994; Ekman & Friesen, 1969; Matsumoto & Ekman, 1989; Matsumoto & Kudoh, 1993). They have concluded that **display rules** are particular to each culture and dictate what kinds of emotional expressions people are supposed to show. As we saw in our discussion of athletes' spontaneous expressions at the Olympics and Paralympics (Tracy & Matsumoto, 2008), the display rules of individualistic cultures discourage the expression of shame in front of others, while the display rules of collectivistic cultures allow (or even encourage) it.

Here is another example: American cultural norms discourage emotional displays in men, such as grief or crying, but allow the facial display of such emotions in women. In Japan, traditional cultural rules dictate that women should not exhibit a wide, uninhibited smile (Ramsey, 1981). Japanese women will often hide a wide smile behind their hands, whereas Western women are allowed—indeed, encouraged—to smile broadly and often (Henley, 1977; La France, Hecht, & Paluck, 2003). In fact, the cultural display rules that govern Japanese nonverbal expression are surprisingly different from Western ones. Japanese norms lead people to cover up negative facial expressions with smiles and laughter and to display fewer facial expressions in general than is true in the West (Argyle, 1986; Aune & Aune, 1996; Gudykunst, Ting-Toomey, &

Affect Blend
A facial expression in which one part of the face registers one emotion while another part of the face registers a different emotion

Display Rules
Culturally determined rules about which nonverbal behaviors are appropriate to display

Nishida, 1996; Richmond & McCroskey, 1995). This is undoubtedly what lies behind the Western stereotype that Asians are "inscrutable" and "hard to read."

There are, of course, other channels of nonverbal communication besides facial expressions. These nonverbal cues are shaped by culture as well. Eye contact and gaze are particularly powerful nonverbal cues. Members of American culture become suspicious when a person doesn't "look them in the eye" while speaking, and they find talking to someone who is wearing dark sunglasses quite disconcerting. However, as you can see in Figure 4.1, in other parts of the world, direct eye gaze is considered invasive or disrespectful. Another form of nonverbal communication is how people use personal space. Imagine you are talking to a person who stands too close to you (or too far away); these deviations from "normal" spacing will affect your impressions of that person. Cultures vary greatly in what is considered normative use of personal space (Hall, 1969). For example, most Americans like to have a bubble of open space, a few feet in radius, surrounding them; in comparison, in some other cultures, strangers think nothing of standing right next to each other, to the point of touching.

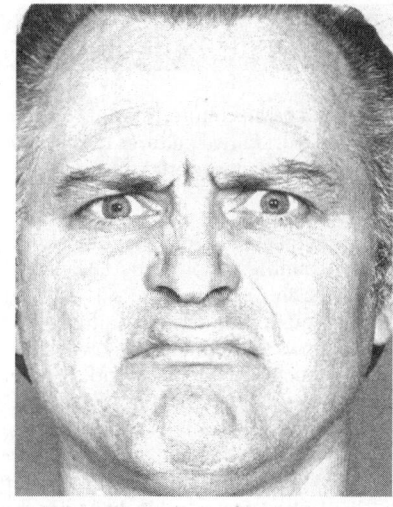

Often people express more than one emotion at the same time. Can you tell which emotions these people are expressing? The answers are printed below.
(Adapted from Ekman & Friesen, 1975)

Answers: The man is expressing a blend of anger and disgust. The woman is expressing a blend of surprise and happiness.

Gestures of the hands and arms are also a fascinating means of communication. Americans are very adept at understanding certain gestures, such as the "OK" sign, in which one forms a circle with the thumb and forefinger and the rest of the fingers curve above the circle, and "flipping the bird," in which one bends all the fingers down at the first knuckle except the longest, middle finger. Gestures like these, for which there are clear, well-understood definitions, are called **emblems** (Ekman & Friesen, 1975; Archer, 1997a). The important point about emblems is that they are not universal; each culture has devised its own emblems, and these need not be understandable to people from other cultures (see Figure 4.1). Thus "flipping the bird" will be a clear communicative sign in American society, whereas in some parts of Europe, you'd need to make a quick gesture with a cupped hand under your chin to convey the same message. President George H. W. Bush once used the "V for victory" sign (where two fingers form a V shape), but he did it backward—the palm of his hand was facing him instead of the audience. Unfortunately, he flashed this gesture to a large crowd in Australia—and in Australia, this emblem is the equivalent of "flipping the bird" (Archer, 1997a)!

Multichannel Nonverbal Communication
多渠道的非语言交流

Except for certain specific situations, such as talking on the telephone, everyday life is made up of multichannel nonverbal social interaction (Archer & Akert, 1998; Rosenthal, Hall, Di Matteo, Rogers, & Archer, 1979). Typically, many nonverbal cues are available to us when we talk to or observe other people. How do we use this information? And how accurately do we use it?

To study multichannel nonverbal decoding, Dane Archer and Robin Akert have constructed a nonverbal communication decoding task that closely mirrors real-life interpretative situations. The Social Interpretations Task (SIT) videotape is composed of 20 scenes of naturally occurring nonverbal behavior (Archer & Akert, 1977a, 1977b, 1980, 1984). Real people, not actors, are seen and heard having real conversations, not scripted ones. The scenes last a minute or so, giving the viewer a slice of a real interaction. Following each scene, the viewer is asked a question about the people in the scene or their relationship to each other. For example, in one scene, two women are seen playing with a baby. The viewer is asked, "Which woman is the mother of the

Emblems
Nonverbal gestures that have well-understood definitions within a given culture; they usually have direct verbal translations, such as the "OK" sign

Cultural Differences in Nonverbal Communication

Many forms of nonverbal behavior are specific to a given culture. Not only do some of the nonverbal behaviors of one culture mean nothing in another, but the same nonverbal behavior can exist in two cultures but have very different meanings in each. Such nonverbal differences can lead to misunderstanding when people from different societies interact. Some of these cultural differences are noted here.

Eye contact and gaze

In American culture, direct eye contact is valued; a person who won't "look you in the eye" is perceived as being evasive or even lying. However, in many parts of the world, direct eye contact is considered disrespectful, especially with superiors. For example, in Nigeria, Puerto Rico, and Thailand, children are taught not to make direct eye contact with their teachers and other adults. Cherokee, Navajo, and Hopi Native Americans use minimal eye contact as well. Japanese use far less direct eye contact than Americans. In contrast, Arabs use a great deal of eye contact, with a gaze that would be considered piercing by people from some other cultures.

Personal space and touching

Societies vary in whether they are high-contact cultures, where people stand close to each other and touch frequently, or low-contact cultures, where people maintain more interpersonal space and touch less often. High-contact cultures include Middle Eastern countries, South American countries, and southern European countries. Low-contact cultures include North American countries, northern European countries, Asian countries, Pakistan, and Native American peoples. Cultures also differ in how appropriate they consider same-sex touching among friends. For example, in Korea and Egypt, men and women hold hands, link arms, or walk hip to hip with their same-sex friends, and these nonverbal behaviors carry no sexual connotation. In the United States, such behavior is much less common, particularly between male friends.

Hand and head gestures

The "OK" sign: The OK sign is formed by making a circle with your thumb and index finger, with your three other fingers extended upward. In the United States, this means "OK." However, in Japan, this hand gesture means "money." In France, it means "zero"; in Mexico, it means "sex." In Ethiopia, it means "homosexuality." Finally, in some South American countries, like Brazil, it is an obscene gesture, carrying the same meaning as the American "flipping the bird" sign, where the middle finger is the only one extended.

The "thumb up" gesture: In the United States, raising one thumb upward with the rest of the fingers in the fist means "OK." Several European countries have a similar meaning for this gesture; for example, in France it means "excellent!" However, in Japan, the same gesture means "boyfriend," while in Iran and Sardinia, it is an obscene gesture.

The "hand-purse" gesture: This gesture is formed by straightening the fingers and thumb of one hand and bringing them together so the tips touch, pointing upwards. This gesture has no clear meaning in American culture. However, in Italy, it means "What are you trying to say?"; in Spain, it means "good"; in Tunisia, it means "slow down"; and in Malta, it means "you may seem good, but you are really bad."

Nodding the head: In the United States, nodding one's head up and down means "yes" and shaking it from side to side means "no." However, in some parts of Africa and India, the opposite is true: nodding up and down means "no," and shaking from side to side means "yes." To complicate this situation even more, in Korea, shaking one's head from side to side means "I don't know" (which in the United States is communicated by a shrug of the shoulders). Finally, Bulgarians indicate disagreement by throwing their heads back and then returning them to an upright position—which is frequently mistaken by Americans as meaning agreement.

FIGURE 4.1

According to covariation theory, we use the consistency, distinctiveness, and level of consensus about person's behavior as mainly caused either by the person's situation or by the person's own characteristics or dispositions.

baby?" A clear criterion for accuracy exists for each of the scenes; one of the women really is the mother of the baby. However, neither of the women states this fact out loud; nor did the women realize this would be the interpretative question paired with their scene.

To get this and the other scenes right, the viewer must pay attention to and interpret the nonverbal behavior of the people in the scenes. Archer and Akert (1980) found that 64 percent of the more than 1,400 people tested were able to decode this scene accurately, far above the chance level of accuracy of 33 percent. People reported using several different channels of nonverbal communication to help them choose the right answer. For example, they compared the tone of voice of the real mother when talking to the baby to the other woman's tone of voice; they noted the body position and posture of the nonmother as she held the baby, as well as the way she held the baby; they relied on eye contact cues, especially the baby's eye contact with the mother versus the nonmother; and they focused on the way the mother touched the baby versus the nonmother's touch.

These photographs depict French nonverbal emblems. These gestures are clearly understood in France but are difficult for an American to interpret. (The one on the left means, "How boring." The one on the right means, "You can't fool me!")

(Adapted from Wylie, 1977)

Further research with the SIT videotape has shown that the important, or diagnostic, nonverbal information is actually diffused throughout each scene (Archer & Akert, 1980; Akert & Panter, 1986). In other words, it is not typically the case that only one significant clue signals the right answer. Instead, useful nonverbal information is present via many channels in each scene. This makes the decoder's job easier: If you fail to notice the eye gaze behavior, you may notice the tone of voice or the unusual gesture and still arrive at an accurate judgment.

To summarize, we can learn quite a lot about people from their nonverbal behavior, including their attitudes, emotions, and personality traits. Nonverbal behavior gives us many bits of information—"data" that we then use to construct our overall impressions or theories about people. But nonverbal cues are just the beginning of social perception. We turn now to the cognitive processes people use when forming impressions of others.

CONNECTIONS 链 接

The E-Mail Dilemma: Communicating without Nonverbal Cues
e-mail的两难：没有非语言线索的交流

There you are, working at 4:00 in the morning on your psychology paper, which is due the next afternoon. You have a question and decide to e-mail your professor, figuring there may be a chance he'll respond the next morning. You add a little joke about "waiting until the last minute" to do your paper, when in fact the complexity of your question should indicate that you've been working on it for days. Next morning, a blistering e-mail arrives from your professor, criticizing you for not taking the assignment seriously. Oh dear. Your professor didn't get that you were joking.

Scenarios like this demonstrate the dilemma of e-mail communication: Words go out, but there are no nonverbal cues to give them additional meaning. Humor, sarcasm, sadness, and other emotions are stripped away and your words stand alone, potentially open to misinterpretation. Sometimes we try to clarify our words by inserting *emoticons* in e-mails, like this one: :-)). Although there are many emoticons in existence (check www.emoticonuniverse.com for several hundred), they can be inappropriate if your message is a formal one, and they are often hard to interpret. What does %-(or ;~/ mean, for example? ("I'm confused," and "I'm unsure," respectively; Kruger, Epley, Parker & Ng, 2005).

Do e-mail writers realize to a sufficient extent that the loss of nonverbal cues can be a problem? Research by Justin Kruger and his colleagues (2005) suggests no. They conducted a study where college students were given a number of topics about which to

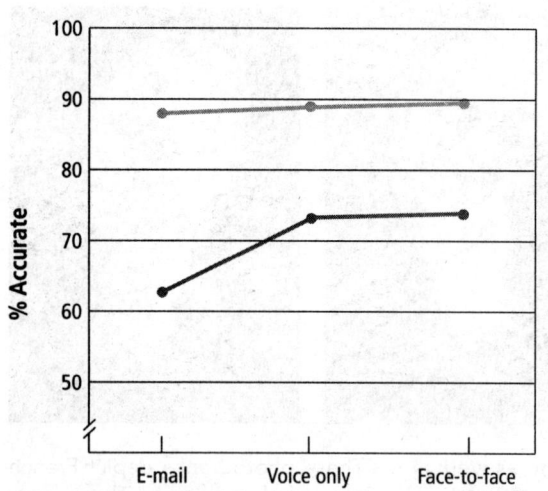

FIGURE 4.2
Accuracy at communicating emotions in three types of messages.

Although message senders were highly confident they could communicate sarcasm, humor, sadness, and seriousness in all of the three types of messages, they were, in fact, most likely to fail to communicate the emotions accurately over e-mail. This occurred whether the e-mail recipients were their friends or strangers.

(Adapted from Kruger, Epley, Parker, & Ng, 2005)

> *Others are to us like the "characters" in fiction, external and incorrigible; the surprises they give us turn out in the end to have been predictable—unexpected variations on the theme of being themselves.*
> —Mary McCarthy

Implicit Personality Theory
A type of schema people use to group various kinds of personality traits together; for example, many people believe that someone who is kind is generous as well

communicate (e.g., "dorm life," "dating") and which were matched to one of four emotions: sarcasm, sadness, anger, or seriousness. Their job was to construct a statement on the topic that successfully conveyed the associated emotion. They communicated their statements either face-to-face with another person; to another person but using their voice only; or via an e-mail. Finally, participants communicated their messages to either a stranger or a close friend.

Before they delivered their statements, participants were asked to what extent they thought they had successfully communicated the emotion in their message. As you can see in Figure 4.2, this "anticipated accuracy" is very high. Participants were very confident of their communicative abilities—from e-mail to face-to-face interactions, they felt they'd done it accurately almost 90 percent of the time. Next, the message recipients were asked to indicate what emotion was in the message: the "actual accuracy." As Figure 4.2 shows, recipients were significantly less likely to get the emotional meaning if the message was communicated via e-mail. To make these results even more worrisome, participants' friends did no better at decoding the correct emotion than did complete strangers! Thus, e-mail writers were overconfident about their ability to communicate emotion with words alone—they thought they had communicated clearly, but in fact, they had not (Kruger et al., 2005).

The moral of the story: Relying on words alone, as occurs in e-mail, always results in an impoverished medium of communication. Be careful. Be very, very careful, when you e-mail. You can easily be misunderstood and those misunderstandings (as we'll see throughout this chapter) can have serious effects on your interactions with others. And remember too, that you are very likely to think your meaning is clear in an e-mail, when in fact, it is only clear to *you*.

Implicit Personality Theories: Filling in the Blanks 内隐人格理论：填补空白

As we saw in Chapter 3, when people are unsure about the nature of the social world, they use their schemas to fill in the gaps. A schema is a mental shortcut: When all we have is a small amount of information, our schemas provide additional information to fill in the gaps (Fiske & Taylor, 1991; Markus & Zajonc, 1985). Thus when we are trying to understand other people, we can use just a few observations of a person as a starting point and then, using our schemas, create a much fuller understanding (Dweck, Chiu, & Hong, 1995; Kim & Rosenberg, 1980). Schemas allow us to form impressions quickly, without having to spend weeks with people to figure out what they are like.

This kind of schema is called an **implicit personality theory:** It consists of our ideas about what kinds of personality traits go together (Asch, 1946; Schneider, 1973; Sedikides & Anderson, 1994; Werth & Foerster, 2002). We use a few known traits to determine what other characteristics a person has. If someone is kind, our implicit personality theory tells us he or she is probably generous as well; similarly, we assume that a stingy person is also irritable. But relying on schemas can also lead us astray. We might make the wrong assumptions about an individual; we might even resort to stereotypical thinking, where our schema, or stereotype, leads us to believe that the individual is like all the other members of his or her group. (We will discuss these issues in more depth in Chapter 13.)

Culture and Implicit Personality Theories 文化与内隐人格理论

Implicit personality theories are developed over time and with experience. Although each of us may have a few idiosyncratic theories about which personality traits go together, we also share many similar theories with one another (Gervey, Chiu, Hong, & Dweck, 1999; Hamilton, 1970; Stapel & Koomen, 2000). This occurs because implicit personality theories are strongly tied to culture. Like other beliefs, they are passed from generation to generation in a society, and one culture's implicit personality theory may be very different from another's (Anderson, 1995; Chiu, Morris, Hong, & Menon, 2000; Cousins, 1989; Vonk, 1995).

For example, when Americans perceive someone as "helpful," they also perceive them as "sincere"; a "practical" person is also "cautious" (Rosenberg, Nelson, & Vivekananthan, 1968). Another strong implicit personality theory in this culture involves physical attractiveness. We presume that "what is beautiful is good"—that people with physical beauty will also have a whole host of other wonderful qualities (Dion, Berscheid, & Walster, 1972; Eagly, Ashmore, Makhijani, & Longo, 1991; Jackson, Hunter, & Hodge, 1995). In China, an implicit personality theory describes a person who embodies traditional Chinese values: creating and maintaining interpersonal harmony, inner harmony, and *ren qin* (a focus on relationships; Cheung et al., 1996).

Cultural variation in implicit personality theories was demonstrated in an intriguing study (Hoffman, Lau, & Johnson, 1986). The researchers noted that cultures have different ideas about personality types—the kinds of people for whom there are simple, agreed-on verbal labels. For example, in Western cultures, saying someone has an "artistic personality" implies that the person is creative, intense, and temperamental and has an unconventional lifestyle. The Chinese, however, do not have a schema or implicit personality theory for an artistic type. Granted, there are Chinese words to describe the individual characteristics of such people, such as creative, but there are no labels like "artistic" or "bohemian" that convey the whole constellation of traits implied by the English term. Conversely, in China, there are categories of personality that do not exist in Western cultures. For example, a *shi gú* person is someone who is worldly, devoted to his or her family, socially skillful, and somewhat reserved.

Hoffman and his colleagues (1986) hypothesized that these cultural implicit personality theories influence the way people form impressions of others. To test this hypothesis, they wrote stories in English and Chinese, describing someone behaving like an artistic type or a *shi gú* type, without using those labels. They gave the English versions to a group of native English speakers who spoke no other languages and to a group of Chinese-English bilinguals. Another group of Chinese-English bilinguals received the versions written in Chinese.

If people were using their cultural theories to understand the stories they read, what would you expect to happen? One measure of the use of theories (or schemas) is the tendency to fill in the blanks—to believe that information fitting the schema was observed when in fact it was not. The researchers asked the participants to write down their impressions of the characters in the stories; they then looked to see whether the participants listed traits that were not in the stories but did fit the artistic or *shi gú* personality type. For example, the term *unreliable* was not used in the "artistic personality type" story but is consistent with that implicit personality theory.

When the native English speakers read about the characters in English, they were much more likely to form an impression that was

Implicit personality theories differ from culture to culture. Westerners assume there is an artistic type of person—someone who is creative, intense, temperamental, and unconventional (for example, the artist Andy Warhol, above). The Chinese have no such implicit personality theory. The Chinese have a category of a *shi gú* person—someone who is worldly, devoted to his or her family, socially skillful, and somewhat reserved (below). Westerners do not have this implicit personality theory.

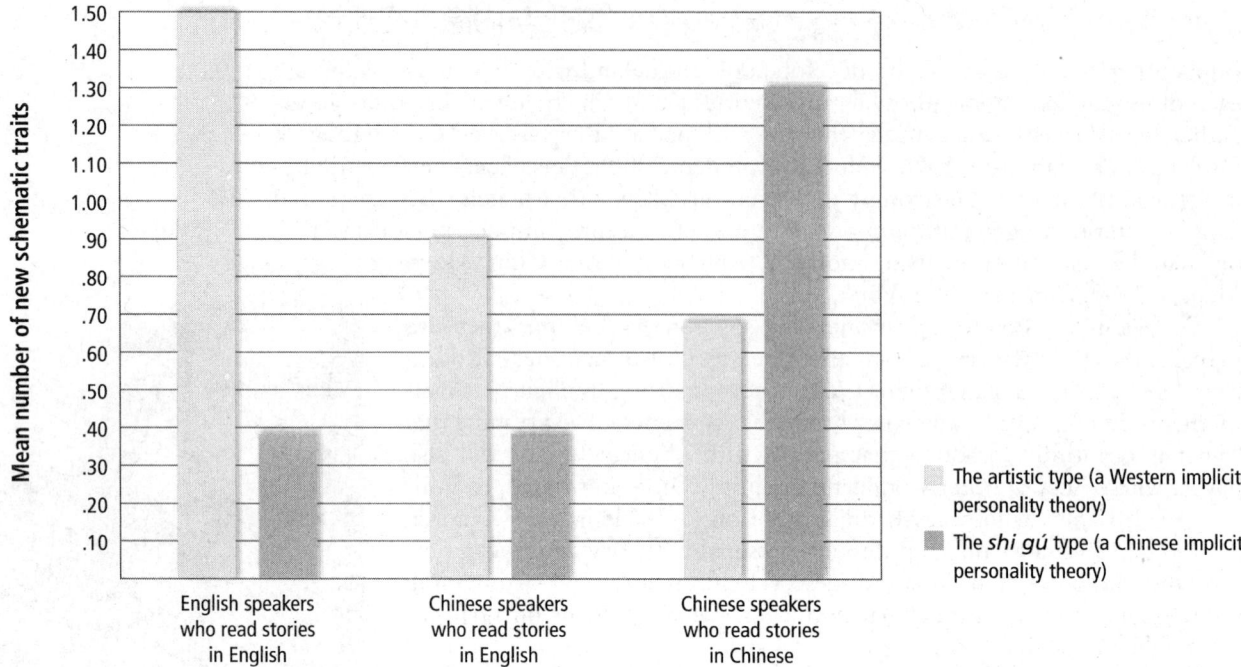

FIGURE 4.3

Implicit personality theories: How our culture and language shape our impressions of others.

People formed an impression of other people that was consistent with the implicit personality theory contained in their language. For example, when Chinese-English bilinguals read stories about people in English, they were likely to form impressions consistent with a Western implicit theory, the artistic personality. When Chinese-English bilinguals read the same stories in Chinese, they were likely to form impressions consistent with a Chinese implicit theory, the shi gú personality.

(Adapted from Hoffman, Lau, & Johnson, 1986)

consistent with the artistic type than with the *shi gú* type (see Figure 4.3). Similarly, when the Chinese-English bilinguals read the descriptions of the characters in English, they too formed an impression that was consistent with the artistic type but not with the *shi gú* type because English provides a convenient label for the artistic type. In comparison, Chinese-English bilinguals who read the descriptions in Chinese showed the opposite pattern of results. Their impression of the *shi gú* character was more consistent with that schema than their impression of the artist was because the Chinese language provides a convenient label or implicit personality theory for this kind of person.

These results are consistent with a well-known argument by Benjamin Whorf (1956) that the language people speak influences the way they think about the world. Characters described identically were perceived differently by the bilingual research participants, depending on the language (and therefore the implicit personality theory) that was used. Thus one's culture and one's language produce widely shared implicit personality theories, and these theories can influence the kinds of inferences people form about one another.

Decoding nonverbal behaviors and relying on implicit personality theories tend to occur automatically—we are not always consciously aware of using this information (Willis & Todorov, 2008). What about those times when we must work consciously to explain another's behavior?

Causal Attribution: Answering the "Why" Question
因果归因：回答"为什么"的问题

We have seen that when we observe other people, we have a rich source of information—their nonverbal behavior—on which to base our impressions. From their nonverbal behavior, we can also make guesses about people's personalities, such as how friendly or outgoing they are. And once we get this far, we use our implicit personality theories to fill in the blanks: If a person is friendly, we generally infer that he or she must be sincere as well.

However, nonverbal behavior and implicit personality theories are not fail-safe indicators of what a person is really thinking or feeling. If you meet an acquaintance and she says, "It's great to see you!" does she really mean it? Perhaps she is acting more thrilled than she really feels, out of politeness. Perhaps she is outright lying and really can't stand you. The point is that even though nonverbal communication is sometimes easy to decode and our implicit personality theories can streamline the way we form impressions, there is still substantial ambiguity as to what a person's behavior really means (De Paulo, 1992; De Paulo, Stone, & Lassiter, 1985; Schneider, Hastorf, & Ellsworth, 1979).

Why did that acquaintance behave as she did? To answer this "why" question, we will use our immediate observations to form more elegant and complex inferences about what people are really like and what motivates them to act as they do. How we go about answering these questions is the focus of **attribution theory**, the study of how we infer the causes of other people's behavior.

> *In the beginning was not the word, not the deed, not the silly serpent. In the beginning was why? Why did she pluck the apple? Was she bored? Was she inquisitive? Was she paid? Did Adam put her up to it? If not, who did?*
>
> —John le Carré, The Russia House, 1989

The Nature of the Attribution Process 归因过程的本质

Fritz Heider (1958) is frequently referred to as the father of attribution theory. His influential book defined the field of social perception, and his legacy is still very much evident in current research (Singer & Frith, 2006; Trope & Gaunt, 2003). Heider discussed what he called "naive" or "commonsense" psychology. In his view, people were like amateur scientists, trying to understand other people's behavior by piecing together information until they arrived at a reasonable explanation or cause (Surian, Caldi, & Sperber, 2007). Heider was intrigued by what seemed reasonable to people and by how they arrived at their conclusions.

One of Heider's most valuable contributions is a simple dichotomy: When trying to decide why people behave as they do—for example, why a father has just yelled at his young daughter—we can make one of two attributions. One option is to make an **internal attribution**, deciding that the cause of the father's behavior was something about him—his disposition, personality, attitudes, or character—an explanation that assigns the causes of his behavior internally. For example, we might decide that the father has poor parenting skills and disciplines his child in inappropriate ways. Alternatively, we might make an **external attribution**, deciding that something in the situation, not in the father's personality or attitudes, caused his behavior. If we conclude that he yelled because his daughter had just stepped into the street without looking, we would be making an external attribution for his behavior.

Notice that our impression of the father will be very different, depending on the type of attribution we make. If we make an internal attribution, we'll have a negative impression of him. If we make an external attribution, we won't learn much about him—after all, most parents would have done the same thing if they were in that situation and their child had just disobeyed them by stepping into the street. Quite a difference!

This internal/external attribution dichotomy plays an extraordinarily important role in even the most intimate parts of our lives. Indeed, spouses in happy, satisfied marriages make very different attributions about their partners than spouses in troubled, distressed

Attribution Theory
A description of the way in which people explain the causes of their own and other people's behavior

Internal Attribution
The inference that a person is behaving in a certain way because of something about the person, such as attitude, character, or personality

External Attribution
The inference that a person is behaving a certain way because of something about the situation he or she is in; the assumption is that most people would respond the same way in that situation

According to Fritz Heider, we tend to see the causes of a person's behavior as internal. For example, when a person on the street asks for money, we are likely to assume that he is at fault for being poor—perhaps lazy or drug-addicted. If we knew the person's situation—perhaps he has lost his job due to a factory closing or has a spouse whose medical bills have bankrupted them—we might come up with a different, external attribution.

marriages. Satisfied spouses tend to make internal attributions for their partners' positive behaviors (e.g., "She helped me because she's such a generous person") and external attributions for their partners' negative behaviors (e.g., "He said something mean because he's so stressed at work this week"). In contrast, spouses in distressed marriages tend to display the opposite pattern: Their partners' positive behaviors are chalked up to external causes (e.g., "She helped me because she wanted to impress our friends"), while negative behaviors are attributed to internal causes (e.g., "He said something mean because he's a totally self-centered jerk"). When an intimate relationship becomes troubled, this second pattern of attributions about one's partner only makes the situation worse and can have dire consequences for the health and future of the relationship (Bradbury & Fincham, 1991; Fincham, Bradbury, Arias, Byrne, & Karney, 1997; Karney & Bradbury, 2000).

Another of Heider's important contributions was his discussion of our preference for internal attributions over external ones. Although either type of attribution is always possible, Heider (1958) noted that we tend to see the causes of a person's behavior as residing in that person. We are perceptually focused on people—they are who we notice—and the situation (the external explanation), which is often hard to see and hard to describe, may be overlooked (Bargh, 1994; Fletcher, Reeder, & Bull, 1990; Gilbert, 1998b; Jones, 1979, 1990; Jones & Davis, 1965; Miller, 1998). You can observe people making attributions in their conversations using the Try It! exercise on the next page.

The Covariation Model: Internal versus External Attributions
共变模式：内部归因与外部归因

The first, essential step in the process of social perception is determining how people decide whether to make an internal or an external attribution. Harold Kelley's major contribution to attribution theory was the idea that we notice and think about more than one piece of information when we form an impression of another person (1967, 1973). For example, let's say you ask your friend to lend you her car, and she says no. Naturally, you wonder why. What explains her behavior? Kelley's theory, called the **covariation model**, says that you will examine multiple instances of behavior, occurring at different times and in different situations, to answer this question. Has your friend refused to lend you her car in the past? Does she lend it to other people? Does she normally lend you other possessions?

Kelley, like Heider before him, assumes that when we are in the process of forming an attribution, we gather information, or data. The data we use, according to Kelley, are how a person's behavior "covaries" or changes across time, place, different actors, and different targets of the behavior. By discovering covariation in people's behavior (e.g., your friend refuses to lend you her car; she agrees to lend it to others), you are able to reach a judgment about what caused their behavior.

When we are forming an attribution, what kinds of information do we examine for covariation? Kelley (1967) identified three key types of information: *consensus*, *distinctiveness*, and *consistency*. Suppose that you are working at your part-time job at the Gap, and you observe your boss yelling at another employee, Hannah, telling her that she's an idiot. Automatically, you ask that attributional question: "Why is the boss yelling at Hannah and being so critical—is it something about the boss, something about Hannah, or something about the situation that surrounds and affects him?"

How would Kelley's (1967, 1972, 1973) model of covariation assessment answer this question? **Consensus information** refers to how other people behave toward the same stimulus—in this case, Hannah. Do other people at work also yell at Hannah and criticize her? **Distinctiveness information** refers to how the actor (the person whose

Covariation Model
A theory that states that to form an attribution about what caused a person's behavior, we systematically note the pattern between the presence or absence of possible causal factors and whether or not the behavior occurs

Consensus Information
Information about the extent to which other people behave the same way toward the same stimulus as the actor does

behavior we are trying to explain) responds to other stimuli. Does the boss yell at and demean other employees in the store? **Consistency information** refers to the frequency with which the observed behavior between the same actor and the same stimulus occurs across time and circumstances. Does the boss yell at and criticize Hannah regularly and frequently, whether the store is filled with customers or empty?

According to Kelley's theory, when these three sources of information combine into one of two distinct patterns, a clear attribution can be made. People are most likely to make an internal attribution (deciding that the behavior was due to something about the boss) when the consensus and distinctiveness of the act are low but its consistency is high (see Figure 4.4). We would be pretty confident that the boss yelled at Hannah because he is a mean and vindictive person if we knew that no one else yells at Hannah, that the boss yells at other employees, and that the boss yells at Hannah every chance he gets. People are likely to make an external attribution (in this case, about Hannah) if consensus, distinctiveness, and consistency are all high. Finally, when consistency is low, we cannot make a clear internal or external attribution and so resort to a special kind of external or situational attribution, one that assumes something unusual or peculiar is going on in these circumstances—for example, the boss just received very upsetting news and lost his temper with the first person he saw.

The covariation model assumes that people make causal attributions in a rational, logical way. People observe the clues, such as the distinctiveness of the act, and then draw a logical inference about why the person did what he or she did. Several studies have confirmed that people often do make attributions the way that Kelley's model says they should (Forsterling, 1989; Gilbert, 1998a; Hewstone & Jaspars, 1987; Hilton, Smith, & Kim, 1995; Orvis, Cunningham, & Kelley, 1975; White, 2002)—with two exceptions. Studies have shown that people don't use consensus information as much as Kelley's theory predicted; they rely more on consistency and distinctiveness information when forming attributions (McArthur, 1972; Wright, Luus, & Christie, 1990). Also, people don't always have the relevant information they need on all three of Kelley's dimensions. For example, you may not have consistency information because this is the first time you have ever asked your friend to borrow her car. In these situations, research has shown that people proceed with the attribution process using the information they do have and, if necessary, making inferences about the missing data (Fiedler, Walther, & Nickel, 1999; Kelley, 1973).

To summarize, the covariation model portrays people as master detectives, deducing the causes of behavior as systematically and logically as Sherlock Holmes would.

Distinctiveness Information
Information about the extent to which one particular actor behaves in the same way to different stimuli

Consistency Information
Information about the extent to which the behavior between one actor and one stimulus is the same across time and circumstances

 **Listen as People Make Attributions** 试一试！听听别人如何进行归因

Forming attributions is a major part of daily life—note the Ann Landers column on page 108. You can watch the attribution process in action too. All it takes is a group of friends and an interesting topic to discuss. Perhaps one of your friends is telling you about something that happened to her that day, or perhaps your group is discussing another person whom everybody knows. As they talk, pay very close attention to what they say. They will be trying to figure out why the person being discussed did what she did or said what he said. In other words, they will be making attributions. Your job is to try to keep track of their comments and label the attributional strategies they are using.

In particular, do they make internal attributions, about a person's character or personality, or do they make situational attributions, about all the other events and variables that make up a person's life? Do your friends seem to prefer one type of attribution over the other? If their interpretation is dispositional, what happens when you suggest another possible interpretation, one that is situational? Do they agree or disagree with you? What kinds of information do they offer as "proof" that their attribution is right? Observing people when they are making attributions in real conversations will show you just how common and powerful this type of thinking is when people are trying to understand each other.

FIGURE 4.4
The covariation model.

Why did the boss yell at his employee Hannah? To decide whether a behavior was caused by internal (dispositional) factors or by external (situational) factors, people use consensus, distinctiveness, and consistency information.

Why did the boss yell at his employee Hannah?			
People are likely to make an *internal attribution*—it was something about the boss—if they see this behavior as	*low* in consensus: The boss is the only person working in the store who yells at Hannah	*low* in distinctiveness: The boss yells at all the employees	*high* in consistency: The boss yells at Hannah almost every time he sees her
People are likely to make an *external attribution*—it was something about Hannah—if they see this behavior as	*high* in consensus: All of the employees yell at Hannah too	*high* in distinctiveness: The boss doesn't yell at any of the other employees	*high* in consistency: The boss yells at Hannah almost every time he sees her
People are likely to think it was something peculiar about the particular circumstances in which the boss yelled at Hannah if they see this behavior as	*low or high* in consensus	*low or high* in distinctiveness	*low* in consistency: This is the first time that the boss has yelled at Hannah

However, as noted in Chapters 3 and 6, people aren't always logical or rational when forming judgments about others. Sometimes they distort information to satisfy their need for high self-esteem (see Chapter 6). At other times they use mental shortcuts that, although often helpful, can lead to inaccurate judgments (see Chapter 3). Unfortunately, the attributions we make are sometimes just plain wrong. In the next section, we will discuss some specific errors or biases that plague the attribution process. One shortcut is very common: The idea that people do what they do because of the kind of people they are, not because of the situation they are in. This has been termed the *correspondence bias*.

The Correspondence Bias: People as Personality Psychologists
一致性偏见：人人都是人格心理学家

One day in December 1955, a black seamstress in Montgomery, Alabama, refused to give up her seat on the city bus to a white man. At the time, segregationist "Jim Crow" laws in the South relegated African Americans to second-class status in all aspects of everyday life. For example, they had to sit in the back 10 rows of the bus; they could sit in the middle section, if it was empty, but they had to give up their seats to white people when the bus got full. The front 10 rows were always reserved for white people only (Feeney, 2005). That day in 1955, Rosa Parks broke the law and refused to give up her seat. Later, she said, "People always say I didn't give up my seat because I was tired, but that wasn't true. I was not tired physically . . . No, the only tired I was, was tired of giving in" (Feeney, 2005, p. A1, B8). Ms. Parks was convicted of violating the segregation laws and fined. In response, African Americans boycotted the Montgomery buses for over a year and mounted a legal challenge, which led to a successful Supreme Court decision in 1956 outlawing segregation on buses. Rosa Parks's brave act was the precipitating event of the Civil Rights Movement (Shipp, 2005).

On October 24, 2005, Rosa Parks died at the age of 92. To commemorate her, the American Public Transportation Association called for December 1 to be the "Tribute to Rosa Parks Day." Buses in major cities across the country designated one seat, behind the driver, to be kept empty for the day in her honor. Signs were posted on the windows adjacent to the seat, with Rosa Parks's photograph and the small caption, "It all started on a bus" to alert riders (Ramirez, 2005).

A New York City journalist rode the buses that day to see if people would honor the request—after all, an empty seat on a big city bus is a coveted item. He found that the vast majority of riders did so, even during rush hour when just finding a place to stand is difficult. However, some people did sit in the special seat (Ramirez, 2005). Now this was an interesting development, both to the journalist and his fellow travelers. What were these people thinking? Why did they do it? It seemed to be a flagrant act of disrespect. How could one not honor Rosa Parks? Were these "sitters" prejudiced, even racist? Were they selfish or arrogant, believing that their personal needs were more important than anything else? In short, dispositional attributions were being made about these sitters, and they were negative attributions about the people's character and attitudes.

Rosa Parks, sitting at the front of the bus, after the Supreme Court ruled bus segregation was illegal.

Being a good reporter, the journalist began asking the sittters why they chose to sit in this special seat. Lo and behold, a situational explanation emerged. They hadn't seen the sign. In fact, the small signs were badly placed and easy to miss in the midst of scheduling announcements (Ramirez, 2005). After the sign was pointed out to sitters, they reacted swiftly. One man "read it quickly, shuddered, then uttered a loud profanity in dismay. He scooted out of the seat. 'I didn't realize it was there . . . It's history . . . It means freedom'" (Ramirez, 2005, p. B1). Another rider, a black man, began to sit down but stopped halfway when he saw the sign. He said to another rider, a black woman, "'But people were sitting here.' The woman said gently, 'They couldn't see the sign.' 'Well,' the man said, peeling away the sign and moving it the edge of the seat, 'they will now'" (Ramirez, 2005, p. B1). Thus, people on the bus were making the wrong attribution about the sitters. The other riders believed that their behavior was due to the kind of people they were (bad ones), instead of being due to the situation, in this case, a too small, badly written, and badly located sign.

The pervasive, fundamental theory or schema most of us have about human behavior is that people do what they do because of the kind of people they are, not because of the situation they are in. When thinking this way, we are more like personality psychologists, who see behavior as stemming from internal dispositions and traits, than like social psychologists, who focus on the impact of social situations on behavior. This tendency to infer that people's behavior corresponds to, or matches, their dispositions and personality has been called the **correspondence bias** (Fiske & Taylor, 1991; Gilbert, 1998b; Gilbert & Jones, 1986; Gilbert & Malone, 1995; Jones, 1979, 1990). The correspondence bias is so pervasive that many social psychologists call it the *fundamental attribution error* (Heider, 1958; Jones, 1990; Ross, 1977; Ross & Nisbett, 1991).

Buses across the United States posted a sign like this one, asking riders to keep one seat empty to honor Rosa Parks.

(Richard Perry/*The New York Times*)

There have been many empirical demonstrations of the tendency to see people's behavior as a reflection of their dispositions and beliefs, rather than as influenced by the situation (Gawronski, 2003; Jones, 1979, 1990; Miller, Ashton, & Mishal, 1990; Miller, Jones, & Hinkle, 1981; Vonk, 1999). For example, in a classic study, Edward Jones and Victor Harris (1967) asked college students to read

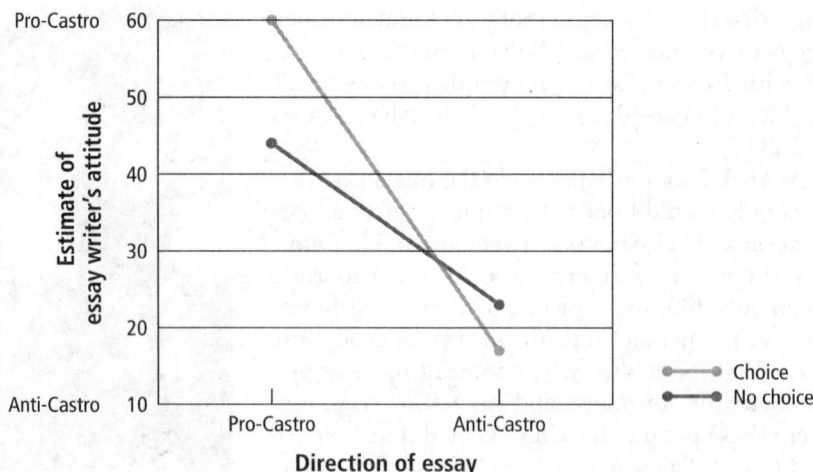

FIGURE 4.5

The correspondence bias.

Even when people knew that the author's choice of an essay topic was externally caused (i.e., in the no-choice condition), they assumed that what he wrote reflected how he really felt about Castro. That is, they made an internal attribution from his behavior.

(Adapted from Jones & Harris, 1967)

an essay written by a fellow student that either supported or opposed Fidel Castro's rule in Cuba and then to guess how the author of the essay really felt about Castro (see Figure 4.5). In one condition, the researchers told the students that the author freely chose which position to take in the essay, thereby making it easy to guess how he really felt. If he chose to write in favor of Castro, clearly he must be sympathetic to Castro. In another condition, however, the students learned that the author had been assigned the position as a participant in a debate. One should not assume, then, that the writer believed what he or she wrote. Yet the participants in this study, and in dozens of others like it, assumed that the author really believed what he wrote, even when they knew he could not choose which position to take. As you can see in Figure 4.5, people moderated their guesses a little bit—there was not as much difference in their estimates of the author's attitude in the pro-Castro and anti-Castro conditions—but they still assumed that the content of the essay reflected the author's true feelings.

> *Be not swept off your feet by the vividness of the impression, but say, "Impression, wait for me a little. Let me see what you are and what you represent".*
> —Epictetus, Discourses

Why is this correspondence bias, the tendency to explain behavior in terms of people's dispositions, often called the fundamental attribution error? It is not always wrong to make an internal attribution; clearly, people often do what they do because of the kind of people they are. However, considerable evidence indicates that social situations can strongly affect behavior; indeed, the major lesson of social psychology is that these influences can be extremely powerful. The point of the correspondence bias is that people tend to underestimate external influences when explaining other people's behavior. Even when the influence of the situation on behavior is obvious, as in the Jones and Harris (1967) experiment, people persist in making internal attributions (Lord, Scott, Pugh, & Desforges, 1997; Newman, 1996; Ross, 1977; Ross, Amabile, & Steinmetz, 1977; Ross & Nisbett, 1991).

The Role of Perceptual Salience in the Correspondence Bias Why do people fall prey to the correspondence bias? One reason is that when we try to explain someone's behavior, our focus of attention is usually on the person, not on the surrounding situation (Baron & Misovich, 1993; Heider, 1944, 1958; Jones & Nisbett, 1972). In fact, the situational causes of another person's behavior are practically invisible to us (Gilbert & Malone, 1995). If we don't know what happened to someone earlier in the day (e.g., she received an F on her midterm), we can't use that situational information to help us understand her current behavior. And even when we know her situation, we still don't know how she interprets it—for example, the F may not have upset her because she's planning to drop the course anyway. If we don't know the meaning of the situation for her, we can't accurately judge its effects on her behavior. Much of the time, in fact, information about the situational causes

Correspondence Bias
The tendency to infer that people's behavior corresponds to (matches) their disposition (personality)

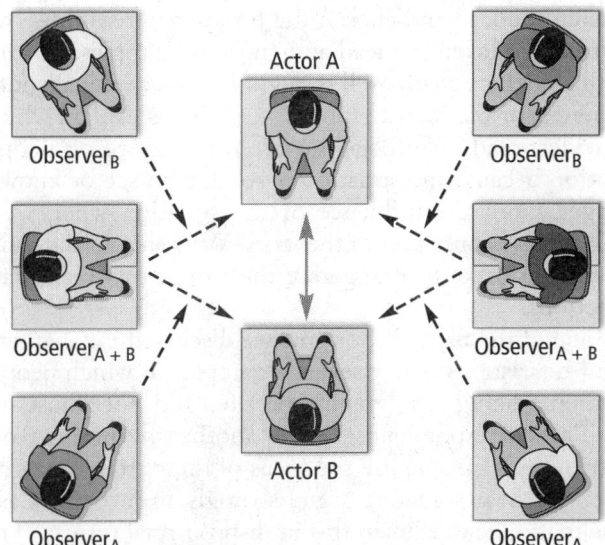

FIGURE 4.6
Manipulating perceptual salience.

This is the seating arrangement for two actors and the six research participants in the Taylor and Fiske study. Participants rated each actor's impact on the conversation. Researchers found that people rated the actor they could see more clearly as having the larger role in the conversation.

(Adapted from Taylor & Fiske, 1975)

of behavior is unavailable or difficult to interpret accurately (Gilbert, 1998b; Gilbert & Malone, 1995).

What information does that leave us? Although the situation may be close to invisible, the individual is extremely "perceptually prominent"—people are what our eyes and ears notice. And what we notice seems to be the reasonable and logical cause of the observed behavior (Heider, 1958). We can't see the situation, so we ignore its importance. People, not the situation, have **perceptual salience** for us; we pay attention to them, and we tend to think that they alone cause their behavior.

Several studies have confirmed the importance of perceptual salience—especially an elegant one by Shelley Taylor and Susan Fiske (1975). In this study, two male students engaged in a "get acquainted" conversation. (They were actually both accomplices of the experimenters and were following a script during their conversation.) At each session, six actual research participants also took part. They sat in assigned seats, surrounding the two conversationalists (see Figure 4.6). Two of them sat on each side of the actors; they had a clear, profile view of both individuals. Two observers sat behind each actor; they could see the back of one actor's head but the face of the other. Thus, who was visually salient—that is, the individual the participants could see better—was cleverly manipulated in this study.

After the conversation, the research participants were asked questions about the two men—for example, who had taken the lead in the conversation and who had chosen the topics to be discussed? What happened? The person they could see better was the person they thought had more impact on the conversation (see Figure 4.7). Even though all the observers heard the same conversation, those who were facing student A

Perceptual Salience

The seeming importance of information that is the focus of people's attention

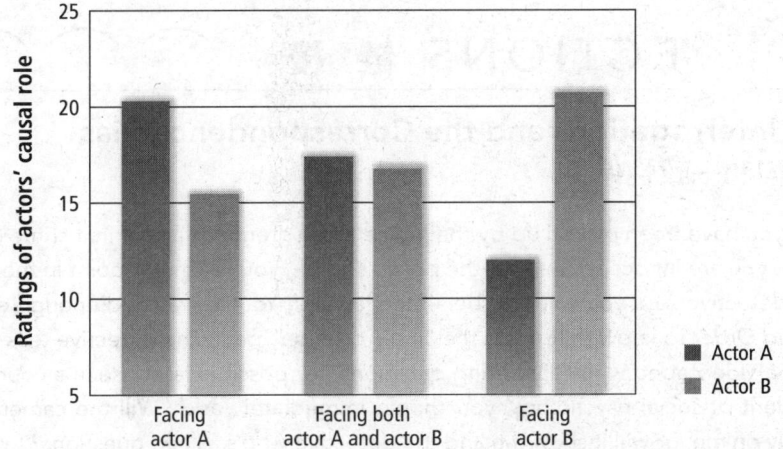

FIGURE 4.7
The effects of perceptual salience.

These are the ratings of each actor's causal role in the conversation. People thought that the actor they could see better had more impact on the conversation.

(Adapted from Taylor & Fiske, 1975)

thought he had taken the lead and chosen the topics, whereas those who were facing student B thought he had taken the lead and chosen the topics. In comparison, those who could see both students equally well thought both were equally influential.

Perceptual salience, or our visual point of view, helps explain why the correspondence bias is so widespread. We focus our attention more on people than on the surrounding situation because the situation is so hard to see or know; we underestimate or even forget about the influence of the situation when we are explaining human behavior. But this is only part of the story. Why should the simple fact that we are focused on a person make us exaggerate the extent to which that person determines his or her actions?

The culprit is one of the mental shortcuts we discussed in Chapter 3: the anchoring and adjustment heuristic. We saw several examples in which people began with a reference point when making a judgment and then did not adjust sufficiently away from that point. The correspondence bias is another by-product of this shortcut. When making attributions, people use the focus of their attention as a starting point. For example, when we hear someone argue strongly in favor of Castro's regime in Cuba, our first inclination is to explain this in dispositional terms: "This person must hold radical political views." We realize that this explanation might not be the whole story, however. We might think, "On the other hand, I know he was assigned this position as part of a debate," and adjust our attributions more toward a situational explanation. However, the problem is that people often don't adjust their judgments enough. In the Jones and Harris (1967) experiment, participants who knew that the essay writer did not have a choice of topics nevertheless thought he believed what he had written, at least to some extent. They adjusted insufficiently from their anchor, the position advocated in the essay (Quattrone, 1982).

The Two-Step Process of Making Attributions   In sum, we go through a **two-step process** when we make attributions (Gilbert, 1989, 1991, 1993; Krull, 1993). We make an internal attribution; we assume that a person's behavior was due to something about that person. We then attempt to adjust this attribution by considering the situation the person was in. But we often don't make enough of an adjustment in this second step. Indeed, when we are distracted or preoccupied, we often skip the second step, making an extreme internal attribution (Gilbert & Hixon, 1991; Gilbert & Osborne, 1989; Gilbert, Pelham, & Krull, 1988). Why? Because the first step (making the internal attribution) occurs quickly and spontaneously, whereas the second step (adjusting for the situation) requires more effort and conscious attention (see Figure 4.8).

We will engage in this second step of attributional processing if we consciously slow down and think carefully before reaching a judgment, if we are motivated to reach as accurate a judgment as possible, or if we are suspicious about the behavior of the target person, for example, believing that he or she is lying or has ulterior motives (Hilton, Fein, & Miller, 1993; Risen & Gilovich, 2007; Webster, 1993).

CONNECTIONS 链 接

Police Interrogations and the Correspondence Bias
警察审问和一致性偏见

Let's say you have been picked up by the police as a potential suspect in a crime (though, of course, you are innocent). Back at the police station, you reach the point in the process where a detective says you will now be "interviewed." You've watched enough episodes of *Law and Order* to know that this is the "interrogation" part. The detective tells you that you will be videotaped while answering questions, for possible later use in a court of law. As a student of social psychology, you should immediately ask, "Will the camera be focused only on me, or will it show me and the detective who's asking questions?" Why, you ask? Because recent research on videotaped police interrogations has shown that percep-

Two-Step Process of Attribution
Analyzing another person's behavior first by making an automatic internal attribution and only then thinking about possible situational reasons for the behavior, after which one may adjust the original internal attribution

tual salience can trigger the correspondence bias, affecting how guilty the suspect is judged to be (Lassiter, 2002).

G. Daniel Lassiter and his colleagues (2007) presented 21 courtroom judges (who also had previous experience as both prosecutors and criminal defense attorneys) and 24 police officers (who had extensive experience conducting interrogations) with a videotaped suspect (actually a confederate) who confesses to a crime. These research participants were shown one of three videotaped camera-perspective versions: The focus was on the suspect only; on the detective only; or there was equal focus on the suspect and the detective. They were then asked to rate how "voluntary" the confession was, as opposed to "coerced." For both the judges and police officers, the videotape that focused only on the suspect produced significantly higher ratings of "voluntariness" than the other two videotape versions (Lassiter, Diamond, Schmidt, & Elek, 2007). The perceptual salience of the suspect, when shown all alone, triggered a correspondence bias, making him appear more guilty than when he was not as perceptually salient. These results are worrisome because videotaping only the suspect is standard operating procedure in real criminal investigations. In fact, only one country in the world thus far, New Zealand, has adopted an "equal-focus" camera perspective (suspect + detective) for videotaped interrogations, and they have done so in response to concerns about attributional bias (Lassiter, Ratcliff, Ware, & Irvin, 2006).

Culture and the Correspondence Bias 文化与一致性偏见

For decades, it was taken for granted that the correspondence bias was universal: People everywhere, we thought, applied this cognitive shortcut when forming attributions (Norenzayan, Choi, & Nisbett, 1999). But social psychologists are focusing more and more on the role of culture in many aspects of social behavior. Given that social

FIGURE 4.8
The two-step process of attribution.

psychology is the study of how the situation affects the individual, we can think of culture as an all-encompassing, higher-level situational variable. You are born into a culture; as you grow up, you learn the rules, norms, and ways of labeling reality that define your culture. In short, culture is one of the biggest "situations" affecting your daily life. In the past decade, social psychologists have explored the correspondence bias cross-culturally. Do people everywhere show the correspondence bias? Or is culture, specifically Western culture, a cause of the correspondence bias? Let's look at the evidence.

North American and some other Western cultures stress individual autonomy. A person is perceived as independent and self-contained; his or her behavior reflects internal traits, motives, and values (Markus & Kitayama, 1991). The intellectual history of this cultural value can be traced from the Judeo-Christian belief in the individual soul and the English legal tradition of individual rights (Menon, Morris, Chiu, & Hong, 1999; Kitayama, Ishii, Imada, Takemura, & Ramaswamy, 2006). In contrast, East Asian cultures such as those in China, Japan, and Korea stress group autonomy. The individual derives his or her sense of self from the social group to which he or she belongs. The intellectual history of this belief derives from the Confucian tradition, for example, the "community man" (*qunti de fenzi*) or "social being" (*shehui de renge*) (Menon et al., 1999, p. 703).

Research has indicated that these differing cultural values affect the kind of information that people notice and pay attention to. As we discussed in Chapter 3, the values inherent in individualistic Western cultures cause people, as they grow up, to develop an *analytic thinking style*. This style involves focusing on the properties of objects (or people) while paying much less attention, if any, to the context or situation that surrounds that object. In contrast, the values of collectivistic cultures, such as those of East Asia (e.g., China, Korea, and Japan) cause people to develop a *holistic thinking style*. Here, people focus on the "whole picture," that is the object (or person) and the context that surrounds that object, as well as on the relationships that exist between them (Nisbett, 2003; Nisbett & Masuda, 2003). These differences in thinking styles influence how we perceive other people, for example, how we decode their facial expressions of emotion.

Imagine you are talking to a group of friends. The expression on one friend's face catches your attention. She's frowning and her mouth is set in a tight line. What is she feeling? The analytic thinking style suggests you would focus on her face alone and reach a decision. The holistic thinking style suggests you would scan the faces of the others in the group, compare them to hers, and then reach a decision. Takahiko Masuda and colleagues (2008) conducted a study on decoding facial expressions much like this example. They presented research participants in the United States and Japan with cartoon drawings of people in groups. One person in each cartoon was the central figure, shown in the foreground. This person had a facial expression that was happy, sad, angry, or neutral. The other people in the group had facial expressions that either matched the central figure or were different. The participants' task was to judge the central person's emotion on a 10-point scale.

The researchers found that the facial expressions on the group members' faces had little effect on Americans' ratings of the central figure. If that figure was smiling broadly, he received a high rating for "happy." It didn't matter what the rest of the group was expressing. In comparison, the facial expressions of the group members had a significant effect on the Japanese participants' ratings of the central figure. A broad smile was interpreted as very happy if the group members were also smiling; the same broad smile was interpreted as significantly less happy if the other group members were looking sad or angry. In short, the meaning of the cartoon character's facial expression changed given his "context"—what the other cartoon characters standing next to him were feeling (Masuda et al., 2008). In addition, the researchers measured the eye-tracking movements of the participants as they looked at the cartoons. The Japanese spent more time looking at the cartoon characters in the background than did the Americans. Both groups began by looking at the central character, but after 1 second, the Japanese started to scan their eyes over the other characters significantly more than did the Americans (Masuda et al., 2008). As Dr. Denise Park puts it, using a camera analogy, "The Americans are more zoom and the East Asians are more panoramic" (Goldberg, 2008, p. C1).

The eye-tracking results in the Masuda and colleagues (2008) study suggest that something very interesting is going on, at a physiological level, in people who engage in analytic versus holistic thinking. Two groups of researchers have investigated this question, using different techniques. Trey Hedden and colleagues (2008) used functional magnetic resonance imaging (fMRI) to examine where in the brain cultural experience affects perceptual processing. Their participants, East Asians and European Americans, underwent fMRI while making judgments about the length of lines inside boxes. Some of the participants were told to ignore the box around each line ("ignore context") and some were told to pay attention to the box around each line ("attend to context"). While participants were equally accurate at judging the lengths of the lines, they showed significantly more brain activity when they had to follow the instructions that were the opposite of their cultural thinking style. That is, American participants showed greater activation in higher-order cortical regions (frontal and parietal areas) when told to pay attention to the context, while East Asian participants showed greater activity in the same brain regions when told to ignore the context. Greater cortical activation means that the participant had to exert more attention (in a sense, had to work harder cognitively) when asked to perceive objects in a way that was not typical for him or her (Hedden, Katay, Aron, Markus, & Gabrieli, 2008).

The second group of researchers used event-related potentials (ERPs) to measure brain activity (Lewis, Goto, & Kong, 2008). While fMRI indicates which brain regions are active, ERPs provide a more fine-grained analysis of the onset and offset of neural firing. These researchers also presented participants with a series of simple perceptual tasks that involved visual information about "targets" and context. In an interesting twist, their participants were all Americans who had grown up in American culture but were of two different ethnic backgrounds: European-American or East Asian-American. The pattern of ERPs indicated that the European-American participants paid more attention to the targets while the East Asian-American participants paid more attention to the context surrounding the targets.

As John Gabrieli puts it, "Culture is not changing how you see the world, but rather how you think and interpret" (Goldberg, 2008, p. C3). Does Western culture, which emphasizes individual freedom and uniqueness, socialize its members to prefer dispositional attributions over situational ones? Are Westerners brought up to look inward to explain their actions rather than looking at the situation? (Dix, 1993; Rholes, Newman, & Ruble, 1990) In comparison, do collectivist (often Eastern) cultures, which emphasize group membership, interdependence, and conformity to group norms, socialize their members to prefer situational dispositions over dispositional ones? In these cultures, are children raised to think that the situation, more than the individual, explains behavior (Fletcher & Ward, 1988; Hong, Morris, Chiu, & Benet-Martinez, 2000; Markus & Kitayama, 1991; Triandis, 1990, 2001)? As a result of this very different socialization, do people in collectivist cultures show less of a correspondence bias than people in individualistic cultures?

The answer is both simple and complex: People in individualist cultures do prefer dispositional attributions about others, relative to people in collectivist cultures, who prefer situational attributions. For example, Joan Miller (1984) asked people of two cultures—Hindus living in India and Americans living in the United States—to think of various examples of behaviors performed by their friends and to explain why those behaviors occurred. The American participants preferred dispositional explanations for the behaviors. They were more likely to say that the causes of their friends' behaviors were the kind of people they were, rather than the situation or context in which the behaviors occurred. In contrast, Hindu participants preferred situational explanations for their friends' behaviors.

But, you might be thinking, perhaps the Americans and Hindus generated different kinds of examples. Perhaps the Hindus thought of behaviors that were really more

Research has shown that when forming attributions, people in collectivistic cultures like Japan are more likely to take situational information into account than are people in individualistic cultures.

situationally caused, whereas the Americans thought of behaviors that were really more dispositionally caused. To test this alternative hypothesis, Miller (1984) took some of the behaviors generated by the Hindu participants and gave them to Americans to explain. The difference in internal and external attributions appeared again: Americans still found internal, dispositional causes for the behaviors that the Hindus had thought were caused by the situation.

Another study that found cultural differences in the prevalence of the correspondence bias compared newspaper articles in Chinese- and English-language newspapers. The researchers targeted two mass murders, one committed by a Chinese graduate student in Iowa and one committed by a Caucasian postal worker in Michigan (Morris & Peng, 1994). They coded all the news articles about the two crimes that appeared in the *New York Times* and the *World Journal*, a Chinese-language U.S. newspaper. The results showed that journalists writing in English made significantly more dispositional attributions about both mass murderers than journalists writing in Chinese did. For example, American reporters described one murderer as a "darkly disturbed man" with a "sinister edge" to his personality. Chinese reporters, when describing the same murderer, emphasized more situational causes, such as "not getting along with his adviser" and his "isolation from the Chinese community."

Thus, people in Western cultures appear to be more like personality psychologists, viewing behavior in dispositional terms. In contrast, people in Eastern cultures seem to be more like social psychologists, considering the situational causes of behavior.

However, it would be a mistake to think that members of collectivist cultures don't ever make dispositional attributions. Of course they do—it's just a matter of degree. Recent research indicates that a tendency to think dispositionally about others—the correspondence bias—appears in many cultures. However, members of collectivistic cultures are more aware of how the situation affects behavior and more likely to take situational effects into account (Choi, Dalal, Kim-Prieto, & Park, 2003; Choi & Nisbett, 1998; Choi, Nisbett, & Norenzayan, 1999; Krull et al., 1999; Miyamoto & Kitayama, 2002). Thus, the difference is that people in collectivist cultures are more likely to go beyond dispositional explanations, including information about the situation as well.

Let's look at the evidence. Several researchers have conducted studies that are variations of the design used by Edward Jones and Victor Harris (1967), which we discussed earlier in this chapter. In this design, a target person is told to write an essay or give a speech after being assigned a specific position (e.g., pro or con) on the topic. Afterward, research participants are asked to rate the target person's real attitude on the topic. Remember, the position of the essay was assigned and not necessarily the target's true attitude. Nonetheless, as we saw earlier, American participants show a correspondence bias between the topic and the speaker and commit the fundamental attribution error: They assume that the attitude expressed by the target person is the person's true attitude. The same thing happens in Korea, Japan, and China: Participants believe the content of the target's speech or essay indicates what he or she is really like (Choi & Nisbett, 1998; Krull et al., 1999; Kashima, Siegel, Tanaka, & Kashima, 1992; Kitayama & Masuda, 1997; Masuda & Kitayama, 1996, 2003).

What if we made the situation more salient in an essay-writing type of study? Would participants from collectivistic cultures show less of a correspondence bias than participants from individualistic cultures? Researchers made the situational information more salient in these studies by having the participants go through the same procedure as the target person they are judging. Like the target, the observers are also assigned to write an essay on a position they did not choose. Sometimes they are also given prepared statements to include in their essays. When later asked to judge the target's attitude, the observers should realize that the target was just as constrained by the situation as they were, so the content of the target's essay shouldn't reveal much about the target. What happens? American participants still show the correspondence bias when judging the target person; they still think the essay tells them something about what the target is really like. But in collectivist cultures, participants take this situational information into account and make far fewer dispositional attributions about the target (Choi & Nisbett, 1998; Kitayama & Masuda, 1997; Masuda & Kitayama, 1996).

Thus, there is indeed something "fundamental" about the correspondence bias—people, regardless of their culture, like to think dispositionally about others. However, people in collectivist cultures like the East Asian ones, because of their values and experience, also seem able to override this dispositionalist tendency. They are more likely than people in Western, individualistic cultures to take situational information into account when forming attributions, especially if the situational information is particularly salient and noticeable (Choi, Dalal, Kim-Prieto, & Park, 2003; Lieberman, Jarcho, & Obayashi, 2005; Trope & Gaunt, 2000).

In conclusion, how can we summarize cultural differences in the attribution process that underlies the correspondence bias? Recall the two-step process we discussed earlier (see Figure 4.8). What are people in collectivist cultures doing differently from people in individualist cultures? At what stage in this process do the two cultures diverge? We think that people everywhere start off at the same point, showing the correspondence bias: They automatically make dispositional attributions about other people. What happens next is that people in collectivistic cultures look to the situation: They revise and correct their first impressions, taking the situation into account. Westerners tend to avoid this second step. Their first impression, the dispositional attribution, sticks (Choi et al., 2003; Hedden, Ketay, Aron, Markus, & Gabrieli, 2008; Knowles, Morris, Chiu, & Hong, 2001; Lewis et al., 2008).

> Resemblances are the shadows of differences. Different people see different similarities and similar differences.
> —Vladimir Nabokov, Pale Fire

The Actor/Observer Difference 当事人与旁观者差异

An interesting twist on the correspondence bias is that it applies unevenly: Whereas we are very likely to find internal causes for other people's behavior, we tend to look beyond ourselves, to the situation, to explain our own.

This creates an interesting attributional dilemma: The same behavior can trigger dispositional attributions in people observing the behavior and situational attributions in the person performing the behavior. For example, we observe a woman yelling at her child in the grocery store. We make the attribution that she's a mean, bad parent. However, when she thinks about her behavior, she attributes it to the anxiety and stress she's under since she lost her job. This difference in attributions is called the **actor/observer difference** (Jones & Nisbett, 1972; Hansen, Kimble, & Biers, 2001; Nisbett, Caputo, Legant, & Marecek, 1973; Robins, Spranka, & Mendelson, 1996; Watson, 1982).

The letter to Ann Landers (see page 108) demonstrates the actor/observer difference. The writer is focusing on the external forces that are affecting her life and shaping her behavior. She would rather focus outside of herself—on what she calls her mother's "obsession"—than on her own reaons for staying in a destructive relationship. Ann Landers, however, will have none of it. She responds with a strong, internal attribution—the woman herself, not her mother's disapproval (the situation), is the cause of her problems. As you might guess, the actor/observer difference can lead to some striking disagreements between people. Why, at times, do the attributions made by actors and observers diverge so sharply?

> Things are seldom as they seem, Skim milk masquerades as cream.
> —W. S. Gilbert, H. M. S. Pinafore

Perceptual Salience Revisited One reason for such divergence is our old friend perceptual salience (Jones & Nisbett, 1972). As we said earlier, just as we notice other people's behavior more than their situation, we notice our own situation more than our own behavior. None of us is so egotistic or self-centered that we walk through life holding up a full-length mirror to observe ourselves constantly. We are looking

Actor/Observer Difference
The tendency to see other people's behavior as dispositionally caused but focusing more on the role of situational factors when explaining one's own behavior

> **Dear Ann Landers:**
>
> I'm writing you in desperation, hoping you can help me with a problem I'm having with my mother.
>
> A little over a year ago, I moved in with my boyfriend despite my mother's protests. She has never liked "Kevin." I'll admit he's far from perfect and we've had our problems. He's an alcoholic, has a bad temper, is mentally abusive, is a compulsive liar and cannot hold a job. I am in debt over my head because of him but my biggest problem is that my mother is obsessed with my situation. I understand her concern, but I can take only so much. . . .
> OVER-MOTHERED
> IN MICHIGAN
>
> *Dear Over-Mothered:*
> *Your mother didn't write to me. You did. So you're the one who is going to get the advice. Get into counseling at once and find out why you insist on hanging on to an alcoholic, abusive, unemployed liar. . . .*

The letter and its response depict actor/observer differences in attribution. Schoeneman and Rubanowitz (1985) examined letters to the "Ann Landers" and "Dear Abby" advice columns and found strong evidence for actor/observer differences. The letter writers tended to attribute their problems to external factors (e.g., this letter writer says her biggest problem is her mother), whereas the advice columnists tended to make dispositional attributions to the letter writers (e.g., "Get into counseling at once").

(Dear Ann Landers. © Creators Syndicate, Inc. Used with permission.)

outward; what is perceptually salient to us is other people, objects, and the events that unfold. We don't pay as much attention to ourselves. Consequently, when the actor and the observer think about what caused a given behavior, they are swayed by the information that is most salient and noticeable to them: the actor for the observer, and the situation for the actor (Malle & Knobe, 1997; Nisbett & Ross, 1980; Ross & Nisbett, 1991; Storms, 1973).

The Role of Information Availability in the Actor/Observer Difference The actor/observer difference occurs for another reason as well. Actors have more information about themselves than observers do. Actors know how they've behaved over the years; they know what happened to them that morning. They are far more aware than observers are of both the similarities and the differences in their behavior over time and across situations (Balcetis & Dunning, 2008; Jones & Nisbett, 1972; Krueger, Ham, & Linford, 1996; Malle & Knobe, 1997). In Kelley's (1967) terms, actors have far more consistency and distinctiveness information about themselves than observers do.

For example, if you are quiet and sit alone at a party, an observer is likely to make a dispositional attribution about you—"That person is quite an introvert." In fact, you may know that this is not the way you usually behave at a party. Perhaps you are shy only at parties where you don't know anyone. Maybe you are just feeling tired or depressed by some recent bad news. It is not surprising, then, that actors' self-attributions often reflect situational factors because they know more about how their behavior varies from one situation to the next than most observers do, who see them in limited contexts.

So far, our discussion of the mental shortcuts people use when making attributions has covered the role of perceptual salience and information availability. But what about a person's needs, desires, hopes, and fears—do these more emotional factors also create biases in our attributions? Are you motivated to see the world in certain ways because these views make you feel better, about both yourself and life in general? The answer is yes. The shortcuts we will discuss have a motivational basis; they are attributions that protect our self-esteem and our belief that the world is a safe and just place.

Self-Serving Attributions 自利归因

Imagine that Alison goes to her chemistry class one day feeling anxious because she's getting her midterm grade that day. The professor returns her exam. Alison turns it over and sees that she has received an A. What will Alison think explains her grade? As you would guess, people tend to take personal credit for their successes but to blame their failures on external events beyond their control. Alison is likely to think that her success was due to the fact that she's good at chemistry and just plain smart.

How can we explain this departure from the typical actor/observer pattern of attributions? The answer is that when people's self-esteem is threatened, they often make **self-serving attributions**. Simply put, these attributions refer to our tendency to take credit for our successes (by making internal attributions) but to blame others or the situation (by making external attributions) for our failures (Carver, De Gregorio, & Gillis, 1980; McAllister, 1996; Miller & Ross, 1975; Pronin, Lin, & Ross, 2002; Robins & Beer, 2001).

A particularly interesting arena for studying self-serving attributions is professional sports. When explaining their victories, athletes and coaches both point overwhelmingly to aspects of their own teams or players. In fact, an analysis of professional athletes' and coaches' explanations for their team's wins and losses found that 80 percent of the attributions for wins were to such internal factors (Lau & Russell, 1980). For example, when explaining why the New York Yankees defeated the Los Angeles Dodgers in game 4 of the 1977 World Series, Yankees manager Billy Martin attributed it to a player on his team: "Pinella has done it all" (Lau & Russell, 1980, p. 32). Losses were more likely to be attributed to external causes, outside of the team's control. For example, the Dodgers attributed their loss not to their inferior ability or poor play, but instead to bad luck or the superior play of the Yankees. Tommy Lasorda, the Dodgers' manager, said, "It took a great team to beat us, and the Yankees definitely are a great team" (p. 32).

Who is more likely to make self-serving attributions? Roesch and Amirkhan (1997) wondered if in the realm of sports, a player's skill, experience, and type of sport (team sports versus solo sports like tennis) affected the type of attribution the player made about a sports outcome. They found that less experienced athletes were more likely to make self-serving attributions than experienced ones. Experienced athletes realize that losses are sometimes their fault and that they can't always take credit for wins. Highly skilled athletes made more self-serving attributions than those with lower ability. The highly talented athlete believes that success is due to his or her prowess, while failure, an unusual and upsetting outcome, is due to teammates or other circumstances of the game. Finally, athletes in solo sports made more self-serving attributions than those in team sports. Solo athletes know that winning and losing rests on their shoulders. You can explore self-serving attributions by sports figures in the Try It! Exercise on page 110.

Why do we make self-serving attributions? Most people try to maintain their self-esteem whenever possible, even if that means distorting reality by changing a thought or belief. (We will discuss this concept at length in Chapter 6.) Here we see a specific attributional strategy that can be used to maintain or raise self-esteem: Just locate "causality"—the reason something happened—where it does you the most good (Greenberg, Pyszczynski, & Solomon, 1982; Snyder & Higgins, 1988; Wann & Schrader, 2000). We are particularly likely to engage in self-serving attributions when we fail at something and we feel we can't improve at it. The external attribution truly protects our self-esteem, as there is little hope we can do better in the future. But if we believe we can improve, we're more likely to attribute our current failure to internal causes and then work on improving (Duval & Silvia, 2002).

A second reason has to do with how we present ourselves to others, a topic we'll explore in the next chapter (Goffman, 1959). We want people to think well of us and to admire us. Telling others that our poor performance was due to some external cause puts a "good face" on failure; many people call this strategy "making excuses" (Greenberg et al., 1982; Tetlock, 1981; Weary & Arkin, 1981).

Sports winners and losers often make very different, self-serving attributions to explain the outcome of the competition.

Self-Serving Attributions
Explanations for one's successes that credit internal, dispositional factors and explanations for one's failures that blame external, situational factors

TRY IT! 试一试！体育专栏中的自利归因
Self-Serving Attributions in the Sports Pages

Do athletes and coaches tend to take credit for their wins but make excuses for their losses? Find out for yourself the next time you read the sports section of the newspaper or watch television interviews after a game. Analyze the sports figures' comments to see what kinds of attributions they make about their performance. Is the pattern a self-serving one?

For example, after a win, does the athlete make internal attributions like "We won because of excellent teamwork; our defensive line really held today" or "My serve was totally on"? After a loss, does the athlete make external attributions like "All the injuries we've had this season have really hurt us" or "That line judge made every call against me"? According to the research, these self-serving attributions should occur more often than the opposite pattern, for example, where a winner says, "We won because the other team played so badly it was like they were dead" (external) or where a loser says, "I played terribly today. I stank" (internal).

Next, see if you can find examples that fit Roesch and Amirkhan's (1997) research. Are self-serving attributions more common among solo-sport athletes than team-sport athletes? Do the athlete "stars" make more self-serving attributions than their less talented colleagues? Finally, think about the three reasons we identify for why people make self-serving attributions (maintaining self-esteem, presenting yourself positively to others, and personal knowledge about your past performances). When a sports figure makes a self-serving attribution, which one of these three motives do you think is at work? For example, if Michael Jordan attributed his team's loss to factors outside of himself, do you think he was protecting his self-esteem, trying to look good in front of others, or making the most logical attribution he could given his experience (i.e., he was so talented, most team losses weren't his fault)?

A third reason people make self-serving attributions has to do with our earlier discussion about the kind of information that is available to people. Let's imagine the attributional process of another student in the chemistry class, Ron, who did poorly on the midterm. Ron knows that he studied very hard for the midterm, that he typically does well on chemistry tests, and that in general he is a very good student. The D on the chemistry midterm comes as a surprise. The most logical attribution Ron can make is that the test was unfair—the D grade wasn't due to a lack of ability or effort. The professor, however, knows that some students did well on the test; given the information that is available to the professor, it is logical for him to conclude that Ron, and not the fact that it was a difficult test, was responsible for the poor grade (Miller & Ross, 1975; Nisbett & Ross, 1980).

People also alter their attributions to deal with other kinds of threats to their self-esteem. One of the hardest things to understand in life is the occurrence of tragic events, such as rapes, terminal diseases, and fatal accidents. Even when they happen to strangers we have never met, they can be upsetting. They remind us that if such tragedies can happen to someone else, they can happen to us. So we take steps to deny this fact. One way we do this is by making **defensive attributions**, which are explanations for behavior that defend us from feelings of vulnerability and mortality.

One form of defensive attribution is to believe that bad things happen only to bad people—or at least, only to people who make stupid mistakes or poor choices. Therefore, bad things won't happen to us because we won't be that stupid or careless. Melvin Lerner (1980, 1998) has called this the **belief in a just world**—the assumption that people get what they deserve and deserve what they get (Hafer, 2000; Hafer & Begue, 2005; Lipkus, Dalbert, & Siegler, 1996).

The just world belief has some sad and even tragic consequences. For example, suppose a female student on your campus was the victim of a date rape by a male fellow student. How do you think you and your friends would react? Would you wonder if she'd done something to trigger the rape? Was she acting suggestively earlier in the evening? Had she invited the man into her room?

Defensive Attributions
Explanations for behavior that avoid feelings of vulnerability and mortality

Belief in a Just World
A form of defensive attribution wherein people assume that bad things happen to bad people and that good things happen to good people

Research by Elaine Walster (1966) and others has focused on such attributions, which these investigators call "blaming the victim" (e.g., Burger, 1981; Lerner & Miller, 1978; Stormo, Lang, & Stritzke, 1997). In several experiments, they have found that the victims of crimes or accidents are often seen as causing their fate. For example, not only do people tend to believe that rape victims are to blame for the rape (Abrams, Viki, Masser, & Bohner, 2003; Bell, Kuriloff, & Lottes, 1994), but also battered wives are often seen as responsible for their abusive husbands' behavior (Summers & Feldman, 1984). By using this attributional bias, the perceiver does not have to acknowledge that there is a certain randomness in life, that an accident or criminal may be waiting just around the corner for an innocent person like oneself. The belief in a just world keeps anxiety-provoking thoughts about one's own safety at bay.

Culture and Other Attributional Biases
文化与其他归因偏见

Continuing to explore the link between culture and attributional biases, social psychologists have examined the self-serving bias and found a strong cultural component to it as well. For example, researchers asked industrial workers and their supervisors in Ghana, Africa, to assign causality for on-the-job accidents. Both groups made very self-serving attributions. Workers blamed factors in the situation, which absolved them of responsibility and blame; for example, they cited work overload, management pressure, and inadequate training. Supervisors blamed the workers—it was their carelessness, lack of skill, and ignorance that led to accidents (Gyekye & Salminen, 2004).

In a recent meta-analysis of 266 studies conducted all over the world, Amy Mezulis and her colleagues (2004) found that the self-serving bias is strongest in the United States and some other Western countries—Canada, Australia and New Zealand. It is also prevalent in Africa, Eastern Europe, and Russia. Within the United States, samples of participants who were of white, Asian, African, Hispanic, and Native American descent did not differ significantly from each other in the degree of self-serving bias. On the other hand, some Asian cultures displayed a markedly low or even absent level of self-serving bias: Japan, the Pacific Islands, and India (Mezulis, Abramson, Hyde, & Hankin, 2004).

In many traditional Asian cultures, the values of modesty and harmony with others are highly valued. For example, Chinese students are expected to attribute their success to other people, such as their teachers or parents, or to other aspects of the situation, such as the high quality of their school (Bond, 1996; Leung, 1996). Their cultural tradition does not encourage them to attribute their success to themselves (such as to their talent or intelligence), as it does in the United States and other Western countries. As you might expect, Chinese research participants took less credit for their successes than U.S. participants did (Anderson, 1999; Lee & Seligman, 1997). Instead, Chinese students attributed their success to aspects of their situation, reflecting the values of their culture.

Do individualistic and collectivistic cultures differ in how they explain Olympic gold-medal success? Prior meta-analytic research has indicated that "cultural products" such as advertising, song lyrics, television shows, and art have content that reflects their culture's values: more individualistic content in Western cultures and more collectivistic content in countries such as Japan, Korea, China, and Mexico (Morling & Lamoreaux, 2008). Hazel Markus and her colleagues (2006) found that this applies to television and newspaper sports commentary as well. They coded Japanese and American media accounts of their country's gold medal winning athletes in the 2000 and 2002 Olympics. They found that U.S. media described the performance of American gold medalists in terms of their unique abilities and talents; in short the athletes had demonstrated that they had "the right stuff" (Markus, Uchida, Omoregie, Townsend, & Kitayama, 2006, p. 110). In comparison, Japanese media described the performance of Japanese gold medalists in much broader terms, including the individual's ability, but also encompassing his or her past experiences of success and failure, and the role of other people such as coaches, teammates, and family in his or her success. Finally, American coverage focused more on positive aspects than negative ones (e.g., "[his] strength keeps him in the running"), consistent with a self-serving attributional style, while Japanese coverage focused more equally on positive and negative aspects (e.g., "Her second Olympics is a regrettable one. She was almost at the top, but she didn't have a perfect performance"; Markus et al., 2006, pp. 106–107). The following two quotes from gold medalists summarize the different ways in which culture influences how one defines and explains one's own behavior:

> *I think I just stayed focused. It was time to show the world what I could do . . . I knew I could beat [her], deep down in my heart I believed it . . . the doubts kept creeping in . . . but I just said, "No, this is my night." (Misty Hyman, American gold medalist in the women's 200-m butterfly).* (Markus et al., 2006, p. 103)

> *Here is the best coach in the world, the best manager in the world, and all of the people who support me—all these things were getting together and became a gold medal. So I think I didn't get it alone, not only by myself (Naoko Takahashi, Japanese gold medalist in the women's marathon).* (Markus et al., 2006, p. 103)

What about failure? Recall that in individualistic cultures like the United States, people tend toward the self-serving bias, looking outside of themselves—to the situation—to explain failure. In collectivist cultures like China, the reverse is true: People attribute failure to internal causes, not to external ones (Anderson, 1999; Oishi, Wyer, & Colcombe, 2000). In fact, in some Asian cultures, such as Japan and Korea, self-critical attributions are extremely common and an important "glue" that holds groups together. When one criticizes one's self (the opposite of a self-serving attribution), others offer sympathy and compassion, which strengthens the interdependence of the group members (Kitayama & Uchida, 2003; Kitayama, Markus, Matsumoto, & Norasakkunkit, 1995).

Recall that the belief in a just world is a defensive attribution that helps people maintain their vision of life as safe, orderly, and predictable. Is there a cultural component to it as well? Adrian Furnham (1993) argues that in a society where most people tend to believe the world is a just place, economic and social inequities are considered "fair." In such societies, people believe that the poor and disadvantaged have less because they deserve less. Thus, the just world attribution can be used to explain and justify injustice. Preliminary research suggests that this is the case: In cultures with extremes of wealth and poverty, just world attributions are more common than in cul-

HOW WOULD YOU USE THIS? 如何学以致用？

You're going to spend your whole life making attributions about other people. You simply can't survive if you don't. You'll need to make decisions about what kind of people they "really" are. Someone you can love? Someone you can't trust? How to do that accurately? That is the question. So much rides on "accuracy" in this area of life, and yet we often have, at best, imperfect knowledge upon which to base our judgments. Here's what you can do: First, remember that attributions come in two "flavors," *internal* and *external*. Remind yourself, often, to think about both as potential causes for another's behavior. If you find yourself overrelying on one type (perhaps falling prey to an attributional *bias*), force yourself to consider the other possibility. Play fair, in other words, when you make attributions. Human behavior is remarkably complex and is often a product of both the individual and the situation. Second, be humble. When you're forming an attribution about another, think of it as a "hypothesis," one that you're working on but are willing to change when new information comes in. Third, acknowledge when you've been right, but also acknowledge when you've been wrong. Incorrect attributions can be an immense learning experience. In fact, we call that "gaining wisdom." So go out there, and be wise!

tures where wealth is more evenly distributed (Dalbert & Yamauchi, 1994; Furnham, 1993; Furnham & Procter, 1989). For example, research participants in India and South Africa received higher scores on the just world belief scale than participants in the United States, Australia, Hong Kong, and Zimbabwe, who had scores in the middle of the scale. The lowest-scoring groups in the sample—those who believed the least in a just world—were the British and the Israelis (Furnham, 1993).

Summary 总结

- **Nonverbal Behavior** Nonverbal communication is used to express emotion, convey attitudes, and communicate personality traits. People can accurately decode subtle nonverbal cues.
  - **Facial Expressions of Emotion** The six major emotions are universal, encoded and decoded similarly by people around the world; they have evolutionary significance. **Affect blends** occur when one part of the face registers one emotion and another part, a different emotion. Mirror neurons are involved in emotional encoding and decoding, and help us experience empathy.
  - **Culture and the Channels of Nonverbal Communication** Other channels of nonverbal communication include eye gaze, touch, personal space, gesture, and tone of voice. **Display rules** are particular to each culture and dictate what kinds of emotional expressions people are supposed to show. **Emblems** are gestures with well-defined meanings and are culturally determined.
  - **Multichannel Nonverbal Communication** Social interaction involves **decoding** (and **encoding**) many channels of nonverbal communication at the same time. Because nonverbal information is diffused across these many channels, we can often rely on one channel to understand what is going on. This increases our ability to make accurate judgments about others.

- **Implicit Personality Theories: Filling in the Blanks** To understand other people, we observe their behavior but we also infer their feelings, traits, and motives. To do so, we use general notions or schemas about which personality traits go together in one person.
  - **Culture and Implicit Personality Theories** These general notions, or schemas, are shared by people in a culture, and are passed from one generation to another.

- **Causal Attribution: Answering the "Why" Question** According to **attribution theory**, we try to determine why people do what they do in order to uncover the feelings and traits that are behind their actions. This helps us understand and predict our social world.
  - **The Nature of the Attribution Process** When trying to decide what causes people's behavior, we can make one of two attributions: an **internal** or dispositional attribution, or an **external**, situational attribution.
  - **The Covariation Model: Internal versus External Attributions** The **covariation model** focuses on observations of behavior across time, place, actors, and targets of the behavior. It examines how the perceiver chooses either an internal or an external attribution. We make such choices by using **consensus**, **distinctiveness**, and **consistency** information.
  - **The Correspondence Bias: People as Personality Psychologists** People also use various mental shortcuts when making attributions, including the use of schemas and theories. One common shortcut is the **correspondence bias**, the tendency to believe that people's behavior corresponds to (matches) their dispositions. A reason for this bias is that a person's behavior has greater **perceptual salience** than does the surrounding situation. The **two-step process of attribution** states that the initial and automatic attribution tends to be dispositional, but it can be altered by situational information at the second step.
  - **Culture and the Correspondence Bias** Although people from individualistic and collectivistic cultures both demonstrate the correspondence bias, members of collectivist cultures are more sensitive to situational causes of behavior and more likely to rely on situational explanations, as long as situational variables are salient. A reliance on holistic versus analytic styles of thinking underlies this effect.
  - **The Actor/Observer Difference** The **actor/observer difference** is an amplification of the correspondence bias: We tend to see other people's behavior as dispositionally caused, although we are more likely to see our own behavior as situationally caused. The actor/observer effect occurs because **perceptual salience** and **information availability** differ for the actor and the observer.
  - **Self-Serving Attributions** People's attributions are also influenced by their personal needs. **Self-serving attributions** occur when people make internal attributions for their successes and external attributions for their failures. **Defensive attributions** help people avoid feelings of mortality. One type of defensive attribution is the **belief in a just world**, where we believe that bad things happen to bad people and good things happen to good people.

- **Culture and Other Attributional Biases** There is evidence for cross-cultural differences in **self-serving** and **defensive attributions**. Typically, the difference occurs between Western, individualistic cultures and Eastern, collectivistic cultures.

CHAPTER 4 TEST 第4章习题

1. Paul Ekman and Walter Friesen traveled to New Guinea to study the meaning of various facial expressions in the primitive South Fore tribe. What major conclusion did they reach?
   a. Facial expressions are not universal because they have different meanings in different cultures.
   b. The six major emotional expressions are universal.
   c. The six major emotional expressions are not universal.
   d. The members of the South Fore used different facial expressions than Westerners to express the same emotion.

2. What is a major assumption of Kelley's covariation model of attribution?
   a. We make quick attributions after observing one instance of someone's behavior.
   b. People make causal attributions using cultural schemas.
   c. People infer the cause of others' behaviors through introspection.
   d. People gather information to make causal attributions rationally and logically.

3. Which of the following psychological phenomena shows least cultural variation?
   a. Self-serving attributions
   b. Implicit personality theories
   c. Anger and fear facial expressions
   d. Correspondence bias

4. Suppose that Mischa has found that when she sits in the first row of discussion classes she gets a better participation grade, regardless of how much she actually participates. Her positioning in front of the teacher could have an effect on how large of a role the teacher thinks Mischa has in discussion due to
   a. the teacher's use of schemas.
   b. perceptual salience.
   c. the teacher's implicit personality theories.
   d. the two-step process of attribution.

5. Mr. Rowe and Ms. Dabney meet on a blind date. They get along well until they get into his black convertible to go to a movie. Ms. Dabney is quiet and reserved for the rest of the evening. It turns out that her brother had recently been in a serious accident in that same type of car and seeing it brought up those unwanted emotions. Mr. Rowe assumes that Ms. Dabney has a cold and reserved personality, thereby demonstrating
   a. a belief in a just world.
   b. the correspondence bias.
   c. perceptual salience.
   d. insufficient justification.

6. Suppose a certain student, Jake, falls asleep during every chemistry class. Suppose further that Jake is the only one who falls asleep in this class and he falls asleep in all of his other classes. According to Kelley's covariation theory of attribution, how will people explain his behavior (falling asleep)?
   a. It is due to something unusual about Jake, because his behavior is low in consensus, high in distinctiveness, and high in consistency.
   b. Chemistry is really a boring class because Jake's behavior is high in consensus, high in distinctiveness, and high in consistency.
   c. It is due to something unusual about Jake, because his behavior is low in consensus, low in distinctiveness, and high in consistency.
   d. It is due to something peculiar about the circumstances on one day, because his behavior is high in consensus.

7. Imagine you are in Hong Kong reading the morning newspaper, and you notice a headline about a double murder that took place overnight. A suspect is in custody. Which of the following headlines is most likely to accompany the story?
   a. Dispute over Gambling Debt Ends in Murder
   b. Crazed Murdered Slays Two
   c. Homicidal Maniac Stalks Innocents
   d. Bloodthirsty Mobster Takes Revenge

8. Ming is from China; Jason is from the United States. Both participate in an experiment in which they take a test, are given feedback, and told that they did very well. They are then asked to make attributions for their performance. Based on cross-cultural research on the self-serving bias, you would expect that
   a. Jason, but not Ming, will say that he succeeded due to his high ability.
   b. neither Ming nor Jason will say that they succeeded due to their high ability.
   c. both Ming and Jason will say that they succeeded due to their high ability.
   d. Ming, but not Jason, will say that he succeeded due to his high ability.

9. Which of the following statements best describes cultural differences in the correspondence bias?
   a. Members of collectivist cultures rarely make dispositional attributions.
   b. Members of Western cultures rarely make dispositional attributions.
   c. Members of collectivist cultures are more likely to go beyond dispositional explanations, including information about the situation as well.

d. Members of Western cultures are more likely to go beyond dispositional explanations, including information about the situation as well.
10. According to the actor/observer difference in attribution, we tend to see
   a. our own behavior as dispositionally caused, but other people's behavior as situationally caused.
   b. our own behavior as situationally caused, but other people's behavior as dispositionally caused.
   c. both our own behavior and other people's behavior as dispositionally caused.
   d. both our own behavior and other people's behavior as situationally caused.

Chapter 4 Answer Key
1-b 2-d 3-c 4-b 5-b 6-c 7-a 8-a 9-c 10-a

For more review plus practice tests, videos, flashcards, writing help and more, log on to MyPsychLab.

5

The Self
Understanding Ourselves in a Social Context

自我：
在社会情境中理解我们自己

OUTLINE 提纲

- **Self-Knowledge**
  - Cultural Differences in Defining the Self
  - Gender Differences in Defining the Self
  - Knowing Ourselves Through Introspection
  - Knowing Ourselves by Observing Our Own Behavior
  - CONNECTIONS: How Should Parents Praise Their Children?
  - Mindsets: Understanding Our Own Abilities
  - Using Other People to Know Ourselves
- **Self-Control: The Executive Function of the Self**
- **Impression Management: All the World's a Stage**
  - Culture, Impression Management, and Self-Enhancement
- **Summary**

G**REAT ATHLETES ARE BORN AND NOT MADE—OR SO IT** seems. "She's a natural," we hear, or "he's one in a million." Talent is important to athletic success, of course, which is why one of your authors became a psychologist instead of a major league baseball pitcher. But is talent everything? Consider Michael Jordan, thought to be the most gifted basketball player who ever lived. Did you know he was cut from his high school team? (Yes, *that* Michael Jordan.) Rather than giving up, he redoubled his efforts, leaving home at six in the morning to practice before school. He eventually made it to the University of North Carolina, which has one of the top basketball programs in the country. But instead of resting on his laurels, Jordan constantly worked on his game. One year, after a disappointing loss that ended North Carolina's season, Jordan went right to the gym and spent hours working on his jump shot. Mia Hamm, considered to be the best women's soccer player in the world, had the same attitude. As a child she constantly challenged herself by playing with older, more accomplished players. When she was 10, she talked herself onto an 11-year-old boys' team and eventually led them in scoring. In college she didn't consider herself to be that good, but as she played against the top players in the country, she found herself "improving faster than I had ever dreamed possible" (Hamm, 1999, p. 4). After playing on teams that won the World Cup and an Olympic Gold Medal, here is what Hamm says about people who call her the best player in the world: "They're wrong. I have the potential, maybe, but I'm still not there" (Hamm, 1999, p. 15).

The point of these stories is not just that "practice makes perfect"—it's about the importance of how we see ourselves and our abilities. Some people view athletic talent as a gift you either have or you don't—the "one in a million" theory. The problem is that when such people do poorly, as every athlete does on occasion, it is a devastating sign that they don't have it. "I'm *not* one in a million and nothing can change that," they think. "So why bother practicing? Maybe I should take a psychology class instead." Others, like Michael Jordan and Mia Hamm, view athletic performance as a skill that can be improved. Failure is a sign that they need to work harder, not that they should give up. As we will see in this chapter, how people view their own abilities and interpret the reasons for their behavior can be crucial determinants of their success.

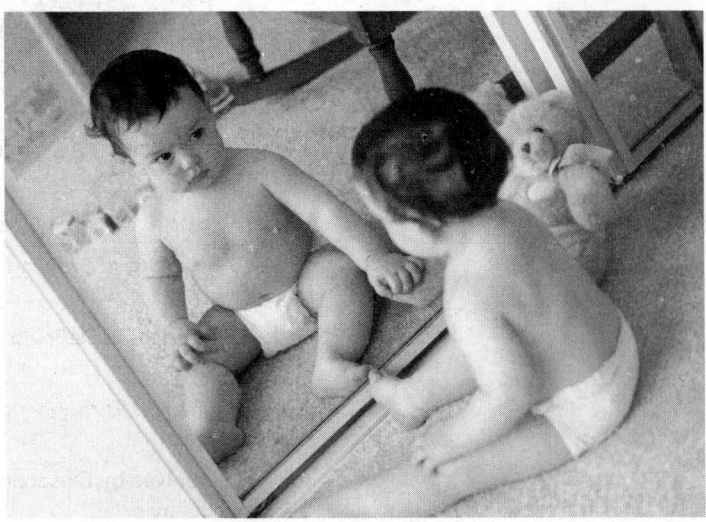

Researchers have examined whether other species have a self-concept, by seeing whether they recognize that an image in a mirror is themselves and not another member of their species. The same procedure has been used with humans, revealing that people develop a self-concept around the age of 18 months.

But how do people come to know themselves? More generally, what is the nature of the self, and how do people discover it? These are the questions to which we turn.

Who are you? How did you come to be this person you call "myself"? The founder of American psychology, William James (1842–1910), described the basic duality of our perception of self. The self is composed of our thoughts and beliefs about ourselves, or what James (1890) called the "known," or, more simply, the "me." The self is also the active processor of information, the "knower," or "I." In modern terms, we refer to the known aspect of the self as the **self-concept**, which is the content of the self (our knowledge about who we are), and to the knower aspect as **self-awareness**, which is the act of thinking about ourselves. These two aspects of the self combine to create a coherent sense of identity: Your self is both a book (full of fascinating content collected over time) and the reader of that book (who at any moment can access a specific chapter or add a new one). In this chapter, we will consider both aspects of the self—the nature of the self-concept and how we come to know ourselves through self-awareness.

A good place to begin is with the question of whether we are the only species with a sense of self. Some fascinating studies suggest that we are not alone in this regard (Gallup, 1997). Researchers placed a mirror in an animal's cage until the mirror became a familiar object. The animal was then briefly anesthetized and an odorless red dye was painted on its brow or ear. What happened when the animal woke up and looked in the mirror? Chimpanzees and orangutans immediately touched the area of their heads marked with the red spot. Dolphins have also shown signs of recognizing themselves in mirrors. When a spot was drawn on their bodies (with a nontoxic marker), the dolphins swam directly to mirrors and twisted their bodies to see the spot (Emery & Clayton, 2005; Reiss & Marino, 2001).

These studies suggest that chimps and orangutans, and possibly gorillas and dolphins, have a rudimentary self-concept. They realize that the image in the mirror is themselves and not another animal, and they recognize that they look different from how they looked before (Gallup, Anderson, & Shillito, 2002; Heschl & Burkart, 2006; Posada & Colell, 2007).

Wondering when a sense of self develops in humans, researchers used a variation of the red-dye test with toddlers and found that self-recognition develops at around 18 months of age (Courage, Edison, & Howe, 2005; Lewis & Ramsay, 2004). As we grow older, this rudimentary self-concept becomes more complex. One way psychologists have studied how people's self-concept changes from childhood to adulthood is to ask people of different ages to answer the simple question "Who am I?" Typically, a child's self-concept is concrete, with references to clear-cut, easily observable characteristics like age, sex, neighborhood, and hobbies. A 9-year-old answered the question this way: "I have brown eyes. I have brown hair. I have brown eyebrows. . . . I'm a boy. I have an uncle that is almost 7 feet tall" (Montemayor & Eisen, 1977, p. 317).

As we mature, we place less emphasis on physical characteristics and more on psychological states (our thoughts and feelings) and on considerations of how other

Self-Concept
The content of the self; that is, our knowledge about who we are

Self-Awareness
The act of thinking about ourselves

people judge us (Hart & Damon, 1986; Livesley & Bromley, 1973; Montemayor & Eisen, 1977). Consider this 12th-grade high school student's answer to the "Who am I?" question:

> I am a human being. . . . I am a moody person. I am an indecisive person. I am an ambitious person. I am a very curious person. I am not an individual. I am a loner. I am an American (God help me). I am a Democrat. I am a liberal person. I am a radical. I am a conservative. I am a pseudoliberal. I am an atheist. I am not a classifiable person (i.e., I don't want to be). (Montemayor & Eisen, 1977, p. 318)

Clearly, this teenager has moved well beyond descriptions of her hobbies and appearance (Harter, 2003). But what exactly does the self do? It serves four important functions: *self-knowledge*, whereby we formulate and organize what we know about ourselves; *self-control*, whereby we make plans and execute decisions; *self-presentation*, whereby we try to put our best foot forward to others, *self-justification*, whereby we try to put our best foot forward to ourselves (Baumeister, 1998; Graziano, Jensen-Campbell, & Finch, 1997; Leary & Tangney, 2003). We will discuss the first three functions of the self in this chapter and discuss self-justification in the next.

When Harvard-educated Masako Owada abandoned her promising career to marry Crown Prince Naruhito of Japan and assumed the traditional roles required of her, many Western women questioned her decision. At issue for many were cultural differences in interdependence versus independence of the self.

Self-Knowledge 自我认知

How do you define who you are? As straightforward as this question might seem, the way in which you answer it likely reveals some fascinating cultural and social processes.

Cultural Differences in Defining the Self 自我定义的文化差异

In June 1993, Masako Owada, a 29-year-old Japanese woman, married Crown Prince Naruhito of Japan. Masako was a brilliant career diplomat in the foreign ministry, educated at Harvard and Oxford. She spoke five languages and was on the fast track to a prestigious job as a diplomat. Her decision to marry the prince surprised many observers because it meant she would have to give up her career. Indeed, she gave up any semblance of an independent life, becoming subservient to the prince and the rest of the royal family and spending much of her time participating in rigid royal ceremonies. Although some people hoped that she would modernize the monarchy, "so far the princess has not changed the imperial family as much as it has changed her" (Girl born to Japan's princess, 2001).

How do you feel about Masako's decision to marry the prince? Your answer may say something about the nature of your self-concept and the culture in which you grew up. In many Western cultures, people have an **independent view of the self**, which is a way of defining oneself in terms of one's own internal thoughts, feelings, and actions and not in terms of the thoughts, feelings, and actions of others (Kitayama & Uchida, 2005; Markus & Kitayama, 1991, 2001; Nisbett, 2003; Oyserman & Lee, 2008; Triandis, 1995). Westerners learn to define themselves as quite separate from other people and to value independence and uniqueness. Consequently, many Western observers were mystified by Masako's decision to marry the crown prince. They assumed that she was coerced into the marriage by a backward, sexist society that did not properly value her worth as an individual with an independent life of her own.

In contrast, many Asian and other non-Western cultures have an **interdependent view of the self**, which is a way of defining oneself in terms of one's relationships to other people and recognizing that one's behavior is often determined by the thoughts, feelings, and actions of others. Connectedness and interdependence between people are valued, whereas independence and uniqueness are frowned on. For example, when asked to complete sentences beginning with "I am . . ." people from Asian cultures are more likely to refer to social groups, such as their family or religious group, than

Independent View of the Self

A way of defining oneself in terms of one's own internal thoughts, feelings, and actions and not in terms of the thoughts, feelings, and actions of other people

Interdependent View of the Self

A way of defining oneself in terms of one's relationships to other people; recognizing that one's behavior is often determined by the thoughts, feelings, and actions of others

> *The squeaky wheel gets the grease.*
> — American proverb
>
> *The nail that stands out gets pounded down.*
> — Japanese proverb

people from Western cultures are (Bochner, 1994; Triandis, 1989). To many Japanese and other Asians, Masako's decision to give up her career was not at all surprising and was a natural consequence of her view of herself as connected and obligated to others, such as her parents and the royal family. What is viewed as positive and normal behavior by one culture may be viewed very differently by another.

Ted Singelis (1994) developed a questionnaire that measures the extent to which people view themselves as interdependent or independent. Sample items from this scale are given in the following Try It! exercise. Singelis administered the questionnaire to students at the University of Hawaii at Manoa and found that Asian Americans agreed more with the interdependence than the independence items, whereas Caucasian Americans agreed more with the independence than the interdependence items.

We do not mean to imply that every member of a Western culture has an independent view of the self and that every member of an Asian culture has an interdependent

---

TRY IT! 试一试！独立性与相互依存性量表
A Measure of Independence and Interdependence

Instructions: Indicate the extent to which you agree or disagree with each of these statements.

	Strongly Disagree						Strongly Agree
1. My happiness depends on the happiness of those around me.	1	2	3	4	5	6	7
2. I will sacrifice my self-interest for the benefit of the group I am in.	1	2	3	4	5	6	7
3. It is important to me to respect decisions made by the group.	1	2	3	4	5	6	7
4. If my brother or sister fails, I feel responsible.	1	2	3	4	5	6	7
5. Even when I strongly disagree with group members, I avoid an argument.	1	2	3	4	5	6	7
6. I am comfortable with being singled out for praise or rewards.	1	2	3	4	5	6	7
7. Being able to take care of myself is a primary concern for me.	1	2	3	4	5	6	7
8. I prefer to be direct and forthright when dealing with people I've just met.	1	2	3	4	5	6	7
9. I enjoy being unique and different from others in many respects.	1	2	3	4	5	6	7
10. My personal identity, independent of others, is very important to me.	1	2	3	4	5	6	7

Note: These questions are taken from a scale developed by Singelis (1994) to measure the strength of people's interdependent and independent views of themselves. The actual scale consists of 12 items that measure interdependence and 12 items that measure independence. We have reproduced 5 of each type of item here: The first 5 are designed to measure interdependence, and the last 5 are designed to measure independence. For scoring instructions, turn to page 147.

(Adapted from Singelis, 1994)

view of the self. Within cultures, there are differences in the self-concept, and as contact between cultures increases, differences between cultures may decrease. It is interesting to note, for example, that Masako's decision to marry the prince was unpopular among at least some young Japanese women, who felt that her choice was not a positive sign of interdependence, but a betrayal of the feminist cause in Japan (Sanger, 1993). Women are joining the workforce in Japan in record numbers, and more women are postponing or forgoing marriage in favor of careers. And the restricted life in the Imperial Household seems to have taken its toll on Princess Masako. In 2004 she stopped making public appearances, and the press office for the royal family announced that she was receiving therapy for depression (Carpenter, 2008).

Nonetheless, the difference between the Western and Eastern sense of self is real and has interesting consequences for communication between the cultures. Indeed, the differences in the sense of self are so fundamental that it is very difficult for people with independent selves to appreciate what it is like to have an interdependent self, and vice versa. Western readers might find it difficult to appreciate the Asian sense of interdependence; similarly, many Japanese find it difficult to comprehend that Americans could possibly know who they are separate from the social groups to which they belong. After giving a lecture on the Western view of the self to a group of Japanese students, one psychologist reported that the students "sighed deeply and said at the end, 'Could this really be true?'" (Kitayama & Markus, 1994, p. 18). To paraphrase William Shakespeare, in Western society the self is the measure of all things. But however natural we consider this conception of the self to be, it is important to remember that it is socially constructed and therefore may differ from culture to culture.

> Introspection is difficult and fallible ... The difficulty is simply that of all observation of whatever kind.
>
> —William James, 1890

Gender Differences in Defining the Self
自我定义的性别差异

Is there any truth to the stereotype that when women get together, they talk about interpersonal problems and relationships, whereas men talk about anything but their feelings (usually sports)? Although this stereotype is clearly an exaggeration, it does have a grain of truth and reflects a difference in women's and men's self-concept (Baumeister & Sommer, 1997; Cross, Bacon, & Morris, 2000; Cross & Madson, 1997; Gabriel & Gardner, 1999, 2004).

Women have more *relational interdependence*, meaning that they focus more on their close relationships, such as how they feel about their spouse or their child. Men have more *collective interdependence*, meaning that they focus on their memberships in larger groups, such as the fact that they are Americans or that they belong to a fraternity (Brewer & Gardner, 1996; Gabriel & Gardner, 1999). Starting in early childhood, American girls are more likely to develop intimate friendships, cooperate with others, and focus their attention on social relationships, whereas boys are more likely to focus on their group memberships (Cross & Madson, 1997). These differences persist into adulthood, such that women focus more on intimacy and cooperation with a small number of close others and are in fact more likely to discuss personal topics and disclose their emotions than men are (Caldwell & Peplau, 1982; Davidson & Duberman, 1982).

Men focus more on their social groups like sports teams. For example, when women and men were asked to describe either a positive or negative emotional event in their lives, women tended to mention personal relationships, such as becoming engaged or the death of a family member (Gabriel & Gardner, 1999). Men talked about events involving larger groups, such as the time they joined a fraternity or their sports team lost an important game (see Figure 5.1). To see how much your self-concept is based on a sense of relational interdependence, answer the questions in the following Try It! exercise on page 122.

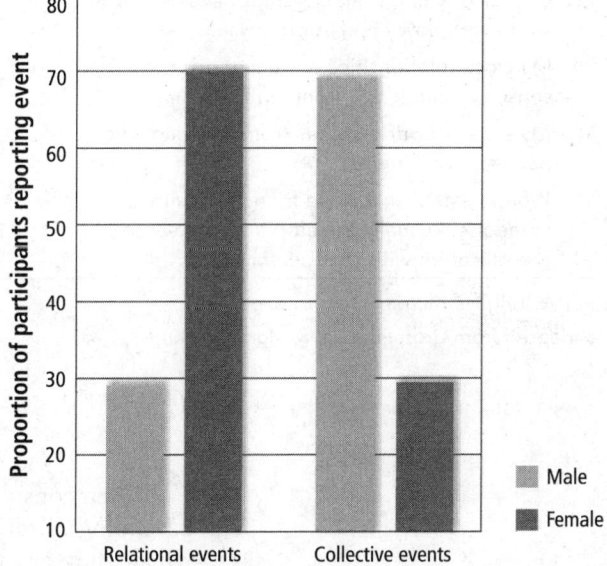

FIGURE 5.1

Gender differences in types of interdependence.

Male and female college students were asked to describe an important emotional event in their lives. Women reported more relational events, ones that had to do with close personal relationships. Men reported more collective events, ones that had to do with their membership in larger groups.

(From Gabriel & Gardner, 1999, p. 648)

试一试！对关系的相互依存性的量表
A Measure of Relational Interdependence

Instructions: Indicate the extent to which you agree or disagree with each of these statements.

	Strongly Disagree						Strongly Agree
1. My close relationships are an important reflection of who I am.	1	2	3	4	5	6	7
2. When I feel close to someone, it often feels to me as if that person is an important part of who I am.	1	2	3	4	5	6	7
3. I usually feel a strong sense of pride when someone close to me has an important accomplishment.	1	2	3	4	5	6	7
4. I think one of the most important parts of who I am can be captured by looking at my close friends and understanding who they are.	1	2	3	4	5	6	7
5. When I think of myself, I often think of my close friends or family also.	1	2	3	4	5	6	7
6. If a person hurts someone close to me, I feel personally hurt as well.	1	2	3	4	5	6	7
7. In general, my close relationships are an important part of my self-image.	1	2	3	4	5	6	7
8. Overall, my close relationships have very little to do with how I feel about myself.	1	2	3	4	5	6	7
9. My close relationships are unimportant to my sense of what kind of person I am.	1	2	3	4	5	6	7
10. My sense of pride comes from knowing who I have as close friends.	1	2	3	4	5	6	7
11. When I establish a close friendship with someone, I usually develop a strong sense of identification with that person.	1	2	3	4	5	6	7

For scoring instructions, turn to page 147.
(Adapted from Cross, Bacon, & Morris, 2000)

When considering gender differences such as these, we need to be cautious: The psychological differences between men and women are far fewer than the ways in which they are the same (Deaux & LaFrance, 1998, Hyde, 2005). Nevertheless, there do appear to be differences in the way women and men define themselves in the United States, with women having a greater sense of relational interdependence than men.

Knowing Ourselves Through Introspection 通过内省来认识自己

We've seen that the culture in which people grow up, and their gender, help shape their self-concept. But how do people come to know the selves that are shaped by culture and gender?

This might seem like a strange question. "Good grief!," you might be thinking. "I don't need a social psychology textbook to tell me that! It's not exactly a surprise; I just think about myself. No big deal." In other words, you rely on **introspection**, looking

Introspection
The process whereby people look inward and examine their own thoughts, feelings, and motives

inward to examine the "inside information" that you, and you alone, have about your thoughts, feelings, and motives. And indeed, you do find some answers when you introspect. But there are two interesting things about introspection: People do not rely on this source of information as often as you might think—actually, people spend very little time thinking about themselves—and even when people do introspect, the reasons for their feelings and behavior can be hidden from conscious awareness (Wilson, 2002; Wilson & Dunn, 2004). In short, self-scrutiny isn't all it's cracked up to be, and if this were our only source of knowledge about ourselves, we would be in trouble.

Focusing on the Self: Self-Awareness Theory

How often do people think about themselves? To find out, researchers asked 107 employees, who ranged in age from 19 to 63 and worked at five different companies, to wear beepers for 1 week. The beepers went off at random intervals between 7:30 A.M. and 10:30 P.M., a total of seven to nine times a day (Csikszentmihalyi & Figurski, 1982). At the sound of the beeper, the participants answered a series of questions about their activities, thoughts, and moods at that time. As you can see in Figure 5.2, people thought about themselves surprisingly little. Only 8 percent of the total thoughts recorded were about the self; more often, the participants thought about work, chores, and time. In fact, the response of "no thoughts" was more frequent than that of thoughts about the self. So although we do engage in introspection at times, it is not a frequent cognitive activity. Mundane thoughts about everyday life, and indeed thoughts about other people and our conversations with them, account for the vast majority of our daily thoughts (see Figure 5.2).

Sometimes, of course, we do turn the spotlight of consciousness on ourselves, particularly when we encounter something in the environment that triggers self-awareness, such as seeing ourselves on videotape or staring at ourselves in a mirror. For example, if you are watching a home video taken by a friend with her new video camera and you are the featured attraction, you will be in a state of self-awareness; you become the focus of your attention. According to **self-awareness theory**, when this happens we evaluate and compare our current behavior to our internal standards and values (Carver, 2003; Duval & Silvia, 2002; Duval & Wicklund, 1972; Phillips & Silva, 2005; Wiekens & Stapel, 2008). In short, we become self-conscious, in the sense that we become objective, judgmental observers of ourselves, seeing ourselves as an outside observer would. Let's say that you feel that you should quit smoking, and one day you catch an image of yourself in a store window smoking a cigarette. How do you think you will feel?

Seeing your reflection will make you aware of the disparity between your behavior and your internal standards. If you can change your behavior to match your internal guidelines (e.g., quit smoking), you will do so. If you feel you can't change your behavior, being in a state of self-awareness will be uncomfortable because you will be confronted with disagreeable feedback about yourself (Duval & Silvia, 2002). Figure 5.3 illustrates how self-awareness makes us conscious of our internal standards and directs our subsequent behavior.

Sometimes people go even further in their attempt to escape the self. Such diverse activities as alcohol abuse, binge eating, and sexual masochism have one thing in common: All are effective ways of turning off the internal spotlight on oneself (Baumeister, 1991). Getting drunk, for example, is one way of avoiding negative thoughts about oneself (at least temporarily). The fact that people regularly engage in such dangerous behaviors, despite their risks, is an indication of how aversive self-focus can be (Hull, 1981; Hull & Young, 1983; Hull, Young, & Jouriles, 1986).

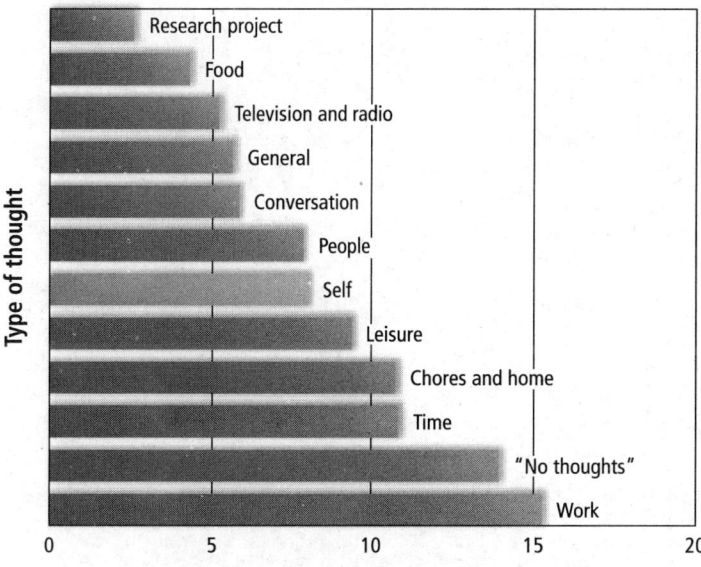

FIGURE 5.2
"What are you thinking about?"

For a week, people wore beepers that went off at random intervals several times a day. Each time the beepers went off, people described what they had just been thinking about. Thoughts about the self were surprisingly infrequent.

(Adapted from Csikszentmihalyi & Figurski, 1982)

But as I looked into the mirror, I screamed, and my heart shuddered: for I saw not myself but the mocking, leering, face of a devil.

—Friedrich Nietzsche, *Thus Spake Zarathustra*

Self-Awareness Theory
The idea that when people focus their attention on themselves, they evaluate and compare their behavior to their internal standards and values

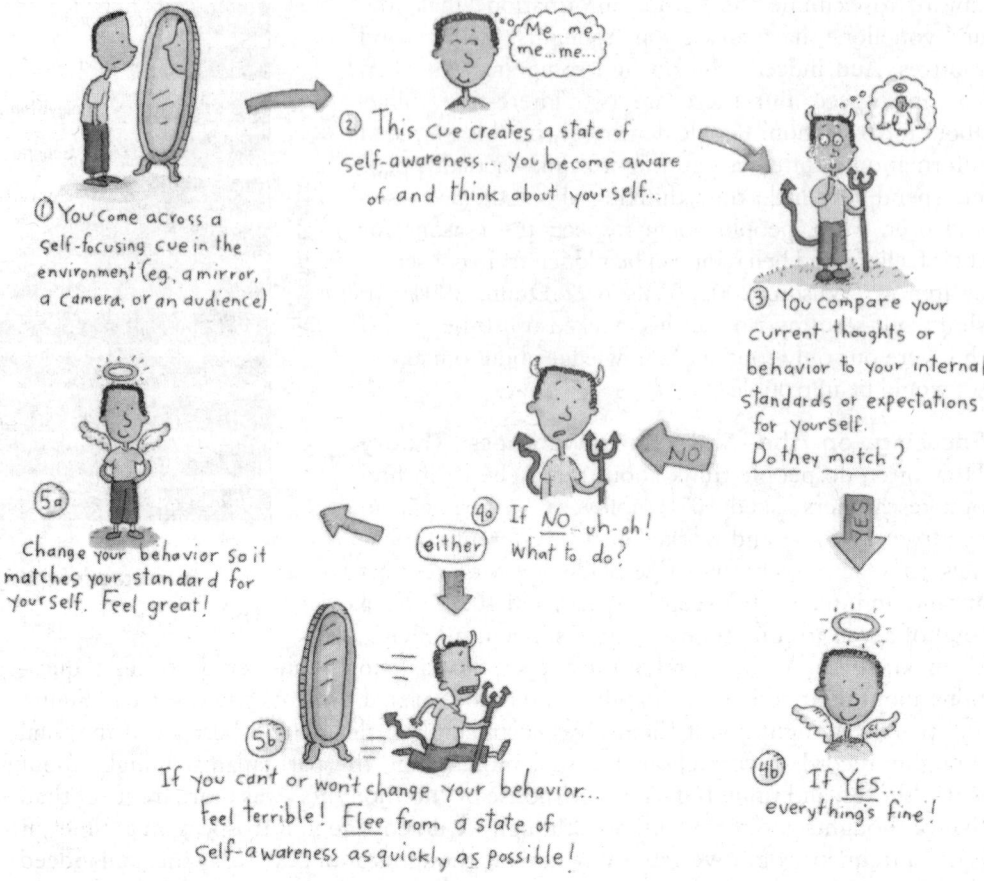

FIGURE 5.3
Self-awareness theory: the consequences of self-focused attention.

When people focus on themselves, they compare their behavior to their internal standards.

(Adapted from Carver & Scheier, 1981)

> I swear to you... that to be overly conscious is a sickness, a real, thorough sickness.
>
> Fyodor Dostoevsky, *Notes from Underground,* 1864

Not all means of escaping the self, however, are so damaging. Many forms of religious expression and spirituality are also effective means of avoiding self-focus (Baumeister, 1991). Further, self-focus is not always aversive. If you have just experienced a major success, focusing on yourself can be pleasant indeed because it highlights your positive accomplishments (Greenberg & Musham, 1981; Silvia & Abele, 2002). Further, self-focus can also be a way of keeping you out of trouble, by reminding you of your sense of right and wrong. For example, several studies have found that when people are self-aware (e.g., in front of a mirror), they are more likely to follow their moral standards, such as avoiding the temptation to cheat on a test (Beaman, Klentz, Diener, & Svanum, 1979; Diener & Wallbom, 1976; Gibbons, 1978). Self-awareness, then, is particularly aversive when it reminds people of their shortcomings, and under these circumstances (e.g., right after doing poorly on a test), people try to avoid it. At other times, however—such as when that little devil is on your shoulder pushing you into temptation—a dose of self-awareness is not such a bad thing because it makes you more aware of your morals and ideals.

Virtually all the work we have described so far, however, has been conducted with samples of people from Western countries (primarily Americans). Given that people who grow up in East Asian cultures tend to have a more interdependent view of the self, defining themselves in terms of their relationships to other people, is it possible that they differ in how self-aware they tend to be? Recent research indicates that the answer is yes. Dov Cohen and his colleagues have found that East Asians are more likely to have an *outside perspective on the self,* viewing themselves through the eyes of other people. People who grow up in Western cultures are more likely to have an *insider perspective on the self,* focusing on their own private experiences without considering how other people see them (Cohen, Hoshino-Browne, & Leung, 2007). To be clear, people in both cultures can adopt either perspective, but the "default" state people tend to adopt differs.

"Steer clear of that group. They're all terribly self-aware."

Another way of saying this is that East Asians may be in a chronic state of self-awareness, because they are more likely to be seeing themselves through the eyes of other people. If so, it follows that the research we have just discussed, in which self-awareness can be induced by placing people in front of mirrors or video cameras, may be true more of Westerners than East Asians. Because East Asians are already self-aware, they should be less influenced by cues such as mirrors. This is exactly what Steve Heine and colleagues found in a recent study (Heine, Takemoto, Moskalenko, Lasaleta, & Henrich, 2008). The participants, who were college students at an American or a Japanese university, were asked to rate how much a series of 20 statements, such as "I am extremely considerate," described them. Then they rated how much each statement characterized how they would ideally like to be. Essentially this task measured how much people believed that they fell short of their ideal selves; for example, whether they thought they were less considerate than they aspired to be. Half of the participants completed this task in front of a mirror and half did not. As we saw earlier, when Westerners see their reflection in the mirror, it triggers an outside perspective whereby they become objective, judgmental observers of themselves, and are more likely to see a disparity between their behavior and their internal standards. The same was true of the Americans in this study; when they completed the questionnaire in front of a mirror, they noticed a bigger discrepancy between their ideal and real selves. The Japanese students, however, where unaffected by whether or not a mirror was in the room. As seen in Figure 5.4, they noticed discrepancies in both conditions; that is, they responded as the Americans did in the mirror condition. As the authors note, their Japanese participants acted as if they had "mirrors in their heads," and did not need an actual mirror to see themselves from an outside perspective (Heine et al., 2008). How self-aware do you tend to be? Complete the Try It! exercise on page 126 to find out.

> I have often wished I had time to cultivate modesty . . . But I am too busy thinking about myself.
>
> —Dame Edith Sitwell

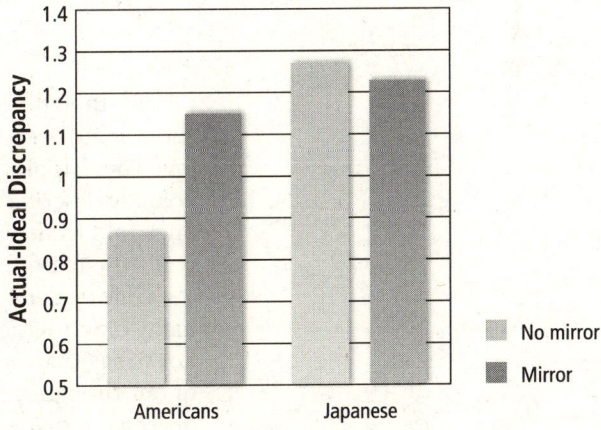

FIGURE 5.4

Effects of mirror on Japanese and American college students

American college students who filled out a questionnaire in front of a mirror noticed more discrepancies between their ideal and actual selves than did American college students who filled out the questionnaire without a mirror present. The presence of a mirror had no effect on the answers of Japanese college students.

Judging Why We Feel the Way We Do: Telling More Than We Can Know Even when we are self-aware and introspect to our heart's content, it can be difficult to know *why* we feel the way we do. Imagine trying to decide why you love someone. Being in love typically makes you feel giddy, euphoric, and preoccupied; in fact, the ancient

试一试！测量你的内在自我意识
Measure Your Private Self-Consciousness

How much do you focus on yourself when you are alone? The following questions are taken from a scale developed by Fenigstein, Scheier, and Buss (1975) to measure private self-consciousness—the consistent tendency to be self-aware.

Instructions: Answer the following questions as honestly as possible on a scale from 1 to 5, where

1 = extremely uncharacteristic (not at all like me)
2 = somewhat uncharacteristic
3 = neither characteristic nor uncharacteristic
4 = somewhat characteristic
5 = extremely characteristic (very much like me)

	1	2	3	4	5
1. I'm always trying to figure myself out.	1	2	3	4	5
2. Generally, I'm not very aware of myself.	1	2	3	4	5
3. I reflect about myself a lot.	1	2	3	4	5
4. I'm often the subject of my own fantasies.	1	2	3	4	5
5. I never scrutinize myself.	1	2	3	4	5
6. I'm generally attentive to my inner feelings.	1	2	3	4	5
7. I'm constantly examining my motives.	1	2	3	4	5
8. I sometimes have the feeling that I'm off somewhere watching myself.	1	2	3	4	5
9. I'm alert to changes in my mood.	1	2	3	4	5
10. I'm aware of the way my mind works when I work through a problem.	1	2	3	4	5

For scoring instructions, turn to page 147.
(Adapted from Fenigstein, Scheier, & Buss, 1975)

Greeks thought love was a sickness. But why do you feel this way? Exactly what is it about your sweetheart that made you fall in love? We know it is something about our loved one's looks, personality, values, and background. But precisely what? How can we possibly describe the special chemistry that exists between two people? A friend of ours once told us he was in love with a woman because she played the saxophone. Was this really the reason? The heart works in such mysterious ways that it is difficult to tell.

Unfortunately, it's not just love that is difficult to explain. As we saw in Chapter 3, many of our basic mental processes occur outside of awareness (Wilson, 2002). This is not to say that we are thinkers without a clue—we are usually aware of the final result of our thought processes (e.g., that we are in love) but often unaware of the cognitive processing that led to the result. It's as if the magician pulled a rabbit out of a hat: You see the rabbit, but you don't know how it got there. How do we deal with this rabbit problem? Even though we often don't know why we feel a certain way, it seems we are always able to come up with an explanation. We are the proud owners of the most powerful brain to evolve on this planet, and we certainly put it to use. Unfortunately, it didn't come with an owner's manual. Introspection may not lead us to the true causes of our feelings and behavior, but we'll manage to convince ourselves that it did. Richard Nisbett and Tim Wilson referred to this phenomenon as "telling more than we can know" because people's explanations of their feelings and behavior often go beyond what they can reasonably know (Nisbett & Ross, 1980; Nisbett & Wilson, 1977; Wilson, 2002).

In one study, for example, college students recorded their daily moods every day for 5 weeks (Wilson, Laser, & Stone, 1982). The students also kept track of things that might predict their daily moods, such as the weather, their workload, and how much sleep they had gotten the night before. At the end of the 5 weeks, the students estimated how much their mood was related to these other variables. An analysis of the actual data showed that in many cases, people were wrong about what predicted their mood. For example, most people believed that the amount of sleep they got predicted how good a mood they were in the next day when in fact this wasn't true: Amount of sleep was unrelated to people's moods. The participants had introspected and found or generated some logical-sounding theories that in fact weren't always right (Niedenthal & Kitayama, 1994; Wegner, 2002; Wilson, 2002).

What these participants had relied on, at least in part, were their **causal theories**. People have many theories about what influences their feelings and behavior (e.g., "My mood should be affected by how much sleep I got last night") and often use these theories to help them explain why they feel the way they do (e.g., "I'm in a bad mood; I'll bet the fact that I got only 6 hours of sleep last night has a lot to do with it"). We learn many of these theories from the culture in which we grow up—ideas such as absence makes the heart grow fonder, people are in bad moods on Mondays, or people who have been divorced are a poor choice for a successful second marriage. The only problem is that, as discussed in Chapter 3, our schemas and theories are not always correct and thus can lead to incorrect judgments about the causes of our actions.

Consider this example of causal theories in action from researchers who have studied them. One night, Dick Nisbett and Tim Wilson were meeting in an office at the University of Michigan. They were trying to think of ways to test the hypothesis that introspection often can't tell us why people feel the way they do and that they rely on causal theories when trying to uncover the reasons for their feelings, judgments, and actions. Brilliant insights were not bubbling forth, and the researchers were frustrated by their lack of progress. Then they realized that a source of their frustration (or so they thought) was the annoying whine of a vacuum cleaner that a custodial worker was operating right outside the office. Because it took them a while to realize that the noise of the vacuum was disrupting their meeting, they experienced what seemed like an inspiration. Maybe distracting background noises were an example of the very kind of occurrence they were looking for—one that would influence people's judgments but, because their causal theories did not adequately cover this possibility, would be overlooked when people explained their behavior.

Nisbett and Wilson (1977) designed a study to test this possibility (after shutting the door). They showed people a documentary in the presence of an annoying noise. About a minute into the film, a construction worker (played by Dick Nisbett) turned on a power saw right outside the door to the room in which the film was shown and ran the machine intermittently for several seconds until Tim Wilson, the experimenter, went to the door and asked him to please stop sawing until the film was over. At the end of the film, the participants rated how much they had enjoyed it; then the experimenter asked them to indicate whether the noise had influenced their evaluations. To see if the noise really did have an effect, there was a control condition in which other participants viewed the film without any distracting noise. The hypothesis was that the noise would lower people's evaluation of the film, but that people would not realize the noise was responsible for their negative evaluation.

Does this seem like a reasonable hypothesis? It did to the researchers, but as it turned out, they were completely wrong. The participants who watched the film with the annoying background noise did not like it any less than those who saw the film without the distracting noise (in fact, they liked the film slightly more). When the participants were asked how much the noise had influenced their ratings, however, their hypothesis agreed with Nisbett and Wilson's. Even though the noise had no detectable effect on people's feelings about the film, it influenced their *explanations* for their feelings: Most reported that the noise had lowered their ratings of the film. In this case, both the participants and the researchers had the same causal theory, but the theory wasn't true—at least not when it came to watching a documentary while hearing construction noise.

> We can never, even by the strictest examination, get completely behind the secret springs of action.
>
> Immanuel Kant

Causal Theories
Theories about the causes of one's own feelings and behaviors; often we learn such theories from our culture (e.g., "absence makes the heart grow fonder")

In an episode of the TV program *Friends*, Ross made a list of the reasons why he liked and disliked Rachel. According to research on self-generated attitude change, the act of making this list might have changed his mind about how he felt.

Reasons-Generated Attitude Change
Attitude change resulting from thinking about the reasons for one's attitudes; people assume their attitudes match the reasons that are plausible and easy to verbalize

We do not mean to imply that people rely solely on their causal theories when introspecting about the reasons for their feelings and behaviors. In addition to culturally learned causal theories, people have a great deal of information about themselves, such as how they have responded in the past and what they happen to have been thinking about before making a choice (Gavanski & Hoffman, 1987; Wilson, 2002). The fact remains, however, that introspecting about our past actions and current thoughts does not always yield the right answer about why we feel the way we do (Wilson & Bar-Anan, 2008).

The Consequences of Introspecting about Reasons In an episode of the old television show *Friends*, Ross faces a dilemma. Rachel, whom he has pursued for years, has finally showed a romantic interest in him, and they shared their first kiss. The problem is that Ross is currently dating Julie, whom he also likes a great deal. What to do? Urged on by his friends Chandler and Joey, Ross makes a list of the things he likes and dislikes about each woman to try to clarify his thoughts. Was this a good idea?

Probably not. Tim Wilson and his colleagues have found that analyzing the reasons for our feelings is not always the best strategy and in fact can make matters worse (Wilson, 2002; Wilson, Dunn, Kraft, & Lisle, 1989; Wilson, Hodges, & LaFleur, 1995). As we have just seen, it is often difficult to know exactly why we feel the way we do about something, so we bring to mind reasons that sound plausible. The reasons that sound plausible, however, may not be the correct reasons. Even worse, we might convince ourselves that these reasons are correct, thereby changing our minds about how we feel to match our reasons.

Consider people like Ross who try to analyze exactly why they feel the way they do about a romantic partner. When people list reasons in this manner, they often change their attitudes toward their partners, at least temporarily (Wilson, Dunn, Bybee, Hyman, & Rotondo, 1984; Wilson & Kraft, 1993). Why? It is difficult to dissect the exact causes of our romantic feelings, so we latch on to reasons that sound good and that happen to be on our minds (remember our friend who claimed he was in love with a woman because she played the saxophone?). In Wilson's studies, people report such reasons as how well they communicate with their dating partner and how similar they are in their interests and backgrounds. Though these reasons may often be correct, people probably overlook other reasons that are not so easy to verbalize, such as the special chemistry that can exist between two people.

The trouble is that reasons that sound plausible to people and are easy to verbalize sometimes imply a different attitude from the one they had before. Suppose that things are going well between you and your dating partner, but you have trouble verbalizing exactly why this is so. What comes to mind is some annoying habit your partner has, such as chewing gum loudly. "That gum smacking is really irritating," you might think. "I'm not sure I can stay with a person who does that." Consequently, you are likely to change your mind about how you feel, resulting in **reasons-generated attitude change**, which is attitude change resulting from thinking about the reasons for your attitudes; you assume that your attitudes match the reasons that are plausible and easy to generate (Wilson & Kraft, 1993). Over time, though, the effects of analyzing reasons tends to wear off, and people's original "hard to explain" attitudes return. Thus, if people make important decisions right after analyzing reasons—such as deciding whether to break up with their boyfriend or girlfriend—they might make a decision they later regret. This is because right after analyzing reasons people tend to focus on the things that are easy to put into words (e.g., the gum chewing) and ignore feelings that are hard to explain (e.g., that special chemistry). But it is the hard-to-explain feelings that often matter in the long run (Halberstadt & Levine, 1997; Reifman, Larrick, Crandall, & Fein, 1996; Sengupta & Fitzsimons, 2004; Wilson, Lindsey, & Schooler, 2000).

In sum, it is often difficult for people to know exactly why they feel the way they do, and it can be dangerous to think too much about one's reasons. If introspection has its limits, how else might we find out what sort of person we are and what our attitudes are? We turn now to another source of self-knowledge—observations of our own behavior.

Knowing Ourselves by Observing Our Own Behavior
通过观察自己的行为来认识自己

Suppose that a friend of yours asks you how much you like classical music. You hesitate because you never listened to classical music much when you were growing up, but lately you have found yourself listening to symphonies every now and then. "Well, I don't know," you reply. "I guess I like some kinds of classical music. Just yesterday, I listened to a Beethoven symphony on the radio while I was driving to work." If so, you used an important source of self-knowledge: observations of one's own behavior (in this case, what you chose to listen to).

Self-perception theory argues that when our attitudes and feelings are uncertain or ambiguous, we infer these states by observing our behavior and the situation in which it occurs (Bem, 1972). Let's consider each part of this theory. First, we infer our inner feelings from our behavior only when we are not sure how we feel. If you've always known that you love classical music, you do not need to observe your behavior to figure this out (Andersen, 1984; Andersen & Ross, 1984). Maybe, though, your feelings are murky; you've never really thought about how much you like it. If so, you are especially likely to use your behavior as a guide to how you feel (Chaiken & Baldwin, 1981; Wood, 1982).

Second, people judge whether their behavior really reflects how they feel or whether it was the situation that made them act that way. If you freely choose to listen to the classical music station—no one makes you do it—you are especially likely to conclude that you listen to that station because you like classical music. If it is your spouse and not you who turned to the station playing Beethoven, you are unlikely to conclude that you listen to classical music in your car because you like it.

Sound familiar? In Chapter 4, we discussed attribution theory—the way in which people infer someone else's attitudes and feelings by observing that person's behavior. According to self-perception theory, people use the same attributional principles to infer their own attitudes and feelings. For example, if you were trying to decide whether a friend likes classical music, you would observe her behavior and explain why she behaved that way. You might notice, for example, that she is always listening to classical music in the absence of any situational pressures or constraints—no one makes her play those Mozart CDs. You would make an internal attribution for her behavior and conclude that she likes Mozart. Self-perception theory says we infer our own feelings in the same way: We observe our behavior and explain it to ourselves; that is, we make an attribution about why we behaved that way (Albarracin & Wyer, 2000; Laird, 2007; Olson & Stone, 2005; Wilson, 2002). A large number of studies have supported self-perception theory, as we will now see.

Intrinsic Versus Extrinsic Motivation Imagine that you are an elementary school teacher who wants your students to develop a love of reading. Not only do you want your students to read more, but you also want them to develop a love of books. How might you go about accomplishing this? It is not going to be easy, because so many other things compete for your students' attention, such as television, video games, and text messaging.

If you are like many educators, you might decide that a good approach would be to reward the children for reading. Maybe that will get them to put down those cell phones and pick up a book—and develop a love of reading in the process. Teachers have always rewarded kids with a smile or a gold star on an assignment, of course, but recently they have turned to more powerful incentives. A chain of pizza restaurants offers elementary school students in some school districts a certificate for a free pizza when they have read a certain number of books (see "Book It!" at www.bookitprogram.com). In others, teachers offer candy, brownies, and toys for academic achievement (Perlstein, 1999).

> *I've always written poems . . . I never know what I think until I read it in one of my poems.*
> —Virginia Hamilton Adair

Self-Perception Theory
The theory that when our attitudes and feelings are uncertain or ambiguous, we infer these states by observing our behavior and the situation in which it occurs

Many programs try to get children to read more by rewarding them. But do these programs increase or decrease a child's love of reading?

Intrinsic Motivation

The desire to engage in an activity because we enjoy it or find it interesting, not because of external rewards or pressures

Extrinsic Motivation

The desire to engage in an activity because of external rewards or pressures, not because we enjoy the task or find it interesting

Overjustification Effect

The tendency for people to view their behavior as caused by compelling extrinsic reasons, making them underestimate the extent to which it was caused by intrinsic reasons

Several years ago, Mel Steely, a professor at West Georgia College, decided to offer underprivileged children an even more lucrative reward. He started a program called Earning by Learning in which low-income children were offered $2 for every book they read. The program has since been expanded to schools in several states, including Florida, North Carolina, Texas, and Washington (Kimel, 2001). In Dallas, for example, more than 66,000 students have read over 650,000 books (see "Earning by Learning of Dallas" at www.eblofdallas.org/).

There is no doubt that rewards are powerful motivators and that pizzas and money will get kids to read more. One of the oldest and most fundamental psychological principles is that giving a reward each time a behavior occurs will increase the frequency of that behavior. Whether it be a rat pressing a bar to obtain a food pellet or a child reading to get a free pizza, rewards can change behavior.

But people are not rats, and we have to consider the effects of rewards on what's inside—people's thoughts about themselves, their self-concept, and their motivation to read in the future. Does being paid to read, for example, change people's ideas about *why* they are reading? The danger of reward programs such as Earning by Learning is that kids will begin to think they are reading to earn money, not because they find reading to be an enjoyable activity in its own right. When the reward programs end and dollars or pizzas are no longer forthcoming, children may actually read less than they did before.

This is especially likely to happen to children who already liked to read. Such children have high **intrinsic motivation**—the desire to engage in an activity because they enjoy it or find it interesting, not because of external rewards or pressures (Durik & Harackiewicz, 2007; Harackiewicz, Durik, & Barron, 2005; Harackiewicz & Elliot, 1993, 1998; Hirt, Melton, McDonald, & Harackiewicz, 1996; Lepper, Corpus, & Iyengar, 2005; Ryan & Deci, 2000). Your reasons for engaging in the activity have to do with you—the enjoyment and pleasure you feel when reading a book. In other words, reading is play, not work.

What happens when the children start getting rewards for reading? Their reading, originally stemming from intrinsic motivation, is now also spurred by **extrinsic motivation**, the desire to engage in an activity because of external rewards or pressures, not because you enjoy the task or find it interesting. According to self-perception theory, rewards can hurt intrinsic motivation. Whereas before many children read because they enjoyed it, now they are reading so that they will get the reward: The unfortunate outcome is that replacing intrinsic motivation with extrinsic motivation makes people lose interest in the activity they initially enjoyed. This result is called the **overjustification effect**, which results when people view their behavior as caused by compelling extrinsic reasons (e.g., a reward), making them underestimate the extent to which their behavior was caused by intrinsic reasons (Deci, Koestner, & Ryan, 1999a, 1999b; Harackiewicz, 1979; Lepper, 1995; Lepper, Henderlong, & Gingras, 1999).

In one study, for example, fourth- and fifth-grade teachers introduced four new math games to their students, and during a 13-day baseline period, they noted how long each child played each math game. As seen in the leftmost line in Figure 5.5,

Copyright © 1995 PEANUTS reprinted by permission of United Features Syndicate, Inc.

the children had some intrinsic interest in the math games initially, in that they played them for several minutes during this baseline period. For the next several days, a reward program was introduced. Now, the children could earn credits toward certificates and trophies by playing the math games. The more time they spent playing the games, the more credits they earned. As the middle line in Figure 5.5 shows, the reward program was effective in increasing the amount of time the children spent on the math games, showing that the rewards were an effective motivator.

The key question is what happened after the program ended and the kids could no longer earn rewards for playing the games. As predicted by the overjustification hypothesis, the children spent significantly less time on the math games than they had initially, before the rewards were introduced (see the rightmost line in Figure 5.5). The researchers determined, by comparing these results to those of a control condition, that it was the rewards that made people like the games less and not the fact that everyone became bored with the games as time went by. In short, the rewards destroyed the children's intrinsic interest in the games; by the end of the study, they were hardly playing the games at all (Greene, Sternberg, & Lepper, 1976).

What can we do to protect intrinsic motivation from the dangers of society's reward system? Fortunately, there are conditions under which overjustification effects can be avoided. Rewards will undermine interest only if interest was high initially (Calder & Staw, 1975; Tang & Hall, 1995). If a child has no interest in reading, then getting him or her to read by offering free pizzas is not a bad idea, because there is no initial interest to undermine.

Also, the type of reward makes a difference. So far, we have discussed **task-contingent rewards**, meaning that people get them only for doing a task, regardless of how well they do it. Sometimes **performance-contingent rewards** are used, whereby the reward depends on how well people perform the task. For example, grades are performance-contingent because you get a high reward (an A) only if you do well. This type of reward is less likely to decrease interest in a task—and may even increase interest—because it conveys the message that you are good at the task (Deci & Ryan, 1985; Sansone & Harackiewicz, 1997). Thus, rather than giving kids a reward for playing math games regardless of how well they do (i.e., a task-contingent reward), it is better to reward them for doing well in math. Even performance-contingent rewards must be used with care because they too can backfire. Although people like the positive feedback these rewards convey, they do not like the apprehension caused by being evaluated (Harackiewicz, 1989; Harackiewicz, Manderlink, & Sansone, 1984). The trick is to convey positive feedback without making people feel nervous and apprehensive about being evaluated.

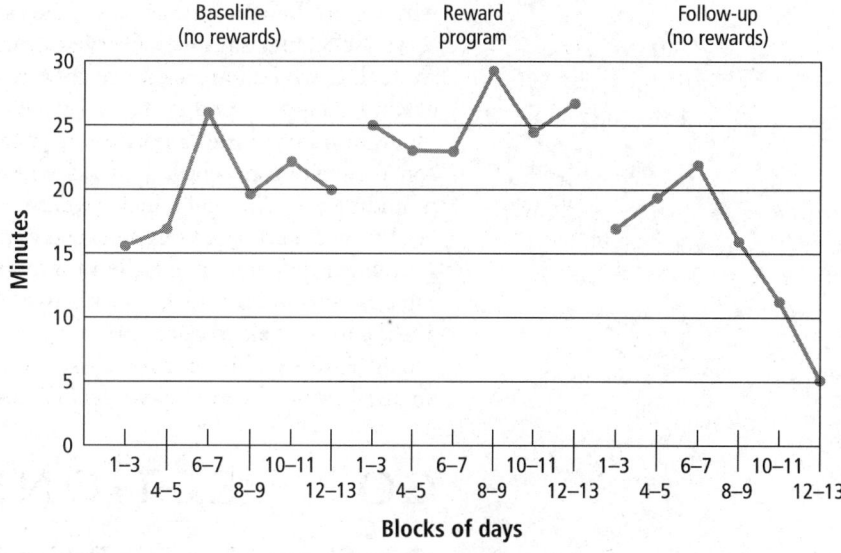

FIGURE 5.5
The overjustification effect.

During the initial baseline phase, researchers measured how much time elementary school children played math games. During the reward program, they rewarded the children with prizes for playing the games. When the rewards were taken away (during the follow-up), the children played the games even less than they had during the baseline phase, indicating that the rewards had lowered their intrinsic interest in the games.

(Adapted from Greene, Sternberg, & Lepper, 1976)

> *I remember that the game [of basketball] lost some of its magical qualities for me once I thought seriously about playing for a living.*
>
> —Bill Russell, 1979

Understanding Our Emotions: The Two-Factor Theory of Emotion Consider how happy, angry, or afraid you feel at any given time. How do you know which emotion you are experiencing? This question probably sounds kind of silly; don't we know how we feel without having to think about it? The way in which we experience emotions, however, has a lot in common with the kinds of self-perception processes we have been discussing.

Stanley Schachter (1964) proposed a theory of emotion that says we infer what our emotions are in the same way that we infer what kind of person we are or how interested we are in math games: In each case, we observe our behavior and then explain

Task-Contingent Rewards
Rewards that are given for performing a task, regardless of how well the task is done

Performance-Contingent Rewards
Rewards that are based on how well we perform a task

why we are behaving that way. The only difference is in the kind of behavior we observe. Schachter says we observe our internal behaviors—how physiologically aroused we feel. If we feel aroused, we then try to figure out what is causing this arousal. For example, suppose you go for a 3-mile run one day and are walking back to your apartment. You go around a corner and nearly walk right into an extremely attractive person from your psychology class whom you are just getting to know. Your heart is pounding and you feel a little sweaty. Is it because love is blossoming between you and your new friend or simply because you just went for a run?

Schachter's theory is called the **two-factor theory of emotion** because understanding our emotional states requires two steps: We must experience physiological arousal, and we must seek an appropriate explanation or label for it. Because our physical states are difficult to label on their own, we use information in the situation to help us make an attribution about why we feel aroused (see Figure 5.6).

CONNECTIONS 链接

How Should Parents Praise Their Children?
父母应怎样赞扬孩子？

If you were to visit a home where parents are helping their children with their homework, you would find the parents doling out a lot of praise, at least in Western cultures. "Nice job on your geography project, Johnny. Your map of South America looks great!" "You got every math problem right, Susie—keep up the good work." Many adults assume that it is beneficial to praise children because it makes them feel good about themselves and enhances their intrinsic motivation. As we saw earlier in this chapter, however, sometimes rewards can actually undermine intrinsic motivation. What should parents do?

The key is the message that the praise conveys (Dweck, 2006; Henderlong & Lepper, 2002; Senko, Durik, & Harackiewicz, 2008). We don't want children to develop a fixed mindset about their abilities, because if they do they won't react well to setbacks ("I guess this C on my spelling test means I'm a lousy speller."). It's better to focus on children's effort ("If you study harder for the next test I bet you'll do better") to encourage a growth mindset, namely the idea that hard work pays off when the going gets tough. When children do well, you shouldn't go overboard and praise them too much for their effort, however, because they might infer that this means they are low on ability, like the player on a basketball team who gets the Best Effort award instead of the Most Valuable Player award. Along with praise for effort, it is a good idea to make children feel that they have gained competence in the area (e.g., "You worked hard on your science project and really learned a lot; you've become quite an expert on plant pesticides"). Note that this praise avoids conveying the fixed mindset (that there is a set amount of ability in this area that people have or don't have). Instead, the praise should convey the message that they gained competence through hard work. This is the mindset that Michael Jordan seemed to have, as seen at the beginning of the chapter. He practiced so hard that he went from a player cut from his high school team to the best player in the world. And by the way, what did his mother tell him when he didn't make his high school team? "I told him to go back and discipline himself," she said. In other words, to work harder—just the right message to foster a growth mindset (Williams, 2001, p. 92).

You may have noticed our comment that parents dole out a lot of praise "in Western cultures." There is some evidence that the situation is different in Eastern cultures, where people have a more interdependent sense of self. Praise is much less frequent in China and Japan because it is viewed as potentially harmful to children's character (Salili, 1996). Also, children in these countries appear to be more intrinsically motivated to begin with and more concerned with the desire to improve their performance (Heine, Lehman, Markus, & Kitayama, 1999; Lewis, 1995). Consequently, praise from adults may not be as necessary to motivate children in these cultures to engage in academic pursuits.

Two-Factor Theory of Emotion
The idea that emotional experience is the result of a two-step self-perception process in which people first experience physiological arousal and then seek an appropriate explanation for it

FIGURE 5.6
The two-factor theory of emotion.

People first experience physiological arousal and then attach an explanation to it.

Imagine that you were a participant in a classic study by Stanley Schachter and Jerome Singer (1962) that tested this theory. When you arrive, the experimenter tells you he is studying the effects of a vitamin compound called Suproxin on people's vision. After a physician injects you with a small amount of Suproxin, the experimenter asks you to wait while the drug takes effect. He introduces you to another participant, who, he says, has also been given some Suproxin. The experimenter gives each of you a questionnaire to fill out, saying he will return in a little while to give you the vision tests.

You look at the questionnaire and notice that it contains some highly personal and insulting questions. For example, one question asks, "With how many men (other than your father) has your mother had extramarital relationships?" (Schachter & Singer, 1962, p. 385). The other participant reacts angrily to these offensive questions, becoming more and more furious, until he finally tears up his questionnaire, throws it on the floor, and stomps out of the room. How do you think you would feel? Would you feel angry as well?

As you've probably guessed, the real purpose of this experiment was not to test people's vision. The researchers set up a situation in which the two crucial variables—arousal and an emotional explanation for that arousal—would be present or absent and then observed which, if any, emotions people experienced. The participants did not really receive an injection of a vitamin compound. Instead, some participants received epinephrine, a hormone produced naturally by the human body that causes arousal (body temperature and heart and breathing rates increase), and the other half received a placebo that had no physiological effects.

Imagine how you would have felt had you received the epinephrine: As you read the insulting questionnaire, you begin to feel aroused. (Remember, the experimenter didn't tell you the shot contained epinephrine, so you don't realize that the injection is making you feel this way.) The other participant—who was actually an accomplice of the experimenter—reacts with rage. You are likely to infer that you are feeling flushed and aroused because you too are angry. You have met the conditions Schachter (1964) argues are necessary to experience an emotion—you are aroused, you have sought out and found a reasonable explanation for your arousal in the situation that surrounds you, and so you become furious. This is indeed what happened—participants who had been given epinephrine reacted much more angrily than participants who had been given the placebo.

A fascinating implication of Schachter's theory is that people's emotions are somewhat arbitrary, depending on what the most plausible explanation for their arousal happens to be. Schachter and Singer (1962) demonstrated this idea in two ways. First, they showed that they could prevent people from becoming angry by providing a nonemotional explanation for why they felt aroused. They did this by informing some of the people who received epinephrine that the injection would increase their heart rate, make their face feel warm and flushed, and cause their hands to shake slightly. When people actually began to feel this way, they inferred that it was not because they were angry but because the injection was taking effect. As a result, these participants did not react angrily to the questionnaire.

> *I could feel all the excitement of losing the big fish going through the transformer and coming out as anger at my brother-in-law.*
>
> —Norman Maclean, *A River Runs Through It*, 1976

Even more impressively, Schachter and Singer showed that they could make participants experience a very different emotion by changing the most plausible explanation for their arousal. In another condition, participants did not receive the insulting questionnaire and the accomplice did not respond angrily. Instead, the accomplice acted in a euphoric, devil-may-care fashion, playing basketball with rolled-up pieces of paper, making paper airplanes, and playing with a Hula-Hoop he found in the corner. How did the real participants respond? If they had received epinephrine but had not been told of its effects, they inferred that they must be feeling happy and euphoric and often joined the accomplice's antics.

The Schachter and Singer experiment has become one of the most famous studies in social psychology because it shows that emotions can be the result of a self-perception process: People look for the most plausible explanation for their arousal. Sometimes the most plausible explanation is not the right one, and so people end up experiencing a mistaken emotion. The people who became angry or euphoric in the Schachter and Singer (1962) study did so because they felt aroused and thought this arousal was due to the obnoxious questionnaire or to the infectious, happy-go-lucky behavior of the accomplice. The real cause of their arousal, the epinephrine, was hidden from them, so they relied on situational cues to explain their behavior.

Misattribution. When people are aroused for one reason, such as occurs when they cross a scary bridge, they often attribute this arousal to the wrong source—such as attraction to the person they are with.

Finding the Wrong Cause: Misattribution of Arousal

To what extent do the results found by Schachter and Singer (1962) generalize to everyday life? (Recall from Chapter 2 that a test of a study's external validity is whether the results hold up outside the lab.) Do people form mistaken emotions in the same way as participants in that study did? In everyday life, one might argue, people usually know why they are aroused. If a mugger points a gun at us and says, "Give me your wallet!" we feel aroused and correctly identify this arousal as fear. If our heart is thumping while we walk on a deserted moonlit beach with the man or woman of our dreams, we correctly label this arousal love or sexual attraction.

Many everyday situations, however, present more than one plausible cause for our arousal, and it is difficult to identify how much of the arousal is due to one source or another. Imagine that you go to see a scary movie with an extremely attractive date. As you are sitting there, you notice that your heart is thumping and you are a little short of breath. Is this because you are wildly attracted to your date or because the movie is terrifying you? It is unlikely that you could say, "Fifty-seven percent of my arousal is due to the fact that my date is gorgeous, 32 percent is due to the scary movie, and 11 percent is due to indigestion from all the popcorn I ate." Because of this difficulty in pinpointing the precise causes of our arousal, we sometimes misidentify our emotions. You might think that most of your arousal is a sign of attraction to your date when in fact a lot of it is due to the movie (or maybe even indigestion).

If so, you have demonstrated **misattribution of arousal**, whereby people make mistaken inferences about what is causing them to feel the way they do (Ross & Olson, 1981; Sinclair, 1994; Thompson, Gold, & Ryckman, 2003; Zillmann, 1978). Consider how this worked in a field experiment by Donald Dutton and Arthur Aron (1974). An attractive young woman asked men visiting a park in British Columbia if they would fill out a questionnaire for her as part of a psychology project on the effects of scenic attractions on people's creativity. When they had finished, she said that she would be happy to explain her study in more detail when she had more time. She tore off a corner of the questionnaire, wrote down her name and phone number, and told the participant to give her a call if he wanted to talk with her some more. How attracted do you think the men were to this woman? Would they telephone her and ask for a date?

This is a hard question to answer. Undoubtedly, it depends on whether the men were dating someone else, how busy they were, and so on. It might also depend, however, on how they interpreted any bodily symptoms they were experiencing. If they were aroused for some extraneous reason, they might mistakenly think some of the arousal is the result of attraction to the young woman. To test this idea, Dutton and Aron (1974) had the woman approach males in the park under two very different circumstances.

In one condition, the men were walking across a 450-foot-long suspension bridge that spanned a deep canyon. The bridge was made of wooden planks attached to wire cables, and as they walked across, they had to stoop to hold on to the low handrail. A little way out over the canyon, the wind tended to catch the bridge and make it wobble from side to side. This is a scary experience, and most people who cross the bridge become more than a little aroused—their heart pounds against their chest, they breathe rapidly, and they begin to perspire. It was at this point that the attractive woman approached a man on the bridge and asked him to fill out her questionnaire. How attracted do you think he felt toward her?

In another condition, the woman waited until men had crossed the bridge and rested for a while on a bench in the park before approaching them. They had a chance to calm down—their hearts were no longer pounding, and their breathing rate had returned to normal. They were peacefully admiring the scenery when the woman asked them to fill out her questionnaire. How attracted were these men to the woman? The prediction from Schachter's two-factor theory is clear: The men approached on the bridge would be considerably more aroused and might mistakenly think some of this arousal is the result of attraction to the beautiful woman. That is exactly what happened. A large proportion of the men approached on the bridge telephoned the woman later to ask her for a date, whereas relatively few of the men approached on the bench telephoned the woman (see Figure 5.7). This type of misattribution of arousal has been found in numerous subsequent studies, in both men and women (e.g., Meston & Frohlich, 2003; Zillmann, 1978). The moral is this: If you encounter an attractive man or woman and your heart is going thump-thump, think carefully about why you are aroused—you might fall in love for the wrong reasons!

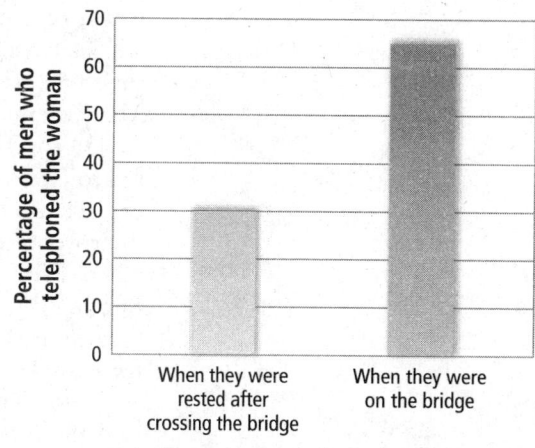

FIGURE 5.7
Misattribution of arousal.

When a woman approached men on a scary bridge and asked them to fill out a questionnaire, a high percentage of them were attracted to her and called her for a date. When the same woman approached men after they had crossed the bridge and had rested, relatively few called her for a date.

(Adapted from Dutton & Aron, 1974)

Misattribution of Arousal
The process whereby people make mistaken inferences about what is causing them to feel the way they do

Interpreting the Social World: Appraisal Theories of Emotion Though many studies have confirmed that people can misattribute the cause of their arousal, sometimes we experience an emotion in a situation in which we don't feel aroused at all. Many events can be viewed in different ways; our emotional reactions depend on how we interpret those events. Suppose that your best friend tells you she was just admitted to one of the top medical schools in the country. What emotion will you feel? A central idea of **appraisal theories of emotion** is that it depends on the way in which you interpret or explain this event, in the absence of any physiological arousal (Ellsworth, 1994; Frijda, 1986; Lazarus, 1995; Ortony, Clore, & Collins, 1988; Roseman & Smith, 2001; Russell & Barrett, 1999; Scherer, Dan, & Flykt, 2006). Two kinds of appraisals are especially important: Do you think the event has good or bad implications for you? And how do you explain what caused the event?

If you have been dreaming all your life about becoming a doctor and you are worried about being admitted to any medical school rather than feeling good about your friend's spectacular acceptance, you might feel envious and resentful: You have interpreted her success as a threat to your own. On the other hand, if you have no desire to go to medical school, you will probably feel happy about her success and may even bask in her reflected glory (Tesser, 1988). The emotion you will feel also depends on how you explain the cause of the event. If you think you contributed to your friend's success (she wouldn't have made it through that tough physics course without your help), you will probably feel pride. (Of course, if you were rejected by that same medical school, you might not feel so happy for the friend who benefited from your help.) If you think she did it entirely on her own, you will probably feel admiration, assuming that you do not feel threatened by her success.

Cognitive appraisals are similar to one of the two factors in Schachter's two-factor theory—the part whereby people try to explain the causes of an event and their reactions to it (see Figure 5.6). The main difference between Schachter's theory and cognitive appraisal theories concerns the role of arousal. According to cognitive appraisal theories, arousal does not always come first; the cognitive appraisals alone are a sufficient cause of emotional reactions. The two theories are not incompatible, however. When people are aroused and not certain where this arousal comes from, how they explain the arousal determines their emotional reaction (Schachter's two-factor theory). When people are not aroused, how they interpret and explain what happens to them determines their emotional reaction (cognitive appraisal theories). The theories agree that one way people learn about themselves is by observing events—including their own behavior—and then trying to explain those events.

Mindsets: Understanding Our Own Abilities 心态：理解我们的能力

As seen in our opening example about Michael Jordan and Mia Hamm, there is another very important kind of self-knowledge—how we explain our own talents and abilities to ourselves. Some people believe that their abilities are set in stone; they either have them or they do not. The psychologist Carol Dweck (2006) calls this a **fixed mindset**—the idea that we have a set amount of an ability that cannot change. According to this view we have a fixed amount of intelligence, athletic ability, musical talent, and so on. Other people have what Dweck calls a **growth mindset**, which is the idea that their abilities are malleable qualities that they can cultivate and grow. Research shows that the mindset people have is crucial to their success: People with the fixed mindset are more likely to give up after setbacks and are less likely to work on and hone their skills; after all, if they fail it must be a sign that they simply don't have what it takes. People with the growth mindset, like Michael Jordan and Mia Hamm, view setbacks as an opportunity to improve through hard work (Cury, da Fonseca, Zahn, & Elliot, 2008).

Mindsets are important not only to athletic performance, but also to how we view any ability, including how good we are at academics. Most students hit a bump in the road when they start college; for you maybe it was a lower grade than you expected on a psychology or math test. How did you react to your disappointing grade? Dweck's

---

Appraisal Theories of Emotion
Theories holding that emotions result from people's interpretations and explanations of events, even in the absence of physiological arousal

Fixed Mindset
The idea that we have a set amount of an ability that cannot change

Growth Mindset
The idea that our abilities are malleable qualities that we can cultivate and grow

In this cartoon, Sally is trying to give her daughter encouragement before she takes her final exams. But, according to research on fixed and growth mindsets, did she say the right thing? As discussed in this chapter, it is better for parents to convey to their children that their abilities are malleable qualities that can grow with hard work (the growth mindset), rather than the idea that abilities are fixed quantities that you either have or do not have.

research shows that the students who have a fixed mindset about intelligence are more likely to give up and do poorly on subsequent tests, whereas those with growth mindsets are more likely to redouble their efforts and do better on subsequent tests. And, she finds that the mindsets themselves can change; people with fixed views can learn to adopt the growth view. Thus, the next time you experience a setback—be it on the athletic field, in your classes, or in your personal relations—you might want to view it as an opportunity to work harder and improve, rather than a sign that you "don't have what it takes."

Using Other People to Know Ourselves 通过他人来认识自己

The self-concept does not develop in a solitary context but is shaped by the people around us. If we never interacted with other people, our own image would be a blur because we would not see ourselves as having selves distinct from other people. Remember the mirror and red-dye test we discussed earlier, used to determine if animals have a self-concept? Variations of this test have been used to show that social contact is indeed crucial to the development of a self-concept. Gordon Gallup (1997) compared the behavior of chimpanzees raised in normal family groupings with that of chimps who were raised alone, in complete social isolation. The socially experienced chimps "passed" the mirror test; after red dye was put on their foreheads and they looked at themselves in a mirror, they immediately used their mirrored image to explore the red areas of their heads. However, the socially isolated chimps did not react to their reflections at all—they did not recognize themselves in the mirror, suggesting that they had not developed a sense of self.

Knowing Ourselves by Comparing Ourselves to Others How do we use others to define ourselves? One way is to measure our own abilities and attitudes by seeing how we stack up against other people. Suppose you work in an office that subscribes to a charity fund: You can deduct from your monthly paycheck whatever you want and have it go to worthy organizations. You decide to donate $50 a month. How generous is this? Should you be feeling particularly proud of your philanthropic nature? One way to answer this question is to compare yourself to others. If you find out that your friend Sue donated only $10 per month, you are likely to feel that you are a very generous person who cares a lot about helping others. If you find out, however, that your friend Sue donated $100 per month, you probably will not view yourself as quite so generous.

This example illustrates **social comparison theory**, which holds that people learn about their own abilities and attitudes by comparing themselves to others (Buunk & Gibbons, 2007; Festinger, 1954; Mussweiler, 2003; Suls & Wheeler, 2000). The theory revolves around two important questions: When do you engage in social comparison? And with whom do you choose to compare yourself? The answer to the first question is that people socially compare when there is no objective standard to measure themselves against and when they experience some uncertainty about themselves

Social Comparison Theory
The idea that we learn about our own abilities and attitudes by comparing ourselves to other people

"Of course you're going to be depressed if you keep comparing yourself with successful people."

in a particular area (Suls & Fletcher, 1983; Suls & Miller, 1977). If the office donation program is new and you are not sure what amount would be generous, you are especially likely to compare yourself to others.

As to the second question—With whom do people compare themselves?—research reveals a surprising answer (Gilbert, Giesler, & Morris, 1995; Mussweiler, Rüter, & Epstude, 2004). People's initial impulse is to compare themselves with anyone who is around, and this initial comparison occurs quickly and automatically (see our discussion of automatic judgment in Chapter 3). After a quick assessment of how our performance compares to others', however, we then decide how appropriate that comparison is, realizing that not all comparisons are equally informative.

Suppose that it is the first day of a college Spanish class and you are wondering about your abilities and how well you will do in the class. With whom should you compare yourself: a student who mentions that she lived in Spain for two years, a student who says she took the course on a lark and has never studied Spanish before, or a student who has a similar background to yours? Not surprisingly, people find it most informative to compare themselves to others who have a similar background in the area in question (Goethals & Darley, 1977; Miller, 1982; Suls, Martin, & Wheeler, 2000). Comparing yourself to a student with a very similar background in Spanish—the one who, like you, took Spanish in high school but has never traveled to a Spanish-speaking country—will be most informative. If that student is doing well in the class, you probably will, too.

If we want to know what excellence is—the top level to which we can aspire—we engage in upward social comparison: We compare ourselves to people who are better than we are on a particular ability (Blanton, Buunk, Gibbons, & Kuyper, 1999). If we want to know the "best of the best" so that we can dream of getting there some day, then clearly we should compare ourselves to the student who lived in Spain and see how well she is doing in the class. In terms of self-knowledge, however, it is often more useful to compare ourselves to someone who is similar to us (Thornton & Arrowood, 1966; Wheeler, Koestner, & Driver, 1982; Zanna, Goethals, & Hill, 1975).

But forming an accurate image of ourselves is only one reason we engage in social comparison—we also use social comparison to boost our egos (Helgeson & Mickelson, 1995). Is it very important to you to believe that you are a fabulous Spanish speaker? Then compare your performance in the class to the student who is taking Spanish for the first time because you will surely have her beat. This use of **downward social comparison**—comparing yourself to people who are worse than you on a particular trait or ability—is a self-protective, self-enhancing strategy (Aspinwall & Taylor, 1993; Buunk, Oldersma, & de Dreu, 2001; Lockwood, 2002; Walton & Cohen, 2003). If you compare yourself to people who are not as well off as you are, you'll feel better about yourself. For example, when interviewed by researchers, the vast majority of cancer patients spontaneously compared themselves to other patients who were more ill than they were, presumably as a way of making them feel more optimistic about the course of their own disease (Wood, Taylor, & Lichtman, 1985).

Another way we can feel better about ourselves is to compare our current performance with our own past performance. In a sense, people use downward social comparison here as well, though the point of comparison is a "past self," not someone else. In one study, people made themselves feel better by comparing their current self with a past self who was worse off. One student, for example, said that her "college self" was more outgoing and sociable than her "high school self," who had been shy and reserved (Ross & Wilson, 2003; Wilson & Ross, 2000).

In short, the nature of our goals affects the comparisons we make. When we want an accurate assessment of our abilities and opinions, we compare ourselves to people

> *There is little satisfaction in the contemplation of heaven for oneself if one cannot simultaneously contemplate the horrors of hell for others.*
>
> —P. D. James, *The Children of Men*, 1992

Downward Social Comparison
Comparing ourselves to people who are worse than we are on a particular trait or ability

who are similar to us. When we want information about what we can strive toward, we make **upward social comparisons**. Finally, when our goal is self-enhancement, we compare ourselves to those who are less fortunate (including our past selves); such downward comparisons make us look better by comparison.

Knowing Ourselves by Adopting Other People's Views As we just saw, sometimes we use other people as a measuring stick to assess our own abilities. When it comes to our views of the social world, however, often we adopt the views our friends hold. Have you ever noticed that people who hang out together tend to see the world in the same way? Maybe the roommates in the apartment across the hall were all supporters of Barack Obama during the 2008 presidential campaign and all enjoy watching *American Idol* together, whereas the roommates in the apartment next door strongly favored John McCain and are big fans of the *The Real World*. One explanation for people holding common views, of course, is that people who have similar views are attracted to each other and are more likely to form social bonds than people who have dissimilar views. In Chapter 10 we will see that indeed, birds of a feather do tend to flock together (Newcomb, 1961).

Another explanation is that under some conditions people adopt the views of the people they hang out with. Charles Cooley (1902) called this the "looking glass self," by which he meant that we see ourselves and the social world through the eyes of other people and often adopt those views. According to more recent research, this is especially true when two people want to get along with each other (Hardin & Higgins, 1996; Lun, Sinclair, Whitchurch, & Glenn, 2007; Sinclair, Huntsinger, Skorinko, & Hardin, 2005). If a close friend thinks that *The Real World* is the best TV show ever made, you will probably like it as well.

Perhaps it is no surprise that friends influence what each other thinks. What is more surprising is that such **social tuning**, the process whereby people adopt another person's attitudes, can happen even when we meet someone for the first time, if we want to get along with that person. And, social tuning can happen unconsciously. Imagine, for example, that you were a participant in a study by Stacey Sinclair and her colleagues (Sinclair, Lowery, Hardin, & Colangelo, 2005). When you arrive, the experimenter acts in either a likable or unlikable manner. In the likable condition she thanks you for participating and offers you some candy from a bowl, whereas in the unlikable condition she pushes the bowl of candy to the side and exclaims, "Just ignore this; some of the experimenters in my lab like to give subjects candy for their participation, but I think you are lucky just to get credit" (Sinclair et al., 2005, p. 588). You then sit at a computer and complete a simple task, on which you press one key every time the word "good" appears on the screen and another whenever the word "bad" appears.

Unbeknownst to you, the computer task is a measure of automatic prejudice. A photograph of a white or black face is flashed very rapidly right before the word "good" or "bad" appears. The faces are flashed so quickly that you do not consciously see them, and the computer measures how long it takes you to respond to the words. Previous research has shown that such subliminal flashes can influence people under controlled laboratory conditions (see Chapter 7 for a discussion of this research). In the present study, the assumption was that if people are prejudiced toward blacks, then they should respond relatively quickly to the word "bad" when it was preceded by a black face and relatively slowly to the word "good" when it was preceded by a black face.

To see if people "tuned" their views to the experimenter, the researchers altered one other thing: In half of the sessions the experimenter wore a T-shirt that expressed antiracism views ("Eracism"), and in half of the sessions she did not. The question was, did people unconsciously adopt the experimenter's antiracist views more when she was likable than when she was not? As seen in Figure 5.8, the answer was yes. When the experimenter was likable, participants showed less automatic prejudice when she was wearing the antiracism T-shirt than when she was not. Without

> Most people are other people. Their thoughts are someone else's opinions, their lives a mimicry, their passions a quotation.
> —Oscar Wilde, 1905

> The truth is, we never know for sure about ourselves . . . Only after we've done a thing do we know what we'll do. . . . [That] is why we have spouses and children and parents and colleagues and friends, because someone has to know us better than we know ourselves.
> —Richard Russo, *Straight Man*, 1997

Upward Social Comparison
Comparing ourselves to people who are better than we are on a particular trait or ability

Social Tuning
The process whereby people adopt another person's attitudes

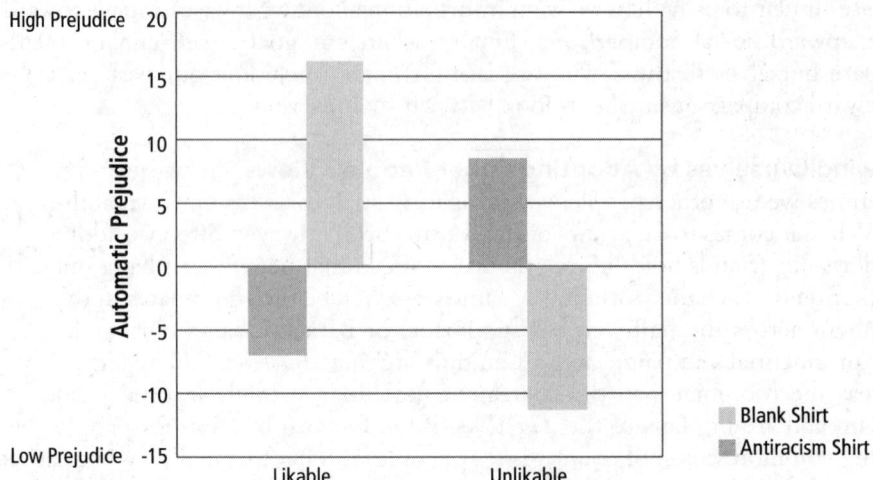

FIGURE 5.8
Social tuning to a likable experimenter.

Participants took a test of automatic prejudice toward blacks, after interacting with an experimenter who was likable or unlikable and wore an antiracism t-shirt or a blank t-shirt. When the experimenter was likable, participants showed less automatic prejudice when she was wearing the antiracism t-shirt than when she was not (the higher the number on the scale, the more the anti-black prejudice). When the experimenter was unlikable, participants reacted against her views: They showed more automatic prejudice when she was wearing the antiracist t-shirt than when she was not. These results show that people tend to automatically adopt the views of people they like, but automatically reject the views of people they do not.

(Adapted from Sinclair, Lowery, Hardin, & Colangelo, 2005)

even knowing it, they "tuned" their views toward hers. What about when she was unlikable? As seen in Figure 5.8, participants seemed to react against her views: They showed more automatic prejudice when she was wearing the antiracist T-shirt than when she was not. These results show that we tend to automatically adopt the views of people we like, but automatically reject the views of people we do not.

Self-Control: The Executive Function of the Self 自我控制：自我的执行功能

Sarah has vowed to take the high road with her ex-boyfriend Jake, letting bygones be bygones and just forgetting about all the stupid things he did. "That's ancient history," she thinks. "Time to move on." One night she runs into Jake at party and wouldn't you know it, there he is with her friend Meghan, whom Jake swore he wasn't interested in. Sarah is sorely tempted to make a scene and tell them both off, but she grits her teeth, puts on her best smile, and acts as if she is the belle of the ball. She is proud of herself, but a little while later she finds herself devouring a bowl of potato chips, even though she had promised herself to eat a healthy diet and shed a few pounds. In this example Sarah is doing something familiar to us all—trying to exert self-control. She succeeds in one case—suppressing her desire to tell off her ex-boyfriend, but fails in another, her desire to eat a healthy diet. What determines how successful we are at exerting self-control?

Another important function of the self is to be the chief executive who makes choices about what to do in the present and plans for the future (Baumeister, Schmeichel, & Vohs, 2007; Carver & Scheier, 1998; Higgins, 1989, 2005; Leary, 2004). We appear to be the only species, for example, that can imagine events that have not yet occurred and engage in long-term planning, and it is the self that does this planning and exerts control over our actions (Gilbert, 2006). Regulating our behavior and choices in optimal ways, of course, can be easier said than done, as anyone who has been on a diet or tried to quit smoking knows.

In Chapter 3 we talked about one form of self-control that does not work very well and often backfires, namely *thought suppression*, whereby we try to push thoughts out of our minds. Often, the more we try not to think about something, such as an ex-boyfriend or the chips on the buffet table, the more those very thoughts keep coming to mind. A better strategy is to go ahead and think about the forbidden topic while trying to exert will power when it comes to acting on those thoughts. Often, of course, this is easier said than done. When are we likely to succeed? The answer, according to the *self-regulatory resource model*, is to make sure that we have plenty of energy when we are trying to control our actions (Baumeister & Hetherington, 1996; Baumeister, Vohs, & Tice, 2007; Schmeichel & Baumeister, 2004). According to this approach self-control requires energy, and spending this energy on one task limits the amount that can be spent on another task, just as going for a 5-mile run makes it difficult to immediately play a game of basketball.

To test this idea, researchers ask participants to exert self-control on one task, to see if this reduces their ability to exert control on a subsequent and completely unrelated task. In one study, for example, people who were instructed to suppress a thought (don't think about a white bear) were worse at trying to regulate their emotions on a second task (try not to laugh while watching a comedy film), compared to people who did not first have to suppress their thoughts (Muraven, Tice, & Baumeister, 1998). Although the tasks were quite different, the researchers suggest that the first one depleted the resource people use to control their behaviors and feelings, making it difficult to engage in a subsequent act of self-control. This is why Sarah found it hard to avoid eating the potato chips—she had used up a lot of energy when checking her impulse to tell off her ex-boyfriend, making it difficult to exert self-control on something else.

Exactly what is this "energy" that we spend when exerting self-control? Recent research suggests that it is the level of glucose in the bloodstream at any given point (Gailliot & Baumeister, 2007). Glucose, a form of sugar, can be thought of as the fuel that supplies energy to the brain, and when people try hard to control their own actions, they need a lot of that fuel. Thus, if they use it up on one task (smiling sweetly to one's ex-boyfriend), there is less blood glucose available to fuel self-control on another task (avoiding the bowl of potato chips). The implications? Eat a healthy, regular diet without skipping meals, because we get blood glucose from food. One study found that people who drank lemonade sweetened with sugar were better able to exert self-control than people who drank lemonade with an artificial sweetener (Masicampo & Baumeister, 2008). Don't go overboard by loading up your diet with sugar, bercause that can have obvious negative effects (e.g., weight gain), and there is only so much your brain can use. But, if you know that you are going to have to grit your teeth and try hard to control yourself in the near future—you know your ex-boyfriend or ex-girlfriend is going to be at the party—eating a little more sugar before you go might not be a bad idea.

> Keep up appearances whatever you do.
>
> Charles Dickens, 1843

Impression Management: All the World's a Stage 印象管理：世界是个大舞台

In 1991, David Duke decided to run for governor of Louisiana as a mainstream conservative Republican. He had some obstacles to overcome in convincing people to vote for him because for most of his adult life he had been a white supremacist and anti-Semite who in 1989 had sold Nazi literature from his office ("Duke," 1991). To improve his appeal, he claimed that he no longer supported Nazi ideology or the Ku Klux Klan, of which he had been a leader (or Grand Wizard) in the 1970s. He also tried to improve his appearance by undergoing facial cosmetic surgery. Duke's campaign rhetoric didn't fool too many Louisiana voters. They perceived the same racist message disguised in new clothes, and he was defeated by the Democratic candidate, Edwin Edwards. In 2003, he was sentenced to 15 months in federal prison for allegedly using funds raised from supporters for personal investments and gambling (Murr & Smalley, 2003).

Impression management in action: In the 1970s, David Duke was a leader in the Ku Klux Klan; in 1991, he ran for governor of Louisiana as a mainstream conservative Republican. A remarkable change occurred in Duke's presentation of self during this time. Besides undergoing facial cosmetic surgery to improve his appearance, he claimed during his campaign that he no longer supported Nazi ideology or the Ku Klux Klan.

Though few politicians attempt as extreme a makeover as David Duke did, managing public opinion is hardly a new concept in politics. President John F. Kennedy presented himself as a healthy, vigorous man ready to face any challenge that came his way when in fact he suffered from degenerative bone disease and chronic back pain and was under heavy medication for much of his presidency (Dallek, 2002).

These are extreme examples of **impression management**, which is the attempt by people to get others to see them the way they want to be seen (Goffman, 1959; Knowles & Sibicky, 1990; Leary, 2004; Murphy, 2007; Schlenker, 2003; Spencer, Fein, Zanna, & Olson, 2003). Just as politicians try to put the best possible spin on their actions and manage the impressions others have of them, so do we in our everyday lives. As Erving Goffman (1959) pointed out, we are all like stage actors who are trying our best to convince the "audience" (the people around us) that we are a certain way, even if we really are not.

People have many different impression management strategies (Jones & Pittman, 1982). One is **ingratiation**—using flattery or praise to make yourself likable to another, often a higher-status person (Brodsky, 2004; Jones & Wortman, 1973; Vonk, 2002). We can ingratiate through compliments, by agreeing with another's ideas, by commiserating and offering sympathy, and so on. If your boss drones on at a staff meeting, nearly putting the entire office to sleep, and you say, "Great job today, Sue. Loved your presentation," you are probably ingratiating. Ingratiation is a powerful technique because we all enjoy having someone be nice to us—which is what the ingratiator is good at. However, such a ploy can backfire if the recipient of your ingratiation senses that you're being insincere (Jones, 1964; Kauffman & Steiner, 1968).

Another strategy, and the one that has attracted the most research attention, is **self-handicapping**. In this case, people create obstacles and excuses for themselves so that if they do poorly on a task, they can avoid blaming themselves. Doing poorly or failing at a task is damaging to your self-esteem. In fact, just doing less well than you expected or than you have in the past can be upsetting, even if it is a good performance. How can you prevent this disappointment? Self-handicapping is a rather surprising solution: You can set up excuses before the fact, just in case you do poorly (Arkin & Oleson, 1998; Jones & Berglas, 1978; McCrea, 2008; Rhodewalt & Vohs, 2005).

Let's say it's the night before the final exam in one of your courses. It's a difficult course, required for your major, and one in which you'd like to do well. A sensible

Impression Management
The attempt by people to get others to see them as they want to be seen

Ingratiation
The process whereby people flatter, praise, and generally try to make themselves likable to another person, often of higher status

Self-Handicapping
The strategy whereby people create obstacles and excuses for themselves so that if they do poorly on a task, they can avoid blaming themselves

strategy would be to eat a good dinner, study for a while, and then go to bed early and get a good night's sleep. The self-handicapping strategy would be to pull an all-nighter, do some heavy partying, and then wander into the exam the next morning bleary-eyed and muddle-headed. If you don't do well on the exam, you have an excuse to offer to others to explain your performance, one that deflects the potential negative, internal attribution they might otherwise make (that you're not smart). If you ace the exam, well, so much the better—you did it under adverse conditions (no sleep), which suggests that you are especially bright and talented.

There are two major ways in which people self-handicap. In its more extreme form, people create obstacles that reduce the likelihood they will succeed on a task so that if they do fail, they can blame it on these obstacles rather than on their lack of ability. The obstacles people have been found to use include drugs, alcohol, reduced effort on the task, and failure to prepare for an important event (Deppe & Harackiewicz, 1996; Kimble & Hirt, 2005; Lucas & Lovaglia, 2005; Spalding & Hardin, 1999). Interestingly, research shows that men are more likely to engage in this kind of self-handicapping than women (McCrea, Hirt, & Milner, 2008).

The second type of self-handicapping is less extreme. Rather than creating obstacles to success, people devise ready-made excuses in case they fail (Baumgardner, Lake, & Arkin, 1985; Greenberg, Pyszczynski, & Paisley, 1984; Hirt, Deppe, & Gordon, 1991). We might not go so far as to pull an all-nighter the night before an important exam, but we might complain that we are not feeling well. People can arm themselves with all kinds of excuses: They blame their shyness, test anxiety, bad moods, physical symptoms, and adverse events from their past.

A problem with preparing ourselves with excuses in advance, however, is that we may come to believe these excuses and hence exert less effort on the task. Why work hard at something if you are going to do poorly anyway? Self-handicapping may prevent unflattering attributions for our failures, but it often has the adverse effect of causing the poor performance we feared to begin with. Further, even if self-handicappers avoid unflattering attributions about their performance (e.g., people thinking they aren't smart), they risk being disliked by their peers. People do not like others

Virtually all politicians try to manage the impressions they convey to the public, sometimes distorting reality. President John F. Kennedy presented himself as a healthy, vigorous man ready to face any challenge that came his way, when in fact he suffered from degenerative bone disease and chronic back pain, and was under heavy medication for much of his presidency.

whom they perceive as engaging in self-handicapping strategies (Hirt, McCrea, & Boris, 2003; Rhodewalt, Sanbonmatsu, Tschanz, Feick, & Waller, 1995). Women are particularly critical of other people who self-handicap. Thus, as we saw earlier, women are less likely to engage in the kind of self-handicapping in which they put obstacles in their way, and are critical of others who do so (McCrea et al., 2008). Why? Research shows that women place more value on trying hard to achieve something than men do and thus are more critical of people who seem not to try hard and then make up excuses for doing poorly.

Culture, Impression Management, and Self-Enhancement
文化、印象管理和自我提升

People in all cultures are concerned with the impression they make on others, but the nature of this concern and the impression management strategies people use differ considerably from culture to culture (Lalwani, Shavitt, & Johnson, 2006). We have seen, for example, that people in Asian cultures tend to have a more interdependent view of themselves than people in Western cultures do. One consequence of this identity is that "saving face," or avoiding public embarrassment, is extremely important in Asian cultures. In Japan, people are very concerned that they have the "right" guests at their weddings and the appropriate number of mourners at the funerals of their loved ones—so concerned, in fact, that if guests or mourners are unavailable, they can go to a local "convenience agency" and rent some. These agencies (*benriya*) have employees who are willing to pretend—for a fee—that they are your closest friends. A woman named Hiroko, for example, worried that too few guests would attend her second wedding. No problem—she rented six, including a man to pose as her boss, at a cost of $1,500. Her "boss" even delivered a flattering speech about her at the wedding (Jordan & Sullivan, 1995). Although such impression management strategies might seem extreme to Western readers, the desire to manage public impressions is just as strong in the West (as seen by David Duke's attempts to change the way the public viewed him).

> *To succeed in the world, we do everything we can to appear successful.*
> —François de La Rochefoucauld, 1678

HOW WOULD YOU USE THIS? 如何学以致用？

This chapter was concerned with the nature of the self and the way in which people come to know their own attitudes, traits, and abilities. What is this topic doing in a book on social psychology, which is concerned with the way in which people's thoughts and behaviors are influenced by other people? Nothing is as personal as our self-knowledge, but as we have seen even our private thoughts and beliefs are formed in a social context. Can you think of examples from your own life in which your views of yourself were shaped by your parents, friends, or teachers? Or, more broadly, by the community and culture in which you live? (See pages 119–122 on cultural and gender influences on the self.) Now let's turn the question around: Can you think of examples in which you have influenced someone else's self-views, such as a sibling, a close friend, or a romantic partner? Suppose, for example, that you have a friend who could use a bit of a confidence boost; he or she has an unrealistically negative view of his or her abilities (e.g., in academics, music, athletics, driving ability, or whatever). Based on what you have learned in this chapter, can you think of a couple of ways in which you might help this person gain confidence? (See, for example, pages 129–131 on intrinsic versus extrinsic motivation and pages 136–137 on mindsets.)

Summary 总 结

The self-concept refers to the content of our knowledge about ourselves, whereas self-awareness refers to the act of thinking about ourselves. In this chapter we examined three functions of the self: *self-knowledge*, whereby we formulate and organize what we know about ourselves; *self-control*, whereby we make plans and execute decisions; and *self-presentation*, whereby we try to put our best foot forward to others.

- **Self-Knowledge** How do we define who we are? There are a number of cultural and social influences on self-knowledge.
  - **Cultural Differences in Defining the Self** People who grow up in Western cultures tend to have an independent view of the self, whereas people who grow up in Asian cultures tend to have an interdependent view of the self.
  - **Gender Differences in Defining the Self** Women tend to have relational interdependence, focusing more on close relationships, whereas men tend to have collective interdependence, focusing on their membership in larger groups.
  - **Knowing Ourselves Through Introspection** According to self-awareness theory, when people focus on themselves, they evaluate and compare their current behavior to their internal standards and values. According to research on "telling more than we can know," when people introspect about why they feel the way they do, they often use causal theories, many of which are learned from one's culture. When people think about the reasons for their attitudes they assume that their attitudes match the reasons that are plausible and easy to verbalize, leading to reasons-generated attitude change.
  - **Knowing Ourselves by Observing Our Own Behavior** Another way that people gain self-knowledge is by observing their own behavior. Self-perception theory argues that when our attitudes and feelings are uncertain or ambiguous, we infer these states by observing our own behavior and the situation in which it occurs. An overjustification effect occurs when people focus on the extrinsic reasons for their behavior and underestimate their intrinsic reasons. According to the two-factor theory of emotion, emotional experience is the result of a two-step self-perception process in which people first experience arousal and then seek an appropriate explanation for it. Sometimes people make mistaken inferences about what is causing them to be aroused. Appraisal theories argue that emotions result from people's interpretations and explanations of events, even in the absence of physiological arousal.
  - **Mindsets: Understanding Our Own Abilities** Some people have a **fixed mindset** about their abilities, which is the idea that they have a set amount of the ability that cannot change. Others have a **growth mindset**, which is the idea that their abilities are malleable qualities that they can cultivate and grow. People with a fixed mindset are more likely to give up after setbacks and are less likely to work on and hone their skills, whereas people with a growth mindset view setbacks as an opportunity to improve through hard work.
  - **Using Other People to Know Ourselves** Our self-concepts are shaped by the people around us. According to social comparison theory, we learn about our own abilities and attitudes by comparing ourselves to other people. In addition, people tend to automatically adopt the attitudes of those they like and want to interact with.

- **Self-Control: The Executive Function of the Self** Self-control requires energy, and spending this energy on one task limits the amount that can be spent on another task. Recent research suggests that the level of glucose in the bloodstream is the mental "fuel" we spend on self-control.

- **Impression Management: All the World's a Stage** People try to get others to see them as they want to be seen.
  - **Culture, Impression Management, and Self-Enhancement** The desire to manage the image we present to others is strong in all cultures, although the kinds of images we want to present depend on the culture in which we live.

CHAPTER 5 TEST 第5章习题

1. Which of the following statements is *least* true, according to research on self-knowledge?
   a. The best way to "know thyself" is to look inward, introspecting about ourselves.
   b. Sometimes the best way to know ourselves is to see what we do.
   c. We often try to figure ourselves out by comparing ourselves to others.
   d. One way we know ourselves is by using theories we learn from our culture.
   e. The way in which we know ourselves is often similar to the way in which we come to know other people.

2. Your friend Jane is interning at a law firm. When you ask her how it's going, she says, "Fine, I'm doing much better than the intern who started a month after me." What kind of social comparison is Jane making?

a. Upward social comparison
b. Downward social comparison
c. Impression comparison
d. Self-knowledge comparison

3. Suppose you meet Jessica, a student in your psychology class who is very friendly, and you like her immediately. She tells you about her recent trip to France and how much she loved it. Later on at a study abroad session, you find yourself drawn to a program in Paris. This would be an example of
   a. reasons-generated attitude change.
   b. self-perception theory.
   c. social tuning.
   d. misattribution of arousal.
   e. upward social comparison.

4. Elise needs to bear down and study for a test but has been distracted by some family problems she has been having of late. According to research on self-control, which of the following would help her concentrate on her studies? She should
   a. go for a run before studying.
   b. eat a small, sugary snack before studying.
   c. try her best not to think about her family troubles while studying.
   d. compare herself to her roommate, who is a straight-A student.

5. Your little sister enjoys taking time out of her day to make bead necklaces. A birthday party is coming up and you decide you want to give a necklace to each person at the party. She offers to make a necklace for each of your friends, but for added motivation, you give her a dollar for each one she makes. Which of the following is most likely to happen?
   a. After the party, your sister will enjoy making beads *more* than she did before, because you used a task-contingent reward.
   b. After the party, your sister will enjoy making beads *more* than she did before, because you used a performance-contingent reward.
   c. After the party, your sister will enjoy making beads *less* than she did before, because you used a task-contingent reward.
   d. After the party, your sister will enjoy making beads *less* than she did before, because you used a performance-contingent reward.

6. According to research on sex differences in how people define themselves,
   a. women have higher collective interdependence in a family setting.
   b. men are low in relational interdependence only in situations that do not call for emotional sensitivity.
   c. women have lower relational independence.
   d. men have more collective interdependence than women.

7. On Halloween, you decide to do an experiment. When the trick-or-treaters arrive at your house, you have them stand in a line on your front porch. You stay outside with the group, and let each child enter your house individually. You tell them they can take *one* piece of candy from the bowl that is sitting on a table. Half of the time you put the candy bowl in front of a big mirror. The other half of the time, there is no mirror present. All of the children may be tempted to take more than one piece of candy. Which children will be *more* likely to give in to temptation?
   a. Those in the mirror condition
   b. Those who are between 7 and 9 years old
   c. Those in the no mirror condition
   d. Those who experience downward social comparison

8. Catherine did very well on her math test. Which of the following statements should her mother tell her to increase the chances that Catherine will not give up on math if it later becomes more difficult for her?
   a. "You really worked hard for this test and your hard work paid off!"
   b. "You are such a smart kid, you excel in everything you do!"
   c. "You are so good in math, you obviously have a gift for this!"
   d. "I'm so glad to see you are doing better than all your classmates!"
   e. "Being good at math is in our family genes."

9. Michael and Pam are friends but have never dated. Michael wants to ask Pam out on a date, with the hope that she will think of him as more than just a friend. Based on research on overjustification and dissonance theory, under which of the following conditions will Pam like Michael the most?
   a. Michael asks her to go to a Dave Matthews concert. Pam loves the Dave Matthews Band but didn't have a ticket, so she accepts enthusiastically.
   b. Michael asks her to go to a Dave Matthews concert. Pam loves the Dave Matthews Band and didn't have a ticket, but she says no because she has a big paper due that week.
   c. Michael asks her to a Valentine's Day dinner at a restaurant that Pam doesn't like very much, and she accepts.
   d. Michael asks her to a Valentine's Day dinner at a very expensive restaurant that Pam loves, and she accepts.

10. According to self-perception theory, which of the following audience members would enjoy the taping of *The Daily Show with Jon Stewart* the most?
    a. David, who sat right in front of the flashing "applause" sign and noticed that he clapped every time the sign said to.
    b. Stephen, who noticed that he was laughing more than other people.
    c. Zita, whose friends nudged her to get her to clap.
    d. Jimmy, who laughed a lot in order to make his friend Eleanor happy.

Answer Key
1-a 2-b 3-c 4-b 5-c 6-d 7-c 8-a 9-c 10-b

Scoring the TRY IT! exercises "试一试！"答案

Page 120

1. To estimate your degree of interdependence, take the average of your answers to questions 1–5. To estimate your degree of independence, take the average of your answers to questions 6–10. On which measure did you come out higher? Singelis (1994) found that Asian Americans agreed more with the interdependence than the independence items, whereas Caucasian Americans agreed more with the independence than the interdependence items.

Page 122

2. To compute your score, first reverse the rating you gave to questions 8 and 9. That is, if you circled a 1, change it to a 7; if you circled a 2, change it to a 6; if you circled a 7, change it to a 1; and so on. Then add up your answers to the 11 questions. High scores reflect more of a tendency to define yourself in terms of relational interdependence. Cross, Bacon, and Morris (2000) found that women tend to score higher than men; in eight samples of college students, women averaged 57.2 and men averaged 53.4.

Page 126

3. Reverse your answers to questions 2 and 5. If you answered 1 to these questions, change it to a 5; if you answered 2, change it to a 4; and so on. Then add your ratings for all 10 questions. The higher your score, the more likely you are to focus your attention on yourself. Fenigstein, Scheier, and Buss (1975) found that the average score was 26 in a sample of college students.

6

The Need to Justify Our Actions

The Costs and Benefits of Dissonance Reduction

合理化行为的需要：

A DECADE AGO, 39 PEOPLE WERE FOUND DEAD AT A luxury estate in Rancho Santa Fe, California—participants in a mass suicide. They were all members of an obscure cult called Heaven's Gate, founded by Marshall Herff Applewhite, a former college professor. Each body was laid out neatly, feet clad in brand-new black Nikes, face covered with a purple shroud. The cult members died willingly and peacefully—and didn't really consider it suicide. They left behind detailed videotapes describing their beliefs and intentions: They believed that the Hale-Bopp Comet, at the time clearly visible in the western sky, was their ticket to a new life in paradise. They were convinced that Hale-Bopp's wake was a gigantic spaceship whose mission was to carry them off to a new incarnation. To be picked up by the spaceship, they first needed to rid themselves of their current "containers." That is, they needed to leave their own bodies by ending their lives. Alas, no spaceship ever came.

Several weeks before the mass suicide, when Hale-Bopp was still too distant to be seen with the naked eye, some members of the cult walked into a specialty store and purchased a very expensive high-powered telescope. They wanted to get a clearer view of the comet and the spaceship that they believed was traveling behind it. A few days later, they made their way back to the store, returned the telescope, and politely asked for their money back. When the store manager asked them if they had problems with the scope, they replied, "Well, gosh, we found the comet, but we can't find anything following it" (Ferris, 1997). Although the store manager tried to convince them that there was nothing wrong with the telescope and that there was nothing following the comet, they remained unconvinced. Their attitude was clear, and given their premise, their logic was impeccable: We know an alien spaceship is following behind the Hale-Bopp Comet. If an expensive telescope failed to reveal that spaceship, there must be something wrong with the telescope.

Their thinking might strike you as strange, irrational, or stupid, but generally speaking, the members of the Heaven's Gate cult were not stupid, irrational, or crazy people. Neighbors who knew them considered them pleasant, smart, reasonable individuals. Moreover, they were expert at using computers and the Internet and earned their living setting up highly innovative Web pages. Clients who worked closely with them were impressed, describing them as unusually bright, talented, and creative. What is the process by which intelligent, sane people can succumb to such fantastic thinking and self-destructive behavior? We will attempt to

OUTLINE 提 纲

- Maintaining a Stable, Positive Self-Image

    The Theory of Cognitive Dissonance

    Rational Behavior versus Rationalizing Behavior

    Decisions, Decisions, Decisions

    Dissonance, the Brain, and Evolution

    Justifying Your Effort

    The Psychology of Insufficient Justification

    Advocacy and Hypocrisy Applied to Social Problems

    Good and Bad Deeds

    Culture and Dissonance

    CONNECTIONS: Dissonance Theory Used by Mainstream Journalist to Explain the Actions of Suicide Bombers

- Some Final Thoughts on Dissonance: Learning from Our Mistakes

- Heaven's Gate Revisited

- Summary

explain their actions near the end of this chapter. For now, we will simply state that their behavior is not unfathomable—it is simply an extreme example of a normal human tendency: the need to justify our actions.

Maintaining a Stable, Positive Self-Image
保持稳定、积极的自我形象

During the past half-century, social psychologists have discovered that one of the most powerful determinants of human behavior stems from our need to preserve a stable, positive self-image (Aronson, 1969, 1998; Tavris & Aronson, 2008; Wicklund & Brehm, 1998). Most of us have moderate to high self-esteem. Like the mythical residents of Garrison Keilor's Lake Wobegon, we need to believe that we are above average. For example, in a survey of a million high school students, only 2 percent stated that they were below average in their leadership ability (Gilovich 1991).

But maintaining this belief is not always easy. As we go through life, we encounter a great many challenges to it. The topic of this chapter is how human beings deal with those challenges.

> *When the heart speaks, the mind finds it indecent to object.*
> —Milan Kundera

The Theory of Cognitive Dissonance 认知失调理论

Most of us have a need to see ourselves as reasonable, moral, and smart. When we are confronted with information implying that we may have behaved in ways that are irrational, immoral, or stupid, we experience a good deal of discomfort. This feeling of discomfort caused by performing an action that runs counter to one's customary (typically positive) conception of oneself is referred to as **cognitive dissonance**. A half-century of research has demonstrated that cognitive dissonance is a major motivator of human thought and behavior. Leon Festinger (1957) was the first to investigate the precise workings of this powerful phenomenon and elaborated his findings into what is arguably social psychology's most important and most provocative theory, the theory of cognitive dissonance. At first, social psychologists believed that cognitive dissonance could be caused by *any* two conflicting cognitions (thoughts or opinions) (Brehm & Cohen, 1962; Festinger, 1957; Festinger & Aronson, 1960). But later research made it clear that not all cognitive inconsistencies are equally upsetting. Rather, we discovered that dissonance is most powerful and most upsetting when people behave in ways that threaten their self-esteem. This is upsetting precisely because it forces us to confront the discrepancy between who we *think* we are and how we have in fact behaved (Aronson, 1968, 1969, 1992, 1998; Greenwald & Ronis, 1978).

Cognitive Dissonance
A drive or feeling of discomfort, originally defined as being caused by holding two or more inconsistent cognitions and subsequently defined as being caused by performing an action that is discrepant from one's customary, typically positive self-conception

Cognitive dissonance always produces discomfort, and in response, we try to reduce it. The process is very similar to the effects of hunger and thirst: Discomfort motivates us to eat or drink. But unlike satisfying hunger or thirst by eating or drinking, the path to reducing dissonance is not always simple or obvious. In fact, it can lead to fascinating changes in the way we think about the world and the way we behave. How can we reduce dissonance? There are three basic ways (see Figure 6.1):

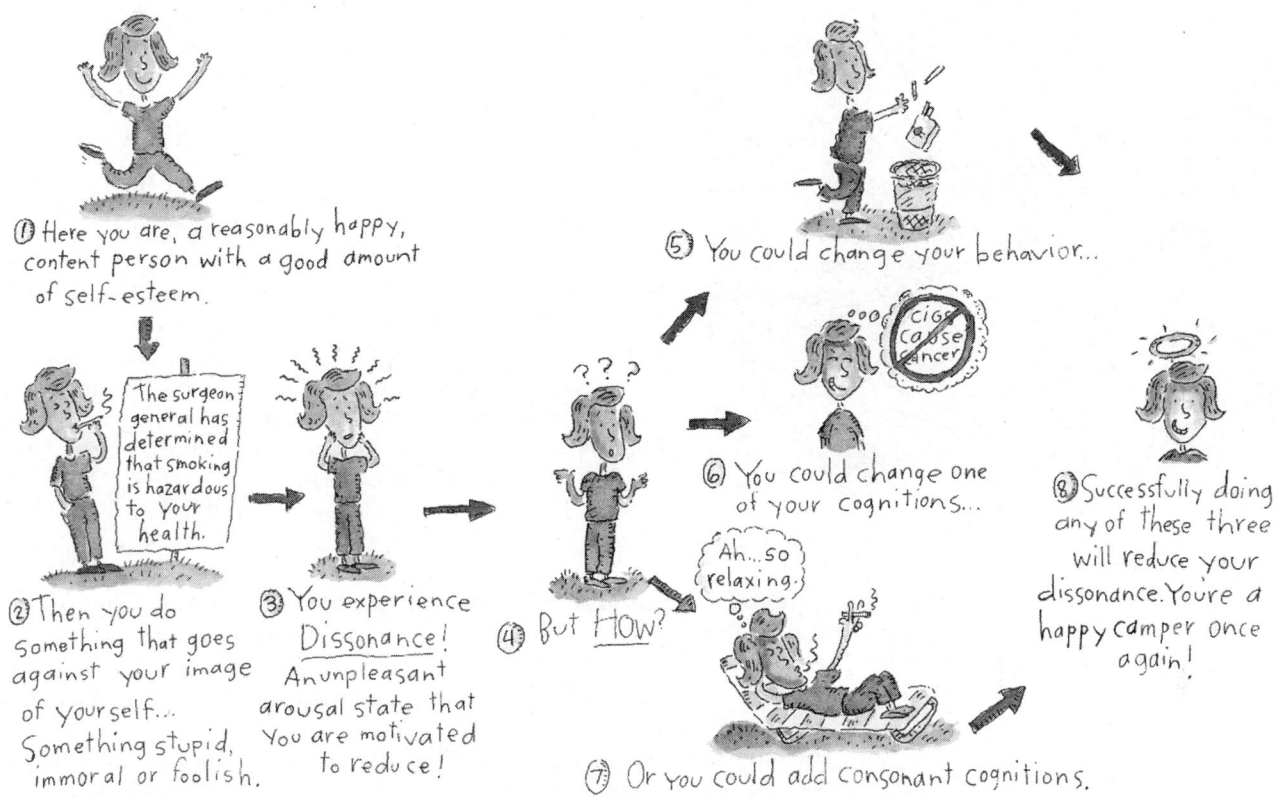

FIGURE 6.1
How we reduce cognitive dissonance.

- By changing our behavior to bring it in line with the dissonant cognition
- By attempting to justify our behavior through changing one of the dissonant cognitions
- By attempting to justify our behavior by adding new cognitions

To illustrate, let's look at a behavior that millions of people engage in several times a day—smoking cigarettes. If you are a smoker, you are likely to experience dissonance because you know that this behavior can lead to a painful, early death. How can you reduce this dissonance? The most direct way is to change your behavior—to give up smoking. Your behavior would then be consistent with your knowledge of the link between smoking and cancer. Though many people have succeeded in doing just that, it's not easy—many have tried to quit and failed. What do these people do? It would be wrong to assume that they simply swallow hard and prepare to die. They don't. Researchers studied the behavior and attitudes of heavy smokers who attended a smoking cessation clinic and succeeded in quitting smoking for a while but then relapsed into heavy smoking again. What do you suppose the researchers discovered? Heavy smokers who tried to quit and failed actually succeeded in lowering their perception of the dangers of smoking. In this way, they could continue to smoke without feeling terrible about it (Gibbons, Eggleston, & Benthin, 1997).

Smokers can come up with some pretty creative ways to justify their smoking. Some succeed in convincing themselves that the data linking cigarette smoking to cancer are inconclusive. Others try to add new cognitions—for example, the erroneous belief that filters trap most of the harmful chemicals and thus reduce the threat of cancer. Some add a cognition that allows them to focus on the vivid exception: "Look at my grandfather. He's 87 years old, and he's been smoking a pack a day since he was 12. That proves it's not always bad for you." Still others add the cognition that smoking is an extremely enjoyable activity, one for which it is worth risking cancer. Others even succeed in convincing themselves that all things considered, smoking is

This youngster may be thinking: "There's nothing wrong with putting on a little extra weight. After all, some professional football players weigh more than 300 pounds and earn millions of dollars a year. Pass the fries."

worth the risk because it relaxes them, reduces nervous tension, and in this way improves their health.

These justifications may sound silly to the nonsmoker. That is precisely our point. As the smokers' rationales show, people experiencing dissonance will often deny or distort reality to reduce it. People who try and fail to lose weight, who refuse to practice safer sex, or who receive bad news about their general health can be equally "creative" in denying risk and reducing their discomfort (Aronson, 1997; Croyle & Jemmott, 1990; Goleman, 1982; Kassarjian & Cohen, 1965; Leishman, 1988). Occasionally, these illusions can be helpful; for example, Shelley Taylor and her colleagues have demonstrated that individuals who harbor unrealistically positive illusions about surviving a terminal illness like AIDS live longer than those who are more "realistic" (Taylor, 1989; Taylor & Armor, 1996; Taylor & Brown, 1988; Taylor & Gollwitzer, 1995). Far more often (as in the case of smoking), such illusions are destructive.

Why We Overestimate the Pain of Disappointment Imagine that you have just interviewed for the job of your dreams. The position is in your field, the salary is fabulous, and your potential coworkers seem like fun-loving people. You expect to be very disappointed if you don't get the job. How long do you think you would feel that way?

By now you know the answer to this question—it depends on how successfully you reduce the dissonance caused by not getting the job. When you get the bad news, you will be disappointed; however, more than likely, you will put a spin on it that makes you feel better. For example, you might decide that the job was a dead-end anyway.

Interestingly, people often do not anticipate how successfully they will reduce dissonance. Several studies by Daniel Gilbert and Tim Wilson suggest that when people think about how they will react to future negative events they show an **impact bias**, whereby they overestimate the intensity and duration of their negative emotional reactions. For example, people overestimate how dreadful they will feel following a romantic breakup or losing a job (Gilbert, Pinel, Wilson, Blumberg, & Wheatley, 1998; Mellers & McGraw, 2001; Wilson & Gilbert, 2005).

Given that people have successfully reduced dissonance in the past, why is it that they are not aware that they will do so in the future? The answer is that the process of *reducing dissonance is largely unconscious*. Indeed, dissonance reduction works better that way (Gilbert et al., 1998). It is *not* very effective to hear ourselves say, "I'll try to make myself feel better by *convincing myself* that the person who just rejected me is an idiot." It is more effective if we *unconsciously* transform our view of the interviewer; we feel better believing that objectively he is an idiot (Bem & McConnell, 1970; Goethals & Reckman, 1973). Because the dissonance reduction process is mostly unconscious, we do not anticipate that it will save us from future angst.

Rational Behavior versus Rationalizing Behavior
理性行为与合理化行为

Most people think of themselves as rational beings, and generally, they are right: We are certainly capable of rational thought. But as we've seen, the need to maintain our self-esteem leads to thinking that is not always rational; rather, it is *rationalizing*. People who are in the midst of reducing dissonance are so involved with convincing themselves that they are right that they frequently end up behaving irrationally and maladaptively.

During the late 1950s, when segregation was still widespread, Edward Jones and Rika Kohler (1959) performed a simple experiment in a southern town. They selected people who were deeply committed to a position on the issue of racial segregation—some strongly supported segregation; others opposed it just as strongly. Next, the re-

Impact Bias

The tendency to overestimate the intensity and duration of our emotional reactions to future negative events

searchers presented these individuals with a series of arguments on both sides of the issue. Some of the arguments on each side were plausible, and others on each side were rather silly. The question was, which of the arguments would people remember best?

If the participants were behaving in a purely rational way, we would expect them to remember the plausible arguments best and the implausible arguments least, regardless of how they felt about segregation. After all, why would anyone want to remember implausible arguments? What does dissonance theory predict? A silly argument that supports your own position arouses some dissonance because it raises doubts about the wisdom of that position or the intelligence of people who agree with it. Likewise, a sensible argument on the other side of the issue also arouses some dissonance because it raises the possibility that the other side might be closer to the truth than you had thought. Because these arguments arouse dissonance, we try not to think about them.

"It certainly is a safe car, and besides, maybe the price of gasoline will drop."

This is exactly what Jones and Kohler found. The participants remembered the plausible arguments agreeing with their own position *and* the *implausible* arguments agreeing with the *opposing* position. Subsequent research has yielded similar results on many issues, from whether or not the death penalty deters people from committing murder to the risks of contracting AIDS through heterosexual contact (e.g., Biek, Wood, & Chaiken, 1996; Edwards & Smith, 1996).

All this research indicates that we humans do not always process information in an unbiased way. Rather, we distort it in a way that fits our preconceived notions. This probably explains why on issues such as politics and religion, people who are deeply committed to a view different from our own will almost never come to see things our way (the proper way!), no matter how powerful and balanced our arguments might be.

Decisions, Decisions, Decisions
决策，决策，还是决策

Every time we make a decision, we experience dissonance. How come? Let's take a close look at the process. Suppose you are about to buy a car, but you are torn between a van and a subcompact. You know that each has advantages and disadvantages: The van would be convenient; you can haul things in it, you can sleep in it during long trips, and it has plenty of power, but it gets poor mileage and it's hard to park. The subcompact is a lot less roomy, and you wonder about its safety. But it is less expensive to buy and operate, it's a lot zippier to drive, and it has a pretty good repair record. Before you decide, you will probably get as much information as you can. Chances are you will read *Consumer Reports* to find out what this expert, unbiased source has to say. You'll talk with friends who own a van or a subcompact. (You may even talk to your parents.) You'll probably visit automobile dealers to test-drive the vehicles to see how each one feels. All this predecision behavior is perfectly rational. Let's assume you decide to buy the subcompact.

What happens next? We predict that your behavior will change in a specific way: You will begin to think more and more about the number of miles to the gallon as though it were the most important thing in the world. Simultaneously, you will almost certainly downplay the fact that you can't sleep in your subcompact. Similarly, you will barely remember that your new car can put you at considerable risk of harm in a collision. How does this shift in thinking happen?

Distorting Our Likes and Dislikes In any decision, whether it is between two cars, two colleges, or two potential lovers, the chosen alternative is seldom entirely positive, and the rejected alternative is seldom entirely negative. So while making the decision, you have your doubts. After the decision, your cognition that you are a smart person is dissonant with all the negative things about the car, college, or lover you chose; that

All sales are final. When will the customer be happier with his or her new TV set: Ten minutes before the purchase? Ten minutes after the purchase?

Postdecision Dissonance

Dissonance aroused after making a decision, typically reduced by enhancing the attractiveness of the chosen alternative and devaluating the rejected alternatives

cognition is also dissonant with all the *positive* aspects of the car, college, or lover you *rejected*. We call this **postdecision dissonance**. Cognitive dissonance theory predicts that to help yourself feel better about the decision, you will do some mental work to try to reduce the dissonance.

What kind of work? An early experiment by Jack Brehm (1956) will clarify. Brehm posed as a representative of a consumer testing service and asked women to rate the attractiveness and desirability of several kinds of appliances, such as toasters and electric coffeemakers. Each woman was told that as a reward for having participated in the survey, she could have one of the appliances as a gift. She was given a choice between two of the products she had rated as being equally attractive. After she made her decision, her appliance was wrapped up and given to her. Twenty minutes later, each woman was asked to rerate all the products. Brehm found that after receiving the appliance of their choice, the women rated its attractiveness somewhat higher than they had the first time. Not only that, but they drastically lowered their rating of the appliance they might have chosen but decided to reject.

In other words, following a decision, to reduce dissonance we change the way we feel about the chosen and unchosen alternatives, cognitively spreading them apart in our own minds in order to make ourselves feel better about the choice we made.

The Permanence of the Decision It stands to reason that the more important the decision, the greater the dissonance. Deciding which car to buy is clearly more important than deciding between a toaster and a coffeemaker; deciding which person to marry is clearly more important than deciding which car to buy. Decisions also vary in terms of how permanent they are—that is, how difficult they are to revoke. It is a lot easier to trade in your new car for another one than it is to get out of an unhappy marriage. The more permanent and less revocable the decision, the greater the need to reduce dissonance.

An excellent place to investigate the significance of irrevocability is the racetrack. Experienced bettors typically spend a lot of time poring over the "dope sheets," trying to decide which horse to put their money on. When they make a decision, they head for the betting windows. While they are standing in line, they have already made their decision, but we would hypothesize that because it is still revocable, they have no urge to reduce dissonance; however, after they get to the window and place their bet—even if it's for only $2—it is absolutely irrevocable. If irrevocability is an important factor, therefore, we would expect bettors to be engaged in much more dissonance reduction a few minutes after placing the bet than a few minutes before placing the bet.

In a simple but clever experiment, social psychologists intercepted people who were on their way to place $2 bets and asked them how certain they were that their horses would win (Knox & Inkster, 1968). The investigators also approached other bettors just as they were leaving the $2 window, after having placed their bets, and asked them the same question. Almost invariably, people who had already placed their bets gave their horses a much better chance of winning than those who had not yet placed their bets did. Because only a few minutes separated one group from another, nothing real had occurred to increase the probability of winning; the only thing that had changed was the finality of the decision—and hence the dissonance it produced.

Moving from the racetrack to the Harvard campus, Gilbert and Ebert (2002) tested the irrevocability hypothesis in a photography class. In their study participants were recruited through an advertisement for students interested in learning photography while taking part in a psychology experiment. Students were informed that they would shoot a roll of film and print two of the photographs. They would rate the two photographs and then get to choose one to keep. The other would be kept for administrative reasons. The students were randomly assigned to one of two conditions:

Condition One: Students were informed that they had the option to exchange photographs within a 5-day period; Condition Two: Students were told that their choice was final. The researchers found that prior to making the choice between the two photographs, the differences in liking between the two photographs was insignificant. Researchers then contacted students 2, 4, and 9 days after they had made their choice to find out if those who had a choice to exchange photographs liked the one they chose more or less than those in the no-choice (irrevocable) condition.

The results of the experiment showed that the students who had the option of exchanging photographs liked the one they finally ended up with less than those who made the final choice on the first day.

An interesting addition to this study was that students were asked to predict whether keeping their options open would make them more or less happy with their decision. They predicted that keeping their option open would make them happier. They were wrong. Apparently people cannot anticipate the fact that the finality of the decision makes them happier.

Creating the Illusion of Irrevocability The irrevocability of a decision always increases dissonance and the motivation to reduce it. Because of this, unscrupulous salespeople have developed techniques for creating the illusion that irrevocability exists. One such technique is called **lowballing** (Cialdini, Cacioppo, Basset, & Miller, 1978; Weyant, 1996). Robert Cialdini, a distinguished social psychologist, temporarily joined the sales force of an automobile dealership to observe this technique closely. Here's how it works: You enter an automobile showroom intent on buying a particular car. Having already priced it at several dealerships, you know you can purchase it for about $18,000. You are approached by a personable, middle-aged man who tells you he can sell you one for $17,679. Excited by the bargain, you agree to write out a check for the down payment so that the salesman can take it to the manager as proof you are a serious customer. Meanwhile, you imagine yourself driving home in your shiny new bargain. But alas, 10 minutes later the salesperson returns, looking forlorn. He tells you that in his zeal to give you a good deal, he miscalculated, and the sales manager caught it. The price of the car actually comes to $18,178. You are disappointed. Moreover, you are pretty sure you can get it a bit cheaper elsewhere. The decision to buy is not irrevocable. And yet in this situation, research by Cialdini and his colleagues (1978) suggests that far more people will go ahead with the deal than if the original asking price had been $18,178, even though the reason for buying the car from this particular dealer—the bargain price—no longer exists. How come?

There are at least three reasons why lowballing works. First, although the customer's decision to buy is certainly reversible, a commitment of sorts does exist. Signing a check for a down payment creates the illusion of irrevocability, even though, if the car buyer really thought about it, he or she would quickly realize it is a nonbinding contract. In the world of high-pressure sales, however, even temporary illusion can have powerful consequences. Second, the feeling of commitment triggered the anticipation of an exciting

Lowballing
An unscrupulous strategy whereby a salesperson induces a customer to agree to purchase a product at a very low cost, subsequently claims it was an error, and then raises the price; frequently, the customer will agree to make the purchase at the inflated price

The Advantage of Finality 试一试！一锤子买卖的好处

Ask five friends who are not in this psychology class the following question: Imagine you are shopping for a particular cell phone and you find it in two stores. In both stores the price for the phones is identical, but in Store A you have the option to exchange the phone within 30 days, while in Store B, all sales are final. One week after your purchase, which situation will make you happier with the cell phone: Store A (with the option to return the phone) or Store B (purchase not revokable)?

After he cheats, he will try to convince himself that everybody would cheat if they had the chance.

event: driving out with a new car. To have had the anticipated event thwarted (by not going ahead with the deal) would have produced dissonance and disappointment. Third, although the final price is substantially higher than the customer thought it would be, it is probably only slightly higher than the price at another dealership. Under these circumstances, the customer in effect says, "Oh, what the heck. I'm here, I've already filled out the forms, I've written out the check—why wait?" Thus, by using dissonance reduction and the illusion of irrevocability, high-pressure salespeople increase the probability that you will decide to buy their product at their price.

The Decision to Behave Immorally Of course, decisions about cars, appliances, racehorses, and even presidential candidates are the easy ones. Often our choices involve moral and ethical issues. When is it OK to lie to a friend, and when is it not? When is an act stealing, and when is it borrowing? Resolving moral dilemmas is a particularly interesting area in which to study dissonance because of the powerful implications for one's self-esteem. Even more interesting is the fact that dissonance reduction following a difficult moral decision can cause people to behave either more *or less* ethically in the future.

Take the issue of cheating on an exam. Suppose you are a college sophomore taking the final exam in a physics course. Ever since you can remember, you have wanted to be a surgeon, and you think that your admission to medical school will depend heavily on how well you do in this physics course. The key question on the exam involves some material you know fairly well, but because so much is riding on this exam, you experience acute anxiety and draw a blank. The minutes tick away. You become increasingly anxious. You simply cannot think. You look up and notice that you happen to be sitting next to the smartest person in the class. You glance at her paper and discover that she is just completing her answer to the crucial question. You know you could easily read her answer if you chose to. Time is running out. What do you do? Your conscience tells you it's wrong to cheat—and yet if you don't cheat, you are certain to get a poor grade. And if you get a poor grade, you are convinced that there goes medical school. You wrestle with your conscience.

Regardless of whether you decide to cheat or not, the threat to your self-esteem arouses dissonance. If you cheat, your belief or cognition "I am a decent, moral person" is dissonant with your cognition "I have just committed an immoral act." If you decide to resist temptation, your cognition "I want to become a surgeon" is dissonant with your cognition "I could have nailed a good grade and admission to medical school, but I chose not to. Wow, was I stupid!"

In this situation, some students would decide to cheat; others would decide not to cheat. What happens to the students' attitudes about cheating after their decision? Suppose that after a difficult struggle, you decide to cheat. How do you reduce the dissonance? According to dissonance theory, it is likely that you would try to justify the action by finding a way to minimize the negative aspects of the action you chose. In this case, an efficient path to reducing dissonance would involve changing your attitude about cheating. You would adopt a more lenient attitude toward cheating, convincing yourself that it is a victimless crime that doesn't hurt anybody, that everybody does it, and so it's not really that bad.

Suppose, by contrast, that after a difficult struggle, you decide not to cheat. How would you reduce your dissonance? Again, you could change your attitude about the morality of the act—but this time in the opposite direction. That is, to justify giving up a good grade, you must convince yourself that cheating is a heinous sin, that it's one of the lowest things a person can do, and that cheaters should be rooted out and severely punished.

How Dissonance Affects Personal Values What has happened is not merely a rationalization of your own behavior, but an actual change in your system of values. People facing this kind of choice will undergo either a softening or a hardening of their attitudes toward cheating on exams, depending on whether or not they decided to cheat. The interesting and important thing to remember is that two people acting in two different ways could have started out with almost identical attitudes toward cheating. One came within an inch of cheating but decided to resist, while the other came within an inch of resisting but decided to cheat. After they had made their decisions, however, their attitudes toward cheating would diverge sharply as a consequence of their actions. (See Figure 6.2)

These speculations were tested by Judson Mills (1958) in an experiment he performed in an elementary school. Mills first measured the attitudes of sixth graders toward cheating. He then had them participate in a competitive exam, with prizes awarded to the winners. The situation was arranged so that it was almost impossible to win without cheating. Mills made it easy for the children to cheat and created the illusion that they could not be detected. Under these conditions, as one might expect, some of the students cheated and others did not. The next day, the sixth graders were again asked to indicate how they felt about cheating. Sure enough, the children who had cheated became more lenient toward cheating, and those who had resisted the temptation to cheat adopted a harsher attitude.

Classic experiments conducted in the laboratory often inspire contemporary research in the real world. A case in point: While conducting research among midlevel business executives in India, two social psychologists came up with some interesting data pertinent to Mills's results (Viswesvaran & Deshpande, 1996). They reasoned that executives who were in the process of making a decision about whether to behave ethically or not were in a vulnerable state: On the one hand, they wanted to behave ethically; on the other hand, they were undoubtedly concerned that they might need to behave unethically in order to succeed. The investigators found that executives who had substantial reason to believe that managerial success could be achieved only through unethical behavior experienced far greater dissonance (in the form of job dissatisfaction) than those who were given no reason to believe this. Our prediction is that if the investigators had returned a year or two later, they would have found a reduction in dissonance in this group; that is, as with Mills's subjects, most of those who behaved unethically would have found a way to justify that behavior after the fact.

Dissonance, the Brain, and Evolution
认知失调、大脑和进化

Neuroscientists have recently shown that cognitive dissonance and its reduction are reflected in the way the brain processes information. In a study of people who were wired up to MRIs while they were trying to process dissonant or consonant information, Drew Westen and his colleagues (2006) found that the reasoning areas of the brain virtually shut down when a person is confronted with dissonant information, and the emotion circuits of the brain light up happily when consonance is restored. As Westen put it, people twirl the "cognitive kaleidoscope" until the pieces fall into the pattern they want to see, and then the brain repays them by activating circuits involved in pleasure—not unlike, he added, what addicts feel when they get a fix.

Experiments by Louisa Egan, Laurie Santos, and Paul Bloom (2007) support the notion that cognitive dissonance developed evolutionarily, suggesting that it has survival value. Recall the study by Brehm (1956) in which homemakers ranked appliances, and then, after getting to keep an appliance of their choice, lowered their ranking of the previously attractive appliance they did not choose. In the Egan, Santos, and Bloom study, monkeys were placed in a similar situation, only they were choosing between different colored M&Ms instead of kitchen appliances. Like the homemakers, they reduced their liking for the color M&Ms not chosen. Additional support for the

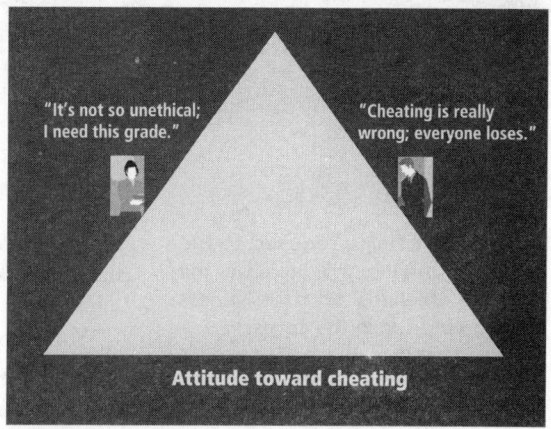
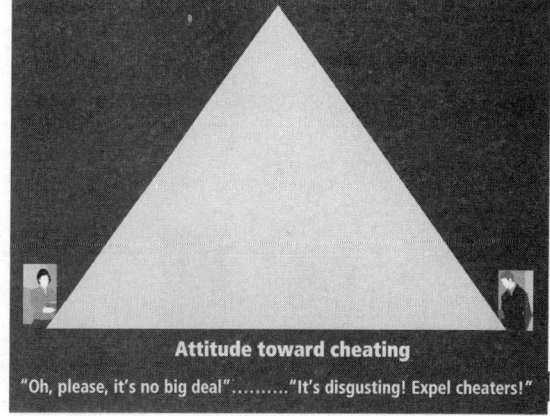

FIGURE 6.2
Cheating pyramid.

Imagine two students taking an exam. Both are tempted to cheat. Initially, their attitudes toward cheating are almost identical. Suppose one cheats and the other does not. Their attitudes will then undergo predictable changes.

(Created by Carol Tavris. Used by permission)

The harsh training required to become a marine will increase the recruits' feelings of cohesiveness and their pride in the corps.

biological basis of cognitive dissonance comes from experiments by Eddie Harmon-Jones, Cindy Harmon-Jones, Meghan Fearn, Jonathan Sigelman, and Peter Johnson (2008). They found evidence that the left frontal cortical activity was involved in the dissonance reduction process.

Justifying Your Effort 合理化你的努力

Most people are willing to work hard to get something they really want. For example, if you are really interested in pursuing a particular career, you are likely to go the extra mile to get it. You'll probably study hard to meet graduate school entrance requirements, study some more for graduate school admissions exams, and submit to a series of stressful interviews.

Let's turn that proposition inside out. Suppose you expend a great deal of effort to get into a particular club and it turns out to be a totally worthless organization, consisting of boring, pompous people engaged in trivial activities. You would feel pretty foolish, wouldn't you? A sensible person doesn't work hard to gain something worthless. Such a circumstance would produce a significant amount of dissonance; your cognition that you are a sensible, adept human being is dissonant with your cognition that you worked hard to get into a dismal club. How would you reduce this dissonance? How would you justify your behavior?

You might start by finding a way to convince yourself that the club and the people in it are nicer, more interesting, and more worthwhile than they appeared to be at first glance. How can one turn boring people into interesting people and a trivial club into a worthwhile one? Easy. Even the most boring people and trivial clubs have some redeeming qualities. Activities and behaviors are open to a variety of interpretations; if we are motivated to see the best in people and things, we will tend to interpret these ambiguities in a positive way. We call this the **justification of effort**—the tendency for individuals to increase their liking for something they have worked hard to attain.

In a classic experiment, Elliot Aronson and Judson Mills (1959) explored the link between effort and dissonance reduction. In their experiment, college students volunteered to join a group that would be meeting regularly to discuss various aspects of the psychology of sex. To be admitted to the group, they volunteered to go through a screening procedure. For one-third of the participants, the procedure was extremely demanding and unpleasant; for one-third, it was only mildly unpleasant; and one-third were admitted to the group without any screening at all.

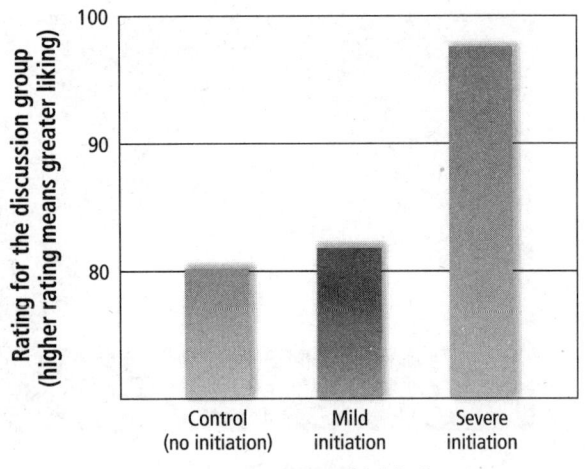

FIGURE 6.3

The tougher the initiation, the more we like the group.

The more effort we put into gaining group membership, the more we like the group we have just joined.

(Adapted from Aronson & Mills, 1959)

Justification of Effort

The tendency for individuals to increase their liking for something they have worked hard to attain

Each participant was then allowed to listen in on a discussion being conducted by the members of the group they would be joining. Although they were led to believe that the discussion was live, they actually heard a prerecorded tape. The taped discussion was arranged so that it was as dull and bombastic as possible. After the discussion was over, each participant was asked to rate it in terms of how much he or she liked it, how interesting it was, how intelligent the participants were, and so forth. The major findings are shown in Figure 6.3.

The results supported the predictions: Participants who underwent little or no effort to get into the group did not enjoy the discussion very much. They were able to see it for what it was—a dull and boring waste of time. They regretted that they had agreed to participate. Participants who went through a severe initiation, however, convinced themselves that the same discussion, though not as scintillating as they had hoped, was dotted with interesting and provocative tidbits and was therefore, in the main, a worthwhile experience. In short, they justified the effort they had expended by interpreting all the ambiguous aspects of the group discussion in the most positive way possible. Similar results have been obtained by other researchers in comparable circumstances (e.g., Cooper, 1980; Gerard & Mathewson, 1966).

It should be clear that we are not suggesting that most people enjoy difficult, unpleasant experiences—they do not. Nor are we suggesting that people enjoy things that are merely associated with unpleasant experiences—they do not. What we are asserting is that if a person agrees to go through a demanding or an unpleasant experience in order to attain some goal or object, that goal or object becomes more attractive. Thus if you were walking to the discussion group and a passing car splashed mud all over you, you would not like that group any better; however, if you volunteered to jump into a mud puddle in order to be admitted to a group that turned out to be trivial and boring, you *would* like the group better. (See the following Try It! exercise.)

TRY IT! Justifying Actions 试一试！合理化你的行为

Think about something that you have gone after in the past that necessitated your going through a lot of trouble or effort. Perhaps you waited for several hours in a long line to get tickets to a concert; perhaps you sat in your car through an incredible traffic jam because it was the only way you could visit a close friend.

1. Specifically, list the things you had to go through to attain your goal.

2. Do you think you might have tried to justify all that effort? Did you find yourself exaggerating the good things about the goal and minimizing any negative aspects of the goal? List some of the ways you might have exaggerated the value of the goal.

3. The next time you find yourself in that kind of situation, you might want to monitor your actions and cognitions carefully to see if there is any self-justification involved.

The Psychology of Insufficient Justification 非充分合理化的心理学

When we were little, we were taught never to tell a lie. Indeed, our elementary school history courses were full of mythical stories (disguised as truths) like that of George Washington and the cherry tree, apparently aimed at convincing us that we had better be truthful if we aspired to the presidency. Alas, there may be some people who have never told a lie, but most of us have yet to meet one. At times, most of us feel that for good reason, we need to be less than perfectly truthful. One such reason involves something else that we were taught—to be kind to one another. Occasionally, to be kind to someone, we find it necessary to tell a lie.

Suppose your friend Jen shows you her expensive new dress and asks your opinion. You think it is atrocious and are about to say so when she tells you that she has already had it altered, which means that she cannot return it. What do you say? Chances are you go through something like the following thought process: "Jen seems so happy and excited about her new dress. She spent a lot of money for it, and she can't take it back. If I if say what I really think, I'll upset her."

So you tell Jen that you like her dress very much. Do you experience much dissonance? We doubt it. There are a great many thoughts that are consonant with having told this lie, as outlined in your reasoning in the preceding paragraph. In effect, your cognition that it is important not to cause pain to people you like provides ample **external justification** for having told a harmless lie.

Counterattitudinal Advocacy What happens if you say something you don't really believe but there isn't a good external justification for being insincere? That is, what if your friend Jen was fabulously wealthy and could easily afford to absorb the cost of her ugly new dress? What if she sincerely wanted to know what you thought? What if

External Justification

A reason or an explanation for dissonant personal behavior that resides outside the individual (e.g., in order to receive a large reward or avoid a severe punishment)

in the past you'd told her that she had bought something awful and your friendship survived? Now the external justifications—the reasons for lying to Jen about the dress—are minimal. If you still withhold your true opinion (saying instead, "Gee, Jen, it's, uh, interesting"), you will experience dissonance. When you can't find external justification for your behavior, you will attempt to find **internal justification**—you will try to reduce dissonance by changing something about yourself (e.g., your attitude or behavior).

How can you do this? You might begin looking harder for positive things about the dress that you hadn't noticed before. If you look hard enough, you will probably find something. Within a short time, your attitude toward the dress will have moved in the direction of the statement you made—and that is how saying becomes believing. This phenomenon is generally referred to as **counterattitudinal advocacy**. It occurs when we claim to have an opinion or attitude that differs from our true beliefs. When we do this with little external justification, that is, without being motivated by something outside of ourselves, what we believe begins to look more and more like the lie we told.

This proposition was first tested in a groundbreaking experiment by Leon Festinger and J. Merrill Carlsmith (1959). College students were induced to spend an hour performing a series of excruciatingly boring and repetitive tasks. The experimenter then told them that the purpose of the study was to determine whether or not people would perform better if they had been informed in advance that the tasks were interesting. They were each informed that they had been randomly assigned to the control condition—that is, they had not been told anything in advance. However, he explained, the next participant, a young woman who was just arriving in the anteroom, was going to be in the experimental condition. The researcher said that he needed to convince her that the task was going to be interesting and enjoyable. Because it was much more convincing if a fellow student rather than the experimenter delivered this message, would the participant do so? Thus, with his request the experimenter induced the participants to lie about the task to another student.

Half of the students were offered $20 for telling the lie (a large external justification), while the others were offered only $1 for telling the lie (a small external justification). After the experiment was over, an interviewer asked the lie-tellers how much they had enjoyed the tasks they had performed earlier in the experiment. The results validated the hypothesis: The students who had been paid $20 for lying—that is, for saying that the tasks had been enjoyable—rated the activities as the dull and boring experiences they were. But those who were paid only $1 for saying the task was enjoyable rated the task as significantly more enjoyable. In other words, people who had received an abundance of external justification for lying told the lie but didn't believe it, whereas those who told the lie without a great deal of external justification succeeded in convincing themselves that what they said was closer to the truth.

Does the same thing happen when important attitudes are involved? Can you induce a person to change an attitude about things that matter? Subsequent research has shown that the Festinger-Carlsmith paradigm has wide ramifications in areas of great significance. Consider an experiment by Arthur R. Cohen (1962), for example. Cohen was a social psychologist at Yale University during a turbulent political period when the city police were often called to the campus to control the behavior of students who were demonstrating against the war in Southeast Asia. Occasionally, the police reacted with excessive force. After one such incident, Cohen visited a dormitory, pretending that he worked for a well-known research institute. He told the students that there were two sides to every issue and that the institute was interested in looking at both sides of the police-student issue. He then asked the students to write forceful essays supporting the behavior of the police. Moreover, he told them he was able to offer them an incentive for writing the essay. Depending on the condition to which the students were assigned, he offered them 50 cents, $1, $5, or $10. (In 1962, $10 bought about 30 beers.) None of the students knew what the others were offered. After the students wrote their essays, Cohen assessed their real attitude toward the actions of the city police.

Internal Justification
The reduction of dissonance by changing something about oneself (e.g., one's attitude or behavior)

Counterattitudinal Advocacy
Stating an opinion or attitude that runs counter to one's private belief or attitude

The results were clear: The smaller the incentive, the more favorable people became toward the city police. In other words, when the students were given a great deal of external justification for writing the essay, they did not need to convince themselves that they really believed what they had written. When they faced the fact that they had written positive things about the police for 50 cents or $1, however, they needed to convince themselves that there may have been some truth in what they had written.

In a similar experiment, researchers approached college students who initially believed that marijuana was harmful and induced them to compose and recite a videotaped speech favoring its use and legalization (Nel, Helmreich, & Aronson, 1969). Some were offered large incentives; others were offered small incentives. Again, the findings were clear: The smaller the incentive, the greater the softening of the attitude toward the use and legalization of marijuana.

In many of these experiments, people behaved without integrity (told a lie) in a manner that also might have harmed another person. For example, if you believe that marijuana is dangerous and you tell someone that it is not, in your own mind, you might be doing that person a great deal of harm. Accordingly, it is reasonable to ask the following question: Is lying enough? Is harming another person a necessary condition for dissonance, or is dissonance produced simply by behaving without integrity, even if no harm results? An experiment by Eddie Harmon-Jones and his colleagues (1996) made it clear that behaving without integrity, in and of itself, produces dissonance. In their experiment, people who drank an awful-tasting beverage and then volunteered to say that it tasted good actually came to believe that it tasted good (compared to the rating of a control group). The way they "said" it tasted good was to write their false opinion down on a small slip of paper, which they then immediately crumpled up and threw away. Thus, even though their lie could not possibly harm anyone, the act of lying produced changes in belief aimed at softening the dissonance and restoring a sense of integrity.

Do you think that he will come to believe the message he is delivering?

Advocacy and Hypocrisy Applied to Social Problems
社会问题中的拥护和伪善

What happens outside the laboratory? Can the experiments on counterattitudinal advocacy be used to tackle social problems? Let's look at race relations and racial prejudice, surely one of our nation's most important and enduring problems. Would it be possible to get people to endorse a policy favoring a minority group and then see if their attitudes become more favorable toward that group? Absolutely.

In an important set of experiments, Mike Leippe and Donna Eisenstadt (1994, 1998) induced white college students to write a counterattitudinal essay publicly endorsing a controversial proposal at their university to double the amount of funds available for academic scholarships for African American students. Because the total amount of funds was limited, this meant cutting by half the amount of scholarship funds available to white students. As you might imagine, this was a highly dissonant situation. How might the students reduce dissonance? The best way would be to convince themselves that they really believed deeply in that policy. Moreover, it is reasonable to suggest that dissonance reduction might generalize beyond the specific policy—that is, the theory would predict that their general attitude toward African Americans would become more favorable and more supportive. And that is exactly what Leippe and Eisenstadt found.

In a similar experiment Leanne Son Hing, Winnie Li, and Mark Zanna (2002) were able to induce hypocrisy among students deemed "aversive racists" (those low in explicit prejudice but high in implicit prejudice) to reduce prejudicial behaviors. In the study the experimental group first wrote essays about why it was important to treat minority students fairly. They were later instructed to write about two situations in which they reacted to an Asian more negatively than they thought they should have. This created feelings of hypocrisy in the experimental group. Subsequently, this group of students showed evidence of a reduction in prejudicial behavior. Specifically, participants in the hypocrisy condition refused to support a budget cut for the Asian Student Association.

The Hypocrisy Paradigm In the past two decades, this aspect of dissonance theory—the induction of hypocrisy— has also been applied to another important social issue—preventing the spread of AIDS. Since the early 1980s, when the first few cases were diagnosed, the virus (known as HIV) that causes AIDS has killed approximately 15 million people across the globe, and in Asia and Africa, the number of infected people keeps rising. The greatest tragedy, perhaps, is that AIDS is largely preventable. By practicing "safe sex," including the use of condoms, people can significantly reduce their risk of contracting the HIV virus. To get this message across, the U.S. government has spent millions of dollars on AIDS information and prevention campaigns. But it turned out that information alone is not enough to prevent people from engaging in risky sexual behavor. As with many things, there is a wide gap between knowing what you should do and actually doing it. For example, although college students know that AIDS is a serious problem, only a small percentage use condoms every time they have sex. The reason seems to be that condoms are inconvenient and unromantic, and they remind people of disease—the last thing they want to be thinking about when preparing to make love. Rather, as researchers have consistently discovered, sexual behavior is often accompanied by denial. In this case, we tend to believe that although AIDS is a problem for most people, we ourselves are not at risk. How can this dangerous belief be overcome?

The hypocrisy paradigm was first used during the 1990s when Elliot Aronson and his students found that it could help solve this problem (Aronson, Fried, & Stone, 1991; Stone, Aronson, Crain, Winslow, & Fried, 1994). The researchers asked two groups of college students to compose a speech describing the dangers of AIDS and advocating the use of condoms every time a person has sex. In one group, the students merely composed the arguments. In the second group, after composing their arguments, they were to recite them in front of a video camera and were told that an audience of high school students would watch the resulting tape. In addition, half the students in each group were made mindful of their own failure to use condoms by making a list of the circumstances in which they had found it particularly difficult, awkward, or impossible to use them.

Essentially, then, the participants in one group—those who made a video for high school students after the experimenter got them to think about their own failure to use condoms—experienced high dissonance. Why? They were made aware of their own hypocrisy: They had to deal with the fact that they were preaching behavior that they themselves were not practicing. To remove the hypocrisy and maintain their self-esteem, they would need to start practicing what they were preaching. And that is exactly what the researchers found: They gave each student the chance to buy condoms very cheaply. The results demonstrated that the students in the hypocrisy condition were far more likely to buy condoms than students in any of the other conditions (see Figure 6.4). To find out if the results were long-lasting, the researchers phoned the students several months after the experiment and found that the effects held up. People in the hypocrisy condition—the students who would have felt the most cognitive dissonance—reported far greater use of condoms than those in the control conditions.

Using a similar research design, Alexandra Peterson, Graeme Haynes, and James Olson (2008) instructed undergraduate smokers to create an antismoking video suggesting that it would be used to encourage high school students to quit smoking. The experiment, like the ones above, was designed to induce dissonance among the participants because their behavior (smoking) contradicted the antismoking position they advocated on the video, causing them to face the inconsistency between their behavior

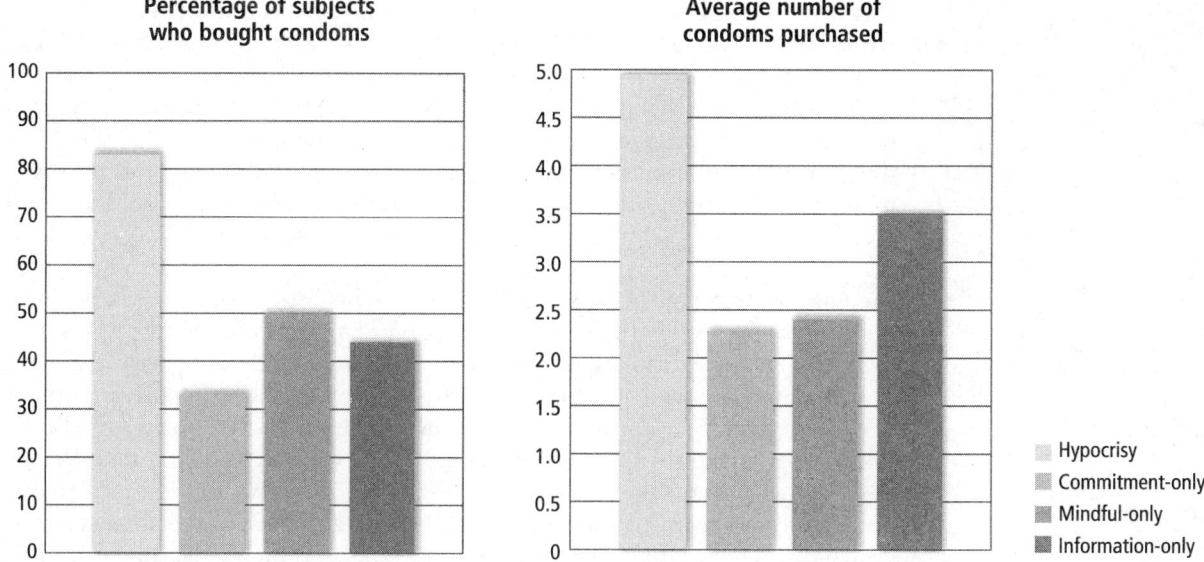

FIGURE 6.4
People who are made mindful of their hypocrisy begin to practice what they preach.
(Adapted from J. Harachiewicz, 1994)

and their words. And indeed the induction of hypocrisy did increase the participants' stated intention to quit smoking.

Peterson's study also measured the relationship between high self-esteem and the intention to make behavioral changes. They found that the higher the participants' self-esteem, the greater was their intention to reduce dissonance in the most direct way, by quitting smoking. This research builds nicely on an earlier study in which drivers were confronted with the dissonant information that their choice to drive, instead of using public transit, was both irrational (took more time) and less responsible (caused greater environmental harm). The researchers found that the respondents with higher self-esteem expressed a willingness to change their behavior—to use public transportation; on the other hand, the drivers with lower self-esteem made rationalizations for their driving, including forming the belief that environmentalists' claims are exaggerated (Holland, Meertens, & Van Vugt, 2002).

Hypocrisy Induction and Road Rage In a related attempt to apply **hypocrisy induction** to change destructive behavior, Seiji Takaku (2006) applied the theory to the problem of road rage. Road rage—situations in which people act out their anger while driving—is responsible for a high percentage of fatal car accidents and approximately $250 billion worth of social costs per year (AAA, 2004). In a series of experiments Takaku tested the effect of induced hypocrisy on reducing road rage. In one study he used video to simulate a highway situation in which a driver is cut off by another driver, a common incident that frequently leads to anger. In the experimental condition, the participant first accidentally cuts off another driver, thus being reminded of the fact that cutting people off is not an indication of a flawed personality, but rather the type of mistake that we are all capable of making. Takaku found that when people are reminded of their own fallibility, they are quicker to go from anger to forgiveness than if this reminder is not induced. This reminder reduces their felt need to retaliate.

The Power of Mild Punishment All societies run, in part, on punishment or the threat of punishment. For example, while cruising down the highway at 75 miles an hour, we know that if a cop spots us, we will pay a substantial fine, and if we get caught often, we will lose our license. So we learn to obey the speed limit when patrol cars are in the vicinity. By the same token, youngsters in school know that if they cheat on an exam and get caught, they could be humiliated by the teacher and severely punished. So they learn not to cheat while the teacher is in the room watching them. But does

Hypocrisy Induction
The arousal of dissonance by having individuals make statements that run counter to their behaviors and then reminding them of the inconsistency between what they advocated and their behavior. The purpose is to lead individuals to more responsible behavior.

A parent can intervene to stop bullying after it takes place, but what might she do to make it less likely to happen in the future?

Insufficient Punishment

The dissonance aroused when individuals lack sufficient external justification for having resisted a desired activity or object, usually resulting in individuals' devaluing the forbidden activity or object

harsh punishment teach adults to want to obey the speed limit? Does it teach youngsters to value honest behavior? We don't think so. Rather, we believe that all it teaches is to try to avoid getting caught.

Let's look at bullying behavior. It is extremely difficult to persuade children that it's not right or enjoyable to beat up smaller children (Olweus, 2002). But theoretically, it is conceivable that under certain conditions they will persuade themselves that such behavior is unenjoyable. Imagine that you are the parent of a 6-year-old boy who often beats up his 4-year-old brother. You've tried to reason with your older son, to no avail. In an attempt to make him a nicer person (and to preserve the health and welfare of his little brother), you begin to punish him for his aggressiveness. As a parent, you can use a range of punishments, from the extremely mild (a stern look) to the extremely severe (a hard spanking, forcing the child to stand in the corner for 2 hours, depriving him of TV privileges for a month). The more severe the threat, the greater the likelihood the youngster will cease and desist—while you are watching him. But he may very well hit his brother again as soon as you are out of sight. In short, just as most drivers learn to watch for the highway patrol while speeding, your 6-year-old still enjoys bullying his little brother; he has merely learned not to do it while you are around to punish him. Suppose that you threaten him with a mild punishment. In either case—under threat of severe punishment or of mild punishment—the child experiences dissonance. He is aware that he is not beating up his little brother, and he is also aware that he would like to beat him up. When he has the urge to hit his brother and doesn't, he implicitly asks himself, "How come I'm not beating up my little brother?" Under severe threat, he has a convincing answer in the form of a sufficient external justification: "I'm not beating him up because if I do, my parents are going to really punish me." This serves to reduce the dissonance.

The child in the mild threat situation experiences dissonance too. But when he asks himself, "How come I'm not beating up my little brother?" he doesn't have a very convincing answer because the threat is so mild that it does not provide a superabundance of justification. In short, this is **insufficient punishment**. The child is refraining from doing something he wants to do, and while he does have some justification for not doing it, he lacks complete justification. In this situation, he continues to experience dissonance; therefore, the child must find another way to justify the fact that he is not aggressing against his kid brother.

The less severe you make the threat, the less external justification there is; the less external justification, the greater the need for internal justification. The child can reduce his dissonance by convincing himself that he doesn't really want to beat up his brother. In time, he can go further in his quest for internal justification and decide that beating up little kids is not fun. We would predict, then, that allowing children the leeway to construct their own internal justification enables them to develop a permanent set of values.

So far, we have been speculating that threats of mild punishment for any behavior will make that behavior less likely than severe threats will. To find out if this is in fact what happens, Elliot Aronson and J. Merrill Carlsmith (1963) devised an experiment with preschoolers. Because very young children were involved, the researchers thought it would be unethical to try to influence important values, like those concerning aggressive behavior. Instead, they attempted to change something that was unimportant to society but very important to the children—their desire for different kinds of toys. The experimenter first asked each child to rate the attractiveness of several toys. He then pointed to a toy that the child considered among the most attractive and told the child that he or she was not allowed to play with it. Half the children were threatened with mild punishment if they disobeyed; the other half were threatened with severe punishment. The experimenter left the room for a few minutes, giving the children the time and opportunity to play with the other toys and to resist the temptation to play with the forbidden toy. None of the children played with the forbidden toy.

Next, the experimenter returned and asked each child to rate how much he or she liked each of the toys. Initially, everyone had wanted to play with the forbidden toy, but during the temptation period, when they had the chance, not one child played with the toy. Clearly, the children were experiencing dissonance. How did they respond to this uncomfortable feeling? The children who had received a severe threat had ample justification for their restraint. They knew why they hadn't played with the toy, and therefore, they had no reason to change their attitude about it. These children continued to rate the forbidden toy as highly desirable; indeed, some even found it more desirable than they had before the threat.

But what about the others? Without much external justification for avoiding the toy—they had little to fear if they played with it—the children in the mild threat condition needed an *internal* justification to reduce their dissonance. They succeeded in convincing themselves that the reason they hadn't played with the toy was that they didn't really like it. They rated the forbidden toy as less attractive than they had when the experiment began. What we have here is a clear example of self-justification leading to self-persuasion in the behavior of very young children. The implications for child rearing are fascinating. Parents who use punishment to encourage their children to adopt desirable values should keep the punishment mild—barely enough to produce a change in behavior—and the values will follow.

Does Self-Persuasion Last? Let's say you've attended a lecture on the evils of cheating. It might have a temporary effect on your attitudes toward cheating. But if a week or two later you found yourself in a highly tempting situation, would your new attitude keep you from cheating? Probably not. Social psychologists know that mere lectures do not usually result in permanent or long-lasting attitude change. But suppose that your experience was similar to the children's in Judson Mills's (1958) experiment on cheating, discussed earlier in this chapter. Here we would expect that your new attitude would endure. The children who were tempted to cheat but resisted came to believe that cheating is bad, not because someone told them so but through **self-persuasion**: They persuaded themselves of this belief to justify the fact that by not cheating, they had given up something they really wanted. Self-persuasion is more permanent than direct attempts at persuasion precisely because, with self-persuasion, the persuasion takes place internally and not because of external coaxing or pressure.

To test the long-lasting effects of attitudes that result from self-justification, Jonathan Freedman (1965) replicated Aronson and Carlsmith's (1963) forbidden toy experiment. Several weeks later, a young woman came to the school, telling the children she was there to administer some paper-and-pencil tests. In fact, she was working for Freedman. Coincidentally, she was administering her tests in the same room Freedman had used for his experiment—the room where the same toys were casually scattered about. After administering the test, she asked the children to wait for her while she scored it in another room. She then casually suggested that the scoring might take a while and that—how lucky!—someone had left some toys around and the children could play with anything they liked.

The results were striking: The overwhelming majority of the children whom Freedman had mildly threatened several weeks earlier decided, on their own, not to play with the forbidden toy. By contrast, the great majority of the children who had been severely threatened played with the forbidden toy. A single mild threat was still very effective several weeks later; the severe threat was not.

Again, the power of this phenomenon rests on the fact that the reason the children didn't play with the toy was not that some adult told them the toy was undesirable: That kind of information would not have had much effect after the adult left. The reason the mild threat persisted for at least several weeks was that *the children were motivated to convince themselves the toy was undesirable*. The results of Freedman's experiment are presented in Figure 6.5.

How can we induce this child to give up playing with an attractive toy?

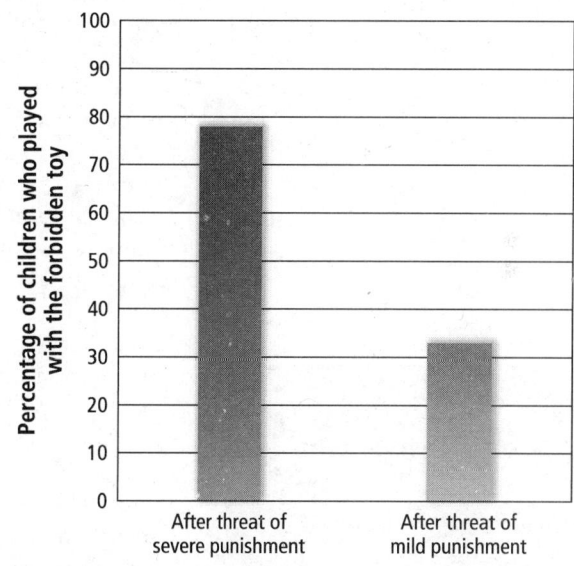

FIGURE 6.5

The forbidden toy experiment.

Several weeks afterward, children who had received a threat of mild punishment were far less likely to play with the forbidden toy than children who had received a threat of severe punishment. Those given a mild threat had to provide their own justification by devaluing the attractiveness of the toy.

(Adapted from Freedman, 1965)

Self-Persuasion

A long-lasting form of attitude change that results from attempts at self-justification

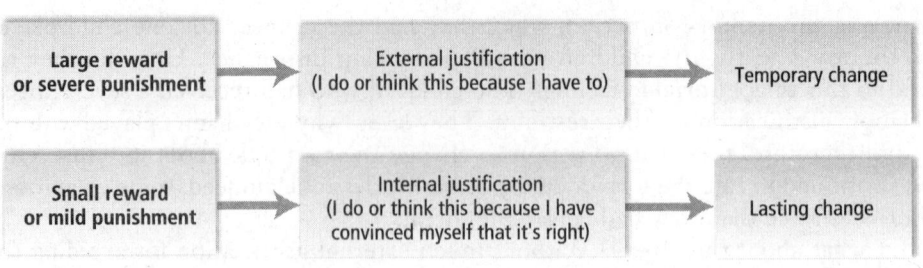

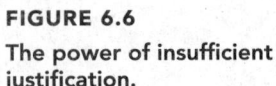

FIGURE 6.6
The power of insufficient justification.

Not Just Tangible Rewards or Punishments As we have seen, a sizable reward or a severe punishment provides strong external justification for an action. So if you want a person to do something or not to do something only once, the best strategy would be to promise a large reward or threaten a severe punishment. But if you want a person to become committed to an attitude or to a behavior, the *smaller* the reward or punishment that will lead to momentary compliance, the *greater* will be the eventual change in attitude and therefore the more permanent the effect. Large rewards and severe punishments, because they are strong external justifications, encourage compliance but prevent real attitude change (see Figure 6.6.)

This phenomenon is not limited to tangible rewards and punishments; justifications can also come in more subtle packages. Take friendship, for example. We like our friends; we trust our friends; we do favors for our friends. Suppose you are at a formal dinner party at the home of a close friend. Your friend is passing around a strange-looking appetizer. "What is it?" you ask. "Oh, it's a fried grasshopper; I'd really like you to try it." She's a good friend and you don't want to embarrass her in front of the other guests, so you pick one up and eat it. How much do you think you will like this new snack food?

Keep that in mind for a moment. Now suppose you are a dinner guest at the home of a person you don't like very much, and he hands you, as an appetizer, a fried grasshopper and tells you that he'd really like you to try it. You comply. Now the crucial question: In which of these two situations will you like the taste of the grasshopper better? Common sense might suggest that the grasshopper would taste better when recommended by a friend. But think about it for a moment; which condition involves less external justification? Common sense notwithstanding, dissonance theory makes the opposite prediction. In the first case, when you ask yourself, "How come I ate that disgusting insect?" you have ample justification: You ate it because your good friend asked you to. In the second case, you don't have this kind of outside justification, so you must create it. Namely, you must convince yourself that you actually *liked* the grasshopper. Although this may seem a rather bizarre example of dissonance-reducing behavior, it's not as far-fetched as you might think. Indeed, Philip Zimbardo and his colleagues conducted an experiment directly analogous to our example (Zimbardo, Weisenberg, Firestone, & Levy, 1965). In this experiment, army reservists were asked to eat fried grasshoppers as part of a research project on survival foods. Reservists who ate grasshoppers at the request of a stern, unpleasant officer increased their liking for grasshoppers far more than those who ate grasshoppers at the request of a well-liked, pleasant officer. Those who complied with the unfriendly officer's request had little external justification for their actions. As a result, they adopted more positive attitudes toward eating grasshoppers in order to justify their otherwise strange and dissonance-arousing behavior.

Good and Bad Deeds 善行与恶行

Whenever we act either kindly or cruelly toward a person, we never quite feel the same way about that person again. (See the following Try It! exercise.)

The Ben Franklin Effect When we like people, we show it by treating them well. The reverse is also true. We might even go out of our way to snub someone we dislike. But what happens when we do a person a favor? In particular, what happens when we are subtly induced to do a favor for a person we do not like—will we like the person

Without realizing it, Ben Franklin may have been the first dissonance theorist.

TRY IT! Good Deeds 试一试！善 行

When you walk down a city street and view people sitting on the sidewalk, panhandling, or pushing their possessions around in a shopping cart, how do you feel about them? Think about it for a few moments, and write down a list of your feelings. If you are like most college students, your list will reflect some mixed feelings. That is, you probably feel some compassion but also think these people are a nuisance, that if they really tried, they could get their lives together. The next time you go to an area that has people panhandling (and/or people digging through the trash) take the initiative and give one of these people $1 and wish them well. Note your feelings. Is there a change in how you perceive these people? How so? Analyze any changes you notice in terms of cognitive dissonance theory.

more? Or less? Dissonance theory predicts that we will like the person more after doing the favor. Can you see why? Jot down your answer in the margin.

This phenomenon has been a part of folk wisdom in several cultures for a very long time. The great Russian novelist Leo Tolstoy wrote about it in 1869, and more than a century before that, Benjamin Franklin confessed to having used this bit of folk wisdom as a political strategy. While serving in the Pennsylvania state legislature, Franklin was disturbed by the political opposition and animosity of a fellow legislator. So he set out to win him over.

> I did not . . . aim at gaining his favour by paying any servile respect to him but, after some time, took this other method. Having heard that he had in his library a certain very scarce and curious book I wrote a note to him expressing my desire of perusing that book and requesting he would do me the favour of lending it to me for a few days. He sent it immediately and I returned it in about a week with another note expressing strongly my sense of the favour. When we next met in the House he spoke to me (which he had never done before), and with great civility; and he ever after manifested a readiness to serve me on all occasions, so that we became great friends and our friendship continued to his death. This is another instance of the truth of an old maxim I had learned, which says, "He that has once done you a kindness will be more ready to do you another than he whom you yourself have obliged."
>
> (Franklin, 1868/1900, pp. 216–217)

Benjamin Franklin was clearly pleased with the success of his blatantly manipulative strategy. But as rigorous scientists, we should not be convinced by his anecdote. We have no way to know whether Franklin's success was due to this particular gambit or simply to his general, all-around charm. To be certain, it is important to design and conduct an experiment that controls for such things as charm. Such a study was conducted by Jon Jecker and David Landy (1969), more than 240 years after Franklin's more casual experiment. In the Jecker and Landy experiment, students participated in an intellectual contest that enabled them to win a substantial sum of money. After the experiment was over, one-third of the participants were approached by the experimenter, who explained that he was using his own funds for the experiment and was running short, which meant he might be forced to close down the experiment prematurely. He asked, "As a special favor to me, would you mind returning the money you won?" The same request was made to a different group of subjects, except this time not by the experimenter but by the departmental secretary, who asked them if they would return the money as a special favor to the (impersonal) psychology department's research fund, which was running low. The remaining participants were not asked to return their winnings at all. Finally, all of the participants were asked to fill out a questionnaire that included an opportunity to rate the experimenter. Participants who had been

> We do not love people so much for the good they have done us as for the good we have done them.
>
> —Leo Tolstoy, 1869

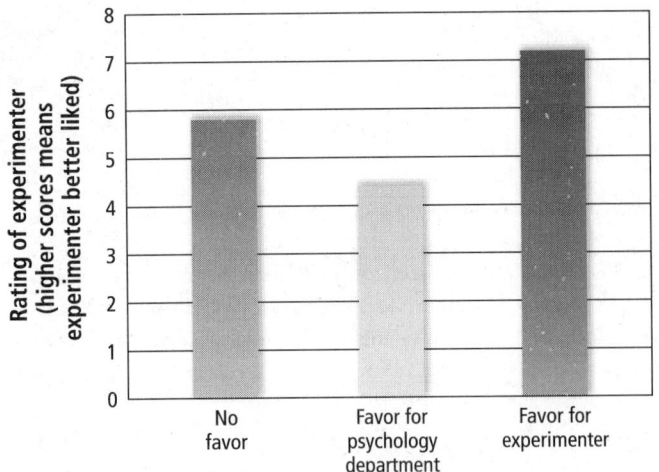

FIGURE 6.7

If we have done someone a favor, we are likely to feel more positively toward that person.

(Adapted from Jecker & Landy, 1969)

cajoled into doing a special favor for the experimenter found him the most attractive; that is, after they did him a favor, they convinced themselves he was a wonderful, deserving fellow. The others thought he was a pretty nice guy but not anywhere near as wonderful as the people who had been asked to do him a favor (see Figure 6.7).

Recall the experiment by Mike Leippe and Donna Eisenstadt in which white students developed more favorable attitudes toward African Americans after having said publicly that they favored preferential treatment for African American students. Can you see how the "Ben Franklin effect" might apply here—how this act of helping might have contributed to their change in attitudes?

Suppose you find yourself in a situation where you have an opportunity to lend a helping hand to an acquaintance, but because you are in a hurry or because it is inconvenient, you decline to help that person. How do you think this act of omission might affect your feelings for this person? This is precisely the kind of situation investigated by Gail Williamson and her colleagues (Williamson, Clark, Pegalis, & Behan, 1996). As you might expect, this refusal led to a decline in the attractiveness of the acquaintance. This was an act of omission. But suppose you actually did harm to another person. What do you suppose might happen then? We will discuss that in the following section.

Hating Our Victims During the height of the war in Vietnam, Elliot Aronson hired a young man to help paint his house.

> The painter was a gentle and sweet-natured person who had graduated from high school, joined the army, and fought in Vietnam. After leaving the army, he took up housepainting and was a good and reliable craftsman and an honest businessman. I enjoyed working with him. One day while we were taking a coffee break, we began to discuss the war and the intense opposition to it, especially at the local university. It soon became apparent that he and I were in sharp disagreement on this issue. He felt that the American intervention was reasonable and just and would "make the world safe for democracy." I argued that it was a terribly dirty war, that we were killing, maiming, and napalming thousands of innocent people—old people, women, children—people who had no interest in war or politics. He looked at me for a long time; then he smiled sweetly and said, "Hell, Doc, those aren't people; those are Vietnamese! They're gooks." He said it matter-of-factly, without obvious rancor or vehemence. I was astonished and chilled by his response. I wondered how it could be that this apparently good-natured, sane, and gentle young man could develop that kind of attitude. How could he dismiss an entire national group from the human race?
>
> Over the next several days, as we continued our dialogue, I got to know more about him. It turned out that during the war he had participated in actions in which Vietnamese civilians had been killed. What gradually emerged was that initially he had been racked by guilt—and it dawned on me that he might have developed this attitude toward the Vietnamese people as a way of assuaging his guilt. That is, if he could convince himself that the Vietnamese were not fully human, it would make him feel less awful about having hurt them, and it would reduce the dissonance between his actions and his self-concept as a decent person.

Clearly, these speculations about the causes of the housepainter's attitude are far from conclusive. While he may have derogated the Vietnamese people as a way of reducing dissonance, the situation is complex; for example, he might always have had a negative and prejudiced attitude toward the Vietnamese, and this might have made it easier for him to behave brutally toward them. To be certain that the justification of cruelty can occur in such situations, it is essential for the social psychologist to temporarily step back from the helter-skelter of the real world and test the proposition in the more controlled setting of the experimental laboratory.

Ideally, if we want to measure attitude change as a result of dissonant cognitions, we should know what the attitudes were before the dissonance-arousing behavior occurred. Such a situation was produced in an experiment performed by Keith Davis and Edward Jones (1960). Each student's participation consisted of watching a young man being interviewed and then, on the basis of this observation, providing him with an analysis of his shortcomings as a human being. Specifically, the participants were told to tell the young man (a confederate of the researchers) that they thought he was a shallow, untrustworthy, boring person. The participants succeeded in convincing themselves that they didn't like the victim of their cruelty—after the fact. In short, after saying things they knew were certain to hurt him, they convinced themselves that he deserved to be hurt. They found him less attractive than they had prior to saying the hurtful things to him.

Let's go back to our housepainter example. Suppose for a moment that all the people he killed and injured in Vietnam had been fully armed enemy soldiers rather than noncombatants. Do you think he would have experienced as much dissonance? We think it is unlikely. When engaged in combat with an enemy soldier, it is a "you or me" situation; if the housepainter had not killed the enemy soldier, the enemy soldier might have killed him. So even though hurting or killing another person is probably never taken lightly, it is not nearly so heavy a burden as it would be if the victim were an unarmed civilian—a child, a woman, an old person.

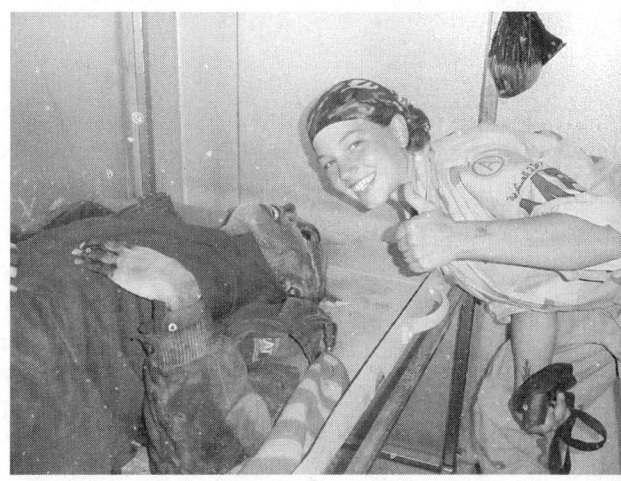

Why does war lead to the dehumanization of the enemy?

These speculations are supported by the results of an experiment by Ellen Berscheid and her colleagues (Berscheid, Boye, & Walster, 1968). College students volunteered for an experiment in which each of them administered a (supposedly) painful electric shock to a fellow student. As one might expect, these students derogated their victim as a result of having administered the shock. Half the students were told there would be a turnabout: The other student would be given the opportunity to retaliate against them at a later time. Those who were led to believe that their victim would be able to retaliate later did not derogate the victim. In short, because the victim was going to be able to even the score, there was very little dissonance, and therefore the harm-doers had no need to belittle their victim in order to convince themselves that he or she deserved it.

There's nothing people can't contrive to praise or condemn and find justification for doing so.

—Moliére, *The Misanthrope*

The results of these laboratory experiments lend credence to our speculations about the behavior of the housepainter; the results suggest that during a war, military personnel have a greater need to derogate civilian victims (because these individuals can't retaliate) than military victims. Moreover, several years after Aronson's encounter with the housepainter, a similar set of events emerged during the court-martial of Lieutenant William Calley for his role in the slaughter of innocent civilians at My Lai in Vietnam. In long and detailed testimony, Calley's psychiatrist made it clear that the lieutenant had come to regard the Vietnamese people as less than human.

As we have seen, systematic research in this area demonstrates that people do not perform acts of cruelty and come out unscathed. We can never be completely certain of how the housepainter, Lieutenant Calley, and thousands of other American military personnel came to regard the Vietnamese as subhuman, but it seems reasonable to assume that when people are engaged in a war where a great number of innocent people are being killed, they might try to derogate the victims to justify their complicity. They might poke fun at them, refer to them as "gooks," and dehumanize them. Ironically, success at dehumanizing the victim virtually guarantees a continuation or even an escalation of the cruelty. It becomes easier to hurt and kill subhumans than to hurt and kill fellow human beings. Reducing dissonance in this way therefore has sobering future consequences: It increases the likelihood that the atrocities people are willing to commit will become greater and greater through an endless chain of violence followed by self-justification (in the form of dehumanizing the victim), followed by greater violence and still more intense dehumanization. In this manner, unbelievable acts of human cruelty—such as the Nazi "Final Solution" that led to the murder of 6 million European Jews—can occur. Unfortunately, atrocities are not a thing of the past but are as recent as today's newspaper.

Culture and Dissonance 文化与失调

We can find the effects of dissonance in almost every part of the world (e.g., Beauvois & Joule, 1996; Sakai, 1999), but it does not always take the same form. Harry Triandis (1995) has argued that in societies where the needs of the group matter more than the needs of the individual, dissonance-reducing behavior might be less prevalent—at least on the surface. In such cultures, we'd be more likely to find behavior aimed at maintaining group harmony and less likely to see self-justification, which is an individual drive. Others have argued that dissonance-reducing behavior may be less extreme in Japan than it is in the West because Japanese culture considers an individual's acceptance of inconsistency to be a sign of maturity and broad-mindedness (Hong, 1992).

It may also be that self-justification does occur in less individualistic societies but is triggered in more communal ways. In a striking set of experiments, Japanese social psychologist Haruki Sakai (1999) investigated dissonance-reducing behavior in Japan by combining his interest in dissonance with his expert knowledge of Japanese community orientation. In a nutshell, what Sakai found was that in Japan, not only does a person reduce dissonance after saying that a boring task is interesting and enjoyable (as in the classic Festinger and Carlsmith experiment), but in addition, if a person merely observes someone he or she knows and likes saying that a boring task is interesting and enjoyable, that will cause the observer to experience dissonance. Consequently, in that situation, the observer's attitudes change. In short, observers bring their evaluation more in line with the lie their friend has told!

CONNECTIONS 链 接

Dissonance Theory Used by Mainstream Journalist to Explain the Actions of Suicide Bombers
主流记者基于认知失调理论对自杀性爆炸事件的解释

Following the catastrophic destruction of the World Trade Center by suicide bombers on September 11, 2001, political analysts struggled to understand how hatred can be so strong that people would destroy themselves to kill thousands of innocent people—when they must have known that their action could not possibly produce any direct political advantage. Most analysts have explained the behavior of the suicide bombers in terms of religious fanaticism. But this explanation does not add much to our understanding. Thomas Friedman, a Pulitzer Prize–winning journalist and an astute observer of the Middle East, has taken a different approach. He has offered a partial answer to this most difficult question based on the theory of cognitive dissonance. Friedman (2002) suggests that there are thousands of young Muslim men all over the Middle East and Europe who are suffering from a loss of dignity. According to Friedman, these young men were

> taught from youth in the mosque that theirs is the most complete and advanced form of the three monotheistic faiths—superior to both Christianity and Judaism—yet who become aware that the Islamic world has fallen behind both the Christian West and the Jewish state in education, science, democracy, and development. This produces a **cognitive dissonance** in these young men—a **cognitive dissonance** that is the original spark for all their rage.... They reconcile this by concluding that the Islamic world has fallen behind the rest of the world either because the Europeans, Americans, and Israelis stole something from the Muslims, or because the Europeans, Americans, and Israelis are deliberately retarding the progress of Muslims, or because those who are leading the Muslim world have drifted away from the true faith and are behaving in un-Islamic ways, but are being kept in power by America.... They see America as the most powerful lethal weapon destroying their religious universe, or at least the universe they would like to build. And that is why they transform America into the ultimate evil, even more than Western Europe, an evil that needs to be weakened and, if possible, destroyed. Even by suicide? Why not? If America is destroying the source of meaning in their lives, then it needs to be destroyed back. (2002, pp. 334–335)

Some Final Thoughts on Dissonance: Learning from Our Mistakes
关于失调的最后几点思考：从我们所犯的错误中学习

Throughout this chapter, we've seen that dissonance-reducing behavior can be useful because it restores our sense of stability and allows us to maintain our self-esteem. But if we human beings were to spend all our time and energy defending our egos, we would never learn from our mistakes. Instead, we would try to ignore them or, worse still, attempt to turn them into virtues. If we do not learn from our mistakes, we will get stuck within the confines of our narrow minds and fail to grow or change.

The first thing we must do is become more aware of the human tendency toward self-justification. But, as we have seen, the process of self-justification is an unconscious one. Nevertheless, once we know that we are prone to justify our actions, we can begin to monitor our thinking and, in effect, "catch ourselves in the act." We can then begin to examine our behavior critically and dispassionately. We then stand a chance of breaking out of the cycle of action followed by self-justification followed by more intense action. For example, suppose that Mary, a college student, has acted unkindly toward her roommate, Sandra. Mary's usual course of action would be to convince herself that Sandra deserved it. To learn from that experience, Mary must be able to resist the need to derogate her victim. Ideally, it would be effective if she were able to stay with the dissonance long enough to say, "OK, I blew it; I did a cruel and stupid thing. But that doesn't necessarily make me a cruel or stupid person. Let me think about why I did what I did, how I can make amends, and how I can learn from the experience so that I don't make a similar mistake again." Admittedly, this is easier said than done—precisely because it involves acknowledging our mistakes and most people have difficulty doing that.

It is hard enough for ordinary people like us to take responsibility for our mistakes. History suggests that it is much harder for political leaders to do so (Tavris & Aronson, 2007). The memoirs of some of our most beleaguered former presidents are full of the kinds of self-serving, self-justifying statements that can best be summarized as "If I had it all to do over again, I would not change very much" (Johnson, 1971; Nixon, 1990; Reagan, 1990).

When we ordinary people get caught up in a cycle of self-justification, we lose an opportunity to learn and to grow. When a political leader gets caught up in that cycle, the consequences can be devastating.

In his memoirs, Robert McNamara (1995), who was secretary of defense and one of President Lyndon Johnson's principal military advisers during the Vietnam War, reveals that he came to the realization that the war was not winnable as early as 1967—eight years before our eventual withdrawal. But he chose to remain silent on this issue—even after leaving office—while the war raged on, incurring tens of thousands of additional American casualties as well as more than one hundred thousand Vietnamese lives. Most knowledgeable analysts believe that to have been a tragic and catastrophic error, arguing that if he had spoken out publicly, it could have shortened the war. To have admitted that the war was not winnable was so very discrepant with so much of his earlier analyses (e.g., "I can see the light at the end of the tunnel")—he chose to keep quiet.

More recently, President George W. Bush wanted to believe that Iraqi leader Saddam Hussein possessed weapons of mass destruction (WMD) which posed a threat to Americans. This led the president and his advisers to interpret CIA reports as definitive proof of Iraq's weapons of mass destruction, even though the reports were ambiguous and were contradicted by other evidence. President Bush's interpretation

These women blew a big lead and lost the game. Will they make excuses or will they learn from their mistakes?

Did President Bush convince himself that invading Iraq was essential?

provided the justification to launch a preemptive war. He was convinced that once our troops entered Iraq they would find these weapons.

After the invasion of Iraq, administration officials, when asked "Where are the WMD?" said that Iraq is a big country and they have them well hidden but asserted that they would be found. As the months dragged on and still no WMD were found, they continued to assert that they would find them. Why? Because they were experiencing enormous dissonance. They had to believe they would find them. Finally, it was officially concluded that there were no WMD. This suggests that at the time of our invasion, Iraq posed no immediate threat to the United States.

Now what? American soldiers and Iraqi civilians were dying every week, and tens of billions of dollars were being drained from the treasury. How did President Bush and his staff reduce dissonance? By *adding new cognitions to justify* the war: Suddenly we learned that the U.S. mission was to liberate the nation from a cruel dictator and give the Iraqi people the blessings of democratic institutions. To a neutral observer, that justification was inadequate (after all, there are a great many brutal dictators in the world). But to President Bush and his advisers, who had been experiencing enormous dissonance, the justification seemed reasonable.

Several commentators have suggested that the Bush administration was dissembling—that they were deliberately trying to deceive the American people. We cannot be certain what was going on in the president's mind. What we do know, based on 50 years of research on cognitive dissonance, is that the president and his advisers may not have been intentionally deceiving the American people, but it is likely that they succeeded in deceiving *themselves*. That is, they may have succeeded in convincing themselves that invading Iraq was worthwhile even in the absence of WMD.

How can a leader avoid falling into the self-justification trap? Historical examples show us that the way out of this process is for leaders to bring in skilled advisers *outside the inner circle* because they are not caught up in the need to reduce dissonance from their earlier decision making. Precisely for this reason, Abraham Lincoln chose a cabinet that included several people who disagreed with his policies (Goodwin, 2005). President Obama has taken a page from Lincoln's playbook. His cabinet consists of individuals with demonstrated effectiveness including several whose political values are more conservative than his own. Although this caused some consternation among his liberal supporters, our guess is that it will make for better decision making and help avoid excessive self-justification.

> Both salvation and punishment for man lie in the fact that, if he lives wrongly, he can befog himself so as not to see the misery of his position.
> —Leo Tolstoy

Heaven's Gate Revisited 再探天门教事件

At the beginning of this chapter, we raised a vital question regarding the followers of Marshall Herff Applewhite of Heaven's Gate. Similar questions were raised in Chapter 1 about the followers of the Reverend Jim Jones and those of David Koresh in Waco, Texas. How could intelligent people allow themselves to be led into what to the overwhelming majority of us is obviously senseless and tragic behavior, resulting in mass suicide? Needless to say, the situation is complex; there were many factors operating, including the charismatic, persuasive power of each of these leaders, the existence of a great deal of social support for the views of the group (from other members of the group), and the relative isolation of each group from dissenting views, producing a closed system—a little like living in a roomful of mirrors.

In addition to these factors, we are convinced that one of the single most powerful forces common to all these groups was the existence of a high degree of cognitive dissonance within the minds of the participants. After reading this chapter, you now realize that when individuals make an important decision and invest heavily in that decision (in terms of time, effort, sacrifice, and commitment), this results in a strong need to justify those actions and that investment. The more they give up and the harder they work, the greater will be the need to convince themselves that their views are correct; indeed, they may even begin to feel sorry for others who do not share their beliefs. The members of the Heaven's Gate cult sacrificed a great deal for their beliefs: They abandoned their friends and families, turned their backs on their professions, relinquished their money and possessions, moved to another part of the world, and worked hard and long for the particular cause they believed in—all increasing their commitment to the belief. Those of us who have studied the theory of cognitive dissonance were not surprised to learn that the Heaven's Gate people, having bought a telescope that failed to reveal a spaceship that wasn't there, concluded that the telescope was faulty. To have believed otherwise would have created too much dissonance to bear. That they went on to abandon their "containers," believing that they were moving on to a higher incarnation, although tragic and bizarre, is not unfathomable. It is simply an extreme manifestation of a process that we have seen in operation over and over again throughout this chapter.

HOW WOULD YOU USE THIS? 如何学以致用?

You have a friend who drives after drinking. You keep telling him that it is dangerous to do it. He says he can handle it. How could you get him to change his behavior? *Hint*: Think about the research on getting students to practice safe sex (use condoms); think about the "hypocrisy paradigm."

Summary 总 结

- **Maintaining a Stable, Positive Self-Image** Most people generally need to see themselves as intelligent, sensible, and decent folks who behave with integrity. Indeed, what triggers the behavior change and cognitive distortion that occur when we try to reduce feelings of dissonance is precisely our need to maintain this picture of ourselves. At first glance, much of the behavior described in this chapter may seem startling—people coming to dislike others more after doing them harm; people liking others more after doing them a favor; people believing a lie they've told only if there is little or no reward for telling it. These behaviors would be difficult for us to understand if it weren't for the insights provided by the theory of cognitive dissonance.
  - **The Theory of Cognitive Dissonance** According to cognitive dissonance theory, people experience discomfort (dissonance) when they behave in ways that are inconsistent with their conception of themselves (self-image). To reduce the dissonance, people either (1) change their behavior to bring it in line with their cognitions about themselves, (2) justify their behavior by changing one of their cognitions, or (3) attempt to justify their behavior by inventing new cognitions.
- **Rational Behavior versus Rationalizing Behavior** Humans often process information in a biased way, one that fits our preconceived notions. The explanation for this is that information or ideas that disagree with our views arouse dissonance. And we humans avoid dissonance even at the expense of rational behavior.
- **Decisions, Decisions, Decisions** Decisions arouse dissonance because they require choosing one thing and not the other. The thought that we may have made the wrong choice causes discomfort because it would threaten our self-image as one who makes good decisions. After the choice is final, the mind diminishes the discomfort through solidifying the case for the item chosen.

Dissonance, the Brain, and Evolution

- **Justifying Your Effort** People tend to increase their liking for something they have worked hard to attain, even if the thing they attained is not something they would otherwise like. This explains, for example, the intense loyalty the initiated feel for their fraternities after undergoing hazing.

- **The Psychology of Insufficient Justification** This effect is wonderfully counterintuitive. When we perform an action because of the ample reward to do it, then the action has little or no effect on our attitudes or beliefs. However, if the reward is not big enough to justify the action, we find ourselves experiencing cognitive dissonance because there is little *external* justification for what we did. This activates an *internal* process to justify the action to ourselves. The internal process of self-justification has a much more powerful effect on an individual's long-term values and behaviors than a situation where the external justifications are evident.

- **Advocacy and Hypocrisy Applied to Social Problems** When someone publicly advocates something that is counter to what they believe or how they actually behave, it arouses dissonance. In the case of an AIDS prevention experiment, participants videotaped speeches about the importance of using condoms and they were made aware of their own failure to use them. To reduce dissonance, they changed their behavior—they purchased condoms. Inducing hypocrisy—making people face the difference between what they say and what they do—is one way to use the human tendency to reduce dissonance to foster socially beneficial behaviors.

- **Good and Bad Deeds** A clever, though manipulative, application of cognitive dissonance theory is to get someone to like you by having them do you a favor. The reason this works is that the person needs to internally justify the fact that they did something for you. The converse is true as well. If one does harm to another, in order to reduce the threat to their self-image that could come from doing a bad deed, they will tend to justify the bad deed by derogating their victim. That is, they will embrace the cognition that the victim deserved the harm or, in more extreme cases, that they are less than human.

- **Culture and Dissonance** Cognitive dissonance is also found to take place in non-Western cultures, but the process and intensity of dissonance reduction does vary, reflecting the difference in cultural norms.

- **Some Final Thoughts on Dissonance: Learning from Our Mistakes** There are times when dissonance reduction is counterproductive because it solidifies negative values and behaviors. Although the process of reducing dissonance is unconscious, it is possible to intervene in the process. The knowledge humans are dissonance-reducing animals can make us more aware of the process. The next time we feel the discomfort of having acted counter to our values, we can consciously pause the self-justification process to reflect on our action.

CHAPTER 6 TEST 第6章习题

1. Based on the Ben Franklin effect, you are most likely to increase your liking for Tony when
    a. Tony lends you $10.
    b. you lend Tony $10.
    c. Tony returns the $10 you loaned him.
    d. Tony finds $10.

2. After spending two years fixing up an old house themselves, which involved many hours of tedious work, Abby and Brian are even more convinced that they made the right choice of house. According to the dissonance theory, this is an example of
    a. counterattitudinal advocacy.
    b. insufficient punishment.
    c. the Ben Franklin effect.
    d. justifying their effort.

3. Your friend Amy asks you what you think of the shoes she just bought. Privately you think they are some of the ugliest shoes you have ever seen, but you tell her you love them. In the past, Amy has always valued your honest opinion and she doesn't care that much about the shoes—they were inexpensive. Because the external justification for your fib was _____, you will probably _____.
    a. high, decide you like the shoes
    b. high, maintain your view that the shoes are ugly
    c. low, decide you like the shoes
    d. low, maintain your view that the shoes are ugly

4. Meghan has been accepted to two top graduate schools. According to cognitive dissonance theory, under which of the following conditions will she experience the most dissonance?
    a. When she is thinking about the pros and cons of both programs before making up her mind.
    b. When she is pretty sure which program she wants to attend but has not yet notified them of her decision.
    c. Right after she decides which program to attend and notifies them of her decision.
    d. Megan will experience an equal amount of dissonance in each of the above three circumstances.

5. You are required to sell $30 entertainment books for a club fundraiser. How could you use the technique of lowballing to improve your sales?
    a. Start by offering the books at $70 each and pretend to bargain with customers, making $30 your "final offer."
    b. Start by selling the books at $25, but once the customer has retrieved his or her checkbook, tell him or her you made a mistake and the books are actually $5 more expensive than you thought.
    c. Offer the customers additional incentives to buy the book (like free cookies with every purchase).

d. Start by selling the books at $40, but tell the customer he or she will get $10 back in the mail in 3 weeks.

6. Suppose you are babysitting for two boys, brothers who are ages 6 and 3. The older child often beats up his younger brother. What would be the most effective way to make him stop?
   a. Threaten the older child with mild punishment, like sitting in time-out for 5 minutes—and hope that he obeys.
   b. Threaten the older child with mild punishment, like sitting in time-out for 5 minutes, and don't worry about whether he obeys.
   c. Threaten the older child with very harsh punishment, like spanking him.
   d. Talk to the younger child about ways he can defend himself.

7. Which of the following techniques relating to *postdecision dissonance* could a clothing store use to increase customer satisfaction?
   a. Cut all prices in half.
   b. Ask customers to make a radio ad saying how great the store is.
   c. Charge a membership fee to shop at the store.
   d. Make all sales final.

8. A school principal who wants to reduce vandalism has several students who are notorious for graffiti give a speech to the entire school about the negative aspects of damaging school property. Which of the following should the principal do to make it most likely that these students will actually stop vandalizing the school, according to research using the hypocrisy paradigm?
   a. He should have every student deliver a speech, not just those who have already committed vandalism.
   b. He should have them deliver speeches about the positive aspects of vandalism as well as the negative aspects.
   c. After they make the speech, he should ask them to remember times they have committed vandalism.
   d. Right after students deliver the speech, he should ask them to volunteer to help clean up the school parking lot.

9. Imagine that before a test, the professor told Jake that if he is caught cheating, he will be expelled. Imagine that the professor told Amanda that if caught cheating, her only punishment will be to write a short paper about why cheating is wrong. If both students don't cheat, what would dissonance theory predict?
   a. Amanda will feel more honest than Jake will.
   b. Jake will feel more honest than Amanda will.
   c. Amanda and Jake will both feel equally honest.
   d. Neither Jake nor Amanda will feel honest because they were both threatened.

10. Bess undergoes treatment for drug addiction. According to cognitive dissonance theory, after she leaves the clinic, Bess is most likely to stay off drugs if the treatment at the clinic was
    a. involuntary (she was ordered to undergo treatment) and a difficult ordeal.
    b. involuntary (she was ordered to undergo treatment) and an easy experience.
    c. voluntary (she chose to undergo treatment) and an easy experience.
    d. voluntary (she chose to undergo treatment) and a very difficult ordeal.

Chapter 6 Answer Key
1-b 2-d 3-c 4-c 5-b 6-a 7-d 8-c 9-a 10-d

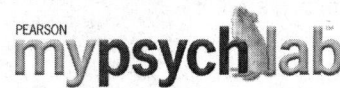

For more review plus practice tests, videos, flashcards, writing help and more, log on to MyPsychLab.

7

Attitudes and Attitude Change

Influencing Thoughts and Feelings

态度与态度改变：

影响思维和情绪

OUTLINE 提纲

- **The Nature and Origin of Attitudes**
  - Where Do Attitudes Come From?
  - Explicit Versus Implicit Attitudes
- **How Do Attitudes Change?**
  - Changing Attitudes by Changing Behavior: Cognitive Dissonance Theory Revisited
  - Persuasive Communications and Attitude Change
  - Emotion and Attitude Change
  - Confidence in One's Thoughts and Attitude Change
- **Resisting Persuasive Messages**
  - Attitude Inoculation
  - Be Alert to Product Placement
  - Resisting Peer Pressure
  - When Persuasion Attempts Boomerang: Reactance Theory
- **When Will Attitudes Predict Behavior?**
  - Predicting Spontaneous Behaviors
  - Predicting Deliberative Behaviors
- **The Power of Advertising**
  - How Advertising Works
  - CONNECTIONS: Do Media Campaigns to Reduce Drug Use Work?
  - Subliminal Advertising: A Form of Mind Control?
  - Advertising, Cultural Stereotypes, and Social Behavior
- **Summary**

I T SEEMS AS IF ADVERTISING HAS MADE INROADS EVERYWHERE we look. Ads are rampant on the Internet, on the inside door of stalls in public restrooms, and on video screens at cash machines and gasoline pumps (Cropper, 1998). But Andrew Fischer, a 20-year-old from Omaha, Nebraska, wins the prize for advertising innovation. Fischer placed an ad on EBay, offering to wear someone's logo or message on his forehead for 30 days (in the form of a nonpermanent tattoo). The bidding was furious (especially after the national press wrote about Fischer) and was finally won by a company called SnoreStop that makes products to keep people from snoring. They paid Fischer a whopping $37,375, and he dutifully imprinted their logo on his forehead (Puente, 2005).

Fischer was not alone in offering his body to advertisers. Jacob Authier, a student at Chapman College in California known as the "Shirtless Guy," wore birthday greetings or political slogans on his chest for a mere $1 each (Pomfret, 2005). And an Internet gambling site paid Elise Harp $8,800 to wear its Web address on her stomach. Harp was 8 months pregnant at the time (Puente, 2005). The human body is not the only strange new venue for advertising. In case you wanted to check out the new TV lineup on CBS, you could open your refrigerator. In the fall of 2006, CBS advertised its new programs on eggshells (Joachim, 2006).

It is easy to laugh at the lengths to which advertisers will go, brushing them off as absurd but harmless attempts to influence us. We should keep in mind, though, that advertising can have powerful effects. Consider the history of cigarette ads. In the nineteenth century, most consumer goods, including tobacco products, were made and sold locally. But as the Industrial Revolution led to the mass production

"How else are we going to pay for the war?"

People have begun offering their own bodies as venues for advertisers. Andrew Fischer received $37,375 to wear a SnoreStop tattoo on his forehead for 30 days. Elise Harp (shown here) received $8,800 to advertise GoldenPalace on her belly.

of many consumer products, manufacturers sought broader markets for their products. Advertising was the natural result. In the 1880s, cigarettes were being mass produced for the first time, and moguls such as James Buchanan Duke began to market their brands aggressively. Duke placed ads for his brands in newspapers, rented space on thousands of billboards, hired famous actresses to endorse his brands, and gave gifts to retailers who stocked his products. Other cigarette manufacturers soon followed suit (Kluger, 1996).

Although these efforts were phenomenally successful—sales of cigarettes skyrocketed in the United States—there was still a vast untapped market, namely women. Until the early twentieth century, men bought 99 percent of cigarettes sold. It was socially unacceptable for women to smoke; those who did were considered to have questionable morals. This began to change with the burgeoning women's rights movement and the fight to achieve the right to vote; ironically, smoking cigarettes became a symbol of women's emancipation (Kluger, 1996). Cigarette manufacturers were happy to encourage this view by targeting women in their advertisements. Because it was unacceptable for women to smoke in public, early cigarette ads never showed a woman actually smoking. Instead, they tried to associate smoking with sophistication and glamour or convey that cigarettes helped control weight ("Reach for a Lucky instead of a sweet"). By the 1960s, cigarette advertisements were making a direct link between women's liberation and smoking, and a new brand was started (Virginia Slims) specifically for this purpose ("You've come a long way, baby"). Women began to purchase cigarettes in droves. In 1955, there were twice as many male as female smokers in the United States. Although the smoking rate has decreased overall, women have almost caught up to men. In 2005, 24 percent of adult men smoked, compared to 18 percent of adult women (National Center for Health Statistics, 2007).

To make up for the shrinking market in the United States, tobacco companies have aggressively marketed cigarettes in other countries. The World Health Organization estimates that 50,000 teenagers a day begin smoking in Asia alone and that smoking may eventually kill *one-quarter* of the young people currently living in Asia (Teves, 2002).

Is advertising responsible? To what extent can advertising shape people's attitudes and behavior? Exactly what is an attitude, anyway, and how is it changed? These questions, which are some of the oldest in social psychology, are the subject of this chapter.

The Nature and Origin of Attitudes
态度的本质与根源

Attitudes

Evaluations of people, objects, and ideas

Each of us *evaluates* our worlds. We form likes and dislikes of virtually everything we encounter; indeed, it would be odd to hear someone say, "I feel completely neutral toward anchovies, chocolate, Radiohead, and Barack Obama." Simply put, **attitudes** are evaluations of people, objects, or ideas (Ajzen & Fishbein, 2005; Crano & Prislin, 2006; Eagly & Chaiken, 2007; Fazio, 2007; Petty, Cacioppo, Strathman, & Priester, 2005). Attitudes are important because they often determine what we do—whether we eat anchovies and chocolate, attend Radiohead concerts, and vote for Barack Obama.

Where Do Attitudes Come From?
态度从何而来？

One provocative answer to the question of where attitudes come from is that some attitudes, at least, are linked to our genes (Guastello & Guastello, 2008; Tesser, 1993). Evidence for this conclusion comes from the fact that identical twins share more attitudes than fraternal twins, even when the identical twins were raised in different homes and never knew each other. One study, for example, found that identical twins had more similar attitudes toward such things as the death penalty and jazz than fraternal twins did (Martin et al., 1986). Now, we should be careful how to interpret this evidence. No one is arguing that there are specific genes that determine our attitudes; it is highly unlikely, for example, that there is a "jazz-loving" gene that determines your music preferences. It appears, though, that some attitudes are an indirect function of our genetic makeup. They are related to things like our temperament and personality, which are directly related to our genes (Olson, Vernon, Harris, & Jang, 2001). People may have inherited a temperament and personality from their parents that made them predisposed to like jazz more than rock-and-roll.

Some attitudes are based more on emotions and values than on facts and figures. Attitudes toward abortion may be such a case.

Even if there is a genetic component, our social experiences clearly play a major role in shaping our attitudes. Social psychologists have focused on these experiences and how they result in different kinds of attitudes. They have identified three components of attitudes: the *cognitive component*, which is the thoughts and beliefs that people form about the attitude object, the *affective component*, which is people's emotional reactions toward the attitude object, and the *behavioral component*, which is how people act toward the attitude object. Importantly, any given attitude can be based more on one type of experience than another (Zanna & Rempel, 1988).

I don't like you, but I love you.
Seems that I'm always thinking of you.
You treat me badly, I love you madly.
You've really got a hold on me.

—Smokey Robinson, "You've Really Got a Hold on Me," 1962

Cognitively Based Attitudes Sometimes our attitudes are based primarily on the relevant facts, such as the objective merits of an automobile. How many miles to the gallon does it get? What are its safety features? To the extent that people's evaluation is based primarily on their beliefs about the properties of an attitude object, we say it is a **cognitively based attitude**. The purpose of this kind of attitude is to classify the pluses and minuses of an object so that we can quickly tell whether we want to have anything to do with it. Consider your attitude toward a utilitarian object like a vacuum cleaner. Your attitude is likely to be based on your beliefs about the objective merits of particular brands, such as how well they vacuum up dirt and how much they cost—not on how sexy they make you feel.

Affectively Based Attitudes An attitude rooted more in emotions and values than on an objective appraisal of pluses and minuses is called an **affectively based attitude** (Breckler & Wiggins, 1989; Zanna & Rempel, 1988). Sometimes we simply like a car, regardless of how many miles to the gallon it gets. Occasionally we even feel great about something—such as another person—in spite of having negative beliefs (see the quote on this page from Smokey Robinson's song "You've Really Got a Hold on Me").

As a guide to which attitudes are likely to be affectively based, consider the topics that etiquette manuals suggest should not be discussed at a dinner party: politics, sex, and religion. People seem to vote more with their hearts than their minds, for example, caring more about how they feel about a candidate than their beliefs about his or

Cognitively Based Attitude
An attitude based primarily on people's beliefs about the properties of an attitude object

Affectively Based Attitude
An attitude based more on people's feelings and values than on their beliefs about the nature of an attitude object

> *We never desire passionately what we desire through reason alone.*
>
> —François de La Rochefoucauld, *Maxims*, 1665

> *That is the way we are made; we don't reason; where we feel, we just feel.*
>
> —Mark Twain, *A Connecticut Yankee in King Arthur's Court*, 1885

Classical Conditioning
The phenomenon whereby a stimulus that elicits an emotional response (e.g., your grandmother) is repeatedly paired with a neutral stimulus that does not (e.g., the smell of mothballs) until the neutral stimulus takes on the emotional properties of the first stimulus

Operant Conditioning
The phenomenon whereby behaviors we freely choose to perform become more or less frequent, depending on whether they are followed by a reward (positive reinforcement) or punishment.

her specific policies (Abelson, Kinder, Peters, & Fiske, 1982; Granberg & Brown, 1989). In fact, it has been estimated that one-third of the electorate knows virtually nothing about specific politicians but nonetheless has strong feelings about them (Redlawsk, 2002; Wattenberg, 1987).

If affectively based attitudes do not come from examining the facts, where do they come from? They have a variety of sources. They can stem from people's values, such as their basic religious and moral beliefs. People's feelings about such issues as abortion, the death penalty, and premarital sex are often based more on their values than on a cold examination of the facts. The function of such attitudes is not so much to paint an accurate picture of the world as to express and validate one's basic value system (Maio & Olson, 1995; Schwartz, 1992; Smith, Bruner, & White, 1956; Snyder & DeBono, 1989). Other affectively based attitudes can result from a sensory reaction, such as liking the taste of chocolate (despite its number of calories), or an aesthetic reaction, such as admiring a painting or the lines and color of a car. Still others can be the result of conditioning (De Houwer, Thomas, & Baeyans, 2001; Walther, 2002).

Classical conditioning works this way: A stimulus that elicits an emotional response is accompanied by a neutral stimulus that does not until eventually the neutral stimulus elicits the emotional response by itself (Olson & Fazio, 2001). For example, suppose that when you were a child, you experienced feelings of warmth and love when you visited your grandmother. Suppose also that her house always smelled faintly of mothballs. Eventually, the smell of mothballs alone will trigger the emotions you experienced during your visits, through the process of classical conditioning (Dawson, Rissling, Schell, & Wilcox, 2007; De Houwer, 2007; Olson & Fazio, 2006).

In **operant conditioning**, behaviors that we freely choose to perform become more or less frequent, depending on whether they are followed by a reward (positive reinforcement) or punishment. How does this apply to attitudes? Imagine that a 4-year-old white girl goes to the playground with her father and begins to play with an African American girl. Her father expresses strong disapproval, telling her, "We don't play with that kind of child." It won't take long before the child associates interacting with African Americans with disapproval, thereby adopting her father's racist attitudes. Attitudes can take on a positive or negative affect through either classical or operant conditioning, as shown in Figure 7.1 (Cacioppo et al., 1992; Kuykendall & Keating, 1990).

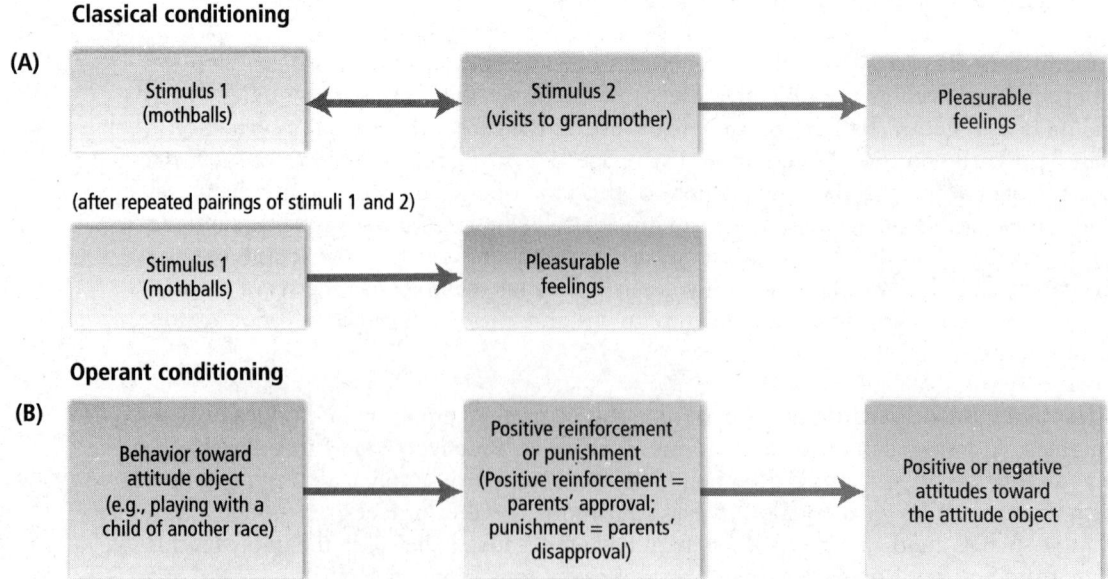

FIGURE 7.1
Classical and operant conditioning of attitudes.
Affectively based attitudes can result from either classical or instrumental conditioning.

Although affectively based attitudes come from many sources, we can group them into one family because they (1) do not result from a rational examination of the issues, (2) are not governed by logic (e.g., persuasive arguments about the issues seldom change an affectively based attitude), and (3) are often linked to people's values, so that trying to change them challenges those values (Katz, 1960; Smith; Bruner, & White, 1956). How can we tell if an attitude is more affectively or cognitively based? See the following Try It! exercise for one way to measure the bases of people's attitudes.

试一试！态度的情感和认知基础
Affective and Cognitive Bases of Attitudes

Fill out this questionnaire to see how psychologists measure the affective and cognitive components of attitudes.

1. Circle the number on each scale that best describes your feelings toward snakes:

hateful	–3	–2	–1	0	1	2	3	love
sad	–3	–2	–1	0	1	2	3	delighted
annoyed	–3	–2	–1	0	1	2	3	happy
tense	–3	–2	–1	0	1	2	3	calm
bored	–3	–2	–1	0	1	2	3	excited
angry	–3	–2	–1	0	1	2	3	relaxed
disgusted	–3	–2	–1	0	1	2	3	acceptance
sorrowful	–3	–2	–1	0	1	2	3	joy

2. Circle the number on each scale that best describes the traits or characteristics of snakes:

useless	–3	–2	–1	0	1	2	3	useful
foolish	–3	–2	–1	0	1	2	3	wise
unsafe	–3	–2	–1	0	1	2	3	safe
harmful	–3	–2	–1	0	1	2	3	beneficial
worthless	–3	–2	–1	0	1	2	3	valuable
imperfect	–3	–2	–1	0	1	2	3	perfect
unhealthy	–3	–2	–1	0	1	2	3	wholesome

Add up your responses to question 1 and, separately, your responses to question 2.

Question 1 measures the affective component of your attitude toward snakes, whereas question 2 measures the cognitive component of attitudes. Most people's attitudes toward snakes are more affectively than cognitively based. If this were true of you, your total score for question 1 should depart more from zero (in a negative direction, for most people) than your total score for question 2.

Now go back and fill out the scales again, substituting "vacuum cleaners" for "snakes." Most people's attitudes toward a utilitarian object such as a vacuum cleaner are more cognitively than affectively based. If this were true of you, your total score for question 2 should depart more from zero than your total score for question 1.

Behaviorally Based Attitudes A **behaviorally based attitude** stems from people's observations of how they behave toward an object. This may seem a little odd—how do we know how to behave if we don't already know how we feel? According to Daryl Bem's (1972) *self-perception theory*, under certain circumstances, people don't know how they feel until they see how they behave. For example, suppose you asked a friend how much she likes to exercise. If she replies, "Well, I guess I like it, because I always seem to be going for a run or heading over to the gym to work out," we would say she has a behaviorally based attitude. Her attitude is based more on an observation of her behavior than on her cognitions or affect.

Behaviorally Based Attitude

An attitude based on observations of how one behaves toward an attitude object

> How can I know what I think till I see what I say?
>
> —Graham Wallas, *The Art of Thought*, 1926

As noted in Chapter 5, people infer their attitudes from their behavior only under certain conditions. First, their initial attitude has to be weak or ambiguous. If your friend already has a strong attitude toward exercising, she does not have to observe her behavior to infer how she feels about it. Second, people infer their attitudes from their behavior only when there are no other plausible explanations for their behavior. If your friend believes she exercises to lose weight or because her doctor has ordered her to, she is unlikely to assume that she runs and works out because she enjoys it. (See Chapter 5 for a more detailed description of self-perception theory.)

Explicit Versus Implicit Attitudes 外显态度与内隐态度

Once an attitude develops, it can exist at two levels. **Explicit attitudes** are ones we consciously endorse and can easily report; they are what we think of as our evaluations when someone asks us a question like "What is your opinion about affirmative action?" People can also have **implicit attitudes**, which are involuntary, uncontrollable, and at times unconscious evaluations (Gawronski & Bodenhausen, 2006; Greenwald & Banaji, 1995; Nosek, 2007; Stanley, Phelps, & Banaji, 2008; Wilson, Lindsey, & Schooler, 2000).

Consider Sam, a white, middle-class college student who genuinely believes that all races are equal and abhors any kind of racial bias. This is Sam's explicit attitude, in the sense that it is his conscious evaluation of members of other races that governs how he chooses to act, for example, consistent with his explicit attitude, Sam recently signed a petition in favor of affirmative action policies at his university. Sam has grown up in a culture in which there are many negative stereotypes about minority groups, however, and it is possible that some of these negative ideas have seeped into him in ways of which he is not fully aware (Devine, 1989a). When he is around African Americans, for example, perhaps some negative feelings are triggered automatically and unintentionally. If so, he has a negative implicit attitude toward African Americans, which is likely to influence behaviors he is not monitoring or controlling, such as how nervous he acts around African Americans (Dovidio, Kawakami, & Gaertner, 2002).

People can have explicit and implicit attitudes toward the same topic. Explicit attitudes are those we consciously endorse and can easily report; implicit attitudes are involuntary, uncontrollable, and at least at times, unconscious. Social psychologists have been especially interested in people's explicit and implicit attitudes toward members of other races.

We will discuss such automatic prejudice in Chapter 13 (see also our discussion of automatic thinking in Chapter 3). For now, we point out that people can have explicit and implicit attitudes toward virtually anything, not just other races. For example, students can believe explicitly that they hate math but have a more positive attitude at an implicit level (Galdi, Arcuri, & Gawronski, 2008; Kawakami, Steele, Cifa, Phills, & Dovidio, 2008; McConnell, Rydell, Strain, & Mackie, 2008; Ranganath & Nosek, 2008).

How do we know? A variety of techniques have been developed to measure people's implicit attitudes, some of which we discussed in Chapter 3. One of the most popular is the Implicit Association Test or IAT (Greenwald, McGhee, & Schwartz, 1998; Nosek, Greenwald, & Banaji, 2005), in which people categorize words or pictures on a computer. Rather than going into detail about how this test works, we encourage you to visit a Web site where you can take the test yourself and read more about how it is constructed (implicit.harvard.edu/implicit).

Research on implicit attitudes is in its infancy and social psychologists are actively investigating the nature of these attitudes, how to measure them, and their relation to explicit attitudes (Albarracín, Hart, & McCulloch, 2006; Fazio & Olson, 2003; Gawronski & Bodenhausen, 2006; Kruglanski & Dechesne, 2006; Petty, Brinol, & DeMarree, 2007). Progress is being made on a variety of fronts, including the question of where implicit attitudes come from. Laurie Rudman, Julie Phelan, and Jessica Heppen (2007), for example, found evidence that implicit attitudes are rooted more in people's childhood experiences whereas explicit attitudes are rooted more in their recent expe-

Explicit Attitudes
Attitudes that we consciously endorse and can easily report

Implicit Attitudes
Attitudes that are involuntary, uncontrollable, and at times unconscious

riences. In one study, the researchers measured college students' implicit and explicit attitudes toward overweight people. They also asked the students to report their current weight and their weight when they were growing up. Participants' implicit attitudes toward overweight people were predicted by their childhood weight, but not their current weight, whereas their explicit attitudes were predicted by their current weight, but not their childhood weight. Consider, for example, someone who was overweight as a child but is of normal weight as an adult. This person's implicit attitude toward overweight people would likely be positive, because it is rooted in his or her childhood experiences with obesity. The person's explicit attitude toward overweight people would likely be negative, because it is based on the fact he or she does not currently have a weight problem. An additional finding from this study was that people whose mother was overweight, and were close to their mothers, had positive implicit attitudes toward overweight people, even if they held negative explicit attitudes. In short, people can often have different attitudes toward the same thing, one rooted more in childhood experiences and the other based more on their adult experiences.

We will return to a discussion of implicit attitudes in Chapter 13 as they apply to stereotyping and prejudice. The focus in the remainder of this chapter will be on how explicit attitudes change and their relation to behavior.

How Do Attitudes Change? 态度是如何改变的?

Attitudes do sometimes change. In America, for example, the popularity of the president often seems to rise and fall with surprising speed. In the weeks before the tragic events of September 11, 2001, only about 50 percent of Americans said that they approved of the job that George W. Bush was doing as president. In the days right after 9/11, his approval rating jumped to 86 percent. After that, his popularity went up and down. Right before the U.S. invasion of Iraq in March 2003 his approval rating had dropped to 57 percent; a month later, it rose to 71 percent. In the waning days of the Bush presidency, as the war dragged on and the economy nosedived, less than 30 percent of Americans approved of President Bush's performance (pollingreport.com/BushJob.htm).

When attitudes change, they often do so in response to social influence. Our attitudes toward everything from a presidential candidate to a brand of laundry detergent can be influenced by what other people do or say. This is why attitudes are of such interest to social psychologists—even something as personal and internal as an attitude is a highly social phenomenon, influenced by the imagined or actual behavior of other people. The entire premise of advertising, for example, is that your attitudes toward consumer products can be influenced by advertising. Remember Andrew Fischer? After he tattooed SnoreStop onto his forehead, Web sales of the product increased by 500 percent (aided by coverage of Fischer's stunt in the national press; Puente, 2005). Let's take a look at the conditions under which attitudes are most likely to change.

Sometimes attitudes change dramatically over short periods of time. In the United States, for example, the popularity of the president often seems to rise and dip with surprising speed. In the weeks before the 9/11 terrorists attacks, for example, about 50 percent of Americans approved of the job President Bush was doing. In the days after the attacks, his approval ratings soared to 82 percent. But by the end of his presidency in 2008, his approval ratings had dipped below 30 percent. As President Obama begins his presidency, we will see whether his approval ratings remain steady or rise and dip like those of previous presidents.

Changing Attitudes by Changing Behavior: Cognitive Dissonance Theory Revisited
通过改变行为来改变态度：重返认知失调理论

We have already discussed one way that attitudes change—when people behave inconsistently with their attitudes and cannot find external justification for their behavior. We refer, of course, to cognitive dissonance theory. As we noted in Chapter 6, people experience dissonance when they do something that threatens their image of themselves as decent, kind, and honest, particularly if there is no way they can explain away this behavior as due to external circumstances.

If you wanted to change some friends' attitude toward smoking, you might succeed by getting them to give antismoking speeches. You would want to make it hard for your friends to find external reasons for giving the speech; for example, you would not want them to justify their actions by saying, "I'm doing it as a special favor for my friend" or "I'm getting paid handsomely for doing it." That is, as we saw in Chapter 6, the goal is to get your friends to find *internal justification* for giving the speech, whereby they reduce the dissonance of giving the speech by deciding that they believe what they are saying. But what if your goal is to change attitudes on a mass scale? Suppose you were hired by the American Cancer Society to come up with an antismoking campaign that could be used nationwide to counteract the kind of tobacco advertisements we discussed at the beginning of this chapter. Although dissonance techniques are powerful, they are very difficult to carry out on a mass scale (e.g., it would be hard to have all American smokers make antismoking speeches under just the right conditions of internal justification). To change as many people's attitudes as possible, you would have to resort to other techniques of attitude change. You would probably construct some sort of **persuasive communication**, which is a communication such as a speech or television advertisement that advocates a particular side of an issue. How should you construct your message so that it would change people's attitudes?

> *By persuading others, we convince ourselves.*
> —Junius

Persuasive Communications and Attitude Change
说服性沟通与态度改变

Suppose the American Cancer Society has given you a six-figure budget to develop your advertising campaign. You have a lot of decisions ahead of you. Should you pack your public service announcement with facts and figures? Or should you take a more emotional approach, including frightening visual images of diseased lungs in your message? Should you hire a movie star to deliver your message or a Nobel Prize–winning medical researcher? Should you take a friendly tone and acknowledge that it is hard to quit smoking, or should you take a hard line and tell smokers to quit cold turkey? You can see the point—constructing a truly persuasive communication is complicated.

Luckily, social psychologists have conducted many studies over the years on what makes a persuasive communication effective, beginning with Carl Hovland and his colleagues (Hovland, Janis, & Kelley, 1953). Drawing on their experiences during World War II, when they worked for the United States armed forces to increase the morale of U.S. soldiers (Stouffer, Suchman, De Vinney, Star, & Williams, 1949), Hovland and his colleagues conducted many experiments on the conditions under which people are most likely to be influenced by persuasive communications. In essence, they studied "who says what to whom," looking at the source of the communication (e.g., how expert or attractive the speaker is), the communication itself (e.g., the quality of the arguments; whether the speaker presents both sides of the issue), and the nature of the audience (e.g., which kinds of appeals work with hostile or friendly audiences). Because these researchers were at Yale University, this approach to the study of persuasive communications is known as the **Yale Attitude Change approach**.

> *Of the modes of persuasion furnished by the spoken word there are three kinds. The first kind depends on the personal character of the speaker; the second on putting the audience into a certain frame of mind; the third on the proof, or apparent proof, provided by the words of the speech itself.*
> —Aristotle, *Rhetoric*

This approach yielded a great deal of useful information on how people change their attitudes in response to persuasive communications; some of this information is summarized in Figure 7.2. As the research mounted, however, a problem became apparent: Many aspects of persuasive communications turned out to be important, but it was not clear which were more important than others—that is, it was unclear when one factor should be emphasized over another.

For example, let's return to that job you have with the American Cancer Society. The marketing manager wants to see your ad next month! If you were to read the many Yale Attitude Change studies, you might find lots of useful information about who should say what to whom in order to construct a persuasive communication.

Persuasive Communication
Communication (e.g., a speech or television ad) advocating a particular side of an issue

Yale Attitude Change Approach
The study of the conditions under which people are most likely to change their attitudes in response to persuasive messages, focusing on "who said what to whom"— the source of the communication, the nature of the communication, and the nature of the audience

> **FIGURE 7.2**
> The Yale Attitude Change Approach.

> ### The Yale Attitude Change Approach
>
> The effectiveness of persuasive communications depends on who says what to whom.
>
> **Who: The Source of the Communication**
>
> - Credible speakers (e.g., those with obvious expertise) persuade people more than speakers lacking in credibility (Hovland & Weiss, 1951; Jain & Posavac, 2000).
> - Attractive speakers (whether due to physical or personality attributes) persuade people more than unattractive speakers do (Eagly & Chaiken, 1975; Petty, Wegener, & Fabrigar, 1997).
>
> **What: The Nature of the Communication**
>
> - People are more persuaded by messages that do not seem to be designed to influence them (Petty & Cacioppo, 1986; Walster & Festinger, 1962).
> - Is it better to present a one-sided communication (one that presents only arguments favoring your position) or a two-sided communication (one that presents arguments for and against your position)? In general, two-sided messages work better, if you are sure to refute the arguments on the other side (Crowley & Hoyer, 1994; Igou & Bless, 2003; Lumsdaine & Janis, 1953).
> - Is it better to give your speech before or after someone arguing for the other side? If the speeches are to be given back to back and there will be a delay before people have to make up their minds, it is better to go first. Under these conditions, there is likely to be a primacy effect, wherein people are more influenced by what they hear first. If there is a delay between the speeches and people will make up their minds right after hearing the second one, it is better to go last. Under these conditions, there is likely to be a recency effect, wherein people remember the second speech better than the first one (Haugtvedt & Wegener, 1994; Miller & Campbell, 1959).
>
> **To Whom: The Nature of the Audience**
>
> - An audience that is distracted during the persuasive communication will often be persuaded more than one that is not (Albarracin & Wyer, 2001; Festinger & Maccoby, 1964).
> - People low in intelligence tend to be more influenceable than people high in intelligence, and people with moderate self-esteem tend to be more influenceable than people with low or high self-esteem (Rhodes & Wood, 1992).
> - People are particularly susceptible to attitude change during the impressionable ages of 18 to 25. Beyond those ages, people's attitudes are more stable and resistant to change (Krosnick & Alwin, 1989; Sears, 1981).

However, you might also find yourself saying, "There's a lot of information here, and I'm not sure where I should place the most emphasis. Should I focus on who delivers the ads? Or should I worry more about the content of the message?"

The Central and Peripheral Routes to Persuasion Some well-known attitude researchers have asked the same questions: When is it best to stress factors central to the communication—such as the strength of the arguments—and when is it best to stress factors peripheral to the logic of the arguments, such as the credibility or attractiveness of the person delivering the speech? (Chaiken, 1987; Chaiken, Wood, & Eagly, 1996; Petty & Cacioppo, 1986; Petty et al., 2005; Petty & Briñol, 2008). The **elaboration likelihood model** of persuasion (Petty & Cacioppo, 1986; Petty et al., 2005), for example, specifies when people will be influenced by what the speech says (i.e., the logic of the arguments) and when they will be influenced by more superficial characteristics (e.g., who gives the speech or how long it is).

The theory states that under certain conditions, people are motivated to pay attention to the facts in a communication, and so they will be most persuaded when these facts are logically compelling. That is, sometimes people elaborate on what they hear, carefully thinking about and processing the content of the communication. Petty and Cacioppo (1986) call this the **central route to persuasion**. Under other conditions, people are not motivated to pay attention to the facts; instead,

Elaboration Likelihood Model
A model explaining two ways in which persuasive communications can cause attitude change: *centrally*, when people are motivated and have the ability to pay attention to the arguments in the communication, and *peripherally*, when people do not pay attention to the arguments but are instead swayed by surface characteristics (e.g., who gave the speech)

Central Route to Persuasion
The case whereby people elaborate on a persuasive communication, listening carefully to and thinking about the arguments, as occurs when people have both the ability and the motivation to listen carefully to a communication

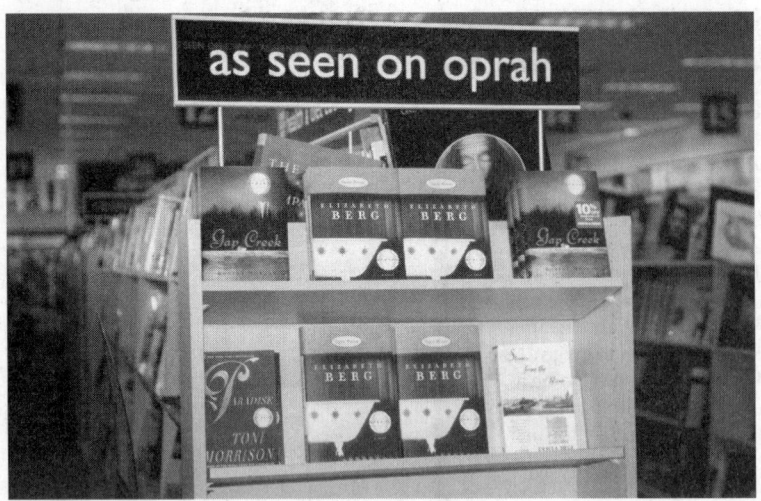

Sometimes attitude change occurs via a peripheral route, whereby people are persuaded by things other than arguments about the facts. For example, sometimes we are swayed more by who delivers a persuasive communication than by the strength of the message. An endorsement by Oprah Winfrey, for example, can turn a book into an instant best seller.

they notice only the surface characteristics of the message, such as how long it is and who is delivering it. Here people will not be swayed by the logic of the arguments because they are not paying close attention to what the communicator says. Instead, they are persuaded if the surface characteristics of the message—such as the fact that it is long or is delivered by an expert or attractive communicator—make it seem like a reasonable one. Petty and Cacioppo call this the **peripheral route to persuasion** because people are swayed by things peripheral to the message itself.

What determines whether people take the central versus the peripheral route to persuasion? The key is whether people have both the motivation and the ability to pay attention to the facts. If people are truly interested in the topic and thus motivated to pay close attention to the arguments, *and* if people have the ability to pay attention—for example, if nothing is distracting them—they are more likely to take the central route (see Figure 7.3).

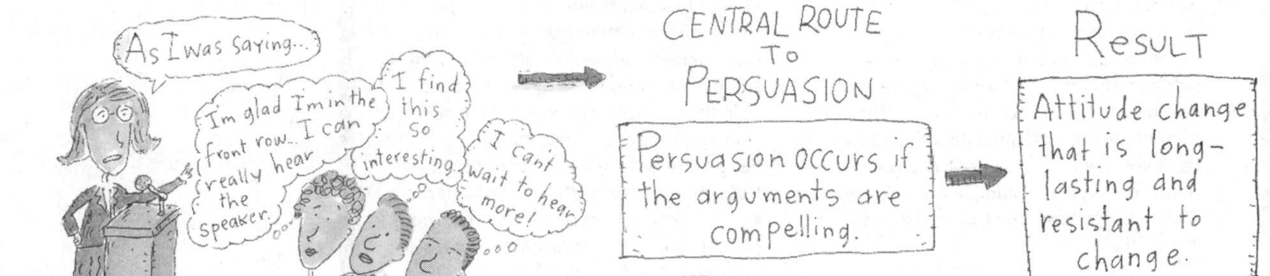

FIGURE 7.3

The elaboration likelihood model.

The elaboration likelihood model describes how people change their attitudes when they hear persuasive communications.

The Motivation to Pay Attention to the Arguments One thing that determines whether people are motivated to pay attention to a communication is the personal relevance of the topic: How important is the topic to a person's well-being? For example, consider the issue of whether Social Security benefits should be reduced. How personally relevant is this to you? If you are a 72-year-old whose sole income is from Social Security, the issue is extremely relevant; if you are a 20-year-old from a well-to-do family, the issue has little personal relevance.

The more personally relevant an issue is, the more willing people are to pay attention to the arguments in a speech, and therefore the more likely people are to take the central route to persuasion. In one study, for example, college students were asked to listen to a speech arguing that all college seniors should be required to pass a comprehensive exam in their major before they graduate (Petty, Cacioppo, & Goldman, 1981). Half of the participants were told that their university was seriously considering requiring comprehensive exams. For these participants, the issue was personally relevant. For the other half, the issue was of the "ho-hum" variety—the students were told that their university might require such exams but would not implement them for 10 years.

The researchers then introduced two variables that might influence whether people would agree with the speech. The first was the strength of the arguments presented. Half of the participants heard arguments that were strong and persuasive (e.g., "The quality of undergraduate teaching has improved at schools with the exams"), whereas the others heard arguments that were weak and unpersuasive (e.g., "The risk of failing the exam is a challenge most students would welcome"). The second was a peripheral cue—the prestige of the speaker. Half of the participants were told that the author of the speech was an eminent professor at Princeton University, whereas the others were told that the author was a high school student.

When deciding how much to agree with the speaker's position, the participants could use one or both of these different kinds of information. They could listen carefully to the arguments and think about how convincing they were, or they could simply go by who said them (i.e., how prestigious the source was). As predicted by the elaboration likelihood model, the way in which people were persuaded depended on the personal relevance of the issue. The left panel of Figure 7.4 shows what happened

> *The ability to kill or capture a man is a relatively simple task compared with changing his mind.*
>
> —Richard Cohen, 1991

Peripheral Route to Persuasion
The case whereby people do not elaborate on the arguments in a persuasive communication but are instead swayed by peripheral cues

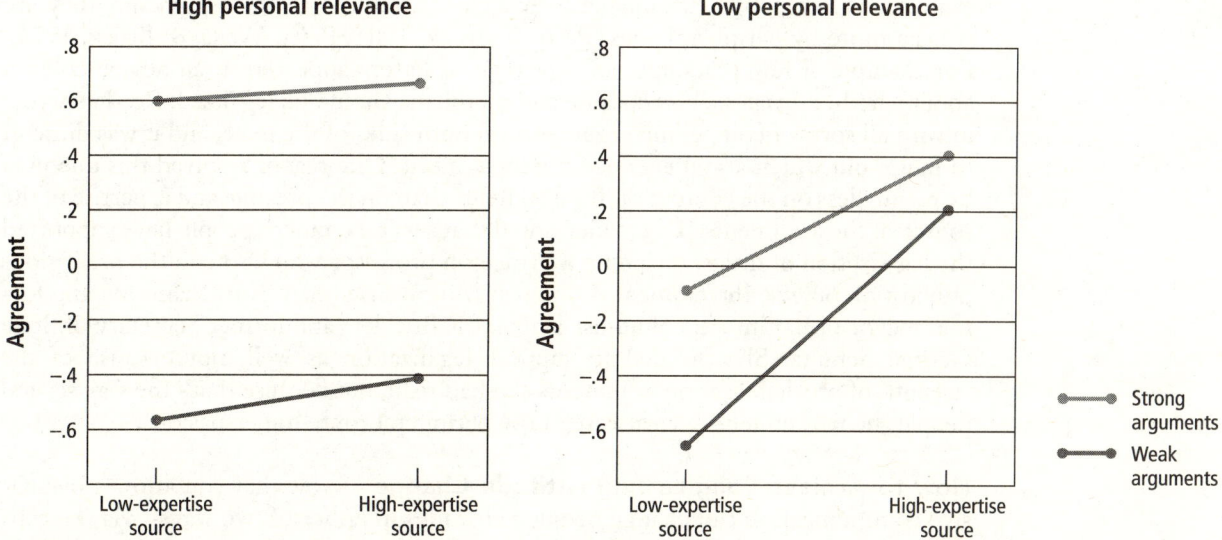

FIGURE 7.4

Effects of personal relevance on type of attitude change.

The higher the number, the more people agreed with the persuasive communication—namely, that their university should adopt comprehensive exams. Left panel: When the issue was highly relevant, people were swayed by the quality of the arguments more than the expertise of the speaker. This is the central route to persuasion. Right panel: When the issue was low in relevance, people were swayed by the expertise of the speaker more than the quality of the arguments. This is the peripheral route to persuasion.

(Adapted from Petty & Cacioppo, 1986, based on Petty, Cacioppo, & Goldman, 1981)

when the issue was highly relevant to the listeners. These students were greatly influenced by the quality of the arguments (i.e., persuasion occurred via the central route). Those who heard strong arguments agreed much more with the speech than those who heard weak arguments. It didn't matter who presented the arguments, the Princeton professor or the high school student. A good argument was a good argument, even if it was written by someone who lacked prestige.

What happens when a topic is of low relevance? As seen in the right panel of Figure 7.4, what mattered was not the strength of the arguments but who the speaker was. Those who heard the strong arguments agreed with the speech only slightly more than those who heard the weak arguments, whereas those who heard the Princeton professor were much more swayed than those who heard the high school student.

This finding illustrates a general rule: When an issue is personally relevant, people pay attention to the arguments in a speech and will be persuaded to the extent that the arguments are sound—the "proof" of the speech, in Aristotle's words. When an issue is not personally relevant, people pay less attention to the arguments. Instead, they will take a mental shortcut, following such peripheral rules as "Prestigious speakers can be trusted" (Chen & Chaiken, 1999; Fabrigar, Priester, Petty, & Wegener, 1998).

> *I'm not convinced by proofs but signs.*
>
> —Coventry Patmore

In addition to the personal relevance of a topic, people's motivation to pay attention to a speech depends on their personality. Some people enjoy thinking things through more than others do; they are said to be high in the **need for cognition** (Cacioppo, Petty, Feinstein, & Jarvis, 1996). This is a personality variable that reflects the extent to which people engage in and enjoy effortful cognitive activities. People high in the need for cognition are more likely to form their attitudes by paying close attention to relevant arguments (i.e., via the central route), whereas people low in the need for cognition are more likely to rely on peripheral cues, such as how attractive or credible a speaker is. The Try It! exercise on the next page can show you how high you are in the need for cognition.

The Ability to Pay Attention to the Arguments Sometimes it is difficult to pay attention to a speech, even if we want to. Maybe we're tired; maybe we're distracted by construction noise outside the window; maybe the issue is too complex and hard to evaluate. When people are unable to pay close attention to the arguments, they are swayed more by peripheral cues (Petty & Brock, 1981; Petty, Wells, & Brock, 1976). For example, a few years ago, an exchange of letters appeared in an advice column about whether drugs such as cocaine and marijuana should be legalized. Readers wrote in with all sorts of compelling arguments on both sides of the issue, and it was difficult to figure out which arguments had the most merit. One reader resolved this dilemma by relying less on the content of the arguments than on the prestige and expertise of the source of the arguments. The reader noted that several eminent people have supported the legalization of drugs, including a Princeton professor who wrote in the prestigious publication *Science*; the eminent economist Milton Friedman; Kurt Schmoke, the former mayor of Baltimore; columnist William F. Buckley; and former Secretary of State George Schultz. She decided to support legalization as well, not because of the strength of pro-legalization arguments she had read, but because that's the way several people she trusted felt—a clear case of the peripheral route to persuasion.

How to Achieve Long-Lasting Attitude Change Now that you know a persuasive communication can change people's attitudes in either of two ways—via the central or the peripheral route—you may be wondering what difference it makes. Does it really matter whether it was the logic of the arguments or the expertise of the source that changed students' minds about comprehensive exams in the Petty and colleagues (1981) study? Given the bottom line—they changed their attitudes—why should any of us care how they got to that point?

If we are interested in creating long-lasting attitude change, we should care a lot. People who base their attitudes on a careful analysis of the arguments will be more likely to maintain this attitude over time, more likely to behave consistently with this

Need for Cognition
A personality variable reflecting the extent to which people engage in and enjoy effortful cognitive activities

TRY IT! The Need for Cognition 试一试！认知需求

Indicate to what extent each statement is characteristic of you, using the following scale:

1 = extremely uncharacteristic of you (not at all like you)
2 = somewhat uncharacteristic
3 = uncertain
4 = somewhat characteristic
5 = extremely characteristic of you (very much like you)

1. I would prefer complex to simple problems. _____
2. I like to have the responsibility of handling a situation that requires a lot of thinking. _____
3. Thinking is not my idea of fun. _____
4. I would rather do something that requires little thought than something that is sure to challenge my thinking abilities. _____
5. I try to anticipate and avoid situations where there is a likely chance I will have to think in depth about something. _____
6. I find satisfaction in deliberating hard and for long hours. _____
7. I only think as hard as I have to. _____
8. I prefer to think about small, daily projects to long-term ones. _____
9. I like tasks that require little thought once I've learned them. _____
10. The idea of relying on thought to make my way to the top appeals to me. _____
11. I really enjoy a task that involves coming up with new solutions to problems. _____
12. Learning new ways to think doesn't excite me very much. _____
13. I prefer my life to be filled with puzzles that I must solve. _____
14. The notion of thinking abstractly is appealing to me. _____
15. I would prefer a task that is intellectual, difficult, and important to one that is somewhat important but does not require much thought. _____
16. I feel relief rather than satisfaction after completing a task that required a lot of mental effort. _____
17. It's enough for me that something gets the job done; I don't care how or why it works. _____
18. I usually end up deliberating about issues even when they do not affect me personally. _____

This scale measures the *need for cognition*, which is a personality variable reflecting the extent to which people engage in and enjoy effortful cognitive activities (Cacioppo et al., 1996). People high in the need for cognition are more likely to form their attitudes by paying close attention to relevant arguments (i.e., via the central route), whereas people low in the need for cognition are more likely to rely on peripheral cues, such as how attractive or credible a speaker is.

Note: Turn to p. 209 for instructions on how to add up your score on this measure.

---

attitude, and more resistant to counterpersuasion than people who base their attitudes on peripheral cues (Chaiken, 1980; Mackie, 1987; Petty, Haugtvedt, & Smith, 1995; Petty & Wegener, 1999). In one study, for example, people changed their attitudes either by analyzing the logic of the arguments or by using peripheral cues. When the participants were telephoned 10 days later, those who had analyzed the logic of the arguments were more likely to have maintained their new attitude—that is, attitudes that changed via the central route to persuasion lasted longer (Chaiken, 1980).

Emotion and Attitude Change 情绪与态度改变

Now you know exactly how to construct your ad for the American Cancer Society, right? Well, not quite. Before people will consider your carefully constructed arguments, you have to get their attention. If you are going to show your antismoking ad on television, for example, how can you be sure people will watch the ad when it comes on, instead of changing the channel or heading for the refrigerator? One way is to grab people's attention by playing to their emotions.

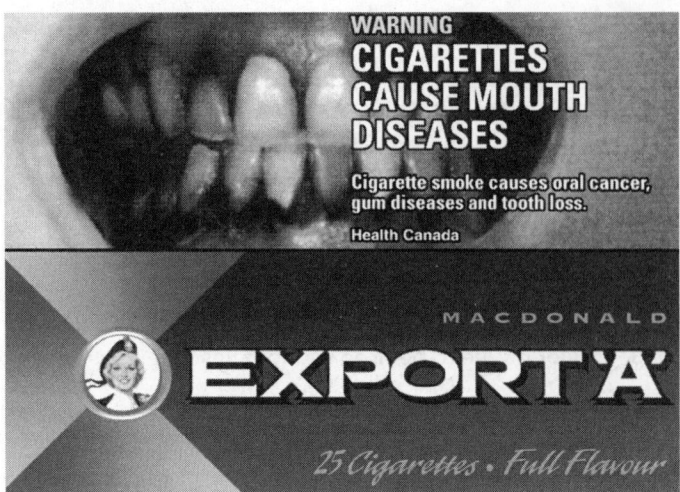

In Canada, all cigarette packs are required to display pictures that warn about the dangers of smoking. Do you think that this ad would scare people into quitting?

Fear-Arousing Communications
Persuasive messages that attempt to change people's attitudes by arousing their fears

Fear-Arousing Communications One way to get people's attention is to scare them—for example, by showing pictures of diseased lungs and presenting alarming data about the link between smoking and lung cancer. This kind of persuasive message—attempting to change people's attitudes by stirring up their fears—is called a **fear-arousing communication**. Public service ads often take this approach by trying to scare people into practicing safer sex, wearing seat belts, and staying away from drugs. For example, since January 2001, cigarette packs sold in Canada have been required to display graphic pictures of diseased gums and other body parts that cover at least 50 percent of the outside label (Carroll, 2003).

Do fear-arousing communications work? It depends on whether the fear influences people's ability to pay attention to and process the arguments in a message. If a moderate amount of fear is created and people believe that listening to the message will teach them how to reduce this fear, they will be motivated to analyze the message carefully and will likely change their attitudes via the central route (Petty, 1995; Rogers, 1983).

Consider a study in which a group of smokers watched a graphic film depicting lung cancer and then read pamphlets with specific instructions about how to quit smoking (Leventhal, Watts, & Pagano, 1967). As shown in the bottom line in Figure 7.5, people in this condition reduced their smoking significantly more than people who were shown only the film or only the pamphlet. Why? Watching the film scared people, and giving them the pamphlet reassured them that there was a way to reduce this fear—by following the instructions on how to quit. Seeing only the pamphlet didn't work very well because there was little fear motivating people to read it carefully. Seeing only the film didn't work very well either because people are likely to tune out a message that raises fear but does not give information

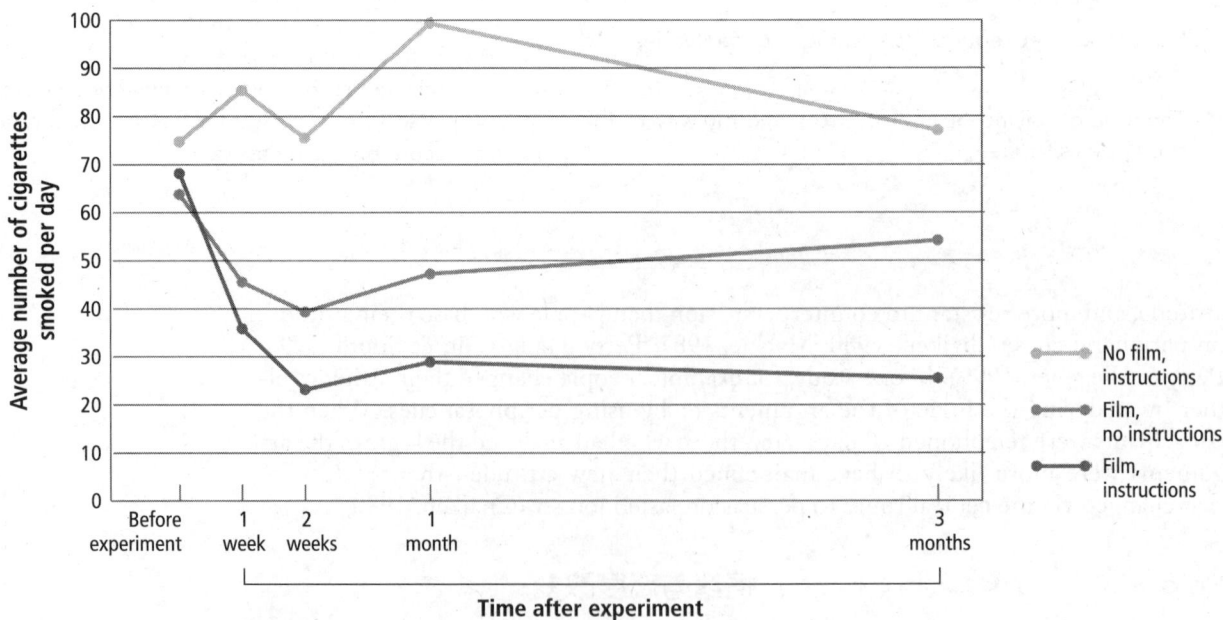

FIGURE 7.5

Effects of fear appeals on attitude change.

People were shown a scary film about the effects of smoking, instructions about how to stop smoking, or both. Those who were shown both reduced the number of cigarettes they smoked the most.

(Adapted from Leventhal, Watts, & Pagano, 1967)

about how to reduce it. This may explain why some attempts to frighten people into changing their attitudes and behaviors fail: They succeed in scaring people but do not provide specific recommendations to help them reduce their fear (Aronson, in press; Hoog, Stroebe, & de Wit, 2005; Ruiter, Abraham, & Kok, 2001).

Fear-arousing appeals will also fail if they are so strong that they overwhelm people. If people are scared to death, they will become defensive, deny the importance of the threat, and be unable to think rationally about the issue (Janis & Feshbach, 1953; Liberman & Chaiken, 1992). So if you have decided to arouse people's fear in your ad for the American Cancer Society, keep these points in mind: Try to create enough fear to motivate people to pay attention to your arguments but not so much fear that people will tune out or distort what you say and include some specific recommendations about how to stop smoking so people will be reassured that paying close attention to your arguments will help them reduce their fear.

"While we're waiting for His Honor, may I offer the jury a selection of hand-dipped Swiss chocolates, compliments of my client?"

Emotions as a Heuristic Another way in which emotions can cause attitude change is by acting as a signal for how we feel about something. According to the **heuristic–systematic model of persuasion** (Chaiken, 1987), when people take the peripheral route to persuasion, they often use heuristics. Recall from Chapter 3 that heuristics are mental shortcuts people use to make judgments quickly and efficiently. In the present context, a heuristic is a simple rule people use to decide what their attitude is without having to spend a lot of time analyzing every little detail about the matter. Examples of such heuristics are "Experts are always right" and "Length equals strength" (i.e., long messages are more persuasive than short ones).

Interestingly, our emotions and moods can themselves act as heuristics to determine our attitudes. When trying to decide what our attitude is about something, we often rely on the "How do I feel about it?" heuristic (Clore & Huntsinger, 2007; Forgas, 1995; Schwarz & Clore, 1988; Storbeck & Clore, 2007). If we feel good, we must have a positive attitude; if we feel bad, it's thumbs down. Now this probably sounds like a pretty good rule to follow, and like most heuristics, it is—most of the time. Suppose you need a new couch and go to a furniture store to look around. You see one in your price range and are trying to decide whether to buy it. If you use the "How do I feel about it?" heuristic, you do a quick check of your feelings and emotions. If you feel great while you're sitting in the couch in the store, you will probably buy it.

The only problem is that sometimes it is difficult to tell where our feelings come from. Is it really the couch that made you feel great, or is it something completely unrelated? Maybe you were in a good mood to begin with, or maybe on the way to the store you heard your favorite song on the radio. The problem with the "How do I feel about it?" heuristic is that we can make mistakes about what is causing our mood, misattributing feelings created by one source (our favorite song) to another (the couch; see Chapter 5 on misattribution; Claypool, Hall, Mackie, & Garcia-Marques, 2008). If so, people might make a bad decision. After you get the new couch home, you might discover that it no longer makes you feel all that great. It makes

Heuristic–Systematic Model of Persuasion
An explanation of the two ways in which persuasive communications can cause attitude change: either systematically processing the merits of the arguments or using mental shortcuts (heuristics), such as "Experts are always right"

Many advertisements attempt to use emotions to persuade people. This ad uses a combination of cuteness (images of stuffed animals) and apprehension ("face up to wake up") to educate parents that it is safest for babies to sleep on their backs.

sense, then, that advertisers and retailers want to create good feelings while they present their product (e.g., by playing appealing music or showing pleasant images), hoping that people will attribute at least some of those feelings to the product they are trying to sell.

Emotion and Different Types of Attitudes The success of various attitude change techniques depends on the type of attitude we are trying to change. As we saw earlier, not all attitudes are created equally; some are based more on beliefs about the attitude object (cognitively based attitudes), whereas others are based more on emotions and values (affectively based attitudes). Several studies have shown that it is best to fight fire with fire: If an attitude is cognitively based, try to change it with rational arguments; if it is affectively based, try to change it with emotional appeals (Fabrigar & Petty, 1999; Haddock, Maio, Arnold, & Huskinson, 2008; Shavitt, 1989; Snyder & DeBono, 1989).

> *It is useless to attempt to reason a man out of a thing he was never reasoned into.*
> —Jonathan Swift

Consider a study of the effectiveness of different kinds of advertisements (Shavitt, 1990). Some ads stress the objective merits of a product, such as an ad for an air conditioner or a vacuum cleaner that discusses its price, efficiency, and reliability. Other ads stress emotions and values, such as ones for perfume or designer jeans that try to associate their brands with sex, beauty, and youthfulness, rather than saying anything about the objective qualities of the product. Which kind of ad is most effective?

To find out, participants looked at different kinds of advertisements. Some were for "utilitarian products," such as air conditioners and coffee. People's attitudes toward such products tend to be formed after an appraisal of the utilitarian aspects of the products (e.g., how energy efficient an air conditioner is) and thus are cognitively based. The other items were "social identity products," such as perfume and greeting cards. People's attitudes toward these types of products tend to reflect a concern with how they appear to others and are more affectively based.

As shown in Figure 7.6, people reacted most favorably to the ads that matched the type of attitude they had. If people's attitudes were cognitively based (e.g., toward air conditioners or coffee), the ads that focused on the utilitarian aspects of these products, such as the features of the air conditioner, were most successful. If people's attitudes were more affectively based (e.g., toward perfume or greeting cards), the ads that focused on values and social identity concerns were most successful. The graph displayed in Figure 7.6 shows the number of favorable thoughts people had in response to the different kinds of ads. Similar results were found on a measure of how much people intended to buy the products. Thus if you ever get a job in advertising, the moral is to know what type of attitude most people have toward your product and then tailor your advertising accordingly.

FIGURE 7.6
Effects of affective and cognitive information on affectively and cognitively based attitudes.

When people had cognitively based attitudes (e.g., toward air conditioners and coffee), cognitively based advertisements that stressed the utilitarian aspects of the products worked best. When people had more affectively based attitudes (e.g., toward perfume and greeting cards), affectively based advertisements that stressed values and social identity worked best. (The higher the number, the more favorable thoughts people listed about the products after reading the advertisements.)

(Adapted from Shavitt, 1990)

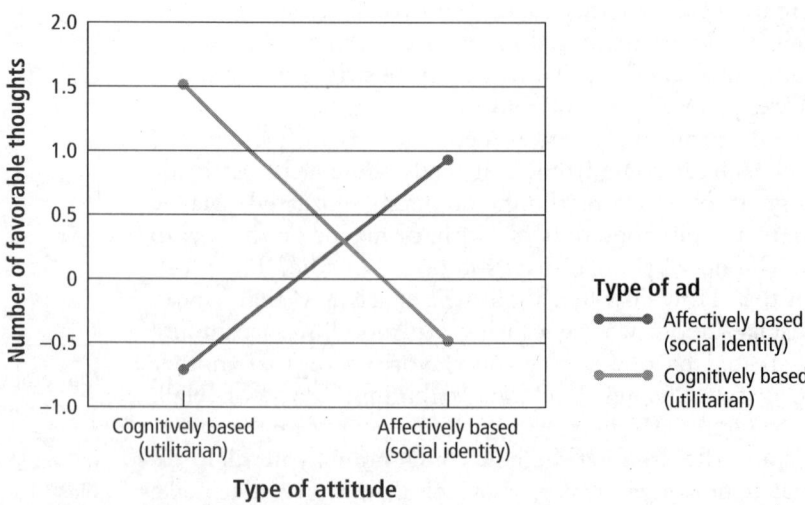

Culture and Different Types of Attitudes Are there differences across cultures in the kinds of attitudes people have toward the same products, reflecting the differences in self-concept we discussed in Chapter 5? As we saw, Western cultures tend to stress independence and individualism, whereas many Asian cultures stress interdependence and collectivism. Maybe these differences influence the kinds of attitudes people have and hence how those attitudes change (Aaker, 2000).

Perhaps people in Western cultures base their attitudes more on concerns about individuality and self-improvement, whereas people in Asian cultures base their attitudes more on concerns about their standing in their social group, such as their families. If so, advertisements that stress individuality and self-improvement might work better in Western cultures, and advertisements that stress one's social group might work better in Asian cultures. To test this hypothesis, researchers created different ads for the same product that stressed independence (e.g., an ad for shoes said, "It's easy when you have the right shoes") or interdependence (e.g., "The shoes for your family") and showed them to both Americans and Koreans (Han & Shavitt, 1994). The Americans were persuaded most by the ads stressing independence, and the Koreans were persuaded by the ads stressing interdependence. The researchers also analyzed actual magazine advertisements in the United States and Korea and found that these ads were in fact different: American ads tended to emphasize individuality, self-improvement, and benefits of the product for the individual consumer, whereas Korean ads tended to emphasize the family, concerns about others, and benefits for one's social group. In general, then, advertisements work best if they are tailored to the kind of attitude they are trying to change.

Do you think this ad will work better with people who have affectively based or cognitively based attitudes toward cars? In general, ads work best if they are tailored to the kind of attitude they are trying to change. Given that this ad seems to be targeting people's emotions (indeed, it doesn't present any information about the car, such as its safety record, gas mileage, or reliability), it will probably work best on people whose attitudes are affectively based.

Confidence in One's Thoughts and Attitude Change
对个人想法的信心与态度改变

Although you know a lot by now about how to craft your persuasive message for the American Cancer Society, there is one other thing you might want to take into account: how confident people are in the thoughts that your message triggers. Suppose your message succeeds in getting smokers to think, "Wow, there are a lot of dangers to smoking I didn't know about." That's all well and good, but you also want to make sure that people have a lot of *confidence* in those thoughts. If they roll their eyes and think, "I'm not so sure about any of that," your message isn't going to have much effect (Petty & Briñol, 2008; Petty, Briñol, & DeMarree, 2007). Although that probably seems straightforward enough, the *way* in which people gain confidence in their thoughts isn't always so obvious. Consider a study by Pablo Briñol and Richard Petty (2003) in which participants were asked to test out the durability of some new headphones. Some were asked to shake their heads from side to side while wearing them, whereas others were asked to nod their heads up and down. While they were doing this the participants listened to an editorial arguing that all students should be required to carry personal identification cards on campus. One final twist was that half of the participants heard strong, persuasive arguments (e.g., the ID cards would make the campus safer for students) whereas the other half heard weak, unconvincing arguments (e.g., if students carried the cards security guards would have more time for lunch).

As you have no doubt gathered, the point of the study was not to test the headphones but to see whether whether shaking or nodding one's head while listening to a persuasive communication influenced how persuaded people were by it. The idea was that even though the head movements had nothing to do with the editorial, they might influence how confident people felt in the arguments they heard. Nodding one's head up and down, as people do when they say "yes," might make them feel more confident than when they shake their head side-to-side, as they do when they say "no." This is exactly

FIGURE 7.7
Effects of confidence in one's own thoughts on persuasion.

People listened to either a strong or weak editorial arguing that all students should carry personal identification cards. Supposedly to test the durability of the headphones, half of the participants nodded their heads up and down while listening to the editorial whereas half shook their heads from side to side. When the arguments were strong, people who nodded their heads up and down (like they were saying "yes") had more confidence in the arguments and were thus more persuaded by them (see the left side of the figure). When the arguments were weak, people who nodded their heads up and down had more confidence that the arguments were unconvincing, and were thus less persuaded by them (see the right side of the figure). In other words, people who nodded their heads up and down, compared to those who shook their heads from side to side, had greater confidence in their thoughts about the message (e.g., "wow, this is really convincing" when the arguments were strong, and "wow, this is really dumb" when the arguments were weak). (Figure adapted from Briñol and Petty, 2003)

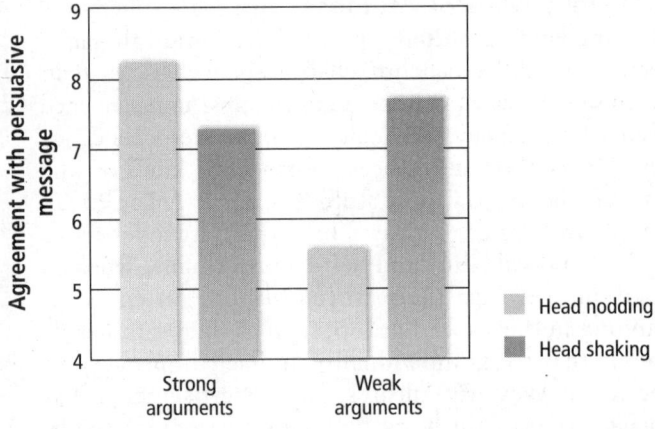

what happened, which had some interesting consequences. When the arguments in the editorial were strong, people who nodded their heads agreed with it more than did people who shook their heads, because the head nodders had more confidence in the strong arguments that they heard (see the left side of Figure 7.7). But, when the arguments were weak, head nodding had the opposite effect. It gave people more confidence that the arguments they heard were, in fact, weak and unconvincing, making them *less* convinced than people who shook their heads from side to side (see the right side of Figure 7.7). The moral? Anything you can do to increase people's confidence in their thoughts about your message will make it more effective, as long as your arguments are strong and convincing (Barden & Petty, 2008).

Resisting Persuasive Messages 抗拒说服信息

By now you are no doubt getting nervous (and not just because the chapter hasn't ended yet). With all these clever methods to change your attitudes, are you ever safe from persuasive communications? Indeed you are, or at least you can be, if you use some strategies of your own. Here's how to make sure all those persuasive messages that bombard you don't turn you into a quivering mass of constantly changing opinion.

Attitude Inoculation 态度的预防免疫

One thing you can do is consider the arguments against your attitude before someone attacks it. The more people have thought about pro and con arguments beforehand using the technique known as **attitude inoculation** (Bernard, Maio, & Olson, 2003; McGuire, 1964), the better they can ward off attempts to change their minds using logical arguments. By considering "small doses" of arguments against their position, people become immune to later, full-blown attempts to change their attitudes. Having considered the arguments beforehand, people are relatively immune to the effects of the later communication, just as exposing people to a small amount of a virus can inoculate them against exposure to the full-blown viral disease. In contrast, if people have not thought much about the issue—that is, if they formed their attitude via the peripheral route—they are particularly susceptible to an attack on that attitude using logical appeals.

In one study, for example, William McGuire (1964) "inoculated" people by giving them brief arguments against *cultural truisms*, beliefs that most members of a society accept uncritically, such as the idea that we should brush our teeth after every meal. Two days later, people came back and read a much stronger attack on the truism, one that contained a series of logical arguments about why brushing your teeth too frequently is a bad idea. The people who had been inoculated against these arguments were much less likely to change their attitudes than a control group who had not been inoculated. Why? The individuals who were inoculated with weak arguments had time to think about why these arguments were false, making them more able to contradict the stronger attack they heard 2 days later. The control group, never having

Attitude Inoculation
Making people immune to attempts to change their attitudes by initially exposing them to small doses of the arguments against their position

thought about how often people should brush their teeth, was particularly susceptible to the strong communication arguing against frequent brushing.

Be Alert to Product Placement 警惕产品内置

It is a typically tense moment on the hit TV show *24*. Terrorists are on the loose and Jack Bauer, the rogue antiterrorist agent, is right behind them. The terrorists are wily foes, however, and have just tried to hack into the computer system at the Counter Terrorist Unit (CTU) headquarters. Chloe, the CTU computer expert, notices the online attack but isn't worried. "The Cisco system is self-defending," she tells her boss, as the camera zooms in on the words "Cisco Security Response System" on her computer screen. It's another product placement moment, in which companies pay television shows to display their products during the show. For awhile Cisco Systems even had a link to the clip from *24* on its Web site (Paul, 2005).

The chief effect of talk on any subject is to strengthen one's own opinions and, in fact, one never knows exactly what he does believe until he is warmed into conviction by the heat of the attack and defense.

—Charles Dudley Warner, *Backlog Studies, 1873*

When an advertisement comes on during a TV show, people often decide to press the mute button on the remote control (or the fast forward button if they have recorded the show). To counteract this tendency to avoid ads, advertisers look for ways of displaying their wares during the show itself. Companies pay the makers of a TV show or movie to incorporate their product into the script (Kang, 2008). In the movie *E.T. the Extra-Terrestrial*, for example, Elliot left a trail of Reese's Pieces to draw out E.T., after which sales of the candy boomed. More than 40 products were shown in the hit movie *Iron Man*, including both Apple and Dell computers, cars made by Audi, Ford, and Rolls Royce, and the magazines *Vanity Fair* and *Rolling Stone*.

One reason product placement can work is that people do not realize that someone is trying to influence their attitudes and behavior. People's defenses are down; when we see E.T. eating Reese's Pieces, we don't think about the fact that someone is trying to influence our attitudes and we don't generate counterarguments (Burkley, 2008; Levitan & Visser, 2008; Wheeler, Briñol, & Hermann, 2007). Children are especially vulnerable. One study, for example, found that the more children in grades 5 to 8 had seen movies in which adults smoked cigarettes, the more positive were their attitudes toward smoking (Sargent et al., 2002; Wakefield, Flay, & Nichter, 2003).

This leads to the question of whether forewarning people that someone is about to try to change their attitudes is an effective tool against product placement, or persuasion more generally. It turns out that it is. Several studies have found that warning people about an upcoming attempt to change their attitudes makes them less susceptible to that attempt. When people are forewarned, they analyze what they see and hear more carefully and as a result are likely to avoid attitude change. Without such warnings, people pay little attention to the persuasive attempts and tend to accept them at face value (Knowles & Linn, 2004; Sagarin, Cialdini, Rice, & Serna, 2002; Wood & Quinn, 2003). So before letting kids watch TV or sending them off to the movies, it is good to remind them that they are likely to encounter several attempts to change their attitudes.

Product placement, in which a commercial product is incorporated into the script of a movie or television show, is becoming more common. In an episode of *24* for example, agent Jack Bauer discusses strategies over his prominently displayed Macintosh PowerBook.

Resisting Peer Pressure 拒绝同伴压力

We've seen that many attacks on our attitudes consist of appeals to our emotions. Can we ward off this kind of opinion change technique, just as we can ward off the effects of logical appeals? This is an important question, because many critical changes in attitudes and behaviors occur not in response to logic but via more emotional appeals. Consider the way in which

> *A companion's words of persuasion are effective.*
> —Homer

many adolescents begin to smoke, drink, or take drugs. Often they do so in response to pressure from their peers, at an age when they are particularly susceptible to such pressure. Indeed, one study found that the best predictor of whether an adolescent smokes marijuana is whether he or she has a friend who does so (Allen, Donohue, & Griffin, 2003; Yamaguchi & Kandel, 1984).

Think about how this occurs. It is not as if peers present a set of logical arguments ("Hey, Jake, did you know that recent studies show that moderate drinking may have health benefits?"). Instead, peer pressure is linked more to people's values and emotions, playing on their fear of rejection and their desire for freedom and autonomy. In adolescence, peers become an important source of social approval—perhaps the most important—and can dispense powerful rewards for holding certain attitudes or behaving in certain ways, such as using drugs or engaging in unprotected sex. What is needed is a technique that will make young people more resistant to attitude change attempts via peer pressure so that they will be less likely to engage in dangerous behaviors.

One possibility is to extend the logic of McGuire's inoculation approach to more affectively based persuasion techniques, such as peer pressure. In addition to inoculating people with doses of logical arguments that they might hear, we could also inoculate them with samples of the kinds of emotional appeals they might encounter.

Consider Jake, a 13-year-old who is hanging out with some classmates, many of whom are smoking cigarettes. The classmates begin to tease Jake about not smoking, calling him a wimp. One of them even lights a cigarette and holds it in front of Jake, daring him to take a puff. Many 13-year-olds, facing such pressure, would cave in. But suppose that we immunized Jake from such social pressures by exposing him to mild versions of them and showing him ways to combat these pressures. We might have him role-play a situation where a friend calls him a chicken for not smoking a cigarette and teach him to respond by saying, "I'd be more of a chicken if I smoked it just to impress you." Would this help him resist the more powerful pressures exerted by his classmates?

Several programs designed to prevent smoking in adolescents suggest that it would. In one, psychologists used a role-playing technique with seventh graders, very much like the one we just described (McAlister, Perry, Killen, Slinkard, & Maccoby, 1980). The researchers found that these students were significantly less likely to smoke 3 years after the study, compared to a control group that had not participated in the program. This result is encouraging and has been replicated in similar programs designed to reduce smoking (Chassin, Presson, & Sherman, 1990; Crone et al., 2003; Hoffman, Monge, Chou, & Valente, 2007).

A number of programs designed to prevent smoking in adolescents have had some success. Many celebrities have lent their names and pictures to the effort, as in this ad featuring Boyz II Men.

When Persuasion Attempts Boomerang: Reactance Theory
当说服产生反作用：抗拒理论

Reactance Theory
The idea that when people feel their freedom to perform a certain behavior is threatened, an unpleasant state of reactance is aroused, which they can reduce by performing the threatened behavior

It is important not to use too heavy a hand when trying to immunize people against assaults on their attitudes. Suppose you want to make sure that your child never smokes. "Might as well err on the side of giving too strong a message," you might think, absolutely forbidding your child to even look at a pack of cigarettes. "What's the harm?" you figure. "At least this way, my child will get the point about how serious a matter this is."

Actually, there is harm to administering strong prohibitions—the stronger they are, the more likely they will boomerang, causing an increase in interest in the prohibited activity. According to **reactance theory** (Brehm, 1966), people do not like to feel that their freedom to do or think whatever they want is being threatened. When they feel that their freedom is threatened, an unpleasant state of reactance is aroused, and people can reduce this reactance by performing the threatened behavior (e.g., smoking).

In one study, for example, researchers placed one of two signs in the bathrooms on a college campus, in an attempt to get people to stop writing graffiti on the restroom walls (Pennebaker & Sanders, 1976). One sign read, "Do not write on these walls under any circumstances." The other gave a milder prohibition: "Please don't write on these walls." The researchers returned two weeks later and observed how much graffiti had been written since they posted the signs. As they predicted, significantly more people wrote graffiti in the bathrooms with the "Do not write . . ." sign than with the "Please don't write . . ." sign. Similarly, people who receive strong admonitions against smoking, taking drugs, or getting their nose pierced become more likely to perform these behaviors to restore their sense of personal freedom and choice (Bushman, 2006; Miller, Lane, Deatrick, Young, & Potts, 2007).

When Will Attitudes Predict Behavior?
态度何时能预测行为？

Remember the advertising campaign you were hired to develop for the American Cancer Society? The reason they and other groups are willing to spend so much money on ad campaigns is because of a simple assumption: When people change their attitudes (e.g., they don't like cigarettes as much) they change their behavior as well (e.g., they stop smoking).

Actually, the relationship between attitudes and behavior is not so simple, as shown in a classic study (LaPiere, 1934). In the early 1930s, Richard LaPiere embarked on a cross-country sightseeing trip with a young Chinese couple. Prejudice against Asians was common in the United States at this time, so at each hotel, campground, and restaurant they entered, LaPiere worried that his friends would be refused service. To his surprise, of the 251 establishments he and his friends visited, only 1 refused to serve them.

Struck by this apparent lack of prejudice, LaPiere decided to explore people's attitudes toward Asians in a different way. After his trip, he wrote a letter to each establishment he and his friends had visited, asking if it would serve a Chinese visitor. Of the many replies, only *one* said it would. More than 90 percent said they definitely would not; the rest were undecided. Why were the attitudes people expressed in writing the reverse of their actual behavior?

LaPiere's study was not, of course, a controlled experiment. As he acknowledged, there are several reasons why his results may not show an inconsistency between people's attitudes and behavior. He had no way of knowing whether the proprietors who answered his letter were the same people who had served him and his friends, and even if they were, people's attitudes could have changed in the months between the time they served the Chinese couple and the time they received the letter. Nonetheless, the lack of correspondence between people's attitudes and what they actually did was so striking that we might question the earlier assumption that behavior routinely follows from attitudes. This is especially the case in light of research performed after LaPiere's study, which also found that people's attitudes can be poor predictors of their behavior (Wicker, 1969).

How can this be? Does a person's attitude toward Asians or political candidates really tell us nothing about how he or she will behave? How can we reconcile LaPiere's findings—and other studies like it—with the fact that many times behavior and attitudes *are* consistent? It turns out that attitudes do predict behavior, but only under certain specifiable conditions (DeBono & Snyder, 1995; Zanna & Fazio, 1982). One key factor is knowing whether the behavior we are trying to predict is spontaneous or planned (Fazio, 1990).

> We give advice but we do not influence people's conduct.
> —François de La Rouchefoucauld, Maxims, 1665

Predicting Spontaneous Behaviors 预测自发行为

Sometimes we act spontaneously, thinking little about what we are about to do. When LaPiere and his Chinese friends entered a restaurant, the manager did not have a lot of time to reflect on whether to serve them; he or she had to make a snap decision.

Similarly, when someone stops us on the street and asks us to sign a petition in favor of a change in the local zoning laws, we usually don't stop and think about it for 5 minutes; we decide whether to sign the petition on the spot.

Attitudes will predict spontaneous behaviors only when they are highly accessible to people (Fazio, 1990, 2007; Kallgren & Wood, 1986). **Attitude accessibility** refers to the strength of the association between an object and an evaluation of it, which is typically measured by the speed with which people can report how they feel about an issue or object (Fazio, 2000). When accessibility is high, your attitude comes to mind whenever you see or think about the attitude object. When accessibility is low, your attitude comes to mind more slowly. It follows that highly accessible attitudes will be more likely to predict spontaneous behaviors because people are more likely to be thinking about their attitude when they are called on to act. But what makes attitudes accessible in the first place? One important determinant is the degree of behavioral experience people have with the attitude object. Some attitudes are based on hands-on experience, such as a person's attitude toward the homeless after volunteering at a homeless shelter. Other attitudes are formed without much experience, such as a person's attitude toward the homeless that is based on reading about them in the newspaper. The more direct experience people have with an attitude object the more accessible their attitude is, and the more accessible it is, the more likely their spontaneous behaviors will be consistent with their attitudes (Glasman & Albarracín, 2006).

Predicting Deliberative Behaviors 预测有意行为

In many circumstances, behavior is not spontaneous, but deliberative and planned. Most of us think seriously about where to go to college, whether to accept a new job, or where to spend our vacation. Under these conditions, the accessibility of our attitude is less important. Given enough time to think about an issue, even people with inaccessible attitudes can bring to mind how they feel. It is only when we have to decide how to act on the spot, without time to think it over, that accessibility matters (Eagly & Chaiken, 1993; Fazio, 1990).

The best-known theory of how attitudes predict deliberative behaviors is the **theory of planned behavior** (Ajzen & Albarracín, 2007; Ajzen & Fishbein, 1980, 2005). According to this theory, when people have time to contemplate how they are going to behave, the best predictor of their behavior is their intention, which is determined by three things: their attitudes toward the specific behavior, their subjective norms, and their perceived behavioral control (see Figure 7.8). Let's consider each of these in turn.

Specific Attitudes The theory of planned behavior holds that only specific attitudes toward the behavior in question can be expected to predict that behavior. In one study, researchers asked a sample of married women for their attitudes toward birth control pills, ranging from the general (their attitude toward birth control) to the specific (their attitude toward using birth control pills during the next two years; see Table 7.1). Two years later, they asked the women whether they had used birth control pills at any time since the last

Attitude Accessibility
The strength of the association between an attitude object and a person's evaluation of that object, measured by the speed with which people can report how they feel about the object

Theory of Planned Behavior
The idea that the best predictors of a person's planned, deliberate behaviors are the person's attitudes toward specific behaviors, subjective norms, and perceived behavioral control

FIGURE 7.8
The theory of planned behavior.
According to this theory, the best predictors of people's planned, deliberative behaviors are their behavioral intentions. The best predictors of their intentions are their attitudes toward the specific behavior, their subjective norms, and their perceived behavioral control of the behavior.

(Adapted from Ajzen, 1985)

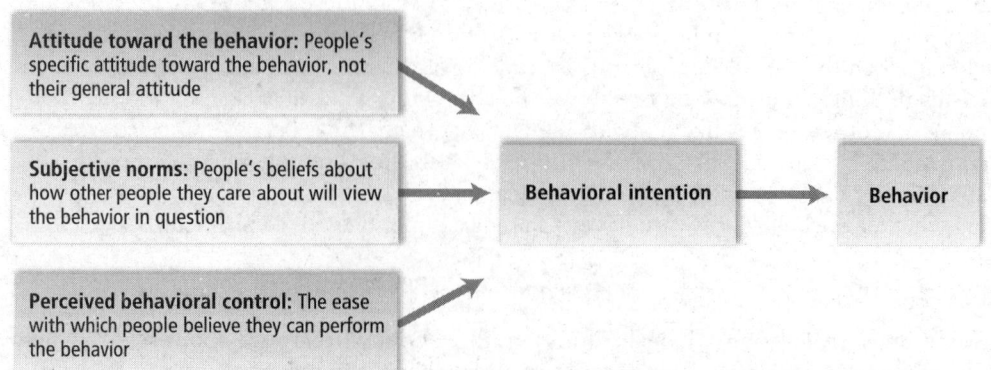

TABLE 7.1	Specific Attitudes Are Better Predictors of Behavior

Different groups of women were asked about their attitudes toward birth control. The more specific the question, the better it predicted their actual use of birth control. *Note:* If a correlation is close to 0, it means that there is no relationship between the two variables. The closer the correlation is to 1, the stronger the relationship between attitudes and behavior.

Attitude Measure	Attitude Behavior Correlation
Attitude toward birth control	.08
Attitude toward birth control pills	.32
Attitude toward using birth control pills	.53
Attitude toward using birth control pills during the next 2 years	.57

Source: Adapted from Davidson & Jaccard, 1979.

interview. As Table 7.1 shows, the women's general attitude toward birth control did not predict their use of birth control at all. This general attitude did not take into account other factors that could have influenced their decision, such as concern about the long-term effects of the pill and their attitude toward other forms of birth control. The more specific the question was about the act of using birth control pills, the better this attitude predicted their actual behavior (Davidson & Jaccard, 1979).

This study helps explain why LaPiere (1934) found such inconsistency between people's attitudes and behaviors. His question to the proprietors—whether they would serve "members of the Chinese race"—was very general. Had he asked a much more specific question—such as whether they would serve an educated, well-dressed, well-to-do Chinese couple accompanied by a white American college professor—the proprietors might have given an answer that was more in line with their behavior.

> *If actions are to yield all the results they are capable of, there must be a certain consistency between them and one's intentions.*
>
> —François de La Rochefoucauld,
> *Maxims*, 1665

Subjective Norms In addition to measuring attitudes toward the behavior, we also need to measure people's subjective norms—their beliefs about how people they care about will view the behavior in question (see Figure 7.8). To predict someone's intentions, knowing these beliefs can be as important as knowing the person's attitudes. For example, suppose we want to predict whether Kristen intends to go to a hip-hop concert, and we know that she doesn't like hip-hop music. We would probably say she won't go. But suppose we also know that Kristen's best friend, Tony, really wants her to go. Knowing this subjective norm—her belief about how a close friend views her behavior—we might make a different prediction.

Perceived Behavioral Control Finally, as seen in Figure 7.8, people's intentions are influenced by the ease with which they believe they can perform the behavior, or perceived behavioral control. If people think it is difficult to perform the behavior, such as remembering to use condoms when having sex, they will not form a strong intention to do so. If people think it is easy to perform the behavior, such as remembering to buy milk on the way home from work, they are more likely to form a strong intention to do so.

Considerable research supports the idea that asking people about these determinants of their intentions—attitudes toward specific behaviors, subjective norms, and perceived behavioral control—increases the ability to predict their planned, deliberative behaviors, such as deciding what job to accept, whether to wear a seat belt, whether to check oneself for disease, and whether to use condoms when having sex (Albarracin, Johnson, Fishbein, & Muellerleile, 2001; Armitage & Conner, 2001; Cooke & Sheeran, 2004; Trafimow & Finlay, 1996).

The Power of Advertising 广告的威力

A curious thing about advertising is that most people think it works on everyone but themselves (Wilson & Brekke, 1994). People typically comment, "There is no harm in watching commercials. Some of them are fun, and they don't have much influence on me." Are they right? This is an important question for social psychology, because most of the research on attitudes and behavior we have discussed so far was conducted in the laboratory with college students. As we saw at the beginning of the chapter, each of us is confronted with hundreds of attempts to change our attitudes every day in the form of advertisements. Do these ads really work, or are companies wasting the billions of dollars a year they are spending on advertising?

> You can tell the ideals of a nation by its advertisements.
> —George Norman Douglas, *South Wind*, 1917

It turns out that people are influenced by advertisements more than they think (Abraham & Lodish, 1990; Liebert & Sprafkin, 1988; Ryan, 1991; Wells, 1997; Wilson, Houston, & Meyers, 1998). The best evidence that advertising works comes from studies using what are called *split cable market tests*. Advertisers work in conjunction with cable television companies and grocery stores, showing a target commercial to a randomly selected group of people. They keep track of what people buy by giving potential consumers special ID cards that are scanned at checkout counters; thus they can tell whether people who saw the commercial for ScrubaDub laundry detergent actually buy more ScrubaDub—the best measure of advertising effectiveness. The results of over 300 split cable market tests indicate that advertising does work, particularly for new products (Lodish et al., 1995).

How Advertising Works 广告如何发挥作用

How does advertising work, and what types of ads work best? The answers follow from our earlier discussion of attitude change. If advertisers are trying to change an affectively based attitude, then as we have seen, it is best to fight emotions with emotions. Many advertisements take the emotional approach—for example, ads for different brands of soft drinks. Given that different brands of colas are not all that different, many people do not base their purchasing decisions on the objective qualities of the different brands. Consequently, soda advertisements do not stress facts and figures. As one advertising executive noted, "The thing about soda commercials is that they actually have nothing to say" ("Battle for Your Brain," 1991). Instead of presenting facts, soft drink ads play to people's emotions, trying to associate feelings of excitement, youth, energy, and sexual attractiveness with the brand.

If people's attitudes are more cognitively based, we need to ask an additional question: How personally relevant is the issue? Does it have important consequences for people's everyday lives, or is it a remote issue that does not directly affect them? Consider, for example, the problem of heartburn. This is not a topic that evokes strong emotions and values in most people—it is more cognitively based. To people who suffer from frequent heartburn, however, the topic clearly has direct personal relevance. In this case, the best way to change people's attitudes is to use logical, fact-based arguments—convince people that your product will reduce heartburn the best or the fastest, and people will buy it (Chaiken, 1987; Petty & Cacioppo, 1986).

THE TOBACCO INDUSTRY FINDS A NEW MARKET

What if you are dealing with a cognitively based attitude that is not of direct personal relevance to people? For example, what if you are trying to sell a heartburn medicine to people who experience heartburn only every now and then and do not consider it a big deal? Here you have a problem because people are unlikely to pay close attention to your advertisement. You might succeed in changing

CONNECTIONS 链 接

Do Media Campaigns to Reduce Drug Use Work?
减少药物使用的媒体宣传有用吗？

Smoking and drinking are common in movies, and sometimes public figures admired by many youth glamorize the use of drugs and alcohol. Advertising, product placement, and the behavior of admired figures can have powerful effects on people's behavior, including tobacco and alcohol use (Pechmann & Knight, 2002; Saffer, 2002). This raises an important question: Do public service ads designed to reduce people's use of drugs such as alcohol, tobacco, and marijuana work?

By now you know that changing people's attitudes and behavior can be difficult, particularly if people are not very motivated to pay attention to a persuasive message or are distracted while trying to pay attention. If persuasive messages are well crafted, they can have an effect, however, and we have seen many successful attempts to change people's attitudes in this chapter. What happens when researchers take these techniques out of the laboratory and try to change real-life attitudes and behavior, such as people's attraction to and use of illegal drugs?

A meta-analysis of studies that tested the effects of a media message (conveyed via television, radio, electronic, and print media) on substance abuse (including illegal drugs, alcohol, and tobacco) in youths was encouraging (Derzon & Lipsey, 2002). After a media campaign that targeted a specific substance, such as tobacco, kids were less likely to use that substance. Television and radio messages had bigger effects than messages in the print media (Ibrahim & Glantz, 2007).

In one particularly impressive study, researchers developed 30-second television spots in which teen actors conveyed the risks of smoking marijuana, such as its effects on people's relationships, level of motivation, and judgment (Palmgreen, Donohew, Lorch, Hoyle, & Stephenson, 2001). The ads were shown for 4-month intervals at different times in two similar communities, Fayette County, Kentucky, and Knox County, Tennessee. The researchers interviewed randomly chosen teenagers in both communities and assessed their attitudes and use of marijuana during the previous 30 days.

The ads had no detectable effect among teenagers who were low in sensation seeking, which is a personality trait having to do with how much people are attracted to novel, emotionally exciting activities. These people did not use marijuana much to begin with, so we would not expect the public service ads to change their behavior. Among the teenagers who were high in sensation seeking, however, the ads had a definite impact. When the ads were shown in Fayette County but not Knox County, the percentage of Fayette teenagers who reported using marijuana in the preceding 30 days dropped from about 38 percent to 28 percent. The percentage of Knox County teenagers who said they used marijuana increased during this same time period. When the ads were shown in Knox County, reported marijuana use also dropped by about 10 percent. These drops were not huge; it is not as if every teenager who saw the ads decided against smoking marijuana. Undoubtedly, some teenagers never saw the ads, and many who did were unaffected. From a public health perspective, however, a 10 percent drop is impressive, providing some hope for the success of media campaigns that promote healthier behavior.

A recent meta-analysis showed that public campaigns to reduce drug use can work. Do you think this ad is effective, based on what you have read in this chapter?

their attitudes via the peripheral route, such as having attractive movie stars endorse your product. The problem here, as we have seen, is that attitude change triggered by simple peripheral cues is not long-lasting (Chaiken, 1987; Petty & Cacioppo, 1986). So if you have a product that does not trigger people's emotions and is not directly relevant to their everyday lives, you are in trouble.

But don't give up. The trick is to *make* your product personally relevant. Let's take a look at some actual ad campaigns to see how this is done. Consider the case of Gerald Lambert, who early in the twentieth century inherited a company that made a surgical antiseptic used to treat throat infections—Listerine. Seeking a wider market for his product, Lambert decided to promote it as a mouthwash. The only problem was that no one at the time used a mouthwash or even knew what one was. So having invented the cure, Lambert invented the disease. Look at the ad for Listerine, which appeared in countless magazines over the years. Even though today we find this ad incredibly sexist, at the time the ad successfully played on people's fears about social rejection and failure. The phrase "Often a bridesmaid, never a bride" became one of the most famous in the history of advertising. In a few cleverly chosen words, it succeeded in making a problem—*halitosis*—personally relevant to millions of people.

Subliminal Advertising: A Form of Mind Control?
阈下广告：一种精神控制方式？

In September 2000, during the heat of the United States presidential campaign between George W. Bush and Al Gore, a man in Seattle was watching a political advertisement on television. At first, the ad looked like a run-of-the-mill political spot, in which an announcer praised the benefits of George W. Bush's prescription drug plan and criticized Al Gore's plan. But the viewer thought that he noticed something odd. He videotaped the ad the next time it ran and played it back at a slow speed, and sure enough, he *had* noticed something unusual: As the announcer said, "The Gore prescription plan: Bureaucrats decide," the word RATS flashed on the screen very quickly—for one-thirtieth of a second at normal viewing speed. The alert viewer notified officials in the Gore campaign, who quickly contacted the press. Soon the country was abuzz about a possible attempt by the Bush campaign to use subliminal messages to create a negative impression of Al Gore. The Bush campaign denied that anyone had deliberately inserted the word RATS, claiming that it was "purely accidental" (Berke, 2000).

The RATS incident was neither the first nor the last controversy over the use of **subliminal messages**, defined as words or pictures that are not consciously perceived but may influence people's judgments, attitudes, and behaviors. In the late 1950s, James

This ad is one of the most famous in the history of advertising. Although today it is easy to see how sexist and offensive it is, when it appeared in the 1930s it succeeded in making a problem (bad breath) personally relevant by playing on people's fears and insecurities about personal relationships. Can you think of contemporary ads that try to raise similar fears?

Subliminal Messages
Words or pictures that are not consciously perceived but may nevertheless influence people's judgments, attitudes, and behaviors

In September 2000, during the U.S. presidential campaign, George W. Bush aired a television ad about his prescription drug plan. As the announcer intoned, "The Gore prescription plan: Bureaucrats decide," the word "RATS" was flashed on the screen for one-thirtieth of a second. Do subliminal messages like this have any effect on people's attitudes?

Vicary supposedly flashed the messages "Drink Coca-Cola" and "Eat popcorn" during a commercial movie and claimed that sales at the concession counter skyrocketed (according to some reports, Vicary made up these claims; Weir, 1984). Wilson Bryan Key (1973, 1989) has written several best-selling books on hidden persuasion techniques, which claim that advertisers routinely implant sexual messages in print advertisements, such as the word *sex* in the ice cubes of an ad for gin, and male and female genitalia in everything from pats of butter to the icing in an ad for cake mix. Key (1973) argues that these images are not consciously perceived but put people in a good mood and make them pay more attention to the advertisement. More recently, gambling casinos in Canada removed a brand of slot machines, after it was revealed that the machines flashed the winning symbols on every spin, at a speed too fast for the players to see consciously (Benedetti, 2007).

Subliminal messages are not just visual; they can be auditory as well. There is a large market for audiotapes that contain subliminal messages to help people lose weight, stop smoking, improve their study habits, raise their self-esteem, and even shave a few strokes off their golf scores. But are subliminal messages effective? Do they really make us more likely to buy consumer products or help us lose weight and stop smoking? Most members of the public believe that subliminal messages can shape their attitudes and behaviors, even though they are not aware that the messages have entered their minds (Zanot, Pincus, & Lamp, 1983). Are they right?

Debunking the Claims about Subliminal Advertising Few of the proponents of subliminal advertising have conducted controlled studies to back up their claims. Fortunately, many studies of subliminal perception have been conducted, allowing us to evaluate the sometimes outlandish claims that are made. Simply stated, there is no evidence that the types of subliminal messages encountered in everyday life have any influence on people's behavior. Hidden commands do not cause us to line up and buy popcorn any more than we normally do, and the subliminal commands on self-help tapes do not (unfortunately!) help us quit smoking or lose weight (Brannon & Brock, 1994; Broyles, 2006; Pratkanis, 1992; Theus, 1994; Trappey, 1996). For example, one study randomly assigned people to listen to a subliminal self-help tape designed to improve people's memory or to one designed to raise their self-esteem (Greenwald, Spangenberg, Pratkanis, & Eskenazi, 1991). Neither of the tapes had any effect on people's memory or self-esteem. Even so, participants were convinced that the tapes had worked, which explains why people spend millions of dollars on subliminal self-help tapes each year. It would be nice if we could all improve ourselves simply by listening to music with subliminal messages, but this study and others like it show that subliminal tapes are no better at solving our problems than patent medicines or visits to an astrologist.

There is no scientific evidence that implanting sexual images in advertising boosts sales of the product. The public is very aware of this subliminal technique, however—so much so that some advertisers have begun to poke fun at subliminal messages in their ads.

Laboratory Evidence for Subliminal Influence You may have noticed that we said that subliminal messages don't work when "encountered in everyday life." There *is* evidence that people can be influenced by subliminal messages under carefully controlled laboratory conditions (Dijksterhuis, Aarts, & Smith, 2005). In one study, for example, Dutch college students saw subliminal flashes of the words "Lipton Ice" (a brand of ice tea) or a nonsense word made of the same letters (Karremans, Stroebe, & Claus, 2006). All the students were then asked whether they would prefer Lipton Ice or a brand of Dutch mineral water if they were offered a drink at that moment. If students were not thirsty at the time, the subliminal flashes had no effect on their drink preference. But if students were thirsty, those who had seen the subliminal flashes of "Lipton Ice" were significantly more likely to chose that drink than were students who had seen subliminal flashes of the nonsense word. Several other laboratory studies have found similar effects of pictures or words flashed at subliminal levels (e.g., Bargh & Pietromonaco, 1982; Bornstein, Leone, & Galley, 1987; Dijksterhuis & Aarts, 2002; Strahan, Spencer, & Zanna, 2002).

Does this mean that advertisers will figure out how to use subliminal messages in everyday advertising? Maybe, but it hasn't happened yet. All the successful demonstrations of subliminal stimuli have been conducted under carefully controlled laboratory conditions that are difficult to reproduce in everyday life. To get subliminal effects, researchers have to make sure that the illumination of the room is just right, that people are seated just the right distance from a viewing screen, and that nothing else is occurring to distract them as the subliminal stimuli are flashed. Further, even in the laboratory, there is no evidence that subliminal messages can get people to act counter to their wishes, values, or personalities (Neuberg, 1988). Under just the right conditions in the laboratory, subliminal messages can make thirsty people choose one pleasant beverage over another. They do not, however, make people march off to the supermarket to buy products they don't want or vote for candidates they despise. Thus it is highly unlikely that the word RATS in the Bush campaign ad converted people from Gore supporters to Bush supporters.

Advertising, Cultural Stereotypes, and Social Behavior
广告、文化的刻板印象与社会行为

Ironically, the hoopla surrounding subliminal messages has obscured the fact that ads are more powerful when people consciously perceive them. We have seen plenty of evidence that the ads people perceive consciously every day can substantially influence their behavior, even though the ads do not contain subliminal messages. It is interesting that people fear subliminal advertising more than regular advertising when it is regular advertising that is more powerful (Wilson, Gilbert, & Wheatley, 1998). The following Try It! exercise will help you see whether this is true of people you know.

Advertising and Mind Control 试一试！广告与思想控制

Here is an exercise on people's beliefs about the power of advertising that you can try on your friends. Ask about 10 friends the following questions—preferably friends who have not had a course in social psychology! See how accurate their beliefs are about the effects of different kinds of advertising.

1. Do you think that you are influenced by subliminal messages in advertising? (Define *subliminal messages* for your friends as words or pictures that are not consciously perceived but nevertheless supposedly influence people's judgments, attitudes, and behaviors.)

2. Do you think that you are influenced by everyday advertisements that you perceive consciously, such as television ads for laundry detergent and painkillers?

3. Suppose you had a choice to listen to one of two speeches that argued against a position you believe in, such as whether marijuana should be legalized. In speech A, a person presents several arguments against your position. In speech B, all of the arguments are presented subliminally—you will not perceive anything consciously. Which speech would you rather listen to, A or B?

Tally the results here:

Question 1	Question 2	Question 3
Yes:	Yes:	Yes:
No:	No:	No:

Turn to page 209 to see if your results match those of actual studies. Show off your knowledge to your friends. Ask them why they are more wary of subliminal messages than everyday advertising when it is everyday ads and not subliminal messages that change people's minds. Why do *you* think that people are most afraid of the kinds of ads that are least effective? What does this say about people's awareness of their own thought processes?

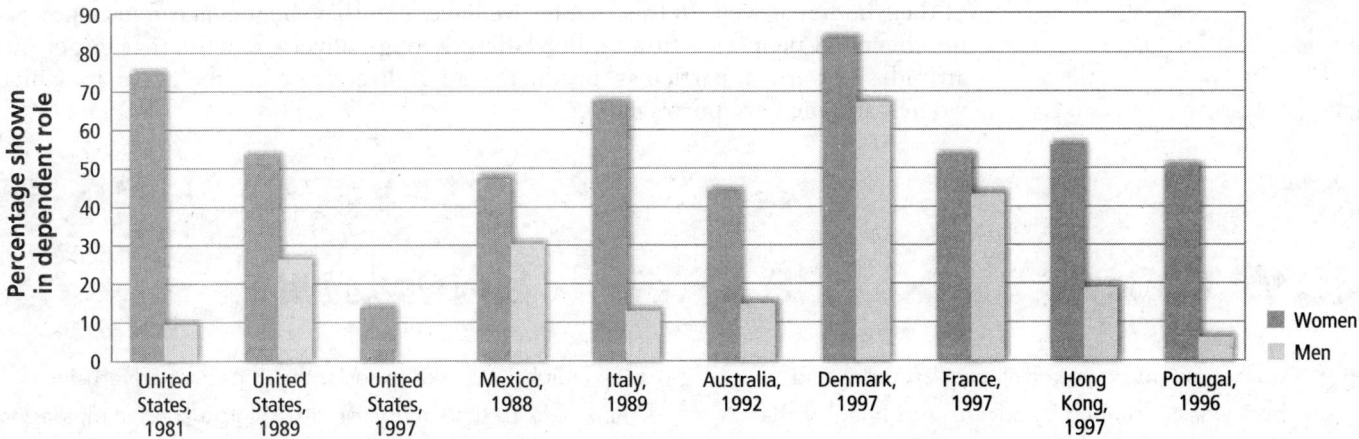

FIGURE 7.9
Portrayals of women and men in television advertising.
The ways in which women and men are portrayed in television commercials have been examined throughout the world. In every country, women were more likely to be portrayed in powerless, dependent roles than men were.

(Adapted from Furnham & Mak, 1999)

Further, advertising influences more than just our consumer attitudes. Advertisements transmit cultural stereotypes in their words and images, subtly linking products with desired images (e.g., Marlboro ads linking cigarettes with the rugged, macho Marlboro Man; beer ads linking beer consumption with sex). Advertisements can also reinforce and perpetuate stereotypical ways of thinking about social groups. Until recently, ads almost always showed groups of whites (token individuals of color are now mixed into the group), couples who are heterosexual, families that are traditional (with a mom, dad, son, and daughter), and so on. You would think that divorced families, the middle-aged and the elderly, people of color, lesbians and gay men, the physically disabled, and others just didn't exist.

Gender stereotypes are particularly pervasive in advertising imagery. Men are doers; women are observers. Several studies have examined television commercials throughout the world and coded how men and women are portrayed. As seen in Figure 7.9, one review found that women were more likely to be portrayed in dependent roles (that is, not in a position of power but dependent on someone else) than men in every country that was examined (Furnham & Mak, 1999).

Well, you might think, television commercials reflect the stereotypes of a society but play little role in shaping those stereotypes or influencing people's attitudes and behavior. Actually, the images conveyed in advertisements are far from harmless. As we will see in Chapter 8, a thin body style for women is glamorized in the media. The women shown in magazines, movies, and television programs are getting thinner all the time, are thinner than women in the actual population, and are often so thin that they would qualify for a diagnosis of anorexia (Fouts & Burggraf, 1999, 2000; Wiseman, Gray, Moismann, & Ahrens, 1992). The message to women and young girls? To be beautiful you must be thin. This message is hitting home; girls and women in America are becoming increasingly dissatisfied with the way they look. In one survey, nearly half of college women said they were unhappy with their bodies (Bearman, Presnell, & Martinez, 2006; Monteath & McCabe, 1997), and this dissatisfaction was unrelated to the women's *actual* body size (Grabe & Hyde, 2006). What's worse, body dissatisfaction has been shown to be a risk factor for eating disorders, low self-esteem, and depression (Grabe, Hyde, & Lindberg, 2007). But is there a causal connection between the way women are depicted in the media and women's feelings about their own bodies? It appears that there is. Experimental studies show that women who are randomly assigned to look at media depitctions of thin women show a dip in their body self-image (Grabe, Ward, & Hyde, 2008). In Chapter 8 we will see that the media has influenced men's images of their bodies as well. In this chapter we have seen that the media can have powerful effects on people's attitudes, both directly (e.g., advertisements that target our attitudes toward a particular product) and indirectly (e.g., the ways in which women and men are portrayed).

HOW WOULD YOU USE THIS? 如何学以致用？

To what extent do you think your attitudes and behavior are shaped by advertising? Imagine that you are watching television and an ad comes on for a particular brand of pain relief medicine. Or, suppose that instead of seeing an ad for this brand, you see it as part of a product placement in a TV show (maybe you see Jack Bauer pop a couple of the pills to ward off a headache caused by fighting terrorists on *24*). It might seem farfetched that seeing an ad or a product placed within a show can dramatically influence what you choose to buy the next time you are at the drug store, but after reading this chapter, can you be so sure? Assuming that you do not want to be at the mercy of the advertising industry, what steps might you take to resist the impact of advertising? Think back to the section on resisting persuasive messages (pages 194–197): Are there strategies you could adopt to avoid being influenced? Of course, you might not think it is worth the effort to muster your defenses against ads for pain relievers. But what about attempts to get you to vote for a particular political candidates or to develop positive attitudes toward cigarettes? None of us, of course, is an automaton that marches completely to the tune of Madison Avenue. It is worth thinking, however, about how much we want to be influenced by advertising and steps we can take to avoid that influence.

Summary 总　结

- **The Nature and Origin of Attitudes** An **attitude** is a person's enduring evaluation of people, objects, and ideas.
  - **Where Do Attitudes Come From?** Although some attitudes may have a weak genetic basis, they are based mostly on our experiences. **Cognitively based attitudes** are based mostly on people's beliefs about the properties of the attitude object. **Affectively based attitudes** are based more on people's emotions and values; they can be created through **classical conditioning** or **operant conditioning**. **Behaviorally based attitudes** are based on people's actions toward the attitude object.
  - **Explicit Versus Implicit Attitudes** Once an attitude develops, it can exist at two levels. **Explicit attitudes** are ones we consciously endorse and can easily report. **Implicit attitudes** are involuntary, uncontrollable, and at times unconscious.

- **How Do Attitudes Change?** Attitudes often change in response to social influence.
  - **Changing Attitudes by Changing Behavior: Cognitive Dissonance Theory Revisited** One way that attitudes change is when people engage in counterattitudinal advocacy for low external justification. When this occurs, people find internal justification for their behavior, bringing their attitudes in line with their behavior.
  - **Persuasive Communications and Attitude Change** Attitudes can also change in response to a **persuasive communication**. According to the **Yale Attitude Change approach,** the effectiveness of a persuasive communication depends on aspects of the communicator, or source of the message; aspects of the message itself (e.g., its content); and aspects of the audience. The **elaboration likelihood model** specifies when people are persuaded more by the

strength of the arguments in the communication and when they are persuaded more by surface characteristics. When people have both the motivation and ability to pay attention to a message, they take the **central route to persuasion,** where they pay close attention to the strength of the arguments. When they have low motivation or ability, they take the **peripheral route to persuasion,** where they are swayed by surface characteristics, such as the attractiveness of the speaker.

- **Emotion and Attitude Change** Emotions influence attitude change in a number of ways. **Fear-arousing communications** can cause lasting attitude change if a moderate amount of fear is aroused and people believe they will be reassured by the content of the message. Emotions can also be used as heuristics to gauge one's attitude; if people feel good in the presence of an object, they often infer that they like it, even if those good feelings were caused by something else. Finally, the effectiveness of persuasive communications also depends on the type of attitude people have. Appeals to emotion and social identity work best if the attitude is based on emotion and social identity.
- **Confidence in One's Thoughts and Attitude Change** People's confidence in their thoughts about an attitude object affects how much they will influenced by a persuasive communication. People's confidence can be affected by such things as whether they are nodding or shaking their head while listening to a persuasive message.

- **Resisting Persuasive Messages** Researchers have studied a number of ways that people can avoid being influenced by persuasive messages.
  - **Attitude Inoculation** One way is to expose people to small doses of arguments against their position, which makes it easier for them to defend themselves against a persuasive message they hear later.
  - **Being Alert to Product Placement** Increasingly, advertisers are paying to have their products shown prominently in TV shows and movies. Forewarning people about attempts to change their attitudes, such as product placement, makes them less susceptible to attitude change.

- **Resisting Peer Pressure** Teaching kids how to resist peer pressure can make them less vulnerable to it.
- **When Persuasion Attempts Boomerang: Reactance Theory** According to reactance theory, people experience an unpleasant state called reactance when their freedom of choice is threatened. Attempts to manage people's attitudes can backfire if they make people feel that their choice is limited.

- **When Will Attitudes Predict Behavior?** Under what conditions will people's attitudes dictate how they actually behave?
  - **Predicting Spontaneous Behaviors** Attitudes predict spontaneous behaviors only when they are relatively accessible. **Attitude accessibility** refers to the strength of the association between an object and an evaluation of it.
  - **Predicting Deliberative Behaviors** According to the **theory of planned behavior**, deliberative (non-spontaneous) behaviors are a function of people's attitude toward the specific act in question, subjective norms (people's beliefs about how others view the behavior in question), and how much people believe they can control the behavior.

- **The Power of Advertising** Advertising has been found to be quite effective at changing people's attitudes, as indicated by split cable market tests, where advertisers show different advertisements to different samples of cable subscribers and then look at what they buy.
  - **How Advertising Works** Advertising works by targeting affectively based attitudes with emotions, by targeting cognitively based attitudes with facts, and by making a product seem personally relevant.
  - **Subliminal Advertising: A Form of Mind Control?** There is no evidence that subliminal messages in advertisements have any influence on people's behavior. Subliminal influences have been found, however, under controlled laboratory conditions.
  - **Advertising, Cultural Stereotypes, and Social Behavior** In addition to changing people's attitudes toward commercial products, advertisements often transmit cultural stereotypes.

CHAPTER 7 TEST 第7章习题

1. All of the following are true about attitudes *except*
   a. they are evaluations of people, objects, and ideas.
   b. they are related to our temperament and personality.
   c. they rarely change over time.
   d. they can be changed with persuasive communications.
   e. under the right conditions they predict people's behavior.

2. Paige wants to buy a puppy. She does some research and decides to buy an English springer spaniel rather than a Great Dane because they are smaller, more active, and good with children. Which type of attitude influenced her decision?
   a. Affectively based attitude
   b. Behaviorally based attitude
   c. Explicitly based attitude
   d. Cognitively based attitude

3. People will be most likely to change their attitudes about smoking if an antismoking advertisement
   a. uses extremely graphic pictures of how smoke can harm the body, and warns of the risks of smoking.
   b. gives people subliminal messages about the risks of smoking as well as recommendations of how to quit.
   c. uses graphic pictures of the damages of smoking on the body and then provides specific recommendations on how to quit smoking.
   d. uses success stories of how people quit smoking.

4. Emilia would be most likely to pay attention to facts about the danger of AIDS during a school assembly *and* remember the facts for a long time if
   a. the speaker emphasized statistical information about AIDS throughout the world.
   b. the speaker emphasized how the disease has spread in her community, and there isn't anything distracting Emilia from listening.
   c. the speaker emphasized how the disease has spread in her community, but at the same time, Emilia's best friend is whispering to her about a big party that weekend.
   d. the speaker is a nationally known expert on AIDS.

5. You are trying to sell a new electronic toothbrush at the airport to busy, distracted travelers. Which of the following is *least* likely to be successful at getting people to buy a toothbrush?
   a. Make up a flier that gives convincing reasons why the toothbrush is so good.
   b. Make a large sign that says, "9 out of 10 dentists recommend this toothbrush!"
   c. Put up a large banner featuring a picture of your friend who looks like Brad Pitt posing with the toothbrush.
   d. Stop people and say, "Do you know that this is the toothbrush that is used the most by Hollywood stars?"

6. According to reactance theory, what of the following public service messages would be *least* likely to get people to wear seatbelts?
   a. "Please wear your seatbelt every time you drive."
   b. "Wear your seatbelt to save lives."
   c. "It's the law—you must wear your seatbelt."
   d. "Buckle up your children—you might save their life."

7. Under which of the following conditions would people be most likely to vote for a political candidate? They
   a. like the candidate's policies but have negative feelings toward him or her.
   b. know little about the candidate's policies but have positive feelings toward him or her.
   c. see subliminal ads supporting the candidate on national television.
   d. see television ads supporting the candidate while they are distracted by their children.

8. All of the following are examples of ways to resist persuasion *except*
   a. making people immune to change of opinions by initially exposing them to small doses of arguments against their position.
   b. warning people about advertising techniques such as product placement.
   c. forbidding people to buy a product.
   d. role-playing using milder versions of real-life social pressures.

9. On a survey, Milo reports that he agrees with wearing a seatbelt. According to the theory of planned behavior, what else will predict whether Milo will wear a seatbelt on a given day?
   a. He generally agrees that safe driving is important.
   b. His best friend, Trevor, was in the car and he also wore a seatbelt.
   c. His attitude toward seatbelts was not very accessible.
   d. Milo believes that it is hard to remember to wear his seatbelt.

10. Suppose that while you are watching a film at a movie theater, the words "Drink Coke" are flashed on the screen at speeds too quick for you to see consciously. According to research on subliminal perception, which of the following is most true?
    a. You will get up and buy a Coke, but only if you are thirsty.
    b. You will get up and buy a Coke, but only if you prefer Coke to Pepsi.
    c. You will be *less* likely to get up and buy a Coke.
    d. You will be no more likely to buy a Coke than if the subliminal messages were not flashed.

Chapter 7 Answer Key
1-c, 2-d, 3-c, 4-b, 5-a, 6-c, 7-b, 8-c, 9-b, 10-d

For more review plus practice tests, videos, flashcards, writing help and more, log on to MyPsychLab.

Scoring the TRY IT! exercises "试一试！"答案

● Page 189

Scoring: First, reverse your responses to items 3, 4, 5, 7, 8, 9, 12, 16, and 17. Do so as follows: If you gave a 1 to these questions, change it to a 5; if you gave a 2, change it to a 4; if you gave a 3, leave it the same; if you gave a 4, change it to a 2; if you gave a 5, change it to a 1. Then add up your answers to all 18 questions.

People who are high in the need for cognition score slightly higher in verbal intelligence but no higher in abstract reasoning. And there are no gender differences in the need for cognition.

● Page 204

Question 1: Wilson, Gilbert, and Wheatley (1998) found that 80 percent of college students preferred not to receive a subliminal message because it might influence them in an undesirable way.

Question 2: Wilson, Gilbert, and Wheatley (1998) found that only 28 percent of college students preferred not to receive a regular everyday TV ad because it might influence them in an undesirable way.

Question 3: When Wilson, Houston, and Meyers (1998) asked college students to choose to listen to the type of speech they thought would influence them the least, 69 percent chose the regular speech and 31 percent chose the subliminal speech. Ironically, it was the regular speech that changed people's minds the most.

8

Conformity
Influencing Behavior

从众：
影响行为

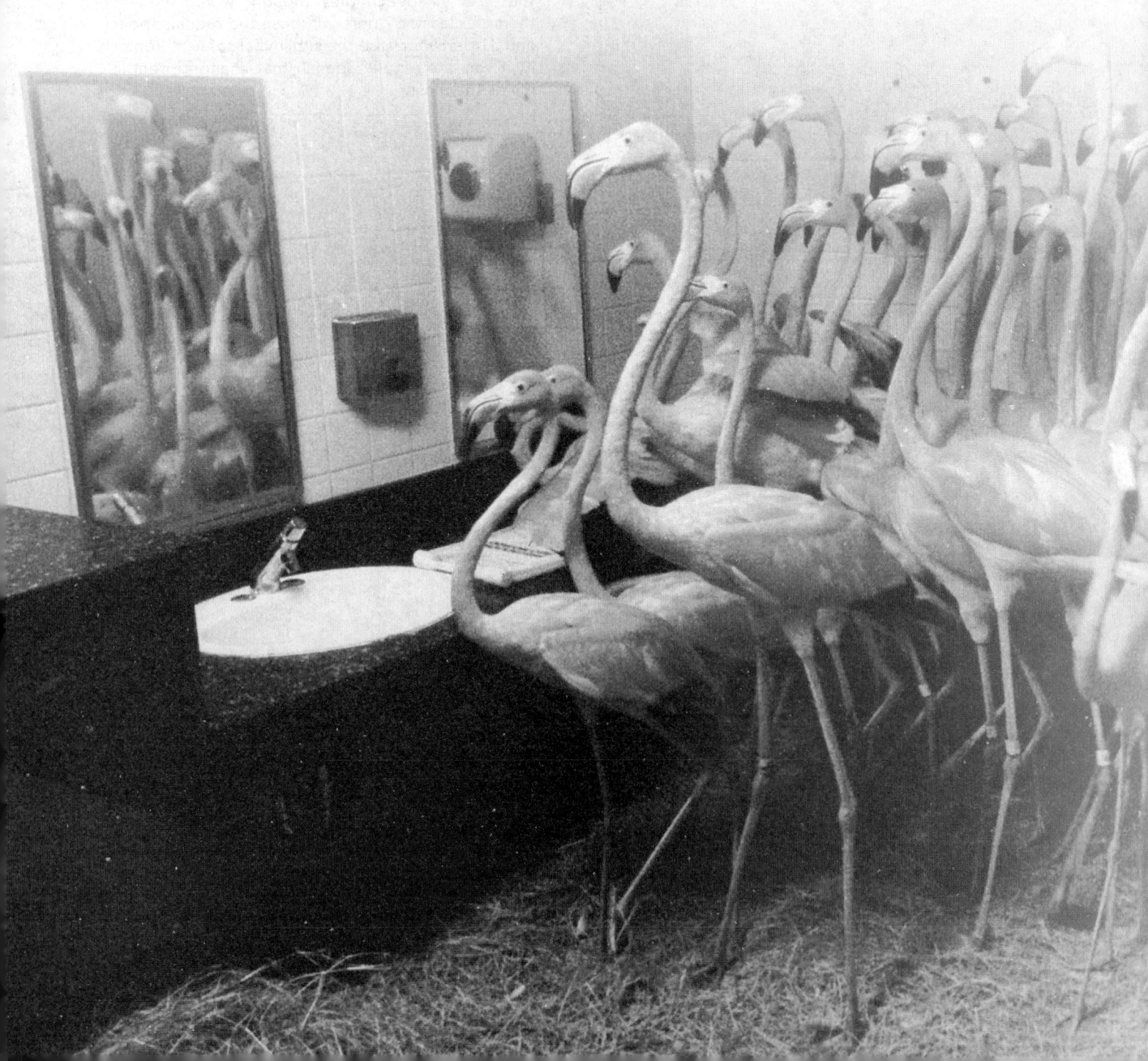

OUTLINE 提纲

- Conformity: When and Why
- Informational Social Influence: The Need to Know What's "Right"
  - The Importance of Being Accurate
  - When Informational Conformity Backfires
  - When Will People Conform to Informational Social Influence?
- Normative Social Influence: The Need to Be Accepted
  - Conformity and Social Approval: The Asch Line Judgment Studies
  - The Importance of Being Accurate, Revisited
  - The Consequences of Resisting Normative Social Influence
  - Normative Social Influence in Everyday Life
  - When Will People Conform to Normative Social Influence?
  - Minority Influence: When the Few Influence the Many
  - CONNECTIONS: The Power of Propaganda
- Using Social Influence to Promote Beneficial Behavior
  - The Role of Injunctive and Descriptive Norms
- Obedience to Authority
  - The Role of Normative Social Influence
  - The Role of Informational Social Influence
  - Other Reasons Why We Obey
  - The Obedience Studies, Then and Now
- Summary

N APRIL 2004, A MAN CALLED THE MCDONALD'S RESTAURANT in Mount Washington, Kentucky, and identified himself as a police detective to the assistant manager, Donna Jean Summers, 51. He told her she had a problem: One of her employees had stolen from the restaurant. He told her he had talked to McDonald's corporate headquarters and to her store manager, whom he named correctly. The policeman gave Ms. Summers a rough description of the perpetrator, a teenage female, and she identified one of her employees (whom we will call Susan, to protect her identity). The police detective told the assistant manager that she needed to search Susan immediately for the stolen money, or else Susan would be arrested, taken to jail, and searched there (Wolfson, 2005).

Now, you might be thinking that this all sounds a bit odd. Ms. Summers said later that she was initially rather confused, but the caller was very authoritative and presented his information in a very convincing manner. And, after all, he was a

policeman. We're supposed to obey the police. During the phone call, Ms. Summers thought she heard police radios in the background.

She called Susan into a small room and locked the door. Susan was 18 and had been a perfect employee for the past several months. The policeman on the phone told Ms. Summers what to do and what to say. Following his instructions, she ordered Susan to take off her clothing, one item at a time, until she was standing naked. Ms. Summers put all the clothes in a bag and put the bag outside the room, as instructed by the caller. Susan was now crying, fearful of the charge of theft and distraught by the strip search. It was 5:00 P.M. Unfortunately for Susan, the next 4 hours would involve even further degradation and sexual abuse, all because of the orders given by the "policeman" on the phone (Barrouquere, 2006).

Susan was not the first fast-food employee victim. Phone calls to restaurant managers, ordering them to abuse their employees, had been occurring around the country since 1999. It just took law enforcement some time to learn about the crimes and put the whole picture together, given that the perpetrator was using a telephone calling card, which is difficult to trace. In all, managers of 70 restaurants, representing a dozen different chains in 32 states, received these phone calls, and obeyed the caller's instructions (Barrouquere, 2006; Gray, 2004; Wolfson, 2005). The caller, as you have probably guessed, was not a policeman but was perpetrating a horrible hoax on hundreds of people.

Susan had been standing, naked, in the small, locked room for an hour. Ms. Summers needed to get back to supervising the cooking area, so the "policeman" told her to find someone else to guard Susan. She called her fiancé, Walter Nix, Jr., 42, who agreed to come over to the restaurant. Mr. Nix locked himself into the room with the increasingly hysterical, terrified, and naked teenager. At this point, the events become even more bizarre. Mr. Nix also believed the caller was who he said he was, and Mr. Nix proved even more obedient. In a series of escalating demands over 3 hours, the "detective" told Mr. Nix to force Susan to acquiesce to various sexual demands. The caller also talked directly to Susan, frightening her with what would happen to her if she didn't obey. "I was scared because they were a higher authority to me. I was scared for my safety because I thought I was in trouble with the law," she said (Wolfson, 2005, p. 3).

Hours later, the caller told Mr. Nix to replace himself with another man. Thomas Simms, a 58-year-old employee, was called into the room. As he put it later, he knew immediately "something is not right about this" (Wolfson, 2005, p. 7). He refused to obey the policeman on the phone. He called in Ms. Summers and convinced her something was wrong. "I knew then I had been had," she said. "I lost it. I begged [Susan] for forgiveness. I was almost hysterical" (Wolfson, 2005, p. 7). At this point, the "detective" hung up the phone. Susan's nightmare was finally over.

After an investigation that involved police detectives in several states, a Florida man, David R. Stewart, 38, was arrested and charged as the telephone hoax "caller." Married and the father of five, Stewart worked as a prison guard and was formerly a mall security guard and a volunteer sheriff's deputy. He was tried in Bullitt, Kentucky, in the fall of 2006. Because the evidence against him was circumstantial, the jury returned a verdict of not guilty. There have been no further fast-food hoax phone calls since his arrest and trial ("ABC News," 2007). The assistant manager, Donna Summers, and her (no longer) fiancé, Walter Nix, Jr., pleaded guilty to various charges. Ms. Summers was sentenced to probation, and Mr. Nix was sentenced to 5 years in prison. Susan, who now suffers from panic attacks, anxiety, and depression, sued the McDonald's corporation for failing to warn employees nationally after the first hoaxes occurred at their restaurants. She was awarded $6.1 million in damages by a Kentucky jury (Barrouquere, 2006; Neil, 2007; Wolfson, 2005). The assistant manager, Donna Summers, also sued McDonald's and was awarded $1.1 million in damages (Neil, 2007).

In one of the saddest comments on this event, Susan's therapist said that Susan followed orders that night because her experience with adults "has been to do what she is told, because good girls do what they are told" (Wolfson, 2005). Every day, people try to influence us to do what they want. The most powerful form of social influence produces obedience and occurs when a legitimate authority figure gives an order. The fast-food restaurant hoax shows us how overly obedient people can be. A more subtle form of social influence involves conformity. Here, others subtly indicate to us what is appropriate and it seems in our best interest to go along. In this chapter, we will focus on the potentially positive and negative effects of these social influence processes.

Conformity: When and Why
从众行为：发生的时机与原因

Which one of the two quotations on the right do you find more appealing? Which one describes your immediate reaction to the word *conformity*? We wouldn't be surprised if you preferred the second quotation. American culture stresses the importance of not conforming (Hofstede, 1986; Kim & Markus, 1999; Markus, Kitayama, & Heiman, 1996). We think of ourselves as a nation of rugged individualists, people who think for themselves, who stand up for the underdog, who go against the tide for what they think is right. This cultural self-image has been shaped by the manner in which our nation was founded, by our system of government, and by our society's historical experience with western expansion—the "taming" of the Wild West (Kitayama, Ishii, Imada, Takemura, & Ramaswamy, 2006; Turner, 1932).

> Do as most do, and [people] will speak well of thee.
>
> —Thomas Fuller

American mythology has celebrated the rugged individualist in many ways. For example, one of the longest running and most successful advertising campaigns in American history features the "Marlboro Man." Since 1955, the photograph of a cowboy alone on the range has been an archetypal image. It has also sold a lot of cigarettes. People who have never seen a horse, let alone the American West, have responded for half a century to this simple, evocative image. Clearly, it tells us something about ourselves that we want and like to hear: that we make up our own minds; that we're not spineless, weak conformists; that we're not puppets, but players (Cialdini, 2005; Pronin, Berger, & Molouki, 2007).

But are we, in fact, nonconforming creatures? Are the decisions we make always based on what we think, or do we sometimes use other people's behavior to help us decide what to do? As we saw in Chapter 6, the mass suicide of the Heaven's Gate cult members suggests that people sometimes conform in extreme and surprising ways—even when making such a fundamental decision as whether or not to take their own lives. But, you might argue, this is an unusual and extreme case. Perhaps the followers of Marshall Applewhite were disturbed people who were somehow predisposed to do what a charismatic leader told them to do. There is, however, another, more chilling possibility: Maybe most of us would have acted the same way had we been exposed to the same long-standing, powerful conformity pressures as the members of Heaven's Gate. According to this view, almost anyone would have conformed in these same extreme circumstances.

> It were not best that we should all think alike; it is difference of opinion that makes horse races.
>
> —Mark Twain

If this statement is true, we should be able to find other situations in which people, put under strong social pressures, conform to a surprising degree. For example, in 1961, activists in the American civil rights movement incorporated Mohandas Gandhi's principles of nonviolent protest into their demonstrations to end segregation. They trained their "Freedom Riders" in the passive acceptance of violent treatment. Thousands of southern African Americans, joined by a smaller number of northern whites, many from

Under strong social pressure, individuals will conform to the group, even when this means doing something immoral. During the Vietnam War, American soldiers massacred several hundred Vietnamese civilians—old men, women, and children—in the village of My Lai. This award-winning photograph of some of the victims chilled the nation. Why did the soldiers commit this atrocity? As you read this chapter, you will see how the social influence pressures of conformity and obedience can cause decent people to commit indecent acts.

Conformity

A change in one's behavior due to the real or imagined influence of other people

college campuses, demonstrated against the segregationist laws of the South. In one confrontation after another, the civil rights activists reacted nonviolently as they were beaten, clubbed, hosed, whipped, raped, and even killed by southern sheriffs and police (Powledge, 1991). Their powerful show of conformity to the ideal of nonviolent protest helped usher in a new era in America's fight for equality—passage of the Civil Rights Act of 1964.

Now consider the case of the My Lai massacre in Vietnam. On the morning of March 16, 1968, at the height of the Vietnam War, a company of American soldiers boarded helicopters that would take them to the village of My Lai. The soldiers were very apprehensive because they had never been in combat before and the village was rumored to be occupied by the 48th Vietcong Battalion, one of the most feared units of the enemy. One of the helicopter pilots radioed that he saw Vietcong soldiers below, and so the American soldiers jumped off the helicopters, rifles blazing. They soon realized that the pilot was wrong—there were no enemy soldiers. Instead, the Americans found several villagers, all women, children, and elderly men, cooking breakfast over small fires. Inexplicably, the leader of the platoon, Lieutenant William Calley, ordered one of the soldiers to kill the villagers. Other soldiers began firing too, and the carnage spread. The Americans rounded up and systematically murdered all the villagers of My Lai. They shoved women and children into a ravine and shot them; they threw hand grenades into huts filled with cowering villagers. Though no one knows the exact number of deaths, the estimates range from 450 to 500 Vietnamese civilians (Hersh, 1970).

In all these examples, people found themselves caught in a web of social influence. In response, they changed their behavior and conformed to the expectations of others (O'Gorman, Wilson, & Miller, 2008). For social psychologists, this is the essence of **conformity**: changing one's behavior due to the real or imagined influence of others (Kiesler & Kiesler, 1969; Aarts & Dijksterhuis, 2003). As these examples show, the consequences of conformity can span a wide range, from usefulness and nobility to hysteria and tragedy. But why did these people conform? Some probably conformed because they did not know what to do in a confusing or unusual situation. The behavior of the people around them served as a cue as to how to respond, and they decided to act in a similar manner. Other people probably conformed because they did not wish to be ridiculed or punished for being different from everybody else. They chose to act the way the group expected them to act so that they wouldn't be rejected or thought less of by group members. Let's see how each of these reasons for conforming operates.

Informational Social Influence: The Need to Know What's "Right"
信息性社会影响：想知道"正确"情况的需要

How should you address your psychology professor—as "Dr. Berman," "Professor Berman," "Ms. Berman," or "Patricia"? How should you vote in the upcoming referendum that would raise your tuition to cover expanded student services? Do you cut a piece of sushi or eat it whole? Did the scream you just heard in the hallway come from a person joking with friends or from the victim of a mugging?

In these and many other situations, we feel uncertain about what to think or how to act. We simply don't know enough to make a good or accurate choice. Luckily, we have a powerful and useful source of knowledge available to us—the behavior of other people. Asking others what they think or watching what they do helps us reach a definition of the situation (Kelley, 1955; Thomas, 1928). When we subsequently act like everyone else, we are conforming, but not because we are weak, spineless individuals with no self-reliance. Instead, the influence of other people leads us to conform because we see them as a source of information to guide our behavior. We conform because we believe that others' interpretation of an ambiguous situation is more accurate than ours and will help us choose an appropriate course of action. This is called **informational social influence** (Cialdini, 2000; Cialdini & Goldstein, 2004; Deutsch & Gerard, 1955).

As an illustration of how other people can be a source of information, imagine that you are a participant in the following experiment by Muzafer Sherif (1936). In the first phase of the study, you are seated alone in a dark room and asked to focus your attention on a dot of light 15 feet away. The experimenter asks you to estimate in inches how far the light moves. You stare earnestly at the light, and yes, it moves a little. You say, "about 2 inches," though it is not easy to tell exactly. The light disappears and then comes back; you are asked to judge again. The light seems to move a little more, and you say, "4 inches." After several of these trials, the light seems to move about the same amount each time—about 2 to 4 inches.

The interesting thing about this task is that the light was not actually moving at all. It looked as if it was moving because of a visual illusion called the autokinetic effect. If you stare at a bright light in a uniformly dark environment (e.g., a star on a dark night), the light will appear to waver back and forth. This occurs because you have no stable reference point to anchor the position of the light. The distance that the light appears to move varies from person to person but becomes consistent for each person over time. In Sherif's experiment, the subjects all arrived at their own stable estimate during the first phase of the study, but these estimates differed from person to person. Some people thought the light was moving only an inch or so; others thought it was moving as much as 10 inches.

Sherif chose to use the autokinetic effect because he wanted a situation that would be ambiguous—where the correct definition of the situation would be unclear to his participants. In the second phase of the experiment, a few days later, the participants were paired with two other people, each of whom had had the same prior experience alone with the light. Now the situation became a truly social one, as all three made their judgments out loud. Remember, the autokinetic effect is experienced differently by different people; some see a lot of movement and some see not much at all. After hearing their partners give judgments that were different from their own, what did people do?

Over the course of several trials, people reached a common estimate, and each member of the group conformed to that estimate. These results indicate that people were using each other as a source of information, coming to believe that the group estimate was the correct one (see Figure 8.1). An important feature of informational social influence is that it can lead to **private acceptance**, when people conform to the behavior of others because they genuinely believe that these other people are right.

> It's always best on these occasions to do what the mob do." "But suppose there are two mobs?" suggested Mr. Snodgrass. "Shout with the largest," replied Mr. Pickwick.
>
> —Charles Dickens, *Pickwick Papers*

Informational Social Influence

The influence of other people that leads us to conform because we see them as a source of information to guide our behavior; we conform because we believe that others' interpretation of an ambiguous situation is more correct than ours and will help us choose an appropriate course of action

Private Acceptance

Conforming to other people's behavior out of a genuine belief that what they are doing or saying is right

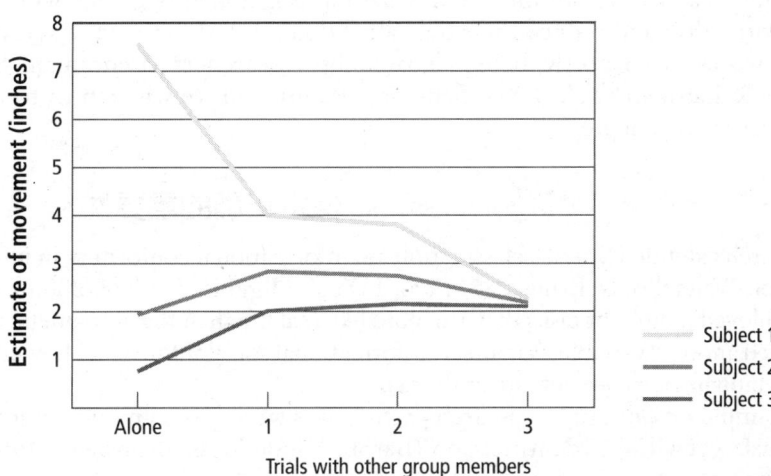

FIGURE 8.1

One group's judgments in Sherif's (1936) autokinetic studies.

People estimated how far a point of light appeared to move in a dark room. When they saw the light by themselves, their estimates varied widely. When they were brought together in groups and heard other people announce their estimates, people conformed to the group's estimate of how much the light moved.

(Adapted from Sherif, 1936)

It might seem equally plausible that people publicly conformed to the group but privately maintained the belief that the light was moving only a small amount. For example, maybe someone privately believed that the light was moving 10 inches but announced that it had moved 3 inches, the group estimate, to avoid looking silly or foolish. This would be a case of **public compliance**, conforming publicly without necessarily believing in what the group is saying or doing. Sherif cast doubt on this interpretation, however, by asking people to judge the lights once more by themselves, after participating in groups. Even though they no longer had to worry about looking silly in front of other participants, they continued to give the answer the group had given earlier. One study even found that people still conformed to the group estimate when they participated individually a year later (Rohrer, Baron, Hoffman, & Swander, 1954). These results suggest that people were relying on each other to define reality and came to privately accept the group estimate.

The power of informational conformity to produce private acceptance has been demonstrated in several areas of life, including energy conservation. For example, Jessica Nolan and her colleagues (2008) gave a sample of California residents information urging them to conserve electrical energy in their homes. The household members received one of four messages. Three of these presented basic reasons to conserve: to protect the environment; to benefit society; or to save money. The fourth message contained a message designed to promote informational conformity: The participants were told that the majority of their neighbors conserved electrical energy. The researchers then measured actual energy usage from the homes' electrical meters. They found that the normative message, containing information about the behavior of one's neighbors, caused people to conserve significantly more energy than did the other three messages (Nolan, Schultz, Cialdini, Goldstein, & Griskevicius, 2008). Similarly, Noah Goldstein, Robert Cialdini, and Vladas Griskevicius (2008) managed to increase hotel guests' compliance with the "reuse your bath towels and save energy" request, a widely used hotel management technique that hasn't proved very popular with guests. The researchers found that an informational sign in the bathroom, stating that the majority of guests in this room reuse their towels, was significantly more effective than the appeal usually used by hotels ("Help save the environment"; Goldstein et al., p. 473).

Finally, using informational conformity to produce private acceptance has been harnessed by administrators at hundreds of colleges and universities in the United States to combat binge drinking in the student body. Over the past few years, a new technique, the "social norms approach," has replaced prior "scare" tactics as a way to convince students to drink less alcohol. The social norms approach directly invokes informational conformity to reduce drinking. Researchers have found that the typical student believes that his or her classmates drink a lot more than they actually do. This method involves giving students accurate information about the (lower) drinking levels on their campus. By reducing ambiguity about drinking norms and giving students a new definition of the situation, it is hoped that they will conform to this information and reduce their own alcohol intake. Whether the social norms approach works is currently being debated by researchers (Lederman, Stewart, Goodhart, & Laitman et al., 2003; Schemo, 2003b), and we will return to this discussion later in the chapter.

The Importance of Being Accurate 保持正确的重要性

Later research extended Sherif's classic study on informational conformity in interesting ways (Baron, Vandello, & Brunsman, 1996; Levine, Higgins, & Choi, 2000). This research employed judgment tasks that are more like real life than the autokinetic effect. It also revealed another variable that affects informational social influence: How important it is to the individual to be accurate at the task.

For example, in one study, research participants were given an involving and ambiguous task: eyewitness identification (Baron, Vandello, & Brunsman, 1996). Just like eyewitnesses of a real crime, the participants were asked to pick "perpetrators"

Public Compliance
Conforming to other people's behavior publicly without necessarily believing in what the other people are doing or saying

out of lineups. For each of the 13 tasks, the participants were first shown a slide of a man—the "perpetrator." Next they saw a slide of a "lineup" composed of four men, one of whom was the perpetrator. In the lineup, the perpetrator was sometimes dressed differently than he had been in the prior slide. The participant's job was to pick out the perpetrator. The task was made very difficult (to the point of ambiguity) by presenting the slides extremely quickly. Participants saw each slide for only half a second.

The eyewitness task took place in a group, consisting of the participant and three confederates. Each of the four said their answers out loud after viewing each pair of slides. On the critical seven trials, where informational social influence would be measured, the three confederates answered before the participant, and all the confederates gave the same wrong answer.

How important it was to the research participants to be accurate at the task was manipulated in the following way. In the high-importance condition, they were told that the task they were about to do was a real test of eyewitness identification ability and would soon be used by police departments and courts to differentiate good eyewitnesses from poor ones. Participants' scores would establish the norm for performance. In addition, those who scored the highest in accuracy would receive $20 from the experimenters. In contrast, in the low-importance condition, the research participants were told that the study was a first attempt to study eyewitness identification and that the slide task was still being developed. The experimenters were interested in getting "useful hints" about how to present the slides to others, and they had no idea what the norm for performance was on the task. Thus as the participants began the task, they were in two very different states of mind. Half thought their performance was very important and would have ramifications for the legal community. They were motivated to do well (and winning $20 would be nice). The other half had few illusions; this was just a regular research study like any other. Their performance didn't seem important to the experimenters.

We can see that the high-importance condition mirrors the concerns of everyday life—your judgments and decisions have consequences, and you're motivated to "get things right." Will that make you more or less susceptible to informational social influence? The researchers found that it makes you *more* susceptible. In the low-importance condition, participants conformed to the confederates' judgments and gave the same wrong answers on 35 percent of the critical trials. In the high-importance condition, participants conformed to the confederates' judgments on 51 percent of the critical trials.

As we've noted, when a situation is ambiguous and choosing the right answer is difficult, we look to others to give us the additional information we need. Baron and his colleagues found that in such situations, the more important the decision is to us, the more we will rely on other people for information and guidance.

Thus, when you aren't sure what to think or do and it is important that you figure out an answer, you are more likely to engage in informational conformity. In an ambiguous situation, this is a good strategy, but it does come with risks: What if the other people are wrong?

Eight thousand pumpkins meet the Eiffel Tower. Halloween is a popular holiday in the United States; in recent years, retailers have increased the "hype" surrounding the holiday because it increases sales of their merchandise during a traditionally slow sales period—October. While the holiday is based on ancient British and Irish traditions surrounding "all Hallows' Eve," Halloween as we know it is a completely American phenomenon. Until October 1997, that is, when "Ah-lo-ween" was introduced to the French public by French retailers. Why? The French economy was in bad shape and retailers needed to come up with an idea that would get people to buy merchandise (Cohen, 1997). Informational social influence led them to borrow the Halloween concept from America, and informational social influence is how the French are literally learning what this holiday is about. As of Halloween 1997, they had no idea of what "treek au treeting" was. For example, one Parisian exclaimed, "I must tell you all this is absolutely bizarre. I suddenly started seeing pumpkins everywhere in my local Monoprix supermarket and I had no idea what was going on" (Cohen, 1997, p. A1). However, by Halloween 2000, informational social influence had done its work. French shops were decorated in black and orange, carved pumpkins were displayed, and nightclubs held costume competitions. By 2002, Halloween had become so popular in France that Christian religious leaders launched a campaign against it, hoping to refocus French attention to All Saints' Day, a religious holiday that occurs a day later (Associated Press, 2002).

The New York Times headlined the War of the Worlds incident. Partly because of informational social influences, many listeners believed that Orson Welles's radio broadcast about an invasion by Martians was true.

When Informational Conformity Backfires
当信息性社会影响导致相反的效果时

A dramatic form of informational social influence occurs during crises, when an individual is confronted with a frightening, potentially dangerous situation to which he or she is ill-equipped to respond (Killian, 1964). The person may have no idea of what is really happening or what he or she should do. When one's personal safety is involved, the need for information is acute—and the behavior of others is very informative.

Consider what happened on Halloween Night in 1938. Orson Welles, the gifted actor and film director, and the Mercury Theater broadcast a radio play based loosely on H. G. Wells's science fiction fantasy *War of the Worlds*. Remember, this was the era before television; radio was a primary source of entertainment, with music, comedy, and drama programs, and the only source for fast-breaking news. That night, the drama that Welles and his fellow actors broadcast—portraying the invasion of Earth by hostile Martians—was so realistic that at least a million listeners became frightened and alerted the police; several thousand were so panic-stricken that they tried to flee the "invasion" in their cars (Cantril, 1940).

Why were so many Americans convinced that what they heard was a real news report of an actual invasion by aliens? Hadley Cantril (1940), who studied this real-life "crisis," suggested two reasons. One was that the play parodied existing radio news shows very well, and many listeners missed the beginning of the broadcast (when it was clearly identified as a play) because they had been listening to the nation's top-rated show, *Charlie McCarthy*, on another station. The other culprit, however, was informational social influence. Many people were listening with friends and family and naturally turned to each other, out of uncertainty, to see whether they should believe what they heard. Seeing looks of concern and worry on their loved ones' faces added to the panic people were beginning to feel. "We all kissed one another and felt we would all die," reported one listener (Cantril, 1940, p. 95).

> *Ninety-nine percent of the people in the world are fools, and the rest of us are in great danger of contagion.*
>
> —Thornton Wilder, *The Matchmaker*

In addition, many frightened listeners misinterpreted actual events so that they fit the news on the radio program: "We looked out the window and Wyoming Avenue was black with cars. People were rushing away, I figured," or "No cars came down my street. Traffic is jammed on account of the roads being destroyed, I thought" (Cantril, 1940, p. 93). When a situation is highly ambiguous and people begin to believe they know what is happening, they will even reinterpret potentially disconfirming evidence so that it fits their definition of the situation.

A late-nineteenth-century social scientist, Gustav Le Bon (1895), was the first researcher to document how emotions and behavior can spread rapidly through a crowd—an effect he called **contagion** (Fowler & Christakis, 2008; Hatfield, Cacioppo, & Rapson, 1993; Levy & Nail, 1993). As we have learned, in a truly ambiguous situation, people will most likely rely on the interpretation of others. Unfortunately, in a truly ambiguous and confusing situation, other people may be no more knowledgeable or accurate than we are. If other people are misinformed, we will adopt their mistakes and misinterpretations. Depending on others to help us define the situation can therefore sometimes lead us into serious inaccuracies.

An example of extreme and misdirected informational social influence is **mass psychogenic illness** (Bartholomew & Wessely, 2002; Colligan, Pennebaker, & Murphy, 1982), the occurrence of similar physical symptoms, with no known physical cause, in a group of people. For example, in 1998, a teacher at a high school in Tennessee reported the smell of gasoline in her classroom; soon she experienced headache, nausea, shortness of breath, and dizziness. As her class was being evacuated, others in the

Contagion
The rapid spread of emotions or behaviors through a crowd

Mass Psychogenic Illness
The occurrence, in a group of people, of similar physical symptoms with no known physical cause

school reported similar symptoms. The decision was made to evacuate the entire school. Everyone watched as the teacher and some students were placed in ambulances. Local experts investigated and could find nothing wrong with the school. Classes resumed—and more people reported feeling sick. Again, the school was evacuated and closed. Experts from numerous government agencies were called in to conduct an environmental and epidemiological investigation. Again, nothing was found to be wrong with the school. When it reopened this time, the epidemic of mysterious illness was over (Altman, 2000).

> *Yes, we must, indeed, all hang together or, most assuredly, we shall all hang separately.*
>
> —Benjamin Franklin at the signing of the Declaration of Independence, 1776

Timothy Jones of the Tennessee Department of Health led a study of this unusual case. In all, more than 170 students, teachers, and staff had gone to the hospital with symptoms for which no organic cause was ever found. Jones and his colleagues (2000) determined that mass psychogenic illness was the cause. This form of contagion usually begins with just one person or a few people reporting physical symptoms; typically, these people are experiencing some kind of stress in their lives. Other people around them construct what seems to be a reasonable explanation for their illness. This explanation, a new definition of the situation, spreads, and more people begin to think that they, too, have symptoms. As the number of afflicted people grows, both the physical symptoms and their supposed explanation become more credible and thus more widespread (Colligan et al., 1982; Kerckhoff & Back, 1968; Singer, Baum, Baum, & Thew, 1982). In the Tennessee high school case, the students who became sick were more likely than students who did not get sick to report having directly observed an ill person during the outbreak or to have known a classmate who was ill. Clearly, the "information" that defined vague symptoms (or even no symptoms) as a frightening, building-caused illness had spread through direct contact. In addition, dramatic and extensive media coverage of the event increased people's anxiety and spread more "information" about what was supposedly happening.

What is particularly interesting about mass psychogenic illness (as well as other peculiar forms of conformity) is the powerful role that the mass media play in its dissemination. Through television, radio, newspapers, magazines, the Internet, and e-mail, information is spread quickly and efficiently to all segments of the population. Whereas in the Middle Ages it took 200 years for the "dancing manias" (a kind of psychogenic illness) to crisscross Europe (Sirois, 1982), today it takes only minutes for most of the inhabitants of the planet to learn about an unusual event. Luckily, the mass media also have the power to quickly squelch these uprisings of contagion by introducing more logical explanations for ambiguous events.

When Will People Conform to Informational Social Influence?
何时人们会顺从信息性社会影响？

Let's review the situations that are the most likely to produce conformity because of informational social influence.

When the Situation Is Ambiguous Ambiguity is the most crucial variable for determining how much people use each other as a source of information. When you are unsure of the correct response, the appropriate behavior, or the right idea, you will be most open to influence from others. The more uncertain you are, the more you will rely on others (Allen, 1965; Renfrow & Gosling, 2006; Tesser, Campbell, & Mickler, 1983; Walther et al., 2002). Situations such as My Lai were ambiguous ones for the people involved, ideal circumstances for informational social influence to take hold. The soldiers were young (typically 18 or 19) and very inexperienced. For most of them, this was their first combat situation. When they saw a few other soldiers begin shooting at the villagers, most of them thought this is what they were supposed to do too, and they joined in.

The *Southern Standard* headlined a frightening and mysterious event at a local Tennessee high school. In fact, an investigation proved that the "poisonings" were a case of mass psychogenic illness.

When the Situation Is a Crisis Crisis, another variable that promotes the use of others as a source of information, often occurs simultaneously with ambiguity. In a crisis situation, we usually do not have time to stop and think about exactly which course of action we should take. We need to act—immediately. If we feel scared and panicky and are uncertain what to do, it is only natural for us to see how other people are responding and to do likewise. Unfortunately, the people we imitate may also feel scared and panicky and not be behaving rationally.

The soldiers at My Lai, for example, expected to experience combat with the Vietcong when they arrived at the village of My Lai. They were undoubtedly scared and on edge. Further, it was not easy to tell who the enemy was. In the Vietnam War, Vietnamese civilians who were sympathizers of the Vietcong were known to have laid mines in the path of U.S. soldiers, fired guns from hidden locations, and thrown or planted grenades. In a guerrilla war like Vietnam, it was often difficult to tell if people were civilians or combatants, allies, or enemies. So when one or two soldiers began firing on the villagers in My Lai, it is perhaps not surprising that others followed suit, believing this to be the proper course of action. Had the soldiers not been in a crisis situation and instead had more time to think about their actions, perhaps the tragedy would have been avoided.

When Other People Are Experts Typically, the more expertise or knowledge a person has, the more valuable he or she will be as a guide in an ambiguous situation (Allison, 1992; Cialdini & Trost, 1998). For example, a passenger who sees smoke coming out of an airplane engine will probably check the flight attendants' reaction rather than their seatmates'; however, experts are not always reliable sources of information. Imagine the fear felt by the young man listening to the *War of the Worlds* broadcast who called his local police department for an explanation, only to learn that the police, too, thought the events described on the radio were actually happening (Cantril, 1940)! (In the Try It! exercise you can explore how the informational social influence variables of ambiguity, crisis, and expertise have operated in your life and your friends' lives.)

试一试！信息性社会影响与突发事件
Informational Social Influence and Emergencies

One of the most interesting examples of informational social influence in action is the behavior of bystanders in emergencies. An emergency is by definition a crisis situation. In many respects, it is an ambiguous situation as well; sometimes there are "experts" present, but sometimes there aren't. In an emergency, the bystander is thinking: What's happening? Is help needed? What should I do? What's everybody else doing?

As you'll recall from the story told by Robin Akert on page 000, trying to decide if an emergency is really happening and if your help is really needed can be very difficult. Bystanders often rely on informational social influence to help them figure out what to do, but as we saw in the story in the book's Preface, if other people are acting as if nothing is wrong, you could be misled by their behavior and interpret the situation as a nonemergency too. In that case, informational social influence has backfired.

To explore informational social influence, gather some stories about people's reactions to emergencies when they were bystanders (not victims). Think about your own experiences, and ask your friends to tell you about emergencies they have been in. As you recollect your own experience or talk to your friends about their experiences, note how informational social influence played a role:

1. How did you (and your friends) decide that an emergency was really occurring? Did you glance at other passersby and watch their response? Did you talk to other people to help you figure out what was going on?

2. After you decided that it was an emergency, how did you decide what to do? Did you do what other people were doing? Did you show or tell them what to do?

3. Were there any experts present, people who knew more about the situation or how to offer assistance? Did you do what the experts told you to do? If you were in the role of expert (or were at least knowledgeable) at the scene of the emergency, did people follow your lead?

The issues raised by these questions are all examples of informational social influence in action.

Normative Social Influence: The Need to Be Accepted
规范性社会影响：希望被接受的需要

In the 1990s in Rio de Janeiro, Brazil, teenage boys and girls engaged in a dangerous and reckless game: "surfing" on the tops of trains, standing with arms outstretched as the trains sped along. Despite the fact that an average of 150 teenagers died each year from this activity and 400 more were injured by falling off the trains or hitting the 3,000-volt electric cable, the surfing continued (Arnett, 1995). More recently, in the United States and Australia, teenagers surfing on speeding cars has become a growing problem. Severe injuries and deaths from car surfing have been reported in Massachusetts, Ohio, Arizona, Wisconsin, and New South Wales, Australia (Daniel & Nelson, 2004).

The desire to be accepted and liked by others can lead to dangerous behavior. Here, Brazilian teenagers "surf" on top of trains because it has become the popular thing to do in their peer group.

Why do some adolescents engage in such risky behavior? Why does anyone follow the group's lead when the resulting behavior is less than sensible and may even be dangerous? We doubt that the Brazilian, American, or Australian teenagers risked their lives due to informational conformity. It is difficult to argue that a boy or girl staring at a train would say, "Gee, I don't know what to do. I guess standing on top of a train going 60 miles an hour makes a lot of sense; everybody else is doing it." This example tells us that something else explains why we conform besides the need for information: We also conform so that we will be liked and accepted by other people (Maxwell, 2002). We conform to the group's **social norms**, which are implicit (and sometimes explicit) rules for acceptable behaviors, values, and beliefs (Deutsch & Gerard, 1955; Kelley, 1955; Miller & Prentice, 1996). Groups have certain expectations about how the group members should behave, and members in good standing conform to these rules. Members who do not are perceived as different, difficult, and eventually deviant.

Deviant members can be ridiculed, punished, or even rejected by other group members (James & Olson, 2000; Kruglanski & Webster, 1991; Levine, 1989; Miller & Anderson, 1979). In Japan, a whole class (even the entire school) will sometimes turn against one student perceived as different. The students will alternate between harassing and shunning the individual. In a highly cohesive, group-oriented culture like Japan, this kind of treatment has had profound and tragic results: Twelve teenage victims of bullying killed themselves in one year (Jordan, 1996). Another social phenomenon in Japan is the *hikikomori*, teenagers (mostly male) who have withdrawn from all social interaction. They spend all their time alone, in their bedrooms in their parents' homes. Some *hikikomori* have remained sequestered for over a decade. Japanese psychologists state that many *hikikomori* were the victims of severe bullying before their withdrawal (Jones, 2006). Recently, researchers in the United States and Great Britain have begun to study "cyberbullying" in middle and secondary schools. This form of bullying, using cell phones and the Internet, is increasingly frequent, affecting as many as 11 percent of middle-school children (Kowalski & Limber, 2007; Smith et al., 2008).

We human beings are by nature a social species. Few of us could live happily as hermits, never seeing or talking to another person. Through interactions with others, we receive emotional support, affection, and love, and we partake of enjoyable experiences. Other people are extraordinarily important to our sense of well-being. Research on individuals who have been isolated for long periods of time indicates that being deprived of human contact is stressful and traumatic (Baumeister & Leary, 1995; Schachter, 1959; Williams, 2001).

Given this fundamental human need for social companionship, it is not surprising that we often conform to be accepted by others. Conformity for normative reasons occurs in situations where we do what other people are doing not because we are using them as a source of information but because we won't attract attention, be made fun

Social Norms
The implicit or explicit rules a group has for the acceptable behaviors, values, and beliefs of its members

of, get into trouble, or be rejected. Thus **normative social influence** occurs when the influence of other people leads us to conform to be liked and accepted by them. This type of conformity results in public compliance with the group's beliefs and behaviors, but not necessarily in private acceptance (Cialdini, Kallgren, & Reno, 1991; Deutsch & Gerard, 1955; Levine, 1999; Nail, McDonald, & Levy, 2000).

You probably don't find it too surprising that people sometimes conform to be liked and accepted by others. You might be thinking, where's the harm? If the group is important to us and wearing the right clothes or using hip words will gain us acceptance, why not go along? But when it comes to more important kinds of behaviors, such as hurting another person, surely we will resist such conformity pressures. And surely we won't conform when we are certain of what the correct way of behaving is and the pressures are coming from a group that we don't care all that much about. Or will we?

Conformity and Social Approval: The Asch Line Judgment Studies
从众与社会认同：阿希线段判断研究

To find out, Solomon Asch (1951, 1956) conducted a series of now classic studies exploring the power of normative social influence. Asch devised the studies assuming that there are limits to how much people will conform. Naturally, people conformed in the Sherif studies (see page 215), he reasoned, because the situation was highly ambiguous—trying to guess how much a light was moving. But when a situation was completely unambiguous, Asch expected that people would act like rational, objective problem solvers. When the group said or did something that contradicted an obvious truth, surely people would resist social pressures and decide for themselves what was going on.

To test his hypothesis, Asch conducted the following study. Had you been a participant, you would have been told that this was an experiment on perceptual judgment and that you would be taking part with seven other students. Here's the scenario: The experimenter shows everyone two cards, one with a single line on it, the other with three lines labeled 1, 2, and 3. He asks each of you to judge and then announce out loud which of the three lines on the second card is closest in length to the line on the first card (see Figure 8.2).

It is crystal clear that the correct answer is the second line. Not surprisingly, each participant says, "Line 2." Your turn comes next to last, and of course you say, "Line 2" as well. The last participant concurs. The experimenter then presents a new set of cards and asks the participants again to make their judgments and announce them out loud. Again, the answer is obvious, and everyone gives the correct answer. At this point, you are probably thinking to yourself, "What a waste of time. I've got a paper due tomorrow. I need to get out of here."

Normative Social Influence
The influence of other people that leads us to conform in order to be liked and accepted by them; this type of conformity results in public compliance with the group's beliefs and behaviors but not necessarily private acceptance of those beliefs and behaviors

FIGURE 8.2

The judgment task in Asch's line studies.

In a study of normative social influence, participants judged which of the three comparison lines on the right was closest in length to the standard line on the left. The correct answer was obvious (as it is here). However, members of the group (actually confederates) gave the wrong answer out loud. Now the participant was in a dilemma: Should he give the right answer and go against the whole group, or should he conform to their behavior and give the obviously wrong answer?

(Adapted from Asch, 1956)

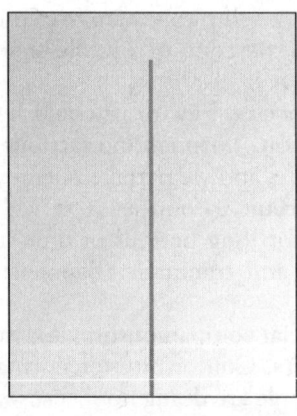
Standard line

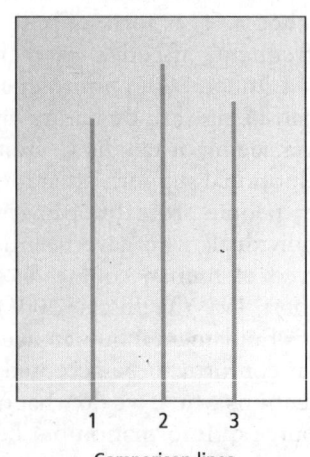
Comparison lines

Participants in an Asch line study. The real participant is seated in the middle. He is surrounded by the experimenter's accomplices, who have just given the wrong answer on the line task.

As your mind starts to wander, something surprising happens. The experimenter presents a third set of lines, and again the answer is obvious—line 3 is clearly the closest in length to the target line. But the first participant announces that the correct answer is line 1! "This guy must be so bored that he fell asleep," you think. Then the second person announces that line 1 is the correct answer. The third, fourth, fifth, and sixth participants agree; then it's your turn to judge. By now startled, you are probably looking at the lines very closely to see if you missed something. But no, line 3 is clearly the right answer. What will you do? Will you bravely blurt out, "Line 3," or will you go along with the group and give the obviously wrong answer, "Line 1"?

As you can see, Asch set up a situation to discover if people would conform even when the right answer was absolutely obvious. In each group, all the participants but one had been told earlier to give the wrong answer on 12 of the 18 trials. What happened? Contrary to what Asch expected, a considerable amount of conformity occurred: Seventy-six percent of the participants conformed on at least one trial. On average, people conformed on about a third of the 12 trials on which the accomplices gave the incorrect answer (see Figure 8.3).

Why did people conform so much of the time? Participants couldn't have needed information from others to help them decide, as in the Sherif study, because the situation was not ambiguous. The right answers were so obvious that when people in a control group made the judgments by themselves, they were accurate more than 98 percent of the time. Instead, normative pressures came into play. Even though the other participants were strangers, the fear of being the lone dissenter was so strong that people conformed, at least occasionally. One participant explained: "Here was a group; they had a definite idea; my idea disagreed; this might arouse anger . . . I was standing out [like] a sore thumb . . . I didn't want particularly to make a fool of myself . . . I felt I was definitely right . . . [but] they might think I was peculiar" (Asch, 1956, Whole No. 416).

These are classic normative reasons for conforming: People know that what they are doing is wrong but go along anyway so as not to feel peculiar or look like a fool. These reasons illustrate an important fact about normative pressures: In contrast to informational social influence, normative pressures usually result in *public compliance without private acceptance*—people go along with the group even if they do not believe in what they are doing or think it is wrong.

What is especially surprising about Asch's results is that people were concerned about looking foolish in front of complete strangers. It is not as if the participants were in danger of being ostracized by a group that was important to them. Nor was there any risk of open punishment or disapproval for failing to conform or of losing the esteem of people they really cared about, such as friends and family members. Yet decades of research indicate that conformity for normative reasons can occur simply because we do not want to risk social disapproval,

It isn't difficult to keep alive, friends—just don't make trouble—or if you must make trouble, make the sort of trouble that's expected.

—Robert Bolt, *A Man for All Seasons*

FIGURE 8.3

Results of the Asch line judgment study.

Participants in the Asch line study showed a surprisingly high level of conformity, given how obvious it was that the group was wrong in its judgments. Seventy-six percent of the participants conformed on at least one trial; only 24 percent of participants never conformed at all (see bar labeled zero). Most participants conformed on one to three of the 12 trials in which the group gave the wrong answer. However, a sizable number of participants conformed to the group's response nearly every time it gave the wrong answer (see the two bars on the right).

(Adapted from Asch, 1957)

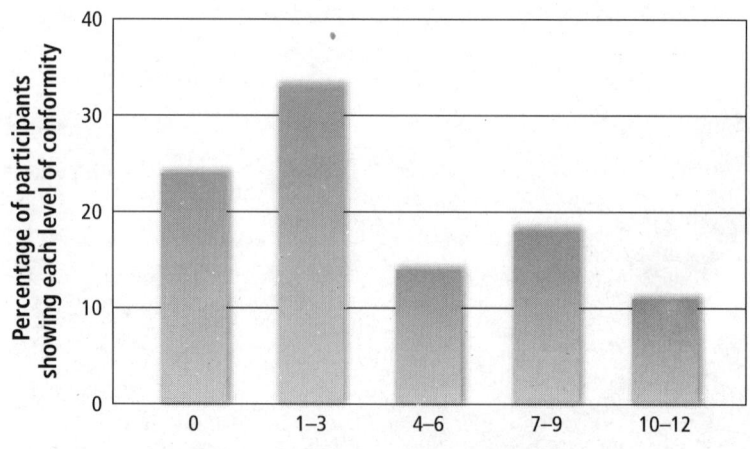

even from complete strangers we will never see again (Crutchfield, 1955; Tanford & Penrod, 1984).

In a variation of his study, Asch (1957) demonstrated the power of social disapproval in shaping a person's behavior. The confederates gave the wrong answer 12 out of 18 times, as before, but this time the participants wrote their answers on a piece of paper instead of saying them out loud. Now people did not have to worry about what the group thought of them because the group would never find out what their answers were. Conformity dropped dramatically, occurring on an average of only 1.5 of the 12 trials (Insko, Smith, Alicke, Wade, & Taylor, 1985; Nail, 1986). As Serge Moscovici (1985) observed, the Asch studies are "one of the most dramatic illustrations of conformity, of blindly going along with the group, even when the individual realizes that by doing so he turns his back on reality and truth" (p. 349).

Research by Gregory Berns and his colleagues has provided biological evidence for just how unpleasant and uncomfortable it is to resist normative social influence (Berns et al., 2005). Berns and his research team used functional magnetic resonance imaging (fMRI) to examine the alterations in brain activity of research participants as they either normatively conformed to a group's judgment or maintained their independence and disagreed with the group.

Instead of judging the lengths of lines, the task in this study involved mental rotation. While in the fMRI scanner, participants were shown an image of the three-dimensional figure, and asked if a second figure (rotated in a different direction) was the same as the first figure or different. They indicated their answers by pushing a button. The task was slightly more difficult than Asch's line judgment task; the baseline error rate, when participants made judgments alone, was 13.8 percent, compared to Asch's (1951, 1956) baseline error rate of 2 percent.

Before being placed in the fMRI, participants met and interacted with the four other participants, who were actually confederates. These four would be doing the same mental rotation task, but only the participant would have his or her brain activity monitored in the fMRI. During the task, the participant completed one-third of the trials with no knowledge of the answers of the other four people. On the remaining two-thirds of the trials, the participant saw the four group members' answers on a visual display. Half the time, the group had all chosen the wrong answer, and the other half of the time, they had all chosen the right answer.

Now, what did the participants do, and most importantly, what areas of their brains were activated when they did it? First, participants did conform to the group's wrong answers some of the time, on average, for 41 percent of the trials. [This level of normative conformity is similar to that found in the Asch (1951, 1956) studies.] On the baseline trials, where the participants answered alone, the fMRI indicated brain activity in the posterior brain areas dedicated to vision and perception. When the participants conformed to the group's wrong answers, activation occurred in the same areas; however, when participants chose to give the right answer and thus disagree with the group and their unanimous wrong answer, the visual/perceptual areas of the brain were not activated. Instead, different areas of the brain became active: The amygdala, an area devoted to negative emotions, and the right caudate nucleus, an area devoted to modulating social behavior (Berns et al., 2005). Thus, this brain-imaging research supports the idea that normative social influence occurs because people feel negative emotions, such as discomfort and tension, when they stand up for their beliefs and go against the group (Spitzer, Fischbacher, Herrnberger, Gron, & Fehr, 2007).

Customs do not concern themselves with right or wrong or reason. But they have to be obeyed; one reasons all around them until [one] is tired, but [one] must not transgress them, it is sternly forbidden.

—Mark Twain

The Importance of Being Accurate, Revisited
回顾：保持正确的重要性

Now, you may be thinking, "OK, so we conform to normative social influence, but hey, only when it's something little. Who cares whether you give the right answer on the line judgment task? It doesn't matter, nothing is at stake, and so it's easier to go along with the group. I wouldn't conform to the group's wrong answer if something important was involved!" And this would be a very good criticism. Recall our discussion of importance in connection with informational social influence; we found that the more important the decision or choice a person has to make is, the more the person conforms for informational reasons in ambiguous situations. What about in nonambiguous situations? Maybe the more important the decision or choice is, the less the person would conform for normative reasons. When it's important to you to be right, are you strong enough to withstand group pressure and disagree with the group?

In the study of eyewitness identification of perpetrators that we discussed earlier, Baron and his colleagues (Baron, Vandello, & Brunsman, 1996) included experimental conditions that triggered normative social influence. Recall that their research participants viewed pairs of slides, one of the perpetrator alone and one of the perpetrator in a lineup. Participants watched the slides in groups with two confederates. When studying informational conformity, the researchers made the task fiendishly difficult and therefore ambiguous—the slides were projected for only half a second. In order to study normative social influence, the researchers made the same task ridiculously easy: The participants viewed each slide for a full 5 seconds, and to make it even easier, they were shown each pair of slides twice. Now the task is analogous to Asch's line-judging task; basically, if you're awake, you'll get the right answer. Baron and colleagues proved that the task was easy by having a control group view the slides alone. The controls answered correctly on 97 percent of the trials, very close to Asch's control group's performance of 98 percent on the line-judging task.

Baron and colleagues again manipulated the importance of the participants' being accurate, in ways we discussed earlier. Half thought it was very important that they give the right answers, and half thought it really didn't matter to the experimenters how they did. Now how will participants respond when the confederates give the obviously wrong answer? Will they, as the participants in the Asch study did, conform to the group on at least some of the trials? Or will the participants who are motivated to do well stand up to the group, ignore their wrong answers and the normative pressure to agree with them, and give the right answers every time?

The researchers found that participants in the low-importance condition conformed to the group on 33 percent of the critical trials. (These findings are very close to Asch's on the line-judgment task.) What happens when it is important to the participants to be accurate? They conform less to the obviously wrong answers of the group; on only 16 percent of the critical trials did they echo the group's blatantly wrong answer. Note, however, that they still conformed sometimes! Instead of standing up to the group, they caved in on at least some trials. These findings underscore the power of normative social influence: Even when the group is wrong, the right answer is obvious, and there are strong incentives to be accurate, some people will find it difficult to risk social disapproval, even from strangers (Baron et al., 1996; Hornsey, Majkut, Terry, & McKimmie, 2003).

Normative social influence most closely reflects the negative stereotype of conformity we referred to earlier. At times, conforming for normative reasons can be spineless and weak; it can have negative consequences. Even in a dangerous situation, like that faced by the Brazilian teenagers who surf on top of trains, you might go ahead and conform because normative social pressures can be difficult to resist. The desire to be accepted is part of human nature, but it can have tragic consequences.

The Consequences of Resisting Normative Social Influence
拒绝规范性社会影响的后果

One way to observe the power of normative social pressure is to see what happens when people manage to resist it. If a person refuses to do as the group asks and thereby violates its norms, what happens? Think about the norms that operate in your group of friends. Some friends have an egalitarian norm for making group decisions. For example, when choosing a movie, everyone gets to state a preference; the choice is then discussed until agreement is reached on one movie. What would happen if, in a group with this kind of norm, you stated at the outset that you only wanted to see *Rebel Without a Cause*? Your friends would be surprised by your behavior; they would also be annoyed with you or even angry. If you continued to disregard the friendship norms of the group by failing to conform to them, two things would most likely happen. First, the group would try to bring you "back into the fold," chiefly through increased communication with you. Teasing comments and long discussions would ensue as your friends tried to figure out why you were acting so strangely and would try to get you to conform to their expectations (Garfinkle, 1967). If these discussions didn't work, your friends would most likely say negative things to you and about you and start to withdraw from you (Festinger & Thibaut, 1951). Now, in effect, you've been rejected (Abrams, Marques, Bown, & Henson, 2000; Hornsey, Jetten, McAuliffe, & Hogg, 2006; Levine, 1989; Marques, Abrams, Paez, & Hogg, 2001; Milgram & Sabini, 1978).

Success or failure lies in conformity to the times.

—Niccolò Machiavelli, *The Prince*

Stanley Schachter (1951) demonstrated how the group responds to an individual who ignores the group's normative influence. He asked groups of college students to read and discuss a case history of "Johnny Rocco," a juvenile delinquent. Most of the students took a middle-of-the-road position about the case, believing that Rocco should receive a judicious mixture of love and discipline. Unbeknown to the participants, however, Schachter had planted an accomplice in the group who was instructed to disagree with the group's recommendations. He consistently argued that Rocco should receive the harshest amount of punishment, regardless of what the other group members argued.

How was the deviant treated? He received the most comments and questions from the real participants throughout the discussion until near the end, when communication with him dropped sharply. The other group members had tried to convince the deviant to agree with them; when it appeared that that wouldn't work, they ignored him. In addition, they punished the deviant. After the discussion, they were asked to fill out questionnaires that supposedly pertained to future discussion meetings of their group. The participants were asked to nominate one group member who should be eliminated from further discussions if the size had to be reduced. They nominated the deviant. They were also asked to assign group members to various tasks in future discussions. They assigned the unimportant or boring jobs, such as taking notes, to the deviant. Social groups are well versed in how to bring a nonconformist into line. No wonder we respond as often as we do to normative pressures! You can find out what it's like to resist normative social influence in the following Try It! exercise.

试一试！违规：揭开规范性社会影响的面纱
Unveiling Normative Social Influence by Breaking the Rules

Every day, you talk to a lot of people—friends, professors, co-workers, and strangers. When you have a conversation (whether long or short), you follow certain interaction "rules" that operate in American culture. These rules for conversation include nonverbal forms of behavior that Americans consider "normal" as well as "polite." You can find out how powerful these norms are by breaking them and noting how people respond to you; their response is normative social influence in action.

For example, in conversation, we stand a certain distance from each other—not too far and not too close. About 2 to 3 feet is typical in this culture. In addition, we maintain a good amount of eye contact when we are listening to the other person; in comparison, when we're talking, we look away from the person more often.

What happens if you break these normative rules? For example, have a conversation with a friend and stand either too close or too far away (e.g., 1 foot or 7 feet). Have a typical, normal conversation with your friend; only the spacing from what you normally use with this person should be different. Note how your friend responds. If you're too close, your friend will probably back away; if you continue to keep the distance small, he or she may act uncomfortable and even terminate your conversation sooner than usual. If you're too far away, your friend will probably come closer; if you back up, he or she may think you are in a strange mood. In either case, your friend's response will probably include looking at you a lot, having a puzzled look on his or her face, acting uncomfortable or confused, and talking less than normal or ending the conversation.

You have acted in a nonnormative way, and your conversational partner is, first, trying to figure out what is going on and, second, responding in a way to get you to stop acting oddly. From this one brief exercise, you will get the idea of what would happen if you behaved oddly all the time—people would try to get you to change, and then they would probably start avoiding or ignoring you.

When you're finished, please "debrief" your friend, explaining the exercise, so that your behavior is understood.

Normative Social Influence in Everyday Life
日常生活中的规范性社会影响

Normative social influence operates on many levels in our daily lives. For example, although few of us are slaves to fashion, we tend to wear what is considered appropriate and stylish at a given time. The wide ties popular in the 1970s gave way to narrow ties in the 1980s; hemlines dropped from mini to maxi and rose again in the 1990s. Normative social influence is at work whenever you notice a look shared by people in a certain group, and no matter what it is, it will look outdated just a few years later until the fashion industry declares it stylish again.

Fads are another fairly frivolous example of normative social influence. Certain activities or objects can suddenly become popular and sweep the country. For example, in the late 1950s, every child had to have a Hula-Hoop or risk social ostracism. College students swallowed live goldfish in the 1930s, crammed as many people as possible into telephone booths in the 1950s, and "streaked" (ran naked) at official gatherings in the 1970s. These fads seem silly now, but ask yourself, could there be "fads" that you are following now?

Social Influence and Women's Body Image A more sinister form of normative social influence involves women's attempts to conform to cultural definitions of an attractive body. Although many, if not most, world societies consider plumpness in females attractive, Western culture and particularly American culture currently value extreme thinness in the female form (Grossbard, Lee, Neighbors, & Larimer, 2009; Jackson, 1992; Weeden & Sabini, 2005).

In 1969, hippie fashions in clothing and hairstyles were all the rage.

FIGURE 8.4

What is the "ideal" female body across cultures?

Researchers divided 54 cultures into groups, depending on the reliability of their food supply. They then determined what was considered the "ideal" female body in each culture. Heavy female bodies were considered the most beautiful in cultures with unreliable or somewhat unreliable food supplies. As the reliability of the food supply increases, the preference for a moderate to heavy body type decreased. Only in cultures where food was very readily available was the slender body valued.

(Adapted from Anderson, Crawford, Nadeau, & Lindberg, 1992)

Ideal body type in the culture (preference indicated in percentages)	Reliability of the food supply in the culture			
	Very unreliable (7 cultures)	Moderately unreliable (6 cultures)	Moderately reliable (36 cultures)	Very reliable (5 cultures)
Heavy body	71%	50%	39%	40%
	100%	83%	78%	60%
Moderate body	29%	33%	39%	20%
Slender body	0%	17%	22%	40%

> *No woman can be too slim or too rich.*
> —Wallis Simpson, Duchess of Windsor

Why should preference for female body type vary by culture? To explore this question, Judith Anderson and her colleagues (Anderson, Crawford, Nadeau, & Lindberg, 1992) analyzed what people in 54 cultures considered the ideal female body: a heavy body, a body of moderate weight, or a slender body. The researchers also analyzed how reliable the food supply was in each culture. They hypothesized that in societies where food was frequently scarce, a heavy body would be considered the most beautiful: These would be women who had enough to eat and therefore were healthy and fertile. As you can see in Figure 8.4, their hypothesis was supported. Heavy women were preferred over slender or moderate ones in cultures with unreliable or somewhat unreliable food supplies. As the reliability of the food supply increases, the preference for heavy-to-moderate bodies decreases. Most dramatic is the increase in preference for the slender body across cultures. Only in cultures with very reliable food supplies (like the United States) was the slender body type highly valued.

What is the American standard for the female body? Has it changed over time? In the 1980s, Brett Silverstein and her colleagues (Silverstein, Perdue, Peterson, & Kelly, 1986) analyzed photographs of women appearing in *Ladies' Home Journal* and *Vogue* magazines from 1901 to 1981. The researchers measured the women's busts and waists in centimeters, creating a bust-to-waist ratio. A high score indicates a heavier, more voluptuous body, while a lower score indicates a thin, lean body type. Their results show a startling series of changes in the cultural definition of female bodily attractiveness during the twentieth century (see Figure 8.5).

At the turn of the twentieth century, an attractive woman was voluptuous and heavy; by the "flapper" period of the 1920s, the correct look for women was rail-thin and flat-chested. The normative body changed again in the 1940s, when World War II "pinup girls" like Betty Grable exemplified a heavier standard. The curvaceous female body remained popular during the 1950s; witness, for example, Marilyn Monroe. However, the "swinging 1960s" fashion look, exemplified by the reed-thin British model Twiggy, introduced a very thin silhouette again. The average bust-to-waist ratio has been very low since 1963, marking the longest period of time in the past century (and continuing now into the twenty-first century) that American women have been exposed to an extremely thin standard of feminine physical attractiveness (Barber, 1998; Wiseman, Gray, Mosimann, & Ahrens, 1992). In fact, a recent meta-analysis of research studies indicates that American women have adopted the "thin is beautiful" standard even more strongly in the 2000s than in the 1990s (Grabe, Ward, & Hyde, 2008).

Interestingly, the standards for physical attractiveness for Japanese women have also undergone changes in recent decades. Since World War II, the preferred look has taken on a "Westernized" element—long-legged, thin bodies or what is called the

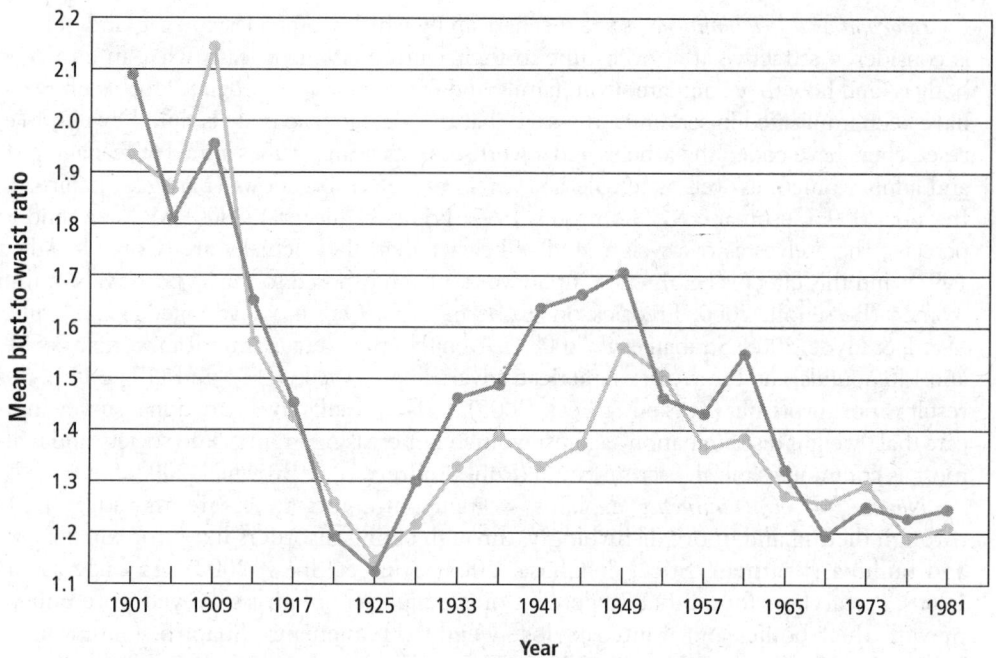

FIGURE 8.5
The mean bust-to-waist ratios of models in *Vogue* and *Ladies' Home Journal*, 1901–1981.

What has been considered an attractive female body changed dramatically during the twentieth century, from heavy women at the beginning of the 1900s to rail-thin women during the 1920s to somewhat heavier and more curvaceous women during the 1940s and 1950s, to a return to very thin women in the 1960s and thereafter.

(Adapted from Silverstein, Perdue, Peterson, & Kelly, 1986)

— *Vogue*
— *Ladies' Home Journal*

"*hattou shin* beauty" (Mukai, Kambara, & Sasaki, 1998). And this cultural shift has had an effect—Japanese women experience strong normative pressures to be thin (Mukai, 1996). In fact, researchers who studied Japanese and American college-aged women found that the Japanese women were even more likely than the American women to perceive themselves as being overweight. They also reported greater dissatisfaction with their bodies than the American women did. All this occurred despite the fact that the Japanese women were significantly thinner than the American women. In addition, these researchers found that participants' "need for social approval" as measured on a questionnaire was a significant predictor of eating disorders for the Japanese women but not for the American women. Japanese culture places a greater emphasis on conformity than American culture, and hence the normative pressure to be thin operates with even more serious consequences for Japanese women (Mukai et al., 1998).

Cultural standards for women's bodies are changeable. Whereas today's female models and movie stars tend to be lean and muscle-toned, the female icons of the 1940s and 1950s, like Marilyn Monroe, were curvaceous, heavier, and less muscular.

Informational social influence is the mechanism by which women learn what kind of body is considered attractive at a given time in their culture. Women learn what an attractive body is (and how they compare) from family and friends and the media. All forms of media have been implicated in sending a message that the ideal female body is thin. For example, researchers have coded the articles and advertisements in magazines aimed at teenage girls and adult women, as well as female characters on television shows (Barriga, Shapiro, & Jhaveri, 2009; Cusumano & Thompson, 1997; Fouts & Burggraf, 2000). Women tend to perceive themselves as overweight and as heavier than they actually are (Cohn & Adler, 1992), and this effect is heightened if they've just been exposed to media portrayals of thin women (Bessenoff, 2006; Fredrickson, Roberts, Noll, Quinn, & Twenge, 1998; Grube, Ward, & Hyde, 2008; Strahan et al., 2008). Given that the average American woman is 5'4" and 140 pounds, and the average American advertising model is 5'11" and 117 pounds, this result is not surprising (Locken & Peck, 2005). In fact, results from a national survey indicate that "weight discrimination" against women is increasing in American society and is almost as common as racial discrimination (Puhl, Andreyeva, & Brownell, 2008).

Normative social influence explains women's attempts to create the ideal body through dieting and, more disturbingly, through eating disorders like anorexia nervosa and bulimia (Bearman, Stice, & Chase, 2003; Stice & Shaw, 2002). As early as the 1960s, researchers found that 70 percent of the high school girls surveyed were unhappy with their bodies and wanted to lose weight (Heunemann, Shapiro, Hampton, & Mitchell, 1966; Sands & Wardle, 2003). The sociocultural pressure for thinness that is currently operating on women is a potentially fatal form of normative social influence. The last time that a very thin standard of bodily attractiveness for women existed, in the mid-1920s, an epidemic of eating disorders appeared (Killen et al., 1994; Silverstein, Peterson, & Perdue, 1986). And it is happening again, but with even younger girls: The American Anorexia Bulimia Association recently released statistics indicating that one-third of 12- to 13-year-old girls are actively trying to lose weight by dieting, vomiting, using laxatives, or taking diet pills (Ellin, 2000). Similarly, recent research has indicated that American girls as young as 7 years old are reporting that they are dissatisfied with their bodies (Dohnt & Tiggeman, 2006; Grabe & Hyde, 2006).

Christian Crandall (1988) has conducted research on conformity pressures and eating disorders—in this case, bulimia, an eating pattern characterized by periodic episodes of uncontrolled binge eating, followed by periods of purging through fasting, vomiting, or using laxatives. Crandall's research participants belonged to two college sororities. He found, first, that each sorority had its own social norm for binge eating. In one sorority, the group norm was that the more one binged, the more popular one was in the group. In the other sorority, popularity was associated with bingeing the right amount—the most popular women binged not too often and not too infrequently, compared to the others.

Did binge eating operate as a form of normative social influence? Yes, it did. Crandall tested the women throughout the school year and found that new members had conformed to the eating patterns of their friends. Probably, the initial conforming behavior was informational, as a new pledge learned from the group how to manage her weight. However, normative conformity processes would then take over as the woman matched her bingeing behavior to the sorority's standard and that of her friends. Not to engage in the behavior or to do it differently from the others could easily have resulted in a loss of popularity and even ostracism.

Social Influence and Men's Body Image What about cultural definitions of an attractive *male* body? Have these changed over time as well? Do men engage in normative conformity too, trying to achieve the perfect-looking body? Until recently, there was very little research on these questions, but studies conducted in the past decade suggest that yes, cultural norms have changed in that men are beginning to come under the same pressure to achieve an ideal body that women have experienced for decades (Cafri et al., 2005; Cafri & Thompson, 2004; Grossbard, Lee, Neighbors, & Lerimer, 2009; Morry & Staska, 2001; Olivardia, Pope, Borowiecki, & Cohane, 2004; Wojtowicz & von Ranson, 2006).

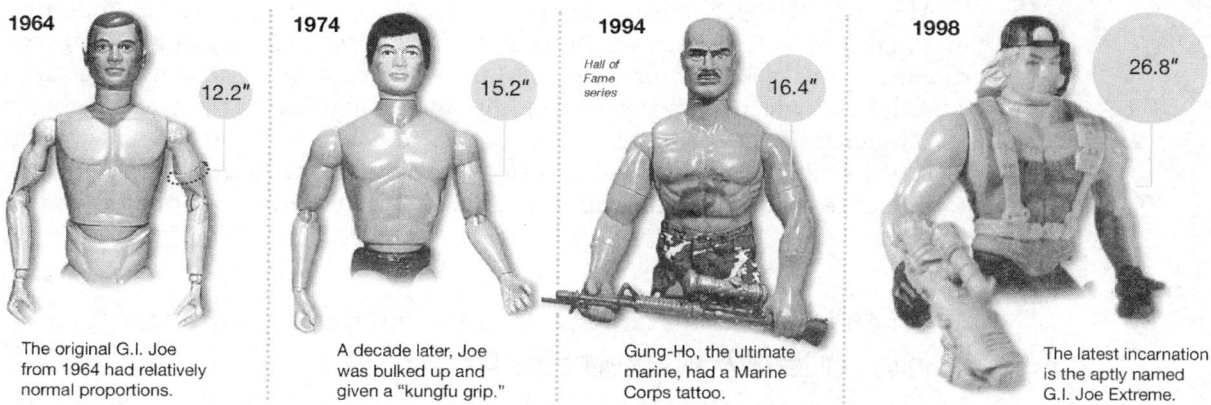

The original G.I. Joe from 1964 had relatively normal proportions.

A decade later, Joe was bulked up and given a "kungfu grip."

Gung-Ho, the ultimate marine, had a Marine Corps tattoo.

The latest incarnation is the aptly named G.I. Joe Extreme.

Has the American cultural ideal of the male body changed over time? Harrison Pope and his colleagues (1999) measured the waist, chest, and biceps of the most popular action figure toys of the last three decades, including G.I. Joe dolls, pictured here. The researchers found that the toy figures had grown much more muscular over time, far exceeding the muscularity of even the largest human bodybuilders. The researchers suggest that such images of the male body may contribute to body image disorders in boys.

Specifically, evidence suggests that sociocultural expectations of attractiveness for males have changed over recent decades, and that the ideal male body is now much more muscular. For example, Harrison Pope and his colleagues (Pope, Olivardia, Gruber, & Borowiecki, 1999) analyzed boys' toys such as G.I. Joe dolls by measuring their waists, chests, and biceps. The changes in the G.I. Joe from 1964 to 1998 are startling, as you can see in the photographs from their research.

They also coded advertisements in two women's magazines, *Glamour* and *Cosmopolitan*, since 1950, for how often male and female models were pictured in some state of undress. For women, the percentage remained at about 20 percent over the decades, but for men a change was clear. In 1950, less than 5 percent of ads showed men in some state of undress; by 1995, that figure had risen to as much as 35 percent (Pope, Phillips, & Olivardia, 2000).

Do these presentations of (nearly) naked—and perfect—male bodies affect male viewers' perceptions of themselves? Ida Jodette Hatoum and Deborah Belle (2004) investigated this question by focusing on the relationship between media consumption and bodily concerns in a sample of college men. They found that reading male-oriented magazines like *Maxim, Details, Esquire, Men's Fitness*, and *Men's Health*, all of which present the "hypermuscular" male body, was significantly correlated with negative feelings about one's own body. In addition, these researchers found that the more men were exposed to these male-directed magazines (as well as to movies), the more they valued thinness in women.

Pope and colleagues (Pope, Gruber et al., 2000) asked men in the United States, France, and Austria to alter a computer image of a male body in terms of fat and muscle until it reflected, first, their own bodies; second, the body they'd like to have; and finally, the body they thought women would find most attractive. The men were quite accurate in their depiction of their own bodies; however, men in all three countries chose an ideal body that had on average 28 more pounds of muscle than their own. This ideal standard was also the body they chose for what they thought women would find attractive. (In fact, when women participants did the task, they chose a very normal, typical-looking male body as their ideal.)

Researchers have found that adolescent and young men report feeling pressure from parents, peers, and the media to be more muscular; they respond to this pressure by developing strategies to achieve the ideal, "six-pack" body (Bergstrom & Neighbors, 2006; McCabe & Ricciardelli, 2003a, 2003b; Ricciardelli &

> You cannot make a man by standing a sheep on its hind-legs. But by standing a flock of sheep in that position you can make a crowd of men.
>
> —Sir Max Beerbohm, *Zuleika Dobson*

McCabe, 2003). For example, results from a number of studies indicate that 21 percent to 42 percent of young men have altered their eating habits in order to gain muscle mass and/or weight, while 12 percent to 26 percent have dieted in order to reduce body fat/weight. An increasing number are also using risky substances such as steroids or ephedrine to achieve a more muscular physique (Cafri et al., 2005). All these data suggest that informational and normative social influence is now operating on men, affecting their perceptions of their bodies' attractiveness.

When Will People Conform to Normative Social Influence?
何时人们会顺从规范性社会影响？

People don't always cave in to peer pressure. Although conformity is commonplace, we are not lemmings who always do what everyone else is doing. And we certainly do not agree on all issues, like abortion, affirmative action, or same-sex marriages. Exactly when are people most likely to conform to normative pressures?

The answer to this question is provided by Bibb Latané's (1981) **social impact theory**. According to this theory, the likelihood that you will respond to social influence from other people depends on three variables:

1. *Strength:* How important to you is the group?
2. *Immediacy:* How close is the group to you in space and time during the attempt to influence you?
3. *Number:* How many people are in the group?

Social impact theory predicts that conformity will increase as strength and immediacy increase. Clearly, the more important a group is to us and the more we are in its presence, the more likely we will be to conform to its normative pressures. For example, the sorority sisters that Crandall (1988) studied experienced a high level of strength and immediacy in their groups, with serious consequences. You can explore a more benign version of normative social influence in the Try It! exercise on p. 234.

Number operates differently. As the size of the group increases, each additional person has less of an influencing effect—going from three people to four makes more of a difference than going from 53 people to 54. If we feel pressure from a group to conform, adding another person to the majority makes much more of a difference if the group consists of 3 rather than 15 people. Latané constructed a mathematical model that captures these hypothesized effects of strength, immediacy, and number and has applied this formula to the results of many conformity studies. It has effectively predicted the actual amount of conformity that occurred (Bourgeois & Bowen, 2001; Latané, 1981; Latané & Bourgeois, 2001; Latané & L'Herrou, 1996).

For example, gay men who lived in communities that were highly involved in AIDS awareness activities (where strength, immediacy, and number would all be high) reported feeling more social pressure to avoid risky sexual behavior and stronger intentions to do so than gay men who lived in less involved communities (Fishbein et al., 1993). Similarly, a sample of heterosexual college students reported that what governed the likelihood of their engaging in risky sexual behavior was the norm for sexual behavior that operated in their group of friends (Winslow, Franzini, & Hwang, 1992).

Let's see in more detail what social impact theory says about the conditions under which people will conform to normative social pressures.

When the Group Size Is Three or More At what point does group size stop influencing conformity? Asch (1955) and later researchers found that conformity increased as the number of people in the group increased, but once the group reached four or five other people, conformity does not increase much (Bond, 2005; Campbell & Fairey, 1989; Gerard, Wilhelmy, & Conolley, 1968)—just as social impact theory suggests (see Figure 8.6). In short, it does not take an extremely large group to create normative social influence. As Mark Twain wrote in *The Adventures of Huckleberry Finn*, "Hain't we got all the fools in town on our side? And ain't that a big enough majority in any town?"

Social Impact Theory
The idea that conforming to social influence depends on the strength of the group's importance, its immediacy, and the number of people in the group

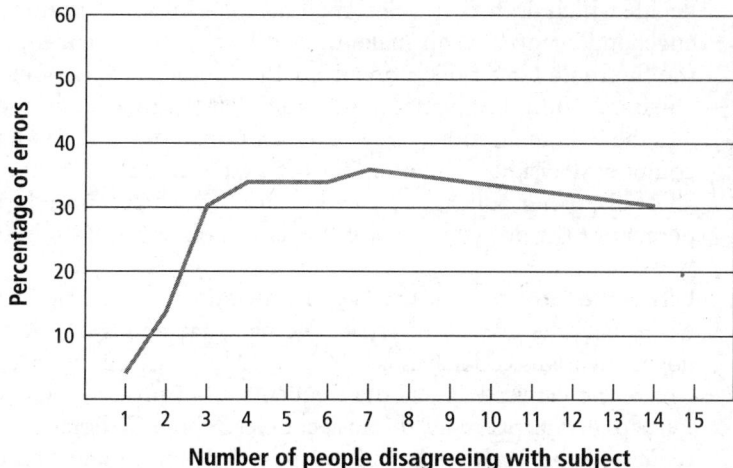

FIGURE 8.6

Effects of group size on conformity.

Asch varied the size of the unanimous majority and found that once the majority numbered four people, adding more people had little influence on conformity.

(Adapted from Asch, 1955)

When the Group Is Important Another tenet of social impact theory is that the strength of the group—defined as how important the group is to us—makes a difference. Normative pressures are much stronger when they come from people whose friendship, love, and respect we cherish because there is a large cost to losing this love and respect. Thus, groups to which we are highly attracted and with which we strongly identify will exert more normative influence on us than groups for which we have little or no attachment (Abrams, Wetherell, Cochrane, Hogg, & Turner, 1990; Guimond, 1999; Hogg, 1992; Nowak, Szamrej, & Latané, 1990; Wolf, 1985). One consequence is that it can be dangerous to have policy decisions made by highly cohesive groups because they care more about pleasing each other and avoiding conflict than arriving at the soundest, most logical decision. We will see several examples of this phenomenon in Chapter 9.

We should note, however, that the very act of conforming normatively to important groups *most* of the time can earn you the right to deviate occasionally without serious consequences. This interesting observation was made by Edwin Hollander (1960, 1985), who stated that conforming to a group over time earns you **idiosyncrasy credits**, much like putting money in the bank. It's as if your past conformity allows you, at some point in the future, to deviate from the group (to "make withdrawls") without getting into too much trouble. If you refuse to lend your car, for example, your friends may not become upset with you if you have followed their friendship norms in other areas in the past, for you've earned the right to deviate from their normative rules in this area.

When One Has No Allies in the Group Normative social influence is most powerfully felt when everyone in the group says or believes the same thing—for example, when your group of friends all believe that *101 Dalmatians* was the greatest movie ever made. Resisting such unanimous social influence is difficult or even impossible—unless you have an ally. If another person disagrees with the group—say, by nominating *Citizen Kane* as the best movie ever—this behavior will help you buck the tide as well.

To test the importance of having an ally, Asch (1955) conducted another version of his conformity experiment. He had six of the seven confederates give the wrong answer and one confederate give the right answer on every trial. Now the subject was not alone. Though still disagreeing with the majority of the group, having one ally helped the subject resist normative pressures. People conformed on an average of only 6 percent of the trials in this study, compared to 32 percent in the version where all of the confederates gave the wrong answer. Several other studies have found that observing another person resist normative social influence emboldens the individual to do the same (Allen & Levine, 1969; Morris & Miller, 1975; Nemeth & Chiles, 1988).

The difficulty of being the lone dissenter is apparent even in the U.S. Supreme Court. After hearing a case, the nine justices first determine, informally, whether they are unanimous or split in their decision. Some justices then write drafts and others

Idiosyncrasy Credits

The tolerance a person earns, over time, by conforming to group norms; if enough idiosyncrasy credits are earned, the person can, on occasion, behave deviantly without retribution from the group

The extent to which conformity is valued varies across cultures. Hunting cultures that prize independence and assertiveness, like the Inuit, show low levels of conformity.

decide which draft they will sign. There are informal attempts at influence, and eventually, all make their decision. A content-analysis of all the Supreme Court decisions from 1953 to 2001 (4,178 decisions, involving 29 different justices) indicated that the most common decision was the 9–0, unanimous one (35 percent of all decisions). And the least common decision? The one that required one justice to disagree with all of his or her colleagues, the 8–1 split, which accounted for only 10 percent of the decisions over 48 years (Granberg & Bartels, 2005).

When the Group's Culture Is Collectivistic "In America, the squeaky wheel gets the grease. In Japan, the nail that stands out gets pounded down" (Markus & Kitayama, 1991, p. 224). Is it true that the society in which one is raised affects the frequency of normative social influence? Perhaps not surprisingly, the answer is yes. Stanley Milgram (1961, 1977) replicated the Asch studies in Norway and France and found that the Norwegian participants conformed to a greater degree than the French participants did. Milgram (1961, p. 51) describes Norwegian society as "highly cohesive" with "a deep feeling of group identification," while French society, in comparison, shows "far less consensus in both social and political life." In another cross-cultural study of normative social influence, people in Lebanon, Hong Kong, and Brazil conformed to a similar extent (both to each other and to the American sample), whereas participants from the Bantu tribe of Zimbabwe conformed to a much greater degree (Whittaker & Meade, 1967). As the researchers point out, conformity has a very high social value in Bantu culture.

试一试！时装：现实中的规范性社会影响
Fashion: Normative Social Influence in Action

You can observe social impact theory in action by focusing on fashion—specifically, the clothes and accessories that you and your group of friends wear, as well as the look of other groups on campus. You can also observe what happens when you break those normative rules for fashion, for example, by dressing in a way that deviates from your group.

When you are with a group of friends and acquaintances, note carefully how everyone is dressed. Pretend that you are from another culture and not acquainted with the norms of this group; this will help you notice details that you might otherwise overlook. For example, what kinds of pants, shoes, shirts, jewelry, and other items are worn by this group? Are there similarities in their haircuts? Can you discover their fashion "rules"?

Next, spend some time on campus "people-watching," specifically observing what other groups of people are wearing. Can you discern different subgroups on your campus, defined by their style of dress? If so, there are different types of normative conformity operating on your campus; groups of friends are dressing according to the rules of their subgroup and not according to the rules of the campus as a whole.

Finally, if you are brave, break the fashion rules of your normative group. You can do this subtly or you can be very obvious. (But do be sensible; don't get yourself arrested!) For example, if you're male, you could wear a skirt around campus. That would definitely attract attention; you will be not conforming to normative influence in a very major way! If you're female, you'll have to get more creative to break the normative rules, since women's fashion includes male-type clothing. You could wear a garbage bag (with holes cut out for your head and arms) over your clothing. In either case, just walk around campus as usual, seeming unaware that you are wearing anything strange at all. How do people react to you? What will your friends say? Will strangers stare at you?

Your group of friends (as well as the students at your school in general) may well have the qualities that social impact theory discusses: The group is important to you, the group has more than three members, and the group is unanimous (which is the case if your group of friends or your college has definite fashion norms). If you stop conforming to this normative social influence, the other group members will exert some kind of pressure on you, trying to get you to return to conformity.

Although Japanese culture is more highly conforming than our own in many areas, two Asch-type studies found that when the group unanimously gave the incorrect answer, Japanese students were less conformist in general than North Americans (Frager, 1970; Williams & Sogon, 1984). In Japan, cooperation and loyalty are directed to the groups to which one belongs and with which one identifies; there is little expectation that one should conform to the behavior of complete strangers, especially in such an artificial setting as a psychology experiment. Similarly, conformity was much higher in a British sample when the participants thought the other group members were psychology majors like themselves rather than art history majors (Abrams et al., 1990). Similarly, German research participants have shown less conformity in the Asch experiment than North Americans (Timaeus, 1968); in Germany, conformity to strangers is less valued than conformity to a few well-defined groups (Moghaddam, Taylor, & Wright, 1993).

> People create social conditions, and people can change them.
>
> —Tess Onwueme

In a meta-analysis of 133 Asch line-judgment studies conducted in 17 countries, researchers found that cultural values affected normative social influence (Bond & Smith, 1996). (The countries were the United States, Canada, Britain, France, the Netherlands, Belgium, Germany, Portugal, Japan, Hong Kong, Fiji, Zimbabwe, Congo (Zaïre), Ghana, Brazil, Kuwait, and Lebanon.) Participants in collectivistic cultures showed higher rates of conformity on the line task than participants in individualistic cultures. In collectivistic cultures, conformity is a valued trait, not a negative one as in the United States. Agreeing with others is not an act of submission or cowardice in collectivist cultures, but an act of tact and sensitivity (Hodges & Geyer, 2006; Smith & Bond, 1999). Because the emphasis is on the group and not the individual, people in collectivistic cultures value normative social influence because it promotes harmony and supportive relationships in the group (Guisinger & Blatt, 1994; Kim, Triandis, Kagitcibasi, Choi, & Yoon, 1994; Markus et al., 1996).

J. W. Berry (1967; Kim & Berry, 1993) explored the issue of conformity as a cultural value by comparing two cultures that had very different strategies for accumulating food. He hypothesized that societies that relied on hunting or fishing would value independence, assertiveness, and adventurousness in their members—traits that were needed to find and bring home food—whereas societies that were primarily agricultural would value cooperativeness, conformity, and acquiescence—traits that made close living and interdependent farming more successful. Berry compared the Inuit people of Baffin Island in Canada, a hunting and fishing society, to the Temne of Sierra Leone in Africa, a farming society, on an Asch-type conformity task. The Temne showed a significant tendency to accept the suggestions of the group, while the Inuit almost completely disregarded them. As one Temne put it, "When the Temne people choose a thing, we must all agree with the decision—this is what we call cooperation"; in contrast, the few times the Inuit did conform to the group's wrong answer, they did so with "a quiet, knowing smile" (Berry, 1967, p. 417).

Finally, there is intriguing evidence that the level of conformity is changing in the United States. For example, replications of the Asch study conducted 25 to 40 years after the original, in Western countries like the United States and Britain, have found that conformity percentages are decreasing (Bond & Smith, 1996; Lalancette & Standing, 1990; Larsen, 1990; Nicholson, Cole, & Rocklin, 1985; Perrin & Spencer, 1981).

Minority Influence: When the Few Influence the Many
少数人的影响：少数人何时能影响多数人

We shouldn't leave our discussion of normative social influence with the impression that the individual never has an effect on the group. As Serge Moscovici (1985, 1994; Moscovici, Mucchi-Faina, & Maass, 1994) says, if groups really did succeed in silencing nonconformists, rejecting deviants, and persuading everyone to go along with the majority point of view, how could change ever be introduced into the system? We would all be like little robots, marching along with everyone else in monotonous synchrony, never able to adapt to changing reality.

> *Never let anyone keep you contained, and never let anyone keep your voice silent.*
>
> —Adam Clayton Powell

Instead, Moscovici (1985, 1994) argues, the individual, or the minority of group members, can influence the behavior or beliefs of the majority. This is called **minority influence**. The key is consistency: People with minority views must express the same view over time, and different members of the minority must agree with one another. If a person in the minority wavers between two different viewpoints or if two individuals express different minority views, the majority will dismiss them as people who have peculiar and groundless opinions. If, however, the minority expresses a consistent, unwavering view, the majority is likely to take notice and may even adopt the minority view (Moscovici & Nemeth, 1974). For example, a minority of scientists began to raise concerns about global warming over 2 decades ago. Today the majority is paying attention; political leaders from the industrialized nations have met to discuss possible worldwide solutions.

In a meta-analysis of nearly one hundred studies, Wendy Wood and her colleagues describe how minority influence operates (Wood, Lundgren, Ouellette, Busceme, & Blackstone, 1994). People in the majority can cause other group members to conform through normative influence. As in the Asch experiments, the conformity that occurs may be a case of public compliance without private acceptance. People in the minority can rarely influence others through normative means—the majority has little concern for how the minority views them. In fact, majority group members may be loath to agree publicly with the minority; they don't want anyone to think that they agree with those unusual, strange views of the minority. Minorities therefore exert their influence on the group via the other principal method, informational social influence. The minority introduces new and unexpected information to the group and causes the group to examine the issues more carefully. Such careful examination may cause the majority to realize that the minority view has merit, leading the group to adopt all or part of the minority's view. In short, majorities often obtain public compliance because of normative social influence, whereas minorities often achieve private acceptance because of informational social influence (De Dreu & De Vries, 2001; Levine, Moreland, & Choi, 2001; Wood, Pool, Leck, & Purvis, 1996.)

CONNECTIONS 链接

The Power of Propaganda 宣传的威力

One example of extraordinary social influence is propaganda, especially as perfected by the Nazi regime in the 1930s. Propaganda is defined as "the deliberate, systematic attempt to shape perceptions, manipulate cognitions, and direct behavior to achieve a response that furthers the desired intent of the propagandist" (Jowett & O'Donnell, 1999, p. 6).

Adolf Hitler was well aware of the power of propaganda as a tool of the state. In *Mein Kampf* (1925), written before he came to power, Hitler stated, "Its task is not to make an objective study of the truth . . . and then set it out before the masses with academic fairness; its task is to serve our right, always and unflinchingly" (pp. 182–183). In 1933, Hitler appointed Joseph Goebbels as head of the newly created Nazi Ministry of Popular Enlightenment and Propaganda. It was a highly efficient agency that permeated every aspect of Germans' lives. Nazis controlled all forms of the media, such as newspapers, films, and radio. They also disseminated Nazi ideology through the extensive use of posters and "spectacles"—lavish public rallies that aroused powerful emotions of loyalty and patriotism in the massive crowds (Jowett & O'Donnell, 1999; Zeman, 1995). Nazi propaganda was taught in schools and further promoted in Hitler Youth groups. The propaganda always presented a consistent, dogmatic message: The German people must take action to protect their racial purity and to increase their *Lebensraum* (living space) through conquest (Staub, 1989).

The concerns with *Lebensraum* led to World War II; the concerns with racial purity led to the Holocaust. How could the German people have acquiesed to the destruction of European Jewry? A major factor was prejudice (which we will discuss further in Chapter 13). Anti-Semitism was not a new or a Nazi idea. It had existed in Germany and in many other parts of

Minority Influence
The case where a minority of group members influences the behavior or beliefs of the majority

the Continent for hundreds of years. Propaganda is most successful when it taps into an audience's preexisting beliefs. Thus, the German people's anti-Semitism could be quite easily strengthened and expanded by Goebbels's ministry. Jews were described in the Nazi propaganda as destroyers of Aryan racial purity and thus a threat to German survival. They were "pests, parasites, bloodsuckers" (Staub, 1989, p. 103) and were compared to "a plague of rats that needed to be exterminated" (Jowett & O'Donnell, 1999, p. 242); however, anti-Semitism is not a sufficient cause in and of itself. Germany was initially no more prejudiced against Jews than its neighboring countries (and the United States) in the 1930s. None of these other countries came up with the concept of a "final solution" as Germany did (Tindale, Munier, Wasserman, & Smith, 2002).

Nazi propaganda permeated every facet of German life in the 1930s and 1940s. Here, huge crowds attend the 1934 Nuremberg rally. Such large public gatherings were a technique frequently used by Goebbels and Hitler to promote loyalty and conformity to the Nazi party.

Although prejudice was an important precursor, more is needed to explain the Holocaust. Clearly, the propaganda operated as persuasive messages leading to attitude change, as we discussed in Chapter 7. But the propaganda also initiated social influence processes. In a totalitarian, fascist regime, the state is the "expert," always present, always right, and always to be obeyed. Propaganda would persuade many Germans through informational conformity. They learned new "facts" (which were really lies) about the Jews and learned new solutions to what the Nazis had defined as the "Jewish problem." The propaganda did an excellent job of convincing Germans that the Jews were a threat. As we saw earlier, people experiencing a crisis are more likely to conform to information delivered by an expert.

But surely, you are thinking, there must have been Germans who did not agree with the Nazi propaganda. Yes, but think about the position they were in. The Nazi ideology so permeated daily life that children and teenagers in Hitler Youth groups were encouraged to spy on their own parents and report them to the Gestapo if they were not "good" Nazis (Staub, 1989). Neighbors, co-workers, salespeople in shops—they could all turn you in if you said or did something that indicated you were not loyal. This situation is ripe for normative conformity, where public compliance occurs without, necessarily, private acceptance. Rejection, ostracism, even torture or death by the Gestapo would all be strong motivators for normative conformity.

Whether people conformed to Nazi propaganda for informational or normative reasons, their conformity allowed the Holocaust to occur. In the early years of the Third Reich, Hitler was very concerned about public resistance to his ideas (Staub, 1989). Unfortunately, because of social influence processes, prejudice, and the totalitarian system, public resistance never arose.

> *To swallow and follow, whether old doctrine or new propaganda, is a weakness still dominating the human mind.*
> —Charlotte Perkins Gilman

Using Social Influence to Promote Beneficial Behavior 利用社会影响以促进有益行为

We have seen how informational and normative conformity occurs. Even in a highly individualistic culture such as the United States, conformity of both types is common. Is there a way that we can use this tendency to conform to affect people's behavior for the common good? Robert Cialdini, Raymond Reno, and Carl Kallgren have developed a model of normative conduct in which social norms (the rules that a society has for acceptable behaviors, values, and beliefs) can be used to subtly induce people to conform to correct, socially approved behavior (Cialdini, Kallgren, & Reno, 1991; Kallgren, Reno, & Cialdini, 2000).

For example, we all know that littering is wrong. When we've finished our Big Mac, do we toss the wrapper on the ground or out the car window? Or do we carry it

Here we see the aftermath of a large festival in Australia. By invoking conformity to social norms, we can encourage people to behave in socially desirable ways, such as refraining from littering.

with us until we come to a trash receptacle? Let's say we wanted to decrease littering or increase voter registration or encourage people to donate blood. How would we go about doing it?

Cialdini and his colleagues (1991) suggest that first we need to focus on what kind of norm is operating in the situation. Only then can we invoke a form of social influence that will encourage people to conform in socially beneficial ways. A culture's social norms are of two types. **Injunctive norms** have to do with what we think other people approve or disapprove of. Injunctive norms motivate behavior by promising rewards (or punishments) for normative (or nonnormative) behavior. For example, an injunctive norm in our culture is that littering is wrong. **Descriptive norms** concern our perceptions of the way people actually behave in a given situation, regardless of whether the behavior is approved or disapproved of by others. Descriptive norms motivate behavior by informing people about what is effective or adaptive behavior. For example, while we all know that littering is wrong (an injunctive norm), we also all know that there are times and situations when people are likely to do it (a descriptive norm)—for example, dropping peanut shells on the ground at a baseball game or leaving your trash behind at your seat in a movie theater. Thus, an injunctive norm is what most people in a culture approve or disapprove; a descriptive norm is what people actually do (Kallgren et al., 2000).

Now let's examine how we can use social influence processes to promote beneficial social behavior.

The Role of Injunctive and Descriptive Norms
命令性规范与描述性规范的作用

In a series of studies, Cialdini, Kallgren, and Reno have explored how injunctive and descriptive norms affect people's likelihood to litter. For example, in one field experiment, patrons of a city library were returning to their cars in the parking lot when a confederate approached them (Reno, Cialdini, & Kallgren, 1993). In one condition, the control group, the confederate just walked by, saying and doing nothing. In the *descriptive norm condition*, the confederate was carrying an empty bag from a fast-food restaurant and dropped the bag on the ground before passing the participant. By littering, the confederate was subtly communicating "what people do in this situation." In the *injunctive norm condition*, the confederate was not carrying anything but instead picked up a littered fast-food bag from the ground before passing the participant. By picking up someone else's litter, the confederate was subtly communicating that "littering is wrong." These three conditions occurred in one of two environments—either the parking lot was heavily littered (by the experimenters, using paper cups, candy wrappers, and so on), or the area was clean and unlittered (cleaned up by the experimenters).

At this point, research participants have been exposed to one of two types of norms about littering or to no norm (the control group), and they've done this in a littered or a clean environment. What about their chance to litter? When they got to their cars, they found a large handbill slipped under the driver's side of the windshield. The handbill appeared on all the other cars too (not surprising, since the experimenters put them there). The participant had two choices at this point: throw the handbill on the ground, littering, or take the handbill to the car and dispose of it later. What will they do? Who refrains from littering?

The control group tells us what percentage of people will litter in this situation. As you can see in Figure 8.7, the researchers found that slightly more than one-third of people threw the handbill on the ground; it didn't matter if the area was already littered or if it was clean. In the descriptive norm condition, the confederate's littering communicated

Injunctive Norms
People's perceptions of what behaviors are approved or disapproved of by others

Descriptive Norms
People's perceptions of how people actually behave in given situations, regardless of whether the behavior is approved or disapproved of by others

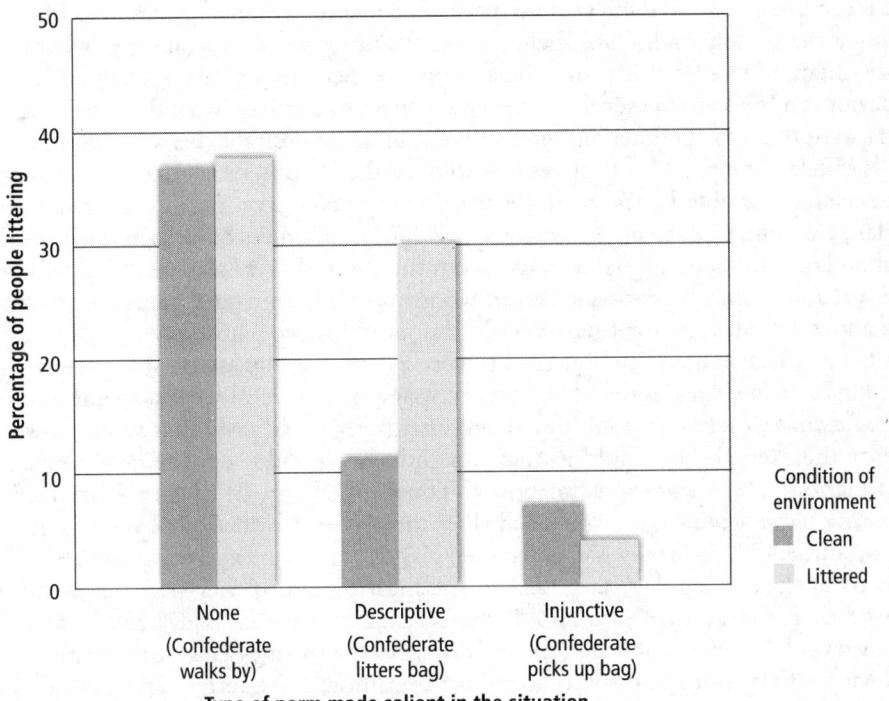

FIGURE 8.7

The effect of injunctive and descriptive norms on littering.

The data for the control group (left) indicate that 37 percent to 38 percent of people litter a handbill found on their car windshield whether the environment (a parking lot) is littered or clean. When a descriptive norm is made salient to them, littering decreases significantly only in the clean environment (middle). When an injunctive norm is made salient, littering decreases significantly in both types of environment, indicating that injunctive norms are more effective at changing behavior.

(Adapted from Reno, Cialdini, & Kallgren, 1993)

two different messages, depending on the condition of the parking lot. In the littered parking lot, the confederate's behavior communicated. "Littering is what most people do here." In the clean parking lot, the confederate's behavior communicated "Littering is not what people do here." Hence we would expect the descriptive norm to reduce littering more in the clean environment than in the littered one, and this is what the researchers found (see Figure 8.7). Finally, what about the injunctive norm condition? This kind of norm supplies the most powerful social influence information: Seeing the confederate picking up someone else's litter invokes the injunctive norm ("Littering is wrong") in both the clean and the littered environments and leads to the lowest amount of littering in the study (see Figure 8.7; Reno et al., 1993.)

Following this and other studies, the researchers concluded that injunctive norms are more powerful than descriptive norms in producing desirable behavior (Kallgren et al., 2000). This should not surprise you because injunctive norms tap into normative conformity—we conform (for example, refrain from littering) because someone's behavior has reminded us that our society disapproves of littering. We will look like selfish slobs if we litter, and we will feel embarrassed or worse if other people see us litter. It's true that norms are always present—we know that littering is bad—but they are not always *salient* to us (Kallgren et al., 2000). To promote socially beneficial behavior, something in the situation needs to draw our attention to the relevant norm so that we think about it. Thus information that communicates *injunctive norms*—what society approves and disapproves of—is the type that needs to be present to create positive behavioral change.

Using Norms to Change Behavior: Beware the "Boomerang Effect" Earlier in this chapter, we discussed the social norms technique for decreasing alcohol binge drinking on college campuses. The idea is that students typically overestimate how much their peers drink each week (Berkowitz, 2004; Lewis, Lee, Patrick, & Fossos, 2007; Perkins, 2007). Thus, telling them, "Students at your school, on average, drink only X number of drinks a week," should lead them to decrease their alcohol intake as they conform informationally to this lower level. However, researchers have noted a major problem with this approach: Sometimes, it "boomerangs." That is, some students, who already drink very little (or not at all), find out what the "average amount" is on their campus and *increase* their own alcohol intake to be like everyone else! In short, the public service message meant to decrease alcohol consumption can actually have the effect of increasing it (Perkins, Haines, & Rice, 2005; Wechsler et al., 2003). For this approach to work, one needs to remember that there are two types of people receiving your message: Those performing the socially undesirable behavior at an *above average* level (and you want to convince them to decrease it), and those who are performing the socially undesirable behavior at a *below average* level (and you want them to continue what they're doing—you don't want them to "boomerang" and start doing the undesirable behavior more).

P. Wesley Shultz and colleagues investigated the "boomerang effect" by focusing on the socially desirable behavior of electrical energy conservation in the home (Shultz, Nolan, Cialdini, Goldstein, & Griskevicius, 2007). Members of households in a neighborhood in California agreed to take part in the study. Their baseline energy usage was measured, and they were divided into two groups: Those whose energy consumption was above the average for their neighborhood and those whose energy consumption was below the average. The households were then randomly assigned to receive one of two kinds of feedback about their energy usage over several weeks. In the *descriptive norm condition*, they were told how much energy they had used that week; how much energy the average household in their neighborhood had used (the descriptive norm information); and suggestions for how to conserve energy. In the *descriptive norm plus injunctive norm condition*, they received all of the above information plus one subtle, but important, addition: If they had consumed less energy than the average household, the researcher drew a "smiley" face next to the information. If they had consumed more energy than the average household, the researcher drew a "sad" face instead. The happy or sad face communicated the *injunctive* part of the message—the recipients were receiving either approval or disapproval for the amount of energy they had used.

The researchers measured energy usage again, weeks later. Did the messages help people to conserve energy? Did those who already used low amounts stray from the path of conservation righteousness and "boomerang," deciding to be like their wasteful neighbors? First, the results indicated that the "descriptive norm" message had a positive effect on those who consumed more energy than average; they cut back and conserved. However, the descriptive norm message did have a boomerang effect on those who consumed less energy than average. Once they learned what their neighbors were doing (using electricity like crazy), they increased their energy usage!

On the other hand, the "descriptive norm plus injunctive norm" message was uniformly successful. Those whose consumption was more than average decreased their usage when they received this message. (Thus, both types of information worked for these households.) Most importantly, those whose consumption was below average to begin with did not boomerang when they received this message—they maintained their low level of energy use, the same level as before the study started. Thus, the smiley face they received reminded them that they were doing the right thing, and they kept on doing it (Schultz et al., 2007).

This study has had a major impact on energy conservation strategies in the United States. The use of smiley and sad faces to give injunctive norm feedback, combined with descriptive norm energy usage information, is now being used by utility companies in 10 major metropolitan areas, including Chicago, Sacramento, and Seattle (Kaufman, 2009).

Obedience to Authority 服从权威

Obedience is a social norm that is valued in every culture. You simply can't have people doing whatever they want all the time—it would result in chaos. Consequently, we are socialized, beginning as children, to obey authority figures who we perceive as legitimate (Blass, 2000; Staub, 1989). We internalize the social norm of obedience such that we usually obey rules and laws even when the authority figure isn't present—you stop at red lights even if the cops aren't parked at the corner; however, obedience can have extremely serious and even tragic consequences. People will obey the orders of an authority figure to hurt or even kill other human beings.

Why did the My Lai massacre occur? In this instance, the reasons that people conform combined to produce an atrocity. The behavior of the other soldiers made the killing seem like the right thing to do (*informational influence*), and the soldiers wanted to avoid rejection by their peers and superior officers (*normative influence*). In addition, some of the soldiers later testified at the congressional investigation of the atrocity that they had received direct orders from their officer, Lieutenant Calley, to shoot the civilians. Thus, the My Lai tragedy occurred in part because some of the soldiers followed the social norm of obedience to authority too readily, without questioning or taking personal responsibility for what they were doing. It was the power of these conformity pressures that led to the tragedy, not personality defects in the soldiers. This makes the incident all the more frightening because it implies that similar incidents can occur with any group if similar pressures of social influence are present. The fast-food restaurant hoax we discussed in the beginning of the chapter is another disturbing example of people following the norm of obedience blindly.

The twentieth century was marked by repeated atrocities and genocides—in Germany and the rest of Europe, Armenia, the Ukraine, Rwanda, Cambodia, Bosnia, Sudan, and elsewhere. One of the most important questions facing the world's inhabitants therefore becomes, where does obedience end and personal responsibility begin? The philosopher Hannah Arendt (1965) was particularly interested in understanding the causes of the Holocaust. How could Hitler's Nazi regime in Germany accomplish the murder of 6 million European Jews? Arendt argued that most participants in the Holocaust were not sadists or psychopaths who enjoyed the mass murder of innocent people but ordinary citizens subjected to complex and powerful social pressures. She covered the trial of Adolf Eichmann, the Nazi official responsible for the transportation of Jews to the death camps, and concluded that he was not the monster that many people made him out to be but a commonplace bureaucrat like any other bureaucrat who did what he was told without questioning his orders (Miller, 1995).

Victims of the Holocaust, Nordhausen, Germany, April 1945. According to social psychologists, most of the German guards and citizens who participated in the Holocaust were not madmen but ordinary people exposed to extraordinary social influences.

Our point is not that Eichmann—or the soldiers at My Lai or the Khmer Rouge in Cambodia or the Serbs in Bosnia—should be excused for the crimes they committed. The point is that it is too easy to explain their behavior as the acts of madmen. It is more fruitful—and more frightening—to view their behavior as the acts of ordinary people exposed to extraordinary social influence. But how can we be sure that the Holocaust, My Lai, and other mass atrocities were not caused solely by evil, psychopathic people but by powerful social forces operating on people of all types? The way to find out is to study social pressure in the laboratory under controlled conditions. We could take a sample of ordinary citizens, subject them to various kinds of social influence, and see to what extent they will conform and obey. Can an experimenter influence ordinary people to commit immoral acts, such as inflicting severe pain on an innocent bystander? Stanley Milgram (1963, 1974, 1976) decided to find out, in what has become the most famous series of studies in social psychology.

Imagine that you were a participant in one of Milgram's studies. You answer an ad in the newspaper asking for participants in a study on memory and learning. When you arrive at the laboratory, you meet another participant, a 47-year-old, somewhat overweight, pleasant-looking fellow. The experimenter, wearing a white lab coat, explains that one of you will play the role of a teacher and the other a learner. You draw a slip of paper out of a hat and discover that you will be the teacher. It turns out that your job is to teach the other participant a list of word pairs (e.g., *blue–box, nice–day*) and then test him on the list. The experimenter instructs you to deliver an electric shock to the learner whenever he makes a mistake because the purpose of the study is to examine the effects of punishment on learning.

You watch as the other participant—the learner—is strapped into a chair in an adjacent room and electrodes are attached to his arm. You are seated in front of a shock generator whose 30 switches deliver varying levels of shock in 15-volt increments, from 15 to 450 volts. There are labels accompanying these switches, from "Slight Shock" to "Danger: Severe Shock" to an ominous "XXX" next to the highest levels (see the photos on the next page). The experimenter tells you that the first time the learner makes a mistake, you

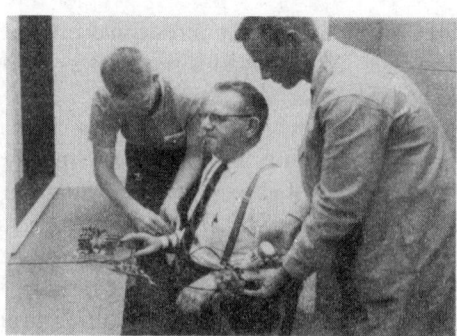

Left: The shock generator used in the Milgram experiments. *Right:* The learner (an accomplice of the experimenter) is strapped into the chair, and electrodes are attached to his arm.

(Adapted from Milgram, 1974)

should give him a shock of 15 volts—the smallest amount—and then increase the amount by 15 volts for each subsequent mistake he makes. So that you will know what the shocks are like, the experimenter gives you a sample shock of 45 volts, which is rather painful.

You read the list of word pairs to the learner and then begin the testing phase. After announcing the first word of a pair, you give four possible answers; the learner responds by pressing one of four switches, which illuminates a light on the answer box in front of you. Everything begins smoothly as the learner gets the first few right. Then he gets some wrong, and as instructed, you deliver the shocks. At this point, you are probably getting concerned about the number and severity of the shocks you will have to give. When you get to the 75-volt level, the learner, whom you can hear over an intercom, emits a painful "Ugh!" Perhaps you pause and ask the experimenter what you should do. "Please continue," he responds. As the learner continues to make mistakes, you deliver a few more shocks. The learner protests, shouting, "Ugh! Experimenter! That's all! Get me out of here!" You look at the experimenter with grave concern. He tells you, "It is absolutely essential that you continue." (See Figure 8.8.)

What would you do? How many people do you think would continue to obey the experimenter and increase the levels of shock until they had delivered the maximum amount, 450 volts?

When this question was posed to psychology majors at Yale University, they estimated that only about 1 percent of the population would go to this extreme. A sample of middle-class adults and a panel of psychiatrists made similar predictions; however, from our discussion of conformity thus far, you are probably not so optimistic. Whereas no one would have believed that such travesties as the Holocaust could have occurred, they did. Most of Milgram's participants succumbed to the pressure of an authority figure. The average maximum shock delivered was 360 volts, and 62.5 percent of the participants went all the way, delivering the 450-volt shock. A full 80 percent of the participants continued giving the shocks even after the learner, who earlier had mentioned that he had a heart condition, screamed, "Let me out of here! Let me out of here! My heart's bothering me. Let me out of here! . . . Get me out of here! I've had enough. I won't be in the experiment any more" (Milgram, 1974, p. 56).

It is important to note that the learner was actually an accomplice of the experimenter who play-acted his role; he did not receive any actual shocks. It is equally important to note that the study was very convincingly done so that people believed they really were shocking the learner. Here is Milgram's description of one participant's response to the teacher role:

> I observed a mature and initially poised businessman enter the laboratory smiling and confident. Within 20 minutes he was reduced to a twitching, stuttering wreck, who was rapidly approaching a point of nervous collapse. He constantly pulled on his earlobe, and twisted his hands. At one point he pushed his fist into his forehead and muttered, "Oh God, let's stop it." And yet he continued to respond to every word of the experimenter, and obeyed to the end. (Milgram, 1963, p. 377)

Why did so many research participants (who ranged in age from the twenties to the fifties and included blue-collar, white-collar, and professional workers) conform to the wishes of the experimenter, to the point where they (at least in their own minds)

Learner's Protests

75 volts: Ugh!
90 volts: Ugh!
105 volts: Ugh! (louder)
120 volts: Ugh! Hey this really hurts.
135 volts: Ugh!!
150 volts: Ugh!!! Experimenter! That's all. Get me out of here. I told you I had heart trouble. My heart's starting to bother me now. Get me out of here, please. My heart's starting to bother me. I refuse to go on. Let me out.
165 volts: Ugh! Let me out! (shouting)
180 volts: Ugh! I can't stand the pain. Let me out of here! (shouting)
195 volts: Ugh! Let me out of here. Let me out of here. My heart's bothering me. Let me out of here! You have no right to keep me here! Let me out! Let me out of here! Let me out! Let me out of here! My heart's bothering me. Let me out! Let me out!
210 volts: Ugh! Experimenter! Get me out of here. I've had enough. I won't be in the experiment any more.
225 volts: Ugh!
240 volts: Ugh!
255 volts: Ugh! Get me out of here.
270 volts: Ugh! (Agonized scream) Let me out of here. Let me out of here. Let me out of here. Let me out. Do you hear? Let me out of here.
285 volts: Ugh! (Agonized scream)
300 volts: Ugh! (Agonized scream) I absolutely refuse to answer any more. Get me out of here. You can't hold me here. Get me out. Get me out of here.
315 volts: Ugh! (Intensely agonized scream) I told you I refuse to answer. I'm no longer part of this experiment.
330 volts: Ugh! (Intense and prolonged agonized scream) Let me out of here. Let me out of here. My heart's bothering me. Let me out, I tell you. (Hysterically) Let me out of here. Let me out of here. You have no right to hold me here. Let me out! Let me out! Let me out of here! Let me out!

Instructions Used by the Experimenter to Achieve Obedience

Prod 1: Please continue *or* Please go on.
Prod 2: The experiment requires that you continue.
Prod 3: It is absolutely essential that you continue.
Prod 4: You have no other choice; you must go on.

The prods were always made in sequence: Only if prod 1 had been unsuccessful could prod 2 be used. If the subject refused to obey the experimenter after prod 4, the experiment was terminated. The experimenter's tone of voice was at all times firm but not impolite. The sequence was begun anew on each occasion that the subject balked or showed reluctance to follow orders.

Special prods. If the subject asked whether the learner was likely to suffer permanent physical injury, the experimenter said:

Although the shocks may be painful, there is no permanent tissue damage, so please go on. [Followed by prods 2, 3, and 4 if necessary.]

If the subject said that the learner did not want to go on, the experimenter replied: Whether the learner likes it or not, you must go on until he has learned all the word pairs correctly. So please go on. [Followed by prods 2, 3, and 4 if necessary.]

FIGURE 8.8

Transcript of the learner's protests in Milgram's obedience study and of the prods used by the experimenter to get people to continue giving shocks.

(Adapted from Milgram, 1963, 1974)

were inflicting great pain on another human being? Why were the college students, middle-class adults, and psychiatrists so wrong in their predictions about what people would do? Each of the reasons that explain why people conform combined in a dangerous way, causing Milgram's participants to obey—just as the soldiers did at My Lai. Let's take a close look at how this worked in the Milgram experiments.

The Role of Normative Social Influence 规范性社会影响的作用

First, it is clear that normative pressures made it difficult for people to refuse to continue. As we have seen, if someone really wants us to do something, it can be difficult to say no. This is particularly true when the person is in a position of authority over us. Milgram's participants probably believed that if they refused to continue, the experimenter would be disappointed, hurt, or maybe even angry—all of which put pressure on them to continue. It is important to note that this study, unlike the Asch study, was set up so that the experimenter actively attempted to get people to conform, giving stern commands such as "It is absolutely essential that you continue." When an authority figure is

FIGURE 8.9
Results of different versions of the Milgram experiment.

Obedience is highest in the standard version, where the participant is ordered to deliver increasing levels of shock to another person (left panel). Obedience drops when other participants model disobedience or when the authority figure is not present (two middle panels). Finally, when no orders are given to increase the shocks, almost no participants do so (right panel). The contrast in behavior between the far-left and far-right panels indicates just how powerful the social norm of obedience is.

(Adapted from Milgram, 1974)

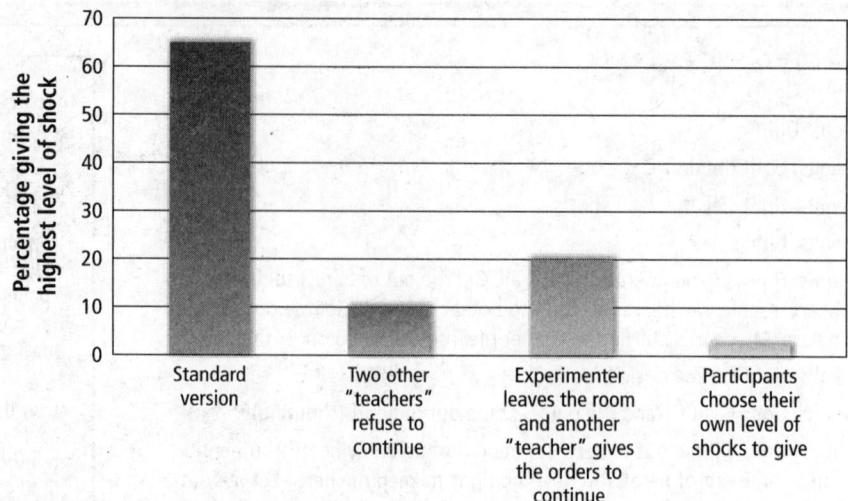

so insistent that we obey, it is difficult to say no (Blass, 1991, 2000, 2003; Hamilton, Sanders, & McKearney, 1995; Meeus & Raaijmakers, 1995; Miller, 1986).

The fact that normative pressures were present in the Milgram experiments is clear from a variation of the study that he conducted. This time, there were three teachers, two of whom were confederates of the experimenter. One confederate was instructed to read the list of word pairs; the other, to tell the learner whether his response was correct. The (real) participant's job was to deliver the shocks, increasing their severity with each error, as in the original experiment. At 150 volts, when the learner gave his first vehement protest, the first confederate refused to continue, despite the experimenter's command that he do so. At 210 volts, the second confederate refused to continue. The result? Seeing their peers disobey made it much easier for the actual participant to disobey too. Only 10 percent of the participants gave the maximum level of shock in this experiment (see Figure 8.9). This result is similar to Asch's finding that people did not conform nearly as much when one accomplice bucked the majority and consistently gave the correct answer.

The Role of Informational Social Influence 信息性社会影响的作用

Despite the power of the normative pressures in Milgram's original study, they are not the sole reason people complied. The experimenter was authoritative and insistent, but he was not pointing a gun at participants and telling them to "conform or else." The participants were free to get up and leave anytime they wanted to. Why didn't they, especially when the experimenter was a stranger they had never met before and probably would never see again?

As we saw earlier, when people are in a confusing situation and unsure of what they should do, they use other people to help define the situation. Informational social influence is especially powerful when the situation is ambiguous, when it is a crisis, and when the other people in the situation have some expertise. The situation Milgram's participants faced was clearly confusing, unfamiliar, and upsetting. It all seemed straightforward enough when the experimenter explained it to them, but then it turned into something else altogether. The learner cried out in pain, but the experimenter told the participant that although the shocks were painful, they did not cause any permanent damage. The participant didn't want to hurt anyone, but he or she had agreed to be in the study and to follow the directions. When in such a state of conflict, it was only natural for the participants to use an expert—the experimenter—to help them decide what was the right thing to do (Hamilton et al., 1995; Krakow & Blass, 1995; Miller, 1986; Miller, Collins, & Brief, 1995).

Another version of the experiment that Milgram performed supports the idea that informational influence was operative. This version was identical to the original one except for three critical changes: First, the experimenter never said which shock levels were to be given, leaving this decision up to the teacher (the real participant). Second, before the study began, the experimenter received a telephone call and had to leave the room. He told the participant to continue without him. Third, there was a confederate playing the role of an additional teacher, whose job was to record how long it took the learner to respond. When the experimenter left, this other teacher said that he had just thought of a good system: How about if they increased the level of shock each time the learner made a mistake? He insisted that the real participant follow this procedure.

Note that in this situation, the expertise of the person giving the commands has been removed: He was just a regular person, no more knowledgeable than the participants themselves. Because he lacked expertise, people were much less likely to use him as a source of information about how they should respond. As seen in Figure 8.9, in this version, compliance dropped from 62.5 percent giving the maximum shock to only 20 percent. (The fact that 20 percent still complied suggests that some people were so uncertain about what to do that they used even a nonexpert as a guide.)

An additional variation conducted by Milgram underscores the importance of authority figures as experts in eliciting such conformity and obedience. In this variation, two experimenters gave the real participants their orders. At 150 volts, when the learner first cried out that he wanted to stop, the two experimenters began to disagree about whether they should continue the study. At this point, 100 percent of the participant-teachers stopped responding. Note that nothing the victim ever did caused all the participants to stop obeying; however, when the authorities' definition of the situation became unclear, the participants broke out of their conforming role.

> *When you think of the long and gloomy history of man, you will find more hideous crimes have been committed in the name of obedience than in the name of rebellion.*
>
> —C. P. Snow

Other Reasons Why We Obey 服从的其他原因

Both normative and informational social influences were very strong in Milgram's experiments; however, these reasons for complying still fall short of fully explaining why people acted so inhumanely. They seem to account for why people initially complied, but after it became increasingly obvious to people what they were doing to the learner, why didn't they realize that what they were doing was terribly wrong and stop? Just as the soldiers at My Lai persisted in killing the villagers long after it was obvious that they were unarmed and defenseless civilians (and just as the fast-food restaurant managers continued to abuse their employees long after the demands of the "policeman" on the phone became bizarre and illegal), many of Milgram's participants pulled the shock levers time after time after time, despite the cries of anguish from a fellow human being.

Conforming to the Wrong Norm To understand this continued compliance, we need to consider additional aspects of the situation. We don't mean to imply that Milgram's participants were completely mindless or unaware of what they were doing. All were terribly concerned about the plight of the victim. The problem was that they were caught in a web of conflicting norms, and it was difficult to determine which one to follow. At the beginning of the experiment, it was perfectly reasonable to heed the norm that says, "Obey expert, legitimate authority figures." The experimenter was confident and knowledgeable, and the study seemed as if it was a reasonable test of an interesting hypothesis. So why not cooperate and do as you are told?

But gradually the rules of the game changed, and this "obey authority" norm was no longer appropriate. The experimenter, who seemed so reasonable before, was now asking people to inflict great pain on their fellow participant. But once people are following one norm, it can be difficult to switch midstream, realizing that this norm is no longer appropriate and that another norm, "Do not inflict needless harm on a fellow human being," should be followed. For example, suppose the experimenter had explained, at the outset, that he would like people to deliver possibly fatal shocks to the other participant. How many people would have agreed? Very few, we suspect, because it would have been clear that this violated an important social and personal norm about inflicting harm on others. Instead, the experimenter pulled a kind of "bait and switch" routine whereby he first made it look like an "obey authority" norm was appropriate and then gradually violated this norm (Collins & Brief, 1995).

It was particularly difficult for people to abandon the "obey authority" norm in the Milgram experiments because of three key aspects of the situation. First, the experiment was fast-paced, preventing the participants from reflecting on what they were doing. They were busy recording the learner's responses, keeping track of which word pairs to test him on next, and determining whether his responses were right or wrong. Given that they had to attend carefully to these details and move along at a fast pace, it was difficult for them to realize that the norm that was guiding their behavior—cooperating with the authority figure—was, after a while, no longer appropriate (Conway & Schaller, 2005; Modigliani & Rochat, 1995). We suspect that if halfway through the experiment, Milgram's participants had been told to take a break and go sit in a room by themselves, many more would have successfully redefined the situation and refused to continue.

Self-Justification It is important to remember that the experimenter asked people to increase the shocks in very small increments. The participants did not go from giving a small shock to giving a potentially lethal one. Instead, at any given point, they faced the decision about whether to increase the amount of shock they had just given by 15 volts. As we saw in Chapter 6, every time a person makes an important or difficult decision, dissonance is produced, with resultant pressures to reduce it. An effective way of reducing dissonance produced by a difficult decision is to decide that the decision was fully justified. But because reducing dissonance provides a justification for the preceding action, in some situations it makes a person vulnerable to pressures leading to an escalation of the chosen activity.

Thus in the Milgram study, the participants' initial agreement to administer the first shock created internal pressure on them to continue to obey. As the participants administered each successive level of shock, they had to justify it in their own minds. After they had justified a particular shock level, it became very difficult for them to decide on a place where they should draw the line and stop. How could they say, in effect, "OK, I gave him 200 volts, but not 215—never 215!" Each succeeding shock and its justification laid the groundwork for the next shock and would have been dissonant with quitting; 215 volts is not that different from 200, and 230 is not that different from 215. Those who did break off the series did so against enormous internal pressure to continue (Darley, 1992; Gilbert, 1981; Miller et al., 1995).

Mika Haritos-Fatouros (1988; see also Staub, 1989) reports that this incremental approach was used by the Greek military dictatorship of the late 1960s to train torturers. In interviews with former torturers, Haritos-Fatouros learned that their first contact with political prisoners was to bring them food and "occasionally" give them some blows. Next, they were put on guard while others conducted torture sessions. Next, they would take part in a few group floggings or beatings. The last step, being in charge of a torture session, "was announced suddenly to the [man] by the commander-in-chief without leaving him any time for reflection" (1988, p. 1117).

The Loss of Personal Responsibility The third reason why it was difficult for participants to abandon the "obey authority" norm in the Milgram experiments is a particularly troubling one. When you are the research participant (or the employee) and the other person is a legitimate authority figure (the Experimenter; the boss; the police officer), you are the "puppet" and they are the ones who pull the strings. They define what it is you are supposed to do, and they are responsible for the end results—after all, it was their idea, you were "just following orders." Milgram (1974) stressed that the loss of a sense of personal responsibility for one's actions was a critical component explaining the results of the obedience studies.

A particularly disturbing job is that of prison guards who are members of the execution team. They must carry out a capital punishment sentence. How do these guards respond to a job where they are told to kill another person? Clearly, they need to reduce their cognitive dissonance. Taking a life is a supremely immoral act, so they will very much need to engage in self-justifcation in order to do it. Michael Osofsky, Albert Bandura, and Philip Zimbardo (2005) studied guards on the execution teams of three southern state prisons, and compared them to their fellow guards who did not conduct executions. All the guards responded anonymously to a questionnaire that asked them to rate their level of agreement with statements such as "Because of the nature of their crime, murderers have lost the right to live," and "Those who carry out state executions should not be criticized for following society's wishes."

The researchers found a highly significant difference in the attitudes of the two types of guards. The execution team guards demonstrated much more "moral disengagement" from their work than did the other guards. The execution team guards denied all personal responsibility for the executions. They strongly felt they were just following orders, in this case, those of a judge and jury. They also engaged in high levels of justification in other areas. As compared to the regular prison guards, they dehumanized the prisoners more, seeing them as lacking important human qualities. They perceived the prisoners as more of a threat to society, such that it was necessary that they be killed. All these attitudes helped the execution guards reduce their qualms about the morality of what they did at work. As one guard put it, "I had a job to do, that's what we did. Our job was to execute this man and we were going to do it in a professional manner" (Osofsky, Bandura, & Zimbardo, 2005, p. 386).

The Obedience Studies, Then and Now 过去和现在的服从研究

Stanley Milgram's study of obedience is widely considered to be one of the most important contributions to the field of psychology (Benjamin & Simpson, 2009). His work, conducted in the early 1960s, was replicated in the following years by researchers in 11 countries, involving approximately 3,000 research participants (Blass, 2009). However, Milgram's research paradigm also ignited a storm of protest (and soul-searching) in the research community over the ethical treatment of research participants.

Milgram's studies were criticized as unethical for several reasons. First, the study involved *deception*. For example, participants were told it was a study on memory and learning, when of course, it was not; participants were told the electric shocks were real, when of course, they were not. Second, there was no true *informed consent* on the part of participants. When they agreed to be in the study, they were not informed as to its true nature and thus their consent to take part was effectively meaningless. Third, their role as teacher caused them *psychological distress*; for many participants, this occurred at a high level. Fourth, the participants were not told that they had the *right to withdraw*; in fact, the experimenter told them the exact opposite, for example, that they "had to continue," taking away their freedom. Fifth, the participants experienced *inflicted insight*. When the study ended, some of them had learned things about themselves (e.g., they would obey orders to hurt someone) that they had not agreed to beforehand (Baumrind, 1964, 1985; Milgram, 1964; Miller, 2009). While the ethical issues surrounding Milgram's experiments were not (as is often believed) the reason ethical guidelines for research participants were created in the United States in 1966 (they were created to protect participants in medical research), these new guidelines made conducting an obedience study increasingly problematic (Benjamin & Simpson, 2009). Between 1976 (in the United States) and 1985 (outside the United States, in Austria), the last obedience studies were conducted using Milgram's procedure (Blass, 2009). Until now.

In 2006, Jerry M. Burger (2009) conducted the first obedience experiment in the United States in 30 years. Much has changed in the country over these decades. Has the likelihood of being obedient, even to the point of inflicting harm, changed as well? In order to conduct this study under modern ethical guidelines, Burger (2009) had to make a number of changes to the procedure. First, he reduced the psychological distress experienced by participants by stopping the study after 150 volts, when the learner is first heard yelling that he wants out and refuses to go on. A meta-analysis of data from eight of Milgram's experiments indicated that when disobedience occurred, it was most likely to happen at this point in the study (Packer, 2008). Thus, Burger could compare obedience versus disobedience up to and at this critical 150-volt juncture and then end the study, without further subjecting those who were obedient at 150 volts to the many, many levels of shock (and stress) that remained. Second, participants were prescreened by a clinical psychologist, and those who were identified as even slightly likely to have a negative reaction to the experience were excluded from the study (38 percent were excluded). Finally, Burger (2009) explicitly and repeatedly told his participants that they could leave the study at any time, as could the learner.

In many other areas, Burger's (2009) experiment was like the original. His experimenter used the same four "prods" that Milgram used (e.g., "It is absolutely essential that you continue") to order participants to continue when they began to disagree. (The meaning that participants would give to these "orders" is unclear given that they had also been told they could withdraw at any time.) Burger's participants, like Milgrim's, were adult residents (in this case, of Santa Clara, California), recruited through newspaper advertisements and flyers. Their age range of 20 to 81 years was broader than Milgram's, though their average age of about 43 years was similar. They were ethnically more diverse than Milgram's participants, and they were also more highly educated: Forty percent of Burger's sample had college degrees and another 20 percent had master's degrees. Both men and women participated as teachers in Burger's study; Milgram had female participants in only one of his many experiments. Finally, because the Milgram obedience studies are quite well known, Burger excluded participants who had taken more than two college-level psychology courses.

What did Burger (2009) find? Are people more disobedient today than they were in Milgram's experiments 45 years ago? After all, during these decades, people learned to "question authority" as they took part in the Civil Rights movement and the anti-Vietnam War movement. They also grew less complacent and accepting of their government at both the state and federal level (Cohen, 2008). Did these cultural experiences translate into a newly empowered, disobedient Milgram participant? Sadly, the answer is no; it did not. Burger (2009) found no significant difference in obedience rates between his participants and Milgram's. After the critical 150-volt shock had been delivered (and the learner cried out to be released), 70 percent of Burger's participants obeyed and were ready to continue (at which point, Burger ended the study). At this same point in the comparable Milgram study, 82.5 percent were obedient and continued; the difference between 70 percent and 82.5 percent is not statistically significant. Similarly, Burger (2009) found no significant difference in obedience between his male and female participants, which was also the case in Milgram's study.

Note that Burger's ethically necessary changes in methodology make a direct comparison to Milgram's results difficult (Miller, 2009). Some of Burger's changes may have increased the likelihood of disobedience; others may have increased the likelihood of obedience. The most profound change that Burger made was stopping the study after 150 volts. While this makes the procedure more ethical, it means we have no idea how many participants, today, would go all the way to the 450-volt shock (Twenge, 2009). The extraordinary power and meaning of the Milgram obedience studies come from participants' choices from 150 volts, continuing step by small step, to the last switch on the shock generator. It is during this part of the obedience paradigm that participants feel the most conflicted, tense, and anxious. It is here that they reveal their response to a moral conflict (Miller, 2009). This is the information that is lost in the present replication. And as such, it reminds us that scientific inquiry has two, sometimes competing, aims: to discover new knowledge, and to do no harm.

It's Not about Aggression Before leaving our discussion of the Milgram studies, we should mention one other possible interpretation of his results: Did the participants act so inhumanely because there is an evil side to human nature, lurking just below the surface, ready to be expressed with the flimsiest excuse? To test this hypothesis, Milgram conducted another version of his study. Everything was the same except that the experimenter told the participants that they could choose any level of shock they wished to give the learner when he made a mistake. Milgram gave people permission to use the highest levels, telling them that there was a lot to be learned from all levels of shock. This instruction should have allowed any aggressive urges to be expressed unchecked. Instead, the participants chose to give very mild shocks (see Figure 8.9). Only 2.5 percent of the participants gave the maximum shock. Thus, the Milgram studies do not show that people have an evil streak that shines through when the surface is scratched (Reeder, Monroe, & Pryor, 2008). Instead, these studies demonstrate that social pressures can combine in insidious ways to make humane people act in an inhumane manner. Let us conclude this chapter with the words of Stanley Milgram:

> Even Eichmann was sickened when he toured the concentration camps, but in order to participate in mass murder he had only to sit at a desk and shuffle papers. At the same time the man in the camp who actually dropped [the poison] into the gas chambers is able to justify his behavior on the grounds that he is only following orders from above. Thus there is fragmentation of the total human act; no one man decides to carry out the evil act and is confronted with its consequences. The person who assumes full responsibility for the act has evaporated. Perhaps this is the most common characteristic of socially organized evil in modern society. (1976, pp. 183–184)

HOW WOULD YOU USE THIS? 如何学以致用?

The topics of conformity and obedience bring to mind the great opening sentence in Charles Dickens's novel *A Tale of Two Cities*: "It was the best of times, it was the worst of times." These types of social influence are incredibly useful in maintaining social order. Without them, life would be chaotic, even dangerous. However, they have their "dark side" as well, even to the point of promoting and enabling genocide. What can you do to protect yourself from the potentially negative effects of social influence? Probably the most difficult is informational conformity; by definition, you conform to others because you don't know what's going on. Therefore, it is very difficult to know if they're wrong. Typically, it's best to rely on an expert instead of a nonexpert, but even this advice can be tricky. Resisting normative conformity is more straightforward. You'll know what the right thing to do is, but will you be able to withstand the disapproval of others? Remember that having an ally will help you to stand up to group pressure. Obedience also presents a fairly straightforward scenario. You'll know when you've been given an order that goes against your ethical or moral beliefs. As with normative conformity, it will be a matter of whether or not you are willing and able to experience the repercussions of your disobedience. Luckily, learning about these types of social influence will make you more aware in the future of when it is appropriate to agree with the group and when it is not.

Summary 总 结

- **Conformity: When and Why** Conformity occurs when people change their behavior due to the real (or imagined) influence of others. There are two main reasons people conform: because of informational and normative social influences.

- **Informational Social Influence: The Need to Know What's "Right"** Informational social influence occurs when people do not know what is the correct (or best) thing to do or say. They look to the behavior of others as an important and needed source of information, and they use it to choose appropriate courses of action for themselves. Informational social influence usually results in private acceptance, wherein people genuinely believe in what other people are doing or saying.

  - **Importance of Being Accurate** In situations where it is important to be accurate, the tendency to conform to other people through informational social influence increases.

  - **When Informational Conformity Backfires** Using other people as a source of information can backfire when they are wrong about what's going on. Contagion occurs when emotions and behaviors spread rapidly throughout a group; one example is **mass psychogenic illness**.

- **When Will People Conform to Informational Social Influence?** People are more likely to conform to informational social influence when the situation is ambiguous, a crisis, or if experts are present.

● **Normative Social Influence: The Need to Be Accepted** Normative social influence occurs when we change our behavior to match that of others because we want to remain a member of the group and continue to gain the advantages of group membership. We conform to the group's **social norms**, implicit or explicit rules for acceptable behaviors, values, and attitudes. Normative social influence usually results in **public compliance** but not private acceptance of other people's ideas and behaviors.

  - **Conformity and Social Approval: The Asch Line Judgment Studies** In a series of classic studies, Solomon Asch found that people would conform, at least some of the time, to the obviously wrong answer of the group.
  - **The Importance of Being Accurate, Revisited** When it is important to be accurate, people are more likely to resist normative social influence and go against the group, giving the right answer.
  - **The Consequences of Resisting Normative Social Influence** Resisting normative social influence can lead to ridicule, ostracism, and even rejection by the group.
  - **Normative Social Influence in Everyday Life** Normative social influence operates on many levels in social life: It influences our eating habits, hobbies, fashion, body image, and so on, and it promotes correct (polite) behavior in society.
  - **When Will People Conform to Normative Social Influence?** **Social impact theory** specifies when normative social influence is most likely to occur by referring to the strength, immediacy, and size of the group. We are more likely to conform when the group is one we care about, when the group members are unanimous in their thoughts or behaviors, when the group has three or more members, and when we are members of collectivist cultures. Past conformity gives people **idiosyncrasy credits**, allowing them to deviate from the group without serious consequences.
  - **Minority Influence: When the Few Influence the Many** Under certain conditions, an individual (or small number of people) can influence the majority. The key is consistency in the presentation of the minority viewpoint.

● **Using Social Influence to Promote Beneficial Behavior** Social influence techniques can be used to promote socially beneficial behavior in others. Communicating **injunctive norms** is a more powerful way to create change than communicating **descriptive norms**. In addition, one must be careful that descriptive norms do not create a "boomerang effect."

  - **The Role of Injunctive and Desciptive Norms**

● **Obedience to Authority** In the most famous series of studies in social psychology, Stanley Milgram examined obedience to authority figures. He found chilling levels of obedience, to the point where a majority of participants administered what they thought were near-lethal shocks to a fellow human being.

  - **The Role of Normative Social Influence** Normative pressures make it difficult for people to stop obeying authority figures. They want to please the authority figure by doing a good job.
  - **The Role of Informational Social Influence** The obedience experiment was a confusing situation for participants, with competing, ambiguous demands. Unclear about how to define what was going on, they followed the orders of the expert.
  - **Other Reasons We Obey** Participants conformed to the wrong norm: They continued to follow the "obey authority" norm when it was no longer appropriate. It was difficult for them to abandon this norm for three reasons: the fast-paced nature of the experiment; the fact that the shock levels increased in small increments; and their loss of a feeling of personal responsibility.
  - **The Obedience Studies, Then and Now** Milgram's research design was criticized on ethical grounds, involving deception, informed consent, psychological distress, the right to withdraw, and inflicted insight. A current U.S. replication of the Milgram study found that the level of obedience in 2009 was not significantly different from that found in the classic 1960s' study. Similarly, there was no difference in obedience between men and women participants in the two different time periods.

CHAPTER 8 TEST 第8章习题

1. All of the following are examples of informational social influence *except*
   a. you are running a race, but because you are unsure of the route, you wait to check which of two roads the other runners follow.
   b. you've just started work at a new job, and a fire alarm goes off; you watch your coworkers to see what to do.
   c. when you get to college you change the way you dress so that you "fit in" better, that is, so that people will like you more.
   d. you ask your adviser which classes you should take next semester.
   e. mass psychogenic illness.

2. Which of the following is most true, according to social impact theory?
   a. People conform more to others who are physically close than to others who are physically distant.
   b. People conform more if the others are important to them.
   c. People conform more to three or more people than to one or two people.

d. All of the above are true, according to social impact theory.
e. Only (a) and (b) are true, according to social impact theory.

3. In Asch's line studies, participants who were alone when asked to report the length of the lines gave the correct answer 98 percent of the time. When they were with the confederates, however (i.e., all of whom gave the wrong answer on some trials), 76 percent of participants gave the wrong answer at least once. This suggests that Asch's studies are an illustration of
   a. public compliance with private acceptance.
   b. the fundamental attribution error.
   c. public compliance without private acceptance.
   d. informational influence.
   e. private compliance.

4. Which of the following situations demonstrates mass psychogenic illness?
   a. You share the happiness a close friend experiences when she learns that she's won the state lottery.
   b. During the past week complaints of dizziness and fainting spells spread throughout the dorm though no physical cause can be identified.
   c. After looking through a medical dictionary you fear that you have three separate illnesses.
   d. Panic spreads throughout a crowd when someone yells "Killer bees!"

5. Whereas _____ may be the mechanism by which women learn what kind of body type is considered attractive, _____ explains their attempts to obtain such a shape through dieting and other means.
   a. contagion influence; minority influence
   b. minority influence; contagion influence
   c. informational social influence; normative social influence
   d. normative social influence; informational social influence

6. Which of the following is most true about informational social influence?
   a. When deciding whether to conform, people should ask themselves whether the other people know more about what is going on than they do.
   b. People should always try to resist it.
   c. People are most likely to conform when other people have the same level of expertise as they do.
   d. Often, people publicly conform but do not privately accept this kind of influence.

7. Brandon knows that society considers underage drinking to be wrong; he also knows, however, that on a Saturday night at his university, many of his friends will engage in this behavior. His belief that most of the public would disapprove of underage drinking is _____, while his perception that many teenagers drink under certain circumstances is _____.
   a. an injunctive norm; a descriptive norm
   b. a descriptive norm; an injunctive norm
   c. a descriptive norm; conformity
   d. an injunctive norm; conformity

8. Tom is a new student at his university. During the first week of classes, he notices a fellow student from one of his classes getting on a bus. Tom decides to follow the student and discovers that this bus takes him right to the building where his class meets. This best illustrates what kind of conformity?
   a. Obedience to authority
   b. Informational social influence
   c. Public compliance
   d. Normative social influence
   e. Mindless conformity

9. Which of the following best describes an example of normative social influence?
   a. Sarah is studying with a group of friends. When comparing answers on the practice test, she discovers they all answered the question differently than she had. Instead of speaking up and telling them she thinks the answer is something else, she agrees with their answer, because she figures they must be right.
   b. Sarah is supposed to bring a bottle of wine to a dinner party she is attending. She doesn't drink wine herself, but figures she can just ask the store clerk for advice on what kind to buy.
   c. Sarah is out to lunch with her boss and coworkers. Her boss tells a joke that makes fun of a certain ethnic group and everyone else laughs. Sarah doesn't think the joke is funny but laughs anyway.
   d. Sarah is flying on an airplane for the first time. She is worried when she hears the engine make a strange noise but feels better after she looks at the flight attendants and sees that they are not alarmed.

10. Which of the following had the least influence on participants' willingness to keep giving shocks in the Milgram studies?
    a. Normative social influence
    b. Activation of the "obey authority" norm
    c. Self-justification
    d. Informational social influence
    e. Participants' aggression

Answer Key
1-c, 2-d, 3-c, 4-b, 5-c, 6-a, 7-a, 8-b, 9-d, 10-e

For more review plus practice tests, videos, flashcards, writing help and more, log on to MyPsychLab.

9

Group Processes
Influence in Social Groups
团体过程：
社会团体的影响

ON MARCH 19, 2003, AN UNSEASONABLY COOL SPRING day in Washington D.C., President George W. Bush convened a meeting with his top advisers in the Situation Room, the nerve center in the basement of the White House. Months of planning had come down to this moment: final approval of the invasion of Iraq. The president first asked whether any of his advisers had any last thoughts or recommendations. When none did, he asked the staff to establish a secure video link with General Tommy Franks, the commander of all U.S. armed forces in the Middle East. Franks and his senior field commanders, who were at Prince Sultan Air Force Base in Saudi Arabia, gave President Bush a final briefing, after which General Franks concluded, "The force is ready to go, Mr. President." President Bush then gave a prepared statement: "For the peace of the world and the benefit and freedom of the Iraqi people, I hereby give the order to execute Operation Iraqi Freedom. May God bless the troops" (Woodward, 2004, p. 379).

With these words, President Bush set in motion a controversial war that will undoubtedly be debated by historians for decades to come. For social psychologists, a fascinating question is how the decision to invade Iraq was made—indeed, how important decisions of any kind are made. Do groups of experts make better decisions, for example, than individuals? The American government has at its disposal a huge number of talented people with expertise in world affairs, national security, human rights, and military intelligence, and it might seem that drawing upon and combining this expertise would lead to the best decisions. Groups don't always make good decisions, however, especially when they are blinded by the desire to maintain cohesiveness or the desire to please a dominant leader. In this chapter, we will focus on questions such as these about the nature of groups and how they influence people's behavior, which are some of the oldest topics in social psychology (Cartwright & Zander, 1968; Kerr & Tindale, 2004; Forsyth, 2000; Levine & Moreland, 1998; Wittenbaum & Moreland, 2008). We will return to a discussion of the Iraq War later in the chapter.

OUTLINE 提纲

- What Is a Group?
  Why Do People Join Groups?
  The Composition and Functions of Groups

- Groups and Individuals' Behavior
  Social Facilitation: When the Presence of Others Energizes Us
  Social Loafing: When the Presence of Others Relaxes Us
  Gender and Cultural Differences in Social Loafing: Who Slacks Off the Most?
  Deindividuation: Getting Lost in the Crowd

- Group Decisions: Are Two (or More) Heads Better Than One?
  Process Loss: When Group Interactions Inhibit Good Problem Solving
  CONNECTIONS: Was the Decision to Invade Iraq a Result of Groupthink?
  Group Polarization: Going to Extremes
  Leadership in Groups

- Conflict and Cooperation
  Social Dilemmas
  Using Threats to Resolve Conflict
  Effects of Communication
  Negotiation and Bargaining

- Summary

What Is a Group? 什么是团体?

Groups have a number of benefits. Other people can be an important source of information. Groups are also an important part of our identity, helping us define who we are, and are a source of social norms, the explicit or implicit rules defining what is acceptable behavior.

Six students studying at a table in the library are not a group. But if they meet to study for their psychology final together, they are. A **group** consists of three or more people who interact and are interdependent in the sense that their needs and goals cause them to influence each other (Cartwright & Zander, 1968; Lewin, 1948). (Two people are generally considered to be a "dyad" rather than a "group"; Levine & Moreland, 2006). Like a president's advisers working together to reach a foreign policy decision, citizens meeting to solve a community problem, or people who have gathered to blow off steam at a party, groups are people who have assembled for some common purpose.

Think for a moment of the number of groups to which you belong. Don't forget to include your family, campus groups (such as clubs or political organizations), community groups (such as churches or synagogues), sports teams, and more temporary groups (such as your classmates in a small seminar). All of these count as groups because you interact with the other members and you are interdependent: You influence them, and they influence you.

Why Do People Join Groups? 人们为什么要加入团体?

Forming relationships with other people fulfills a number of basic human needs—so basic, in fact, that there may be an innate need to belong to groups. Some researchers argue that in our evolutionary past, there was a substantial survival advantage to establishing bonds with other people (Baumeister & Leary, 1995). People who bonded together were better able to hunt for and grow food, find mates, and care for children. Consequently, they argue, the need to belong has become innate and is present in all societies. Consistent with this view, people in all cultures are motivated to form relationships with other people and to resist the dissolution of these relationships (Gardner, Pickett, & Brewer, 2000; Manstead, 1997). People monitor their status in groups and look for any sign that they might be rejected (Kerr & Levine, 2008; Leary & Baumeister, 2000; Pickett & Gardner, 2005; Twenge, 2008). One study found that people who were asked to recall a time when they had been rejected by other people estimated that the temperature of the room was 5 degrees lower than did people who were asked to recall a time when they were accepted by other people (Zhong & Leonardelli, in press). Social rejection is, literally, chilling.

Another important function of groups is that they help us define who we are. As we saw in Chapter 8, other people can be an important source of information, helping us resolve ambiguity about the nature of the social world (Darley, 2004). All groups make assumptions about the nature of the social world, and thus provide us with a lens through which we can understand the world and our place in it (Hogg, Hohman, & Rivera, 2008). Thus, groups become an important part of our identity—witness the number of times people wear shirts with the name of one of their groups (e.g., a campus organization) emblazoned on it. Groups also help establish social norms, the explicit or implicit rules defining what is acceptable behavior.

The Composition and Functions of Groups 团体的组成与功能

The groups to which you belong probably vary in size from a few members to several dozen members. Most groups, however, have three to six members (Desportes & Lemaine, 1988; Levine & Moreland, 1998; McPherson, 1983). This is due in part to our definition of groups as involving interaction between members. If groups become too large, you cannot interact with all the members; for example, the college or university that you attend is not a group because you are unlikely to meet and interact with every other student.

Group
Three or more people who interact and are interdependent in the sense that their needs and goals cause them to influence each other

Another important feature of groups is that the members tend to be alike in age, sex, beliefs, and opinions (George, 1990; Levine & Moreland, 1998; Magaro & Ashbrook, 1985). There are two reasons for the homogeneity of groups. First, many groups tend to attract people who are already similar before they join (Feld, 1982). As we'll see in Chapter 10, people are attracted to others who share their attitudes and thus are likely to recruit fellow group members who are similar to them. Second, groups tend to operate in ways that encourage similarity in the members (Moreland, 1987). This can happen in a number of important ways, some of which we discussed in Chapter 8.

Social Norms   As we saw in Chapter 8, *social norms* are a powerful determinant of our behavior. All societies have norms about which behaviors are acceptable, some of which all members are expected to obey (e.g., we should be quiet in libraries) and some of which vary from group to group (e.g., rules about what to wear to weddings and funerals). If you belong to a fraternity or sorority, you can probably think of social norms that govern behavior in your group, such as whether alcoholic beverages are consumed and how you are supposed to feel about rival fraternities or sororities. It is unlikely that other groups to which you belong share these norms. The power of norms to shape behavior becomes clear when we violate them too often: We are shunned by other group members and, in extreme cases, pressured to leave the group (Marques, Abrams, & Serodio, 2001; Schachter, 1951; see also Chapter 8).

Social Roles   Most groups have a number of well-defined **social roles**, which are shared expectations in a group about how particular people are supposed to behave (Hare, 2003). Whereas norms specify how all group members should act, roles specify how people who occupy certain positions in the group should behave. A boss and an employee in a business occupy different roles and are expected to act in different ways in that setting. Like social norms, roles can be very helpful because people know what to expect from each other. When members of a group follow a set of clearly defined roles, they tend to be satisfied and perform well (Barley & Bechky, 1994; Bettencourt & Sheldon, 2001).

There are, however, potential costs to social roles. People can get so far into a role that their personal identities and personalities get lost. Suppose that you agreed to take part in a 2-week psychology experiment in which you were randomly assigned to play the role of a prison guard or a prisoner in a simulated prison. You might think that the role you were assigned to play would not be very

Social Roles
Shared expectations in a group about how particular people are supposed to behave

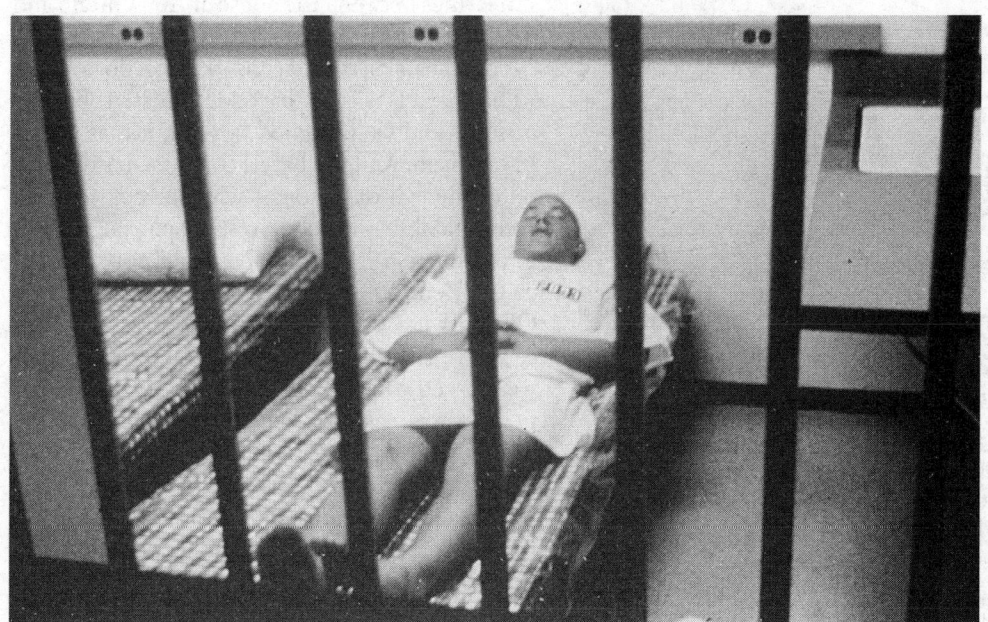

Philip Zimbardo and his colleagues randomly assigned students to play the role of prisoner or guard in a mock prison. The students assumed these roles all too well. Those playing the role of guard became quite aggressive, and those playing the role of prisoner became passive, helpless, and withdrawn. People got into their roles so much that their personal identities and sense of decency somehow got lost.

important; after all, everyone knows that it is only an experiment and that people are just pretending to be guards or prisoners. Philip Zimbardo and his colleagues, however, had a different hypothesis. They believed that social roles can be so powerful that they "take over" our personal identities to the point that we become the role we are playing.

To see if this is true, Zimbardo and colleagues conducted an unusual study. They built a mock prison in the basement of the psychology department at Stanford University and paid students to play the role of guard or prisoner (Haney, Banks, & Zimbardo, 1973; Zimbardo, 2007). The role students played was determined by the flip of a coin. The guards were outfitted with a uniform of khaki shirts and pants, a whistle, a police nightstick, and reflecting sunglasses, and the prisoners were outfitted with a loose-fitting smock with an identification number stamped on it, rubber sandals, a cap made from a nylon stocking, and a locked chain attached to one ankle.

The researchers planned to observe the students for 2 weeks to see whether they began to act like real prison guards and prisoners. As it turned out, the students quickly assumed these roles—to such an extent that the researchers ended the experiment after only 6 days. Many of the guards became quite abusive, thinking of creative ways of verbally harassing and humiliating the prisoners. The prisoners became passive, helpless, and withdrawn. Some prisoners, in fact, became so anxious and depressed that they had to be released from the study earlier than the others. Remember, everyone knew that they were in a psychology experiment and that the prison was only make-believe. The roles of guard and prisoner were so compelling and powerful, however, that this simple truth was often overlooked. People got so far into their roles that their personal identities and sense of decency somehow got lost.

Prison Abuse at Abu Ghraib Does all this sound familiar? In 2004, it came to light that American military guards had been abusing prisoners in Abu Ghraib, a prison in Iraq (Hersch, 2004). A report written by U. S. Major General Taguba, who investigated the claims of abuse, documented numerous cases of physical beatings, sexual abuse, and psychological humiliation. The American public was shocked by pictures of U.S. soldiers smiling as they stood in front of naked Iraqi prisoners, as if they were posing in front of local landmarks for the folks back home.

Most groups have a number of well-defined social roles, which are shared expectations in a group about how particular people are supposed to behave. Roles can be very helpful, because people know what to expect from each other. However, people can get so far into a role that their personal identities and personalities get lost, sometimes with tragic consequences. Some people think that the abuse at the Abu Ghraib prison in Iraq was due to soldiers getting too far into their roles as prison guards.

Did a few bad apples happen to end up in the unit guarding the prisoners? Not according to Phillip Zimbardo (2007), who has analyzed the similarities between the abuse at Abu Ghraib and the prison study he conducted 30 years earlier. "What's bad is the barrel," Zimbardo argued. "The barrel is the barrel I created by my prison—and we put good boys in, just as in this Iraqi prison. And the barrel corrupts. It's the barrel of the evil of prisons—with secrecy, with no accountability—which gives people permission to do things they ordinarily would not" (quoted in O'Brien, 2004). The military guards at Abu Ghraib were under tremendous stress, had received scant training, had little supervision, and were asked to set their own rules for interrogation. It was easy to dehumanize the prisoners, given that the guards didn't speak their language and that many of the prisoners were naked (due to shortage of prison suits). "You start looking at these people as less than human," said one guard, "and you start doing things to 'em that you would never dream of" (Zimbardo, 2007, p. 352).

This is not to say that the soldiers should be completely excused for their actions. The abuse came to light when 24-year-old Joe Darby, an Army Reservist at Abu Ghraib, reported what was happening, and as in Zimbardo's study, there were some guards who treated the prisoners well. Thus, not everyone was caught in the web of their social roles, unable to resist. But as much as we would like to think that we would be one of these heroes, the lesson from the Zimbardo prison study—and Milgram's studies of obedience, discussed in Chapter 8—is that most of us would be unable to resist the social influences in these powerful situations, and, perhaps, perform acts we thought we were incapable of.

Gender Roles Not all social roles involve such extreme behavior, of course. Even in everyday life, however, roles can be problematic when they are arbitrary or unfair. All societies, for example, have expectations about how people who occupy the roles of women and men should behave. In many cultures, women are expected to assume the role of wife and mother and have limited opportunities to pursue other careers. In the United States and other countries, these expectations are changing, and women have more opportunities than ever before. Conflict can result, however, when expectations change for some roles but not for others assumed by the same person. In India, for example, women were traditionally permitted to take only the roles of wife, mother, agricultural laborer, and domestic worker. As their rights have improved, women are increasingly working at other professions. At home, though, many husbands still expect their wives to assume the traditional role of child rearer and household manager, even if their wives have other careers. Conflict results, because many women are expected to "do it all"—maintain a career, raise the children, clean the house, and attend to their husband's needs (Brislin, 1993; Wax, 2008). Such conflicts are not limited to India; many American readers will find this kind of role conflict all too familiar (Eagly & Diekman, 2003; Kite, Deaux, & Haines, 2008; Reid, Cooper, & Banks, 2008; Rudman, 1998).

Changing roles do more than cause us conflict; they can actually affect our personalities. In a historical study, researchers tracked women's social status in the United States between 1931 and 1993 and compared those results to women's ratings of their own assertiveness (Twenge, 2001). Women's status improved between the years of 1931 and 1945. During this time, women increasingly earned college degrees and worked outside the home; by 1945, for example, over half of all college degrees were earned by women. If World War II increased opportunities for women while men were away fighting, when the men came home, so did the women. During the years 1946 to 1967, the stay-at-home mom became the norm; women increasingly dropped out of the workforce, and fewer women went to college. In 1950, for example, about 25 percent of college degrees were earned by women. Between 1968 and 1993, women's status improved as the feminist movement took hold in the United States. By the early 1990s, women were again earning more college degrees than men.

As seen in Figure 9.1, women's ratings of assertiveness mirrored these societal trends. As women's role in the United States changed from independent to dependent, their ratings of assertiveness dropped. As they became more independent, their ratings of assertiveness increased. The roles that people assume in groups, and in society at large, are powerful determinants of their feelings, behavior, and personality (Eagly & Steffen, 2000; Eagly, Diekman, Johannesen-Schmidt, & Koenig, 2004). The Try It! exercise on the next page describes a way you can experience this for yourself.

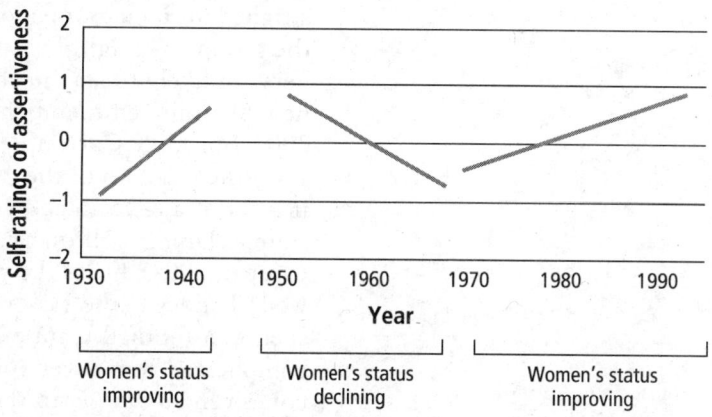

FIGURE 9.1

Relationship between Women's Status and Their Ratings of Their Assertiveness.

Researchers compared women's ratings of their own assertiveness with societal trends in women's social status. Women's status improved in the United States between 1931 and 1945, and as seen by the line on the far left, so did women's ratings of their own assertiveness. Women's status decreased between 1945 and 1967, and as seen by the line in the middle, their ratings of assertiveness decreased during the same time period. Women's status increased again between 1968 and 1993, and as seen by the line on the far right, their ratings of their assertiveness increased during this time period. These results suggest that the social roles people occupy in society influence how they view themselves.

(Adapted from Twenge, 2001)

试一试！当你违背角色时会怎样？
What Happens When You Violate a Role?

Pick a behavior that is part of the role for your gender in your culture, and deliberately violate it. For example, if you are male in the United States, you might decide to put on makeup or carry a purse to your next class. If you are female, you might wear a jacket and tie to a party. Keep a journal describing how others react to you. More than likely, you will encounter a good deal of social disapproval, such as people staring at you or questioning your behavior. For this reason, you want to avoid role violations that are too extreme.

The social pressure that is brought to bear on people who do not conform to their roles explains why it can be so difficult to break out of the roles to which we are assigned, even when they are arbitrary. Of course, there is safety in numbers; when enough people violate role expectations, others do not act nearly as negatively, and the roles begin to change. For example, it is now much more acceptable for men to wear earrings than it was 20 years ago. To illustrate this safety in numbers, enlist the help of several same-sex friends and violate the same role expectation together. Again, note carefully how people react to you. Did you encounter more or less social disapproval in the group than you did as an individual?

Group Cohesiveness Another important aspect of group composition is how cohesive the group is. The qualities of a group that bind members together and promote mutual liking are known as **group cohesiveness** (Dion, 2000; Friedkin, 2004; Hogg, 1993; Holtz, 2004). If a group has formed primarily for social reasons, such as a group of friends who like to go to the movies together on weekends, then the more cohesive the group is, the better. This is pretty obvious; would you rather spend your free time with a bunch of people who don't care much for each other or a tight-knit bunch of people who feel committed to you and the other members of the group? As might be expected, the more cohesive a group is, the more its members are likely to stay in the group, take part in group activities, and try to recruit new like-minded members (Levine & Moreland, 1998; Pickett, Silver, & Brewer, 2002; Sprink & Carron, 1994).

If the function of the group is to work together and solve problems, however, as it is for a sales team at a company or a military unit, then the story is not quite so simple. Doing well on a task causes a group to become more cohesive (Mullen & Cooper, 1994), but is the reverse true? Does cohesiveness cause a group to perform well? It does if the task requires close cooperation between the group members, such as a football team executing a difficult play or a military unit carrying out a complicated maneuver (Gully, Devine, & Whitney, 1995). Sometimes, however, cohesiveness can get in the way of optimal performance, if maintaining good relations among group members becomes more important than finding good solutions to a problem. Is it possible, for example, that the cohesiveness felt by President Bush and his advisers got in the way of clear thinking about whether to invade Iraq? We will return to this question later in the chapter, when we discuss group decision making.

Groups and Individuals' Behavior
团体与个人行为

Group Cohesiveness
Qualities of a group that bind members together and promote liking between members

Do you act differently when other people are around? Simply being in the presence of other people can have a variety of interesting effects on our behavior. We will begin by looking at how a group affects your performance on something with which you are very familiar—taking a test in a class.

Social Facilitation: When the Presence of Others Energizes Us
社会促进：他人在场为我们增添活力

It is time for the final exam in your psychology class. You have spent countless hours studying the material, and you feel ready. When you arrive, you see that the exam is scheduled in a tiny room already packed with students. You squeeze into an empty desk, elbow to elbow with your classmates. The professor arrives and says that if any students are bothered by the close quarters, they can take the test by themselves in one of several smaller rooms down the hall. What should you do?

The question is whether being with other people will affect your performance (Geen, 1989; Guerin, 1993; Kent, 1994; Sanna, 1992). The presence of others can mean one of two things: (1) performing a task with coworkers who are doing the same thing you are or (2) performing a task in front of an audience that is not doing anything but observing you. Note that the question is a basic one about the mere presence of other people, even if they are not part of a group that is interacting. Does the simple fact that other people are around make a difference, even if you never speak or interact with them in any way?

To answer this question, we need to talk about insects—cockroaches, in fact. Believe it or not, a classic study using cockroaches as research participants suggests an answer to the question of how you should take your psychology test. Robert Zajonc and his colleagues (Zajonc, Heingartner, & Herman, 1969) built a contraption to see how a cockroach's behavior was influenced by the presence of its peers. The researchers placed a bright light (which cockroaches dislike) at the end of a runway and timed how long it took a roach to escape the light by running to the other end, where it could scurry into a darkened box (see the left side of Figure 9.2). The question was, did roaches perform this simple feat faster when they were by themselves or when they were in the presence of other cockroaches?

You might be wondering how the researchers managed to persuade other cockroaches to be spectators. They simply placed other roaches in clear plastic boxes next to the runway. These roaches were in the bleachers, so to speak, observing the solitary cockroach do its thing (see Figure 9.2). As predicted, the individual cockroaches performed the task faster when other roaches were there than when they were by themselves.

We would not give advice on how you should take your psychology test based on one study that used cockroaches. But the story does not end here. Dozens of studies have been done on the effects of the mere presence of other people, involving human beings as well as other species, such as ants and birds (e.g., Aiello & Douthitt, 2001;

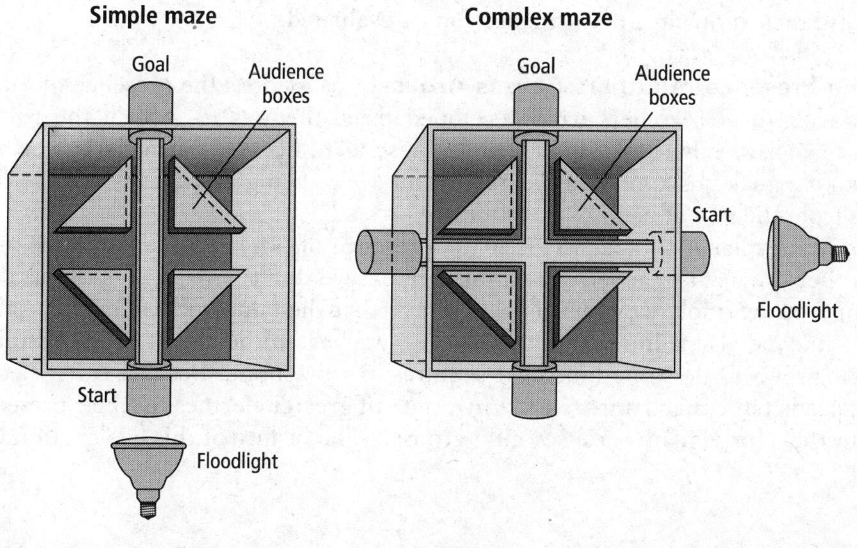

> *Mere social contact begets . . . a stimulation of the animal spirit that heightens the efficiency of each individual workman.*
>
> —Karl Marx, *Das Kapital*, 1867

FIGURE 9.2
Cockroaches and social facilitation.

In the maze on the left, cockroaches had a simple task: to go from the starting point down the runway to the darkened box. They performed this feat faster when other roaches were watching than when they were alone. In the maze on the right, the cockroaches had a more difficult task. It took them longer to solve this maze when other roaches were watching than when they were alone.

(Adapted from Zajonc, Heingartner, & Herman, 1969)

Research on social facilitation finds that people do better on a well-learned task when in the presence of others than when they are alone. If students have studied hard and know the material well, they might be better off taking an exam in a room with lots of other people.

Social Facilitation
The tendency for people to do better on simple tasks and worse on complex tasks when they are in the presence of others and their individual performance can be evaluated

Rajecki, Kidd, & Ivins, 1976; Thomas, Skitka, Christen, & Jurgena, 2002). The findings of these studies are remarkably consistent: As long as the task is a relatively simple, well-learned one—as escaping a light is for cockroaches—the mere presence of others improves performance. For example, in one of the first social psychology experiments ever done, Norman Triplett (1898) asked children to wind up fishing line on a reel, either by themselves or in the presence of other children. They did so faster when in the presence of other children than when by themselves.

Simple Versus Difficult Tasks Before concluding that you should stay in the crowded classroom to take your exam, we need to consider a different set of findings. Remember that we said the presence of others enhances performance on simple, well-learned tasks. Escaping a light is old hat for a cockroach, and winding fishing line on a reel is not difficult, even for a child. What happens when we give people a more difficult task to do and place them in the presence of others? To find out, Zajonc and his colleagues (1969) included another condition in the cockroach experiment. This time, the cockroaches had to solve a maze that had several runways, only one of which led to the darkened box (see the right side of Figure 9.2). When working on this more difficult task, the opposite pattern of results occurred: The roaches took *longer* to solve it when other roaches were present than when they were alone. Many other studies have also found that people and animals do worse in the presence of others when the task is difficult (e.g., Bond & Titus, 1983; Geen, 1989).

Arousal and the Dominant Response In an influential article, Robert Zajonc (1965) offered an elegant theoretical explanation for why the presence of others facilitates a well-learned response but inhibits a less practiced or new response. The presence of others increases physiological arousal (i.e., our bodies become more energized). Also when such arousal exists, it is easier to perform a dominant response (e.g., something we're good at) but harder to do something complex or learn something new. Consider, for example, a behavior that is second nature to you, such as riding a bicycle or writing your name. Arousal, caused by the presence of other people watching you, should make it even easier to perform these well-learned tasks. But let's say you have to do something more complex, such as learning a new sport or working on a difficult math problem. Now arousal will lead you to feel flustered and do less well than if you were alone (Schmitt, Gilovich, Goore, & Joseph, 1986). This phenomenon became known as **social facilitation**, which is the tendency for people to do better on simple tasks and worse on complex tasks when they are in the presence of others and their individual performance can be evaluated.

Why the Presence of Others Causes Arousal Why does the presence of others lead to arousal? Researchers have developed three theories to explain the role of arousal in social facilitation: Other people cause us to become particularly alert and vigilant, they make us apprehensive about how we're being evaluated, and they distract us from the task at hand.

The first explanation suggests that the presence of other people makes us more alert. When we are by ourselves reading a book, we don't have to pay attention to anything but the book; we don't have to worry that the lamp will ask us a question. When someone else is in the room, however, we have to be alert to the possibility that he or she will do something that requires us to respond. Because other people are less predictable than lamps, we are in a state of greater alertness in their presence. This alertness, or vigilance, causes mild arousal. The beauty of this explanation (the one preferred by Zajonc, 1980) is that it explains both the animal and the human studies. A solitary cockroach need not worry about what the cockroach in the next room is doing; however, it needs to be alert when in the presence of another member of its species—and the same goes for human beings.

The second explanation focuses on the fact that people are not cockroaches and are often concerned about how other people are evaluating them. When other people can see how you are doing, the stakes are raised: You feel as if the other people are evaluating you and will feel embarrassed if you do poorly and pleased if you do well. This concern about being judged, called *evaluation apprehension*, can cause mild arousal. According to this view, then, it is not the mere presence of others but the presence of others who are evaluating us that causes arousal and subsequent social facilitation (Blascovich, Mendes, Hunter, & Salomon, 1999; Bond, Atoum, & Van Leeuwen, 1996; Muller & Butera, 2007; Seta & Seta, 1995).

The third explanation centers on how distracting other people can be (Baron, 1986; Muller, Atzeni, & Fabrizio, 2004). It is similar to Robert Zajonc's (1980) notion that we need to be alert when in the presence of others, except that it focuses on the idea that any source of distraction—be it the presence of other people or noise from the party going on in the apartment upstairs—will put us in a state of conflict because it is difficult to pay attention to two things at the same time. This divided attention produces arousal, as any parent knows who has ever tried to read the newspaper while his or her 2-year-old clamors for attention. Consistent with this interpretation, nonsocial sources of distraction, such as a flashing light, cause the same kinds of social facilitation effects as the presence of other people (Baron, 1986).

We have summarized research on social facilitation in the top half of Figure 9.3 (we will discuss the bottom half in a moment). This figure illustrates that there is more than one reason that the presence of other people is arousing. The consequences of

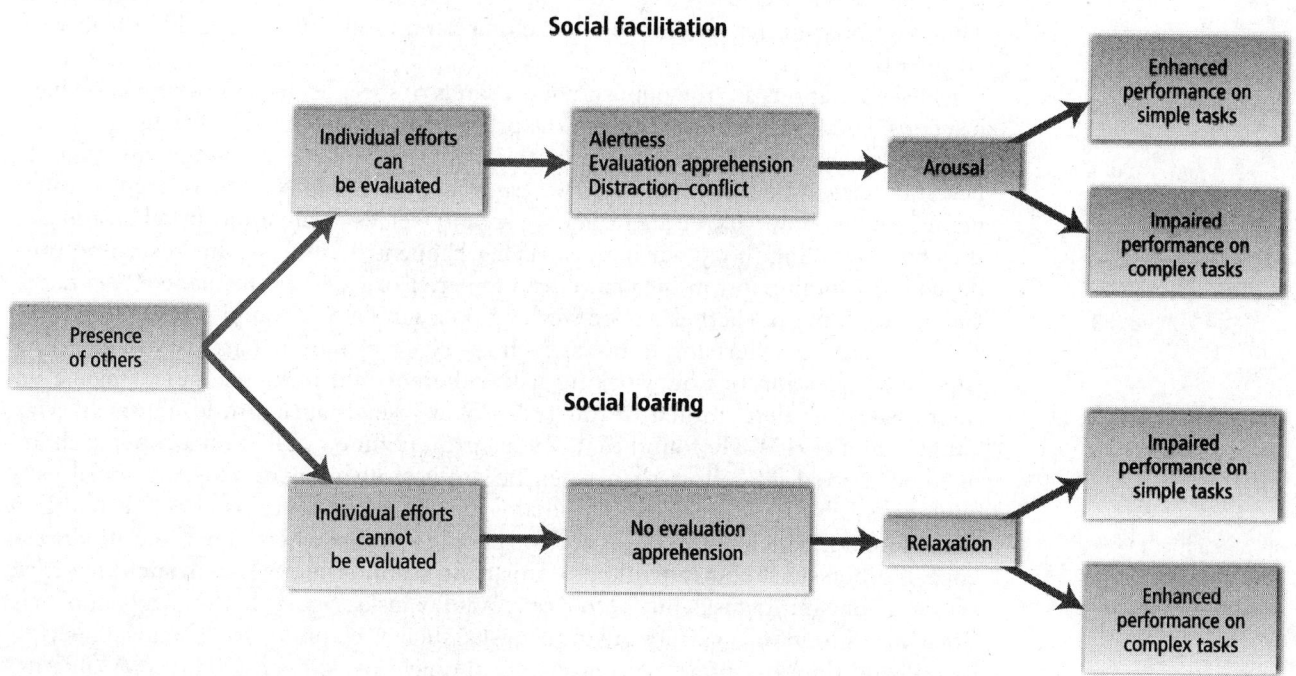

FIGURE 9.3

Social facilitation and social loafing.

The presence of others can lead to social facilitation or social loafing. The important variables that distinguish the two are evaluation, arousal, and the complexity of the tasks.

(Adapted from Cottrell, Wack, Sekerak, & Ritter, 1968)

> *Which of us ... is to do the hard and dirty work for the rest—and for what pay?*
>
> —John Ruskin

this arousal, however, are the same: When people are around other people, they do better on tasks that are simple and well learned, but they do worse on tasks that are complex and require them to learn something new.

Where, then, should you take your psychology exam? We recommend that you stay with your classmates, assuming you know the material well, so that it is relatively simple for you to recall it. The arousal produced by being elbow to elbow with your classmates should improve your performance. But when you study for an exam—that is, when you learn new material—you should do so by yourself, away from other people. In this situation, the arousal caused by others will make it more difficult to concentrate. And oh yes, it is not only the presence of real people who can influence our behavior—so can the presence of our favorite TV characters as well. In a recent study, college students performed a simple or complex task while a picture of their favorite TV character or some other TV character was displayed on a computer screen. When the TV character was people's favorite—such as George from *Grey's Anatomy*—it was as if a real person was in the room: People did better on the simple task but worse on the complex task. When the TV character wasn't people's favorite, their performance was unaffected (Gardner & Knowles, 2008).

Social Loafing: When the Presence of Others Relaxes Us
社会懈怠：他人在场使我们放松

When you take your psychology exam, your individual efforts will be evaluated (you will be graded on the test). This is typical of the research on social facilitation we have reviewed: People are working on something (either alone or in the presence of others), and their individual efforts are easily observed and evaluated. When people are in the presence of others, however, their individual efforts often cannot be distinguished from those of the people around them. Such is the case when you clap after a concert (no one can tell how loudly you are clapping) or when you play an instrument in a marching band (your instrument blends in with all the others).

These situations are the opposite of the kinds of social facilitation settings we have just considered. In social facilitation, the presence of others puts the spotlight on you, making you aroused. But if being with other people means we can merge into a group, becoming less noticeable than when we are alone, we should become relaxed. Because no one can tell how well we are doing, we should feel less evaluation apprehension and thus be less willing to try our hardest. What happens then? Will this relaxation produced by becoming lost in the crowd lead to better or worse performance? Again, the answer depends on whether we are working on a simple or a complex task.

Let's first consider simple tasks, such as trying to pull as hard as you can on a rope. The question of how working with others would influence performance on such a task was first studied in the 1880s by a French agricultural engineer, Max Ringelmann (1913). He found that when a group of men pulled on a rope, each individual exerted less effort than when he did it alone. A century later, social psychologists Bibb Latané, Kipling Williams, and Stephen Harkins (1979) called this **social loafing**, which is the tendency for people to relax when they are in the presence of others and their individual performance cannot be evaluated, such that they do worse on simple tasks but better on complex tasks. Social loafing in groups has since been found on a variety of simple tasks, such as clapping your hands, cheering loudly, and thinking of as many uses for an object as you can (Karau & Williams, 2001; Shepperd & Taylor, 1999).

What about complex tasks? Recall that when performance in a group cannot be identified, people become more relaxed. Recall also our earlier discussion of the effects of arousal on performance: Arousal enhances performance on simple tasks but impairs performance on complex tasks. By the same reasoning, becoming relaxed impairs performance on simple tasks—as we have just seen—but improves performance

Social Loafing
The tendency for people to relax when they are in the presence of others and their individual performance cannot be evaluated, such that they do worse on simple tasks but better on complex tasks.

on complex tasks (Jackson & Williams, 1985). This process is illustrated on the bottom part of Figure 9.3.

Gender and Cultural Differences in Social Loafing: Who Slacks Off the Most? 社会懈怠的性别和文化差异：谁最偷懒？

Jane and John are working with several classmates on a class project, and no one can assess their individual contributions. Who is more likely to slack off and let the other do most of the work, John or Jane? If you said John, you are probably right. In a review of more than 150 studies of social loafing, the tendency to loaf was found to be stronger in men than in women (Karau & Williams, 1993). As discussed in Chapter 5, women tend to be higher than men in *relational interdependence*, which is the tendency to focus on and care about personal relationships with other individuals. Perhaps it is this focus that makes women less likely to engage in social loafing when in groups (Eagly, 1987; Wood, 1987).

Research has also found that the tendency to loaf is stronger in Western cultures than Asian cultures, which may be due to the different self-definitions prevalent in these cultures (Karau & Williams, 1993). Asians are more likely to have an *interdependent view of the self*, which is a way of defining oneself in terms of relationships to other people (see Chapter 5). This self-definition may reduce the tendency toward social loafing when in groups. We should not, however, exaggerate these gender and cultural differences. Women and members of Asian cultures do engage in social loafing when in groups; they are just less likely to do so than men or members of Western cultures (Chang & Chen, 1995).

To summarize, you need to know two things to predict whether the presence of others will help or hinder your performance: whether your individual efforts can be evaluated and whether the task is simple or complex. If your performance can be evaluated, the presence of others will make you alert and aroused. This will lead to social facilitation effects, where people do better on simple tasks but worse on complex tasks (see the top of Figure 9.3). If your efforts cannot be evaluated (i.e., you are one cog in a machine), you are likely to become more relaxed. This leads to social loafing effects, where people do worse on simple tasks but better on complex ones (see the bottom of Figure 9.3).

These findings have numerous implications for the way in which groups should be organized. On the one hand, if you are a manager who wants your employees to work on a relatively simple problem, a little evaluation apprehension is not such a bad thing—it should improve performance. You shouldn't place your employees in groups where their individual performance cannot be observed, because social loafing (lowered performance on simple tasks) is likely to result. On the other hand, if you want your employees to work on a difficult, complex task, then lowering their evaluation apprehension—by placing them in groups in which their individual performance cannot be observed—is likely to result in better performance.

The robes and hoods of the Ku Klux Klan cloak its members in anonymity; their violent behavior is consistent with research on deindividuation.

Deindividuation: Getting Lost in the Crowd
去个体化：迷失在人群中

If you are going to make people more anonymous, you should be aware of other consequences of being a face in the crowd. So far, we have discussed the ways in which a group affects how hard people work and how successfully they learn new things. Being in a group can also cause **deindividuation**, which is the loosening of normal constraints

Deindividuation
The loosening of normal constraints on behavior when people can't be identified (such as when they are in a crowd)

on behavior when people can't be identified (such as when they are in a crowd; Lea, Spears, & de Groot, 2001). In other words, getting lost in a crowd can lead to an unleashing of behaviors that we would never dream of doing by ourselves. Throughout history, there have been many examples of groups of people committing horrendous acts that no individual would do on his or her own. The massacre at My Lai during the Vietnam War, when a group of American soldiers systematically murdered hundreds of defenseless women, children, and elderly men (see Chapter 8), was one such instance. In Europe, mobs of soccer fans sometimes attack and bludgeon each other. In the United States, hysterical fans at rock concerts have trampled each other to death. And the United States has a shameful history of whites—often cloaked in the anonymity of white robes—lynching African Americans.

Brian Mullen (1986) content-analyzed newspaper accounts of 60 lynchings committed in the United States between 1899 and 1946 and discovered an interesting fact: The more people there were in the mob, the greater the savagery and viciousness with which they killed their victims. Similarly, Robert Watson (1973) studied 24 cultures and found that warriors who hid their identities before going into battle—for example, by using face and body paint—were significantly more likely to kill, torture, or mutilate captive prisoners than warriors who did not hide their identities.

Deindividuation Makes People Feel Less Accountable Why does deindividuation lead to impulsive (and often violent) acts? One reason is that people feel less accountable for their actions because it reduces the likelihood that any individual will be singled out and blamed (Diener, 1980; Postmes & Spears, 1998; Zimbardo, 1970). In Harper Lee's novel *To Kill a Mockingbird*, for example, a mob of white Southerners assembled to lynch Tom Robinson, a black man falsely accused of rape. Here was a classic case of deindividuation: It was night, the men were dressed alike, and it was difficult to tell one from another. But then Scout, Atticus's 8-year-old daughter, recognized one of the farmers and greeted him by name. She unwittingly performed a brilliant social psychological intervention by increasing the extent to which the mob felt like individuals who were accountable for their actions. And indeed, the mob disbanded and went home at that point.

Deindividuation Increases Obedience to Group Norms In a meta-analysis of more than 60 studies, researchers found that becoming deindividuated also increases the extent to which people obey the group's norms (Postmes & Spears, 1998). Sometimes the norms of a specific group of which we are a member conflict with the norms of other groups or of society at large. When group members are together and deindividuated, they are more likely to act according to the group norms than the other norms. In *To Kill a Mockingbird*, for example, the norms of the lynch mob were to take the law into their own hands, but clearly these norms conflicted with other rules and laws (e.g., "Thou shalt not kill"). Because of the conditions promoting deindividuation, they were about to act on the group's norms and ignore the others until Scout stepped in and reminded them that they were individuals. Thus it is not just that deindividuation reduces the likelihood that one person will stand out and be blamed but also that it increases adherence to the specific group's norms.

If you can keep your head when all about you are losing theirs . . . .
—Rudyard Kipling, "If," 1909

Consequently, deindividuation does not always lead to aggressive or antisocial behavior—it depends on what the norm of the group is. Imagine that you are at a raucous college party at which everyone is dancing wildly to very loud music. To the extent that you feel deindividuated—it is dark, and you are dressed similarly to other people—you are more likely to join the group and let loose on the dance floor. Thus it is the specific norm of the group that determines whether deindividuation will lead to positive or negative behaviors (Gergen, Gergen, & Barton, 1973; Johnson & Downing, 1979). If the group is angry and the norm is to act violently, deindividuation will make people in the group act aggressively. If we are at a party and the norm is to eat a lot, being deindividuated will increase the likelihood that we will eat the entire bowl of guacamole.

Deindividuation in Cyberspace Have you ever participated in an Internet blog, in which people post anonymous comments about some issue or event? If so, you have probably witnessed deindividuation at work, whereby people feel less inhibited about what they write because of their anonymity. In January 2006, the *Washington Post* had to temporarily shut down its Web site post.blog (blogs.washingtonpost.com/washpostblog/) after the site was deluged with postings from angry readers, many of whom wrote obscene or insulting comments. The flap was over the claim by a *Washington Post* reporter that the lobbyist Jack Abramoff "had made substantial campaign contributions to both major parties" (Farhi, 2006, p. A8). The *Post* later published a correction, noting that Abramoff had contributed mostly to the Republican Party. But not before its Web site was flooded with responses not fit for a family newspaper.

Before blogs and Internet chat rooms became popular, angry readers could have written letters to the editor or vented their feelings to their coworkers at the water cooler. In both cases, their discourse would have likely been more civil, free of the profanities used by many of the people who posted comments on post.blog—in no small part because people are not anonymous in these settings (most newspapers require people to sign letters to the editor). The Internet has provided new ways in which people can communicate with each other anonymously, and just as research on deindividuation predicts, in these settings people often feel free to say things they would never dream of saying if they could be identified (Lee, 2004). There are advantages, of course, to free and open discussion of difficult topics, but the cost seems to be a reduction in common civility, as the editors of post.blog discovered.

Group Decisions: Are Two (or More) Heads Better Than One?
团体决策：两人（或者更多人）的决策一定优于单独决策吗？

We have just seen that the presence of other people influences individual behavior in a number of interesting ways. We turn now to one of the major functions of groups: to make decisions. Most important decisions in the world today are made by groups because it is assumed that groups make better decisions than individuals. In the American judicial system, many verdicts are determined by groups of individuals (juries), not single individuals (for a discussion of jury decision making, see Social Psychology in Action 3, "Social Psychology and the Law"). The United States Supreme Court is made up of nine justices, not just one member of the judiciary. Similarly, governmental and corporate decisions are often made by groups of people who meet to discuss the issues, and U.S. presidents have a cabinet and the National Security Council to advise them.

> *Nor is the people's judgement always true: The most may err as grossly as the few.*
>
> —John Dryden, *Absalom and Achitophel*, 1682

Is it true that two (or more) heads are better than one? Most of us assume the answer is yes. A lone individual may be subject to all sorts of whims and biases, whereas several people together can exchange ideas, catch each other's errors, and reach better decisions. We have all taken part in group decisions in which we listened to someone else and thought to ourselves, "Hmm, that's a really good point—I never would have thought of that." In general, groups do better than individuals if they rely on the person with the most expertise (Davis & Harless, 1996), and if people are motivated to search for the answer that is best for the entire group and not just for themselves (De Dreu, Nijstad, & van Knippenberg, 2008). Sometimes, though, two or more heads are not better than one, or at least no better than two heads working alone (Kerr & Tindale, 2004). Several factors can cause groups to make worse decisions than individuals.

Process Loss: When Group Interactions Inhibit Good Problem Solving 过程损失：团体互动抑制了良好的解决办法

One problem is that a group will do well only if the most talented member can convince the others that he or she is right—which is not always easy, given that many of us bear a strong resemblance to mules when it comes to admitting we are wrong

(Henry, 1995; Laughlin, 1980; Maier & Solem, 1952). You undoubtedly know what it's like to try to convince a group to follow your idea, be faced with opposition and disbelief, and then have to sit there and watch the group make the wrong decision. This is called **process loss**, which is any aspect of group interaction that inhibits good problem solving (Hurley & Allen, 2007; Steiner, 1972). Process loss can occur for a number of reasons. Groups might not try hard enough to find out who the most competent member is and instead rely on someone who really doesn't know what he or she is talking about. The most competent member might find it difficult to disagree with everyone else in the group (recall our discussion of normative social pressures in Chapter 8). Other causes of process loss involve communication problems within the group—in some groups, people don't listen to each other; in others, one person is allowed to dominate the discussion while the others tune out (Sorkin, Hays, & West, 2001; Watson, Johnson, Kumar, & Critelli, 1998).

Failure to Share Unique Information Another interesting example of process loss is the tendency for groups to focus on what its members already know in common, failing to discuss information that only some members have (Geitemeyer & Schulz-Hardt, 2003; Stasser & Titus, 1985; Wittenbaum & Park, 2001). In any group, members share some common knowledge but also know unique things not shared by other members. Suppose, for example, that you were meeting with three other people to decide whether to support a particular candidate for Student Council president. You all share some information about the candidate, such as the fact that she was president of her sophomore class and is an economics major. But each of you has unique information as well. Maybe you are the only one who knows that she was punished for underage drinking in her first-year dorm, whereas one of the other group members is the only one who knows that she volunteers every week at a local homeless shelter. Obviously, the four of you will make the best decision if you share with each other everything you know about the candidate. But there is a funny thing about groups: They tend to focus on the information they share and ignore facts known to only some members of the group. One study, for example, simulated the situation we just described, in which students decided who was most qualified to be Student Council president (Stasser & Titus, 1985). In the shared information condition, each participant was given the same packet of information to read, data indicating that candidate A was the best choice for office. As seen at the top of Figure 9.4, all participants in this condition knew that candidate A had eight positive qualities and four negative qualities, making him superior to the other candidates. Not surprisingly, when this group met to discuss the candidates, almost all of the members chose candidate A.

In the unshared information condition, each participant received a different packet of information. As seen at the bottom of Figure 9.4, each person knew that candidate A had two positive qualities and four negative qualities; however, the two positive qualities cited in each person's packet were unique—different from those listed in other participants' packets. Everyone learned that candidate A had the same four negative qualities; thus if the participants shared with each other the information that was in their packets, they would learn that candidate A had a total of eight positive qualities and four negative qualities—just as people in the shared information condition knew. Most of the groups in the unshared information condition never realized that candidate A had more good than bad qualities, however, because they focused on the information they shared rather than on the information they did not. As a result, few of these groups chose candidate A.

Subsequent research has focused on ways to get groups to focus more on unshared information (Campbell & Stasser, 2006; Postmes, Spears, & Cihangir, 2001; Scholten, Knippenberg, Nijstad, & De Dreu, 2007; Stasser & Birchmeier, 2003). Unshared information is more likely to be brought up later in the discussion, suggesting that group discussions should last long enough to get beyond what everyone already knows (Fraidin, 2004; Larson, Christensen, Franz, & Abbott, 1998). Another approach is to assign different group members to specific areas of expertise so that they know that

Process Loss
Any aspect of group interaction that inhibits good problem solving

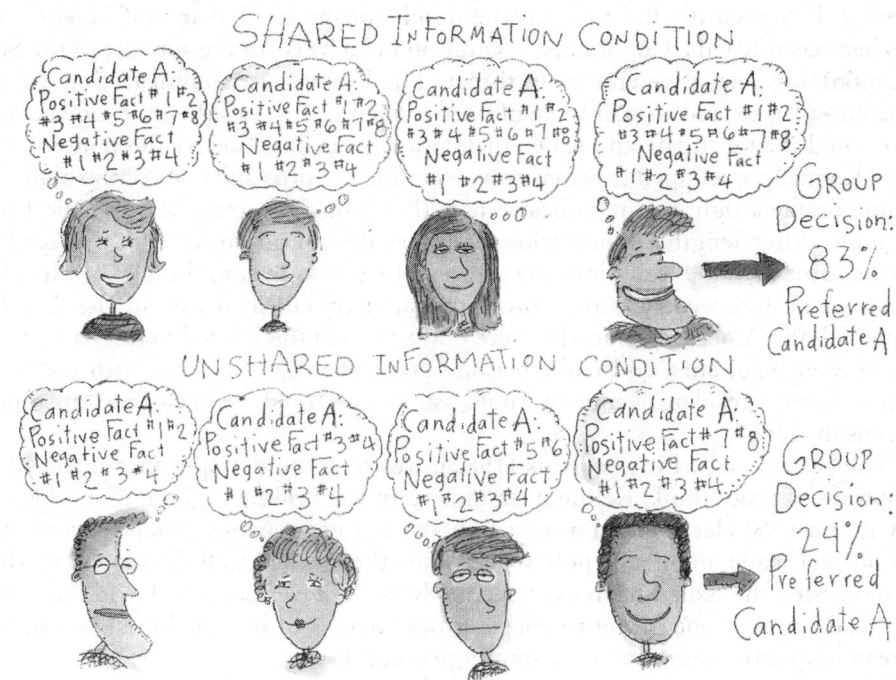

FIGURE 9.4

When people are in groups, do they share information that only they know?

Participants in a study met to discuss candidates for an election. In the shared information condition (top half of figure), each person was given the same positive and negative facts about the candidates. Candidate A was clearly the superior candidate, and most groups preferred him. In the unshared information condition (bottom half of figure), each person was given the same four negative facts about candidate A as well as two unique positive facts. In discussion, these people focused on the information they all shared and failed to mention their unique information; these groups were less likely to see candidate A as superior.

(Adapted from Stasser & Titus, 1985)

they alone are responsible for certain types of information. If only one doctor's job is to monitor the blood tests, he or she is more likely to bring up this information and other members are more likely to pay attention to it (Stasser, Stewart, & Wittenbaum, 1995; Stewart & Stasser, 1995).

This last lesson has been learned by many couples, who know to rely on each other's memories for different kinds of information. One member of a couple might be responsible for remembering the times of social engagements, whereas the other might be responsible for remembering when to pay the bills (Wegner, Erber, & Raymond, 1991). The combined memory of two people that is more efficient than the memory of either individual is called **transactive memory** (Hollingshead, 2001; Wegner, 1995). By learning to specialize their memories and knowing what their partner is responsible for, couples often do quite well in remembering important information. The same can be true of groups, if they develop a system whereby different people are responsible for remembering different parts of a task (Ellis, Porter, & Wolverton, 2008; Lewis, Belliveau, Herndon, & Keller, 2007; Moreland, 1999). In sum, the tendency for groups to fail to share important information known to only some of the members can be overcome if people learn who is responsible for what kinds of information and take the time to discuss these unshared data (Stasser, 2000).

Groupthink: Many Heads, One Mind Earlier we mentioned that group cohesiveness can get in the way of clear thinking and good decision making. Using real-world events, Irving Janis (1972, 1982) developed an influential theory of group decision making that he called **groupthink**, a kind of thinking in which maintaining group cohesiveness and solidarity is more important than considering the facts in a realistic manner. According to Janis's theory, groupthink is most likely to occur when certain preconditions are met, such as when the group is highly cohesive, isolated from contrary opinions, and ruled by a directive leader who makes his or her wishes known. One of his examples was the decision by President John F. Kennedy and his advisers to invade Cuba. It might seem odd, from our twenty-first-century perspective, that a tropical island 90 miles off the coast of Florida was considered a major

The only sin which we never forgive in each other is difference of opinion.

—Ralph Waldo Emerson, *Society and Solitude*, 1870

Transactive Memory

The combined memory of two people that is more efficient than the memory of either individual

Groupthink

A kind of thinking in which maintaining group cohesiveness and solidarity is more important than considering the facts in a realistic manner

threat to U.S. security. But this was the middle of the Cold War, and Fidel Castro, who had recently led a Communist revolution in Cuba (with the support of the Soviet Union), was seen as an enormous threat. The Eisenhower administration had formulated a plan to land a small force of CIA-trained Cuban exiles on the Cuban coast, who would then instigate and lead a mass uprising against Castro. Soon after taking office Kennedy assembled his advisers to examine the pros and cons of the plan. The group became a tightly knit, cohesive unit that brought a great deal of expertise to the topic. After lengthy deliberation, they decided to go ahead, and on April 17, 1961, a force of 1,400 exiles invaded an area of Cuba known as the Bay of Pigs. Disaster quickly followed. Castro's forces captured or killed nearly all the invaders. Friendly Latin American countries were outraged that the United States had invaded one of their neighbors, and Cuba became even more closely allied with the Soviet Union. Later, President Kennedy would ask, "How could we have been so stupid?" (Sorenson, 1966).

The reason, according to Janis (1982), was that the decision met many of the symptoms of groupthink. Kennedy and his team were riding high on their close victory in the 1960 election and were a tight-knit, homogeneous group. Because they had not yet made any major policy decisions, they lacked well-developed methods for discussing the issues. Moreover, Kennedy made it clear that he favored the invasion, and he asked the group to consider only details of how it should be executed instead of questioning whether it should proceed at all.

When these preconditions of groupthink are met, several symptoms appear (see Figure 9.5). The group begins to feel that it is invulnerable and can do no wrong. People do not voice contrary views (they exercise self-censorship) because they are afraid of ruining the group's high morale or because they fear being criticized by the others. For example, Arthur Schlesinger, one of Kennedy's advisers, reported that he had severe doubts about the Bay of Pigs invasion but did not express these concerns during the discussions out of a fear that "others would regard it as presumptuous of him, a college professor, to take issue with august heads of major government institutions" (Janis, 1982, p. 32). If anyone does voice a contrary viewpoint, the rest of the group is quick to criticize, pressuring the person to conform to the majority view. Schlesinger did share some of his doubts with Dean Rusk, the secretary of state. When Robert Kennedy, the attorney general and the president's brother, got wind of this, he took Schlesinger aside at a party and told him that the president had made up his mind to go ahead with the invasion and that his friends should support him. This kind of behavior creates an illusion of unanimity, where it looks as if everyone agrees. On the day the group voted on whether to invade, President Kennedy asked all those present for their opinion—except Arthur Schlesinger.

The perilous state of groupthink causes people to implement an inferior decision-making process. As seen at the far right in Figure 9.5 for example, the group does not consider the full range of alternatives, does not develop contingency plans, and does not adequately consider the risks of its preferred choice. Can you think of other governmental decisions that were plagued by groupthink? Janis (1972, 1982) discusses several, such as the failure of the U.S. military commanders in Pearl Harbor to anticipate the Japanese attack in 1941; President Truman's decision to invade North Korea in 1950, despite

"All those in favor say 'Aye.'"
"Aye." "Aye." "Aye." "Aye."
"Aye." "Aye."

© The New Yorker Collection, 1979 Henry Martin from cartoonbank.com. All Rights Reserved.

Antecedents of groupthink	Symptoms of groupthink	Defective decision making
The group is highly cohesive: The group is valued and attractive, and people very much want to be members. **Group isolation:** The group is isolated, protected from hearing alternative viewpoints. **A directive leader:** The leader controls the discussion and makes his or her wishes known. **High stress:** The members perceive threats to the group. **Poor decision-making procedures:** No standard methods to consider alternative viewpoints.	**Illusion of invulnerability:** The group feels it is invincible and can do no wrong. **Belief in the moral correctness of the group:** "God is on our side." **Stereotyped views of out-group:** Opposing sides are viewed in a simplistic, stereotyped manner. **Self-censorship:** People decide themselves not to voice contrary opinions so as not to "rock the boat." **Direct pressure on dissenters to conform:** If people do voice contrary opinions, they are pressured by others to conform to the majority. **Illusion of unanimity:** An illusion is created that everyone agrees, for example, by not calling on people known to disagree. **Mindguards:** Group members protect the leader from contrary viewpoints.	Incomplete survey of alternatives Failure to examine risks of the favored alternative Poor information search Failure to develop contingency plans

FIGURE 9.5

Groupthink: Antecedents, symptoms, and consequences.

Under some conditions, maintaining group cohesiveness and solidarity is more important to a group than considering the facts in a realistic manner (see "Antecedents"). When this happens, certain symptoms of groupthink occur, such as the illusion of invulnerability (see "Symptoms"). These symptoms lead to defective decision making.

(Adapted from Janis, 1982)

explicit warnings from the Chinese that they would attack with massive force; President Johnson's decision to escalate the Vietnam War in the mid-1960s; and the Watergate coverup by President Nixon and his advisers. A nonpolitical example was the decision in 1986 by NASA to go ahead with the launch of the space shuttle *Challenger* despite the objections of engineers who said that the freezing temperatures presented a severe danger to the rubber O-ring seals. The seals failed during the launch, causing the rocket to explode, killing all aboard. All these decisions were plagued by many of the symptoms and consequences of groupthink, outlined in Figure 9.5 (Esser & Lindoerfer, 1989).

A lot of water has gone over the dam since the theory of groupthink was first proposed, and a number of researchers have put it to the test (Paulus, 1998; Mullen, Anthony, Salas, & Driskell, 1994; Tetlock, Peterson, McGuire, Chang, & Field, 1992; Turner, Pratkanis, Probasco, & Leve, 2006; Turner, Pratkanis, & Struckman, 2007). The upshot of this research is that defective group decision making may be more common than the original theory assumed. The groupthink theory held that a specific set of conditions had to be met in order for groupthink to occur, namely the antecedents listed on the left side of Figure 9.5 (e.g., the group has to be highly cohesive). It now appears that groupthink can occur even when some of these antecedents are missing. It may be enough for people to identify strongly with the group, have clear norms about what the group is supposed to do, and have low confidence that the group can solve the problem (Baron, 2005; Henningsen, Henningsen, Eden, & Cruz, 2006). It is thus all the more important that groups be aware of the potential for groupthink and take steps to avoid it.

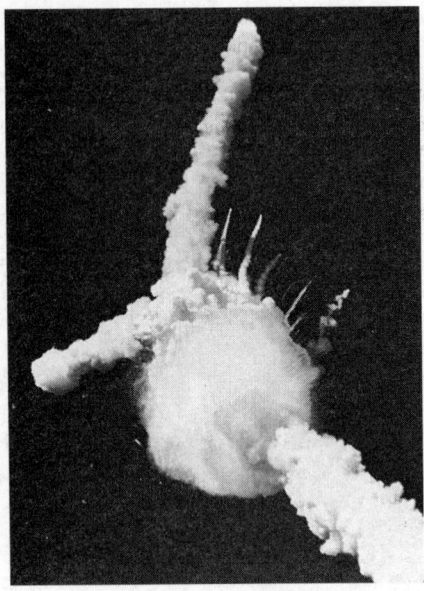

The decision to launch the space shuttle *Challenger*, which tragically exploded due to defective O-ring seals, appears to have been the result of groupthink on the part of NASA officials, who disregarded engineers' concerns about the quality of the seals.

Avoiding the Groupthink Trap A wise leader can take several steps to ensure that his or her group is immune to the groupthink style of decision making (Flowers, 1977; McCauley, 1989; Zimbardo & Andersen, 1993).

- **Remain impartial.** The leader should not take a directive role but should remain impartial.
- **Seek outside opinions.** The leader should invite outside opinions from people who are not members of the group and who are thus less concerned with maintaining group cohesiveness.
- **Create subgroups.** The leader should divide the group into subgroups that first meet separately and then meet together to discuss their different recommendations.
- **Seek anonymous opinions.** The leader might also take a secret ballot or ask group members to write down their opinions anonymously; doing so would ensure that people give their true opinions, uncensored by a fear of recrimination from the group.

Fortunately, President Kennedy learned from his mistakes with the Bay of Pigs decision, and when he encountered his next major foreign policy decision, the Cuban missile crisis, he took many of these steps to avoid groupthink. When his advisers met to decide what to do about the discovery that the Soviet Union had placed nuclear-tipped missiles in Cuba, pointed towards the United States, Kennedy often absented himself from the group so as not to inhibit discussion. He also brought in outside experts (e.g., Adlai Stevenson) who were not members of the in-group. That Kennedy successfully negotiated the removal of the Soviet missiles was almost certainly due to the improved methods of group decision making he adopted.

CONNECTIONS 链 接

Was the Decision to Invade Iraq a Result of Groupthink?
出兵伊拉克的决定是团体思维的结果吗?

It is risky, perhaps, to analyze the decision to invade Iraq without the perspective of time. We leave it to future historians to assess the wisdom of President Bush's decision to wage war with Iraq and whether it was the result of groupthink processes. Here we offer the opinion of some current politicians and political observers, organized in terms of the antecedents, symptoms, and consequences of groupthink (see Figure 9.5):

Antecedents of Groupthink

Highly Cohesive Group. President Bush was known for having a tightly knit, cohesive inner circle of advisers, many of whom were long-time friends who were reluctant to criticize the president (Baker, 2005).

High Stress. No one knew, in the aftermath of the 9/11 terrorists attacks, whether other attacks would occur soon. Some thought the White House was the next target.

Poor Decision-Making Procedures. Scott McClelland, President Bush's former press secretary, notes that "during the buildup to war, the president's advisers allowed his own hands to be tied, putting Bush in a position where *avoiding* conflict was more difficult than launching it" (McClelland, 2008, p. 143).

Symptoms of Groupthink

Belief in the Moral Correctness of the Group. Madeleine Albright, who was secretary of state under President Bill Clinton, said that she "worked for two presidents who were men of faith, and they did not make their religious views part of American policy.... President Bush's certitude about what he believes in, and the division between good and evil, is, I think, different... The absolute truth is what makes Bush so worrying to some of us" (Goddard, 2006).

Illusion of Unanimity. McClelland, the former press secretary, notes that once President Bush made his view known "it was rarely questioned," because "that is what Bush expected and made known to his top advisers" (p. 128). There was not quite an illusion of unanimity, because Secretary of State Colin Powell voiced doubts about the war. But he was the only adviser to do so. National Security Adviser Condoleezza Rice, says McClelland, was "more interested in accommodating the president's instincts and ideas than in questioning them or educating him" (McClelland, 2008, p. 144).

Mindguards. Paul O'Neill, the former treasury secretary in the Bush administration, observed that Vice President Cheney and others were "a praetorian guard that encircled the president" and shielded him from views that disagreed with the administration ("Bush sought 'way' to invade Iraq," 2004).

Defective Decision Making

Poor Information Search. Several members of Congress and officials in the intelligence community argued that the Bush administration engaged in the "cherry picking" of intelligence, focusing only on data that supported the decision to invade Iraq (Pincus, 2006). McClelland agrees, noting that "as the campaign [to sell the war] accelerated, caveats and qualifications were downplayed or dropped altogether. Contradictory intelligence was largely ignored or simply disregarded" (p. 144). Even worse, says McClelland, people in the Bush administration began to believe their own claims; that is, they "confused their propaganda campaign with the realities of the war-making campaign" (p. 135).

Failure to Develop Contingency Plans. The former press secretary also believes that the Bush team failed to develop contingency plans in case the war did not go as planned: "The White House forestalled any debate about the fundamental goals and long-term plans for such an invasion... the president and his advisers avoided having to discuss the big issues of what would happen after the invasion" (p. 143).

To be fair, there are other ways in which the decision to invade Iraq did not meet the conditions of groupthink. A key antecedent is that there be a highly directive leader, and President Bush does not appear to have been a controlling, intimidating leader who dominated group discussions. We leave it to future historians to decide whether, on balance, the decision to invade Iraq resulted from sound decision-making processes or suffered from the consequences of groupthink.

Group Polarization: Going to Extremes 团体极化：走向极端

Maybe you are willing to grant that groups sometimes make poor decisions. Surely, though, groups will usually make less risky decisions than a lone individual will—one individual might be willing to bet the ranch on a risky proposition, but if others help make the decision, they will interject reason and moderation. Or will they? The question of whether groups or individuals make more risky decisions has been examined in numerous studies. Participants are typically given the Choice Dilemmas Questionnaire (CDQ), a series of stories that presents a dilemma for the main character and asks the reader to choose how much probability of success there would have to be before the reader would recommend the risky alternative (Kogan & Wallach, 1964). An example of a CDQ item about a chess player appears in the following Try It! exercise. People choose their answers alone and then meet in a group to discuss the options, arriving at a unanimous group decision for each dilemma.

Many of the initial studies found, surprisingly, that groups make riskier decisions than individuals do. For example, when deciding alone, people said that the chess player should make the risky gambit only if there were at least a 30 percent chance of success. But after discussing the problem with others in a group, people said that the chess player should go for it even if there were only a 10 percent chance of success (Wallach, Kogan, & Bem, 1962). Findings such as these became known as the *risky shift*. But further research has made clear that such shifts are not the full story. It turns out that groups tend to make decisions that are more extreme in the same direction as the individual's initial predispositions, which happened to be risky in the case of the chess problem. What would happen if people were initially inclined to be conservative? In cases such as these, groups tend to make even more conservative decisions than individuals do.

Consider this problem: Roger, a young married man with two children, has a secure but low-paying job and no savings. Someone gives him a tip about a stock that will triple in value if the company's new product is successful but will plummet if the new product fails. Should Roger sell his life insurance policy and invest in the company? Most people recommend a safe course of action here: Roger should buy the stock only if the new product is very certain to succeed. When they talk it over in a group, they become even more conservative, deciding that the new product would have to have a nearly 100 percent chance of success before they would recommend that Roger buy stock in the company.

TRY IT! Choice Dilemmas Questionnaire 试一试！选择困境问卷

You'll need four or five friends for this exercise. First, copy the following questionnaire and give it to each of your friends to complete individually, without talking to anyone else. Then bring them all together and ask them to discuss the dilemma and arrive at a unanimous decision. They should try to reach a consensus such that every member of the group agrees at least partly with the final decision. Finally, compare people's initial decisions (made alone) with the group decision. Who made the riskier decisions on average, people deciding by themselves or the group?

The Choice Dilemmas Questionnaire

A low-ranked participant in a national chess tournament, playing an early match against a highly favored opponent, has the choice of attempting or not attempting a deceptive but risky maneuver that might lead to quick victory if it is successful or almost certain defeat if it fails. Indicate the lowest probability of success that you would accept before recommending that the chess player play the risky move.

_____ 1 chance in 10 of succeeding

_____ 3 chances in 10 of succeeding

_____ 5 chances in 10 of succeeding

_____ 7 chances in 10 of succeeding

_____ 9 chances in 10 of succeeding

_____ I would not recommend taking the chance.

Remember, groups tend to make riskier decisions than individuals on problems such as these. Did you find the same thing? Why or why not? If the group did make a riskier decision, was it due more to the persuasive arguments interpretation discussed in the text, the social comparison interpretation, or both?

(Adapted from Wallach, Kogan, & Bem, 1962)

The tendency for groups to make decisions that are more extreme than the initial inclination of its members—toward greater risk if people's initial tendency is to be risky and toward greater caution if people's initial tendency is to be cautious—is known as **group polarization** (Brown, 1965; Palmer & Loveland, 2008; Rodrigo & Ato, 2002; Teger & Pruitt, 1967)

Group polarization occurs for two main reasons. According to the persuasive arguments interpretation, all individuals bring to the group a set of arguments, some of which other individuals have not considered, supporting their initial recommendation. For example, one person might stress that cashing in the life insurance policy is an unfair risk to Roger's children, should he die prematurely. Another person might not have considered this possibility; thus he or she becomes more conservative as well. A series of studies supports this interpretation of group polarization, whereby each member presents arguments that other members had not considered (Burnstein & Sentis, 1981; Burnstein & Vinokur, 1977).

According to the social comparison interpretation, when people discuss an issue in a group, they first check out how everyone else feels. What does the group value—being risky or being cautious? To be liked, many people then take a position that is similar to everyone else's but a little more extreme. In this way, the individual supports the group's values and also presents himself or herself in a positive light—a person in the vanguard, an impressive thinker. Both the persuasive arguments and the social comparison interpretations of group polarization have received research support (Blaskovich, Ginsburg, & Veach, 1975; Brown, 1986; Isenberg, 1986; Zuber, Crott, & Werner, 1992).

Leadership in Groups 团体中的领导

A critical question we have not yet considered is the role of the leader in group decision making. The question of what makes a great leader has intrigued psychologists, historians, and political scientists for some time (Bass, 1990; Chemers, 2000; Fiedler, 1967; Hogg, 2007; Hollander, 1985; Klenke, 1996; Simonton, 1987). One of the best-known answers to this question is the **great person theory**, which maintains that certain key personality traits make a person a good leader, regardless of the nature of the situation the leader faces.

If the great person theory is true, we ought to be able to isolate the key aspects of personality that make someone a great leader. Is it a combination of intelligence, charisma, and courage? Is it better to be introverted or extroverted? Should we add a dollop of ruthlessness to the mix as well, as Niccolò Machiavelli suggested in 1513 in his famous treatise on leadership, *The Prince*? Or do highly moral people make the best leaders?

> *There is properly no history, only biography.*
>
> —Ralph Waldo Emerson, *Essays, History*, 1841

Leadership and Personality Numerous studies have found weak relationships between personality and leadership abilities. Compared to nonleaders, for example, leaders tend to be slightly more intelligent, extroverted, driven by the desire for power, charismatic, socially skilled, open to new experiences, confident in their leadership abilities, less neurotic, and have a moderate degree of assertiveness (Ames & Flynn, 2007; Chemers, Watson, & May, 2000; Hogg, 2007; Judge, Bono, Ilies, & Gerhardt, 2002; Van Vugt, 2006). What is most telling, however, is the absence of strong relationships. Surprisingly few personality characteristics correlate strongly with leadership effectiveness, and the relationships that have been found tend to be modest. For example, Dean Simonton (1987, 2001) gathered information about 100 personal attributes of all U.S. presidents, such as their family backgrounds, educational experiences, occupations, and personalities. Only 3 of these variables—height, family size, and the number of books a president published before taking office—correlated with how effective the presidents were in office. Tall presidents, those from small families, and those who have published books are most likely to become effective leaders, as rated by historians. The other 97 characteristics, including personality traits, were not related to leadership effectiveness at all.

Group Polarization
The tendency for groups to make decisions that are more extreme than the initial inclinations of its members

Great Person Theory
The idea that certain key personality traits make a person a good leader, regardless of the situation

What determines whether someone is a great leader, such as Martin Luther King, Jr.? Is it a certain constellation of personality traits, or is it necessary to have the right person in the right situation at the right time?

Transactional Leaders
Leaders who set clear, short-term goals and reward people who meet them

Transformational Leaders
Leaders who inspire followers to focus on common, long-term goals

Contingency Theory of Leadership
The idea that leadership effectiveness depends both on how task-oriented or relationship-oriented the leader is and on the amount of control and influence the leader has over the group

Task-Oriented Leader
A leader who is concerned more with getting the job done than with workers' feelings and relationships

Relationship-Oriented Leader
A leader who is concerned primarily with workers' feelings and relationships

Leadership Styles Although great leaders may not have specific kinds of personalities, they do appear to adopt specific kinds of leadership styles. **Transactional leaders** set clear, short-term goals and reward people who meet them. **Transformational leaders**, on the other hand, inspire followers to focus on common, long-term goals (Bass, 1998; Burns, 1978). Transactional leaders do a good job of making sure the needs of the organization are met and that things run smoothly. It is transformational leaders, however, who think outside the box, identify important long-term goals, and inspire their followers to toil hard to meet these goals.

Interestingly, these leadership styles are not closely linked with personality traits; it is not as if people are "born" to be one or the other type of leader (Judge, Colbert, & Ilies, 2004). Further, these styles are not mutually exclusive; in fact, the most effective leader is one who adopts both styles (Judge & Piccolo, 2004). If no one was minding the day-to-day operation of an organization, and people were not being rewarded for meeting short-term objectives, the organization would suffer. At the same time it is important to have a charismatic leader who inspires people to think about long-term objectives as well.

The Right Person in the Right Situation As you know by now, one of the most important tenets of social psychology is that to understand social behavior, it is not enough to consider personality traits alone—we must take the social situation into account as well. The inadequacy of the great person theory does not mean that personal characteristics are irrelevant to good leadership. Instead, being good social psychologists, we should consider both the nature of the leader and the situation in which the leading takes place.

A business leader, for example, can be highly successful in some situations, but not in others. Consider Steve Jobs, who, at age 21, founded the Apple Computer Company with Stephen Wozniak. Jobs was anything but an M.B.A. type of corporate leader. A product of the 1960s' counterculture, he turned to computers only after experimenting with LSD, traveling to India, and living on a communal fruit farm. In the days when there were no personal computers, Jobs's offbeat style was well suited to starting a new industry. Within 5 years, he was the leader of a billion-dollar company. But Jobs's unorthodox style was ill-suited to managing a large corporation in a competitive market. Apple's earnings began to suffer, and in 1985, Jobs was forced out (Patton, 1989). Undeterred, Jobs cofounded Pixar in 1986, the first major company to make computer-generated animation, and sold it to the Disney Company in 2006 for $7.4 billion. And in the 1990s the Apple company faced some of the same technological challenges it did at its inception, having to revamp the operating system for its Macintosh computers and regain market share. Whom did Apple hire to lead this new challenge? Steve Jobs, of course (Markoff, 1996).

A comprehensive theory of leadership thus needs to focus on characteristics of the leader, the followers, and the situation. The best-known theory of this type is the **contingency theory of leadership**, which argues that leadership effectiveness depends both on how task-oriented or relationship-oriented the leader is and on the amount of control and influence the leader has over the group (Fiedler, 1967, 1978). There are basically two kinds of leaders, the theory argues: those who are **task-oriented**, concerned more with getting the job done than with workers' feelings and relationships, and those who are **relationship-oriented**, concerned more with workers' feelings and relationships. Task-oriented leaders do well in *high-control work situations*, when the leader has excellent interpersonal relationships with subordinates, his or her position in the company is clearly perceived as powerful, and the work needing to be done by the group is structured and well defined. They also do well in *low-control work situations*, when the leader has poor relationships with subordinates and the work needing to be done is not clearly defined. What about relationship-oriented leaders? They are most effective in *moderate-control work situations*. Under these conditions, the wheels are turning fairly smoothly, but some attention to the squeakiness caused by poor relationships and hurt feelings is needed. The leader who can soothe such feelings will

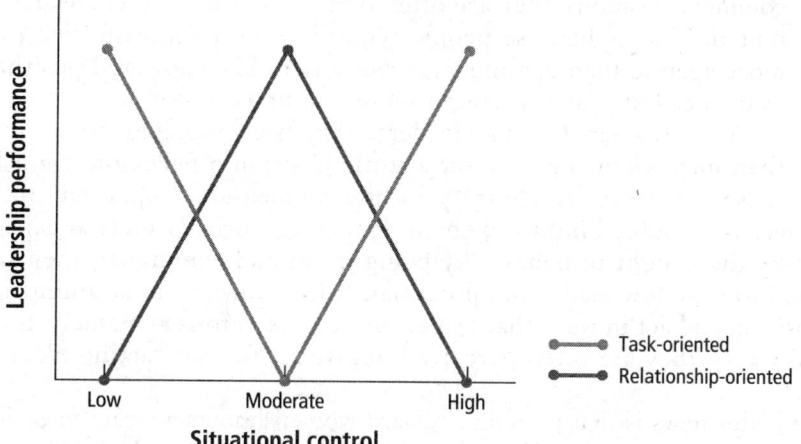

FIGURE 9.6

Fiedler's contingency theory of leadership.

According to Fiedler, task-oriented leaders perform best when situational control is high or low, whereas relationship-oriented leaders perform best when situational control is moderate.

be most successful (see Figure 9.6). The contingency theory of leadership has been supported in studies of numerous types of leaders, including business managers, college administrators, military commanders, and postmasters (Chemers, 2000; Peters, Hartke, & Pohlmann, 1985; Schriesheim, Tepper, & Tetrault, 1994; Van Vugt & DeCremer, 1999).

Gender and Leadership An old adage says that because of sex discrimination, a woman has to be "twice as good as a man" to advance in an organization. No doubt barriers to advancement are breaking down. In the past few years, for example, a woman (Hillary Clinton) came close to winning the Democratic nomination for president, and a woman (Sarah Palin) ran for vice president on the Republican ticket for the first time. Unfortunately, the barriers have not completely disappeared. In 2008, only 12 of the CEOs of Fortune 500 companies were women. More than 85 percent of the boards of directors of these companies were men, as were more than 84 percent of the corporate officers (Catalyst, 2008). Things are not much different in Europe. In the top 50 companies in the European Union, only 11 percent of the top executives are women (European Commission, 2007).

Not only is it difficult for women to attain top leadership positions in business, but also when they do they are often put in precarious positions where it is difficult to succeed. Michelle Ryan and her colleagues have identified what they call a "glass cliff" (Ryan, Haslam, Hersby, Kulich, & Atkins, 2008). Even when women have broken through the "glass ceiling" into top leadership positions, they are more likely than men to be put in charge of units that are in crisis and in which the risk of failure is high. Ryan and her colleagues found this to be true in studies of hiring in real-world companies, as well as in controlled laboratory studies in which people read descriptions of companies and recommended people for leadership positions. Participants were more likely to recommend a woman when an organziational unit was in crisis and a man when the unit was running smoothly—which makes it more likely that women will fail in their leadership positions.

One reason for the "glass cliff" is that women are perceived as better at crisis management, particularly when there are interpersonal problems that need to be dealt with. For example, women are expected to be more *communal* (concerned with the welfare of others, warm, helpful, kind, affectionate) and men are expected to be more *agentic* (assertive, controlling, dominant, independent, self-confident). But these expectations can have some pernicious effects in the way that women are evaluated (Carli & Eagly, 1999; Eagly, Johannesen-Schmidt, & van Engen, 2003; Eagly & Karau, 2002; Eagly, Karau, & Makhijani, 1995). If women behave in the way they are "supposed" to according to societal norms (namely, in a

Research shows that women seeking leadership roles can find themselves in a double bind. If they conform to society's expectations about how they ought to behave, by being warm and communal, they are often perceived to have low leadership potential. If they become leaders and act in ways that leaders are expected to act, namely in agentic, forceful ways, they are often perceived negatively for not "acting like a woman should."

> *Leadership cannot really be taught. It can only be learned.*
>
> —Harold Geneen, 1984

communal fashion), they are often perceived as having less leadership potential. This is because people typically expect successful leaders to be more agentic than communal, especially in high-powered positions such as the head of a large corporation or a military leader.

After women become leaders, they are evaluated more negatively than men when they exhibit agentic leadership behavior, again because these behaviors are contrary to how women are "supposed" to behave. Thus there is a double bind for women: If they conform to societal expectations about how they ought to behave, by being warm and communal, they are often perceived to have low leadership potential. If they succeed in attaining a leadership position and act in ways that leaders are expected to act—namely, in agentic, forceful ways—they are often perceived negatively for not "acting like a woman should."

The better news is that prejudice toward women leaders appears to be lessening over time. In a Gallup poll conducted in 1953, 66 percent of people said that they preferred a man as a boss and only 5 percent preferred a woman (25 percent had no preference). In a similar poll conducted in 2002, 32 percent preferred a man as a boss, 19 percent preferred a woman, and 49 percent had no preference. Further, there is some evidence that people are becoming more accepting of women who act in stereotypical "male" ways (Twenge, 1997) and that there is a growing recognition that effective leaders must be able to act in stereotypical female (communal) ways as well as stereotypical male (agentic) ways (Eagly & Karau, 2002).

> *I wonder men dare trust themselves with men.*
>
> —William Shakespeare, *The Life of Timon of Athens*

Conflict and Cooperation 冲突与合作

We have just examined how people work together to make decisions; in these situations, group members have a common goal. Often, however, people have incompatible goals, placing them in conflict with each other. This can be true of two individuals, such as romantic partners who disagree about who should clean the kitchen, or two groups, such as a labor union and company management who disagree over wages and working conditions. It can also be true of nations, such as the long-standing conflict between Israel and its Arab neighbors or between the Shiites, Sunnis, and Kurds in Iraq. The opportunity for interpersonal conflict exists whenever two or more people interact. Sigmund Freud (1930) went so far as to argue that conflict is an inevitable by-product of civilization because the goals and needs of individuals often clash with the goals and needs of their fellow human beings. The nature of conflict, and how it can be resolved, has been the topic of a great deal of social psychological research (Cohen & Insko, 2008; Deutsch, 1973; Levine & Thompson, 1996; Pruitt, 1998; Thibaut & Kelley, 1959).

Many conflicts are resolved peacefully, with little rancor. Couples can find a way to resolve their differences in a mutually acceptable manner, and labor disputes are sometimes settled with a handshake. All too often, however, conflict erupts into open hostilities. The divorce rate in the United States is distressingly high. People sometimes resort to violence to resolve their differences, as shown by the high rate of murders in the United States, which has been called "the murder capital of the civilized world." Warfare between nations remains an all-too-common solution to international disputes. In fact, when wars over the past 5 centuries are examined, the twentieth century ranks first in the severity of wars (defined as the number of deaths per war) and second in their frequency (Levy & Morgan, 1984). Between 1972 and 1976, fewer than 2,000 people were killed by terrorists. Unfortunately this number has been increasing rapidly; between 2002 and 2006, the number exceeded 30,000 (Cohen & Insko, 2008). Obviously it is of great importance to find ways of resolving conflicts peacefully.

Social Dilemmas 社会困境

What is best for an individual is not always best for the group as a whole. Consider a recent publishing venture by the novelist Stephen King. He wrote two installments of a novel called *The Plant* and posted them on the Internet, asking readers to pay $1 per installment. The deal he offered was simple: If at least 75 percent of the people who downloaded the installments paid the fee, he would keep writing and posting new installments. If fewer than 75 percent of the people paid, he would stop writing, and people would never get the rest of the novel.

King had devised a classic **social dilemma**, a conflict in which the most beneficial action for an individual will, if chosen by most people, be harmful to everyone (Weber, Kopelman, & Messick, 2004). It was to any individual's financial advantage to download King's novel free of charge and let other people pay. However, if too many people took this approach, everyone would lose, because King said he would stop writing the novel.

At first, people acted for the good of all; more than 75 percent paid for the first installment. As with many other social dilemmas, however, people eventually acted in their own self-interest, to the detriment of all. The number of people who paid for their later installments dropped below 75 percent, and King stopped posting new ones, saying on his Web site that the novel is "on hiatus."

There are many perspectives on how people respond to social dilemmas, including sociological studies of social movements and historical, economic, and political analyses of international relations. The social psychological approach is unique in its attempt to study these conflicts experimentally, testing both their causes and resolutions in the laboratory.

One of the most common ways of studying social dilemmas in the laboratory is with a game called the *prisoner's dilemma*. In this game, two people have to choose one of two options without knowing what the other person will choose. The number of points they win depends on the options chosen by both people. Suppose that you were playing the game with a friend. As shown in the following Try It! exercise you have to choose option X or option Y, without knowing which option your friend will choose. Your payoff—the amount of money you win or lose—depends on the choices of both you and your friend. For example, if both you and your friend choose option X, you both win $3. If, however, you choose option Y and your friend chooses option X, you win $6 and your friend loses $6. Which option would you choose?

Many people begin by choosing option Y. At worst, you will lose $1, and at best, you will win the highest possible amount, $6. Choosing option X raises the possibility that both sides will win some money, but this is also a risky choice. If your partner chooses Y while you choose X, you stand to lose a great deal. Because people often do not know how much they can trust their partners, option Y frequently seems like the safest choice (Rapoport & Chammah, 1965). The rub is that both players will probably think this way, ensuring that both sides lose (see the lower right-hand corner of the figure in the Try It! exercise).

People's actions in these games seem to mirror many conflicts in everyday life. To find a solution desirable to both parties, people must trust each other. Often they do not, and this lack of trust leads to an escalating series of competitive moves so that in the end no one wins (Batson & Ahmad, 2001; Insko & Schopler, 1998; Kelley & Thibaut, 1978; Pruitt, 1998). Two countries locked in an arms race may feel that they cannot afford to disarm out of fear that the other side will take advantage of their weakened position. The result is that both sides add furiously to their stockpile of weapons, neither gaining superiority over the other and both spending

Sometimes people are able to resolve conflicts peacefully, such as a couple that has an amicable divorce. Other times conflicts escalate into rancor and violence. Social psychologists have performed experiments to test ways in which conflict resolution is most likely to occur.

Social Dilemma
A conflict in which the most beneficial action for an individual will, if chosen by most people, have harmful effects on everyone

The Prisoner's Dilemma 试一试！囚徒困境

	Your Options	
Your Friend's Options	Option X	Option Y
Option X	You win $3 Your friend wins $3	You win $6 Your friend loses $6
Option Y	You lose $6 Your friend wins $6	You lose $1 Your friend loses $1

Play this version of the prisoner's dilemma game with a friend. First, show the table to the friend, and explain how the game works: On each trial of the game, you and your friend can choose option X or option Y, without knowing what the other will choose. You should each write your choice on folded pieces of paper that are opened at the same time. The numbers in the table represent imaginary money that you and your friend win or lose on each trial. For example, if you choose option X on the first trial and your friend chooses option Y, you lose an imaginary $6 and your friend wins an imaginary $6. If both of you choose option Y, you both lose an imaginary $1. Play the game for 10 trials, and keep track of how much each of you wins or loses. Did you and your friend choose the cooperative option (option X) or the competitive option (option Y) more often? Why? Did a pattern of trust or mistrust develop over the course of the game?

money they could use to solve domestic problems (Deutsch, 1973). Such an escalation of conflict is also seen all too often among couples who are divorcing. Sometimes the goal seems more to hurt the other person than to further one's own needs (or the children's). In the end, both suffer because, metaphorically speaking, they both choose option Y too often.

Increasing Cooperation in the Prisoner's Dilemma Such escalating conflict, though common, is not inevitable. Many studies have found that when people play a prisoner's dilemma game, they will, under certain conditions, adopt the more cooperative response (option X), ensuring that both sides end up with a positive outcome. Not surprisingly, if people are playing the game with a friend or if they expect to interact with their partner in the future, they are more likely to adopt a cooperative strategy that maximizes both their profits and their partner's (Cohen & Insko, 2008). In addition, growing up in some societies, such as Asian cultures, seems to foster a more cooperative orientation than growing up in the West does (Bonta, 1997; Markus & Kitayama, 1991). Finally, subtly changing the norms about what kind of behavior is expected can have large effects on how cooperative people are. One study found that simply changing the name of the game from the "Wall Street Game" to the "Community Game" increased the percentage of people who cooperated from 33 percent to 71 percent (Liberman, Samuels, & Ross, 2004). Another, conducted with Chinese college students in Hong Kong, found that showing people symbols of Chinese culture before the game (e.g., a Chinese dragon) made people more cooperative, whereas showing people symbols of American culture (e.g., an American flag) made them more competitive (Wong & Hong, 2005).

To increase cooperation, you can also try the **tit-for-tat strategy**, which is a way of encouraging cooperation by at first acting cooperatively but then always responding the way your opponent did (cooperatively or competitively) on the previous trial. This strategy communicates a willingness to cooperate and an unwillingness to sit back and be exploited if the partner does not cooperate. The tit-for-tat strategy is usually successful in getting the other person to respond with the cooperative, trusting response (Axelrod, 1984; Messick & Liebrand, 1995; Parks & Rumble, 2001; Sheldon, 1999; Van Lange, Ouwerkerk, & Tazelaar, 2002). The analogy to the arms race would be to match not only any military buildup made by an unfriendly nation, but also any conciliatory gesture, such as a ban on nuclear testing.

Tit-for-Tat Strategy
A means of encouraging cooperation by at first acting cooperatively but then always responding the way your opponent did (cooperatively or competitively) on the previous trial

Another proven strategy is to allow individuals rather than opposing groups to resolve a conflict, because two individuals who play the prisoner's dilemma are more likely to cooperate than two groups who play the same game (Schopler & Insko, 1999). The reason for this is that people are more likely to assume that another individual is cooperative at heart and can be trusted but that most groups of individuals will, given the opportunity, stab us in the back. Does this mean that world leaders would be more cooperative when negotiating one-on-one than when groups of advisers from the two nations meet? Possibly. In 1985, Ronald Reagan and Mikhail Gorbachev, the leaders of the United States and the Soviet Union, met in Switzerland for the first time to discuss arms reduction. After formal meetings between the leaders and their aides stalled, Reagan and Gorbachev took a walk to a boathouse accompanied only by translators. According to some reports, the two men came close to agreeing to dismantle all of their nuclear missiles—until their aides got wind of this "preposterous" idea and squelched it (Korda, 1997).

Other Kinds of Social Dilemmas A number of other kinds of social dilemmas have been studied as well. A **public goods dilemma** occurs when individuals must contribute to a common pool to maintain the public good, such as paying taxes for public schools. It is to each individual's advantage to pay as little as possible, but if everyone adopts this strategy, everyone suffers.

The **commons dilemma** is a situation in which everyone takes from a common pool of goods that will replenish itself if used in moderation but will disappear if overused. This dilemma got its name from an example in which there is a common grassy area in the middle of a town on which all residents are permitted to let their sheep graze. This is a classic social dilemma because it is to each individual farmer's benefit to let his or her sheep graze as much as possible, but if all farmers do this, the commons will be overgrazed and the grass will disappear (Hardin, 1968). Modern examples include the use of limited resources such as water and energy. Individuals benefit by using as much as they need, but if everyone does so, shortages often result. We discuss commons dilemmas in Social Psychology in Action 1, in the context of how to get people to avoid environmentally damaging behaviors.

Using Threats to Resolve Conflict 用威胁解决冲突

When involved in a conflict, many of us are tempted to use threats to get the other party to cave in to our wishes, believing that we should, in the words of Teddy Roosevelt, "speak softly and carry a big stick." Parents commonly use threats to get their children to behave, and teachers often threaten their students with demerits or a visit to the principal. More alarming is the increasing number of youths in the United States who carry weapons and use them to resolve conflicts that used to be settled with a playground scuffle. Threats are commonly used on an international scale as well, to further the interests of one nation over another (Turner & Horvitz, 2001).

A classic series of studies by Morton Deutsch and Robert Krauss (1960, 1962) indicates that threats are not an effective means of reducing conflict. These researchers developed a game in which two participants imagined they were in charge of trucking companies named Acme and Bolt. The goal of each company was to transport merchandise as quickly as possible to a destination. The participants were paid 60 cents for each "trip" but had 1 cent subtracted for every second it took them to make the trip. The most direct route for each company was over a one-lane road on which only one truck could travel at a time. This placed the two companies in direct conflict, as seen in Figure 9.7. If Acme and Bolt both tried to take the one-lane road, neither truck could pass, and both would lose money. Each company could take an alternate route, but this was much longer, guaranteeing they would lose at least 10 cents on each trial.

After a while, most participants worked out a solution that allowed both trucks to make a modest amount of money. They took turns waiting until the other party

Public Goods Dilemma

A social dilemma in which individuals must contribute to a common pool in order to maintain the public good

Commons Dilemma

A social dilemma in which everyone takes from a common pool of goods that will replenish itself if used in moderation but will disappear if overused

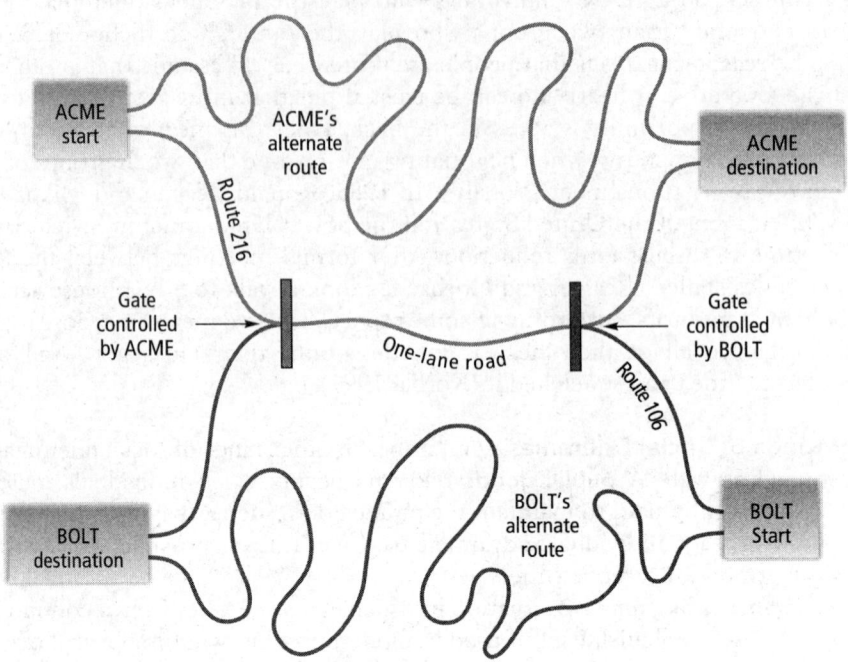

FIGURE 9.7
The trucking game.

Participants play the role of the head of either Acme or Bolt Trucking Company. In order to earn money, they have to drive their truck from the starting point to their destination as quickly as possible. The quickest route is the one-lane road, but both trucks cannot travel on this road at the same time. In some versions of the studies, participants were given gates they used to block the other's progress on the one-lane road.

(Adapted from Russett, 1962)

> *My own belief is that Russian and Chinese behavior is as much influenced by suspicion of our intentions as ours is by suspicion of theirs. This would mean that we have great influence over their behavior—that, by treating them as hostile, we assure their hostility.*
>
> —J. William Fulbright

crossed the one-lane road; then they would take that route as well. In another version of the study, the researchers gave Acme a gate that could be lowered over the one-lane road, thereby blocking Bolt from using that route. You might think that using force—the gate—would increase Acme's profits, because all Acme had to do was to threaten Bolt to "stay off the one-lane road or else." In fact, quite the opposite happened. When one side had the gate, both participants lost more than when neither side had the gate—as seen in the left panel of Figure 9.8. This figure shows the total amount earned or lost by both sides. (Acme won slightly more than Bolt when it had the gate but won substantially more when neither side had a gate.) Bolt did not like to be threatened and often retaliated by parking its truck on the one-lane road, blocking the other truck's progress. Meanwhile, the seconds ticked away, and both sides lost money.

What would happen if the situation were more equitable, with both sides having gates? Surely they would learn to cooperate very quickly, recognizing the stalemate that would ensue if both of them used their gates—right? To the contrary (as you can see in the left panel of Figure 9.8), both sides lost more money in the bilateral threat condition than in any of the others. The owners of the trucking companies both threatened to use their gates and did so with great frequency.

Effects of Communication 沟通的作用

There is a way in which the Deutsch and Krauss trucking game does not approximate real life: The two sides were not allowed to communicate with each other. Would the two adversaries work out their differences if they could talk them over?

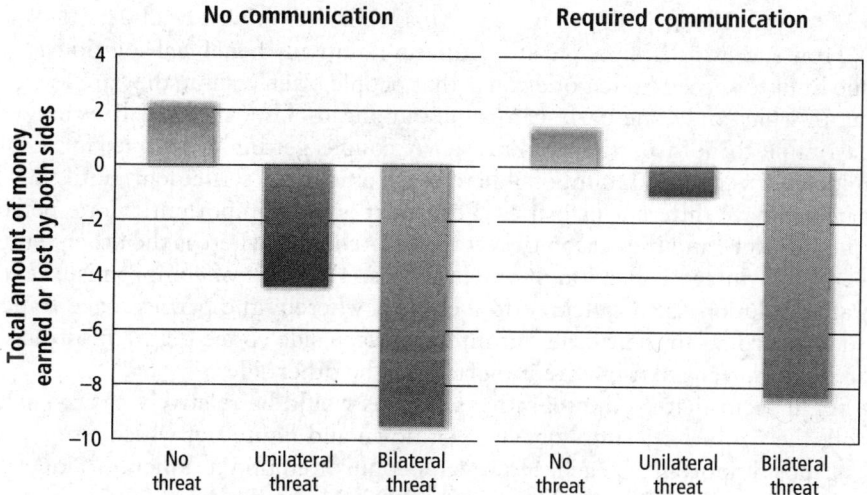

FIGURE 9.8
Results of the trucking game studies.

The left-hand panel shows the amount of money the participants made (summed over Acme and Bolt) when they could not communicate. When threats were introduced by giving one or both sides a gate, both sides lost more money. The right-hand panel shows the amount of money the participants made when they were required to communicate on every trial. Once again, giving them gates reduced their winnings.

(Adapted from Russett, 1962)

To find out, Deutsch and Krauss ran a version of their study in which the participants were required to communicate on every trial. Surely if people talked to each other, they would cooperate more. But as seen in the right panel of Figure 9.8, no dramatic increase in profits occurred. Making people communicate reduced losses somewhat when Acme alone had the gate (the unilateral threat condition) but failed to increase cooperation in either of the two other conditions (no threat; bilateral threat). Overall, requiring people to communicate did not raise profits dramatically. Why not?

The problem with the communication in the trucking studies is that it did not foster trust. In fact, people used the intercom to threaten each other. Krauss and Deutsch demonstrated this fact in a later version of their trucking study in which they specifically instructed people in how to communicate, telling them to work out a solution that was fair to both parties—that they would be willing to accept if they were in the other person's shoes. Under these conditions, verbal communication increased the amount of money both sides won because it fostered trust instead of adding fuel to the competitive fires (Deutsch, 1973, 1990; Krauss & Deutsch, 1966; Pruitt, 1998).

Negotiation and Bargaining 协商与讨价还价

In the laboratory games we have discussed so far, people's options are limited. They have to choose option X or Y in the prisoner's dilemma, and they have only a couple of ways of getting their truck to its destination in the trucking game. In everyday life, we often have a wide array of options. Consider two people haggling over the price of a car. Both the buyer and the seller can give in to all of the other's demands, to some of them, or to none of them. Either party can walk away from the deal at any time. Given that there is considerable latitude in how people can resolve the conflict, communication between the parties is all the more important. By talking, bargaining, and negotiating, people can arrive at a satisfactory settlement. **Negotiation** is a form of communication between opposing sides in a conflict in which offers and counteroffers are made and a solution occurs only when both parties agree (De Dreu, Beersma,

Negotiation
A form of communication between opposing sides in a conflict in which offers and counteroffers are made and a solution occurs only when both parties agree

Steinel, & Van Kleef, 2007; Galinsky, Mussweiler, & Medvec, 2002; Thompson, 2005). How successful are people at negotiating mutually beneficial solutions?

One limit to successful negotiation is that people often assume they are locked in a conflict in which only one party can come out ahead. They don't realize that a solution favorable to both parties is available. A couple getting a divorce, for example, might lock horns and find it impossible to reach a financial settlement, until they realize that they have different priorities. Perhaps it is most important to one person to keep the furniture and the season tickets to the orchestra, whereas the other wants the china and the vintage collection of vinyl records. This type of compromise, called an **integrative solution**, is an outcome to a conflict whereby the parties make trade-offs on issues according to their different interests; each side concedes the most on issues that are unimportant to it but are important to the other side.

It might seem that such integrative solutions would be relatively easy to achieve. After all, the two parties simply have to sit down and figure out which issues are the most important to each. However, people often find it difficult to identify integrative solutions (DeDreu et al., 2007; Moran & Ritov, 2007; Thompson, 1997). For example, the more people have at stake in a negotiation, the more biased their perceptions of their opponent. They will tend to distrust proposals made by the other side and to overlook interests they have in common (O'Connor & Carnevale, 1997; Ross & Ward, 1995, 1996). This is one reason people often use neutral mediators to solve labor disputes, legal battles, and divorce proceedings: Mediators are often in a better position to recognize that there are mutually agreeable solutions to a conflict (Carnevale, 1986; Kressel & Pruitt, 1989; Ross & LaCroix, 1996).

What about the role of communication in negotiation? As we saw earlier, communication is only helpful if it allows parties to develop trust. It appears that this is easier in old-fashioned face-to-face negotiations than in electronic communication such as email, instant messaging, text messaging, and video conferencing. These techniques have many advantages, of course, but a disadvantage is that it is harder to get to know people and learn to trust them. A meta-analysis of several studies found that negotiations conducted over electronic media were more hostile, and resulted in lower profits, than face-to-face negotiations (Stuhlmacher & Citera, 2005).

The bottom line? When you are negotiating with someone, it is important to keep in mind that integrative solutions are often available. Try to gain the other side's trust, and communicate your own interests in an open manner (ideally in person, or with the help of a mediator). Remember that the way you construe the situation is not necessarily the same as the way the other party construes the situation. You may well discover that the other side communicates its interests more freely as a result, increasing the likelihood that you will find a solution beneficial to both parties.

> Yet there remains another wall. This wall constitutes a psychological barrier between us, ... [a] barrier of distorted and eroded interpretation of every event and statement. . . . I ask, why don't we stretch our hands with faith and sincerity so that together we might destroy this barrier?
>
> —Former Egyptian president Anwar al-Sadat, speaking before the Israeli Knesset, 1977

Integrative Solution
A solution to a conflict whereby the parties make trade-offs on issues according to their different interests; each side concedes the most on issues that are unimportant to it but important to the other side

Neutral mediators often help solve labor disputes, legal battles, and divorce proceedings. Mediators are often in a better position to recognize that there are mutually agreeable solutions to a conflict.

HOW WOULD YOU USE THIS? 如何学以致用？

Chances are you will soon find yourself in a group that needs to make a decision. Perhaps you are an officer in a student organization that is making budget decisions, part of a team of students deciding how to proceed on a class project, or a member of a fraternity or sorority deciding whom to admit. Based on what you have learned in this chapter, will you act any differently to make sure that your group makes the best decision? What kinds of *process loss* should you be alert to, for example, that might impede good decision making? (See page 265.) How can you make sure that people share information that others don't have? (See page 266.) Is it possible that you and your friends will be subject to *groupthink*, and if so, how can you prevent it? (See page 267.) Lastly, can you predict who is likely to become the leader in your groups and how effective they will be? What should you do to increase the chances that you will be chosen as the leader? (See pages 273–276.) Good luck!

Summary 总 结

- **What Is a Group?** A **group** consists of three or more people who interact with each other and are interdependent.
  - **Why Do People Join Groups?** The *need to belong* to groups may be innate. Groups also serve as a source of information about the social world and are an important part of our social identities. People are very sensitive to rejection from groups and do what they can to avoid it.
  - **The Composition and Functions of Groups** Groups tend to consist of homogeneous members, in part because groups have *social norms* that people are expected to obey. Groups also have well-defined social roles, shared expectations about how people are supposed to behave. People can get so far into a social role that their personal identities and personalities get lost. Group cohesiveness, qualities of a group that bind members together and promote liking between members, is another important property of groups that influences the group's performance.

- **Groups and Individuals' Behavior** Research has compared the performance of people who are by themselves versus in groups.
  - **Social Facilitation: When the Presence of Others Energizes Us** When people's individual efforts on a task can be evaluated, the mere presence of others leads to social facilitation: Their performance is enhanced on simple tasks but impaired on complex tasks.
  - **Social Loafing: When the Presence of Others Relaxes Us** When people's individual efforts *cannot* be evaluated, the mere presence of others leads to relaxation and social loafing: Performance is impaired on simple tasks but enhanced on complex tasks.
  - **Gender and Cultural Differences in Social Loafing: Who Slacks Off the Most?** Social loafing is more prevalent among men than women, and more prevalent in Western than Asian cultures.
  - **Deindividuation: Getting Lost in the Crowd** The mere presence of others can also lead to deindividuation, which is the loosening of normal constraints on behavior when people are in crowds.

- **Group Decisions: Are Two (or More) Heads Better Than One?** Research has compared how people make decisions when they are by themselves versus in groups.
  - **Process Loss: When Group Interactions Inhibit Good Problem Solving** Groups make better decisions than individuals if they are good at pooling ideas and listening to the expert members of the group. Often, however, process loss occurs, which is any aspect of group interaction that inhibits good decision making. For example, groups often focus on the information they have in common and fail to share unique information. Tightly knit, cohesive groups are also prone to groupthink, which occurs when maintaining group cohesiveness and solidarity becomes more important than considering the facts in a realistic manner.
  - **Group Polarization: Going to Extremes** Group polarization causes groups to make more extreme decisions in the direction toward which its members were initially leaning; these group decisions can be more risky or more cautious, depending on which attitude is valued in the group.

- **Leadership in Groups** There is little support for the great person theory, which argues that good leadership is a matter of having the right personality traits. Leaders do adopt specific kinds of leadership styles, such as transactional or transformational. Leadership effectiveness is a function of both the kind of person a leader is and the nature of the work situation. Although strides have been made, women are still underrepresented in leadership positions. Women who become leaders often face a "glass cliff" whereby they are put in charge of work units that are in crisis and in which the risk of failure is high. Further, there is a double bind for women leaders: If they conform to societal expectations about how they ought to behave, by being warm and communal, they are often perceived as having low leadership potential. If they succeed in attaining a leadership position and act in ways that leaders are expected to act—namely, in agentic, forceful ways—they are often perceived negatively for not "acting like a woman should."

- **Conflict and Cooperation** Research has examined how people resolve conflicts when they have incompatible goals.
  - **Social Dilemmas** These occur when the most beneficial action for an individual will, if chosen by most people, have harmful effects on everyone. A commonly studied social dilemma is the prisoner's dilemma, in which two people must decide whether to look out for only their own interests or for their partner's interests as well. Creating trust is crucial in solving this kind of conflict.
  - **Using Threats to Resolve Conflict** Research has found that using threats tends to escalate rather than resolve conflicts.
  - **Effects of Communication** Communication resolves conflict only when it promotes trust.
  - **Negotiation and Bargaining** When two sides are negotiating and bargaining it is important to look for an integrative solution, whereby each side concedes the most on issues that are unimportant to it but are very important to its adversary.

CHAPTER 9 TEST 第9章习题

1. Why are groups homogeneous (alike in age, sex, beliefs, and opinions)?
   a. People who are already similar to each other will join.
   b. Evolutionary pressures caused people with similar genes to join groups.
   c. Groups encourage similarity in their members.
   d. (a) and (c).
   e. (a), (b), and (c).

2. Group cohesiveness is best defined as
   a. shared expectations in a group about how people are supposed to behave.
   b. qualities that bind members together and promote liking between members.
   c. expectations about the roles and behaviors of men and women.
   d. the tendency for people to do better on simple tasks and worse on complex tasks in the presence of others.

3. You are trying to decide whether to take a test in a lecture hall where you will be surrounded by lots of other people, or in a room by yourself. Assuming you have studied for the test and know the material, you should take the test in the _____ because it will result in _____.
   a. hallway; social loafing
   b. hallway; social facilitation
   c. classroom; social loafing
   d. hallway; deindividuation
   e. classroom; social facilitation

4. The tendency to engage in social loafing is stronger in _____ than _____; it is also stronger in _____ than _____.
   a. men, women; Asian cultures, Western cultures
   b. women, men; Asian cultures, Western cultures
   c. men, women; Western cultures, Asian cultures
   d. women, men; Western cultures, Asian cultures

5. On his way back from class, Matt encounters an angry mob ready to storm the dining hall to demand better food. Matt likes the food as it is and wants to stop the mob. What would be the most effective solution?
   a. Increasing group cohesiveness by inviting the entire mob to his house for tea.
   b. Passing out blue shirts for everyone to wear.
   c. Reducing process loss in the group by making sure that its most expert members have the most influence.
   d. Finding a friend in the group, calling out her name, and talking to her loudly about an upcoming test.

6. Four psychology students working on a group project together are trying to figure out how they should avoid groupthink when making decisions about which information to include in their project. Which of these ideas would be the *least* helpful?
   a. Bonding by going to see a movie together before starting the project.
   b. Assigning each group member to be responsible for a different chapter in their textbook so they cover all the details.
   c. Having a student not in their group review the project.
   d. Designating a leader to oversee the project, but the leader is nondirective and encourages people to give honest feedback.

7. Bill and Pam, a married couple, are buying a house and have narrowed their choice down to two options. Bill remembers that one house had a beautiful kitchen; Pam, however, remembers that there were roaches in the broom closet. By sharing this information with each other, Pam and Bill are using _____ to avoid _____.
    a. mindguards; groupthink
    b. social roles; deindividuation
    c. transactive memory; process loss
    d. subgroups; group polarization

8. Which of the following is *least likely* to lead to process loss in a group?
    a. A group leader has high charisma but very little expertise.
    b. The group members have never met before.
    c. Group members do not share information that others lack.
    d. Some members in the group do not listen to each other.
    e. The most competent member doesn't feel free to speak up.

9. Which of the following is an example of a commons dilemma?
    a. Each fisherman is better off fishing as much as he can, but if they all do that, the fish will be depleted and all fishermen will suffer.
    b. People may leave a concert before the clapping starts and secure a fast exit from the concert hall, but if everybody does that, it won't be any faster to get out of the hall.
    c. Individuals are better off not paying taxes because even if they don't pay taxes, they will still be able to benefit from parks and highways that were paid for with taxes collected from others.
    d. When the check is going to be shared at dinner, each individual in a group is better off ordering a more expensive meal, but if everybody does that, everybody will end up paying more.

10. When is communication most effective for resolving conflict?
    a. When people communicate through electronic means (e.g., over email).
    b. When it is required.
    c. When the stakes are high for people on both sides of a conflict.
    d. When a mediator is used.

Answer Key: 1-d, 2-b, 3-e, 4-c, 5-d, 6-a, 7-c, 8-b, 9-a, 10-d

For more review plus practice tests, videos, flashcards, writing help and more, log on to MyPsychLab.

10

Interpersonal Attraction
From First Impressions to Close Relationships

人际吸引：
从第一印象到亲密关系

OUTLINE 提纲

- **What Causes Attraction?**
  - The Person Next Door: The Propinquity Effect
  - Similarity
  - Reciprocal Liking
  - Physical Attractiveness and Liking
  - Theories of Interpersonal Attraction: Social Exchange and Equity
- **Close Relationships**
  - Defining Love
  - Culture and Love
- **Love and Relationships**
  - Evolution and Love: Choosing a Mate
  - CONNECTIONS: Does Ovulation Affect Perceptions of Male Attractiveness?
  - Attachment Styles in Intimate Relationships
  - CONNECTIONS: This Is Your Brain . . . In Love
  - Social Exchange in Long-Term Relationships
  - Equity in Long-Term Relationships
- **Ending Intimate Relationships**
  - The Process of Breaking Up
  - The Experience of Breaking Up
- **Summary**

IN THE VILLAGE OF JUNIGAU, NEPAL, 100 MILES SOUTHWEST of Kathmandu, young men and women have the same hopes and goals as their peers around the world—to find someone to love and with whom to share their life. But the path they follow to matrimony is strikingly different from that of people in Western countries like the United States. In Nepalese villages, dating is forbidden, and even casual meetings between young men and women are considered inappropriate. Traditionally, one's future spouse is chosen by one's parents, who focus on the potential suitor's social standing: family, caste, and economic resources. In these arranged marriages, the bride and groom often speak to each other for the first time on their wedding day. It is not unusual for the bride to cry during the ceremony and for the groom to look stunned and resigned (Goode, 1999). Despite what might seem an inauspicious beginning, many of these unions turn out to be very successful. The high divorce rate in the United States suggests that the Western process of choosing one's own mate is not necessarily the most successful way!

After the ceremony, the bride moves in with her husband's family, where she is considered of low status. She has to perform the hardest work and is expected to wash her husband's feet every morning and then drink the washwater (a tradition that some women have abandoned in recent years; Goode, 1999).

It is not just the process of finding a romantic partner that varies around the world, but even how "love" is defined and experienced. As we have discussed throughout this book, Western and Eastern cultures vary in their definitions of the needs of individuals and of the group or the society. Western societies are individualistic, emphasizing that the individual is autonomous, self-sufficient, and defined by his or her personal qualities. Eastern cultures are collectivistic, emphasizing loyalty to the group and defining the individual through membership in the group (Hofstede, 1984; Kim & Markus, 1999; Markus, Kitayama, & Heiman, 1996; Triandis, 1995).

Social psychologists have noted that romantic love is an important, even crucial basis for marriage in individualistic societies but has less value in collectivistic ones. In individualistic societies, romantic love is a heady, highly personal experience. One immerses oneself in the new partner, virtually ignoring friends and family for a while. The decision regarding whom to become involved with or marry is for the most part a personal one. In comparison, in collectivistic societies, the individual in love must consider the wishes of family and other group members, which sometimes includes agreeing to an arranged marriage (Dion & Dion, 1988, 1993; Fiske, Kitayama, Markus, & Nisbett, 1998; Levine, Sato, Hashimoto, & Verma, 1995).

Nevertheless, Western ways of finding a partner have permeated collectivistic cultures through the media, and these media portrayals have had an effect (Hatfield & Rapson, 2002). In Nepal, for example, prospective brides and grooms now write letters to each other, getting to know each other a bit before the wedding. In their letters, they do not communicate romantic love as Westerners idealize it. Instead, they discuss serious economic issues that suggest what their future life together will be like, as well as reassure each other they they are trustworthy and honest (Goode, 1999). Even further from tradition is the outcome of these letters: The couple may choose to "elope," marrying at the groom's home (if they have his family's blessing). The couple still must get the bride's family's acceptance of the marriage after the fact; otherwise, the bride can be disinherited.

Similarly, South Asians in London have taken the finding of mates into their own hands to a certain extent. Traditionally, Indians and Pakistanis in Britain, as in their homelands, have viewed marriage as a union between families, not individuals. As one young Indian woman put it, marriage "is not based on love, which can fizzle out," but on similarities in education, income, family standing, religion, and character (Alvarez, 2003, p. 3). Nevertheless, modern Western-style courtship techniques, including "speed dating," are changing traditional ways of meeting (see the photograph on page 286.) Speed dating involves meeting many potential mates in a public setting for a few minutes of conversation with each; Hindus are seated at one table and Muslims at another. Someone who strikes a speed dater's fancy is quickly taken home to "meet the parents." Although this ritual occurs in individualistic cultures too, it has far deeper ramifications in collectivistic cultures. In this new version of an arranged marriage, the South Asian suitors play an important role in the beginning, but the families of both still make the ulitmate decision (Alvarez, 2003).

Thus, even something as basic to the human condition as falling in love and choosing a life partner shows the effects of social psychology: the influence of the situation—in this case, one's culture. In this chapter, we will explore what makes us feel attracted to other people, whether as friends or lovers, and how relationships develop and progress.

What Causes Attraction? 产生吸引的原因

When social psychologist Ellen Berscheid asked people of various ages what made them happy, at or near the top of their lists were making and maintaining friendships and having positive, warm relationships (Berscheid, 1985; Berscheid & Peplau, 1983; Berscheid & Reis, 1998). The absence of meaningful relationships with other people makes people feel lonely, worthless, hopeless, helpless, powerless, and alienated (Baumeister & Leary, 1995; Hartup & Stevens, 1997; Peplau & Perlman, 1982; Stroebe & Stroebe, 1996). In fact, the social psychologist Arthur Aron states that a central human motivation is "self-expansion." This is the desire to overlap or blend with another person, so that you have access to that person's knowledge, insights, and experience and thus broaden and deepen your own experience of life (Aron, Aron, & Norman, 2004; Aron, Mashuk, & Aron, 2004). In this chapter, we will discuss the antecedents of attraction, from the initial liking of two people meeting for the first time to the love that develops in close relationships.

> Contrary to popular belief, I do not believe that friends are necessarily the people you like best; they are merely the people who got there first.
>
> —Sir Peter Ustinov, *Dear Me*, 1977

The Person Next Door: The Propinquity Effect

住在隔壁的人：时空接近效应

One of the simplest determinants of interpersonal attraction is proximity (sometimes called *propinquity*). The people who, by chance, are the ones you see and interact with the most often are the most likely to become your friends and lovers (Berscheid & Reis, 1998).

Now, this might seem obvious. But the striking thing about proximity and attraction, or the **propinquity effect**, as social psychologists call it, is that it works in a very narrow sense. For example, consider a classic study conducted in a housing complex for married students at MIT. Leon Festinger, Stanley Schachter, and Kurt Back (1950) tracked friendship formation among the couples in the various apartment buildings. For example, one section of the complex, Westgate West, was composed of 17 two-story buildings, each having 10 apartments. The residents had been assigned to their apartments at random, as a vacancy opened up, and nearly all of them were strangers when they moved in. The researchers asked the residents to name their three closest friends in the entire housing project. Just as the propinquity effect would predict, 65 percent of the friends mentioned lived in the same building, even though the other buildings were not far away.

Even more striking was the pattern of friendships within a building. Each Westgate West building was designed like the drawing in Figure 10.1: Most of the front doors were only 19 feet apart, and the greatest distance between apartment doors was only 89 feet. The researchers found that 41 percent of the next-door neighbors indicated they were close friends, 22 percent of those who lived two doors apart said so, and only 10 percent of those who lived on opposite ends of the hall indicated they were close friends.

Festinger and his colleagues (1950) demonstrated that attraction and propinquity rely not only on actual physical distance but also on "functional distance." Functional distance refers to certain aspects of architectural design that make it more likely that some people will come into contact with each other more often than with others. For example, consider the friendship choices of the residents of apartments 1 and 5 in Figure 10.1. Living at the foot of the stairs and in one case near the mailboxes meant that these couples saw a great deal of upstairs residents. Sure enough, apartment dwellers in apartments 1 and 5 throughout the complex had more friends upstairs than dwellers in the other first-floor apartments did. (You can map out propinquity effects in your life with the following Try It! exercise.)

Close friendships are often made in college, in part because of prolonged propinquity.

Propinquity Effect
The finding that the more we see and interact with people, the more likely they are to become our friends
(Jonathan Player/*The New York Times*.)

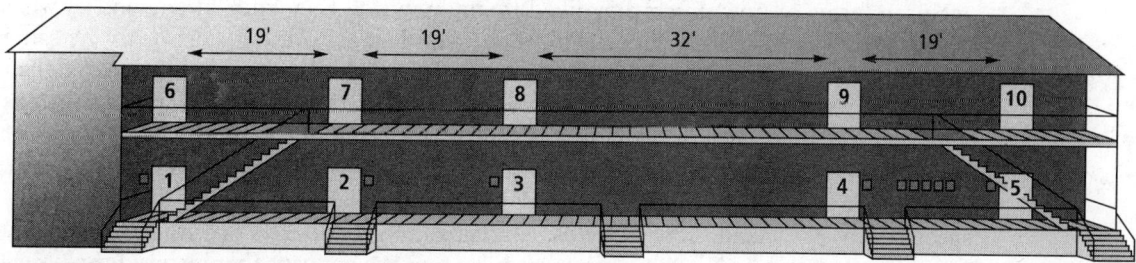

FIGURE 10.1
The floor plan of a Westgate West building.

All the buildings in the housing complex had the same floor plan.

(Adapted from Festinger, Schachter, & Back, 1950)

试一试！在生活中体验时空接近效应
Mapping the Effect of Propinquity in Your Life

In this exercise, you will be examining the relationship between who your friends and acquaintances are and the places where you spend time regularly. Does propinquity explain who your friends are?

First, pick a physical space to focus on. You could choose your dormitory, your apartment building, or the building where you work. (We'll use a dormitory as an example.) Draw a rough floor plan of your dormitory floor. Include the location of all the dorm room doors, the stairs or elevator, the restroom, living room, and so on. Mark your room with a large X. (You can decide whether you need to draw just your floor or more of the building.)

Second, think about who your close friends on the floor are. Mark their dorm rooms with the number 1. Next, think about who your friends are; mark their rooms with a 2. Finally, think about your acquaintances—people you say hello to or chat with briefly now and then. Mark their rooms with a 3.

Now examine the pattern of friendships on your map. Are your friends clustered near your room in physical space? Are the dorm rooms with the numbers 1 and 2 among the closest to your room in physical space? Are they physically closer to your room than the ones with number 3? And what about the dorm rooms that didn't get a number (meaning that you don't really know these people or interact with them)—are these rooms the farthest from yours?

Finally, examine your propinquity map for the presence of functional distance as well. Do aspects of the architectural design of your dorm make you more likely to cross paths with some dorm members more than others? For example, the location of the restroom, kitchen, living room, stairs or elevator, and mailboxes can play an important role in propinquity and friendship formation. These are all places that you go to frequently; when walking to and from them, you pass some people's rooms and not others'. Are the people who live along your path the ones you know the best? If so, propinquity has played an important role in determining the people with whom you have formed relationships!

The propinquity effect works because of familiarity, or the **mere exposure effect**: The more exposure we have to a stimulus, the more apt we are to like it. We see certain people a lot, and the more familiar they become, the more friendship blooms. Of course, if the person in question is an obnoxious jerk, then, not surprisingly, the more exposure you have, the greater your dislike (Norton, Frost, & Ariely, 2007). But in the absence of such negative qualities, familiarity breeds attraction and liking (Bornstein, 1989; Griffin & Sparks, 1990; Moreland & Beach, 1992; Lee, 2001).

A good example of the propinquity and mere exposure effects is your college classroom. All semester long, you see the same people. Does this increase your liking for them? Researchers tested this hypothesis with German college students by randomly assigning them to seats in the classroom for the semester, during the first day of class (Back, Schmukle, & Egloff, 2008). That first day, they had the class rate each class member on how likeable they thought each was, and to what extent they would like to get to know each person. These initial ratings indicated that students who sat in neighboring seats or in the same row had higher initial attraction scores than those seated far apart. A year later, they asked these students to rate the members of their original class again, in terms of how much they liked them, how well they knew them, and to what degree they were friends. Once again, those who had sat side-by-side, or in the same row, the prior semester were significantly more likely to be friends a year later than those who sat far apart. The propinquity effect means that some of our relationships develop simply because we really were "at the right place, at the right time."

A final note on propinquity involves how it operates in a computer-mediated world. We can get to know people who are very far away physically but very close in cyberspace (Chan & Cheng, 2004; Dodds, Muhamad, & Watts, 2003). Jure Leskovec and Eric Horvitz conducted a fascinating study testing the concept that inspired the popular game, "Six Degrees of Kevin Bacon." A "degree of separation" is a measure of social distance between people. You are 1 degree away from everyone you know, 2 degrees away from everyone they know, and so on. These researchers analyzed the Microsoft

Mere Exposure Effect
The finding that the more exposure we have to a stimulus, the more apt we are to like it

Messenger instant-messaging network in June 2006, composing approximately half the world's instant-messaging traffic. They looked at who sent each other text messages and then calculated how many different people in a "chain" it would take, on average, to connect two users to each other. After making calculations for 30 billion conversations among 240 million people, they found that the average length of people in the chain was 7 and that 90 percent of the pairs could be connected in 8 "hops" (Leskovec & Horvitz, 2007). Thus, 6 (or 7) degrees of separation appear to explain quite well how interconnected people are in this media age.

Similarity 相似性

As we saw, propinquity increases familiarity, which leads to liking, but something more is needed to fuel a growing friendship or a romantic relationship. (Otherwise, every pair of roommates would be best friends!) That "fuel" is *similarity*—a match between our interests, attitudes, values, background, or personality and those of another person. Folk wisdom captures this idea in the expression "Birds of a feather flock together" (the concept of *similarity*). But folk wisdom also has another saying, "Opposites attract" (the concept of *complementarity*, or that we are attracted to people who are our opposites). Luckily, we don't have to remain forever confused by contradictory advice from old sayings; research evidence proves that it is overwhelmingly similarity and not complementarity that draws people together (AhYun, 2002; Berscheid & Reis, 1998; Byrne, 1997; McPherson, Smith-Lovin, & Cook, 2001).

"I don't care if she is a tape dispenser. I love her."

Copyright © The New Yorker Collection 1998 Sam Gross from cartoonbank.com. All Rights Reserved.

Opinions and Personality A large body of research indicates that the more similar someone's opinions are to yours, the more you will like the person (e.g., Byrne & Nelson, 1965; Lutz-Zois, Bradley, Mihalik, & Moorman-Eavers, 2006). For example, in a classic study, Theodore Newcomb (1961) randomly assigned male college students at the University of Michigan to be roommates in a particular dormitory at the start of the school year. Would similarity predict friendship formation? The answer was yes: Men became friends with those who were demographically similar (e.g., shared a rural background), as well as with those who were similar in attitudes and values (e.g., were also engineering majors or also held liberal political views). It's not just attitudes or demographics that are important. Similar personality characteristics also promote liking and attraction. For example, in a study of gay men's relationships, men sought men with similar personalities. Those who scored high on a test of stereotypical male traits desired a partner who was most of all logical—a stereotypical masculine trait. Gay men who scored high on a test of stereotypical female traits desired a partner who was most of all expressive—a stereotypical feminine trait (Boyden, Carroll, & Maier, 1984). Similar personality characteristics are important for heterosexual couples and for friends as well (Acitelli, Kenny, & Weiner, 2001; Caspi & Harbener, 1990; Gonzaga, Campos, & Bradbury, 2007; Klohnen & Luo, 2003).

An administrator in the Housing Office of Barnard College sorts through roommate applications, placing them in piles according to their similar answers to questions about living habits and interests.

(Willie J. Allen Jr./*The New York Times*.)

Interpersonal Style We are also attracted to people whose interpersonal style and communication skills are similar to ours. In one study, people were attracted to peers who were similar to them in how they thought about people and how they liked to talk about interpersonal interactions (Burleson & Samter, 1996). High-skill people saw social interactions as complicated and complex; they focused on the psychological aspects of the interaction and valued communication with others that included this psychological component. Low-skill people saw social interactions in a more straightforward, less complicated way; they focused on the instrumental aspects of the interaction (e.g., what can be accomplished and what actually happened) and were less interested in the personalities or motivation of the participants. Pairs of friends had similar levels of communication skill—low with low, high with high. In fact, researchers have found that relationships with people who do not share your interpersonal communication style are frustrating and less likely to flourish (Burleson, 1994; Duck & Pittman, 1994). This is probably a great predictor of satisfaction in relationships and marriage—and of breakups and divorce!

Interests and Experiences   Finally, similarity operates in another, more subtle way. The situations that you choose to be in are, by definition, populated by people who have chosen them for similar reasons. You're sitting in a social psychology class, surrounded by people who also chose to take social psychology this semester. You sign up for salsa dance lessons; the others in your class are there because they too want to learn Latin dancing. Thus we choose to enter into certain types of social situations where we then find similar others. For example, in a study of the patterns of students' friendships that focused on the effects of "tracking" (grouping students by academic ability), researchers found that students were significantly more likely to choose friends from their track than from outside it (Kubitschek & Hallinan, 1998). Clearly, propinquity and initial similarity play a role in the formation of these friendships. However, the researchers add that similarity plays yet another role: Over time, students in the same academic track share many of the same experiences, which are different from the experiences of those in other tracks. Thus new similarities are created and discovered between them, fueling the friendships.

Some Final Comments about Similarity   Here are two additional points about similarity. First, while similarity is a very important variable in close relationships, it is important to make a distinction between "actual" (or real) similarity and "perceived" similarity, that is, the degree to which one *believes* oneself is similar to another (Morry, 2007). In a recent meta-analysis, R. Matthew Montoya and his colleagues found that in long-term relationships, "perceived" similarity predicted liking and attraction better than "actual" similarity did. Thus, feeling similar to another is still important, in fact, so much so that we will create beliefs about the similarity between ourselves and intimate others, believing such similarities exist even when they don't (Montoya, Horton, & Kirchner, 2008).

Second, a *lack* of similarity does appear to play an important role in one type of relationship. When we begin a romantic relationship, we typically want a serious, committed relationship—but sometimes, we just want a "fling." David Amodio and Carolin Showers (2005) found that whether it was similarity or complementarity that was important depended on the level of commitment that research participants felt toward their romantic partner and their relationship. If participants wanted a committed relationship, they chose a similar partner; however, if they felt a low level of commitment to the relationship, they favored dissimilar partners. Thus, in low commitment relationships, we may purposefully choose someone who is strikingly different from us. A relationship with this sort of person represents an "adventure" or an "exploration," as we experience someone totally different and new; however, as we'll see as we progress through this chapter, relationships based on differences, rather than similarities, can be very difficult to maintain.

Reciprocal Liking   互惠式的好感

We all like to be liked. In fact, just knowing that someone likes us fuels our attraction to the person. Liking is so powerful that it can even make up for the absence of similarity. For example, in one experiment, when a young woman expressed interest in male research participants simply by maintaining eye contact, leaning toward them, and listening attentively, the men expressed great liking for her despite the fact that they knew she disagreed with them on important issues (Gold, Ryckman, & Mosley, 1984). Whether the clues are nonverbal or verbal, perhaps the most crucial determinant of whether we will like person A is the extent to which we believe person A likes us (Berscheid & Walster, 1978; Kenny, 1994b; Kenny & La Voie, 1982; Kubitschek & Hallinan, 1998; Montoya & Insko, 2008).

Reciprocal liking sometimes happens because of a self-fulfilling prophecy, as we discussed in Chapter 3. Researchers demonstrated this process by conducting the following experiment (Curtis & Miller, 1986). College students participated in the study in pairs; they had not known each other before meeting at the study. One member of each pair was randomly chosen to receive special information. The researchers led some to believe that the other student liked them and led others to believe that the other student disliked them. The pairs of students were then allowed to meet and talk to each other again. Just as predicted, those who thought they were liked behaved in more likable ways with their partner; they disclosed more about themselves, disagreed less about the topic under discussion, and generally behaved in a warmer, more pleasant manner than the individuals who thought they were disliked. Moreover, those who believed they were liked came to be liked by the other student to a far greater extent than those who believed they were disliked. In short, the partner tended to mirror the behaviors of the person with whom he or she was paired.

> *Life is to be fortified by many friendships. To love, and to be loved, is the greatest happiness of existence.*
> *Love to faults is always blind,*
> *Always is to joy inclin'd.*
> —William Blake, *Love to Faults*

Physical Attractiveness and Liking 外表的吸引力与好感

Propinquity, similarity, and reciprocal liking are not the only determinants of who we will come to like. How important is physical appearance to our first impressions of people? In field experiments investigating people's actual behavior (rather than what they say they will do), people overwhelmingly go for physical attractiveness. For example, in a classic study, Elaine Walster Hatfield and her colleagues (Walster, Aronson, Abrahams, & Rottman, 1966) randomly matched 752 incoming students at the University of Minnesota for a blind date at a dance during freshman orientation week. Although the students had previously taken a battery of personality and aptitude tests, the researchers paired them up at random. On the night of the dance, the couples spent a few hours together dancing and chatting. They then evaluated their date and indicated the strength of their desire to date that person again. Of the many possible characteristics that could have determined whether they liked each other—such as their partner's intelligence, independence, sensitivity, or sincerity—the overriding determinant was physical attractiveness.

What's more, there was no great difference between men and women on this score. This is an interesting point, for while several studies have found that men and women pay equal attention to the physical attractiveness of others (Duck, 1994a, 1994b; Lynn & Shurgot, 1984; Speed & Gangestad, 1997; Woll, 1986), other studies have reported that men value attractiveness more than women do (Buss, 1989; Buss & Barnes, 1986; Howard, Blumstein, & Schwartz, 1987). A meta-analysis of many studies found that while both sexes value attractiveness, men value it somewhat more (Feingold, 1990); however, this gender difference was greater when men's and women's attitudes were being measured than when their actual behavior was being measured. Thus it may be that men are more likely than women to *say* that physical attractiveness is important to them in a potential friend, date, or mate, but when it comes to actual behavior, the sexes are more similar in their response to the physical attractiveness of others.

> *It is only shallow people who do not judge by appearances.*
> —Oscar Wilde, *The Picture of Dorian Gray*, 1891

Recent research continues to find that men and women rank physical attractiveness as equally important. Two researchers focused on an important distinction: They asked male and female participants to rate the desirability of 23 traits (including physical attractiveness) in a potential sexual partner (i.e., in a short-term, uncommitted relationship) and in a potential marriage partner (i.e., in a committed, long-term relationship; Regan & Berscheid, 1997). Both sexes ranked physical attractiveness as the most highly desirable characteristic in a potential sexual partner. (Only when it came to rating a marriage partner did men rate physical attractiveness higher than women did, though it was not one of the top characteristics desired by men.) In other studies, both genders rated physical attractiveness as the single most important characteristic that triggers sexual desire (Graziano, Jensen-Cambell, Shebilske, & Lundgren, 1993; Regan & Berscheid, 1995).

Finally, the powerful role that physical appearance plays in attraction is not limited to heterosexual relationships. When gay men participated in a "blind date" study like the one described earlier, they responded just as the heterosexual men and women had in the earlier study: The physical attractiveness of their dates was the strongest predictor of their liking for them (Sergios & Cody, 1985).

What Is Attractive? Is physical attractiveness "in the eye of the beholder," or do we all share some of the same notions of what is beautiful and handsome? From early childhood on, the media tell us what is beautiful, and they tell us that this definition of beauty is associated with goodness. For example, illustrators of most traditional children's books, as well as the people who draw the characters in Disney movies, have taught us that the heroines—as well as the princes who woo and win them—all look alike. For example, the heroines all have regular features; small, pert noses; big eyes; shapely lips; blemish-free complexions; and slim, athletic bodies—pretty much like Barbie dolls.

> *Oh, what vileness human beauty is, corroding, corrupting everything it touches.*
> —Orestes, 408 B.C.

Bombarded as we are with media depictions of attractiveness, it is not surprising to learn that we share a set of criteria for defining beauty (Fink & Penton-Voak, 2002; Tseëlon, 1995). Look at the photographs on the next page of entertainers who are considered very attractive in Western culture. Can you describe the facial characteristics that have earned them this label? Michael Cunningham (1986) designed a creative study to determine these standards of beauty. He asked college men to rate the attractiveness of 50 photographs of women, taken from a college yearbook and from an international beauty pageant program. Cunningham then carefully measured the relative size of the facial features in each photograph. He found that high attractiveness ratings were associated with female faces with large eyes, a small nose, a small chin, prominent cheekbones and narrow cheeks, high eyebrows, large pupils, and a big smile. Researchers then examined women's ratings of male beauty in the same way (Cunningham, Barbee, & Pike, 1990). They found that men's faces with large eyes, prominent cheekbones, a large chin, and a big smile received higher attractiveness ratings.

There is some overlap in the men's and women's ratings. Both sexes admire large eyes in the opposite sex; these are considered a "babyface" feature, for newborn mammals have very large eyes for the size of their faces. Babyface features are thought to be attractive because they elicit feelings of warmth and nurturance in perceivers—think of our typical response to babies, kittens, and puppies (e.g., Berry, 1995; McArthur & Berry, 1987; Zebrowitz, 1997; Zebrowitz & Montepare, 1992). Both sexes also admire prominent cheekbones in the opposite sex, an adult feature that is found only in the faces of those who are sexually mature. Note that the female face that is considered beautiful has more babyface features (small nose, small chin) than the handsome male face, suggesting that beauty in the female is associated more with childlike qualities than male beauty is.

Cultural Standards of Beauty Are people's perceptions of what is beautiful or handsome similar across cultures? The answer is a surprising yes (Cunningham, Roberts, Barbee, Druen, & Wu, 1995; Jones & Hill, 1993; McArthur & Berry, 1987; Rhodes et al., 2001). Even though racial and ethnic groups do vary in specific facial features, people from a wide range of cultures agree on what is physically attractive in the human face. Researchers asked participants from various countries, ethnicities, and racial groups to rate the physical attractiveness of photographed faces of people who also represented various countries, ethnicities, and racial groups. The participants' ratings agreed to a remarkable extent. For example, one review of this literature

Today's popular actors, such as Natalie Portman, Jessica Alba, Ziyi Zhang, Halle Berry, Benjamin Bratt, Patrick Dempsey, Daniel Dae Kim, and Will Smith represent facial standards of beauty for men and women.

found that the correlations between participants' ratings ranged from 0.66 to 0.93 (Langlois & Roggman, 1990), which are very strong correlations (see Chapter 2). A meta-analysis of many studies by Judith Langlois and her colleagues (2000) also found evidence for cross-cultural agreement in what constitutes a beautiful or handsome face. Although people's judgments vary across large groups a consensus emerges: Perceivers think some faces are just better looking than others, regardless of cultural background (Berscheid & Reis, 1998).

How can we explain these results? Researchers have suggested that humans came to find certain dimensions of faces attractive during the course of our evolution (Langlois & Roggman, 1990; Langlois, Roggman, & Musselman, 1994). We know, for example, that even infants prefer photographs of attractive faces to unattractive ones, and infants prefer the same photographs adults prefer (Langlois, Ritter, Roggman, & Vaughn, 1991; Langlois, Roggman, & Rieser-Danner, 1990). One aspect of facial beauty that is preferred in both men and women is symmetry, where the placement and size of the features on one side of the face match those on the other. People are

Beauty is a greater recommendation than any letter of introduction.

—Aristotle, fourth century B.C.

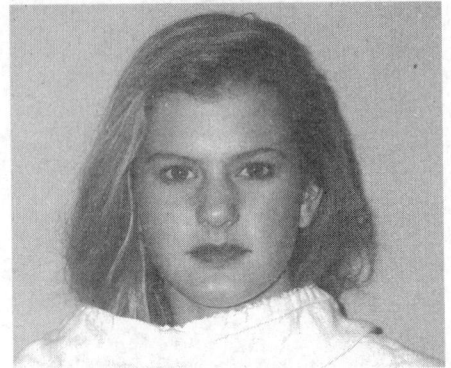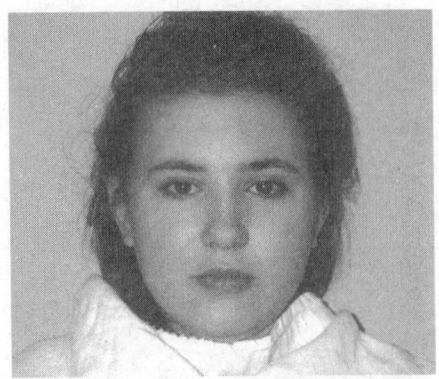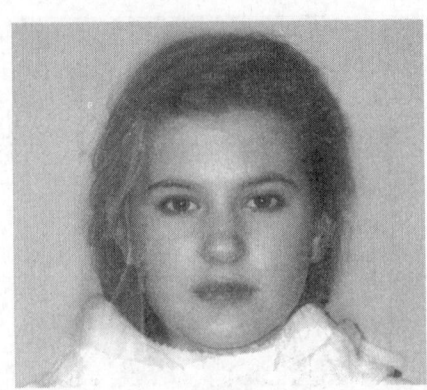

Physical attractiveness of composite faces. Langlois and Roggman (1990) created composites of faces using a computer. Pictured here is the first step in the process: The first two women's photos are merged to create the "composite person" at the far right. This composite person has facial features that are the mathematical average of the facial features of the two original women.

(From Langlois, Roggman, & Musselman, 1994)

more attracted to symmetrical faces than to asymmetrical ones (Little et al., 2008; Langlois et al., 2000; Rhodes, 2006). Evolutionary psychologists suggest that symmetrical features are markers of good health and reproductive fitness, and thus a human preference for facial symmetry exists because it is an indicator of "good genes" (Grammer & Thornhill, 1994). A series of studies explored this preference by creating "composite" photographs of faces. Two photographs of faces were combined, digitally, to create one composite that was the mathematical average of the features of the two faces. This process was continued until 32 faces had been combined into one composite. When shown to research participants, these final composite photographs were judged as more attractive than were all the separate faces that had created them, and this was true for both male and female photographs (Langlois & Roggman, 1990; Langlois et al., 1994). This "average" composite face was more attractive because it had lost some of the atypical or asymmetrical variation that was present in the individual faces.

Does this mean that we find "average" faces the most attractive? Clearly not, for we respond to the physical appearance of movie stars and models because their looks are "above average" compared to most humans. David Perret and his colleagues made this point clear in the following study (Perret, May, & Yoshikawa, 1994). They created composite faces of two types: One composite was based on 60 photographs that had each been rated as "average" in attractiveness. The other composite was based on 60 photographs that had each been rated as "highly" attractive. Composites of these two types were made using photographs of Caucasian women, Caucasian men, Japanese women, and Japanese men. Research participants in Great Britain and Japan then rated all the composite faces for attractiveness.

The researchers found, first, that the "highly attractive" composites were rated significantly more attractive than the "average attractive" composites. Second, the Japanese and British participants showed the same pattern when judging the faces, reinforcing the idea that similar perceptions of facial attractiveness exist cross-culturally and exist for ethnic groups that are the same or different from one's own. Finally, what did those "highly attractive" composites look like? Their facial shapes, whether Japanese or Caucasian, matched the descriptions for men and women that Michael Cunningham and his colleagues (Cunningham, 1986; Cunningham, Barbee, & Pike, 1990) found in their research. For example, the Japanese and Caucasian "highly attractive" female composites had higher cheekbones, a thinner jaw, and larger eyes relative to the size of the face than the "average attractive" composites did (Perrett et al., 1994).

The Power of Familiarity The crucial variable that explains interpersonal attraction may actually be familiarity (Berscheid & Reis, 1998). We've seen that "averaging" many faces together produces one face that looks typical, familiar, and physically attractive (see also Halberstadt & Rhodes, 2000). Recent research has found evidence for an even more startling effect for familiarity: When research participants rated the attractiveness of faces, they preferred the faces that most resembled their own! The researchers then computer-morphed a picture of each participant's face (without the participant's knowledge) into that of a person of the opposite sex. When they presented this photo to participants, they gave the photo of their opposite-sex "clone" even higher ratings of attractiveness (Little & Perrett, 2002). This preference for the familiar appears to be shared amongst people in close relationships. Research participants who were members of the same family or close friends agreed much more with each other when they rated photographs of faces for attractiveness than they did with strangers. It appears that while there is variation in people's "personal taste" as to whom they consider handsome or beautiful, their taste is very much shared with those with whom they are most familiar and close (Bronstad & Russell, 2007).

Familiarity also underlies the other concepts we've discussed thus far: propinquity (people we see frequently become familiar through mere exposure), similarity (people who are similar to us will also seem familiar to us), and reciprocal liking (people who like each other get to know and become familiar with each other). All these attraction variables may be expressions of our "underlying preference for the familiar and safe over the unfamiliar and potentially dangerous" (Berscheid & Reis, 1998, p. 210).

Assumptions about Attractive People It's important to realize that beauty "matters"—even when it shouldn't. We're attracted to that which is beautiful, and that can lead to inequity in everyday life. A particularly chilling example of the unfair benefit of beauty was discovered by Lina Badr and Bahia Abdallah (2001), who rated the facial physical attractiveness and health status of premature infants born in hospitals in Beirut, Lebanon. They found that physical attractiveness significantly predicted the health outcomes of these infants above and beyond the contribution of factors such as their medical condition. The more attractive the infant, the more quickly he or she gained weight and the shorter his or her stay in the hospital. The reason? Neonatal nurses responded more to the "prettier" infants and gave them better care.

Physical attractiveness confers many other benefits as well. People of above-average looks tend to earn 10 percent to 15 percent more than those of below-average appearance (French, 2002; Hammermesh & Biddle, 1994; Mobius & Rosenblat, 2006). Attractiveness even helps people win elections. Panu Poutvaara and his colleagues (2006) presented a large number of photographs of Finnish political candidates to research participants in many other countries (who would have no prior knowledge of these candidates) and asked them to rate the politicians on attractiveness, as well as on other attributes. They found that the participants' ratings of attractiveness were the best predictors of the actual number of votes each candidate had gotten in the real elections. The effect was present for both male and female politicians, though stronger for the females. A higher "beauty rating" implied an increase of between 2.5 and 2.8 percentage points in the vote total for female candidates, and between 1.5 and 2.1 percentage points for male candidates, amounts that could matter in a close election (Poutvaara, Berggren, & Jordahl, 2006).

Many studies have found that physical attractiveness affects the attributions people make about the attractive. Specifically, people attribute positive qualities to beautiful people that have nothing to do with their looks. This tendency is called the "what is beautiful is good" stereotype (Ashmore & Longo, 1995; Calvert, 1988; Dion, Berscheid, & Walster, 1972; Moore, Graziano, & Millar, 1987). Meta-analyses have revealed that physical attractiveness has the largest effect on both men's and women's attributions when they are judging social competence: The beautiful are thought to be more sociable, extroverted, and popular than the less attractive (Eagly, Ashmore, Makhijani, & Longo, 1991; Feingold, 1992b). They are also seen as more sexual, happier, and more assertive.

Do these stereotypes about beautiful people operate across cultures? The answer appears to be yes (Anderson, Adams, & Plaut, 2008; Chen, Shaffer, & Wu, 1997). For example, college students in Seoul, South Korea, were asked to rate a number of yearbook photographs that varied in physical attractiveness (Wheeler & Kim, 1997). Both male and female participants thought the more physically attractive people would also be

In Western cultures, where independence is valued, the "beautiful" stereotype includes traits of personal strength. In more collectivistic Asian cultures, beautiful people are assumed to have traits such as integrity and concern for others.

TABLE 10.1 How Culture Affects the "What Is Beautiful Is Good" Stereotype

The "what is beautiful is good" stereotype has been explored in both an individualistic culture (North America) and a collectivistic culture (Asia). Male and female research participants in the United States and Canada and in South Korea rated photographs of people with varying degrees of physical attractiveness. Their responses indicated that some of the traits that make up the stereotype are the same across cultures, while other traits that are associated with the stereotype are different in the two cultures. In both cultures, the physically attractive are seen as having more of the characteristics that are valued in that culture than the less physically attractive have.

Traits Shared in the Korean, American, and Canadian Stereotype

sociable	extraverted	likable
happy	popular	well-adjusted
friendly	mature	poised
sexually warm and responsive		

Additional Traits Present in the American and Canadian Stereotype

strong	assertive	dominant

Additional Traits Present in the Korean Stereotype

sensitive	empathic	generous
honest	trustworthy	

Sources: Eagly, Ashmore, Makhijani, & Longo (1991); Feingold (1992b); Wheeler & Kim (1997).

more socially skilled, friendly, and well adjusted—the same group of traits that North American participants thought went with physical attractiveness (see Table 10.1). But Korean and North American students differed in some of the other traits they assigned to the beautiful, highlighting what is important and valuable in each culture (Markus et al., 1996; Triandis, 1995). For the American and Canadian students, who live in individualistic cultures that value independence, individuality, and self-reliance, the "beautiful" stereotype included traits of personal strength. These traits were not part of the Korean "beautiful" stereotype. Instead, for the Korean students, who live in a collectivistic culture that values harmonious group relations, the "beautiful" stereotype included integrity and concern for others, traits that were not part of the North American stereotype (see Table 10.1).

Interestingly, the stereotype that the beautiful are particularly gifted in the area of social competence has some research support; highly attractive people do develop good social interaction skills and report having more satisfying interactions with others than the less attractive do (Feingold, 1992b; Langlois et al., 2000; Reis et al., 1982). Undoubtedly, this "kernel of truth" in the stereotype occurs because the beautiful, from a young age, receive a great deal of social attention that in turn helps them develop good social skills. You probably recognize the self-fulfilling prophecy at work here (see Chapter 3): The way we treat people affects how they behave and ultimately how they perceive themselves.

Can a "regular" person be made to act like a "beautiful" one through the self-fulfilling prophecy? To find out, researchers gave college men a packet of information about another research participant, including her photograph (Snyder, Tanke, & Berscheid, 1977). The photograph was rigged; it was either of an attractive woman or of an unattractive woman. The men were told that they would have a telephone conversation with this woman (in this experimental condition, only verbal communication—no gestures or facial expressions—was used). The experimental purpose of the photograph was to invoke the men's stereotype that "what is beautiful is good"—that the woman would be more warm, likable, poised, and fun to talk to if she was physically attractive than if she was unattractive. In fact, the photograph the men were given was not a photo of the woman with whom they spoke. Did the men's beliefs create reality?

Yes—the men who thought they were talking to an attractive woman responded to her in a warmer, more sociable manner than the men who thought they were talking to an unattractive woman. Not only that, but the men's behavior influenced how the women themselves responded. When independent observers listened to a tape recording of only the woman's half of the conversation (without looking at the photograph), they rated the women whose male partners thought they were physically attractive as more attractive, confident, animated, and warm than the women whose male partners thought they were unattractive. In short, because the male partner thought he was talking to an attractive woman, he spoke to her in a way that brought out her best and most sparkling qualities.

This study was later replicated with the roles switched: Women participants looked at a photograph of an attractive or an unattractive man and then spoke with him on the phone (Andersen & Bem, 1981). The men were unaware of the women's belief about them, and just as in the original study, the women acted on their "prophecy" and the unknowing men responded accordingly. These data remind us that it is a myth that physical attractiveness affects women's lives more than men's. Three meta-analyses that have examined the effect of attractiveness on behavior and perceptions across hundreds of studies have found no gender differences: Physical attractiveness is as important a factor in men's lives as women's (Eagly et al., 1991; Feingold, 1992b; Langlois et al., 2000).

> *Don't threaten me with love, baby. Let's go walking in the rain.*
> —Billie Holiday

Theories of Interpersonal Attraction: Social Exchange and Equity 人际吸引理论：社会交换理论和公平理论

So far, we've examined the determinants of attraction that concern aspects of the situation (propinquity, repeated exposure), the individual's attributes (physical attractiveness, similarity, self-esteem), and the individual's behavior (conveying liking). We turn now to theories of interpersonal attraction that link these phenomena together.

Social Exchange Theory   Many of the variables we have discussed can be thought of as examples of social rewards. It is pleasing to have our attitudes validated; thus the more similar a person's attitudes are to ours, the more rewarded we feel. Likewise, it is rewarding to be around someone who likes us and is physically attractive. One way of summarizing much of our discussion so far is to say that the more social rewards a person provides us with (and the fewer costs), the more we will like the person. The flip side of this equation is that if a relationship costs (e.g., in terms of emotional turmoil) far more than it gives (e.g., in terms of validation or praise), chances are that it will not last.

This simple notion that relationships operate on an economic model of costs and benefits, much like the marketplace, has been expanded by psychologists and sociologists into complex theories of social exchange (Blau, 1964; Homans, 1961; Kelley & Thibaut, 1978; Secord & Backman, 1964; Thibaut & Kelley, 1959). **Social exchange theory** holds that how people feel (positively or negatively) about their relationships will depend on (1) their perception of the rewards they receive from the relationship, (2) their perception of the costs they incur, and (3) their perception of what kind of relationship they deserve and the probability that they could have a better relationship with someone else. In other words, we buy the best relationship we can get, one that gives us the most value for our emotional dollar. The basic concepts of social exchange theory are reward, cost, outcome, and comparison level.

Rewards are the positive, gratifying aspects of the relationship that make it worthwhile and reinforcing. They include the kinds of personal characteristics and behaviors of our relationship partner that we have already discussed and our ability to acquire external resources by virtue of knowing this person (e.g., gaining access to money, status, activities, or other interesting people; Lott & Lott, 1974). For example, in Brazil, friendship is openly used as an exchange value. Brazilians will readily admit that they need a *pistolão* (literally, a big, powerful handgun), meaning they need a person who will use his or her personal connections to help them get what they want (Rector & Neiva, 1996). Costs are, obviously, the other side of the

> *Love is often nothing but a favorable exchange between two people who get the most of what they can expect, considering their value on the personality market.*
> —Erich Fromm, *The Sane Society*, 1955

Social Exchange Theory
The idea that people's feelings about a relationship depend on their perceptions of the rewards and costs of the relationship, the kind of relationship they deserve, and their chances for having a better relationship with someone else

coin, and all friendships and romantic relationships have some costs attached to them (such as putting up with those annoying habits and characteristics of the other person). The outcome of the relationship is a direct comparison of its rewards and costs; you can think of it as a mathematical formula where outcome equals rewards minus costs. (If you come up with a negative number, your relationship is not in good shape.)

How satisfied you are with your relationship depends on another variable—your **comparison level**, or what you expect the outcome of your relationship to be in terms of costs and rewards (Kelley & Thibaut, 1978; Thibaut & Kelley, 1959). Over time, you have amassed a long history of relationships with other people, and this history has led you to have certain expectations as to what your current and future relationships should be like. Some people have a high comparison level, expecting lots of rewards and few costs in their relationships. If a given relationship doesn't match this expected comparison level, they will be unhappy and unsatisfied. In contrast, people who have a low comparison level would be happy in the same relationship because they expect relationships to be difficult and costly.

Finally, your satisfaction with a relationship also depends on your perception of the likelihood that you could replace it with a better one—or your **comparison level for alternatives**. There are a lot of people out there; could a relationship with a different person give you a better outcome or greater rewards for fewer costs than your current one? People who have a high comparison level for alternatives, either because they believe the world is full of fabulous people dying to meet them or because they know of a fabulous person dying to meet them, are more likely to get into circulation and make a new friend or find a new lover. People with a low comparison level for alternatives will be more likely to stay in a costly relationship because to them, what they have is not great but is better than their expectation of what they could find elsewhere (Simpson, 1987).

Social exchange theory has received a great deal of empirical support; friends and romantic couples do pay attention to the costs and rewards in their relationships, and these affect how positively people feel about the status of the relationship (Bui, Peplau, & Hill, 1996; Le & Agnew, 2003; Rusbult, 1983; Rusbult, Martz, & Agnew, 1998).

Equity Theory Some researchers have criticized social exchange theory for ignoring an essential variable in relationships—the notion of fairness, or equity. Proponents of **equity theory** argue that people are not just out to get the most rewards for the least cost; they are also concerned about equity in their relationships, wherein the rewards and costs they experience and the contributions they make to the relationship are roughly equal to those of the other person (Homans, 1961; Walster, Walster, & Berscheid, 1978). These theorists describe equitable relationships as the happiest and most stable. In comparison, inequitable relationships result in one person feeling overbenefited (getting a lot of rewards, incurring few costs, having to devote little time or energy to the relationship) or underbenefited (getting few rewards, incurring a lot of costs, having to devote a lot of time and energy to the relationship).

According to equity theory, both underbenefited and overbenefited partners should feel uneasy about this state of affairs, and both should be motivated to restore equity to the relationship. This makes sense for the underbenefited person (who wants to continue feeling miserable?), but why should the overbenefited individual want to give up what social exchange theory indicates is a cushy deal—lots of rewards for little cost and little work? Some theorists argue that equity is a powerful social norm—people will eventually feel uncomfortable or even guilty if they get more than they deserve in a relationship. Being overbenefited just doesn't seem as bad as being underbenefited, however, and research has borne out that inequity is perceived as more of a problem by the underbenefited individual (Buunk & Schaufeli, 1999; Guerrero, La Valley, & Farinelli, 2008; Sprecher & Schwartz, 1994; Van Yperen & Buunk, 1990).

> *Friendship is a scheme for the mutual exchange of personal advantages and favors.*
> —François de La Rochefoucauld, Maxims, 1665

Comparison Level
People's expectations about the level of rewards and punishments they are likely to receive in a particular relationship

Comparison Level for Alternatives
People's expectations about the level of rewards and punishments they would receive in an alternative relationship

Equity Theory
The idea that people are happiest with relationships in which the rewards and costs experienced and the contributions made by both parties are roughly equal

Close Relationships 亲密关系

After getting to this point in the chapter, you should be in a pretty good position to make a favorable first impression the next time you meet someone. Suppose you want Claudia to like you. You should hang around her so that you become familiar, act in ways that are rewarding to her, emphasize your similarity to her, and let her know you enjoy her company. But what if you want to do more than make a good impression? What if you want to have a close friendship or a romantic relationship?

Until recently, social psychologists had little to say in answer to this question; research on interpersonal attraction focused almost exclusively on first impressions. Why? Primarily because close, long-term relationships are much more difficult to study scientifically than first impressions. As we saw in Chapter 2, random assignment to different conditions is the hallmark of an experiment. When studying first impressions, a researcher can randomly assign you to a get-acquainted session with someone who is similar or dissimilar to you. But a researcher can't randomly assign you to the similar or dissimilar "lover" condition and make you have a relationship! In addition, the feelings and intimacy associated with close relationships can be difficult to measure. Psychologists face a daunting task when trying to measure such complex feelings as love and passion.

This scene from the movie *Twilight* exemplifies the early stages of love.

Defining Love 爱的定义

Despite the difficulties in studying close relationships, social psychologists have made some interesting discoveries about the nature of love, how it develops, and how it flourishes. Let's begin with perhaps the most difficult question: What, exactly, is love? Early attempts to define love distinguished between liking and loving, showing that as you might expect, love is something different from "lots of liking," and it isn't just sexual desire either (Rubin, 1970).

Companionate versus Passionate Love For Shakespeare's Romeo and Juliet, love was passionate, turbulent, and full of longing. Your grandparents, if they've remained married for a long time, probably exemplify a calmer, more tranquil kind of love. We use the word *love* to describe both of these relationships, though each seems to be of a different kind (Berscheid & Meyers, 1996, 1997; Fehr, 1994; Fehr & Russell, 1991; Vohs & Baumeister, 2004).

Social psychologists have recognized that a good definition of love must include the passionate, giddy feelings of romantic love as well as the deep, long-term devotion of a long-married couple, lifelong friends, or siblings. In defining love, then, we generally distinguish between *companionate love* and *passionate love* (Hatfield, 1988; Hatfield & Rapson, 1993; Hatfield & Walster, 1978). **Companionate love** consists of feelings of intimacy and affection we have for someone that are not accompanied by passion or physiological arousal. People can experience companionate love in nonsexual relationships, such as close friendships, or in sexual relationships, where they experience great feelings of intimacy (companionate love) but not a great deal of the heat and passion they may once have felt.

Passionate love involves an intense longing for another person, characterized by the experience of physiological arousal, the feeling of shortness of breath and a thumping heart in our loved one's presence (Fisher, 2004; Regan & Berscheid, 1999). When things are going well—the other person loves us too—we feel great fulfillment and ecstasy. When things are not going well—our love is unrequited—we feel great sadness and despair. Cross-cultural research comparing an individualistic culture (the United States) and a collectivistic culture (China) indicates that American couples tend to value passionate love more than Chinese couples do, and Chinese couples tend to value companionate love more than American couples do (Gao, 1993; Jankowiak, 1995; Ting-Toomey & Chung, 1996). In comparison, the Taita of Kenya, in East Africa, value both

> Love is something so divine,
> Description would but make it less;
> 'Tis what I feel, but can't define,
> 'Tis what I know, but can't express.
>
> —Beilby Porteus

> Try to reason about love, and you will lose your reason.
>
> —French proverb

Companionate Love
The intimacy and affection we feel when we care deeply for a person but do not experience passion or arousal in the person's presence

Passionate Love
An intense longing we feel for a person, accompanied by physiological arousal; when our love is reciprocated, we feel great fulfillment and ecstasy, but when it is not, we feel sadness and despair

TABLE 10.2 Cross-Cultural Evidence for Passionate Love Based on Anthropological Research in 166 Societies

Cultural Area	Passionate Love Present	Passionate Love Absent
Mediterranean	22 (95.7%)	1 (4.3%)
Sub-Saharan Africa	20 (76.9%)	6 (23.1%)
Eurasia	32 (97.0%)	1 (3.0%)
Insular Pacific	27 (93.1%)	2 (6.9%)
North America	24 (82.8%)	5 (17.2%)
South and Central America	22 (84.6%)	4 (15.4%)

Source: Data from Jankowiak & Fischer (1992).

equally; they conceptualize romantic love as a combination of companionate love and passionate love. The Taita consider this the best kind of love, and achieving it is a primary goal in their society (Bell, 1995). Reviewing the anthropological research on 166 societies, William Jankowiak and Edward Fischer (1992) found evidence for passionate love in 147 of them, as you can see in Table 10.2.

Elaine Hatfield and Susan Sprecher (1986) developed a questionnaire to measure passionate love. As measured by this scale, passionate love consists of strong, uncontrollable thoughts; intense feelings; and overt acts toward the target of one's affection. Find out if you are experiencing (or have experienced) passionate love by filling out the questionnaire in the following Try It! exercise.

TRY IT! Passionate Love Scale 试一试！激情之爱量表

These items ask you to describe how you feel when you are passionately in love. Think of the person whom you love most passionately right now. If you are not in love right now, think of the last person you loved passionately. If you have never been in love, think of the person you came closest to caring for in that way. Choose your answers remembering how you felt when your feelings were the most intense.

For each of the 15 items, choose the number between 1 and 9 that most accurately describes your feelings. The answer scale ranges from 1, not at all true, to 9, definitely true. Write the number you choose next to each item.

```
1   2   3   4   5   6   7   8   9
↑               ↑               ↑
Not at all true  Moderately true  Definitely true
```

1. I would feel deep despair if _____ left me.
2. Sometimes I feel I can't control my thoughts; they are obsessively on _____.
3. I feel happy when I am doing something to make _____ happy.
4. I would rather be with _____ than anyone else.
5. I'd get jealous if I thought _____ were falling in love with someone else.
6. I yearn to know all about _____.
7. I want _____—physically, emotionally, mentally.
8. I have an endless appetite for affection from _____.
9. For me, _____ is the perfect romantic partner.
10. I sense my body responding when _____ touches me.
11. _____ always seems to be on my mind.
12. I want _____ to know me—my thoughts, my fears, and my hopes.
13. I eagerly look for signs indicating _____'s desire for me.
14. I possess a powerful attraction for _____.
15. I get extremely depressed when things don't go right in my relationship with _____.

Scoring: Add up your scores for the 15 items. The total score can range from a minimum of 15 to a maximum of 135. The higher your score, the more your feelings for the person reflect passionate love; the items to which you gave a particularly high score reflect those components of passionate love that you experience most strongly.

(Adapted from Hatfield & Sprecher, 1986)

Culture and Love 文化和爱

Although love is a universal emotion, how we experience it (and what we expect from close relationships) is linked to culture. For example, the Japanese describe *amae* as an extremely positive emotional state in which one is a totally passive love object, indulged and taken care of by one's romantic partner, much like a mother–infant relationship. *Amae* has no equivalent word in English or in any other Western language; the closest is the word *dependency*, an emotional state that Western cultures consider unhealthy in adult relationships (Dion & Dion, 1993; Doi, 1988; Farrer, Tsuchiya, & Bagrowicz, 2008).

Similarly, the Chinese concept of *gan qing* differs from the Western view of romantic love. *Gan qing* is achieved by helping and working for another person; for example, a "romantic" act would be fixing someone's bicycle or helping someone learn new material (Gao, 1996). In Korea, a special kind of relationship is expressed by the concept of *jung*. Much more than "love," *jung* is what ties two people together. Couples in new relationships may feel strong love for each other, but they have not yet developed strong *jung*—that takes time and many mutual experiences. Interestingly, *jung* can develop in negative relationships too—for example, between business rivals who dislike each other. *Jung* may unknowingly grow between them over time, with the result that they will feel that a strange connection exists between them (Lim & Choi, 1996; Kline, Horton, & Zhang, 2008).

Although people all over the world experience love, how love is defined varies across cultures.

Phillip Shaver and his colleagues (Shaver, Wu, & Schwartz, 1992) wondered if romantic or passionate love was associated with the same emotions in different cultures. They asked research participants in the United States, Italy, and China to sort more than a hundred emotional words into categories; their analysis indicated that love has similar and different meanings cross-culturally. The most striking difference was the presence of a "sad love" cluster in the Chinese sample. The Chinese had many love-related concepts that were sad, such as words for "sorrow-love," "tenderness-pity," and "sorrow-pity." Although this "sad love" cluster made a small appearance in the U.S. and Italian samples, it was not perceived as a major aspect of love in these Western societies.

Other researchers wondered what the lyrics of popular American and Chinese (Mainland China and Hong Kong) love songs would reveal about the experience of love in each culture (Rothbaum & Tsang, 1998). Finding that the Chinese love songs had significantly more references to suffering and to negative outcomes than the American love songs, the researchers looked to the Chinese concept of *yuan*. This is the belief that interpersonal relations are predestined. According to the traditional Buddhist belief in *karma*, fate determines what happens in a relationship. The romantic partners have little control over this process (Goodwin, 1999). If a relationship is not working, it cannot be saved; one must accept fate and the suffering that accompanies it (Rothbaum & Tsang, 1998). Although Chinese songs were sadder than American ones, there was no difference in the intensity with which love was described in the two countries. The researchers found that love in Chinese songs was as "passionate and erotic" as love expressed in American songs.

Love is or it ain't. Thin love ain't love at all.

—Toni Morrison

How romantic love is defined and experienced can vary across individualistic and collectivistic cultures, as we discussed earlier. Researchers have found that Canadian college students have different attitudes about love, depending on their ethnocultural background: Asian (Chinese, Korean, Vietnamese, Indian, Pakistani), Anglo-Celtic (English, Irish, Scottish), or European (Scandinavian, Spanish, German, Polish). In comparison to their peers, the Asian respondents were significantly more likely to identify with a companionable, friendship-based romantic love, a "style of love that would not disrupt a complex network of existing family relationships" (Dion & Dion, 1993, p. 465). Similarly, in West African settings, relationships with one's parents, siblings, and other relatives are seen as more important and consequential than the more recent relationship one has formed with one's spouse. In many areas of West Africa, happily married couples do not live together in the same house, nor do they expect to sleep together every night. In stark contrast to the pattern of intimate relationships in individualistic cultures, their connection and obligation to their extended family members take precedence over those to their spouse. In individualistic cultures, the opposite is typically true (Adams, Anderson, & Adonu, 2004). Finally, researchers surveyed college students in 11 countries around the world, asking them, "If a man (woman) had all the qualities you desired, would you marry this person if you were not in love with him (her)?" These researchers found that marrying for love was most important to participants in Western and Westernized countries (e.g., the United States, Brazil, England, and Australia) and of least importance to participants in less developed Eastern countries (i.e., India, Pakistan, and Thailand; Levine et al., 1995).

The results of these studies indicate that the concept of romantic love is to some extent culturally specific (Dion & Dion, 1996; Gao & Gudykunst, 1995; Hatfield & Rapson, 2002; Hatfield & Sprecher, 1995; Sprecher, Aron et al., 1994). Love can vary in definition and behavior in different societies. We all love, but we do not necessarily all love in the same way—or at least we don't describe it in the same way (Landis & O'Shea, 2000). As noted earlier, anthropologists found evidence of romantic (passionate) love in 147 of the 166 cultures sampled (Jankowiak, 1995; Jankowiak & Fischer, 1992); it was present even in societies "that do not accept" romantic love "or embrace it as a positive ideal" (Jankowiak, 1995, p. 4).

Thus it appears that romantic love is nearly universal in the human species, but cultural rules alter how that emotional state is experienced, expressed, and remembered (Carillo, 2001; Farrer, 2002; Higgins, Zheng, Liu, & Sun, 2002; Jackson, Chen, Guo, & Gao, 2006). For example, Shuangyue Zhang and Susan Kline (2009) found two major differences in American and Chinese dating couples' decisions to marry. Chinese students placed a heavier emphasis on two concepts central to their collectivistic culture, *xiao* (the obedience and devotion shown by children to their parents) and *guanxi* (relationships as a network of connections), when describing how they would decide whether or not to marry their partners, while American students placed importance on receiving support, care, and "living a better life." As Robert Moore (1998) noted in summarizing his research in the People's Republic of China, "Young Chinese do fall deeply in love and experience the same joys and sorrows of romance as young Westerners do. But they do so according to standards that require . . . the individual [to] sacrifice personal interests for the sake of the family . . . This means avoiding fleeting infatuations, casual sexual encounters, and a dating context [where] family concerns are forgotten" (p. 280).

Love and Relationships 爱情和人际关系

Are the causes of love similar to the causes of initial attraction? How do the factors we discussed earlier as determinants of first impressions play out in intimate relationships? And do other variables come into play when we are developing and maintaining a close relationship?

Evolution and Love: Choosing a Mate 进化和爱：选择配偶

The poet Robert Browning asked, "How do I love thee? Let me count the ways." For psychologists, the question is "Why do I love thee?" For many, the answer lies in an **evolutionary approach to love**. The basic tenet of evolutionary biology is that an animal's "fitness" is measured by its reproductive success—that is, its capability to pass on its genes to the next generation. Reproductive success is not just part of the game; it *is* the game. This biological concept has been applied to social behavior by psychologists, who define **evolutionary psychology** as the attempt to explain social behavior in terms of genetic factors that evolved over time according to the principles of natural selection. Has human behavior evolved in specific ways to maximize reproductive success? Evolutionary psychologists say yes; they argue that men and women have very different agendas due to their differing roles in producing offspring.

Evolutionary Approach to Love

A theory derived from evolutionary biology that holds that men and women are attracted to different characteristics in each other (men are attracted by women's appearance; women are attracted by men's resources) because this maximizes their chances of reproductive success

Evolutionary Psychology

The attempt to explain social behavior in terms of genetic factors that evolved over time according to the principles of natural selection

For women, reproduction is costly in terms of time, energy, and effort: They must endure the discomforts of pregnancy and birth and then care for their infants until maturity. Reproducing, then, is a serious business, so women, the theory goes, must consider carefully when and with whom to reproduce. In comparison, reproduction has few costs for men. The evolutionary approach to love concludes that reproductive success for the two sexes translates into two very different behavior patterns: Throughout the animal world, males' reproductive success is measured by the quantity of their offspring. They pursue frequent pairings with many females in order to maximize the number of their surviving progeny. In contrast, females' reproductive success lies in successfully raising each of their offspring to maturity. They pair infrequently and only with a carefully chosen male because the cost of raising and ensuring the survival of each offspring is so high (Berkow, 1989; Symons, 1979).

Men seek to propagate widely, whereas women seek to propagate wisely.

—Robert Hinde

Now, what does this have to do with falling in love? David Buss and his colleagues state that this evolutionary approach explains the different strategies of men and women in romantic relationships (Buss, 1985, 1988a, 1996a, 1996b; Buss & Schmitt, 1993). Buss (1988b) explains that finding (and keeping) a mate requires one to display one's resources—the aspects of oneself that will appear attractive to potential mates. This approach argues that across millennia, human beings have been selected through evolution to respond to certain external cues in the opposite sex. Women, facing high reproductive costs, will look for a man who can supply the resources and support she needs to bear a child. Men will look for a woman who appears capable of reproducing successfully. More specifically, men will respond to the physical appearance of women because age and health denote reproductive fitness, and women will respond to the economic and career achievements of men because these variables represent resources they and their offspring will need (Buss, 1988b).

Many studies have found support for these predictions. For example, Buss and his colleagues (Buss, 1989; Buss et al., 1990) asked more than nine thousand adults in 37 countries how important and desirable various characteristics were in choosing a marriage partner. In general, the women participants valued ambition, industriousness, and good earning capacity in a potential mate more than the men did. The men valued physical attractiveness in a mate more than the women did, a finding echoed in other research. [It should be noted, however, that the top characteristics on both men's and women's lists were the same, involving such characteristics as honesty, trustworthiness, and a pleasant personality (Buss & Barnes, 1986; Hatfield & Sprecher, 1995; Regan & Berscheid, 1997; Sprecher, Sullivan, & Hatfield, 1994).] As we discussed earlier, men are more likely than women to say that physical attractiveness is important to them in a potential date (Feingold, 1990). Other survey studies have indicated that men prefer spouses who are younger than they are (youth indicating greater reproductive fitness), while women prefer spouses around their own age (Buss, 1989; Kenrick & Keefe, 1992). When college students were asked to imagine that their romantic partner had been sexually unfaithful or emotionally unfaithful, the men were more upset by the sexual infidelity scenario than the women were, while the women were relatively more upset by the emotional infidelity story (Buss, Larsen, Westen, & Semmelroth, 1992).

An elaboration of the evolutionary approach to love and mate selection has been offered by Steven Gangestad and David Buss (1993). If physical attractiveness in women is preferred by men because it signals reproductive fitness, female physical attractiveness should be particularly valued in regions of the world where disease is very common—the idea being that the physically attractive are both healthy and possibly resistant to local diseases. Gangestad and Buss found that in areas of the world where disease-transmitting parasites are prevalent, people did indicate a stronger preference for physically attractive mates than in areas with a low prevalence of parasites; however, this preference for the physically attractive mate was just as strong among women as it was among men. Thus this study offers support for the fundamental points of the evolutionary approach but calls into question the proposed gender difference between men and women regarding attractiveness in mate selection (Weeden & Sabini, 2005).

She's beautiful and therefore to be woo'd.

—William Shakespeare

CONNECTIONS 链 接

Does Ovulation Affect Perceptions of Male Attractiveness?
排卵是否会影响对男性吸引力的知觉？

The basic point of the evolutionary approach to love is that strategies evolved in our ancestral environments which helped males and females produce healthy offspring, perpetuating the species. These strategies are still with us—affecting us, unconsciously, when we decide with whom to become involved intimately. Recent research has focused on whether women's perceptions of male facial attractiveness vary due to where they are in their menstrual cycles (Penton-Voak & Perrett, 2000). Evolutionarily speaking, a woman should be most interested in a man with "good genes" when she is ovulating, and thus at the peak period of possible conception. Do women prefer more "masculine" looking men when they are ovulating than when they are not?

Victor Johnston and his colleagues (2001) studied this question by first creating photographs of a composite male and female face. They then created a QuickTime movie where a computer program "morphed" these faces from one extreme of a "very masculine" face, continuing on through many faces to an androgynous face (with both male and female facial features), and continuing on through many more faces to the extreme of a "very feminine" face. The task of the female heterosexual research participants was to use the slider control to move back and forth across these many faces and choose the one male face (and the one female face) that was the "most attractive" and the "most masculine" (or "feminine"). The participants did this task twice, at two different points in their menstrual cycle. The researchers found that the women's ratings varied depending on where they were in terms of ovulation. Those who did the task during their time of highest conception risk (a few days prior to ovulation) chose as the most attractive male face one that was significantly more masculine looking than when they were at the point in their cycles with the lowest conception risk. In comparison, their choice of the most attractive female face did not vary at these two times, only their choice for the most attractive male face. More masculine facial features are indicators of testosterone and are believed to be associated with good health. Thus, these results indicate that women, unconsciously, respond to a more masculinized face than an average male face when their ability to conceive is high, but not when it is low (Johnston, Hagel, Franklin, Fink, & Grammer, 2001).

Steven Gangestad and his colleagues (2007) also explored the effect of the ovulatory cycle on women's perceptions of male attractiveness. Heterosexual female research participants watched videotapes of men being interviewed and rated them on their attractiveness as a *short-term mate* (i.e., for a short-term sexual affair) and as a *long-term mate* (i.e., for a long-term relationship). Using questionnaires, the researchers estimated the women's conception risk at the time of the study. A second group of female participants rated the men on a series of traits that prior research had found were preferred in *long-term mates* (warmth; intelligence; good father potential; financial success potential; sexual faithfulness; social respectability) and on traits preferred in *short-term mates* (physical attractiveness; muscularity; confrontativeness with other men; arrogance; social respectability; Li & Kenrick, 2006; Schmitt, 2005).

The researchers found, first, that who women found attractive was strongly influenced by whether they were making short-term or long-term judgments. The men who were perceived as most attractive as short-term mates had higher ratings of muscularity, physical attractiveness, confrontativeness, and arrogance. The men who were perceived as most attractive as long-term mates had higher ratings of warmth, intelligence, faithfulness, and potential for parenting and financial success. Second, those women participants who were at the most fertile stage of their menstrual cycle (i.e., high in conception risk) preferred as short-term mates those men who appeared more muscular, physically attractive, confrontative, arrogant, and socially respected, as compared to women who were low in conception risk. In comparison, women at the most fertile stage of their cycle did not differ from women at the least fertile stage in preferences for long-term mates. These findings suggest that women have "short-" and "long-term" strategies when selecting partners, and that they appear to particularly value male indicators of "good genes" when they are fertile and evaluating men as potential short-term mates (Gangested, Garver-Apgar, Simpson, & Cousins, 2007).

The evolutionary approach to love has attracted its share of debate. For example, an alternative explanation is that there were evolutionary advantages for females to have multiple sexual partners too, not just for males. With multiple partners, females would have increased the odds of getting resources and protection for their offspring, as well as benefiting from genetic diversity. With multiple partners, females could have chosen an attractive male with "good genes" with whom to procreate and another male with whom to raise the offspring (Campbell, 2002; Gangestad & Simpson, 2000; Gangestad & Thornhill, 1998). It has also been argued that men may value physical attractiveness in a partner simply because they have been taught to value it; they have been conditioned by decades of advertising and media images to value beauty in women and to have a recreational approach to sex (Hatfield & Rapson, 1993). Similarly, research has found that women value physical attractiveness as much as men when they are considering a potential sexual partner as opposed to a potential marriage partner (Regan & Berscheid, 1997; Simpson & Gangestad, 1992). Finally, some researchers note that the preference for different qualities in a mate can be explained without resorting to evolutionary principles: Around the world, women have less power, status, wealth, and other resources than men do. If women need to rely on men to achieve economic security, they must consider this characteristic when choosing a husband (Rosenblatt, 1974). Thus in the framework of equity theory, female youth and beauty are considered a fair exchange for male career and economic success.

Steven Gangestad (1993) tested this hypothesis by correlating the extent to which women in several countries had access to financial resources and the extent to which women reported male physical attractiveness as an important variable in a mate. (In this study, parasite prevalence was controlled, so it was not a factor in the results.) He found an association between the two: The more economic power women had in a given culture, the more women were interested in a physically attractive man. In the United States, women have access to economic resources (e.g., education, well-paid jobs, high-status occupations) to a greater extent than most other women in the world. How does this affect American mate preferences? A recent survey of nearly one thousand young adults in the Northeast found that similarity in physical attractiveness and wealth was a stronger predictor of mate choice than the "beauty for money" exchange. People from wealthy families wanted a partner who was also wealthy, whether they were male or female. Similarly, men and women who were physically attractive wanted to find their match: a beautiful or handsome mate (Buston & Emlen, 2003). As you can see, when discussing human mate preference, it is difficult to disentangle "nature" (inborn preferences) from "nurture" (cultural norms and gender roles; Fitness, Fletcher, & Overall, 2003).

Attachment Styles in Intimate Relationships
亲密关系中的依恋类型

Most of the influences on love and intimacy we have discussed so far have been in the here-and-now of a relationship: the attractiveness and similarity of the partners, how they treat each other, and so on. The evolutionary approach takes the long view—that how people act today is based on behavior patterns that evolved from our species' hominid past. Another recent theory of love takes the middle ground, stating that our behavior in adult relationships is based on our experiences in the early years of life with our parents or caregivers. This approach focuses on attachment styles and draws on the groundbreaking work of John Bowlby (1969, 1973, 1980) and Mary Ainsworth (Ainsworth, Blehar, Waters, & Wall, 1978) on how infants form bonds with their primary caregivers (e.g., their mothers or fathers). According to the theory of **attachment styles**, the kinds of bonds we form early in life influence the kinds of relationships we form as adults.

Ainsworth and her colleagues (1978) identified three types of relationships between infants and their mothers. Infants with a **secure attachment style** typically have caregivers who are responsive to their needs and who show positive emotions when interacting with them. These infants trust their caregivers, are

Attachment Styles
The expectations people develop about relationships with others, based on the relationship they had with their primary caregiver when they were infants

Secure Attachment Style
An attachment style characterized by trust, a lack of concern with being abandoned, and the view that one is worthy and well liked

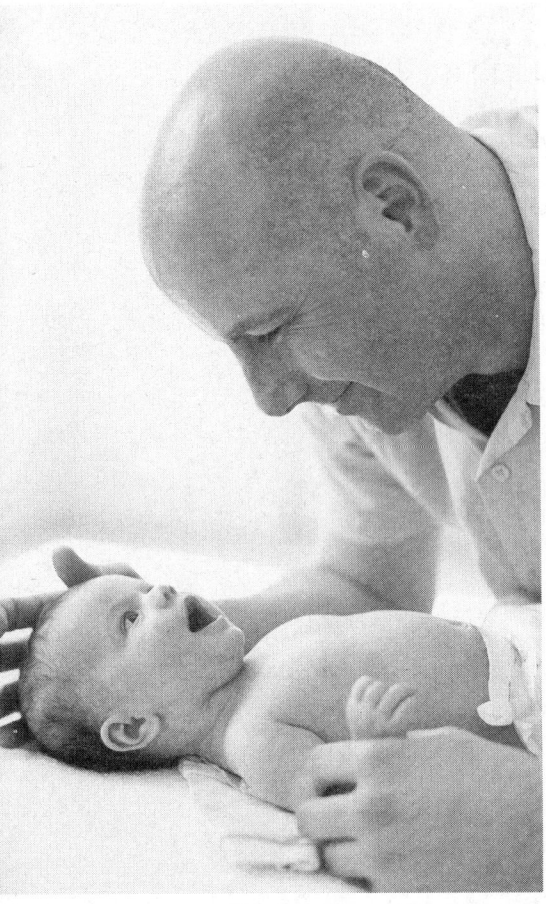

Attachment theory predicts that the attachment style we learn as infants and young children stays with us throughout life and generalizes to all of our relationships with other people.

Avoidant Attachment Style

An attachment style characterized by a suppression of attachment needs, because attempts to be intimate have been rebuffed; people with this style find it difficult to develop intimate relationships

Anxious/Ambivalent Attachment Style

An attachment style characterized by a concern that others will not reciprocate one's desire for intimacy, resulting in higher-than-average levels of anxiety

not worried about being abandoned, and come to view themselves as worthy and well liked. Infants with an **avoidant attachment style** typically have caregivers who are aloof and distant, rebuffing the infants' attempts to establish intimacy. These infants desire to be close to their caregiver but learn to suppress this need, as if they know that attempts to be intimate will be rejected. People with this style find it difficult to develop intimate relationships. Infants with an **anxious/ambivalent attachment style** typically have caregivers who are inconsistent and overbearing in their affection. These infants are unusually anxious because they can never predict when and how their caregivers will respond to their needs.

The key assumption of attachment theory is that the particular attachment style we learn as infants and young children becomes our working model or schema (as we discussed in Chapter 3) for what relationships are like. This early childhood relationship schema typically stays with us throughout life and generalizes to all our relationships with other people (Fraley & Shaver, 2000; Hartup & Laursen, 1999; Mikulincer & Shaver, 2003, 2007). Thus, people who had a secure relationship with their parents or caregivers are able to develop mature, lasting relationships as adults; people who had avoidant relationships with their parents are less able to trust others and find it difficult to develop close, intimate relationships; and people who had anxious/ambivalent relationships with their parents want to become close to their adult partners but worry that their partners will not return their affections (Collins & Feeney, 2000; 2004a; Rholes, Simpson & Friedman, 2006; Simpson, Collins, Tran, & Hayden, 2007). This has been borne out in numerous studies that measure adults' attachment styles with questionnaires or interviews and then correlate these styles with the quality of their romantic relationships.

For example, researchers asked adults to choose one of the three statements shown in Table 10.3 according to how they typically felt in romantic relationships (Hazan & Shaver, 1987). Each of these statements was designed to capture the three kinds of attachment styles we have described. The researchers also asked people questions about their current relationships. The results of this study—and several others like it—were consistent with an attachment theory perspective. Securely attached adults report that they easily become close to other people, readily trust others, and

TABLE 10.3 Measuring Attachment Styles

As part of a survey of attitudes toward love published in a newspaper, people were asked to choose the statement that best described their romantic relationships. The attachment style each statement was designed to measure and the percentage of people who chose each alternative are indicated.

Style	%	Statement
Secure style	56%	"I find it relatively easy to get close to others and am comfortable depending on them and having them depend on me. I don't often worry about being abandoned or about someone getting too close."
Avoidant style	25%	"I am somewhat uncomfortable being close to others; I find it difficult to trust them completely, difficult to allow myself to depend on them. I am nervous when anyone gets close, and often love partners want me to be more intimate than I feel comfortable being."
Anxious style	19%	"I find that others are reluctant to get as close as I would like. I often worry that my partner doesn't really love me or won't stay with me. I want to merge completely with another person, and this desire sometimes scares people away."

Adapted from Hazen & Shaver, 1986.

CONNECTIONS 链 接

This Is Your Brain . . . In Love 恋爱中的大脑

Falling in love is an extraordinary feeling—you are giddy, euphoric, full of energy, and close to obsessed with your new beloved. These powerful emotions, experienced by people in many different cultures, suggest that romantic love may have evolved as a primary component of the human mating system. Is something special happening in our brains when we fall in love?

To find out, a team of researchers recruited college students in the greater New York area who described themselves as currently being "intensely in love" (Aron et al., 2005). They asked these research participants to bring two photographs to the experimental session: one of their beloved, and one of an acquaintance of the same age and sex as their beloved. After filling out some questionnaires (including the Passionate Love Scale on page 302), the participants were ready for the main event. They slid into a functional MRI scanner, which records increases and decreases in blood flow in the brain. These changes in blood flow indicate which parts of the brain have neural activity at any given time. While the participant was in the scanner, the experimenters alternated projecting on a screen one photograph and then the other, interspersed with a mathematical distraction task.

"I am *so* attracted to you right now."

©2006 Harry Bliss. Distributed by Tribune Media Services, Inc.

The researchers found that two specific areas, deep within the brain, were activated when participants looked at the photographs of their romantic partner and were not activated when they looked at the photograph of their acquaintance or engaged in the math task. Furthermore, those participants who self-reported higher levels of romantic love showed greater activation in these areas when looking at their beloved than those who reported lower levels (Aron et al., 2005). These two brain areas were the ventral tegmental area (VTA) and the caudate nucleus, which communicate with each other as part of a circuit. A great deal is already known about what causes these areas of the brain to fire and what kind of processing they do—and now, this knowledge can be applied to the experience of passionate love.

Specifically, prior research has found that the VTA becomes highly active when people ingest cocaine—a drug that induces feelings of pleasure, euphoria, restlessness, sleeplessness, and loss of appetite (reactions that are reminiscent of falling in love, as well). The VTA, rich in the neurotransmitter dopamine, also fires when people eat chocolate. Thus, the VTA is a major "reward" and "motivation" center of the brain, as is the caudate nucleus. For example, functional MRI studies of gamblers' brains as they gambled showed greatly increased activity in these dopamine-rich areas when they won, a rewarding (and motivating) event for them (Aron et al., 2005). Thus when people say that falling in love is "like a drug" or "like winning the lottery," they're right. All these experiences activate the same areas of the brain: dopamine-rich centers of pleasure, reward, and motivation (Bartels & Zeki, 2000, 2004; Fisher, 2004).

have satisfying romantic relationships. People with an avoidant style report that they are uncomfortable becoming close to others, find it hard to trust others, and have less satisfying romantic relationships. And people with an anxious/ambivalent style tend to have less satisfying relationships but of a different type: They are likely to be obsessive and preoccupied with their relationships, fearing that their partners do not want to be as intimate or as close as they desire them to be (Feeney, Noller, & Roberts, 2000;

> *In my very own self, I am part of my family.*
> —D. H. Lawrence

Feeney, Cassidy, & Ramos-Marcuse, 2008; Hazan & Shaver, 1994a, 1994b; Simpson & Rholes, 1994).

Many researchers have reported similar findings: Securely attached individuals have the most enduring, long-term romantic relationships of the three attachment types. They experience the highest level of commitment to the relationship as well as the highest level of satisfaction with their relationships. The anxious/ambivalently attached individuals have the most short-lived romantic relationships of the three. They enter into romantic relationships the most quickly, often before they know their partners well. (For example, a study conducted at a marriage license bureau found that anxious men acquired marriage licenses after a shorter courtship than either secure or avoidant men; Senchak & Leonard, 1992.) They are also the most upset and angriest of the three types when their love is not reciprocated. Finally, avoidant individuals are the least likely to enter into a romantic relationship and the most likely to report never having been in love. They maintain their distance in relationships and have the lowest level of commitment to their relationships of the three types (Campbell, Simpson, Boldry, & Kashy, 2005; Feeney & Noller, 1990; Keelan, Dion, & Dion, 1994).

Finally, attachment styles have also been found to affect men's and women's behavior in an experimental setting (Collins, Ford, Guichard, & Allard, 2006; Simpson, Rholes, & Nelligan, 1992). For example, researchers brought heterosexual dating couples into the lab and measured their attachment styles using a questionnaire (Collins & Feeney, 2004b). They then asked one member of each couple to give a speech on the "value of a college education," which would be videotaped and later judged for quality. The other member of the couple was asked to sit in a waiting room while his or her partner prepared and gave the speech. The couples were told they would be allowed to communicate with each other, with the waiting partner sending a couple of notes to the speech-giver.

Unbeknown to the participants, they had been randomly assigned to one of two conditions: The waiting partner would send very suppportive notes, or less supportive notes, to his or her partner. In fact, the experimenters had written the notes themselves, and they asked the waiting partners to copy the notes so they would be in their handwriting. The speech-giving partner received two notes, one while he or she prepared the speech, and the other after he or she had given the speech. The supportive notes were: "Don't worry, just say how you feel and what you think and you'll do great," and "I liked your speech. That was a hard thing to do and you did a really good job." The two less supportive notes were: "Try not to say anything too embarrassing—especially since so many people will be watching your tape," and "Your speech was a little hard to follow, but I guess you did the best you could under the circumstances."

Now, how would you react to messages like these from your romantic partner? And how might your attachment style affect your perceptions? Collins and Feeney (2004b) found that there were no differences between the participants in terms of their reactions to the notes when they received supportive ones. Everyone felt supported by their partners, and there were no differences given their attachment styles; however, when participants received the less supportive notes, significant differences in reactions occurred. The first note, received while they were preparing their speech, was perceived the most negatively by highly avoidant participants. The second note, received after they'd given their speech, was perceived the most negatively by highly anxious particpants. In both cases, these participants reported that the note was upsetting, disappointing, and made them feel angry.

Thus while securely attached participants reacted calmly to the less supportive messages, avoidant and anxious participants saw the same comments in a much more negative light. Avoidant individuals believe that people they are close to cannot be relied on for support or nurturance. Receiving the somewhat unsupportive note at a time when they needed support—preparing the speech—was particularly upsetting to them. Anxious individuals believe that people close to them are unpredictable and likely to reject them. Receiving the somewhat unsupportive note at a time when they needed positive feedback—after giving the speech—was particularly upsetting to them. In comparison, secure individuals took the somewhat unsupportive notes in stride, interpreting them as more neutral in tone than the avoidant or anxious participants (Collins & Feeney, 2004b).

Attachment Style Combinations You can see how attachment style can affect communication in a relationship as well as the attributions that partners make about each other (Collins & Feeney, 2004b; Simpson, Winterheld, Rholes, & Orina, 2007). For example, what would happen if an anxious person became involved with an avoidant one? Research has found that anxious and avoidant people become couples because they both match each other's relationship schema: Anxious people expect to be more invested in their relationships than their partners, and avoidant people expect to be less committed than their partners (Kirkpatrick & Davis, 1994). *Voilà!* Expectations met! But are these relationships happy ones? Not really; anxious-avoidant pairs report little satisfaction with their relationships and negative, problematic communication patterns (Kane et al., 2007; Morgan & Shaver, 1999).

You would probably expect that romantic relationships made up of these pairs would also be short-lived, but there's an interesting twist here. One type of anxious-avoidant pair had very stable relationships: anxious women involved with avoidant men (Kirkpatrick & Davis, 1994). Their relationships were as stable over a four-year period as those of the secure woman–secure man couples in the sample. The researchers suggest that gender stereotypes play an important role in maintaining anxious woman–avoidant man relationships. Anxious women display stereotypically feminine traits in their relationships: They invest a lot of energy in the relationship, they demonstrate concern about how the relationship is doing, and they engage in "caretaking" behavior toward their partners. Avoidant men display stereotypically masculine traits in their relationships: They invest little energy in the relationship, they show and share little emotion in the relationship, and they avoid discussions about the relationship. Although these couples have far less positive relationships than secure–secure couples, they believe that the problems are due to their partner's gender—"He's just being a guy" or "Women are like that." Thus they tolerate their partner's behavior because it fits their stereotype or schema for the opposite sex. And what of romantic couples where the man is anxious and the woman is avoidant? Researchers have found that these relationships don't last long. Each partner views the other's behavior as especially troubling and negative because it deviates so far from the stereotypical pattern of gender behavior (Morgan & Shaver, 1999).

Attachment theory does not mean that if people had unhappy relationships with their parents, they are doomed to repeat this same kind of unhappy relationship with everyone they ever meet (Simms, 2002). For example, some researchers have recontacted their research participants months or years after the original studies and asked them to take the attachment style scale again. They have found that 25 percent to 30 percent of their participants had changed from one attachment style to another (Feeney & Noller, 1996; Kirkpatrick & Hazan, 1994). People can and do change; their experiences in relationships can help them learn new and more healthy ways of relating to others than what they experienced as children. In fact, it may be that people can develop more than one attachment style over time, as a result of their various experiences in close relationships (Baldwin & Fehr, 1995). At any given time, the attachment style that they display is the one that is called into play by their partner's behavior and the type of relationship that they've created as a couple. Thus people may respond to situational variables in their relationships, displaying a more secure attachment style in one relationship and a more anxious one in another (Fraley, 2002; Hammond & Fletcher, 1991; Simpson, Rholes, Campbell & Wilson, 2003).

The Genetic Contribution to Attachment Styles Your attachment style is clearly shaped by your "environment"—your caregivers as a child, and the friends and romantic partners with whom you interact as an adult. Do your genes affect your attachment style too? Two recent studies explored just this question. Omri

Gillath and colleagues (2008) collected saliva samples from their research participants, from which their DNA was extracted. DNA sequences were amplified and tested for the presence and number of specific alleles related to the neurotransmitters dopamine and serotonin. The researchers also had participants rate themselves on attachment anxiety and avoidance. They found that the presence of a particular dopamine allele pattern was significantly related to attachment anxiety, and a particular serotonin allele pattern was significantly related to attachment avoidance. The strength of these relationships indicated that genes accounted for about 20 percent of the variability in attachment anxiety and avoidance (Gillath, Shaver, Baek, & Chun, 2008). Thus, a person's genotype may predispose him or her to a specific attachment style, which will be then be further affected, one way or the other, by influences in the environment.

M. Brent Donnellan and his colleagues (2008) conducted a "twin" study, where they compared the anxiety and avoidance attachment scores of monozygotic (MZ) twins (identical twins) and dizygotic (DZ) twins (fraternal twins) who were in their twenties. Each pair of twins had grown up together and had presumably experienced similar caregiving. Of course, MZ twins share the same genes, while DZ twins are no more similar genetically than any two siblings. Using behavioral genetic statistical modeling to compare MZ and DZ twins, the researchers determined that genetic effects accounted for 45 percent of the variability in attachment anxiety, and 39 percent of the variability in attachment avoidance. Most of the remaining variability was due to the environment, but not the "shared" environment of the childhood home. Instead, the researchers found that "nonshared" aspects of the environment affected the participants' scores on attachment anxiety and avoidance. Nonshared experiences (meaning, not shared by one's twin) would principally involve the relationships that the participants had had as adults (Donnellan, Burt, Levendosky, & Klump, 2008). This is another indicator that attachment styles can be fluid and are capable of change over the course of a lifetime. While we await more research on the heritability of attachment styles, it currently appears that one's genes account for 20 percent to 45 percent of the anxious and avoidant styles, with one's environment accounting for the rest.

Social Exchange in Long-Term Relationships
长期人际关系中的社会交换

What, after all, is our life but a great dance in which we are all trying to fix the best going rate of exchange?
—Malcolm Bradbury, 1992

According to the rule of social exchange, if we want other people to like us, we must dole out social rewards to them (Blau, 1964; Homans, 1961). Research has shown ample support for social exchange theory in intimate relationships in cultures as different as Taiwan and the Netherlands (Lin & Rusbult, 1995; Le & Agnew, 2003; Rusbult & Van Lange, 1996; Van Lange et al., 1997). For example, college-age dating couples focused much more on rewards during the first three months of their relationships (Rusbult, 1983). If the relationships were perceived as offering a lot of rewards, the people reported feeling happy and satisfied. The perception of rewards continued to be important over time. At 7 months, couples who were still together believed their rewards had increased over time. The perception and importance of costs came into play a few months into the relationships; this is when the glow created by all those rewards begins to be dimmed by the realization that costs are involved too. Not surprisingly, satisfaction with the relationship decreased markedly over time for those who reported that costs were increasing in their relationships. Thus rewards are always important to the outcome; costs become increasingly important over time.

Of course, we know that many people do not leave their partners, even when they are dissatisfied and their other alternatives look bright. Research indicates that we need to consider at least one additional factor to understand close relationships—a person's level of investment in the relationship (Impett, Beals, & Peplau, 2001–2002; Rusbult, Olsen, Davis, & Hannon, 2001; Goodfriend & Agnew, 2008). In her **investment model** of close relationships, Caryl Rusbult (1983) defines investments as anything people have put into a relationship that will be lost if they leave it. Examples include tangible things, such as financial resources and possessions (e.g., a house), as

Investment Model
The theory that people's commitment to a relationship depends not only on their satisfaction with the relationship in terms of rewards, costs, and comparison level and their comparison level for alternatives but also on how much they have invested in the relationship that would be lost by leaving it

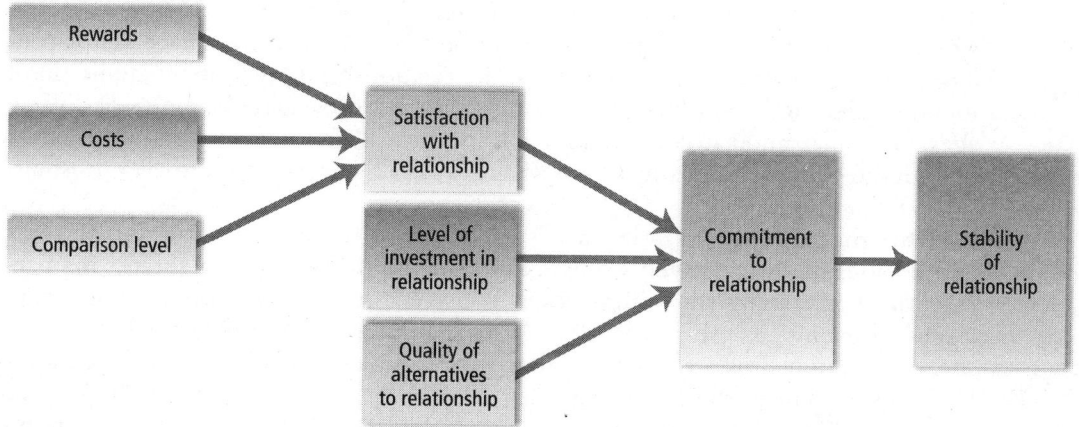

FIGURE 10.2

The investment model of commitment.

People's commitment to a relationship depends on several variables. First, their *satisfaction* with the relationship is based on their comparing their *rewards* to their *costs* and determining if the outcome exceeds their general expectation of what they should get in a relationship (or *comparison level*). Next, their *commitment* to the relationship depends on three variables: how *satisfied* they are, how much they feel they have *invested* in the relationship, and whether they have good *alternatives* to this relationship. These commitment variables in turn predict how *stable* the relationship will be. For example, a woman who feels her relationship has more costs and fewer rewards than she considers acceptable would have a low satisfaction. If she also felt she had little invested in the relationship and a very attractive person had just asked her for a date, she would have a low level of commitment. The end result is low stability; most likely, she will break up with her current partner.

(Adapted from Rusbult, 1983)

well as intangible things, such as the emotional welfare of one's children, the time and emotional energy spent building the relationship, and the sense of personal integrity that will be lost if one gets divorced. As seen in Figure 10.2, the greater the investment individuals have in a relationship, the less likely they are to leave, even if satisfaction is low and other alternatives look promising. In short, to predict whether people will stay in an intimate relationship, we need to know (1) how satisfied they are with the relationship, (2) what they think of the alternatives, and (3) how great their investment in the relationship is.

To test this model, Rusbult (1983) asked college students involved in heterosexual dating relationships to fill out questionnaires for 7 months. Every 3 weeks or so, people answered questions about each of the components of the model shown in Figure 10.2. Rusbult also kept track of whether the students stayed in the relationships or broke up. As you can see in Figure 10.3, people's satisfaction, alternatives,

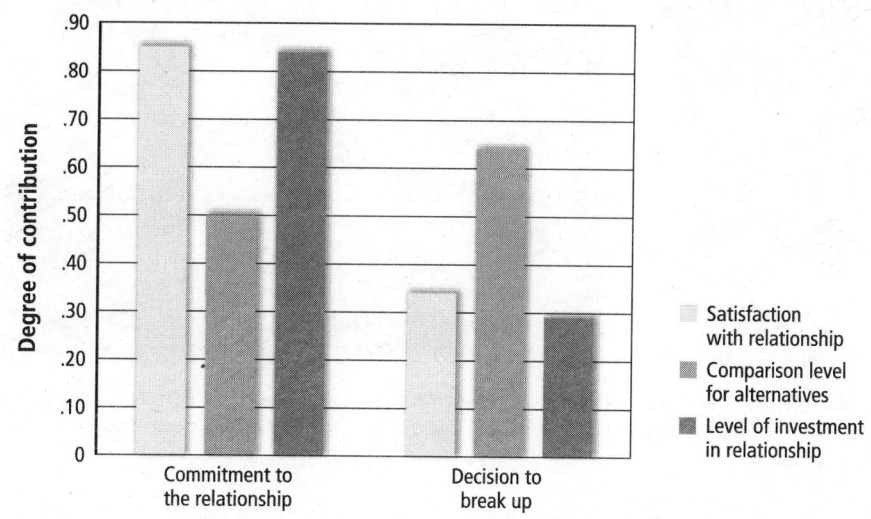

FIGURE 10.3

A test of the investment model.

This study examined the extent to which college students' satisfaction with a relationship, their comparison level for alternatives, and their investment in the relationship predicted their commitment to the relationship and their decision about whether to break up with their partner. The higher the number, the more each variable predicted commitment and breakup, independent of the two other variables. All three variables were good predictors of how committed people were and whether or not they broke up.

(Adapted from Rusbult, 1983)

and investments all predicted how committed they were to the relationship and whether it lasted. (The higher the number on the scale, the more each factor predicted the commitment to and length of the relationship.) Subsequent studies have found results similar to those shown in Figure 10.3 for married couples of diverse ages, for lesbian and gay couples, for close (nonsexual) friendships, and for residents of both the United States and Taiwan (Kurdek, 1992; Lin & Rusbult, 1995; Rusbult, 1991; Rusbult & Buunk, 1993).

Does the same model hold for destructive relationships? To find out, Rusbult and a colleague interviewed women who had sought refuge at a shelter for battered women, asking them about their abusive romantic relationships and marriages (Rusbult & Martz, 1995). Why had these women stayed in these relationships, even to the point where some of them returned to the abusive male partner when they left the shelter? As the theory would predict, feelings of commitment to the abusive relationship were greater among women who had poorer economic alternatives to the relationship, were more heavily invested in the relationship (e.g., were married, had children), and were less dissatisfied with the relationship (i.e., reported receiving less severe forms of abuse). In long-term relationships, then, commitment is based on more than just the amount of rewards and punishments people dole out; it also depends on people's perceptions of their investments in, satisfaction with, and alternatives to the relationship.

> The friendships which last are those wherein each friend respects the other's dignity to the point of not really wanting anything from him.
> —Cyril Connolly

Equity in Long-Term Relationships 长期人际关系中的公平性

Does equity theory operate in long-term relationships the same way it does in new or less intimate relationships? Not exactly: The more we get to know someone, the more reluctant we are to believe that we are simply exchanging favors and the less inclined we are to expect immediate compensation for a favor done. In casual relationships, we trade "in kind"—you lend someone your class notes, he buys you a beer. But in intimate relationships, we trade very different resources, so determining if equity has been achieved can be difficult. Does "dinner at an expensive restaurant on Monday balance out three nights of neglect due to a heavy workload" (Hatfield & Rapson, 1993, p. 130)? In other words, long-term, intimate relationships seem to be governed by a looser give-and-take notion of equity rather

Close relationships can have either exchange or communal properties. Family relationships are typically communal; friendships are typically based on exchange, although they can become communal over time.

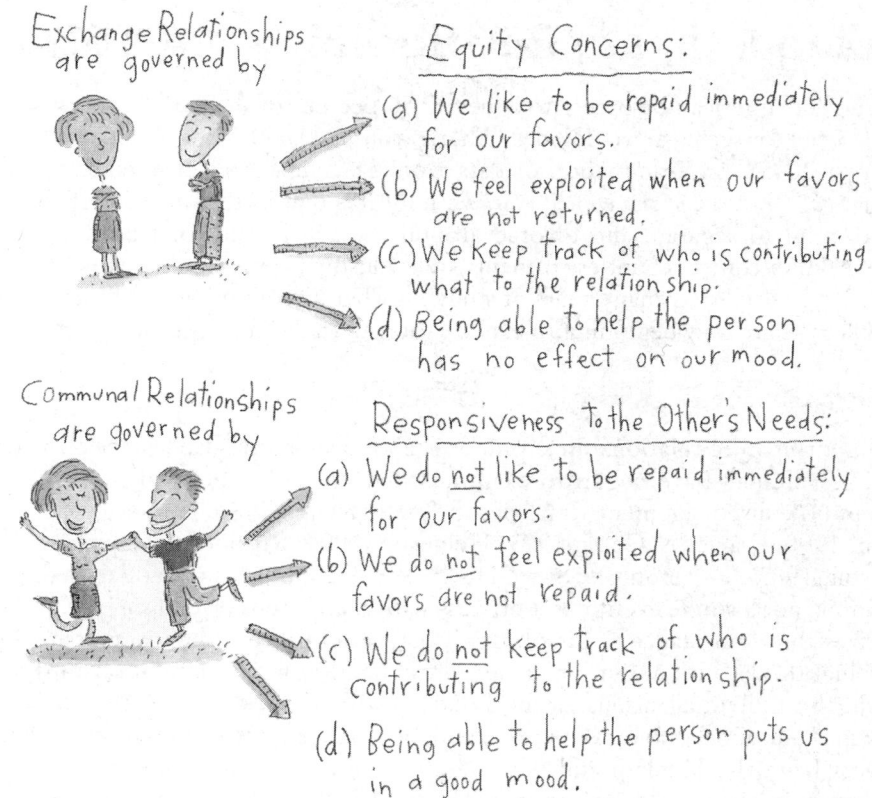

FIGURE 10.4
Exchange versus communal relationships.

than a rigid tit-for-tat strategy (Kollack, Blumstein, & Schwartz, 1994; Laursen & Hartup, 2002; Vaananen, Buunk, Kivimaki, Pentti, & Vahtera, 2005).

According to Margaret Clark and Judson Mills (1993), interactions between new acquaintances are governed by equity concerns and are called **exchange relationships**. As you can see in Figure 10.4, in exchange relationships, people keep track of who is contributing what and feel taken advantage of when they feel they are putting more into the relationship than they are getting out of it.

In comparison, interactions between close friends, family members, and romantic partners are governed less by an equity norm and more by a desire to help each other in times of need. In these **communal relationships**, people give in response to the other's needs, regardless of whether they are paid back (Clark, 1984, 1986; Clark & Mills, 1993; Mills & Clark, 1982, 1994, 2001; Vaananen et al., 2005). Communal interactions are the hallmark of intimate relationships. Research comparing heterosexual couples to same-sex couples has found that they are equally committed and communal in their relationships. If anything, gay men and lesbians report greater compatibility and less conflict than heterosexual couples do (Balsam, Beauchaine, Rothblum, & Solomon, 2008; Roisman, Clausell, Holland, Fortuna, & Elieff, 2008).

Are people in communal relationships completely unconcerned with equity? No. As we saw earlier, people do feel distressed if they believe their intimate relationships are inequitable (Canary & Stafford, 2001; Walster et al., 1978); however, equity takes on a somewhat different form in communal relationships than it does in less intimate ones. In communal relationships, the partners are more relaxed about what constitutes equity at any given time; they believe that things will eventually balance out and a rough kind of equity will be achieved over time (Lemay & Clark, 2008; Lemay, Clark, & Feeney, 2007). If this is not the case—if they come to feel there is an imbalance—the relationship may end.

Exchange Relationships
Relationships governed by the need for equity (i.e., for an equal ratio of rewards and costs)

Communal Relationships
Relationships in which people's primary concern is being responsive to the other person's needs

Ending Intimate Relationships 亲密关系的结束

The current American divorce rate is nearly 50 percent of the current marriage rate and has been for the past two decades (Thernstrom, 2003; National Center for Health Statistics, 2005). An examination of data from 58 human societies, taken from the *Demographic Yearbook of the United Nations*, indicates that in the majority of societies, couples tend to separate and divorce around the fourth year of marriage (Fisher, 2004). And, of course, countless romantic relationships between unmarried individuals end every day. After many years of studying what love is and how it blooms, social psychologists are now beginning to explore the end of the story—how it dies.

The Process of Breaking Up 分手的过程

Ending a romantic relationship is one of life's more painful experiences. In recent years, researchers have begun to examine what makes people end their relationships and the disengagement strategies they use (Baxter, 1986; Femlee, Sprecher, & Bassin, 1990; Frazier & Cook, 1993; Helgeson, 1994; Rusbult & Zembrodt, 1983; Simpson, 1987). For example, Steve Duck (1982) reminds us that relationship dissolution is not a single event but a process with many steps (see Figure 10.5). Duck theorizes that four stages of dissolution exist, ranging from the intrapersonal (the individual thinks a lot about his or her dissatisfaction with the relationship) to the dyadic (the individual discusses the breakup with the partner) to the social (the breakup is announced to other people) and back to the intrapersonal (the individual recovers from the breakup and forms an account, or version, of how and why it happened). In terms of the last stage in the process, John Harvey and his colleagues (Harvey, 1995; Harvey, Flanary, & Morgan, 1986; Harvey, Orbuch, & Weber, 1992) have found that the version of "why the relationship ended" that we present to close friends can be very different from the official (i.e., cleaned-up) version that we present to co-workers or neighbors. Take a moment to examine the stages outlined in Figure 10.5; see if they mirror your experience.

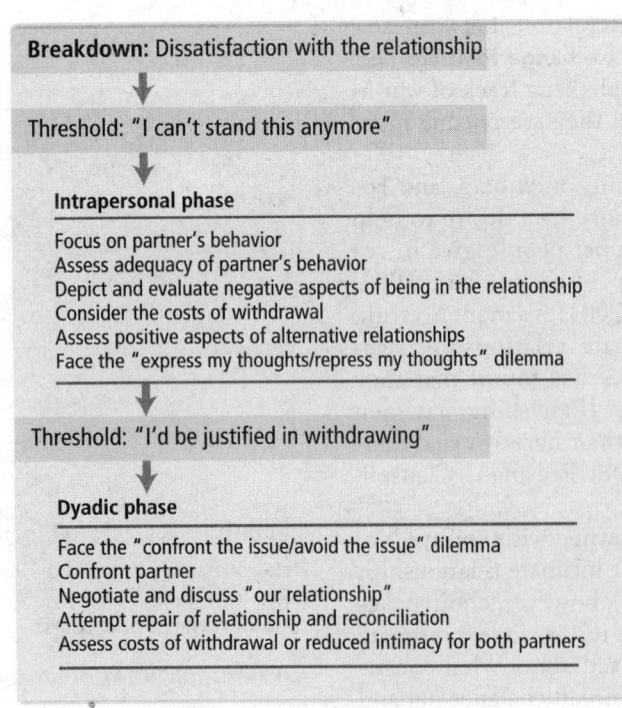
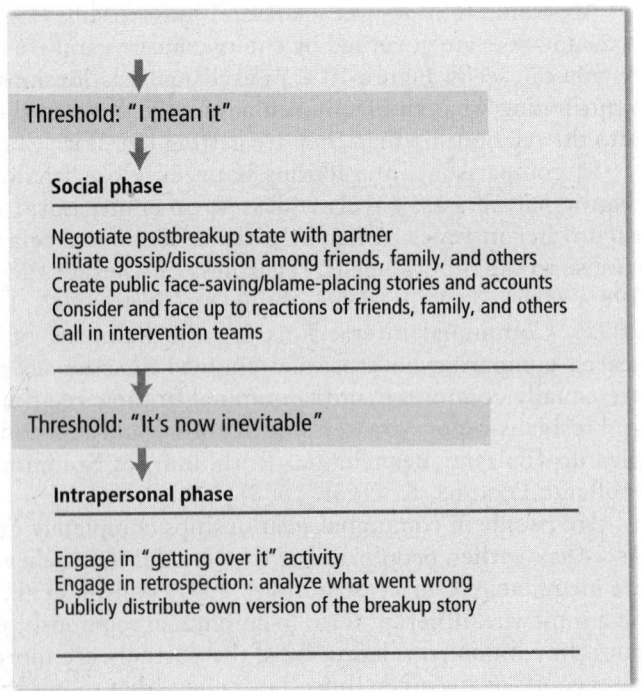

FIGURE 10.5

Steps in dissolving close relationships.

(Adapted from Duck, 1982)

Why relationships end has been studied from several angles. One approach has used the investment model, which we discussed earlier (Bui et al., 1996; Drigotas & Rusbult, 1992). Caryl Rusbult's work on social exchange theory has led her to identify four types of behavior that occur in troubled relationships (Rusbult, 1987; Rusbult & Zembrodt, 1983). The first two types are destructive behaviors: actively harming the relationship (e.g., abusing the partner, threatening to break up, actually leaving) and passively allowing the relationship to deteriorate (e.g., refusing to deal with problems, ignoring the partner or spending less time together, putting no energy into the relationship). The other two responses are positive, constructive behaviors: actively trying to improve the relationship (e.g., discussing problems, trying to change, going to a therapist) and passively remaining loyal to the relationship (e.g., waiting and hoping that the situation will improve, being supportive rather than fighting, remaining optimistic).

"Somehow I remember this one differently."

© 2003 The New Yorker Collection, Steve Duenes from cartoonbank.com. All Rights Reserved.

Rusbult and her colleagues have found that destructive behaviors harm a relationship a lot more than constructive behaviors help it. Furthermore, when one partner acts destructively, the other partner tends to accommodate this behavior by responding constructively to save the relationship. When both partners act destructively, the relationship typically ends (Rusbult, Johnson, & Morrow, 1986; Rusbult, Yovetich, & Verette, 1996).

Another approach to studying why relationships end focuses on what attracts people to someone in the first place. In this research, college men and women were asked to focus on a romantic relationship that had ended and to list the qualities that first attracted them to the person and the characteristics they ended up disliking the most about the person (Femlee, 1995, 1998a, 1988b). Thirty percent of these breakups were examples of "fatal attractions." The very qualities that were initially so attractive became the very reasons why the relationship ended. For example, "He's so unusual and different" became "He and I have nothing in common." "She's so exciting and unpredictable" became "I can never count on her." This type of breakup reminds us again of the importance of similarity between partners, as a characteristic of successful relationships.

If a romantic relationship is in bad shape, can we predict who will end it? Much has been made about the tendency in heterosexual relationships for women to end relationships more often than men (Rubin, Peplau, & Hill, 1981). Recent research has found, however, that neither sex ends romantic relationships more frequently than the other (Akert, 1998; Hagestad & Smyer, 1982; Rusbult et al., 1986).

The Experience of Breaking Up 分手的体验

Can we predict the different ways people will feel when their relationship ends? One key is the role people play in the decision to end the relationship (Akert, 1998; Helgeson, 1994; Lloyd & Cate, 1985). For example, Robin Akert asked 344 college-age men and women to focus on their most important romantic relationship that had ended and to respond to a questionnaire focusing on their experiences during the breakup. One question asked to what extent they or their partner had been responsible for the decision to break up. Participants who indicated a high level of responsibility for the decision were labeled breakers; those who reported a low level of responsibility, breakees; and those who shared the decision making with their partners about equally, mutuals.

Akert found that the role people played in the decision to end the relationship was the single most powerful predictor of their breakup experiences. Not surprisingly, breakees were miserable—they reported high levels of loneliness, depression, unhappiness, and

Relationships can end for many reasons. For example, in "fatal attractions," the very qualities that once attracted you ("He's so mature and wise") can become the very reason you break up ("He's too old").

Love is like war; easy to begin but very hard to stop.

—H. L. Mencken

anger, and virtually all reported experiencing physical disorders in the weeks after the breakup as well. Breakers found the end of the relationship the least upsetting, the least painful, and the least stressful of the three. Although breakers did report feeling guilty and unhappy, they had the fewest negative physical symptoms (39 percent), such as headaches, stomachaches, and eating and sleeping irregularities.

The mutual role, which carries with it a component of shared decision making, helped individuals evade some of the negative emotional and physical reactions to breaking up. Mutuals were not as upset or hurt as breakees, but they were not as unaffected as breakers. Some 60 percent of the mutuals reported physical symptoms, indicating that a mutual conclusion to a romantic relationship is a more stressful experience than simply deciding to end it on one's own. Finally, gender played a role in the emotional and physical responses of the respondents, with women reporting somewhat more negative reactions to breaking up than men.

Do people want to stay friends when they break up? It depends on the role one plays in the breakup, as well as one's gender. Akert (1998) found that men are not very interested in remaining friends with their ex-girlfriends when they are in either the breaker or the breakee role, although women are more interested in remaining friends, especially when they are the breakees (see Figure 10.6). Interestingly, the mutual role is the one where men's and women's interest in future friendship matches the most. These data suggest that when men experience either great control (breaker) or little control (breakee) over the ending of the relationship, they tend to want to "cut their losses" and move on, severing ties with their ex-partner. In comparison, women tend to want to continue feeling connected to their ex-partner, hoping to reshape the intimate relationship into a platonic friendship. The mutual breakup is the one in which each partner effectively plays the breaker and breakee roles simultaneously. This equality in roles appears to be important in producing an equivalent interest in future friendship for men and women (see Figure 10.6).

The breakup moral? If you find yourself in a romantic relationship and your partner seems inclined to break it off, try to end it mutually. Your experience will be less traumatic because you will share some control over the process (even if you don't want it to happen). Unfortunately for your partner, if you are about to be in the role of breaker, you will experience less pain and suffering if you continue to play that role; however, changing your role from breaker to mutual would be an act of kindness toward your soon-to-be ex–loved one.

FIGURE 10.6

Importance of remaining friends after the breakup.

After ending a romantic relationship, do people want to remain friends with their ex-partner? It depends on both the role they played in the decision to break up and on their gender. Women are more interested than men in staying friends when they are in the breakee or breaker role; men and women are equally interested in staying friends when the relationship ends by mutual decision.

(Akert, 1998)

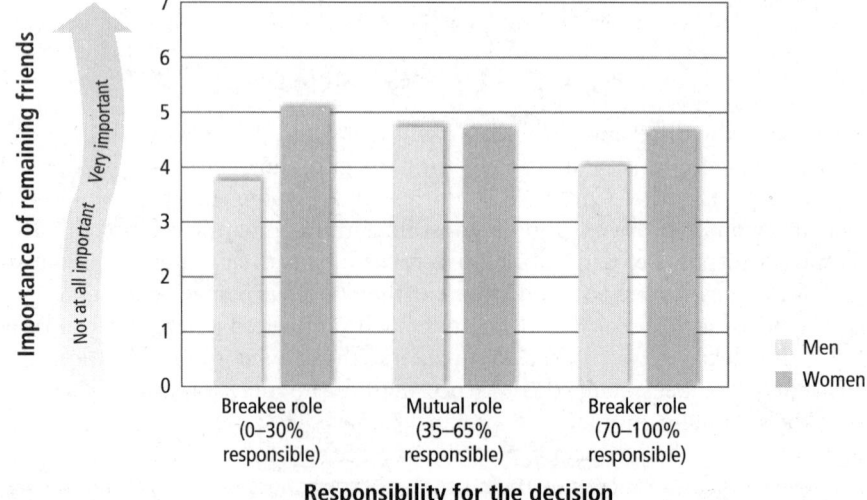

HOW WOULD YOU USE THIS? 如何学以致用？

If there was ever a chapter in a textbook that had something to say about your "real" life, this is probably it. Romantic relationships and friendships are an integral part of our lives, and wonderful as they are, they are also frequently confusing and even upsetting. While the information in this chapter could help you when you're "falling in love," you'll probably be too distracted by your new partner to even think about research studies on attraction. However, when things go bad, this information can really be of help. Apply the various terms and theories to your predicament—do they help shed some light on what is going on? For example, are you and your friend or romantic partner seeing the relationship differently, perhaps one of you as an "exchange" and the other as "communal?" Does one or the other of you have an attachment style that is causing problems? Are the two of you dissimilar in areas that are important to you? Are there cultural differences that might explain what's going on? If your loved one is thinking of ending the relationship, is it because he or she has a viable "comparison level for alternatives?" Finally, as a last bit of advice, try to make your break up "mutual."

Summary 总 结

- **What Causes Attraction?**
    - **The Person Next Door: The Propinquity Effect** In the first part of this chapter, we discussed the variables that cause initial attraction between two people. One such variable is physical proximity, or the **propinquity effect:** People who you come into contact with the most are the most likely to become your friends and lovers. This occurs because of the **mere exposure effect:** Exposure to any stimulus produces liking for it.
    - **Similarity** Similarity between people, whether in attitudes, values, personality traits, or demographic characteristics, is also a powerful cause of attraction and liking. Similarity is a more powerful predictor of attraction than complementarity, the idea that opposites attract.
    - **Reciprocal Liking** In general, we like others who behave as if they like us.
    - **Physical Attractiveness and Liking** Physical attractiveness also plays an important role in liking. People from different cultures perceive facial attractiveness quite similarly. The "what is beautiful is good" stereotype indicates that people assume that physical attractiveness is associated with other desirable traits.
    - **Theories of Interpersonal Attraction: Social Exchange and Equity** Social exchange theory states that how people feel about their relationships depends on their perception of the rewards they receive and the costs they incur. In order to determine whether people will stay in a relationship, we also need to know their **comparison level**—their expectations about the outcomes of their relationship—and their **comparison level for alternatives**—their expectations about how happy they would be in other relationships. **Equity theory** states that the most important determinant of satisfaction is the amount of equity in the relationship.

- **Close Relationships**
    - **Defining Love** One definition of love makes a distinction between **companionate love**—feelings of intimacy that are not accompanied by intense longing and arousal—and **passionate love**—feelings of intimacy that are accompanied by intense longing and arousal.
    - **Culture and Love** Although love is a universal emotion, cultural variations in the definition of love do occur. Love has a somewhat different emphasis in collectivistic and individualistic cultures.

- **Love and Relationships**
    - **Evolution and Love: Choosing a Mate Evolutionary psychology** explains love in terms of genetic factors that evolved over time according to the principles of natural selection. Men and women are attracted to different characteristics in each other because this maximizes their reproductive success.
    - **Attachment Styles in Intimate Relationships** People's past relationships with their parents are a significant determinant of the quality of their close relationships as adults; there is evidence that there is a genetic determinant as well. There are three types of attachment relationships: **secure, avoidant,** and **anxious/ambivalent.**

- **Social Exchange in Long-Term Relationships** Whether a couple will stay together depends on each person's level of investment in and satisfaction with the relationship, as well as each person's comparison level and comparison level for alternatives.
- **Equity in Long-Term Relationships** The equity of rewards and costs is different in long-term relationships (typically **communal relationships**) than in short-term relationships (typically **exchange relationships**).

- **Ending Intimate Relationships**
  - **The Process of Breaking Up** The breaking-up process is composed of stages. Strategies for responding to problems in a romantic relationship include both constructive and destructive behaviors. Fatal attractions occur when the qualities in a person that once were attractive become the very qualities that repel.
  - **The Experience of Breaking Up** A powerful variable that predicts how a person will weather the breakup is the role he or she plays in the decision to terminate the relationship.

CHAPTER 10 TEST 第10章习题

1. Sam has his eye on Julie and wants her to like him. According to research in social psychology, which of the following is *least* likely to work? He should
   a. emphasize how similar their attitudes are.
   b. arrange to work with her on a class project so that he can spend time with her.
   c. emphasize that they have complementary personalities; after all, "opposites attract."
   d. make himself look as physically attractive as he can.

2. Rachel is considered physically attractive by her American classmates because of her large eyes and small nose, "baby face" characteristics. In another culture she would most likely be considered
   a. unattractive because her features are not unique.
   b. unattractive because people's perceptions of beauty differ across cultures.
   c. attractive because people's perceptions of beauty are similar across cultures.
   d. attractive because she appears exotic to people of other cultures attractive if that culture has a high standard of living (e.g., is fairly wealthy).

3. Which of the following is *false*?
   a. People in communal relationships tend to keep track of who is contributing what to the relationship.
   b. People find "average" faces to be more attractive than unusual faces.
   c. People like others who like them.
   d. The more we see and interact with people, the more we will like them.

4. Kate and Jamie are dating. According to the *investment model of close relationships*, which of the following is *least* likely to influence their commitment to the relationship?
   a. Their satisfaction with the relationship
   b. Their level of investment in the relationship
   c. The availability and quality of alternative partners
   d. Their perception that what they are putting into the relationship is roughly the same as what they are getting out of it

5. _____ involves intense longing for another person, accompanied by physiological arousal whereas _____ is the intimacy and affection we feel without arousal.
   a. passionate love; infatuation
   b. companionate love; passionate love
   c. infatuation; companionate love
   d. passionate love; companionate love

6. Which of the following romantic couples are likely to stay together the longest?
   a. An anxious woman with an avoidant man
   b. An anxious man with an avoidant woman
   c. An anxious woman with an anxious man
   d. An avoidant woman with an avoidant man

7. Matthew and Eric have been friends since the beginning of the school year. According to equity theory, their friendship will suffer if
   a. Eric is much more likely to help Matthew out when he needs it than Matthew is to help Eric.
   b. Eric has a "makeover" and becomes more attractive than Matthew.
   c. Eric and Matthew stop having similar interests.
   d. Eric and Matthew are romantically interested in the same person.

8. Elliot worries that his girlfriend doesn't really love him and smothers her with attention. According to social psychological research, Elliot probably has a(n) _____ attachment style, because when he was an infant his caregivers were _____.
   a. Avoidant/aloof and distant
   b. avoidant/inconsistent and overbearing
   c. anxious-ambivalent/aloof and distant
   d. anxious-ambivalent/inconsistent and overbearing
   e. secure/responsive to his needs

9. You are evaluating whether or not you want to break up with your significant other of one month. While the relationship gives you lots of rewards and has few costs, you have recently met someone new who you anticipate will give you even more rewards for even fewer costs. Your dilemma stems from the fact that you have a _____ and a _____.
   a. low satisfaction level; high comparison level for alternatives
   b. high satisfaction level; high comparison level for alternatives
   c. low satisfaction level; low comparison level for alternatives

d. low satisfaction level; high equity level
e. high satisfaction level; low equity level

10. According to social psychological research, women who are at the point in their menstrual cycle when they are most likely to become pregnant (around the time of ovulation) find
    a. "feminine" looking men to be more attractive than "masculine" looking men.
    b. "masculine" looking men to be more attractive than "feminine" looking men.
    c. "masculine" and "feminine" looking men to be equally unattractive; they like men who are a blend of the two the best.
    d. "masculine" and "feminine" looking men to be equally attractive.

Answer Key
1-c, 2-c, 3-a, 4-d, 5-d, 6-a, 7-a, 8-d, 9-b, 10-b

For more review plus practice tests, videos, flashcards, writing help and more, log on to MyPsychLab.

11

Prosocial Behavior
Why Do People Help?

亲社会行为：
为什么人们助人？

OUTLINE 提纲

- **Basic Motives Underlying Prosocial Behavior: Why Do People Help?**
  - Evolutionary Psychology: Instincts and Genes
  - Social Exchange: The Costs and Rewards of Helping
  - Empathy and Altruism: The Pure Motive for Helping
- **Personal Qualities and Prosocial Behavior: Why Do Some People Help More Than Others?**
  - Individual Differences: The Altruistic Personality
  - Gender Differences in Prosocial Behavior
  - Cultural Differences in Prosocial Behavior
  - Religion and Prosocial Behavior
  - The Effects of Mood on Prosocial Behavior
- **Situational Determinants of Prosocial Behavior: When Will People Help?**
  - Environment: Rural versus Urban
  - Residential Mobility
  - The Number of Bystanders: The Bystander Effect
  - The Nature of the Relationship: Communal versus Exchange Relationships
- **How Can Helping Be Increased?**
  - Increasing the Likelihood That Bystanders Will Intervene
  - Positive Psychology and Prosocial Behavior
  - CONNECTIONS: Increasing Volunteerism
- **Summary**

SEPTEMBER 11, 2001, WAS TRULY A DAY OF INFAMY IN American history, with terrible loss of life at the World Trade Center, the Pentagon, and the field in Pennsylvania where United Air Lines flight 93 crashed. It was also a day of incredible courage and sacrifice by people who did not hesitate to help their fellow human beings. Many people lost their lives while helping others, including 403 New York firefighters and police officers who died trying to rescue people from the World Trade Center.

Many of the heroes of September 11 were ordinary citizens who found themselves in extraordinary circumstances. Imagine that you were working in the World Trade Center towers when they were hit by the planes and how strong the desire must have been to flee and seek personal safety. This is exactly what William Wik's wife urged him to do when he called her from the 92nd floor of the South Tower shortly after the attacks. "No, I can't do that; there are still people here," he replied (Lee, 2001, p. 28). Wik's body was found in the rubble of the South Tower after it collapsed; he was wearing work gloves and holding a flashlight.

Abe Zelmanowitz worked on the 27th floor of the North Tower and could easily have walked down the stairs to safety when the plane struck the floors above. Instead he stayed behind with his friend Ed Beyea, a quadriplegic, waiting for help to carry him down the stairs. Both died when the tower collapsed.

Rick Rescorla was head of security for the Morgan Stanley brokerage firm. After the first plane hit the North Tower, Rescorla and the other employees in the South Tower were instructed to remain at their desks. Rescorla, who had spent years studying the security of the towers, had drilled his employees repeatedly in what to do in an emergency like this—find a partner, avoid the elevators, and evacuate the building. He invoked this plan immediately, and when the plane hit the South Tower, he was on the 44th floor supervising the evacuation, yelling instructions through a bullhorn. After most of the Morgan Stanley employees made it out of the building, Rescorla decided to do a final sweep of the offices to make sure no one was left behind and he perished when the South Tower collapsed. Rescorla is credited with saving the lives of the 3,700 employees he guided to safety (Stewart, 2002).

And then there were the passengers on United flight 93. Based on phone calls made from the plane in the fateful minutes after it was hijacked, it appears that several passengers, including Todd Beamer, Jeremy Glick, and Thomas Burnett, all fathers of young children, stormed the cockpit and struggled with the terrorists. They could not prevent the plane from crashing, killing everyone on board, but they did prevent an even worse tragedy. The plane was headed for Washington, D.C., with the White House or the U.S. Capitol the likely target.

Basic Motives Underlying Prosocial Behavior: Why Do People Help?
亲社会行为的基本动机：为什么人们助人？

How can we explain acts of great self-sacrifice and heroism when people are also capable of acting in uncaring, heartless ways? In this chapter, we will consider the major causes of **prosocial behavior**—any act performed with the goal of benefiting another person (Penner, Dovidio, Piliavin, & Schroeder, 2005). We are particularly concerned with prosocial behavior that is motivated by **altruism**, which is the desire to help another person even if it involves a cost to the helper. Someone might act in a prosocial way out of self-interest, hoping to get something in return. Altruism is helping purely out of the desire to benefit someone else, with no benefit (and often a cost) to oneself, such as the heroes of September 11, who gave their lives while helping strangers.

We begin by considering the basic origins of prosocial behavior and altruism: Is the willingness to help a basic impulse with genetic roots? Must it be taught and nurtured in childhood? Is there a pure motive for helping? Or do people typically help only when there is something in it for them? Let's see how psychologists have addressed these centuries-old questions (Dovidio, Piliavin, Schroeder, & Penner, 2006).

Evolutionary Psychology: Instincts and Genes
进化心理学：本能与基因

According to Charles Darwin's (1859) theory of evolution, natural selection favors genes that promote the survival of the individual (see Chapter 10). Any gene that furthers our survival and increases the probability that we will produce offspring is likely to be passed on from generation to generation. Genes that lower our chances of survival, such as those causing life-threatening diseases, reduce the chances that we will produce offspring and thus are less likely to be passed on. Evolutionary biologists like E. O. Wilson (1975) and Richard Dawkins (1976) have used these principles of evolutionary theory to explain such social behaviors as aggression and altruism. Several psychologists have pursued these ideas, spawning the field of *evolutionary psychology*, which is the attempt to explain social behavior in terms of genetic factors that evolved over time according to the principles of natural selection (Buss, 2005; Dunbar & Barrett, 2007; Pinker, 2002; Tooby & Cosmides, 2005). In Chapter 10, we discussed how evolutionary psychology attempts to explain love and attraction; here we discuss how it attempts to explain prosocial behavior (McCullough, Kimeldorf, & Cohen, 2008; McAndrew, 2002).

Darwin realized early on that there was a problem with evolutionary theory: How can it explain altruism? If people's overriding goal is to ensure their own survival, why would they ever help others at a cost to themselves? It would seem that over the course of human evolution, altruistic behavior would disappear, because people who acted that way would, by putting themselves at risk, produce fewer offspring than people who acted selfishly. Genes promoting selfish behavior should be more likely to be passed on—or should they?

Kin Selection One way that evolutionary psychologists attempt to resolve this dilemma is with the notion of **kin selection**, the idea that behaviors that help a genetic relative are favored by natural selection (Hamilton, 1964; Meyer, 1999). People can increase the chances that their genes will be passed along not only by having their own children, but also by ensuring that their genetic relatives have children. Because a person's blood relatives share some of his or her genes, the more that person ensures their survival, the greater the chance that his or her genes will flourish in future generations. Thus natural selection should favor altruistic acts directed toward genetic relatives.

Prosocial Behavior
Any act performed with the goal of benefiting another person

Altruism
The desire to help another person even if it involves a cost to the helper

Kin Selection
The idea that behaviors that help a genetic relative are favored by natural selection

According to evolutionary psychology, prosocial behavior occurs in part because of kin selection.

In one study, for example, people reported that they would be more likely to help genetic relatives than nonrelatives in life-and-death situations, such as a house fire. People did not report that they would be more likely to help genetic relatives when the situation was non-life-threatening, which supports the idea that people are most likely to help in ways that ensure the survival of their own genes. Interestingly, both males and females, and both American and Japanese participants, followed this rule of kin selection in life-threatening situations (Burnstein, Crandall, & Kitayama, 1994).

Of course, in this study, people reported what they thought they would do; this doesn't prove that in a real fire they would indeed be more likely to save their sibling than their cousin. Anecdotal evidence from real emergencies, however, is consistent with these results. Survivors of a fire at a vacation complex reported that when they became aware there was a fire, they were much more likely to search for family members before exiting the building than they were to search for friends (Sime, 1983).

Evolutionary psychologists are not suggesting that people consciously weigh the biological importance of their behavior before deciding whether to help: We don't compute the likelihood that our genes will be passed on before deciding whether to help someone push his or her car out of a ditch. According to evolutionary theory, however, the genes of people who follow this "biological importance" rule are more likely to survive than the genes of people who do not. Over the millennia, kin selection may have become ingrained in human behavior.

Altruism based on kin selection is the enemy of civilization. If human beings are to a large extent guided to favor their own relatives and tribe, only a limited amount of global harmony is possible.

—E. O. Wilson, 1978

The Reciprocity Norm To explain altruism, evolutionary psychologists also point to the **norm of reciprocity**, which is the expectation that helping others will increase the likelihood that they will help us in the future. The idea is that as human beings were evolving, a group of completely selfish individuals, each living in his or her own cave, would have found it more difficult to survive than a group who had learned to cooperate. Of course, if people cooperated too readily, they might have been exploited by an adversary who never helped in return. Those who were most likely to survive, the argument goes, were people who developed an understanding with their neighbors about reciprocity: "I will help you now, with the agreement that when I need help, you will return the favor." Because of its survival value, such a norm of reciprocity may have become genetically based (Cosmides & Tooby, 1992; de Waal, 1996; Shackelford & Buss, 1996; Trivers, 1971). Some researchers suggest that the emotion of *gratitude*—the positive feelings that are caused by the perception that one has been helped by others—evolved in order to regulate reciprocity (Bartlett & DeSteno, 2006; McCullough, Kimeldorf, & Cohen, 2008). That is, if someone helps us we feel gratitude, which motivates us to return the favor in the future. The following Try It! exercise describes how the reciprocity norm can work to increase helping in everyday life.

Learning Social Norms Nobel laureate Herbert Simon (1990) offered another link between evolution and altruism. He argued that it is highly adaptive for individuals to learn social norms from other members of a society. People who are the best learners of the norms and customs of a society have a survival advantage because over the centuries, a culture learns such things as which foods are poisonous and how best to cooperate, and the person who learns these rules is more likely to survive than the person who does not. Consequently, through natural selection, the ability to learn social norms has become part of our genetic makeup. One norm that people learn is the value of helping others—considered a valuable norm in virtually all societies. In short, people are genetically programmed to learn social norms, and one of these norms is altruism (Hoffman, 1981; Kameda, Takezawa, & Hastie, 2003).

Group Selection Classic evolutionary theory argues that natural selection operates on individuals: People who have traits that make them more likely to survive are more likely to reproduce and pass those traits on to future generations. Some argue that

Norm of Reciprocity
The expectation that helping others will increase the likelihood that they will help us in the future

natural selection also operates at the level of the group. Imagine two neighboring villages, for example, that are often at war with each other. Village A is made up entirely of selfish individuals who refuse to help each other, by, say, keeping watch to see if the other village is staging an invasion. Village B, on the other hand, has selfless sentries who put their lives at risk by alerting their comrades of an invasion. Which *group* is more likely to win the war and pass on its genes to later generations? The one with members who are altruistic members, of course, even though the *individual* sentries are at danger and likely to be captured and killed. Because people in Village B are more likely to survive than people in Village A, the trait of altruism is passed on to future generations. Though the idea of group selection is controversial and not supported by all biologists, it has prominent proponents (Wilson, Van Vugt, & O'Gorman, 2008; Wilson & Wilson, 2007).

TRY IT! 试一试！互惠规范能促进帮助行为吗？
Does the Reciprocity Norm Increase Helping?

Have you ever gotten a fund-raising appeal from a charity that included a little gift, such as address labels with your name on it? If so, did the gift make you more inclined to donate money to the charity? If so, you were subject to the reciprocity norm—because the charity did something for you, you felt more obligated to do something for the charity. The same norm applies when stores offer free samples of a product they are selling. It can feel rude not to reciprocate by buying the product, even though these are strangers trying to sell us something, and not friends doing us a favor. What about in everyday life? Can you think of times that the reciprocity norm influenced how likely you were to help a friend? Have you found that doing a favor for a friend makes it more likely that your friend will do a favor for you? Give this a try and see if it works.

In sum, evolutionary psychologists believe that people help others because of factors that have become ingrained in our genes: kin selection, the norm of reciprocity, and the ability to learn and follow social norms. As we saw in Chapter 10, evolutionary psychology is a challenging and creative approach to understanding prosocial behavior, though it does have its critics (Batson, 1998; Buller, 2005; Caporael & Brewer, 2000; Wood & Eagly, 2002). How, for example, can evolutionary theory explain why complete strangers sometimes help each other, even when there is no reason for them to assume that they share some of the same genes or that their favor will ever be returned? It seems absurd to say that the heroes of September 11, who lost their lives

Calvin and Hobbes by Bill Watterson

CALVIN AND HOBBES Copyright © 1995 Watterson. Reprinted with permission of UNIVERSAL PRESS SYNDICATE. All rights reserved.

while saving others, somehow calculated how genetically similar they were to the others before deciding to help. Further, just because people are more likely to save family members than strangers from a fire does not necessarily mean that they are genetically programmed to help genetic relatives. It may simply be that they cannot bear the thought of losing a loved one and so go to greater lengths to save the ones they love over people they have never met. We turn now to other possible motives behind prosocial behavior that do not necessarily originate in people's genes.

Let him who neglects to raise the fallen, fear lest, when he falls, no one will stretch out his hand to lift him up.

—Saadi, The Orchard, 1257

Social Exchange: The Costs and Rewards of Helping
社会交换：助人的成本与报酬

Although some social psychologists disagree with evolutionary approaches to prosocial behavior, they share the view that altruistic behavior can be based on self-interest. In fact, *social exchange theory* (see Chapter 10) argues that much of what we do stems from the desire to maximize our rewards and minimize our costs (Cook & Rice, 2003; Homans, 1961; Lawler & Thye, 1999; Thibaut & Kelley, 1959). The difference from evolutionary approaches is that social exchange theory doesn't trace this desire back to our evolutionary roots, nor does it assume that the desire is genetically based. Social exchange theorists assume that just as people in an economic marketplace try to maximize the ratio of their monetary profits to their monetary losses, people in their relationships with others try to maximize the ratio of social rewards to social costs.

Helping can be rewarding in a number of ways. As we saw with the norm of reciprocity, it can increase the likelihood that someone will help us in return. Helping someone is an investment in the future, the social exchange being that someday, someone will help us when we need it. Helping can also relieve the personal distress of a bystander. Considerable evidence indicates that people are aroused and disturbed when they see another person suffer and that they help at least in part to relieve their own distress (Dovidio, 1984; Dovidio, Piliavin, Gaertner, Schroeder, & Clark, 1991; Eisenberg & Fabes, 1991). By helping others, we can also gain such rewards as social approval from others and increased feelings of self-worth.

The other side of the coin, of course, is that helping can be costly. Helping decreases when the costs are high, such as when it would put us in physical danger, result in pain or embarrassment, or simply take too much time (Dovidio et al., 1991; Piliavin, Dovidio, Gaertner, & Clark, 1981; Piliavin, Piliavin, & Rodin, 1975). Perhaps Abe Zelmanowitz, who stayed behind with his friend Ed Beyea in the World Trade Center, found the prospect of walking away and letting his friend die too distressing. Basically, social exchange theory argues that true altruism, in which people help even when doing so is costly to them, does not exist. People help when the benefits outweigh the costs.

I once saw a man out of courtesy help a lame dog over a stile, and [the dog] for requital bit his fingers.

—William Chillingworth

If you are like many of our students, you may think this is an overly cynical view of human nature. Is true altruism, motivated only by the desire to help someone else, really such a mythical act? Must we trace all prosocial behavior, such as large charitable gifts made by wealthy individuals, to the self-interest of the helper? Well, a social exchange theorist might reply, there are many ways in which people can obtain gratification, and we should be thankful that one way is by helping others. After all, wealthy people could decide to get their pleasure only from lavish vacations, expensive cars, and meals at fancy restaurants. We should applaud their decision to give money to the disadvantaged, even if, ultimately, it is just a way for them to feel good about themselves. Prosocial acts are doubly rewarding in that they help both the giver and the recipient of the aid. Thus it is to everyone's advantage to promote and praise such acts.

Still, many people are dissatisfied with the argument that all helping stems from self-interest. How can it explain why people give up their lives for others, as many of the heroes of September 11th did? According to some social psychologists, people do have hearts of gold and sometimes help only for the sake of helping.

What seems to be generosity is often no more than disguised ambition.

—François de la Rochefoucauld, Maxims, 1665

Empathy and Altruism: The Pure Motive for Helping
移情与利他主义：助人的纯粹动机

C. Daniel Batson (1991) is the strongest proponent of the idea that people often help purely out of the goodness of their hearts. Batson acknowledges that people sometimes help others for selfish reasons, such as to relieve their own distress at seeing another person suffer. But he also argues that people's motives are sometimes purely altruistic, in that their only goal is to help the other person, even if doing so involves some cost to them. Pure altruism is likely to come into play, he maintains, when we feel **empathy** for the person in need of help, putting ourselves in the shoes of another person and experiencing events and emotions the way that person experiences them (Batson, Ahmad, Powell, & Stocks, 2008).

Suppose that while you are food shopping, you see a man holding a baby and a bag full of diapers, toys, and rattles. As he reaches for a box of Wheat Chex, the man drops the bag, and everything spills onto the floor. Will you help him pick up his things? According to Batson, it depends first on whether you feel empathy for him. If you do, you will help, regardless of what you have to gain. Your goal will be to relieve the other person's distress, not to gain something for yourself. This is the crux of Batson's **empathy-altruism hypothesis**: When we feel empathy for another person, we will attempt to help the person for purely altruistic reasons, regardless of what we have to gain.

If you do not feel empathy, then, Batson says, social exchange concerns come into play. What's in it for you? If there is something to be gained, such as obtaining approval from the man or from onlookers, you will help the man pick up his things. If you will not profit from helping, you will go on your way without stopping. Batson's empathy-altruism hypothesis is summarized in Figure 11.1.

Empathy
The ability to put oneself in the shoes of another person and to experience events and emotions (e.g., joy and sadness) the way that person experiences them

Empathy-Altruism Hypothesis
The idea that when we feel empathy for a person, we will attempt to help that person purely for altruistic reasons, regardless of what we have to gain

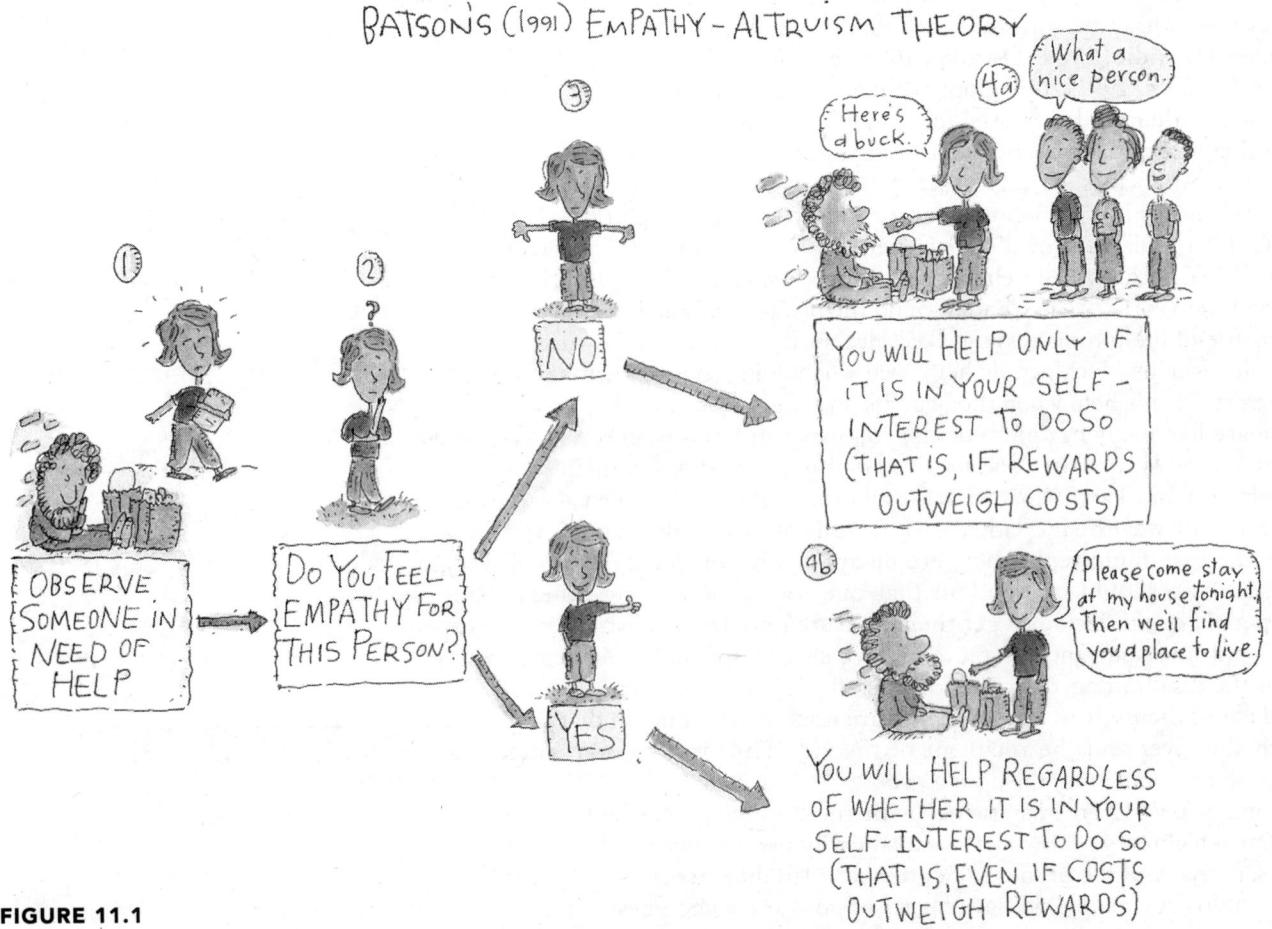

FIGURE 11.1
Batson's (1991) empathy-altruism theory.

Batson and his colleagues would be the first to acknowledge that it can be very difficult to isolate the exact motives behind complex social behaviors. If you saw someone help the man pick up his possessions, how could you tell whether the person was acting out of empathic concern or to gain some sort of social reward? Consider a famous story about Abraham Lincoln. One day, while riding in a coach, Lincoln and a fellow passenger were debating the very question we are considering: Is helping ever truly altruistic? Lincoln argued that helping always stems from self-interest, whereas the other passenger took the view that true altruism exists. Suddenly the men were interrupted by the screeching of a pig who was trying to save her piglets from drowning in a creek. Lincoln ordered the coach to stop, jumped out, ran down to the creek, and lifted the piglets to the safety of the bank. When he returned, his companion said, "Now, Abe, where does selfishness come in on this little episode?" "Why, bless your soul, Ed," Lincoln replied. "That was the very essence of selfishness. I should have had no peace of mind all day had I gone on and left that suffering old sow worrying over those pigs. I did it to get peace of mind, don't you see?" (Sharp, 1928, p. 75).

As this example shows, an act that seems truly altruistic is sometimes motivated by self-interest. How, then, can we tell which is which? Batson and his colleagues have devised a series of clever experiments to unravel people's motives (Batson, Ahmad, & Stocks, 2004; Batson & Powell, 2003). Imagine that you were an introductory psychology student in one of these studies (Toi & Batson, 1982). You are asked to evaluate some tapes of new programs for the university radio station, one of which is called *News from the Personal Side*. There are lots of different pilot tapes for this program, and you are told that only one person will be listening to each tape. The one you hear is an interview with a student named Carol Marcy. She describes a bad automobile accident in which both of her legs were broken and talks about how hard it has been to keep up with her class work as a result of the accident, especially because she is still in a wheelchair. Carol says she is especially concerned about how far she has fallen behind in her introductory psychology class and mentions that she will have to drop the class unless she can find another student to tell her what she has missed.

After you listen to the tape, the experimenter hands you an envelope marked "To the student listening to the Carol Marcy pilot tape." The experimenter says she doesn't know what's in the envelope but was asked by the professor supervising the research to hand it out. You open the envelope and find a note from the professor, saying that he was wondering if the student who listened to Carol's tape would be willing to help her out with her psychology class. Carol was reluctant to ask for help, he says, but because she is so far behind in the class, she agreed to write a note to the person listening to her tape. The note asks if you could meet with her and share your introductory psychology lecture notes.

As you have probably guessed, the point of the study was to look at the conditions under which people agreed to help Carol. The researchers pitted two motives against each other—self-interest and empathy. They varied how much empathy people felt toward Carol by telling different participants to adopt different perspectives when listening to the tape. In the high-empathy condition, people were told to try to imagine how Carol felt about what happened to her and how it changed her life. In the low-empathy condition, people were told to try to be objective and not be concerned with how Carol felt. As expected, people in the high-empathy condition reported feeling more sympathy for Carol than people in the low-empathy condition did.

The researchers also varied how costly it would be *not* to help Carol. In one condition, participants learned that she would start coming back to class the following week and happened to be in the same psychology section as they were; thus they would see her every time they went to class and would be reminded that she needed help. This was the high-cost condition because it would be unpleasant to refuse to help Carol and then run into her every week in class. In the low-cost

> It is one of the beautiful compensations of this life that no one can sincerely try to help another without helping himself.
>
> —Charles Dudley Warner, 1873

FIGURE 11.2
Altruism versus self-interest.

Under what conditions did people agree to help Carol with the work she missed in her introductory psychology class? When empathy was high, people helped regardless of the costs and rewards (i.e., regardless of whether they would encounter her in their psychology class). When empathy was low, people were more concerned with the rewards and costs for them— they helped only if they would encounter Carol in their psychology class and thus feel guilty about not helping.

(Adapted from Toi & Batson, 1982)

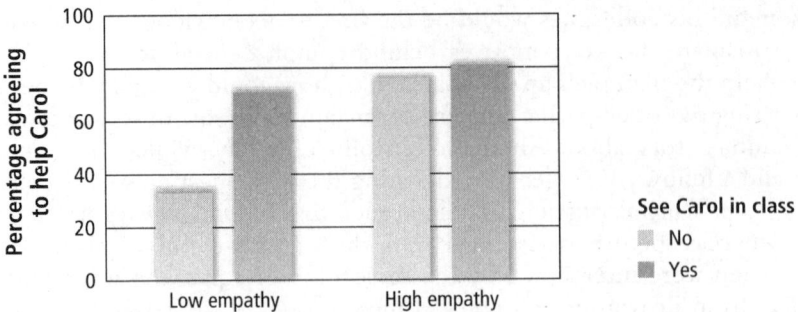

condition, people learned that Carol would be studying at home and would not be coming to class; thus they would never have to face her in her wheelchair and feel guilty about not helping her.

When deciding whether to help Carol, did people take into account the costs involved? According to the empathy-altruism hypothesis, people should have been motivated purely by altruistic concerns and helped regardless of the costs—if empathy was high (see Figure 11.1). As you can see in the right side of Figure 11.2, this prediction was confirmed: In the high-empathy condition, about as many people agreed to help when they thought they would see Carol in class as when they thought they would not see her in class. This suggests that people had Carol's interests in mind and not their own. In the low-empathy condition, however, many more people agreed to help when they thought they would see Carol in class than when they thought they would not see her in class (see the left side of Figure 11.2). This suggests that when empathy was low, social exchange concerns came into play, in that people based their decision to help on the costs and benefits to themselves. They helped when it was in their interests to do so (i.e., when they would see Carol in her wheelchair and feel guilty for not helping) but not otherwise (i.e., when they thought they would never see her again).

These results suggest that true altruism exists when people experience empathy toward the suffering of another. But what makes people feel empathy in the first place? Recent research points to two determinants. One is how securely attached we are feeling at the moment. As we saw in Chapter 10, *attachment styles* refer to people's expectations about the nature of relationships with others, based on the relationships they had with their primary caregiver when they were infants. The *secure attachment style* is characterized by trust, a lack of concern with being abandoned, and the view that one is worthy and well liked. Although people have different attachment styles, it is also the case that any of us can feel more secure in some situations than others. And how secure people feel has been shown to influence how much empathy they feel toward someone in need and how likely they are to help that person. In one series of studies, some participants were primed with a secure attachment mindset, by writing about people they turned to when they felt distressed. Compared to participants who wrote about other topics, those primed with secure attachment were more likely to feel empa-

Study: Cavemen helped disabled

United Press International
NEW YORK—The skeleton of a dwarf who died about 12,000 years ago indicates that cave people cared for physically disabled members of their communities, a researcher said yesterday.

The skeleton of the 3-foot-high youth was initially discovered in 1963 in a cave in southern Italy but was lost to anthropologists until American researcher David W. Frayer reexamined the remains and reported his findings in the British journal Nature.

Frayer, a professor of anthropology at the University of Kansas at Lawrence, said in a telephone interview that the youth "couldn't have taken part in normal hunting of food or gathering activities so he was obviously cared for by others."

Archaeologists have found the remains of other handicapped individuals who lived during the same time period, but their disabilities occurred when they were adults, Frayer said.

"This is the first time we've found someone who was disabled since birth....", Frayer said. He said there was no indication that the dwarf, who was about 17 at the time of his death, had suffered from malnutrition or neglect.

He was one of six individuals buried in the floor of a cave and was found in a dual grave in the arms of a woman, about 40 years old.

This touching story of early hominid prosocial behavior is intriguing to think about in terms of different theories of prosocial behavior. Evolutionary psychologists might argue that the caregivers helped the dwarf because he was a relative and that people are programmed to help those who share their genes (kin selection). Social exchange theory would maintain that the dwarf's caregivers received sufficient rewards from their actions to outweigh the costs of caring for him. The empathy-altruism hypothesis would hold that the caregivers helped out of strong feelings of empathy and compassion for him—an interpretation supported by the article's final paragraph.

Helping behavior is common in virtually all species of animals, and sometimes it even crosses species lines. In August 1996, a 3-year-old boy fell into a pit containing seven gorillas at the Brookfield, Illinois, zoo. Binti, a 7-year-old gorilla, immediately picked up the boy. After cradling him in her arms, she placed the boy near a door where zookeepers could get to him. Why did she help? Evolutionary psychologists would argue that prosocial behavior is selected for and thus becomes part of the genetic makeup of the members of many species. Social exchange theorists would argue that Binti had been rewarded for helping in the past. In fact, because she had been rejected by her mother, she had received training in parenting skills from zookeepers, in which she was rewarded for caring for a doll (Bils & Singer, 1996).

thy toward another student who was in need and to help that student—even when it was costly to them to help (Mikulincer, Shaver, Gillath, & Nitzberg, 2005). Thus, when people are feeling particularly secure about their own attachment, they have a greater capacity to feel empathy toward others.

Another determinant of empathy is whether we have recently been included or excluded by a group of people we care about. In a recent series of studies, participants who were excluded from a group were less likely to donate money to charity, volunteer their time, or help someone clean up after a mishap (knocking over a cup of pencils). The reason was *not* that social rejection put people in a bad mood—in fact, people who were rejected seemed to experience a temporary inability to feel anything too deeply. This had the advantage of protecting people's feelings; by shutting down emotionally people avoided the pain of being rejected by others. But it also made them less able to feel empathy toward someone who needed their help (DeWall & Baumeister, 2006; Twenge, Baumeister, DeWall, Ciarocco, & Bartels, 2007). In sum, in order to feel empathy people must feel that another person is in need, value that person's welfare, and take the perspective of that person (Batson, Eklund, Chermok, Hoyt, & Ortiz, 2007), and that is *more* likely to occur when people are feeling securely attached, and *less* likely to occur if people have recently been rejected by others.

As we learned from Abraham Lincoln and the pigs, however, unraveling people's exact motives for helping someone is a formidable task, and the empathy-altruism hypothesis has sparked a lively debate. Some researchers have questioned whether people who experience empathy help purely out of concern for the person in need or, like Abe Lincoln, offer help to relieve their own distress at seeing someone suffer (e.g., Cialdini, Brown, Lewis, Luce, & Neuberg, 1997; Maner et al., 2002; Preston & De Waal, 2002).

To sum up, we've identified three basic motives underlying prosocial behavior:

1. Helping is an instinctive reaction to promote the welfare of those genetically similar to us (evolutionary psychology).
2. The rewards of helping often outweigh the costs, so helping is in our self-interest (social exchange theory).
3. Under some conditions, powerful feelings of empathy and compassion for the victim prompt selfless giving (the empathy-altruism hypothesis).

Each of these approaches has its supporters and critics.

Personal Qualities and Prosocial Behavior: Why Do Some People Help More Than Others?
个人品质与亲社会行为：为什么一些人比其他人更多助人？

If basic human motives were all there was to it, why are some people so much more helpful than others? Clearly, we need to consider the personal qualities that distinguish the helpful person from the selfish one.

Individual Differences: The Altruistic Personality
个体差异：利他人格

> On reflecting at dinner that he had done nothing to help anybody all day, he uttered these memorable and praise-worthy words: "Friends, I have lost a day."
>
> —Suetonius, *Lives of the Twelve Caesars*, first century A.D.

When you read the descriptions of the September 11 heroes at the beginning of this chapter, did you think about the personalities of the people we described? It is natural to assume that William Wik, Abe Zelmanowitz, Rick Rescorla, and the passengers of United flight 93 were cut from a different cloth—selfless, caring people who would never dream of ignoring someone's pleas for help. Psychologists have been interested in the nature of the **altruistic personality**, the qualities that cause an individual to help others in a wide variety of situations (Eisenberg, Spinrad, & Sadovsky, 2006; Mikulincer & Shaver, 2005; Penner, 2002).

Although some people are obviously more helpful than others, personality alone does not determine behavior—the pressures of the situation matter as well (as we have seen throughout this book). Predicting how helpful people will be is no exception. Studies of both children and adults, for example, find that people with high scores on personality tests of altruism are not that much more likely to help than those with lower scores (Batson, 1998; Magoo & Khanna, 1991; Piliavin & Charng, 1990). Why not? We need to consider several other critical factors as well, such as the situational pressures that are affecting people, their gender, the culture in which they grew up, how religious they are, and even their current mood (Graziano, Habashi, Sheese, & Tobin, 2007).

Gender Differences in Prosocial Behavior 亲社会行为中的性别差异

Consider two scenarios. In one, someone performs a dramatic, heroic act, like storming the cockpit of United flight 93 to fight the terrorists. In the other, someone is involved in a long-term helping relationship, such as assisting a disabled neighbor with chores around the house. Are men or women more likely to help in each situation?

The answer is males in the first situation and females in the second (Eagly & Crowley, 1986; Eagly & Koenig, 2006). In virtually all cultures, norms prescribe different traits and behaviors for males and females, learned as boys and girls are growing up. In Western cultures, the male sex role includes being chivalrous and heroic; females are expected to be nurturant and caring and to value close, long-term relationships. Indeed, of the 7,000 people who received medals from the Carnegie Hero Fund Commission for risking their lives to save a stranger, 91 percent have been men. In contrast, women are more likely than men to provide social support to their friends and to engage in volunteer work that involves helping others (Eagly & Koenig, 2006; McGuire, 1994; Monin, Clark, & Lemay, 2008). Cross-cultural evidence suggests the same pattern. In a survey of adolescents in seven countries, more girls than boys reported doing volunteer work in their communities (Flanagan, Bowes, Jonsson, Csapo, & Sheblanova, 1998).

Clearly, some people have more of an altruistic personality than others, causing them to engage in more prosocial behavior. Personality, however, is not the whole story; the nature of the social situation also determines whether people help.

Altruistic Personality
The qualities that cause an individual to help others in a wide variety of situations

Cultural Differences in Prosocial Behavior 亲社会行为中的文化差异

Let's look again at Western and non-Western cultures (see Chapter 5). Does an independent view of the self versus a more interdependent, group-oriented outlook affect people's willingness to help others? Because people with an interdependent view of the self are more likely to define themselves in terms of their social relationships and have more of a sense of "connectedness" to others, we might predict that they'd be more likely to help a person in need.

However, people in all cultures are more likely to help someone they define as a member of their **in-group**, the group with which an individual identifies. People everywhere are less likely to help someone they perceive to be a member of an **out-group**, a group with which they do not identify (Brewer & Brown, 1998; Stürmer, Synder, & Omoto, 2005; see also Chapter 13). Cultural factors come into play in determining how strongly people draw the line between in-groups and out-groups. In many interdependent cultures, the needs of in-group members are considered more important than those of out-groups, and consequently, people in these cultures are more likely to help in-group members than members of individualistic cultures are (Leung & Bond, 1984; Miller, Bersoff, & Harwood, 1990; Moghaddam, Taylor, & Wright, 1993). However, because the line between "us" and "them" is more firmly drawn in interdependent cultures, people in these cultures are *less* likely to help members of out-groups than people in individualistic cultures are (Kemmelmeier, Jambor, & Letner, 2006; Leung & Bond, 1984; Triandis, 1994). Thus to be helped by other people, it is important that they view you as a member of their in-group—as "one of them"—and this is especially true in interdependent cultures (Ting & Piliavin, 2000).

A particular cultural value that strongly relates to prosocial behavior is *simpatía*. Prominent in Spanish-speaking countries, *simpatía* refers to a range of social and emotional traits, including being friendly, polite, good-natured, pleasant, and helpful toward others (interestingly, it has no direct English translation). One study tested the hypothesis that helping would be higher in cultures that value *simpatía* (Levine, 2003; Levine, Norenzayan, & Philbrick, 2001). The researchers staged helping incidents in large cities in 23 countries and observed what people did. In one scenario, for example, a researcher posing as a blind person stopped at a busy intersection and observed whether pedestrians offered help in crossing or informed the researcher when the light turned green.

If you look at Table 11.1, you'll see that the percentage of people who helped (averaged across the different incidents) varied. On average, people in countries that value *simpatía* helped more than in countries that did not, 83 percent to 66 percent. The researchers noted that these results are only suggestive, because the five Latin American and Spanish countries differed from the others in ways other than the value they placed on *simpatía*. And some countries not known for their *simpatía* had high rates of helping. Nevertheless, if a culture strongly values friendliness and prosocial behavior, people may be more likely to help strangers on city streets (Janoff-Bulman & Leggatt, 2002).

Religion and Prosocial Behavior 宗教和亲社会行为

Most religions teach some version of the Golden Rule, urging us to do unto others as we would have others do unto us. Are religious people more likely to follow this advice than nonreligious people? That is, does religion foster prosocial behavior? The answer is yes on some measures, but not all. People who attend religious services report on surveys that they give more money to charity, and engage in more volunteer work, than do people who do not attend religious services (Brooks, 2006). When it comes to what people actually do, however—not just what they report on surveys—the story is a little more complicated. Religious people are more likely to help (e.g., raising money for a sick child) in situations in which helping makes them look good to themselves or others. They are not more likely to help, however, in private situations in which no one will know that they helped (Batson, Schoenrade, & Ventis, 1993). In terms of Batson's empathy-altruism hypothesis that we discussed earlier, religious people do not appear to feel more empathy toward others, though they are more likely to help when it is in their best interests to do so (Norenzayan & Shariff, 2008).

Whereas men are more likely to perform chivalrous and heroic acts, women are more likely to be helpful in long-term relationships that involve greater commitment.

In-Group
The group with which an individual identifies as a member

Out-Group
Any group with which an individual does not identify

TABLE 11.1	Helping in Twenty-Three Cities

In 23 cities around the world, researchers observed how many people helped in three situations: helping a person with a leg brace who dropped a pile of magazines, helping someone who did not notice that he or she had dropped a pen, and helping a blind person across a busy intersection. The percentages in the table are averaged across the three situations. The cities in boldface are in countries that have the cultural value of *simpatía*, which prizes friendliness, politeness, and helping others.

City	Percent Helping %
Rio de Janeiro, Brazil	93
San José, Costa Rica	91
Lilongwe, Malawi	86
Calcutta, India	83
Vienna, Austria	81
Madrid, Spain	79
Copenhagen, Denmark	78
Shanghai, China	77
Mexico City, Mexico	76
San Salvador, El Salvador	75
Prague, Czech Republic	75
Stockholm, Sweden	72
Budapest, Hungary	71
Bucharest, Romania	69
Tel Aviv, Israel	68
Rome, Italy	63
Bangkok, Thailand	61
Taipei, Taiwan	59
Sofia, Bulgaria	57
Amsterdam, Netherlands	54
Singapore	48
New York, United States	45
Kuala Lumpur, Malaysia	40

(Adapted from Levine, Norenzayan, & Philbrick, 2001)

The Effects of Mood on Prosocial Behavior
心境对亲社会行为的影响

Imagine that you are at your local shopping mall. As you walk from one store to another, a fellow in front of you drops a manila folder and papers go fluttering in all directions. He looks around in dismay, then bends down and starts picking up the papers. Would you stop and help him? The answer might depend on what your current mood happens to be.

Effects of Positive Moods: Feel Good, Do Good In a classic study, researchers wanted to see whether people's mood influenced shoppers' likelihood of helping a stranger, much like the example we just gave (Isen & Levin, 1972). To find out, they temporarily boosted some shoppers' moods in a clever way—they left dimes in the coin-return slot of a public telephone at the mall and then waited for someone to find the coins. (Note the year this study was done—there were no cell phones, so more people used pay phones. Also, 10 cents then would be like finding 50 cents today.) As the lucky shoppers left the phone with their newly found dime, a research assistant played the role of the man with the manila folder. He intentionally dropped the folder a few feet in front of the shopper to see whether he or she would stop and help him pick up his papers. It turned out that finding the dime had a dramatic effect on helping. Only 4 percent of the people who did not find a dime helped the man pick up his papers, whereas a whopping 84 percent of the people who found a dime stopped to help.

This "feel good, do good" effect has been replicated many times with different ways of boosting people's mood (including doing well on a test, receiving a gift, thinking happy thoughts, and listening to pleasant music; North, Tarrant, & Hargreaves, 2004) and with many different kinds of helping (including contributing money to charity, helping someone find a lost contact lens, tutoring another student, donating blood, and helping co-workers on the job; Carlson, Charlin, & Miller, 1988; Isen, 1999; Salovey, Mayer, & Rosenhan, 1991).

Being in a good mood can increase helping for three reasons. First, good moods make us look on the bright side of life. That is, when we're in a good mood, we tend to see the good side of other people, giving them the benefit of the doubt. A victim who might normally seem clumsy or annoying will, when we are feeling cheerful, seem like a decent, needy person who is worthy of our help (Carlson et al., 1988; Forgas & Bower, 1987). Second, helping other people is an excellent way of prolonging our good mood. If we see someone who needs help, then being a Good Samaritan spawns even more good feelings, and we can walk away feeling terrific. In comparison, not helping when we know we should is a surefire "downer," deflating our good mood (Clark & Isen, 1982; Isen, 1987; Lyubomirsky, Sheldon, & Schkade, 2005). (See the following Try It! exercise for another example of how helping others improves our moods.) Finally, good moods increase the amount of attention we pay to ourselves, and this factor in turn makes us more likely to behave according to our values and ideals (see Chapter 3). Because most of us value altruism and because good moods increase our attention to this value, good moods increase helping behavior (Berkowitz, 1987; Carlson et al., 1988; Salovey & Rodin, 1985).

TRY IT! Do Good, Feel Good? 试一试！心情好，做好事？

Suppose you found a $20 bill on the ground and could spend it on yourself (e.g., buy yourself a nice lunch) or on someone else (e.g., treat a friend to lunch). Which would you rather do? If your goal is to improve your mood, the answer might surprise you—spend it on your friend! Research by Dunn, Aknin, and Norton (2008) found that people who spent money on others were happier than people who spent money on themselves. Try this yourself the next time you have a little money to spend. Rather than buying yourself a treat, try treating a friend or donating the money to charity. You might be surprised by how good you feel!

Feel Bad, Do Good What about when we are in a bad mood? Suppose that when you saw the fellow in the mall drop his folder, you were feeling down. Would this influence the likelihood that you would help the man pick up his papers? One kind of bad mood clearly leads to an increase in helping—feeling guilty (Baumeister, Stillwell, & Heatherton, 1994; Estrada-Hollenbeck & Heatherton, 1998). People often act on the idea that good deeds cancel out bad deeds. When they have done something that has made them feel guilty, helping another person balances things out, reducing their guilty feelings. For example, one study found that churchgoers were more likely to donate money to charities before attending confession than afterward, presumably because confessing to a priest reduced their guilt (Harris, Benson, & Hall, 1975). Thus if you just realized you had forgotten your best friend's birthday and you felt guilty about it, you would be more likely to help the fellow in the mall, to repair your guilty feelings.

If you want others to be happy, practice compassion. If you want to be happy, practice compassion.

—The Dalai Lama

But suppose you just had a fight with a friend or just found out you did poorly on a test and you were feeling sad. Given that feeling happy leads to greater helping, it might seem that feeling sad would decrease helping. Surprisingly, however, sadness can also lead to an increase in helping, at least under certain conditions (Carlson & Miller, 1987; Salovey et al., 1991). When people are sad, they are motivated to engage in activities that make them feel better (Cialdini & Fultz, 1990; Cialdini et al., 1987; Wegener & Petty, 1994). To the extent that helping is rewarding, it can lift us out of the doldrums.

Situational Determinants of Prosocial Behavior: When Will People Help?
亲社会行为的情境决定因素：什么时候人们会助人？

Personality, gender, culture, and mood all contribute a piece to the puzzle of why people help others, but they do not complete the picture. To understand more fully why people help, we also need to consider the social situation in which people find themselves.

Environment: Rural versus Urban 环境：乡村与城市

Suppose you are walking down the street one day when you see a man suddenly fall down and cry out with pain. He rolls up his pants leg, revealing a bandaged shin that is bleeding heavily. What would you do? When this event was staged in small towns, about half the people who walked by stopped and offered to help the man. In large cities, only 15 percent of passersby stopped to help (Amato, 1983). Other studies have found that people in small towns are more likely to help when asked to find a lost child, give directions, and return a lost letter. Helping has been found to be more prevalent in small towns in several countries, including the United States, Canada, Israel, Australia, Turkey, Great Britain, and the Sudan (Hedge & Yousif, 1992; Steblay, 1987).

> *Do not wait for extraordinary circumstances to do good actions; try to use ordinary situations.*
> —John Paul Richter, 1763

Why are people more likely to help in small towns? One possibility is that people who grow up in a small town are more likely to internalize altruistic values. If this were the case, people who grew up in small towns would be more likely to help, even if they were visiting a big city. Alternatively, the immediate surroundings might be the key and not people's internalized values. Stanley Milgram (1970), for example, suggested that people living in cities are constantly bombarded with stimulation and that they keep to themselves in order to avoid being overwhelmed by it. According to this **urban overload hypothesis**, if you put urban dwellers in a calmer, less stimulating environment, they would be as likely as anyone else to reach out to others. Research has supported the urban overload hypothesis more than the idea that living in cities makes people less altruistic by

Urban Overload Hypothesis
The theory that people living in cities are constantly being bombarded with stimulation and that they keep to themselves to avoid being overwhelmed by it

People are less helpful in big cities than in small towns, not because of a difference in values but because the stress of urban life causes them to keep to themselves.

nature. To predict whether people will help, it is more important to know whether they are currently in a rural or urban area than it is to know where they happened to grow up (Levine, Martinez, Brase, & Sorenson, 1994; Steblay, 1987).

Residential Mobility 居民流动性

It is not only where you live that matters, but how often you have moved from one place to another. In many areas of the world, it is common for people to move far away from where they were raised (Hochstadt, 1999). In the year 2000, for example, nearly one in five Americans (18 percent) were living in a different state than they were in 1995 ("Migration and Geographic Mobility," 2003), and in many urban areas, fewer than half of the residents were living in the same house as they were in 1995 (Oishi et al., 2007). As it turns out, people who have lived for a long time in one place are more likely to engage in prosocial behaviors that help the community. Living for a long time in one place leads to a greater attachment to the community, more interdependence with one's neighbors, and a greater concern with one's reputation in the community (Baumeister, 1986, Oishi et al., 2007). For all these reasons, long-time residents are more likely to engage in prosocial behaviors. Oishi et al. (2007), for example, found that people who had lived for a long time in the Minneapolis-St. Paul area were more likely to purchase "critical habitat" license plates, compared to people who had recently moved to the area. (These license plates cost an extra $30 a year and provide funds for the state to purchase and manage natural habitats.)

Many states offer special license plates for an extra charge, with the funds going to help the environment, wildlife, or other statewide needs. Research on residential mobility found that people who had lived for a long time in the Minneapolis-St. Paul area were more likely to purchase "critical habitat" license plates, such as the one in this picture, than were people who had recently moved to the area.

Perhaps it is not surprising that people who have lived in one place for awhile feel more of a stake in their community. Oishi et al. (2007) also found, though, that this increase in helping can arise quite quickly even in a one-time laboratory setting. Imagine you are in a study in which you are playing a trivia contest against four other students, in which the winner will win a $10 gift certificate. The experimenter says that people in the group can help each other if they want, but that doing so might lower the helper's chances of winning the prize. As the game progresses one of your fellow group members keeps sighing and commenting that he doesn't know the answers to the questions. Would you offer him some help, or let him continue to struggle on his own?

The answer, it turns out, depends on how long you have been in the group with the struggling student. In the actual study by Oishi and colleagues there was a total of four tasks (the trivia contest was the last one). Half the participants remained together and worked on all the tasks throughout the study, whereas the other half switched to a new group after each task. Thus, in the former condition people had more of an opportunity to get to know each other and form a sense of community, whereas the latter group was more analogous to moving from one community to another. As the researchers predicted, people in the "stable community" condition were more likely to help their struggling companion than were people in the "transient" group condition. Another reason that people might be less helpful in big cities, then, is that residential mobility is higher in cities than in rural areas. People are more likely to have just moved to a city and thus feel less of a stake in the community.

The Number of Bystanders: The Bystander Effect
旁观者数目：旁观者效应

Remember Kitty Genovese? We have just seen one reason why her neighbors turned a deaf ear to her cries for help: The murder took place in New York City, one of the most densely populated areas in the world. Perhaps her neighbors had moved to the city recently, or maybe they were so overloaded with urban stimulation that they dismissed Genovese's cries as one small addition to the surrounding din. Although it is true that people help less in urban environments, that isn't the only reason Genovese's neighbors failed to help. Her desperate cries surely must have risen above the everyday noises of garbage trucks and car horns. And there have been cases where people ignored the pleas of their neighbors even in small towns. In Fredericksburg, Virginia, a convenience store clerk was beaten in front of customers who did nothing to help, even after the assailant had fled and the clerk lay bleeding on the floor (Hsu, 1995). Fredericksburg and its surrounding county have only about 90,000 residents.

Bibb Latané and John Darley (1970) are two social psychologists who taught at universities in New York at the time of the Genovese murder. As we discussed in Chapter 2, they too were unconvinced that the only reason her neighbors failed to help was the stresses and stimulation of urban life. They focused on the fact that so many people heard her cries. Paradoxically, they thought, it might be that the greater the number of bystanders who observe an emergency, the less likely any one of them is to help. As Latané (1987) put it, "We came up with the insight that perhaps what made the Genovese case so fascinating was itself what made it happen—namely, that not just one or two, but thirty-eight people had watched and done nothing" (p. 78). We should add that some have recently doubted the veracity of the Kitty Genovese story, such as whether there really were 38 people who heard her cries and whether no one helped (Manning, Levine, & Collins, 2007). That was the story of the murder at the time, however, and the account that inspired Latané and Darley's research.

In a series of now classic experiments, Latané and Darley (1970) found that in terms of receiving help, there is no safety in numbers. Think back to the seizure experiment we discussed in Chapter 2. In that study, people sat in individual cubicles, participating in a group discussion of college life (over an intercom system) with students in other cubicles. One of the other students suddenly had a seizure, crying out for help, choking, and finally falling silent. There was actually only one real participant in the study. The other "participants," including the one who had the seizure, were prerecorded voices. The point of the study was to see whether the real participant would attempt to help the seizure victim by trying to find him or by summoning the experimenter or whether, like Kitty Genovese's neighbors, the person would simply sit there and do nothing.

As Latané and Darley anticipated, the answer depended on how many people the participant thought witnessed the emergency. When people believed they were the only ones listening to the student having the seizure, most of them (85 percent) helped within 60 seconds. By two and a half minutes, 100 percent of the people who thought they were the only bystander had offered assistance (see Figure 11.3). In comparison, when the research participants believed there was one other student listening, fewer helped—

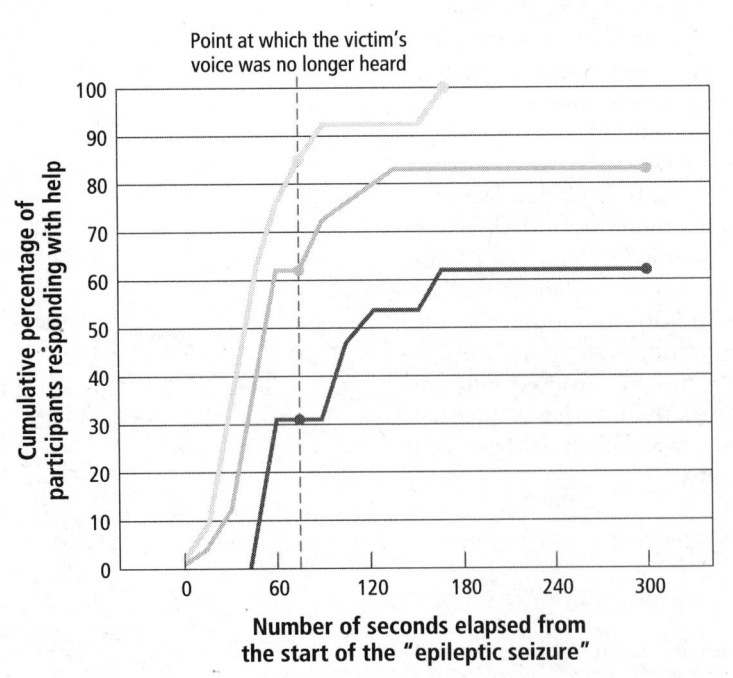

FIGURE 11.3

Bystander intervention: The presence of bystanders reduces helping.

When people believed they were the only one witnessing a student having a seizure—when they were the lone bystander—most of them helped him immediately, and all did within a few minutes. When they believed that someone else was listening as well—that there were two bystanders—they were less likely to help and did so more slowly. And when they believed that four others were listening—that there were five bystanders—they were even less likely to help.

(Adapted from Darley & Latané, 1968)

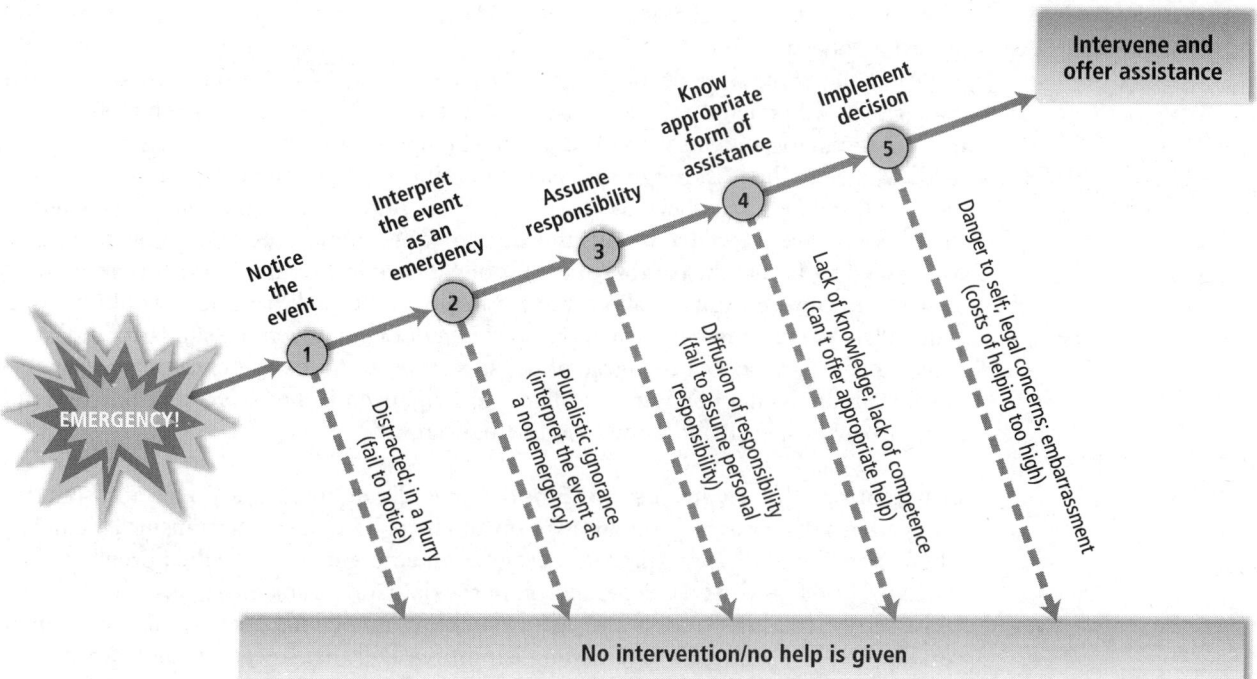

FIGURE 11.4

Bystander intervention decision tree: Five steps to helping in an emergency.

Latané and Darley (1970) showed that people go through five decision-making steps before they help someone in an emergency. If bystanders fail to take any one of the five steps, they will not help. Each step, as well as the possible reasons for why people decide not to intervene, is outlined here.

(Adapted from Latané & Darley, 1970)

only 62 percent within 60 seconds. As you can see in Figure 11.3, helping occurred more slowly when there were two bystanders and never reached 100 percent, even after 6 minutes, when the experiment was ended. Finally, when the participants believed there were four other students listening in addition to themselves, the percentage of people who helped dropped even more dramatically. Only 31 percent helped in the first 60 seconds, and after 6 minutes, only 62 percent had offered help. Dozens of other studies, conducted in the laboratory and in the field, have found the same thing: The greater the number of bystanders who witness an emergency, the less likely any one of them is to help the victim—a phenomenon called the **bystander effect**.

Why is it that people are less likely to help when others are present? Latané and Darley (1970) developed a step-by-step description of how people decide whether to intervene in an emergency (see Figure 11.4). Part of this description is an explanation of how the number of bystanders can make a difference. But let's begin with the first step—whether people notice that someone needs help.

Noticing an Event If you are hurrying down a crowded street, you might not notice that someone has collapsed in a doorway. Obviously, if people don't notice that an emergency situation exists, they will not intervene and offer to help. What determines whether people notice an emergency? John Darley and Daniel Batson (1973) demonstrated that something as seemingly trivial as how much of a hurry people are in can make more of a difference than what kind of person they are. These researchers conducted a study that mirrored the parable of the Good Samaritan, wherein many passersby failed to stop to help a man lying unconscious at the side of the road. The research participants were people we might think would be extremely altruistic—seminary students preparing to devote their lives to the ministry. The students were asked to walk to another building, where the researchers would record them making a brief speech. Some were told that they were late and should hurry to keep their appointment. Others were told that there was no rush because the assistant in the other building was running a few minutes behind schedule. As they walked to the other building, each of the students passed a man who was slumped in a doorway. The man (an accomplice of the experimenters) coughed and groaned as each student walked by. Did the seminary students stop and offer to help him? If they were not in a hurry, most of them (63 percent) did. If they were hurrying to keep their appointment,

Bystander Effect

The finding that the greater the number of bystanders who witness an emergency, the less likely any one of them is to help

however, only 10 percent stopped to help. Many of the students who were in a hurry did not even notice the man.

Surely if people were deeply religious, they would be less influenced by such a small matter as how hurried they were. Surprisingly, though, Darley and Batson (1973) found that the seminary students who were the most religious were no more likely to help than those who were the least religious. What about if they were thinking about helping people in need? The researchers also varied the topic of the speech they asked the students to give: Some were asked to discuss the kinds of jobs seminary students preferred; others were asked to discuss the parable of the Good Samaritan. You might think that seminary students who were thinking about the parable of the Good Samaritan would be especially likely to stop and help a man slumped in a doorway, given the similarity of this incident to the parable, but the topic of the speech made little difference in whether they helped. Students in a hurry were unlikely to help, even if they were very religious and about to give a speech about the Good Samaritan.

Interpreting the Event as an Emergency Even if people do notice someone slumped in a doorway, they might not stop and help. The next determinant of helping is whether the bystander interprets the event as an emergency—as a situation where help is needed (see Figure 11.4). Is the person in the doorway drunk or seriously ill? If we see white smoke coming out of a vent, is it something innocuous, such as mist from an air conditioner, or a sign that the building is on fire? Did that scream we just heard come from someone having a good time at a party, or is someone being attacked? If people assume that nothing is wrong when an emergency is taking place, they will not help.

When other bystanders are present, people are more likely to assume that an emergency is something innocuous. To understand why, think back to our discussion of informational social influence in Chapter 8. This type of social influence occurs when we use other people to help us define reality. When we are uncertain about what's going on, such as whether the smoke we see is a sign of a fire, one of the first things we do is look around to see how other people are responding. If other people look up, shrug, and go about their business, we are likely to assume there is nothing to worry about. If other people look panic-stricken and yell, "Fire!" we immediately assume the building is indeed on fire. As we saw in Chapter 8, it's often a good strategy to use other people as a source of information when we are uncertain about what's going on. The danger is that sometimes no one is sure what is happening. Since an emergency is often a sudden and confusing event, bystanders tend to freeze, watching and listening with blank expressions as they try to figure out what's going on. When they glance at each other, they see an apparent lack of concern on the part of everyone else. This results in a state of **pluralistic ignorance**, whereby people think that everyone else is interpreting a situation in a certain way, when in fact they are not. When an emergency occurs, for example, bystanders often assume that nothing is wrong because no one else looks concerned—even though everyone is worried and concerned.

Consider another classic experiment by Latané and Darley (1970). You are participating in a study of people's attitudes toward the problems of urban life, and you arrive at the appointed time. A sign tells you to fill out a questionnaire while you're waiting for the study to begin, so you take a seat and get started. Then you notice something odd: White smoke is trickling into the room through a small vent in the wall. Before long, the room is so filled with smoke that you can barely see the questionnaire. What will you do?

In fact, there was no real danger—the experimenters were pumping smoke into the room to see how people would respond to this potential emergency. Not surprisingly, when people were alone, most of them took action. Within 2 minutes, 50 percent of the participants left the room and found the experimenter down the hall, reporting that there may have been a fire in the building; by 6 minutes, 75 percent of the participants had left the room to alert the experimenter.

But what would happen if people were not alone? Given that 75 percent of the participants who were by themselves reported the smoke, it would seem that the larger

Pluralistic Ignorance
The case in which people think that everyone else is interpreting a situation in a certain way, when in fact they are not.

the group, the greater the likelihood that someone would report the smoke. In fact, this can be figured mathematically: If there is a 75 percent chance that any one person will report the smoke, then there is a 98 percent chance that at least one person in a three-person group will do so.

To find out if there really is safety in numbers, Latané and Darley (1970) included a condition in which three participants took part at the same time. Everything was identical except that three people sat in the room as the smoke began to seep in. Surprisingly, in only 12 percent of the three-person groups did someone report the smoke within 2 minutes, and in only 38 percent of the groups did someone report the smoke within 6 minutes. In the remaining groups, the participants sat there filling out questionnaires even when they had to wave away the smoke with their hands to see what they were writing. What went wrong?

Emergency situations can be confusing. Does this man need help? Have the bystanders failed to notice him, or has the behavior of the others led each of them to interpret the situation as a nonemergency—an example of pluralistic ignorance?

Unsure whether the smoke signaled an emergency, participants used each other as a source of information. If the people next to you glance at the smoke and then continue filling out their questionnaires, you will feel reassured that nothing is wrong; otherwise, why would they be acting so unconcerned? The problem is that they are probably looking at you as well, and if you seem untroubled, they too are reassured that everything is OK. In short, each group member is reassured because they assume that everyone else knows more about what's going on than they do. And when the event is ambiguous—as when smoke is coming from a vent—people in groups will convince each other that nothing is wrong (Clark & Word, 1972; Solomon, Solomon, & Stone, 1978).

Assuming Responsibility Sometimes it is obvious that an emergency is occurring, as when Kitty Genovese cried out, "Oh my God, he stabbed me! Please help me! Please help me!" (Rosenthal, 1964, p. 33). Genovese's neighbors must have believed that something terrible was happening and that she desperately needed help. That they did nothing indicates that even if we interpret an event as an emergency, we have to decide that it is *our* responsibility—not someone else's—to do something about it. Here again the number of bystanders is a crucial variable.

Think back to the Latané and Darley (1968) seizure experiment in which participants believed they were the only one listening to the student while he had a seizure. The responsibility was totally on their shoulders. If they didn't help, no one would, and the student might die. As a result, in this condition most people helped almost immediately, and all helped within a few minutes.

But what happens when there are many witnesses? A **diffusion of responsibility** occurs: Each bystander's sense of responsibility to help decreases as the number of witnesses increases. Because other people are present, no single bystander feels a strong personal responsibility to act. Recall from our earlier discussion that helping often entails costs—we might be putting ourselves in danger or end up looking foolish by overreacting or doing the wrong thing. Why should we risk these costs when many other people who can help are present? The problem is that everyone is likely to feel the same way, making all the bystanders less likely to help. This is particularly true if people cannot tell whether someone else has already intervened. When participants in the seizure experiment believed that other students were witnesses as well, they couldn't tell whether another student had already helped because the intercom system allowed only the voice of the student having the seizure to be transmitted. Each student probably assumed that he or she did not have to help because surely someone else had already done so. Similarly, Kitty Genovese's neighbors had no way of knowing whether someone else had called the police. Most likely, they assumed there was no need to do so because someone else had already made the call. Tragically, everyone assumed it was somebody else's responsibility to act, and Genovese was left to fight her assailant alone. The sad irony of Genovese's murder is that she probably would be alive today if fewer people had heard her cries for help.

Diffusion of Responsibility
The phenomenon whereby each bystander's sense of responsibility to help decreases as the number of witnesses increases

Knowing How to Help Even if people have made it this far in the helping sequence, another condition must still be met (step 4 in Figure 11.4): They must decide what kind of help is appropriate. Suppose that on a hot summer day, you see a woman collapse in the street. No one else seems to be helping, and so you decide it is up to you. But what should you do? Has the woman had a heart attack? Is she suffering from heatstroke? Should you call an ambulance, administer CPR, or try to get her out of the sun? If people don't know what form of assistance to give, obviously they will be unable to help.

Deciding to Implement the Help Finally, even if you know exactly what kind of help is appropriate, there are still reasons why you might decide not to intervene. For one thing, you might not be qualified to deliver the right kind of help. Even if the woman is complaining of chest pains, indicating a heart attack, you may not know how to give her CPR. Or you might be afraid of making a fool of yourself, of doing the wrong thing and making matters worse, or even of placing yourself in danger by trying to help. Consider the fate of three television network technicians who in 1982 saw a man beating a woman in a New York parking lot, tried to intervene, and were shot and killed by the assailant. Even when we know what kind of intervention is needed, we have to weigh the costs of trying to help.

What about helping situations that are not emergencies? The Latané and Darley model applies here as well. Consider an Internet chat room, in which someone needs help figuring out how to use the software. Are people less likely to help each other as the number of people in the chat room increases? Researchers in one study entered chat groups on Yahoo! Chat, in which 2 to 19 people were discussing a wide variety of topics (Markey, 2000). The researchers posed as either a male or female participant and typed this request for help: "Can anyone tell me how to look at someone's profile?" (p. 185). (A profile is a brief biographical description that each person in the chat group provides.) The message was addressed either to the group as a whole or to one randomly selected person in the chat room. Then the researchers timed how long it took someone in the group to respond to the request for help.

When the request was addressed to the group as a whole, Latané and Darley's results were replicated closely: The more people there were in the chat room, the longer it took for anyone to respond to the request for help. But when the request was directed to a specific person, that person responded quickly, regardless of the size of the group. These results suggest that the diffusion of responsibility was operating. When a general request for help is made, a large group makes people feel that they do not have much responsibility to respond. When addressed by name, though, people are more likely to feel a responsibility to help, even when many others are present.

Even if people are by themselves, however, they can still experience a diffusion of responsibility. In a recent study, people who were asked to think about going out to dinner with 10 friends were less likely to donate money to charity or volunteer to help with another experiment than people who were asked to think about going out to dinner with one friend (Garcia, Weaver, Moskowitz, & Darley, 2002). Simply imagining ourselves in a group is enough to make us feel less responsible for helping others.

The Nature of the Relationship: Communal versus Exchange Relationships
关系的性质：共有关系与交换关系

A great deal of research on prosocial behavior has looked at helping between strangers, such as Latané and Darley's research on bystander intervention. Although this research is very important, most helping in everyday life occurs between people who know each other well, such as family members and close friends. In Chapter 10, we distinguished between communal and exchange relationships. *Communal relationships* are those in which people's primary concern is with the welfare of the other person (e.g., a child), whereas *exchange relationships* are governed by concerns about equity—that what you put into the relationship equals what you get out of it. How does helping occur in communal relationships?

Margaret Clark and Judson Mills (Mills, Clark, Ford, & Johnson, 2004; Mills & Clark, 2001) argue that people in communal relationships are concerned less with the benefits they will receive by helping and more with simply satisfying the needs of the other person. When parents are deciding whether to help their children, for example, they seldom think, "Well, what have they done for me lately?" Unlike in exchange relationships, in which people are concerned with what they are getting in return from other people, in communal relationships people are concerned primarily with the welfare of the other person (Clark, 1984; Clark & Grote, 1998; Clark, Mills, & Corcoran, 1989).

Does this mean that people are more helpful toward friends than strangers? Yes—at least under most circumstances. We are more likely to have communal relationships with friends and are therefore more likely to help even when there is nothing in it for us. In fact, we like to help a partner in a communal relationship more than a partner in an exchange relationship (Williamson, Clark, Pegalis, & Behan, 1996). There is, however, an interesting exception to this rule. Research by Abraham Tesser (1988) on self-esteem maintenance has shown that when a task is not important to us, we do indeed help friends more than strangers. But suppose that the most important thing in the world for you is to be a doctor, that you are struggling to pass a difficult premed physics course, and that two other people in the class—your best friend and a complete stranger—ask you to lend them your notes from a class they missed. According to Tesser's research, you will be more inclined to help the stranger than your friend (Tesser, 1991; Tesser & Smith, 1980). Why? Because it hurts to see a close friend do better than we do in an area of great importance to our self-esteem. Consequently, we are less likely to help a friend in these important areas than in areas we don't care as much about.

In communal relationships, such as those between parents and their children, people are concerned less with who gets what and more with how much help the other person needs.

TRY IT! The Lost Letter Technique 试一试！遗失信件技术

Here's a simple technique you can use to test your own hypotheses about prosocial behavior. This procedure, called the "lost letter technique", involves leaving stamped envelopes on the ground and seeing whether people pick them up and mail them. Stanley Milgram (1969), who first used this technique, found that people were more likely to mail letters addressed to organizations they supported; for example, 72 percent of letters addressed to "Medical Research Associates" were mailed, whereas only 25 percent of letters addressed to "Friends of the Nazi Party" were mailed (all were addressed to the same post office box so that Milgram could count how many were returned).

You can use the lost letter technique to test some of the hypotheses about helping behavior we have discussed in this chapter or hypotheses that you come up with on your own. Put your address on the letters so that you can count how many are returned, but vary where you put the letters or to whom they are addressed. For example, drop some letters in a small town and in an urban area to see whether people in small towns are more likely to mail them (be sure to mark the envelopes in some way that will let you know where they were dropped; e.g., put a little pencil mark on the back of the ones dropped in small towns). Did you replicate the finding of previous studies that people living in small towns are more likely to mail the letters (Bridges & Coady, 1996; Hansson & Slade, 1977)? Or you might vary the ethnicity of the name of the person on the address to see if people are more likely to help members of some ethnic groups more than others. Be creative!

After deciding what you want to vary (e.g., the ethnicity or gender of the addressee), be careful to place envelopes of both types (e.g., those addressed to males and females) in similar locations. It is best to use a fairly large number of letters (e.g., a minimum of 15 to 20 in each condition) to get reliable results. Obviously, you should not leave more than one letter in the same location. You might want to team up with some classmates on this project so that you can split the cost of the stamps.

How Can Helping Be Increased?
怎样增加助人行为？

We would all be better off if prosocial behavior were more common than it is. How can we get people, when faced with an emergency, to act more like Abe Zelmanowitz and less like Kitty Genovese's neighbors?

Before addressing this question, we should point out that people do not always want to be helped. Imagine that you are sitting at a computer terminal at the library and are struggling to learn a new e-mail system. You can't figure out how to send and receive mail and are becoming increasingly frustrated as the computer responds with messages like "Invalid Command." A confident-looking guy whom you know only slightly walks over to you and looks over your shoulder for a few minutes. "You have a lot to learn," he says. "Let me show you how this baby works." How would you react? You might feel some gratitude, but you will probably also feel some resentment. His offer of help comes with a message: "You are too stupid to figure this out for yourself." Because receiving help can make people feel inadequate and dependent, they do not always react positively when someone offers them aid. People do not want to appear incompetent, and so they often decide to suffer in silence, even if doing so lowers their chances of successfully completing a task (Brown, Nesse, & Vinokur, 2003; Nadler, 2002; Nadler, Ellis, & Bar, 2003; Schneider, Major, Luhtanen, & Crocker, 1996).

> *When death, the great reconciler, has come, it is never our tenderness that we repent of, but our severity.*
> —George Eliot (Marian Evans), *Adam Bede*, 1859

Nevertheless, the world would be a better place if more people helped those in need. How can we increase everyday acts of kindness, such as looking out for an elderly neighbor or volunteering to read to kids at the local school? The answer to this question lies in our discussion of the causes of prosocial behavior. For example, we saw that several personal characteristics of potential helpers are important, and promoting those factors can increase the likelihood that these people will help (Clary, Snyder, Ridge, Miene, & Haugen, 1994; Snyder, 1993). But even kind, altruistic people will fail to help if certain situational constraints are present, such as being in an urban environment or witnessing an emergency in the presence of numerous bystanders.

Increasing the Likelihood That Bystanders Will Intervene
增加旁观者干预的可能性

There is evidence that simply being aware of the barriers to helping in an emergency can increase people's chances of overcoming those barriers. A few years ago at Cornell University, several students intervened to prevent another student from committing suicide. As is often the case with emergencies, the situation was very confusing, and at first, the bystanders were not sure what was happening or what they should do. The student who led the intervention said that she was reminded of a lecture she had heard on bystander intervention in her introductory psychology class a few days before and realized that if she didn't act, no one would (Savitsky, 1998). Or consider an incident at Vassar College not long ago, where students saw someone being attacked by a mugger. Like Kitty Genovese's neighbors, most of them did nothing, probably because they assumed that somebody else had already called the police. One of the students, however, immediately called the campus police because she was struck by how similar the situation was to the studies on bystander intervention she had read about in her social psychology course—even though she had taken the class more than a year earlier (Coats, 1998).

These are not controlled experiments, of course, and we cannot be certain that these helpful people were spurred on by what they had learned in their psychology classes. Fortunately this question has been addressed experimentally (Beaman, Barnes, Klentz, & McQuirk, 1978). The researchers randomly assigned students to listen to a lecture on Latané and Darley's (1970) bystander intervention research or a lecture on an unrelated topic. Two weeks later, all the students participated in what they thought was a completely unrelated sociology study, during which they encountered a student lying on the floor. Was he in need of help? Had he fallen and injured himself, or was he simply a student who had fallen asleep after pulling an all-nighter? As we have seen, when in an ambiguous situation such as this, people look to see how other people are reacting. Because an accomplice of the experimenter (posing as another participant) intentionally acted unconcerned, the natural thing to do was to assume that nothing was wrong. This is exactly what most participants did if they had not heard the lecture about bystander intervention research; in this condition, only 25 percent of them stopped to help the student. However, if the participants had heard the lecture about bystander intervention, 43 percent stopped to help the student. Thus, knowing how we can be unwittingly influenced by others can by itself help overcome this type of social influence. We can only hope that knowing about other barriers to prosocial behavior will make them easier to overcome as well.

Positive Psychology and Prosocial Behavior
积极心理学与亲社会行为

In recent years, a new field known as *positive psychology* has emerged (Seligman, 2002; Seligman, Steen, & Park, 2005). Martin Seligman, an influential clinical psychologist, observed that much of psychology—particularly clinical psychology—had focused on mental disorders, largely ignoring how to define and nurture psychological health. Psychology should not just be the study of "disease, weakness, and damage," he argued, but the study of "strength and virtue" (2002, p. 4). Largely through Seligman's efforts, many psychologists are now focusing on such topics as the nature of healthy human functioning, how to define and categorize human strengths, and how to improve people's lives (Snyder & Lopez, 2007).

The positive psychology movement is a useful and necessary corrective to the emphasis on mental illness in clinical psychology and has led to many fascinating research programs. As we have seen in this book, though, social psychology has not concentrated solely on negative behaviors. For many years, there have been active social psychological research programs on such topics as how people develop intrinsic interest in an activity (Chapter 5), how people maintain high self-esteem (Chapter 6), and how people form impressions of and lasting relationships with others (Chapter 10). To be sure, social psychology has documented many negative behaviors that can result from powerful social influences, such as obedience to authority and other kinds of conformity (Chapter 8). By studying the basic ways in which humans process information about themselves and their social worlds, however, it has been possible to understand both the dark and bright side of human behavior, such as when people will help others and when they will not.

An excellent example of the social psychological approach is the topic of this chapter, the study of the conditions under which people help or fail to help their fellow humans. Is this the study of positive psychology or a focus on the dark side? Both, because social psychologists study the condition under which people are likely to help (e.g., when people feel empathy toward another) and the conditions under which they are likely to fail to help (e.g., when they experience a diffusion of responsibility).

As noted earlier, Daniel Batson and his colleagues have been the strongest proponents of the idea that many people have a pure, unselfish motive for helping others and will do so when they feel empathy (Batson, Ahmad, Lishner, & Tsang, 2002). In the experiment we reviewed earlier, for example, when people felt empathy toward a classmate who had been in an automobile accident, they were willing to help her regardless of whether there was a cost to them of doing so (see Figure 11.2). Research on empathy and prosocial behavior is an excellent example of the way in which social psychologists have been interested in positive psychology, the study of people's strengths and virtues.

Why did this person help, even when several other bystanders witnessed the same emergency? Perhaps this person had learned about the barriers to bystander intervention in a social psychology class.

CONNECTIONS 链接

Increasing Volunteerism 增加志愿主义

There are many important kinds of prosocial behavior besides intervening in emergencies, including volunteerism and community service. Social psychologists have studied this kind of helping as well, whereby people commit to helping strangers on a more long-term basis (Snyder, Omoto, & Lindsay, 2004; Omoto, 2005; Penner, 2004).

Surveys of Western European and North American countries have found that many people engage in volunteer work, with the highest rate in the United States (47 percent; Ting & Piliavin, 2000). Of course, that means that even in the United States, more than half of the population is not volunteering, raising the question of how to increase people's willingness to spend time helping others. Some institutions have responded by requiring their members to perform community service. Some high schools, colleges, and businesses, for example, require their students or employees to engage in volunteer work.

These programs have the benefit of increasing the pool of volunteers available to help community organizations such as homeless shelters, medical clinics, and day-care centers. But the question arises as to the effect of such "mandatory volunteerism" on the motivation of the people who do the helping. Many of these organizations assume that they are increasing the likelihood that their members will volunteer in the future, even after they leave the organizations. That is, making people volunteer is assumed to foster volunteerism by enlightening people about its benefits.

As we discussed in Chapter 5, however, giving people strong external reasons for performing an activity can actually undermine their intrinsic interest in that activity. This is called the *overjustification effect:* People see their behavior as caused by compelling extrinsic reasons (e.g., being required to do volunteer work), making them underestimate the extent to which their behavior was caused by intrinsic reasons (e.g., that they like to do volunteer work). Consistent with this research, the more that people feel they are volunteering because of external requirements, the less likely they are to volunteer freely in the future (Batson, Coke, Jasnoski, & Hanson, 1978; Bringle, 2005; Kunda & Schwartz, 1983; Stukas, Snyder, & Clary, 1999). The moral is that organizations should be careful about how heavy-handedly they impose requirements to volunteer. If people feel that they are complying only because they have to, they may actually become less likely to volunteer in the future. Encouraging people to volunteer while preserving the sense that they freely chose to do so has been shown to increase people's sense of well-being and their intentions to volunteer again in the future (Piliavin, 2008; Stukas et al., 1999).

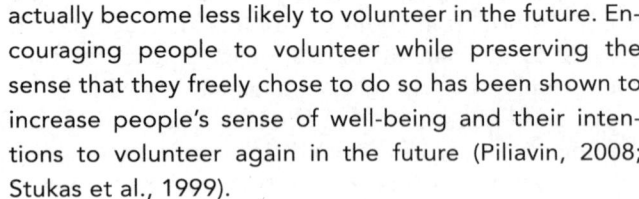

An increasing number of schools and businesses are requiring people to perform community service. These programs can actually lower interest in volunteering if people feel they are doing so because of an external requirement. Encouraging people to volunteer while preserving the sense that they freely choose to do so is likely to increase people's intentions to volunteer again in the future.

HOW WOULD YOU USE THIS? 如何学以致用？

We hope it never happens, but suppose you are injured in an accident in a public place and need help. Based on what you have learned in this chapter, how could you make sure that someone comes to your aid as soon as possible? As we saw in the section on the bystander effect, the trick is to make sure people notice that you need help, interpret it as an emergency, and assume that they (and not someone else) is responsible for helping. One way to avoid a diffusion of responsibility is to point to one person and ask for their help. That is, instead of shouting, "Will someone please help me?", single out one person—"Hey, you in the blue shirt and sunglasses—could you please call 911?" That makes one person feel responsible and also communicates to him or her how to help. Based on what you have read in this chapter, you should also know more about what to do if you witness an emergency—don't assume that someone else will help. By the way, you might be interested to know that contrary to what happened in the last episode of the TV show *Seinfeld*, there are no laws in the United States obligating people to help a stranger in need. Many states do have Good Samaritan laws that make it hard for a victim to sue a bystander who tries to help but causes further injury. These laws don't give bystanders complete protection, but they are meant to increase the likelihood that people will come to each other's aid.

Summary 总 结

- **Basic Motives Underlying Prosocial Behavior: Why Do People Help?** This chapter examined the causes of **prosocial behavior**, acts performed with the goal of benefiting another person. What are the basic origins of prosocial behavior?
    - **Evolutionary Psychology: Instincts and Genes** Evolutionary theory explains prosocial behavior in four ways. The first is **kin selection**, the idea that behaviors that help a genetic relative are favored by natural selection. The second is the **norm of reciprocity**, which is the expectation that helping others will increase the likelihood that they will help us in the future. The third is that it is adaptive for people to learn social norms of all kinds, and one of these norms is the value of helping others. The fourth is **group selection**, the idea that social groups with altruistic members are more likely to survive in competition with other groups.
    - **Social Exchange: The Costs and Rewards of Helping** Social exchange theory argues that prosocial behavior is not necessarily rooted in our genes. Instead, people help others in order to maximize social rewards and minimize social costs.
    - **Empathy and Altruism: The Pure Motive for Helping** People can be motivated by **altruism**, the desire to help another person even if it involves a cost to the helper. According to the **empathy-altruism hypothesis**, when people feel empathy toward another person (they experience events and emotions the other person experiences), they attempt to help that person purely for altruistic reasons. People are especially likely to experience empathy when they are feeling securely attached, and especially likely not to experience empathy when they have been rejected by other people.

- **Personal Qualities and Prosocial Behavior: Why Do Some People Help More Than Others?** Basic motives are not all there is to understanding prosocial behavior. We need to understand why some people are more helpful than others.
    - **Individual Differences: The Altruistic Personality** Although some people have personality qualities that make them more likely to help than others, personality factors have not been shown to be strong predictors of who will help across a variety of social situations.
    - **Gender Differences in Prosocial Behavior** In many cultures, the male sex role includes helping in chivalrous and heroic ways, whereas the female sex role includes helping in close, long-term relationships.
    - **Cultural Differences in Prosocial Behavior** People in all cultures are more likely to help someone they define as a member of their **in-group**, the group with which an individual identifies. People everywhere are less likely to help someone they perceive to be a

member of an **out-group,** a group with which they do not identify. Cultural factors come into play in determining how strongly people draw the line between in-groups and out-groups.

- **Religion and Prosocial Behavior** People who are religious report on surveys that they help more than do people who are not religious, and they actually do help more in situations in which helping makes them look good to themselves or others. They are not more likely to help, however, in private situations in which no one will know that they helped.
- **The Effects of Mood on Prosocial Behavior** People are more likely to help if they are in especially good moods, but also if they are in especially bad moods.

◉ **Situational Determinants of Prosocial Behavior: When Will People Help?** To understand why people help others, we also need to consider the nature of the social situation.

- **Environment: Rural versus Urban** People are less likely to help in dense, urban settings because of the **urban overload hypothesis**—the idea that people living in cities are constantly bombarded with stimulation and that they keep to themselves in order to avoid being overwhelmed by it.
- **Residential Mobility** People who have lived for a long time in one place are more likely to engage in prosocial behaviors than people who have recently moved to an area.
- **The Number of Bystanders: The Bystander Effect** In order to help in an emergency people must meet five conditions: They must notice the event, interpret it as an emergency, assume responsibility, know the appropriate form of assistance, and implement their decision to help. As the number of bystanders who witness an emergency increases, the more difficult it is to meet two of these conditions—interpreting the event as an emergency and assuming responsibility. This produces the **bystander effect**: The larger the number of bystanders, the less likely any one of them is to help.
- **The Nature of the Relationship: Communal versus Exchange Relationships** People in *exchange relationships*—those governed by concerns about equity—are concerned primarily with the benefits they will receive by helping others. People in *communal relationships*—those in which the primary concern is the welfare of the other person—are less concerned with the benefits they will receive and more with simply satisfying the needs of the other person.

◉ **How Can Helping Be Increased?** Prosocial behavior can be increased in a number of ways.

- **Increasing the Likelihood That Bystanders Will Intervene** Research shows that teaching people about the barriers to bystander intervention increases the likelihood that they will help in emergencies.
- **Positive Psychology and Prosocial Behavior** A new field called positive psychology has emerged that focuses on people's strengths and virtues, instead of mental disease. The social psychological approach is to investigate the conditions under which people act in positive (e.g., helpful) and negative (e.g., unhelpful) ways. Many of these conditions were discussed in this chapter. For example, people will help at a cost to themselves when they feel empathy toward a person in need. When they do not feel empathy, they will help only when it is in their self-interest.

CHAPTER 11 TEST 第11章习题

1. Which of the following is *not* a way that evolutionary theory explains prosocial behavior?
   a. Social exchange
   b. Kin selection
   c. The reciprocity norm
   d. Group selection
   e. Learning social norms

2. Amy is walking across campus and sees someone on her hands and knees looking for a ring that slipped off her finger. Which of the following is *false*, according to the empathy-altruism hypothesis? Amy
   a. feels empathy toward the person, so she will probably stop and help the stranger look for the ring, regardless of whether it is in her self-interest to do so.
   b. feels empathy toward the person, but she doesn't think she has much to gain by helping, so she decides not to help the person look for the ring.
   c. doesn't feel empathy toward the person, but recognizes her as a TA in her English class. Amy really wants to get a good grade in that English class, so she will probably stop and help her TA look for the ring.
   d. doesn't feel empathy toward the person and doesn't think she has much to gain by helping, so she decides not to help the person look for the ring.

3. Which of the following is *not* a reason that being in a good mood tends to increase prosocial behavior?
   a. Good moods make us frame situations more positively and thus we are more likely to give people the benefit of the doubt.
   b. Helping prolongs good moods.
   c. Good moods make us pay more attention to social norms, so we will be more aware of the altruism norm.
   d. Good moods increase how much attention we pay to ourselves, which makes us more likely to act according to our values.

4. Frank has recently graduated from college and moves from New York City back to the small town in Connecticut where he was born. He now finds that he is much more inclined to engage in prosocial behavior. What is the most likely reason for this change?
   a. Growing up in a small town caused him to internalize altruistic values.

b. The change in his immediate surroundings changed his likelihood of helping.
c. College students are less likely to help because they are more susceptible to the bystander effect.
d. Frank is more likely to engage in negative-state relief when he is in the small town.

5. Luke listened to a lecture in his history class that he found very confusing, but at the end of the class when the professor asked whether there was anything students didn't understand, Luke didn't raise his hand. Because there were no other hands raised, Luke assumed that other students had understood the material and that he just didn't pay enough attention. In fact many students hadn't understood the material and were in the same situation as Luke. This is an example of
   a. jigsaw classroom.
   b. self-fulfilling prophecy.
   c. ultimate attribution error.
   d. pluralistic ignorance.
   e. normative conformity.

6. Research on prosocial behavior finds that religious people
   a. help others more than nonreligious people in virtually all ways.
   b. report on surveys that they help the same amount as do nonreligious people.
   c. actually help more than nonreligious people only if it puts them in a good light to themselves or others.
   d. actually help others less than do nonreligious people.

7. People in interdependent cultures, compared to Westerners, are
   a. more likely to help in-group members, but less likely to help out-group members.
   b. more likely to help out-group members.
   c. more likely to engage in prosocial behavior.
   d. less likely to engage in heroic acts, but more likely to engage in sustained helping.

8. Meghan lives in a single room in a college dormitory. Late one night she hears a scream coming from just outside her dorm. She is pretty sure that the person needs help because the person yelled, "Help me! I think I broke my leg!" Meghan goes back to sleep, only to find out the next day that the person was on the ground for 45 minutes before someone helped. Which of the following best explains why Meghan didn't help?
   a. Informational influence.
   b. A diffusion of responsibility.
   c. She didn't interpret it as an emergency.
   d. Pluralistic ignorance.

9. Which of the following is true about prosocial behavior?
   a. How often people have moved from one place to another influences how helpful they are.
   b. There is no effect of personality on prosocial behavior.
   c. Being in a bad mood decreases prosocial behavior.
   d. Only people in non-Western societies are more likely to help members of their in-group.

10. Which of the following is not true about prosocial behavior?
    a. When people are put in a good mood, they are more likely to help.
    b. People in stable communities are more likely to help than people in communities with high residential mobility.
    c. When people are put in a bad mood, they are more likely to help.
    d. Having an altruistic personality is a strong predictor of helping behavior.
    e. Helping in-group members more than out-group members is more common in interdependent cultures than in independent cultures.

Chapter 11 Answer Key
1-a, 2-b, 3-c, 4-b, 5-d, 6-c, 7-a, 8-b, 9-a, 10-d

For more review plus practice tests, videos, flashcards, writing help and more, log on to MyPsychLab.

12 Aggression

Why Do We Hurt Other People? Can We Prevent It?

侵犯：
我们为什么伤害他人？
能防止吗？

ON APRIL 20, 1999, THE CORRIDORS AND CLASSROOMS of Columbine High School in Littleton, Colorado, reverberated with the sound of gunshots. Two students, Eric Harris and Dylan Klebold, armed with assault weapons and explosives, had gone on a rampage, killing a teacher and several of their fellow students. They then turned their guns on themselves. After the smoke cleared, 15 people lay dead (including the shooters) and 23 others were hospitalized, some with severe wounds. It was the worst school massacre in American history. As horrendous as it was, we now know that the toll could have been much higher. The two shooters made videotapes a few weeks before the massacre, and from these we have learned that they actually prepared 95 explosive devices that failed to go off. Of these, one set was placed a few miles from the school, intended to explode first and distract police by keeping them busy away from the school.

A second set was intended to explode in the cafeteria, killing a large number of students and causing hundreds to evacuate the building in terror, with Harris and Klebold waiting to gun them down. They planted a third set of explosives in their own cars in the school parking lot, timed to explode after the police and paramedics had arrived on the scene as a way of further increasing the number of casualties and creating even more chaos. The videotape shows the perpetrators gleefully predicting that before the day was over, they would have killed 250 people.

The Columbine massacre was the deadliest of nine multivictim school shootings that took place in the United States during a period of two and a half years. In the sad aftermath of a school shooting—especially one as terrible as Columbine—the country needed someone or something to blame. Almost everyone wondered, were these youngsters crazy? If they were crazy, why didn't their parents and teachers notice their pathology before it erupted into violence? How could reasonably observant parents not know that their sons kept guns in their bedrooms and were manufacturing bombs in their garage? And where were the school authorities? Didn't the teachers notice behaviors that would have predicted such violence? Some people even wondered if schools should give students personality tests to identify the ones most likely to commit acts of this kind.

OUTLINE 提纲

- **What Is Aggression?**
  - Is Aggression Inborn or Learned?
  - Is Aggression Instinctual? Situational? Optional?
  - Aggression and Culture
- **Neural and Chemical Influences on Aggression**
  - Gender and Aggression
  - Alcohol and Aggression
  - Pain, Discomfort, and Aggression
- **Social Situations and Aggression**
  - Frustration and Aggression
  - Being Provoked and Reciprocating
  - Aggressive Objects as Cues
  - Endorsement, Imitation, and Aggression
  - Violence in the Media: TV, Movies, and Video Games
  - Does Violence Sell?
  - Violent Pornography and Violence against Women
- **How to Reduce Aggression**
  - Does Punishing Aggression Reduce Aggressive Behavior?
  - CONNECTIONS: Curbing Bullying: A Case Study in Reducing Aggression at School
  - Catharsis and Aggression
  - The Effect of War on General Aggression
  - What Are We Supposed to Do with Our Anger?
  - Dehumanization: The Opposite of Empathy
  - CONNECTIONS: Teaching Empathy in School
- **Could the Columbine Massacre Have Been Prevented?**
- **Summary**

Certain observers quickly concluded that the major cause of such violence is the easy availability of guns, claiming that if we could only control the use and sale of guns, we could eliminate the problem. Others were quick to blame the Supreme Court for outlawing prayer in the schools—wouldn't prayer prevent this sort of outrage? Still others pointed to the prevalence of violence in films, on TV, and in video games. If we could ban violent entertainment, wouldn't that make our schools safe again? And some people felt that these outrageous acts grew out of a general lack of respect among teenagers in our culture. One state legislature responded to the massacre by actually passing a law requiring students to call their teachers "sir" or "ma'am" as a way of showing respect—as if respect can be mandated (Aronson, 2000).

The Columbine tragedy is a stark reminder that humans are capable of acts of extreme aggression. It also underscores the importance of our trying to understand the causes of aggression so that the awful losses suffered at Columbine are not repeated elsewhere.

In this chapter, we will focus on aggression and try to understand what causes it. Are human beings instinctively aggressive? Can normal people be inspired to commit violence by the example of violent characters on TV or in films or by the easy availability of weapons of destruction? Can a society, a school, or a parent do anything to reduce aggression? If so, specifically, what? These are social psychological questions of the utmost importance. Needless to say, we don't have all the answers. But we do have some of them. By the time you get to the end of this chapter, we hope you will have gained some insight into those issues.

What Is Aggression? 什么是侵犯？

For social psychologists, aggressive action is intentional behavior aimed at causing either physical or psychological pain. It should not be confused with assertiveness—even though most people loosely refer to others as "aggressive" if they stand up for their rights, write letters to the editor complaining about real or imagined injustices, or are real "go-getters." Similarly, in a sexist society, a woman who simply speaks her mind or takes the initiative and invites a man to dinner might be called aggressive by some. Our definition is far more specific: **Aggression** is intentional action aimed at doing harm or causing pain. The action might be physical or verbal; it might succeed in its goal or not. It is still aggression. So if someone throws a beer bottle at your head and you duck so that the bottle misses your head, it was still an aggressive act. The important thing is the intention. By the same token, if a drunk driver unintentionally runs you down while you're attempting to cross the street, that is not an act of aggression, even though the damage would be far greater than that caused by the beer bottle that missed.

It is also useful to distinguish between hostile aggression and instrumental aggression (Berkowitz, 1993). **Hostile aggression** is an act of aggression stemming from feelings of anger and aimed at inflicting pain or injury. In **instrumental aggression**, there is an intention to hurt the other person, but the hurting takes place as a means to some goal other than causing pain. For example, in a professional football game, a defensive lineman will usually do whatever it takes to thwart his opponent (the blocker) and tackle the ball carrier. This typically includes intentionally inflicting pain on his opponent if doing so is useful in helping him get the blocker out of the way so that he can get to the ball carrier. This is instrumental aggression. By contrast, if he believes his opponent has been playing dirty, he might become angry and go out of his way to hurt his opponent, even if doing so does not increase his opportunity to tackle the ball carrier. This is hostile aggression.

Aggression
Intentional behavior aimed at doing harm or causing pain to another person

Hostile Aggression
Aggression stemming from feelings of anger and aimed at inflicting pain

Instrumental Aggression
Aggression as a means to some goal other than causing pain

Is Aggression Inborn or Learned? 侵犯是天生的还是后天习得的?

For centuries, scientists, philosophers, and other serious thinkers have been arguing about the human capacity for aggression; some are convinced that aggression is an inborn, instinctive human trait. Others are just as certain that aggressive behavior must be learned (Baron & Richardson, 1994; Berkowitz, 1993; Geen, 1998). The seventeenth-century political philosopher Thomas Hobbes viewed human beings as naturally self-interested creatures who seek their own well-being, even if this leads to aggressing against others. Hobbes stated that life in a state of nature (i.e., without civil society) would be "solitary, poor, nasty, brutish, and short" (*Leviathan*, 1651). This leads to a general state of anxiety in which most fear a premature death at the hands of other people; therefore, he argued, people join into society to gain security from others. A century later, Jean-Jacques Rousseau argued the opposite. Humans, he wrote in 1762, are by nature compassionate loners. But, according to Rousseau, unlike animals, human behavior is not determined by instinct; human behavior is malleable; it changes with changes in the societies within which humans live. Therefore, Rousseau suggests that the brutish traits that Hobbes attributes to human nature are actually caused by the type of society that Hobbes's contemporaries lived in and not essential human nature.

Man's inhumanity to man makes countless thousands mourn.

—Robert Burns, Man Was Made to Mourn

Hobbes's more pessimistic view was elaborated in the twentieth century by Sigmund Freud (1930), who theorized that humans are born with an instinct toward life, which he called **Eros**, and an equally powerful instinct toward death, which he called **Thanatos**. About the death instinct, Freud wrote: "It is at work in every living being and is striving to bring it to ruin and to reduce life to its original condition of inanimate matter" (p. 67). Freud believed that aggressive energy must come out somehow, lest it continue to build up and produce illness. Freud's notion can best be characterized as a "hydraulic theory"—the analogy is to water pressure building up in a container: Unless energy is released, it will produce some sort of explosion.

According to Freud, society performs an essential function in regulating these instincts and in helping people *sublimate* them, that is, turn the energy into acceptable or useful behavior. For example, Freud believed that the energy behind artistic creation or the innovations that built cities were sublimations of aggressive (or sexual) energy.

Eros
The instinct toward life, posited by Freud

Thanatos
According to Freud, an instinctual drive toward death, leading to aggressive actions

Is Aggression Instinctual? Situational? Optional?
侵犯行为是本能的、情境性的还是选择性的?

The Evolutionary Argument In recent years evolutionary psychologists (Buss, 2004, 2005) have entered the discussion by arguing that aggression is genetically programmed into men because it enables them to perpetuate their genes. Males are theorized to aggress for two reasons: First, males behave aggressively to establish dominance over other males. The idea here is that the female will choose the male who is most likely to provide the best genes and the greatest protection and resources for their offspring. Second, males aggress "jealously" to ensure that their mate(s) are not copulating with others. This ensures their paternity.

The evolutionary perspective receives tangential support from crime statistics which show that males are most likely to engage in violence during their peak reproductive years—their teens and 20s (Wilson & Daly, 1985; Geen, 1998). Among these young males violence is typically initiated by seemingly trivial matters related to "respect." For the males involved the stakes seem high: They believe they are fighting for their status in

Boys are more likely than girls, the world over, to roughhouse and pummel each other. Is this evidence of physical play or of "aggression"?

the group. Jealousy is another major reason males aggress against each other and their mates (Wilson, Daly, & Weghorst, 1982; Schützwohl & Koch, 2004).

In most contemporary societies, social dominance, and hence access to females, is still largely (but certainly not entirely) based on status. But, nowadays, status has taken on a different meaning. In most societies the ability to physically intimidate the other males in the group is no longer the primary attribute that attracts females. Rather, power is now based on attributes related to success such as high-status careers, wealth, and celebrity. This suggests that among our prehistoric ancestors, women might have found someone like heavyweight boxer Mike Tyson unbelievably attractive, while in contemporary times, women might favor someone like Donald Trump or Bill Gates. Mr. Gates probably would not be able to hold his own one-on-one with Mr. Tyson, but he has some qualities that today's women might find more appealing than Mr. Tyson's brute strength and physical aggressiveness. These speculations from evolutionary social psychologists are interesting and provocative, but ultimately . . . well, speculative.

Fighting and Its Attractiveness 试一试！打架及其吸引力

Interview several of your male friends and ask them to reflect on their childhood and adolescent experiences with physical fighting or simply being challenged to fight. Ask them what they think was at stake in the fight. How difficult was it to back down? Ask them to elaborate on their answers.

Now interview several of your female friends. Ask them the same questions you asked the men. Are their responses wildly different from those of the men? How come? Now ask the women to think about men they know in terms of possible relationships. Determine to what extent they consider physical aggressiveness to be attractive. Ask them to elaborate on their response. Do your findings support the evolutionary argument?

Aggression among the Lower Animals As we suggested earlier, the research supporting the evolutionary perspective is provocative, but inconclusive because it is impossible to conduct a definitive experiment. Accordingly, scientists have turned to experiments with nonhuman species to gain additional insight into the extent to which aggression may be hardwired. To take one example, consider the common belief about cats and rats. Most people assume that cats will instinctively stalk and kill rats. Half a century ago biologist Zing Yang Kuo (1961) attempted to demonstrate that this was a myth. He performed a simple little experiment: He raised a kitten in the same cage with a rat. Not only did the cat refrain from attacking the rat, but the two became close companions. Moreover, when given the opportunity, the cat refused either to chase or to kill other rats; thus the benign behavior was not confined to this one buddy but generalized to rats the cat had never met.

Although this experiment is charming, it fails to prove that aggressive behavior is not instinctive; it merely demonstrates that the aggressive instinct can be inhibited by early experience. What if an organism grows up without any contact with other organisms? Will it or won't it show aggressive tendencies? It turns out that rats raised in isolation (i.e., without any experience in fighting other rats) will attack a fellow rat when one is introduced into the cage; moreover, the isolated rats use the same pattern of threat and attack that experienced rats use (Eibl-Eibesfeldt, 1963). So even though aggressive behavior can be modified by experience (as shown by Kuo's experiment), aggression apparently does not need to be learned.

We can gain still greater insight into our own biological heritage by observing the behavior of those animals with whom we have the most genetic similarity. Our closest relatives in the animal kingdom are two primates: the chimpanzees and the bonobos (also known as pygmy chimpanzees). Both species have 98 percent of their DNA in common with human beings. The chimpanzee is known for the aggressive behavior of its male members (Watts, Muller, Amsler, Mbabazi, & Mitani, 2006. It is the only nonhuman species in which groups of male members hunt and kill other members of their own kind. Wrangham, Wilson, and Muller (2006) found that chimps kill each other at about the same rate that humans in hunter-gatherer societies kill each other. Based on the research on chimpanzees, we might conclude that humans, especially males, are genetically programmed for aggressive behavior.

However, living across the river from the chimpanzees (and therefore out of their reach) are the bonobos, our equally close genetic relative. Unlike the chimpanzee, the bonobo is known for its nonaggressive behavior. In fact, bonobos are often referred to as the "make love, not war" ape. Prior to engaging in activities that could otherwise lead to conflict, bonobos engage in sex. This sexual activity functions to diffuse potential conflict (De Waal, 1995). For example, when the group arrives at a feeding ground, they first engage in sexual play and then proceed to eat peacefully. In contrast, when chimps arrive at a feeding ground, they compete aggressively for the food. Also, unlike the chimps, bonobos form into female-dominated societies and are known for their sensitivity to others in their group (Parish & de Waal, 2000).

The bonobo is a rare exception. The near universality of aggression strongly suggests that aggressiveness has evolved and has been maintained because it has survival value (Lore & Schultz, 1993; Buss, 2004). At the same time, these researchers underscore the point that nearly all organisms also seem to have evolved strong inhibitory mechanisms that enable them to suppress aggression when it is in their best interests to do so. Aggression is an optional strategy. It is determined by the animal's previous social experiences as well as by the specific social context in which the animal finds itself.

Aggression and Culture 侵犯与文化

Most social psychologists agree that aggression is an optional strategy. Moreover, where humans are concerned, because of the complexity and importance of our social interactions, the social situation becomes even more important than it is among the lower organisms (Bandura, 1973; Berkowitz, 1968, 1993; Lysak, Rule, & Dobbs, 1989). We humans seem to have an inborn tendency to respond to certain provocative stimuli by striking out against the perpetrator (Berkowitz, 1993). But whether or not the aggressive action is actually expressed depends on a complex interplay between these innate tendencies, a variety of learned inhibitory responses, and the precise nature of the social situation. For example, although it is true that many animals, from insects to apes, will usually attack another animal that invades their territory, we *cannot* conclude, as some popular writers have, that human beings are likewise programmed to protect their territory and behave aggressively in response to specific stimuli. Instead, much evidence supports the view of most social psychologists that for humankind, innate patterns of behavior are infinitely modifiable and flexible. Cross-cultural studies have found, in fact, that human cultures vary widely in their degree of aggressiveness. European history, when condensed, consists of one major war after another. In contrast, recent findings reveal that cultures imbedded with cooperative, collectivist values had lower levels of aggression than European societies (Bergeron & Schneider, 2005). Similarly, certain "primitive" tribes, such as the Lepchas of Sikkim, the Pygmies of Central Africa, and the Arapesh of New Guinea, live in apparent peace and harmony, with acts of aggression being extremely rare (Baron & Richardson, 1994).

The forest Teduray, a hunter-gatherer culture in the Philippine rainforest, have established institutions and norms specifically designed to prevent intragroup violence. In their societies, people are expected to pay special attention to the effect of their actions on the feelings of others. When a situation arises, such as adultery, in which there is significant risk that anger will lead to violence, specific members of a Teduray village work to placate the injured individuals. The Teduray acknowledge that humans

When people say that aggression is "natural," they often point to our primate relatives. Chimpanzees (top) are indeed pretty belligerent and aggressive, but bonobos (bottom) would rather make love than war.

The early economies of the American South and West created a "culture of honor" in which men were literally quick on the trigger if they thought another man was about to smear their reputation—or rustle their cattle.

are violent by nature but believe that intragroup violence is not the way to live. They will, however, engage in violence to protect themselves from aggression from outside groups (Schlegel, 1998).

Changes in Aggression across Time Within a given culture, changing social conditions frequently lead to striking changes in aggressive behavior. For example, for hundreds of years, the Iroquois of North America lived peacefully as a hunting nation, without engaging in aggressive behavior against other tribes. But in the seventeenth century, barter with the newly arrived Europeans brought the Iroquois into direct competition with the neighboring Hurons over furs, which dramatically increased in value, because they could now be traded for manufactured goods. A series of skirmishes with the Hurons ensued, and within a short time, the Iroquois developed into ferocious warriors. It would be hard to argue that they were spectacular warriors because of uncontrollable aggressive instincts; rather, their aggressiveness almost certainly came about because a social change produced increases in competition (Hunt, 1940).

Regionalism and Aggression In our own society, there are some striking regional differences in aggressive behavior and in the kinds of events that trigger violence. For example, Richard Nisbett (1993) has shown that homicide rates for white southern males are substantially higher than those for white northern males, especially in rural areas. But this is true only for "argument-related" homicides. Nisbett's research shows that southerners do not endorse violence more than northerners when survey questions are expressed in general terms; however, southerners are more inclined to endorse violence for protection and in response to insults. This pattern suggests that the "culture of honor" may have begun with (and may be characteristic of) particular economic and occupational circumstances, especially the herding society of the early South and the old West, where protection of the herd was vital. If you own cattle, constant vigilance is impossible; therefore, to protect your cattle you would want to have the reputation as a person of honor who will behave aggressively against thieves and rustlers.

In a follow-up study, Nisbett and his colleagues (Cohen, Nisbett, Bowdle, & Schwarz, 1996) conducted a series of experiments in which they demonstrated that these norms characteristic of a "culture of honor" manifest themselves in the cognitions, emotions, behaviors, and physiological reactions of contemporary southern white males enrolled at the University of Michigan. In these experiments, each participant was "accidentally" bumped into by the experimenter's confederate, who then insulted him by calling him a denigrating name. Compared with northern white males (who tended to simply shrug off the insult), southerners were more likely to think their masculine reputation was threatened, became more upset (as shown by a rise in cortisol levels in their bloodstream), were more physiologically primed for aggression (as shown by a rise in testosterone levels in their bloodstream), became more cognitively primed for aggression, and were ultimately more likely to engage in aggressive and dominant behavior following the incident.

Neural and Chemical Influences on Aggression 神经生化因素对侵犯的影响

Aggressive behaviors in human beings, as well as in the lower animals, are associated with an area in the core of the brain called the **amygdala**. When the amygdala is stimulated, docile organisms become violent; similarly, when neural activity in that area is blocked, violent organisms become docile (Moyer, 1976). But there is flexibility here also: The impact of neural mechanisms can be modified by social factors, even in nonhumans. For example, if a male monkey is in the presence of other less dominant

Amygdala

An area in the core of the brain that is associated with aggressive behaviors

monkeys, he will attack the other monkeys when the amygdala is stimulated. But if the amygdala is stimulated while the monkey is in the presence of more dominant monkeys, he will not attack but will run away instead.

Certain chemicals have been shown to influence aggression. For example, **serotonin**, a chemical substance that occurs naturally in the midbrain, seems to have an *inhibiting* effect on impulsive aggression. In animals, when the flow of serotonin is disrupted, increases in aggressive behavior frequently follow; among humans, researchers have found that violent criminals have particularly low levels of naturally produced serotonin (Davidson, Putnam, & Larson, 2000). Moreover, in laboratory experiments on normal people, when the natural production of serotonin is interrupted, aggressive behavior increases (Bjork, Dougherty, Moeller, Cherek, & Swann, 1999).

Too little serotonin can lead to increases in aggression, but so can too much **testosterone**, a male sex hormone. Laboratory animals injected with testosterone became more aggressive (Moyer, 1983), and there is a parallel finding in humans: Naturally occurring testosterone levels are significantly higher among prisoners convicted of violent crimes than among those convicted of nonviolent crimes. Also, after incarceration, prisoners with higher testosterone levels violated more prison rules, especially those involving overt confrontation (Dabbs, Carr, Frady, & Riad, 1995; Dabbs, Ruback, Frady, Hopper, & Sgoutas, 1988). Similarly, juvenile delinquents have higher testosterone levels than college students (Banks & Dabbs, 1996). Comparing fraternities at a given college, those generally considered most rambunctious, less socially responsible, and "cruder" were found to have the highest average testosterone levels (Dabbs, 2000; Dabbs, Hargrove, & Heusel, 1996).

The studies above are correlational in nature. It is conceivable that the cause of higher testosterone levels is situational; that is, being in an aggressive context leads to greater production of testosterone (Thompson, Dabbs, & Frady, 1990; Mazur & Dabbs, 1992; Gladue, Boechler, & McCaul, 1989). How would one study the effect of testosterone levels in a more systematic way? The opportunity for a "natural experiment" is presented by individuals who choose to change their sex through modifying their testosterone levels. Men choosing to become women have their testosterone lowered; women choosing to become men have their testosterone raised. What happens to their levels of aggression? As one might expect, those who became men became more aggressive; those who became women became less aggressive (Van Goozen et al., 1995; Cohen-Ketteinis & Van Goozen, 1997). As suggestive as this study is, it lacks the rigor of a true experiment in which the participants are not aware of experimental manipulations and expected results. In this "natural experiment" the participants knew their hormones were being manipulated, and they expected to become either more masculine or more feminine. Clearly, an ideal experiment would require that hormone levels be manipulated without the individual knowing whether they were being raised or lowered and without the anticipation of developing new feelings. But, needless to say, such a study would exceed the boundaries of ethics by a wide margin!

Gender and Aggression 性别与侵犯

If testosterone level affects aggressiveness, does that mean that men are more aggressive than women? Apparently so. In a classic survey of research on children, Eleanor Maccoby and Carol Jacklin (1974) demonstrated that boys appear to be more aggressive than girls. For example, in one study, the investigators closely observed children at play in a variety of cultures, including the United States, Switzerland, and Ethiopia. Among boys, there was far more "nonplayful" pushing, shoving, and hitting than among girls (Deaux & La France, 1998).

But the research on gender differences is a bit more complicated than it might seem on the surface. For example, although research shows that young boys tend to be more overtly aggressive than young girls (in the sense that they lash out directly at the target person), girls tend to express their aggressive feelings more covertly—by gossiping, engaging in more backbiting, and spreading false rumors about the target person (Coie et al., 1999; Dodge & Schwartz, 1997; McFadyen-Ketchum, Bates, Dodge,

Serotonin
A chemical in the brain that may inhibit aggressive impulses

Testosterone
A hormone associated with aggression

& Pettit, 1996). Moreover, a meta-analysis of 64 separate experiments found that although it is true that men are far more aggressive than women under ordinary circumstances, the gender difference becomes much smaller when men and women are actually provoked (Bettencourt & Miller, 1996).

In other words, in everyday life situations, when nothing special is going on, men behave far more aggressively than women; but when people are subjected to frustration or insult, women will react almost as aggressively as men. Our interpretation of these data is that men are more likely to interpret ambiguous situations as provocative than women are—and are therefore more likely to react aggressively in what we would consider everyday situations. A good example is road rage: Many men seem to regard being cut off in traffic as a personal insult or a threat to their masculinity and respond aggressively. Women are more likely to take such occurrences in stride.

This might help explain why the great majority of people arrested for aggressive offenses are men. Women are arrested typically for property crimes (forgery, fraud, larceny) rather than violent crimes (murder, aggravated assault). Are males naturally predisposed to be more physically aggressive than females, or have they learned to behave that way? In short, does biology or social learning have the greater influence? We cannot be sure, but there is some evidence of a biological difference. Specifically, in the United States, the enormous social changes affecting women during the past 45 years have not produced increases in the incidence of violent crimes committed by women relative to those committed by men. In fact, the data indicate that women have shown a far greater increase in *nonviolent* crimes relative to that shown by men (Wilson & Herrnstein, 1985).

Again, this does not necessarily mean that aggressiveness among women is rare, but women are much less likely to behave aggressively in nonprovocative circumstances than men are. Furthermore, when women do commit acts of overt aggression, they tend to feel more guilt or anxiety about such acts than men do (Eagly & Steffen, 1986).

Does Culture Make a Difference? Sex differences in aggressive behaviors tend to hold up across cultures. In one study, teenagers from 11 different countries, mostly in Europe and Asia, read stories involving conflict among people and were asked to write their own endings (Archer & McDaniel, 1995). In every one of the 11 countries, young men showed a greater tendency toward violent solutions to conflict than young women did.

From these data, we can conclude that there are biochemical differences between men and women, but biochemical differences were not the only cause of these findings. Although within a given culture, men showed consistently higher levels of aggression than women, culture also played a major role. For example, women from Australia and New Zealand showed greater evidence of aggressiveness than men from Sweden and Korea did.

Violence among Intimate Partners Finally, we must address the enormous gender difference in violence committed against intimate partners. Of all the violent crimes against women in a typical year, some 22 percent were committed by their intimate male partners; for men, the figure is 3 percent. Husbands are far more likely to murder their wives than vice versa. For example, in 1998, of the 3,419 women killed in the United States, 32 percent died at the hands of a husband, boyfriend, former husband, or former boyfriend. The shocking frequency of women being murdered by intimate partners prompted one senior health official to remark: "Women worry when they go out; perhaps they should worry when they stay in" (Goode, 2000, p. F1).

Again, these data do not prove that testosterone is the sole cause of this gender difference. When dealing with such a complex phenomenon, there is probably more than one simple cause. The gender difference in intimate homicide could be due, at least in part, to testosterone. In addition, it could be at least partly social—the reflection of a sexist society in which some men may come to feel entitled to exercise

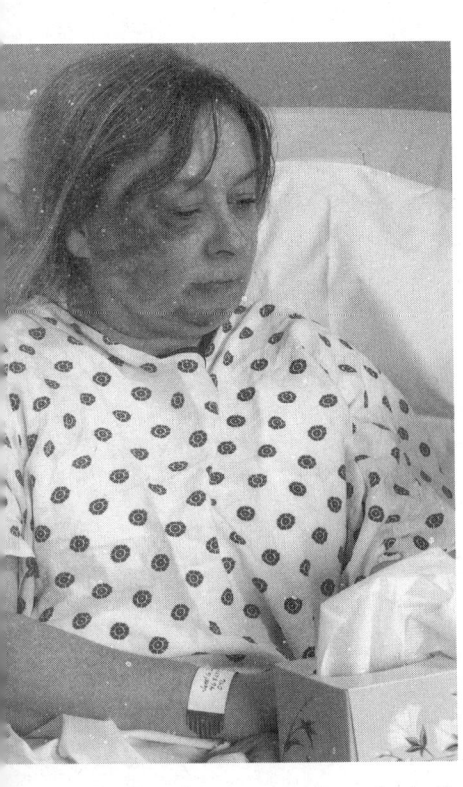

Why do some men physically abuse their partners?

power and control over women (Eisenstat & Bancroft, 1999). It may also be explained by the evolutionary psychology perspective in which male jealousy once functioned to improve the survival chances of men's progeny (Geen, 1998; Buss, 2004). Nevertheless, even if the cause is partly biological, it does not excuse violent behavior, nor does it mean that such behavior cannot be altered by a social intervention—as we shall see.

Alcohol and Aggression 酒精与侵犯

As most socially active college students know, alcohol is a social lubricant that lowers our inhibitions against acting in ways frowned on by society, including acts of aggression (Desmond, 1987; Taylor & Leonard, 1983). The link between alcohol and aggressive behavior is well known among researchers, and it appears even among people who have not been provoked and who do not usually behave aggressively when sober (Bailey & Taylor, 1991; Bushman & Cooper, 1990; White, 1997; Yudko, Blanchard, Henne, & Blanchard, 1997). This might explain why fistfights frequently break out in bars and nightclubs and why family violence is often associated with alcohol abuse.

"Oh that wasn't me talking, it was the alcohol talking."

Copyright © The New Yorker Collection 1975 Dana Fradon from cartoonbank.com. All Rights Reserved.

Why can alcohol increase aggressive behavior? Alcohol often serves as a disinhibitor—it reduces our social inhibitions, making us less cautious than we usually are (MacDonald, Zanna, & Fong, 1996). But it is more than that. Alcohol appears to disrupt the way we usually process information (Bushman, 1993, 1997; Bushman & Cooper, 1990). This means that intoxicated people often respond to the earliest and most obvious aspects of a social situation and tend to miss the subtleties. For example, in practical terms, if you are sober and someone steps on your toe, you would notice that the person didn't do it on purpose. But if you were drunk, you might miss the subtlety of the situation and respond as if he had purposely stomped on your foot. Accordingly (especially if you are a male), you might slug him. This is typical of the kinds of ambiguous situations that males might interpret as provocative—especially under the influence of alcohol. In fact, crime statistics reveal that most people arrested for murder, assault, and other violent crimes were legally drunk at the time of their arrest (Greenfield & Henneberg, 2001). In addition, controlled laboratory experiments demonstrate that when individuals ingest enough alcohol to make them legally drunk, they tend to respond more violently to provocations than those who have ingested little or no alcohol (Bushman, 1993; Lipsey, Wilson, Cohen, & Derzon, 1997; Taylor & Leonard, 1983).

Pain, Discomfort, and Aggression 疼痛、不适与侵犯

If an animal is in pain and cannot flee the scene, it will almost invariably attack; this is true of rats, mice, hamsters, foxes, monkeys, crayfish, snakes, raccoons, alligators, and a host of other creatures (Azrin, 1967; Hutchinson, 1983). In those circumstances, animals will attack members of their own species, members of different species, or anything else in sight, including stuffed dolls and tennis balls. Do you think this is true of human beings as well? A moment's reflection might help you guess that it may very well be. Most of us feel a flash of irritation when we stub a toe or hit our thumb with a hammer and know the feeling of wanting to lash out at the nearest available target. Indeed, in a series of experiments, students who underwent the pain of having their hand immersed in very cold water were far more likely to act aggressively against other students (Berkowitz, 1983).

By the same token, many theorists have speculated that other forms of bodily discomfort, such as heat, humidity, air pollution, and offensive odors, lower the threshold for aggressive behavior (Stoff & Cairns, 1997). During the late 1960s and early 1970s, when tensions in the United States ran high over the war in Vietnam and racial injustice, national leaders worried about "the long, hot summer." The

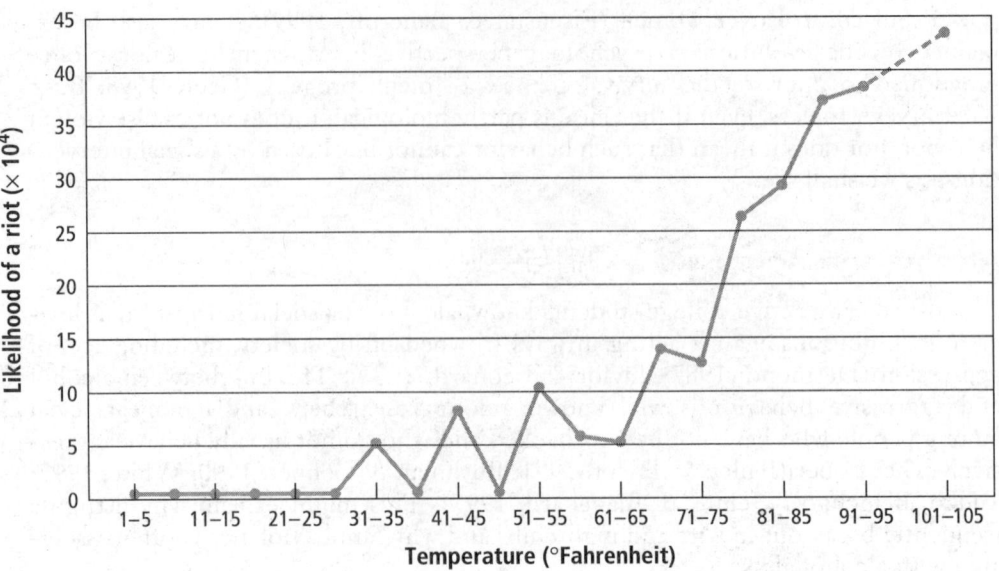

FIGURE 12.1

The long, hot summer.

Warm temperatures increase the likelihood that violent riots and other aggressive acts will occur.

(Adapted from Carlsmith & Anderson)

phrase was a code for the fear that the summer's heat would cause simmering tensions to explode. Their fears were justified. An analysis of disturbances in 79 cities between 1967 and 1971 found that riots were far more likely to occur on hot days than on cold ones (Carlsmith & Anderson, 1979) (see Figure 12.1). Similarly, in major American cities, from Houston, Texas, to Des Moines, Iowa, the hotter it is on a given day, the greater the likelihood that violent crimes will occur (Anderson & Anderson, 1984; Harries & Stadler, 1988).

As you know by now, one must be cautious about interpreting events that take place in natural settings, outside the laboratory. For example, the scientist in you might be tempted to ask whether increases in aggression are due to the temperature itself or merely to the fact that more people are apt to be outside (getting in one another's way) on hot days than on cold or rainy days. So how might we determine that it's the heat that caused the aggression and not merely the greater opportunity for contact? We can bring the phenomenon into the laboratory; in fact, it is remarkably easy to do so. In one such experiment, students took the same test under different conditions: Some worked in a room at normal room temperature while others worked in a room where the temperature reached 90 degrees (Griffitt & Veitch, 1971). The students in the hot room not only reported feeling more aggressive but also expressed more hostility toward a stranger whom they were asked to describe and rate. Similar results have been reported by a number of investigators (Anderson, Anderson, & Deuser, 1996; Rule, Taylor, & Dobbs, 1987).

Additional evidence from the natural world helps bolster our belief in the relationship between heat and aggression. Not only are violent crimes more frequent during hotter years than cooler ones (Anderson, Bushman, & Groom, 1997), but even on the baseball field, heat and hostility seem to go together. In major league baseball games, significantly more batters are hit by pitched balls when the temperature rises above 90 degrees (Reifman, Larrick, & Fein, 1988). And in the desert city of Phoenix, Arizona, drivers in non-air-conditioned cars are more likely to honk their horns in traffic jams than drivers in air-conditioned cars (Kenrick & MacFarlane, 1986). See the Try It!

Most scientists agree that the climate will heat up due to the increase of greenhouse gasses in the atmosphere. Based on what you have read in this chapter, would you predict that global warming might have an effect on aggression as well? The answer appears to be yes. In a recent analysis, Craig Anderson, the world's leading expert on the effects of climate and aggression, predicted that global warming is almost certain to produce a major increase in the rate of violent crime (Anderson, 2009).

TRY IT! Heat, Humidity, and Aggression 试一试！炎热、潮湿与侵犯

The next time you find yourself caught in a traffic jam, try doing a simple, naturalistic replication of the Kenrick and MacFarlane (1986) experiment. Consider the following hypothesis: The greater the heat and humidity, the greater the aggression.

- Take notes on how much aggression you notice (in the form of horn honking).
- Note the heat and humidity that day.
- The next two or three times you get caught in a traffic jam, do the same thing.

Can you discern a relationship between heat and humidity and horn honking?

Social Situations and Aggression
社会情境与侵犯

We've seen the effects of body chemistry, alcohol, and unpleasant physical experiences such as pain and heat on aggression. Aggression can also be caused by unpleasant social situations. Imagine that your friend Sam is driving you to the airport so that you can fly home for the Christmas holidays. Sam has picked you up a bit later than you feel comfortable with; he accuses you of being overly anxious and assures you that he knows the route well and that you will arrive there with plenty of time to spare. Halfway to the airport, you are standing still in bumper-to-bumper traffic. Sam assures you that there is plenty of time—but this time he sounds less confident. After a few minutes, your palms are sweating. You open the car door and survey the road ahead: Not a car is moving as far ahead as you can see. You get back in the car, slam the door, and glare at Sam. He smiles lamely and says, "How was I supposed to know there would be so much traffic?" Should he be prepared to duck?

Frustration and Aggression 挫折感与侵犯

As this all-too-familiar story suggests, frustration is a major cause of aggression. Frustration occurs when a person is thwarted on the way to an expected goal or gratification. All of us have felt frustrated from time to time—at least three or four times a week—if not three or four times a day! Research has shown that frustration can increase the probability of an aggressive response. This tendency is referred to as **frustration-aggression theory**, which holds that people's perception that they are being prevented from attaining a goal will increase the probability of their responding aggressively (Dollard, Doob, Miller, Mowrer, & Sears, 1939). This does not mean that frustration always leads to aggression—but it frequently does, especially when the frustration is decidedly unpleasant, unwelcome, and uncontrollable.

In a classic experiment by Roger Barker, Tamara Dembo, and Kurt Lewin (1941), young children were led to a roomful of attractive toys that were kept out of their reach by a wire screen. After a long wait, the children were finally allowed to play with the toys. In a control condition, a different group of children were allowed to play with the toys immediately, without first being frustrated. These children played joyfully with the toys, but the frustrated group, when finally given access to the toys, were extremely destructive: Many smashed the toys, threw them against the wall, stepped on them, and so forth.

Frustration-Aggression Theory

The idea that frustration—the perception that you are being prevented from attaining a goal—increases the probability of an aggressive response

Is road rage caused by frustration with stupid drivers who get in the way? If so, how come not every driver gets as angry as this guy?

Several things can increase frustration and, accordingly, will increase the probability that some form of aggression will occur. One such factor involves your closeness to the goal or the object of your desire. The closer the goal, the greater the expectation of pleasure that is thwarted; the greater the expectation, the more likely the aggression. This was demonstrated in a field experiment (Harris, 1974). A confederate cut in line in front of people who were waiting in a variety of places—for movie tickets, outside crowded restaurants, and at the checkout counter of a supermarket. On some occasions, the confederate cut in front of the second person in line; at other times, the confederate cut in front of the twelfth person. The results were clear: The people standing behind the intruder were much more aggressive when the confederate cut into the second place in line.

Aggression also increases when the frustration is unexpected (Kulik & Brown, 1979). Experimenters hired students to telephone strangers and ask for donations to a charity. The students worked on a commission basis—they received a small fraction of each dollar pledged. Some of the students were led to expect a high rate of contributions; others, to expect far less success. The experiment was rigged so that none of the potential donors agreed to make a contribution. What happened? The callers with high expectations were more verbally aggressive toward the non-donors, speaking more harshly and slamming down the phone with more force than the callers with low expectations.

As we've said, frustration does not always produce aggression. Rather, it seems to produce anger or annoyance and a readiness to aggress if other things about the situation are conducive to aggressive behavior (Berkowitz, 1978, 1988, 1989, 1993; Gustafson, 1989). What are those other things? Well, one obvious other thing would be the size and strength of the person responsible for your frustration, as well as that person's ability to retaliate. It is undoubtedly easier to slam the phone down on a reluctant donor who is miles away and has no idea who you are than to take out your anger against your frustrator if he turned out to be the middle linebacker of the Green Bay Packers and was staring you right in the face. Similarly, if the frustration is understandable, legitimate, and unintentional, the tendency to aggress will be reduced. For example, in one experiment, when a confederate "unwittingly" sabotaged the problem solving of his teammates because his hearing aid stopped working, the resulting frustration did not lead to a measurable degree of aggression (Burnstein & Worchel, 1962).

It should be clear that frustration is not the same as deprivation. For example, children who simply don't have toys do not aggress more than children who do. In the toy experiment, frustration and aggression occurred because the children had every reason to expect to play with the toys, and their reasonable expectation was thwarted; this thwarting was what caused the children to behave destructively.

Accordingly, the Reverend Jesse Jackson pointed out that the race riots of 1967 and 1968 occurred in the middle of rising expectations and increased, though inadequate, social spending. In short, Jackson was suggesting that thwarted expectations were largely responsible for the frustration and aggression of the rioters. This is consistent with the observations of psychiatrist Jerome Frank (1978), who noted that the most serious riots in that era occurred not in the geographic areas of greatest poverty but in Los Angeles and Detroit, where things were not nearly as bad for African Americans as they were in most other large urban centers. The point is that things were bad relative to the rioters' perception of how white people were doing and relative to the positive changes many African Americans had a right to expect. Thus, what causes aggression is not deprivation but *relative deprivation:* the perception that you (or your group) have less than you deserve, less than what you have been led to expect, or less than what people similar to you have.

A similar phenomenon occurred in Eastern Europe in 1991, when serious rebellion against the Soviet Union took place only after the chains had been loosened somewhat. In the same vein, Primo Levi (1986), a survivor of Auschwitz, contended that even in concentration camps, the few instances of rebellion were performed not by the inmates at the very bottom of the camp totem pole—the suffering victims of unrelenting horror—but "by prisoners who were privileged in some way" (p. 203).

Being Provoked and Reciprocating 被激怒和报复

Suppose you are working at your part-time job behind the counter, flipping hamburgers in a crowded fast-food restaurant. Today, you are working harder than usual because the other short-order cook went home sick, and the customers are lining up at the counter, clamoring for their burgers. In your eagerness to speed up the process, you spin around too fast and knock over a large jar of pickles that smashes on the floor just as the boss enters the workplace. "Boy, are you clumsy!" he screams. "I'm gonna dock your pay $10 for that one; grab a broom and clean up, you moron! I'll take over here!" You glare at him. You'd love to tell him what he can do with this lousy job!

Aggression frequently stems from the need to reciprocate after being provoked by aggressive behavior from another person. Although the Christian plea to "turn the other cheek" is wonderful advice, most people don't take it, as has been illustrated in countless experiments in and out of the laboratory. Typical of this line of research is an experiment by Robert Baron (1988) in which participants prepared an advertisement for a new product; their ad was then evaluated and criticized by an accomplice of the experimenter. In one condition, the criticism, though strong, was done in a gentle and considerate manner ("I think there's a lot of room for improvement"); in the other condition, the criticism was given in an insulting manner ("I don't think you could be original if you tried"). When provided with an opportunity to retaliate, those people who were treated harshly were far more likely to do so than those in the "gentle" condition.

Nothing is more costly, nothing is more sterile, than revenge.

—Winston Churchill

But even when provoked, people do not always reciprocate. We ask ourselves, was the provocation intentional or not? When convinced it was unintentional, most of us will not reciprocate (Kremer & Stephens, 1983). Similarly, if there are mitigating circumstances, counteraggression will not occur. But to curtail an aggressive response, these mitigating circumstances must be known at the time of the provocation (Johnson & Rule, 1986). In one study, students were insulted by the experimenters' assistant. Half of them were first told that the assistant was upset after receiving an unfair low grade on a chemistry exam; the other students received this information only after the insult was delivered. All subjects later had an opportunity to retaliate by choosing the level of unpleasant noise with which to zap the assistant. Those students who knew about the mitigating circumstances before being insulted delivered less intense bursts of noise. Why the difference? At the time of the insult, the informed students simply did not take it personally and therefore had no need to retaliate. This interpretation is bolstered by evidence of their physiological arousal: At the time of the insult, the heartbeat of the insulted students did not increase as rapidly if they knew about the assistant's unhappy state of mind beforehand.

Aggressive Stimulus
An object that is associated with aggressive responses (e.g., a gun) and whose mere presence can increase the probability of aggression

Aggressive Objects as Cues 攻击性物体的提示作用

Certain stimuli seem to impel us to action. Is it conceivable that the mere presence of an **aggressive stimulus**—an object that is associated with aggressive responses—might increase the probability of aggression?

In a classic experiment by Leonard Berkowitz and Anthony Le Page (1967), college students were made angry. Some of them were made angry in a room in which a gun was left lying around (ostensibly from a previous experiment), and others were made angry in a room in which a neutral object (a badminton racket) was substituted for the gun. Participants were then given the opportunity to administer what they believed were electric shocks to a fellow college student. Those individuals who had been made angry in the presence of the gun administered more intense electric shocks than those made angry in the presence of the racket (see Figure 12.2). The basic findings have been replicated a great many times in the United States

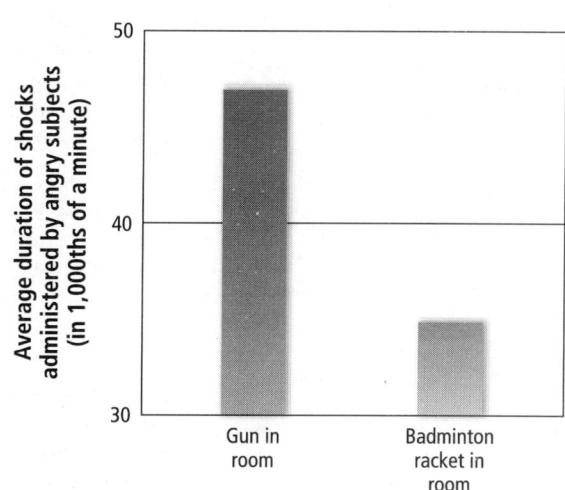

FIGURE 12.2
The trigger can pull the finger.

Aggressive cues, such as weapons, tend to increase levels of aggression.

(Adapted from Berkowitz & Le Page, 1967)

and Europe (Frodi, 1975; Turner & Leyens, 1992; Turner, Simons, Berkowitz, & Frodi, 1977). These findings are provocative and point to a conclusion opposite to a familiar slogan often used by opponents of gun control that "guns don't kill; people do." Guns do kill. As Leonard Berkowitz (1981, p. 12) put it, "An angry person can pull the trigger of his gun if he wants to commit violence; but the trigger can also pull the finger or otherwise elicit aggressive reactions from him, if he is ready to aggress and does not have strong inhibitions against such behavior."

 **Insults and Aggression** 试一试！侮辱和侵犯

Think about the last time you were insulted.

- Who insulted you?
- What were the circumstances?
- Did you take it personally or not?

- How did you respond?

  How does your behavior relate to the material you have just finished reading?

Consider Seattle, Washington, and Vancouver, British Columbia. They are twin cities in a lot of ways; they have similar climates, populations, economies, general crime rates, and rates of physical assault. They differ in two respects: (1) Vancouver severely restricts handgun ownership; Seattle does not, and (2) the murder rate in Seattle is more than twice as high as that in Vancouver (Sloan et al., 1988). Is one thing the cause of the other? We cannot be sure. But the laboratory experiments just described strongly suggest that the ubiquitous presence of aggressive stimuli such as guns in the United States could be a factor.

This speculation receives additional support from a cross-national study that found that the homicide rate in countries around the world is highly correlated with the availability of handguns (Archer & Gartner, 1984). Britain, for example, where handguns are banned, has one-fourth the population of the United States and one-sixteenth as many homicides.

In a large-scale follow-up study, Archer and his colleagues (Archer, 1994; Archer & McDaniel, 1995) asked teenagers from the United States and 10 other countries to read stories involving conflict among people and to predict the outcome of the conflict. The results? American teenagers were more likely to anticipate a violent conclusion to the conflict than teenagers from other countries. Moreover, the violent conclusions drawn by American teenagers were far more likely to be "lethal, gun-laden and merciless" (Archer, 1994, p. 19). The conclusions are undeniable: Lethal violence, especially involving guns, is simply a major part of American society—and therefore plays a major role in the expectations and fantasies of American youngsters.

Endorsement, Imitation, and Aggression 社会赞许、模仿和侵犯

As you have learned, most people take their cues from others. For example, if we want to know whether aggressive behavior is okay, we will look to see what others are doing or what others are saying about it. Thus, if a respected person or institution endorses aggression, it will have an impact on the attitudes and behavior of a great many people. To take one example, in a recent study, Brad Bushman and his colleagues explored the impact of religiously sanctioned stories of violence and aggression. As one might expect, they found that when a violent story was attributed to the Bible and when, in that story, God sanctioned the violence, the reader was more likely to behave aggressively afterward. It is interesting to note that the effect held for nonreligious as well as religious participants (Bushman, Ridge, Das, Key, & Busath, 2007).

When it comes to the imitation of aggression, the influence of others is not confined to prestigious institutions like religion. Almost anyone will do. This is especially true for children. Children frequently learn to solve conflicts aggressively by imitating adults and their peers, especially when they see that the aggression is rewarded. For example, in most sports the more aggressive players usually achieve the greatest fame (and the highest salaries), and the more aggressive teams win more games. In sports, it usually doesn't pay to be a gentle soul—as famed baseball manager Leo Durocher once pointed out, "Nice guys finish last!" The data bear him out. In professional hockey, for example, those players most frequently sent to the penalty box for overly aggressive play also scored the most goals and earned the highest salaries (McCarthy & Kelly, 1978). And it is not surprising that an excellent film on the life of the great middleweight boxing champion Jake LaMotta was called *Raging Bull*. To the extent that athletes serve as role models for children and adolescents, what is being modeled might be that fame and fortune go hand in hand with excessive aggressiveness.

Guns to the left of me, guns to the right of me. Does the easy availability of guns in the United States contribute to the frequency and intensity of violence?

The people children imitate the most, of course, are their parents. And if the parents were abused as children, this can set a chain of abuse in motion. Indeed, a large percentage of physically abusive parents were themselves abused by their own parents when they were kids (Silver, Dublin, & Lourie, 1969; Strauss & Gelles, 1980). Many experts speculate that when children are physically abused by their parents, they learn that violence is an acceptable way to socialize their own kids. But of course, that is not the only conclusion one might draw from these family data.

We've seen that aggression has a strong inborn component, so might aggressive parents simply breed aggressive children? How can one determine whether or not imitation might be operating here? As you might guess, a laboratory study could provide useful evidence. In a classic series of experiments, Albert Bandura and his associates (Bandura, Ross, & Ross, 1961, 1963) demonstrated the power of social learning.

Social learning theory holds that we learn social behavior (e.g., aggression) by observing others and imitating them. The basic procedure in the Bandura experiments was to have an adult knock around a plastic, air-filled "Bobo" doll (the kind that bounces back after it's been knocked down). The adult would smack the doll around with the palm of a hand, strike it with a mallet, kick it, and yell aggressive things at it. The kids were then allowed to play with the doll. In these experiments, the children imitated the aggressive models and treated the doll in an abusive way. Children in a control condition, who did not see the aggressive adult in action, almost never unleashed any aggression against the hapless doll. Moreover, the children who watched the aggressive adult used identical actions and identical aggressive words as the adult. And many went beyond mere imitation—they also engaged in novel forms of aggressive behavior. This research offers strong support for our belief that aggressive behavior is often learned by the simple process of watching and imitating the behavior of others.

Children have never been very good at listening to their elders, but they have never failed to imitate them.

—James Baldwin, *Nobody Knows My Name*

Violence in the Media: TV, Movies, and Video Games
媒体中的暴力：电视、电影和电子游戏

If just watching people behave aggressively causes children to mistreat dolls, what does watching violence on television do to them—to all of us? And what about violent video games in which children participate in the destruction of cities and the lopping off of heads and limbs of characters on their computer screens?

Social Learning Theory
The idea that we learn social behavior (e.g., aggression) by observing others and imitating them

Children learn aggressive behavior through imitation. In this classic study, the experimenter modeled some rather violent treatment of the doll—and the children imitated her perfectly.

Effects on Children Most American children are immersed in TV violence. Immersed in it? They are marinated in it! Social psychologist Leonard Eron told a Senate committee that by the time the average American child finishes elementary school, he or she would have seen 8,000 murders and more than 100,000 other acts of violence (Eron, 2001). Violence is difficult to avoid. Dozens of studies (e.g., Seppa, 1997) have demonstrated that 58 percent of all TV programs contain violence—and of those, 78 percent contain not a shred of remorse, criticism, or penalty for that violence. Indeed, some 40 percent of the violent incidents seen on TV during a particular year were initiated by characters portrayed as heroes or other attractive role models for children (Cantor et al., 2001).

Exactly what do children learn from watching violence on TV? A number of long-term studies have indicated that the more violence individuals watch on TV as children, the more violence they exhibit later as teenagers and young adults (Eron, 1982, 1987; Eron, Huesmann, Lefkowitz, & Walder, 1996). In a typical study of this kind, teenagers are asked to recall which shows they watched on TV when they were kids and how frequently they watched them. Next, the shows are independently rated by judges as to how violent they are. Finally, the general aggressiveness of the teenagers is independently rated by their teachers and classmates. Not only is there a high correlation between the amount of violent TV watched and the viewer's subsequent aggressiveness, but also the impact accumulates over time—that is, the strength of the correlation increases with age.

> *Television has brought murder back into the home—where it belongs.*
>
> —Alfred Hitchcock, 1965

Although these are fairly powerful data, they do not definitively prove that watching a lot of violence on TV causes children to become violent teenagers. After all, it is at least conceivable that the aggressive kids were born with a tendency to enjoy violence and that this enjoyment manifests itself in both their aggressive behavior and their liking for watching violence on TV. Once again, we see the value of the controlled experiment in helping us sort out what causes what. To demonstrate conclusively that watching violence on TV actually causes violent behavior, the relationship must be shown experimentally.

Because this is an issue of great importance to society, it has been well researched. Although not all the research is consistent, the overwhelming thrust of the experimental evidence demonstrates that watching violence does indeed increase the frequency of aggressive behavior in children (for reviews of the literature, see Cantor et al., 2001; Geen, 1994, 1998; Huesmann & Miller, 1994; Wood, Wong, & Chachere, 1991). For example, in an early experiment on this issue, Robert Liebert and Robert Baron (1972) exposed a group of children to an extremely violent TV episode of a police drama. In a control condition, a similar group of children was exposed to an exciting but nonviolent TV sporting event for the same length of time. Each child was then allowed to play in another room with a group of other children. Those who had watched the violent police drama showed far more aggression against their playmates than those who had watched the sporting event.

A subsequent experiment by Wendy Josephson (1987) showed, as one might expect, that watching TV violence has the greatest impact on youngsters who are somewhat prone to violence to begin with. In this experiment, youngsters were exposed to either a film depicting a great deal of police violence or an exciting, nonviolent film about bike racing. The youngsters then played a game of floor hockey. Watching the violent film had the effect of increasing the number of aggressive acts committed during the hockey game—primarily by the youngsters who had previously been rated as highly aggressive by their teachers. These kids hit others with their sticks, threw elbows, and yelled aggressive things at their opponents to a much greater extent than either the kids rated as nonaggressive who had also watched the violent film or the kids rated as aggressive who had watched the nonviolent film. Thus it may be that watching media violence in effect serves to give aggressive kids permission to express their aggression. Josephson's experiment suggests that youngsters who do not have aggressive tendencies to begin with do not necessarily act aggressively—at least not on the basis of seeing only one violent film.

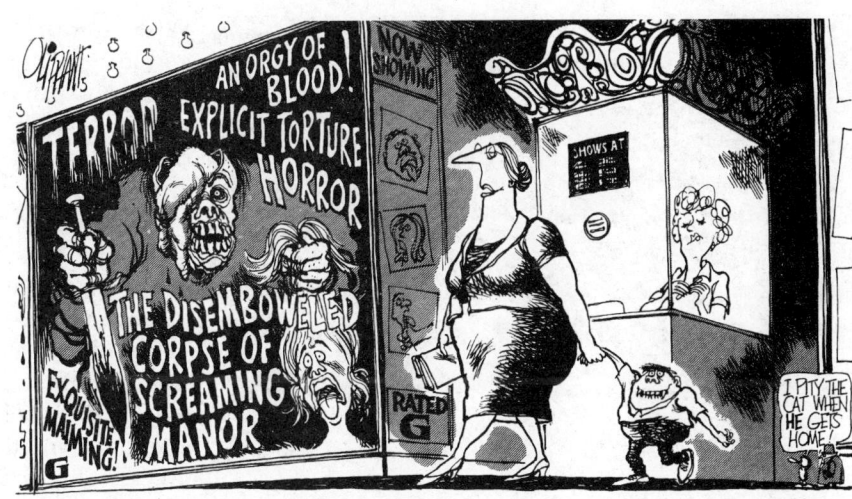

"At last, a movie without all those filthy sex scenes!"

OLIPHANT Copyright © 1973. Reprinted with permission of UNIVERSAL PRESS SYNDICATE. All Rights Reserved.

That last phrase is an important one because it may be that even children who are not inclined toward aggression will become more aggressive if exposed to a steady diet of violent films over a long period. That is exactly what was found in field experiments performed in Belgium by J. Philippe Leyens and his colleagues (Leyens, Camino, Parke, & Berkowitz, 1975; Parke, Berkowitz, Leyens, West, & Sebastian, 1977). In these experiments, groups of children were exposed to differing amounts of media violence over a longer period than is typical of "one-shot" laboratory experiments. In these field experiments, the great majority of the kids (even those without strong aggressive tendencies) who were exposed to a high degree of media violence over a long period were more aggressive than those who watched more benign programs.

As noted earlier, the average 12-year-old has seen an estimated 100,000 acts of televised violence (Signorielli, Gerbner, & Morgan, 1995). We mention this because we believe that one of the crucial factors involved in the findings on the behavior of children exposed to violence, in addition to social learning and imitation, is the simple phenomenon of *priming*. That is, just as exposing children to rifles and other weapons left lying around the house or the laboratory has a tendency to increase the probability of an aggressive response when children subsequently are frustrated or hurt, exposing children to an endless stream of violence in films and on TV might have a similar tendency to prime an aggressive response.

Playing violent video games seems to have the same kind of impact on children that watching TV violence does. In one study, violent video game playing was positively correlated with aggressive behavior and delinquency in children, and the relationship was stronger for children who had been more prone to violence beforehand (Anderson & Dill, 2000). In a second study, the researchers showed that the relationship was more than correlational. Exposing a random sample of children to a graphically violent video game had a direct and immediate impact on their aggressive thoughts and behavior (Anderson & Dill, 2000). Douglas and J. Ronald Gentile argue that video games are especially effective at teaching aggression because they accomplish three elements of "best" instructional practices: teaching the same content across several contexts, practice distributed over time, and the induction of emotional/physiological responses (Gentile & Gentile, 2008).

Does playing violent games, like paintball, make adults more prone to real violence?

What about Adults? So far, we've focused on children—and for good reason. Youngsters are by definition much more malleable than adults—their attitudes and behaviors are almost certainly deeply influenced by the things they view. Moreover, children are not as adept as adults at distinguishing between reality and fantasy. But the effects of media violence on violent behavior are not limited to children.

Media violence has a major impact on the aggressive behavior of adolescents and young adults as well. In a recent longitudinal study, researchers monitored the behavior of more than 700 families over a period of 17 years. Their findings are striking: They found a significant association between the amount of time spent watching television during adolescence and early adulthood and the likelihood of subsequent violent acts against others. This association was significant *regardless of parental education, family income, and neighborhood violence*. Moreover, unlike most laboratory experiments on aggression that must use rather pallid measures of aggression (such as administering fake electric shocks or loud noises to the victim), this study, because it took place in the real world over a long period of time, allowed for the examination of severe aggressive behavior like assault and armed robbery (Johnson, 2002).

On numerous occasions, adult violence seems to be a case of life imitating art. To cite just one example, in 1991 a man drove his truck through the window of a crowded cafeteria in Killeen, Texas, emerged from the cab, and began shooting people at random. By the time the police arrived, he had killed 22 people, making this the most destructive shooting spree in American history. He then turned the gun on himself. In his pocket, police found a ticket stub to *The Fisher King*, a film depicting a deranged man firing a shotgun into a crowded bar, killing several people.

> *At last, a movie without all those filthy sex scenes! Death has been tidied up, cleansed of harmful ingredients, and repackaged in prime-time segments that pander to baser appetites but leave no unpleasant aftertaste. The Caesars of network television permit no mess on the living room floor.*
>
> —Donald Goddard, 1977

Did seeing the film cause the violent act? We cannot be sure. But we do know that violence in the media can and does have a profound impact on the behavior of adults. David Phillips (1983, 1986) scrutinized the daily homicide rates in the United States and found that they almost always increased during the week following a heavyweight boxing match. Moreover, the more publicity surrounding the fight, the greater the subsequent increase in homicides. Still more striking, the race of prizefight losers was related to the race of victims of murders after the fights: After white boxers lost fights, there was a corresponding increase in murders of white men but not of black men. After black boxers lost fights, there was a corresponding increase in murders of black men but not of white men. Phillips's results are far too consistent to be dismissed as a fluke. Moreover, his findings have received strong confirmation from a meta-analysis of research showing that across a wide range of ages, there is a reliable relationship between viewing violence on TV and the antisocial behavior of the viewer (Paik & Comstock, 1994). Again, these data should not be construed as indicating that all people or even a sizable percentage of people are motivated to commit violence through watching media violence. But the fact that some people are influenced—and that the results can be tragic—cannot be denied.

The Numbing Effect of TV Violence Repeated exposure to difficult or unpleasant events tends to have a numbing effect on our sensitivity to those events. In one experiment, researchers measured the physiological responses of several young men while they were watching a rather brutal and bloody boxing match (Cline, Croft, & Courier, 1973). Those who watched a lot of TV in their daily lives seemed relatively indifferent to the mayhem in the ring—that is, they showed little physiological evidence of excitement, anxiety, or other arousal. They were unmoved by the violence. But those who typically watched relatively little TV showed major physiological arousal—the violence really agitated them.

Studies have also found that viewing television violence can subsequently numb people's reactions when they face real-life aggression (Thomas, Horton, Lippincott, & Drabman, 1977). The researchers had their subjects watch either a violent police drama or an exciting but nonviolent volleyball game. After a short break, the subjects were allowed to observe a verbally and physically aggressive interaction between two preschoolers. Those who had watched the police show responded less emotionally than those who had watched the volleyball game. It seems that viewing the initial violence served to desensitize them to further acts of violence—they were not upset by an incident that by all rights should have upset them. Although such a reaction may psychologically protect us from upset, it may also have the unintended effect of increasing our indifference to victims of violence and perhaps render us more accepting of violence as an aspect of life in the modern world. In a follow-up experiment, Margaret Thomas (1982) took this reasoning a step further. She demonstrated that college students exposed to a great deal of TV violence not only showed physiological evidence of greater acceptance of violence but in addition, when subsequently given the opportunity to administer electric shocks to a fellow student, they administered more powerful electric shocks than those in the control condition.

Does watching violent movies make children more aggressive?

In a related fashion, researchers have shown that people who participate in violent video games are more likely to be oblivious to the needs of others. In one experiment, Brad Bushman and Craig Anderson (in press) ran an experiment in which participants had the opportunity to help an injured person. Those who previously had been playing a violent video game took much longer to respond than those who were playing a nonviolent game.

Conversely, Douglas Gentile and his colleagues found that video games with prosocial content lead to an increase in prosocial behavior (Gentile et al., in press). The researchers' explanation for this is, in part, that the prosocial games prime the scripts of helping behavior in much the same way that the violent video games prime a more aggressive script. **Scripts** are ways of behaving socially that we learn implicitly from the culture.

How Does Media Violence Affect Our View of the World? If I am watching all this murder and mayhem on the TV screen, wouldn't it be logical for me to conclude that it simply isn't safe to leave the house—especially after dark? That is precisely what many heavy TV viewers do conclude (Gerbner, Gross, Morgan, Signorielli, & Shanahan, 2002). Adolescents and adults who are heavy TV viewers (who watch more than 4 hours per day) are more likely than light TV viewers (who watch less than 2 hours per day) to have an exaggerated view of the degree of violence taking place outside their own home. Moreover, heavy TV viewers have a much greater fear of being personally assaulted.

Why Does Media Violence Affect Viewers' Aggression? As suggested throughout this discussion, there are at least five distinct reactions that explain why exposure to violence via the media might increase aggression:

1. **"If they can do it, so can I."** When people see characters on TV behaving violently, it may simply weaken their previously learned inhibitions against violent behavior.

2. **"Oh, so that's how you do it!"** When people see characters on TV behaving violently, it might trigger imitation, providing them with ideas as to how they might go about it.

Scripts
Ways of behaving socially that we learn implicitly from our culture

3. **"Those feelings I am having must be real anger rather than simply a stressful day."** Watching violence may put people more in touch with their feelings of anger and make an aggressive response more likely simply through priming, as discussed in Chapter 4. Having recently viewed violence on TV, someone might interpret his or her own feelings of mild irritation as intense anger and then be more likely to lash out.
4. **"Ho-hum, another brutal beating; what's on the other channel?"** Watching a lot of mayhem seems to reduce both our sense of horror about violence and our sympathy for the victims, making it easier for us to live with violence and perhaps easier for us to act aggressively.
5. **"I had better get him before he gets me!"** If watching a lot of TV makes people think the world is a dangerous place, they might be more apt to be hostile to a stranger who approaches them on the street.

Does Violence Sell? 暴力能提高销售吗？

Everyone knows that violence on TV is popular. People might complain about all that mayhem, but most people also seem to enjoy watching it. What message does that send to advertisers? Perhaps it would lead them to conclude that violence sells. Not so fast. The ultimate goal of advertising is not simply to get a lot of people to tune in to the ad; rather, it is to present the product in such a way that the public will end up purchasing it over a long period of time. What if it turns out that certain kinds of shows produce so much mental turmoil that the sponsor's product is soon forgotten? If people cannot remember the name of the product, seeing the show will not lead them to buy it. In a striking experiment, Brad Bushman and Angelica Bonacci (2002) got people to watch TV shows that were either violent, sexually explicit, or neutral. Each of the shows contained the same nine ads. Immediately after seeing the show, the researchers asked the viewers to recall the brands and to pick them out from photos of supermarket shelves. Twenty-four hours later, they telephoned the viewers and asked them to recall the brands they had seen during the viewing. The people who saw the ads during the viewing of a neutral (nonviolent, non sexually explicit) show were able to recall the advertised brands better than the people who saw the violent show or the sexually explicit show. This was true both immediately after viewing and 24 hours after viewing, and was true for both men and women of all ages. It seems that watching media violence and sex impair the memory of viewers. In terms of maximizing sales, advertisers might be well advised to sponsor nonviolent shows.

Violent Pornography and Violence against Women
暴力色情与对女性的暴力

A particularly troubling aspect of aggression in the United States involves violence expressed by some men against women in the form of rape. According to national surveys, during the past 3 decades, almost half of all rapes or attempted rapes do not involve assaults by a stranger but are instances of "date rape," in which the victim is acquainted with or even dating the assailant. Many date rapes occur because the male refuses to take no for an answer. Why does this happen?

Part of the answer lies in the "sexual scripts" adolescents learn as they grow toward sexual maturity. The sexual scripts adolescents are exposed to suggest that the traditional female role is to resist the male's sexual advances and the male's role is to be persistent (Check & Malamuth, 1983; White, Donat, & Humphrey, 1995). This may explain why, in one survey of high school students, although 95 percent of the males and 97 percent of the females agreed that the man should stop his sexual advances as soon as the woman says no, nearly half of those same students also believed that when a woman says "no," she doesn't always mean it (Monson, Langhinrichsen-Rohling, & Binderup, 2002). During the 1990s, this confusion prompted several colleges to suggest that dating couples negotiate an explicit contract about their sexual conduct and limitations at the very beginning of the date. Given the problems associated with sexual scripts and the emotionally destructive consequences of miscommunication, it is understandable that college administrators would have resorted to these extreme precautions. But social critics (e.g., Roiphe, 1994) lambasted these measures on the grounds that they encouraged fear and paranoia, destroyed the spontaneity of romance, and reduced the excitement of dating to something resembling a field trip to a lawyer's office. The measures were eventually dropped.

Coincidental with the increase in date rape has been an increase in the availability of magazines, films, videos, and the Internet depicting vivid, explicit sexual behavior. For better or worse, in recent years our society has become increasingly freer and more tolerant of pornography. If viewing aggression in films and on television contributes to aggressiveness, doesn't it follow that viewing pornographic material could increase the incidence of rape? Although this possibility has been presented as a fact by certain self-appointed guardians of morality, scientific research suggests that it is still an open question. Because pornography is a hot-button issue, research findings often get distorted or ignored in the heat of rhetoric. In 1970, after studying the existing evidence, the Presidential Commission on Obscenity and Pornography concluded that explicit sexual material, in and of itself, does not contribute to sexual crimes, violence against women, or other antisocial acts. But as you will recall, in Chapter 2 we discussed the fact that in 1985, the attorney general's commission disagreed with the findings of the earlier report and concluded that pornography has a major impact on violent crimes against women. Which commission was right?

As is often the case in such politically motivated disputes, the truth is more complex than either of these conclusions. Careful scientific research suggests an important distinction between simple pornography and violent pornography. By "violent pornography," we mean exactly what you might think: pornographic material that contains an element of violence against women.

Over the past 25 years, a team of researchers has conducted careful studies, in both naturalistic and laboratory settings, to determine the effects of violent pornography. Taken as a whole, these studies indicate that exposure to violent pornography promotes greater acceptance of sexual violence toward women and is almost certainly a factor associated with actual aggressive behavior toward women (Dean & Malamuth, 1997; Donnerstein & Linz, 1994; Malamuth, Linz, Heavey, Barnes, & Acker, 1995). In one experiment (Donnerstein & Berkowitz, 1981), male subjects were angered by a female accomplice. They were then shown one of three films—an aggressive-erotic one involving rape, a purely erotic one without violence, or a film depicting nonerotic violence against women. After viewing one of these films, the men took part in a supposedly unrelated experiment that involved teaching the female accomplice by means of administering electric shocks to her whenever she gave incorrect answers. They were also allowed to choose whatever level of shock they wished to use. (As with other experiments using this procedure, no shocks were actually received.) Only the men who had earlier seen the violent pornographic film subsequently administered intense shocks to the female accomplice. There is also evidence that under these conditions, subjects who view violent pornographic films will administer more intense shocks to a female confederate than to a male confederate (Donnerstein, 1980). This indicates that viewing pornographic violence against women does tend to focus aggressive feelings on women as a target.

In a similar experiment, male college students watched one of two erotic films (Malamuth, 1981). One version showed two mutually consenting adults making love; in the other version, the male raped the woman. After watching the film, the men were asked to engage in sexual fantasy. What would you predict? Men who had watched the rape version of the film created more violent sexual fantasies than those who had watched the mutual-consent version. Further, just as we saw with violence, prolonged exposure to depictions of sexual violence against women makes viewers more accepting of this kind of violence and less sympathetic toward the victim (Linz, Donnerstein, & Penrod, 1984). Interestingly, this applies to female viewers as well as male viewers.

All of this does not mean that viewing nonviolent pornographic films has zero impact on aggressive feelings directed toward women. Here the data are mixed: Some researchers have found no relationship, and some have found small effects.

Trying to make sense out of the mixed results, a team of psychologists analyzed data from 30 studies (a meta-analysis; see Chapter 2). They found that exposure to violent pornographic material produced a high degree of aggression against women (Allen, D'Alessio, & Brezgel, 1995). They also found that nonviolent pornographic material had a small but measurable effect on aggressive behavior against women. Making this issue even more complex, they found, too, that men who were exposed to images of nude women not engaged in sexual activity were actually less prone to commit violence against women than men in control conditions. Given the complexity of the data, the only firm conclusion we are able to draw at this time is that only violent pornography presents a clear and unambiguous problem for our society.

How to Reduce Aggression 如何减少侵犯

"Stop hitting your brother!" "Turn off the TV and go to your room!" Trying to curb the aggressive behavior of their children, most parents use some form of punishment. Some deny privileges; others use force, believing in the old saying, "Spare the rod and spoil the child." How well does punishment work?

Does Punishing Aggression Reduce Aggressive Behavior?
惩罚能减少侵犯行为吗?

Punishment is a complex event, especially as it relates to aggression. On the one hand, you might think that punishing any behavior, including aggression, would reduce its frequency. On the other hand, if the punishment takes the form of an aggressive act, the punishers are actually modeling aggressive behavior for the person whose aggressive behavior they are trying to stamp out and might induce that person to imitate their action. This seems to be true—for children. As we have seen, children who grow up with punitive, aggressive parents tend to be prone toward violence when they grow up (Vissing, Straus, Gelles, & Harrop, 1991).

> *All punishment is mischief; all punishment itself is evil.*
>
> —Jeremy Bentham, *Principles of Morals and Legislation*, 1789

Moreover, as we saw in Chapter 6, several experiments with preschoolers demonstrated that the threat of relatively severe punishment for committing a transgression does not make the transgression less appealing to the child. On the other hand, the threat of mild punishment—of a degree just powerful enough to get the child to stop the undesired activity temporarily—leads the child to try to justify his or her restraint and, as a result, can make the behavior less appealing (Aronson & Carlsmith, 1963; Freedman, 1965).

Using Punishment on Violent Adults The criminal justice system of most cultures administers harsh punishments both as retribution and as a means of deterring violent crimes like murder, manslaughter, and rape. Does the threat of harsh punishments for violent crimes make such crimes less likely? Do people who are about to commit violent crimes say to themselves, "I'd better not do this because if I get caught, I'm going to jail for a long time; I might even be executed"? The scientific evidence is mixed. Laboratory experiments indicate that punishment can indeed act as a deterrent (Bower & Hilgard, 1981), but only if two "ideal conditions" are met: Punishment must be both prompt and certain. It must follow quickly after the violence occurred, and it must be unavoidable. In the real world, these ideal conditions are almost never met, especially in a complex society with a high crime rate and a slow criminal justice system like our own. In most American cities, the probability that a person who commits a violent crime will be apprehended, charged, tried, and convicted is not high. Moreover, given the volume of cases in our courts, as well as the necessary cautions with which the criminal justice system must operate, promptness is almost impossible. Typically, punishment is delayed by months or even years. Consequently, in the complex world of criminal justice, severe punishment is unlikely to have the kind of deterrent effect that it does in the controlled conditions of the laboratory.

Given these realities, severe punishment is not likely to deter violent crime. Countries that invoke the death penalty for murder do not have fewer murders per capita

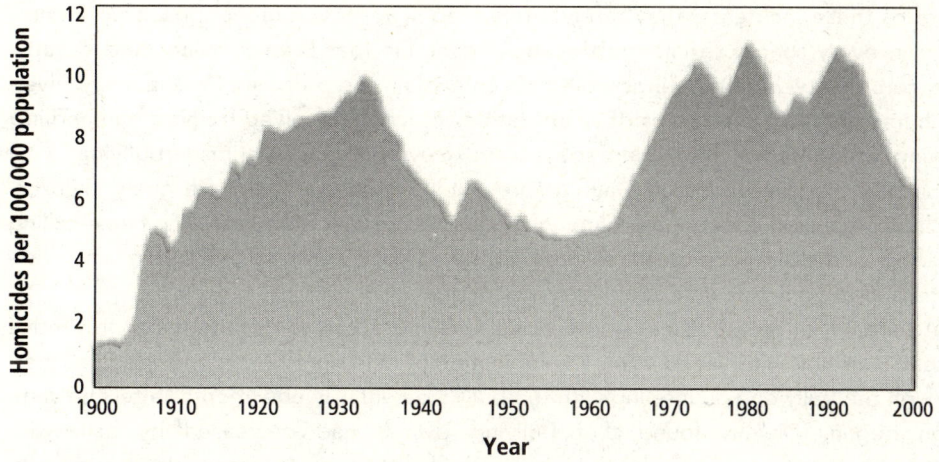

FIGURE 12.3
U.S. homicide rate, 1900–2000.

What accounts for the rise and fall in homicide rates? In the past century, there was a peak in the 1930s and again in the 1980s, but the rate has been dropping in the past 10 years.

(National Center for Vital Statistics, 2002)

than those without it. Similarly, U.S. states that have abolished the death penalty have not had an increase in capital crimes, as some experts predicted (Archer & Gartner, 1984; Nathanson, 1987). Ruth Peterson and William Bailey (1988) examined a period in the United States just after a national hiatus on the death penalty, resulting from a Supreme Court ruling that it constituted cruel and unusual punishment. When the Court reversed itself in 1976, there was no indication that the return to capital punishment produced a decrease in homicides. During the past 30 years, the homicide rate in the United States has fluctuated between 6 and 10 murders per year for every 100,000 people in the population (see Figure 12.3). This statistic is striking when one compares it to other industrialized countries like Germany, England, and France, where the homicide rate has remained stable at less than 1 per 100,000. Similarly, a study by the National Academy of Sciences (see Berkowitz, 1993) demonstrated that consistency and certainty of punishment were far more effective deterrents of violent behavior than severe punishment.

CONNECTIONS 链 接

Curbing Bullying: A Case Study in Reducing Aggression at School
阻止恃强凌弱：一项减少学校中侵犯行为的个案研究

These findings were confirmed by psychologist Dan Olweus (1991, 1995a, 1995b, 1996, 1997) in a pioneering intervention aimed at curbing bullying in Norway in which he used a combination of education and mild punishment. This remarkable effort blanketed the entire country. This action was prompted by the Norwegian government's concern over the suicides of three young victims of bullying and the attempted suicide of several others. Take the example of Henry, a sixth grader:

> On a daily basis, Henry's classmates called him "Worm," broke his pencils, spilled his books on the floor, and mocked him whenever he answered a teacher's questions. Finally, a few boys took him to the bathroom and made him lie, face down, in the urinal drain. After school that day he tried to kill himself. His parents found him unconscious, and only then learned about his torment.

(Olweus, 1991, p. 413).

At the request of the government, Olweus surveyed all of Norway's 90,000 schoolchildren. He concluded that bullying was serious and widespread, that teachers and parents were only dimly aware of bullying incidents, and that even when adults were aware of these incidents, they rarely intervened. The government sponsored a campaign in every school to change the social dynamic that breeds bullies and victims. First, community-wide meetings were held to explain the problem. Parents were given brochures detailing symptoms of victimization. Teachers received training on handling bullying. Students watched videotapes to evoke sympathy for victims of bullying.

Second, classes discussed ways to prevent bullying and befriend lonely children. Teachers organized cooperative learning groups and moved quickly to stop name-calling and other aggression that escalates into bullying. Principals ensured that lunchrooms, bathrooms, and playgrounds were adequately supervised.

A third set of measures came into play if bullying occurred despite these preventive steps. Counselors intervened using a combination of mild punishment and intensive therapy with the bully and counseling with the bully's parents. Twenty months after the campaign began, Olweus found that bullying overall had decreased by half, with improvements at every grade level. He concluded, "It is no longer possible to avoid taking action about bullying problems at school using lack of awareness as an excuse—it all boils down to a matter of will and involvement on the part of adults" (1991, p. 415).

Schoolyard bullying and taunting make life miserable for many children.

Catharsis and Aggression 宣泄与侵犯

Conventional wisdom suggests that one way to reduce feelings of aggression is to do something aggressive. "Get it out of your system" has been a common piece of advice for a great many years. So if you are feeling angry (the belief goes), yell, scream, curse, throw a dish at the wall. Express the anger, the wisdom goes, and it won't build up into something truly uncontrollable. This common belief is based on an oversimplification of the psychoanalytic notion of **catharsis** (see Dollard, Doob, Miller, Mowrer, & Sears, 1939; Freud, 1933) that has filtered down to the popular culture. As we noted earlier, Freud held a "hydraulic" idea of aggressive impulses; he believed that unless people were allowed to express their aggression in relatively harmless ways, the aggressive energy would be dammed up, pressure would build, and the energy would seek an outlet, either exploding into acts of extreme violence or manifesting itself as symptoms of mental illness.

Freud was a brilliant and complex thinker whose conclusions and advice were never simplistic. Unfortunately, his theory of catharsis has been boiled down to the dictum that youngsters should be taught to vent their anger. The idea is that blowing off steam will not only make angry people feel better but also serve to make them less likely to engage in subsequent acts of destructive violence. Does this square with the data?

The Effects of Aggressive Acts on Subsequent Aggression When frustrated or angry, many of us do feel less tense after blowing off steam by yelling, cursing, or perhaps even hitting someone. But does aggression reduce the need for further aggression? Does playing competitive games, for example, serve as a harmless outlet for aggressive energies (Menninger, 1948)? Generally, the answer is no. In fact, the reverse is true: Competitive games often make participants and observers more aggressive.

Arthur Patterson (1974) measured the hostility of high school football players, rating them both 1 week before and 1 week after the football season. If it were true that the intense competitiveness and aggressive behavior that are part of playing football serve to reduce the tension caused by pent-up aggression, the players would be expected to exhibit a decline in hostility over the course of the season. Instead, the results showed that feelings of hostility *increased* significantly.

What about watching aggressive games? Will that reduce aggressive behavior? A Canadian sports psychologist tested this proposition by measuring the hostility of spectators at an especially violent hockey game (Russell, 1983). As the game progressed, the spectators became increasingly belligerent; toward the end of the final period, their level

Catharsis

The notion that "blowing off steam"—by performing an aggressive act, watching others engage in aggressive behaviors, or engaging in a fantasy of aggression—relieves built-up aggressive energies and hence reduces the likelihood of further aggressive behavior

of hostility was extremely high and did not return to the pregame level until several hours after the game was over. Similar results have been found among spectators at football games and wrestling matches (Arms, Russell, & Sandilands, 1979; Branscombe & Wann, 1992; Goldstein & Arms, 1971). As with participating in an aggressive sport, watching one also increases aggressive behavior. Finally, does direct aggression against the source of your anger reduce further aggression? Again, the answer is no (Geen, 1998; Geen & Quanty, 1977). Actually, by far the most common finding resembles the research on watching violence: When people commit acts of aggression, such acts increase the tendency toward future aggression. For example, in an experiment by Russell Geen and his associates (Geen, Stonner, & Shope, 1975), college students were paired with another student who was actually a confederate of the experimenters. First, the student was angered by the confederate; during this phase, which involved the exchanging of opinions on various issues, the student was given phony electric shocks when his partner disagreed with his opinion. Next, during a bogus study of "the effects of punishment on learning," the student acted as a teacher while the confederate served as learner. On the first learning task, some of the students were required to deliver electric shocks to the confederate each time he made a mistake; others merely recorded his errors. On the next task, all the students were given the opportunity to deliver shocks. If a cathartic effect were operating, we would expect the students who had previously given shocks to the confederate to administer fewer and less intense shocks the second time. This didn't happen; in fact, those students who had previously delivered shocks to the confederate expressed even greater aggression when given the subsequent opportunity to attack him.

Outside the lab, in the real world, we see the same phenomenon: Verbal acts of aggression are followed by further attacks (Ebbesen, Duncan, & Konecni, 1975). All in all, the weight of the evidence does not support the catharsis hypothesis.

Something of vengeance I had tasted for the first time; an aromatic wine it seemed, on swallowing, warm and racy; its after-flavour, metallic and corroding, gave me a sensation as if I had been poisoned.

—Charlotte Brontë, *Jane Eyre*, 1847

Blaming the Victim of Our Aggression When somebody angers us, venting our hostility against that person does seem to relieve tension and make us feel better, at least temporarily—assuming the person we vent on doesn't decide to vent back on us. But "feeling better" should not be confused with a reduction in hostility. With human beings, aggression is dependent not merely on tensions—what a person feels—but also on what a person thinks.

Imagine yourself in the experiments just described. After you've administered what you think are shocks to another person or expressed hostility against your ex-boss, it becomes easier to do so a second time. Aggressing the first time can reduce your inhibitions against committing other such actions; in a sense, the aggression is legitimized, making it easier to carry out such assaults. Further, and more important, the main thrust of the research on this issue indicates that committing an overt act of aggression against a person changes your feelings about that person, increasing your negative feelings toward the target and making future aggression against that person more likely.

Does this material begin to sound familiar? It should. As we saw in Chapter 6, harming someone sets in motion cognitive processes aimed at justifying the act of cruelty. Specifically, when you hurt another person, you experience cognitive dissonance. The cognition "I have hurt Charlie" is dissonant with the cognition "I am a decent, reasonable person." A good way for you to reduce dissonance is somehow to convince yourself that hurting Charlie was not a bad thing to do. You can accomplish this by ignoring Charlie's virtues and emphasizing his faults, by convincing yourself that Charlie is a bad person who deserved to be hurt. This would especially hold if the target was an innocent victim of your aggression. Thus, as in experiments described in Chapter 6 (Davis & Jones,

Fans watching aggressive sports do not become less aggressive; in fact, they may become more aggressive than if they hadn't watched at all.

> *In war, the state is sanctioning murder. Even when the war is over, this moral corruption is bound to linger for many years.*
>
> —Erasmus, 1514

1960; Glass, 1964), participants inflicted either psychological or physical harm on an innocent person who had done them no prior harm. Participants then derogated their victims, convincing themselves they were not nice people and therefore deserved what they got. This reduces dissonance, all right—and it also sets the stage for further aggression, for once a person has succeeded in derogating someone, it makes it easier to do further harm to the victim in the future.

What happens if the victim isn't totally innocent? For example, what if the victim has done something that hurt or disturbed you and therefore deserves your retaliation? Here the situation becomes more complex and more interesting. One of several experiments to test this idea was performed several years ago (Kahn, 1966). A young man posing as a medical technician, taking some physiological measurements from college students, made derogatory remarks about the students. In one experimental condition, the participants were allowed to vent their hostility by expressing their feelings about the technician to his employer—an action that looked as though it would get the technician into serious trouble, perhaps even cost him his job. In another condition, participants did not have the opportunity to express any aggression against the person who had aroused their anger. Those who were allowed to express their aggression subsequently felt greater dislike and hostility for the technician than those who were inhibited from expressing their aggression did. In other words, expressing aggression did not inhibit the tendency to aggress; rather, it tended to *increase* it—even when the target was not simply an innocent victim.

These results suggest that when people are angered, they frequently engage in overkill. In this case, costing the technician his job is much more devastating than the minor insult delivered by the technician. The overkill produces dissonance in much the same way that hurting an innocent person produces dissonance: If there is a major discrepancy between what the person did to you and the force of your retaliation, you must justify that discrepancy by derogating the object of your wrath.

If our reasoning is correct, it might help explain why it is that when two nations are at war, few members of the victorious nation feel much sympathy for the victims of the nation's actions. For example, near the end of World War II, American planes dropped atomic bombs on Hiroshima and Nagasaki. More than one hundred thousand civilians—including a great many children—were killed, and countless thousands suffered severe injuries. Shortly thereafter, a poll taken of the American people indicated that less than 5 percent felt we should not have used those weapons, whereas 23 percent felt we should have used many more of them before giving Japan the opportunity to surrender. Why would so many Americans favor the death and disfigurement of civilians? Our guess is that in the course of the war, a sizable proportion of Americans gradually adopted increasingly negative attitudes toward the Japanese that made it increasingly easy to accept the fact that we were causing them a great deal of misery. The more misery we inflicted on them, the more these Americans derogated them—leading to an endless spiral of aggression and the justification of aggression, even to the point of favoring a delay in the ending of the war so that still more destruction might be inflicted.

How could this be? Are Americans such callous, unsympathetic people? We don't believe so. You now have the tools to begin to understand the mechanics of how that phenomenon comes about. This spiral of self-justification was bolstered by the way the Japanese people were depicted in American newspapers and magazines as well as in Hollywood films: as sneaky, treacherous, diabolical, and evil (see Chapter 7). After all, they did attack Pearl Harbor without provocation. It is important to note that in our government's information and propaganda campaigns, these traits were specifically attributed to the Japanese people as a whole, not simply their leaders or their military.

During World War II, Americans depicted the Japanese enemy as being vampires and other creatures. Dehumanizing images as shown in this poster helped justify the use of the atom bomb on Hiroshima and Nagasaki, causing the deaths of hundreds of thousands of civilians.

Of course, the nature of the propaganda and the details of the justification spiral will vary according to the specific events and the political objectives of the war. With this in mind, it is interesting to compare the war against Japan with the Iraq war of 2003. In World War II, our aim was to defeat Japan as quickly and as totally as possible. The Allies were fighting for our lives. The thinking of our leaders was that if this meant breaking the will of the Japanese people by indiscriminately bombing heavily populated cities, so be it. Indeed, during World War II, the intentional bombing of densely populated cities was a strategy employed by both sides. London, Berlin, Tokyo, Rotterdam, and Dresden were heavily bombed, resulting in a huge loss of civilian life (Aron, 2002).

In contrast, in 2003 the stated American objective was not to conquer Iraq or to break the will of its people but merely to get rid of Saddam Hussein and his weapons of mass destruction. Accordingly, our leaders deemed it important to win the hearts and minds of the people of Iraq so that they would welcome us as liberators and cooperate with us as we endeavored to put a more democratic regime in place. This necessitated a serious attempt to limit "collateral damage" (a chilling military euphemism for the unintentional killing and maiming of noncombatants) and to inform the American people that Iraqi civilians were not the enemy but rather were innocent victims of their ruthless dictator. Because our military killed relatively few civilians, Americans felt no inclination to dislike or derogate the Iraqi people as a whole—only the supporters of Saddam and the insurgents. Unfortunately, as the situation continues to deteriorate and more innocent civilians are killed, the general attitude is almost certain to change. This is the inevitable consequence of a prolonged occupation.

> *To jaw-jaw is better than to war-war.*
> —Winston Churchill, 1954

The Effect of War on General Aggression 战争对总体侵犯性的影响

We all know that war is hell, but the consequences of war extend far beyond the battlefield. When a nation is at war, the circumstance has a major impact on the aggressive feelings of its citizens. Specifically, when a nation is at war, its people are more likely to commit aggressive acts against one another (Archer & Gartner, 1976, 1984). Crime rates for 110 countries from 1900 on show that compared with similar nations that remained at peace, after a country had fought a war, its homicide rates rose substantially (see Figure 12.4). This is consistent with everything we have been saying about the social causes of aggression. In a sense, when a nation is at war, it's like one big, violent TV drama. Just as with overexposure to TV violence, the fact that a nation is at war (1) weakens the population's inhibitions against aggression, (2) leads to imitation of aggression, (3) makes aggressive responses more acceptable, and (4) numbs our senses to the horror of cruelty and destruction, making us less sympathetic toward the victims. In addition, being at war serves to legitimize violence as a way to address difficult problems. This phenomenon is likely to be more powerful now than ever before because thanks to satellite transmission, we and our children can watch the war unfold, from the comfort of our homes, 24 hours a day.

What Are We Supposed to Do with Our Anger?
我们应该怎么处理愤怒？

If violence leads to self-justification, which in turn breeds more violence, what are we to do with our angry feelings toward someone? Stifling anger and sulking around the house, hoping someone will read our mind, doesn't

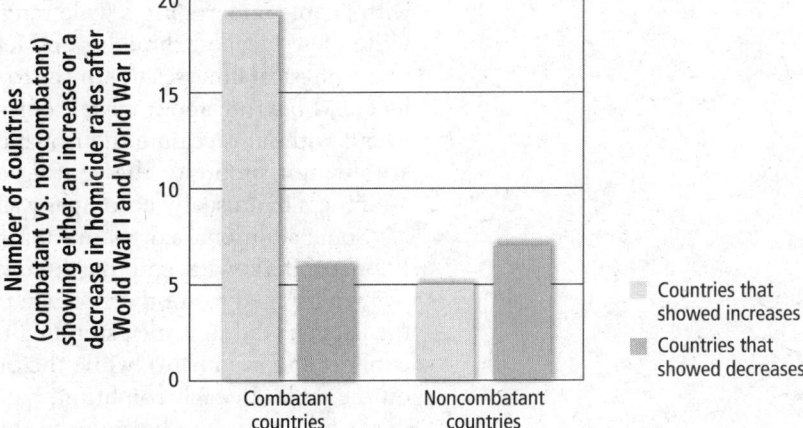

FIGURE 12.4
The effects of war on combatants versus noncombatants.
Immediately after a war, combatant countries are more likely to show an increase in violent crimes than are countries not involved in a war. How would you explain this?

seem to be a good solution, and neither are brooding and ruminating by ourselves, which just prolong and intensify the anger (Rusting & Nolen-Hoeksema, 1998). But if keeping our feelings bottled up and expressing them are both harmful, what are we supposed to do? The answer is simpler than it might seem.

First, it is possible to control our anger by actively enabling it to dissipate. "Actively enabling" means using such simple devices as counting to 10 before shooting your mouth off (as Thomas Jefferson recommended). Taking deep breaths or engaging in a distracting activity (working a crossword puzzle, listening to soothing music, taking a bike ride, or even doing a good deed) are good ways of actively enabling the anger to fade away. If this sounds suspiciously like something your grandmother could have told you, well, that's because it is! Your grandmother often knows what she is talking about. But there is more to anger than merely controlling it, as you will see.

Venting versus Self-Awareness Dissipating anger is not always best for you or for a relationship. If your close friend or spouse does something that makes you angry, you may want to express that anger in a way that helps you gain insight into yourself and the dynamics of the relationship. But for that to happen, the anger must be expressed in a nonviolent and nondemeaning way. You can do this (after counting to 10!) by making a clear, calm, and simple statement indicating that you are feeling angry and describing, nonjudgmentally, precisely what your friend or spouse did to bring about those feelings. Such a statement in itself will probably relieve tension and make the angered person feel better. At the same time, because you haven't actually harmed the target of your anger, such a response does not set in motion the cognitive processes that would lead you to justify your behavior by ridiculing or derogating your friend. Moreover, when such feelings are expressed among friends or acquaintances in a clear, open, nonpunitive manner, greater mutual understanding and a strengthening of the friendship can result. It almost seems too simple. Yet we have found such behavior to be a reasonable option that will have more beneficial effects than shouting, name-calling, and throwing dishes, on the one hand, or suffering in silence as you grin and bear it, on the other (Aronson, 2008).

> *I was angry with my friend; I told my wrath, my wrath did end.*
>
> —William Blake

Although it is probably best to reveal your anger to the friend who provoked it, at least if you are hoping to resolve the problem between you, sometimes it is helpful to write down your feelings in a journal. Just write your "deepest thoughts and feelings" about the event that has distressed you. Try to do this for 20 minutes a day for a few days, and then reread what you have written. Can you see the situation differently? Do solutions offer themselves that you hadn't thought of? In experiments with people undergoing a wide range of traumatic events, those who were induced to write their "deepest thoughts and feelings" about the event felt healthier and suffered fewer physical illnesses 6 months to a year later than either people who suffered in silence, who wrote about trivial topics, or who wrote about the details of the traumatic events without revealing their own underlying feelings. The benefits of "opening up" are due not simply to the venting of feeling, but primarily to the insights and self-awareness that usually accompany such self-disclosure (Pennebaker, 1990).

Some additional corroboration for this suggestion comes from an experiment by Leonard Berkowitz and Bartholomeu Troccoli (1990). In this experiment, young women listened to another woman talk about herself as part of a job interview. Half of the listeners did so while extending their nondominant arm, unsupported (causing discomfort and mild pain), while the others listened with their arms resting comfortably on the table. In each condition, half of the participants were asked to rate their feelings while they were listening to the job interview; according to the researchers, this procedure provided those participants with a vehicle for understanding their discomfort and a way to gain insight into it. The results were striking: The participants who felt pain and discomfort during the interview but were not given the opportunity to process it later had the most negative feelings toward the interviewee—and the more unpleasant the experience was for them, the more negative they felt toward the interviewee. By contrast, the participants who were given the opportunity to process their pain were able to avoid being unfairly harsh to the interviewee.

Defusing Anger through Apology Earlier, we noted that when people had been frustrated by someone and then learned that the person simply couldn't do any better, that frustration was less likely to bubble over into anger or aggression. This suggests that one way to reduce aggression is for the individual who caused the frustration to take responsibility for the action, apologize for it, and indicate that it is unlikely to happen again. Suppose you are taking a friend to a concert that starts at 8:00 P.M. She's been looking forward to it, and you've arranged to be at her house at 7:30. You leave your house with barely enough time to get there and discover that you have a flat tire. By the time you change the tire and get to her house, you are already 20 minutes late for the concert. Imagine her response if you (a) casually walk in, smile, and say, "Hey, it probably wouldn't have been such a good concert anyway. Lighten up; it's not a big deal" or (b) run in clearly upset, show her your dirty hands, explain what happened, tell her you left your house in time to make it but got a flat, apologize sincerely, and vow to make it up to her.

We would predict that your friend would be prone toward aggression in the first case but not in the second, and a host of experiments support our prediction (Baron, 1988, 1990; Ohbuchi & Sato, 1994; Weiner, Amirkhan, Folkes, & Verette, 1987). Typically, any apology sincerely given and in which the perpetrator took full responsibility was effective at reducing aggression.

With this in mind, Elliot Aronson has speculated about the great advantages that might be gained by equipping automobiles with "apology" signals. Picture the scene: You stop at a stop sign and then proceed, but too late you realize that the right of way wasn't really yours. What happens? In most urban centers, the offended driver will honk angrily at you or open the window and give you that ancient near-universal symbol of anger and contempt that consists of the middle finger pointed skyward (Wagner & Armstrong, 2003). Because nobody likes to be the recipient of such abuse, you might be tempted to honk back—and the escalating anger and aggression produce classic road rage. Such escalation might be avoided, though, if in addition to the horn (which throughout the world is most often used as an instrument of aggression), every car were equipped with an apology signal—perhaps at the push of a button, a little flag could pop up, saying, "Oops! Sorry!" In the foregoing scenario, had you pushed such a button as soon as you became aware of your transgression, you might have defused the cycle of anger and retaliation. One of our Eastern European readers wrote to tell us that in Poland and Hungary people apologize by using their emergency flashing lights; in the United States some motorists tap their chest as if to say "my fault." If and when these techniques become widely used, road rage may become a thing of the past.

The Modeling of Nonaggressive Behavior We've seen that children will be more aggressive (toward dolls as well as other children) if they've seen people behaving aggressively in similar situations. What if we reverse things and expose children to nonaggressive models—to people who, when provoked, expressed themselves in a restrained, rational, pleasant manner? This has been tested in several experiments (Baron, 1972; Donnerstein & Donnerstein, 1976; Vidyasagar & Mishra, 1993) and found to work. In those experiments, children first watched youngsters behaving nonaggressively when provoked. Later, when the children were put in a situation in which they themselves were provoked, they were much less likely to respond aggressively than children who had not seen the nonaggressive models.

> Man must evolve for all human conflict a method which rejects revenge, aggression, and retaliation.
>
> —Martin Luther King Jr., Nobel Prize acceptance speech, 1964

Training in Communication and Problem-Solving Skills It is impossible to go through life—or sometimes to get through the day—without feeling frustrated, annoyed, angry, or conflicted. Feeling angry is part of being human, but anger itself is not the problem. The problem is the *expression* of anger in violent or cruel ways. Yet we are not born knowing how to express anger or annoyance constructively and nonviolently. Indeed, it seems almost natural to lash out when we are angry. In most societies, it is precisely the people who lack proper social skills who are most prone to violent solutions to interpersonal problems (Toch, 1980). One way to reduce violence, then, is to teach people such techniques as how to communicate anger or criticism in constructive ways, how to negotiate and compromise when conflicts arise, and how to be more sensitive to the needs and desires of others.

Martin Luther King Jr. pioneered the use of nonviolence as a way of fighting the unjust laws of segregation. He was arrested often, as here, attempting to eat at a segregated diner.

There is some evidence that such formal training can be an effective means of reducing aggression (Studer, 1996). For example, in a classic experiment by Joel Davitz (1952), children were allowed to play in groups of four. Some of these groups were taught constructive ways to relate to one another and were rewarded for such behavior; others were rewarded for aggressive or competitive behavior. Next, the children were deliberately frustrated. They were told that they would see some entertaining movies and would be allowed to have fun. The experimenter began to show a movie and to hand out candy bars, but then he abruptly stopped the movie at the point of highest interest and took the candy bars away. Now the children were allowed to play freely as the researchers watched for aggressive or constructive behavior. The results? Children who had been trained for constructive behavior showed far more constructive activity and far less aggressive behavior than those in the other group. Many elementary and secondary schools now train students to employ nonaggressive strategies for resolving conflict (Eargle, Guerra, & Tolan, 1994; Educators for Social Responsibility, 2001).

Building Empathy Let's look at horn blowing again. Picture the following scene: A long line of cars is stopped at a traffic light at a busy intersection; the light turns green; the lead car hesitates for 10 seconds. What happens? Almost inevitably, there will be an eruption of horn honking. In a controlled experiment, Robert Baron (1976) found that when the lead car failed to move after the light turned green, almost 90 percent of the drivers of the second car honked their horn in a relentless, aggressive manner. As part of the same experiment, a pedestrian crossed the street between the first and the second car while the light was still red and was out of the intersection by the time the light turned green.

As you might imagine, this did not have an effect on the behavior of the drivers of the next car in line—almost 90 percent honked their horn when the light turned green. But in another condition, the pedestrian was on crutches. He hobbled across the street before the light turned green. In this condition, only 57 percent of the drivers honked their horn. How come? Seeing a person on crutches evoked feelings of empathy, which you will recall from Chapter 11 is the ability to put oneself in the shoes of another person and vicariously experience some of the same feelings that person is experiencing. In this instance, when the feeling of empathy was evoked, it infused the consciousness of the potential horn honkers and decreased their urge to be aggressive.

In a similar vein, Seiji Takaku (2006) performed a clever experiment in which he studied a situation in which road rage could be dissipated if drivers were made aware of the fact that they are capable of the same "reckless" mistakes as the person they got angry at. Takaku set up a driving simulation in which the driver first made the mistake of cutting someone off prior to becoming the victim of another driver's recklessness. In the conditions in which the participants had the experience of their own mistakes, they were more likely to be forgiving of the driver who cut them off. Thus, becoming aware of our own fallibility creates greater empathy for other drivers and, thus, creates the possibility of reducing road rage (see Chapter 6 on using the induction of hypocrisy to change behavior).

Dehumanization: The Opposite of Empathy
去人性化：同情心的反面

Most people find it difficult to inflict pain on a stranger unless they can find a way to dehumanize their victim (Caselman, 2007; Feshbach & Feshbach, 1969; N. D. Feshbach, 1978; S. Feshbach, 1971). Thus, when the United States was fighting wars against Asians (Japanese in the 1940s, Koreans in the 1950s, Vietnamese in the 1960s), military personnel frequently referred to them as "gooks." We see this as a dehumanizing rationalization for acts of cruelty; it's easier to commit violent acts against someone you think is subhuman than against a fellow human being. This kind of rationalization guarantees that we will continue to aggress against that person. Once we accept that our enemy is not really human, it lowers our inhibitions for committing all kinds of atrocities.

Understanding the process of dehumanization is the first step toward reversing it. Specifically, if it is true that most individuals must dehumanize their victims in order to commit an extreme act of aggression, then by building empathy among people, aggressive acts should be more difficult to commit. The research data lend strong support to this contention. In one study, students who had been trained to empathize—that is, to take the perspective of the other person—behaved far less aggressively toward that person than students who had not received the training (Richardson, Hammock, Smith, & Gardner, 1994). In a similar study, Japanese students were told to shock another student as part of a learning experiment (Ohbuchi & Baba, 1988; Ohbuchi, Ohno, & Mukai, 1993). In one condition, the "victims" first revealed something personal about themselves; in the other condition, they were not given this opportunity. Participants gave less severe shocks to the "victim" who had revealed personal information.

CONNECTIONS 链接

Teaching Empathy in School 学校里的同情心教育

"What would the world look like to you if you were as small as a cat?" "What birthday present would make each member of your family happiest?" These questions form the basis of some of the exercises for elementary school children in Los Angeles who participated in a 30-hour program designed by Norma Feshbach, who has pioneered the teaching of empathy in elementary schools. Thinking hard about the answers to such questions expands children's ability to put themselves in another's situation. In addition, the children listened to stories and then retold them from the point of view of each of the different characters in each story. The children played the role of each of the characters. The performances were videotaped. The children then viewed the tapes and analyzed how people look and sound when they express different feelings.

Children who are taught to put themselves in others' shoes often have higher self-esteem, are more generous, and are less aggressive than children who lack skills of empathy.

At the end of the program, the children not only had learned to be more empathic but also showed higher self-esteem, greater generosity, more positive attitudes, and less aggressiveness than students who had not participated in the program.

At first glance, such a program may seem unrelated to academics. Yet role playing and close analysis of stories is just what students do when putting on a play or analyzing a piece of literature. Interestingly, in reminiscing about his childhood, the Nobel Prize–winning physicist Richard Feynman reported that his father challenged his intellect by asking him to pretend he was a tiny creature living in their living room carpet. To deal with that challenge, Feynman needed, in effect, to crawl into the skin and persona of that tiny creature and get a feel for what his life would be like in those circumstances. Such questions also encourage the kind of cognitive flexibility taught in corporate creativity programs. Accordingly, it should not surprise us when Norma Feshbach reports that students who have learned to develop greater empathic ability also tend to have higher academic achievement (Feshbach, 1989, 1997).

Could the Columbine Massacre Have Been Prevented?
哥伦比亚屠杀本来可以避免吗？

At the beginning of this chapter, we described the massacre at Columbine High School as well as other recent school shootings and discussed some of the speculations about what might have caused those horrifying events. The key question is, could those events have been prevented? Before we can hope to prevent such events, we must have some idea as to their cause. After reading this chapter, perhaps you can see that several factors might have been involved—factors such as the easy availability of guns and the prevalence of violence in the media and in video games. But these factors are almost certainly not the root cause of these shootings. It is also possible that the shooters were crazy. In his analysis of the Columbine massacre, Elliot Aronson (2000), while acknowledging that these violent acts were pathological, suggested that it would be a serious mistake to dismiss them as "simply" the result of individual pathology and let it go at that. Such an explanation leads nowhere because Harris and Klebold (as well as the other recent school shooters) were functioning quite effectively. They were getting good grades, attended class regularly, and did not present serious behavior problems to their parents or to the school authorities. True, they were loners and they did dress in a strange manner. But this was typical of hundreds of other students at Columbine High School. In short, their pathological behavior was not readily predictable from their day-to-day interactions with parents, teachers, or friends. It was not even detected by Eric Harris's psychiatrist (whose care Harris was under for a mild depression). This was not due to negligence on the part of these adults; it was due to the fact that Harris and Klebold's observable behavior was not far from the norm.

But more important, to dismiss this horrifying deed as "merely" the result of mental illness would lead us to miss something of vital importance, something that might help us prevent similar tragedies in the future: the power of the social situation. Specifically, Aronson (2000) argued that the spate of school shootings is merely the pathological tip of a very large iceberg.

Harris and Klebold were almost certainly reacting in an extremely pathological manner to a general school atmosphere that creates an environment of exclusion, mockery, and taunting, making life difficult for a sizable number of students. Most high schools are cliquish places where students are shunned if they are the "wrong" race or the "wrong" ethnic group, if they come from the wrong side of the tracks, wear the wrong clothes, are too short, too fat, too tall, or too thin.

After the shootings, Columbine students recalled that Harris and Klebold suffered greatly by being taunted and bullied by the in-group. Indeed, one student, a member of the in-group, justified this behavior by saying:

> Most kids didn't want them there. They were into witchcraft. They were into voodoo. Sure we teased them. But what do you expect with kids who come to school with weird hairdos and horns on their hats? If you want to get rid of someone, usually you tease 'em. So the whole school would call them homos . . .

(Gibbs & Roche, 1999, p. 154)

The image that many young people can identify with is that of a lone student, standing in the cafeteria with a tray full of food, searching the crowded room in vain for a friendly face who might welcome the student to join a group at a table. Describing the alienating nature of the underlying social atmosphere is not intended to excuse the behavior of Harris and Klebold, merely to try to understand it so that we might prevent further occurrences of this kind.

This specific analysis of what might have been going on in the young men's minds is supported by the videocassette they left behind, which depicts them angrily talking about the insults and bullying they endured at Columbine. According to psychiatrist James Gilligan (1996), the director of mental health for the Massachusetts prison system, the motivation behind the vast majority of rampage killings is an attempt to transform feelings of shame and humiliation into feelings of pride. "Perhaps now we will get the respect we deserve," said Klebold on the videotape, brandishing a sawed-off shotgun.

Aronson's analysis received more general support from the dozens of messages submitted to Internet chat groups in the immediate aftermath of the Columbine massacre. The overwhelming majority expressed anguish and unhappiness, describing how awful it feels to be rejected and taunted by more popular classmates. Several months before the Harris-Klebold videotapes were released, many of the writers were convinced that Harris and Klebold must have had similar experiences of rejection and exclusion. We hasten to note that none of these teenagers condoned the shootings, yet their Internet postings revealed a surprisingly high degree of understanding and empathy for the suffering the two adolescents must have endured. Most students suffer in silence—but they do suffer. Some contemplate suicide; according to recent research, 20 percent of all high school students have seriously contemplated suicide (Aronson, 2000). Thus far, blessedly few go so far over the edge that they blast away at their fellow students.

A typical Internet posting was written by a 16-year-old girl, who said: "I know how they feel. Parents need to realize that a kid is not overreacting all the time they say that no one accepts them. Also, all of the popular conformists need to learn to accept everyone else. Why do they shun everyone who is different?" If Aronson's analysis of the Columbine massacre is correct, it should be possible to make our schools safer by bringing about a change in the negative, exclusionary social atmosphere. If one could achieve this, not only would it make the schools safer, but it would make them more pleasant, more exciting, and more humane as well. A clue as to how this might come about comes from two lines of research discussed in this chapter: the success of Dan Olweus's program to reduce bullying in the schools of Norway and Norma Feshbach's successful attempt to build empathy among schoolchildren in the United States. These and other successful programs will be discussed in greater detail in the following chapter.

HOW WOULD YOU USE THIS? 如何学以致用？

Imagine that you have a younger brother who is a sophomore in high school. In a phone conversation with your parents, you learn that he seems to be having a problem with anger management. He has been getting into fistfights with some of his classmates and has even beaten up on smaller boys. Your father has recommended that he try out for the high school football team as a way of "burning off" some of his excess aggressive energy. Your mother is not sure that this is a good idea. They say to you, "You have taken courses in psychology, what would you recommend?"

What questions would you ask them about your brother's hobbies and activities? Based on what you learn, what would you recommend?

Summary 总 结

- **What Is Aggression?** Aggression is intentional behavior aimed at doing harm or causing pain to another person. Hostile aggression is defined as having as one's goal the harming of another; instrumental aggression uses inflicting harm as a means to some other end.
  - **Is Aggression Inborn or Learned?** Over the centuries philosophers and psychologists have argued about whether or not humans are aggressive by nature. Some argued that it is in human nature to be aggressive, whereas others argued that humans are fundamentally malleable and thus the qualities of a society determine how aggressive its members are.
  - **Is Aggression Instinctual? Situational? Optional?** Evolutionary psychologists argue that aggression is inherited because of its survival value—that is, it increased the individual's chances of reproducing. Observations of other species suggest that animals are naturally aggressive; however, there is substantial variation in the degree of aggressiveness of our two closest animal relatives—chimpanzees and bonobos. Social psychologists argue that although aggressive behavior may be hardwired into humans, it is influenced by situational and cultural factors and is infinitely modifiable.
  - **Aggression and Culture** There is a great deal of variation in the levels of aggression of individuals living in different cultures. It is also the case that within a given society, for example, the Iroquois, the degree of aggressiveness can change across time because of changes in the situation faced by the tribe. The key point here is that multiple factors shape whether or not a culture tends to nurture aggressive behavior.

- **Neural and Chemical Influences on Aggression** The area in the brain called the amygdala is thought to control aggression. Evidence suggests that the chemical serotonin serves to inhibit aggressive behavior and that testosterone is positively correlated with aggressive behavior.
  - **Gender and Aggression** Men are much more likely than women to behave aggressively in provocative situations. Men are also more likely to interpret a given situation as provocative; however, gender differences are reduced when women are actually provoked. Crime statistics show that males commit violent crimes at much higher rates than females. Within heterosexual couples husbands are far more likely to murder their wives than vice versa.
  - **Alcohol and Aggression** Alcohol can increase aggressive behavior because it serves as a disinhibitor—it reduces one's social inhibitions. Research suggests that alcohol disrupts the way people usually process information so that they may respond to the most obvious aspects of a social situation and fail to pick up the more subtle elements of the situation.
  - **Pain, Discomfort, and Aggression** When people experience pain they are far more likely to act aggressively. Discomfort, such as heat, humidity, and offensive odors, increases the likelihood of hostile and violent behavior.
- **Social Situations and Aggression** Many social situations lead to aggression including sports events and situations that cause frustration, such as traffic jams.
  - **Frustration and Aggression** The frustration-aggression theory states that frustration can increase the probability of an aggressive response. Frustration is more likely to produce aggression if one is thwarted on the way to a goal in a manner that is either illegitimate or unexpected. Also, relative deprivation—the feeling that you have less than what you deserve or less than people similar to you have—can lead to frustration and aggressive behavior.
  - **Being Provoked and Reciprocating** Individuals frequently aggress to reciprocate for the aggressive behavior of others. This response is reduced if there are mitigating circumstances.
  - **Aggressive Objects as Cues** Research suggests that the mere presence of a violent object in a situation increases the degree of aggressive behavior. In a classic study participants angered in the presence of a gun administered more intense electric shocks to their "victim" than those angered in the same setting in which a tennis racket was substituted for the gun.
  - **Endorsement, Imitation, and Aggression** Social learning theory holds that we learn social behavior (e.g., aggression) by observing others and imitating them. People, especially children, learn to respond to conflict aggressively by observing aggressive behavior in adults and peers.
  - **Violence in the Media** Most children are exposed to a great deal of violence through watching TV and movies and playing violent video games. Long-term studies show that the more TV violence observed by children, the greater the amount of violence they exhibit as teenagers and young adults. Children are particularly susceptible to violent media because they are less able (than adults) to distinguish between reality and fiction. Exposure to violent media, however, has also been shown to increase violent behavior in adults.
  - **Does Violence Sell?** Research shows that viewing violence impairs the memory of viewers, and therefore, people are less likely to remember a product advertised on a violent TV program.
  - **Violent Pornography and Violence against Women** Exposure to violent pornography increases acceptance of sexual violence toward women.
- **How to Reduce Aggression**
  - **Does Punishing Aggression Reduce Aggressive Behavior?** If the punishment is itself aggressive, it actually models such behavior to children and may engender greater aggressiveness in the child. Further, severe punishment may actually enhance the attractiveness of the transgression to the child; however, mild punishment, because it triggers cognitive dissonance in the child, has been shown to be more effective in changing behaviors. For punishment to serve as a deterrent to crime it must be both prompt and certain.
  - **Catharsis and Aggression** The theory of catharsis would predict that venting one's anger or watching others behave aggressively would serve to make one less likely to engage in subsequent acts of aggression. Research shows the contrary: Acting aggressively or observing aggressive events (such as a football game) actually increases the likelihood of future aggressive behavior. At a national level, violent acts against another nation lead to increasingly negative attitudes towards that nation and greater willingness to inflict further violence because it triggers the tendency to justify that action.
  - **The Effect of War on General Aggression** When a nation is at war, even one that is far away, its people are more likely to commit aggressive acts against one another.
  - **What Are We Supposed to Do with Our Anger?** Typically, venting anger causes more harm than good. It is more effective to become aware of the anger and then to deal with it in ways that are more constructive. It is often the case that a cycle of anger and aggression can be diffused through apology.
  - **Dehumanization: The Opposite of Empathy?**
- **Could the Columbine Massacre Have Been Prevented?** A humiliating social atmosphere prevalent in high schools was one of the major root causes of the Columbine massacre. Changing the atmosphere of schools is an effective way to reduce the frequency of such occurrences.

CHAPTER 12 TEST 第12章习题

1. _____ aggression stems from feelings of anger and is aimed at inflicting pain whereas _____ aggression serves as a means to some goal other than pain.
   a. hostile; instrumental
   b. direct; passive
   c. instrumental; hostile
   d. passive; direct

2. A lack of which of the following brain chemicals is associated with aggression?
   a. Dopamine
   b. Norepinephrine
   c. Serotonin
   d. Testosterone

3. Which of the following gender differences in aggression is *false*?
   a. Young boys tend to be more overtly aggressive than young girls.
   b. Girls tend to express their aggressive feelings more covertly, such as by gossiping.
   c. Gender differences in aggression become much smaller when men and women are subjected to frustration or insults.
   d. When women do commit acts of overt aggression, they tend to feel less guilt or anxiety about such acts than men do.

4. Which of the following people is most likely to act aggressively toward someone who insults him?
   a. Ray, who grew up in Texas
   b. Randy, who grew up in California
   c. Richard, who grew up in Massachusetts
   d. Ricky, who grew up in Michigan

5. Under which of the following conditions is John *least* likely to be aggressive?
   a. His boss tells him he isn't going to get a raise he was promised.
   b. He likes to look at nonviolent pictures of nude women who are not involved in sexual activity.
   c. When driving to work, another driver deliberately cuts in front of him during a traffic jam.
   d. He has consumed enough alcohol to make him legally drunk and a stranger bumps into him in a crowded restaurant.

6. Which of the following is *false*?
   a. Watching violence on television increases the frequency of aggressive behavior in children.
   b. Watching violence on television increases the frequency of aggressive behavior in adolescents and young adults.
   c. Playing violent video games seems to have the same kind of impact on children that watching TV violence does.
   d. Viewing television violence can numb people's reactions when they see violence in real life.
   e. Television advertising works better when it is shown during violent shows than nonviolent shows.

7. Jim has recently been convicted in a highly publicized assault case. When asked by the press, he offers many reasons for his aggressiveness. Which of the following of Jim's arguments would a social psychologist find the *least* convincing (based upon research on aggression)?
   a. "There was a gun in the room when it happened."
   b. "I used to watch my older brother beat up neighborhood kids."
   c. "I had just been fired from a job I really wanted."
   d. "I grew up in a very cold climate in Minnesota."
   e. "I watched a lot of violent television growing up."

8. Brandon is furious at Whit for forgetting his birthday. To diffuse his anger, Brandon should
   a. think about other times Whit annoyed him and then confront Whit with all the evidence.
   b. write about his feelings privately for 20 minutes a day for a few days.
   c. vent his anger by watching a football game before confronting Whit.
   d. vent his anger by talking about Whit to a friend before confronting Whit.
   e. play a violent video game.

9. John is an easily angered man who displays a lot of aggression toward other people. If one of his New Year's resolutions is to be less aggressive, what would be the *best* approach for him to take?
   a. He should surround himself with the things that make him mad so he gets used to them and they no longer evoke the same anger responses.
   b. He should really focus on the thing that angers him and release all his feelings at once toward that object.
   c. He should try to empathize with the person who is making him angry and apologize for his aggressive behavior.
   d. He should try and set up a system of punishment for himself so that every time he displays anger, he is punished for it.

10. Suppose you want to reduce the chances that your children will act in aggressive ways toward other people. Which of the following is *least* likely to work?
    a. Be a good role model; that is, do not act aggressively in front of your children.
    b. Limit the amount of violence your children see on television.
    c. Do not let them play video games that involve aggression and violence.
    d. Encourage them to feel empathy toward other people.
    e. Encourage them to play sports where they can vent their frustrations on the playing field.

Chapter 12 Answer Key
1-a, 2-c, 3-d, 4-a, 5-b, 6-e, 7-d, 8-b, 9-c, 10-e

For more review plus practice tests, videos, flashcards, writing help and more, log on to MyPsychLab.

13 Prejudice
Causes and Cures
偏见：
原因与消除

OUTLINE 提纲

- **Prejudice: The Ubiquitous Social Phenomenon**
  Prejudice and Self-Esteem
  A Progress Report
- **Prejudice Defined**
  Stereotypes: The Cognitive Component
  Discrimination: The Behavioral Component
- **What Causes Prejudice?**
  The Way We Think: Social Cognition
  How We Assign Meaning: Attributional Biases
  Blaming the Victim
  Prejudice and Economic Competition: Realistic Conflict Theory
  The Way We Conform: Normative Rules
  Subtle Sexism
- **How Can Prejudice Be Reduced?**
  The Contact Hypothesis
  When Contact Reduces Prejudice: Six Conditions
  Why Early Desegregation Failed
  CONNECTIONS: Cooperation and Interdependence: The Jigsaw Classroom
  Why Does Jigsaw Work?
  CONNECTIONS: A Letter from "Carlos"
- **Summary**

IN THE 1930S, WHEN THURGOOD MARSHALL WAS A YOUNG lawyer working for the National Association for the Advancement of Colored People (NAACP), he was sent to a small town in the South to defend a black man who was accused of a serious crime. When he arrived, he was shocked and dismayed to learn that the defendant was already dead—lynched by an angry white mob. With a heavy heart, Marshall returned to the railroad station to wait for a train back to New York. While waiting, he realized he was hungry and noticed a small food stand on the platform. Walking toward the stand, he debated whether to go right up to the front and order a sandwich (as was his legal right) or to go around to the back of the stand (as was the common practice for African Americans in the South at that time). But before he reached the stand, he was approached by a large, heavyset white man who looked at him suspiciously. Marshall took him to be a lawman of some sort because he walked with an air of authority and had a bulge in his pants pocket that could only have been made by a handgun.

"Hey, boy," the man shouted at Marshall. "What are you doing here?" "I'm just waiting for a train," Marshall replied. The man scowled, took a few steps closer, glared at him menacingly, and said, "I didn't hear you. What did you say, boy?"

Marshall realized that his initial reply had not been sufficiently obsequious. "I beg your pardon, sir, but I'm waiting for a train." There was a long silence, during which the man slowly looked Marshall up and down, and then said, "And you'd better catch that train, boy—and soon, because in this town, the sun has never set on a live nigger."

As Marshall later recalled, at that point his debate about how to get the sandwich proved academic. He decided not to get a sandwich at all but to catch the very next train out—no matter where it was headed. Besides, somehow he didn't feel hungry anymore. (Williams, 1998)

Thurgood Marshall went on to become chief counsel for the NAACP; in 1954, he argued the case of *Brown* v. *Board of Education* before the U.S. Supreme Court. His victory there put an end to legalized racial segregation in public schools. Subsequently, Marshall was appointed to the Supreme Court, where he served with distinction until his retirement in 1991. We are not sure what became of the man with the bulge in his pocket.

The Supreme Court decision of 1954 set the stage for a flurry of civil rights legislation in the following decades, which opened the doors to equal opportunity for underprivileged minorities in the United States. In 2008 the citizens of our country

What does Obama's election suggest about the direction of racial prejudice in the United States?

elected an African American to the highest office in the land. This was a watershed event that could not have been predicted in 1954, when the overwhelming majority of Americans were opposed to the desegregation of schools. Of course, it would be naïve to assume that the election of Barack Obama heralds the end of racial prejudice in this country. But the importance of Obama's election cannot be overstated. Indeed, even his candidacy has already had important ramifications. To cite just one example, researchers found that Obama's candidacy produced a sharp reduction in bias against blacks (Plant, Devine et al., 2009). During the run-up to the election, in the presidential debates and countless additional televised appearances, a great many Americans were able to see this highly intelligent, articulate, poised African American in action. According to Plant and her colleagues, this exposure made it difficult for them to maintain whatever negative stereotypes they may have held about African Americans in general.

But prejudice remains a serious problem. Of all the social behaviors we discuss in this book, prejudice is among the most common and the most dangerous. Prejudice touches nearly everyone's life. We are all victims or potential victims of stereotyping and discrimination, for no other reason than our membership in an identifiable group, whether on the basis of ethnicity, religion, gender, national origin, sexual orientation, body size, or disability—to name a few. Even though manifestations of prejudice today tend to be both less frequent and less flagrant than they used to be, prejudice continues to exact a heavy toll on its victims. There are still hate crimes, church burnings, and countless miscellaneous acts of prejudice-induced violence, as well as "lesser" outrages like the futility of trying to get a cab to stop for you late at night in an American metropolis if you happen to be a black man (Fountain, 1997).

Moreover, on a wide variety of important social issues, a huge racial divide exists in this country in terms of attitude and experience. Although sophisticated observers have long been aware of this divide, it was brought home with stunning force in the mid-1990s during the murder trial of O. J. Simpson. The trial captured the rapt attention of millions of Americans, but from the outset, it seemed as if white Americans and black Americans were watching two different trials. Overwhelmingly, whites believed Simpson was guilty; and overwhelmingly, blacks found the evidence unconvincing at best.

We cannot be sure whether this huge difference was due to differences among the racial groups in their respective experiences with the criminal justice system or differences in the degree to which they found the defendant to be attractive and sympathetic (Toobin, 1995). In order to understand this phenomenon and others like it, we must take a long look at prejudice as a social psychological phenomenon.

Prejudice: The Ubiquitous Social Phenomenon 偏见：普遍的社会现象

It would be wrong to conclude that only minority groups are the targets of prejudice at the hands of the dominant majority. Of course, this aspect of prejudice is both powerful and poignant. But the truth is that prejudice is ubiquitous; in one form or another, it affects us all. Prejudice is a two-way street; it often flows from the minority group to the majority group as well as in the other direction. And any group can be a target of prejudice.

Let us take one of the most superordinate groups to which you belong—your nationality. As you well know, Americans are not universally loved, respected, and admired; at one time or another, we Americans have been the target of prejudice in just about every corner of the world. In the 1960s and 1970s, North Vietnamese Communists referred to Americans as the "running dogs of capitalist imperialism." In the twenty-first century, the majority of people living in the Middle East think of America as a ruthless, power-hungry, amoral nation, referring to us as "the great Satan." In our own hemisphere, many of our neighbors to the south consider us overfed economic and military bullies.

On a more subtle level, even our political allies do not always see us accurately. For example, in research on stereotyping, it turns out that British citizens tend to label Americans as intrusive, pushy, and excessively patriotic. This is not a recent development: Historian Simon Schama (2003) points out that the British and other Europeans have held such stereotypes of Americans for at least two hundred years. But stereotyping cuts both ways: Americans tend to label the British as cold, unemotional, and detached. Similarly, during the United Nations debates prior to the invasion of Iraq in 2002, the French viewed Americans as brash and bellicose, while Americans viewed the French as cowardly appeasers.

Your nationality is only one of a number of aspects of your identity that can cause you to be labeled and discriminated against. Racial and ethnic identity is a major focal point for prejudiced attitudes. Some white or European American groups also experience prejudice: Note the long-standing negative stereotypes used over the past century to describe Italian Americans and Irish Americans. Other aspects of your identity also leave you vulnerable to prejudice—for example, your gender, your sexual orientation, and your religion. Your appearance or physical state can arouse prejudice as well; obesity, disabilities, and diseases such as AIDS, for example, cause people to be treated unfairly by others.

Or consider the old stereotype that blondes are ditzy bimbos. Finally, even your profession or hobbies can lead to your being stereotyped. We all know the "dumb jock" and the "computer nerd" stereotypes. Some people have negative attitudes about blue-collar workers; others, about bankers and Wall Street executives. The point is that none of us emerges completely unscathed by prejudice; it is a problem common to all humankind.

In addition to being widespread, prejudice is dangerous. Simple dislike of a group can be relentless and can escalate to extreme hatred, to thinking of its members as less than human, and to torture, murder, and even genocide. But even when murder or genocide is not the culmination of prejudiced beliefs, the targets of prejudice will suffer in less dramatic ways. One frequent consequence of being the target of relentless prejudice is a diminution of one's self-esteem. As we discussed in Chapter 6, self-esteem is a vital aspect of a person's life. Who we think we are is a key determinant of how we behave and who we become. A person with low self-esteem will, by definition, conclude that he or she is unworthy of a good education, a decent job, an exciting romantic partner, and so on. Thus a person with low self-esteem is more likely to be unhappy and unsuccessful than a person with well-grounded high self-esteem. In a democracy, such a person is also less likely to take advantage of available opportunities.

A little black girl yearns for the blue eyes of a little white girl, and the horror at the heart of her yearning is exceeded only by the evil of fulfillment.

—Toni Morrison, *The Bluest Eye*

Prejudice and Self-Esteem 偏见和自尊

For the targets of relentless prejudice, the seeds of low self-esteem are usually sown early in life. In a classic experiment social psychologists Kenneth Clark and Mamie Clark (1947) demonstrated that African American children—some of them only 3 years old—were already convinced that it was not particularly desirable to be black. In this experiment, the children were offered a choice between playing with a white doll and playing with a black doll. The great majority of them rejected the black doll, feeling that the white doll was prettier and generally superior.

In his argument before the Supreme Court in 1954, Thurgood Marshall cited this experiment as evidence that psychologically, segregation did irreparable harm to the

If an African American girl believes that white dolls are more desirable than black dolls, should we be concerned about her self-esteem?

Is this roughly the stereotypical image that comes to mind when you are asked to imagine a New York City cab driver?

self-esteem of African American children. Taking this evidence into consideration, the Court ruled that separating black children from white children on the basis of race alone "generates a feeling of inferiority as to their status in the community that may affect their hearts and minds in a way unlikely ever to be undone. Separate educational facilities are therefore inherently unequal" (Justice Earl Warren, speaking for the majority in the case of *Brown v. Board of Education of Topeka*, 1954).

Lowered self-esteem has affected other oppressed groups as well. For example, Philip Goldberg (1968) demonstrated that like African Americans, women in this culture had learned to consider themselves intellectually inferior to men. In his experiment, Goldberg asked female college students to read scholarly articles and to evaluate them in terms of their competence and writing style. For some students, specific articles were signed by male authors (e.g., "John T. McKay"), while for others, the same articles were signed by female authors (e.g., "Joan T. McKay"). The female students rated the articles much higher if they were attributed to a male author than if the same articles were attributed to a female author. In other words, these women had learned their place; they regarded the output of other women as inferior to that of men, just as the African American youngsters learned to regard black dolls as inferior to white dolls. This is the legacy of a prejudiced society.

A Progress Report 发展的报告

Clark and Clark's experiment was conducted more than 60 years ago; Goldberg's, over 40. Significant changes have taken place in American society since then. For example, the number of blatant acts of overt prejudice and discrimination has decreased sharply, legislation on affirmative action opened the door to greater opportunities for women and minorities, and the media have increased our exposure to women and minorities doing important work in positions of power and influence. As one might expect, these changes are reflected in the gradual increase in the self-esteem of people in these groups, an increase underscored by the fact that most recent research has failed to replicate the results of those earlier experiments. African American children have gradually become more content with black dolls than they were in the late 1930s (Gopaul-McNicol, 1987; Porter, 1971; Porter & Washington, 1979, 1989), and people no longer discriminate against a piece of writing simply because it is attributed to a woman (Swim, 1994; Swim, Borgida, Maruyama, & Myers, 1989). Similarly, recent research suggests that there might not be any major differences in global self-esteem between blacks and whites or between men and women (Aronson, Quinn, & Spencer, 1998; Crocker & Major, 1989; Steele, 1992, 1997). Although this progress is real, it would be a mistake to conclude that prejudice has ceased to be a serious problem in the United States. As mentioned earlier in this chapter, prejudice exists in countless subtle and not-so-subtle ways. For the most part, in America, prejudice has gone underground and become less overt (Pettigrew, 1985, 1998; Vala, 2009). During the past half-century, social psychologists have contributed greatly to our understanding of the psychological processes underlying prejudice and have begun to identify and demonstrate some possible solutions. What is prejudice? How does it come about? How can it be reduced?

Prejudice Defined 偏见的定义

Prejudice is an attitude. As we discussed in Chapter 7, attitudes are made up of three components: an affective or emotional component, representing both the type of emotion linked with the attitude (e.g., anger, warmth) and the extremity of the attitude (e.g., mild uneasiness, outright hostility); a cognitive component, involving the beliefs or thoughts (cognitions) that make up the attitude; and a behavioral component, relating to one's actions—people don't simply hold attitudes; they usually act on them as well.

Prejudice refers to the general attitude structure and its affective (emotional) component. Technically, there are positive and negative prejudices. For example, you could be prejudiced against Texans or prejudiced in favor of Texans. In one case, your emotional reaction is negative; when a person is introduced to you as "This is Bob from Texas," you will expect him to act in particular ways that you associate with "those obnoxious Texans." Conversely, if your emotional reaction is positive, you will be delighted to meet another one of "those wonderful, uninhibited Texans," and you'll expect Bob to demonstrate many positive qualities, such as warmth and friendliness. While prejudice can involve either positive or negative affect, social psychologists (and people in general) use the word *prejudice* primarily when referring to negative attitudes about others. In this context, **prejudice** is a hostile or negative attitude toward people in a distinguishable group, based *solely* on their membership in that group. For example, when we say that someone is prejudiced against blacks, we mean that he or she is primed to behave coolly or with hostility toward blacks and that he or she feels that all blacks are pretty much the same. Thus the characteristics this individual assigns to blacks are negative and applied to the group as a whole. The individual traits or behaviors of the individual target of prejudice will either go unnoticed or be dismissed.

As headlines show, many groups are victims of prejudice.

Stereotypes: The Cognitive Component
"刻板印象"：认知要素

Close your eyes for a moment and imagine the looks and characteristics of the following people: a high school cheerleader, a New York cab driver, a Jewish doctor, a black musician. Our guess is that this task was not difficult. We all walk around with images of various "types" of people in our heads. The distinguished journalist Walter Lippmann (1922), who was the first to introduce the term *stereotype*, described the distinction between the world out there and stereotypes—"the little pictures we carry around inside our heads." Within a given culture, these pictures tend to be remarkably similar. For example, we would be surprised if your image of the high school cheerleader was anything but bouncy, peppy, pretty, nonintellectual, and (of course!) female. We would also be surprised if the Jewish doctor or the New York cab driver in your head was female—or if the black musician was playing classical music.

It goes without saying that there are male cheerleaders, women doctors who are Jewish, and black classical musicians. Deep down, we know that New York cab drivers come in every size, shape, race, and gender. But we tend to categorize according to what we regard as normative. And within a given culture, what people regard as normative is very similar, in part because these images are perpetuated and broadcast widely by the media of that culture. Stereotyping, however, goes a step beyond simple categorization. A **stereotype** is a generalization about a group of people in which identical characteristics are assigned to virtually all members of the group, regardless of actual variation among the members. When formed, stereotypes are resistant to change on the basis of new information.

But be aware that stereotyping is a cognitive process, not an emotional one. Stereotyping does not necessarily lead to intentional acts of abuse. Often stereotyping is merely a technique we use to simplify how we look at the world—and we all do it to some extent. For example, Gordon Allport (1954) described stereotyping as "the law of least effort." According to Allport, the world is just too complicated for us to have a highly differentiated attitude about everything. Instead, we maximize our cognitive time and energy by developing elegant, accurate attitudes about some topics while relying on simple, sketchy beliefs for others. (Recall the many facets of social cognition that we discussed in Chapter 3.) Given our limited capacity for processing information,

Prejudice
A hostile or negative attitude toward a distinguishable group of people, based solely on their membership in that group

Stereotype
A generalization about a group of people in which certain traits are assigned to virtually all members of the group, regardless of actual variation among the members

it is reasonable for human beings to behave like "cognitive misers"—to take shortcuts and adopt certain rules of thumb in our attempt to understand other people (Fiske, 1989b; Fiske & Depret, 1996; Jones, 1990; Taylor, 1981). To the extent that the resulting stereotype is based on experience and is at all accurate, it can be an adaptive shorthand way of dealing with complex events. However, if the stereotype blinds us to individual differences within a class of people, it is maladaptive, unfair, and potentially abusive. (See the Try It! exercise.)

> **TRY IT!** **Stereotype and Aggression** 试一试！刻板印象和攻击
>
> Close your eyes. Imagine a very aggressive construction worker. How is this person dressed, where is this person located, and what, specifically, is this person doing to express aggression? Write it all down, being specific about the person's actions.
>
> Now imagine a very aggressive lawyer. How is this person dressed, where is this person located, and what, specifically, is this person doing to express aggression? Write it all down, being specific about the person's actions.
>
> If you are like the experimental subjects in a research study, your stereotype of the construction worker and of the lawyer would have influenced the way you construed the term *aggression*: Most of the study subjects imagined the construction worker using physical aggression and the lawyer using verbal aggression (Kunda, Sinclair, & Griffin, 1997).

Sports, Race, and Attribution The potential abuse of stereotyping's mental shortcuts can be blatant and obvious—as when one ethnic group is considered lazy or another ethnic group is considered greedy. But the potential abuse can be more subtle—and it might even involve a stereotype about a positive attribute. For example, in 1992, Twentieth Century Fox produced an amusing film about two-on-two street basketball called *White Men Can't Jump*. The implication is that African American men are better at basketball than white men. Well, it turns out that over 75 percent of the players in the National Basketball Association have been African American (Gladwell, 1997; Hoose, 1989). This figure is far greater than one would expect from comparative population statistics (approximately 13 percent of the U.S. population is African American).

So what here is abusive to the minority? What's wrong with the implication that black men can jump? The abuse enters when we ignore the overlap in the distributions—that is, when we ignore the fact that a great many African American kids are not adept at basketball and a great many white kids are. Thus if we meet a young African American man and are astonished at his ineptitude on the basketball court, we are, in a very real sense, denying him his individuality. And there is ample evidence that this kind of potentially abusive stereotyping occurs (Brinson & Robinson, 1991). In a clever experiment, college students listened to a 20-minute audiotape recording of a college basketball game. They were asked to focus on one of the players, Mark Flick, and were allowed to look at a folder containing information about him, including a photograph—allegedly of Flick. Half of the participants saw a photo of an African American male; the others saw a photo of a white male. After listening to the game, the students rated Flick's performance. Their ratings reflected the prevailing stereotypes: Students who believed Flick was African American rated him as having more athletic ability and as having played a better game than those who thought he was white. Those who thought he was white rated him as having greater hustle and greater basketball sense (Stone, Perry, & Darley, 1997).

Stereotypes, Attribution, and Gender A particularly interesting manifestation of stereotyping takes place in the perception of gender differences. Almost universally, women are thought to be more nurturant and less assertive than men (Deaux & Lewis, 1984). It is possible that this perception may be entirely role-related—that is, women have traditionally been assigned the role of homemaker and thus may be seen as more nurturant (see Deaux & La France, 1998). At the other end of the continuum, evolutionary social psychologists (Buss, 1995, 1996b; Buss & Kenrick, 1998) suggest that female behavior and male behavior differ in precisely those domains in which the sexes have faced different adaptive problems. From a Darwinian perspective, there are powerful biological reasons why women might have evolved as more nurturant than men. Specifically, among our ancient ancestors, for anatomical reasons, women were always the early caregivers of infants; women who were not nurturant did not have many babies who survived; therefore, their nonnurturing genes were less likely to be passed on.

Although there is no clear way of determining whether or not caregiving is more likely to be part of a woman's genetic nature than a man's, it does turn out that the cultural stereotype is not far from reality. Research has shown that compared to men, women do tend to manifest behaviors that can best be described as more socially sensitive, friendlier, and more concerned with the welfare of others, while men tend to behave in ways that are more dominant, controlling, and independent (Eagly, 1994; Eagly & Wood, 1991; Swim, 1994). Indeed, if anything, some of the data indicate that the stereotype tends to underestimate the actual gender differences (Swim, 1994). Again, as with our basketball example, considerable overlap exists between men and women on these characteristics. Nonetheless, as Eagly (1995, 1996) has argued, the differences are too consistent to be dismissed as unimportant.

Needless to say, the phenomenon of gender stereotyping often does not reflect reality and can cut deeply. In one experiment, for example, when confronted with a highly successful female physician, male undergraduates perceived her as being less competent and having had an easier path toward success than a successful male physician (Feldman-Summers & Kiesler, 1974). Female undergraduates saw things differently: Although they saw the male physician and the female physician as being equally competent, they saw the male as having had an easier time of it. Both males and females attributed higher motivation to the female physician. It should be noted that attributing a high degree of motivation to a woman can be one way of implying that she has less skill than her male counterpart (i.e., "She's not very smart, but she tries hard").

This possibility comes into clear focus when we examine a similar study (Deaux & Emsweiler, 1974). Male and female

"No, this is not Mel's secretary. This is Mel."

students were shown a highly successful performance on a complex task by a fellow student and were asked how it came about. When a man succeeded, both male and female students attributed his achievement almost entirely to his ability; when it was a woman who succeeded, students of *both* genders thought the achievement was largely a matter of luck. Apparently, if the sexual stereotype is strong enough, even members of the stereotyped group tend to buy it.

Again, this research was done three decades ago. American society has undergone a great many changes since then. Have these changes affected the stereotypes held of women? Not so you'd notice. In a careful analysis of some 58 more recent experiments Janet Swim and Lawrence Sanna (1996) found that the results were remarkably consistent with the earlier research. Specifically, they found that if a man was successful on a given task, observers of both sexes attributed his success to ability; if a woman was successful at that same task, observers attributed her success to hard work. If a man failed on a given task, observers attributed his failure either to bad luck or to lower effort; if a woman failed, observers felt the task was simply too hard for her ability level.

Even as children, girls have a tendency to downplay their own ability. In one experiment, while fourth-grade boys attributed their own successful outcomes on a difficult intellectual task to their ability, girls tended to derogate their own successful performance. Moreover, this experiment also showed that while boys had learned to protect their egos by attributing their own failures to bad luck, girls took more of the blame for failures on themselves (Nichols, 1975). In a subsequent study, the tendency girls have to downplay their own ability appeared most prevalent in traditionally male domains like math (Stipek & Gralinski, 1991). Specifically, junior high school girls attributed their success on a math exam to luck, while boys attributed their success to ability. Girls also showed less feelings of pride than boys following success on a math exam.

These self-defeating beliefs do not develop in a vacuum. They can be influenced by the attitudes of our society in general and, most powerfully, by the most important people in the young girl's life—her parents. In this regard, Janis Jacobs and Jacquelynne Eccles (1992) explored the influence of mothers' gender-stereotypical beliefs on the way these same mothers perceived the abilities of their 11- and 12-year-old sons and daughters. The researchers then tested to see what impact this might have on the children's perceptions of their own abilities. As you might predict, mothers who held the strongest gender-stereotypical beliefs also believed that their own daughters had relatively low math ability and that their sons had relatively high math ability. Mothers who did not hold stereotypical beliefs did not see their daughters as less able in math than their sons. How did the mothers' beliefs affect the beliefs of their children? The daughters of women with strong gender stereotypes believed that they had poor math ability; the opposite was true as well: Mothers who did not hold strong gender stereotypes had daughters without this self-defeating mind-set. This is an interesting variation on the self-fulfilling prophecy discussed in Chapters 3 and 4: Here, if your mother doesn't expect you to do well, chances are you will not do as well as you otherwise might.

Discrimination: The Behavioral Component   "歧视"：行为要素

This brings us to the final component of prejudice—the action component. Stereotypical beliefs often result in unfair treatment. We call this **discrimination:** an unjustified negative or harmful action toward the members of a group simply because of their membership in that group.

If you are a fourth-grade math teacher and you have the stereotypical belief that little girls are hopeless at math, you might be less likely to spend as much time in the classroom coaching a girl than coaching a boy. If you are a police officer and you have the stereotypical belief that African Americans are more violent than whites, this might affect your behavior toward a specific black man you are trying to arrest.

Discrimination
Unjustified negative or harmful action toward a member of a group simply because of his or her membership in that group

In one study, researchers compared the treatment of patients in a psychiatric hospital run by an all-white professional staff (Bond, DiCandia, & McKinnon, 1988). The results of the study are illustrated in Figure 13.1. The researchers examined the two most common methods used by staff members to handle patients' violent behavior: secluding the individual in a timeout room and restraining the individual in a straitjacket and administering tranquilizing drugs. An examination of hospital records over 85 days revealed that the harsher method—physical and chemical restraint—was used with black patients nearly four times as often as with white patients. This was the case despite the virtual lack of differences in the number of violent incidents committed by the black and the white patients. Moreover, this discriminatory treatment occurred even though the black patients, on being admitted to the hospital, had been diagnosed as slightly less violent than the white patients.

This study did uncover an important positive finding: After several weeks, reality managed to overcome the effects of the existing stereotype. The staff eventually noticed that the black and the white patients did not differ in their degree of violent behavior, and they began to treat black and white patients equally. Although this is encouraging, the overall meaning of the study is both clear and disconcerting: The existing stereotype resulted in undeserved, harsher initial treatment of black patients by trained professionals. At the same time, the fact that reality overcame the stereotype is a tribute to the professionalism of the staff because, as we shall see, in most cases deeply rooted prejudice, stereotypes, and discrimination are not easy to change.

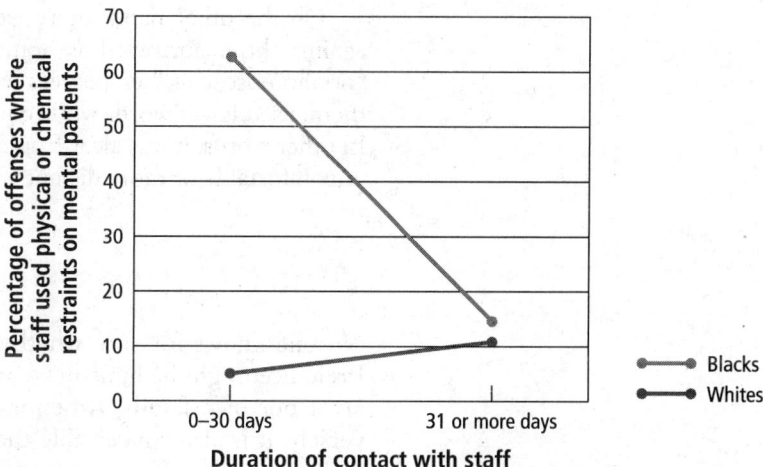

FIGURE 13.1

Use of extreme measures against black mental patients.

During the first 30 days of confinement, there appeared to be an assumption that blacks would be more violent than whites.

(Adapted from Bond, DiCandia, & McKennon, 1988)

Discrimination against Homosexuals In the summer of 2003, the Supreme Court struck down state laws against sodomy, echoing the softening attitudes towards homosexuality in American society. Nevertheless, several studies during the past two decades have shown that homosexuals face a good deal of discrimination and antipathy in their day-to-day lives (Fernald, 1995; Franklin, 2000; Herek, 1991).

Unlike women, ethnic minorities, and people with disabilities, homosexuals are not protected by national laws banning discrimination in the workplace, and only 11 states have such laws. So it would seem that homosexuals would be vulnerable to job discrimination. If you were applying for a job, how would you be treated by your potential employers if they had prior information that you were a homosexual? Would they refuse to hire you? Would they treat you with less warmth than they treat heterosexuals?

In a field experiment, Michelle Hebl and her colleagues (Hebl, Foster, Mannix, & Dovidio, 2002) tried to find out. Sixteen college students (eight males and eight females), who were actually confederates of the experimenters, applied for jobs at local stores. In some of their interviews, they were portrayed as being homosexual; in others, they were not. To standardize the interactions, the applicants were all dressed similarly in jeans and pullover jackets.

The researchers looked at two kinds of discrimination: formal discrimination and interpersonal discrimination. To gauge formal discrimination, they sought to determine if there were differences in what the employer said about the availability of jobs, differences in whether the employer allowed them to fill out a job application, differences in whether or not they received a callback, and differences in the employer's response to a request to use the bathroom. There was no evidence of discrimination against those portrayed as homosexuals. The employers could not be accused of treating "homosexual" applicants unjustly.

> *Prejudices are the props of civilization.*
>
> —Andre Gide, 1939

On the other hand, there were strong indications of interpersonal discrimination against those portrayed as homosexuals. Compared to the way they interacted with "nonhomosexuals," employers were less verbally positive, spent less time interviewing them, used fewer words while chatting with them, and made less eye contact with them. In other words, it was clear from their behavior that the potential employers were either uncomfortable or more distant with people they believed to be homosexual.

What Causes Prejudice? 偏见的起因

No one knows for sure whether or not prejudice is part of our biological makeup. Prejudice might be built-in—part of our biological survival mechanism inducing us to favor our own family, tribe, or race and to express hostility toward outsiders. Conversely, it is also conceivable that humans are naturally inclined to be friendly, open, and cooperative. If this were the case, prejudice would not come naturally. Rather, the culture (parents, community, the media) might intentionally or unintentionally instruct us to assign negative qualities to people who are different from us.

While social psychologists do not agree on whether or not humans are naturally prejudiced, most would agree that *the specifics* of prejudice must be learned. Even when young children pick up their parents' prejudices, they do not necessarily retain those prejudices in adulthood. Indeed, when researchers examined the similarity of attitudes and values of parents and their adult children, they discovered an interesting pattern (Rohan & Zanna, 1996). They found that when parents held egalitarian attitudes and values, their adult children did as well. But when parents held prejudice-related attitudes and values, their adult children were less likely to hold the same views. Why would this be true? It is likely that the discrepancy occurs because the culture as a whole is more egalitarian than the bigoted parents. So when children of bigoted parents leave home (e.g., to go off to college), they are more likely to be exposed to competing views.

At the same time, it is reasonably clear that children can be taught prejudice. Jane Elliot (1977), a third-grade teacher in Riceville, Iowa, was concerned that her young students' lives were too sheltered. The children all lived in rural Iowa, they were all white, and they were all Christian. Elliot felt it was important for their development to give them some direct experience about what stereotyping and discrimination felt like from both sides. To achieve this end, she divided her class by eye color. She told her students that blue-eyed people were superior to brown-eyed people—smarter, nicer, more trustworthy, and so on. The brown-eyed youngsters were required to wear special cloth collars around their necks so that they would be instantly recognizable as a member of the inferior group. She gave special privileges to the blue-eyed youngsters: They got to play longer at recess, could have second helpings at the cafeteria, were praised in the classroom, and so on. How did the children respond?

In just hours, Elliot created a microcosm of a prejudiced society in her classroom. The children had been a cooperative, cohesive group, but once the seeds of divisiveness were planted, there was trouble. The "superior" blue-eyed kids made fun of the brown-eyed kids, refused to play with them, tattled on them to the teacher, thought up new restrictions and punishments for them, and even started a fistfight in the schoolyard. The "inferior" brown-eyed kids became self-conscious, depressed, and demoralized. They performed poorly on classroom tests that day.

The next day, Elliot switched the stereotypes about eye color. She said she'd made a dreadful mistake—that brown-eyed people were really the superior ones. She told the brown-eyed kids to put their collars on the blue-eyed kids.

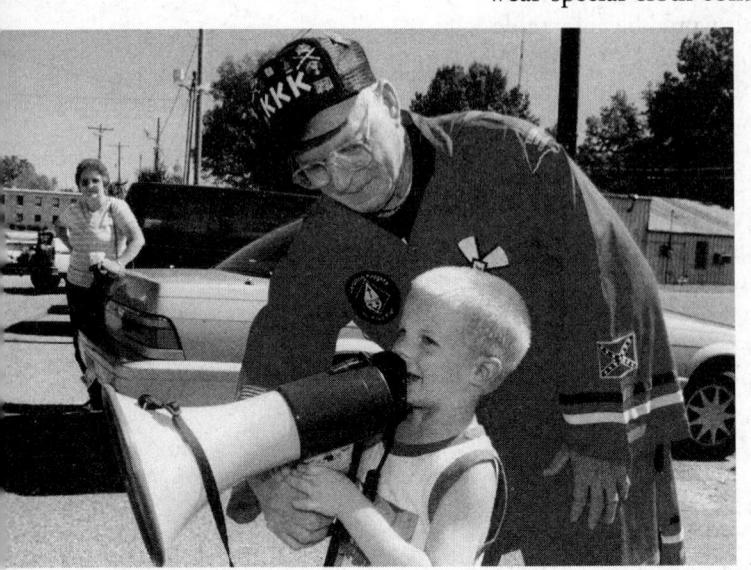

Children often learn prejudice from parents and grandparents.

They gleefully did so. The tables had turned—and the brown-eyed kids exacted their revenge.

On the morning of the third day, Elliot explained to her students that they had been learning about prejudice and discrimination and how it feels to be a person of color in this society. The children discussed the two-day experience and clearly understood its message. In a follow-up, Elliot met with these students at a class reunion, when they were in their mid-twenties. Their memories of the exercise were startlingly clear—they reported that the experience had had a powerful and lasting impact on their lives. They felt that they were less prejudiced and more aware of discrimination against others because of this childhood experience.

> *The world is full of pots jeering at kettles.*
>
> —Francois de la Rochefoucauld, *Maxims*, 1665

The Way We Think: Social Cognition 我们的思维方式：社会认知

Our first explanation for what causes prejudice is that it is the inevitable by product of the way we process and organize information—in other words, it is the dark side of human social cognition (see Chapter 3). Our tendency to categorize and group information, to form schemas and use them to interpret new or unusual information, to rely on potentially inaccurate heuristics (shortcuts in mental reasoning), and to depend on what are often faulty memory processes—all of these aspects of social cognition can lead us to form negative stereotypes and to apply them in a discriminatory way. Let's examine this dark side of social cognition more closely.

Social Categorization: Us versus Them The first step in prejudice is the creation of groups—putting some people into one group based on certain characteristics and others into another group based on their different characteristics. This kind of categorization is the underlying theme of human social cognition (Brewer & Brown, 1998; Rosch & Lloyd, 1978; Taylor, 1981; Wilder, 1986). For example, we make sense out of the physical world by grouping animals and plants into taxonomies based on their physical characteristics; similarly, we make sense out of our social world by grouping people according to other characteristics, including gender, nationality, ethnicity, and so on. When we encounter people with these characteristics, we rely on our perceptions of what people with similar characteristics have been like in the past to help us determine how to react to someone else with the same characteristics (Andersen & Klatzky, 1987). Thus social categorization is both useful and necessary; however, this simple cognitive process has profound implications.

For example, in Jane Elliot's third-grade classroom, children grouped according to eye color began to act differently based on that social categorization. Blue-eyed children, the superior group, stuck together and actively promoted and used their higher status and power in the classroom. They formed an in-group, defined as the group with which an individual identifies. The blue-eyed kids saw the brown-eyed ones as outsiders—different and inferior. To the blue-eyed children, the brown-eyed kids were the out-group, the group with which the individual does not identify.

In-Group Bias Kurt Vonnegut captures the in-group versus out-group concept beautifully in his novel *Cat's Cradle* (1963). A woman discovers that a person she has just met, casually, on a plane is from Indiana. Even though they have almost nothing else in common, a bond immediately forms between them:

"My God," she said, "are you a Hoosier?"

I admitted I was.

"I'm a Hoosier too," she crowed. "Nobody has to be ashamed of being a Hoosier."

"I'm not," I said. "I never knew anybody who was." (pp. 42–43)

What is the mechanism that produces this in-group bias—positive feelings and special treatment for people we have defined as being part of our in-group and negative feelings and unfair treatment for others simply because we have defined them as

Wearing our school colors is a way of demonstrating that we are a member of the in-group.

being in the out-group? The British social psychologist Henri Tajfel (1982a) discovered that the major underlying motive is self-esteem: Individuals seek to enhance their self-esteem by identifying with specific social groups. Yet self-esteem will be enhanced only if the individual sees these groups as superior to other groups. Thus, for members of the Ku Klux Klan, it is not enough to believe that the races should be kept separate; they must convince themselves of the supremacy of the white race in order to feel good about themselves.

To get at the pure, unvarnished mechanisms behind this phenomenon, Tajfel and his colleagues have created entities that they refer to as *minimal groups* (Tajfel, 1982a; Tajfel & Billig, 1974; Tajfel & Turner, 1979). In these experiments, complete strangers are formed into groups using the most trivial criteria imaginable. For example, in one experiment, participants watched a coin toss that randomly assigned them to either group X or group W. In another experiment, participants were first asked to express their opinions about artists they had never heard of and were then randomly assigned to a group that appreciated either the "Klee style" or the "Kandinsky style," ostensibly due to their picture preferences. The striking thing about this research is that despite the fact that the participants were strangers before the experiment and didn't interact with one another during it, they behaved as if those who shared the same meaningless label were their dear friends or close kin. They liked the members of their own group better; they rated the members of their in-group as more likely to have pleasant personalities and to have done better work than out-group members. Most striking, the participants allocated more money and other rewards to those who shared their label and did so in a rather hostile, cutthroat manner—for example, when given a clear choice, they preferred to give themselves only two dollars, if it meant giving the out-group person one dollar, over giving themselves three dollars, if that meant the out-group member received four dollars (Brewer, 1979; Hogg & Abrams, 1988; Mullen, Brown, & Smith, 1992; Wilder, 1981).

In short, even when the reasons for differentiation are minimal, being in the in-group makes you want to win against members of the out-group and leads you to treat the latter unfairly because such tactics build your self-esteem. And when your group does win, it strengthens your feelings of pride and identification with that group. How do you feel about being a student of your university following a winning or losing football season? You probably think it doesn't matter much—and it probably doesn't, in the long run. But Robert Cialdini and his colleagues (1976; Cialdini, 1993) discovered something very interesting. They simply counted the number of college insignia T-shirts and sweatshirts worn to classes on the Monday following a football game at seven different universities. The results? You guessed it: Students were more likely to wear their university's insignia after victory than after defeat.

Out-Group Homogeneity Besides the in-group bias, another consequence of social categorization is the perception of **out-group homogeneity**, the belief that "they" are all alike (Linville, Fischer, & Salovey, 1989; Quattrone, 1986). In-group members tend to perceive those in the out-group as more similar to each other (homogeneous) than they really are, as well as more homogeneous than the in-group members are. Does your college have a traditional rival, whether in athletics or academics? If so, as an in-group member, you probably value your institution more highly than this rival (thereby raising and protecting your self-esteem), and you probably perceive students at this rival school to be more similar to each other (e.g., as a given type) than you perceive students at your own college to be.

Consider a study of students in two rival universities: Princeton and Rutgers (Quattrone & Jones, 1980). The rivalry between these colleges is based on athletics, academics, and even class consciousness (Princeton is private and Rutgers is public). Male research participants at the two schools watched videotaped scenes in which

Out-Group Homogeneity
The perception that individuals in the out-group are more similar to each other (homogeneous) than they really are, as well as more similar than the members of the in-group are

three different young men were asked to make a decision—for example, in one videotape, an experimenter asked a man whether he wanted to listen to rock music or classical music while he participated in an experiment on auditory perception. The participants were told that the man was either a Princeton or a Rutgers student, so for some of them the student in the videotape was an in-group member and for others an out-group member. Participants had to predict what the man in the videotape would choose. After they saw the man make his choice (e.g., rock or classical music), they were asked to predict what percentage of male students at that institution would make the same choice. Did the predictions vary due to the in- or out-group status of the target men? As you can see in Figure 13.2, the results support the out-group homogeneity hypothesis: When the target person was an out-group member, the participants believed his choice was more predictive of what his peers would choose than when he was an in-group member (a student at their own school). In other words, if you know something about one out-group member, you are more likely to feel you know something about all of them. Similar results have been found in a wide variety of experiments in the United States, Europe, and Australia (Duck, Hogg, & Terry, 1995; Hartstone & Augoustinos, 1995; Judd & Park, 1988; Ostrom & Sedikides, 1992; Park & Rothbart, 1982).

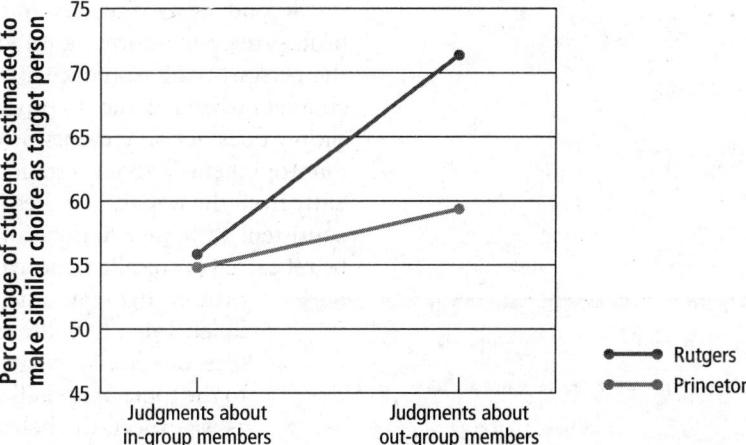

FIGURE 13.2
Judgments about in-group and out-group members.

After watching the target person make a choice between two alternatives, participants were asked to estimate what percentage of students at their school (in-group) and their rival school (out-group) would make the same choice. An out-group homogeneity bias was found: Students' estimates for out-group members were higher (greater similarity) than for in-group members.

(Adapted from Quattrone & Jones, 1980)

The Failure of Logic If you've ever argued with people holding deep-seated prejudices, you know how hard it is to get them to change their minds. Even people who are usually sensible and reasonable about most topics become relatively immune to rational, logical arguments when it comes to the topic of their prejudice. Why is this so? There are two reasons, involving the affective and cognitive aspects of an attitude. First, it is primarily the emotional aspect of attitudes that makes a prejudiced person so hard to argue with; logical arguments are not effective in countering emotions. The difficulty of using reason to change prejudiced attitudes is beautifully illustrated by Gordon Allport in his landmark book *The Nature of Prejudice* (1954). Allport reports a dialogue between Mr. X and Mr. Y:

> *Mr. X:* The trouble with the Jews is that they only take care of their own group.
>
> *Mr. Y:* But the record of the Community Chest campaign shows that they gave more generously, in proportion to their numbers, to the general charities of the community than did non-Jews.
>
> *Mr. X:* That shows they are always trying to buy favor and intrude into Christian affairs. They think of nothing but money; that is why there are so many Jewish bankers.
>
> *Mr. Y:* But a recent study shows that the percentage of Jews in the banking business is negligible, far smaller than the percentage of non-Jews.
>
> *Mr. X:* That's just it; they don't go in for respectable business; they are only in the movie business or run night clubs. (pp. 13–14)

Because Mr. X is emotionally caught up in his beliefs about Jews, his responses are not logical. In effect, the prejudiced Mr. X is saying, "Don't trouble me with facts; my mind is made up." Rather than refuting the powerful data presented by Mr. Y, he distorts the facts so that they support his hatred of Jews, or he simply ignores them and initiates a new line of attack. The prejudiced attitude remains intact, despite the fact that the specific arguments Mr. X began with are now lying in tatters at his feet.

> *Our minds thus grow in spots; and like grease spots, the spots spread. But we let them spread as little as possible; we keep unaltered as much of our old knowledge, as many of our old prejudices and beliefs, as we can.*
>
> —William James, 1907

Second, as we discussed in earlier chapters, an attitude tends to organize the way we process relevant information about the targets of that attitude. This presents difficulties for the person trying to reduce a friend's prejudice. None of us is a 100 percent reliable accountant when it comes to processing social information we care about. The human mind simply does not tally events objectively. Accordingly, individuals who hold specific opinions (or schemas) about certain groups will process information about those groups differently from the way they process information about other groups. Specifically, information consistent with their notions about these target groups will be given more attention, will be rehearsed (or recalled) more often, and will therefore be remembered better than information that contradicts these notions (Bodenhausen, 1988; Dovidio, Evans, & Tyler, 1986; O'Sullivan & Durso, 1984; Wyer, 1988). These are the familiar effects of *schematic processing* that we discussed in Chapter 4. Applying these effects to the topic of prejudice, we can see that whenever a member of a group behaves as we expect, the behavior confirms and even strengthens our stereotype. Thus stereotypes become relatively impervious to change; after all, proof that they are accurate is always out there—when our beliefs guide us to see it.

> *The mind of a bigot is like the pupil of the eye; the more light you pour upon it, the more it will contract.*
>
> —Oliver Wendell Holmes Jr., 1901

The Persistence of Stereotypes Stereotypes reflect cultural beliefs—within a given society, they are easily recognized descriptions of members of a particular group. For example, we all know the stereotype of the woman driver or the overemotional female. Even if we don't believe these stereotypes, we can easily recognize them as common beliefs held by others. For example, in a series of studies conducted at Princeton University over a span of 36 years (1933–1969), students were asked to assign traits to members of various ethnic and national groups (Gilbert, 1951; Karlins, Coffman, & Walters, 1969; Katz & Braly, 1933). The participants could do so easily, and to a large extent they agreed with each other. They knew the stereotypes, even for groups about whom they had little real knowledge, such as Turks. Table 13.1 shows

TABLE 13.1	Some Common Stereotypes Held by Princeton Students over the Years		
Note the general stability as well as changes in these stereotypes.			
Group	**1933**	**1951**	**1969**
Americans	industrious	materialistic	materialistic
	intelligent	intelligent	ambitious
	materialistic	industrious	pleasure-loving
	ambitious	pleasure-loving	industrious
	progressive	individualistic	conventional
Japanese	intelligent	imitative	industrious
	industrious	sly	ambitious
	progressive	extremely	efficient
	shrewd	nationalistic	intelligent
	sly	treacherous	progressive
Jews	shrewd	shrewd	ambitious
	mercenary	intelligent	materialistic
	industrious	industrious	intelligent
	grasping	mercenary	industrious
	intelligent	ambitious	shrewd
Negroes (African Americans)	superstitious	superstitious	musical
	lazy	musical	happy-go-lucky
	happy-go-lucky	lazy	lazy
	ignorant	ignorant	pleasure-loving
	musical	pleasure-loving	ostentatious
Adapted from Gilbert (1951); Karlins, Coffman, & Walters (1969); Katz & Braly (1933).			

some of the results of these studies. Note how negative the early stereotypes were in 1933 and how they became somewhat less negative over time. What is particularly interesting about these studies is that participants in 1951 began to voice discomfort with the task (discomfort that didn't exist in 1933). By 1969, many participants not only felt discomfort but also seemed reluctant to admit that these stereotypes even existed because they did not believe the stereotypes themselves (Karlins et al., 1969). A quarter of a century later, Patricia Devine and Andrew Elliot (1995) showed that the stereotypes were not really fading at all; virtually all the participants were fully aware of the negative stereotypes of African Americans, whether they believed them personally or not.

The Activation of Stereotypes This brings us to an intriguing social cognition puzzle: If you know a stereotype, will it affect your cognitive processing about a target person, even if you neither believe the stereotype nor consider yourself prejudiced against this group? Imagine this scenario: You are a member of a group, judging another person's performance. Someone in your group makes an ugly, stereotypical comment about the individual. Will the comment affect your judgment of his or her performance? "No," you are probably thinking. "I'd disregard it completely." But would you be able to do so? Is it possible that the comment would trigger in your mind all the other negative stereotypes and beliefs about people in that group and affect your judgment about this particular person?

"It's a cat calendar, so it may not be all that accurate."

Copyright © The New Yorker Collection 1995 Jack Ziegler from cartoonbank.com. All Rights Reserved

Attempting to find out, researchers had two confederates, one African American and one white, stage a debate about nuclear energy for groups of participants (Greenberg & Pyszczynski, 1985). For half the groups, the African American debater presented far better arguments and clearly won the debate; for the other half, the white debater performed far better and won the debate. The participants were asked to rate both debaters' skill; however, just before subjects were to do this, the critical experimental manipulation occurred. A confederate planted in the group did one of three things: (1) He made a highly racist remark about the African American debater—"There's no way that nigger won the debate"; (2) he made a nonracist remark about the African American debater—"There's no way the pro (or con) debater won the debate"; or (3) he made no comment at all.

The researchers reasoned that if those participants who heard the racist comment were able to disregard it completely, they would not rate the African American debater any differently from the way participants in the other conditions, who had not heard such a comment, rated him. Was that the case? Figure 13.3 clearly shows that the answer is no. The data compared the ratings of skill given to the African American and white debaters when they were each in the losing role. As you can see, the participants rated the African American and white debaters as equally skillful when no comment was made; similarly, when a nonracist, nonstereotypical comment was made about the African American debater, he was rated as being just as skillful as the white debater. After the racist comment evoked racial

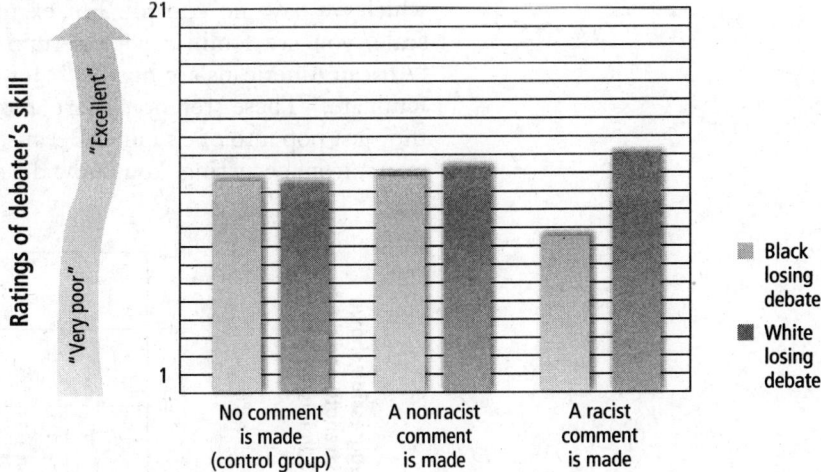

FIGURE 13.3
Activation of stereotypical belief.

When a derogatory comment was made about the black debater, it activated the latent stereotype held by the observers, causing them to lower their rating of his performance.
(Adapted from Greenberg & Pyszczynski, 1985)

stereotypes, however, participants rated the African American debater *significantly lower* than participants in the other groups did. Why? The derogatory comment activated other negative stereotypes about African Americans so that those who heard it rated the same performance by the debater as less skilled than those who had not heard the racist remark. This phenomenon has been referred to as implicit prejudice—where negative stereotyping operates below the person's level of conscious awareness (Greenwald, Nosek, & Banaji, 2003).

In a similar study, all it took was one negative action by one African American (actually a confederate of the experimenters) to activate the negative stereotypes against blacks and to discourage the participants from wanting to interact with a different African American (Henderson-King & Nisbett, 1996). These findings suggest that in most of us, stereotypes lurk just beneath the surface. It doesn't take much to activate the stereotype, and once activated, it can have dire consequences for how a particular member of that out-group is perceived and treated.

This process is demonstrated powerfully by an experiment by Rogers and Prentice-Dunn (1981): White students were told they would be inflicting electric shock on another student, the "learner," whom they were told was either white or African American, as part of an apparent study of biofeedback. The students initially gave a lower intensity of shock to black learners than to white ones—reflecting a desire, perhaps, to show they were not prejudiced. The students then overheard the learner making derogatory comments about them, which, naturally, made them angry. Now, given another opportunity to inflict electric shock, the students who were working with a black learner administered higher levels of shock than did students who worked with a white one (see Figure 13.4). The same result appears in studies of how English-speaking Canadians behave toward French-speaking Canadians, straights toward homosexuals, non-Jewish students toward Jews, and men toward women. Participants successfully suppress their negative feelings under normal conditions, but as soon as they become angry or frustrated, or their self-esteem wobbles, they express their implicit prejudice directly because now they can *justify* it. *I'm not a bad or prejudiced person, but hey! He insulted me!*

Automatic and Controlled Processing of Stereotypes How does this activation process work? Patricia Devine and her colleagues argue that members of society share an archive of accessible stereotypes, even if they do not believe them. Devine differentiates between the automatic processing of information and the controlled processing of information (Devine, 1989a; Devine, Plant, Amodio, Harmon-Jones, & Vance, 2002; Zuwerink, Montieth, Devine, & Cook, 1996). An automatic process is one over which we have no control. For example, even if you score very low on a prejudice scale, you are familiar with certain stereotypes that exist in the culture, such as "African Americans are hostile," "Jews are materialistic," or "homosexual men are effeminate." These stereotypes are automatically triggered under certain conditions—they just pop into one's mind. Because the process is automatic, you can't control it or stop it from occurring. You know the stereotypes, and they simply come to mind—say,

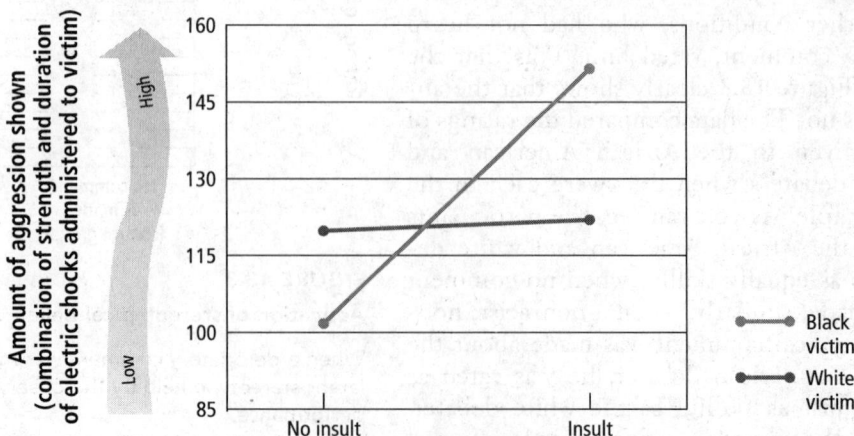

FIGURE 13.4
The unleashing of prejudice against African Americans.

(Adapted from Rogers & Prentice-Dunn, 1981)

when you are meeting someone or rating a person's performance. For people who are not deeply prejudiced, however, their control processes can suppress or override these stereotypes. For example, such a person can think, "Hey, that stereotype isn't fair and it isn't right—African Americans are no more hostile than whites. Ignore the stereotype about this person's ethnicity."

What Devine's theory suggests, therefore, is a two-step model of cognitive processing: The automatic processing brings up information—in this case, stereotypes—but the controlled (or conscious) processing can refute or ignore it. But what happens if you are busy, overwhelmed, distracted, or not paying much attention? You may not initiate that controlled level of processing, meaning that the information supplied by the automatic process—the stereotype—is still in your mind and unrefuted. Devine (1989a) set out to study exactly this process: A stereotype is automatically activated when a member of an out-group is encountered, and the stereotype can be ignored through conscious processing—for example, by people who are not prejudiced (see Figure 13.5).

First, Devine administered a test of prejudice to a large number of students and, according to their scores, divided them into high-prejudice and low-prejudice groups. Next, she demonstrated that regardless of prejudice, both groups possessed equal knowledge of racial stereotypes. Next came the test of automatic and conscious processing: She flashed stereotyped words (e.g., *black, hostile, lazy, welfare*) and neutral words (e.g., *however, what, said*) on a screen so quickly that the words were just below the participants' perceptual (conscious) awareness. They saw something, but they weren't sure what—that is, their conscious processing couldn't identify the words; however, their automatic processing could recognize the words; how could Devine be sure?

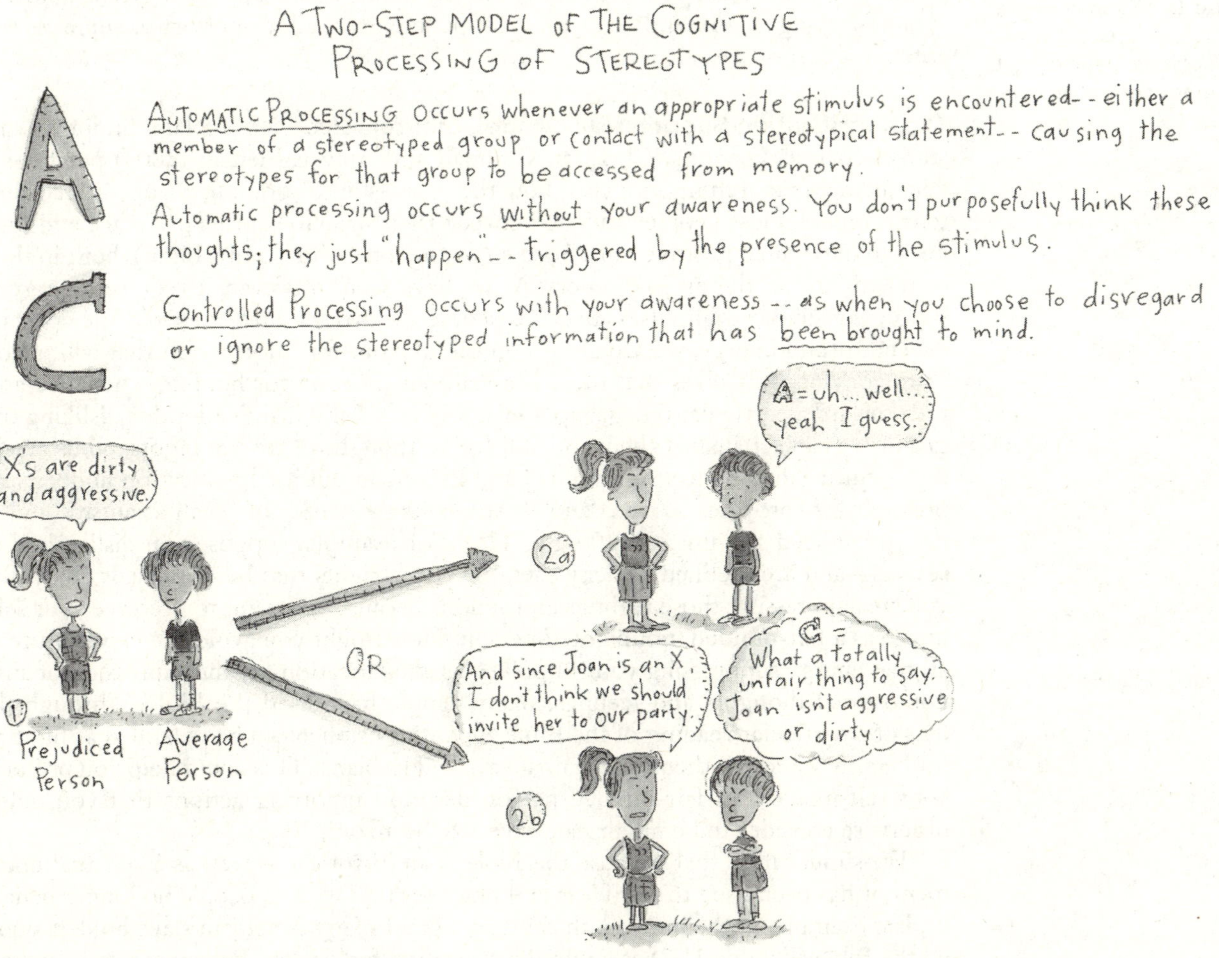

FIGURE 13.5

A two-step model of the cognitive processing of stereotypes.

According to Patricia Devine's theory, we exhibit both automatic and controlled processing of information. So even though your automatic response to this man might reflect prejudice, you could override the stereotypes behind that response by more controlled processing.

After flashing the words, she asked the participants to read a story about "Donald" (his ethnicity was not mentioned) and to rate their impressions of him. Donald was described somewhat ambiguously; he did some things in the story that could be interpreted either positively or negatively. The participants who had seen the words reflecting the stereotype of black Americans interpreted Donald significantly more negatively than those who had seen the neutral words did. Thus for one group the negative stereotype had been primed (activated unconsciously through automatic processing); without their awareness, the participants were affected by these hostile and negative words, as indicated in their ratings of the Donald character. Because these stereotypes were operating outside their conscious cognitive control, white students who were low in prejudice were just as influenced by the cultural stereotype (e.g., that blacks are hostile) as the prejudiced students.

In her final experiment, Devine gave the students a task that involved their conscious processing: She asked them to list all the words they could think of that are used to describe black Americans. The high-prejudice students listed significantly more negative words than the low-prejudice students did. In other words, the less prejudiced participants used their conscious processing to edit out the negative stereotype and therefore were able to respond in a manner that was relatively free of its influence.

Devine's work sheds a lot of light on stereotyping and the ways in which people deal with it. According to Devine, almost all white people in American society have learned the negative stereotype of African Americans. This negative stereotype is therefore activated automatically in just about everyone. Accordingly, to avoid behaving in a prejudiced way, most people exert a lot of effort to suppress this automatic response.

The Justification-Suppression Model of Prejudice To explain findings from studies such as Devine's, Christian Crandall and Amy Eshleman (2003) put forth a convincing, overarching model of how the expression of prejudice works. According to this model, most people struggle between their urge to express prejudice and their need to maintain a positive self-concept (as someone who is not a bigot), both in their own eyes and in the eyes of others. As we have seen, however, it requires energy to suppress prejudiced impulses. Because people are programmed to avoid the constant expenditure of energy, we are always on the lookout for information that will enable us to convince ourselves that there is a valid justification for holding a negative attitude toward a particular out-group. Once we find a valid justification for disliking this group, we can act against them and still feel as though we are not bigots—thus avoiding cognitive dissonance. As Crandall and Eshleman put it, "Justification undoes suppression, it provides cover, and it protects a sense of egalitarianism and a non-prejudiced self-image" (2003, p. 425). For example, suppose you dislike homosexuals—and are inclined to deny them the same rights that heterosexuals enjoy. But you are suppressing those feelings and actions because you want to preserve your self-image as a fair-minded, nonbigoted person. How might you avoid the expenditure of all that energy suppressing your impulse? As a justification for the expression of anti-homosexual thoughts and feelings, many people have used the Bible. Through the lens of a particular reading of the Bible, an antigay stance can be defended as fighting for "family values" rather than against gays and lesbians. This could help you preserve your self-image as a fair-minded person despite supporting actions that you might otherwise consider to be unfair (see Myers & Scanzoni, 2006).

We should note that because the Bible is an historical as well as a spiritual document, it has been used to justify several practices that we as a people no longer believe in. For example, in the nineteenth century, a great many American slave holders quoted the Bible (Exodus 21:7) as a moral justification for slavery. Prominent among these was the Reverend Thornton Stringfellow of Virginia, a distinguished theologian, who wrote a treatise (1841) designed to "rebut the palpable ignorance" of Northerners who were denouncing slavery as a sin. On the contrary, he wrote, "From Abraham's day, until the coming of Christ, a period of two thousand years, this institution found favor with God." He went on to argue that Jesus accepted slavery and never spoke out against it. Needless to say, biblical teachings about love and justice have also informed and motivated the proliferation of hospitals, the founding of universities, and the fight to abolish slavery. As Gordon Allport (1954, p. 444) wrote, "The role of religion is paradoxical. It makes prejudice and it unmakes prejudice."

The Illusory Correlation Another way that our cognitive processing perpetuates stereotypical thinking is through the phenomenon of **illusory correlation** (Fiedler, 2000; Garcia-Marques & Hamilton, 1996; Shavitt, Sanbonmatsu, Smittipatana, & Posavac, 1999). When we expect two things to be related, we fool ourselves into believing that they are—even when they are actually unrelated. Many illusory correlations exist in our society. For example, there is a common belief that couples who haven't been able to have children will conceive a child after they adopt a child—apparently because after the adoption, they feel less anxious and stressed. Guess what: This correlation is entirely illusory. Occasionally, an "infertile" couple does conceive after adopting a child, but this occurs with no greater frequency than for "infertile" couples who do not adopt. The former event, because it is so charmingly vivid, simply makes more of an impression on us when it happens, creating the illusory correlation (Gilovich, 1991).

What does all this have to do with prejudice and stereotypes? Illusory correlations are most likely to occur when the events or people are distinctive or conspicuous—that is, when they are different from the run-of-the-mill, typical social scene we are accustomed to (Hamilton, 1981; Hamilton, Stroessner, & Mackie, 1993). Minority group members—for example, as defined by race—are, by definition, distinctive because fewer of them are present in the society. Other groups who are not distinctive in terms of numbers—such as women, who make up 50 percent of the species—may nonetheless become distinctive or conspicuous because of a nonstereotypical profession or talent—for example, a woman member of the U.S. Senate. David Hamilton and Robert Gifford (1976) have shown that such distinctiveness leads to the creation of and belief in an illusory correlation—a relationship between the distinctive target person and the behavior he or she displays. This illusory correlation is then applied to all members of the target group.

Illusory Correlation
The tendency to see relationships, or correlations, between events that are actually unrelated

Is the stereotype of African American women changing?

How does this work in everyday life? Let's say you don't know many Jews, so for you, interacting with a Jew is a distinctive event and for you, Jews in general are distinctive people. Let's say you meet a Jewish individual who is an investment banker. Let's say you meet a second Jew who is an economist. An illusory correlation between Jews and money is created. If you also are aware of the stereotype that Jews are materialistic, the correlation you perceived based on your personal experiences seems all the more sound. The result is that in the future, you will be more likely to notice situations in which Jews are behaving materialistically, you will be less likely to notice situations in which Jews are not behaving materialistically, and you will be less likely to notice situations in which non-Jews are behaving materialistically. You will have processed new information guided by your illusory correlation, seeing what you expect to see. You will also have strengthened your illusory correlation, confirming in your mind that your stereotype is right (Hamilton & Sherman, 1989; Mullen & Johnson, 1988).

A fanatic is one who can't change his mind and won't change the subject.
—Winston Churchill, 1944

We should note that illusory correlations are created in a far more passive fashion, too. It is not necessary to have personal experience with people in a distinctive group—television, newspapers, and other media create illusory correlations when they portray women, minorities, and other groups in stereotypical roles (Busby, 1975; Deaux & La France, 1998; Friedman, 1977; McArthur & Resko, 1975).

Can We Change Stereotypical Beliefs? How do you get people to change their negative stereotypical beliefs? Would simply providing them with accurate information refute their stereotypes? Unfortunately, it's not that simple. Let's say your next-door neighbor believes that Asian Americans are unpatriotic. What if you informed him that the most highly decorated combat unit in World War II was composed solely of Asian Americans? Would this information affect your neighbor's stereotypes?

Not necessarily. Researchers have found that when people are presented with an example or two that seems to refute their existing stereotype, most of them do not change their general belief. Indeed, in one experiment, some people presented with this kind of disconfirming evidence actually *strengthened* their stereotypical belief because the disconfirming evidence challenged them to come up with additional reasons for holding on to that belief (Kunda & Oleson, 1997).

It *is* possible to change a stereotype; a great deal depends on how the disconfirming information is presented. Research has shown that when you present people with only two or three powerful disconfirming pieces of evidence, it is not effective because participants simply dismiss the disconfirming examples as "the exceptions that prove the rule." But when the participants are bombarded with many examples that are inconsistent with the stereotype, they gradually modify their beliefs (Webber & Crocker, 1983).

To sum up this discussion, two points need to be emphasized: (1) We all stereotype others to some extent—it is part of being a cognitive miser—and (2) emotional attitudes are harder to change than nonemotional ones. Thus a strongly prejudiced person engages in stereotyping in a deeper, more thorough manner than the rest of us. Through this process, prejudiced attitudes become like a fortress—a closed circuit of cognitions, if you will—and this fortress drastically reduces the effectiveness of logical argument or scattered pieces of disconfirming information.

The cause is hidden, but the result is known.
—Ovid, first century C.E.

How We Assign Meaning: Attributional Biases
如何赋予意义：归因偏差

As we discussed in Chapter 4, people and situations don't come with neon signs telling us everything we need to know about them. Instead, we must rely on one aspect of social cognition—attributional processes—to try to understand why people behave as they do. Just as we form attributions to make sense out of one person's behavior, we also make attributions about whole groups of people. As you shall see, the attributional biases we discussed in Chapter 4 come back to haunt us now in a far more damaging and dangerous form: prejudice and discrimination.

Dispositional versus Situational Explanations One reason stereotypes are so insidious and persistent is the human tendency to make dispositional attributions—that is, to leap to the conclusion that a person's behavior is due to some aspect of his or her personality rather than to some aspect of the situation. This is the familiar fundamental attribution error we discussed in Chapter 4. Although attributing people's behavior to their dispositions is often accurate, human behavior is also shaped by situational forces. Relying too heavily on dispositional attributions, therefore, often leads us to make attributional mistakes. Given that this process operates on an individual level, you can only imagine the problems and complications that arise when we overzealously act out the fundamental attribution error for a whole group of people—an out-group.

Can the image of an articulate African American president on the world stage change the old stereotype?

Stereotypes are dispositional attributions—negative ones. Thomas Pettigrew (1979) has called our tendency to make dispositional attributions about an individual's negative behavior to an entire group of people the **ultimate attribution error.** For example, some of the stereotypes that characterize anti-Semitism are the result of Christians committing the fundamental attribution error when interpreting the behavior of Jews. These stereotypes have a long history, extending over several centuries. When the Jews were first forced to flee their homeland during the third Diaspora, some 2,500 years ago, they were not allowed to own land or become artisans in the new regions in which they settled. Needing a livelihood, some eventually took to lending money—one of the few professions to which they were allowed easy access. This choice of occupation was a by-product of restrictive laws in which Christians were not allowed to charge interest to Christians, but Jews were allowed to. However, the fact that Jews could lend money for interest but Christians could not led to a dispositional attribution about Jews: They were interested only in dealing with money and not in "honest" labor, like farming. As this attribution became an ultimate attribution error, Jews were labeled conniving, vicious parasites of the kind dramatized and immortalized by Shakespeare in the character of Shylock in *The Merchant of Venice* or of Fagin in Dickens's *Oliver Twist*. This dispositional stereotype undoubtedly contributed to the barbarous consequences of anti-Semitism in Europe during the 1930s and 1940s, when Hitler's Nazi regime murdered 6 million European Jews, and has persisted even in the face of clear, disconfirming evidence such as that produced by the birth of the state of Israel, where Jews have tilled the soil and made the desert bloom.

Similarly, as we have seen, many Americans hold a stereotype about African American and Hispanic men that involves aggression and the potential for violence—a very powerful dispositional attribution. In one study, college students, playing the role of jurors in a mock trial, were more likely to find a defendant guilty of a given crime simply if his name was Carlos Ramirez rather than Robert Johnson (Bodenhausen, 1988). Thus, any situational information or extenuating circumstances that might have explained the defendant's actions were ignored when the powerful dispositional attribution was stereotypically triggered—in this case, by the Hispanic name.

In another study, researchers set up another dispositional versus situational possibility. College students read fictionalized files on prisoners who were being considered for parole and used that information to make a parole decision (Bodenhausen & Wyer, 1985). Sometimes the crime matched the common stereotype of the offender—for example, when a Hispanic male, Carlos Ramirez, committed assault and battery, or when an upper-class Anglo-American, Ashley Chamberlaine, committed embezzlement. In other instances, the crimes were inconsistent with the stereotypes. When the prisoners' crimes were consistent with participants' stereotypes, the students' recommendations for parole were harsher. Most of the students also ignored additional information that was relevant to a parole decision but was inconsistent with the stereotype, such as evidence of good behavior in prison.

Ultimate Attribution Error
The tendency to make dispositional attributions about an entire group of people

These results indicate that when people conform to our stereotype, we tend to blind ourselves to clues about why they might have behaved as they did. Instead, we assume that something about their character or disposition, and not their situation or life circumstances, caused their behavior. In other words, when the fundamental attribution error rears its ugly head, we make dispositional attributions (based on our stereotypical beliefs about an ethnic or racial group) and not situational ones.

Stereotype Threat There is a statistical difference in academic test performance among various cultural groups in this country. In general, although there is considerable overlap, Asian Americans as a group perform slightly better than Anglo-Americans, who in turn perform better than African Americans. Why does this occur? There may be any number of explanations—economic, cultural, historical, political. One important reason recently discovered has to do with anxiety produced by negative stereotypes. In a striking series of experiments, Claude Steele, Joshua Aronson, and their colleagues have demonstrated that at least one major contributing factor is clearly situational and is based on a phenomenon they call **stereotype threat** (Aronson et al., 1998, 1999; Steele, 1997; Steele & Aronson, 1995a, 1995b). Specifically, when African American students find themselves in highly evaluative educational situations, most tend to experience apprehension about confirming the existing negative cultural stereotype of "intellectual inferiority." In effect, they are saying, "If I perform poorly on this test, it will reflect poorly on me and on my race." This extra burden of apprehension in turn interferes with their ability to perform well in these situations. For example, in one of their experiments, Steele and Aronson administered a difficult verbal test, the GRE, individually to African American and white students at Stanford University. Half the students of each race were led to believe that the investigator was interested in measuring their intellectual ability; the other half were led to believe that the investigator was merely trying to develop the test itself—and because the test was not yet valid or reliable (recall the discussion in Chapter 2), they were assured that their performance would mean nothing in terms of their actual ability. The results confirmed the researchers' speculations. White students performed equally well regardless of whether or not they believed the test was being used as a diagnostic tool. The African American students who believed their abilities were not being measured performed as well as the white students. But the African American students who thought the test *was* measuring their abilities did not perform as well as the white students or as well as the African Americans in the other group. In subsequent experiments in the same series, Steele and Aronson also found that if race is made more salient, the decrease in performance among African Americans is even more pronounced.

The effects of stereotype threat generalize to other performance domains. Jeff Stone and his colleagues (1999) found that when a game of miniature golf was framed as a measure of "sport strategic intelligence," black athletes performed worse than whites. But when the game was framed as a measure of "natural athletic ability" the pattern reversed, and the black athletes outperformed the whites.

Stereotype threat applies to gender as well (Spencer, Steele, & Quinn, 1999). The common stereotype has it that men are better at math than women are. In this experiment, when women were led to believe that a particular test was designed to show differences in math abilities between men and women, they did not perform as well as men. In another condition, when women were told that the same test had nothing to do with male-female differences, they performed as well as men. The phenomenon even shows itself among white males if you put them in a similarly threatening situation. For example, Joshua Aronson and his colleagues (1999) demonstrated that white males performed less well on a math exam when they thought they would be compared with Asian males—a group that they considered to have superior math ability. Furthermore, Brown and Pinel (2002) have shown that the more conscious individuals are of the stereotype, the greater is the effect on their performance.

> *I will look at any additional evidence to confirm the opinion to which I have already come.*
> —Lord Molson, British politician

> *We all decry prejudice, yet all are prejudiced.*
> —Herbert Spencer, 1873

Stereotype Threat
The apprehension experienced by members of a group that their behavior might confirm a cultural stereotype

How can the effects of stereotype threat be reversed? Aronson and his colleagues reasoned in the following way: If merely thinking about a stereotype can harm performance, then some kind of alternative mind-set can help performance—by countering the stereotype. For example, in one condition of a recent experiment, Matthew McGlone and Joshua Aronson (2006) did a very simple thing: They reminded the test takers before taking a difficult test of spatial ability that they were students at a "selective northeastern liberal arts college." This reminder was enough to completely eliminate the male-female gap they observed in the control condition, in which the test takers were merely reminded of the fact that they were "residents of the Northeast." The "I'm-a-good-student" mind-set effectively countered the women-aren't-good-at-math stereotype, leading to significantly better spatial performance for the female test takers. Similar results were found for advanced calculus students at the university level (Good, Aronson, & Harder, 2007) and with middle-school students on actual standardized tests (Good, Aronson, & Inzlicht, 2003). Research shows the performance-enhancing benefit of other counter-stereotype mind-sets as well: being reminded that abilities are improvable rather than fixed (Aronson, Fried, & Good, 2002; Good, Aronson, & Inzlicht, 2003)—and even the mind-set that anxiety on standardized tests is normal for members of stereotyped groups (Aronson & Williams, 2009; Johns, Schmader, & Martens, 2005). An understanding of stereotype threat, then, can be useful for improving performance on tests and other evaluations.

Stereotype threat occurs when people feel they are being evaluated against an existing negative cultural stereotype.

Laboratory experiments have shown that when black students are exposed to successful African American role models their performance improves (Marx & Roman, 2002; McIntyre, Paulson, & Lord, 2003). Moving from the laboratory into the actual world, consider the possible impact of President Obama's election. Obama not only models intelligence and achievement, his election demonstrates, for the first time in American history, that there may be no limit to what an African American might accomplish. This has led some journalists to speculate that Obama's election might reduce stereotype threat and thus have a positive impact on the test performance of African American students (Dillon, New York Times, 1-23-2009). However, in a well-controlled experiment, Joshua Aronson and his colleagues found no such effect. The researchers speculate that Obama—law school professor and first black president—may be outside the range of an effective role model; that is, he may be seen as having abilities that are so stellar that typical students can't identify with him (Aronson et. al., 2009, in press).

Blaming the Victim 责怪受害者

Try as they might, it is hard for people who have rarely been discriminated against to fully understand what it's like to be a target of prejudice. Well-intentioned members of the dominant majority will sympathize with the plight of African Americans, Hispanic Americans, Asian Americans, Jews, women, homosexuals, and other groups that are targets of discrimination, but true empathy is difficult for those who have routinely been judged on the basis of their own merit and not their racial, ethnic, religious, or other group membership. And when empathy is absent, it is sometimes hard to avoid falling into the trap of **blaming the victim** for his or her plight. This may take the form of the "well-deserved reputation." It goes something like this: "If the Jews have been victimized throughout their history, they must have been doing something to deserve it." Such suggestions constitute a demand that members of the out-group conform to more stringent standards of behavior than those set for the majority.

Ironically, as we discussed in Chapter 4, this tendency to blame victims for their victimization—attributing their predicaments to deficits in their abilities and character—is typically motivated by an understandable desire to see the world as a fair and just place, one where people get what they deserve and deserve what they get. Most

Blaming the Victim
The tendency to blame individuals (make dispositional attributions) for their victimization, typically motivated by a desire to see the world as a fair place

people, when confronted with evidence of an unfair outcome that is otherwise difficult to explain, find a way to blame the victim (Crandall et al., 2001; Lerner, 1980, 1991; Lerner & Grant, 1990). For example, in one experiment, two people worked equally hard on the same task, and by the flip of a coin, one received a sizable reward and the other received nothing. After the fact, observers tended to reconstruct what happened and convinced themselves that the unlucky person must have worked less hard. Similarly, negative attitudes toward the poor and the homeless—including blaming them for their own plight—are more prevalent among individuals who display a strong belief in a just world (Furnham & Gunter, 1984).

How does the belief in a just world lead to derogation of a victim and the perpetuation of prejudice? When something bad happens to another person (as when someone is mugged or raped), we will undoubtedly feel sorry for the person but at the same time will feel relieved that this horrible thing didn't happen to us. We will also feel scared that such a thing might happen to us in the future. How can we cope with these fears and worries? We can protect ourselves from the fear we feel by convincing ourselves that the person must have done something to cause the tragedy. We feel safe, then, because we would have behaved more cautiously (Jones & Aronson, 1973).

Most of us are very good at reconstructing situations after the fact to support our belief in a just world. It simply requires making a dispositional attribution—to the victim—and not a situational one—to the scary, random events that can happen to anyone at any time. In a fascinating experiment, college students who were provided with a description of a young woman's friendly behavior toward a man judged that behavior as completely appropriate (Janoff-Bulman, Timko, & Carli, 1985). Another group of students was given the same description, plus the information that the encounter ended with the young woman being raped by the man. This group rated the young woman's behavior as inappropriate; she was judged as having brought the rape on herself.

Such findings are not limited to American college students reading hypothetical cases. In a survey conducted in England, a striking 33 percent of the respondents believed that victims of rape are almost always to blame for it (Wagstaff, 1982).

How can we account for such harsh attributions? Most of us find it frightening to think that we live in a world where people, through no fault of their own, can be raped, discriminated against, deprived of equal pay for equal work, or denied the basic necessities of life. By the same token, if 6 million Jews are exterminated for no apparent reason, it is, in some strange way, comforting to believe that they must have done something to bring those events on themselves. The irony is overwhelming: Such thinking makes the world seem safer to us.

Self-Fulfilling Prophecies All other things being equal, if you believe that Amy is stupid and treat her accordingly, chances are that she will not say a lot of clever things in your presence. This is the well-known **self-fulfilling prophecy**, discussed in Chapter 3. How does this come about? If you believe that Amy is stupid, you probably will not ask her interesting questions, and you will not listen intently while she is talking; indeed, you might even look out the window or yawn. You behave this way because of a simple expectation: Why waste energy paying attention to Amy if she is unlikely to say anything smart or interesting? This is bound to have an important impact on Amy's behavior, for if the people she is talking to aren't paying much attention, she will feel uneasy and will probably clam up and not come out with all the poetry and wisdom within her. This serves to confirm the belief you had about her in the first place. The circle is closed; the self-fulfilling prophecy is complete.

Researchers demonstrated the relevance of this phenomenon to stereotyping and discrimination in an elegant experiment (Word, Zanna, & Cooper, 1974). White college undergraduates were asked to interview several job applicants; some of the applicants were white, and others were African American. Unwittingly, the college students displayed discomfort and lack of interest when interviewing African American applicants. They sat farther away, tended to stammer, and ended the interview far sooner than when they were interviewing white applicants. Can you guess how this behavior might have affected the African American applicants? To find out, the researchers

---

Self-Fulfilling Prophecy

The case whereby people (1) have an expectation about what another person is like, which (2) influences how they act toward that person, which (3) causes that person to behave in a way consistent with people's original expectations

FIGURE 13.6
An experiment demonstrating self-fulfilling prophecies.

conducted a second experiment in which they systematically varied the behavior of the interviewers (actually confederates) so that it coincided with the way the real interviewers had treated the African American or white interviewees in the first experiment. But in the second experiment, all of the interviewees were white. The researchers videotaped the proceedings and had the applicants rated by independent judges. They found that those applicants who were interviewed the way African Americans had been interviewed in the first experiment were judged to be far more nervous and far less effective than those who were interviewed the way whites had been interviewed in the first experiment. In sum, these experiments demonstrate clearly that when African Americans are interviewed by whites, they are unintentionally placed at a disadvantage and are likely to perform less well than their white counterparts (see Figure 13.6).

On a societal level, the insidiousness of the self-fulfilling prophecy goes even further. Suppose that there is a general belief that a particular group is irredeemably stupid, uneducable, and fit only for menial jobs. Why waste educational resources on them? Hence they are given inadequate schooling. Thirty years later, what do you find? An entire group that with few exceptions is fit only for menial jobs. "See? I was right all the while," says the bigot. "How fortunate that we didn't waste our precious educational resources on such people!" The self-fulfilling prophecy strikes again.

Prejudice and Economic Competition: Realistic Conflict Theory
偏见和经济竞争:"现实冲突理论"

One of the most obvious sources of conflict and prejudice is competition—for scarce resources, for political power, and for social status. Indeed, whatever problems result from the simple in-group versus out-group phenomenon, they will be magnified by real economic, political, or status competition. **Realistic conflict theory** holds that limited resources lead to conflict among groups and result in prejudice and discrimination (J. W. Jackson, 1993; Sherif, 1966; White, 1977). Thus, prejudiced attitudes tend to increase when times are tense and conflict exists over mutually exclusive goals. For example, prejudice has existed between Anglos and Mexican American migrant workers over a limited number of jobs, between Arabs and Israelis over disputed territory, and between northerners and southerners over the abolition of slavery.

Realistic Conflict Theory
The idea that limited resources lead to conflict between groups and result in increased prejudice and discrimination

Economic competition drives a good deal of prejudice. When unemployment rises, so does resentment against minorities.

Economic and Political Competition In his classic study of prejudice in a small industrial town, John Dollard (1938) was among the first to document the relationship between discrimination and economic competition. At first, there was no discernible hostility toward the new German immigrants; prejudice flourished, however, as jobs grew scarce:

> Local whites largely drawn from the surrounding farms manifested considerable direct aggression toward the newcomers. Scornful and derogatory opinions were expressed about these Germans, and the native whites had a satisfying sense of superiority toward them. ... The chief element in the permission to be aggressive against the Germans was rivalry for jobs and status in the local woodenware plants. The native whites felt definitely crowded for their jobs by the entering German groups and in case of bad times had a chance to blame the Germans, who by their presence provided more competitors for the scarcer jobs. There seemed to be no traditional pattern of prejudice against Germans unless the skeletal suspicion against all out-groupers (always present) can be invoked in its place.

Similarly, the prejudice, violence, and negative stereotyping directed against Chinese immigrants in the United States fluctuated wildly throughout the nineteenth century as a result of changes in economic competition. Chinese who joined the California gold rush, competing directly with white miners, were described as "depraved and vicious," "gross gluttons," and "bloodthirsty and inhuman" (Jacobs & Landau, 1971, p. 71). Only a few years later, however, when they were willing to accept backbreaking work as laborers on the transcontinental railroad—work few white Americans were willing to do—they were regarded as sober, industrious, and law-abiding. They were so highly regarded, in fact, that Charles Crocker, one of the great tycoons financing the railroad, wrote, "They are equal to the best white men . . . They are very trusty, very intelligent, and they live up to their contracts" (p. 81). With the end of the Civil War came an influx of former soldiers into an already tight job market. This was immediately followed by a dramatic increase in negative attitudes toward the Chinese: The stereotype changed to criminal, conniving, crafty, and stupid (Jacobs & Landau, 1971).

These changes suggest that when times are tough and resources are scarce, in-group members will feel more threatened by the out-group, and incidents of prejudice, discrimination, and violence toward out-group members will increase. How might the hypothesis be tested?

In a classic experiment, Muzafer Sherif and his colleagues (1961) tested group conflict theory using the natural environment of a Boy Scout camp. The participants in the camp were normal, well-adjusted 12-year-old boys who were randomly assigned to one of two groups, the Eagles or the Rattlers. Each group stayed in its own cabin; the cabins were located quite a distance apart to reduce contact between the two groups. The youngsters were placed in situations designed to increase the cohesiveness of their own group. This was done by arranging enjoyable activities such as hiking and swimming and by having the campers work with their group on various building projects, preparing group meals, and so on.

After feelings of cohesiveness developed within each group, the researchers set up a series of competitive activities in which the two groups were pitted against each other—for example, in games like football, baseball, and tug-of-war, where prizes were awarded to the winning team. These competitive games aroused feelings of conflict and tension between the two groups. In addition, the investigators created other situations to further intensify the conflict. For example, a camp party was arranged, but each group was told it started at a different time, thereby ensuring that the Eagles would arrive well before the Rattlers. The refreshments at the party consisted of two different kinds of food: Half the food was fresh, appealing, and appetizing, while the other half was squashed, ugly, and unappetizing. As you'd expect, the early-arriving

Eagles ate well, and the latecoming Rattlers were not happy with what they found. They began to curse at the exploitive group. Because the Eagles believed they deserved what they got (first come, first served), they resented the name-calling and responded in kind. Name-calling escalated into food throwing, and within a short time, punches were thrown and a full-scale riot ensued.

Following this incident, the investigators tried to reverse the hostility they had promoted. Competitive games were eliminated, and a great deal of nonconflictual social contact was initiated. Once hostility had been aroused, however, simply eliminating the competition did not eliminate the hostility. Indeed, hostility continued to escalate, even when the two groups were engaged in such benign activities as watching movies together. Eventually, the investigators did manage to reduce the hostility between the two groups; exactly how will be discussed at the end of this chapter.

"And see that you place the blame where it will do the most good."

The New Yorker Collection 1994. Bernard Schoenbaum from cartoonbank.com. All Rights Reserved.

The Role of the Scapegoat A special case of the conflict-competition theory is the *scapegoat theory* (Allport, 1954; Gemmill, 1989; Miller & Bugelski, 1948). As indicated earlier, if times are tough and things are going poorly, individuals have a tendency to lash out at members of an out-group with whom they compete directly for scarce resources. But there are situations in which a logical competitor does not exist. For example, in Germany following World War I, inflation was out of control, and people were extremely poor, demoralized, and frustrated. When the Nazis gained power in the 1930s, they managed to focus the frustration of the German population on the Jews, an easily identifiable, powerless out-group. The Jews were not the reason the German economy was in such bad shape, but who was? It's hard to fight back against world events or one's government—particularly when one's government is evading responsibility by blaming someone else. Thus the Nazis created the illusion that if the Jews could be punished, deprived of their civil rights, and ultimately eliminated, all of the problems then plaguing Germany would disappear. The Jews served as a convenient scapegoat because they were easily identifiable and were not in a position to defend themselves or strike back (Berkowitz, 1962).

The research on **scapegoating** shows that individuals, when frustrated or unhappy, tend to displace aggression onto groups that are disliked, are visible, and are relatively powerless. Moreover, the form the aggression takes depends on what is allowed or approved by the in-group in question. Since the 1940s and 1950s, lynchings of African Americans and pogroms against Jews have diminished dramatically because these are now deemed illegal by the dominant culture. But not all progress is linear. In the past decade, we have seen many eastern European countries emerge from the shadow of the former Soviet Union. But the new freedoms in the region have been accompanied by increased feelings of nationalism ("us versus them") that have in turn intensified feelings of rancor and prejudice against out-groups. In the Baltic States and the Balkans, the rise in nationalistic feelings has led to the outbreak of hostility and even war among Serbs, Muslims, and Croats, Azerbaijanis and Armenians, and other groups. And there is evidence that anti-Semitism is on the rise again in Eastern Europe (Poppe, 2001; Singer, 1990).

In recent years homosexuals have become an increasingly convenient scapegoat. The Reverend Jerry Falwell issued the following warning: "If you and I do not speak up now, this homosexual steamroller will literally crush all decent men, women, and children who get in its way . . . and our nation will pay a terrible price" (Falwell, quoted in *The Columbia Spectator*, April 4, 2006). The Reverend Pat Robertson declared: "When lawlessness is abroad in the land, the same thing will happen here that happened in Nazi Germany. Many of those people involved with Adolph Hitler were Satanists. Many of them were homosexuals. The two things seem to go together" (Pat Robertson, 700 Club, January 21, 1993). Ironically, of course, far from being in league with Hitler, homosexuals were a prime target of Nazi hostility.

Scapegoating
The tendency for individuals, when frustrated or unhappy, to displace aggression onto groups that are disliked, visible, and relatively powerless

The Way We Conform: Normative Rules 从众行为：规范性标准

We've seen that prejudice is created and maintained by many forces in the social world. Some operate within the individual, such as the ways we process information and assign meaning to observed events; some operate on whole groups of people, such as the effects of competition, conflict, and frustration. Our final explanation for what causes prejudice also occurs on the group level—conformity to normative standards or rules in the society. As we discussed in Chapter 8, conformity is a frequent part of social life, whether we conform to gain information (informational conformity) or to fit in and be accepted (normative conformity). Again, a relatively innocuous social behavior—in this case, conformity—becomes particularly dangerous and debilitating when the conforming involves prejudiced beliefs and behaviors.

When Prejudice Is Institutionalized Norms are beliefs held by a society as to what is correct, acceptable, and permissible. Obviously, norms vary widely across cultures. Important regional differences in norms also occur within the same country. For example, not long ago, racial segregation in hotels, eating places, motion picture theaters, drinking fountains, and toilet facilities was normative in the American South but not in the North. Indeed, it can be said that prior to 1954, segregation controlled most aspects of social life in the South. These norms do not have to be taught directly. Simply by living in a society where stereotypical information abounds and where discriminatory behavior is the norm, the vast majority of us will unwittingly develop prejudiced attitudes and discriminatory behavior to some extent. We call this institutional discrimination or, more specifically, **institutionalized racism** and **institutionalized sexism**. For example, if you grow up in a society where few minority group members and women have professional careers and where most people in these groups hold menial jobs, simply living in that society will increase your likelihood of developing certain (negative) attitudes about the inherent abilities of minorities and women. This state of affairs can come about without anyone actively teaching you that minorities and women are inferior and without any law or decree banning minorities and women from college faculties, boardrooms, or medical schools. Instead, social barriers have created a lack of opportunity for these groups that makes their success extremely unlikely.

How does normative prejudice work? In Chapter 8, we discussed the strong tendency to go along with the group to fulfill the group's expectations and gain acceptance, a phenomenon known as **normative conformity**. Being a nonconformist can be painful. As Thomas Pettigrew (1958, 1985, 1991) has noted, many people consequently adopt prejudiced attitudes and engage in discriminatory behaviors in order to conform to, or fit in with, the prevailing majority view of their culture. It's as if people say, "Hey, everybody else thinks Xs are inferior; if I behave cordially toward Xs, people will think I'm weird. They won't like me. They'll say bad things about me. I don't need the hassle. I'll just go along with everybody else." Pettigrew argues convincingly that although economic competition, frustration, and social cognition processes do account for some prejudice, by far the greatest determinant of prejudice is slavish conformity to social norms.

For example, Ernest Campbell and Thomas Pettigrew (1959) studied the ministers of Little Rock, Arkansas, after the 1954 Supreme Court decision struck down school segregation. Most ministers favored integration and equality for all American citizens, but they kept these views to themselves. They were afraid to support desegregation from their pulpits because they knew that their white congregations were violently opposed to it. Going against the prevailing norm would have meant losing church members and contributions, and under such normative pressure, even ministers found it difficult to do the right thing.

Another way to determine the role of normative conformity is to track changes in prejudice and discrimination over time. As social norms change, so should the strength of prejudiced attitudes and the amount of discriminatory behavior. For example, what happens when people move from one part of the country to another? If conformity is a factor in prejudice, we would expect individuals to show dramatic

---

Institutionalized Racism
Racist attitudes that are held by the vast majority of people living in a society where stereotypes and discrimination are the norm

Institutionalized Sexism
Sexist attitudes that are held by the vast majority of people living in a society where stereotypes and discrimination are the norm

Normative Conformity
The tendency to go along with the group in order to fulfill the group's expectations and gain acceptance

What a difference a decade makes! On the left, in 1963, Governor George Wallace defies a federal order by physically blocking the entrance of the first black student to the University of Alabama. On the right, 10 years later, Governor Wallace happily congratulates the University of Alabama homecoming queen.

increases in their prejudice when they move to an area in which the norm is more prejudicial and to show dramatic decreases when they move to an area in which the norm is less prejudicial. And that is just what happens.

Researchers have found that people who had recently moved to New York City and had come into direct contact with an anti-Semitic norm became more anti-Semitic themselves. Similarly, when southerners entered the army and came into contact with a less prejudiced set of social norms, their prejudice against African Americans gradually decreased (Pettigrew, 1958; Watson, 1950). Researchers in a small mining town in West Virginia found even more dramatic evidence of shifting norms: Over the years, African American miners and white miners developed a pattern of living that consisted of total integration while they were under the ground and total segregation while they were above the ground (Minard, 1952; Reitzes, 1952).

Moreover, surveys conducted over the past 6 decades make it clear that what is going on inside the minds of Americans has changed a great deal. For example, in 1942, the overwhelming majority of white Americans believed that it was a good idea to have separate sections for African American and white people on buses. Two out of every three white Americans surveyed believed that schools should be segregated. In the South, the numbers were even more striking: In 1942, fully 98 percent of the white population was opposed to desegregating schools (Hyman & Sheatsley, 1956). In contrast, by 1988, only 3 percent of white Americans said they wouldn't want their child to attend school with black children. That is a dramatic change indeed!

Shifting cultural norms are well illustrated by the two photographs depicting Governor George Wallace of Alabama. In one, the governor, along with his state militia, is blocking the doors of the University of Alabama as the first African American students seek to register for college. Only the intervention of heavily armed federal troops caused Governor Wallace to back down. And yet just a decade later, the normative climate of Alabama had changed to the extent that Governor Wallace could be seen—as in the second photograph—congratulating the young African American woman whom the University of Alabama student body had chosen to be homecoming queen (Knopke, Norrell, & Rogers, 1991).

"Modern" Prejudice As the norm swings toward tolerance for out-groups, many people simply become more careful—outwardly acting unprejudiced yet inwardly maintaining their stereotyped views. This phenomenon is known as **modern racism**. People have learned to hide prejudice in order to avoid being labeled as racist, but when the situation becomes "safe," their prejudice will be revealed (Dovidio & Gaertner, 1996; McConahay, 1986).

Modern Racism
Outwardly acting unprejudiced while inwardly maintaining prejudiced attitudes

For example, although it is true that few Americans say they are generally opposed to school desegregation, it is interesting that most white parents oppose busing their own children to achieve racial balance. When questioned, these parents insist that their opposition has nothing to do with prejudice; they simply don't want their kids to waste a lot of time on a bus. But as John McConahay (1981) has shown, most white parents are quite tranquil about busing when their kids are simply being bused from one white school to another; most show vigorous opposition only when the busing is interracial.

Given the properties of modern prejudice, it can best be studied with subtle or unobtrusive measures (Crosby, Bromley, & Saxe, 1980). One team of researchers created an ingenious contraption to get at the real attitudes—not simply the socially desirable ones—of their research participants (Jones & Sigall, 1971). They showed research participants an impressive-looking machine, described as a kind of lie detector. In fact, this "bogus pipeline" was just a pile of electronic hardware whose dials the experimenter could secretly manipulate. Here's how researchers use the pipeline: Participants are randomly assigned to one of two conditions in which they indicate their attitudes either on a paper-and-pencil questionnaire (where it is easy to give socially correct responses) or by using the bogus pipeline (where they believe the machine will reveal their true attitudes if they lie). The researchers found that students' responses showed more racial prejudice when the bogus pipeline was used (Sigall & Page, 1971; Roese & Jamieson, 1993). Similarly, college men and women expressed almost identical positive attitudes about women's rights and women's roles in society on a paper-and-pencil measure. When the bogus pipeline was used, however, most of the men displayed far less sympathy to women's issues than the women did (Tourangeau, Smith, & Rasinski, 1997).

Subtle and Blatant Prejudice in Western Europe We've been discussing prejudice and stereotyping in the United States, but Americans have no franchise on prejudice. Examples of blatant prejudice abound in daily newspaper headlines: ethnic cleansing in Bosnia, violent conflict between Arabs and Jews in the Middle East, mass murder between warring tribes in Rwanda. This prejudice exists in "modern" forms as well (Pettigrew, 1998; Pettigrew et al., 1998). A transnational study, for example, found both blatant and more "modern," subtle racism in France, the Netherlands, and Great Britain (Meertens & Pettigrew, 1997; Pettigrew & Meertens, 1995).

The researchers showed that the difference between blatant and subtle racism is important and has interesting consequences. One of their major findings is that although the targets of prejudice differ in the three countries, the behavior of the native population toward recent immigrants can be predicted from their scores on both blatant and subtle measures of prejudice. For example, in all three countries, people who score high on the blatant prejudice scale want to send immigrants back to their home country and wish to restrict their meager rights even further. Those who score low on both scales want to improve the rights of immigrants, are prepared to take action to help them remain in the country, and are willing to act forcefully to improve relations between immigrants and natives. Those who score high on the subtle racism scale but low on the blatant scale tend to reject immigrants in ways that are more covert and socially acceptable. Specifically, although they will not act to send immigrants back to their home country, they will also not do anything to help improve their relations with the immigrant population, nor will they join any attempt to increase that population's civil rights (Pettigrew, 1998).

> *It is never too late to give up our prejudices.*
> —Henry David Thoreau, 1854

Subtle Sexism 内隐性别歧视

Subtle forms of prejudice can also be directed toward women. As we have seen, not all prejudice consists of feelings of antipathy toward the target group. Because we live in a patriarchal society, many men have feelings of ambivalence toward women. Peter Glick and Susan Fiske (2001) have shown that this ambivalence can take one of two forms: *hostile sexism* or *benevolent sexism*. Hostile sexists hold stereotypical views of women that suggest that women are inferior to men (e.g., that they are less intelligent, less competent, and so on). Benevolent sexists hold stereotypically positive views of women. Indeed, their views are actually chivalrous in nature. As we suggested earlier, harboring stereotypically positive feelings about a group (as is true of benevolent sexists) can be damaging to the target because it is limiting. But benevolent sexism goes a bit further. According to Glick and Fiske, underneath it all, benevolent sexists (like hostile sexists) assume that women are the weaker sex. Benevolent sexists tend to idealize women romantically, may admire them as wonderful cooks and mothers, and want to protect them when they do not need protection. Thus in the final analysis, both hostile sexism and benevolent sexism—for different reasons—serve to justify relegating women to traditional stereotyped roles in society.

How Can Prejudice Be Reduced?
如何消除偏见？

Sometimes subtle, sometimes brutally overt, prejudice is indeed ubiquitous. Does this mean that prejudice is an essential aspect of human social interaction and will therefore always be with us? We social psychologists do not take such a pessimistic view. We tend to agree with Thoreau that "it is never too late to give up our prejudices." People can change. But how? What can we do to eliminate or at least reduce this noxious aspect of human social behavior?

Because stereotypes and prejudice are based on false information, for many years social observers believed that education was the answer: All we needed to do was expose people to the truth and their prejudices would disappear. But this has proved a naive hope (Lazarsfeld, 1940). After reading this chapter to this point, you can see why this might be the case. Because of the underlying emotional aspects of prejudice, as well as some of the cognitive ruts we get into (e.g., attributional biases, biased expectations, and illusory correlations), stereotypes based on misinformation are difficult to modify simply by providing people with the facts. But there is hope. As you may have experienced, repeated contact with members of an out-group can modify stereotypes and prejudice. But mere contact is not enough; it must be a special kind of contact. What exactly does this mean?

The Contact Hypothesis 接触假说

In 1954, when the U.S. Supreme Court outlawed segregated schools, social psychologists were excited and optimistic. Because segregation lowered the self-esteem of minority children, most social psychologists believed that desegregating the schools would lead to increases in these youngsters' self-esteem. It was hoped, too, that school desegregation would be the beginning of the end of prejudice. The idea was that contact between children of different races and ethnicities would eventually erode prejudice.

There was good reason for this optimism because not only did it make sense theoretically, but empirical evidence also supported the power of contact among races. Recent studies have supported this idea (Van Laar, Levin & Sidanius, 2008). Indeed, as early as 1951, Morton Deutsch and Mary Ellen Collins examined the attitudes of white Americans toward African Americans in two public housing projects that differed in their degree of racial integration. In one, black and white families had been randomly assigned to separate buildings in the same project. In the other project, black and white families lived in the same building. After several months, white residents in the integrated project reported a greater positive change in their attitudes toward blacks than residents of the segregated project did, even though the former had not chosen to live in an integrated building initially.

Although contact among the races is generally a good thing (Pettigrew & Tropp, 2006; Pettigrew & Tropp, in press), the desegregation of schools did not work as smoothly as most knowledgeable people had expected. Indeed, far from producing the hoped-for harmony,

"I wish we could have met under different circumstances..."

school desegregation frequently led to tension and turmoil in the classroom. In his careful analysis of the research examining the impact of desegregation, Walter Stephan (1978, 1985) was unable to find a single study demonstrating a significant increase in self-esteem among African American children, and 25 percent of the studies showed a significant decrease in their self-esteem following desegregation. In addition, prejudice was not reduced. Stephan (1978) found that in 53 percent of the studies, prejudice actually increased; in 34 percent of the studies, no change in prejudice occurred. And if one had taken an aerial photograph of the schoolyards of most desegregated schools, one would have found that there was very little true integration: White kids tended to cluster with white kids, black kids tended to cluster with black kids, Hispanic kids tended to cluster with Hispanic kids, and so on (Aronson, 1978; Aronson & Gonzalez, 1988; Aronson & Thibodeau, 1992; Schofield, 1986). Clearly, in this instance, mere contact did not work as we had hoped.

> We must recognize that beneath the superficial classification of sex and race the same potentialities exist, recurring generation after generation only to perish because society has no place for them.
>
> —Margaret Mead, *Male and Female*, 1943

What went wrong? Why did desegregated housing work better than desegregated schools? Let's take a closer look at the contact hypothesis. Clearly, not all kinds of contact will reduce prejudice and raise self-esteem. For example, in the South, blacks and whites have had a great deal of contact, dating back to the time when Africans first arrived on American shores; however, prejudice flourished nonetheless. Obviously, the kind of contact they were having—as master and slave—was not the kind that would reduce prejudice. In his strikingly prescient masterwork *The Nature of Prejudice*, Gordon Allport (1954) stated the contact hypothesis this way:

> Prejudice may be reduced by equal-status contact between majority and minority groups in the pursuit of common goals. The effect is greatly enhanced if this contact is sanctioned by institutional supports (i.e., by law, custom or local atmosphere), and provided it is of a sort that leads to the perception of common interests and common humanity between members of the two groups. (p. 281)

In short, prejudice will decrease when two conditions are met: Both groups are of equal status and both share a common goal. Note that implicit in the Deutsch and Collins (1951) housing study was the fact that the two groups were of equal status in the project and that no obvious issues of conflict existed between them. Decades of research have substantiated Allport's early claim that these conditions must be met before contact will lead to a decrease in prejudice between groups (Cook, 1985). Let's now turn to a discussion of these conditions.

When Contact Reduces Prejudice: Six Conditions
接触减少偏见的六个条件

Remember Sherif and colleagues' (1961) study at the boys' camp, involving the Eagles and the Rattlers? When conflict and competition were instigated, stereotyping and prejudice resulted. As part of the study, Sherif and his colleagues also staged several events at the camp to reduce the prejudice they had created. Their findings tell us a great deal about what contact can and cannot do.

First, the researchers found that once hostility and distrust were established, simply removing the conflict and the competition did not restore harmony. In fact, bringing the two groups together in neutral situations actually *increased* their hostility and distrust. The children in these groups had trouble with each other even when they were simply watching a movie together.

How did Sherif succeed in reducing their hostility? He placed the two groups of boys in situations where they experienced **mutual interdependence**, the need to depend on each other to accomplish a goal that is important to each group. For example, the investigators set up an emergency situation by damaging the water supply system. The only way the system could be repaired was if all the Rattlers and Eagles cooperated immediately. On another occasion, the camp truck broke down while the boys were on a camping trip. To get the truck going again, it was necessary to pull it up a rather steep hill. This could be accomplished only if all the youngsters pulled together, regardless of whether they were Eagles or Rattlers. Eventually, these sorts of situations brought about a diminution of hostile feelings and negative

Mutual Interdependence
The situation that exists when two or more groups need each other and must depend on each other to accomplish a goal that is important to each of them

stereotyping among the campers. In fact, after these cooperative situations were introduced, the number of boys who said their closest friend was in the other group increased dramatically (see Figure 13.7). Thus, two of the key factors in the success of contact are *mutual interdependence* and a *common goal* (Amir, 1969, 1976).

The third condition is *equal status*. At the boys' camp (Sherif et al., 1961) and in the public housing project (Deutsch & Collins, 1951), the group members were very much the same in terms of status and power. No one was the boss, and no one was the less powerful employee. When status is unequal, interactions can easily follow stereotypical patterns. The whole point of contact is to allow people to learn that their stereotypes are inaccurate; contact and interaction should lead to disconfirmation of negative, stereotyped beliefs. If status is unequal between the groups, their interactions will be shaped by that status difference—the bosses will act like stereotypical bosses, the employees like stereotypical subordinates—and no one will learn new, disconfirming information about the other group (Pettigrew, 1969; Wilder, 1984).

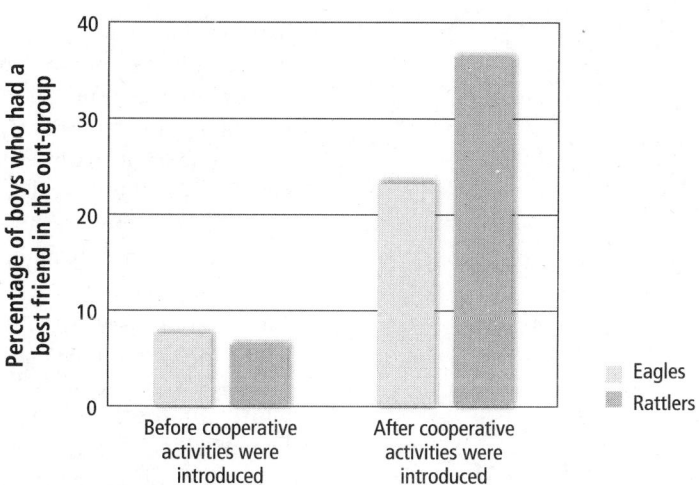

FIGURE 13.7
Intergroup relations.

Intergroup tensions were eased only after members engaged in cooperative activities.

(Adapted from Sherif, Harvey, White, Hood, & Sherif, 1961)

Fourth, contact must occur in a *friendly, informal setting* where in-group members can interact with out-group members on a one-to-one basis (Brewer & Miller, 1984; Cook, 1984; Wilder, 1986). Simply placing two groups in contact in a room where they can remain segregated will do little to promote their understanding or knowledge of each other.

Fifth, through friendly, informal interactions with *multiple members* of the out-group, an individual will learn that his or her beliefs about the out-group are wrong. It is crucial for the individual to believe that the out-group members he or she comes to know are typical of their group; otherwise, the stereotype can be maintained by labeling one out-group member as the exception (Wilder, 1984). For example, a study of male police officers assigned female partners in Washington, DC., found that although the men were satisfied with their female partners' performance, they still opposed hiring women police officers. Their stereotypes about women's ability to do police work hadn't changed; in fact, they matched those of male officers with male partners (Milton, 1971). Why? They perceived their partner as an exception.

Sixth and last, contact is most likely to lead to reduced prejudice when *social norms that promote and support equality among groups* are operating in the situation (Amir, 1969; Wilder, 1984). Social norms are powerful; here they can be harnessed to motivate people to reach out to members of the out-group. For example, if the boss or the professor creates and reinforces a norm of acceptance and tolerance at work or in the classroom, group members will change their behavior to fit the norm.

To sum up, suspicious or even hostile groups will reduce their stereotyping, prejudice, and discriminatory behavior when these six conditions of contact are met (Aronson & Bridgeman, 1979; Cook, 1984; Riordan, 1978):

1. Mutual interdependence
2. A common goal
3. Equal status
4. Informal, interpersonal contact
5. Multiple contacts
6. Social norms of equality

Why Early Desegregation Failed
早期种族混合教育为什么会失败

Knowing now what conditions must exist for contact to work, we can better understand the problems that occurred when schools were first desegregated. Imagine a typical scenario. Carlos, a Mexican American sixth grader, has been attending schools

Under what conditions will contact reduce prejudice?

in an underprivileged neighborhood his entire life. Because the schools in his neighborhood were not well equipped or well staffed, his first five years of education were somewhat deficient. Suddenly, without much warning or preparation, he is bused to a school in a predominantly white, middle-class neighborhood.

As you know from experience, the traditional classroom is a highly competitive environment. The typical scene involves the teacher asking a question; immediately, several hands go into the air as the children strive to show the teacher that they know the answer. When a teacher calls on one child, several others groan because they've missed an opportunity to show the teacher how smart they are. If the child who is called on hesitates or comes up with the wrong answer, there is a renewed and intensified flurry of hands in the air, perhaps even accompanied by whispered, derisive comments directed at the student who failed. Carlos finds he must compete against white, middle-class students who have had better preparation than he and who have been reared to hold white, middle-class values, which include working hard in pursuit of good grades, raising one's hand enthusiastically whenever the teacher asks a question, and so on. In effect, Carlos has been thrust into a highly competitive situation for which he is unprepared and in which payoffs are made for abilities he has not yet developed. He is virtually guaranteed to lose. After a few failures, Carlos, feeling defeated, humiliated, and dispirited, stops raising his hand and can hardly wait for the bell to ring to signal the end of the school day.

In the typical desegregated classroom, to use Allport's (1954) terminology, the students were not of equal status and were not pursuing common goals. Indeed, one might say that they were in a tug-of-war on an uneven playing field. When one examines the situation closely, it is easy to see why Stephan (1978) found a general decrease in the self-esteem of minority children following desegregation. Moreover, given the competitive atmosphere of the classroom, it is likely that the situation would have exacerbated whatever stereotypes existed before desegregation. Specifically, given that the minority kids were not prepared for the competitiveness of the classroom, it is not surprising that some of the white kids quickly concluded that the minority kids were stupid, unmotivated, and sullen—just as they had suspected (Wilder & Shapiro, 1989). Moreover, it is likely that the minority kids might conclude that the white kids were arrogant showoffs. This is an example of the self-fulfilling prophecy we discussed earlier.

How could we change the atmosphere of the classroom so that it comes closer to Gordon Allport's prescription for the effectiveness of contact? Specifically, how could we get white students and minority students to be of equal status, mutually dependent, and in pursuit of common goals?

CONNECTIONS 链接

Cooperation and Interdependence: The Jigsaw Classroom
合作与互倚：拼图教室

In 1971, Austin, Texas, desegregated its schools. Within just a few weeks, African American, white, and Mexican American children were in open conflict; fistfights broke out in the corridors and schoolyards. Austin's school superintendent called on Elliot Aronson, then a professor at the University of Texas, to find a way to create a more harmonious environment. After spending a few days observing the dynamics of several classrooms, Aronson and his graduate students were reminded of the situation that existed in the Sherif and colleagues (1961) camp experiment. With the findings of that study in mind, they developed a technique that created an interdependent classroom atmosphere designed to place the students of various racial and ethnic groups in pursuit of common goals. They called it the **jigsaw classroom** because it resembled the assembling of a jigsaw puzzle (Aronson, 1978; Aronson & Gonzalez, 1988; Aronson & Patnoe, 1997; Walker & Crogan, 1998; Wolfe & Spencer, 1996).

Here is how the jigsaw classroom works: Students are placed in diverse six-person learning groups. The day's lesson is divided into six segments, and each student is assigned one segment of the written material. For example, if the students are to learn the life of Eleanor

Roosevelt, her biography is broken into six parts and distributed to the six students, each of whom has possession of a unique and vital part of the information, which, like the pieces of a jigsaw puzzle, must be put together before anyone can view the whole picture. Each student must learn his or her own section and teach it to the other members of the group, who do not have any other access to that material. Therefore, if Debbie wants to do well on the exam about the life of Eleanor Roosevelt, she must pay close attention to Carlos (who is reciting on Roosevelt's girlhood years), to Shamika (who is reciting on Roosevelt's years in the White House), and so on.

Unlike the traditional classroom, where students are competing against each other, the jigsaw classroom has students depending on each other. In the traditional classroom, if Carlos, because of anxiety and discomfort, is having difficulty reciting, the other students can easily ignore him (or even put him down) in their zeal to show the teacher how smart they are. But in the jigsaw classroom, if Carlos is having difficulty reciting, it is now in the best interests of the other students to be patient, make encouraging comments, and even ask friendly, probing questions to make it easier for Carlos to bring forth the knowledge within him.

When the classroom is structured so that students of various ethnic groups work together cooperatively, prejudice decreases and self-esteem increases.

Through the jigsaw process, the children begin to pay more attention to each other and to show respect for each other. As you might expect, a child like Carlos would respond to this treatment by simultaneously becoming more relaxed and more engaged; this would inevitably produce an improvement in his ability to communicate. In fact, after a couple of weeks, the other students were struck by their realization that Carlos was a lot smarter than they had thought he was. They began to like him. Carlos began to enjoy school more and began to see the Anglo students in his group not as tormentors, but as helpful and responsible teammates. Moreover, as he began to feel increasingly comfortable in class and started to gain more confidence in himself, Carlos's academic performance began to improve. As his academic performance improved, so did his self-esteem. The vicious circle had been broken; the elements that had been causing a downward spiral were changed, and the spiral moved dramatically upward.

The formal data gathered from the jigsaw experiments were clear and striking: Compared to students in traditional classrooms, students in jigsaw groups showed a decrease in prejudice and stereotyping and an increase in their liking for their groupmates, both within and across ethnic boundaries. In addition, children in the jigsaw classrooms performed better on objective exams and showed a significantly greater increase in self-esteem than children in traditional classrooms. Children in the jigsaw classrooms also showed far greater liking for school than those in traditional classrooms. Moreover, children in schools where the jigsaw technique was practiced showed substantial evidence of true integration—in the schoolyard, there was far more intermingling among the various races and ethnic groups than on the grounds of schools using more traditional classroom techniques.

Two are better than one because they have a good reward for their toil. For if they fail, one will lift up his fellow, but woe to him who is alone when he falls and has not another to lift him up. Again, if two lie together, they are warm; but how can one be warm alone?

—Ecclesiastes 4:9–12

Why Does Jigsaw Work? 拼图教室法为什么有效

One reason for the success of this technique is that the process of participating in a cooperative group breaks down in-group versus out-group perceptions and allows the individual to develop the cognitive category of "oneness" wherein no one is excluded from group membership (Gaertner, Mann, Dovidio, & Murrell, 1990). In addition, the cooperative strategy places people in a "favor-doing" situation. Recall that in Chapter 6, we discussed an experiment by Mike Leippe and Donna Eisenstadt (1994, 1998) demonstrating that people who acted in a way that benefited others subsequently came to feel more favorably toward the people they helped, a finding also echoed in Chapter 11.

Jigsaw Classroom

A classroom setting designed to reduce prejudice and raise the self-esteem of children by placing them in small, desegregated groups and making each child dependent on the other children in the group to learn the course material and do well in the class

There is at least one additional reason why jigsaw learning produces such positive interpersonal outcomes: The process of working cooperatively encourages the development of empathy. Here's why. In the competitive classroom, the goal is simply to show the teacher how smart you are. You don't have to pay much attention to the other students in your classroom. But to participate effectively in the jigsaw classroom, each student needs to pay close attention to whichever member of the group is reciting. In doing so, the participants begin to learn that great results can accrue if each of their classmates is approached in a way that is tailored to fit his or her special needs. For example, Alicia may learn that Carlos is a bit shy and needs to be prodded gently, while Trang is so talkative that she might need to be reined in occasionally. Peter can be joked with, but Darnell responds only to serious suggestions.

If our analysis is sound, it should follow that working in jigsaw groups would lead to the sharpening of a youngster's general empathic ability—a change that will reduce the tendency to rely on stereotypes. To test this notion, Diane Bridgeman conducted a clever experiment with 10-year-old children. Just prior to her experiment, half of the children had spent 2 months participating in jigsaw classes and half in traditional classrooms. In her experiment, Bridgeman (1981) showed the children a series of cartoons aimed at testing children's ability to empathize—to put themselves in the shoes of the cartoon characters. For example, in one cartoon, the first panel shows a little boy looking sad as he waves good-bye to his father at the airport. In the next panel, a letter carrier delivers a package to the boy. In the third panel, the boy opens the package, finds a toy airplane inside, and bursts into tears. Bridgeman asked the children why they thought the little boy burst into tears at the sight of the airplane. Nearly all of the children could answer correctly—because the toy airplane reminded him of how much he missed his father. Then Bridgeman asked the crucial question: "What did the letter carrier think when he saw the boy open the package and start to cry?"

Most children of this age make a consistent error; they assume that everyone knows what they know. Thus the youngsters in the control group thought that the letter carrier would know the boy was sad because the gift reminded him of his father leaving. But the children who had participated in the jigsaw classroom responded differently. Because of their experience with jigsaw, they had developed the ability to take the perspective of the letter carrier—to put themselves in his shoes—and they realized that he would be confused at seeing the boy cry over receiving a nice present because the letter carrier hadn't witnessed the farewell scene at the airport. (See the following Try It! exercise.)

TRY IT! Jigsaw-Type Group Study 试一试！拼图式的学习小组

The next time a quiz is coming up in one of your courses, try to organize a handful of your classmates into a jigsaw-type group for purposes of studying for the quiz.

Assign each person a segment of the reading. That person is responsible for becoming the world's greatest expert on that material. That person will organize the material into a report that will be given to the rest of the group. The rest of the group will feel free to ask questions to make sure they fully understand the material. At the end of the session, ask the group members the following questions:

1. Compared to studying alone, was this more or less enjoyable?

2. Compared to studying alone, was this more or less efficient?

3. How are you feeling about each of the people in the group, compared to how you felt about them prior to the session?

4. Would you like to do this again?

You should realize that this situation is probably a lot less powerful than the jigsaw groups described in this book. Why?

Offhand, this might not seem very important. After all, who cares whether kids have the ability to figure out what is in the mind of a cartoon character? In point of fact, we should all care—a great deal. Recall our discussion of the Columbine tragedy in Chapter 12. In that chapter, we suggested how important empathy is in curbing aggression. The extent to which children can develop the ability to see the world from the perspective of another human being has profound implications for interpersonal relations in general. When we develop the ability to understand what another person is going through, it increases the probability that our heart will open to that person. Once our heart opens to another person, it becomes virtually impossible to feel prejudice against that person, to bully that person, to taunt that person, to humiliate that person. Our guess is that if the jigsaw strategy had been used in Columbine High School and in the elementary and middle schools feeding into Columbine, the tragedy would have been averted.

The Gradual Spread of Cooperative Learning The jigsaw approach was first tested in 1971; since then, educational researchers have developed a variety of similar cooperative techniques (Cook, 1985; Johnson & Johnson, 1987; Slavin & Cooper, 1999). The striking results Aronson and his colleagues obtained have now been successfully replicated in hundreds of classrooms in all regions of the country and abroad (Jurgen-Lohmann, Borsch, & Giesen, 2001; Sharan, 1980). Cooperative learning is now generally accepted by educational researchers as one of the most effective ways of improving race relations, building empathy, and improving instruction in our schools (Deutsch, 1997; McConahay, 1981; Slavin, 1996). What began as a simple experiment in one school system is slowly becoming an important force in the field of public education. Unfortunately, the operative word in the preceding sentence is *slowly*. The educational system, like all other bureaucracies, tends to resist change. As the Columbine massacre illustrates, this slowness can have tragic consequences (Aronson, 2000, 2004).

CONNECTIONS 链 接

A Letter from "Carlos" 来自"卡洛斯"的一封信

In 1982 Elliot Aronson received the following letter:

Dear Professor Aronson:

I am a senior at _____University. Today I got a letter admitting me to the Harvard Law School. This may not seem odd to you, but let me tell you something. I am the 6th of 7 children my parents had—and I am the only one who ever went to college, let alone graduate, or go to law school.

By now, you are probably wondering why this stranger is writing to you and bragging to you about his achievements. Actually, I'm not a stranger although we never met. You see, last year I was taking a course in social psychology and we were using a book you wrote, *The Social Animal,* and when I read about prejudice and jigsaw it all sounded very familiar—and then, I realized that I was in that very first class you ever did jigsaw in—when I was in the 5th grade. And as I read on, it dawned on me that I was the boy that you called Carlos. And then I remembered you when you first came to our classroom and how I was scared and how I hated school and how I was so stupid and didn't know anything. And you came in—it all came back to me when I read your book—you were very tall—about 6 1/2 feet—and you had a big black beard and you were funny and made us all laugh.

And, most important, when we started to do work in jigsaw groups, I began to realize that I wasn't really that stupid. And the kids I thought were cruel and hostile became my friends and the teacher acted friendly and nice to me and I actually began to love school, and I began to love to learn things and now I'm about to go to Harvard Law School.

You must get a lot of letters like this but I decided to write anyway because let me tell you something. My mother tells me that when I was born I almost died. I was born at home and the cord was wrapped around my neck and the midwife gave me mouth to mouth and saved my life. If she was still alive, I would write to her too, to tell her that I grew up smart and good and I'm going to law school. But she died a few years ago. I'm writing to you because, no less than her, you saved my life too.

Sincerely,

Summary 总 结

- **Prejudice: The Ubiquitous Social Phenomenon**
  Prejudice is a widespread phenomenon, present in all societies of the world. What varies across societies are the particular social groups that are the victims of prejudice and the degree to which societies enable or discourage discrimination.
  - **Prejudice and Self-Esteem** Often, but not always, prejudice leads to feelings of inferiority on the part of those who are the recipients of prejudiced expressions.
  - **A Progress Report** The intensity of the expression of prejudice in the United States has lessened over the last several decades. As would be predicted, the self-esteem of individuals in discriminated-against groups has also improved. Although this progress is real, prejudice is still a significant social problem.
- **Prejudice Defined** Social psychologists define **prejudice** as a hostile or negative attitude toward a distinguishable group of people based solely on their group membership.
  - **Stereotypes: The Cognitive Component** Stereotypes, while related to prejudice, are different. While prejudice is defined in terms of a negative attitudinal and emotional response, stereotypes denote both the positive and negative traits that people assign to members solely by virtue of their membership in a particular social group.
  - **Discrimination: The Behavioral Component** Discrimination denotes actual behavior. It is defined as an unjustified negative or harmful action towards members of a group solely because of their membership in that group.
- **What Causes Prejudice?** As a broad-based and powerful attitude, prejudice has many causes. We discussed four aspects of social life that bring about prejudice: the way we think, the way we assign meaning or make attributions, the way we allocate resources, and the way we conform to social rules. Prejudice is enabled by the human tendency to organize people into in-groups and out-groups.
  - **The Way We Think: Social Cognition** The processes of social cognition are important in the creation and maintenance of stereotypes and prejudice. Categorization of people into groups leads to the perception of in-groups and out-groups. In-group bias means that we will treat members of our own group more positively than members of the out-group. Another consequence of categorization is the perception of out-group homogeneity.
  - **How We Assign Meaning: Attributional Biases** The fundamental attribution error applies to prejudice—we tend to overestimate the role of dispositional forces when making sense out of others' behavior. Stereotypes can be described as the ultimate attribution error—making negative dispositional attributions about an entire out-group. When out-group members act nonstereotypically, we tend to make situational attributions about them, thereby maintaining our stereotypes.
  - **Blaming the Victim**
  - **Prejudice and Economic Competition** Realistic conflict theory states that prejudice is the inevitable by-product of real conflict between groups for limited resources—whether involving economics, power, or status. Competition for resources leads to derogation of and discrimination against the competing out-group. **Scapegoating** is a process whereby frustrated and angry people tend to displace their aggression from its real source to a convenient target—an out-group that is disliked, visible, and relatively powerless.
  - **The Way We Conform: Normative Rules** Institutionalized racism and institutionalized sexism are norms operating throughout the society's structure. Normative conformity, or the desire to be accepted and "fit in," leads many people to go along with stereotyped beliefs and not challenge them. Modern racism is an example of a shift in normative rules about prejudice: Nowadays, people have learned to hide their prejudice in situations where it would lead them to be labeled as racist.
  - **Subtle Sexism**
- **How Can Prejudice Be Reduced?** The most important way to reduce prejudice is through contact—bringing in-group and out-group members together; however, mere contact is not enough and can even exacerbate existing negative attitudes. Instead, contact situations must include the following six conditions: mutual interdependence; a common goal; equal status; informal, interpersonal contact; multiple contacts; and social norms of equality.
  - **The Contact Hypothesis**
  - **When Contact Reduces Prejudice: Six Conditions**
  - **Why Early Desegregation Failed**
  - **Why Does Jigsaw Work?**

CHAPTER 13 TEST 第13章习题

1. According to realistic conflict theory, prejudice and discrimination are likely to increase when:
   a. a country has a history of institutionalized racism
   b. the person who holds the stereotypes is frustrated
   c. people know that their close friends are prejudiced
   d. there is competition over jobs in a country
   e. prejudice is explicit rather than implicit

2. Rebecca is covering her college's football game against its archrival for the school newspaper. At the game, she interviews several students from her college, but decides she only needs to interview one or two students from the rival school to understand the general opinion of students at that rival school. Rebecca is demonstrating:
   a. in-group bias
   b. a perception of out-group homogeneity
   c. the ultimate attribution error
   d. blaming the victim

3. Because the number of blatant acts of prejudice and discrimination in the United States has declined sharply, and because affirmative action has provided women and minorities access to opportunities previously withheld, there has been
   a. a subtle but powerful backlash against members of these groups
   b. a gradual reduction in the self-esteem of men and members of the majority group
   c. a gradual increase in the self-esteem of women and minority group members
   d. a gradual increase in the self-esteem of majority group members

4. Suppose you're a bartender and observe occasional fights at your establishment. Although you don't know very many people with visible tattoos, it seems to you that people with tattoos are more likely to get into fights than people without tattoos. But you are wrong; people with visible tattoos have not been more likely to get into fights. Based on the research discussed in this chapter, your faulty memory is most likely due to:
   a. illusory correlation
   b. the subliminal priming of stereotypic information
   c. automatic activation of your stereotype
   d. realistic conflict theory

5. According to social psychological research, racism in America today:
   a. has almost completely disappeared
   b. results in low self-esteem for both the racists and those whom they discriminate against
   c. has decreased more at the controlled level than at the automatic level
   d. has remained the same at the controlled level

6. At a party, Sam makes negative comments about gays and lesbians. According to research in social psychology, which of the following is *least* likely to explain Sam's behavior?
   a. Sam recently found out he had done poorly on an important test and was experiencing low self-esteem
   b. Sam's friends often make similar comments and he conformed for normative reasons
   c. When Sam was growing up his parents often made negative comments about gays and lesbians
   d. Sam had high self-esteem and felt very secure about his own sexuality
   e. Sam recently applied for a job but Sam learned that an openly gay man got the job instead of him

7. According to social psychological research, which of the following is *least* likely to prevent Sam from making similar negative comments about gays and lesbians in the future?
   a. A woman Sam likes tells him that she disapproves of his negative comments
   b. Sam finds out that a member of a rival fraternity is gay
   c. Bob, a close friend of Sam's and a member of his fraternity, tells Sam that he (Bob) is gay
   d. Sam is assigned a lab partner in a biology class who is openly gay. In order to get a good grade in the class Sam must cooperate with his partner

8. Melissa, a high school senior, doesn't get in to the college she wants to attend. She blames this on affirmative action, and starts to act aggressively toward the minority students at her school. Melissa's aggression can best be explained by:
   a. out-group homogeneity
   b. the ultimate attribution error
   c. scapegoating
   d. the illusory correlation phenomenon

9. Which of the following is *least* true about race and stereotyping, from a social psychological perspective?
   a. Evolutionary theory holds that different human races have different genetic makeups that cause them to adopt different social behaviors
   b. People often look for information that will allow them to convince themselves that there is a valid justification for holding a negative attitude toward a particular group
   c. Stereotype threat has been found to lower the performance of African Americans and women
   d. Categorizing people is a convenient way of learning about and remembering things about them

10. Increasing contact between groups will reduce prejudice if all of the following conditions are met except one. Which one?
    a. Mutual interdependence
    b. Higher status of the minority group
    c. Multiple contacts
    d. Informal, interpersonal contact
    e. Social norms of equality

Chapter 13 Answer Key
1-d, 2-b, 3-c, 4-a, 5-c, 6-d, 7-b, 8-c, 9-a, 10-b

For more review plus practice tests, videos, flashcards, writing help and more, log on to MyPsychLab.

SOCIAL PSYCHOLOGY IN ACTION

1 Making a Difference with Social Psychology

Attaining a Sustainable Future

实践中的社会心理学之一：

获得可持续的未来

OUTLINE 提纲

- **Applied Research in Social Psychology**
  Capitalizing on the Experimental Method
  Social Psychology to the Rescue
- **Using Social Psychology to Achieve a Sustainable Future**
  Resolving Social Dilemmas
  Conveying and Changing Social Norms
  Keeping Track of Consumption
  Introducing a Little Competitiveness
  Inducing Hypocrisy
  Removing Small Barriers to Achieve Big Changes
- **Happiness and a Sustainable Lifestyle**
  What Makes People Happy?
  Money, Materialism, and Happiness
  Do People Know What Makes Them Happy?
- **Summary**

THE RESIDENTS OF SHISHMAREF, A VILLAGE OFF THE western coast of Alaska, recently voted to abandon their island and move to the mainland, at a total cost of $200–$300 million dollars. The cause? Global warming, which in this part of the world is not a theoretical issue, but a very real problem. About 15 years ago, the villagers noticed that the sea around the island was freezing later each fall and thawing earlier each spring, which made the island more vulnerable to sea surges during storms. In the fall of 1997, a storm washed away a 125-foot strip of land on the northern edge of the island. Four years later, 12-foot waves threatened the entire island, which rises to only 21 feet above sea level. Many feel that it is only a matter of time before the entire village is destroyed (Kolbert, 2006; "Alaskan village," 2008)

Planet Earth has always had a supply of "greenhouse" gases that capture heat from the sun and keep the earth warm. But ever since the Industrial Revolution in the eighteenth century, humans have been adding to these gases—chiefly carbon dioxide (CO_2), which is released when we burn fossil fuels (e.g., in power plants, factories, and automobiles). The amount of CO_2 we are now releasing far exceeds the amount that the earth can absorb naturally. As a result, the global temperature has been rising at an accelerating rate. In fact, since the year 2001, we have experienced seven of the eight warmest years ever recorded ("Global warming," 2008).

The village of Shismaref may signal the beginning of worldwide havoc due to global warming. Shelf ice in Antartica and Greenland has begun to melt at an alarming rate and may cause a 20-foot increase in sea levels over the next few decades. That might not seem like much, but it would cause the abandonment of many of the world's greatest cities and displace as many as 2 billion people (Weart, 2003). Further, many scientists believe that the frequency and severity of hurricanes are getting worse because of a rise in ocean temperatures. Hurricane Katrina may not have been a fluke, but a sign of what we can expect in coming years. In fact, the frequency of severe hurricanes has nearly doubled in the past 30 years. All told, deaths attributable to global warming may reach 300,000 people a year by 2030 (www.climatecrisis.net/thescience/).

Unfortunately, global warming is not the only environmental problem that human beings are causing. We are using natural resources (such as oil and coal) at an alarming rate. The United States imports 62 percent of its oil, a figure that is rising while worldwide demand for oil is increasing ("Where is our oil coming from?," 2008). And yet, scientists estimate that we already have or soon will reach

Because of global warming, the sea around the village of Shishmaref, Alaska, has been freezing later each fall and thawing earlier each spring. This makes the island more vulnerable to sea surges, which are destroying the island. This house, for example, was upended by a storm. Villagers fear that it is only a matter of time before the entire island is submerged.

the point of maximum oil production (Jones, 2003). Where to put our trash is another problem. In 1987 a barge called the *Mobro 4000* set out in search of a place to dump its cargo of trash from New York City because landfills in that area were overflowing. It made ports of call in North Carolina, Florida, Alabama, Mississippi, Louisiana, Mexico, Belize, and the Bahamas, but no one was willing to dump New York's trash in their landfills. Finally, after a 6,000-mile voyage, the *Mobro 4000* returned home, and local authorities convinced a landfill outside of New York City to incinerate and bury the trash. Where else is our trash going? Researchers recently discovered that a huge patch of the Pacific Ocean (an area larger than the United States) has become an enormous garbage dump. The problem is that a great deal of plastic material is produced and discarded into rivers and oceans near coastlines. Because the plastic is not biodegradable, it floats along currents into the north Pacific, which has become the final resting place for used toothbrushes, disposable lighers, plastic bags, and umbrella handles ("Plastic oceans," 2008).

The root cause of all of these environmental problems is that there are so many of us—nearly 7 billion people. As seen in Figure SPA-1.1, the human population was pretty steady until the Industrial Revolution, at which point people began to reproduce like crazy. Around that time the English clergyman Thomas Malthus warned that the human population was expanding so rapidly that soon there would not be enough food to feed everyone. He was wrong about when such a calamity would occur, largely because of technological advances in agriculture that have vastly improved grain yields. As the food supply dwindles, however, the number of malnourished people in the world increases: By some estimates, one out of every eight people in the world is hungry (Bunch, 2004). Malthus's timing may have been a little off, but many scientists fear that his predictions are becoming truer every day.

What can we do? Basically there are three solutions: First, we can try to curb population growth. The good news is that the rate of growth has slowed in the last few decades, though the population is still expanding (Rosenberg, 2006). Second, we can hope that improved technology bails us out, such as the development of more efficient grains and renewable energy sources such as wind and solar power. Although wonderful advances are being made in these areas, they are unlikely to solve environ-

In 1987, a barge called the *Mobro 4000* left New York City in search of a place to dump its load of trash. After traveling 6,000 miles and finding no takers, it returned to New York and dumped it in an overflowing landfill outside of the city.

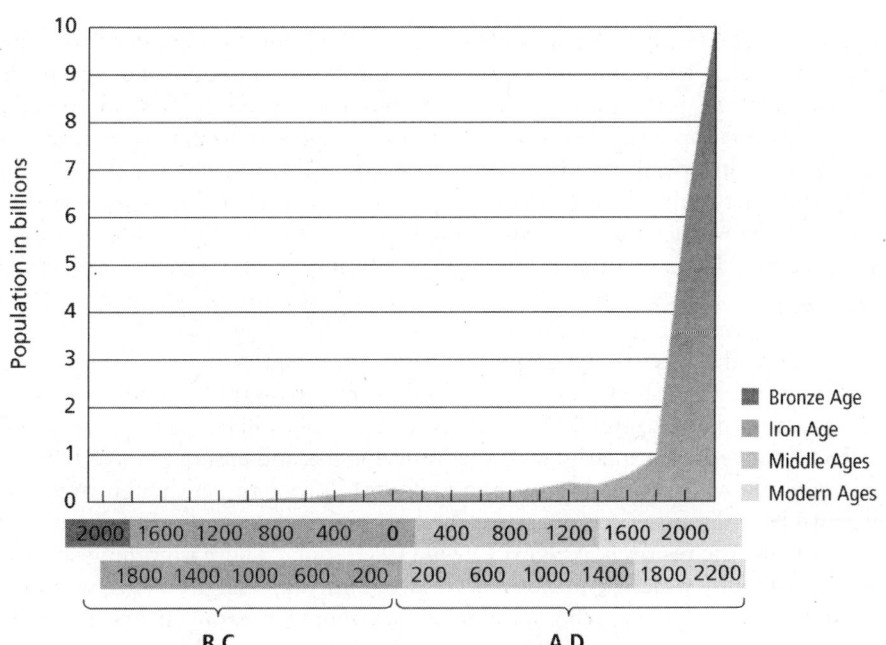

FIGURE SPA-1.1

The growth of world population.

The size of the human race increased only very gradually until the Industrial Revolution in the 18th century. It has been growing exponentially ever since.

mental problems on their own. Finally, people can adopt a more sustainable lifestyle by using fewer of the world's resources. This is easier said than done, of course; no one likes to be told that they have to consume less, and entrenched habits are hard to change. But if change we must, how can we encourage people to act in more environmentally responsible ways?

By now you know that this is a classic social psychological question. In earlier chapters we talked about how people form and change attitudes, how people are influenced by other people's behavior, the power of social norms, and so on. We turn now to a general discussion of how social psychology can be used to address social and psychological problems, followed by a specific discussion of research on getting people to adopt more sustainable lifestyles. Then, in the following chapters, we discuss two other major areas of applied social psychological research, namely health and the law, respectively.

"Gentlemen, it's time we gave some serious thought to the effects of global warming."

The New Yorker Collection, 1999. Mick Stevens from cartoonbank.com. All Rights Reserved.

Applied Research in Social Psychology
社会心理学的应用性研究

Since its inception, the field of social psychology has been interested in applying what it knows to solve practical problems. Kurt Lewin (1946), generally recognized as the founder of empirical social psychology, made three key points:

- Social psychological questions are best tested with the experimental method
- These studies can be used to understand basic psychological processes and to develop theories about social influence
- Social psychological theories and methods can be used to address pressing social problems

We already touched on these issues elsewhere in the book. In Chapter 2 we saw the importance of using the experimental method to test causal hypotheses, and in subsequent chapters we saw how social psychological research has increased our understanding of important theoretical questions, such as how people think about themselves and the social world, respond to social influence, change their attitudes, and help and hurt their fellow humans. Much of this research also dealt directly with important applied issues, such as school violence, racism, bystander intervention, and decision making. To many of us in the field, the beauty of social psychology is that by its very nature it addresses both basic and applied questions about human behavior. Research on stereotyping and prejudice, for example, investigates basic theoretical questions about the ways in which people form impressions of each other, as well as applied questions about how stereotyping and prejudice might be reduced.

As we discussed in Chapter 2, though, a distinction can still be made between *basic research* that is concerned primarily with theoretical issues and *applied research* that is concerned primarily with addressing specific real-world problems. Although much of the research we have discussed so far has touched on practical problems, it falls squarely in the category of basic research. As Kurt Lewin (1951) said, "There is nothing so practical as a good theory," by which he meant that to solve difficult social problems, we must first understand the underlying psychological dynamics of human nature and social influence. Increasingly, though, social psychologists are conducting studies designed specifically to address practical problems. In fact, social psychologists are better equipped to study applied problems than many other disciplines, for reasons we now discuss.

Capitalizing on the Experimental Method 利用实验法

One of the most important lessons of social psychology is the value of conducting experiments to answer questions about social influence. Nowhere is this more important than in finding ways to solve applied questions, such as getting people to reduce energy consumption. Only by conducting experiments (as opposed to observational or correlational studies; see Chapter 2) can we hope to discover which solutions will work the best.

Most people seem to understand this lesson in other domains, such as research on medical treatments. Suppose that a chemist found a new compound that seems to be an effective pain killer—the initial studies with rats look very promising, but studies with people have not yet been conducted. Should we allow a drug company to go ahead and market the drug to people? Not so fast, most of us would think. Who knows how safe the drug is for humans; it might turn out to have dangerous side effects, as seems to have been the case with the pain killer Vioxx. There should be extensive clinical trials in humans, in which people are randomly assigned to receive the new drug or a placebo, to see whether it really does reduce pain, and whether it has any serious side effects. Indeed, federal law requires extensive testing and approval by the FDA before drugs become available to the public.

We have laxer standards when it comes to testing psychological and social "treatments." If someone wants to try a new energy conservation technique, a new educational initiative, or a program to reduce prejudice, they can usually do so without a lot of rigorous testing of the intervention. A company might try a new program to reduce energy usage or institute a mandatory diversity training program, for example, before such techniques have been tested experimentally.

Well, you might think, what's the harm? Trying a new energy conservation program hardly puts people at risk, and we certainly don't want to inhibit innovation by subjecting people to cumbersome testing guidelines. And, can't we find out whether these interventions work by interviewing people afterward or seeing whether their behavior changes (e.g., do they use less energy after the conservation program)? Unfortunately, it's not so simple. It is difficult to test the effectiveness of an intervention without a randomly assigned control group, and failing to conduct such tests can have serious consequences.

Assessing the Effectiveness of Interventions As an example, consider a psychological intervention that has been widely implemented across the world to help people who have experienced traumatic events, such as rescue workers who witness multiple deaths in a natural disaster or plane crash. The basic idea of the program, called Critical Incident Stress Debriefing (CISD), is to bring people together as soon as possible after the trauma for a 3- to-4 hour session, in which participants describe their experiences in detail and discuss their emotional reactions to the events. This cathartic experience is supposed to prevent later psychiatric symptoms, including post-traumatic stress disorder (PTSD). Numerous fire and police departments have made CISD the treatment of choice for officers who witness terrible human tragedies. It is also widely used with civilians who experience traumatic events. Following the September 11, 2001, terrorists attacks, more than 9,000 counselors rushed to New York City to help survivors deal with the trauma and stress and prevent post-traumatic stress disorder, many using psychological debriefing techniques.

Psychological debriefing makes sense, doesn't it? An ounce of prevention is worth a pound of cure, and getting people to openly discuss their reactions to traumas, rather than bottling them up, seems like a good thing. "Seems like" and "really is" are not the same thing, however, and an interesting thing about CISD is that it was widely implemented before social scientists conducted rigorous tests of its effectiveness.

Think for a moment about how you might go about conducting such a test. Perhaps a good place to start would be to ask people who go through CISD what they think of it. Several studies have done just that, and found that participants often report that CISD was helpful. In one study, for example, 98 percent of police officers who had witnessed traumatic events and underwent psychological debriefing reported that they were satisfied with the procedure.

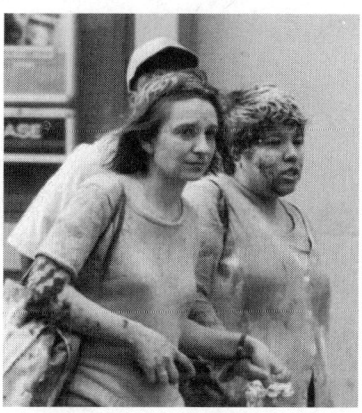

Following the September 11, 2001, terrorists attacks, more than 9,000 counselors rushed to New York City to help survivors deal with the trauma and stress and prevent post-traumatic stress disorder. Many used a technique called Critical Incident Stress Debriefing. Was this technique adequately tested before it was widely used? Does it work or actually do harm? (See the text for the answer.)

As we saw in Chapter 5, however, self-knowledge is not all that it's cracked up to be, and we should be careful about accepting these kinds of self-reports on face value. People might feel pressure to say a program that has been endorsed by their employers was helpful. More fundamentally, people might genuinely believe that the intervention was helpful, but they could be relying on theories that are incorrect. A firefighter might think, "Well, it was painful to have to rehash the fire and the deaths that I witnessed; I really would have rather gone home and played with my kids and forgotten about it. But, I guess it will help me in the long run to have talked it through now." The thing is, participants can't know how they would be feeling if they had *not* undergone the CISD procedure. Maybe firefighters who go home and play with their kids *do* feel better and are at no greater risk for problems down the road.

The only way to find out is to conduct an experiment in which some people are randomly assigned to undergo CISD and others are not, and then giving everyone a battery of psychological measures—ideally over a long period of time. This kind of experiment was finally conducted at various sites to test the effectiveness of CISD. The results have not been encouraging. In a comprehensive review of the literature, Harvard psychologist Richard McNally and his colleagues concluded that there is "no convincing evidence" that psychological debriefing techniques prevent post-traumatic stress disorders (McNally, Bryant, & Ehlers, 2003, p. 72).

Potential Risks of Social Interventions Even if CISD doesn't work as well as people said it did, what's the big deal? Surely getting people together to talk about their experiences can't do any harm. But here's another problem with social and psychological interventions: People use common sense to assess their effectiveness, and common sense is sometimes wrong. Not only has CISD been found to be ineffective at preventing PTSD, it may in fact do harm. In one study, participants who had been severely burned and admitted to the hospital were randomly assigned to receive CISD or to a control group that did not. All participants completed various psychological measures over the next several months and were interviewed at home by a researcher who was unaware of whether they had undergone CISD. The results were sobering: Thirteen months after the intervention, the CISD group had a significantly *higher* incidence of post-traumatic stress disorder, scored *higher* on psychological measures of anxiety and depression, and reported significantly *less* contentedness with their lives (Carlier, Voerman, & Gersons, 2000). Similar results have been found of studies testing the effectiveness of CISD with emergency workers. In their review of the literature, McNally and colleagues (2003) noted that "some evidence suggests that it [CISD] may impede natural recovery" and recommended that "for scientific and ethical reasons, professionals should cease compulsory debriefing of trauma-exposed people" (p. 72).

It turns out that right after a traumatic event, when people are experiencing considerable negative emotions, may not be the best time to focus on the event and discuss it with others. Instead, as we will see in Chapter SPA-2, people are often quite resilient when left alone (Bonanno, 2004). Forcing people to talk about and relive traumatic experiences may make people more likely to remember those experiences later. If people don't succeed in recovering on their own, they might do better to let some time pass before reliving the trauma, at a point when they have distance from it and can think about the event more objectively (Pennebaker, 2001).

Think of the consequences of implementing CISD so widely before it was adequately tested. Not only has it been a colossal waste of time, effort, and money but also thousands of police, fire, and rescue workers have been forced to undergo a debriefing procedure that may have harmed more of them than it helped. If this were a medical intervention, there would be a huge public outcry (followed by the inevitable lawsuits).

Social Psychology to the Rescue 社会心理救援

Social psychologists are in a unique position to find solutions to applied problems and to avoid fiascos like the widespread use of CISD. First, the field of social psychology is a rich source of theories about human behavior that people can draw upon to devise solutions to problems. Second, of equal importance, social psychologists know how to perform rigorous experimental tests of these solutions to see if they work (Wilson, 2005).

We encountered an excellent example of such an approach in Chapter 13 in our discussion of the contact hypothesis to reduce prejudice, the idea that bringing social groups together—under the right conditions—will reduce prejudice and stereotyping. More than 700 studies have tested the contact hypothesis, and the bottom line is that increasing contact between hostile groups works, but only under certain conditions, namely mutual interdependence; sharing a common goal; equal status; informal; interpersonal contact; multiple contacts; and social norms of equality (Pettigrew & Tropp, 2006).

Elliot Aronson and his colleagues drew on this work to devise an educational intervention, the Jigsaw Classroom (also discussed in Chapter 13), in which children of different backgrounds and races are placed in groups in which they have to interact and cooperate to earn good grades. Compared to children in traditional classrooms, children who take part in jigsaw groups show a decrease in prejudice and stereotyping, feel better about themselves and their school, and perform better on exams. Jigsaw techniques have been widely adopted in classrooms throughout the United States and other countries. We mention this research again because it is a prototypical example of a successful social psychological intervention, which grew out of solid theoretical work and was tested rigorously before being adopted—contrary to our example of CISD debriefing techniques.

There are many other examples of successful applied research by social psychologists, which we will discuss here and in the next two chapters. We return now to the issue with which we began this chapter, how to get people to act in ways that will help ensure a sustainable future.

Using Social Psychology to Achieve a Sustainable Future 利用社会心理学实现可持续发展

Social psychologists have adopted a variety of approaches to get people to act in more environmentally responsible ways. The approaches were inspired by social psychological theories and used the experimental method to see if the approach is successful (Abrahamse, Steg, & Vlek, 2005; Geller, 2002; Oskamp, 1995, 2000).

Resolving Social Dilemmas 解决社会困境

Be honest: When you think about the topic of energy conservation, how do you feel? If you are like us, you know you should conserve energy and reduce CO_2 emissions, but the prospect of changing your habits doesn't sound very appealing. It involves personal sacrifice, such as using our cars less, turning down the thermostat in the winter and up in the summer, and buying fewer consumer goods. "Why do I have to do these things," you might think. "After all, I'm just one person and why should I be the one to sacrifice?"

Good question. What we have here is a classic *social dilemma*, a conflict in which the most beneficial action for an individual will, if chosen by most people, have harmful effects on everyone (see Chapter 9). It is in everyone's self-interest to use as much energy as he or she wants; after all, one person's contribution to global warming is miniscule. But if we all adopt that attitude, we all suffer the consequences.

Of particular relevance to energy conservation is a type of social dilemma called the *commons dilemma*, a situation in which everyone takes from a common pool of goods that will replenish itself if used in moderation but will disappear if overused. Examples include the use of limited resources such as water and energy. Individuals benefit by using as much as they need, but if everyone does so, shortages result (Brucks & Van Lange, 2008; Dawes, 1980; Hardin, 1968; Levine & Moreland, 1998; Weber, Kopelman, & Messick, 2004). How can we resolve social dilemmas, convincing people to act for the greater good of everyone, rather than purely out of self-interest?

Social psychologists have devised some fascinating laboratory games to try to answer this question. In a typical study, the experimenter gathers a group of seven participants and gives them all a stake of money, such as $6. Participants are told that they can keep the money or donate some or all of it to the rest of the group. If they make a donation, the experimenter will double the amount and give it to the other group members. For example, if you donate your entire $6, it will be doubled to $12 and divided evenly among the six other participants. If other group members donate their money to the pot, it will be doubled and you will get a share. What would you do in this situation? If you are like most participants, you will keep your six bucks (Orbell, van de Kragt, & Dawes, 1988). It's risky to give away the money, because if everyone else keeps theirs, you will end up with nothing. "I'll hold on to what I have," most people think, "because at least I'll end up with something." The problem with this strategy is that because most people adopted it, everyone suffered. That is, the total pool of money to be divided remained low because few people allowed the experimenter to double the money by donating it to the group. As with many other social dilemmas, most people looked out for themselves, and as a result, everyone lost.

How can we convince people to trust their fellow group members, cooperating in such a way that everyone benefits? It is notoriously difficult to resolve social dilemmas, as indicated by the difficulty of getting people to conserve water when there are droughts, recycle their waste goods, and clean up a common area in a dormitory or apartment. Research has found that simply allowing the group to talk with each other for 10 minutes dramatically increases the number of people who donate money to the group (Orbell et al., 1988). Communication works in two ways. First, when people make a public commitment to help, it is harder to back down. Second, when people communicate, they are more likely to establish a sense of group identity and solidarity, which makes them more likely to act for the good of the group (Weber et al., 2004). Another way to increase cooperation is for one person to set an example by cooperating consistently and without exception. When people observe someone else acting in such a selfless manner, they contribute more to the group as a result (Weber & Murnighan, 2008). How else might we encourage people to adopt a more sustainable life style?

Conveying and Changing Social Norms
传递并改变社会规范

One approach is to try to remind people of social norms, the rules a group has for the acceptable behaviors, values, and beliefs of its members. As we discussed in Chapter 8, people follow two kinds of norms: *injunctive norms*, which

How can we encourage people to act in selfless ways that help the environment? One way is to set an example by acting that way ourselves. When people observe someone else acting in a selfless manner, they are likely to follow suit and cooperate as well.

"Help!"

Copyright © The New Yorker Collection 1991 Mike Stevens from cartoonbank.com. All Rights Reserved.

are people's perceptions of what behaviors are approved or disapproved of by others, and *descriptive norms*, which are people's perceptions of how people actually behave. If people believe that a certain kind of behavior is strongly frowned upon by their social group, and they observe that others are obeying the norm, they are likely to follow the norm as well (Christensen, Rothgerber, Wood, & Matz, 2004; Cialdini, 2003).

Robert Cialdini and his colleagues have illustrated the power of social norms in preventing people from littering. Compared to other environmental problems, littering may not seem to be all that serious a matter. Although billboards implore us to "Keep America Beautiful," many people seem to think it isn't a big deal to leave their paper cup at the side of the road instead of in a trash barrel. Unfortunately, those paper cups add up. In California, for example, $41 million of tax money is spent per year cleaning up litter ("Litter bugs," 2005). The stuff we discard is polluting our water systems, endangering wildlife, and costing us millions of dollars.

In Chapter 8, we discussed a field experiment by Reno and his colleagues (1993) in which an experimental accomplice conveyed an injunctive norm against littering by picking up a fast-food bag that had been discarded on the ground. The researchers hypothesized that seeing the accomplice pick up the fast-food bag would be a vivid reminder of the injunctive norm—littering is bad, and other people disapprove of it—and hence would lower people's inclination to litter. They were right; almost no one who saw the accomplice pick up the fast-food bag took a handbill that had been placed on the windshield of their car and tossed it on the ground. In a control condition, in which there was no fast-food bag on the ground and the accomplice simply walked by, 37 percent threw the handbill on the ground.

> We live in an environment whose principal product is garbage.
>
> —Russell Baker, 1968

What is the best way to communicate *descriptive* norms against littering? The most straightforward way, it would seem, would be to clean up all the litter in an environment, to illustrate that "no one litters here." In general, this is true: The less litter there is in an environment, the less likely people are to litter (Huffman, Grossnickle, Cope, & Huffman, 1995; Krauss, Freedman, & Whitcup, 1978; Reiter & Samuel, 1980). There is, however, an interesting exception to this finding. Cialdini, Reno, and Kallgren (1990) figured that seeing one conspicuous piece of litter on the ground, spoiling an otherwise clean environment, would be a better reminder of descriptive norms than seeing a completely clean environment. The single piece of trash sticks out like a sore thumb, reminding people that no one has littered here except one thoughtless person. In contrast, if there is no litter on the ground, people might be less likely to think about what the descriptive norm is. Ironically, then, littering may be more likely to occur in a totally clean environment than in one containing a single piece of litter.

To test this hypothesis, the researchers stuffed students' mailboxes with handbills and then observed, from a hidden vantage point, how many of the students dropped the handbills on the floor (Cialdini et al., 1990). In one condition, the researchers cleaned up the mailroom so that there were no other pieces of litter to be seen. In another condition, they placed one very noticeable piece of litter on the floor—a hollowed-out piece of watermelon. In a third condition, they not only put the watermelon rind on the floor but also spread out dozens

Besides being unsightly, litter can cost millions of dollars to clean up. Social psychologists have found that emphasizing different kinds of social norms against littering is an effective way to prevent it.

of discarded handbills. As predicted, the lowest rate of littering occurred in the condition where there was a single piece of trash on the floor (see Figure SPA-1.2). The single violation of a descriptive norm highlighted the fact that no one had littered but the one doofus who had dropped the watermelon rind on the floor. Now that people's attention was focused on the descriptive norm against littering, virtually none of the students littered. The highest percentage of littering occurred when the floor was littered with lots of handbills; here it was clear that there was a descriptive norm in favor of littering, and many of the students followed suit.

Another way of conveying descriptive norms is simply to tell people what most others do, particularly in situations in which you can't directly observe others' behavior. If you have ever stayed in a hotel, for example, you might have seen a sign asking you to reuse your towels, because washing towels every day wastes environmental resources (e.g., water and electricity). Do these appeals work? Not as much as conveying a descriptive norm about what people *actually* do. Researchers found that the standard appeal to help the environment worked less well than one that said, "Join Your Fellow Guests in Helping to Save the Environment" and said that 75 percent of guests reuse their towels (Goldstein, Cialdini, & Griskevicius, 2008). The simple message that "other people do it" can be enough to get people to do the right thing (Nolan, Schultz, Cialdini, Goldstein, & Griskevicius, 2008). If you would like to try to use descriptive norms in an experiment of your own, see the following Try It! exercise.

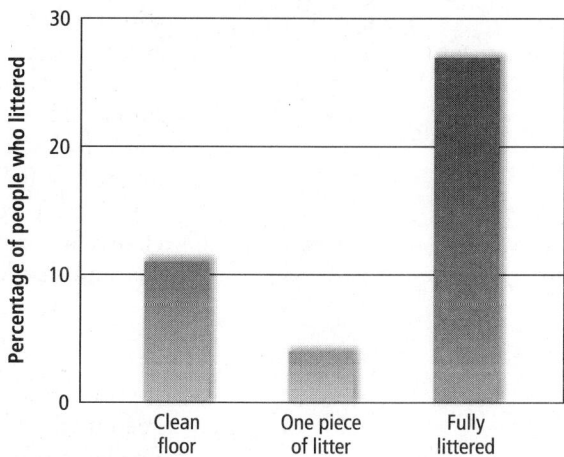

FIGURE SPA-1.2
Descriptive norms and littering.

Who littered the least—people who saw that no one else had littered, people who saw one piece of litter on the floor, or people who saw several pieces of litter? As shown in the figure, it was people who saw one piece of litter. Seeing the single piece of litter was most likely to draw people's attention to the fact that most people had not littered, making people less likely themselves to litter.

(Adapted from Cialdini, Reno, & Kallgren, 1990)

 试一试！通过描述性规范减少乱丢垃圾的行为
Reducing Littering with Descriptive Norms

See if you can use the findings from the Goldstein and colleagues' (2008) hotel study to get people to act in more environmentally friendly ways. For example, you could make different kinds of signs urging people to recycle their bottles and cans in a dormitory. In some locations (randomly chosen, of course), you might convey descriptives norms by saying, "Join Your Fellow Students in Helping to Save the Environment—75% of Residents of This Dorm Recycle Their Bottles and Cans." In other locations the signs could simply say, "Help to Save the Environment—Recycle Your Bottles and Cans." You can then keep track of how much people recycle in each location. Be creative and try different kinds of signs!

Clearly, drawing people's attention to both injunctive and descriptive norms can nudge them into acting in more environmentally responsible ways. But what happens when there are no norms for acting in environmentally responsible ways, or even norms for behaving in the opposite manner? Suppose, for example, that you are a member of a fraternity or sorority in which many people drive gas-guzzling SUVs. Perhaps that is the vehicle of choice for you and your peers; maybe it's even a sign of status and prestige. No one likes to "break the rules," and though you might have been thinking about trading in your Jeep Grand Cherokee for a car with a hybrid engine, you worry about what your friends will say.

But would it really be so bad? Sometimes people overestimate the consequences of violating an injunctive norm, in other words, how much our friends would really care if we traded in our SUV. Research shows that college students overestimate other injunctive norms, such as what their friends think about drinking alcohol. Many college students believe that their peers are more in favor of drinking than they actually are

(Borsari & Carey, 2005). The same might be true about cars—people might not care as much as you think about what kind of car you drive.

Even if your friends would look disparagingly at your purchase of a hybrid car, someone has to be the first to change an injunctive norm. As we saw in Chapter 8, it is easier to buck the tide if we can get just one other person to go along with us, so you might first try to convince a friend who is looking to buy a car to consider a hybrid. If this doesn't work, just go for it. You might be surprised by how much you alone can change a norm, especially if you keep reminding people how much you are saving on gas, and that SUVs are not nearly as safe as people think they are (Gladwell, 2005).

Keeping Track of Consumption 追踪消费

A problem with some environmental social dilemmas is that it is not easy for people to keep track of how much of a resource they are using, such as gas, electricity, or water. During a drought, for example, people may be asked to conserve water, but it is not easy for them to monitor how many gallons a month they are using. One pair of researchers reasoned that making it easy for people to keep track of their water consumption would make it easier for them to act on their concern for the greater good (Van Vugt & Samuelson, 1999). They compared two communities in the Hampshire region of England during a severe drought in the summer of 1995. The houses in one community had been equipped with water meters that allowed residents to monitor how much water they were consuming. The houses in the other community did not have meters. As expected, when people felt that the water shortage was severe, those in the metered houses consumed less water than those in the unmetered houses.

What if we got people to keep track of the energy they were saving, rather than the energy they were consuming? For example, what if we asked drivers to keep track of the miles they *avoided* driving, by walking, riding a bike, taking public transportation, or getting a ride with a friend? Making people more mindful of opportunities to avoid driving might make people more willing to leave their car at home. To find out, Graham, Koo, and Wilson (in press) asked college students to keep track of the number of miles they avoided driving and to record that figure on a Web site every other day for 2 weeks. As predicted, students who kept track of the miles they saved drove their cars less than did students in a control group who did not keep track of the miles they saved. This finding is consistent with research showing that simply keeping track of one's behavior is the first step to changing it.

Graham and colleagues (in press) also examined whether giving the students different kinds of feedback about the miles they saved would influence their driving habits. After students entered how many miles they had avoided driving, some received feedback about how much money they had saved on gas and maintenance costs. Others received feedback about savings in air pollution (e.g., how many carbon dioxide and hydrocarbon emissions weren't emitted). Some got both kinds of feedback. It turned out that this latter group—that learned both how much money they had saved and how much pollution wasn't emitted—was especially likely to avoid driving their cars. Keeping track of one's behavior that avoids environmental damage, and receiving concrete feedback about the savings, turned out to be an effective way to get college students to drive their cars less. (If you would like to try this on your own, you can download a spreadsheet with instructions how to use it at: people.virginia.edu/~tdw/Driving.file.htm).

Introducing a Little Competitiveness 适当引入竞争

Other researchers have demonstrated that a little competitiveness helps people conserve energy in the workplace (Siero, Bakker, Dekker, & Van Den Burg, 1996). At one unit of a factory in the Netherlands, the employees were urged to engage in energy-saving behaviors. For example, announcements were placed in the company magazine asking people to close windows during cold weather and to turn off lights when leaving a room. In addition, the employees got weekly feedback on their behavior; graphs were posted that showed how much they had improved their energy-saving behaviors, such as how often they had turned off the lights. This intervention resulted in modest improvement. By the end of the program, for example, the number of times people left the lights on decreased by 27 percent.

Another unit of the factory took part in an identical program, with one difference: In addition to receiving weekly feedback on their own energy-saving actions, they received feedback about how the other unit was doing. The researchers hypothesized that this social comparison information would motivate people to do better than their colleagues in the other unit. As seen in Figure SPA-1.3, they were right. By the end of the program, the number of times people left lights on had decreased by 61 percent. Engaging people's competitive spirit can have a large impact on their behavior (Staats, Harland, & Wilke, 2004).

Inducing Hypocrisy 诱导伪善

In many areas water is becoming an increasingly scarce resource. Part of the reason is population growth in areas that have limited water supplies, such as the Southwestern United States. Another cause is droughts, which are becoming increasingly frequent as the temperature of the earth rises. Thirty years ago 10 percent to 15 percent of the earth was drought-stricken; today, that figure is closer to 30 percent ("Drought's growing reach," 2005). It is thus important to find ways to encourage people to conserve water, especially when drought conditions exist.

Several years ago, when California was experiencing severe water shortages, the administrators at one campus of the University of California realized that an enormous amount of water was being wasted by students using the university athletic facilities. The administrators posted signs in the shower rooms of the gymnasiums, exhorting students to conserve water by taking briefer, more efficient showers. The signs appealed to the students' conscience by urging them to take brief showers and to turn off the water while soaping up. The administrators were confident the signs would be effective because the vast majority of students at this campus were ecology-minded and believed in preserving natural resources; however, systematic observation revealed that fewer than 15 percent of the students complied with the conservation message on the posted signs.

The administrators were puzzled—perhaps the majority of the students hadn't paid attention to the signs? After all, a sign on the wall is easy to ignore. So administrators made each sign more obtrusive, putting it on a tripod at the entrance to the showers so that the students needed to walk around the sign in order to get into the shower room. Although this increased compliance slightly (19 percent turned off the shower while soaping up), it apparently made a great many students angry—the sign was continually being knocked over and kicked around, and a large percentage of students took inordinately long showers, apparently as a reaction against being told what to do. The sign was doing more harm than good, puzzling the administrators even more. Time to call in the social psychologists.

Elliot Aronson and his students (Dickerson, Thibodeau, Aronson, & Miller, 1992) decided to apply a technique they had used successfully to get people to practice safer sex (see a description of this study in Chapter 6). The procedure involved intercepting female students who were on their way from the swimming pool to the women's shower room, introducing the experimental manipulations and then having a research assistant casually follow them into the shower room, where she unobtrusively timed their showers. Research participants in one condition were asked to respond to a brief questionnaire about their water use, a task designed to make them mindful of how they sometimes wasted water while showering. In another condition, research participants made a public commitment, exhorting others to take steps to conserve water.

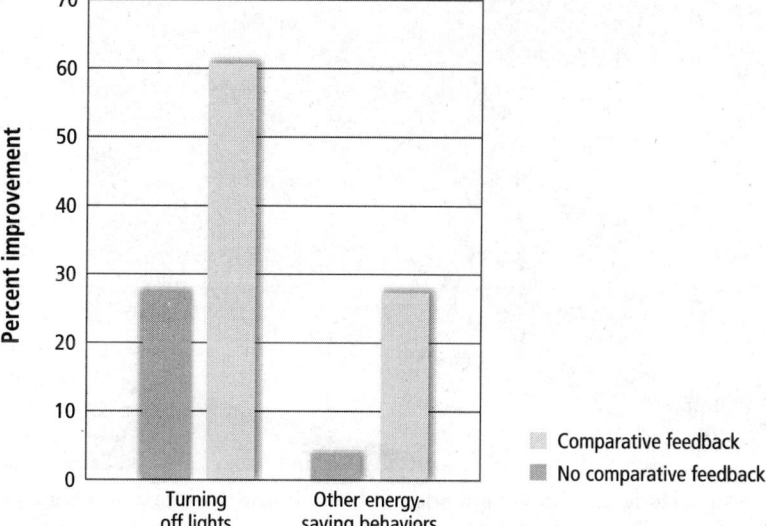

FIGURE SPA-1.3
Effects of comparative feedback on energy-saving behaviors.

Two units of a factory were urged to conserve energy and received feedback about how their unit was doing. Only one of the units, however, received comparative feedback about how it was doing relative to the other unit. As seen in the graph, this second unit improved its behavior the most, especially by turning off lights more.

(Adapted from Siero, Bakker, Dekker, & Van Den Burgh, 1996)

In an age where man has forgotten his origins and is blind even to his most essential needs for survival, water along with other resources has become the victim of his indifference.

—Rachel Carson, *The Silent Spring*, 1962

College students who were made aware that they were advocating water conservation behaviors they themselves were not practicing changed their behavior by taking shorter showers.

Specifically, these participants were asked to sign their names to a public poster that read, "Take Shorter Showers. Turn Shower Off While Soaping Up. If I Can Do It, So Can YOU!" In the crucial condition—the "hypocrisy" condition—the participants did both; that is, they were made mindful of their own wasteful behavior, and they indicated publicly (on the poster) that they were practicing water conservation. In short, they were made aware that they were preaching behavior they themselves were not practicing. Just as in the condom study described in Chapter 6, those participants who were made to feel like hypocrites changed their behavior so that they could feel good about themselves. In this case, they took very brief showers. Indeed, the procedure was so effective that the average time students in this condition spent showering was reduced to 3.5 minutes. The hypocrisy procedure has been found to increase other environmentally sound practices as well, such as recycling (Fried & Aronson, 1995).

Removing Small Barriers to Achieve Big Changes
消除小障碍，实现大变化

Sometimes the best way to change people's behavior is simply to make it easy for them to do so. Consider recycling. To reduce the amount of trash that ends up in landfills, many cities are encouraging their residents to recycle materials such as glass, paper, and aluminum. But as you know, it can be inconvenient to do so; in some areas, you have to load your car with boxes of cans and bottles and drop them off at a recycling center, which might be several miles from your house. Other cities have curbside recycling, whereby a truck picks up recycling materials that you set out at the curb on a designated day. Even here, though, you have to remember to separate your cans and bottles from the rest of the trash and find a place to store them until the pickup day. We thus have another social dilemma—a behavior (recycling) that, while good for us all, is effortful and unpleasant for individuals. As you might imagine, several social psychologists have turned their attention to ways of getting people to recycle more.

There have been two general approaches to this problem. First, some psychologists have focused on ways of changing people's attitudes and values in a pro-environment direction, with the assumption that their behavior will follow suit. This assumption is consistent with social psychological research on attitudes, which has found that under many conditions, people's attitudes are good predictors of their behavior (see Chapter 7). Several studies have found that people's attitudes toward recycling are in fact good predictors of their recycling behaviors, suggesting that a mass media campaign that targets people's attitudes is a good way to go (Knussen, Yule, & MacKenzie, 2004; Oskamp, Burkhardt, Schultz, Hurin, & Zelezny, 1998; Valle, Rebelo, & Reis, 2005).

Sometimes, however, we fail to act consistently with our attitudes, despite our best intentions. Perhaps the recycling center is too far away or we just can't find the time to sort our trash, even though we know we should. Kurt Lewin (1947), one of the founders of social psychology, made the observation that big social changes can sometimes occur by removing small barriers from people's environments (Ross & Nisbett, 1991). When it comes to recycling, it might be better simply to make it hassle-free, such as instituting curbside recycling, than to try to change people's attitudes toward the environment. A number of studies have found this to be true. Increasing the number of recycling bins in a community, instituting curbside recycling, and allowing residents to mix materials, instead of having to sort them, have all been found to increase people's recycling behaviors (Domina & Koch, 2002; Ludwig, Gray, & Rowell, 1998; Schultz, Oskamp, & Mainieri, 1995).

Consider a natural experiment that was conducted in Fairfax County, Virginia (Guagnano, Stern, & Dietz, 1995). Curbside recyling had recently begun in the county, but only about a quarter of the residents had received plastic bins in which to put their recyclable materials. Others had to find their own containers in which to put their bottles and cans. Now, it might seem as if this would not be much of an impedi-

Sometimes the best way to change people's behavior is simply to make it easy for them to do so. When cities provide curbside recycling pickup, and provide the bins, even people who do not have strong pro-environmental attitudes are likely to recycle.

ment to recycling; if people really cared about the environment, they should be able to find their own box. As Lewin argued, however, sometimes little barriers have big effects, and indeed, the people who had the bins were much more likely to recycle. The researchers also measured people's attitudes toward recycling to see if those with positive attitudes were more likely to recycle than those who were not. Interestingly, people's attitudes predicted behavior only when they did *not* possess a recycling bin. When there was a barrier preventing easy compliance—people had to search through the garage to find a suitable box—only those with positive attitudes made the effort to circumvent the barrier. When there was no barrier—people had a convenient container provided by the county—attitudes did not matter as much. People were likely to conform even if they did not have strong pro-environmental attitudes. One study, for example, found that providing office workers with a recycling box that they could keep next to their desks dramatically increased the amount of paper they recycled (Holland, Aarts, & Langendam, 2006). The simple convenience of putting paper in a box next to their desk—as opposed to taking it to a central location—was enough to alter people's behavior. Of course, we can't make every behavior easy to perform. How else can we nudge people into doing the right thing? The same study found that it works to get people to form **implementation intentions**, which are people's specific plans about where, when, and how they will fulfill a goal. The researchers also measured the extent to which people recycled plastic cups, which had to be taken to a central location (that is, the workers did not have boxes in their offices in which they could deposit used cups). Workers in the implementation intention condition were first asked to visualize and write down exactly when, where, and how they would recycle their cups, whereas workers in a control condition were not. People in the former condition recycled nearly four times as many cups as those in the latter, suggesting that the best-laid plans of mice and men often go awry (to paraphrase the poet Robert Burns), *unless* we first visualize how we are going to make those plans come true.

Now that you have read about several approaches for changing people's behavior in ways that help the environment, you are in a position to try them out yourself. See the following Try It! exercise for suggestions on how to do this.

implementation intentions
People's specific plans about where, when, and how they will fulfill a goal.

试一试！改变破坏环境的行为
TRY IT! Changing Environmentally Damaging Behaviors

Use the techniques discussed in this chapter to change people's behavior in ways that help the environment. Here's how to proceed.

1. Choose the behavior you want to change. You might try to reduce the amount of electricity used in your dorm, increase the amount that you and your roommates recycle, or increase water conservation.

2. Choose the technique you will use to change the behavior. For example, you might use the comparative feedback technique used by Frans Siero and colleagues (1996) to increase energy conservation. Encourage two areas of your dormitory to reduce energy usage or to recycle, and give each feedback about how it is doing relative to the other area. (To do this, you will have to have an easy, objective way of measuring people's behavior, such as the number of lights that are left on at night or the number of cans that are recycled.) Or you might try the hypocrisy technique used by Elliot Aronson and colleagues (Dickerson et al., 1992) to increase water conservation, whereby you ask people to sign a public poster that encourages recycling and have them fill out a questionnaire that makes them mindful of times they have failed to recycle. Be creative, and feel free to use more than one technique.

3. Measure the success of your intervention. Find an easy way to measure people's behavior, such as the amount that they recycle. Assess their behavior before and after your intervention. Best of all, include a control group of people who do not receive your intervention (randomly assigned, of course). In the absence of such a control group, it will be difficult to gauge the success of your intervention; for example, if people's behavior changes over time, you won't be able to tell if it is because of your intervention or some other factor (e.g., an article on recycling that happened to appear in the newspaper). By comparing the changes in behavior in your target group to the control group, you will have a better estimate of the success of your intervention.

Happiness and a Sustainable Lifestyle
幸福和可持续的生活方式

The research we have been discussing thus far might seem sobering or even depressing. There are lots of environmental problems and drastic steps are necessary to prevent them. We need to cut back on our use of energy, buy less, recycle more, and in general tighten our belts. This doesn't sound like a recipe for a happy life, does it? Actually, it might be. We end this chapter on a positive note by discussing research showing that consumption isn't nearly what it's cracked up to be, when it comes to being happy. It is entirely possible to adopt a sustainable lifestyle and be a very happy person.

What Makes People Happy? 让人们幸福的是什么？

A good place to start is with the question of what makes people happy. This is a complicated question, of course, and part of the recipe for happiness is outside of our control. Most psychologists agree, for example, that happiness is partly genetic; some of us are born with a happier temperament than others (Lykken & Tellegen, 1996). Further, environmental circumstances outside of our control, such as huge political upheavals in a country, can have a big impact on happiness (Inglehart & Klingemann, 2000). Nonetheless, research shows that there are things that people *can* control that influence their happiness. Three of the most important factors are having satisfying relationships with other people, pursuing something you love, and helping others.

Satisfying Relationships Perhaps the best predictor of whether someone is happy is the quality of his or her social relationships. In one study, for example, extremely happy college students were compared to their less-happy peers, and the main thing that set them apart was that happy people spent more time with other people and were more satisfied with their relationships (Diener & Seligman, 2003). Now, being a good social psychologist you know that this is a correlational finding, and that there are three possible explanations for it: Good social relationships make people happy, happy people are more likely to have good relationships, or a third variable, such as being extraverted, makes people happier and more likely to have good relationships. These possibilities are not mutually exclusive; in fact, we suspect that all three are true. But researchers generally agree that having high-quality relationships is a major source of happiness (Baumeister & Leary, 1995; Diener & Biswas-Diener, 2008; Diener & Oishi, 2005).

Very happy people are more likely to spend time with other people and are more satisfied with their relationships than are less happy people.

Flow: Becoming Engaged in Something You Enjoy Think back to a time when you worked very hard to achieve a highly valued goal and your efforts paid off. Perhaps you were on a sports team that won a championship, or in an orchestra that performed a concert to rave reviews. Now think back to when you were the happiest: After you achieved the goal, for example, the game ended and you were the champions—or while you were working toward the goal, for example, during the game, when you were playing well and your team was ahead, but you didn't know for sure whether you would win? Although it can be incredibly gratifying to have our dreams come true, there is evidence that people are happier when they are working at something they enjoy and making progress (Haidt, 2006).

There are a couple of reasons for this. First, when people are working toward a goal they are often in a highly desired state called *flow*, which occurs when people are "lost" in a task that is challenging, but attainable (Csikszentiomihalyi, 1997). Flow is what people feel when they are highly absorbed in a task and have the sense that they are making progress, such as when they are playing sports, engaged in creative activities such as writing, composing, or performing, or simply working on an enjoyable puzzle. Flow is such a pleasurable and absorbing state that people often lose track of how much time has passed and exactly where they are. When people achieve their goal—the game is over, or they complete a work of art—the flow stops. People may be very gratified with what they have accomplished, but they are no longer "lost" in the pursuit of their goal (Keller & Bless, 2008).

Second, when people are working toward a goal but are not certain that they will obtain it, it is hard to think about anything else. The uncertainty about the outcome focuses their attention on the task and other matters fade from view. After a goal is obtained, however, people's thoughts invariably turn to other matters—such as how much homework they have and the fact that they need to do their laundry. People usually adapt quickly to their successes, in the sense that sooner or later, their accomplishment comes to seem normal, perhaps even expected, and not something that they think about all that much. In short, pursuing something in an enjoyable way often makes us happier than getting it.

> *Things won are done; joy's soul lies in the doing.*
> —Shakespeare, *Troilus and Cressida*, I.ii.287

Helping Others A good way to be happy and feel better about yourself is to help other people. Lyubomirsky, Sheldon, and Schkade (2005), for example, asked college students to perform five acts of kindness toward others, all in one day. Examples included giving blood, visiting an elderly relative, and helping friends with their homework. Most college students are incredibly busy and this probably seemed like an imposition at first; imagine you had to come up with five acts of kindness and perform them by the end of the day. As it happened, though, the people who were randomly assigned to this condition reported that they were happier than people randomly assigned to a control group and just went about their normal routines. In fact, the "acts of kindness" group maintained this elevated happiness for several weeks. Or, consider a study by Dunn, Aknin, and Norton (2008). They gave passersby an envelope containing a small amount of cash and asked them to spend it on themselves or on someone else by 5:00 P.M. that afternoon. When the researchers telephoned people that evening, the ones that were the happiest were those who had been instructed to spend the money on someone else. Doing a good deed for others made people happier than treating themselves to a small gift.

Helping others can make people happy in a couple of ways. First, it is a way of connecting people to others and enhancing social relationships, which we've already seen is an important source of happiness. Second, people who help others are likely to come to view themselves in a more positive light, namely as the "kind of person" who is altruistic and cares about others (see our discussion of self-perception theory in Chapter 5).

Money, Materialism, and Happiness 金钱，物质主义和幸福

You may have noticed some important omissions from our recipe for happiness: accumulating money, buying lots of stuff, and in general using a lot of the world's resources. Research shows that the relationship between the amount of money people make and how happy they are is weak at best. People who are very poor and have trouble getting food and shelter are, not surprisingly, less happy than others. After people have the basic necessities of life, however, having more money doesn't increase happiness much at all (Diener & Seligman, 2004; Howell & Howell, 2008; Kahneman, Krueger, Schkade, Schwarz, & Stone, 2006). Consider Figure SPA-1.4 that plots the rise in the gross national product in the United States, from 1940 to 2000. As seen in the top line in the graph Americans have become dramatically wealthier over time. As seen in the bottom line, however, happiness has remained remarkably stable.

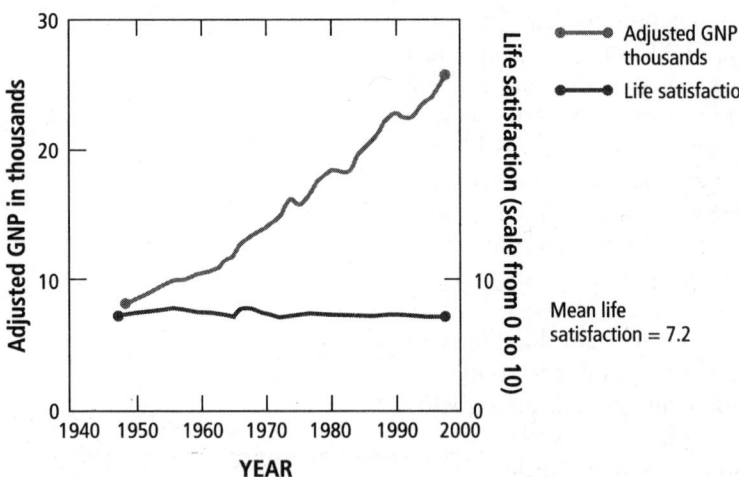

FIGURE SPA-1.4

Life satisfaction in the United States and the gross national product (1940–2000).

People in the United States have become much wealthier in the last 60 years; however, the average amount of life satisfaction people report has remained remarkably steady.

(Adapted from Diener & Seligman, 2004)

Further, there is evidence that people who are materialistic—those who place a high value on money and possessions—are less happy than people who place less value on money and possessions. One reason for this is that people who are materialistic have less satisfying social relationships (Banerjee & Dittmar, 2008; Nickerson, Schwarz, Diener, & Kahneman, 2003). Does this mean that money itself is the problem? Not necessarily. If people used money to obtain the things that really do increase happiness, such as high-quality social relationships, the meaningful pursuit of goals, and helping others—then so much the better. The point is that people who do not have much money can also achieve these things (Frank, 1999).

Do People Know What Makes Them Happy? 人们知道让他们幸福的是什么吗?

An interesting point about research on what makes people happy is that many of us haven't figured it out on our own. Research on *affective forecasting* has found that people often make systematic mistakes about what will make them happy in the future (Gilbert, 2007; Gilbert & Wilson, 2007; Wilson & Gilbert, 2003). When it comes to understanding the recipe for happiness, some people even get it backwards.

When we talk with our undergraduate advisees about their career plans, for example, many of them mention that their goal is to make a lot of money. They are not alone: Most college freshmen, on an annual survey conducted by UCLA and the American Council of Education, rate "to be able to make more money" as one of the most important reasons for going to college ("The American freshman," 2006). There is nothing wrong with wanting to achieve a comfortable lifestyle, of course. But as we have discussed, money itself does not make people happy, especially if it breeds materialism.

We also saw that one of the best predictors of happiness is having satisfying social relationships. And yet, Americans are becoming increasingly isolated from each other. In the last few decades people have become less likely to go to church, attend public meetings, get together to play cards, or entertain friends in their homes (Putnam, 2000). In 1985, about 75 percent of the people surveyed said that they had a close friend with whom they could talk about their problems, but by 2004, only half the people said they had such a friend (Vedantam, 2006).

In short, people often strive for things that are unlikely to make them happier (e.g., earning lots of money) and overlook things that will make them happier (e.g., spending time with close friends and loved ones). And, ironically, striving for money and more consumption is a source of many environmental problems, whereas the things that really make people happy (e.g., social relationships) are not. When it comes to achieving a sustainable lifestyle, the kinds of changes we may need to make can be done without sacrificing the things that truly make people happy.

Suppose, for example, you could choose between two lives. In Life A you live in a huge house in the suburbs and earn $250,000 a year, which you spend on lots of nice things: beautiful furniture, expensive cars, designer clothes. The downside is that you have a long commute to a job you don't really enjoy very much; you are an attorney, say, and spend most of your time researching how large cor-

If people earn enough to buy the basic necessities of life, earning more money does not make them happier. People who are materialistic—those who place a high value on money and possessions—tend to be less happy than people who place less value on money and possessions.

porations can pay fewer taxes. In Life B you live in an apartment and earn $40,000 a year. You don't own a car; most days you ride your bicycle or walk the short distance to your job as a teacher. You can't wait to get to work each morning because you love what you do, especially when you see your efforts to help kids pay off. You have lots of friends at the school where you teach as well as a tightly knit group of friends from college with whom you get together nearly every weekend. You have many interests and hobbies that keep you busy; you recently started taking salsa dance lessons, for example, and you volunteer with a literacy group that teaches adults how to read.

These are extreme examples, of course, and you might argue that we have stacked the deck toward Life B (there is no reason, for example, that our tax attorney couldn't take salsa lessons as well). But we hope the point is clear: Life B includes the recipe for happiness, namely lots of satisfying social relationships, plenty of flow experiences (at work and during leisure time), and ample opportunities to help others. Life A satisfies none of these things. Further, Life A is much less sustainable than Life B, in terms of the amount of resources a person living it would consume—the energy required to heat and cool the huge house, the gasoline needed to commute to work, the resources needed to produce all the consumer items the person buys. The environmental problems we face are severe, but the good news is that we can meet the challenges without sacrificing the things that make us truly happy.

Summary 总 结

- **Applied Research in Social Psychology** By its very nature, social psychology addresses both basic and applied questions about human behavior. Social psychologists have conducted a good deal of applied research on important social and psychological issues, such as how people can adopt a more sustainable lifestyle.
  - **Capitalizing on the Experimental Method** One of the most important lessons of social psychology is the value of conducting experiments to answer questions about social influence. This lesson is important when testing the effectiveness of interventions designed to solve an applied problem. Some interventions have backfired and had negative effects because they were not adequately tested.
  - **Social Psychology to the Rescue** Social psychologists are in a unique position to find solutions to applied problems. First, the field of social psychology is a rich source of theories about human behavior that people can draw upon to devise solutions to problems. Second, social psychologists know how to perform rigorous experimental tests of these solutions to see if they work.
- **Using Social Psychology to Achieve a Sustainable Future** The human population is expanding at an exponential rate with severe environmental consequences. Famine and malnutrition are spreading, natural resources are being depleted, and global warming is an alarming, immediate problem. Social psychologists have devised a number of different approaches to encourage people to adopt a more sustainable lifestyle.

- **Resolving Social Dilemmas** Energy conservation is a type of social dilemma called a *commons dilemma*, a situation in which everyone takes from a common pool of goods that will replenish itself if used in moderation but will disappear if overused. It is in any individual's interest to consume as much as possible, but if everyone acts that way everyone loses—there are no resources left. Social psychologists have studied the conditions under which people are most likely to act for the common good, such as encouraging people to communicate with each other.
- **Conveying and Changing Social Norms** Another approach is to remind people of both **injunctive** and **descriptive norms** against environmentally damaging acts, such as littering. For example, communicating descriptive norms—that other people act in environmentally-friendy ways—has been shown to reduce the extent to which passersby litter and increase the extent to which hotel room guests reuse their towels.
- **Keeping Track of Consumption** One simple technique is to make it easier for people to know how much energy they are using, for example, by providing them with water meters that are easy to read. College students who kept track of the number of miles they avoided driving their cars (e.g., by walking or taking the bus) drove their cars less.
- **Introducing a Little Competitiveness** Units in a company that were competing with each other to conserve energy were more successful than units that were encouraged to save but did not compete.

- **Inducing Hypocrisy** It works to arouse dissonance in people by making them feel that they are not practicing what they are preaching—for example, that even though they believe in water conservation, they are taking long showers.
- **Removing Small Barriers to Achieve Big Changes** Removing barriers that make pro-environmental behaviors difficult, such as instituting curbside recycling and providing people with recycling bins, has been shown to be effective. It also helps to get people to form **implementation intentions**, which are people's specific plans about where, when, and how they will fulfill a goal, such as the goal to recycle.

- **Happiness and a Sustainable Lifestyle** It is possible to adopt a sustainable lifestyle and be a happy person.
  - **What Makes People Happy?** Happiness is partly a matter of the temperament with which we are born and partly a matter of environmental conditions outside of our control, such as the political stability of the government. Three things we can control also influence our happiness: the quality of our social relationships, opportunities for "flow" experiences, and helping others.
  - **Money, Materialism, and Happiness** After people have the basic necessities of life, having more money doesn't increase happiness much at all. Further, people who are materialistic—those who place a high value on money and possessions—tend to be less happy than people who place less value on money and possessions.
  - **Do People Know What Makes Them Happy?** When it comes to understanding the recipe for happiness, some people get it backward—they focus too much on wealth and materialism and too little on social relationships, flow, and helping others. The moral is that people can achieve a sustainable lifestyle without sacrificing the things that make people truly happy.

CHAPTER SPA-1 TEST 第14章习题

1. According to what you read in this chapter, which of the following is likely to be *least* effective at solving environmental problems?
    a. Finding more efficient ways of getting rid of the trash human beings generate
    b. Slowing the population growth of human beings
    c. Developing new technologies such as more efficient grains and renewable energy sources such as wind and solar power
    d. Getting people to adopt a more sustainable lifestyle by using fewer of the world's resources

2. Which of the following statements is *least* true about the social psychological approach to solving applied problems?
    a. Applied questions are best tested with the experimental method.
    b. There is nothing as practical as a good theory.
    c. Social psychological theories and methods can be used to address pressing social problems.
    d. Given how pressing many problems are, it is a good idea to implement solutions before we are able to test them experimentally.

3. All of the following will help solve social dilemmas *except*:
    a. appealing to people's self-interest by telling them that if they don't cooperate they will suffer in the long run.
    b. allowing people to talk with each other before deciding how to act.
    c. having one person set an example by cooperating consistently and without exception.
    d. having people commit publicly to acting in a cooperative way.

4. Suppose you want people in your apartment building to stop throwing their junk mail on the floor of the mailroom. Which of the following would be *least* likely to work?
    a. Set an example by picking up the litter yourself when people are watching.
    b. Post a sign informing people that there is a recycling center on the other side of town that accepts junk mail.
    c. Clean up all the litter in the mailroom, but leave one very noticeable piece of trash on the floor.
    d. Post a sign in the mailroom that says, "Join Your Fellow Residents in Helping to Keep Things Clean—90% of Residents Recycle Their Junk Mail."

5. Suppose you live in a dorm and want to get people who live there to act in more environmentally responsible ways, such as recycling more. Which of the following would be *least* likely to work, according to social psychological research?
    a. Measure how much the dorm recycles each month, and post graphs of these figures where everyone can see them.
    b. Set up a competition with another dorm whereby the one that recycles more each month wins free pizzas.
    c. Make a point of taking soda cans out of the trash and putting them in a recycling bin in a public area where lots of people can see you do this.
    d. Give people statistics about how much recycling saves energy and prevents landfills from overflowing.

6. Suppose you wanted to get people to use less electricity where you work by getting them to turn off lights when they leave. Which of the following is likely to work the best, based on research in social psychology?
    a. Get people to sign a public pledge that they will turn off lights when they leave.
    b. Ask people to write about times when they forgot to turn off lights when they left.
    c. Ask people to do both—sign the public pledge and write about times they didn't turn off the lights.
    d. Ask people to sign the public pledge and write about times they did turn off the lights when they left.

7. Which of the following is *least* likely to make people happy?
   a. Helping other people
   b. Having satisfying relationships with other people
   c. Earning enough money to be able to afford a lot of luxury possessions
   d. Having "flow" activities in which people become highly engaged

8. Which of the following is most true about research on happiness?
   a. People have a pretty good idea of what will make them happy in the future.
   b. One of the best predictors of happiness is having satisfying social relationships, but Americans are becoming increasingly isolated from each other.
   c. When choosing a career, the most important thing to consider is how much money you will earn.
   d. Acting in ways that will help the environment will probably make people less happy.

Answer Key
1-a, 2-d, 3-a, 4-b, 5-d, 6-c, 7-c, 8-b

For more review plus practice tests, videos, flashcards, writing help and more, log on to MyPsychLab.

SOCIAL PSYCHOLOGY IN ACTION

2 Social Psychology and Health
实践中的社会心理学之二：
社会心理学与健康

OUTLINE 提纲

- **Stress and Human Health**
  - Resilience
  - Perceived Stress and Health
  - Feeling in Charge: The Importance of Perceived Control
  - Knowing You Can Do It: Self-Efficacy
  - Explaining Negative Events: Learned Helplessness
  - Optimism: Looking on the Bright Side
- **Coping with Stress**
  - Gender Differences in Coping with Stress
  - Social Support: Getting Help from Others
  - Opening Up: Making Sense of Traumatic Events
- **Prevention: Promoting Healthier Behavior**
  - Preventable Health Problems
  - Social Psychological Interventions: Targeting Safer Sex
- **Summary**

JOANNE HILL SUFFERED AN UNIMAGINABLE AMOUNT OF loss over a four-year period. It began when her husband Ken died of heart failure at the age of 55. That was soon followed by the deaths of her brother, stepfather, mother, aunt, two uncles, two cousins, her cousin's partner, her stepmother, and finally, her son, who died suddenly of a heart attack at the age of 38. Joanne was involved in the care of several of these loved ones before they died; her mother suffered from Alzheimer's and breast cancer and broke her hip twice, her brother Richard died of lung cancer, her aunt Becky from liver cancer. "Everyone I loved seemed to need help," she said (Hill, 2002, p. 21).

How could anyone endure so much loss? Surely any one of these tragedies would stop us in our tracks, and suffering so many in such a short time would surely push most of us to the breaking point, taking a severe toll on our physical and emotional well-being. But rather than crawling under a rock, Joanne made it through what she calls her "Locust Years" with remarkable strength, grace, and resilience. She was the executor of several of her relatives' estates and dealt successfully with complicated legal issues. She provided help and support to numerous friends and family members. She went back to college, traveled to Europe, and wrote a book about her experiences. Life is "filled with both bright sunny places and dark stormy times," she says. "Within each I looked for the golden nuggets of wisdom and truth that helped me grow stronger, happier and healthier" (Hill, n.d.).

Maybe Joanne is one of those rare people who was born with a huge reservoir of inner strength, allowing her to weather any storm. But she didn't always find it so easy to deal with life's slings and arrows. She struggled with depression in childhood and beyond, became addicted to prescription medication early in her marriage, and suffered from debilitating physical ailments—so many that she had difficulty buying life insurance. "Today," she reports in her book, "in spite of one trauma after another for several years, I am healthy in body and whole in mind. Not because of Lady Luck, but because I decided to make different choices" (p. 133). Hill attributes her survival to a series of "rainbow remedies" that she learned, through hard experience, to apply to her life.

This chapter is concerned with the application of psychology to physical and mental health, which is a flourishing area of research. We will focus primarily on topics that connect social psychology and health: how people cope with stress in their lives, the relationship between their coping styles and their physical and mental health, and how we can get people to behave in healthier ways. Along the way we will return to Joanne Hill's story, discuss her "rainbow remedies," and see that at least some of them are backed up by research in social psychology and health.

Stress and Human Health 压力与人类健康

There is more to our physical health than germs and disease—we also need to consider the amount of stress in our lives and how we deal with that stress (Chida & Hamer, 2008; Inglehart, 1991; Koolhaas, de Boer, & Buwalda, 2006). Early research in this area documented some extreme cases in which people's health was influenced by stress. Consider these examples, reported by psychologist W. B. Cannon (1942):

- A New Zealand woman eats a piece of fruit and then learns that it came from a forbidden supply reserved for the chief. Horrified, her health deteriorates, and the next day she dies—even though it was a perfectly fine piece of fruit.
- A man in Africa has breakfast with a friend, eats heartily, and goes on his way. A year later, he learns that his friend had made the breakfast from a wild hen, a food strictly forbidden in his culture. The man immediately begins to tremble and is dead within 24 hours.
- An Australian man's health deteriorates after a witch doctor casts a spell on him. He recovers only when the witch doctor removes the spell.

These examples probably sound bizarre, like something you would read in *Ripley's Believe It or Not*. But let's shift to the present in the United States, where many similar cases of sudden death occur following a psychological trauma. When people undergo a major upheaval in their lives, such as losing a spouse, declaring bankruptcy, or being forced to resettle in a new culture, their chance of dying increases (Morse, Martin, & Moshonov, 1991). Soon after a major earthquake in the Los Angeles area on January 17, 1994, there was an increase in the number of people who died suddenly of heart attacks (Leor, Poole, & Kloner, 1996). And many people experienced psychological and physical problems after the terrorist attacks on September 11, 2001 (Schlenger et al., 2002; Silver, Holman, McIntosh, Poulin, & Gil-Rivas, 2002). One study measured the heart rates of a sample of adults in New Haven, Connecticut, the week after the attacks. Compared to a control group of people studied before the attacks, the post–September 11 sample showed lower heart rate variability, which is a risk factor for sudden death (Gerin et al., 2005; Lampert, Baron, McPhearson, & Lee, 2002). On the other hand, as we will see in a moment, studies of the long-term effects of the 9/11 attacks have found relatively little evidence of prolonged negative reactions. What exactly are the effects of stress on our psychological and physical health, and how can we learn to cope most effectively?

Resilience 恢复力

The first thing to note is that humans are remarkably resilient. To be sure, we all must contend with the blows life deals us, including day-to-day hassles and major, life-altering events. And although it is true that such events can have negative effects on psychological and physical health, many people, such as Joanne Hill, cope with them extremely well. Researchers have examined people's reactions over time to major life events, including the death of loved ones and the 9/11 terrorist attacks. The most common response to such traumas is **resilience**, which can be defined as mild, transient reactions to stressful events, followed by a quick return to normal, healthy functioning (Bonanno, 2004, 2005; Bonanno & Mancini, 2008).

Resilience
Mild, transient reactions to stressful events, followed by a quick return to normal, healthy functioning

Take life's most difficult challenge, dealing with the loss of a loved one. For years, mental health professionals assumed that the "right" way to grieve was to go through an intense period of sadness and distress, in which people confronted and worked through their feelings, eventually leading to acceptance of the loss. People who did not show symptoms of extreme distress were said to be in a state of denial that would lead to greater problems down the road. When researchers looked systematically at how people respond to the death of loved ones, however, an interesting fact emerged: Many people never experienced significant distress and recovered quickly (Wortman & Silver, 1989). Studies of bereaved spouses, for example, typically find that fewer than half show signs of significant, long-term distress (Bonanno, Boerner, Wortman, 2008; Bonanno, Moskowitz, Papa, & Folkman, 2005). The remainder, like Joanne Hill, show no signs of depression and are able to experience positive emotions.

Although one might think that such people are in a state of denial, or that they were never very attached to their spouses, there is no evidence for these possibilities. Rather, there is increasing evidence that although life's traumas can be quite painful, many people have the resources to recover from them quickly. The same pattern has been found in people's responses to other highly stressful events, such as emergency workers' reactions to the bombing of the federal building in Oklahoma City in 1995, and New Yorkers' reactions to the 9/11 terrorist attacks. Surprisingly few people show prolonged, negative reactions to these tragedies (McNally, & Breslau, 2008; Seery, Silver, Holman, Ence, & Chu, 2008; Updegraff, Silver, & Holman, 2008). Nonetheless, some people do have severe negative reactions to stressful events. What determines whether people bounce back quickly or buckle under stress?

People are surprisingly resilient in the face of stressful events. Studies of reactions to the 9/11 terrorist attacks, for example, have found that relatively few people showed long-term signs of depression or other mental health problems.

Effects of Negative Life Events Among the pioneers in research on stress was Hans Selye (1956, 1976), who defined *stress* as the body's physiological response to threatening events. Selye focused on how the human body adapts to threats from the

Some of these events are happy, yet they cause stress. Which of these situations might cause you to experience stress?

environment, regardless of the source, be it a psychological or physiological trauma. Later researchers have examined what it is about a life event that makes it threatening. Holmes and Rahe (1967), for example, suggested that stress is the degree to which people have to change and readjust their lives in response to an external event. The more change that is required, the greater the stress we experience. For example, if a spouse or partner dies, just about every aspect of a person's life is disrupted, leading to a great deal of stress. This definition of stress applies to happy events as well, if the event causes big changes in one's daily routine. Graduating from college is a happy occasion, but it can be stressful because it is often accompanied by a separation from friends and adapting to a new situation, such as looking for a job, working full time, or going to graduate school.

To assess the amount of change in people's lives, Holmes and Rahe (1967) developed a measure called the Social Readjustment Rating Scale. Here's how the scale works: Participants get a list of life events, such as "divorce" and "trouble with boss," each of which has been assigned a certain number of points, depending on how stressful it is (e.g., "divorce" gets 73 points, whereas "trouble with boss" gets 23). People check the events that have happened to them in the past year and add up the points associated with these events, to get an overall "life change" score. Several studies have found that the higher the people's score, the worse their mental and physical health (Almeida, 2005; Dohrenwend, 2006; Seta, Seta, & Wang, 1990).

The original scale is a bit dated and did not include events that many college students find stressful, such as taking final exams. The Try It! exercise contains a version that was recently developed specifically for college students. Go ahead and take it and figure out your score. How did you do? When the authors who developed the scale gave it to a sample of undergraduates, they found that the average score was 1,247 (Renner & Mackin, 1998).

It seems pretty obvious that the amount of stress people are experiencing, the more likely they are to feel anxious and get sick. But the findings aren't all that straightforward. For example, as discussed earlier, some people are quite resilient when experiencing stressful events. One problem, as you may have recognized, is that most studies in this area use correlational designs, not experimental designs. Just because life changes are correlated with health problems does not mean that the life changes caused the health problems (see Chapter 2 on correlation and causality). Some researchers have argued persuasively for the role of "third variables," whereby certain kinds of people are more likely to be experiencing difficult life changes and to report that they are ill (Schroeder & Costa, 1984; Watson & Pennebaker, 1989). According to these researchers, it is not life changes that cause health problems. Instead, people with certain personality traits, such as the tendency to experience negative moods, are more likely to experience life difficulties and to have health problems.

Another problem with inventories such as Holmes and Rahe's is that they focus on stressors experienced by the middle class and underrepresent stressors experienced by the poor and members of minority groups. Variables such as poverty and racism are potent causes of stress (Clark, Anderson, Clark, & Williams, 1999; Jackson et al., 1996; Gibbons, Gerrard, & Cleveland, 2004; Giscombé & Lobel, 2005). Moreover, the way in which these variables influence health is not always obvious. It might not surprise you to learn that the more racism minority groups experience, the worse their health. It might come as more of a surprise to learn that majority groups who express the most racist attitudes also experience diminished health (Jackson & Inglehart, 1995). Racism is often associated with hostility and aggression, and there is evidence that hostility is related to health problems such as coronary heart disease. Clearly, to understand the relationship between stress and health, we need to understand better such community and cultural variables as poverty and racism.

TRY IT! The College Life Stress Inventory 试一试！大学生生活压力量表

Instructions: Copy the "stress rating" number into the last column for any event that has happened to you in the past year; then add these scores.

Event	Stress Rating	Your Score
Being raped	100	_____
Finding out that you are HIV-positive	100	_____
Being accused of rape	98	_____
Death of a close friend	97	_____
Death of a close family member	96	_____
Contracting a sexually transmitted disease (other than AIDS)	94	_____
Concerns about being pregnant	91	_____
Finals week	90	_____
Concerns about your partner being pregnant	90	_____
Oversleeping for an exam	89	_____
Flunking a class	89	_____
Having a boyfriend or girlfriend cheat on you	85	_____
Ending a steady dating relationship	85	_____
Serious illness in a close friend or family member	85	_____
Financial difficulties	84	_____
Writing a major term paper	83	_____
Being caught cheating on a test	83	_____
Drunk driving	82	_____
Sense of overload in school or work	82	_____
Two exams in one day	80	_____
Cheating on your boyfriend or girlfriend	77	_____
Getting married	76	_____
Negative consequences of drinking or drug use	75	_____
Depression or crisis in your best friend	73	_____
Difficulties with parents	73	_____
Talking in front of a class	72	_____
Lack of sleep	69	_____
Change in housing situation (hassles, moves)	69	_____
Competing or performing in public	69	_____
Getting in a physical fight	66	_____
Difficulties with a roommate	66	_____
Job changes (applying, new job, work hassles)	65	_____
Declaring a major or concerns about future plans	65	_____
A class you hate	62	_____
Drinking or use of drugs	61	_____
Confrontations with professors	60	_____
Starting a new semester	58	_____
Going on a first date	57	_____
Registration	55	_____
Maintaining a steady dating relationship	55	_____
Commuting to campus or work, or both	54	_____
Peer pressures	53	_____
Being away from home for the first time	53	_____
Getting sick	52	_____
Concerns about your appearance	52	_____
Getting straight A's	51	_____
A difficult class that you love	48	_____
Making new friends; getting along with friends	47	_____
Fraternity or sorority rush	47	_____
Falling asleep in class	40	_____
Attending an athletic event (e.g., football game)	20	_____
Sum of Your Score		_____

Perceived Stress and Health 知觉压力与健康

There is another problem with measures such as the College Life Stress Inventory: They violate a basic principle of social psychology, namely that subjective situations have more of an impact on people than objective situations (Dohrenwend, 2006; Griffin & Ross, 1991). Of course, some situational variables are hazardous to our health regardless of how we interpret them (Jackson & Inglehart, 1995; Taylor, Repetti, & Seeman, 1997). Children growing up in smog-infested areas such as Los Angeles, for example, have been found to have 10 to 15 percent less efficiency in their lungs than children who grow up in less polluted areas (Peters et al., 1999). Nonetheless, some environmental events are open to interpretation and seem to have negative effects only on people who construe these events in certain ways. To some students, writing a term paper is a major hassle; for others, it's a minor inconvenience (or even an enjoyable experience). For some people, a major life change such as getting divorced is a liberating escape from an abusive relationship; for others, it is a devastating personal failure. As recognized by Richard Lazarus (1966, 2000) in his pioneering work on stress, it is subjective, not objective, stress that causes problems. An event is stressful for people only if they interpret it as stressful; thus we can define **stress** as the negative feelings and beliefs that occur whenever people feel unable to cope with demands from their environment (Lazarus & Folkman, 1984).

Consider the number of losses Joanne Hill experienced in a 4-year period. If she had filled out the Holmes and Rahe's Social Readjustment Rating Scale, she would have scored a very high number of life change units. According to the theory, she should have been experiencing a great deal of stress, enough to put her at great risk for severe physical problems. The fact that she made it through with such grace and strength suggests that there are limits to trying to predict people's reactions from a count of the number of stressful events in their lives. We need to take into account how different people *interpret* disruptions and challenges in their lives.

Studies using this subjective definition of stress confirm the idea that negative life experiences are bad for our health. In fact, stress caused by negative interpretations of events can directly affect our immune systems, making us more susceptible to disease. Consider the common cold. When people are exposed to the virus that causes a cold, only 20 percent to 60 percent of them become sick. Is it possible that stress is one determinant of who these 20 percent to 60 percent will be? To find out, researchers asked volunteers to spend a week at a research institute in southern England (Cohen, Tyrrell, & Smith, 1991, 1993). As a measure of stress, the participants listed recent events that had had a negative impact on their lives. (Consistent with our definition of stress, the participants listed only events they perceived as negative.)

The researchers then gave participants nasal drops that contained either the virus that causes the common cold or saline (salt water). The participants were subsequently quarantined for several days so that they had no contact with other people. The results? The people who were experiencing a great deal of stress in their lives were more likely to catch a cold from the virus (see Figure SPA-2.1). Among people who reported the least amount of stress, about 27 percent came down with a cold. This rate increased steadily the more stress people reported, topping out at a rate of nearly 50 percent in the group that was experiencing the most stress. This effect of stress was found even when several other factors that influence catching a cold were taken into account, such as the time of year people participated and the participants' age, weight, and gender. This study, along with others like it, shows that the more stress people experience, the lower their immunity to disease (Cohen et al., 2008; O'Leary, 1990; Stone et al., 1993).

You may have noticed that the Cohen and colleagues study used a correlational design; this must make us cautious about its interpretation. The amount of stress people were experiencing was measured and correlated with the likelihood that people caught a cold. It is possible that stress itself did not lower people's immunity but rather that some variable correlated with stress did. It would have been ethically impermissible, of course, to conduct an experimental study in which people were randomly assigned to

Stress
The negative feelings and beliefs that arise whenever people feel unable to cope with demands from their environment

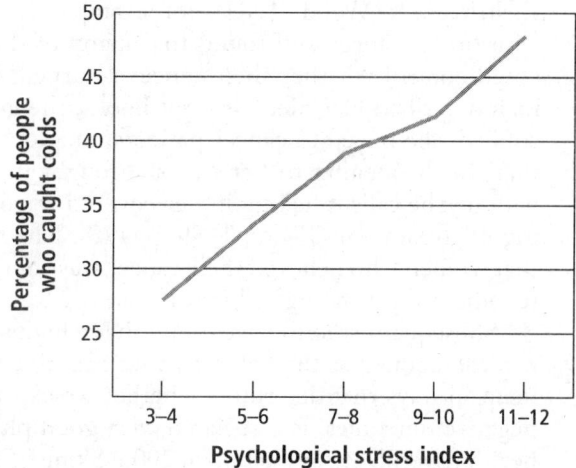

**FIGURE SPA-2.1
Stress and the likelihood of catching a cold.**

People were first exposed to the virus that causes the common cold and then isolated. The greater the amount of stress they were experiencing, the greater the likelihood that they caught a cold from this virus.

(Adapted from Cohen, Tyrrell, & Smith, 1991)

a condition in which they experienced a great deal of prolonged stress. There are studies, however, in which people's immune responses are measured before and after undergoing mildly stressful tasks in the laboratory, such as solving mental arithmetic problems continuously for 6 minutes or giving speeches on short notice. Even relatively mild stressors such as these can lead to a suppression of the immune system (Cacioppo, 1998; Cacioppo et al., 1998).

The finding that stress negatively affects health raises an important question: What exactly is it that makes people perceive a situation as stressful? One important determinant is the amount of control they believe they have over the event.

Feeling in Charge: The Importance of Perceived Control
自主感：知觉控制感的重要性

> There are times in life when we feel so out of control that helplessness and hopelessness become constant companions. But choice, like breath, is something that is part of us. *We always have a choice*. (Hill, 2002, p. 128)

Suppose you read a series of statements and had to choose the one in each pair that you thought was more true. For example, do you think that, "people's misfortunes result from mistakes they make," or that "many of the unhappy things in people's lives are partly due to bad luck?" Which of these two do you think is more true: "In the case of the well-prepared student there is rarely if ever such a thing as an unfair test," or "Many times exam questions tend to be so unrelated to course work that studying is really useless." These statements are part of a test of **internal-external locus of control** (Rotter, 1966), which is the tendency to believe that things happen because we control them versus believing that good and bad outcomes are out of our control. The first statement in each pair above reflects an internal locus of control, which is the belief that people can control their fates. The second statement in each pair reflects an external locus of control, which is the belief that our fates are more a matter of happenstance.

Research by Jean Twenge and her colleagues (Twenge, Zhang, & Im, 2004) has found that between the years 1960 and 2002, college students in the United States have scored more and more on the external end of the locus of control scale. That is, as seen in Figure SPA-2.2, college students are becoming more convinced that good and bad things in life are outside of their control.

The reasons for this trend are not entirely clear; it may be part of an increased sense of alienation and distrust among new generations in the United States (Fukuyama, 1999; Putnam, 2000). Whatever the reasons, research in social psychology suggests that the tendency to feel less control over one's fate is not good for our psychological and physical health. Shelley Taylor and her colleagues (Taylor,

Internal-External Locus of Control

The tendency to believe that things happen because we control them versus believing that good and bad outcomes are out of our control

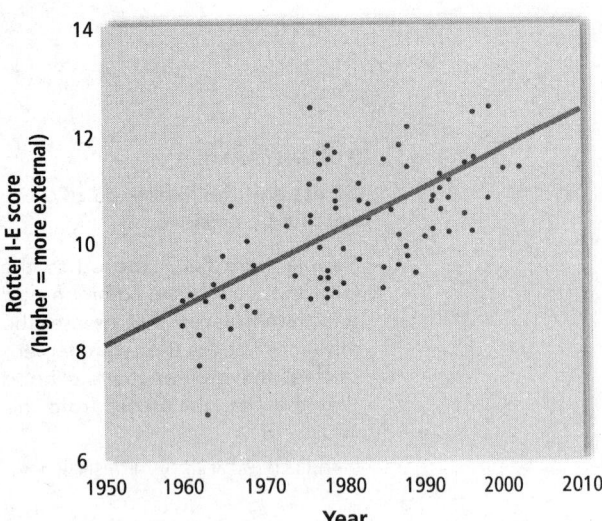

FIGURE SPA-2.2

Beliefs in internal-external locus of control in college students over time.

As seen in the graph, in the past 50 years there is a trend whereby college students in the United States endorse more external beliefs about locus of control. This means that they increasingly believe that good and bad things in life are outside of their control.

(Adopted from Twenge, Zhang, & Im, 2004)

Perceived Control

The belief that we can influence our environment in ways that determine whether we experience positive or negative outcomes

Lichtman, & Wood, 1984), for example, interviewed women with breast cancer and found that many of them believed they could control whether their cancer returned. Here is how one man described his wife: "She got books, she got pamphlets, she studied, she talked to cancer patients. She found out everything that was happening to her and she fought it. She went to war with it. She calls it 'taking in her covered wagons and surrounding it'" (quoted in Taylor, 1989, p. 178). The researchers found that women who believed their cancer was controllable were better adjusted psychologically (Folkman & Moskowitz, 2000).

Subsequent studies have found that a high sense of **perceived control**, defined as the belief that we can influence our environment in ways that determine whether we experience positive or negative outcomes, is associated with good physical and mental health (Averill, 1973; Lachman, 2006; Skinner, 1995; Thompson, 1999). For example, among people who had undergone a coronary angioplasty because of diseased arteries, those who had a high sense of control over their futures were less likely to experience subsequent heart problems than people with a low sense of control (Helgeson, 2003; Helgeson & Fritz, 1999). Joanne Hill recognized this lesson; one of her rainbow remedies is that the "Power of Choice is an empowering remedy that truly makes the difference whether we survive and thrive, or wither and die" (Hill, n.d.).

Increasing Perceived Control in Nursing Homes Some of the most dramatic effects of perceived control have been found in studies of older people in nursing homes. Many people who end up in nursing homes and hospitals feel they have lost control of their lives (Raps, Peterson, Jonas, & Seligman, 1982). People are often placed in long-term care facilities against their wishes and, when there, have little say in what they do, whom they see, or what they eat. Two psychologists believed that boosting their feelings of control would help such people (Langer & Rodin, 1976). They asked the director of a nursing home in Connecticut to convey to the residents that contrary to what they might think, they had a lot of responsibility for their own lives. Here is an excerpt of his speech:

> Take a minute to think of the decisions you can and should be making. For example, you have the responsibility of caring for yourselves, of deciding whether or not you want to make this a home you can be proud of and happy in. You should be deciding how you want your rooms to be arranged—whether you want it to be as it is or whether you want the staff to help you rearrange the furniture. You should be deciding how you want to spend your time.... If you are unsatisfied with anything here, you have the influence to change it.... These are just a few of the things you could and should be deciding and thinking about now and from time to time every day. (Langer & Rodin, 1976, pp. 194–195)

The director went on to say that a movie would be shown on two nights the next week and that the residents should decide which night they wanted to attend. Finally, he offered each resident a gift of a house plant, emphasizing that it was up to the resident to decide whether to take one (they all did) and to take care of it. The director also gave a speech to residents assigned to a comparison group. This speech was different in one crucial way—all references to making decisions and being responsible for oneself were deleted. He emphasized that he wanted the residents to be happy, but he did not say anything about the control they had over their lives. He said that a movie would be shown on two nights the next week but that the residents would be assigned to see it on one night or the other. He gave plants to these residents as well but said that the nurses would take care of the plants.

The director's speech might not seem like a major change in the lives of the residents. The people in the induced control group heard one speech about the responsibility they had for their lives and were given one plant to water. That doesn't seem like very strong stuff, does it? But to an institutionalized person who feels helpless and constrained, even a small boost in control can have a dramatic effect. Indeed, the residents in the induced control group became happier and more active than residents in the comparison group (Langer & Rodin, 1976). Most dramatically of all, the intervention improved the residents' health and reduced the likelihood that they would die in the next year and a half (Rodin & Langer, 1977). Eighteen months after the director's speech, 15 percent of the residents in the induced control group had died, compared to 30 percent in the comparison condition (see the left side of Figure SPA-2.3).

Giving senior citizens a sense of control over their lives has been found to have positive benefits, both physically and psychologically.

Another researcher increased feelings of control in residents of nursing homes in a different way (Schulz, 1976). Undergraduates visited the residents of a North Carolina nursing home once a week for 2 months. In the induced control condition, the residents decided when the visits would occur and how long they would last. In a randomly assigned comparison condition, it was the students, not the residents, who decided when the visits would occur and how long they would last. Thus the residents received visits in both conditions, but in only one could they control the visits' frequency and duration. This may seem like a minor difference, but again, giving the residents some semblance of control over their lives had dramatic effects. After 2 months, those in the induced control condition were happier, healthier, more active, and taking fewer medications than those in the comparison group.

Schulz returned to the nursing home several months later to assess the long-term effects of his intervention, including its effect on mortality rates. Based on the results of the Langer and Rodin (1976) study, we might expect that the residents who could control the students' visits would be healthier and more likely still to be alive than the residents who could not. But there is a crucial difference between the two studies: The residents in the Langer and Rodin study were given an enduring sense of control, whereas the residents in the Schulz study experienced control and then lost it. Langer and Rodin's participants could continue to choose which days to participate in different activities, continue to take care of their plant, and continue to feel they could make a difference in what happened to them, even after the study ended. By contrast, when Schulz's study was over, the student visits ended. The residents who could control the visits suddenly had that control removed.

Unfortunately, Schulz's intervention had an unintended effect: After the program ended, the people in the induced control group did worse (Schulz & Hanusa, 1978). Compared to people in the comparison group, they were more likely to have experienced deteriorating health and zest for life, and they were more likely to have died (see

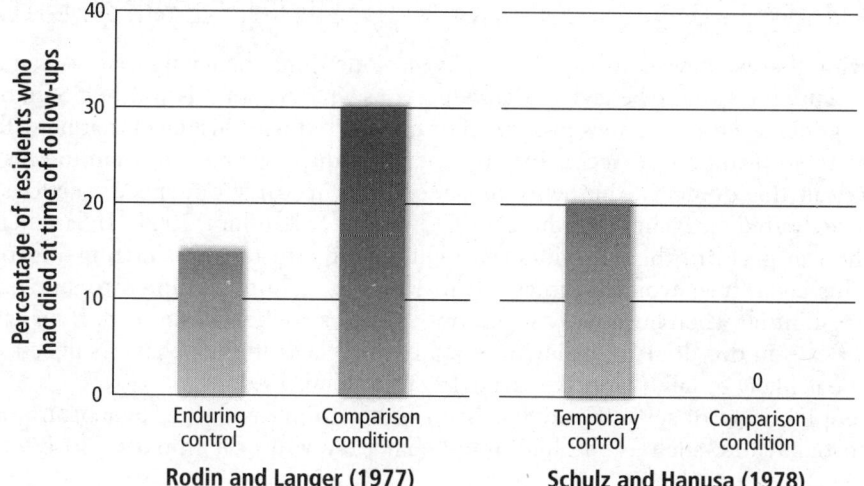

FIGURE SPA-2.3
Perceived control and mortality.

In two studies, elderly residents in nursing homes were made to feel more in control of their lives. In one (Rodin & Langer, 1977), the intervention endured over time, so that people continued to feel in control. As seen on the left side of the figure, this intervention had positive effects on mortality rates. Those who received it were more likely to be alive eighteen months later than those who did not. In the other study (Schulz & Hanusa, 1978), the intervention was temporary. Being given control and then having it taken away had negative effects on mortality rates, as seen on the right side of the figure.

(Adapted from Rodin & Langer, 1977; Schulz & Hanusa, 1978)

the right side of Figure SPA-2.3). This study has sobering implications for the many college-based volunteer programs in which students visit residents of nursing homes, prisons, and mental hospitals. These programs might be beneficial in the short run but do more harm than good after they end.

Disease, Control, and Well-Being We end this discussion with some words of caution. First, the relationship between perceived control and distress is more important to members of Western cultures than members of Asian cultures. One study found that Asians reported that perceived control was less important to them than Westerners did and that there was less of a relationship between perceived control and psychological distress in Asians than in Westerners (Sastry & Ross, 1998). The researchers argue that in Western cultures, where individualism and personal achievement are prized, people are more likely to be distressed if they feel that they cannot personally control their destinies. A lowered sense of control is less of an issue in Asian cultures, they argue, because Asians place greater value on collectivism and putting the social group ahead of individual goals.

Second, even in Western societies, there is a danger in exaggerating the relationship between perceived control and health. The social critic Susan Sontag (1978, 1988) has perceptively observed that when a society is plagued by a deadly but poorly understood disease, such as tuberculosis in the nineteenth century and AIDS today, the illness is often blamed on some kind of human frailty, such as a lack of faith, a moral weakness, or a broken heart. As a result, people sometimes blame themselves for their illnesses, even to the point where they do not seek effective treatment. Even though it helps people to feel that they are in control of their illnesses, the downside of this strategy is that if they do not get better, they may blame themselves for failing to recover. Tragically, diseases such as cancer can be fatal no matter how much control a person feels. It only adds to the tragedy if people with serious diseases feel a sense of moral failure, blaming themselves for a disease that is unpredictable and incurable.

For people living with serious illnesses, keeping some form of control even when their health is failing has benefits. Researchers have found that even when people who are seriously ill with cancer or AIDS feel no control over the disease, many of them believe they could control the consequences of the disease, such as their emotional reactions and some of the physical symptoms of the disease, such as how tired they felt. And the more people felt they could control the consequences of their disease, the better adjusted they were, even if they knew they could not control the eventual course of their illness. In short, it is important to feel in control of something, even if it is not the disease itself. Maintaining such a sense of control is likely to improve one's psychological well-being, even if one's health fails (Heckhausen & Schulz, 1995; Morling & Evered, 2006; Thompson, 2002).

Knowing You Can Do It: Self-Efficacy 知道自己能做得到：自我效能

Believing that we have control over our lives is one thing; believing that we can actually execute the specific behaviors that will get us what we want is another. Sam might have a general sense that he is in control of his life, but will this mean that he will find it easy to stop smoking? According to Albert Bandura, we have to examine his **self-efficacy** in this domain—the belief in one's ability to carry out specific actions that produce desired outcomes (Bandura, 1997; Benight & Bandura, 2004). If Sam believes that he can perform the behaviors that will enable him to quit smoking—throwing away his cigarettes, avoiding situations in which he is most tempted to smoke, distracting himself when he craves a cigarette—chances are he will succeed. If he has low self-efficacy in this domain, believing that he can't perform the behaviors necessary to quit, he is likely to fail (Carey & Carey, 1993; Holden, 1991).

People's level of self-efficacy has been found to predict a number of important health behaviors, such as the likelihood that they will quit smoking, lose weight,

Self-Efficacy
The belief in one's ability to carry out specific actions that produce desired outcomes

lower their cholesterol, and exercise regularly (Bandura, 1997; Koestner et al., 2006; Hyde, Hankins, Deale, & Marteau, 2008; Maddux, 1995; Sullivan, O'Connor, & Burris, 2006). Again, it is not a general sense of control that predicts these behaviors, but the confidence that one can perform the specific behaviors in question. A person might have high self-efficacy in one domain, such as high confidence that she can lose weight, but low self-efficacy in another domain, such as low confidence that she can quit smoking.

Self-efficacy helps in two ways. First, it influences our persistence and effort at a task. People with low self-efficacy tend to procrastinate and give up easily, whereas those with high self-efficacy set higher goals, try harder, and persist more in the face of failure—thereby increasing the likelihood that they will succeed (Cervone & Peake, 1986; Litt, 1988; Steel, 2007). Second, self-efficacy influences the way our bodies react while we are working toward our goals. For example, people with high self-efficacy experience less anxiety while working on a difficult task, and their immune systems function more optimally (Bandura, Cioffi, Taylor, & Brouillard, 1988; Wiedenfeld et al., 1990). In short, self-efficacy operates as a kind of self-fulfilling prophecy. The more you believe that you can accomplish something, such as quitting smoking, the greater the likelihood that you will.

Other people can help us gain self-efficacy. In one study, for example, participants took part in a 14-week program to help them quit smoking (Blittner, Goldberg, & Merbaum, 1978). The program was especially successful if the researchers first instilled self-efficacy by telling people that they had been chosen for the study because they had "strong willpower and great potential to control and conquer their desires and behavior" (p. 555). The people in this condition did not really have stronger willpower than anyone else because they were randomly assigned to receive the self-efficacy feedback. The *belief* that they were likely to succeed, however, led to greater success. More people in the self-efficacy condition quit smoking than in a condition that underwent the same treatment but without the self-efficacy instructions or a control condition that did not receive any treatment (see Figure SPA-2.4). Believing that we can do something has a powerful influence on whether we succeed.

Explaining Negative Events: Learned Helplessness
解释负性事件：习得性无助

What happens when we experience a setback? Despite believing in ourselves, perhaps we failed to quit smoking or did poorly on a midterm. Another important determinant of our physical and mental health is how we explain to ourselves why a negative event occurred. Consider two college students who both got poor grades on their first calculus test. Student A says to herself, "I'll bet the professor deliberately made the test difficult, to motivate us to do better. I'll just have to study harder. If I really buckle down for the next test, I'll do better." Student B says to himself, "Wow, I guess I can't really cut it here at State U. I was worried that I wasn't smart enough to make it in college, and boy, was I ever right." Which student do you think will do better on the next test? Clearly the first one because she has explained her poor performance in a way that is more flattering to herself and makes her feel more in control. In contrast, the second student is expressing **learned helplessness**, pessimism that results from attributing a negative event to stable, internal, and global factors (Abramson, Seligman, & Teasdale, 1978; Peterson & Park, 2007; Seligman, 1975).

If we think a negative event had a stable cause, we've made a **stable attribution**—we believe that the event was caused by things that will not change over time (e.g., our intelligence), as opposed to factors that can change over time (e.g., the amount of effort we

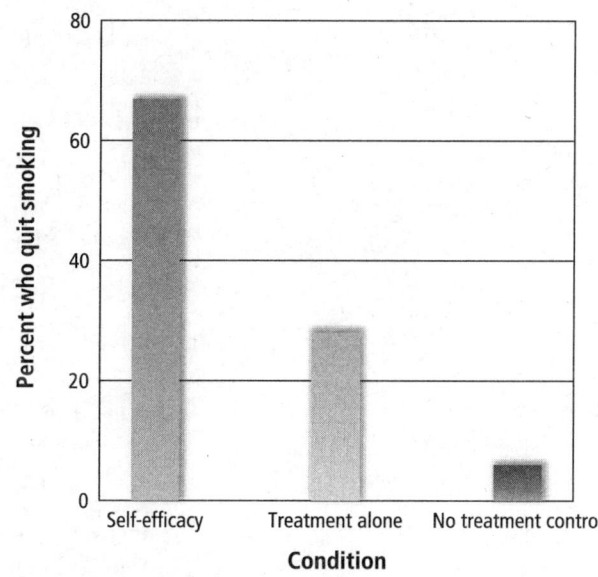

FIGURE SPA-2.4
The role of self-efficacy in smoking cessation.

Adult smokers were randomly assigned to one of three conditions. In the self-efficacy condition, people were told that they were selected for the study because they had great potential to quit. They then underwent a fourteen-week smoking cessation program. People in the treatment-alone condition participated in the same program but were told that they had been randomly selected for it. People in the no-treatment control did not take part in the program. At the end of the fourteen-week period, substantially more people in the self-efficacy condition had quit smoking. Believing that one has the ability to carry out beneficial behaviors—having high self-efficacy—is an important determinant of whether people succeed.

(Adapted from Blittner, Goldberg, & Merbaum, 1978)

Learned Helplessness

The state of pessimism that results from attributing a negative event to stable, internal, and global factors

Stable Attribution

The belief that an event is caused by factors that will not change over time (e.g., your intelligence), as opposed to factors that will change over time (e.g., the amount of effort you put into a task)

FIGURE SPA-2.5
The theory of learned helplessness.

Explaining a negative event in a pessimistic manner leads to learned helplessness (depression, lowered effort, poor learning).

Internal Attribution
The belief that an event is caused by things about you (e.g., your own ability or effort), as opposed to factors that are external to you (e.g., the difficulty of a test)

Global Attribution
The belief that an event is caused by factors that apply in a large number of situations (e.g., your intelligence, which will influence your performance in many areas) rather than factors that are specific and apply in only a limited number of situations (e.g., your musical ability, which will affect your performance in music courses but not in other courses)

put into a task). Explaining a negative event as due to an internal cause—that is, making an **internal attribution**—means we believe that something about us caused the event (e.g., our own ability or effort), as opposed to factors that are external to us (e.g., the difficulty of a test). Finally, explaining an event as due to a global cause—that is, making a **global attribution**—is the belief that the event is caused by factors that apply in a large number of situations (e.g., our general intelligence, which will influence our performance in many areas) rather than factors that are specific and apply in only a limited number of situations (e.g., how good we are at math, which will affect our performance in math courses but not in other courses). According to learned helplessness theory, making stable, internal, and global attributions for negative events leads to hopelessness, depression, reduced effort, and difficulty in learning (see Figure SPA-2.5).

Student B, for example, believes that the cause of his poor grade is stable (being unintelligent will last forever), internal (something about him is to blame), and global (being unintelligent will affect him in many situations other than calculus classes). This kind of explanation will lead to learned helplessness, thereby producing depression, reduced effort, and the inability to learn new things. Student A, by contrast, believes that the cause of her poor grade is unstable (the professor will make the tests easier, and she can study harder next time), external (the professor intentionally made the test hard), and specific (the things that caused her poor calculus grade are unlikely to affect anything else, such as her grade in English). People who explain bad events in this more optimistic way are less likely to be depressed and more likely to do better on a broad range of tasks (Hyde, Mezulis, & Abramson, 2008; Peterson & Seligman, 1984; Sweeney, Anderson, & Bailey, 1986).

For example, consider professional bicyclist Lance Armstrong, who showed a remarkable comeback after recovering from testicular cancer. In his first races after his recovery he did fairly well, finishing 14th in a 5-day race through Spain and 19th in an 8-day race from Nice to Paris. He was used to winning, however, and initially explained his failure to do so like this: "Well, I've just been through too much. I've been through three surgeries, three months of chemo, and a year of hell, and that's the reason I'm not riding well. My body is just never going to be the same" (Armstrong, 2000, p. 188). Note that he attributed his poor performance to a cause that was internal (his lowered physical abilities), stable (a condition that would not change), and global (a condition that would influence many aspects of his life, not just one race). Had he persisted in explaining his performance in this way, surely he never would have gone on to win the Tour de France seven consecutive times. Instead, he had the insight to recognize that every cyclist has ups and downs and no one wins every race. "What I really should have been saying," Armstrong realized, "was, 'Hey, it's just a bad day'"—an attribution to a cause that was external (the particular circumstances, not something about him), unstable (something likely to change), and specific (something limited to that one situation).

Students who realize that poor academic performance in the first year of college is common and likely to improve will probably do better than students who believe that poor performance is due to personal shortcomings that are unlikely to change.

Learned helplessness theory is intimately related to attribution theory (see Chapter 4). Attribution theorists assume that your attitudes and behaviors depend on how you interpret the causes of events, an assumption that learned helplessness shares. Note that we do not know the real reason our hypothetical students did poorly on their calculus test. Instead, learned helplessness theory states that it is more important to consider people's perceptions of these causes. The real causes, of course, are not irrelevant. Students who truly lack ability in calculus are likely to do poorly on future calculus tests. Often in life, however, what actually causes our behavior is not so clearcut or fixed. In such situations, people's attributions about the causes of their problems can be very important.

To explore this link between learned helplessness and academic performance, Tim Wilson and Patricia Linville (1982, 1985) conducted a study with first-year college students. They assumed that many first-year students experience academic difficulties because of a damaging pattern of attributions. Due to the difficulty of adjusting to a new academic and social environment, the first year of college has its rough spots for nearly everyone. The problem is, many first-year students do not realize how common such adjustment problems are and assume that their problems are due to personal predicaments that are unlikely to change—just the kind of attribution that leads to learned helplessness.

Wilson and Linville tried to combat this pessimism by convincing students that the causes of poor performance are often temporary. At Duke University, first-year students who were concerned about their academic performance took part in what they thought was a survey of college experiences. In the treatment condition, the students watched videotaped interviews of four upper-class students, each of whom, during the interviews, mentioned that his or her grades were poor or mediocre during the first year but had improved significantly since then. The students were also given statistics indicating that academic performance is often poor in the first year of college but improves thereafter. The researchers hypothesized that this simple message would help prevent learned helplessness, increasing the students' motivation to try harder and removing needless worries about their abilities. Judging by the students' future performance, this is just what happened. Compared to students in a control group who participated in the study but did not watch the videotaped interviews or see the statistics, students in the treatment condition improved their grades more in the following year and were less likely to drop out of college. Similar results have been found in studies in other countries, such as Canada and Belgium (Menec et al., 1994; Van Overwalle & DeMetsenaere, 1990; Wilson, Damiani, & Shelton, 2002).

DILBERT reprinted by permission of United Media Feature Syndicate, Inc.

Because people's attributions were not measured in the Wilson and Linville (1982) study, we can only infer that the students improved their academic performance because of a beneficial change in their attributions. Other studies have directly measured people's attributions and found that those who explain bad events in optimistic ways are less depressed, are in better health, and do better in school and in their careers (Dweck, 1999; Nolen-Hoeksema, Girgus, & Seligman, 1986; Snyder, Irving, & Anderson, 1991).

Optimism: Looking on the Bright Side   乐观：从光明面看

Some people are by nature optimistic, generally expecting the best out of life, whereas others always see the dark underside. Is this personality variable related to how people cope with stressful events? It turns out that optimistic people react better to stress and are generally healthier than pessimists (Carver & Scheier, 2003; Fischer & Chalmers, 2008; Nes & Segerstrom, 2006; Smith, 2006). To get an idea of how optimistic you tend to be, complete the following Try It! exercise.

TRY IT! The Life Orientation Test   试一试！生活定向测验

Please indicate the extent of your agreement with each of the following ten statements, using the following scale:

0 = strongly disagree   1 = disagree   2 = neither agree nor disagree   3 = agree   4 = agree strongly

Be as accurate and honest as you can on all items, and try not to let your answer to one question influence your answer to other questions. There are no right or wrong answers.

1. In uncertain times, I usually expect the best.   _____
2. It's easy for me to relax.   _____
3. If something can go wrong for me, it will.   _____
4. I'm always optimistic about my future.   _____
5. I enjoy my friends a lot.   _____
6. It's important for me to keep busy.   _____
7. I hardly ever expect things to go my way.   _____
8. I don't get upset too easily.   _____
9. I rarely count on good things happening to me.   _____
10. Overall, I expect more good things to happen to me than bad.   _____

Scoring instructions appear on page 471.

(Adapted from Scheier, Carver, & Bridges, 1994)

The good news is that most people have been found to have an optimistic outlook on life. In fact, most people seem to be unrealistically optimistic about their lives (Armor & Taylor, 1998; Taylor & Brown, 1988, 1994). In a typical study, college students estimated how likely a variety of events were to happen to them, compared to how likely these events were to happen to their peers (Harris, Griffin, & Murray, 2008; Lench & Ditto, 2008; Weinstein, 1980). The events included both positive things, such as liking a postgraduation job and living past 80, and negative things, such as getting divorced and contracting lung cancer. People were overly optimistic: Nearly everyone thought that the good events were more likely to happen to them than their peers and that the negative events were less likely to happen to them than their peers (we know that people were wrong, on average, because it is not possible that everyone could be more likely than others to experience the good things and avoid the bad things).

This kind of unrealistic optimism would be a problem if it caused people to make serious mistakes about their prospects in life. Obviously, it would not be a good idea to convince ourselves that we will never get lung cancer and therefore we're free to smoke as much as we want. Most people seem to have a healthy balance of optimism and reality monitoring. We manage to put a positive spin on many aspects of our lives, which leads to increased feelings of control and self-efficacy. At the same time, most people are able to keep their optimistic biases in check when they face a real challenge and to take steps to deal with that challenge (Armor & Taylor, 1998; Sweeny, Carroll, & Shepperd, 2006). As Joanne Hill put it, "An optimistic outlook doesn't keep away the crises that wreak havoc on our lives" (2002, p. 114). With so many losses in her life she was burdened with numerous stressful duties, including the dispersal of belongings and the guardianships of sick family members. She didn't try to deny or minimize the seriousness of each new challenge but rather tried to put as positive a spin on it as she could. Indeed, one of her "rainbow remedies" is, "Accentuate the Positive brings sunshine back into our lives, bringing us optimal emotional well-being" (Hill, n.d.).

In summary, our feelings of control and self-efficacy, the kinds of attributions we make for our performance, and our dispositional optimism are important determinants of our psychological and physical health. The power of our minds over our bodies is, of course, limited. But research shows that people's psychological reactions to life events, such as the amount of control they feel they have over negative events and how they explain them, can have a big influence on their mental and physical health.

> *Twixt the optimist and the pessimist the difference is droll: The optimist sees the doughnut but the pessimist sees the hole.*
>
> —McLandburgh Wilson, 1915

Coping with Stress 压力的应对

No one always feels in control, of course, and sometimes it is difficult to avoid being pessimistic after something bad happens. The death of a loved one, an acrimonious divorce, and the loss of a job are extremely stressful events. Considerable research indicates that people exhibit various reactions, or **coping styles**, in the face of threatening events (Aspinwall & Taylor, 1997; Lazarus & Folkman, 1984; Lehman, Davis, De Longis, & Wortman, 1993; Moos & Holahan, 2003; Salovey et al., 2000; Taylor & Aspinwall, 1993). We examine a few coping styles here, beginning with research on gender differences in the ways people respond to stress.

Gender Differences in Coping with Stress 应对压力的性别差异

If you have ever been to a dog park, you know that dogs respond in one of two ways when they are attacked: Sometimes they respond in kind, and a dogfight occurs. Other times the dog who is attacked will take off as fast as it can, tail between its legs. Walter Cannon (1932) termed this the **fight-or-flight response**, defined as responding to stress by either attacking the source of the stress or fleeing from it. For years, the fight-or-flight response has been viewed as the way in which all mammals respond to stress. When under threat, mammals are energized by the release of hormones such as

Coping Styles
The ways in which people react to threatening events

Fight-or-Flight Response
Responding to stress by either attacking the source of the stress or fleeing from it

Females are somewhat more likely than males to develop intimate friendships, cooperate with others, and focus their attention on social relationships, particularly when under stress. Shelley Taylor and her colleagues (2000) have referred to this as a tend-and-befriend strategy, responding to stress with nurturant activities designed to protect oneself and one's offspring (tending) and creating social networks that provide protection from threats (befriending).

Tend-and-Befriend Response
Responding to stress with nurturant activities designed to protect oneself and one's offspring (tending) and creating social networks that provide protection from threats (befriending)

Social Support
The perception that others are responsive and receptive to one's needs

norepinephrine and epinephrine, and like the dogs in the park, they either go on the attack or retreat as quickly as they can.

That, at least, has been the accepted story for many years. Shelley Taylor and her colleagues (Taylor et al., 2000; Taylor, 2006) pointed out a little-known fact about research on the fight-or-flight syndrome: Most of it has been done on males (particularly male rats). Taylor and her colleagues argue that the fight-or-flight response does not work well for females because they typically play a greater role in caring for children. Fighting is not always a good option for a pregnant female or one tending offspring. Similarly, fleeing is difficult when an adult is responsible for the care of young children or in the later months of pregnancy.

Consequently, Taylor and her colleagues argue, a different way of responding to stress has evolved in females, the **tend-and-befriend response**. Instead of fighting or fleeing, women respond to stress with nurturant activities designed to protect oneself and one's offspring (tending) and creating social networks that provide protection from threats (befriending). Tending has a number of benefits for both the mother and the child (e.g., a quiet child is less likely to be noticed by predators, and nurturing behavior leads to lower stress and improved immune functioning in mammals). Befriending involves the creation of close ties with other members of the species, which also confers a number of advantages. A close-knit group can exchange resources, watch out for predators, and share child care. As we saw in Chapter 5, human females are more likely than males to develop intimate friendships, cooperate with others, and focus their attention on social relationships. This is especially so when people are under stress; under these circumstances, women are more likely to seek out others, particularly other women (Kivlighan, Granger, & Booth, 2005; Tamres, Janicki, & Helgeson, 2002; Zwolinski, 2008).

We should be careful not to oversimplify gender differences such as these. Although gender differences in coping do exist, the magnitude of these differences is not very large (Tamres et al., 2002). Further, seeking social support can benefit both women and men—as seen in the next section.

Social Support: Getting Help from Others
社会支持：获得他人的帮助

Joanne Hill could not have gotten through her "locust years" without the support of a good many family and friends. When she got the devastating news that her son had died, she was at a gathering of the National Speakers Association (NSA). Joanne turned immediately to her friend Mitchell, a man who had survived both a motorcycle accident and a plane crash. Although badly scarred and wheelchair bound, Mitchell had overcome his adversity and become a successful public speaker. He held Joanne's hand and shared her grief and insisted on riding with her to the airport. The president of the NSA and her husband took charge of the travel arrangements and Barbara, a woman Joanne had met just a couple of days earlier at the convention, insisted on accompanying her home. As Joanne writes,

> In my darkest hour, I was surrounded by people ... As word spread of the devastating news, some of the speakers came to my room to hug me and give me an encouraging word. In the days and months to come, many messages of support, hope, and love came from NSA members all over the continent ... Strangers became friends, adding their support to those most dear to me at home, my family and long-time friends. (Hill, 2002, p. 7)

Social support, perceiving that others are responsive and receptive to one's needs, is very helpful for dealing with stress (Helgeson & Cohen, 1996; Stroebe & Stroebe, 1996; Uchino, Cacioppo, & Keicolt-Glaser, 1996; Taylor, 2007). Clearly, Joanne Hill made it through the trauma of so many losses with "a little help from her friends," to paraphrase the Beatles. Does social support help people physically as well as emotionally? There is some evidence that it does. In one of the most dramatic studies, women with advanced breast cancer were randomly assigned to a social support condition or a control condition (Spiegel, Bloom, Kraemer, & Gottheil, 1989). People in the social support condition met weekly with other patients and doctors to discuss their problems and fears, whereas people in the control group did not have access to this support system. Not only did the social support improve women's moods and reduce their fears, but it also lengthened their lives by an average of 18 months. Other studies have shown that interventions designed to increase social support and decrease stress in cancer patients improve the functioning of their immune systems (Antoni & Lutgendorf, 2007; Andersen et al., 2004; McGregor et al., 2004). And social support seems to prolong the lives of healthy people: In a study of a large sample of American men and women in the years 1967–1969, men with a low level of social support were two to three times more likely to die over the next dozen years than men with a high level of social support (House, Robbins, & Metzner, 1982). Women with a low level of social support were one and a half to two times more likely to die than women with a high level of social support (Berkman & Syme, 1979; Schwarzer & Leppin, 1991; Stroebe & Stroebe, 1996). Interestingly, it is not just receiving social support but giving it that is beneficial: A recent study of people 65 and over found that those who *gave* support to others, such as helping family members with child care or doing errands for a neighbor, lived longer than people who did not (Brown, Nesse, & Vinokur, 2003). To get an idea of the amount of social support you feel is available in your life, complete the Try It! exercise that follows.

 **Social Support** 试一试！社会支持

This list contains statements that may or may not be true about you. For each statement that is probably true about you, circle T; for each that is probably not true about you, circle F.

You may find that many of the statements are neither clearly true nor clearly false. In these cases, try to decide quickly whether probably true (T) or probably false (F) is more descriptive of you. Although some questions will be difficult to answer, it is important that you pick one alternative or the other. Circle only one of the alternatives for each statement.

Read each item quickly but carefully before responding. This is not a test, and there are no right or wrong answers.

1. There is at least one person I know whose advice I really trust.   T   F
2. There is really no one I can trust to give me good financial advice.   T   F
3. There is really no one who can give me objective feedback about how I'm handling my problems.   T   F
4. When I need suggestions for how to deal with a personal problem, I know there is someone I can turn to.   T   F
5. There is someone I feel comfortable going to for advice about sexual problems.   T   F
6. There is someone I can turn to for advice about handling hassles over household responsibilities.   T   F
7. I feel that there is no one with whom I can share my most private worries and fears.   T   F
8. If a family crisis arose, few of my friends would be able to give me good advice about how to handle it.   T   F
9. There are very few people I trust to help solve my problems.   T   F
10. There is someone I could turn to for advice about changing my job or finding a new one.   T   F

Scoring instructions appear on page 471.

(Adapted from Cohen, Mermelstein, Kamarack, & Hoberman, 1985)

It may seem obvious that social support is beneficial, but it turns out that there are some interesting qualifications in when and how it helps. First, when things are tough, the kind of social support we get matters. To illustrate, imagine that you are struggling in one of your classes and attend a study session for the final exam. Sarah, a friend of yours in the group, greets you by saying, "I know you aren't doing very well in this class so how about if we all focus on the material you don't understand and give you an extra hand." On the one hand you appreciate the support and extra help. But who likes being singled out as the "dumb person"? As we saw in Chapter 11, people don't like receiving help when it comes with the message, "you are too incompetent to do it yourself." Now suppose that Sarah was a little more subtle in her support. She knows that you are having trouble with the material in the last chapter of the textbook, but rather than singling you out, she says, "A lot of us are struggling with the material in Chapter 16—I know I am. How about if we focus on that?" She steers help your way without singling you out or communicating that you are incompetent.

Research by Niall Bolger and his colleagues (Bolger & Amarel, 2007; Bolger, Zuckerman, & Kessler, 2000) has demonstrated that the latter kind of help, which they call *invisibile support*, is much more effective. This kind of support provides people with assistance without communicating that they are incompetent. The former type of help, which they call *visible support*, is a two-edged sword, because it singles out the beneficiary as needy and as someone who can't help him- or herself. The moral? If you have a friend who is under a great deal of stress, find a way to help him or her unobstrusively without making a big deal of it.

Second, social support operates differently in different cultures. Who do you think is more likely to seek support from other people when things get tough: members of Western cultures that stress individualism and independence, or members of East Asian cultures that stress collectivism and interdependence? It might seem as though cultures that stress collectivism would be more likely to seek help from each other, but research by Shelley Taylor, Heejung Kim, and David Sherman has found just the opposite: When under stress, members of East Asian cultures are *less* likely to seek social support than are members of Western cultures (Kim, Sherman, & Taylor, in press; Taylor et al., 2004; Taylor, Welch, Kim, & Sherman, 2007). The reason? Members of collectivistic cultures are concerned that seeking support from others will disrupt the harmony of the group and open them up to criticism from others.

Does this mean that members of collectivistic cultures receive less support from others and benefit less from it when they do receive it? Not at all—the main difference is in *how* people in different cultures seek and obtain social support. Because members of collectivistic cultures are concerned with upsetting group harmony and criticism from others, they are less likely to ask directly for help in a way that shows they are having problems. For example, they are less likely to say to a friend, "Hey, I'm having a hard time here, can you give me a hand?" They do benefit from interacting with supportive others, as long as they do not have to disclose that they are having problems (Kim et al., in press).

Opening Up: Making Sense of Traumatic Events
敞开心扉：弄清创伤性事件的意义

When something traumatic happens to you, is it best to try to bury it as deep as you can and never talk about it, or to spend time thinking about the event and discuss it with others? Although folk wisdom has long held that it is best to open up, only recently has this assumption been put to the test. James Pennebaker and his colleagues (Pennebaker, 1990, 1997; 2004; Sloan, Marx, Epstein, & Dobbs, 2008; Smyth & Pennebaker, 2008) have conducted a number of interesting experiments on the value of writing about traumatic events. Pennebaker and Beale (1986), for example, asked college students to write, for 15 minutes on each of 4 consecutive nights, about a traumatic event that had happened to them. Students in a control condition wrote for the same amount of time about a trivial event. The traumas that people chose to write about included tragedies such as rape and the death of a sibling. Writing about these events was certainly upsetting in the short run: Students who wrote about traumas reported more negative moods and showed greater increases in blood pressure. But there were also dramatic long-term benefits: The same students were less likely to visit the student health center during the next 6 months, and they reported having fewer illnesses. Similarly, first-year college students who wrote about the problems of entering college and survivors of the Holocaust who disclosed the most about their World War II experiences improved their health over the next several months (Pennebaker, Barger, & Tiebout, 1989; Pennebaker, Colder, & Sharp, 1990).

Research by James Pennebaker (1990) shows that there are long-term health benefits to writing or talking about one's personal traumas.

What is it about opening up that leads to better health? People who write about negative events construct a more meaningful narrative or story that explains the events. Pennebaker (1997) has analyzed the hundreds of pages of writing his participants provided and found that the people who improved the most were those who began with rather incoherent, disorganized descriptions of their problem and ended with coherent, organized stories that explained the event and gave it meaning. After an event is explained, people do not have to think about it as much. Further, people might be less inclined to try to suppress thoughts about the event. Trying to suppress negative thoughts can lead to a preoccupation with those very thoughts because the act of trying not to think about them can actually make us think about them more (Wegner, 1994). Writing about or confiding in others about a traumatic event may help people gain a better understanding of the event and thus move forward with life. Subsequent research has shown that this kind of understanding is especially likely to occur when people take a step back and analyze a negative life event as an observer would, rather than immersing themselves in the event and trying to relive it (Ayduk & Kross, 2008; Kross & Ayduk, 2008). If you would like to try the writing exercise, instructions can be found at homepage.psy.utexas.edu/homepage/Faculty/Pennebaker/Home2000/WritingandHealth.html

In sum, research shows that humans are often remarkably resilient in the face of adversity, particularly if they can maintain a sense of control and self-efficacy, and explain negative events as due to external, unstable, specific causes. Seeking social support can help, as can adopting an optimistic outlook on life. If people continue to be troubled by stressful events, it may help to use Pennebaker's writing technique to help make sense of what happened and what it means.

Prevention: Promoting Healthier Behavior
预防之道：改善健康习惯

In addition to helping people reduce stress, it is important to find ways to help people change their health habits more directly. What sort of problems might we target?

Preventable Health Problems 可预防的健康问题

Many serious health problems are preventable, if people adopted different habits and avoided risky behaviors. According to one estimate, the causes of half the deaths in the United States each year are preventable (Mokdad, Marks, Stroup, & Gerberding, 2004). More than 33 million people are currently infected with the HIV virus, and in 2007, 2.7 million were infected ("Report on the global AIDS epidemic, " 2008). As seen in Figure SPA-2.6, most cases are in Sub-Saharan Africa, although no continent is free of the disease. Most of these cases could have been avoided if people had used condoms during sexual intercourse, yet many people are not taking the precautions they should. One survey in the United States, for example, found that 23 percent of single, sexually active adults never use condoms when having vaginal sex (Oglesby, 2004).

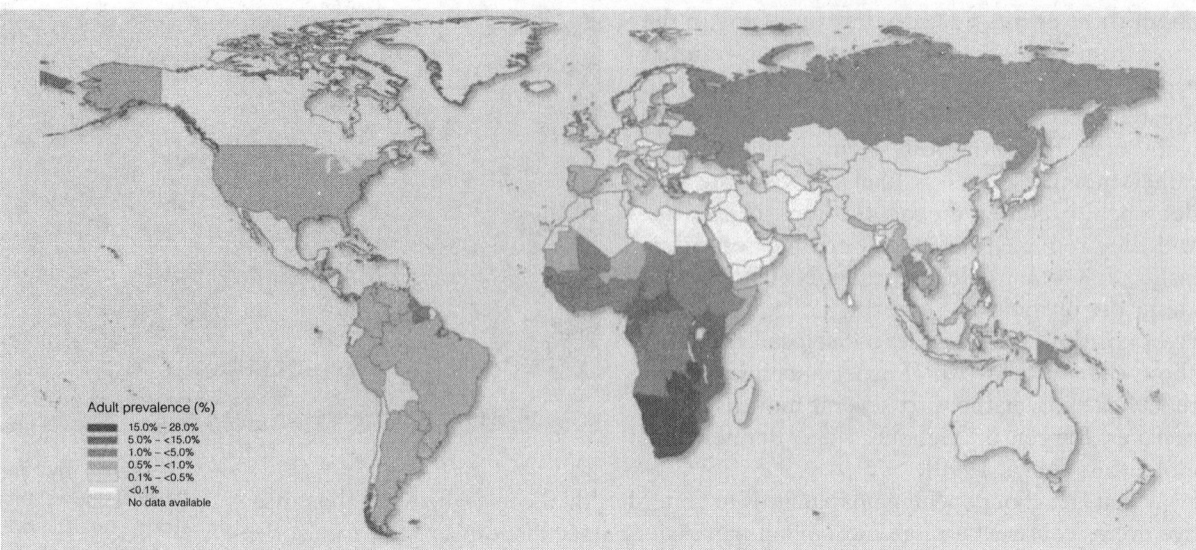

FIGURE SPA-2.6
A global view of HIV infection, 2007.

People could improve their health behaviors in many other areas as well, such as alcohol consumption, smoking, and overeating. Binge drinking, defined as five or more drinks on one occasion for men and four or more for women (Wechsler & Austin, 1998), is a problem on many college campuses. Binge drinkers are more likely to have a number of health problems, including high blood pressure, heart disease, liver disease, meningitis, and sexually transmitted diseases. They are also more likely to be in car accidents, die by drowning, have unwanted pregnancies, experience domestic violence, and have difficulty performing sexually (Naimi et al., 2003; "Quick stats," 2008).

Americans are doing a good job of improving one unhealthy habit, namely smoking cigarettes. Smoking rates have been declining steadily in the United States. For example, in 1995, 35 percent of high school students reported that they smoked, but in 2007 only 20 percent reported that they smoked ("National trends in risk behaviors," 2008). Nonetheless, tobacco use remains the number 1 cause of preventable deaths in the United States. What is number 2? It might surprise you to learn that it is obesity, an area in which Americans are not doing such a good job. A staggering 66 percent of Americans are overweight, which is associated with such health problems as high blood pressure, diabetes, heart disease, and cancer of the breast, prostate, and colon ("Prevalence of overweight," 2006).

We realize that we have just maligned what many people consider to be the chief pleasures of life: sex, eating, drinking, and smoking. Health problems resulting from these behaviors are prevalent precisely because they are so pleasurable—in some cases (e.g., smoking), addictive. It is thus a challenge to find ways to change people's attitudes and behaviors in ways that lead to better health habits. How might we do so?

Social Psychological Interventions: Targeting Safer Sex
社会心理学干预：更安全的性行为

By now you know that this is a classic social psychological issue. In Chapter 7, for example, we discussed theories of attitude change and social influence, and it should be possible to put these theories into action to help people to act in healthier ways. Indeed, there is a great deal of research on this very question, and social psychologists have had

"Maybe we shouldn't have kicked all our bad habits."
© Vahan Shirvanian/www.CartoonStock.com

considerable success in designing programs to get people to use condoms, quit smoking, drink less, and engage in a variety of preventive behaviors, such as using sunscreens (Baum, Revenson, & Singer, 2001; Noar, Benac, & Harris, 2007; Salovey & Rothman, 2003). Here we will focus on interventions designed to reduce HIV infections, primarily by getting people to use condoms.

As we discussed earlier in this chapter, for example, a key to getting people to change their behavior is instilling a sense of self-efficacy, which is the belief in one's ability to carry out specific actions that produce desired outcomes. In the 1990s, the National Institute of Mental Health sponsored an intervention to get people to engage in safer sex that targeted people's self-efficacy in the domain of condom use, namely their beliefs that they could bring up the topic in a conversation with a potential sexual partner and convince their partner that they should use condoms (NIMH Multisite HIV Prevention Trial Group, 1998). The intervention also taught people how to use condoms and attempted to increase their motivation to do so. Specifically, participants were recruited from waiting rooms of clinics that treated sexually transmitted diseases in seven cities in the United States and were randomly assigned to an intervention or control condition. Participants in the intervention condition attended seven sessions over a 2-week period, in which they watched videotapes, listened to presentations, and engaged in role-playing exercises, all with the goal of increasing their sense of self-efficacy about condom use, their motivation to use condoms, and their knowledge about how to use them. Participants in the control condition attended a 1-hour AIDS education session. All participants completed a battery of measures at 3-, 6-, and 12-month intervals, including a question about the number of times they used condoms during sex.

As seen in Figure SPA-2.7, people in both conditions reported an increase in condom use, but the increase was significantly larger in the intervention condition. And, there was evidence that the intervention worked by improving people's sense of self-efficacy, their knowledge about how to use condoms, and their motivation to do so (NIMH Multisite HIV Prevention Trial Group, 2001).

A review of the more than 350 interventions designed to promote safer sex confirmed that they work to increase people's self-efficacy about condom use (Albarracín, Durantini, Earl, Gunnoe, & Leeper, 2008;. Albarracín, Durantini, & Earl, 2006; Albarracín et al., 2005; Noguchi, Albarracín, Durantini, & Glasman, 2007). Other approaches work as well, such as interventions based on the theory of planned behavior (discussed in Chapter 7), which try to increase the (a) desirability of condom use; (b) perceived normative pressures to use condoms; and (c) perceptions that condom use is controllable.

Another type of intervention that has been successful is one that frames the message in terms of gains (e.g., "If you use condoms, you can stay healthy and avoid sexually transmitted diseases") instead of losses (e.g., "If you don't use condoms, you could get AIDS"). It might seem as if these different messages would have the same effect; after all, they convey the same information—that it's a good idea to use condoms. It turns out, though, that framing messages in terms of gains versus losses can make a big difference (Rothman, Wlaschin, Bartels, Latimer, & Salovey, 2008; Rothman & Salovey, 1997). When trying to get people to behave in positive ways that will *prevent* disease, it is best to use a "gain frame," emphasizing what they have to gain by engaging in these behaviors (e.g., the benefits of using condoms or sunscreen; Higgins, 1998; Rothman, Salovey, Antone, Keough, & Martin, 1993). When trying to get people to *detect* the presence of a disease, it is best to use a "loss frame," emphasizing what they have to lose by avoiding this behavior (e.g., the costs of not using condoms or not examining one's skin for cancer; Meyerowitz & Chaiken, 1987; Rothman, 2000).

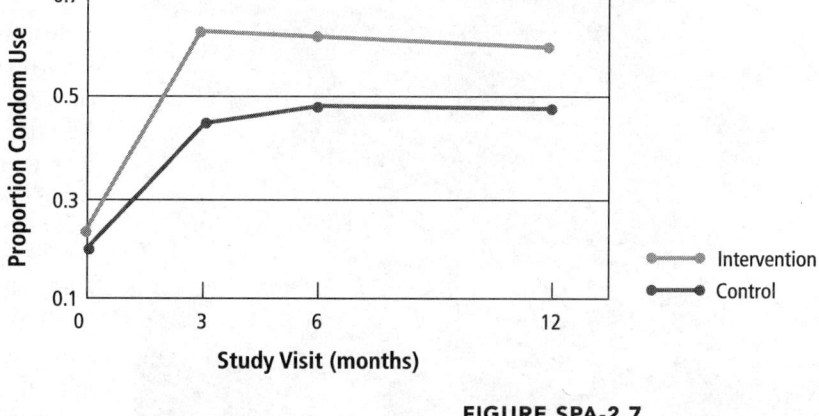

FIGURE SPA-2.7

Effects of an intervention on the proportion of times people reported using condoms during sex.

People visiting clinics that treat sexually transmitted diseases were randomly assigned either to an intervention condition (that tried to increase their self-efficacy about using condoms, their knowledge about condom use, and their motivation to use condoms) or to a control condition. People in the intervention condition showed a significant increase in the proportion of times they reported using condoms, even 12 months after the study began.

From: NIMH Multisite HIV Prevention Trial Group. (1998, June 19). The NIMH Multisite HIV Prevention Trial: Reducing HIV sexual risk behavior. *Science,* 280, 1889–1894.

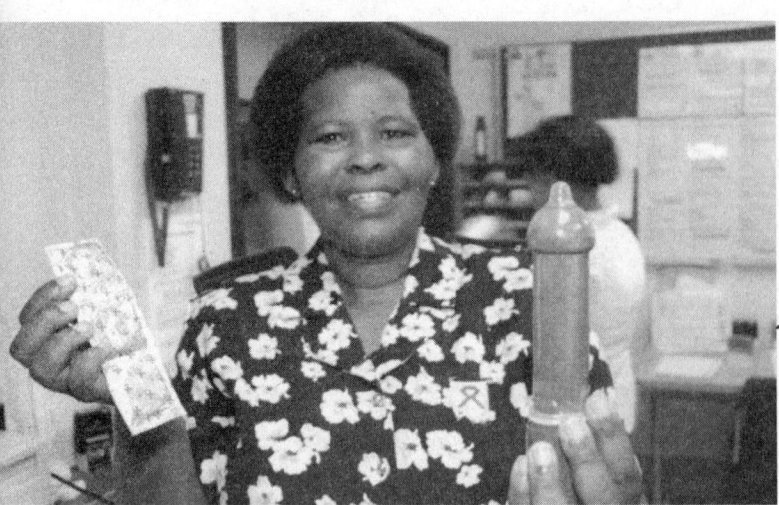

Many serious health problems are preventable, such as those resulting from unsafe sex, smoking, and overeating. Social psychologists have designed many successful interventions to improve health habits, such as programs that encourage people to use condoms.

Why does the way in which a message is framed make a difference? It may change the way we think about our health (Rothman & Salovey, 1997). A loss frame focuses our attention on the possibility that we might have a problem that can be dealt with by performing detection behaviors (e.g., examining our skin for cancer). A gain frame focuses our attention on the fact that we are in a good state of health and that to stay that way, we should perform preventive behaviors (e.g., using sunscreen when exposed to the sun and condoms when having sex).

These findings may explain why some safer-sex interventions have not been successful: ones that use fear appeals that emphasize the negative consequences of not using condoms (Albaracín et al., 2005). In one study, for example, a scary ad about AIDS actually led to riskier sexual behavior in a sample of gay men, possibly because it produced so much fear that it made the men feel helpless and as if contracting AIDS were inevitable (Rosser, 1991). Inducing fear about AIDS emphasizes what people have to lose, which as we have just seen, is ineffective in getting people to engage in preventive behaviors, such as using condoms. Further, as we discussed in Chapter 7, fear appeals can backfire if they scare people so much that they stop listening to the message.

In sum, social psychologists have discovered several ways in which to help people adopt better health habits. Perhaps you can think of ways to adopt some of these approaches in your own life. To see how you might go about this, complete the following Try It! exercise.

TRY IT! Changing Your Health Habits 试一试！改变你的健康习惯

Pick a health habit of yours and try to improve it, using the principles we have discussed in this chapter. For example, you might try to lose a few pounds, exercise more, or cut down on your smoking. This is not easy, of course—if it were, we would all be svelte, physically fit nonsmokers! We suggest that you start small with a limited goal; try to increase your exercise by one or two hours a week, or aim to lose 5 pounds, or smoke fewer cigarettes each day. Here are some specific suggestions as to how to change your behavior:

- Increase your feelings of control over your behavior, particularly your self-efficacy in this domain. One way to do this is to start small. If you are trying to lose weight, for example, begin slowly with some easy-to-control behaviors. You might start by eliminating one food or beverage from your diet that you do not like all that much but is fattening. Suppose you drink a 200-calorie fruit juice five times a week. Replacing the juice with water will save 52,000 calories a year, which is equivalent to 13 pounds! The idea is to gain mastery over your behavior slowly, improving your feelings of self-efficacy. When you've mastered one behavior, try another. You can do it!

- If you experience a setback, such as eating two pieces of cake at a birthday party when you really didn't mean to or not going to the gym when you planned to, avoid a damaging pattern of attributions. Do not assume that the setback was due to internal, stable, global causes—this will cause learned helplessness. Remember, almost everyone fails the first time they try to diet or quit smoking. It often takes people several attempts; therefore, a setback or two are not due to something unchangeable about you. Keep trying.

- It can be stressful to change a firmly ingrained habit, and it is at times of stress that social support is most important. Talk with your friends and family about your attempts to change your behavior. Seek their advice and support. Even better, convince several friends to try these techniques with you. Make it a group project in which you and your friends support each other's efforts to alter your behavior.

Summary 总 结

- **Stress and Human Health** The relationship between stress and human health has received a great deal of attention from social psychologists.
  - **Resilience** People have been found to be surprisingly resilient when they experience negative events, often showing only mild, transient reactions, followed by a quick return to normal, healthy functioning.
  - **Effects of Negative Life Events** Nonetheless, stressful events can have debilitating effects on people's psychological and physical health. Some studies calculate the number of stressful events people are experiencing and use that to predict their health.
  - **Perceived Stress and Health** Stress is best defined as the negative feelings and beliefs that arise when people feel unable to cope with demands from their environment. The more stress people experience, the more likely they are to get sick (e.g., catch a cold).
  - **Feeling in Charge: The Importance of Perceived Control** People perceive negative events as stressful if they feel they cannot control them. In the last 40 years, college students have increasingly adopted an external locus of control, which is the tendency to believe that good and bad outcomes are out of their control. The less control people believe they have, the more likely it is that the event will cause them physical and psychological problems. For example, the loss of control experienced by many older people in nursing homes can have negative effects on their health.
  - **Knowing You Can Do It: Self-Efficacy** It is also important for people to have high **self-efficacy** in a particular domain, which is the belief in their ability to carry out specific actions that produce desired outcomes.
  - **Explaining Negative Events: Learned Helplessness** The way in which people explain the causes of negative events is also critical to how stressful those events will be. When bad things happen, **learned helplessness** results if people make **stable, internal,** and **global attributions** for those events.
  - **Optimism: Looking on the Bright Side** Optimistic people tend to react better to stress and to be healthier.

- **Coping with Stress** Coping styles refer to the ways in which people react to stressful events.
  - **Gender Differences in Coping with Stress** Men are more likely to react to stress with a **fight-or-flight reaction**, responding to stress by either attacking the source of the stress or fleeing from it. Women are more likely to react to stress with a **tend-and-befriend reaction**, responding to stress with nurturant activities designed to protect themselves and their offspring (tending) and creating social networks that provide protection from threats (befriending).
  - **Social Support: Getting Help from Others** Social support—the perception that other people are responsive to one's needs—is beneficial for men and women. The form of social support, however, is important. People react better to invisible than visible support. People from individualistic cultures react well when they directly ask for support, whereas people from collectivistic cultures react well when they get support without disclosing that they are having problems.
  - **Opening Up: Making Sense of Traumatic Events** Other researchers focus on ways of coping with stress that everyone can adopt. Several studies show that opening up, by writing or talking about one's problems, has long-term health benefits.

- **Prevention: Promoting Healthier Behavior** It also important to find ways to help people change their health habits more directly.
  - **Preventable Health Problems** Many serious health problems are preventable. HIV infections are at crisis proportions, particularly in Sub-Saharan Africa. The number one and two causes of preventable deaths in the United States are tobacco use and obesity.
  - **Social Psychological Interventions: Targeting Safer Sex** Social psychologists have designed many successful interventions to improve health habits. For example, many studies have succeeded in getting people to practice safer sex. They have used social psychological principles such as increasing self-efficacy and framing the message in terms of gains instead of losses. Fear appeals have not been found to be effective in promoting safer sex.

CHAPTER SPA-2 TEST 第15章习题

1. After her husband died, Rachel did not experience significant distress and recovered quickly. Which is most true, according to research in psychology?
   a. Because Rachel did not go through the proper stages of grief, she will probably have mental health problems later.
   b. Because Rachel did not experience extreme grief, she was probably in a troubled marriage and did not love her husband very much.
   c. Although life's traumas can be quite painful, many people have the resources to recover from them quickly.
   d. Rachel is showing "delayed grief syndrome" and will probably experience grief later.

2. Bob's grandmother died recently and he just found out that his girlfriend cheated on him. He is also in the middle of final exams. According to research on stress and health, which is most true?
   a. Because Bob is experiencing so many negative life events, he is likely to get sick.
   b. These life events will be stressful for Bob only if he interprets them as stressful, in other words, if he feels unable to cope with the events.
   c. When under stress, a person's immune system is stimulated. Therefore, Bob is less likely to get sick now than he normally would.
   d. If Bob feels more in control of these events than he really is, he is especially likely to get sick.

3. Lindsay does an internship at a nursing home. According to research discussed in this chapter, which of the following would be most likely to benefit the residents?
   a. Lindsay encourages the residents to talk to her about any stressful issues in their lives.
   b. Lindsay allows the residents to choose what time she will come to visit them, and when her internship ends, she decides to keep visiting the residents when they ask her to.
   c. Lindsay allows the residents to choose what time she will come to visit them, but when her internship ends, she doesn't visit the nursing home anymore.
   d. Lindsay gives the residents a plant and makes sure to water it for them.

4. In the classic children's book *The Little Engine That Could*, the steam engine keeps repeating, "I think I can—I think I can," and sure enough, she is able to meet the challenges she faces. The book teaches readers (young and old) about which social psychological construct?
   a. External locus of control
   b. Flight (but not fight) response
   c. Fight (but not flight) response
   d. Self-efficacy

5. Which of the following is most true, according to social psychological research?
   a. It is best to view the world as accurately as possible.
   b. It is best to be pessimistic about our chances of success in life, because that motivates us to try harder.
   c. It is beneficial to be optimistic about our prospects in life, as long as that doesn't prevent us from taking steps to deal with challenges in our lives.
   d. We should be optimistic about our prospects in life, even if that keeps us from acting in healthy ways.

6. To his surprise, Michael does poorly on the first exam he takes in college. Under which of the following conditions is he *least* likely to do well on the next test?
   a. He attributes his poor grade to external, specific, unstable factors.
   b. He believes he can control how well he does on the next test.
   c. He has a feeling of self-efficacy about his performance on the next test.
   d. He is pretty certain that he will do poorly on the next test.

7. Kate has had a hard time getting over her parents' divorce. According to social psychological research, which of the following would probably help Kate the most?
   a. She should spend 15 minutes a night, on 4 consecutive nights, writing about her feelings about the divorce.
   b. She should try to attribute the divorce to internal, global, stable things about herself.
   c. She should avoid talking about the divorce with her closest friends because it would probably just depress them.
   d. She should focus on the fact that she has low self-efficacy to improve her relationship with her parents.

8. All of the following interventions but one have proven effective in getting people to practice safer sex by using condoms. Which one has *not* been shown to work?
   a. Getting people to attribute their use of condoms to external, specific, unstable factors about themselves
   b. Increasing people's sense of self-efficacy about the use of condoms
   c. Interventions based on the theory of planned behavior that try to increase the desirability of condom use, the perceived normative pressures to use condoms, and perceptions that condom use is controllable
   d. Using a "gain frame" message (e.g., "If you use condoms, you can stay healthy and avoid sexually transmitted diseases") instead of a "loss frame" message

Answer Key
1-c, 2-b, 3-b, 4-d, 5-c, 6-d, 7-a, 8-a

For more review plus practice tests, videos, flashcards, writing help and more, log on to MyPsychLab.

Scoring the TRY IT! exercises "试一试！"答案

⊙ Page 460

1. First, reverse your answers to questions 3, 7, and 9. That is, for these questions, change 0 to 4, 1 to 3, 3 to 1, and 4 to 0. Then add these reversed scores to the scores you gave to questions 1, 4, and 10. (Ignore questions 2, 5, 6, and 8; they were filler items.)

2. This measure of dispositional optimism was created by Scheier, Carver, and Bridges (1994). According to these researchers, the higher your score, the more optimistic your approach to life. The average score for college students in their study was 14.3, with no significant differences between women and men. Several studies have found that optimistic people cope better with stress and are generally healthier than their pessimistic counterparts.

⊙ Page 463

1. You get 1 point each time you answered true (T) to questions 1, 4, 5, 6, and 10 and 1 point for each time you answered false (F) to questions 2, 3, 7, 8, and 9.

2. This scale was developed to measure what the researchers call appraisal social support, or "the perceived availability of someone to talk to about one's problems" (Cohen, Mermelstein, Kamarack, & Hoberman, 1985, pp. 75–76). One of the findings was that when people were not under stress, those low in social support had no more physical symptoms than people high in social support did. When people were under stress, however, those low in social support had more physical symptoms than people high in social support did. Another finding was that women scored reliably higher on the social support scale than men did. If you scored lower than you would like, you might want to consider reaching out to others more when you are under stress.

SOCIAL PSYCHOLOGY IN ACTION 3

Social Psychology and the Law
实践中的社会心理学之三:
社会心理学与法律

OUTLINE 提纲

- **Eyewitness Testimony**
  - Why Are Eyewitnesses Often Wrong?
  - Judging Whether Eyewitnesses Are Mistaken
  - Judging Whether Witnesses Are Lying
  - Can Eyewitness Testimony Be Improved?
  - The Recovered Memory Debate
- **Juries: Group Processes in Action**
  - How Jurors Process Information During the Trial
  - Confessions: Are They Always What They Seem?
  - Deliberations in the Jury Room
- **Why Do People Obey the Law?**
  - Do Severe Penalties Deter Crime?
  - Procedural Justice: People's Sense of Fairness
- **Summary**

Y OU BE THE JURY AND DECIDE HOW YOU WOULD VOTE, after hearing the following testimony from an actual case in Texas. On a cold, dark night in November 1976, police officer Robert Wood and his partner spotted a car driving with its headlights off. Wood signaled the car to pull over, got out, and walked up to the driver's side. He intended only to tell the driver to turn on his lights, but he never got the chance. Before Wood could even speak, the driver pointed a handgun at Wood and shot him, killing him instantly. Wood's partner emptied her revolver at the car as it sped away, but the killer escaped.

A month later, the police picked up a suspect, 16-year-old David Harris. Harris admitted that he had stolen a neighbor's car and revolver the day before the murder, that this was the car Officer Wood had pulled over that night, and that he was in the car when the murder occurred. Harris denied, however, that he was the one who shot Wood. He said he had picked up a hitchhiker by the name of Randall Adams and had let Adams drive. It was Adams, he claimed, who reached under the seat, grabbed the revolver, and shot the officer.

When the police questioned Randall Adams, he admitted he had gotten a ride from David Harris but said Harris had dropped him off at his motel 3 hours before the murder occurred. It was Harris, he claimed, who was the murderer. Who was telling the truth? It was Harris's word against Adams's—until the police found three eyewitnesses who corroborated Harris's story. Emily and Robert Miller testified that they drove by just before Officer Wood was shot. Though it was very dark, they said they got a good look at the driver of the car, and both identified him as Randall Adams. "When he rolled down the window, that's what made his face stand out," said Robert Miller. "He had a beard, mustache, kind of dishwater blond hair" (Morris, 1988). David Harris was clean-shaven, and at the time of the murder, Randall Adams did indeed fit Miller's description (see the photo on the next page). Michael Randell, a salesman, also happened to be driving by right before the murder and claimed to have seen two people in the car. He too said the driver had long hair and a mustache.

Who do you think committed the murder? The real jury believed the eyewitnesses and convicted Adams, sentencing him to death. However, as Adams languished in jail, waiting for the courts to hear his appeals, several experts began to doubt that he was guilty. New evidence came to light (largely because of a film made about the case, *The Thin Blue Line*), and it is now almost certain that David Harris was the murderer. Harris was later convicted of another murder and while on death row strongly implied that he, not Randall Adams, had shot Officer Wood.

Randall Adams (top) and David Harris (bottom). The fact that eyewitnesses said the murderer had long hair and a mustache was the main reason Adams was convicted of murdering Officer Wood.

An appeals court finally overturned Adams's conviction. He was a free man—after spending 12 years in prison for a crime he did not commit.

If Adams was innocent, why did the eyewitnesses say that the driver of the car had long hair and a mustache? And why did the jury believe them? How common are such miscarriages of justice? In this chapter, we will discuss the answers to these questions, focusing on the role social psychological processes play in the legal system.

Let's begin with a brief review of the American justice system. When someone commits a crime and the police arrest a suspect, a judge or a grand jury decides whether there is enough evidence to press formal charges. If there is, lawyers for the defense and the prosecution gather evidence and negotiate with each other. As a result of these negotiations, the defendant often pleads guilty to a lesser charge. About a quarter of the cases go to trial, in which a jury or a judge decides the defendant's fate. There are also civil trials, where one party (the plaintiff) brings a complaint against another (the defendant) for violating the former's rights in some way.

All these steps in the legal process are related to central social psychological questions. For example, first impressions of the accused and of the witnesses have a powerful effect on police investigators and the jury; attributions about what caused the criminal behavior are made by police, lawyers, jurors, and the judge; prejudiced beliefs and stereotypical ways of thinking affect those attributions; attitude change and persuasion techniques abound in the courtroom as lawyers for each side argue their case and jurors later debate with one another; and the processes of social cognition affect the jurors' decision making when deciding guilt or innocence. Social psychologists have studied the legal system a great deal in recent years, both because it offers an excellent applied setting in which to study basic psychological processes and because of its immense importance in daily life. If you, through no fault of your own, become the accused in a court trial, what do you need to know to convince the system of your innocence?

We will begin our discussion with eyewitness testimony, the most troubling aspect of the Randall Adams case. We saw in Chapter 4 that although people do form accurate impressions of others, systematic biases can come into play, leading to serious misunderstandings. A closely related question is, how accurate are people at identifying someone who has committed a crime?

Eyewitness Testimony 目击者证词

The American legal system assigns a great deal of significance to eyewitness testimony. If an eyewitness fingers you as the culprit, you are quite likely to be convicted, even if considerable circumstantial evidence indicates that you are innocent. Randall Adams was convicted largely because of the eyewitnesses who identified him, even though in other ways the case against him was weak. Unfortunately, wrongful convictions based on faulty eyewitness identification are not uncommon. According to the Innocence Project, there have been over 225 cases in which someone has been exonerated with DNA evidence after being convicted of a crime and spending an average of 12 years in prison. In 75 percent of these cases, the conviction was based on faulty eyewitness identification (www.innocenceproject.org). In short, the most common cause of an innocent person's being convicted of a crime is an erroneous eyewitness (Brandon & Davies, 1973; Sporer, Koehnken, & Malpass, 1996; Wells & Hasel, 2008; Wells, Memon, & Penrod, 2006).

Systematic experiments have confirmed that jurors and law enforcement professionals rely heavily on eyewitness testimony when they are deciding whether someone is guilty. Unfortunately, jurors also tend to overestimate the accuracy of eyewitnesses

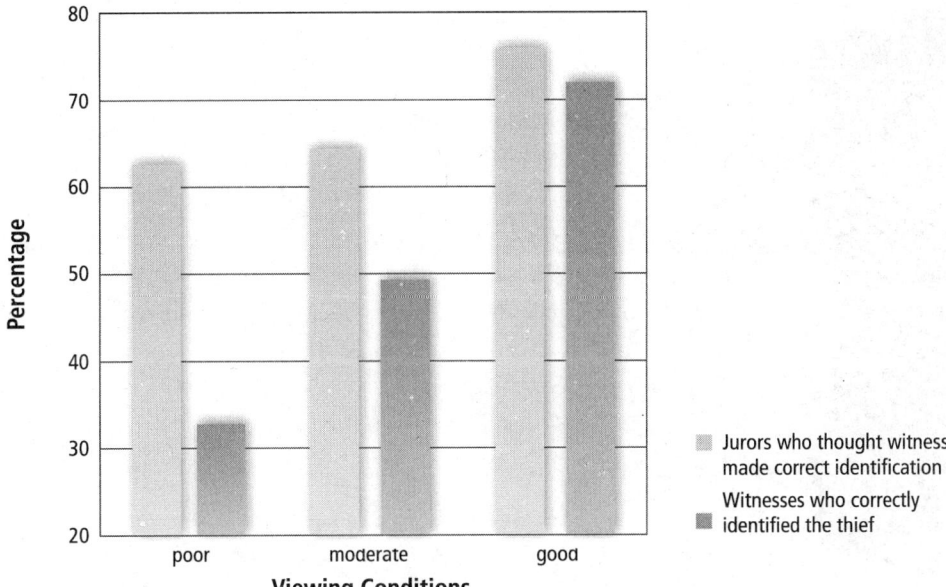

FIGURE SPA-3.1
The accuracy of eyewitness identification.

The accuracy of eyewitness identification depends on the viewing conditions at the time the crime was committed. As in this study, however, most jurors believe that witnesses can correctly identify the criminal even when viewing conditions are poor.

(Adapted from Lindsay, Wells, & Rumpel, 1981)

(Ellsworth & Mauro, 1998; Loftus, 1979; Wells & Hasel, 2008). Rod Lindsay and his colleagues (Lindsay, Wells, & Rumpel, 1981) conducted a clever experiment that illustrates both of these points. The researchers first staged the theft of a calculator in front of unsuspecting students and then saw how accurately the students could pick out the "thief" from a set of six photographs. In one condition, identifying the thief was difficult because he had worn a knit cap pulled over his ears and was in the room for only 12 seconds. In the second condition, the thief had worn the knit cap higher on his head, revealing some of his hair, so that it was easier to identify him. In the third condition, the thief had worn no hat and stayed in the room for 20 seconds, making it easiest to identify him.

The first set of results is as we'd expect: The more visual information available about the thief, the higher the percentage of students who correctly identified him in the photo lineup (see the right-hand bars in Figure SPA-3.1). In the next stage of the experiment, a researcher playing the role of lawyer questioned the students about their eyewitness identifications, just as a real lawyer would cross-examine witnesses in a trial. These question-and-answer sessions were videotaped. A new group of participants, playing the role of jurors, watched the videotapes of these cross-examinations and rated the extent to which they believed the witnesses had correctly identified the thief. As shown by the left-hand bars in Figure SPA-3.1, the jurors overestimated the accuracy of the witnesses, especially in the condition where the thief was difficult to identify.

Why Are Eyewitnesses Often Wrong? 为何目击者经常指认错误?

The problem is that our minds are not like video cameras, which can record an event, store it over time, and play it back later with perfect accuracy. Think back to our discussion of social perception in Chapter 4, the study of how we form impressions of and make inferences about other people. We saw that a number of distortions can occur. Because eyewitness identification is a form of social perception, it is subject to similar problems, particularly those involving memory. To be an accurate eyewitness, a person must successfully complete three stages of memory processing: acquisition, storage, and retrieval of the events witnessed. **Acquisition** refers to the process whereby people notice and pay attention to information in the environment. Because people cannot perceive everything that is happening around them, they acquire only a subset of the information available in the environment. **Storage** refers to the process by which people store in memory information they have acquired from the environment. **Retrieval** refers to the process by which people recall information stored in their memories (see Figure SPA-3.2). Eyewitnesses can be inaccurate because of problems at any of these three stages.

Acquisition
The process by which people notice and pay attention to information in the environment; because people cannot perceive everything that is happening around them, they acquire only a subset of the information available in the environment

Storage
The process by which people store in memory information they have acquired from the environment

Retrieval
The process by which people recall information stored in their memories

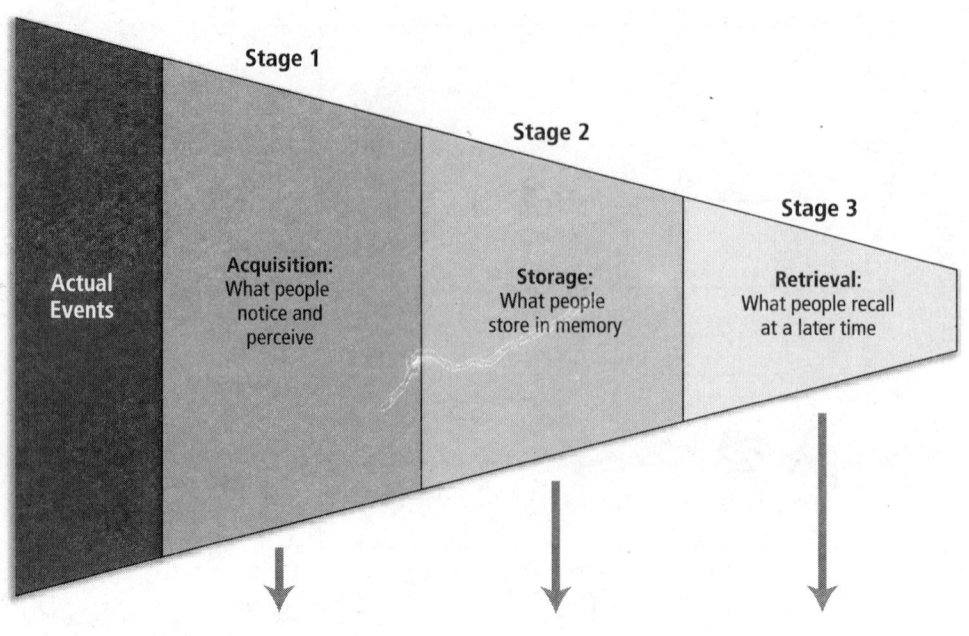

FIGURE SPA-3.2

Acquisition, storage, and retrieval.

To be an accurate eyewitness, people must complete three stages of memory processing. Errors may creep in at each of the three stages.

Acquisition A number of factors limit the amount of information about a crime that people take in, such as how much time they have to watch an event and the nature of the viewing conditions. As obvious as this may sound, people sometimes forget how these factors limit eyewitness reports of crimes. Crimes usually occur under the very conditions that make acquisition difficult: quickly, unexpectedly, under poor viewing conditions (e.g., at night), and under considerable stress. These conditions certainly describe the scene of the murder of Officer Wood. Eyewitnesses were driving down a dimly lit road, passed a pulled-over car, when the unexpected happened—shots were fired and a policeman crumpled to the ground. How well could they see? How much information could they take in, in the few seconds it took to drive by?

Consider a more recent case: In October 1997, four young men in Fairbanks, Alaska, went on a rampage, attacking passersby at random. By the end of the night they had killed a teenage boy and severely wounded an older man, Franklin Dayton. Eventually four suspects were arrested and convicted of the crimes, largely on the basis of eyewitness testimony of Fairbanks resident Arlo Olson. Mr. Olson testified that he seen the defendants attack Mr. Dayton from "a couple of blocks away"—a distance that was later determined to be 450 feet, one-and-a-half lengths of a football field.

How much should we trust Mr. Olson's testimony? To answer this question, Geoffrey Loftus and Erin Harley (2005) calculated the amount of detail that is lost in the perception of a face, as distance increases. As an illustration, look at the photographs of Julia Roberts on the next page. The one on the left is how Ms. Roberts's face would appear if she were standing 5.4 feet away from you. No problem recognizing her here; perhaps you would ask her for her autograph. The middle picture is how her face would appear if she were standing 43 feet away from you. In this case you might think, "Hm, that woman looks kind of like Julia Roberts; maybe I'll get a closer look." The picture on the right is how Ms. Roberts would appear if she were standing 172 feet away. Here it would probably never dawn on you that a famous celebrity was in the vicinity.

How easy is it to recognize Julia Roberts from these photos? These images are how she would appear from a distance of 5.4 feet, 43 feet, and 172 feet.

When Loftus and Harley (2005) showed photographs like these to research participants, they found that accuracy in identifying the celebrities began to drop when the simulated distance exceeded 25 feet. At 34 feet, only 75 percent of the participants recognized the face, and at 77 feet, only 25 percent of the participants did so. It thus seems unlikely that Arlo Olson could have identified the suspects in the Fairbanks murder case from a distance of 450 feet.

We should also remember that when eyewitnesses are the victims of a crime, they will be terribly afraid, and this alone can make it difficult to take in everything that is happening. The more stress people are under, the worse their memory for people involved in and the details of a crime (Deffenbacher, Bornstein, & Penrod, 2004). Another reason why victims of crimes have a poor memory for a suspect is that they focus their attention mostly on any weapon they see and less on the suspect's features (Hope & Wright, 2007; Loftus, Loftus, & Messo, 1987; Pickel, 2007). If someone points a gun at you and demands your money, your attention is likely to be more on the gun than on whether the robber has blue or brown eyes.

The information people notice and pay attention to is also influenced by what they expect to see. Consider our friend Alan, a social psychologist who is an expert on social perception. One Sunday, Alan was worried because his neighbor, a frail woman in her 80s, did not appear for church. After knocking on her door repeatedly and receiving no response, Alan jimmied open a window and searched her house. Soon his worst fears were realized: The woman was lying dead on the floor of her bedroom.

Shaken, Alan went back to his house and telephoned the police. A detective spent a great deal of time in the woman's house, after which he asked Alan some pointed questions, such as whether he had noticed any suspicious activity in the past day or two. Alan was confused by this line of questioning and finally burst out, "Why are you asking me these questions? Isn't it obvious that my neighbor died of old age? Shouldn't we be notifying her family?" Now it was the detective's turn to look puzzled. "Aren't you the one who discovered the body?" he asked. Alan said he was. "Well," said the detective, "didn't you notice that her bedroom had been ransacked, that there was broken glass everywhere, and that there was a belt tied around her neck?"

It turned out that Alan's neighbor had been strangled by a man who had come to spray her house for insects. There had been a fierce struggle, and the fact that the woman was murdered could not have been more obvious. But Alan saw none of the signs. He was worried that his elderly neighbor had passed away. When he discovered that she had in fact died, he was quite upset, and the farthest thing from his mind was that she had been murdered. As a result, he saw what he expected and failed to see what he did not expect. When the police later showed him photographs of the crime scene, he felt as though he had never been there. He recognized almost nothing.

> *When an actual perceptual fact is in conflict with expectation, expectation may prove a stronger determinant of perception and memory than the situation itself.*
>
> —Gordon Allport and Leo Postman, 1947

Suppose you were watching a video of two groups of people passing a basketball back and forth and counting the number of passes one team threw to the other. Would you notice the fact that a person dressed in a gorilla suit entered the scene, faced the camera, and thumped her chest? Only 50 percent of the participants noticed the gorilla in a study by Simons and Chabris (1999). People often fail to notice changes in their environments that are unexpected, especially if they are concentrating on something else (e.g., counting the passes). (From Simons & Chabris, 1999).

Own-Race Bias
The fact that people are better at recognizing faces of their own race than those of other races

Research has confirmed that people are poor at noticing the unexpected. In one study, participants watched a videotape of two teams passing a basketball back and forth and counted the number of times one team passed the ball to the other. Thirty-five seconds into the film, something weird happened: A woman in a gorilla suit walked into the middle of the basketball game, turned toward the camera, thumped her chest, and then walked away. Meanwhile, the basketball players continued with their passing game. Although it seems as if everyone would notice such a bizarre interruption, only half did. The other half simply didn't see the gorilla at all (Simons & Chabris, 1999). Given that crimes are almost always highly unexpected events, it is no surprise that people often fail to notice key details in the crime scene (Rensink, 2002; Simons & Ambinder, 2005).

Even if we notice a person or event, we might not remember it very well if we are unfamiliar with it. For example, people are better at recognizing faces that are of the same race as they are, a phenomenon known as **own-race bias**. Whites are better at recognizing white faces than black or Asian faces, blacks are better at recognizing black than white faces, and Asians are better at recognizing Asian than white faces (Brigham, Bennett, Meissner, & Mitchell, 2007; Johnson & Fredrickson, 2005; Levin, 2000). One study found a similar effect with age: College students were better at recognizing faces of people their own age than faces of middle-aged people, whereas middle-aged people were better at recognizing faces of people their own age than faces of college students (Wright & Stroud, 2002).

Own-race bias is due in part to the fact that people have more contact with members of their own race, allowing them to learn better how to distinguish one individual from another (Meissner & Brigham, 2001b). One study found that 3-month-old babies looked longer at same-race faces than other-race faces, but only if they lived in an environment in which they had little contact with other races (Bar-Haim, Ziv, Lamy, & Hodes, 2006). Another study looked at how well three different groups could recognize white and Asian faces: White residents of France, Koreans who grew up in Korea, and Koreans who had been adopted by white French families when they were children. As expected, the first two groups showed the own-race bias: The whites had better recall for white faces, and the Koreans had better recall for Asian faces. What about the Koreans who grew up in white families? They had better memory for the white faces, which is consistent with the idea that we remember better faces that are of the race we have the most contact with (Sangrigoli, Argenti, Ventureyra, & Sehonen, 2005).

Another reason for the own-race bias is that when people examine same-race faces, they pay close attention to individuating features that distinguish that face from others, such as the height of the cheekbones or the contour of the forehead. When people examine different-race faces, however, they are drawn more to features that distinguish that face from their own race, rather than individuating features (Levin, 2000). Daniel Levin, a researcher who has investigated this hypothesis, puts it like this: "When a white person looks at another white person's nose, they're likely to think to themselves, 'That's John's nose.' When they look at a black person's nose, they're likely to think, 'That's a black nose'" (quoted in Carpenter, 2000, p. 44). Because people usually have less experience with features that characterize individuals of other races, they find it more difficult to tell members of that race apart.

Storage We have just seen that several variables limit what people perceive and thus what they are able to store in their memories. After a piece of information is in memory, it might seem as if it stays there, unaltered, until we recall it at a later time. Many people think memory is like a photograph album. We record a picture of an event, such as the face of a robber, and place it in the memory "album." In reality, few of us have photographic memories. Memories, like real photographs, fade with age. Further, it is tempting to believe that a picture, once stored, cannot be altered or retouched, and that details cannot be added to or subtracted from the image. If the robber we saw was clean-shaven, surely we will not pencil in a mustache at some later time. Hence the fact that the witnesses who testified at the Randall Adams trial remembered that the driver of the car had long hair and a mustache seems like pretty incriminating evidence against Randall Adams.

Unfortunately, memories are far from indelible. People can get mixed up about where they heard or saw something; memories in one "album" can get confused with memories in another. As a result, people can have quite inaccurate recall about what they saw. This is the conclusion reached after years of research on **reconstructive memory**, the distortion of memories of an event by information encountered after the event occurred (Davis & Loftus, 2007; Hirt, McDonald, & Erikson, 1995; Loftus, 1979, 2005; McDonald & Hirt, 1997). According to this research, information we obtain after witnessing an event can change our memories of the event.

In a classic study, Elizabeth Loftus showed students 30 slides depicting different stages of an automobile accident. The content of one slide varied; some students saw a car stopped at a stop sign, and others saw the same car stopped at a yield sign. After the slide show, the students were asked several questions about the car accident they had "witnessed." The key question varied how the traffic sign was described. In one version, the question asked, "Did another car pass the red Datsun while it was stopped at the stop sign?" In the other version, the question asked, "Did another car pass the red Datsun while it was stopped at the yield sign?" Thus for half the participants, the question described the traffic sign as they had in fact seen it. But for the other half, the wording of the question subtly introduced new information—for example, that they had seen a stop sign, when in fact they had seen a yield sign. Would this small change (akin to what might occur when witnesses are being questioned by police investigators or attorneys) influence people's memories of the actual event?

All the students were shown the two pictures reproduced below and asked which one they had originally seen. Most people (75 percent) who were asked about the sign they had actually seen chose the correct picture; that is, if they had seen a stop sign and were asked about a stop sign, most of them correctly identified the stop sign photograph (note that 25 percent made a crucial mistake on what would seem to be an easy question). However, of those who had received the misleading question, only 41 percent chose the correct photograph (Loftus, Miller, & Burns, 1978).

In subsequent experiments, Loftus and her colleagues have found that misleading questions can change people's minds about how fast a car was going, whether broken glass was at the scene of an accident, whether a traffic light was green or red, and—of relevance to the Randall Adams trial—whether a robber had a mustache (Loftus, 1979). Her studies show that the way in which the police and lawyers question witnesses can change the witnesses' reports about what they saw. (There is some suspicion that in the Randall Adams case, the police may have led the witnesses by asking questions that implicated Adams and not Harris. At the time of the murder, Harris was a juvenile and could not receive the death penalty for killing a police officer; Adams was in his 30s and was eligible for the death penalty. According to this reasoning, Adams was a "better" suspect in the eyes of the police.)

> *Give us a dozen healthy memories, well-formed, and . . . we'll guarantee to take any one at random and train it to become any type of memory we might select—hammer, screwdriver, wrench, stop sign, yield sign, Indian chief—regardless of its origin or the brain that holds it.*
>
> —Elizabeth Loftus and Hunter Hoffman, 1989

Reconstructive Memory
The process whereby memories of an event become distorted by information encountered after the event occurred

Students saw one of these pictures and then tried to remember whether they had seen a stop sign or a yield sign. Many of those who heard leading questions about the street sign made mistaken reports about which sign they had seen. (From Loftus, Miller, & Burns, 1978)

Police distributed this sketch of "John Doe No. 2," a suspect in the Oklahoma City bombing in April 1995. The sketch was based on a description given by a mechanic in a truck rental office, who said that he saw Timothy McVeigh and the man in the sketch rent a truck. The employee later acknowledged, however, that he was confused and had actually described a man who had been in the office the day before McVeigh and who had nothing to do with the bombing. This appears to be a classic source monitoring error. The employee had an actual memory of the person he described but was mistaken about where he had seen the person.

Source Monitoring
The process whereby people try to identify the source of their memories

Misleading questions can cause a problem with **source monitoring**, the process people use to try to identify the source of their memories (Johnson, Hashtroudi, & Lindsay, 1993; Johnson, Verfaellie, & Dunlosky, 2008; Qin, Ogle, & Goodman, 2008). People who saw a stop sign but received the misleading question about a yield sign now have two pieces of information in memory, the stop sign and the yield sign. This is all well and good as long as they remember where these memories came from: the stop sign from the accident they saw earlier and the yield sign from the question they were asked later. The problem is that people often get mixed up about where they heard or saw something, mistakenly believing that the yield sign looks familiar because they saw it during the slide show. This process is similar to the misattribution effects we discussed in Chapter 5, when people are unsure about what has caused their arousal. It's easy to get confused about the source of our memories as well. When information gets stored in memory, it is not always well "tagged" as to where it came from.

The implications for legal testimony are sobering. Eyewitnesses who are asked misleading questions often report seeing things that were not really there. In addition, eyewitnesses might be confused as to why a suspect looks familiar. It is likely, for example, that the eyewitnesses in the Randall Adams trial saw pictures of Adams in the newspaper before they testified about what they saw the night of the murder. When asked to remember what they saw that night, they might have become confused because of a source monitoring error. They remembered seeing a man with long hair and a mustache, but they may have gotten mixed up about where they had seen his face before.

Another source monitoring error may have occurred in the Oklahoma City bombing incident. On April 19, 1995, a bomb went off in the Alfred P. Murrah Federal Building in Oklahoma City, killing 168 people. Timothy McVeigh was later convicted of the crime and received the death penalty. But did he act alone? Tom Kessinger, a mechanic in a truck rental office, said that he saw McVeigh and another man rent a Ryder truck the day before the blast. Kessinger described the second suspect, who became known as "John Doe No. 2," as a large, muscular man wearing a black tee-shirt and a baseball hat. A worldwide search for this suspect ensued, but the police were never able to find him, triggering suspicion that one of the bombers was still at large. It later came to light, though, that Kessinger had made a source monitoring error. Feeling pressure to identify McVeigh's companion, Kessinger mixed him up with a man who had been in the office the day before McVeigh, Private Todd Bunting from Fort Riley, Kansas, who had nothing to do with the bombing (Thomas, 1997).

Retrieval Suppose that the police have arrested a suspect and want to see if you, the eyewitness, can identify the person. Typically, the police arrange a lineup at the police station, where you will be asked whether one of several people is the perpetrator. Sometimes you will be asked to look through a one-way mirror at an actual lineup of the suspect and some foils (people known not to have committed the crime). Other times you will be asked to examine videotapes of a lineup or photographs of the suspect and the foils. In each case, if a witness identifies a suspect as the culprit, the suspect is likely to be charged and convicted of the crime. After all, the argument goes, if an eyewitness saw the suspect commit the crime and then picked the suspect out of a lineup later, that's pretty good evidence the suspect is the guilty party.

Just as there are problems with acquisition and storage of information, so too can there be problems with how people retrieve information from their memories (Charman & Wells, 2007; Malpass, Tredoux, & McQuiston-Surrett, 2007; Wells, Memon, & Penrod, 2006; Wells, 2008; Wells & Hasel, 2008). In fact, identification errors from lineups are the most common cause of wrongful convictions in the United States

(Wells et al., 1998). A number of things other than the image of a person that is stored in memory can influence whether eyewitnesses will pick someone out of a lineup. Witnesses often choose the person in a lineup who most resembles the criminal, even if the resemblance is not very strong.

Suppose that a 19-year-old woman committed a robbery and the police mistakenly arrest you, a 19-year-old woman, for the crime. They put you in a lineup and ask witnesses to pick out the criminal. Which do you think would be more fair: if the other people in the lineup were a 20-year-old man, a 3-year-old child, and an 80-year-old woman, or if the other people were all 19-year-old women? In the former case, the witnesses might pick you only because you are the one who most resembles the actual criminal (Buckhout, 1974). In the latter case, it is much less likely that the witnesses will mistake you for the criminal because everyone in the lineup is the same age and sex as the culprit (Wells, 1993; Wells & Luus, 1990).

To avoid this "best guess" problem, where witnesses pick the person who looks most like the suspect, as well as other problems with lineup identifications, social psychologists recommend that police follow these steps:

- **Make sure everyone in the lineup resembles the witness's description of the suspect.** Doing so will minimize the possibility that the witness will simply choose the person who looks most like the culprit (Wells et al., 1998).

- **Tell the witnesses that the person suspected of the crime may or may not be in the lineup.** If witnesses believe the culprit is present, they are much more likely to choose the person who looks most like the culprit, rather than saying that they aren't sure or that the culprit is not present. As a result, false identifications are more likely to occur when people believe the culprit is in the lineup (Clark, 2005; Malpass & Devine, 1981; Steblay, 1997; Wells et al., 1998, 2000).

- **Do not always include the suspect in an initial lineup.** If a witness picks out someone as the culprit from a lineup that includes only foils, you will know the witness is not reliable (Wells, 1984).

- **Make sure that the person conducting the lineup does not know which person in the lineup is the suspect.** This avoids the possibility that the person will unintentionally communicate to the witness who the suspect is (Wells et al., 1998).

- **Present pictures of people sequentially instead of simultaneously.** Doing so makes it more difficult for witnesses to compare all the pictures, choosing the one that most resembles the criminal, even when the criminal is not actually in the lineup (Lindsay & Wells, 1985; Meissner, Tredoux, & Parker, 2005; Steblay, Dysart, Fulero, & Lindsay, 2001).

- **Present witnesses with both photographs of people and sound recordings of their voices.** Witnesses who both see and hear members of a lineup are much more likely to identify the person they saw commit a crime than people who only see the pictures or only hear the voice recordings (Melara, De Witt-Rickards, & O'Brien, 1989).

- **Don't use composite face programs.** Sometimes witnesses are asked to reconstruct the face of a suspect, using computer programs that are designed for this purpose. Typically, the faces that witnesses generate with these programs do not look much like the actual suspect. Even worse, research shows that people who generate faces with these programs subsequently have a worse memory for the suspect than people who do not (Wells, Charman, & Olson, 2005; Wells & Hasel, 2007). Focusing on specific features of a face, such as what the chin looked like, appears to interfere with people's original memory for the face.

- **Don't count on witnesses knowing whether their selections were biased.** To determine whether a witness's selection was biased, attorneys or judges sometimes ask them, for example, "Do you think your choice of suspect was influenced by how the pictures were presented or what the police told you?" Unfortunately, people are not so good at answering these questions. People don't have sufficient access to their thought processes to detect whether they were biased (Charman & Wells, 2008; Nisbett & Wilson, 1977).

"Take your time, Mrs. Scradler, and tell us which of these men you saw looking in your second-story window."

CLOSE TO HOME Copyright © 2002 John McPherson. Reprinted with permission of UNIVERSAL PRESS SYNDICATE. All Rights Reserved.

Judging Whether Eyewitnesses Are Mistaken
判断目击证人是否犯错

Suppose you are a police detective or a member of a jury who is listening to a witness describe a suspect. How can you tell whether the witness's memory is accurate or whether the witness is making one of the many mistakes in memory we have just documented? It might seem that the answer to this question is pretty straightforward: Pay careful attention to how confident the witness is. Consider the case of Jennifer Thompson, who was raped when she was a 22-year-old college student. During the rape, Thompson reports, she "studied every single detail on the rapist's face" to help her identify him. She was determined that if she survived, she was going to make sure he was caught and went to prison. After the ordeal, she went to the police station and looked through hundreds of police photos. When she saw Ronald Cotton's picture, she was certain that he was the rapist. "I knew this was the man. I was completely confident. I was sure."

The police brought Cotton in and put him in a lineup, and Thompson picked him out without hesitation. Certain that Cotton was the man who had raped her, she testified against him in court. "I was sure. I knew it. I had picked the right guy." On the basis of her convincing testimony, Cotton was sentenced to life in prison.

A few years later, the police asked Thompson to go to court and look at another man, Bobby Poole, who had been bragging in prison that he had committed the rape. When asked if she recognized him, Thompson replied, "I have never seen him in my life. I have no idea who he is."

As the years passed, and Cotton remained in jail for the rape, DNA testing became more widely available. The police decided to see if evidence from the case matched Cotton or Poole's DNA. In 1995, 11 years after the crime, the police informed Thompson of the results: "I was standing in my kitchen when the detective and the district attorney visited. They were good and decent people who were trying to do their jobs—as I had done mine, as anyone would try to do the right thing. They told me: 'Ronald Cotton didn't rape you. It was Bobby Poole.' " (Thompson, 2000, p. 15). Cotton was released from prison after serving 11 years for a crime he did not commit.

Does Certainty Mean Accuracy? One reason Cotton was convicted in the first place was that Thompson was so certain that he was the man who had raped her. It is only natural for jurors and law enforcement officers to go by how confident a witness is; surely witnesses who are confident are more likely to be correct. The U.S. Supreme Court concurred with this reasoning, ruling that the amount of confidence witnesses express is a good indicator of their accuracy (*Neil* v. *Biggers*, 1972).

Nevertheless, numerous studies have shown that a witness's confidence is only modestly related to his or her accuracy (Brewer & Weber, 2008; Brewer & Wells, 2006; Olsson, 2000; Wells, Olson, & Charman, 2002). When law enforcement officials and jurors assume that a witness who is very confident is also correct, they can make serious mistakes. For example, in the Lindsay and colleagues (1981) experiment we discussed earlier, witnesses who saw the crime under poor viewing conditions (in which the thief wore the cap over his ears) had as much confidence in their identifications as witnesses who saw the crime under moderate or good viewing conditions, even though they were considerably less accurate (see Figure SPA-3.1 on page 475).

> *No subjective feeling of certainty can be an objective criterion for the desired truth.*
>
> —Hugo Münsterberg, *On the Witness Stand*, 1908

Why isn't confidence always a sign of accuracy? One reason is that the things that influence people's confidence are not necessarily the same things that influence their accuracy (Busey, Tunnicliff, Loftus, & Loftus, 2000). After identifying a suspect, for example, a person's confidence increases if he or she finds out that other witnesses identified the same suspect and decreases if he or she finds out that other witnesses identified a different suspect (Penrod & Cutler, 1999; Wells & Bradfield, 1998). This change in confidence cannot influence the accuracy of the identification the person made earlier. Therefore, just because a witness is confident does not mean that he or she is accurate, as the cases of Randall Adams and Ronald Cotton illustrate so tragically. However, confidence in combination with another way of responding might indeed suggest that people are accurate—namely, if people identify a face quickly.

Responding Quickly In a study by David Dunning and Lisa Beth Stern (1994), participants watched a film in which a man stole some money from a woman's wallet, picked the man out of a photo lineup, and then described how they had made up their minds. Accurate witnesses tended to say that they didn't really know how they recognized the man, that his face just "popped out" at them. Inaccurate witnesses tended to say that they used a process of elimination, deliberately comparing one face to another. Ironically, taking more time and thinking more carefully about the pictures were associated with making more mistakes. We should thus be more willing to believe a witness who says, "I knew it was the defendant as soon as I saw him in the lineup," than one who says, "I compared everyone in the lineup to each other, thought about it, and decided it was the defendant"—particularly if the first witness made his or her judgment in 10 seconds or less (Dunning & Perretta, 2002). Subsequent research found that combining the speed with which people respond and their confidence is the best way to assess accuracy (Weber, Brewer, Wells, Semmler, & Keast, 2004). People who made their choice within 10 seconds *and* expressed very high confidence in their judgment were especially likely to be correct.

The Problem with Verbalization It might seem that another way to improve the accuracy of eyewitness identification would be to tell people to write down a description of the suspect as soon as they can to help them remember what they saw. Studies by Jonathan Schooler and Tonya Engstler-Schooler (1990), however, show that trying to put an image of a face into words can make people's memory worse. They showed students a film of a bank robbery and asked some of the students to write detailed descriptions of the robber's face (the verbalization condition). The others spent the same amount of time completing an unrelated task (the no-verbalization condition). All students then tried to identify the robber from a photo lineup of eight faces. The results? Only 38 percent of the people in the verbalization condition correctly identified the robber, compared to 64 percent of the people in the no-verbalization condition.

Schooler and Engstler-Schooler (1990; see also Chin & Schooler, 2008) suggest that trying to put a face into words is difficult and impairs memory for that face. Using the word *squinty* to describe a robber's eyes, for example, might be a general description of what his eyes looked like but probably does not capture the subtle contours of his eyes, eyelids, eyelashes, eyebrows, and upper cheeks. When you see the photo lineup, you look for eyes that are squinty, and doing so interferes with your attention to the finer details of the faces. If you ever witness a crime, then, you should not try to put into words what the criminal looked like. And if you hear a witness say that he or she wrote down a description of the criminal and then took a while deciding whether the person was present at a lineup, you might doubt the accuracy of the witness's identification.

To sum up, several factors make eyewitness testimony inaccurate, leading to all too many false identifications. Perhaps the legal system in the United States should rely less on eyewitness testimony than it now does. In the legal systems of some countries, a suspect cannot be convicted on the basis of a sole eyewitness; at least two independent witnesses are needed. Adopting this more stringent standard in the United States might mean that some guilty people go free, but it would avoid many false convictions. To see how accurate you and your friends are at eyewitness testimony and to illustrate some of the pitfalls, do the following Try It! exercise.

试一试！目击者证词的准确性
The Accuracy of Eyewitness Testimony

Try this demonstration with a group of friends who you know will be gathered in one place, such as a dorm room or an apartment. The idea is to stage an incident in which someone comes into the room suddenly, acts in a strange manner, and then leaves. Your friends will then be asked to recall as much as they can about this person to see if they are good eyewitnesses. Here are some specific instructions about how you might do this.

1. Take one friend, whom we will call the actor, into your confidence before you do this exercise. Ideally, the actor should be a stranger to the people who will be the eyewitnesses. The actor should suddenly rush into the room where you and your other friends are gathered and act in a strange (but nonthreatening) manner. For example, the actor could hand someone a flower and say, "The flower man cometh!" Or he or she could go up to each person and say something unexpected, like "Meet me in Moscow at the mosque." Ask the actor to hold something in his or her hand during this episode, such as a pencil, shoelace, or banana.

2. *Important note*: The actor should not act in a violent or threatening way or make the eyewitnesses uncomfortable. The goal is to act in unexpected and surprising ways, not to frighten people.

3. After a few minutes, the actor should leave the room. Inform your friends that you staged this event as a demonstration of eyewitness testimony and that if they are willing, they should try to remember, in as much detail as possible, what occurred. Ask them to write down answers to these questions:

   a. What did the actor look like? Write down a detailed description.
   b. What did the actor say? Write down his or her words as best as you can remember.
   c. How much time did the actor spend in the room?
   d. Did the actor touch anyone? If yes, who?
   e. What was the actor holding in his or her hand?

4. After all participants have answered these questions, ask them to read their answers aloud. How much did they agree? How accurate were people's answers? Discuss with your friends why they were correct or incorrect in their descriptions.

Note: This demonstration will work best if you have access to a video camera and can record the actor's actions. That way, you can play the tape to assess the accuracy of the eyewitnesses' descriptions. If you cannot videotape it, keep track of how much time elapsed so that you can judge the accuracy of people's time estimates.

Judging Whether Witnesses Are Lying 判断证人是否撒谎

There is yet another reason eyewitness testimony can be inaccurate: Even if witnesses have very accurate memories for what they saw, they might deliberately lie when on the witness stand. After Randall Adams was tried and convicted, new evidence suggested that some of the eyewitnesses who testified against him had lied. One witness may have struck a deal with the police, agreeing to say what they wanted her to say in return for lenient treatment of her daughter, who had been arrested for armed robbery. If this witness was lying, why couldn't the jurors tell?

We've all had the sense that someone was lying to us; perhaps they keep averting their eyes, or something just doesn't ring true about what they were saying. Were we right? How accurate are people at detecting deception? Not very, as it turns out. In a typical study, participants watch videos or listen to audiotapes of people who are telling the truth half the time and lying half the time, and try to distinguish the lies from the truths. In a review of over 250 such studies, Bond and DePaulo (2006) found that whereas people were better than chance at telling lies from truths, their level of accuracy was not impressive: On average, people were correct only 54 percent of the time (where 50 percent would be guessing at chance levels).

> *If falsehood, like truth, had only one face, we would be in better shape. For we would take as certain the opposite of what the liar said. But the reverse of truth has a hundred thousand shapes.*
>
> —Montaigne, *Essays*, 1595

Interestingly, people with a lot of experience in dealing with liars (e.g., law enforcement agents and employees of the CIA) are no more accurate at detecting deception than college students. It is harder to detect whether someone is lying than we might think—even if we are a seasoned police officer or judge. In fact, there is surprisingly little evidence that some people are better at detecting lies than others. Some people are better at *telling* lies—but when it comes to *detecting* lies, it simply does not appear to be the case that some people have learned to detect them better than others (Bond & DePaulo, 2008).

Can Polygraph Machines Tell If People Are Lying? Because it is so difficult for humans to tell if someone is lying, researchers have developed machines to do the job. The **polygraph**, or "lie detector," is a machine that measures people's physiological responses, such as heart rate and breathing rate. The assumption is that when people lie, they become anxious, and this anxiety can be detected by increases in heart rate, breathing rate, and so on.

Although polygraphs can detect whether someone is lying at levels better than chance, they are far from infallible.

How well do these tests work? A few years ago, the U.S. Department of Energy asked a board of distinguished scientists to address this question, and after an extensive review the board published a summary of its findings (National Research Council, 2003). The polygraph, they concluded, reveals whether someone is lying or telling the truth at levels better than chance. The accuracy rate, averaging over dozens of studies, was .86—that is, people were correctly labeled as lying or telling the truth 86 percent of the time.

Although this might seem like an impressive rate of accuracy, it still allows for a substantial number of errors, including false positives, where people who are telling the truth are incorrectly labeled as liars (Ellsworth & Mauro, 1998, Iacono, 2008; National Research Council, 2003). Think of it this way: If you were wrongly accused of a serious crime, would you be willing to take a test that had a 14 percent chance of landing you in prison? Because of these high error rates, polygraph evidence is inadmissible in most court trials. The National Research Council summarized it like this: "Almost a century of research in scientific psychology and physiology provides little basis for the expectation that a polygraph test could have extremely high accuracy" (p. 212).

Researchers continue to try to develop better lie detectors, using such measures as patterns of brain waves, involuntary eye movements, and blood flow in the face using high-definition thermal imaging technology (Knight, 2004; Pavlidis, Eberhardt, & Levine, 2002). So far, however, none of these measures has proved to be any better than the polygraph (National Research Council, 2003; Sip, Roepstorff, McGregor, & Frith, 2008). A concern with all physiological measures of deception is whether guilty people can learn to beat the tests. There is some evidence that people can deliberately act in ways that reduce the validity of the results of polygraph tests, such as biting their tongue and doing mental arithmetic. The search continues, but there is still no perfect lie detection machine that can always differentiate lies from the truth.

To see how well you and your friends can tell whether someone is lying, do the following Try It! exercise. How did you do? It would be nice if there were a foolproof method of telling whether or not someone is lying. Randall Adams would never have had to endure 12 long years in prison for a crime he did not commit. Many psychologists doubt, though, that such a test will ever be developed; the nuances of human behavior are too rich and complex to allow foolproof tests of honesty.

Polygraph

A machine that measures people's physiological responses (e.g., their heart rate); polygraph operators attempt to tell if someone is lying by observing that person's physiological responses while answering questions

TRY IT! Lie Detection 试一试！测谎

The purpose of this exercise, which should be done with a group of friends, is to see how well people can tell if someone is lying. Ask for a volunteer to be the speaker and the others to be the audience. The speaker's job will be to lie about how much he or she likes five high school acquaintances and to tell the truth about how much he or she likes five other high school acquaintances. The audience's job is to try to guess when the speaker is telling the truth and when he or she is lying. Here are some specific instructions:

Instructions for the speaker: Make a list of 10 people you knew in high school, and think about how much you like each person. Randomly choose 5 people and put a T next to their names. These are the people about whom you will be truthful. Put an L next to the other names. These are the people about whom you will lie. Take a few minutes to think about what you will say. When you are ready, describe your feelings toward each person (truthfully or not) to the audience. Give a few sentences about each person.

Instructions for the audience: The speaker will be describing her or his feelings toward 10 high school acquaintances. He or she will be telling the truth about half the people and lying about the other half. Listen carefully and try to guess when the speaker is telling the truth and when he or she is lying. You may use any cues you want to make your decision. Write down the numbers 1 to 10, and put "truth" or "lie" next to the number corresponding to each person the speaker describes.

Variation: Have half the audience members sit with their backs to the speaker so that they can hear but not see him or her. The other half should face the speaker. Which group was better at detecting when the speaker was lying? Bella DePaulo, Dan Lassiter, and Julie Stone (1983) found that people who were instructed to pay special attention to a speaker's tone of voice did better at lie detection than people instructed to pay attention to how the speaker looked. When people can see a speaker, they tend to focus on facial cues that they think are good indications of lying but in fact are not. The group of people who cannot see the speaker might rely more on his or her tone of voice and thus may be more accurate.

Note: Turn to page 497 for instructions on scoring.

Can Eyewitness Testimony Be Improved?
目击者的证词能够得到改进吗？

We have seen a number of ways in which eyewitness testimony can go wrong. Given the importance of such testimony in criminal trials, are there ways to improve it? Two general approaches have been tried, but neither has proved very successful.

The first involves hypnosis. You may have seen movies in which a witness to a terrible crime has no memory of what occurred—until he or she is put under hypnosis. Then, while in a trancelike state, the person is able to describe the murderer in great detail. Unfortunately, this is one area where the movies do not reflect real life. Not only does hypnosis fail to improve memory, it can also make people more susceptible to suggestion, making them believe that they saw things that they did not. Even worse, people tend to become more confident in their memories after they have been hypnotized, even if they are no more accurate (Lynn, Lock, Loftus, Krackow, & Lilienfeld, 2003; Mazzoni & Lynn, 2007). This is dangerous because as we saw earlier, juries often use confidence as a gauge of a witness's accuracy, even though confidence is not strongly related to accuracy.

The second way people have tried to increase eyewitness accuracy is with the use of the **cognitive interview** (Geiselman & Fischer, 1989). With this technique, a trained interviewer tries to improve eyewitnesses' memories by focusing their attention on the details and context of the event. This is done chiefly by asking the person to recall the event several times from different starting points (e.g., from the beginning of the event and from the middle of the event) and by asking the person to create a mental image of the scene. The investigator also attempts to establish rapport with witnesses and urges them to give lengthy, detailed responses. Research on this technique has been mixed. Its designers claim that it improves witness's recall (Fisher & Schreiber, 2007), whereas others claim that it can increase errors and confabulations of memory, especially when used with children (Whitehouse, Orne, & Dinges, 2005). It will take further research to determine whether the cognitive interview reliably improves the accuracy of eyewitness reports.

The Recovered Memory Debate
关于恢复性记忆的争论

Another form of eyewitness memory has received a great deal of attention: the case in which a person recalls having been the victim of a crime, typically sexual abuse, after many years of being consciously unaware of that fact. Not surprisingly, the accuracy of such **recovered memories** has been hotly debated (McNally, 2003; Pezdek & Banks, 1996; Schooler & Eich, 2000).

One well-known case occurred in 1988 in Olympia, Washington, when Paul Ingram's daughters accused him of sexual abuse, satanic rituals, and murder, events they claimed to have recalled suddenly years after they occurred. The police could find no evidence for the crimes, and Ingram initially denied that they had ever occurred. Eventually, though, he became convinced that he, too, must have repressed his past behavior and that he must have committed the crimes, even though he could not remember having done so. According to experts who have studied this case, Ingram's daughters genuinely believed that the abuse and killing had occurred—but they were wrong. What they thought they remembered were actually false memories (Wright, 1994).

The question of the accuracy of recovered memories is controversial. On one side are writers such as Ellen Bass and Laura Davis (1994), who claim that it is not uncommon for women who were sexually abused to repress these traumas so that they have absolutely no memory of them. The abuse and its subsequent repression, according to this view, are responsible for many psychological problems, such as depression and eating disorders. Later in life, often with the help of a psychotherapist, these events can be "recovered" and brought back into memory. On the other side of the controversy are academic psychologists and others who argue that the accuracy of recovered memories cannot be accepted on faith (e.g., Loftus, Garry, & Hayne, 2008; McNally, Clancy, & Barrett, 2005; Ofshe & Watters, 1994; Schacter, 1996; Wegner, Quillian, & Houston, 1996). These writers acknowledge that sexual abuse and other childhood traumas are a terrible problem and are more common than we would like to think. They further agree that claims of sexual abuse should be investigated fully and that when sufficient evidence of guilt exists, the person responsible for the abuse should be prosecuted.

But here's the problem: What is "sufficient evidence"? Is it enough that someone remembers, years later, that she or he has been abused, in the absence of any other evidence of abuse? According to many researchers, the answer is no, because of a **false memory syndrome**: People can recall a past traumatic experience that is objectively false but that they believe is true (Kihlstrom, 1996). There is evidence that people can acquire vivid memories of events that never occurred, especially if another person—such as a psychotherapist—suggests that the events occurred (Johnson & Raye, 1981; Loftus, Garry, & Hayne, 2008; Schooler & Eich, 2000). In addition to numerous laboratory demonstrations of false memories, evidence from everyday life also indicates that memories of abuse can be false. Often these memories are contradicted by objective evidence (e.g., no evidence of satanic murders can be found); sometimes people who suddenly acquire such memories decide later that the events never occurred; and sometimes the memories are so bizarre (e.g., that people were abducted by aliens) as to strain credulity. Unfortunately, some psychotherapists do not sufficiently consider that by suggesting past abuse, they may be planting false memories rather than helping clients remember real events.

In Olympia, Washington, in 1988, Paul Ingram was accused by his daughters of sexual abuse, satanic rituals, and murder. His daughters claimed to have suddenly recalled these events years after they occurred. According to experts who studied the case, Ingram's daughters genuinely believed the abuse and killing occurred, but in fact they were wrong: What they thought they remembered were actually false memories. Ingram eventually became convinced that he too must have repressed his past behavior and that he must have committed the crimes. Due to his "confession," he is currently serving a prison sentence.

Recovered Memories
Recollections of a past event, such as sexual abuse, that had been forgotten or repressed

False Memory Syndrome
Remembering a past traumatic experience that is objectively false but nevertheless accepted as true

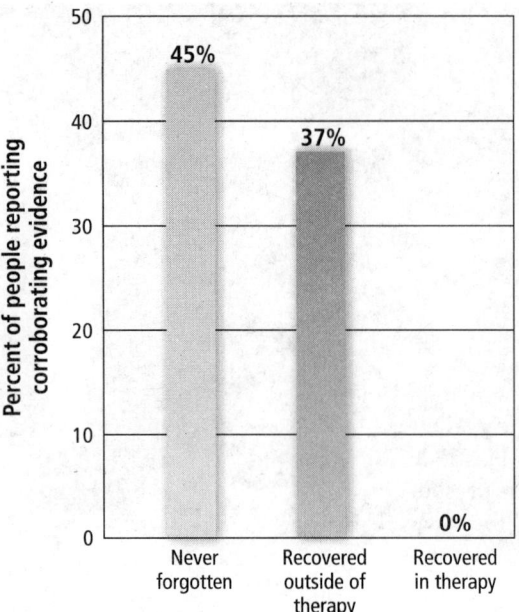

FIGURE SPA-3.3
People who said they had been victims of childhood sexual abuse: percentage reporting corroborating evidence.

People who reported that they had been sexually abused in childhood were divided into three groups: those who had never forgotten the abuse, those who had recovered a memory of the abuse outside of psychotherapy, and those who had recovered a memory of the abuse in psychotherapy. All participants reported whether there was any corroborating evidence of the abuse, such as the perpetrator confessing. As seen in the figure, people who recovered memories of abuse in psychotherapy were less likely to report corroborating evidence.

(Adapted from Geraerts et al., 2007)

'Tis with our judgments as our watches, None go just alike, yet each believes his own.

—Alexander Pope, *Essay on Criticism*, 1711

This is not to say, however, that all recovered memories are false. Although scientific evidence for repression and recovery—the idea that something can be forgotten for years and then recalled with great accuracy—is sparse, there may be instances in which people do suddenly remember traumatic events that really did occur (Schooler, 1999). Thus any claim of abuse should be taken with the utmost seriousness. That said, we might want to be especially wary of memories of sexual abuse that are elicited by a psychotherapist. To examine the basis of these memories, Elke Geraerts and her colleagues (2007) placed advertisements in the newspaper to recruit people who had memories of childhood sexual abuse. The researchers divided the sample into two groups: those who had continuous memories (that is, they had never forgotten their abuse) and those who had recovered a memory of abuse (that is, who said there was a time when they believed they had not been a victim of abuse, but then recalled that they had been abused). The latter group was further divided into those who recovered their memory of abuse outside of psychotherapy and those who recovered their memory of abuse in psychotherapy. All participants were asked to report any knowledge they had of corroborating evidence for the abuse, such as whether other individuals had reported being abused by the same perpetrator or the perpetrator confessed to the abuse. Although not perfect, the reported existence of corroborating information gives some indication of whether the memories were accurate.

As seen in Figure SPA-3.3, people whose memories of sexual abuse had been recovered in therapy were *least* likely to be able to provide corroborating evidence of the abuse; in fact, no one in this group did so. Does this prove that everyone who recovered a memory of abuse with the help of a psychotherapist was incorrect and that no such abuse occurred? Certainly not; we can't be sure how accurate people's memories were. The results suggest, however, that it can be dangerous for therapists to encourage their clients to recall memories of abuse. They may be implanting false memories in some cases, rather than eliciting memories of actual abuse. Claims of abuse cannot be taken on faith, especially if they are the result of suggestions from other people.

Juries: Group Processes in Action
陪审团：团体判决过程

Ultimately, it is not a polygraph that decides whether witnesses are telling the truth, but a judge or jury. Juries are of particular interest to social psychologists because the way they reach verdicts is directly relevant to social psychological research on group processes and social interaction. The right to be tried by a jury of one's peers has a long tradition in English and American law. Trial by jury was an established institution in England at the beginning of the seventeenth century, and the people who founded the first permanent English settlement in North America, at Jamestown, Virginia, carried this tradition with them (though this right was not granted to Native Americans or other nonwhites or to a few rebellious English settlers who were summarily hanged). In the United States today, everyone has the right, under most circumstances, to be tried by a jury.

Despite this tradition, the jury system has often come under attack. In the Randall Adams trial, it is now clear that the jury reached the wrong decision. One study found that judges who presided over criminal jury trials disagreed with the verdict rendered by the jury a full 25 percent of the time (Kalven & Zeisel, 1966). More recent observers have also criticized the jury system, questioning the ability of jurors to understand complex evidence and reach a dispassionate verdict (Arkes & Mellers, 2002; Devine, Clayton, Dunford, Seying, & Pryce, 2001). As noted by a former dean of the Harvard Law School, "Why should anyone think that 12 persons brought in from the street, selected in various ways for their lack of general ability, should have any special capacity for deciding controversies between persons?" (Kalven & Zeisel, 1966, p. 5).

The jury system has its staunch supporters, of course, and few people argue that it should be abolished. The point is that it is not a perfect system and that based on research in social psychology, there are ways we might expect it to go wrong (Levett, Danielsen, Kovera, & Cutler, 2005; Winter & Greene, 2007).

How Jurors Process Information During the Trial
审判过程中陪审员对信息的处理

How do individual jurors think about the evidence they hear during a trial? As we saw in Chapter 3, people often construct theories and schemas to interpret the world around them, and the same is true of jurors (Hart, 1995; Kuhn, Weinstock, & Flaton, 1994; Smith, 1991). Some psychologists suggest that jurors decide on one story that best explains all the evidence; they then try to fit this story to the possible verdicts they are allowed to render, and if one of those verdicts fits well with their preferred story, they are likely to vote to convict on that charge (Hastie, 2008; Hastie & Pennington, 2000). This possibility has important implications for how lawyers present their cases. Lawyers typically present the evidence in one of two ways. In the first, called *story order*, they present the evidence in the sequence in which the events occurred, corresponding as closely as possible to the story they want the jurors to believe. In the second, called *witness order*, they present witnesses in the sequence they think will have the greatest impact, even if this means that events are described out of order. For example, a lawyer might save his or her best witness for last so that the trial ends on a dramatic, memorable note, even if this witness describes events that occurred early in the alleged crime.

If you were a lawyer, in which order would you present the evidence? You can probably guess which order researchers in this area hypothesized would be the most successful. If jurors are ultimately swayed by the story or schema they think best explains the sequence of events, the best strategy should be to present the evidence in story order and not witness order. To test their hypothesis, researchers asked mock jurors to listen to a simulated murder trial and varied the order in which the defense attorney and the prosecuting attorney presented their cases (Pennington & Hastie, 1988). In one condition, both used story order whereas in another condition, both used witness order. In other conditions, one attorney used story order and the other used witness order.

The results provided clear and dramatic support for the story order strategy. As seen in Table SPA-3.1, when the prosecutor used story order and the defense used witness order, the jurors were most likely to believe the prosecutor—78 percent voted to convict the defendant. When the prosecutor used witness order and the defense used story order, the tables were turned—only 31 percent voted to convict. One reason the conviction rate in felony trials in America is so high—approximately 80 percent—may be that in real trials, prosecutors usually present evidence in story order, whereas defense attorneys usually use witness order. If you are a budding lawyer, remember this when you are preparing for your first trial!

Confessions: Are They Always What They Seem? 认罪：它们总是像看起来那样吗？

Imagine that you are a member of a jury at a murder trial. The prosecution presents what seems to be some pretty damning evidence, namely a videotape of the defendant confessing to the crime. "OK, I admit it," you hear the defendant say, "I was the one who pulled the trigger." More than likely you would vote to convict. Why would the defendant admit to the crime if he was innocent? Many cases never even go to trial, because the defendant pleads guilty after confessing to the crime.

> A court is no better than each... of you sitting before me on this jury. A court is only as sound as its jury, and a jury is only as sound as the [people] who make it up.
>
> —Harper Lee, *To Kill a Mockingbird*, 1960

"Your Honor, we're going to go with the prosecution's spin."

Copyright © The New Yorker Collection 1997 Mike Twohy from cartoonbank.com. All Rights Reserved..

TABLE SPA-3.1 How Should Lawyers Present Their Cases?

Lawyers can present their cases in a variety of ways. This study found that story order, in which lawyers present the evidence in the order that corresponds most closely to the story they want the jurors to believe, works best.

Percentage of People Voting to Convict the Defendant

Prosecution Evidence	Defense Evidence	
	Story Order (%)	Witness Order (%)
Story order	59	78
Witness order	31	63

(Adapted from Pennington & Hastie, 1988)

Confessions, however, are not always what they seem. Consider the case of a woman who was raped and brutally beaten while jogging in New York City's Central Park in 1989. The woman was in a coma for several days and when she awoke she had no memory of the attack. Soon, however, the police arrested five African American and Hispanic teenagers who had been in the park that night. The boys confessed to the crime and provided lurid details of what happened. Four of the confessions were videotaped and played at the trial, and largely on this basis all of the teenagers were convicted and given long prison sentences.

The only problem is that it is now clear that the boys were innocent. Thirteen years later Matias Reyes, in prison for three rapes and a murder, confessed to the crime, claiming he had acted alone. His DNA matched semen recovered from the victim (none of the teenagers' DNA matched), and he gave details of the crime scene that were known only to the police. In 2002 a judge vacated the convictions of all five boys.

If the boys were innocent, then why did they confess to the crime? Research by Saul Kassin (2007, 2008) and others has shown that the interrogation process can go wrong in ways that elicit false confessions, even to the point where innocent suspects come to believe that they actually did commit the crime. One problem is that police investigators are often convinced that the suspect is guilty, and this belief biases how they conduct the interrogation. They ask leading questions, isolate suspects and put them under considerable stress, claim that an eyewitness has identified the suspect, and sometimes make false promises. The suspects in the Central Park jogger case, for example, were questioned for up to 30 hours, and the police detectives implied that they could go home if they would sign a confession (Kassin, 2007, 2008). After many hours of prolonged interrogation, innocent people can become so psychologically fatigued that they don't know what to think and may even come to believe that they are guilty. This is all well and good if the suspect really is guilty, and if the techniques succeed in making him confess. As we saw earlier, however, people—even trained investigators—are not very good at telling whether someone is lying, which means that innocent people are sometimes subjected to these techniques. In fact, in a large number of cases in which DNA evidence exonerated defendants who had been falsely convicted of a crime, the defendant had confessed ("False confessions," 2006).

One solution to coerced confessions is requiring that interrogations be videotaped, so a jury can view the recording and judge for themselves whether the defendant was coerced into admitting things he or she didn't do. In 2003, the state of Illinois passed a law requiring that all police interrogations of suspects

"For me, a confession is much too autobiographical."

The problem with some confessions is that they are NOT autobiographical at all, but false.

© The New Yorker Collection. 2002 Frank Cotham from cartoonbank.com. All Rights Reserved.

in homicide cases be electronically recorded. Although this is a step forward, it raises another potential problem. Almost all videos of interrogations focus on the suspect, rather than on the interrogator asking the questions. Well, of course they do, you might think; the whole point is to judge how the suspect is responding to the questioning, so it is no surprise that the camera focuses on him or her. The dedicated student of social psychology, however, will recognize this as a problem. As we discussed in Chapter 4, people's judgments about the causes of another person's behavior are influenced by what is visually salient to them. When we focus our attention on one person in a group, we tend to think that that person is having a disproportionately large influence on the conversation.

Research by Dan Lassiter (2004; Ware, Lassiter, Patterson, & Ransom, 2008) has shown that the same thing is true when people watch video recordings of confessions. He showed people a video of the same confession from different camera angles, and asked them to judge how voluntary or coerced the confession was. People thought that the confession was most voluntary (i.e., the least coerced) when the camera focused on the suspect; here people had the sense that the suspect was in charge of what was happening. When the camera showed both the suspect and the interrogator, people thought the confession was less voluntary. And, when the camera focused only on the interrogator, people thought the confession was the least voluntary (the most coerced). Remember, everyone heard the same confession; all that differed was their visual perspective. In part because of this research, at least one state (Wisconsin) now requires that both the suspect and the questioner be shown in videotaped interviews.

People sometimes confess to crimes they did not commit when they are subjected to long, stressful interrogations.

Deliberations in the Jury Room 陪审室内的商议

As any lawyer can tell you, a crucial part of the jury process occurs out of sight, when jurors deliberate before deciding on the verdict. Even if most jurors are inclined to vote to convict, there might be a persuasive minority who change their fellow jurors' minds. Sometimes this can be a minority of one, as in the classic movie *Twelve Angry Men*. When the film begins, a jury has just finished listening to the evidence in a murder case, and all the jurors except one vote to convict the defendant. But over the course of the next 90 minutes, the lone holdout, played by Henry Fonda, persuades his peers that there is reason to doubt that the young Hispanic defendant is guilty. At first, the other jurors pressure Fonda to change his mind (using techniques of normative and informational conformity, as discussed in Chapter 8), but in the end, reason triumphs, and the other jurors come to see that Fonda is right.

As entertaining as this movie is, research indicates that it does not reflect the reality of most jury deliberations (Devine et al., 2001; Ellsworth & Mauro, 1998; Kalven & Zeisel, 1966; MacCoun, 1989). In the Randall Adams trial, for example, a majority of the 12-person jury (7 men and 5 women) initially voted to convict Adams. After 8 hours of deliberations, the majority prevailed: The holdouts changed their minds, and the jury voted unanimously to convict. In a study of more than two hundred juries in actual criminal trials, researchers found that in 97 percent of the cases, the jury's final decision was the same as the one favored by a majority of the jurors on the initial vote (Kalven & Zeisel, 1966). Thus just as we saw in Chapter 8 on conformity, majority opinion usually carries the day, bringing dissenting jurors into line. If jury deliberation is stacked toward the initial majority opinion, why not just abandon the deliberation process, letting the jury's initial vote determine a defendant's guilt or innocence? For two reasons, this would not be a good idea. First, forcing juries to reach a unanimous verdict makes them consider the evidence more carefully, rather than simply assuming that their initial impressions of the case were correct (Hastie, Penrod, &

In the classic movie *Twelve Angry Men*, Henry Fonda convinces all of his fellow jurors to change their minds about a defendant's guilt. In real life, however, such cases of a minority in a jury convincing the majority to change its mind are rare.

Pennington, 1983). Second, even if minorities seldom succeed in persuading the majority to change their minds about guilt or innocence, minorities often do change people's minds about how guilty a person is. In criminal trials, juries usually have some discretion about the type of guilty verdict they can reach. In a murder trial, for example, they can often decide whether to convict the defendant of first-degree murder, second-degree murder, or manslaughter. One study found that people on a jury who have a minority point of view often convince the majority to change their minds about the specific verdict to render (Pennington & Hastie, 1990). Thus while a minority of jurors are unlikely to convince a majority of jurors to change their verdict from first-degree murder to not guilty, they might well convince the majority to change the verdict to second-degree murder.

Why Do People Obey the Law? 公民为何守法？

Ultimately, the success of the legal system depends on keeping people out of it. We should, of course, find ways to improve the accuracy of eyewitness testimony and help juries make better decisions. Even more important, though, is finding ways of preventing people from committing crimes in the first place. How might we get people to obey the law?

Do Severe Penalties Deter Crime? 严惩能够阻止犯罪吗？

The crime rate has been decreasing in the United States. Since 1991, for example, the per capita rate of violent crime has decreased every year but two, and the per capita rate of property crimes has decreased every year but one (Federal Bureau of Investigation, 2009). A striking illustration of this trend was seen in a power blackout in the northeastern United States and Canada in August 2003. During previous blackouts, such as the one in New York City in 1977, crime rates skyrocketed when people broke into and looted many businesses. In the blackout of 2003, the crime rate was actually lower in New York, Detroit, and Cleveland than on typical summer days ("During blackout, fewer crimes," 2003).

Why has the crime rate gone down? Some experts have attributed these promising trends to, among other things, stiffer penalties for crimes. It makes perfect sense that the harsher the penalty for a crime, the less likely people are to commit it. As we have seen many times in this book, however, common sense is not always correct, and in the case of crime and prison sentences, the story is not as straightforward as it might seem. Some analysts have suggested that the drop in violent crime is due not to stiffer penalties, but to the fact that the population of adolescents and young adults, who are most responsible for violent crimes, has been declining in recent years.

How can we tell which of these interpretations is correct? Unfortunately, it is not easy. Unlike many of the other questions we have posed in this book, this one cannot be answered by randomly assigning people to different experimental conditions. It would be not be feasible, for example, to take a group of people convicted of drunk driving and randomly assign half of them to get 10-year prison sentences and the other half to get 1-year sentences. The next best thing to an experiment, though, is to compare groups of people who have been naturally assigned to one "condition" or the other, such as residents of a state that has a severe penalty for drunk driving and residents of a state that has a milder penalty for drunk driving. Such data are imperfect, of course, because the residents of the two states might differ in other important ways. Nonetheless, these studies can be informative about the relationship between the severity of penalties and crime rates.

Let's begin with a theory that argues that stiff penalties do prevent crimes. **Deterrence theory** argues that people refrain from criminal activity because of the threat of legal punishment, as long as the punishment is perceived as severe, certain, and

The rates of many kinds of crime have been dropping in the United States. For example, during the blackout in New York City in 1977, many people broke into and looted businesses. During the blackout in the United States and Canada in August 2003, however, shown here, few crimes were committed; in fact, the crime rate was lower than on a typical summer day.

swift (Carlsmith, Darley, & Robinson, 2002; Pratt, Cullen, Blevins, Daigle, & Madensen, 2006; Williams & Hawkins, 1986). Undoubtedly, this theory is correct under some circumstances. Imagine, for example, that you are driving to an important appointment one day and get snarled in a traffic jam on the interstate. At last the traffic clears, but unless you hurry, you will be late. "Maybe I'll speed up just a little," you think, as the speedometer creeps up to 75. Your decision to exceed the speed limit was probably based on a consideration of the facts that (1) you are unlikely to get caught and that (2) if you do, the penalty won't be all that severe. But suppose you knew that the interstate is always patrolled by the state police, and that the penalty for speeding is a 5-year prison sentence. Chances are you would not dare to let your foot press too hard on the accelerator.

In this example, we have made a couple of important assumptions. First, we assumed that you know what the penalties for speeding are. Second, we assumed that you have good control over your behavior and that whether you speed is a rational decision that you make after reflecting about the consequences. For many crimes, these assumptions do not hold. Surveys have found that many people are ignorant of the penalties for different crimes; if they do not know what they are, obviously, the penalties cannot act as a deterrent. (To see how well you know the penalties for various federal crimes, complete the Try It! exercise on page 494.) Further, other types of crimes are not based on a rational decision process. Many murders, for example, are impulsive crimes of passion committed by people in highly emotional states, not by people who carefully weigh the pros and cons. In general, severe penalties will work only when people know what they are, believe they are relatively certain to be caught, and are able to weigh the consequences dispassionately before deciding whether to commit a crime (Freeman & Watson, 2006; Williams, 2005).

Increasing the certainty of being caught for drunk driving, by checking the blood alcohol level of all motorists stopped at sobriety checkpoints, is associated with fewer alcohol-related accidents.

To illustrate these points, let's consider two very different kinds of crimes: drunk driving and murder. The decision about whether to drink and drive is one that most of us can control; when we go to a party or a bar and know that we will be driving home afterward, we can decide how much we will drink. Given that this decision is a fairly rational one under most circumstances, we would expect that severe and certain penalties would act as a deterrent. To test this hypothesis, investigators have compared the number of alcohol-related motor vehicle accidents in states with severe versus mild drunk-driving laws or in communities that have instituted tough drunk-driving policies with communities in the same state that have not. These studies find that increasing the severity of penalties for drunk driving is not related, by itself, to fewer alcohol-related accidents. Consistent with deterrence theory, however, increasing the certainty of being caught for drunk driving (e.g., by checking the blood alcohol level of all motorists stopped at sobriety checkpoints) and the speed with which punishment is administered (e.g., by suspending people's driver's licenses when they are arrested for driving under the influence) are associated with fewer alcohol-related accidents (Tippetts, Voas, & Fell, 2005; Voas, Holder, & Gruenewald, 1999 Wagenaar & Maldonado-Molina, 2007; Wagenaar et al., 2007).

Now consider a very different crime and a very different penalty—murder and capital punishment. A majority of Americans support the death penalty for murder, in part because they believe that it acts as a deterrent. There is no more severe penalty than death, of course, and if the death penalty prevents even a few murders, it might be worthwhile—or so the argument goes. To see if this argument is correct, a number of studies have compared the murder rates in American states that have the death penalty with those that do not, compared the murder rates in American states before and after they adopted the death penalty, and compared the murder rates in other countries before and after they adopted the death penalty. The results are unambiguous: There is no evidence that the death penalty prevents murders (Archer & Gartner, 1984; Bedau, 1997; Donohue & Wolfers, 2006; Ellsworth & Mauro, 1998).

Deterrence Theory
The hypothesis that the threat of legal punishment causes people to refrain from criminal activity as long as the punishment is perceived as relatively severe, certain, and swift

试一试！你了解各种联邦罪名的量刑吗？
Are You Aware of the Penalties for Federal Crimes?

Deterrence theory holds that legal penalties will prevent crimes if people perceive them to be severe, certain, and swift. If people are unaware that a crime has a severe penalty, those penalties cannot act as a deterrent. Are you aware, for example, of which federal crimes are punishable by death? Take the following quiz to find out.

Which of the Following Federal Crimes Are Punishable by Death?

Crime	Punishable by Death?	
1. Drug trafficking in large quantities where no death results	No	Yes
2. Attempted killing of a public officer by a drug kingpin	No	Yes
3. Attempting to kill a juror or witness in a case involving a continuing criminal enterprise	No	Yes
4. Carjacking that results in death	No	Yes
5. Kidnapping that results in death	No	Yes
6. Train sabotage that results in death	No	Yes
7. Smuggling aliens where death results	No	Yes
8. Aircraft hijacking that results in death	No	Yes
9. Assassination of a member of Congress	No	Yes
10. Assassination of a major-party vice-presidential candidate	No	Yes
11. Assassination of a cabinet officer	No	Yes
12. Assassination of a Supreme Court justice	No	Yes
13. Assassination of the president	No	Yes
14. Espionage	No	Yes
15. Treason	No	Yes

For the answers, turn to page 497.

Opponents of the death penalty point out that, as we mentioned, most murders are crimes of passion that are not preceded by a rational consideration of the consequences. Because people are not considering the consequences of their actions, the death penalty does not act as a deterrent. Further, an astonishing number of mistakes have been made whereby innocent people have been sentenced to death. Since the death penalty was reinstated in the United States in 1976, one person has been freed from death row (often due to DNA evidence that was unavailable at the trial) for every seven people who have been executed. In January 2003, Illinois Governor George Ryan, an advocate of capital punishment, commuted the sentences of all death row prisoners in Illinois to life in prison because he was so concerned about the fairness of the process and the possibility that innocent people had been sentenced to death. No one knows how many innocent people have been executed in the United States. Given our earlier discussion of eyewitness testimony, however, it is sobering to realize that some defendants have been convicted and executed on the basis of the testimony of one eyewitness. For example, Gary Graham was put to death in Texas due largely to the testimony of a single witness who got only a brief look at him from her car more than 30 feet away. Two other witnesses who got a much better look claimed that Graham was not the killer, but they were not interviewed by Graham's court-appointed attorney. And as we saw at the beginning of this chapter, Randall Adams was almost executed for a crime he didn't commit, based on the faulty reports of eyewitnesses.

Proponents of the death penalty argue that these flaws in the system can be corrected now that tests of DNA evidence are more widely available. Further, as argued by deterrence theory, severe penalties must be applied with certainty and speed. The last of these conditions is almost never met in the case of capital punishment.

The time between a conviction for murder and the execution of the murderer is often many years because of the slowness of the judicial system and the many avenues of appeal open to prisoners on death row. Were the process speeded up, this argument goes, the death penalty would act as a deterrent.

Although this is an empirical question, there is reason to doubt that the death penalty would act as a deterrent, even if it were applied swiftly. We refer to a few studies that have found that executions are followed not by a decrease but an increase in murders (Archer & Gartner, 1984; Bailey & Peterson, 1997; Sakamoto, Sekiguchi, & Shinkyu, 2003). This might seem like a bizarre finding; why would the execution of a convicted murderer increase the likelihood that someone else would commit murder? If you recall our discussion in Chapter 12, though, on aggression, the finding makes sense. As we saw, observing someone else commit a violent act weakens people's inhibitions against aggression, leads to imitation of aggression, and numbs their sense of horror over violence. Could it be that observing the government put someone to death lowers other people's inhibitions, making them more likely to commit murders? Though the data are not conclusive, this argument makes social psychological sense—and there is some evidence to support it (Bailey & Peterson, 1997).

Procedural Justice: People's Sense of Fairness
程序公平：人们对公平的理解

We have just seen that one reason people obey the law is that they fear being caught and punished. An even more important reason, however, is because of their moral values about what constitutes good behavior. People will obey a law if they think it is just, even if it is unlikely that they will be caught for breaking it. For example, many people are honest on their tax returns because they think cheating is wrong, not because they fear being caught for cheating.

If you were a lawmaker, you could therefore try to prevent crime in two ways. You could increase the penalties for breaking the law and the probability that people will be caught, or you could try to convince people that the law is just and fair. As we have seen, the former approach is difficult and sometimes ineffective. If we wanted to prevent people from driving through red lights, we could increase the penalties for doing so and make sure that we stationed a police officer at every intersection. But it would be far simpler to convince people that it is wrong to run red lights so that they comply with the law even when no police officers are around.

American legislators suffer from a monumental illusion in their belief that long prison sentences will reduce the crime rate.

—Jack Gibbs, 1985

What determines whether people think a law is just? One important factor is their perception of the fairness of legal proceedings. **Procedural justice** refers to people's judgments about the fairness of the procedures used to determine outcomes, such as whether they are innocent or guilty of a crime (Clayton & Opotow, 2003; Kelley & Thibaut, 1978; Napier & Tyler, 2008; Skitka, 2002). People who feel that they have been treated fairly are more likely to comply with the law than people who feel that they have been treated unfairly (Tyler, 1990). Consider, for example, what happens when the police are called because of a domestic assault. What determines whether the person accused of assault will repeat this crime in the future? Surprisingly, it is not whether suspects are arrested or threatened with punishment; it is whether they feel that they were treated fairly by the police ("Misconceptions," 1997).

In sum, social psychological research indicates that the American legal system can go wrong in a number of ways: Juries rely heavily on eyewitness testimony when in fact such testimony is often in error; determining when witnesses are telling the truth is difficult, even with the use of polygraphs; and because juries are groups of people who try to reach consensus by discussing, arguing, and bargaining, the kinds of conformity pressures and group processes we discussed in Chapters 8 and 9 can lead to faulty decisions. By illuminating these problems in their research, however, social psychologists can help initiate change in the legal system—change that will lead to greater fairness and equity and to a greater sense of procedural justice. Most important of all, heeding psychological research on these questions might reduce the number of cases in which people like Randall Adams and Ronald Cotton languish in prison for crimes they did not commit.

Procedural Justice
People's judgments about the fairness of the procedures used to determine outcomes, such as whether they are innocent or guilty of a crime

Summary 总 结

- **Eyewitness Testimony** Eyewitness testimony is often of questionable accuracy, because of the way people naturally observe and remember unexpected events.
  - **Why Are Eyewitnesses Often Wrong?** A number of factors bias the acquisition, storage, and retrieval of what people observe, sometimes leading to the false identification of criminals. For example, research on own-race bias shows that people find it more difficult to recognize members of other races than members of their own race. Research on reconstructive memory indicates that errors in source monitoring can occur when people become confused about where they saw or heard something. Recognizing the problems people have retrieving information from memory, social psychologists have issued guidelines for how police lineups should be conducted.
  - **Judging Whether Eyewitnesses Are Mistaken** There is no sure fire way of telling whether a witness is making an accurate or inaccurate identification, although there is some evidence that people who identify a suspect from an array of pictures within 10 seconds *and* express very high confidence in their choice are especially likely to be correct.
  - **Judging Whether Witnesses Are Lying** Humans are not very good at telling whether another person is lying. The polygraph can detect lying at above-chance levels, but is not perfect and often yields inaccurate results.
  - **Can Eyewitness Testimony Be Improved?** Not only does hypnosis fail to improve people's memory, it also makes them more susceptible to suggestion and increases their confidence in their memories. A new interview technique called the cognitive interview offers some promise in improving accuracy, but more research is needed to test its effectiveness.
  - **The Recovered Memory Debate** How valid are recovered memories, the sudden recollection of events, such as sexual abuse, that had been forgotten or repressed? Although recovered memories may be true in some instances, they can also be the result of false memory syndrome, whereby people come to believe the memory is true when it actually is not. False memories are especially likely to occur when another person, such as a psychotherapist, suggests to us that an event really occurred.

- **Juries: Group Processes in Action** Juries are of particular interest to social psychologists because the way they reach verdicts is directly relevant to social psychological research on group processes and social interaction. Jurors are susceptible to the same kinds of biases and social pressures we documented in earlier chapters.
  - **How Jurors Process Information During the Trial** During a trial, jurors attempt to make sense out of the testimony and often decide on one story that explains all of the evidence. Juries are thus most swayed by lawyers who present the evidence in a way that tells a consistent story.
  - **Confessions: Are They Always What They Seem?** The interrogation techniques used by the police can sometimes produce false confessions. The video recording of interrogations is a safeguard against this, although focusing the camera solely on the suspect increases the likelihood that viewers will think he or she voluntarily confessed.
  - **Deliberations in the Jury Room** During deliberations, jurors with minority views are often pressured into conforming to the view of the majority; thus verdicts usually correspond to the initial feelings of the majority of jurors.
  - **Why Do People Obey the Law?** It is important to examine people's perception of the legal system, because these perceptions have a lot to do with how likely people are to obey the law.
  - **Do Severe Penalties Deter Crime?** Deterrence theory holds that people refrain from criminal activity if they view penalties as severe, certain, and swift. Deterrence theory may be correct about crimes that are the result of rational thought but is unlikely to apply to crimes of passion that are not rational, such as many murders. There is no evidence, for example, that the death penalty deters murders, and there is even some evidence that it increases the murder rate.
  - **Procedural Justice: People's Sense of Fairness** People are more likely to obey the law if their sense of procedural justice is high; that is, if they believe that the procedures used to determine their guilt or innocence are fair.

CHAPTER SPA-3 TEST 第16章习题

1. Which of the following is *least* true about eyewitness testimony?
   a. Jurors and law enforcement professionals rely heavily on eyewitness testimony when they are deciding whether someone is guilty.
   b. Jurors tend to overestimate the accuracy of eyewitnesses.
   c. People are better at recognizing faces of people of their own race than faces of people of different races.
   d. Writing down a description of someone you saw will make it easier for you to recognize that person later.

2. Alicia was working the night shift at a convenience store. A man came in, pulled out a gun, and demanded that Alicia give him all the money in the cash register. When the police interview Alicia about the crime, what would she most likely be able to tell them?
   a. The kind of gun the man had
   b. The type of clothes the man wore
   c. The height of the man
   d. The color of the man's eyes

3. You are an assistant district attorney trying to decide which suspect to try for a burglary case. Each of five eyewitnesses picked a different suspect from a photo lineup. Based on social psychological research, which eyewitness would you find most credible?
   a. Beth, who carefully compared each of the faces against the others
   b. Edward, who wrote down a description of the suspect right after the robbery
   c. Larry, who took longer than the other witnesses to pick his suspect
   d. Diana, who reported that the suspect's face just "popped out" at her
   e. Fran, who said that she was "extremely confident" that she was correct

4. Which of the following is *not* a recommendation social psychologists have made about how the police should conduct lineups?
   a. Make sure everyone in the lineup resembles the witness's description of the suspect.
   b. Tell the witness that the person suspected of the crime may or may not be in the lineup.
   c. Before seeing the lineup, have the witness reconstruct the face of the suspect, using face composite computer programs.
   d. Do not always include the suspect in an initial lineup.
   e. Don't count on witnesses knowing whether their selections were biased.

5. Research has supported each of the following statements about recovered memories except one. Which one?
   a. People can recall a past traumatic experience that is objectively false but that they believe is true.
   b. People who recover memories of sexual abuse in psychotherapy are almost always correct that the abuse really occurred.
   c. There may be instances in which people do suddenly remember traumatic events that really did occur.
   d. People who recovered memories of sexual abuse, while in psychotherapy, were less likely to report corroborating evidence for the abuse than were people who recovered memories of sexual abuse outside of psychotherapy.

6. Which of the following recommendations have social psychologists made to the legal profession?
   a. The police should try as hard as they can to get suspects to confess to a crime, because if the suspects confess they are surely guilty.
   b. Lawyers should present witnesses in the sequence they think will have the greatest impact, even if this means that events of the case are described out of order.
   c. The police should videotape all interrogations and make sure that the camera angle shows both the interrogator and the suspect.
   d. The results of polygraph (lie detector) tests should be allowed in trials because these tests are extremely accurate.

7. Which of the following statements about getting people to obey the law is *false*?
   a. People don't know what the penalties are for many crimes.
   b. Some crimes are impulsive crimes of passion and not the result of rational decisions.
   c. There is good evidence that the death penalty decreases the likelihood that other people will commit murders.
   d. People will obey a law if they think it is just, even if it is unlikely that they will be caught for breaking it.

8. Erin gets a ticket for failing to come to a complete stop at a stop sign. She believes she did stop and decides to go to court to contest the charge. According to research on procedural justice, under which of the following conditions will Erin be most satisfied with her experience at court?
   a. After listening carefully to Erin's testimony, the judge upholds the ticket and rules against Erin. Erin feels, though, that the judge treated her fairly.
   b. The judge dismisses the ticket because the police officer who gave Erin the ticket failed to appear to testify.
   c. The judge refuses to listen to Erin's testimony but dismisses the ticket because other cases are running over and taking up too much time.
   d. The judge refuses to listen to Erin's testimony and upholds the ticket, telling Erin that she should be more careful next time. He does, however, compliment her on her appearance.

Answer Key: 1-d, 2-a, 3-d, 4-c, 5-b, 6-c, 7-c, 8-a

For more review plus practice tests, videos, flashcards, writing help and more, log on to MyPsychLab.

TRY IT! "试一试！"答案

● **Page 486**
When the speaker is done, he or she should reveal when he or she was telling the truth versus lying. The audience members should tally how often they were right. People would be correct half the time just by guessing; scores that are substantially above 50 percent may indicate that you are good at detecting deception. Compare notes about what kinds of cues you paid attention to in the speaker. What did the person do that made you think he or she was telling a lie?

● **Page 494**
All the crimes listed are punishable by death (Bedau, 1997).

Glossary 重要词汇

Accessibility The extent to which schemas and concepts are at the forefront of people's minds and are therefore likely to be used when we are making judgments about the social world

Acquisition The process by which people notice and pay attention to information in the environment; because people cannot perceive everything that is happening around them, they acquire only a subset of the information available in the environment

Actor/Observer Difference The tendency to see other people's behavior as dispositionally caused but focusing more on the role of situational factors when explaining one's own behavior

Affect Blend A facial expression in which one part of the face registers one emotion while another part of the face registers a different emotion

Affectively Based Attitude An attitude based more on people's feelings and values than on their beliefs about the nature of an attitude object

Aggression Intentional behavior aimed at doing harm or causing pain to another person

Aggressive Stimulus An object that is associated with aggressive responses (e.g., a gun) and whose mere presence can increase the probability of aggression

Altruism The desire to help another person even if it involves a cost to the helper

Altruistic Personality The qualities that cause an individual to help others in a wide variety of situations

Amygdala An area in the core of the brain that is associated with aggressive behaviors

Analytic Thinking Style A type of thinking in which people focus on the properties of objects without considering their surrounding context; this type of thinking is common in Western cultures

Anxious/Ambivalent Attachment Style An attachment style characterized by a concern that others will not reciprocate one's desire for intimacy, resulting in higher-than-average levels of anxiety

Applied Research Studies designed to solve a particular social problem

Appraisal Theories of Emotion Theories holding that emotions result from people's interpretations and explanations of events, even in the absence of physiological arousal

Archival Analysis A form of the observational method in which the researcher examines the accumulated documents, or archives, of a culture (e.g., diaries, novels, magazines, and newspapers)

Attachment Styles The expectations people develop about relationships with others, based on the relationship they had with their primary caregiver when they were infants

Attitude Accessibility The strength of the association between an attitude object and a person's evaluation of that object, measured by the speed with which people can report how they feel about the object

Attitude Inoculation Making people immune to attempts to change their attitudes by initially exposing them to small doses of the arguments against their position

Attitudes Evaluations of people, objects, and ideas

Attribution Theory A description of the way in which people explain the causes of their own and other people's behavior

Automatic Thinking Thinking that is nonconscious, unintentional, involuntary, and effortless

Availability Heuristic A mental rule of thumb whereby people base a judgment on the ease with which they can bring something to mind

Avoidant Attachment Style An attachment style characterized by a suppression of attachment needs, because attempts to be intimate have been rebuffed; people with this style find it difficult to develop intimate relationships

Base Rate Information Information about the frequency of members of different categories in the population

Basic Research Studies that are designed to find the best answer to the question of why people behave as they do and that are conducted purely for reasons of intellectual curiosity

Behaviorally Based Attitude An attitude based on observations of how one behaves toward an attitude object

Behaviorism A school of psychology maintaining that to understand human behavior, one need only consider the reinforcing properties of the environment—that is, how positive and negative events in the environment are associated with specific behaviors

Belief in a Just World A form of defensive attribution wherein people assume that bad things happen to bad people and that good things happen to good people

Blaming the Victim The tendency to blame individuals (make dispositional attributions) for their victimization, typically motivated by a desire to see the world as a fair place

Bystander Effect The finding that the greater the number of bystanders who witness an emergency, the less likely any one of them is to help

Catharsis The notion that "blowing off steam"—by performing an aggressive act, watching others engage in aggressive behaviors, or engaging in a fantasy of aggression—relieves built-up aggressive energies and hence reduces the likelihood of further aggressive behavior

Causal Theories Theories about the causes of one's own feelings and behaviors; often we learn such theories from our culture (e.g., "absence makes the heart grow fonder")

Central Route to Persuasion The case whereby people elaborate on a persuasive communication, listening carefully to and thinking about the arguments, as occurs when people have both the ability and the motivation to listen carefully to a communication

Classical Conditioning The phenomenon whereby a stimulus that elicits an emotional response (e.g., your grandmother) is repeatedly paired with a neutral stimulus that does not (e.g., the smell of mothballs) until the neutral stimulus takes on the emotional properties of the first stimulus

Cognitive Dissonance A drive or feeling of discomfort, originally defined as being caused by holding two or more inconsistent cognitions and subsequently defined as being caused by performing an action that is discrepant from one's customary, typically positive self-conception

Cognitive Interview A technique whereby a trained interviewer tries to improve eyewitnesses' memories by focusing their attention on the details and context of the event

Cognitively Based Attitude An attitude based primarily on people's beliefs about the properties of an attitude object

Commons Dilemma A social dilemma in which everyone takes from a common pool of goods that will replenish itself if used in moderation but will disappear if overused

Communal Relationships Relationships in which people's primary concern is being responsive to the other person's needs

Companionate Love The intimacy and affection we feel when we care deeply for a person but do not experience passion or arousal in the person's presence

Comparison Level People's expectations about the level of rewards and punishments they are likely to receive in a particular relationship

Comparison Level for Alternatives People's expectations about the level of rewards and punishments they would receive in an alternative relationship

Conformity A change in one's behavior due to the real or imagined influence of other people

Consensus Information Information about the extent to which other people behave the same way toward the same stimulus as the actor does

Consistency Information Information about the extent to which the behavior between one actor and one stimulus is the same across time and circumstances

Construal The way in which people perceive, comprehend, and interpret the social world

Contagion The rapid spread of emotions or behaviors through a crowd

Contingency Theory of Leadership The idea that leadership effectiveness depends both on how task-oriented or relationship-oriented the leader is and on the amount of control and influence the leader has over the group

Controlled Thinking Thinking that is conscious, intentional, voluntary, and effortful

Coping Styles The ways in which people react to threatening events

Correlation Coefficient A statistical technique that assesses how well you can predict one variable from another—for example, how well you can predict people's weight from their height

Correlational Method The technique whereby two or more variables are systematically measured and the relationship between them (i.e., how much one can be predicted from the other) is assessed

Correspondence Bias The tendency to infer that people's behavior corresponds to (matches) their disposition (personality)

Counterattitudinal Advocacy Stating an opinion or attitude that runs counter to one's private belief or attitude

Counterfactual Thinking Mentally changing some aspect of the past as a way of imagining what might have been

Covariation Model A theory that states that to form an attribution about what caused a person's behavior, we systematically note the pattern between the presence or absence of possible causal factors and whether or not the behavior occurs

Cover Story A description of the purpose of a study, given to participants, that is different from its true purpose, used to maintain psychological realism

Cross-Cultural Research Research conducted with members of different cultures, to see whether the psychological processes of interest are present in both cultures or whether they are specific to the culture in which people were raised

Debriefing Explaining to participants, at the end of an experiment, the true purpose of the study and exactly what transpired

Deception Misleading participants about the true purpose of a study or the events that will actually transpire

Decode To interpret the meaning of the nonverbal behavior other people express, such as deciding that a pat on the back was an expression of condescension and not kindness

Defensive Attributions Explanations for behavior that avoid feelings of vulnerability and mortality

Deindividuation The loosening of normal constraints on behavior when people can't be identified (such as when they are in a crowd)

Dependent Variable The variable a researcher measures to see if it is influenced by the independent variable; the researcher hypothesizes that the dependent variable will depend on the level of the independent variable

Descriptive Norms People's perceptions of how people actually behave in given situations, regardless of whether the behavior is approved or disapproved of by others

Deterrence Theory The hypothesis that the threat of legal punishment causes people to refrain from criminal activity as long as the punishment is perceived as relatively severe, certain, and swift

Diffusion of Responsibility The phenomenon whereby each bystander's sense of responsibility to help decreases as the number of witnesses increases

Discrimination Unjustified negative or harmful action toward a member of a group simply because of his or her membership in that group

Display Rules Culturally determined rules about which nonverbal behaviors are appropriate to display

Distinctiveness Information Information about the extent to which one particular actor behaves in the same way to different stimuli

Downward Social Comparison Comparing ourselves to people who are worse than we are on a particular trait or ability

Elaboration Likelihood Model A model explaining two ways in which persuasive communications can cause attitude change: *centrally*, when people are motivated and have the ability to pay attention to the arguments in the communication, and *peripherally*, when people do not pay attention to the arguments but are instead swayed by surface characteristics (e.g., who gave the speech)

Emblems Nonverbal gestures that have well-understood definitions within a given culture; they usually have direct verbal translations, such as the "OK" sign

Empathy The ability to put oneself in the shoes of another person and to experience events and emotions (e.g., joy and sadness) the way that person experiences them

Empathy-Altruism Hypothesis The idea that when we feel empathy for a person, we will attempt to help that person purely for altruistic reasons, regardless of what we have to gain

Encode To express or emit nonverbal behavior, such as smiling or patting someone on the back

Equity Theory The idea that people are happiest with relationships in which the rewards and costs experienced and the contributions made by both parties are roughly equal

Eros The instinct toward life, posited by Freud

Ethnography The method by which researchers attempt to understand a group or culture by observing it from the inside, without imposing any preconceived notions they might have

Evolutionary Approach to Love A theory derived from evolutionary biology that holds that men and women are attracted to different characteristics in each other (men are attracted by women's appearance; women are attracted by men's resources) because this maximizes their chances of reproductive success

Evolutionary Psychology The attempt to explain social behavior in terms of genetic factors that evolved over time according to the principles of natural selection

Exchange Relationships Relationships governed by the need for equity (i.e., for an equal ratio of rewards and costs)

Experimental Method The method in which the researcher randomly assigns participants to different conditions and ensures that these conditions are identical except for the independent variable (the one thought to have a causal effect on people's responses)

Explicit Attitudes Attitudes that we consciously endorse and can easily report

External Attribution The inference that a person is behaving a certain way because of something about the situation he or she is in; the assumption is that most people would respond the same way in that situation

External Justification A reason or an explanation for dissonant personal behavior that resides outside the individual (e.g., in order to receive a large reward or avoid a severe punishment)

External Validity The extent to which the results of a study can be generalized to other situations and to other people

Extrinsic Motivation The desire to engage in an activity because of external rewards or pressures, not because we enjoy the task or find it interesting

False Memory Syndrome Remembering a past traumatic experience that is objectively false but nevertheless accepted as true

Fear-Arousing Communications Persuasive messages that attempt to change people's attitudes by arousing their fears

Field Experiments Experiments conducted in natural settings rather than in the laboratory

Fight-or-Flight Response Responding to stress by either attacking the source of the stress or fleeing from it

Fixed Mindset The idea that we have a set amount of an ability that cannot change

Frustration-Aggression Theory The idea that frustration—the perception that you are being prevented from attaining a goal—increases the probability of an aggressive response

Fundamental Attribution Error The tendency to overestimate the extent to which people's behavior is due to internal, dispositional factors, and to underestimate the role of situational factors

Gestalt Psychology A school of psychology stressing the importance of studying the subjective way in which an object appears in people's minds rather than the objective, physical attributes of the object

Global Attribution The belief that an event is caused by factors that apply in a large number of situations (e.g., your intelligence, which will influence your performance in many areas) rather than factors that are specific and apply in only a limited number of situations (e.g., your musical ability, which will affect your performance in music courses but not in other courses)

Great Person Theory The idea that certain key personality traits make a person a good leader, regardless of the situation

Group Three or more people who interact and are interdependent in the sense that their needs and goals cause them to influence each other

Group Cohesiveness Qualities of a group that bind members together and promote liking between members

Group Polarization The tendency for groups to make decisions that are more extreme than the initial inclinations of its members

Groupthink A kind of thinking in which maintaining group cohesiveness and solidarity is more important than considering the facts in a realistic manner

Growth Mindset The idea that our abilities are malleable qualities that we can cultivate and grow

Heuristic–Systematic Model of Persuasion An explanation of the two ways in which persuasive communications can cause attitude change: either systematically processing the merits of the arguments or using mental shortcuts (heuristics), such as "Experts are always right"

Hindsight Bias The tendency for people to exaggerate how much they could have predicted an outcome after knowing that it occurred

Holistic Thinking Style A type of thinking in which people focus on the overall context, particularly the ways in which objects relate to each other; this type of thinking is common in East Asian cultures (e.g., China, Japan, and Korea)

Hostile Aggression Aggression stemming from feelings of anger and aimed at inflicting pain

Hypocrisy Induction The arousal of dissonance by having individuals make statements that run counter to their behaviors and then reminding them of the inconsistency between what they advocated and their behavior. The purpose is to lead individuals to more responsible behavior.

Idiosyncrasy Credits The tolerance a person earns, over time, by conforming to group norms; if enough idiosyncrasy credits are earned, the person can, on occasion, behave deviantly without retribution from the group

Illusory Correlation The tendency to see relationships, or correlations, between events that are actually unrelated

Impact Bias The tendency to overestimate the intensity and duration of our emotional reactions to future negative events

Implementation Intentions People's specific plans about where, when, and how they will fulfill a goal

Implicit Attitudes Attitudes that are involuntary, uncontrollable, and at times unconscious

Implicit Personality Theory A type of schema people use to group various kinds of personality traits together; for example, many people believe that someone who is kind is generous as well

Impression Management The attempt by people to get others to see them as they want to be seen

In-Group The group with which an individual identifies as a member

Independent Variable The variable a researcher changes or varies to see if it has an effect on some other variable

Independent View of the Self A way of defining oneself in terms of one's own internal thoughts, feelings, and actions and not in terms of the thoughts, feelings, and actions of other people

Individual Differences The aspects of people's personalities that make them different from other people

Informational Social Influence The influence of other people that leads us to conform because we see them as a source of information to guide our behavior; we conform because we believe that others' interpretation of an ambiguous situation is more correct than ours and will help us choose an appropriate course of action

Informed Consent Agreement to participate in an experiment, granted in full awareness of the nature of the experiment, which has been explained in advance

Ingratiation The process whereby people flatter, praise, and generally try to make themselves likable to another person, often of higher status

In- Group The group with which an individual does not identify

Injunctive Norms People's perceptions of what behaviors are approved or disapproved of by others

Institutional Review Board (IRB) A group made up of at least one scientist, one nonscientist, and one member not affiliated with an institution that reviews all psychological research at that institution and decides whether it meets ethical guidelines; all research must be approved by the IRB before it is conducted

Institutionalized Racism Racist attitudes that are held by the vast majority of people living in a society where stereotypes and discrimination are the norm

Institutionalized Sexism Sexist attitudes that are held by the vast majority of people living in a society where stereotypes and discrimination are the norm

Instrumental Aggression Aggression as a means to some goal other than causing pain

Insufficient Punishment The dissonance aroused when individuals lack sufficient external justification for having resisted a desired activity or object, usually resulting in individuals' devaluing the forbidden activity or object

Integrative Solution A solution to a conflict whereby the parties make trade-offs on issues according to their different interests; each side concedes the most on issues that are unimportant to it but important to the other side

Interdependent View of the Self A way of defining oneself in terms of one's relationships to other people; recognizing that one's behavior is often determined by the thoughts, feelings, and actions of others

Interjudge Reliability The level of agreement between two or more people who independently observe and code a set of data; by showing that two or more judges independently come up with the same observations, researchers ensure that the observations are not the subjective, distorted impressions of one individual

Internal Attribution The inference that a person is behaving in a certain way because of something about the person, such as attitude, character, or personality

Internal Justification The reduction of dissonance by changing something about oneself (e.g., one's attitude or behavior)

Internal Validity Making sure that nothing besides the independent variable can affect the dependent variable; this is accomplished by controlling all extraneous variables and by randomly assigning people to different experimental conditions

Internal-External Locus of Control The tendency to believe that things happen because we control them versus believing that good and bad outcomes are out of our control

Intrinsic Motivation The desire to engage in an activity because we enjoy it or find it interesting, not because of external rewards or pressures

Introspection The process whereby people look inward and examine their own thoughts, feelings, and motives

Investment Model The theory that people's commitment to a relationship depends not only on their satisfaction with the relationship in terms of rewards, costs, and comparison level and their comparison level for alternatives but also on how much they have invested in the relationship that would be lost by leaving it

Jigsaw Classroom A classroom setting designed to reduce prejudice and raise the self-esteem of children by placing them in small, desegregated groups and making each child dependent on the other children in the group to learn the course material and do well in the class

Judgmental Heuristics Mental shortcuts people use to make judgments quickly and efficiently

Justification of Effort The tendency for individuals to increase their liking for something they have worked hard to attain

Kin Selection The idea that behaviors that help a genetic relative are favored by natural selection

Learned Helplessness The state of pessimism that results from attributing a negative event to stable, internal, and global factors

Lowballing An unscrupulous strategy whereby a salesperson induces a customer to agree to purchase a product at a very low cost, subsequently claims it was an error, and then raises the price; frequently, the customer will agree to make the purchase at the inflated price

Mass Psychogenic Illness The occurrence, in a group of people, of similar physical symptoms with no known physical cause

Mere Exposure Effect The finding that the more exposure we have to a stimulus, the more apt we are to like it

Meta-Analysis A statistical technique that averages the results of two or more studies to see if the effect of an independent variable is reliable

Minority Influence The case where a minority of group members influence the behavior or beliefs of the majority

Misattribution of Arousal The process whereby people make mistaken inferences about what is causing them to feel the way they do

Modern Racism Outwardly acting unprejudiced while inwardly maintaining prejudiced attitudes

Mere Exposure Effect The finding that the more exposure we have to a stimulus, the more apt we are to like it

Mutual Interdependence The situation that exists when two or more groups need each other and must depend on each other to accomplish a goal that is important to each of them

Natural Selection The process by which heritable traits that promote survival in a particular environment are passed along to future generations, because organisms with that trait are more likely to produce offspring

Need for Cognition A personality variable reflecting the extent to which people engage in and enjoy effortful cognitive activities

Negotiation A form of communication between opposing sides in a conflict in which offers and counteroffers are made and a solution occurs only when both parties agree

Nonverbal Communication The way in which people communicate, intentionally or unintentionally, without words; nonverbal cues include facial expressions, tone of voice, gestures, body position and movement, the use of touch, and gaze

Norm of Reciprocity The expectation that helping others will increase the likelihood that they will help us in the future

Normative Conformity The tendency to go along with the group in order to fulfill the group's expectations and gain acceptance

Normative Social Influence The influence of other people that leads us to conform in order to be liked and accepted by them; this type of conformity results in public compliance with the group's beliefs and behaviors but not necessarily private acceptance of those beliefs and behaviors

Observational Method The technique whereby a researcher observes people and systematically records measurements or impressions of their behavior

Operant Conditioning The phenomenon whereby behaviors we freely choose to perform become more or less frequent, depending on whether they are followed by a reward (positive reinforcement) or punishment

Out-Group Any group with which an individual does not identify

Out-Group Homogeneity The perception that individuals in the out-group are more similar to each other (homogeneous) than they really are, as well as more similar than the members of the in-group are

Overconfidence Barrier The fact that people usually have too much confidence in the accuracy of their judgments

Overjustification Effect The tendency for people to view their behavior as caused by compelling extrinsic reasons, making them underestimate the extent to which it was caused by intrinsic reasons

Own-Race Bias The fact that people are better at recognizing faces of their own race than those of other races

Passionate Love An intense longing we feel for a person, accompanied by physiological arousal; when our love is reciprocated, we feel great fulfillment and ecstasy, but when it is not, we feel sadness and despair

Perceived Control The belief that we can influence our environment in ways that determine whether we experience positive or negative outcomes

Perceptual Salience The seeming importance of information that is the focus of people's attention

Performance-Contingent Rewards Rewards that are based on how well we perform a task

Peripheral Route to Persuasion The case whereby people do not elaborate on the arguments in a persuasive communication but are instead swayed by peripheral cues

Persuasive Communication Communication (e.g., a speech or television ad) advocating a particular side of an issue

Pluralistic Ignorance The case in which people think that everyone else is interpreting a situation in a certain way, when in fact they are not

Polygraph A machine that measures people's physiological responses (e.g., their heart rate); polygraph operators attempt to tell if someone is lying by observing that person's physiological responses while answering questions

Postdecision Dissonance Dissonance aroused after making a decision, typically reduced by enhancing the attractiveness of the chosen alternative and devaluating the rejected alternatives

Prejudice A hostile or negative attitude toward a distinguishable group of people, based solely on their membership in that group

Priming The process by which recent experiences increase the accessibility of a schema, trait, or concept

Private Acceptance Conforming to other people's behavior out of a genuine belief that what they are doing or saying is right

Probability Level (p-value) A number calculated with statistical techniques that tells researchers how likely it is that the results of their experiment occurred by chance and not because of the independent variable or variables; the convention in science, including social psychology, is to consider results *significant* (trustworthy) if the probability level is less than 5 in 100 that the results might be due to chance factors and not the independent variables studied

Procedural Justice People's judgments about the fairness of the procedures used to determine outcomes, such as whether they are innocent or guilty of a crime

Process Loss Any aspect of group interaction that inhibits good problem solving

Propinquity Effect The finding that the more we see and interact with people, the more likely they are to become our friends

Prosocial Behavior Any act performed with the goal of benefiting another person

Psychological Realism The extent to which the psychological processes triggered in an experiment are similar to psychological processes that occur in everyday life.

Public Compliance Conforming to other people's behavior publicly without necessarily believing in what we are doing or saying

Public Goods Dilemma A social dilemma in which individuals must contribute to a common pool in order to maintain the public good

Random Assignment to Condition A process ensuring that all participants have an equal chance of taking part in any condition of an experiment; through random assignment, researchers can be relatively certain that differences in the participants' personalities or backgrounds are distributed evenly across conditions

Random Selection A way of ensuring that a sample of people is representative of a population by giving everyone in the population an equal chance of being selected for the sample

Reactance Theory The idea that when people feel their freedom to perform a certain behavior is threatened, an unpleasant state of reactance is aroused, which they can reduce by performing the threatened behavior

Realistic Conflict Theory The idea that limited resources lead to conflict between groups and result in increased prejudice and discrimination

Reasons-Generated Attitude Change Attitude change resulting from thinking about the reasons for one's attitudes; people assume their attitudes match the reasons that are plausible and easy to verbalize

Reconstructive Memory The process whereby memories of an event become distorted by information encountered after the event occurred

Recovered Memories Recollections of a past event, such as sexual abuse, that had been forgotten or repressed

Relationship-Oriented Leader A leader who is concerned primarily with workers' feelings and relationships

Replications Repeating a study, often with different subject populations or in different settings

Representativeness Heuristic A mental shortcut whereby people classify something according to how similar it is to a typical case

Resilience Mild, transient reactions to stressful events, followed by a quick return to normal, healthy functioning

Retrieval The process by which people recall information stored in their memories

Scapegoating The tendency for individuals, when frustrated or unhappy, to displace aggression onto groups that are disliked, visible, and relatively powerless

Schemas Mental structures people use to organize their knowledge about the social world around themes or subjects and that influence the information people notice, think about, and remember

Scripts Ways of behaving socially that we learn implicitly from our culture

Secure Attachment Style An attachment style characterized by trust, a lack of concern with being abandoned, and the view that one is worthy and well liked

Self-Awareness The act of thinking about ourselves

Self-Awareness Theory The idea that when people focus their attention on themselves, they evaluate and compare their behavior to their internal standards and values

Self-Concept The content of the self; that is, our knowledge about who we are

Self-Efficacy The belief in one's ability to carry out specific actions that produce desired outcomes

Self-Esteem People's evaluations of their own self-worth—that is, the extent to which they view themselves as good, competent, and decent

Self-Fulfilling Prophecy The case whereby people have an expectation about what another person is like, which influences how they act toward that person, which causes that person to behave consistently with people's original expectations, making the expectations come true

Self-Handicapping The strategy whereby people create obstacles and excuses for themselves so that if they do poorly on a task, they can avoid blaming themselves

Self-Perception Theory The theory that when our attitudes and feelings are uncertain or ambiguous, we infer these states by observing our behavior and the situation in which it occurs

Self-Persuasion A long-lasting form of attitude change that results from attempts at self-justification

Self-Serving Attributions Explanations for one's successes that credit internal, dispositional factors and explanations for one's failures that blame external, situational factors

Serotonin A chemical in the brain that may inhibit aggressive impulses

Social Cognition How people think about themselves and the social world; more specifically, how people select, interpret, remember, and use social information to make judgments and decisions

Social Comparison Theory The idea that we learn about our own abilities and attitudes by comparing ourselves to other people

Social Dilemma A conflict in which the most beneficial action for an individual will, if chosen by most people, have harmful effects on everyone

Social Exchange Theory The idea that people's feelings about a relationship depend on their perceptions of the rewards and costs of the relationship, the kind of relationship they deserve, and their chances for having a better relationship with someone else

Social Facilitation The tendency for people to do better on simple tasks and worse on complex tasks when they are in the presence of others and their individual performance can be evaluated

Social Impact Theory The idea that conforming to social influence depends on the strength of the group's importance, its immediacy, and the number of people in the group

Social Influence The effect that the words, actions, or mere presence of other people have on our thoughts, feelings, attitudes, or behavior

Social Learning Theory The idea that we learn social behavior (e.g., aggression) by observing others and imitating them

Social Loafing The tendency for people to relax when they are in the presence of others and their individual performance cannot be evaluated, such that they do worse on simple tasks but better on complex tasks

Social Norms The implicit or explicit rules a group has for the acceptable behaviors, values, and beliefs of its members

Social Perception The study of how we form impressions of and make inferences about other people

Social Psychology The scientific study of the way in which people's thoughts, feelings, and behaviors are influenced by the real or imagined presence of other people

Social Roles Shared expectations in a group about how particular people are supposed to behave

Social Support The perception that others are responsive and receptive to one's needs

Social Tuning The process whereby people adopt another person's attitudes

Source Monitoring The process whereby people try to identify the source of their memories

Stable Attribution The belief that an event is caused by factors that will not change over time (e.g., your intelligence), as opposed to factors that will change over time (e.g., the amount of effort you put into a task)

Stereotype A generalization about a group of people in which certain traits are assigned to virtually all members of the group, regardless of actual variation among the members

Stereotype Threat The apprehension experienced by members of a group that their behavior might confirm a cultural stereotype

Storage The process by which people store in memory information they have acquired from the environment

Stress The negative feelings and beliefs that arise whenever people feel unable to cope with demands from their environment

Subliminal Messages Words or pictures that are not consciously perceived but may nevertheless influence people's judgments, attitudes, and behaviors

Surveys Research in which a representative sample of people are asked (often anonymously) questions about their attitudes or behavior

Task-Contingent Rewards Rewards that are given for performing a task, regardless of how well the task is done

Task-Oriented Leader A leader who is concerned more with getting the job done than with workers' feelings and relationships

Tend-and-Befriend Response Responding to stress with nurturant activities designed to protect oneself and one's offspring (tending) and creating social networks that provide protection from threats (befriending)

Testosterone A hormone associated with aggression

Thanatos According to Freud, an instinctual drive toward death, leading to aggressive actions

Theory of Planned Behavior The idea that the best predictors of a person's planned, deliberate behaviors are the person's attitudes toward specific behaviors, subjective norms, and perceived behavioral control

Thought Suppression The attempt to avoid thinking about something we would prefer to forget

Tit-for-Tat Strategy A means of encouraging cooperation by at first acting cooperatively but then always responding the way your opponent did (cooperatively or competitively) on the previous trial

Transactional Leaders Leaders who set clear, short-term goals and reward people who meet them

Transactive Memory The combined memory of two people that is more efficient than the memory of either individual

Transformational Leaders Leaders who inspire followers to focus on common, long-term goals

Two-Factor Theory of Emotion The idea that emotional experience is the result of a two-step self-perception process in which people first experience physiological arousal and then seek an appropriate explanation for it

Two-Step Process of Attribution Analyzing another person's behavior first by making an automatic internal attribution and only then thinking about possible situational reasons for the behavior, after which one may adjust the original internal attribution

Ultimate Attribution Error The tendency to make dispositional attributions about an entire group of people

Upward Social Comparison Comparing ourselves to people who are better than we are on a particular trait or ability

Urban Overload Hypothesis The theory that people living in cities are constantly being bombarded with stimulation and that they keep to themselves to avoid being overwhelmed by it

Yale Attitude Change Approach The study of the conditions under which people are most likely to change their attitudes in response to persuasive messages, focusing on "who said what to whom"—the source of the communication, the nature of the communication, and the nature of the audience

References 参考文献

Aarts, H., Custers, R., & Holland, R. W. (2007). The nonconscious cessation of goal pursuit: When goals and negative affect are coactivated. *Journal of Personality and Social Psychology, 92*, 165–178.

Aarts, H., & Dijksterhuis, A. (2003) The silence of the library: Environment, situational norm, and social behavior. *Journal of Personality and Social Psychology, 84*, 18–28.

Abelson, R. P., Kinder, D. R., Peters, M. D., & Fiske, S. T. (1982). Affective and semantic components in political person perception. *Journal of Personality and Social Psychology, 42*, 619–630.

Abraham, M. M., & Lodish, L. M. (1990). Getting the most out of advertising and promotion. *Harvard Business Review, 68*, 50–60.

Abrahamse, W., Steg, L., & Vlek, C. (2005). A review of intervention studies aimed at household energy conservation. *Journal of Environmental Psychology, 25*, 273–291.

Abrams, D., Marques, J. M., Bown, N., & Henson, M. (2000). Pro-norm and anti-norm deviance within and between groups. *Journal of Personality and Social Psychology, 78*, 906–912.

Abrams, D., Viki, G. T., Masser, B., & Bohner, G. (2003). Perceptions of stranger and acquaintance rape: The role of benevolent and hostile sexism in victim blame and rape proclivity. *Journal of Personality and Social Psychology, 84*, 111–125.

Abrams, D., Wetherell, M., Cochrane, S., Hogg, M. A., & Turner, J. C. (1990). Knowing what to think by knowing who you are: Self-categorization and the nature of norm formation, conformity and group polarization. *British Journal of Social Psychology, 29*, 97–119.

Adams, G., Anderson, S. L., & Adonu, J. K. (2004). The cultural grounding of closeness and intimacy. In D. J. Mashek & A. Aron (Eds.), *Handbook of closeness and intimacy* (pp. 321–342). Mahwah, NJ: Erlbaum.

Abramson, L., Seligman, M., & Teasdale, J. (1978). Learned helplessness in humans: Critique and reformulation. *Journal of Abnormal Psychology, 87*, 49–74.

Adler, J. (1997, March 22). It's a wise father who knows . . . *Newsweek*, p. 73.

Adolphs, R. (2003). Cognitive neuroscience of human social behavior. *Nature Review. Neuroscience, 4*, 165–178.

Aiello, J. R., & Douthitt, E. A. (2001). Social facilitation from Triplett to electronic performance monitoring. *Group Dynamics: Theory, Research, and Practice, 5*, 163–180.

Ainsworth, M. D. S., Blehar, M. C., Waters, E., & Wall, S. (1978). *Patterns of attachment: A psychological study of the strange situation*. Hillsdale, NJ: Erlbaum.

Ajzen, I. (1985). From intentions to actions: A theory of planned behavior. In J. Kuhl & J. Beckmann (Eds.), *Action control: From cognition to behavior* (pp. 11–39). Heidelberg, Germany: Springer-Verlag.

Ajzen, I., & Fishbein, M. (1980). *Understanding attitudes and predicting social behavior*. Englewood Cliffs, NJ: Prentice Hall.

Ajzen, I., & Fishbein, M. (2005). The influence of attitudes on behavior. In D. Albarracín, B. T. Johnson, & M. P. Zanna (Eds.), *The handbook of attitudes* (pp. 173–221). Mahwah, NJ: Erlbaum.

Akert, R. M. (1998). *Terminating romantic relationships: The role of personal responsibility and gender*. Unpublished manuscript, Wellesley College.

Akert, R. M., Chen, J., & Panter, A. T. (1991). *Facial prominence and stereotypes: The incidence and meaning of face-ism in print and television media*. Unpublished manuscript. Wellesley College.

Akert, R. M., & Panter, A. T. (1986). Extraversion and the ability to decode nonverbal communication. *Personality and Individual Differences, 9*, 965–972.

Akrami, N., Hedlund, L., & Ekehammar, B. (2007). Personality scale response latencies as self-schema indicators: The inverted-u effect revisited. *Personality and Individual Differences, 43*, 611–618

Alaskan village copes with real-life impacts of global climate change (2008, July 10). Online News Hour. Retrieved on December 30, 2008, from www.pbs.org/newshour/bb/environment/july-dec08/alaskawarming_07-10.html

Albarracín, D., Durantini, M., Earl, A., Gunnoe, J., & Leeper, J. (2008). Beyond the most willing audiences: A meta-intervention to increase exposure to HIV-prevention programs by vulnerable populations. *Health Psychology, 27*, 638–644.

Albarracín, D., Durantini, M. R., & Earl, A. N. (2006). Empirical and theoretical conclusions of an analysis of outcomes of HIV-prevention interventions. *Current Directions in Psychological Science, 15*, 73–78.

Albarracín, D., Gillette, J. C., Earl, A. N., Glasman, L. R., Durantini, M. R., & Ho, M. (2005). A test of major assumptions about behavior change: A comprehensive look at the effects of passive and active HIV-prevention interventions since the beginning of the epidemic. *Psychological Bulletin, 131*, 856–897.

Albarracín, D., Johnson, B. T., Fishbein, M., & Muellerleile, P. A. (2001). Theories of reasoned action and planned behavior as models of condom use: A meta-analysis. *Psychological Bulletin, 127*, 142–161.

Albarracín, D., & Wyer, R. S., Jr. (2000). The cognitive impact of past behavior: Influences on beliefs, attitudes, and future behavioral decisions. *Journal of Personality and Social Psychology, 79*, 5–22.

Albarracín, D., & Wyer, R. S., Jr. (2001). Elaborative and nonelaborative processing of a behavior-related communication. *Personality and Social Psychology Bulletin, 27*, 691–705.

Allen, M., D'Alessio, D., & Brezgel, K. (1995). *A meta-analysis summarizing the effects of pornography*: Vol. 2. *Aggression after exposure*. Thousand Oaks, CA: Sage.

Allen, M., Donohue, W. A., & Griffin, A. (2003). Comparing the influence of parents and peers on the choice to use drugs. *Criminal Justice and Behavior, 30*, 163–186.

Allen, V. L. (1965). Situational factors in conformity. In L. Berkowitz (Ed.), *Advances in experimental social psychology* (Vol. 2, pp. 133–175). New York: Academic Press.

Allen, V. L., & Levine, J. M. (1969). Consensus and conformity. *Journal of Personality and Social Psychology, 5*, 389–399.

Almeida, D. (2005). Resilience and vulnerability to daily stressors assessed via diary methods. *Current Directions in Psychological Science, 14*, 64–68.

Allison, P. D. (1992). The cultural evolution of beneficient norms. *Social Forces, 71*, 279–301.

Allport, G. W. (1954). *The nature of prejudice*. Reading, MA: Addison-Wesley.

Allport, G. W. (1985). The historical background of social psychology. In G. Lindzey & E. Aronson (Eds.), *The handbook of social psychology* (3rd ed., Vol. 1, pp. 1–46). New York: McGraw-Hill.

Altman, L. K. (2000, January 18). Mysterious illnesses often turn out to be mass hysteria. *New York Times*, pp. D7, D12.

Alvarez, L. (2003, June 22). Arranged marriages get a little rearranging. *New York Times*, p. 3.

Amato, P. R. (1983). Helping behavior in urban and rural environments: Field studies based on a taxonomic organization of helping episodes. *Journal of Personality and Social Psychology, 45*, 571–586.

Ambady, N., Bernieri, F. J., & Richeson, J. A. (2000). Toward a histology of social behavior: Judgmental accuracy from thin slices of the behavioral stream. In M. P. Zanna (Ed.), *Advances in experimental social psychology* (Vol. 32, pp. 201–271). San Diego, CA: Academic Press.

Ambady, N., & Rosenthal, R. (1992). Thin slices of expressive behavior as predictors of interpersonal consequences: A meta-analysis. *Psychological Bulletin, 111*, 256–274.

Ambady, N., & Rosenthal, R. (1993). Half a minute: Predicting teacher evaluations from thin slices of nonverbal behavior and physical attractiveness. *Journal of Personality and Social Psychology, 64*, 431–441.

American Psychological Association. (1992). Ethical principles of psychologists and code of conduct. *American Psychologist, 47*, 1597–1611.

American Psychological Association. (2002). *Ethical principles of psychologists and code of conduct*. Retrieved from www.apa.org/ethics

Ames, D. R., & Flynn, F. J. (2007). What breaks a leader: The curvilinear relation between assertiveness and leadership. *Journal of Personality and Social Psychology, 92*, 307–324.

Amir, I. (1969). Contact hypothesis in ethnic relations. *Psychological Bulletin, 71*, 319–342.

Amir, I. (1976). The role of intergroup contact in change of prejudice and ethnic relations. In P. A. Katz (Ed.), *Towards the elimination of racism* (pp. 245–308). New York: Pergamon Press.

Amodio, D. M., & Showers, C. J. (2005). 'Similarity breeds liking' revisited: The moderating role of commitment. *Journal of Social and Personal Relationships, 22*, 817–836.

Andersen, B., Farrar, W. B., Golden-Kreutz, D. M., Glaser, R., Emery, C. F., & Crespin, T. R. (2004). Psychological, behavioral, and immune changes after a psychological intervention: A clinical trial. *Journal of Clinical Oncology, 22*, 3570–3580.

Andersen, S. M. (1984). Self-knowledge and social inference: II. The diagnosticity of cognitive/affective and behavioral data. *Journal of Personality and Social Psychology, 46*, 294–307.

Andersen, S. M., & Bem, S. L. (1981). Sex typing and androgyny in dyadic interaction: Individual differences in responsiveness to physical attractiveness. *Journal of Personality and Social Psychology, 41*, 74–86.

Andersen, S. M., & Klatzky, R. L. (1987). Traits and social stereotypes: Levels of categorization in person perception. *Journal of Personality and Social Psychology, 53*, 235–246.

Andersen, S. M., & Ross, L. D. (1984). Self-knowledge and social inference: I. The impact of cognitive/affective and behavioral data. *Journal of Personality and Social Psychology, 46*, 280–293.

Anderson, C. (2009; personal communication). Some Speculations about Global Warming and Aggression.

Anderson, C. A. (1995). Implicit personality theories and empirical data: Biased assimilation, belief perseverance and change, and covariation detection sensitivity. *Social Cognition, 13*, 25–48.

Anderson, C. A. (1999). Attributional style, depression, and loneliness: A cross-cultural comparison of American and Chinese students. *Personality and Social Psychology Bulletin, 25*, 482–499.

Anderson, C. A., Anderson, B., & Deuser, W. (1996). Examining an affective aggression framework: Weapon and temperature effects on aggressive thoughts, affect, and attitudes. *Personality and Social Psychology Bulletin, 22*, 366–376.

Anderson, C. A., & Anderson, D. C. (1984). Ambient temperature and violent crime: Tests of the linear and curvilinear hypotheses. *Journal of Personality and Social Psychology, 46*, 91–97.

Anderson, C. A., & Bushman, B. J. (1997). External validity of "trivial" experiments: The case of laboratory aggression. *Review of General Psychology, 1*, 19–41.

Anderson, C. A., Bushman, B. J., & Groom, R. W. (1997). Hot years and serious and deadly assault: Empirical tests of the heat hypothesis. *Journal of Personality and Social Psychology, 73*, 1213–1223.

Anderson, C. A., & Dill, K. E. (2000). Video games and aggressive thoughts, feelings, and behavior in the laboratory and in life. *Journal of Personality and Social Psychology, 78*, 772–790.

Anderson, C. A., Lepper, M. R., & Ross, L. (1980). The perseverance of social theories: The role of explanation in the persistence of discredited information. *Journal of Personality and Social Psychology, 39*, 1037–1049.

Anderson, N. B. (1989). Racial differences in stress-induced cardiovascular reactivity and hypertension: Current status and substantive issues. *Psychological Bulletin, 105*, 89–105.

Angier, N. (2006, January 3). The cute factor. *New York Times*, pp. D1–D8.

Antoni, M. H., & Lutgendorf, S. (2007). Psychosocial factors and disease progression in cancer. *Current Directions in Psychological Science, 16*, 42–46.

Archer, D. (1991). *A world of gestures: Culture and nonverbal communication* [Videotape and manual]. Berkeley: University of California Extension Center for Media and Independent Learning.

Archer, D. (1994). American violence: How high and why? *Law Studies, 19*, 12–20.

Archer, D. (1997a). Unspoken diversity: Cultural differences in gestures. *Qualitative Sociology, 20*, 79–105.

Archer, D. (1997b). *A world of differences: Understanding cross-cultural communication* [Videotape and manual]. Berkeley: University of California Extension Center for Media and Independent Learning.

Archer, D., & Akert, R. M. (1977a, October). How well do you read body language? *Psychology Today*, pp. 68–69, 72, 119–120.

Archer, D., & Akert, R. M. (1977b). Words and everything else: Verbal and nonverbal cues in social interaction. *Journal of Personality and Social Psychology, 35*, 443–449.

Archer, D., & Akert, R. M. (1980). The encoding of meaning: A test of three theories of social interaction. *Sociological Inquiry, 50*, 393–419.

Archer, D., & Akert, R. M. (1984). Problems of context and criterion in nonverbal communication: A new look at the accuracy issue. In M. Cook (Ed.), *Issues in person perception* (pp. 114–144). New York: Methuen.

Archer, D., & Akert, R. M. (1998). *The interpretation of behavior: Verbal and nonverbal factors in person perception*. New York: Cambridge University Press.

Archer, D., & Gartner, R. (1976). Violent acts and violent times: A comparative approach to postwar homicide rates. *American Sociological Review, 41*, 937–963.

Archer, D., & Gartner, R. (1984). *Violence and crime in cross-national perspective*. New Haven, CT: Yale University Press.

Archer, D., Iritani, B., Kimes, D. D., & Barrios, M. (1983). Face-ism: Five studies of sex differences in facial prominence. *Journal of Personality and Social Psychology, 45*, 725–735.

Archer, D., & McDaniel, P. (1995). Violence and gender: Differences and similarities across societies. In R. B. Ruback & N. A. Weiner (Eds.), *Interpersonal violent behaviors: Social and cultural aspects* (pp. 63–88). New York: Springer-Verlag.

Arendt, H. (1965). *Eichmann in Jerusalem: A report on the banality of evil*. New York: Viking.

Argyle, M. (1975). *Bodily communication*. New York: International Universities Press.

Argyle, M. (1986). Rules for social relationships in four cultures. *Australian Journal of Psychology, 38*, 309–318.

Arkes, H. R., & Mellers, B. A. (2002). Do juries meet our expectations? *Law and Human Behavior, 26*, 625–639.

Arkin, R. M., & Maruyama, G. M. (1979). Attribution, affect, and college exam performance. *Journal of Educational Psychology, 71*, 85–93.

Arkin, R. M., & Oleson, K. C. (1998). Self-handicapping. In J. M. Darley & J. Cooper (Eds.), *Attribution and social interaction: The legacy of Edward E. Jones* (pp. 313–341). Washington, DC: American Psychological Association.

Armitage, C. J., & Conner, M. (2001). Social cognitive determinants of blood donation. *Journal of Applied Social Psychology, 31*, 1431–1457.

Armor, D. A., & Taylor, S. E. (1998). Situated optimism: Specific outcome expectancies and self-regulation. In M. P. Zanna (Ed.), *Advances in experimental social psychology* (Vol. 30, pp. 309–379). San Diego, CA: Academic Press.

Arms, R. L., Russell, G. W., & Sandilands, M. L. (1979). Effects on the hostility of spectators of viewing aggressive sports. *Social Psychology Quarterly, 42*, 275–279.

Armstrong, L. (2000). *It's not about the bike: My journey back to life.* New York: Putnam.

Arnett, J. (1995). The young and the reckless: Adolescent reckless behavior. *Current Directions in Psychological Science, 4*, 67–71.

Aron, A., & Aron, E. N. (1996). Self and self-expansion in relationships. In G. J. O. Fletcher & J. Fitness (Eds.), *Knowledge structures in close relationships: A social psychological approach* (pp. 325–344). Mahwah, NJ: Erlbaum.

Aron, A., Aron, E. N., & Norman, C. (2004). Self-expansion model of motivation and cognition in close relationships and beyond. In M. B. Brewer & M. Hewstone (Eds.), *Self and social identity* (pp. 99–123) Malden, MA: Blackwell Publ.

Aron, A., Dutton, D. G., Aron, E. N., & Iverson, A. (1989). Experiences of falling in love. *Journal of Social and Personal Relationships, 6*, 243–257.

Aron, A., Fisher, H., Mashek, D. J., Strong, G., Li, H., & Brown, L. L. (2005). Reward, motivation, and emotion systems associated with early-stage intense romantic love. *Journal of Neurophysiology, 94*, 327–337.

Aron, A. P., Mashek, D. J., & Aron, E. N. (2004). Closeness as including other in the self. In D. J. Mashek & A. Aron (Eds.), *Handbook of closeness and intimacy* (pp. 27–42). Mahwah, NJ: Erlbaum.

Aron, A., & Rodriguez, G. (1992). Scenarios of falling in love among Mexican, Chinese, and Anglo-Americans. In A. Aron (Chair), *Ethnic and cultural differences in love*. Symposium conducted at the Sixth International Conference on Personal Relationships, Orono, ME.

Aron, A., & Westbay, L. (1996). Dimensions of the prototype of love. *Journal of Personality and Social Psychology, 70*, 535–551.

Aron, R. (2002). *The dawn of universal history*. New York: Perseus Books.

Aronson, E. (1968). Dissonance theory: Progress and problems. In R. P. Abelson, E. Aronson, W. J. McGuire, T. M. Newcomb, M. J. Rosenberg, & P. H. Tannenbaum (Eds.), *Theories of cognitive consistency: A sourcebook* (pp. 5–27). Chicago: Rand McNally.

Aronson, E. (1969). The theory of cognitive dissonance: A current perspective. In L. Berkowitz (Ed.), *Advances in experimental social psychology* (Vol. 4, pp. 1–34). New York: Academic Press.

Aronson, E. (1978). *The Jigsaw Classroom*. Beverly Hills: Sage.

Aronson, E. (1992). The return of the repressed: Dissonance theory makes a comeback. *Psychological Inquiry, 3*, 303–311.

Aronson, E. (1997). The theory of cognitive dissonance: The evolution and vicissitudes of an idea. In C. McGarty & S. A. Haslam (Eds.), *The message of social psychology: Perspectives on mind in society* (pp. 20–35). Malden, MA: Blackwell.

Aronson, E. (1998). Dissonance, hypocrisy, and the self-concept. In E. Harmon-Jones & J. S. Mills (Eds.), *Cognitive dissonance theory: Revival with revisions and controversies* (pp. 21–36). Washington, DC: American Psychological Association.

Aronson, E. (1999). *The social animal* (8th ed.). New York: Worth/Freeman.

Aronson, E. (2000). *Nobody left to hate: Teaching compassion after Columbine*. New York: Worth/Freeman.

Aronson, E. (2002). Drifting my own way: Following my nose and my heart. In R. Sternberg (Ed.), *Psychologists defying the crowd: Stories of those who battled the establishment and won* (pp. 132–148). Washington, DC: American Psychological Association.

Aronson, E. (2007). The evolution of cognitive dissonance theory: A personal appraisal. In A. Pratkanis, *The science of social influence*. New York: Psychology Press.

Aronson, E. (2007). *The social animal*. New York: W. H. Freeman.

Aronson, E. (2008) *The social animal*. New York: W. H. Freeman.

Aronson, E. (2009, in press). *The Rollercoaster: An autobiography*. New York: Basic Books.

Aronson, E. (in press). Fear, denial, and sensible action in the face of disasters. *Social Research*.

Aronson, E., & Bridgeman, D. (1979). Jigsaw groups and the desegregated classroom: In pursuit of common goals. *Personality and Social Psychology Bulletin, 5*, 438–446.

Aronson, E., & Carlsmith, J. M. (1962). Performance expectancy as a determinant of actual performance. *Journal of Abnormal and Social Psychology, 65*, 178–182.

Aronson, E., & Carlsmith, J. M. (1963). Effect of severity of threat in the devaluation of forbidden behavior. *Journal of Abnormal and Social Psychology, 66*, 584–588.

Aronson, E., & Carlsmith, J. M. (1968). Experimentation in social psychology. In G. Lindzey & E. Aronson (Eds.), *The handbook of social psychology* (Vol. 2, pp. 1–79). Reading, MA: Addison-Wesley.

Aronson, E., Ellsworth, P. C., Carlsmith, J. M., & Gonzalez, M. H. (1990). *Methods of research in social psychology* (2nd ed.). New York: McGraw-Hill.

Aronson, E., Fried, C., & Stone, J. (1991). Overcoming denial and increasing the intention to use condoms through the induction of hypocrisy. *American Journal of Public Health, 81*, 1636–1638.

Aronson, E., & Gonzalez, A. (1988). Desegregation, jigsaw, and the Mexican-American experience. In P. A. Katz & D. Taylor (Eds.), *Towards the elimination of racism: Profiles in controversy* (pp. 310–330). New York: Plenum.

Aronson, E., & Linder, D. (1965) Gain and loss of esteem as determinants of interpersonal attractiveness. *Journal of Experimental Social Psychology, 1, 156–171*.

Aronson, E., & Mills, J. S. (1959). The effect of severity of initiation on liking for a group. *Journal of Abnormal and Social Psychology, 59*, 177–181.

Aronson, E., & Patnoe, S. (1997). *Cooperation in the classroom: The jigsaw method*. New York: Longman.

Aronson, E., Stephan, C., Sikes, J., Blaney, N., & Snapp, M. (1978). *The jigsaw classroom*. Beverly Hills, CA: Sage.

Aronson, E., & Thibodeau, R. (1992). The jigsaw classroom: A cooperative strategy for reducing prejudice. In J. Lynch, C. Modgil, & S. Modgil (Eds.), *Cultural diversity in the schools* (pp. 110–118). London: Falmer Press.

Aronson, E., Wilson, T. D., & Brewer, M. B. (1998). Experimental methods. In D. T. Gilbert, S. T. Fiske, & G. Lindzey (Eds.), *The handbook of social psychology* (4th ed., Vol. 1, pp. 99–142). New York: McGraw-Hill.

Aronson, J. (2009, in press). Jigsaw, social psychology, and the nurture of human intelligence. In *The scientist and the humanist: A festschrift in honor of elliot aronson*. New York: Taylor & Francis.

Aronson, J., Fried, C. B., & Good, C. (2002). Reducing the effects of stereotype threat on African American college students by shaping theories of intelligence. *Journal of Experimental Social Psychology, 38*, 113–125.

Aronson, J., Jannone, S., McGlone, M., & Johnson-Campbell, T. (2009, in press). The Obama effect: An experimental test, *Journal Experimental Social Psychology*.

Aronson, J. (in press). Jigsaw and stereotype threat. In Gonzales et al. (Eds.).

Aronson, J. & Williams, J. (2009). Stereotype Threat: Forewarned is Forearmed. Manuscript under review.

Aronson, J. M., Cohen, G., & Nail, P. R. (1999). Self-affirmation theory: An update and appraisal. In E. Harmon-Jones & J. S. Mills (Eds.), *Cognitive dissonance: Progress on a pivotal theory in social psychology* (pp. 127–147). Washington, DC: American Psychological Association.

Aronson, J. M., Lustina, M. J., Good, C., Keough, K., Steele, C. M., & Brown, J. (1999). When white men can't do math: Necessary and sufficient factors in stereotype threat. *Journal of Experimental Social Psychology, 35*, 29–46.

Aronson, J. M., Quinn, D., & Spencer, S. (1998). Stereotype threat and the academic underperformance of women and minorities. In J. K. Swim & C. Stangor (Eds.), *Stigma: The target's perspective* (pp. 83–103). San Diego, CA: Academic Press.

Arthur, K. (2006, April 11). A new fugue for handicappers: Interactive and unpredictable, 'American Idol.' *New York Times*, p. B3.

Asch, S. E. (1946). Forming impressions of personality. *Journal of Abnormal and Social Psychology, 41*, 258–290.

Asch, S. E. (1951). Effects of group pressure upon the modification and distortion of judgment. In H. Guetzkow (Ed.), *Groups, leadership, and men* (pp. 76–92). Pittsburgh, PA: Carnegie Press.

Asch, S. E. (1955). Opinions and social pressure. *Scientific American, 193*, 31–35.

Asch, S. E. (1956). Studies of independence and conformity: A minority of one against a unanimous majority. *Psychological Monographs, 70* (9, Whole No. 416).

Asch, S. E. (1957). An experimental investigation of group influence. In Walter Reed Army Institute of Research, *Symposium on preventive and social psychiatry* (pp. 15–17). Washington, DC: U.S. Government Printing Office.

Ashmore, R. D., & Longo, L. C. (1995). Accuracy of stereotypes: What research on physical attractiveness can teach us. In Y.-T. Lee, L. J. Jussim, & C. R. McCauley (Eds.), *Stereotype accuracy: Toward appreciating group difference* (pp. 63–86). Washington, DC: American Psychological Association.

Aspinwall, L. G., & Taylor, S. E. (1993). Effects of social comparison direction, threat, and self-esteem on affect, evaluation, and expected success. *Journal of Personality and Social Psychology, 64*, 708–722.

Aspinwall, L. G., & Taylor, S. E. (1997). A stitch in time: Self-regulation and proactive coping. *Psychological Bulletin, 121*, 417–436.

Associated Press (2002, November 1). "Halloween is debated by French." *Boston Globe*, p. A20.

Aune, K. S., & Aune, R. K. (1996). Cultural differences in the self-reported experience and expression of emotions in relationships. *Journal of Cross-Cultural Psychology, 27*, 67–81.

Averill, J. R. (1973). Personal control over aversive stimuli and its relationship to stress. *Psychological Bulletin, 80*, 286–303.

Axelrod, R. (1984). *The evolution of cooperation*. New York: Basic Books.

Ayduk, Ö., & Kross, E. (2008). Enhancing the pace of recovery: Self-distanced analysis of negative experiences reduces blood pressure reactivity. *Psychological Science, 19*, 229–231.

Azrin, N. H. (1967, May). Pain and aggression. *Psychology Today*, pp. 27–33.

Babad, E. (1993). Pygmalion—25 years after interpersonal expectations in the classroom. In P. D. Blank (Ed.), *Interpersonal expectations: Theory, research, and applications* (pp. 125–153). New York: Cambridge University Press.

Badr, L. K., & Abdallah, B. (2001). Physical attractiveness of premature infants affects outcome at discharge from the NICU. *Infant Behavior and Development, 24*, 129–133.

Bailey, D. S., & Taylor, S. P. (1991). *Journal of research in personality*, vol. 25, no 3, pp. 334–342.

Bailey, W. C., & Peterson, R. D. (1997). Murder, capital punishment, and deterrence: A review of the literature. In H. A. Bedau (Ed.), *The death penalty in America: Current controversies* (pp. 135–161). New York: Oxford University Press.

Baker, P. (2005, October 4). Once more, Bush turns to his inner circle. *Washington Post*, p. A01.

Baldwin, M. W., & Fehr, B. (1995). On the instability of attachment style ratings. *Personal Relationships, 2*, 247–261.

Baldwin, M. W., Keelan, J. P. R., Fehr, B., Enns, V., & Koh-Rangarajoo, E. (1996). Social-cognitive conceptualizations of attachment working models: Availability and accessibility effects. *Journal of Personality and Social Psychology, 71*, 94–109.

Bandura, A. (1973). *Aggression: A social learning analysis*. Englewood Cliffs, NJ: Prentice Hall.

Bandura, A. (1997). *Self-efficacy: The exercise of control*. New York: Freeman.

Bandura, A., Cioffi, D., Taylor, C. B., & Brouillard, M. E. (1988). Perceived self-efficacy in coping with cognitive stressors and opioid activation. *Journal of Personality and Social Psychology, 55*, 479–488.

Bandura, A., Ross, D., & Ross, S. (1961). Transmission of aggression through imitation of aggressive models. *Journal of Abnormal and Social Psychology, 63*, 575–582.

Bandura, A., Ross, D., & Ross, S. (1963). Imitation of film-mediated aggressive models. *Journal of Abnormal and Social Psychology, 66*, 3–11.

Banerjee, R., & Dittmar, H. (2008). Individual differences in children's materialism: The role of peer relations. *Personality and Social Psychology Bulletin, 34*, 17–31.

Banks, T., & Dabbs, J. M., Jr. (1996). Salivary testosterone and cortisol in delinquent and violent urban subculture. *Journal of Social Psychology, 136*, 49–56.

Barber, N. (1998). Secular changes in standards of bodily attractiveness in American women: Different masculine and feminine ideals. *Journal of Psychology, 132*, 87–94.

Bargh, J. A. (1994). The four horsemen of automaticity: Awareness, intention, efficiency, and control in social cognition. In R. S. Wyer Jr. & T. K. Srull (Eds.), *Handbook of social cognition* (Vol. 1, pp. 1–40). Hillsdale, NJ: Erlbaum.

Bargh, J. A. (1996). Automaticity in social psychology. In E. T. Higgins & A. W. Kruglanski (Eds.), *Social psychology: Handbook of basic principles* (pp. 169–183). New York: Guilford Press.

Bargh, J. A., & Ferguson, M. J. (2000). Beyond behaviorism: On the automaticity of higher mental processes. *Psychological Bulletin, 126*, 925–945.

Bargh, J. A., Gollwitzer, P. M., Lee-Chai, A., Barndollar, K., & Trötschel, R. (2001). The automated will: Nonconscious activation and pursuit of behavioral goals. *Journal of Personality and Social Psychology, 81*, 1014–1027.

Bargh, J. A., & Morsella, E. (2008). The unconscious mind. *Perspectives on Psychological Science, 3*, 73–79.

Bargh, J. A., & Pietromonaco, P. (1982). Automatic information processing and social perception: The influence of trait information presented outside of conscious awareness on impression formation. *Journal of Personality and Social Psychology, 43*, 437–449.

Bar-Haim, Y., Ziv, T., Lamy, D., & Hodes, R. M. (2006). Nature and nurture in own-race face processing. *Psychological Science, 17*, 159–163.

Barker, R., Dembo, T., & Lewin, K. (1941). Frustration and aggression: An experiment with young children. *University of Iowa Studies in Child Welfare, 18*, 1–314.

Barley, S. R., & Bechky, B. A. (1994). In the backrooms of science: The work of technicians in science labs. *Work and Occupations, 21*, 85–126.

Baron, R. A. (1972). Reducing the influence of an aggressive model: The restraining effects of peer censure. *Journal of Experimental Social Psychology, 8*, 266–275.

Baron, R. A. (1976). The reduction of human aggression: A field study on the influence of incompatible responses. *Journal of Applied Social Psychology, 6,* 95–104.

Baron, R. A. (1988). Negative effects of destructive criticism: Impact on conflict, self-efficacy, and task performance. *Journal of Applied Psychology, 73,* 199–207.

Baron, R. A. (1990). Countering the effects of destructive criticism: The relative efficacy of four interventions. *Journal of Applied Psychology, 75,* 235–245.

Baron, R. A. (1997). The sweet smell of . . . helping: Effects of pleasant ambient fragrance on prosocial behavior in shopping malls. *Personality and Social Psychology Bulletin, 23,* 498–503.

Baron, R. A., & Richardson, D. R. (1994). *Human aggression* (2nd ed.). New York: Plenum.

Baron, R. M., & Misovich, S. J. (1993). Dispositional knowing from an ecological perspective. *Personality and Social Psychology Bulletin, 19,* 541–552.

Baron, R. S. (1986). Distraction/conflict theory: Progress and problems. In L. Berkowitz (Ed.), *Advances in experimental social psychology* (Vol. 19, pp. 1–40). Orlando, FL: Academic Press.

Baron, R. S. (2005). So right it's wrong: Groupthink and the ubiquitous nature of polarized group decision making. In M. P. Zanna (Ed.), *Advances in experimental social psychology* (Vol. 37, pp. 219–253). San Diego, CA: Academic Press.

Baron, R. S., Vandello, J. A., & Brunsman, B. (1996). The forgotten variable in conformity research: Impact of task importance on social influence. *Journal of Personality and Social Psychology, 71,* 915–927.

Barrouquere, B. (2006, June 15). "A call, a hoax, a nationwide search for the man on the phone." Associated Press. Retrieved on August 25, 2006, from *0-web.lexis-nexis.com*

Bartholomew, R. E., & Wessely, S. (2002). Protean nature of mass sociogenic illness: From possessed nuns to chemical and biological terrorism. *British Journal of Psychiatry, 180,* 300–306.

Bartlett, F. C. (1932). *Remembering.* Cambridge: Cambridge University Press.

Bartlett, M. Y., & DeSteno, D. (2006). Gratitude and prosocial behavior: Helping when it costs you. *Psychological Science, 17,* 319–325.

Bass, B. M. (1990). *Bass and Stogdill's handbook of leadership: Theory, research, and managerial applications* (3rd ed.). New York: Free Press.

Bass, B. M. (1998). *Transformational leadership: Industry, military, and educational impact.* Mahwah, NJ: Erlbaum.

Bass, E., & Davis, L. (1994). *The courage to heal: A guide for women survivors of childhood sexual abuse* (3rd ed.). New York: HarperCollins.

Batson, C., Ahmad, N., Powell, A., & Stocks, E. (2008). Prosocial motivation. In J. Y. Shah & W. L. Gardner (Eds.), *Handbook of motivation science* (pp. 135–149). New York: Guilford Press.

Batson, C., Eklund, J., Chermok, V., Hoyt, J., & Ortiz, B. (2007). An additional antecedent of empathic concern: Valuing the welfare of the person in need. *Journal of Personality and Social Psychology, 93,* 65–74.

Batson, C. D. (1991). *The altruism question: Toward a social-psychological answer.* Hillsdale, NJ: Erlbaum.

Batson, C. D. (1993). Communal and exchange relationships: What's the difference? *Personality and Social Psychology Bulletin, 19,* 677–683.

Batson, C. D. (1998). Altruism and prosocial behavior. In D. T. Gilbert, S. T. Fiske, & G. Lindzey (Eds.), *The handbook of social psychology* (4th ed., Vol. 2, pp. 282–316). New York: McGraw-Hill.

Batson, C. D., & Ahmad, N. (2001). Empathy-induced altruism in a prisoner's dilemma II: What if the target of empathy has defected? *European Journal of Social Psychology, 31,* 25–36.

Batson, C. D., Ahmad, N., Lishner, D. A., & Tsang, J. (2002). Empathy and altruism. In C. R. Snyder & S. J. Lopez (Eds.), *Handbook of positive psychology* (pp. 485–498). New York: Oxford University Press.

Batson, C. D., Ahmad, N., & Stocks, E. L. (2004). Benefits and liabilities of empathy-induced altruism. In A. G. Miller (Ed.), *The social psychology of good and evil* (pp. 359–385). New York: Guilford.

Batson, C. D., Coke, J. S., Jasnoski, M. L., & Hanson, M. (1978). Buying kindness: Effect of an extrinsic incentive for helping on perceived altruism. *Personality and Social Psychology Bulletin, 4,* 86–91.

Batson, C. D., Polycarpou, M. P., Harmon-Jones, E., Imhoff, H. J., Mitchener, E. C., Bednar, L. L., Klein, T. R., & Highberger, L. (1997). Empathy and attitudes: Can feeling for a member of a stigmatized group improve feelings toward the group? *Journal of Personality and Social Psychology, 72,* 105–118.

Batson, C. D., & Powell, A. A. (2003). Altruism and prosocial behavior. In T. Millon & M. J. Lerner (Eds.), *Handbook of psychology: Personality and social psychology* (Vol. 5, pp. 463–484). New York: Wiley.

Batson, C. D., Sager, K., Garst, E., Kang, M., Rubchinsky, K., & Dawson, K. (1997). Is empathy-induced helping due to self-other merging? *Journal of Personality and Social Psychology, 73,* 495–509.

Batson, C. D., Schoenrade, P., & Ventis, W. L. (1993). *Religion and the individual.* New York: Oxford University Press.

Battle for your brain. (1991, August). *Consumer Reports,* pp. 520–521.

Baum, A., Revenson, T. A., & Singer, J. E. (Eds). (2001). *Handbook of health psychology.* Boulder, CO: NetLibrary.

Baumeister, R. F. (1986). *Identity: Cultural change and the struggle for self.* New York: Oxford University Press.

Baumeister, R. F. (1991). *Escaping the self: Alcoholism, spirituality, masochism, and other flights from the burden of selfhood.* New York: Basic Books.

Baumeister, R. F. (1998). The self. In D. T. Gilbert, S. T. Fiske, & G. Lindzey (Eds.), *The handbook of social psychology* (4th ed., Vol. 1, pp. 680–740). New York: McGraw-Hill.

Baumeister, R. F., Schmeichel, B. J., & Vohs, K. D. (2007). Self-regulation and the executive function: The self as controlling agent. In E. T. Higgins & A. W. Kruglanski (Eds.), *Social psychology: Handbook of basic principles* (2nd ed., pp 516–534). New York: Guilford.

Baumeister, R. F., & Hetherington, T. F. (1996). Self-regulation failure: An overview. *Psychological Inquiry, 7,* 1–15.

Baumeister, R. F., & Leary, M. R. (1995). The need to belong: Desire for interpersonal attachment as a fundamental human motivation. *Psychological Bulletin, 117,* 497–529.

Baumeister, R. F., & Sommer, K. L. (1997). What do men want? Gender differences and two spheres of belongingness: Comment on Cross and Madson (1997). *Psychological Bulletin, 122,* 38–44.

Baumeister, R. F., Stillwell, A. M., & Heatherton, T. F. (1994). Guilt: An interpersonal approach. *Psychological Bulletin, 115,* 243–267.

Baumeister, R., Vohs, K., & Tice, D. (2007). The strength model of self-control. *Current Directions in Psychological Science, 16,* 351–355.

Baumgardner, A. H., Lake, E. A., & Arkin, R. M. (1985). Claiming mood as a self-handicap. *Personality and Social Psychology Bulletin, 11,* 349–357.

Baxter, L. A. (1986). Gender differences in the heterosexual relationship rules embedded in break-up accounts. *Journal of Social and Personal Relationships, 3,* 289–306.

Beach, S. R. H., Tesser, A., Mendolia, M., & Anderson, P. (1996). Self-evaluation maintenance in marriage: Toward a performance ecology of the marital relationship. *Journal of Family Psychology, 10,* 379–396.

Beaman, A. L., Barnes, P. J., Klentz, B., & McQuirk, B. (1978). Increasing helping rates through informational dissemination: Teaching pays. *Personality and Social Psychology Bulletin, 4,* 406–411.

Beaman, A. L., Klentz, B., Diener, E., & Svanum, S. (1979). Objective self-awareness and transgression in children: A field study. *Journal of Personality and Social Psychology, 37,* 1835–1846.

Beauvois, J., & Joule, R. (1996). *A radical dissonance theory.* London: Taylor & Francis.

Bedau, H. A. (Ed.). (1997). *The death penalty in America: Current controversies*. New York: Oxford University Press.

Beer, J., & Ochsner, K. (2006). Social cognition: A multi level analysis. *Brain Research, 1079*, 98–105.

Bell, J. (1995). Notions of love and romance among the Taita of Kenya. In W. Jankowiak (Ed.), *Romantic passion: A universal experience?* (pp. 152–165). New York: Columbia University Press.

Bell, S. T., Kuriloff, P. J., & Lottes, I. (1994). Understanding attributions of blame in stranger-rape and date-rape situations: An examination of gender, race, identification, and students' social perceptions of rape victims. *Journal of Applied Social Psychology, 24*, 1719–1734.

Bem, D. J. (1972). Self-perception theory. In L. Berkowitz (Ed.), *Advances in experimental social psychology* (Vol. 6, pp. 1–62). New York: Academic Press.

Bem 2, D. J., and Mcconnell, H. K. (1970). Testing the self-perception explanation of dissonance phenomena: On the salience of premanipulation attitudes. *Journal of Personality and Social Psychology* 1970, Vol. 14, No. 1, 23–31.

Bender, B. (2003, June 15). Scandals rock military academies. *Boston Globe*, p. A10.

Benight, C. C., & Bandura, A. (2004). Social cognitive theory of posttraumatic recovery: The role of perceived self-efficacy. *Behaviour Research and Therapy, 42*, 1129–1148.

Bergeron, N., & Schneider, BH. (2005). Explaining cross-national differences in peer-directed aggression: A quantitative synthesis. *Aggressive Behavior, 31*, 116–137.

Berke, R. L. (2000, September 12). Democrats see, and smell, "rats" in GOP ad. New York Times on the Web, *www.nytimes.com*

Berkman, L. F., & Syme, S. L. (1979). Social networks, host resistance, and mortality: A nine-year follow-up study of Alameda County residents. *American Journal of Epidemiology, 109*, 186–204.

Berkow, J. H. (1989). *Darwin, sex, and status: Biological approaches to mind and culture*. Toronto, Ontario, Canada: University of Toronto Press.

Berkowitz, L. (1962). *Aggression: A social psychological analysis*. New York: McGraw-Hill.

Berkowitz, L. (1968, September). Impulse, aggression, and the gun. *Psychology Today*, pp. 18–22.

Berkowitz, L. (1978). Whatever happened to the frustration-aggression hypothesis? *American Behavioral Scientist, 21*, 691–708.

Berkowitz, L. (1981, June). How guns control us. *Psychology Today*, pp. 11–12.

Berkowitz, L. (1983). Aversively simulated aggression. *American Psychologist, 38*, 1135–1144.

Berkowitz, L. (1987). Mood, self-awareness, and willingness to help. *Journal of Personality and Social Psychology, 52*, 721–729.

Berkowitz, L. (1988). Frustrations, appraisals, and aversively stimulated aggression. *Aggressive Behavior, 14*, 3–11.

Berkowitz, L. (1989). Frustration-aggression hypothesis: Examination and reformulation. *Psychological Bulletin, 106*, 59–73.

Berkowitz, L. (1993). *Aggression: Its causes, consequences, and control*. New York: McGraw-Hill.

Berkowitz, L., & Le Page, A. (1967). Weapons as aggression-eliciting stimuli. *Journal of Personality and Social Psychology, 7*, 202–207.

Berkowitz, L., & Troccoli, B. (1990). Feelings, direction of attention, and expressed evaluations of others. *Cognition and Emotion, 4*, 305–325.

Bernard, M. M., Maio, G. R., & Olson, J. M. (2003). The vulnerability of values to attack: Inoculation of values and value-relevant attitudes. *Personality and Social Psychology Bulletin, 29*, 63–75.

Berns, G. S., Chappelow, J., Zink, C. F., Pagnoni, G., Martin-Skurski, M. E., & Richards, J. (2005). Neurobiological correlates of social conformity and independence during mental rotation. *Biological Psychiatry, 58*, 245–253.

Berry, D. S. (1995). Beyond beauty and after affect: An event perception approach to perceiving faces. In R. A. Eder (Ed.), *Craniofacial anomalies: Psychological perspectives* (pp. 14–29). New York: Springer-Verlag.

Berry, J. W. (1967). Independence and conformity in subsistence-level societies. *Journal of Personality and Social Psychology, 7*, 415–418.

Berscheid, E. (1985). Interpersonal attraction. In G. Lindzey & E. Aronson (Eds.), *The handbook of social psychology* (3rd ed., Vol. 3, pp. 413–484). New York: McGraw-Hill.

Berscheid, E., Boye, D., & Walster, E. (1968). Retaliation as a means of restoring equity. *Journal of Personality and Social Psychology, 10*, 370–376.

Berscheid, E., & Meyers, S. A. (1996). A social categorical approach to a question about love. *Personal Relationships, 3*, 19–43.

Berscheid, E., & Meyers, S. A. (1997). The language of love: The difference a preposition makes. *Personality and Social Psychology Bulletin, 23*, 347–362.

Berscheid, E., & Peplau, L. A. (1983). The emerging science of relationships. In H. H. Kelley, E. Berscheid, A. Christensen, J. H. Harvey, T. L. Huston, G. Levinger, E. McClintock, L. A. Peplau, & D. R. Peterson (Eds.), *Close relationships* (pp. 1–19). New York: Freeman.

Berscheid, E., & Reis, H. T. (1998). Attraction and close relationships. In D. T. Gilbert, S. T. Fiske, & G. Lindzey (Eds.), *The handbook of social psychology* (4th ed., Vol. 2, pp. 193–281). New York: McGraw-Hill.

Berscheid, E., & Walster, E. (1978). *Interpersonal attraction*. Reading, MA: Addison-Wesley.

Bettencourt, B. A., & Miller, N. (1996). Gender differences in aggression as a function of provocation: A meta-analysis. *Psychological Bulletin, 119*, 422–447.

Bettencourt, B. A., & Sheldon, K. (2001). Social roles as mechanism for psychological need satisfaction within social groups. *Journal of Personality and Social Psychology, 81*, 1131–1143.

Bhanot, R., & Jovanovic, J. (2005). Do parents' academic gender stereotypes influence whether they intrude on their children's homework? *Sex Roles, 52*, 597–607.

Bickman, L. (1974). The social power of a uniform. *Journal of Applied Social Psychology, 4*, 47–61.

Biehl, M., Matsumoto, D., Ekman, P., Hearn, V., Heider, K., Kudoh, T., & Ton, V. (1997). Matsumoto and Ekman's Japanese and Caucasian facial expressions of emotion (JACFEE): Reliability and cross-national differences. *Journal of Nonverbal Behavior, 21*, 3–21.

Biek, M., Wood, W., & Chaiken, S. (1996). Working knowledge, cognitive processing, and attitudes: On the determinants of bias. *Personality and Social Psychology Bulletin, 22*, 547–556.

Biesanz, J. C., Neuberg, S. L., Smith, D. M., Asher, T., & Judice, T. N. (2001). When accuracy-motivated perceivers fail: Limited attentional resources and the reemerging self-fulfilling prophecy. *Personality and Social Psychology Bulletin, 27*, 621–629.

Bjork, J. M., Dougherty, D. M., Moeller, F. G., Cherek, D. R., & Swann, A. C. (1999). The effects of tryptophan depletion and loading on laboratory aggression in men: Time course and a food-restricted control. *Psychopharmacology, 142*, 24–30.

Blank, H., Musch, J., & Pohl, R. F. (2007). Hindsight bias: On being wise after the event. *Social Cognition, 25*, 1–9

Blank, P. D. (1993). Interpersonal expectations in the courtroom: Studying judges' and juries' behavior. In P. D. Blank (Ed.), *Interpersonal expectations: Theory, research, and applications* (pp. 64–87). New York: Cambridge University Press.

Blanton, H., Buunk, B. P., Gibbons, F. X., & Kuyper, H. (1999). When better-than-others compare upward: Choice of comparison and comparative evaluation as independent predictors of academic performance. *Journal of Personality and Social Psychology, 76*, 420–430.

Blanton, H., Pelham, B. W., De Hart, T., & Carvallo, M. (2001). Overconfidence as dissonance reduction. *Journal of Experimental Social Psychology, 37,* 373–385.

Blascovich, J., Ginsburg, G. P., & Veach, T. L. (1975). A pluralistic explanation of choice shifts on the risk dimension. *Journal of Personality and Social Psychology, 31,* 422–429.

Blascovich, J., Mendes, W. B., Hunter, S. B., & Salomon, K. (1999). Social "facilitation" as challenge and threat. *Journal of Personality and Social Psychology, 77,* 68–77.

Blass, T. (1991). Understanding behavior in the Milgram obedience experiment. *Journal of Personality and Social Psychology, 60,* 398–413.

Blass, T. (2000). *Obedience to authority: Current perspectives on the Milgram paradigm.* Mahwah, NJ: Erlbaum.

Blass, T. (2003). The Milgram paradigm after 35 years: Some things we now know about obedience to authority. *Journal of Applied Social Psychology, 29,* 955–978.

Blau, P. M. (1964). *Exchange and power in social life.* New York: Wiley.

Bless, H., Strack, F., & Walther, E. (2001). Memory as a target of social influence? Memory distortions as a function of social influence and metacognitive knowledge. In J. P. Forgas & W. D. Kipling (Eds.), *Social influence: Direct and indirect processes* (pp. 167–183). Philadelphia: Psychology Press.

Blittner, M., Goldberg, J., & Merbaum, M. (1978). Cognitive self-control factors in the reduction of smoking behavior. *Behavior Therapy, 9,* 553–561.

Bochner, S. (1994). Cross-cultural differences in the self-concept: A test of Hofstede's individualism/collectivism distinction. *Journal of Cross-Cultural Psychology, 25,* 273–283.

Bodenhausen, G. V. (1988). Stereotypic biases in social decision making and memory: Testing process models of stereotype use. *Journal of Personality and Social Psychology, 55,* 726–737.

Bodenhausen, G. V., & Wyer, R. S., Jr. (1985). Effects of stereotypes on decision making and information processing strategies. *Journal of Personality and Social Psychology, 48,* 267–282.

Bolger, N., & Amarel, D. (2007). Effects of social support visibility on adjustment to stress: Experimental evidence. *Journal of Personality and Social Psychology, 92,* 458–475.

Bolger, N., Zuckerman, A., & Kessler, R. C. (2000). Invisible support and adjustment to stress. *Journal of Personality and Social Psychology, 79,* 953–961.

Bonanno, G. (2005). Resilience in the face of potential trauma. *Current Directions in Psychological Science, 14,* 135–138.

Bonanno, G. A. (2004). Loss, trauma, and human resilience: Have we underestimated the human capacity to thrive after extremely aversive events. *American Psychologist, 59,* 20–28.

Bonanno, G. A., Moskowitz, J. T., Papa, A., & Folkman, S. (2005). Resilience to loss in bereaved spouses, bereaved parents, and bereaved gay men. *Journal of Personality and Social Psychology, 88,* 827–843.

Bonanno, G., & Mancini, A. (2008). The human capacity to thrive in the face of potential trauma. *Pediatrics, 121,* 369–375.

Bonanno, G., Boerner, K., & Wortman, C. (2008). Trajectories of grieving. In M. S. Stroebe, R. O. Hansson, H. Schut, W. Stroebe, & E. Van den Blink (Eds.), *Handbook of bereavement research and practice: Advances in theory and intervention* (pp. 287–307). Washington, DC: American Psychological Association.

Bond, C., & DePaulo, B. (2008). Individual differences in judging deception: Accuracy and bias. *Psychological Bulletin, 134,* 477–492.

Bond, C., Di Candia, C., & McKinnon, J. R. (1988). Response to violence in a psychiatric setting. *Personality and Social Psychology Bulletin, 14,* 448–458.

Bond, C. F., Jr., Atoum, A. O., & Van Leeuwen, M. D. (1996). Social impairment of complex learning in the wake of public embarrassment. *Basic and Applied Social Psychology, 18,* 31–44.

Bond, C. F. Jr., & DePaulo, B. M. (2006). Accuracy of deception judgments. *Personality and Social Psychology Review, 10,* 214–234.

Bond, C. F., Jr., & Titus, L. J. (1983). Social facilitation: A meta-analysis of 241 studies. *Psychological Bulletin, 94,* 264–292.

Bond, M. H. (Ed.). (1988). *The cross-cultural challenge to social psychology.* Newbury Park, CA: Sage.

Bond, M. H. (1991). Chinese values and health: A culture-level examination. *Psychology and Health, 5,* 137–152.

Bond, M. H. (1996). Chinese values. In M. H. Bond (Ed.), *The handbook of Chinese psychology* (pp. 208–226). Hong Kong: Oxford University Press.

Bond, R. (2005). Group size and conformity. *Group Processes and Intergroup Relations, 8,* 331–354.

Bond, R., & Smith, P. B. (1996). Culture and conformity: A meta-analysis of studies using Asch's (1952b, 1956) line judgment task. *Psychological Bulletin, 119,* 111–137.

Bonta, B. D. (1997). Cooperation and competition in peaceful societies. *Psychological Bulletin, 121,* 299–320.

Bornstein, R. F. (1989). Exposure and affect: Overview and meta-analysis of research, 1968–1987. *Psychological Bulletin, 106,* 265–289.

Bornstein, R. F., Leone, D. R., & Galley, D. J. (1987). The generalizability of subliminal mere exposure effects: Influence of stimuli perceived without awareness on social behavior. *Journal of Personality and Social Psychology, 53,* 1070–1079.

Borsari, B., & Carey, K. B. (2005). Descriptive and injunctive norms in college drinking: A meta-analytic integration. *Journal of Studies on Alcohol, 64,* 331–341.

Bourgeois, M. J., & Bowen, A. (2001). Self-organization of alcohol-related attitudes and beliefs in a campus housing complex: An initial investigation. *Health Psychology, 20,* 434–437.

Bower, G. H., & Hilgard, E. R. (1981). *Theories of learning* (15th ed.). Englewood Cliffs, NJ: Prentice Hall.

Bowlby, J. (1969). *Attachment and loss:* Vol. 1. *Attachment.* New York: Basic Books.

Bowlby, J. (1973). *Attachment and loss:* Vol. 2. *Separation: Anxiety and anger.* New York: Basic Books.

Bowlby, J. (1980). *Attachment and loss:* Vol. 3. *Loss.* New York: Basic Books.

Boyden, T., Carroll, J. S., & Maier, R. A. (1984). Similarity and attraction in homosexual males: The effects of age and masculinity-femininity. *Sex Roles, 10,* 939–948.

Bradbury, T. N., & Fincham, F. D. (1991). A contextual model for advancing the study of marital relationships. In G. J. O. Fletcher & F. D. Fincham (Eds.), *Cognition in close relationships* (pp. 127–147). Hillsdale, NJ: Erlbaum.

Bradfield, A., & Wells, G. L. (2005). Not the same old hindsight bias: Outcome information distorts a broad range of retrospective judgments. *Memory & Cognition, 33,* 120–130.

Brandon, R., & Davies, C. (1973). *Wrongful imprisonment: Mistaken convictions and their consequences.* London: Allen & Unwin.

Brannon, L. A., & Brock, T. C. (1994). The subliminal persuasion controversy. In S. Shavitt & T. C. Brock (Eds.), *Persuasion: Psychological insights and perspectives* (pp. 279–293). Needham Heights, MA: Allyn & Bacon.

Branscombe, N. R., Owen, S., Garstka, T. A., & Coleman, J. (1996). Rape and accident counterfactuals: Who might have done otherwise, and would it have changed the outcome? *Journal of Applied Social Psychology, 26,* 1042–1067.

Branscombe, N. R., & Wann, D. L. (1992). Physiological arousal and reactions to outgroup members during competitions that implicate an important social identity. *Aggressive Behavior, 18,* 85–93.

Breckler, S. J., & Wiggins, E. C. (1989). On defining attitude and attitude theory: Once more with feeling. In A. R. Pratkanis, S. J. Breckler, &

A. G. Greenwald (Eds.), *Attitude structure and function* (pp. 407–427). Hillsdale, NJ: Erlbaum.

Brehm, J. W. (1956). Postdecision changes in the desirability of alternatives. *Journal of Abnormal and Social Psychology, 52,* 384–389.

Brehm, J. W. (1966). *A theory of psychological reactance.* New York: Academic Press.

Brehm, J. W., & Cohen, A. R. (1962). *Explorations in cognitive dissonance.* New York: Wiley.

Brewer, M. B. (1979). In-group bias in the minimal intergroup situation: A cognitive-motivational analysis. *Psychological Bulletin, 86,* 307–324.

Brewer, M. B., & Brown, R. J. (1998). Intergroup relations. In D. T. Gilbert, S. T. Fiske, & G. Lindzey (Eds.), *The handbook of social psychology* (4th ed., Vol. 2, pp. 554–594). New York: McGraw-Hill.

Brewer, M. B., & Gardner, W. L. (1996). Who is this "we"? Levels of collective identity and self-representations. *Journal of Personality and Social Psychology, 71,* 83–93.

Brewer, M. B., & Miller, N. (1984). Beyond the contact hypothesis: Theoretical perspectives on desegregation. In N. Miller & M. B. Brewer (Eds.), *Groups in contact: The psychology of desegregation* (pp. 281–302). New York: Academic Press.

Brewer, N., & Weber, N. (2008). Eyewitness confidence and latency: Indices of memory processes not just markers of accuracy. *Applied Cognitive Psychology, 22,* 827–840.

Brewer, N., & Wells, G. L. (2006). The confidence-accuracy relationship in eyewitness identification: Effects of lineup instructions, foil similarity, and target-absent base rates. *Journal of Experimental Psychology: Applied, 12,* 11–30.

Bridgeman, D. L. (1981). Enhanced role taking through cooperative interdependence: A field study. *Child Development, 52,* 1231–1238.

Bridges, F. S., & Coady, N. P. (1996). Affiliation, urban size, urgency, and cost of responses to lost letters. *Psychological Reports, 79,* 775–780.

Brigham, J., Bennett, L., Meissner, C., & Mitchell, T. (2007). The influence of race on eyewitness memory. In R. C. L. Lindsay, D. F. Ross, D. J. Read, & M. P. Toglia (Eds.). *The handbook of eyewitness psychology*, Vol II: *Memory for people* (pp. 257–281). Mahwah, NJ: Erlbaum.

Bringle, R. G. (2005). Designing interventions to promote civic engagement. In A. M. Omoto (Ed.), *Processes of community change and social action* (pp. 167–187). Mahwah, NJ: Erlbaum.

Brinson, L., & Robinson, E. (1991). The African-American athlete: A psychological perspective. In L. Diamant (Ed.), *Psychology of sports, exercise, and fitness* (pp. 249–259). New York: Hemisphere.

Brislin, R. (1993). *Understanding culture's influence on behavior.* Fort Worth, TX: Harcourt Brace.

Brodsky, S. L. (2004). Ingratiation. In S. L. Brodsky (Ed.), *Coping with cross-examination and other pathways to effective testimony* (pp. 134–137). Washington, DC: American Psychological Association.

Brooke, J. (2000, January 20). Canada proposes scaring smokers with pictures on the packs. New York Times on the Web, *www.nytimes.com*

Brooks, A. (2006). *Who really cares? The surprising truth about compassionate conservatism.* New York: Basic Books.

Brophy, J. E. (1983). Research on the self-fulfilling prophecy and teacher expectations. *Journal of Educational Psychology, 75,* 631–661.

Brown, R. (1965). *Social psychology.* New York: Free Press.

Brown, R. (1986). *Social psychology* (2nd ed.). New York: Free Press.

Brown, R. P., & Pinel, E. C. (2002). Stigma on my mind: Individual differences in the experience of stereotype threat. *Journal of Experimental Social Psychology, 39,* 626–633.

Brown, S. L., Nesse, R. M., & Vinokur, A D. (2003). Providing social support may be more beneficial than receiving it: Results from a prospective study of mortality. *Psychological Science, 14,* 320–327.

Brucks, W., & Van Lange, P. (2008). No control, no drive: How noise may undermine conservation behavior in a commons dilemma. *European Journal of Social Psychology, 38,* 810–822.

Bruschke, J., & Loges, W. E. (2004). *Free press vs. fair trials: Examining publicity's role in trial outcomes.* Mahwah, NJ: Erlbaum.

Buchmann, C., & DiPrete, T. (2006). The growing female advantage in college completion: The role of family background and academic achievement. *American Sociological Review, 71*(4), 515–541

Buckhout, R. (1974). Eyewitness testimony. *Scientific American, 231,* 23–31.

Buehler, R., & Griffin, D. W. (1994). Change-of-meaning effects in conformity and dissent: Observing construal processes over time. *Journal of Personality and Social Psychology, 67,* 984–996.

Buehler, R., Griffin, D. W., & Ross, M. (2002). Inside the planning fallacy: The causes and consequences of optimistic time preferences. In T. Gilovich, D. W. Griffin, & D. Kahneman (Eds.), *Heuristics and biases: The psychology of intuitive judgment* (pp. 250–270). New York: Cambridge University Press.

Bugliosi, V. T. (1997). *Outrage: The five reasons why O. J. Simpson got away with murder.* New York: Dell.

Bui, K.-V. T., Peplau, L. A., & Hill, C. T. (1996). Testing the Rusbult model of relationship commitment and stability in a 15-year study of hetereosexual couples. *Personality and Social Psychology Bulletin, 22,* 1244–1257.

Buller, D. J. (2005). *Adapting minds: Evolutionary psychology and the persistent quest for human nature.* Cambridge, MA: MIT Press.

Bunch, S. (2004). Hunger 2004: Are we on track to end hunger? Bread for the World Institute. Retrieved on June 21, 2006 from: *www.bread.org/learn/hunger-reports/hunger-report-pdfs/hunger-report-2004/Exectuive-Summary.pdf*

Burger, J. M. (1981). Motivational biases in the attribution of responsibility for an accident: A meta-analysis of the defensive-attribution hypothesis. *Psychological Bulletin, 90,* 496–512.

Burleson, B. R. (1994). Friendship and similarities in social-cognitive and communicative abilities: Social skill bases of interpersonal attraction in childhood. *Personal Relationships, 1,* 371–389.

Burleson, B. R., & Samter, W. (1996). Similarity in the communication skills of young adults: Foundations of attraction, friendship, and relationship satisfaction. *Communication Reports, 9,* 127–139.

Burns, J. M. (1978). *Leadership.* New York: Harper & Row.

Burnstein, E., Crandall, C. S., & Kitayama, S. (1994). Some neo-Darwinian decision rules for altruism: Weighing cues for inclusive fitness as a function of the biological importance of the decision. *Journal of Personality and Social Psychology, 67,* 773–789.

Burnstein, E., & Sentis, K. (1981). Attitude polarization in groups. In R. E. Petty, T. M. Ostrom, & T. C. Brock (Eds.), *Cognitive responses in persuasion* (pp. 197–216). Hillsdale, NJ: Erlbaum.

Burnstein, E., & Vinokur, A. (1977). Persuasive argumentation and social comparison as determinants of attitude polarization. *Journal of Experimental Social Psychology, 13,* 315–332.

Burnstein, E., & Worchel, P. (1962). Arbitrariness of frustration and its consequences for aggression in a social situation. *Journal of Personality, 30,* 528–540.

Busby, L. J. (1975). Defining the sex-role standard in commercial network television programming directed at children. *Journalism Quarterly, 51,* 690–696.

Busey, T. A., Tunnicliff, J., Loftus, G. R. & Loftus, E. F. (2000). Accounts of the confidence-accuracy relation in recognition memory. *Psychonomic Bulletin and Review, 7,* 26–48.

Bush sought 'way' to invade Iraq? (2004, Jan. 11). Retrieved on March 8, 2006, from *www.cbsnews.com/stories/2004/01/09/60minutes/main592330.shtml*

Bushman, B. J. (1993). Human aggression while under the influence of alcohol and other drugs: An integrative research review. *Current Directions in Psychological Science, 2,* 148–152.

Bushman, B. J. (1997). Effects of alcohol on human aggression: Validity of proposed explanations. In M. Galanter (Ed.), *Recent developments in alcoholism:* Vol. 13. *Alcohol and violence: Epidemiology, neurobiology, psychology, family issues* (pp. 227–243). New York: Plenum.

Bushman, B. J. (2002). Does venting anger feed or extinguish the flame? Catharsis, rumination, distraction, anger, and aggressive responding. *Personality and Social Psychology Bulletin, 28,* 724–731.

Bushman, B. J., & Anderson, C. A. (in press). Comfortably numb: Desensitizing effects of violent media on helping others. *Psychological Science.*

Bushman, B. J., & Bonacci, A. M. (2002). Violence and sex impair memory for television ads. *Journal of Applied Psychology, 87,* 557–564.

Bushman, B. J., & Cooper, H. M. (1990). Alcohol and human aggression: An integrative research review. *Psychological Bulletin, 107,* 341–354.

Bushman, B. J., Ridge, R. D., Das, E., Key, C. W., & Busath, G. L. (2007). When God sanctions killing: The effect of scriptural violence on aggression., *Psychological Science, 18*(3), 204–207.

Buss D. (2005) *The handbook of evolutionary psychology.* New Jersey: John Wiley & Sons.

Buss, D. M. (1985). Human mate selection. *American Scientist, 73,* 47–51.

Buss, D. M. (1988a). The evolution of human intrasexual competition. *Journal of Personality and Social Psychology, 54,* 616–628.

Buss, D. M. (1988b). Love acts: The evolutionary biology of love. In R. J. Sternberg & M. L. Barnes (Eds.), *The psychology of love* (pp. 110–118). New Haven, CT: Yale University Press.

Buss, D. M. (1989). Sex differences in human mate preferences: Evolutionary hypotheses tested in 37 cultures. *Behavioral and Brain Sciences, 12,* 1–49.

Buss, D. M. (1995). Evolutionary psychology: A new paradigm for psychological science. *Psychological Inquiry, 6,* 1–30.

Buss, D. M. (1996a). The evolutionary psychology of human social strategies. In E. T. Higgins & A. W. Kruglanski (Eds.), *Social psychology: Handbook of basic principles* (pp. 3–38). New York: Guilford Press.

Buss, D. M. (1996b). Sexual conflict: Evolutionary insights into feminism and the "battle of the sexes." In D. M. Buss & N. M. Malamuth (Eds.), *Sex, power, conflict: Evolutionary and feminist perspectives* (pp. 296–318). New York: Oxford University Press.

Buss, D. M. (2004). *Evolutionary psychology: The new science of the mind,* 2nd ed. Boston: Allyn & Bacon.

Buss, D. M. (Ed.). (2005). *The handbook of evolutionary psychology.* Hoboken, NJ: Wiley.

Buss, D. M., Abbott, M., Angleitner, A., Biaggio, A., Blanco-Villasenor, A., Bruchon-Schweitzer, M., et al. (1990). International preferences in selecting mates: A study of 37 cultures. *Journal of Cross-Cultural Psychology, 21,* 5–47.

Buss, D. M., & Barnes, M. L. (1986). Preferences in human mate selection. *Journal of Personality and Social Psychology, 50,* 559–570.

Buss, D. M., & Kenrick, D. T. (1998). Evolutionary social psychology. In D. T. Gilbert, S. T. Fiske, & G. Lindzey (Eds.), *The handbook of social psychology* (4th ed., Vol. 2, pp. 982–1026). New York: McGraw-Hill.

Buss, D. M., Larsen, R. J., Westen, D., & Semmelroth, J. (1992). Sex differences in jealousy: Evolution, physiology, and psychology. *Psychological Science, 3,* 251–255.

Buss, D. M., & Schmitt, D. P. (1993). Sexual strategies theory: An evolutionary perspective on human mating. *Psychological Bulletin, 100,* 204–232.

Buss, D. M., & Shackelford, T. K. (1997). From vigilance to violence: Mate retention tactics in married couples. *Journal of Personality and Social Psychology, 72,* 346–361.

Buston, P. M., & Emlem, S. T. (2003). Cognitive processes underlying human mate choice: The relationship between self-perception and mate preference in Western society. *Proceedings of the National Academy of Sciences, 100,* 8805–8810.

Butler, D., & Geis, F. L. (1990). Nonverbal affect responses to male and female leaders: Implications for leadership evaluations. *Journal of Personality and Social Psychology, 58,* 48–59.

Buunk, A., & Gibbons, F. (2007). Social comparison: The end of a theory and the emergence of a field. *Organizational Behavior and Human Decision Processes, 102,* 3–21.

Buunk, B. P., Oldersma, F. L., & de Dreu, C. K. W. (2001). Enhancing satisfaction through downward comparison: The role of relational discontent and individual differences in social comparison orientation. *Journal of Experimental Social Psychology, 37,* 452–467.

Buunk, B. P., & Schaufeli, W. B. (1999). Reciprocity in interpersonal relationships: An evolutionary perspective on its importance for health and well-being. In W. Stroebe & M. Hewstone (Eds.), *European Review of Social Psychology* (Vol. 10, pp. 259–291). New York: Wiley.

Buunk, B. P., & Van Yperen, N. W. (1991). Referential comparisons, relational comparisons, and exchange orientation: Their relation to marital satisfaction. *Personality and Social Psychology Bulletin, 17,* 709–717.

Byrne, D. (1997). An overview (and underview) of research and theory within the attraction paradigm. *Journal of Social and Personal Relationships, 14,* 417–431.

Byrne, D., & Clore, G. L. (1970). A reinforcement model of evaluative processes. *Personality, 1,* 103–128.

Byrne, D., & Nelson, D. (1965). Attraction as a linear function of positive reinforcement. *Journal of Personality and Social Psychology, 1,* 659–663.

Cacioppo, J. T. (1998). Somatic responses to psychological stress: The reactivity hypothesis. In M. Sabourin & F. Craik (Eds.), *Advances in psychological science: Biological and cognitive aspects* (Vol. 2, pp. 87–112). Hove, England: Psychology Press.

Cacioppo, J. T., Berntson, G. G., Malarkey, W. B., Kiecolt-Glaser, J. K., Sheridan, J. F., Poehlmann, K. M., Burleson, M. H., Ernst, J. M., Hawkley, L. C., & Glaser, R. (1998). Autonomic, neuroendocrine, and immune responses to psychological stress: The reactivity hypothesis. In S. M. McCann & J. M. Lipton (Eds.), *Annals of the New York Academy of Sciences* (Vol. 840, pp. 664–673). New York: New York Academy of Sciences.

Cacioppo, J. T., Petty, R. E., Feinstein, J., & Jarvis, B. (1996). Dispositional differences in cognitive motivation: The life and times of individuals low versus high in need for cognition. *Psychological Bulletin, 119,* 197–253.

Cafri, G., & Thompson, J. K. (2004). Measuring male body image: A review of the current methodology. *Psychology of Men and Masculinity, 5,* 18–29.

Cafri, G., Thompson, J. K., Ricciardelli, L., McCabe, M., Smolak, L., & Yesalis, C. (2005). Pursuit of the muscular ideal: Physical and psychological consequences and putative risk factors. *Clinical Psychology Review, 25,* 215–239.

Calder, B. J., & Staw, B. M. (1975). Self-perception of intrinsic and extrinsic motivation. *Journal of Personality and Social Psychology, 31,* 599–605.

Caldwell, M., & Peplau, L. A. (1982). Sex differences in same-sex friendship. *Sex Roles, 8,* 721–732.

Calvert, J. D. (1988). Physical attractiveness: A review and reevaluation of its role in social skill research. *Behavioral Assessment, 10,* 29–42.

Camille, N., Coricelli, G., Sallet, J., Pradat-Diehl, P., Duhamel, J., & Sirigu, A. (2004). The involvement of the orbitofrontal cortex in the experience of regret. *Science, 304,* 1167–1170.

Campbell, A. (2002). *A mind of her own.* New York: Oxford University Press.

Campbell, D. T. (1967). Stereotypes and the perception of group differences. *American Psychologist, 22,* 817–829.

Campbell, D. T., & Stanley, J. C. (1967). *Experimental and quasi-experimental designs for research*. Chicago: Rand McNally.

Campbell, E. Q., & Pettigrew, T. F. (1959). Racial and moral crisis: The role of Little Rock ministers. *American Journal of Sociology, 64*, 509–516.

Campbell, J. D., & Fairey, P. J. (1989). Informational and normative routes to conformity: The effect of faction size as a function of norm extremity and attention to the stimulus. *Journal of Personality and Social Psychology, 57*, 457–468.

Campbell, J., & Stasser, G. (2006). The influence of time and task demonstrability on decision-making in computer-mediated and face-to-face groups. *Small Group Research, 37*, 271–294.

Campbell, L., Simpson, J. A., Boldry, J., & Kashy, D. A. (2005). Perceptions of conflict and support in romantic relationships: The role of attachment anxiety. *Journal of Personality and Social Psychology, 88*, 510–531.

Canary, D. J., & Stafford, L. (2001). Equity in the preservation of personal relationships. In J. Harvey & A. Wenzel (Eds.), *Close romantic relationships: Maintenance and enhancement* (pp. 133–151). Mahwah, NJ: Erlbaum.

Cannon, W. B. (1932). *The wisdom of the body*. New York: Norton.

Cannon, W. B. (1942). "Voodoo" death. *American Anthropologist, 44*, 169–181.

Cantor, J., Bushman, B. J., Huesmann, L. R., Groebel, J., Malamuth, N. M., Impett, E. A., Donnerstein, E., & Smith, S. (2001). Some hazards of television viewing: Fears, aggression, and sexual attitudes. In D. G. Singer & J. L. Singer (Eds.), *Handbook of children and the media* (pp. 207–307). Thousand Oaks, CA: Sage.

Cantril, H. (1940). *The invasion from Mars: A study in the psychology of panic*. New York: Harper & Row.

Caporael, L. R., & Brewer, M. B. (2000). Metatheories, evolution, and psychology: Once more with feeling. *Psychological Inquiry, 11*, 23–26.

Carey, B. (2006, February 14). "In music, others' tastes may help shape your own." *New York Times*, p. D7.

Carey, K. B., & Carey, M. P. (1993). Changes in self-efficacy resulting from unaided attempts to quit smoking. *Psychology of Addictive Behaviors, 7*, 219–224.

Carli, L. L. (1999). Cognitive reconstruction, hindsight, and reactions to victims and perpetrators. *Personality and Social Psychology Bulletin, 25*, 966–979.

Carli, L. L., & Eagly, A. H. (1999). Gender effects on social influence and emergent leadership. In G. N. Powell (Ed.), *Handbook of gender and work* (pp. 203–222). Thousand Oaks, CA: Sage.

Carlier, I. V. E., Voerman, A. E., & Gersons, B. P. R. (2000). The influence of occupational debriefing on post-traumatic stress symptomatology in traumatized police officers. *British Journal of Medical Psychology, 73*, 87–98.

Carlsmith, J. M., & Anderson, C. A. (1979). Ambient temperature and the occurrence of collective violence: A new analysis. *Journal of Personality and Social Psychology, 37*, 337–344.

Carlsmith, K. M., Darley, J. M., & Robinson, P. H. (2002). Why do we punish? Deterrence and just deserts as motives for punishment. *Journal of Personality and Social Psychology, 83*, 284–299.

Carlson, M., Charlin, V., & Miller, N. (1988). Positive mood and helping behavior: A test of six hypotheses. *Journal of Personality and Social Psychology, 55*, 211–229.

Carlson, M., & Miller, N. (1987). Explanation of the relationship between negative mood and helping. *Psychological Bulletin, 102*, 91–108.

Carnevale, P. J. (1986). Strategic choice in mediation. *Negotiation Journal, 2*, 41–56.

Carpenter, J. (2008, February 9). Agony of Japan's Diana. *Express*, p. 38.

Carpenter, S. (2000, December). Why do "they all look alike"? *Monitor on Psychology*, pp. 44–45.

Carr, J. L., & VanDeusen, K. M. (2004). Risk factors for male sexual aggression on college campuses. *Journal of Family Violence, 19*, 279–289.

Carroll, J. R. (2003, August 26). Proponents push for more graphic cigarette label warnings in U.S. Retrieved on December 28, 2005, from www.usatoday.com/news/health/2003-08-26-tobacco-gns_x.htm

Carter, B. (2000, August 24). "CBS is surprise winner in ratings contest." *New York Times*, p. A22.

Carter, B. (2003, May 19). Even as executives scorn the genre, TV networks still rely on reality. *New York Times*, pp. C1, C7.

Cartwright, D. (1979). Contemporary social psychology in historical perspective. *Social Psychology Quarterly, 42*, 82–93.

Cartwright, D., & Zander, A. (Eds.). (1968). *Group dynamics: Research and theory* (3rd ed.). New York: Harper & Row.

Caruso, E. (2008). Use of experienced retrieval ease in self and social judgments. *Journal of Experimental Social Psychology, 44*, 148–155.

Carver, C. S. (2003). Self-awareness. In M. R. Leary & J. P. Tangney (Eds.), *Handbook of self and identity* (pp. 179–196). New York: Guilford Press.

Carver, C. S., De Gregorio, E., & Gillis, R. (1980). Ego-defensive attribution among two categories of observers. *Personality and Social Psychology Bulletin, 6*, 4–50.

Carver, C. S., & Scheier, M. (2003). Optimism. In S. J. Lopez & C. R. Snyder (Eds.), *Positive psychological assessment: A handbook of models and measures* (pp. 75–89). Washington DC: American Psychological Association.

Carver, C. S., & Scheier, M. F. (1981). *Attention and self-regulation: A control-theory approach to human behavior*. New York: Springer-Verlag.

Carver, C. S., & Scheier, M. F. (1998). *On the self-regulation of behavior*. New York: Cambridge University Press.

Caselman, T., (2007). *Teaching children empathy*. New York: YouthLight.

Caspi, A., & Harbener, E. S. (1990). Continuity and change: Assortive marriage and the consistency of personality in adulthood. *Journal of Personality and Social Psychology, 58*, 250–258.

Catalyst. (2008). *Catalyst Expanding Opportunities for Women and Business*. Retrieved on September 3, 2008, from www.catalyst.org/publication/132/us-women-in-business.

Cervone, D., & Peake, P. (1986). Anchoring, efficacy, and action: The influence of judgmental heuristics on self-efficacy judgments and behavior. *Journal of Personality and Social Psychology, 50*, 492–501.

Chaiken, S. (1980). Heuristic versus systematic information processing and the use of source versus message cues in persuasion. *Journal of Personality and Social Psychology, 39*, 752–766.

Chaiken, S. (1987). The heuristic model of persuasion. In M. P. Zanna, J. M. Olson, & C. P. Herman (Eds.), *Social influence: The Ontario Symposium* (Vol. 5, pp. 3–39). Hillsdale, NJ: Erlbaum.

Chaiken, S., & Baldwin, M. W. (1981). Affective-cognitive consistency and the effect of salient behavioral information on the self-perception of attitudes. *Journal of Personality and Social Psychology, 41*, 1–12.

Chaiken, S., Wood, W., & Eagly, A. H. (1996). Principles of persuasion. In E. T. Higgins & A. W. Kruglanski (Eds.), *Social psychology: Handbook of basic principles* (pp. 702–742). New York: Guilford Press.

Chan, D. K.-S., & Cheng, G. H.-L. (2004). A comparison of offline and online friendship qualities at different stages of relationship development. *Journal of Personal and Social Relationships, 21*, 305–320.

Chang, C., & Chen, J. (1995). Effects of different motivation strategies on reducing social loafing. *Chinese Journal of Psychology, 37*, 71–81.

Chapman, G. B., & Johnson, E. J. (2002). Incorporating the irrelevant: Anchors in judgments of belief and value. In T. Gilovich, D. W. Griffin, & D. Kahneman (Eds.), *Heuristics and biases: The psychology of intuitive judgment* (pp. 120–138). New York: Cambridge University Press.

Charman, S., & Wells, G. (2007). Applied lineup theory. *The handbook of eyewitness psychology*, Vol II: *Memory for people* (pp. 219–254). Mahwah, NJ: Erlbaum.

Charman, S., & Wells, G. (2008). Can eyewitnesses correct for external influences on their lineup identifications? The actual/counterfactual assessment paradigm. *Journal of Experimental Psychology: Applied, 14*, 5–20.

Chassin, L., Presson, C. G., & Sherman, S. J. (1990). Social psychological contributions to the understanding and prevention of adolescent cigarette smoking. *Personality and Social Psychology Bulletin, 16*, 133–151.

Check, J. V., & Malamuth, N. M. (1983). Sex role stereotyping and reactions to depictions of stranger versus acquaintance rape. *Journal of Personality and Social Psychology, 45*, 344–356.

Chemers, M. M. (2000). Leadership research and theory: A functional integration. *Group Dynamics: Theory, Research, and Practice, 4*, 27–43.

Chemers, M. M., Watson, C. B., & May, S. T. (2000). Dispositional affect and leadership effectiveness: A comparison of self-esteem, optimism, and efficacy. *Personality and Social Psychology Bulletin, 26*, 267–277.

Chen, M., & Bargh, J. A. (1997). Nonconscious behavioral confirmation processes: The self-fulfilling consequences of automatic stereotype activation. *Journal of Experimental Social Psychology, 33*, 541–560.

Chen, N. Y., Shaffer, D. R., & Wu, C. H. (1997). On physical attractiveness stereotyping in Taiwan: A revised sociocultural perspective. *Journal of Social Psychology, 137*, 117–124.

Chen, S., & Andersen, S. M. (1999). Relationships from the past in the present: Significant-other representations and transference in interpersonal life. In M. P. Zanna (Ed.), *Advances in experimental social psychology* (Vol. 31, pp. 123–190). San Diego, CA: Academic Press.

Chen, S., & Chaiken, S. (1999). The heuristic-systematic model in its broader context. In S. Chaiken & Y. Trope (Eds.), *Dual-process theories in social psychology* (pp. 73–96). New York: Guilford Press.

Cheung, F. M., Leung, K., Fang, R. M., Song, W. Z., Zhang, J. X., & Zhang, J. P. (1996). Development of the Chinese Personality Assessment Inventory (CPAI). *Journal of Cross-Cultural Psychology, 27*, 181–199.

Chida, Y., & Hamer, M. (2008). Chronic psychosocial factors and acute physiological responses to laboratory-induced stress in healthy populations: A quantitative review of 30 years of investigations. *Psychological Bulletin, 134*, 829–885.

Chin, J., & Schooler, J. (2008). Why do words hurt? Content, process, and criterion shift accounts of verbal overshadowing. *European Journal of Cognitive Psychology, 20*, 396–413.

Chiu, C., Morris, M. W., Hong, Y., & Menon, T. (2000). Motivated cultural cognition: The impact of implicit cultural theories on dispositional attribution varies as a function of need for closure. *Journal of Personality and Social Psychology, 78*, 247–259.

Choi, I., Dalal, R., Kim-Prieto, C., & Park, H. (2003). Culture and judgment of causal relevance. *Journal of Personality and Social Psychology, 84*, 46–59.

Choi, I., & Nisbett, R. E. (1998). Situational salience and cultural differences in the correspondence bias and in the actor-observer bias. *Personality and Social Psychology Bulletin, 24*, 949–960.

Choi, I., Nisbett, R. E., & Norenzayan, A. (1999). Causal attribution across cultures: Variation and universality. *Psychological Bulletin, 125*, 47–63.

Christensen, L. (1988). Deception in psychological research: When is its use justified? *Personality and Social Psychology Bulletin, 14*, 664–675.

Christensen, P. N., Rothgerber, H., Wood, W., & Matz, D. C. (2004). Social norms and identity relevance: A motivational approach to normative behavior. *Personality and Social Psychology Bulletin, 30*, 1295–1309.

Cialdini, R. B. (1993). *Influence: Science and practice* (3rd ed.). New York: HarperCollins.

Cialdini, R. B. (2000). *Influence: Science and practice* (4th ed.). Boston: Allyn & Bacon.

Cialdini, R. B. (2003). Crafting normative messages to protect the environment. *Current Directions in Psychological Science, 12*, 105–109.

Cialdini, R. B., Borden, R. J., Thorne, A., Walker, M. R., Freeman, S., & Sloan, L. R. (1976). Basking in reflected glory: Three (football) field studies. *Journal of Personality and Social Psychology, 34*, 366–375.

Cialdini, R. B., Brown, S. L., Lewis, B. P., Luce, C., & Neuberg, S. L. (1997). Reinterpreting the empathy-altruism relationship: When one into one equals oneness. *Journal of Personality and Social Psychology, 73*, 481–494.

Cialdini, R. B., Cacioppo, J. T., Basset, R., & Miller, J. (1978). Low-ball procedure for producing compliance: Commitment, then cost. *Journal of Personality and Social Psychology, 36*, 463–476.

Cialdini, R. B., & Fultz, J. (1990). Interpreting the negative mood-helping literature via "mega"-analysis: A contrary view. *Psychological Bulletin, 107*, 210–214.

Cialdini, R. B., & Goldstein, N. J. (2004). Social influence: Compliance and conformity. *Annual Review of Psychology, 55*, 591–621.

Cialdini, R. B., Kallgren, C. A., & Reno, R. R. (1991). A focus theory of normative conduct: A theoretical refinement and reevaluation of the role of norms in human behavior. In M. P. Zanna (Ed.), *Advances in experimental social psychology* (Vol. 24, pp. 201–234). San Diego, CA: Academic Press.

Cialdini, R. B., Reno, R. R., & Kallgren, C. A. (1990). A focus theory of normative conduct: Recycling the concept of norms to reduce littering in public places. *Journal of Personality and Social Psychology, 58*, 1015–1026.

Cialdini, R. B., Schaller, M., Houlihan, D., Arps, K., Fultz, J., & Beaman, A. L. (1987). Empathy-based helping: Is it selflessly or selfishly motivated? *Journal of Personality and Social Psychology, 52*, 749–758.

Cialdini, R. B., & Trost, M. R. (1998). Social influence: Social norms, conformity, and compliance. In D. T. Gilbert, S. T. Fiske, & G. Lindzey (Eds.), *The handbook of social psychology* (4th ed., Vol. 2, pp. 151–192). New York: McGraw-Hill.

Clark, K., & Clark, M. (1947). Racial identification and preference in Negro children. In T. M. Newcomb & E. L. Hartley (Eds.), *Readings in social psychology* (pp. 169–178). New York: Holt.

Clark, M. S. (1984). Record keeping in two types of relationships. *Journal of Personality and Social Psychology, 47*, 549–577.

Clark, M. S. (1986). Evidence of the effectiveness of manipulations of communal and exchange relationships. *Personality and Social Psychology Bulletin, 12*, 414–425.

Clark, M. S., & Grote, N. K. (1998). Why aren't indices of relationship costs always negatively related to indices of relationship quality? *Personality and Social Psychology Review, 2*, 2–17.

Clark, M. S., & Isen, A. M. (1982). Toward understanding the relationship between feeling states and social behavior. In A. H. Hastorf & A. M. Isen (Eds.), *Cognitive social psychology* (pp. 73–108). New York: Elsevier.

Clark, M. S., Mills, J., & Corcoran, D. M. (1989). Keeping track of needs and inputs of friends and strangers. *Personality and Social Psychology Bulletin, 15*, 533–542.

Clark, R., Anderson, N. B., Clark, V. R., & Williams, D. R. (1999). Racism as a stressor for African Americans. *American Psychologist, 54*, 805–816.

Clark, R. D., III, & Maass, A. (1988). The role of social categorization and perceived source credibility in minority influence. *European Journal of Social Psychology, 18*, 347–364.

Clark, R. D., III, & Word, L. E. (1972). Why don't bystanders help? Because of ambiguity? *Journal of Personality and Social Psychology, 24*, 392–400.

Clark, S. E. (2005). A re-examination of the effects of biased lineup instructions in eyewitness identification. *Law and Human Behavior, 29*, 575–604.

Clary, E. G., Snyder, M., Ridge, R. D., Miene, P. K., & Haugen, J. A. (1994). Matching messages to motives in persuasion: A functional approach to promoting volunteerism. *Journal of Applied Social Psychology, 24,* 1129–1149.

Clayton, S., & Opotow, S. (2003). Justice and identity: Changing perspectives on what is fair. *Personality and Social Psychology Review, 7,* 298–310.

Cline, V. B., Croft, R. G., & Courrier, S. (1973). Desensitization of children to television violence. *Journal of Personality and Social Psychology, 27,* 360–365.

Coats, E. (1998, March 20). Bystander intervention [E-mail response to G. Mumford, Tobacco update]. Retrieved from *www.stolaf.edu/cgi-bin/mailarchivesearch.pl?directory=/home/www/people/huff/SPSP&listname=archive98*

Cochran, J. L., & Rutten, T. (1998). *Journey to justice.* New York: Ballantine Books.

Cohen, A. R. (1962). An experiment on small rewards for discrepant compliance and attitude change. In J. W. Brehm & A. R. Cohen (Eds.), *Explorations in cognitive dissonance* (pp. 73–78). New York: Wiley.

Cohen, D., Hoshino-Browne, E., & Leung, A. (2007). Culture and the structure of personal experience: Insider and outsider phenomenologies of the self and social world. In M. P. Zanna (Ed.), *Advances in experimental social psychology* (Vol 39, pp. 1–67). San Diego, CA: Elsevier Academic Press.

Cohen, D., & Nisbett, R. E. (1996). *Culture of honor: The psychology of violence in the South.* Boulder, CO: Westview Press.

Cohen, D., Nisbett, R. E., Bowdle, B. F., & Schwarz, N. (1996). Insult, aggression, and the southern culture of honor: An "experimental ethnography." *Journal of Personality and Social Psychology, 70,* 945–960.

Cohen, J. (2001, January 18). On the Internet, love really is blind. *New York Times,* pp. E1, E7.

Cohen, R. (1997, October 31). AH-lo-ween: An American holiday in Paris? *New York Times,* pp. A1; A4.

Cohen, S., Alper, C., Doyle, W., Adler, N., Treanor, J., & Turner, R. (2008). Objective and subjective socioeconomic status and susceptibility to the common cold. *Health Psychology, 27,* 268–274.

Cohen, S., Evans, G. W., Krantz, D. S., Stokols, D., & Kelly, S. (1981). Aircraft noise and children: Longitudinal and cross-sectional evidence on adaptation to noise and the effectiveness of noise abatement. *Journal of Personality and Social Psychology, 40,* 331–345.

Cohen, S., Mermelstein, R., Kamarack, T., & Hoberman, H. (1985). Measuring the functional components of social support. In I. G. Sarason & B. R. Sarason (Eds.), *Social support: Theory, research, and applications* (pp. 73–94). The Hague, Netherlands: Martines Nijhoff.

Cohen, S., Tyrrell, D. A. J., & Smith, A. P. (1991). Psychological stress in humans and susceptibility to the common cold. *New England Journal of Medicine, 325,* 606–612.

Cohen, S., Tyrrell, D. A. J., & Smith, A. P. (1993). Negative life events, perceived stress, negative affect, and susceptibility to the common cold. *Journal of Personality and Social Psychology, 64,* 131–140.

Cohen, T. R., & Insko, C. A. (2008). War and peace: Possible approaches to reducing intergroup conflict. *Perspectives on Psychological Science, 3,* 87–93.

Cohen-Kettenis, P. T., & Van Goozen, S. H. M. (1997). Sex reassignment of adolescent transsexuals: A follow-up study. *Journal of the American Academy of Child and Adolescent Psychiatry, 36,* 263–271.

Cohn, L. D., & Adler, N. E. (1992). Female and male perceptions of ideal body shapes. *Psychology of Women Quarterly, 16,* 69–79.

Coie, J. D., Cillessen, A. H. N., Dodge, K. A., Hubbard, J. A., Schwartz, D., Lemerise, E. D., & Bateman, H. (1999). It takes two to fight: A test of relational factors and a method for assessing aggressive dyads. *Developmental Psychology, 35,* 1179–1188.

Colligan, M. J., Pennebaker, J. W., & Murphy, L. R. (Eds.). (1982). *Mass psychogenic illness: A social psychological analysis.* Hillsdale, NJ: Erlbaum.

Collins, B. E., & Brief, D. E. (1995). Using person-perception vignette methodologies to uncover the symbolic meanings of teacher behaviors in the Milgram paradigm. *Journal of Social Issues, 51,* 89–106.

Collins, N. L., & Feeney, B. C. (2000). A safe haven: An attachment theory perspective on support seeking and caregiving in intimate relationships. *Journal of Personality and Social Psychology, 78,* 1053–1073.

Collins, N. L., & Feeney, B. C. (2004a). An attachment theory perspective on closeness and intimacy. In D. J. Mashek & A. Aron (Eds.), *Handbook of closeness and intimacy* (pp. 163–187). Mahwah, NJ: Lawrence Erlbaum Associates.

Collins, N. L., & Feeney, B. C. (2004b). Working models of attachment shape perceptions of social support: Evidence from experimental and observational studies. *Journal of Personality and Social Psychology, 87,* 363–383.

Collins, N. L., Ford, M. B., Guichard, A. C., & Allard, L. M. (2006). Working models of attachment and attribution processes in intimate relationships. *Personality and Social Psychology Bulletin, 32,* 201–219.

Collins, W. A., & Sroufe, L. A. (1999). Capacity for intimate relationships: A developmental construction. In W. Furman, C. Feiring, & B. B. Brown (Eds.), *Contemporary perspectives on adolescent romantic relationships.* New York: Cambridge University Press.

Conway, L. G. III, & Schaller, M. (2005). When authorities' commands backfire: Attributions about consensus and effects on deviant decision making. *Journal of Personality and Social Psychology, 89,* 311–326.

Cook, K., & Rice, E. (2003). Social exchange theory. In J. Delamater (Ed.), *Handbook of social psychology* (pp. 53–76). New York: Kluwer Academic/Plenum.

Cook, S. W. (1984). Cooperative interaction in multiethnic contexts. In N. Miller & M. B. Brewer (Eds.), *Groups in contact: The psychology of desegregation.* New York: Academic Press.

Cook, S. W. (1985). Experimenting on social issues: The case of school desegration. *American Psychologist, 40,* 452–460.

Cooke, R., & Sheeran, P. (2004). Moderation of cognition-intention and cognition-behaviour relations: A meta-analysis of properties of variables from the theory of planned behaviour. *British Journal of Social Psychology, 43,* 159–186.

Cooley, C. H. (1902). *Human nature and social order.* New York: Scribners.

Cooper, J. (1980). Reducing fears and increasing assertiveness: The role of dissonance reduction. *Journal of Experimental Social Psychology, 47,* 738–748.

Correll, J., Park, B., Judd, C., Wittenbrink, B., Sadler, M., & Keesee, T. (2007). Across the thin blue line: Police officers and racial bias in the decision to shoot. *Journal of Personality and Social Psychology, 92,* 1006–1023.

Correll, J., Park, B., Judd, C. M., & Wittenbrink, B. (2002). The police officer's dilemma: Using ethnicity to disambiguate potentially threatening individuals. *Journal of Personality and Social Psychology, 83,* 1314–1329.

Cosmides, L., & Tooby, J. (1992). Cognitive adaptations for social exchange. In J. H. Barkow, L. Cosmides, & J. Tooby (Eds.), *The adapted mind: Evolutionary psychology and the generation of culture* (pp. 163–228). New York: Oxford University Press.

Costanzo, M., & Archer, D. (1989). Interpreting the expressive behavior of others: The interpersonal perceptions task. *Journal of Nonverbal Behavior, 13,* 223–245.

Cottrell, N. B., Wack, K. L., Sekerak, G. J., & Rittle, R. (1968). Social facilitation in dominant responses by the presence of an audience and the mere presence of others. *Journal of Personality and Social Psychology, 9,* 245–250.

Courage, M. L., Edison, S. C., & Howe, M. L. (2004). Variability in the early development of visual self-recognition. *Infant Behavior and Development, 27,* 509–532.

Cousins, S. D. (1989). Culture and self-perception in Japan and the United States. *Journal of Personality and Social Psychology, 56,* 124–131.

Crandall, C. S. (1988). Social contagion of binge eating. *Journal of Personality and Social Psychology, 55,* 588–598.

Crandall, C. S., D'anello, S., Sakalli, N., Lazarus, E., Wieczorkowska, G., & Feather, N. T. (2001). An attribution-value model of prejudice: Anti-fat attitudes in six nations. *Personality and Social Psychology Bulletin, 27,* 30–37.

Crandall, C. S., & Eshleman, A. (2003). A justification-suppression model of the expression and experience of prejudice. *Psychological Bulletin, 129*(3), 414–446.

Crandall, C. S., & Greenfield, B. S. (1986). Understanding the conjunction fallacy: A conjunction of effects? *Social Cognition, 4,* 408–419.

Crocker, J., & Major, B. (1989). Social stigma and self-esteem: The self-protective properties of stigma. *Psychological Review, 96,* 608–630.

Cropper, C. M. (1998, February 26). Nowhere to hide: Ads crop up in unlikely places. New York Times on the Web, *www.nytimes.com*

Crosby, F., Bromley, S., & Saxe, L. (1980). Recent unobtrusive studies of black and white discrimination and prejudice: A literature review. *Psychological Bulletin, 87,* 546–563.

Cross, S. E., Bacon, P. L., & Morris, M. L. (2000). The relational-interdependent self-construal and relationships. *Journal of Personality and Social Psychology, 78,* 791–808.

Cross, S. E., & Madson, L. (1997). Models of the self: Self-construals and gender. *Psychological Bulletin, 122,* 5–37.

Crowley, A. E., & Hoyer, W. D. (1994). An integrative framework for understanding two-sided persuasion. *Journal of Consumer Research, 20,* 561–574.

Croyle, R. T., & Jemmott, J. B., III. (1990). Psychological reactions to risk factor testing. In J. A. Skelton & R. T. Croyle (Eds.), *The mental representation of health and illness* (pp. 121–157). New York: Springer-Verlag.

Crutchfield, R. A. (1955). Conformity and character. *American Psychologist, 10,* 191–198.

Csikszentmihalyi, M. (1997). *Finding flow*. New York: Basic Books.

Csikszentmihalyi, M., & Figurski, T. J. (1982). Self-awareness and aversive experience in everyday life. *Journal of Personality, 50,* 15–28.

Cunningham, M. R. (1986). Measuring the physical in physical attractiveness: Quasi-experiments on the sociobiology of female facial beauty. *Journal of Personality and Social Psychology, 50,* 925–935.

Cunningham, M. R., Barbee, A. P., & Pike, C. L. (1990). What do women want? Facialmetric assessment of multiple motives in the perception of male facial physical attractiveness. *Journal of Personality and Social Psychology, 59,* 61–72.

Cunningham, M. R., Roberts, A. R., Barbee, A. P., Druen, P. B., & Wu, C. (1995). "Their ideas of beauty are, on the whole, the same as ours": Consistency and variability in the cross-cultural perception of female physical attractiveness. *Journal of Personality and Social Psychology, 68,* 261–279.

Curtis, R. C., & Miller, K. (1986). Believing another likes or dislikes you: Behaviors making the beliefs come true. *Journal of Personality and Social Psychology, 51,* 284–290.

Curtiss, S. (1977). *Genie: A psycholinguistic study of a modern-day "wild child."* New York: Academic Press.

Cury, F., Da Fonseca, D., Zahn, I., & Elliot, A. (2008). Implicit theories and IQ test performance: A sequential mediation analysis. *Journal of Experimental Social Psychology, 44,* 783–791.

Cusumano, D. L., & Thompson, J. K. (1997). Body image and body shape ideals in magazines: Exposure, awareness, and internalization. *Sex Roles, 37,* 701–721.

Dabbs, J. M., Jr. (2000). *Heroes, rogues, and lovers*. New York: McGraw-Hill.

Dabbs, J. M., Jr., Carr, T. S., Frady, R. L., & Riad, J. K. (1995). Testosterone, crime, and misbehavior among 692 male prison inmates. *Personality and Individual Differences, 18,* 627–633.

Dabbs, J. M., Jr., Hargrove, M. F., & Heusel, C. (1996). Testosterone differences among college fraternities: Well-behaved vs. rambunctious. *Personality and Individual Differences, 20,* 157–161.

Dabbs, J. M., Jr., Ruback, R. B., Frady, R. L., Hopper, C. H., & Sgoutas, D. S. (1988). Saliva testosterone and criminal violence among women. *Personality and Individual Differences, 7,* 269–275.

Dalbert, C., & Yamauchi, L. A. (1994). Belief in a just world and attitudes toward immigrants and foreign workers: A cultural comparison between Hawaii and Germany. *Journal of Applied Social Psychology, 24,* 1612–1626.

Dallek, R. (2002, December). The medical ordeals of JFK. *Atlantic,* pp. 49–58.

Daniels, M., & Nelson, K. (2004, 20 August). In search of rush teens risk lives surfing on cars. *Boston Globe,* pp. B1, B4.

Darley, J. (2004). Social comparison motives in ongoing groups. In M. B. Brewer & M. Hewstone (Eds.), *Emotion and motivation* (pp. 281–297). Malden, MA: Blackwell.

Darley, J. M. (1992). Social organization for the production of evil. *Psychological Inquiry, 3,* 199–218.

Darley, J. M., & Akert, R. M. (1993). *Biographical interpretation: The influence of later events in life on the meaning of and memory for earlier events*. Unpublished manuscript, Princeton University.

Darley, J. M., & Batson, C. D. (1973). From Jerusalem to Jericho: A study of situational and dispositional variables in helping behavior. *Journal of Personality and Social Psychology, 27,* 100–108.

Darley, J. M., & Latané, B. (1968). Bystandar intervention in emergencies: Diffusion of responsibility. *Journal of Personality and Social Psychology, 8,* 377–383.

Darwin, C. R. (1859). *The origin of species*. London: Murray.

Darwin, C. R. (1872). *The expression of the emotions in man and animals*. London: Murray.

Davidson, A. R., & Jaccard, J. J. (1979). Variables that moderate the attitude-behavior relation: Results of a longitudinal survey. *Journal of Personality and Social Psychology, 37,* 1364–1376.

Davidson, L., & Duberman, L. (1982). Friendship: Communication and interactional patterns in same-sex dyads. *Sex Roles, 8,* 809–822.

Davidson, R., Putnam, K., & Larson, C. (2000). Dysfunction in the neural circuitry of emotion regulation: A possible prelude to violence. *Science, 289,* 591–594.

Davis, C. G., Lehman, D. R., Wortman, C. B., Silver, R. C., & Thompson, S. C. (1995). The undoing of traumatic life events. *Personality and Social Psychology Bulletin, 21,* 109–124.

Davis, D., & Loftus, E. F. (2007). Internal and external sources of misinformation in adult witness memory. In M. P. Toglia, J. D. Read, D. F. Ross, & R. C. L. Lindsay (Eds.) *The handbook of eyewitness psychology, Vol I: Memory for events* (pp. 195–237). Mahwah, NJ: Erlbaum.

Davis, D. D., & Harless, D. W. (1996). Group versus individual performance in a price-searching experiment. *Organizational Behavior and Human Decision Processes, 66,* 215–227.

Davis, K. E., & Jones, E. E. (1960). Changes in interpersonal perception as a means of reducing cognitive dissonance. *Journal of Abnormal and Social Psychology, 61,* 402–410.

Davis, M. H., & Stephan, W. G. (1980). Attributions for exam performance. *Journal of Applied Social Psychology, 10,* 235–248.

Davitz, J. (1952). The effects of previous training on post-frustration behavior. *Journal of Abnormal and Social Psychology, 47,* 309–315.

Dawes, R. M. (1980). Social dilemmas. *Annual Review of Psychology, 31,* 169–193.

Dawkins, R. (1976). *The selfish gene*. New York: Oxford University Press.

Dean, K. E., & Malamuth, N. M. (1997). Characteristics of men who aggress sexually and of men who imagine aggressing: Risk and moderating variables. *Journal of Personality and Social Psychology, 72,* 449–455.

Deaux, K., & Emsweiler, T. (1974). Explanations of successful performance of sex-linked tasks: What is skill for the male is luck for the female. *Journal of Personality and Social Psychology, 29,* 80–85.

Deaux, K., & La France, M. (1998). Gender. In D. T. Gilbert, S. T. Fiske, & G. Lindzey (Eds.), *The handbook of social psychology* (4th ed., Vol. 1, pp. 788–828). New York: McGraw-Hill.

Deaux, K., & Lewis, L. (1984). Structure of gender stereotypes: Interrelationships among components and gender label. *Journal of Personality and Social Psychology, 46,* 991–1004.

DeWall, C. N., & Baumeister, R. F. (2006). Alone but feeling no pain Effects of social exclusion on physical pain tolerance and pain threshold, affective forecasting, and interpersonal empathy. *Journal of Personality and Social Psychology, 91,* 1–15.

De Bono, K. G., & Snyder, M. (1995). Acting on one's attitudes: The role of a history of choosing situations. *Personality and Social Psychology Bulletin, 21,* 629–636.

Deci, E. L., Koestner, R., & Ryan, R. M. (1999a). A meta-analytic review of experiments examining the effects of extrinsic rewards. *Psychological Bulletin, 125,* 627–668.

Deci, E. L., Koestner, R., & Ryan, R. M. (1999b). The undermining effect is a reality after all—extrinsic rewards, task interest, and self-determination: Reply to Eisenberger, Pierce, and Cameron (1999) and Lepper, Henderlong, and Gingras (1999). *Psychological Bulletin, 125,* 692–700.

Deci, E. L., & Ryan, R. M. (1985). *Intrinsic motivation and self-determination in human behavior.* New York: Plenum.

De Dreu, C. K. W., & De Vries, N. K. (Eds.). (2001). *Group consensus and minority influence: Implications for innovation.* Oxford, England: Blackwell Publishers.

De Dreu, C., Beersma, B., Steinel, W., & Van Kleef, G. (2007). The psychology of negotiation: Principles and basic processes. In A. W. Kruglanski & E. T. Higgins (Eds.), *Social psychology: Handbook of basic principles* (2nd ed., pp. 608-629). New York: Guilford Press.

De Dreu, C., Nijstad, B., & van Knippenberg, D. (2008). Motivated information processing in group judgment and decision making. *Personality and Social Psychology Review, 12,* 22–49.

Deffenbacher, K. A., Bornstein, B. H., & Penrod, S. D. (2004). A meta-analytic review of the effects of high stress on eyewitness memory. *Law and Human Behavior, 28,* 687–706.

De Houwer, J., Thomas, S., & Baweyens, F. (2001). Associative learning of likes and dislikes: A review of 25 years of research on human evaluative conditioning. *Psychological Bulletin, 127,* 853–869.

De Marco, P. (1994, September 28). "Dear diary." *New York Times,* p. C2.

Dennett, D. C. (1991). *Consciousness explained.* Boston: Little, Brown.

De Paulo, B. M. (1992). Nonverbal behavior and self-presentation. *Psychological Bulletin, 111,* 203–243.

DePaulo, B. M., & Friedman, H. S. (1998). Nonverbal communication. In D. T. Gilbert, S. T. Fiske, & G. Lindzey (Eds.), *The handbook of social psychology* (vol. 2, 4th ed., pp. 3-40). New York: McGraw-Hill.

De Paulo, B. M., Kenny, D. A., Hoover, C. W., Webb, W., & Oliver, P. (1987). Accuracy of person perception: Do people know what kinds of impressions they convey? *Journal of Personality and Social Psychology, 52,* 303–315.

De Paulo, B. M., Lassiter, G. D., & Stone, J. I. (1983). Attentional determinants of success at detecting deception and truth. *Personality and Social Psychology Bulletin, 8,* 273–279.

De Paulo, B. M., Stone, J. L., & Lassiter, G. D. (1985). Deceiving and detecting deceit. In B. R. Schlenker (Ed.), *The self and social life* (pp. 323–370). New York: McGraw-Hill.

Deppe, R. K., & Harackiewicz, J. M. (1996). Self-handicapping and intrinsic motivation: Buffering intrinsic motivation from the threat of failure. *Journal of Personality and Social Psychology, 70,* 868–876.

Dershowitz, A. M. (1997). *Reasonable doubts: The criminal justice system and the O. J. Simpson case.* New York: Touchstone.

Derzon, J. H., & Lipsey, M. W. (2002). A meta-analysis of the effectiveness of mass communication for changing substance-use knowledge, attitudes, and behavior. In W. D. Crano & M. Burgoon (Eds.), *Mass media and drug prevention: Classic and contemporary theories and research* (pp. 231–258). Mahwah, NJ: Erlbaum.

Desmond, E. W. (1987, November 30). Out in the open. *Time,* pp. 80–90.

Desportes, J. P., & Lemaine, J. M. (1998). The sizes of human groups: An analysis of their distributions. In D. Canter, J. C. Jesuino, L. Soczka, & G. M. Stephenson (Eds.), *Environmental social psychology* (pp. 57–65). Dordrecht, Netherlands: Kluwer.

Deutsch, M. (1973). *The resolution of conflict: Constructive and destructive processes.* New Haven, CT: Yale University Press.

Deutsch, M. (1990). Cooperation, conflict, and justice. In S. A. Wheelan, E. A. Pepitone, & V. Abt (Eds.), *Advances in field theory* (pp. 149–164). Newbury Park, CA: Sage.

Deutsch, M. (1997, April). *Comments on cooperation and prejudice reduction.* Paper presented at the symposium Reflections on 100 Years of Social Psychology, Yosemite National Park, CA.

Deutsch, M., & Collins, M. E. (1951). *Interracial housing: A psychological evaluation of a social experiment.* Minneapolis: University of Minnesota Press.

Deutsch, M., & Gerard, H. G. (1955). A study of normative and informational social influence upon individual judgment. *Journal of Abnormal and Social Psychology, 51,* 629–636.

Deutsch, M., & Krauss, R. M. (1960). The effect of threat upon interpersonal bargaining. *Journal of Abnormal and Social Psychology, 61,* 181–189.

Deutsch, M., & Krauss, R. M. (1962). Studies of interpersonal bargaining. *Journal of Conflict Resolution, 6,* 52–76.

Devine, D. J., Clayton, L. D., Dunford, B. B., Seying, R., & Pryce, J. (2001). Jury decision making: 45 years of empirical research on deliberating groups. *Psychology, Public Policy, and Law, 7,* 622–727.

Devine, P. G. (1989a). Automatic and controlled processes in prejudice: The roles of stereotypes and personal beliefs. In A. R. Pratkanis, S. J. Breckler, & A. G. Greenwald (Eds.), *Attitude structure and function* (pp. 181–212). Hillsdale, NJ: Erlbaum.

Devine, P. G. (1989b). Stereotypes and prejudice: Their automatic and controlled components. *Journal of Personality and Social Psychology, 56,* 680–690.

Devine, P. G., & Elliot, A. (1995). Are racial stereotypes really fading? The Princeton trilogy revisited. *Personality and Social Psychology Bulletin, 21,* 1139–1150.

Devine, P. G., Plant, E. A., Amodio, D. M., Harmon-Jones, E., & Vance, S. L. (2002). The regulation of explicit and implicit race bias: The role of motivations to respond without prejudice. *Journal of Personality and Social Psychology, 82*(5), 835–848.

Devos-Comby, L., & Salovey, P. (2002). Applying persuasion strategies to alter HIV-relevant thoughts and behavior. *Review of General Psychology, 6,* 287–304.

De Waal, F. B. M. (1995, March). Bonobo sex and society: The behavior of a close relative challenges assumptions about male supremacy in human evolution. *Scientific American,* pp. 82–88.

De Waal, F. B. M. (1996). *Good natured: The origins of right and wrong in humans and other animals.* Cambridge, MA: Harvard University Press.

Dickerson, C., Thibodeau, R., Aronson, E., & Miller, D. (1992). Using cognitive dissonance to encourage water conservation. *Journal of Applied Social Psychology, 22,* 841–854.

Diener, E. (1980). Deindividuation: The absence of self-awareness and self-regulation in group members. In P. B. Paulus (Ed.), *Psychology of group influence* (pp. 209–242). Hillsdale, NJ: Erlbaum.

Diener, E., & Biswas-Diener, R. (2008). *Happiness: Unlocking the mysteries of psychological wealth.* Boston: Wiley-Blackwell.

Diener, E., & Oishi, S. (2005). The nonobvious social psychology of happiness. *Psychological Inquiry, 16,* 162–167.

Diener, E., & Seligman, M. E. P. (2004). Beyond money: Toward an economy of well-being. *Psychological Science in the Public Interest, 5*, 1–31.

Diener, E., & Wallbom, M. (1976). Effects of self-awareness on antinormative behavior. *Journal of Research in Personality, 10*, 107–111.

Dietz, P. D., & Evans, B. E. (1982). Pornographic imagery and prevalence of paraphilia. *American Journal of Psychiatry, 139*, 1493–1495.

Dijksterhuis, A. (2004). Think different: The merits of unconscious thought in preference development and decision making. *Journal of Personality and Social Psychology, 87*, 586–598.

Dijksterhuis, A., Aarts, H., & Smith, P. K. (2005). The power of the subliminal: On subliminal persuasion and other potential applications. In R. R. Hassin, J. S. Uleman, & J. A. Bargh (Eds.), *The new unconscious* (pp. 77–106). New York: Oxford University Press.

Dijksterhuis, A., & Aarts, H. (2002). *The power of the subliminal: On subliminal persuasion and other potential applications.* Unpublished manuscript.

Dijksterhuis, A., & Nordgren, L. F. (2005). A theory of unconscious thought. Vol. I, pp. 95–109. University of Amsterdam.

Dijksterhuis, A., & Nordgren, L. (2006). A theory of unconscious thought. *Perspectives on Psychological Science, 1*, 95–109.

Dijksterhuis, A., & van Knippenberg, A. (1996). The knife that cuts both ways: Facilitated and inhibited access to traits as a result of stereotype activation. *Journal of Experimental Social Psychology, 32*, 271–288.

Dill, J. C., & Anderson, C. A. (1995). Effects of frustration justification on hostile aggression. *Aggressive Behavior, 21*, 359–369.

Dillon, S. (2009, 23 January). Study sees an Obama effect as lifting black test-takers. *New York Times.*

Dion, K. K., & Dion, K. L. (1993). Individualistic and collectivistic perspectives on gender and the cultural context of love and intimacy. *Journal of Social Issues, 49*, 53–69.

Dion, K. K., & Dion, K. L. (1996). Cultural perspectives on romantic love. *Personal Relationships, 3*, 5–17.

Dion, K. L. (2000). Group cohesion: From "fields of forces" to multidimensional construct. *Group Dynamics, 4*, 7–26.

Dion, K. L., & Dion, K. K. (1988). Romantic love: Individual and cultural perspectives. In R. J. Sternberg & M. L. Barnes (Eds.), *The psychology of love* (pp. 264–289). New Haven, CT: Yale University Press.

Dion, K. L., & Dion, K. K. (1993). Gender and ethnocultural comparisons in styles of love. *Psychology of Women Quarterly, 17*, 463–473.

Dion, K., Berscheid, E., & Walster, E. (1972). What is beautiful is good. *Journal of Personality and Social Psychology, 24*, 285–290.

Dionne, E. J. Jr. (2005, June 21). How Cheney fooled himself. *Washington Post*, p. A21.

Dix, T. (1993). Attributing dispositions to children: An interactional analysis of attribution in socialization. *Personality and Social Psychology Bulletin, 19*, 633–643.

Dobbs, M. (2008, June 22). Cool crisis management? It's a myth. Ask JFK. *Washington Post*, pp. B1, B4.

Dodge, K. A., & Schwartz, D. (1997). Social information processing mechanisms in aggressive behavior. In D. M. Stoff & J. Breiling (Eds.), *Handbook of antisocial behavior* (pp. 171–180). New York: Wiley.

Dohrenwend, B. (2006). Inventorying stressful life events as risk factors for psychopathology: Toward resolution of the problem of intracategory variability. *Psychological Bulletin, 132*, 477–495.

Doi, T. (1988). *The anatomy of dependence.* New York: Kodansha International.

Dollard, J. (1938). Hostility and fear in social life. *Social Forces, 17*, 15–26.

Dollard, J., Doob, L., Miller, N., Mowrer, O. H., & Sears, R. R. (1939). *Frustration and aggression.* New Haven, CT: Yale University Press.

Domina, T., & Koch, K. (2002). Convenience and frequency of recycling: Implications for including textiles in curbside recycling programs. *Environment and Behavior, 34*, 216–238.

Donnerstein, E. (1980). Aggressive erotica and violence against women. *Journal of Personality and Social Psychology, 39*, 269–277.

Donnerstein, E., & Berkowitz, L. (1981). Victim reactions in aggressive erotic films as a factor in violence against women. *Journal of Personality and Social Psychology, 41*, 710–724.

Donnerstein, E., & Donnerstein, M. (1976). Research in the control of interracial aggression. In R. G. Green & E. C. O'Neal (Eds.), *Perspectives on aggression* (pp. 133–168). New York: Academic Press.

Donnerstein, E., & Linz, D. G. (1994). Sexual violence in the mass media. In M. Costanzo & S. Oskamp (Eds.), *Violence and the law* (pp. 9–36). Thousand Oaks, CA: Sage.

Donohue, J. & Wolfers, J. J. (2006). Uses and abuses of empirical evidence in the death penalty debate. *Stanford Law Review, 58*, 791–845.

Dovidio, J. F. (1984). Helping behavior and altruism: An empirical and conceptual overview. In L. Berkowitz (Ed.), *Advances in experimental social psychology* (Vol. 17, pp. 361–427). New York: Academic Press.

Dovidio, J. F., Evans, N., & Tyler, R. B. (1986). Racial stereotypes: The contents of their cognitive representations. *Journal of Experimental Social Psychology, 22*, 22–37.

Dovidio, J. F., & Gaertner, S. L. (1996). Affirmative action, unintentional racial biases, and intergroup relations. *Journal of Social Issues, 52*, 51–75.

Dovidio, J. F., Kawakami, K., & Gaertner, S. L. (2002). Implicit and explicit prejudice and interracial interaction. *Journal of Personality and Social Psychology, 82*, 62–68.

Dovidio, J. F., Piliavin, J. A., Gaertner, S. L., Schroeder, D. A., & Clark, R. D., III. (1991). The arousal cost-reward model and the process of intervention. In M. S. Clark (Ed.), *Review of personality and social psychology* (Vol. 12, pp. 86–118). Newbury Park, CA: Sage.

Dovidio, J. F., Piliavin, J. A., Schroeder, D. A., & Penner, L. A. (2006). *The social psychology of prosocial behavior.* Mahwah, NJ: Erlbaum.

Draper, R. (2008). *Dead certain.* New York: Free Press.

Drigotas, S. M., & Rusbult, C. E. (1992). Should I stay or should I go? A dependence model of breakups. *Journal of Personality and Social Psychology, 62*, 62–87.

Driving while black. (1999, March 15). *U.S. News and World Report*, p. 72.

Drought's growing reach: NCAR study points to global warming as key factor (2005). The National Center for Atmospheric Research. Retrieved on June 20, 2006, from: *www.ucar.edu/news/releases/2005/drought_research.shtml*

Drummond, T. (1999, June 14). It's not just in New Jersey: Cops across the nation often search people because of their race, a study says. *Time*, p. 61.

Duck, J., Hogg, M., & Terry, D. (1995). Me, us, and them: Political identification and the third-person effect in the 1993 Australian federal election. *European Journal of Social Psychology, 25*, 195–215.

Duck, S. W. (1982). A typography of relationship disengagement and dissolution. In S. W. Duck (Ed.), *Personal relationships 4: Dissolving personal relationships* (pp. 1–32). London: Academic Press.

Duck, S. W. (1994a). *Meaningful relationships: Talking, sense, and relating.* Thousand Oaks, CA: Sage.

Duck, S. W. (1994b). Stratagems, spoils, and a serpent's tooth: On the delights and dilemmas of personal relationships. In B. H. Spitzberg & W. Cupach (Eds.), *The dark side of interpersonal communication* (pp. 3–24). Hillsdale, NJ: Erlbaum.

Duck, S. W., & Pittman, G. (1994). Social and personal relationships. In M. L. Knapp & G. R. Miller (Eds.), *Handbook of interpersonal communication* (2nd ed., pp. 676–695). Thousand Oaks, CA: Sage.

Duke, the ex-Nazi who would be governor. (1991, November 10). *New York Times*, pp. 1, 26.

Dunbar, R., & Barrett, L. (Eds.). (2007). *Oxford handbook of evolutionary psychology.* New York: Oxford University Press.

Dunn, E., Aknin, L., & Norton, M. (2008). Spending money on others promotes happiness. *Science, 319*, 1687–1688.

Dunn, E. W., Wilson, T. D., & Gilbert, D. T. (2003). Location, location, location: The misprediction of satisfaction in housing lotteries. *Personality and Social Psychology Bulletin, 29,* 1421–1432.

Dunning, D., & Perretta, S. (2002). Automaticity and eyewitness accuracy: A 10- to 12-second rule for distinguishing accurate from inaccurate positive identifications. *Journal of Applied Psychology, 87,* 951–962.

Dunning, D., & Stern, L. B. (1994). Distinguishing accurate from inaccurate eyewitness identifications via inquiries about decision processes. *Journal of Personality and Social Psychology, 67,* 818–835.

Durik, A., & Harackiewicz, J. (2007). Different strokes for different folks: How individual interest moderates the effects of situational factors on task interest. *Journal of Educational Psychology, 99,* 597–610.

During blackout, fewer crimes than on a typical NYPD day. (2003, August 16). Retrieved from *www.wnbc.com/news/2409267/detail.html*

Dutton, D. G., & Aron, A. P. (1974). Some evidence for heightened sexual attraction under conditions of high anxiety. *Journal of Personality and Social Psychology, 30,* 510–517.

Duval, T. S., & Silvia, P. J. (2001). *Self-awareness and causal attributions: A dual-systems theory.* Boston: Kluwer Academic.

Duval, T. S., & Silvia, P. J. (2002). Self-awareness, probability of improvement, and the self-serving bias. *Journal of Personality and Social Psychology, 82,* 49–61.

Duval, T. S., & Wicklund, R. A. (1972). *A theory of objective self-awareness.* New York: Academic Press.

Dweck, C. S. (1999). *Self-theories: Their role in motivation, personality, and development.* Philadelphia: Psychology Press.

Dweck, C. S. (2006). *Mindset: The new psychology of success.* New York: Random House.

Dweck, C. S., Chiu, C., & Hong, Y. (1995). Implicit theories and their role in judgments and reactions: A world from two perspectives. *Psychological Inquiry, 6,* 267–285.

Eagly, A. H. (1987). *Sex differences in social behavior: A social-role interpretation.* Hillsdale, NJ: Erlbaum.

Eagly, A. H. (1994). On comparing women and men. *Feminism and Psychology, 4,* 513–522.

Eagly, A. H. (1995). The science and politics of comparing women and men. *American Psychologist, 50,* 145–158.

Eagly, A. H. (1996). Differences between women and men: Their magnitude, practical importance, and political meaning. *American Psychologist, 51,* 158–159.

Eagly, A. H., Ashmore, R. D., Makhijani, M. G., & Longo, L. C. (1991). What is beautiful is good, but . . .: A meta-analytic review of research on the physical attractiveness stereotype. *Psychological Bulletin, 110,* 109–128.

Eagly, A. H., & Chaiken, S. (1975). An attribution analysis of communicator characteristics on opinion change: The case of communicator attractiveness. *Journal of Personality and Social Psychology, 32,* 136–244.

Eagly, A. H., & Chaiken, S. (1993). *The psychology of attitudes.* Fort Worth, TX: Harcourt Brace.

Eagly, A. H., & Crowley, M. (1986). Gender and helping behavior: A meta-analytic review of the social psychological literature. *Psychological Bulletin, 100,* 283–308.

Eagly, A. H., & Diekman, A. B. (2003). The malleability of sex differences in response to changing social roles. In L. G. Aspinwall & U. M. Staudinger (Eds.), *A psychology of human strengths: Fundamental questions and future directions for a positive psychology* (pp. 103–115). Washington, D.C.: American Psychological Association.

Eagly, A. H., Diekman, A. B., Johannesen-Schmidt, M. C., & Koenig, A. M. (2004). Gender gaps in sociopolitical attitudes: A social psychological analysis. *Journal of Personality and Social Psychology, 87,* 796–816.

Eagly, A. H., Johannesen-Schmidt, M. C., & van Engen, M. L. (2003). Transformational, transactional, and laissez-faire leadership styles: A meta-analysis comparing women and men. *Psychological Bulletin, 129,* 569–591.

Eagly, A. H., & Karau, S. J. (2002). Role congruity theory of prejudice toward female leaders. *Psychological Review, 109,* 573–598.

Eagly, A. H., Karau, S. J., & Makhijani, M. G. (1995). Gender and the effectiveness of leaders: A meta-analysis. *Psychological Bulletin, 117,* 125–145.

Eagly, A. H., & Koenig, A. M. (2006). Social role theory of sex differences and similarities: Implication for prosocial behavior. In K. Dindia & D. J. Canary (Eds.), *Sex differences and similarities in communication* (2nd ed., pp. 161–177). Mahwah, NJ: Erlbaum.

Eagly, A. H., & Steffen, V. J. (1986). Gender and aggressive behavior: A meta-analytic review of the social psychological literature. *Psychological Bulletin, 100,* 309–330.

Eagly, A. H., & Steffen, V. J. (2000). Gender stereotypes stem from the distribution of women and men into social roles. In C. Stangor (Ed.), *Stereotypes and prejudice: Essential readings* (pp. 142–160). Philadelphia: Psychology Press.

Eagly, A. H., & Wood, W. (1991). Explaining sex differences in social behavior: A meta-analytic perspective. *Personality and Social Psychology Bulletin, 17,* 306–315.

Eargle, A., Guerra, N., & Tolan, P. (1994). Preventing aggression in inner-city children: Small group training to change cognitions, social skills, and behavior. *Journal of Child and Adolescent Group Therapy, 4,* 229–242.

Ebbesen, E., Duncan, B., & Konecni, V. (1975). Effects of content of verbal aggression: A field experiment. *Journal of Experimental and Social Psychology, 11,* 192–204.

Eberhardt, J. L., Goff, P. A., Purdie, V. J., & Davies, P. G. (2004). Seeing black: Race, crime, and visual processing. *Journal of Personality and Social Psychology, 87,* 876–893.

Educators for Social Responsibility. (2001). *About the Resolving Conflict Creatively Program.* Retrieved from *www.esrnational.org/about-rccp.html*

Edwards, H. (1973, July). The black athletes: 20th-century gladiators in white America. *Psychology Today,* pp. 43–52.

Edwards, K., & Smith, E. (1996). A disconfirmation bias in the evaluation of arguments. *Journal of Personality and Social Psychology, 71,* 5–24.

Egan, L. C, Santos, L. R., & Bloom, P. (2007). The origins of cognitive dissonance: Evidence from children and monkeys. *Psychological Science, 18,* 978–983.

Ehrlinger, J., Gilovich, T., & Ross, L. (2005). Peering into the bias blind spot: People's assessments of bias in themselves and others. *Personality and Social Psychology Bulletin, 31,* 680–692.

Eibl-Eibesfeldt, I. (1963). Aggressive behavior and ritualized fighting in animals. In J. H. Masserman (Ed.), *Science and psychoanalysis:* Vol. 6. *Violence and war* (pp. 8–17). New York: Grune & Stratton.

Eibl-Eibesfeldt, I. (1975). *Ethology: The biology of behavior.* New York: Holt, Rinehart & Winston.

Eisenberg, N., & Fabes, R. A. (1991). Prosocial behavior and empathy: A multimethod developmental perspective. In M. S. Clark (Ed.), *Review of personality and social psychology* (Vol. 12, pp. 34–61). Newbury Park, CA: Sage.

Eisenberg, N., Spinrad, T. L., & Sadovsky, A. (2006). Empathy-related responding in children. In M. Killen & J. G. Smetana (Eds.), *Handbook of moral development* (pp. 517–549). Mahwah, NJ: Erlbaum.

Eisenstat, S. A., & Bancroft, L. (1999). Domestic violence. *New England Journal of Medicine, 341,* 886–892.

Ekman, P. (1965). Communication through nonverbal behavior: A source of information about an interpersonal relationship. In S. S. Tomkins & C. E. Izard (Eds.), *Affect, cognition, and personality* (pp. 390–442). New York: Springer-Verlag.

Ekman, P. (1993). Facial expression and emotion. *American Psychologist, 48,* 384–392.

Ekman, P., & Davidson, R. J. (Eds.). (1994). *The nature of emotion: Fundamental questions*. New York: Oxford University Press.

Ekman, P., & Friesen, W. V. (1969). The repertoire of nonverbal behavior: Categories, origins, usage, and coding. *Semiotica, 1,* 49–98.

Ekman, P., & Friesen, W. V. (1971). Constants across cultures in the face and emotion. *Journal of Personality and Social Psychology, 17,* 124–129.

Ekman, P., & Friesen, W. V. (1975). *Unmasking the face*. Englewood Cliffs, NJ: Prentice Hall.

Ekman, P., Friesen, W. V., O'Sullivan, M., Chan, A., Diacoyanni-Tarlatzis, I., Heider, K., et al. (1987). Universals and cultural differences in the judgments of facial expressions of emotions. *Journal of Personality and Social Psychology, 53,* 712–717.

Ekman, P., O'Sullivan, M., & Matsumoto, D. (1991). Confusions about content in the judgment of facial expression: A reply to "Contempt and the relativity thesis." *Motivation and Emotion, 15,* 169–176.

Elfenbein, H. A., & Ambady, N. (2002). On the universality and cultural specificity of emotion recognition: A meta-analysis. *Psychological Bulletin, 128,* 203–235.

Ellin, A. (2000, September 17). Dad, do you think I look too fat? *New York Times,* p. 7.

Elliot, J. (1977). The power and pathology of prejudice. In P. Zimbardo & F. Ruch (Eds.), *Psychology and life* (9th ed.). Glenview, IL: Scott, Foresman.

Ellis, J. (2002). *Founding brothers*. New York: Vintage.

Ellis, A. P. J., Porter, C. O. L. H., & Wolverton, S. A. (2008). Learning to work together: An examination of transactive memory system development in teams. In V. I. Sessa & M. London (Eds.), *Work group learning: Understanding, improving and assessing how groups learn in organizations* (pp. 91–115). New York: Erlbaum.

Ellsworth, P. C. (1994). William James and emotion: Is a century of fame worth a century of misunderstanding? *Psychological Review, 101,* 222–229.

Ellsworth, P. C., & Mauro, R. (1998). Psychology and law. In D. T. Gilbert, S. T. Fiske, & G. Lindzey (Eds.), *The handbook of social psychology* (4th ed., Vol. 2, pp. 684–732). New York: McGraw-Hill.

Emery, N. J, & Clayton, N. S. (2005). Animal cognition. In. J. J. Bolhuis (Ed.), *Behavior of animals: Mechanisms, function, and evolution* (pp. 170–196). Malden, MA: Blackwell.

Englich, B., & Mussweiler, T. (2001). Sentencing under uncertainty: Anchoring effects in the courtroom. *Journal of Applied Social Psychology, 31,* 1535–1551.

Epley, E., & Huff, C. (1998). Suspicion, affective response, and education benefit as a result of deception in psychology research. *Personality and Social Psychology Bulletin, 24,* 759–768.

Epley, N., & Gilovich, T. (2004). Are adjustments insufficient? *Personality and Social Psychology Bulletin, 30,* 447–460.

Epley, N., & Gilovich, T. (2005). When effortful thinking influences judgmental anchoring: Differential effects of forewarning and incentives on self-generated and externally provided anchors. *Journal of Behavioral Decision Making, 18,* 199–212.

Eron, L. D. (1982). Parent-child interaction, television violence, and aggression of children. *American Psychologist, 37,* 197–211.

Eron, L. D. (1987). The development of aggressive behavior from the perspective of a developing behaviorism. *American Psychologist, 42,* 425–442.

Eron, L. D. (2001). Seeing is believing: How viewing violence alters attitudes and aggressive behavior. In A. C. Bohart & D. J. Stipek (Eds.), *Constructive and destructive behavior: Implications for family, school, and society* (pp. 49–60). Washington, DC: American Psychological Association.

Eron, L. D., Huesmann, L. R., Lefkowitz, M. M., & Walder, L. O. (1996). Does television violence cause aggression? In D. F. Greenberg (Ed.), *Criminal careers* (Vol. 2, pp. 311–321). Aldershot, England: Dartmouth.

Esser, J. K., & Lindoerfer, J. S. (1989). Groupthink and the space shuttle *Challenger* accident: Toward a quantitative case analysis. *Journal of Behavioral Decision Making, 2,* 167–177.

Estrada-Hollenbeck, M., & Heatherton, T. F. (1998). Avoiding and alleviating guilt through prosocial behavior. In J. Bybee (Ed.), *Guilt and children* (pp. 215–231). San Diego, CA: Academic Press.

European Commission. (2007). *Decision-making in the Top 50 Publicly Quoted Companies*. Retrieved September 3, 2008, from europa.eu.int/comm/employment_social/women_men_stats/out/measures_out438_en.htm.

Fabrigar, L. R., & Petty, R. E. (1999). The role of affective and cognitive bases of attitudes in susceptibility to affectively and cognitively based persuasion. *Personality and Social Psychology Bulletin, 25,* 363–381.

Fabrigar, L. R., Priester, J. R., Petty, R. E., & Wegener, D. T. (1998). The impact of attitude accessibility on elaboration of persuasive messages. *Personality and Social Psychology Bulletin, 24,* 339–352.

False Confessions (2006). Accessed on June 9, 2006, from: www.innocenceproject.org/causes/falseconfessions.php

Farhi, P. (2006, Jan. 21). Deluge shuts down post blog; ombudsman's column had sparked profane responses. *Washington Post* (p. A08).

Farhi, P. (2006, Jan. 21). Deluge shuts down Post blog. *Washington Post,* p. A08.

Fazio, R. H. (1990). Multiple processes by which attitudes guide behavior: The MODE model as an integrative framework. In M. P. Zanna (Ed.), *Advances in experimental social psychology* (Vol. 23, pp. 75–109). San Diego, CA: Academic Press.

Fazio, R. H., & Olson, M. A. (2003). Implicit measures in social cognition research: Their meaning and uses. *Annual Review of Psychology, 54,* 297–327.

Fazio, R. H., Jackson, J. R., Dunton, B. C., & Williams, C. J. (1995). Variability in automatic activation as an unobtrusive measure of racial attitudes: A bona fide pipeline? *Journal of Personality and Social Psychology, 69,* 1013–1027.

Federal Bureau of Investigation (2009). Headline archives Retrieved on march 10, 2009 from http://www.fbi.gov/page2/jan09/ucr_statistics011209.html.

Feeney, J. A., & Noller, P. (1990). Attachment style as a predictor of adult romantic relationships. *Journal of Personality and Social Psychology, 58,* 281–291.

Feeney, J. A., & Noller, P. (1996). *Adult attachment*. Thousand Oaks, CA: Sage.

Feeney, J. A., Noller, P., & Roberts, N. (2000). Attachment and close relationships. In C. Hendrick & S. S. Hendrick (Eds.), *Close relationships: A sourcebook* (pp. 185–201). Thousand Oaks, CA: Sage.

Feeney, M. (2005, October 25). Rosa Parks, civil rights icon, dead at 92. *Boston Globe,* pp. A1, B8.

Fehr, B. (1994). Prototype-based assessment of laypeople's views of love. *Personal Relationships, 1,* 309–331.

Fehr, B. (2001). The life cycle of friendship. In C. Hendrick & S. S. Hendrick (Eds.), *Close relationships: A sourcebook* (pp. 71–82). Thousand Oaks, CA: Sage.

Fehr, B., & Russell, J. A. (1991). The concept of love viewed from a prototype perspective. *Journal of Personality and Social Psychology, 60,* 425–438.

Fein, S., McCloskey, A. L., & Tomlinson, T. M. (1997). Can the jury disregard that information? The use of suspicion to reduce the prejudicial effects of pretrial publicity and inadmissable testimony. *Personality and Social Psychology Bulletin, 23,* 1215–1226.

Feingold, A. (1990). Gender differences in effects of physical attractiveness on romantic attraction: A comparison across five research paradigms. *Journal of Personality and Social Psychology, 59,* 981–993.

Feingold, A. (1992a). Gender differences in mate selection preferences: A test of the parental investment model. *Psychological Bulletin, 112,* 125–139.

Feingold, A. (1992b). Good-looking people are not what we think. *Psychological Bulletin, 111*, 304–341.

Feld, S. L. (1982). Social structural determinants of similarity among associates. *American Sociological Review, 47*, 797–801.

Feldman-Summers, S., & Kiesler, S. B. (1974). Those who are number two try harder: The effect of sex on attributions of causality. *Journal of Personality and Social Psychology, 38*, 846–855.

Femlee, D. H. (1995). Fatal attractions: Affection and disaffection in intimate relationships. *Journal of Social and Personal Relationships, 12*, 295–311.

Femlee, D. H. (1998a). "Be careful what you wish for . . .": A quantitative and qualitative investigation of "fatal attractions." *Personal Relationships, 5*, 235–253.

Femlee, D. H. (1998b). Fatal attractions: Contradictions in intimate relationships. In J. H. Harvey (Ed.), *Perspectives on loss: A sourcebook* (pp. 113–124). Philadelphia: Brunner/Mazel.

Femlee, D. H., Sprecher, S., & Bassin, E. (1990). The dissolution of intimate relationships: A hazard model. *Social Psychology Quarterly, 53*, 13–30.

Fenigstein, A., Scheier, M. F., & Buss, A. H. (1975). Public and private self-consciousness: Assessment and theory. *Journal of Consulting and Clinical Psychology, 43*, 522–527.

Fernald, J. L. (1995). Interpersonal heterosexism. In B. Lott & D. Maluso (Eds.), *The social psychology of interpersonal discrimination* (pp. 80–117). New York: Guilford Press.

Ferris, T. (1997, April 14). The wrong stuff. *New Yorker*, p. 32.

Feshbach, N. D. (1978, March). *Empathy training: A field study in affective education*. Paper presented at the meetings of the American Educational Research Association, Toronto, Ontario, Canada.

Feshbach, N. D. (1989). Empathy training and prosocial behavior. In J. Groebel & R. A. Hinde (Eds.), *Aggression and war: Their biological and social bases* (pp. 101–111). New York: Cambridge University Press.

Feshbach, N. D. (1997). Empathy—the formative years: Implications for clinical practice. In A. C. Bohart & L. S. Greenberg (Eds.), *Empathy reconsidered: New directions in psychotherapy* (pp. 33–59). Washington, DC: American Psychological Association.

Feshbach, N. D., & Feshbach, S. (1969). The relationship between empathy and aggression in two age groups. *Developmental Psychology, 1*, 102–107.

Feshbach, S. (1971). Dynamics and morality of violence and aggression: Some psychological considerations. *American Psychologist, 26*, 281–292.

Festinger, L. (1954). A theory of social comparison processes. *Human Relations, 7*, 117–140.

Festinger, L. (1957). *A theory of cognitive dissonance*. Stanford, CA: Stanford University Press.

Festinger, L., & Aronson, E. (1960). The arousal and reduction of dissonance in social contexts. In D. Cartwright & A. Zander (Eds.), *Group dynamics* (pp. 214–231). Evanston, IL: Row & Peterson.

Festinger, L., & Carlsmith, J. M. (1959). Cognitive consequences of forced compliance. *Journal of Abnormal and Social Psychology, 58*, 203–211.

Festinger, L., & Maccoby, N. (1964). On resistance to persuasive communications. *Journal of Abnormal and Social Psychology, 68*, 359–366.

Festinger, L., Riecken, H. W., & Schachter, S. (1956). *When prophecy fails*. Minneapolis: University of Minnesota Press.

Festinger, L., Schachter, S., & Back, K. (1950). *Social pressures in informal groups: A study of human factors in housing*. New York: Harper.

Festinger, L., & Thibaut, J. (1951). Interpersonal communication in small groups. *Journal of Abnormal and Social Psychology, 46*, 92–99.

Fiedler, F. (1967). *A theory of leadership effectiveness*. New York: McGraw-Hill.

Fiedler, F. (1978). The contingency model and the dynamics of the leadership process. In L. Berkowitz (Ed.), *Advances in experimental social psychology* (Vol. 11, pp. 59–112). Orlando, FL: Academic Press.

Fiedler, K. (2000). Illusory correlations: A simple associative algorithm provides a convergent account of seemingly divergent paradigms. *Review of General Psychology, 4*, 25–58.

Fiedler, K., Walther, E., & Nickel, S. (1999). Covariation-based attribution: On the ability to assess multiple covariations of an effect. *Personality and Social Psychology Bulletin, 25*, 607–622.

Fincham, F. D., Bradbury, T. N., Arias, I., Byrne, C. A., & Karney, B. R. (1997). Marital violence, marital distress, and attributions. *Journal of Family Psychology, 11*, 367–372.

Fine, G. A., & Elsbach, K. D. (2000). Ethnography and experiment in social psychological theory building: Tactics for integrating qualitative field data with quantitative lab data. *Journal of Experimental Social Psychology, 36*, 51–76.

Fink, B., & Penton-Voak, I. (2002). Evolutionary psychology of facial attractiveness. *Current Directions in Psychological Science, 11*, 154–158.

Finney, P. D. (1987). When consent information refers to risk and deception: Implications for social research. *Journal of Social Behavior and Personality, 2*, 37–48.

Fischer, R., & Chalmers, A. (2008). Is optimism universal? A meta-analytical investigation of optimism levels across 22 nations. *Personality and Individual Differences, 45*, 378–382.

Fischhoff, B. (2007). An early history of hindsight research. *Social Cognition, 25*, 10–13.

Fishbein, M., Chan, D., O'Reilly, K., Schnell, D., Wood, R., Beeker, C., & Cohn, C. (1993). Factors influencing gay men's attitudes, subjective norms, and intentions with respect to performing sexual behaviors. *Journal of Applied Social Psychology, 23*, 417–438.

Fisher, J. D., & Fisher, W. A. (2000). Theoretical approaches to individual-level changes in HIV risk behavior. In J. L. Peterson & C. C. DiClemente (Eds.), *Handbook of HIV prevention* (pp. 3-55). New York: Kluwer Academic/Plenum Press.

Fisher, R. P., & Schreiber, N. (2007). Interview protocols to improve eyewitness memory. In M. P. Toglia, J. D. Read, D. F. Ross, & R. C. L. Lindsay (Eds.) *The handbook of eyewitness psychology*, Vol I: *Memory for events* (pp. 53–80). Mahwah, NJ: Erlbaum.

Fisher, W. A., & Barak, A. (2001). Internet pornography: A social psychological perspective on Internet sexuality. *Journal of Sex Research, 38*, 312–323.

Fiske, S. T. (1989b). *Interdependence and stereotyping: From the laboratory to the Supreme Court (and back)*. Address presented at the annual meeting of the American Psychological Association, New Orleans.

Fiske, S. T., & Depret, E. (1996). Control, interdependence, and power: Understanding social cognition in its social context. *European Review of Social Psychology, 7*, 31–61.

Fiske, S. T., & Taylor, S. E. (1991). *Social cognition* (2nd ed.). New York: McGraw-Hill.

Flanagan, C. A., Bowes, J. M., Jonsson, B., Csapo, B., & Sheblanova, E. (1998). Ties that bind: Correlates of adolescents' civic commitments in seven countries. *Journal of Social Issues, 54*, 457–475.

Fletcher, G. J. O., Reeder, G. D., & Bull, V. (1990). Bias and accuracy in attitude attribution: The role of attributional complexity. *Journal of Experimental Social Psychology, 26*, 275–288.

Fletcher, G. J. O., & Ward, C. (1988). Attribution theory and processes: A cross-cultural perspective. In M. H. Bond (Ed.), *The cross-cultural challenge to social psychology* (pp. 230–244). Newbury Park, CA: Sage.

Flowers, M. L. (1977). A lab test of some implications of Janis's groupthink hypothesis. *Journal of Personality and Social Psychology, 35*, 888–897.

Fointiat, V., Grosbras, J-M., Michel, S., & Somat, A. (2001). Encouraging young adults to drive carefully. The use of the hypocrisy paradigm. *Promoting Public Health*, Chambery (France), May, 10–12.

Folkman, S., & Moskowitz, J. T. (2000). The context matters. *Personality and Social Psychology Bulletin, 26*, 150–151.

Forer, B. R. (1949). The fallacy of personal validation: A classroom demonstration of gullibility. *Journal of Abnormal and Social Psychology, 44*, 118–123.

Forgas, J. P. (1995). Mood and judgment: The Affect Infusion Model (AIM). *Psychological Bulletin, 117*, 39–66.

Forgas, J. P., & Bower, G. H. (1987). Mood effects on person-perception judgments. *Journal of Personality and Social Psychology, 53*, 53–60.

Förster, J., Liberman, N., & Friedman, R. (2007). Seven principles of goal activation: A systematic approach to distinguishing goal priming from priming of non-goal constructs. *Personality and Social Psychology Review, 11*(3), 211–233.

Forster, J., Liberman, N., & Higgins, E. T. (2005). Accessibility from active and fulfilled goals. *Journal of Experimental Social Psychology, 41*, 220–239.

Forsterling, F. (1989). Models of covariation and attribution: How do they relate to the analogy of analysis of variance? *Journal of Personality and Social Psychology, 57*, 615–625.

Forsyth, D. R. (2000). One hundred years of group research: Introduction to the special issue. *Group Dynamics, 4*, 3–6.

Fountain, J. W. (1997, May 4). No fare. *Washington Post*, p. F1.

Fouts, G., & Burggraf, K. (1999). Television situation comedies: Female body images and verbal reinforcements. *Sex Roles, 40*, 473–479.

Fox, C. (2006). The availability heuristic in the classroom: How soliciting more criticism can boost your course ratings. *Judgment and Decision Making, 1*, 86–90.

Frager, R. (1970). Conformity and anticonformity in Japan. *Journal of Personality and Social Psychology, 15*, 203–210.

Fraidin, S. N. (2004). When is one head better than two? Interdependent information in group decision making. *Organizational Behavior and Human Decision Processes, 93*, 102–113.

Fraley, R. C. (2002). Attachment stability from infancy to adulthood: Meta-analysis and dynamic modeling of developmental mechanisms. *Personality and Social Psychology Review, 6*, 123–151.

Fraley, R. C., & Shaver, P. R. (2000). Adult romantic attachment: Theoretical developments, emerging controversies, and unanswered questions. *Review of General Psychology, 4*, 132–154.

France: An event not hallowed. (2001, November 1). *New York Times*, p. A14.

Frank, J. D. (1978). *Psychotherapy and the human predicament: A psychosocial approach* (P. E. Dietz, Ed.). New York: Schocken Books.

Frank, R. H. (1999). *Luxury fever: Why money fails to satisfy even in an era of success*. New York: Free Press.

Franklin, B. (1900). *The autobiography of Benjamin Franklin* (J. Bigelow, Ed.). Philadelphia: Lippincott. (Originally published 1868)

Franklin, K. (2000). Antigay Behaviors Among Young Adults. *Journal of interpersonal violence*, vol. 15., 339–362

Frazier, P. A., & Cook, S. W. (1993). Correlates of distress following heterosexual relationship dissolution. *Journal of Social and Personal Relationships, 10*, 55–67.

Fredrickson, B. L., Roberts, T., Noll, S. M., Quinn, D. M., & Twenge, J. M. (1998). That swimsuit becomes you: Sex differences in self-objectification, restrained eating, and math performance. *Journal of Personality and Social Psychology, 75*, 269–284.

Freedman, J. L. (1965). Long-term behavioral effects of cognitive dissonance. *Journal of Experimental Social Psychology, 1*, 145–155.

Freeman, J., & Watson, B (2006). An application of Stafford and Warr's reconceptualisation of deterrence to a group of recidivist drink drivers. *Accident Analysis & Prevention, 38*, 462–471.

Freud, S. (1930). *Civilization and its discontents* (J. Riviere, Trans.). London: Hogarth Press.

Freud, S. (1933). *New introductory lectures on psychoanalysis*. New York: Norton.

Fried, C., & Aronson, E. (1995). Hypocrisy, misattribution, and dissonance reduction: A demonstration of dissonance in the absence of aversive consequences. *Personality and Social Psychology Bulletin, 21*, 925–933.

Friedkin, N. (2004). Social Cohesion. *Annual Review of Sociology, 30*, 409–425.

Friedman, L. (1977). *Sex-role stereotyping in the mass media: An annotated bibliography*. New York: Garland Press.

Friedman, T. (2002). *Longitudes and attitudes: Exploring the world after September 11*. New York: Farrar, Straus & Giroux.

Frijda, N. H. (1986). *The emotions*. Cambridge: Cambridge University Press.

Frodi, A. (1975). The effect of exposure to weapons on aggressive behavior from a cross-cultural perspective. *International Journal of Psychology, 10*, 283–292.

Fukuyama, F. (1999). *The great disruption: Human nature and the reconstitution of social order*. New York: Free Press.

Fulero, S. M. (2002). Afterword: The past, present, and future of applied pretrial publicity research. *Law and Human Behavior, 26*, 127–133.

Fumento, M. (1997, September 12). Why we need a new war on weight. *USA Weekend*, pp. 4–6.

Funder, D. C. (1995). On the accuracy of personality judgments: A realistic approach. *Psychological Review, 102*, 652–670.

Funder, D. C., & Colvin, C. R. (1988). Friends and strangers: Acquaintanceship, agreement, and the accuracy of personality judgment. *Journal of Personality and Social Psychology, 55*, 149–158.

Furnham, A. (1993). Just world beliefs in twelve societies. *Journal of Social Psychology, 133*, 317–329.

Furnham, A., & Gunter, B. (1984). Just world beliefs and attitudes toward the poor. *British Journal of Social Psychology, 23*, 265–269.

Furnham, A., & Mak, T. (1999). Sex-role stereotyping in television commercials: A review and comparison of fourteen studies done on five continents over 25 years. *Sex Roles, 41*, 413–437.

Furnham, A., & Procter, E. (1989). Beliefs in a just world: Review and critique of the individual difference literature. *British Journal of Social Psychology, 28*, 365–384.

Fury, G., Carlson, E. A., & Sroufe, L. A. (1997). Children's representations of attachment relationships in family drawings. *Child Development, 68*, 1154–1164.

Gabriel, S., & Gardner, W. L. (1999). Are there "his" and "hers" types of interdependence? The implications of gender differences in collective versus relational interdependence for affect, behavior, and cognition. *Journal of Personality and Social Psychology, 77*, 642–655.

Gaertner, S. L., Mann, J. A., Dovidio, J. F., & Murrell, A. J. (1990). How does cooperation reduce intergroup bias? *Journal of Personality and Social Psychology, 59*, 692–704.

Galati, D., Miceli, R., & Sini, B. (2001). Judging and coding facial expression of emotions in congenitally blind children. *International Journal of Behavioral Development, 25*, 268–278.

Galinsky, A. D., Mussweiler, T., & Medvec, V. H. (2002). Disconnecting outcomes and evaluations: The role of negotiator focus. *Journal of Personality and Social Psychology, 83*, 1131–1140.

Gallese, V., Fadiga, L., Fogassi, L., & Rizzolatti, G. (1996). Action recognition in the premotor cortex. *Brain, 119*(2), 593–609.

Gailliot, M., & Baumeister, R. (2007). The physiology of willpower: Linking blood glucose to self-control. *Personality and Social Psychology Review, 11*, 303–327.

Gallup, G. (1997). On the rise and fall of self-conception in primates. In J. G. Snodgrass & R. L. Thompson (Eds.), *The self across psychology: Self-recognition, self-awareness, and the self concept* (pp. 73–82). New York: New York Academy of Sciences.

Gallup, G. G., Jr., Anderson, J. R., & Shillito, D. J. (2002). The mirror test. In M. Bekoff & C. Allen (Eds.), *Cognitive animal: Empirical and theoretical perspectives on animal cognition* (pp. 325–333). Cambridge, MA: MIT Press.

Gangestad, S. W. (1993). Sexual selection and physical attractiveness: Implications for mating dynamics. *Human Nature, 4,* 205–235.

Gangestad, S. W., & Buss, D. M. (1993). Pathogen prevalence and human mate preferences. *Ethology and Sociobiology, 14,* 89–96.

Gao, G. (1993, May). *An investigation of love and intimacy in romantic relationships in China and the United States.* Paper presented at the annual conference of the International Communication Association, Washington, DC.

Gao, G. (1996). Self and other: A Chinese perspective on interpersonal relationships. In W. B. Gudykunst, S. Ting-Toomey, & T. Nishida (Eds.), *Communication in personal relationships across cultures* (pp. 81–101). Thousand Oaks, CA: Sage.

Gao, G., & Gudykunst, W. B. (1995). Attributional confidence, perceived similarity, and network involvement in Chinese and European American romantic relationships. *Communication Quarterly, 43,* 431–445.

Garcia, L. T., & Milano, L. (1990). A content analysis of erotic videos. *Journal of Psychology and Human Sexuality, 3,* 95–103.

Garcia, S., Stinson, L., Ickes, W. J., Bissonnette, V., & Briggs, S. (1991). Shyness and physical attractiveness in mixed-sex dyads. *Journal of Personality and Social Psychology, 61,* 35–49.

Garcia, S. M., Weaver, K., Moskowitz, G. B., & Darley, J. M. (2002). Crowded minds: The implicit bystander effect. *Journal of Personality and Social Psychology, 83,* 843–853.

Garcia-Marques, L., & Hamilton, D. L. (1996). Resolving the apparent discrepancy between the incongruency effect and the expectancy-based illusory correlation effect: The TRAP model. *Journal of Personality and Social Psychology, 71,* 845–860.

Gardner, W., & Gabriel, S. (2004). Gender differences in relational and collective interdependence: Implications for self-views, social behavior, and subjective well-being. In A. H. Eagly, A. E. Beall, & R. J. Sternberg (Eds.), *The psychology of gender* (2nd ed., pp. 169–191). New York: Guilford Press.

Gardner, W., & Knowles, M. L. (2008). Love makes you real: Favorite television characters are perceived as "real" in a social facilitation paradigm. *Social Cognition, 26,* 156–168.

Gardner, W. L., & Gabriel, S. (2004). Gender differences in relational and collective interdependence: Implications for self-views, social behavior, and subjective well-being. In A. H. Eagly, A. E. Beall, & R. J. Sternberg (Eds.), *Psychology of gender* (2nd ed., pp. 169–191). New York: Guilford.

Gardner, W. L., Pickett, C. L., & Brewer, M. B. (2000). Social exclusion and selective memory: How the need to belong influences memory for social events. *Personality and Social Psychology Bulletin, 26,* 486–496.

Garfinkle, H. (1967). *Studies in ethnomethodology.* Englewood Cliffs, NJ: Prentice Hall.

Gates, H. L., Jr. (1995, October 23). Thirteen ways of looking at a black man. *New Yorker,* pp. 56–65.

Gavanski, I., & Hoffman, C. (1987). Awareness of influences on one's own judgments: The roles of covariation detection and attention. *Journal of Personality and Social Psychology, 52,* 453–463.

Gawronski, B. (2003). Implicational schemata and the correspondence bias: On the diagnostic value of situationally constrained behavior. *Journal of Personality and Social Psychology, 84,* 1154–1171.

Gawronski, B. (2003b). On difficult questions and evident answers: Dispositional inference from role-constrained behavior. *Personality and Social Psychology Bulletin, 29,* 1459–1475.

Gawronski, B., & Bodenhausen, G.V. (2006). Associative and propositional processes in evaluation: An integrative review of implicit and explicit attitude change. *Psychological Bulletin, 132(5),* 692-731.

Geen, R. G. (1989). Alternative conceptions of social facilitation. In P. B. Paulus (Ed.), *Psychology of group influence* (2nd ed., pp. 15–51). Hillsdale, NJ: Erlbaum.

Geen, R. G. (1994). Television and aggression: Recent developments in research and theory. In D. Zillmann, J. Bryant, & A. C. Huston (Eds.), *Media, children, and the family: Social scientific, psychodynamic, and clinical perspectives* (pp. 151–162). Hillsdale, NJ: Erlbaum.

Geen, R. G. (1998). Aggression and antisocial behavior. In D. T. Gilbert, S. T. Fiske, & G. Lindzey (Eds.), *The handbook of social psychology* (4th ed., Vol. 2, pp. 317–356). New York: McGraw-Hill.

Geen, R. G., & Quanty, M. (1977). The catharsis of aggression: An evaluation of a hypothesis. In L. Berkowitz (Ed.), *Advances in experimental social psychology* (Vol. 10, pp. 1–36). New York: Academic Press.

Geen, R. G., Stonner, D., & Shope, G. (1975). The facilitation of aggression by aggression: A study in response inhibition and disinhibition. *Journal of Personality and Social Psychology, 31,* 721–726.

Geiselman, R. E., & Fisher, R. P. (1989). The cognitive interview technique for victims and witnesses of crime. In D. C. Raskin (Ed.), *Psychological methods in criminal investigation and evidence* (pp. 191–215). New York: Springer-Verlag.

Geitemeier, T., & Schulz-Hardt, S. (2003). Preference-consistent evaluation of information in the hidden profile paradigm: Beyond group-level explanations for the dominance of shared information in group decisions. *Journal of Personality and Social Psychology, 84,* 322–339.

Geller, E. S. (2002). The challenge of increasing proenvironmental behavior. In R. B. Bechtel & A. Churchman (Eds.), *Handbook of environmental psychology* (pp. 525–540). New York: Wiley.

Gemmill, G. (1989). The dynamics of scapegoating in small groups. *Small Group Behavior, 20,* 406–418.

Gentile, D. A., Anderson, C. A., Yukawa, N., Saleem, M., Lim, K. M., Shibuya, A., etal, (in press). The effects of prosocial video games on prosocial behaviors: International evidence from correlational, longitudinal, and experimental studies. *Personality and Social Psychology Bulletin.*

Gentile, D. A., & Gentile, J. R. (2008). Violent video games as exemplary teachers: A conceptual analysis. *Journal of Youth and Adolescence, 37(2),* 127–141.

George, J. M. (1990). Personality, affect, and behavior in groups. *Journal of Applied Psychology, 75,* 107–116.

Geraerts, E., Schooler, J., Merckelbach, H., Jelicic, M., Hauer, B., & Ambadar, Z. (2007). The reality of recovered memories: Corroborating continuous and discontinuous memories of childhood sexual abuse. *Psychological Science, 18,* 564–568.

Gerard, H. B. (1953). The effect of different dimensions of disagreement on the communication process in small groups. *Human Relations, 6,* 249–271.

Gerard, H. B., & Mathewson, G. C. (1966). The effects of severity of initiation on liking for a group: A replication. *Journal of Experimental Social Psychology, 2,* 278–287.

Gerard, H. B., Wilhelmy, R. A., & Conolley, E. S. (1968). Conformity and group size. *Journal of Personality and Social Psychology, 8,* 79–82.

Gerbner, G., Gross, L., Morgan, M., Signorielli, N., & Shanahan, J. (2002). Growing up with television: Cultivation processes. In J. Bryant & D. Zillmann (Eds.), *Media effects: Advances in theory and research* (pp. 43–67). Mahwah, NJ: Erlbaum.

Gerdes, E. P. (1979). College students' reactions to social psychological experiments involving deception. *Journal of Social Psychology, 107,* 99–110.

Gergen, K. J., Gergen, M. M., & Barton, W. H. (1973, July). Deviance in the dark. *Psychology Today,* pp. 129–130.

Gerin, W., Chaplin, W., Schwartz, J. E., Holland, J., Alter, R., Wheeler, R., Duong, D., & Pickering, T. G. (2005). Sustained blood pressure increase after an acute stressor: The effects of the 11 September 2001 attack on the New York City World Trade Center. *Journal of Hypertension, 23*, 279–84.

Gervey, B. M., Chiu, C., Hong, Y., & Dweck, C. S. (1999). Differential use of person information in decisions about guilt versus innocence: The role of implicit theories. *Personality and Social Psychology Bulletin, 25*, 17–27.

Ghiselin, M. T. (1996). Differences in male and female cognitive abilities: Sexual selection or division of labor? *Behavioral and Brain Sciences, 19*, 254–255.

Gibbons, F. X. (1978). Sexual standards and reactions to pornography: Enhancing behavioral consistency through self-focused attention. *Journal of Personality and Social Psychology, 36*, 976–987.

Gibbons, F. X., Eggleston, T. J., & Benthin, A. C. (1997). Cognitive reactions to smoking relapse: The reciprocal relation between dissonance and self-esteem. *Journal of Personality and Social Psychology, 72*, 184–195.

Gibbons, F. X., Gerrard, M., & Cleveland, M. J. (2004). Perceived discrimination and substance use in African American parents and their children: A panel study. *Journal of Personality and Social Psychology, 86*, 517–529. www.obesity.org/subs/fastfacts/obesity_what2.shtml

Gibbs, N., & Roche, T. (1999, December 20). The Columbine tapes. *Time*, p. 154.

Gifford, R. (1991). Mapping nonverbal behavior on the interpersonal circle. *Journal of Personality and Social Psychology, 61*, 279–288.

Gifford, R. (1994). A lens-mapping framework for understanding the encoding and decoding of interpersonal dispositions in nonverbal behavior. *Journal of Personality and Social Psychology, 66*, 398–412.

Gigerenzer, G. (2000). *Adaptive thinking: Rationality in the real world.* Oxford: Oxford University Press.

Gigerenzer, G. (2008). Why heuristics work. *Perspectives on Psychological Science, 3*, 20–29

Gilbert, D. (2008). *Stumbling on happiness.* New York: Vintage.

Gilbert, D. T. (1989). Thinking lightly about others: Automatic components of the social inference process. In J. S. Uleman & J. A. Bargh (Eds.), *Unintended thought* (pp. 189–211). New York: Guilford Press.

Gilbert, D. T. (1991). How mental systems believe. *American Psychologist, 46*, 107–119.

Gilbert, D. T. (1993). The assent of man: Mental representation and the control of belief. In D. M. Wegner & J. W. Pennebaker (Eds.), *The handbook of mental control* (pp. 57–87). Englewood Cliffs, NJ: Prentice Hall.

Gilbert, D. T. (1998a). Ordinary personology. In D. T. Gilbert, S. T. Fiske, & G. Lindzey (Eds.), *The handbook of social psychology* (4th ed., Vol. 2, pp. 89–150). New York: McGraw-Hill.

Gilbert, D. T. (1998b). Speeding with Ned: A personal view of the correspondence bias. In J. M. Darley & J. Cooper (Eds.), *Attribution and social interaction* (pp. 5–36). Washington, DC: American Psychological Association.

Gilbert, D. T. (2006). *Stumbling on happiness.* New York: Knopf.

Gilbert, D. T. (2007). *Stumbling on happiness.* New York: Vintage.

Gilbert, D. T., Ebert, E. J. (2002). Decisions and Revisions: The Affective Forecasting of Changeable Outcomes. *Journal of Personality and Social Psychology.* Copyright 2002 by the American Psychological Association, Inc. 2002, Vol. 82, No. 4, 503–514.

Gilbert, D. T., Giesler, R. B., & Morris, K. A. (1995). When comparisons arise. *Journal of Personality and Social Psychology, 69*, 227–236.

Gilbert, D. T., & Hixon, J. G. (1991). The trouble of thinking: Activation and applications of stereotypical beliefs. *Journal of Personality and Social Psychology, 60*, 509–517.

Gilbert, D. T., & Jones, E. E. (1986). Perceiver-induced constraint: Interpretations of self-generated reality. *Journal of Personality and Social Psychology, 50*, 269–280.

Gilbert, D. T., & Malone, P. S. (1995). The correspondence bias. *Psychological Bulletin, 117*, 21–38.

Gilbert, D. T., & Osborne, R. E. (1989). Thinking backward: Some curable and incurable consequences of cognitive busyness. *Journal of Personality and Social Psychology, 57*, 940–949.

Gilbert, D. T., & Wilson, T. D. (2007). Prospection: Experiencing the future. *Science, 317*, 1351–1354.

Gilbert, D. T., Pelham, B. W., & Krull, D. S. (1988). On cognitive busyness: When person perceivers meet persons perceived. *Journal of Personality and Social Psychology, 54*, 733–740.

Gilbert, G. M. (1951). Stereotype persistence and change among college students. *Journal of Abnormal and Social Psychology, 46*, 245–254.

Gilbert, M. (2000, August 18). Spice of life. *Boston Globe*, pp. D1, D8.

Gilbert, S. J. (1981). Another look at the Milgram obedience studies: The role of the gradated series of shocks. *Personality and Social Psychology Bulletin, 4*, 690–695.

Gilligan, J. (1996). *Violence: Our deadly epidemic and its causes.* New York: Putnam.

Gilovich, T. (1991). *How we know what isn't so: The fallibility of human reasoning in everyday life.* New York: Free Press.

Gilovich, T., & Griffin, D. W. (2002). Introduction: Heuristics and biases, now and then. In T. Gilovich, D. W. Griffin, & D. Kahneman (Eds.), *Heuristics and biases: The psychology of intuitive judgment* (pp. 1–18). New York: Cambridge University Press.

Gilovich, T., Medvec, V. H., & Chen, S. (1995). Commission, omission, and dissonance reduction: Coping with regret in the "Monty Hall" problem. *Personality and Social Psychology Bulletin, 21*, 182–190.

Gilovich, T., & Medvec, V. H. (1995). The experience of regret: What, when, and why. *Psychological Review, 102*, 379–395.

Gilovich, T., & Savitsky, K. (2002). Like goes with like: The role of representativeness in erroneous and pseudoscientific beliefs. In T. Gilovich, D. W. Griffin, & D. Kahneman (Eds.), *Heuristics and biases: The psychology of intuitive judgment* (pp. 617–624). New York: Cambridge University Press.

Girl born to Japan's princess. (2001, December 1). *New York Times*, p. 8.

Girotto, V., Ferrante, D., Pighin, S., & Gonzalez, M. (2007). Postdecisional counterfactual thinking by actors and readers. *Psychological Science, 18*, 510–515.

Giscombé, C., & Lobel, M. (2005). Explaining disproportionately high rates of adverse birth outcomes among African Americans: The impact of stress, racism, and related factors in pregnancy. *Psychological Bulletin, 131*, 662–683.

Gladue, B. A., Boechler, M., & McCaul, K. D. (1989). Hormonal response to competition in human males. *Aggressive Behavior, 15*, 409–422.

Gladwell, M. (1997, May 19). The sports taboo. *New Yorker*, pp. 50–55.

Gladwell, M. (2004, January 12). Big and bad: How the S.U.V. ran over automotive safety. *New Yorker*, p. 28.

Gladwell, M. (2005, January 12). Big and bad: How the S.U.V. ran over automotive safety, *The New Yorker*.

Glass, D. C. (1964). Changes in liking as a means of reducing cognitive discrepancies between self-esteem and aggression. *Journal of Personality, 32*, 531–549.

Gleick, E. (1997, April 7). Planet Earth about to be recycled. Your only chance to survive—leave with us. *Time*, pp. 28–36.

Glick, P., & Fiske, S. (2001). An ambivalent alliance: Hostile and benevolent sexism as complementary justifications for gender inequality. *American Psychologist, 56*, 109–118.

"Global warming: Frequently asked questions." National Oceanic and Atmospheric Administration National Climatic Data Center.

Retrieved on November 4, 2008, from www.ncdc.noaa.gov/oa/climate/globalwarming.html#q3.

Goddard, B. (2006). God on our side. TheHill.com. Retrieved September 7, 2008, from thehill.com/ben-goddard/god-on-our-side-2006-06-08.html

Goethals, G. R., & Darley, J. M. (1977). Social comparison theory: An attributional approach. In J. M. Suls & R. L. Miller (Eds.), *Social comparison processes: Theoretical and empirical perspectives* (pp. 259–278). Washington, DC: Hemisphere/Halsted.

Goethals, G. R., & Reckman, R. F. (1973). *The Perception of Consistency in Attitudes*. Journal of Experimental Social Psychology 9, 6, 491–501, Nov 73.

Goffman, E. (1959). *Presentation of self in everyday life*. Garden City, NY: Anchor/Doubleday.

Gold, J. A., Ryckman, R. M., & Mosley, N. R. (1984). Romantic mood induction and attraction to a dissimilar other: Is love blind? *Personality and Social Psychology Bulletin, 10*, 358–368.

Goldberg, P. (1968, April). Are women prejudiced against women? *Trans-Action*, pp. 28–30.

Goldinger, S. D., Kleider, H. M., Azuma, T., & Beike, D. R. (2003). "Blaming the victim" under memory load. *Psychological Science, 14*, 81–85.

Goldstein, J. H., & Arms, R. L. (1971). Effect of observing athletic contests on hostility. *Sociometry, 34*, 83–90.

Goldstein, N. J., Cialdini, R. B., & Griskevicius, V. (2008). A room with a viewpoint: Using social norms to motivate environmental conservation in hotels. Journal of Consumer Research, 35, 472–482.

Goleman, D. (1982, January). Make-or-break resolutions. *Psychology Today*, p. 19.

Good, C., Aronson, J., & Harder, J. (2007). *Problems in the pipeline: Women's achievement in high-level math courses*. Journal of Applied Developmental Psychology, 29, 17–28.

Good, C., Aronson, J., & Harder, J. (2008). Problems in the pipeline: Women's achievement in high-level math courses. *Journal of Applied Developmental Psychology, 29*, 17–28.

Good, C., Aronson, J., & Inzlicht, M. (2003). Improving adolescents' standardized test performance: An intervention to reduce the effects of stereotype threat. *Journal of Applied Developmental Psychology, 24*, 645–662.

Goode, E. (1999, February 9). Arranged marriage gives way to courtship by mail. *New York Times*, p. D3.

Goode, E. (2000, February 15). When women find love is fatal. *New York Times*, pp. F1 ff.

Goodwin, D.K. (2006) *Team of Rivals*. New York: Simon & Schuster

Goodwin, R. (1999). *Personal relationships across cultures*. New York: Routledge.

Gopaul-McNicol, S. A. A. (1987). A cross-cultural study of the effects of modeling, reinforcement, and color meaning word association on doll color preference of black preschool children and white preschool children in New York and Trinidad. *Dissertation Abstracts International, 48*, 340–341.

Gossett, J. L., & Byrne, S. (2002). "Click here": A content analysis of Internet rape cites. *Gender and Society, 16*, 689–709.

Graham, J., Koo, M., & Wilson, T. D. (in press). Conserving energy by inducing people to drive less. *Journal of Applied Social Psychology*.

Granberg, D., & Bartels, B. (2005). On being a lone dissenter. *Journal of Applied Social Psychology, 35*, 1849–1858.

Granberg, D., & Brown, T. (1989). On affect and cognition in politics. *Social Psychology Quarterly, 52*, 171–182.

Gray, S. (2004, March 30). Bizarre hoaxes on restaurants trigger lawsuits. *Wall Street Journal*, Retrieved on June 5, 2006, from online.wsj.com/article_print/SB108061045899868615.html

Graziano, W. G., Habashi, M. M., Sheese, B. E., & Tobin, R. M. (2007). Agreeableness, empathy, and helping: A person × situation perspective. *Journal of Personality and Social Psychology, 93*, 583–599

Graziano, W. G., Jensen-Campbell, L. A., & Finch, J. F. (1997). The self as a mediator between personality and adjustment. *Journal of Personality and Social Psychology, 73*, 392–404.

Graziano, W. G., Jensen-Campbell, L. A., Shebilske, L. J., & Lundgren, S. R. (1993). Social influence, sex differences, and judgments of beauty: Putting the interpersonal back in interpersonal attraction. *Journal of Personality and Social Psychology, 65*, 522–531.

Greenberg, J., & Musham, C. (1981). Avoiding and seeking self-focused attention. *Journal of Research in Personality, 15*, 191–200.

Greenberg, J., & Pyszczynski, T. (1985). The effect of an overheard slur on evaluations of the target: How to spread a social disease. *Journal of Experimental Social Psychology, 21*, 61–72.

Greenberg, J., Pyszczynski, T., & Paisley, C. (1984). The role of extrinsic incentives in the use of test anxiety as an anticipatory attributional defense: Playing it cool when the stakes are high. *Journal of Personality and Social Psychology, 47*, 1136–1145.

Greenberg, J., Pyszczynski, T., & Solomon, S. (1982). The self-serving attributional bias: Beyond self-presentation. *Journal of Experimental Social Psychology, 18*, 56–67.

Greene, D., Sternberg, B., & Lepper, M. R. (1976). Overjustification in a token economy. *Journal of Personality and Social Psychology, 34*, 1219–1234.

Greenfield, L. A., & Henneberg, M. A. (2001). Alcohol involvement in crime. *Alcohol Research and Health, 25*, 20–32.

Greenwald, A. G., & Banaji, M. R. (1995). Implicit social cognition: Attitudes, self-esteem, and stereotypes. *Psychological Review, 102*, 4–27.

Greenwald, A. G., McGhee, D. E., & Schwartz, J. L. K. (1998). Measuring individual differences in implicit cognition: The Implicit Association Test. *Journal of Personality and Social Psychology, 74*, 1464–1480.

Greenwald, A. G., Nosek, B. A., & Banaji, M. R. (2003). Understanding and using the Implicit Association Test: I. An improved scoring algorithm. *Journal of Personality and Social Psychology, 85*(2), 197-216.

Greenwald, A. G., & Ronis, D. L. (1978). Twenty years of cognitive dissonance: Case study of the evolution of a theory. *Psychological Review, 85*, 53–57.

Greenwald, A. G., Spangenberg, E. R., Pratkanis, A. R., & Eskenazi, J. (1991). Double-blind tests of subliminal self-help audiotapes. *Psychological Science, 2*, 119–122.

Greitemeyer, T., & Schulz-Hardt, S. (2003). Preference-consistent evaluation of information in the hidden profileparadigm: Beyond group-level explanations for the dominance of shared information in group decisions. *Journal of Personality and Social Psychology, 84*, 322–339.

Griffin, D., & Kahneman, D. (2003). Judgmental heuristics: Human strengths or human weaknesses? In L. G. Aspinwall & U. M. Staudinger (Eds.), *A psychology of human strengths: Fundamental questions and future directions for a positive psychology* (pp. 165–178). Washington, DC: American Psychological Association.

Griffin, D. W., Gonzalez, R., & Varey, C. (2001). The heuristics and biases approach to judgment under uncertainty. In A. Tesser & N. Schwarz (Eds.), *Blackwell handbook of social psychology: Intraindividual processes* (pp. 127–133). Oxford, England: Blackwell.

Griffin, D. W., & Ross, L. (1991). Subjective construal, social inference, and human misunderstanding. In L. Berkowitz (Ed.), *Advances in experimental social psychology* (Vol. 24, pp. 319–359). San Diego, CA: Academic Press.

Griffin, E., & Sparks, G. G. (1990). Friends forever: A longitudinal exploration of intimacy in same-sex pairs and platonic pairs. *Journal of Social and Personal Relationships, 7*, 29–46.

Griffitt W, Veitch R (1971) Hot and crowded: influences of population density and temperature on interpersonal affective behavior. *Journal of Personality and Social Psychology.* 1971 Jan; 17(1):92-8.

Guagnano, G. A., Stern, P. C., & Dietz, T. (1995). Influences on attitude-behavior relationships: A natural experiment with curbside recycling. *Environment and Behavior, 27,* 699–718.

Gudykunst, W. B. (1988). Culture and intergroup processes. In M. H. Bond (Ed.), *The cross-cultural challenge to social psychology* (pp. 165–181). Newbury Park, CA: Sage.

Gudykunst, W. B., Ting-Toomey, S., & Nishida, T. (1996). *Communication in personal relationships across cultures.* Thousand Oaks, CA: Sage.

Guerin, B. (1993). *Social facilitation.* Cambridge: Cambridge University Press.

Guimond, S. (1999). Attitude change during college: Normative or informational social influence? *Social Psychology of Education, 2,* 237–261.

Guisinger, S., & Blatt, S. J. (1994). Individuality and relatedness: Evolution of a fundamental dialect. *American Psychologist, 49,* 104–111.

Gully, S. M., Devine, D. J., & Whitney, D. J. (1995). A meta-analysis of cohesion and performance: Effects of level of analysis and task interdependence. *Small Groups Research, 26,* 497–520.

Gustafson, R. (1989). Frustration and successful vs. unsuccessful aggression: A test of Berkowitz's completion hypothesis. *Aggressive Behavior, 15,* 5–12.

Gyekye, S. A., & Salminen, S. (2004). Causal attributions of Ghanaian industrial workers in accident occurrence. *Journal of Applied Social Psychology, 34*(11), 2324–2342.

Hafer, C. L. (2000). Investment in long-term goals and commitment to just means drive the need to believe in a just world. *Personality and Social Psychology Bulletin, 26,* 1059–1073.

Hafer, C. L., & Begue (2005). Experimental research on just-world theory: Problems, developments, and future challenges. *Psychological Bulletin, 131*(1), 128–167.

Hagestad, G. O., & Smyer, M. A. (1982). Dissolving long-term relationships: Patterns of divorcing in middle age. In S. W. Duck (Ed.), *Personal relationships:* Vol. 4. *Dissolving personal relationships* (pp. 155–188). London: Academic Press.

Haidt, J. (2006). *The happiness hypothesis: Finding modern truth in ancient wisdom.* New York: Basic Books.

Haidt, J., & Keltner, D. (1999). Culture and facial expression: Open-ended methods find more faces and a gradient of recognition. *Cognition and Emotion, 13,* 225–266.

Halberstadt, J. B., & Levine, G. L. (1997). *Effects of reasons analysis on the accuracy of predicting basketball games.* Unpublished manuscript, Indiana University.

Halberstadt, J. B., & Rhodes, G. (2000). The attractiveness of nonface averages: Implications for an evolutionary explanation of the attractiveness of average faces. *Psychological Science, 11,* 285–289.

Hall, E. T. (1969). *The hidden dimension.* Garden City, NY: Doubleday.

Halpern, D., Benbow, C., Geary, D., Gur, R., Hyde, J., & Gernsbache, M. (2007). The science of sex differences in science and mathematics. *Psychological Science in the Public Interest, 8*(1), 1–51.

Hamilton, D. L. (1970). The structure of personality judgments: Comments on Kuusinen's paper and further evidence. *Scandinavian Journal of Psychology, 11,* 261–265.

Hamilton, D. L. (1981). Illusory correlation as a basis for stereotyping. In D. L. Hamilton (Ed.), *Cognitive processes in stereotyping and intergroup behavior* (pp. 563–571). Hillsdale, NJ: Erlbaum.

Hamilton, D. L., & Gifford, R. K. (1976). Illusory correlation in interpersonal perception: A cognitive basis of stereotypic judgments. *Journal of Experimental Social Psychology, 12,* 392–407.

Hamilton, D. L., & Sherman, S. J. (1989). Illusory correlations: Implications for stereotype theory and research. In D. Bar-Tal, C. F. Graumann, A. W. Kruglanski, & W. Stroebe (Eds.), *Stereotypes and prejudice: Changing conceptions* (pp. 59–82). New York: Springer-Verlag.

Hamilton, D. L., Stroessner, S., & Mackie, D. M. (1993). The influence of affect on stereotyping: The case of illusory correlations. In D. M. Mackie & D. L. Hamilton (Eds.), *Affect, cognition, and stereotyping: Interactive processes in group perception* (pp. 39–61). San Diego, CA: Academic Press.

Hamilton, V. L., Sanders, J., & McKearney, S. J. (1995). Orientations toward authority in an authoritarian state: Moscow in 1990. *Personality and Social Psychology Bulletin, 21,* 356–365.

Hamilton, W. D. (1964). The genetical evolution of social behavior. *Journal of Theoretical Biology, 7,* 1–52.

Hamm, M. (1999). *Go for the goal: A champion's guide to winning in soccer and life.* New York: HarperCollins.

Hammond, J. R., & Fletcher, G. J. O. (1991). Attachment styles and relationship satisfaction in the development of close relationships. *New Zealand Journal of Psychology, 20,* 56–62.

Han, S., & Shavitt, S. (1994). Persuasion and culture: Advertising appeals in individualistic and collectivistic societies. *Journal of Experimental Social Psychology, 30,* 326–350.

Haney, C., Banks, C., & Zimbardo, P. (1973). Interpersonal dynamics in a simulated prison. *International Journal of Criminology and Penology, 1,* 69–97.

Hansen, C. H., & Hansen, R. D. (1988). Finding the face in the crowd: An angry superiority effect. *Journal of Personality and Social Psychology, 54,* 917-924.

Hansen, E. M., Kimble, C. E., & Biers, D. W. (2000). Actors and observers: Divergent attributions of constrained unfriendly behavior. *Social Behavior and Personality, 29,* 87–104.

Hansson, R. O., & Slade, K. M. (1977). Altruism toward a deviant in a city and small town. *Journal of Applied Social Psychology, 7,* 272–279.

Harackiewicz, J. M. (1979). The effects of reward contingency and performance feedback on intrinsic motivation. *Journal of Personality and Social Psychology, 37,* 1352–1363.

Harackiewicz, J. M. (1989). Performance evaluation and intrinsic motivation processes: The effects of achievement orientation and rewards. In D. M. Buss & N. Cantor (Eds.), *Personality psychology: Recent trends and emerging directions* (pp. 128–137). New York: Springer-Verlag.

Harackiewicz, J. M., Durik, A. M., & Barron, K. E. (Eds.). (2005). *Multiple goals, optimal motivation, and the development of interest.* New York: Cambridge University Press.

Harackiewicz, J. M., & Elliot, A. J. (1993). Achievement goals and intrinsic motivation. *Journal of Personality and Social Psychology, 65,* 904–915.

Harackiewicz, J. M., & Elliot, A. J. (1998). The joint effects of target and purpose goals on intrinsic motivation: A mediational analysis. *Personality and Social Psychology Bulletin, 24,* 675–689.

Harackiewicz, J. M., Manderlink, G., & Sansone, C. (1984). Rewarding pinball wizardry: Effects of evaluation and cue value on intrinsic interest. *Journal of Personality and Social Psychology, 47,* 287–300.

Hardin, C. D., & Higgins, E. T. (Eds.). (1996). *Shared reality: How social verification makes the subjective objective.* New York: Guilford Press.

Hardin, G. (1968). The tragedy of the commons. *Science, 162,* 1243–1248.

Hare, A. P. (2003). Roles, relationships, and groups in organizations: Some conclusions and recommendations. *Small Group Research, 34,* 123–154.

Hare, B., & Tomasello, M. (2005). Human-like social skills in dogs? *Trends in Cognitive Sciences, 9*(9), 439–444.

Haritos-Fatouros, M. (1988). The official torturer: A learning model for obedience to the authority of violence. *Journal of Applied Social Psychology, 18*, 1107–1120.

Harmon-Jones, E., Brehm, J. W., Greenberg, J., Simon, L., & Nelson, D. E. (1996). Evidence that the production of aversive consequences is not necessary to create cognitive dissonance. *Journal of Personality and Social Psychology, 70*, 5–16.

Harmon-Jones, E., Harmon-Jones, C., Fearn, M., (2008) Action orientation, relative left frontal cortical activation, and spreading of alternatives. A test of the Action based Model of Dissonance.

Harmon-Jones, E., & Winkielman, P. (Eds.). (2007). *Social neuroscience: Integrating biological and psychological explanations of social behavior*. New York: Guilford.

Harries, K. D., & Stadler, S. J. (1988). Heat and violence: New findings from Dallas field data, 1980–1981. *Journal of Applied Social Psychology, 18*, 129–138.

Harrigan, J. A., & O'Connell, D. M. (1996). How do you feel when feeling anxious? Facial displays of anxiety. *Personality and Individual Differences, 21*, 205–212.

Harris, B. (1986). Reviewing 50 years of the psychology of social issues. *Journal of Social Issues, 42*, 1–20.

Harris, C. R. (2003). A review of sex differences in jealousy, including self-report data, psychophysiological responses, interpersonal violence, and morbid jealousy. *Personality and Social Psychology Review, 7*, 102–128.

Harris, C. R., & Pashler, H. (2004). Attention and the processing of emotional words and names: Not so special after all. *Psychological Science, 15*, 171–178.

Harris, M. B. (1974). Mediators between frustration and aggression in a field experiment. *Journal of Experimental and Social Psychology, 10*, 561–571.

Harris, M. B., Benson, S. M., & Hall, C. (1975). The effects of confession on altruism. *Journal of Social Psychology, 96*, 187–192.

Harris, M. B., & Perkins, R. (1995). Effects of distraction on interpersonal expectancy effects: A social interaction test of the cognitive busyness hypothesis. *Social Cognition, 13*, 163–182.

Harris, P., Griffin, D., & Murray, S. (2008). Testing the limits of optimistic bias: Event and person moderators in a multilevel framework. *Journal of Personality and Social Psychology, 95*, 1225–1237.

Harrison, J. A., & Wells, R. B. (1991). Bystander effects on male helping behavior: Social comparison and diffusion of responsibility. *Representative Research in Social Psychology, 19*, 53–63.

Hart, A. J. (1995). Naturally occurring expectation effects. *Journal of Personality and Social Psychology, 68*, 109–115.

Hart, D., & Damon, W. (1986). Developmental trends in self-understanding. *Social Cognition, 4*, 388–407.

Harter, S. (1993). Causes and consequences of low self-esteem in children and adolescents. In R. F. Baumeister (Ed.), *Self-esteem: The puzzle of low self-regard* (pp. 87–116). New York: Plenum.

Harter, S. (2003). The development of self-representations during childhood and adolescence. In M. R. Leary & J. P. Tangney (Eds.), *Handbook of self and identity* (pp. 610–642). New York: Guilford Press.

Hartstone, M., & Augoustinos, M. (1995). The minimal group paradigm: Categorization into two versus three groups. *European Journal of Social Psychology, 25*, 179–193.

Hartup, W. W., & Laursen, B. (1999). Relationships as developmental contexts: Retrospective themes and contemporary issues. In W. A. Collins & B. Laursen (Eds.), *Relationships as developmental contexts: Minnesota Symposia on Child Psychology* (Vol. 30, pp. 13–35). Mahwah, NJ: Erlbaum.

Hartup, W. W., & Stevens, N. (1997). Friendships and adaptation in the life course. *Psychological Bulletin, 121*, 355–370.

Harvey, J. H. (1995). *Odyssey of the heart: The search for closeness, intimacy, and love*. New York: Freeman.

Harvey, J. H., Flanary, R., & Morgan, M. (1986). Vivid memories of vivid loves gone by. *Journal of Personal and Social Relationships, 3*, 359–373.

Harvey, J. H., Orbuch, T. L., & Weber, A. L. (1992). The convergence of the attribution and accounts concepts in the study of close relationships. In J. H. Harvey, T. L. Orbuch, & A. L. Weber (Eds.), *Attributions, accounts, and close relationships* (pp. 1–18). New York: Springer-Verlag.

Hassebrauck, M., & Buhl, T. (1996). Three-dimensional love. *Journal of Social Psychology, 136*, 121–122.

Hassin, R. R., Aarts, H., Eitam, B., Custers, R., & Kleiman, T. (in press). Non-conscious goal pursuit and the effortful control of behavior. In E. Morsella, P. M. Gollwitzer & J. A. Bargh (Eds.), *The psychology of action* (Vol. 2). New York: Oxford University Press.

Hassin, R. R., Uleman, J. S., & Bargh, J. A. (Eds.) (2005). *The new unconscious*. New York: Oxford University Press.

Hastie, R., & Pennington, N. (2000). Explanation-based decision making. In T. Connolly & H. R. Arkes (Eds.), *Judgment and decision making: An interdisciplinary reader* (2nd ed., pp. 212–228). New York: Cambridge University Press.

Hastie, R., Penrod, S. D., & Pennington, N. (1983). *Inside the jury*. Cambridge, MA: Harvard University Press.

Hastie, R. (2008). What's the story? Explanations and narratives in civil jury decisions. In B, H. Bornstein, R. L. Wiener, R. Schopp, & S. L. Willborn (Eds.), *Civil juries and civil justice: Psychological and legal perspectives* (pp. 23–34). New York: Springer.

Hatfield, E. (1988). Passionate and companionate love. In R. J. Sternberg & M. L. Barnes (Eds.), *The psychology of love* (pp. 191–217). New Haven, CT: Yale University Press.

Hatfield, E., Cacioppo, J. T., & Rapson, R. L. (1993). *Emotional contagion*. New York: Cambridge University Press.

Hatfield, E., & Rapson, R. L. (1993). *Love, sex, and intimacy: Their psychology, biology, and history*. New York: HarperCollins.

Hatfield, E., & Rapson, R. L. (1996). *Love and sex: Cross-cultural perspectives*. Needham Heights, MA: Allyn & Bacon.

Hatfield, E., & Rapson, R. L. (2002). Passionate love and sexual desire: Cultural and historical perspectives. In A. L. Vangelisti, H. T. Reis, & M. A. Fitzpatrick (Eds.), *Stability and change in relationships* (pp. 306–324). New York: Cambridge University Press.

Hatfield, E., & Sprecher, S. (1986). Measuring passionate love in intimate relationships. *Journal of Adolescence, 9*, 383–410.

Hatfield, E., & Sprecher, S. (1995). Men's and women's preferences in marital partners in the United States, Russia, and Japan. *Journal of Cross-Cultural Psychology, 26*, 728–750.

Hatfield, E., & Walster, G. W. (1978). *A new look at love*. Reading, MA: Addison-Wesley.

Hatoum, I. J., & Belle, D. (2004). Mags and abs: Media consumption and bodily concerns in men. *Sex Roles, 51*, 397–407.

Haugtvedt, C. P., & Wegener, D. T. (1994). Message order effects in persuasion: An attitude strength perspective. *Journal of Consumer Research, 21*, 205–218.

Hays, C. L. (2003, June 5). Martha Stewart indicted by U.S. on obstruction. *New York Times*, pp. A1, C4.

Hazan, C., & Shaver, P. (1987). Romantic love conceptualized as an attachment process. *Journal of Personality and Social Psychology, 52*, 511–524.

Hazan, C., & Shaver, P. (1994a). Attachment as an organizational framework for research on close relationships. *Psychological Inquiry, 5*, 1–22.

Hazan, C., & Shaver, P. (1994b). Deeper into attachment theory. *Psychological Inquiry, 5*, 68–79.

Hazelwood, J. D., & Olson, J. M. (1986). Covariation information, causal questioning, and interpersonal behavior. *Journal of Experimental Social Psychology, 22*, 276–291.

Hebl, M., Foster, J., Bigazzi, J., Mannix, L., & Dovidio, J. (2002). Formal and interpersonal discrimination: A field study of bias toward homosexual applicants. *Personality and Social Psychology Bulletin, 28*, 815–825.

Heckhausen, J., & Schulz, R. (1995). A life-span theory of control. *Psychological Review, 102*, 284–304.

Hedge, A., & Yousif, Y. H. (1992). Effects of urban size, urgency, and cost on helpfulness. *Journal of Cross-Cultural Psychology, 23*, 107–115.

Hedges, L. V., & Nowell, A. (1995). Sex differences in mental test scores, variability, and numbers of high-scoring individuals. *Science, 269*, 41–45.

Heider, F. (1944). Social perception and phenomenal causality. *Psychological Review, 51*, 358–374.

Heider, F. (1958). *The psychology of interpersonal relations*. New York: Wiley.

Heine, S., Proulx, T., & Vohs, K. (2006). The meaning maintenance model: on the coherence of social motivations. *Personality and Social Psychology Review, 10*, 88–110.

Heine, S. J. (2008). *Cultural psychology*. New York: Norton.

Heine, S. J., Kitayama, S., & Lehman, D. R. (2001). Cultural differences in self-evaluation: Japanese readily accept negative self-relevant information. *Journal of Cross-Cultural Psychology, 32*, 434–443.

Heine, S. J., Lehman, D. R., Peng, K., & Greenholtz, J. (2002). What's wrong with cross-cultural comparisons of subjective Likert scales?: The reference-group effect. *Journal of Personality and Social Psychology, 82*, 903–918.

Heine, S. J., Takemoto, T., Moskalenko, S., Lasaleta, J., & Henrich, J. (2008). Mirrors in the head: Cultural variation in objective self-awareness. *Personality and Social Psychology Bulletin. 34*, 879–887.

Helgeson, V. S. (1994). Long-distance romantic relationships: Sex differences in adjustment and breakup. *Personality and Social Psychology Bulletin, 20*, 254–265.

Helgeson, V. S. (2003). Cognitive adaptation, psychological adjustment, and disease progression among angioplasty patents: 4 years later. *Health Psychology, 22*, 30–38.

Helgeson, V. S., & Cohen, S. (1996). Social support and adjustment to cancer: Reconciling descriptive, correlational, and intervention research. *Health Psychology, 15*, 135–148.

Helgeson, V. S., & Fritz, H. L. (1999). Cognitive adaptation as a predictor of new coronary events after percutaneous transluminal coronary angioplasty. *Psychosomatic Medicine, 61*, 488–495.

Helgeson, V. S., & Mickelson, K. D. (1995). Motives for social comparison. *Personality and Social Psychology Bulletin, 21*, 1200–1209.

Henderlong, J., & Lepper, M. R. (2002). The effects of praise on children's intrinsic motivation: A review and synthesis. *Psychological Bulletin, 128*, 774–795.

Henderson-King, E., & Nisbett, R. E. (1996). Anti-black prejudice as a function of exposure to the negative behavior of a single black person. *Journal of Personality and Social Psychology, 71*, 654–664.

Henley, N. M. (1977). *Body politics: Power, sex, and nonverbal communication*. Englewood Cliffs, NJ: Prentice Hall.

Henningsen, D., Henningsen, M., Eden, J., & Cruz, M. (2006). Examining the symptoms of groupthink and retrospective sensemaking. *Small Group Research, 37*, 36–64.

Henry, R. A. (1995). Using relative confidence judgments to evaluate group effectiveness. *Basic and Applied Social Psychology, 16*, 333–350.

Hersch, S. M. (2004, May 10). Torture at Abu Ghraib. *New Yorker*.

Hersh, S. M. (1970). *My Lai 4: A report on the massacre and its aftermath*. New York: Vintage Books.

Heschl, A., & Burkart, J. (2006). A new mark test for mirror self-recognition in non-human primates. *Primates, 47*, 187–198.

Heunemann, R. L., Shapiro, L. R., Hampton, M. C., & Mitchell, B. W. (1966). A longitudinal study of gross body composition and body conformation and their association with food and activity in the teenage population. *American Journal of Clinical Nutrition, 18*, 325–338.

Hewitt, J., & Alqahtani, M. A. (2003). Differences between Saudi and U.S. students in reaction to same- and mixed-sex intimacy shown by others. *Journal of Social Psychology, 143*, 233–242.

Hewstone, M., & Jaspars, J. (1987). Covariation and causal attribution: A logical model of the intuitive analysis of variance. *Journal of Personality and Social Psychology, 53*, 663–672.

Higgins, E. T. (1987). Self-discrepancy: A theory relating self and affect. *Psychological Review, 94*, 319–340.

Higgins, E. T. (1989). Self-discrepancy theory: What patterns of self-beliefs cause people to suffer? In L. Berkowitz (Ed.), *Advances in experimental social psychology* (Vol. 22, pp. 93–136). New York: Academic Press.

Higgins, E. T. (1996a). Knowledge application: Accessibility, applicability, and salience. In E. T. Higgins & A. R. Kruglanski (Eds.), *Social psychology: Handbook of basic principles* (pp. 133–168). New York: Guilford Press.

Higgins, E. T. (1996b). The "self-digest": Self-knowledge serving self-regulatory functions. *Journal of Personality and Social Psychology, 71*, 1062–1083.

Higgins, E. T. (1998). Promotion and prevention: Regulatory focus as a motivational principle. In M. P. Zanna (Ed.), *Advances in experimental social psychology* (Vol. 30, pp. 1–46). San Diego, CA: Academic Press.

Higgins, E. T. (1999). Self-discrepancy: A theory relating self and affect. In R. F. Baumeister (Ed.), *The self in social psychology* (pp. 150–181). Philadelphia: Psychology Press.

Higgins, E. T. (2005). Value from regulatory fit. *Current Directions in Psychological Science, 14*, 209–213.

Higgins, E. T., & Bargh, J. A. (1987). Social cognition and social perception. *Annual Review of Psychology, 38*, 369–425.

Higgins, E. T., Bond, R. N., Klein, R., & Strauman, T. (1986). Self-discrepancies and emotional vulnerability: How magnitude, accessibility, and type of discrepancy influence affect. *Journal of Personality and Social Psychology, 51*, 5–15.

Higgins, E. T., & Brendl, C. M. (1995). Accessibility and applicability: Some "activation rules" influencing judgment. *Journal of Experimental Social Psychology, 31*, 218–243.

Higgins, E. T., Klein, R., & Strauman, T. (1987). Self-discrepancies: Distinguishing among self-states, self-state conflicts, and emotional vulnerabilities. In K. M. Yardley & T. M. Honess (Eds.), *Self and identity: Psychosocial perspectives* (pp. 173–186). New York: Wiley.

Higgins, E. T., Rholes, W. S., & Jones, C. R. (1977). Category accessibility and impression formation. *Journal of Experimental Social Psychology, 13*, 141–154.

Hill, J. K. (2002). *Rainbow remedies for life's stormy times*. South Bend, IN: Moorhill Communications.

Hill, J. K. (n. d.). How I survived the deaths of twelve family members. Retrieved on December 21, 2008, from www.resiliencycenter.com/stories/2002stories/0201hill.shtml

Hilton, D. J., Smith, R. H., & Kim, S. H. (1995). Process of causal explanation and dispositional attribution. *Journal of Personality and Social Psychology, 68*, 377–387.

Hilton, J. L., Fein, S., & Miller, D. T. (1993). Suspicion and dispositional inference. *Journal of Personality and Social Psychology, 19*, 501–512.

Hinds, M. de C. (1993, October 19). Not like the movie: 3 take a dare and lose. *New York Times*, pp. A1, A22.

Hirt, E. R., Deppe, R. K., & Gordon, L. J. (1991). Self-reported versus behavioral self-handicapping: Empirical evidence for a theoretical distinction. *Journal of Personality and Social Psychology, 61*, 981–991.

Hirt, E. R., Kardes, F. R., & Markman, K. D. (2004). Activating a mental simulation mind-set through generation of alternatives: Implications for debiasing in related and unrelated domains. *Journal of Experimental Social Psychology, 40,* 374–383.

Hirt, E. R., McCrea, S. M., & Boris, H. I. (2003). "I know you self-handicapped last exam": Gender differences in reactions to self-handicapping. *Journal of Personality and Social Psychology, 84,* 177–193.

Hirt, E. R., McDonald, H. E., & Erikson, G. A. (1995). How do I remember thee? The role of encoding set and delay in reconstructive memory processes. *Journal of Experimental Social Psychology, 31,* 379–409.

Hirt, E. R., Melton, J. R., McDonald, H. E., & Harackiewicz, J. M. (1996). Processing goals, task interest, and the mood-performance relationship: A mediational analysis. *Journal of Personality and Social Psychology, 71,* 245–261.

Hitler, A. (1925). *Mein kampf.* Boston: Houghton Mifflin.

Hochstadt, S. (1999). *Mobility and modernity: Migration in Germany, 1820–1989.* Ann Arbor: University of Michigan Press.

Hodges, B. H., & Geyer, A. L. (2006). A nonconformist account of the Asch experiments: Values, pragmatics, and moral dilemmas. *Personality and Social Psychology Review, 10,* 2–19.

Hodson, R. (2004). A meta-analysis of workplace ethnographies: Race, gender, and employee attitudes and behavior. *Journal of Contemporary Ethnography, 33,* 4–38.

Hoffman, C., Lau, I., & Johnson, D. R. (1986). The linguistic relativity of person cognition: An English-Chinese comparison. *Journal of Personality and Social Psychology, 51,* 1097–1105.

Hoffman, H. G., Granhag, P. A., See, S. T. K., & Loftus, E. F. (2001). Social influences on reality-monitoring decisions. *Memory and Cognition, 29,* 394–404.

Hoffman, M. L. (1981). Is altruism a part of human nature? *Journal of Personality and Social Psychology, 40,* 121–137.

Hofstede, G. (1984). *Culture's consequences: International differences in work-related values.* Newbury Park, CA: Sage.

Hofstede, G. (1986). Cultural differences in teaching and learning. *International Journal of Intercultural Relations, 10,* 301–320.

Hogg, M. A. (1992). *The social psychology of group cohesiveness: From attraction to social identity.* London: Harvester-Wheatsheaf.

Hogg, M. A. (1993). Group cohesiveness: A critical review and some new directions. In W. Stroebe & M. Hewstone (Eds.), *European review of social psychology* (Vol. 4, pp. 85–111). Chichester, England: Wiley.

Hogg, M. A. (2001). A social identity theory of leadership. *Personality and Social Psychology Review, 5,* 184–200.

Hogg, M. A. (2007). Social psychology of leadership. In A. W. Kruglanski & E. T. Higgins (Eds.), *Handbook of basic principles* (2nd ed., pp. 716–733.). New York: Guilford.

Hogg, M. A., & Abrams, D. (1988). *Social identifications.* London: Routledge.

Hogg, M. A., Hohman, Z. P., & Rivera, J. E. (2008). Why do people join groups? Three motivational accounts from social psychology. *Social and Personality Psychology Compass, 2* (www.blackwell-compass.com/subject/socialpsychology/)

Holden, G. (1991). The relationship of self-efficacy appraisals to subsequent health related outcomes: A meta-analysis. *Social Work in Health Care, 16,* 53–93.

Holland, R. W., Aarts, H., & Langendam, D. (2006). Breaking and creating habits on the working floor: A field-experiment on the power of implementation intentions. *Journal of Experimantal Social Psychology, 42,* 776–783.

Holland, R. W., Meertens, R. M., & Van Vugt, M. (2002). Dissonance on the road: Self-esteem as a moderator of internal and external self-justification strategies. *Personality and Social Psychology Bulletin, 28,* 1713–1724.

Hollander, E. P. (1960). Competence and conformity in the acceptance of influence. *Journal of Abnormal and Social Psychology, 61,* 361–365.

Hollander, E. P. (1985). Leadership and power. In G. Lindzey & E. Aronson (Eds.), *Handbook of social psychology* (3rd ed., Vol. 2, pp. 485–537). New York: McGraw-Hill.

Hollingshead, A. B. (2001). Cognitive interdependence and convergent expectations in transactive memory. *Journal of Personality and Social Psychology, 81,* 1080–1089.

Holmes, T. H., & Rahe, R. H. (1967). The Social Readjustment Rating Scale. *Journal of Psychosomatic Research, 11,* 213–218.

Holtz, R. (2004). Group cohesion, attitude projection, and opinion certainty: Beyond interaction. *Group Dynamics: Theory, Research, and Practice, 8,* 112–125.

Homans, G. C. (1961). *Social behavior: Its elementary forms.* New York: Harcourt Brace.

Hong, G. Y. (1992). *Contributions of "culture-absent "cross-cultural psychology.* Paper presented at the annual meeting of the Society for Cross-Cultural Research, Santa Fe, NM.

Hong, Y., Morris, M. W., Chiu, C., & Benet-Martinez, V. (2000). Multicultural minds: A dynamic constructivist approach to culture and cognition. *American Psychologist, 55,* 709–720.

Hoog, N., Stroebe, W., & de Wit, J. B. F. (2005). The impact of fear appeals on processing and acceptance of action recommendations. *Personality and Social Psychology Bulletin, 31,* 24–33.

Hoose, P. M. (1989). *Necessities: Racial barriers in American sports.* New York: Random House.

Hope, L., Memon, A., & McGeorge, P. (2004). Understanding pretrial publicity: Predecisional distortion of evidence by mock jurors. *Journal of Experimental Psychology: Applied, 10,* 111–119.

Hope, L., & Wright, D. (2007). Beyond unusual? Examining the role of attention in the weapon focus effect. *Applied Cognitive Psychology, 21,* 951–961.

Hornsey, M. J., Jetten, J., McAuliffe, B. J., & Hogg, M. A. (2006). The impact of individualist and collectivist group norms on evaluations of dissenting group members. *Journal of Experimental Social Psychology, 42,* 57–68.

Hornsey, M. J., Majkut, L., Terry, D. J., & McKimmie, B. M. (2003). On being loud and proud: Non-conformity and counter-conformity to group norms. *British Journal of Social Psychology, 42,* 319–335.

House, J., Juster, F. T., Kahn, R. L., Schuman, H., & Singer, E. (Eds). (2004). *A telescope on society: Survey research and social science at the University of Michigan and beyond.* Ann Arbor: University of Michigan Press.

House, J. S., Robbins, C., & Metzner, H. L. (1982). The association of social relationships and activities with mortality: Prospective evidence from the Tecumseh Community Health Study. *American Journal of Epidemiology, 116,* 123–140.

Hovland, C. I., Janis, I. L., & Kelley, H. H. (1953). *Communication and persuasion: Psychological studies of opinion change.* New Haven, CT: Yale University Press.

Hovland, C. I., & Sears, R. R. (1940). Minor studies in aggression: 6. Correlation of lynchings with economic indices. *Journal of Psychology, 9,* 301–310.

Howard, J. A., Blumstein, P., & Schwartz, P. (1987). Social or evolutionary theories? Some observations on preferences in human mate selection. *Journal of Personality and Social Psychology, 53,* 194–200.

Howell, R., & Howell, C. (2008). The relation of economic status to subjective well-being in developing countries: A meta-analysis. *Psychological Bulletin, 134,* 536–560.

Hsu, S. S. (1995, April 8). Fredericksburg searches its soul after clerk is beaten as 6 watch. *Washington Post,* pp. A1, A13.

Huesmann, L. R., & Miller, L. S. (1994). Long-term effects of repeated exposure to media violence in childhood. In L. R. Huesmann (Ed.),

Aggressive behavior: Current perspectives (pp. 153–186). New York: Plenum.

Huffman, K. T., Grossnickle, W. F., Cope, J. G., & Huffman, K. P. (1995). Litter reduction: A review and integration of the literature. *Environment and Behavior, 27*, 153–183.

Hui, C. H., & Triandis, H. C. (1986). Individualism-collectivism: A study of cross-cultural researchers. *Journal of Cross-Cultural Psychology, 17*, 225–248.

Hull, J. G. (1981). A self-awareness model of the causes and effects of alcohol consumption. *Journal of Personality and Social Psychology, 40*, 586–600.

Hull, J. G., & Young, R. D. (1983). Self-consciousness, self-esteem, and success-failure as determinants of alcohol consumption in male social drinkers. *Journal of Personality and Social Psychology, 44*, 1097–1109.

Hull, J. G., Young, R. D., & Jouriles, E. (1986). Applications of the self-awareness model of alcohol consumption: Predicting patterns of use and abuse. *Journal of Personality and Social Psychology, 51*, 790–796.

Hunt, G. T. (1940). *The wars of the Iroquois.* Madison: University of Wisconsin Press.

Hurley, D., & Allen, B. P. (1974). The effect of the number of people present in a nonemergency situation. *Journal of Social Psychology, 92*, 27–29.

Hurley, E., & Allen, B. (2007). Asking the how questions: Quantifying group processes behaviors. *Journal of General Psychology, 134*, 5–21.

Huston, A., & Wright, J. (1996). Television and socialization of young children. In T. M. MacBeth (Ed.), *Tuning in to young viewers: Social science perspectives on television* (pp. 37–60). Thousand Oaks, CA: Sage.

Hutchinson, R. R. (1983). The pain-aggression relationship and its expression in naturalistic settings. *Aggressive Behavior, 9*, 229–242.

Hyde, J., Hankins, M., Deale, A., & Marteau, T. (2008). Interventions to increase self-efficacy in the context of addiction behaviours: A systematic literature review. *Journal of Health Psychology, 13*, 607–623.

Hyde, J., Mezulis, A., & Abramson, L. (2008). The ABCs of depression: Integrating affective, biological, and cognitive models to explain the emergence of the gender difference in depression. *Psychological Review, 115*, 291–313.

Hyde, J. S. (2005). The gender similarities hypothesis. *American Psychologist, 60*, 581–592.

Hyman, J. J., & Sheatsley, P. B. (1956). Attitudes toward desegregation. *Scientific American, 195*(6), 35–39.

Iacono, W. G.. (2008). Polygraph testing. In E. Borgida and S. T. Fiske (Eds.), *Beyond common sense: Psychological science in the courtroom* (pp. 219–235). Malden, MA: Blackwell.

Ickes, W. J., Patterson, M. L., Rajecki, D. W., & Tanford, S. (1982). Behavioral and cognitive consequences of reciprocal versus compensatory responses to preinteraction expectancies. *Social Cognition, 1*, 160–190.

Impett, E. A., Beals, K. P., & Peplau, L. A. (2001–2002). Testing the investment model of relationship commitment and stability in a longitudinal study of married couples. *Current Psychology, 20*, 312–326.

Imrich, D. J., Mullin, C., & Linz, D. G. (1995). Measuring the extent of prejudicial pretrial publicity in major American newspapers: A content analysis. *Journal of Communication, 45*, 94–117.

Inglehart, M. R. (1991). *Reactions to critical life events: A social psychological analysis.* New York: Praeger.

Inglehart, R., & Klingemann, H. (2000). Genes, culture, democracy, and happiness. In E. Diener & E. M. Suh (Eds.), *Culture and subjective well-being* (pp. 165–183). Cambridge, MA: MIT Press.

Insko, C. A., & Schopler, J. (1998). Differential trust of groups and individuals. In C. Sedikides & J. Schopler (Eds.), *Intergroup cognition and intergroup behavior* (pp. 75–107). Mahwah, NJ: Erlbaum.

Insko, C. A., Smith, R. H., Alicke, M. D., Wade, J., & Taylor, S. (1985). Conformity and group size: The concern with being right and the concern with being liked. *Personality and Social Psychology Bulletin, 11*, 41–50.

Isen, A. M. (1987). Positive affect, cognitive processes, and social behavior. In L. Berkowitz (Ed.), *Advances in experimental social psychology* (Vol. 20, pp. 203–253). San Diego, CA: Academic Press.

Isen, A. M. (1999). Positive affect. In T. Dalgleish & M. J. Power (Eds.), *Handbook of cognition and emotion* (pp. 521–539). Chichester, England: Wiley.

Isen, A. M., & Levin, P. A. (1972). Effect of feeling good on helping: Cookies and kindness. *Journal of Personality and Social Psychology, 21*, 384–388.

Isenberg, D. J. (1986). Group polarization: A critical review and meta-analysis. *Journal of Personality and Social Psychology, 50*, 1141–1151.

Izard, C. E. (1994). Innate and universal facial expressions: Evidence from developmental and cross-cultural research. *Psychological Bulletin, 115*, 288–299.

Jackson, J. M., & Williams, K. D. (1985). Social loafing on difficult tasks: Working collectively can improve performance. *Journal of Personality and Social Psychology, 49*, 937–942.

Jackson, J. S., Brown, T. N., Williams, D. R., Torres, M., Sellers, S. L., & Brown, K. (1996). Racism and the physical and mental health status of African Americans: A thirteen-year national panel study. *Ethnicity and Disease, 6*, 132–147.

Jackson, J. S., & Inglehart, M. R. (1995). Reverberation theory: Stress and racism in hierarchically structured communities. In S. E. Hobfoll & M. W. De Vries (Eds.), *Extreme stress and communities: Impact and intervention* (pp. 353–373). Dordrecht, Netherlands: Kluwer.

Jackson, J. W. (1993). Realistic group conflict theory: A review and evaluation of the theoretical and empirical literature. *Psychological Record, 43*, 395–413.

Jackson, L. A. (1992). *Physical appearance and gender: Sociobiological and sociocultural perspectives.* Albany: State University of New York Press.

Jackson, L. A., Hunter, J. E., & Hodge, C. N. (1995). Physical attractiveness and intellectual competence: A meta-analytic review. *Social Psychology Quarterly, 58*, 108–122.

Jacobs, J., & Eccles, J. (1992). The impact of mothers' gender-role stereotypic beliefs on mothers' and children's ability perceptions. *Journal of Personality and Social Psychology, 63*, 932–944.

Jacobs, P., & Landau, S. (1971). *To serve the devil* (Vol. 2). New York: Vintage Books.

Jacowitz, K. E., & Kahneman, D. (1995). Measures of anchoring in estimation tasks. *Personality and Social Psychology Bulletin, 21*, 1161–1166.

Jain, S. P., & Posavac, S. S. (2001). Prepurchase attribute verifiability, source credibility, and persuasion. *Journal of Consumer Psychology, 11*, 169–180.

James, C. (2000, August 25). Machiavelli meets TV's reality: Unreal. *New York Times*, p. B28.

James, L. M., & Olson, J. M. (2000). Jeer pressure: The behavioral effects of observing ridicule of others. *Personality and Social Psychology Bulletin, 26*, 474–485.

James, W. (1890). *The principles of psychology.* New York: Henry Holt.

Janis, I. L. (1972). *Victims of groupthink.* Boston: Houghton Mifflin.

Janis, I. L. (1982). *Groupthink: Psychological studies of policy decisions and fiascoes* (2nd ed.). Boston: Houghton Mifflin.

Janis, I. L., & Feshbach, S. (1953). Effects of fear-arousing communications. *Journal of Abnormal and Social Psychology, 49*, 78–92.

Jankowiak, W. R. (1995). Introduction. In W. R. Jankowiak (Ed.), *Romantic passion: A universal experience?* (pp. 1–19). New York: Columbia University Press.

Jankowiak, W. R., & Fischer, E. F. (1992). A cross-cultural perspective on romantic love. *Ethnology, 31*, 149–155.

Janoff-Bulman, R., & Leggatt, H. K. (2002). Culture and social obligation: When "shoulds" are perceived as "wants." *Journal of Research in Personality, 36*, 260–270.

Janoff-Bulman, R., Timko, C., & Carli, L. L. (1985). Cognitive biases in blaming the victim. *Journal of Experimental Social Psychology, 21*, 161–177.

Jecker, J., & Landy, D. (1969). Liking a person as a function of doing him a favor. *Human Relations, 22*, 371–378.

Joachim, D. S. (2006, July 17). For CBS's fall lineup, check inside your refrigerator. *New York Times.* Retrieved Jan. 20, 2009 from: http://www.nytimes.eom/2006/07/l7/business/media/17adco.html?scp=l&sq=joachim+cbs&st=cse

Johns, M., Schmader, T., & Martens, A. (2005). Knowing is half the battle: Teaching stereotype threat as a means of improving women's math performance. *Psychological Science, 16*, 175–179.

Johnson, D. M. (1945). The phantom anesthetist of Mattoon: A field study of mass hysteria. *Journal of Abnormal and Social Psychology, 40*, 175–186.

Johnson, D. W., & Johnson, R. T. (1987). *Learning together and alone: Cooperative, competitive, and individualistic learning* (2nd ed.). Englewood Cliffs, NJ: Prentice Hall.

Johnson, F. L., & Arles, E. J. (1983). Conversational patterns among same-sex pairs of late-adolescent close friends. *Journal of Genetic Psychology, 142*, 225–238.

Johnson, J. G., Cohen, P., Smailes, E. M., Kasen, S., & Brook, J. (2002). Television viewing and aggressive behavior during adolescence and adulthood. *Science, 295*, 2468–2471.

Johnson, K. J., & Fredrickson, B. L. (2005). We all look the same to me: Positive emotions eliminate the own-race bias in face recognition. *Psychological Science, 16*, 875–881.

Johnson, L. B. (1971). *The vantage point: Perspectives of the presidency, 1963–69.* New York: Holt, Rinehart and Winston.

Johnson, M., Verfaellie, M., & Dunlosky, J. (2008,). Introduction to the special section on integrative approaches to source memory. *Journal of Experimental Psychology: Learning, Memory, and Cognition, 34*, 727–729.

Johnson, M. K., Hashtroudi, S., & Lindsay, D. S. (1993). Source monitoring. *Psychological Bulletin, 114*, 3–28.

Johnson, M. K., & Raye, C. L. (1981). Reality monitoring. *Psychological Review, 88*, 67–85.

Johnson, R. D., & Downing, R. L. (1979). Deindividuation and valence of cues: Effects of prosocial and antisocial behavior. *Journal of Personality and Social Psychology, 37*, 1532–1538.

Johnson, T. E., & Rule, B. G. (1986). Mitigating circumstance information, censure, and aggression. *Journal of Personality and Social Psychology, 50*, 537–542.

Jones, C., & Aronson, E. (1973). Attribution of fault to a rape victim as a function of the respectability of the victim. *Journal of Personality and Social Psychology, 26*, 415–419.

Jones, D., & Hill, K. (1993). Criteria of facial attractiveness in five populations. *Human Nature, 4*, 271–296.

Jones, E. E. (1964). *Ingratiation: A social psychological analysis.* New York: Appleton-Century-Crofts.

Jones, E. E. (1979). The rocky road from acts to dispositions. *American Scientist, 34*, 107–117.

Jones, E. E. (1990). *Interpersonal perception.* New York: Freeman.

Jones, E. E., & Berglas, S. (1978). Control of attributions about the self through self-handicapping strategies: The appeal of alcohol and the role of underachievement. *Personality and Social Psychology Bulletin, 4*, 200–206.

Jones, E. E., & Davis, K. E. (1965). From acts to dispositions: The attribution process in social psychology. In L. Berkowitz (Ed.), *Advances in experimental social psychology* (Vol. 2, pp. 219–266). New York: Academic Press.

Jones, E. E., & Harris, V. A. (1967). The attribution of attitudes. *Journal of Experimental Social Psychology, 3*, 1–24.

Jones, E. E., & Kohler, R. (1959). The effects of plausibility on the learning of controversial statements. *Journal of Abnormal and Social Psychology, 57*, 315–320.

Jones, E. E., & Nisbett, R. E. (1972). The actor and the observer: Divergent perceptions of the causes of behavior. In E. E. Jones, D. E. Kanouse, H. H. Kelley, R. E. Nisbett, S. Valins, & B. Weiner (Eds.), *Attribution: Perceiving the causes of behavior* (pp. 79–94). Morristown, NJ: General Learning Press.

Jones, E. E., & Pittman, T. S. (1982). Toward a general theory of strategic self-presentation. In J. Suls (Ed.), *Psychological perspectives on the self* (pp. 231–262). Hillsdale, NJ: Erlbaum.

Jones, E. E., & Sigall, H. (1971). The bogus pipeline: A new paradigm for measuring affect and attitude. *Psychological Bulletin, 76*, 349–364.

Jones, E. E., & Wortman, C. B. (1973). *Ingratiation: An attributional approach.* Morristown, NJ: General Learning Press.

Jones, G. (2003, Oct. 2). World oil and gas 'running out.' CNN.com/World. Retrieved on June 21, 2006, from: *edition.cnn.com/2003/WORLD/europe/10/02/global.warming/*

Jones, M. (2006, January 15). "Shutting themselves in." *New York Times* (Jan. 15), Sec. 6, pp. 46–51.

Jones, T. F., Craig, A. S., Hoy, D., Gunter, E. W., Ashley, D. L., Barr, D. B., et al. (2000). Mass psychogenic illness attributed to toxic exposure at a high school. *New England Journal of Medicine, 342*, 96–100.

Jordan, M. (1996, January 15). In Japan, bullying children to death. *Washington Post*, pp. A1, A15.

Jordan, M., & Sullivan, K. (1995, September 8). A matter of saving face: Japanese can rent mourners, relatives, friends, even enemies to buff an image. *Washington Post*, pp. A1, A28.

Josephson, W. D. (1987). Television violence and children's aggression: Testing the priming, social script, and disinhibition prediction. *Journal of Personality and Social Psychology, 53*, 882–890.

Jowett, G. S., & O'Donnell, V. (1999). *Propaganda and persuasion.* Thousand Oaks, CA: Sage.

Judd C. M. & Park B. (1988). Out-group homogeneity: judgments of variability at the individual and group levels. *Journal of personality and social psychology*. 1988, vol. 54, n°5, pp. 778–788.

Judge rules ACLU discrimination suit against Continental Airlines can go forward. (2002). Retrieved from *www.aclu.org/RacialEquality/RacialEquality.cfm?ID=10994&c=133*

Judge, T. A., Bono, J. E., Ilies, R., & Gerhardt, M. W. (2002). Personality and leadership: A qualitative and quantitative review. *Journal of Applied Psychology, 87*, 765–780.

Judge, T. A., Colbert, A. E., & Ilies, R. (2004). Intelligence and leadership: A quantitative review and test of theoretical propositions. *Journal of Applied Psychology, 89*, 542–552.

Judge, T. A., & Piccolo, R. F. (2004). Transformational and transactional leadership: A meta-analytic test of their relative validity. *Journal of Applied Psychology, 89*, 755–768.

Jürgen-Lohmann, J., Borsch, F., & Giesen, H. (2001). Kooperatives Lernen an der Hochschule: Evaluation des Gruppenpuzzles in Seminaren der Pädagogischen Psychologie. *Zeitschrift für Pädagogische Psychologie, 15*, 74–84.

Juslin, P., Winman, A., & Hansson, P. (2007). The naïve intuitive statistician: A naïve sampling model of intuitive confidence intervals. *Psychological Review, 114*, 678–703.

Jussim, L. (2005). Accuracy in social perception: criticisms, controversies, criteria, components, and cognitive processes. *Advances in experimental social psychology* (Vol. 37, pp. 1–93). San Diego, CA: Elsevier Academic Press.

Jussim, L., & Eccles, J. S. (1992). Teacher expectations: II. Construction and reflection of student achievement. *Journal of Personality and Social Psychology, 63*, 947–961.

Jussim, L., & Harber, K. (2005). Teacher expectations and self-fulfilling prophecies: Knowns and unknowns, resolved and unresolved controversies. *Personality and Social Psychology Review, 9*, 131–155.

Kahn, J. P. (2003, June 7). How the mighty have fallen. *Boston Globe*, p. D1; D7.

Kahn, M. (1966). The physiology of catharsis. *Journal of Personality and Social Psychology, 3*, 278–298.

Kahneman, D., & Frederick, S. (2002). Representativeness revisited: Attribute substitution in intuitive judgment. In T. Gilovich, D. W. Griffin, & D. Kahneman (Eds). *Heuristics and biases: The psychology of intuitive judgment* (pp. 49–81). New York: Cambridge University Press.

Kahneman, D., Kruger, A. B., Schkade, D., Schwarz, N., & Stone, A. A. (2006). Would you be happier if you were richer? A focusing illusion. *Science, 312*, 1908–1910.

Kahneman, D., & Miller, D. T. (1986). Norm theory: Comparing reality to its alternatives. *Psychological Review, 93*, 136–153.

Kahneman, D., & Tversky, A. (1973). On the psychology of prediction. *Psychological Review, 80*, 237–251.

Kallgren, C. A., Reno, R. R., & Cialdini, R. B. (2000). A focus theory of normative conduct: When norms do and do not affect behavior. *Personality and Social Psychology Bulletin, 26*, 1002–1012.

Kallgren, C. A., & Wood, W. (1986). Access to attitude-relevant information in memory as a determinant of attitude-behavior consistency. *Journal of Experimental Social Psychology, 22*, 328–338.

Kalven, H., Jr., & Zeisel, H. (1966). *The American jury*. Boston: Little, Brown.

Kameda, T., Takezawa, M., & Hastie, R. (2003). The logic of social sharing: An evolutionary game analysis of adaptive norm development. *Personality and Social Psychology Review, 7*, 2–19.

Kang, N., & Kwak, N. (2003). A multilevel approach to civic participation: Individual length of residence, neighborhood residential stability, and their interactive effects with media use. *Communication Research, 30*, 80–106.

Kappas, A. (1997). The fascination with faces: Are they windows to our soul? *Journal of Nonverbal Behavior, 21*, 157–162.

Karau, S. J., & Williams, K. D. (1993). Social loafing: A meta-analytic review and theoretical integration. *Journal of Personality and Social Psychology, 65*, 681–706.

Karau, S. J., & Williams, K. D. (2001). Understanding individual motivation in groups: The collective effort model. In M. E. Turner (Ed.), *Groups at work—theory and research: Applied social research* (pp. 113–141). Mahwah, NJ: Erlbaum.

Karlins, M., Coffman, T. L., & Walters, G. (1969). On the fading of social stereotypes: Studies in three generations of college students. *Journal of Personality and Social Psychology, 13*, 1–16.

Karney, B. R., & Bradbury, T. N. (2000). Attributions in marriage: State or trait? A growth curve analysis. *Journal of Personality and Social Psychology, 78*, 295–309.

Kashima, Y., Siegel, M., Tanaka, K., & Kashima, E. S. (1992). Do people believe behaviors are consistent with attitudes? Towards a cultural psychology of attribution process. *British Journal of Social Psychology, 31*, 111–124.

Kassarjian, H., & Cohen, J. (1965). Cognitive dissonance and consumer behavior. *California Management Review, 8*, 55–64.

Kassin, S. (2007). Internalized false confessions. In M. P. Toglia, J. D. Read, D. F. Ross, & R. C. L. Lindsay (Eds.) *The handbook of eyewitness psychology*, Vol I: *Memory for events* (pp. 175–192). Mahwah, NJ: Erlbaum.

Kassin, S. (2008). Expert testimony on the psychology of confessions: A pyramidal framework of the relevant science. In E. Borgida and S. T. Fiske (Eds.)., *Beyond common sense: Psychological science in the courtroom* (pp. 195–218). Malden, MA: Blackwell.

Katz, D. (1960). The functional approach to the study of attitudes. *Public Opinion Quarterly, 24*, 163–204.

Katz, D., & Braly, K. W. (1933). Racial stereotypes of 100 college students. *Journal of Abnormal and Social Psychology, 28*, 280–290.

Kauffman, D. R., & Steiner, I. D. (1968). Conformity as an ingratiation technique. *Journal of Experimental Social Psychology, 4*, 404–414.

Keelan, J. P. R., Dion, K. L., & Dion, K. K. (1994). Attachment style and hetereosexual relationships among young adults: A short-term panel study. *Journal of Social and Personal Relationships, 11*, 201–214.

Keller, J., & Bless, H. (2008). Flow and regulatory compatibility: An experimental approach to the flow model of intrinsic motivation. *Personality and Social Psychology Bulletin, 34*, 196–209.

Kelley, H. H. (1950). The warm-cold variable in first impressions of persons. *Journal of Personality, 18*, 431–439.

Kelley, H. H. (1955). The two functions of reference groups. In G. E. Swanson, T. M. Newcomb, & E. L. Hartley (Eds.), *Readings in social psychology* (2nd ed., pp. 410–414). New York: Henry Holt.

Kelley, H. H. (1967). Attribution theory in social psychology. In D. Levine (Ed.), *Nebraska Symposium on Motivation* (Vol. 15, pp. 192–238). Lincoln: University of Nebraska Press.

Kelley, H. H. (1972). Attribution in social interaction. In E. E. Jones, D. E. Kanouse, H. H. Kelley, R. E. Nisbett, S. Valins, & B. Weiner (Eds.), *Attribution: Perceiving the causes of behavior* (pp. 1–26). Morristown, NJ: General Learning Press.

Kelley, H. H. (1973). The process of causal attribution. *American Psychologist, 28*, 107–128.

Kelley, H. H. (1983). Love and commitment. In H. H. Kelley, E. Berscheid, A. Christensen, J. H. Harvey, T. L. Huston, G. Levinger, et al. (Eds.), *Close relationships* (pp. 265–314). New York: Freeman.

Kelley, H. H., & Thibaut, J. (1978). *Interpersonal relations: A theory of interdependence*. New York: Wiley.

Keltner, D., & Shiota, M. N. (2003). New displays and new emotions: A commentary on Rozin and Cohen. *Emotion, 3*, 86–91.

Kemmelmeier, M., Jambor, E., & Letner, J. (2006). Individualism and good works: Cultural variation in giving and volunteering across the United States. *Journal of Cross-Cultural Psychology, 37*, 327–344

Kenny, D. A. (1994b). Using the social relations model to understand relationships. In R. Erber & R. Gilmour (Eds.), *Theoretical frameworks for personal relationships* (pp. 111–127). Hillsdale, NJ: Erlbaum.

Kenny, D. A., Albright, L., Malloy, T. E., & Kashy, D. A. (1994). Consensus in interpersonal perception: Acquaintance and the Big Five. *Psychological Bulletin, 116*, 245–258.

Kenny, D. A., & La Voie, L. (1982). Reciprocity of interpersonal attraction: A confirmed hypothesis. *Social Psychology Quarterly, 45*, 54–58.

Kenrick, D. T., & Keefe, R. C. (1992). Age preferences in mate reflect sex differences in human reproductive strategies. *Behavioral and Brain Sciences, 15*, 75–133.

Kenrick, D. T., & MacFarlane, S. W. (1986). Ambient temperature and horn honking: A field study of the heat/aggression relationship. *Environment and Behavior, 18*, 179–191.

Kent, M. V. (1994). The presence of others. In A. P. Hare, H. H. Blumberg, M. F. Davies, & M. V. Kent (Eds.), *Small group research: A handbook* (pp. 81–105). Norwood, NJ: Ablex.

Kerckhoff, A. C., & Back, K. W. (1968). *The June bug: A study of hysterical contagion*. New York: Appleton-Century-Crofts.

Kerr, N., & Levine, J. (2008). The detection of social exclusion: Evolution and beyond. *Group Dynamics: Theory, Research, and Practice, 12*, 39–52.

Kerr, N. L., & Tindale, R. S. (2004). Groups performance and decision making. *Annual Review of Psychology, 55*, 623–655.

Key, W. B. (1973). *Subliminal seduction.* Englewood Cliffs, NJ: Signet Books.

Key, W. B. (1989). *Age of manipulation: The con in confidence and the sin in sincere.* New York: Henry Holt.

Kiesler, C. A., & Kiesler, S. B. (1969). *Conformity.* Reading, MA: Addison-Wesley.

Kihlstrom, J. F. (1996). The trauma-memory argument and recovered memory therapy. In K. Pezdek & W. P. Banks (Eds.), *The recovered memory/false memory debate* (pp. 297–311). San Diego, CA: Academic Press.

Killen, J. D., Taylor, C. B., Hayward, C., Wilson, D. M., Haydel, K. F., Hammer, L. D., et al. (1994). Pursuit of thinness and onset of eating disorder symptoms in a community sample of adolescent girls: A three-year prospective analysis. *International Journal of Eating Disorders, 16,* 227–238.

Killian, L. M. (1964). Social movements. In R. E. L. Farris (Ed.), *Handbook of modern sociology* (pp. 426–455). Chicago: Rand McNally.

Kim, H., & Markus, H. R. (1999). Deviance or uniqueness, harmony or conformity? A cultural analysis. *Journal of Personality and Social Psychology, 77,* 785–800.

Kim, H. S., Sherman, D. K., & Taylor, S. E. (in press). Culture and social support. *American Psychologist.*

Kim, M. P., & Rosenberg, S. (1980). Comparison of two structural models of implicit personality theory. *Journal of Personality and Social Psychology, 38,* 375–389.

Kim, U., & Berry, J. W. (1993). *Indigenous psychologies: Research and experience in cultural context.* Newbury Park, CA: Sage.

Kim, U., Triandis, H. C., Kagitcibasi, C., Choi, S. C., & Yoon, G. (Eds.). (1994). *Individualism and collectivism: Theory, method, and applications.* Thousand Oaks, CA: Sage.

Kimble, C. E., & Hirt, E. R. (2005). Self-focus, gender, and habitual self-handicapping: Do they make a difference in behavioral self-handicapping? *Social Behavior and Personality, 33,* 43–56.

Kimel, E. (2001, Aug. 2). Students earn cash for summer reading. *Sarasota Herald Tribune,* p. BV2.

Kinder, D. R., & Sears, D. O. (1981). Prejudice and politics: Symbolic racism versus racial threats to the good life. *Journal of Personality and Social Psychology, 40,* 414–431.

Kirkpatrick, L. A., & Davis, K. E. (1994). Attachment style, gender, and relationship stability: A longitudinal analysis. *Journal of Personality and Social Psychology, 66,* 502–512.

Kirkpatrick, L. A., & Hazan, C. (1994). Attachment styles and close relationships: A four-year prospective study. *Personal Relationships, 1,* 123–142.

Kitayama, S., & Cohen, D. (Eds.). (2007). *Handbook of cultural psychology.* New York: Guilford.

Kitayama, S., & Markus, H. R. (1994). Culture and the self: How cultures influence the way we view ourselves. In D. Matsumoto (Ed.), *People: Psychology from a cultural perspective* (pp. 17–37). Pacific Grove, CA: Brooks/Cole.

Kitayama, S., Markus, H. R., Matsumoto, H., & Norasakkunkit, V. (1997). Individual and collective processes in the construction of the self: Self-enhancement in the United States and self-criticism in Japan. *Journal of Personality and Social Psychology, 72,* 1245–1267.

Kitayama, S., & Masuda, T. (1997). *Cultural psychology of social inference: The correspondence bias in Japan.* Unpublished manuscript, Kyoto University.

Kitayama, S., & Uchida, Y. (2003). Explicit self-criticism and implicit self-regard: Evaluating self and friend in two cultures. *Journal of Experimental Social Psychology, 39,* 476–482.

Kitayama, S., & Uchida, Y. (2005). Interdependent agency: An alternative system for action. In R. M. Sorrentino & D. Cohen (Eds.), *Cultural and social behavior: The Ontario Symposium* (Vol 10, pp. 137–164). Mahwah, NJ: Erlbaum.

Kite, M. E., Deaux, K., & Haines, E. L. (2008). Gender stereotypes. In F. L. Denmark & M. A. Paludi (Eds.), *Psychology of women: A handbook of issues and theories* (2nd ed., pp. 205–236). Westport, CT: Praeger.

Kivlighan, K., Granger, D., & Booth, A. (2005). Gender differences in testosterone and cortisol response to competition. *Psychoneuroendocrinology, 30,* 58–71.

Klein, R. (2005, November 12). President steps up attack on war critics. *The Boston Globe.* Retrieved on March 8, 2006, from www.boston.com/news/nation/washington/articles/2005/11/12/president_steps_up_attack_on_war_critics/

Klenke, K. (1996). *Women and leadership: A contextual perspective.* New York: Springer-Verlag.

Kluger, R. (1996). *Ashes to ashes: America's hundred-year cigarette war, the public health, and the unabashed triumph of Philip Morris.* New York: Knopf.

Knapp, M., & Hall, J. A. (2006). *Nonverbal communication in human interaction.* Belmont, CA: Thomson Wadsworth.

Knight, J. (2004). The truth about lying. *Nature, 428,* 692–694.

Knopke, H., Norrell, R., & Rogers, R. (1991). *Opening doors: Perspectives on race relations in contemporary America.* Tuscaloosa: University of Alabama Press.

Knowles, E. D., Morris, M. W., Chiu, C., & Hong, Y. (2001). Culture and the process of person perception: Evidence for automaticity among East Asians in correcting for situational influences on behavior. *Personality and Social Psychology Bulletin, 27,* 1344-1356.

Knowles, E. S., & Sibicky, M. E. (1990). Continuity and diversity in the stream of selves: Metaphorical resolutions of William James's one-in-many-selves paradox. *Personality and Social Psychology Bulletin, 16,* 676–687.

Knox, R., & Inkster, J. (1968). Postdecision dissonance at post time. *Journal of Personality and Social Psychology, 8,* 319–323.

Knussen, C., Yule, F., & MacKenzie, J. (2004). An analysis of intentions to recycle household waste: The roles of past behaviour, perceived habit, and perceived lack of facilities. *Journal of Environmental Psychology, 24,* 237–246.

Koehler, J. J. (1993). The base rate fallacy myth. *Psycoloquy, 4,* 49.

Koehler, J. J. (1996). The base rate fallacy reconsidered: Descriptive, normative, and methodological challenges. *Behavioral and Brain Sciences, 19,* 1–53.

Koehnken, G., Malpass, R. S., & Wogalter, M. S. (1996). Forensic applications of line-up research. In S. L. Sporer, R. S. Malpass, & G. Koehnken (Eds.), *Psychological issues in eyewitness identification* (pp. 205–231). Mahwah, NJ: Erlbaum.

Koestner, R., Horberg, E., Gaudreau, P., Powers, T., Di Dio, P., Bryan, C., et al. (2006). Bolstering implementation plans for the long haul: The benefits of simultaneously boosting self-concordance or self-efficacy. *Personality and Social Psychology Bulletin, 32,* 1547–1558. Retrieved on December 27, 2008, from doi:10.1177/0146167206291782

Kogan, N., & Wallach, M. A. (1964). *Risk-taking: A study in cognition and personality.* New York: Henry Holt.

Kolbert, E. (2006). *Field notes from a catastrophe: Man, nature, and climate change.* New York: Bloomsbury.

Kollack, P., Blumstein, P., & Schwartz, P., (1994). The judgment of equity in intimate relationships. *Social Psychology Quarterly, 57,* 340–351.

Koolhaas, J. M., de Boer, S. F., & ; Buwalda, B. (2006). Stress and adaptation. *Current Directions in Psychological Science, 15,* 109–112.

Korda, M. (1997, October 6). Prompting the president. *New Yorker,* pp. 88–95.

Kowert, P. A. (2002). *Groupthink or deadlock: When do leaders learn from their advisors?* Albany: State University of New York Press.

Krakow, A., & Blass, T. (1995). When nurses obey or defy inappropriate physician orders: Attributional differences. *Journal of Social Behavior and Personality, 10,* 585–594.

Kramer, G. P., Kerr, N. L., & Carroll, J. S. (1990). Pretrial publicity, judicial remedies, and jury bias. *Law and Human Behavior, 14,* 409–438.

Krauss, R. M., & Deutsch, M. (1966). Communication in interpersonal bargaining. *Journal of Personality and Social Psychology, 4,* 572–577.

Krauss, R. M., Freedman, J. L., & Whitcup, M. (1978). Field and laboratory studies of littering. *Journal of Experimental Social Psychology, 14,* 109–122.

Kremer, J. F., & Stephens, L. (1983). Attributions and arousal as mediators of mitigation's effects on retaliation. *Journal of Personality and Social Psychology, 45,* 335–343.

Kressel, K., & Pruitt, D. G. (1989). A research perspective on the mediation of social conflict. In K. Kressel & D. G. Pruitt (Eds.), *Mediation research: The process and effectiveness of third party intervention* (pp. 394–435). San Francisco: Jossey-Bass.

Krosnick, J. A., & Alwin, D. F. (1989). Aging and susceptibility to attitude change. *Journal of Personality and Social Psychology, 57,* 416–425.

Kross, E., & Ayduk, O. (2008). Facilitating adaptive emotional analysis: Distinguishing distanced-analysis of depressive experiences from immersed-analysis and distraction. *Personality and Social Psychology Bulletin, 34,* 924–938.

Krueger, J., Ham, J. J., & Linford, K. (1996). Perceptions of behavioral consistency: Are people aware of the actor-observer effect? *Psychological Science, 7,* 259–264.

Kruger, K., Epley, N., Packer, J., & Ng, Z. (2005). Egocentricism over e-mail: Can we communicate as well as we think? *Journal of Personality and Social Psychology, 89* (6), 925–936.

Krull, D. S. (1993). Does the grist change the mill? The effect of the perceiver's inferential goal on the process of social inference. *Personality and Social Psychology Bulletin, 19,* 340–348.

Krull, D. S., & Dill, J. C. (1996). On thinking first and responding fast: Flexibility in social inference processes. *Personality and Social Psychology Bulletin, 22,* 949–959.

Krull, D. S., Loy, M. H., Lin, J., Wang, C., Chen, S., & Zhao, X. (1999). The fundamental correspondence bias in individualist and collectivist cultures. *Personality and Social Psychology Bulletin, 25,* 1208–1219.

Kubitschek, W. N., & Hallinan, M. T. (1998). Tracking and students' friendships. *Social Psychology Quarterly, 61,* 1–15.

Kuhl, J. (1987). Action control: The maintenance of motivational states. In F. Halisch & J. Kuhl (Eds.), *Motivaiton, intention, and volition* (pp. 279–291). New York: Springer.

Kuhn, D., Weinstock, M., & Flaton, R. (1994). How well do jurors reason? Competence dimensions of individual variation in a juror reasoning task. *Psychological Science, 5,* 289–296.

Kulik, J. A., & Brown, R. (1979). Frustration, attribution of blame, and aggression. *Journal of Experimental Social Psychology, 15,* 183–194.

Kunda, Z. (1999). *Social cognition: Making sense of people.* Cambridge, MA: MIT Press.

Kunda, Z., & Oleson, K. C. (1997). When exceptions prove the rule: How extremity of deviance determines the impact of deviant examples on stereotypes. *Journal of Personality and Social Psychology, 72,* 965–979.

Kunda, Z., & Schwartz, S. H. (1983). Undermining intrinsic moral motivation: External reward and self-presentation. *Journal of Personality and Social Psychology, 45,* 763–771.

Kunda, Z., Sinclair, L., & Griffin, D. W. (1997). Equal ratings but separate meanings: Stereotypes and the construal of traits. *Journal of Personality and Social Psychology, 72,* 720–734.

Kuo, Z. Y. (1961). *Instinct.* Princeton, NJ: Van Nostrand.

Kurdek, L. A. (1992). Relationship stability and relationship satisfaction in cohabitating gay and lesbian couples: A prospective longitudinal test of the contextual and interdependence models. *Journal of Social and Personal Relationships, 9,* 125–142.

Kuykendall, D., & Keating, J. P. (1990). Altering thoughts and judgments through repeated association. *British Journal of Social Psychology, 29,* 79–86.

Lachman, M. (2006). Perceived control over aging-related declines: Adaptive beliefs and behaviors. *Current Directions in Psychological Science, 15,* 282–286.

La France, M., Hecht, M. A., & Paluck, E. L. (2003). The contingent smile: A meta-analysis of sex differences in smiling. *Psychological Bulletin, 129,* 305–334.

Laird, J. (2007). *Feelings: The perception of self.* New York, Oxford University Press.

Lalancette, M. F., & Standing, L. (1990). Asch fails again. *Social Behavior and Personality, 18,* 7–12.

Lalwani, A., Shavitt, S., & Johnson, T. (2006). What is the relation between cultural orientation and socially desirable responding? *Journal of Personality and Social Psychology, 90,* 165–178.

Lambert, A. J., Burroughs, T., & Nguyen, T. (1999). Perceptions of risk and the buffering hypothesis: The role of just world beliefs and right-wing authoritarianism. *Personality and Social Psychology Bulletin, 25,* 643–656.

Lampert, R., Baron, S. J., McPherson, C. A., & Lee, F. A. (2002). Heart rate variability during the week of September 11, 2001. *Journal of the American Medical Association, 288,* 575.

Landman, J. (1993). *Regret: The persistence of the possible.* New York: Oxford University Press.

Lane, K. A., Banaji, M. R., & Nosek, B. A. (2007). Understanding and using the implicit association test: IV: What we know (so far) about the method. In B. Wittenbrink & N. Schwarz (Eds.), *Implicit measures of attitudes* (pp. 59–102). New York: Guilford.

Langer, E. J. (1975) The illusion of control. *Journal of Personality and Social Psychology, 32,* 311–328.

Langer, E. J., & Rodin, J. (1976). The effects of choice and enhanced personal responsibility for the aged: A field experiment. *Journal of Personality and Social Psychology, 34,* 191–198.

Langlois, J. H., Kalakanis, L., Rubenstein, A. J., Larson, A., Hallam, M., & Smoot, M. (2000). Maxims or myths of beauty? A meta-analytic and theoretical review. *Psychological Bulletin, 126,* 390–423.

Langlois, J. H., Ritter, J. M., Roggman, L. A., & Vaughn, L. S. (1991). Facial diversity and infant preferences for attractive faces. *Developmental Psychology, 27,* 79–84.

Langlois, J. H., & Roggman, L. A. (1990). Attractive faces are only average. *Psychological Science, 1,* 115–121.

Langlois, J. H., Roggman, L. A., & Musselman, L. (1994). What is average and what is not average about attractive faces? *Psychological Science, 5,* 214–220.

Langlois, J. H., Roggman, L. A., & Rieser-Danner, L. A. (1990). Infants' differential social responses to attractive and unattractive faces. *Developmental Psychology, 26,* 153–159.

La Piere, R. T. (1934). Attitudes vs. actions. *Social Forces, 13,* 230–237.

Larsen, K. S. (1990). The Asch conformity experiment: Replication and transhistorical comparisons. *Journal of Social Behavior and Personality, 5,* 163–168.

Larson, J. R., Jr., Christensen, C., Franz, T. M., & Abbott, A. S. (1998). Diagnosing groups: The pooling, management, and impact of shared and unshared case information in team-based medical decision making. *Journal of Personality and Social Psychology, 75,* 93–108.

Lassiter, G. D. (2004). *Interrogations, confessions, and entrapment.* New York: Kluwer Academic/Plenum.

Latané, B. (1981). The psychology of social impact. *American Psychologist, 36,* 343–356.

Latané, B. (1987). From student to colleague: Retracing a decade. In N. E. Grunberg, R. E. Nisbett, J. Rodin, & J. E. Singer (Eds.), *A distinctive approach to psychological research: The influence of Stanley Schachter* (pp. 66–86). Hillsdale, NJ: Erlbaum.

Latané, B., Williams, K., & Harkins, S. (2006). Many hands make light the work: The causes and consequences of social loafing. In J. M. Levine & R. L. Moreland (Eds.), *Small groups* (pp. 297–308). New York: Psychology Press.

Latané, B., & Bourgeois, M. J. (2001). Successfully simulating dynamic social impact: Three levels of prediction. In J. P. Forgas & K. D. Williams (Eds.), *Social influence: Direct and indirect processes* (pp. 61–76). Philadelphia: Psychology Press.

Latané, B., & Dabbs, J. M. (1975). Sex, group size, and helping in three cities. *Sociometry, 38*, 108–194.

Latané, B., & Darley, J. M. (1968). Group inhibition of bystander intervention. *Journal of Personality and Social Psychology, 10*, 215–221.

Latané, B., & Darley, J. M. (1970). *The unresponsive bystander: Why doesn't he help?* Englewood Cliffs, NJ: Prentice Hall.

Latané, B., & L'Herrou, T. (1996). Spatial clustering in the conformity game: Dynamic social impact in electronic games. *Journal of Personality and Social Psychology, 70*, 1218–1230.

Latané, B., & Nida, S. (1981). Ten years of research on group size and helping. *Psychological Bulletin, 89*, 308–324.

Lau, R. R., & Russell, D. (1980). Attributions in the sports pages: A field test of some current hypotheses about attribution research. *Journal of Personality and Social Psychology, 39*, 29–38.

Laughlin, P. R. (1980). Social combination processes of cooperative problem-solving groups as verbal intellective tasks. In M. Fishbein (Ed.), *Progress in social psychology* (Vol. 1, pp. 127–155). Hillsdale, NJ: Erlbaum.

Laursen, B., & Hartup, W. W. (2002). The origins of reciprocity and social exchange in friendships. In L. Brett & W. G. Graziano (Eds.), *Social exchange in development: New directions for child and adolescent development* (pp. 27–40). San Francisco: Jossey-Bass/Pfeiffer.

Lawler, E. J., & Thye, S. R. (1999). Bringing emotions into social exchange theory. *Annual Review of Sociology, 25*, 217–244.

Lazarsfeld, P. (Ed.). (1940). *Radio and the printed page*. New York: Duell, Sloan & Pearce.

Lazarus, R. S. (1966). *Psychological stress and the coping process*. New York: McGraw-Hill.

Lazarus, R. S. (1995). Vexing research problems inherent in cognitive-mediational theories of emotion—and some solutions. *Psychological Inquiry, 6*, 183–196.

Lazarus, R. S. (2000). Toward better research on stress and coping. *American Psychologist, 55*, 665–673.

Lazarus, R. S., & Folkman, S. (1984). *Stress, appraisal, and coping*. New York: Springer-Verlag.

Le Bon, G. (1895). *The crowd*. London: Unwin.

Le, B., & Agnew, C. R. (2003). Commitment and its theorized determinants: A meta-analysis of the investment model. *Personal Relationships, 10*, 37–57.

Leary, M. R. (2004). *The curse of the self: Self-awareness, egotism, and the quality of human life*. New York: Oxford University Press.

Leary, M. R. (2004). The self we know and the self we show: Self-esteem, self-presentation, and the maintenance of interpersonal relationships. In M. B. Brewer & M. Hewstone (Eds.), *Emotion and motivation* (pp. 204–224). Malden, MA: Blackwell.

Leary, M. R., & Baumeister, R. F. (2000). The nature and function of self-esteem: Sociometer theory. In M. P. Zanna (Ed.), *Advances in experimental social psychology* (Vol. 32, pp. 1–62). San Diego, CA: Academic Press.

Leary, M. R., & Tangney, J. P. (2003). The self as an organizing construct in the behavioral and social sciences. In M. R. Leary & J. P. Tangney (Eds.), *Handbook of self and identity* (pp. 3–14). New York: Guilford Press.

Lea, M., & Spears, R. (1995). Love at first byte: Building personal relationships over computer networks. In J. T. Wood & S. W. Duck (Eds.), *Understudied relationships: Off the beaten track* (pp. 197–233). Thousand Oaks, CA: Sage.

Lea, M., Spears, R., & de Groot, D. (2001). Knowing me, knowing you: Anonymity effects on social identity processes within groups. *Personality and Social Psychology Bulletin, 27*, 526–537.

Leathers, D. G. (1997). *Successful nonverbal communication: Principles and applications*. Needham Heights, MA: Allyn & Bacon.

Lederman, L. C., Stewart, L. P., Goodheart, F. W., & Laitman, L. (2003). A case against "binge" as a term of choice: Convincing college students to personalize messages about dangerous drinking. *Journal of Health Communication, 8*, 79–91.

Lee, A. Y. (2001). The mere exposure effect: An uncertainty reduction explanation revisited. *Personality and Social Psychology Bulletin, 27*, 1255–1266.

Lee, E. (2004). Effects of visual representation on social influence in computer-mediated communication: Experimental tests of the social identity model of deindividuation effects. *Human Communication Research, 30*, 234–259.

Lee, H. (1960). *To kill a mockingbird*. New York: Warner Books.

Lee, R. W. (2001). Citizen heroes. *New American, 17*, 19–32.

Lee, Y., & Seligman, M. E. P. (1997). Are Americans more optimistic than the Chinese? *Personality and Social Psychology Bulletin, 23*, 32–40.

Lehman, D. R., Davis, C. G., De Longis, A., & Wortman, C. B. (1993). Positive and negative life changes following bereavement and their relations to adjustment. *Journal of Social and Clinical Psychology, 12*, 90–112.

Lehman, D. R., Lempert, R. O., & Nisbett, R. E. (1988). The effects of graduate training on reasoning: Formal discipline and thinking about everyday-life events. *American Psychologist, 43*, 431–442.

Leippe, M. R., & Eisenstadt, D. (1994). Generalization of dissonance reduction: Decreasing prejudice through induced compliance. *Journal of Personality and Social Psychology, 67*, 395–413.

Leippe, M. R., & Eisenstadt, D. (1998). A self-accountability model of dissonance reduction: Multiple modes on a continuum of elaboration. In E. Harmon-Jones & J. S. Mills (Eds.), *Cognitive dissonance theory: Revival with revisions and controversies*. Washington, DC: American Psychological Association.

Leishman, K. (1988, February). Heterosexuals and AIDS. *Atlantic*, pp. 39–57.

Lemieux, R., & Hale, J. L. (1999). Intimacy, passion, and commitment in young romantic relationships: Successfully measuring the triangular theory of love. *Psychological Reports, 85*, 497–503.

Lench, H., & Ditto, P. (2008). Automatic optimism: Biased use of base rate information for positive and negative events. *Journal of Experimental Social Psychology, 44*, 631–639.

Leor, J., Poole, W. K., & Kloner, R. A. (1996). Sudden cardiac death triggered by an earthquake. *New England Journal of Medicine, 334*, 413–419.

Lepper, M. R. (1995). Theory by numbers? Some concerns about meta-analysis as a theoretical tool. *Applied Cognitive Psychology, 9*, 411–422.

Lepper, M. R. (1996). Intrinsic motivation and extrinsic rewards: A commentary on Cameron and Pierce's meta-analysis. *Review of Educational Research, 66*, 5–32.

Lepper, M. R., Corpus, J. H., & Iyengar, S. S. (2005). Intrinsic and extrinsic motivational orientations in the classroom: Age differences and academic correlates. *Journal of Educational Psychology, 97*, 184–196.

Lepper, M. R., Greene, D., & Nisbett, R. E. (1973). Undermining children's intrinsic interest with extrinsic reward: A test of the overjustification hypothesis. *Journal of Personality and Social Psychology, 28*, 129–137.

Lepper, M. R., Henderlong, J., & Gingras, I. (1999). Understanding the effects of extrinsic rewards on intrinsic motivation—uses and abuses of meta-analysis: Comment on Deci, Koestner, and Ryan (1999). *Psychological Bulletin, 125,* 669–676.

Lerner, J. S., & Tetlock, P. E. (1999). Accounting for the effects of accountability. *Psychological Bulletin, 125,* 255–275.

Lerner, M. J. (1980). *The belief in a just world: A fundamental decision.* New York: Plenum.

Lerner, M. J. (1991). The belief in a just world and the "heroic motive": Searching for "constants" in the psychology of religious ideology. *International Journal for the Psychology of Religion, 1,* 27–32.

Lerner, M. J. (1998). The two forms of belief in a just world. In L. Montada & M. J. Lerner (Eds.), *Responses to victimization and belief in a just world.* (pp. 247–269). New York: Plenum Press.

Lerner, M. J., & Grant, P. R. (1990). The influences of commitment to justice and ethnocentrism on children's allocations of pay. *Social Psychology Quarterly, 53,* 229–238.

Lerner, M. J., & Miller, D. T. (1978). Just world research and the attribution process: Looking back and ahead. *Psychological Bulletin, 85,* 1030–1051.

Leung, K. (1996). Beliefs in Chinese culture. In M. H. Bond (Ed.), *The handbook of Chinese psychology* (pp. 247–262). Hong Kong: Oxford University Press.

Leung, K., & Bond, M. H. (1984). The impact of cultural collectivism on reward allocation. *Journal of Personality and Social Psychology, 47,* 793–804.

Leventhal, H., Watts, J. C., & Pagano, F. (1967). Effects of fear and instructions on how to cope with danger. *Journal of Personality and Social Psychology, 6,* 313–321.

Levett, L. M., Danielsen, E. M., Kovera, M. B., & Cutler, B. L. (2005). The psychology of jury and juror decision making. In N. Brewer & K. D. Williams (Eds.), *Psychology and law: An empirical perspective* (pp. 365–406). New York: Guilford.

Levi, P. (1986). *"Survival in Auschwitz" and "The Reawakening": Two memoirs.* New York: Summit Books.

Levin, D. T. (2000). Race as a visual feature: Using visual search and perceptual discrimination tasks to understand face categories and the cross-race recognition deficit. *Journal of Experimental Psychology: General, 129,* 559–574.

Levine, J. M. (1989). Reaction to opinion deviance in small groups. In P. B. Paulus (Ed.), *Psychology of group influence* (2nd ed., pp. 187–231). Hillsdale, NJ: Erlbaum.

Levine, J. M., Higgins, E. T., & Choi, H.-S. (2000). Development of strategic norms in groups. *Organizational Behavior and Human Decision Processes, 82,* 88–101.

Levine, J. M., & Moreland, R. L. (1998). Small groups. In D. T. Gilbert, S. T. Fiske, & G. Lindzey (Eds.), *The handbook of social psychology* (4th ed., Vol. 2, pp. 415–469). New York: McGraw-Hill.

Levine, J. M., & Moreland, R. L. (2006). Small groups: An overview. In J. M. Levine & R. L. Moreland (Eds.), *Small groups* (pp. 1–10). New York: Psychology Press.

Levine, J. M., Moreland, R. L., & Choi, S. (2001). Group socialization and newcomer innovation. In M. Hogg & S. Tindale (Eds.), *Blackwell handbook of social psychology: Group Processes* (pp. 86–106). Oxford, England: Blackwell Publishers.

Levine, J. M., & Russo, E. M. (1987). Majority and minority influence. In C. Hendrick (Ed.), *Group processes: Review of personality and social psychology* (Vol. 8, pp. 13–54). Newbury Park, CA: Sage.

Levine, J. M., & Thompson, L. (1996). Conflict in groups. In E. T. Higgins & A. W. Kruglanski (Eds.), *Social psychology: Handbook of basic principles* (pp. 745–776). New York: Guilford Press.

Levine, R. A., & Campbell, D. T. (1972). *Ethnocentrism: Theories of conflict, ethnic attitudes, and group behavior.* New York: Wiley.

Levine, R., Sato, S., Hashimoto, T., & Verma, J. (1995). Love and marriage in eleven cultures. *Journal of Cross-Cultural Psychology, 26,* 554–571.

Levine, R. V. (2003). The kindness of strangers: People's willingness to help someone during a chance encounter on a city street varies considerably around the world. *American Scientist, 91,* 226–233.

Levine, R. V., Martinez, T. S., Brase, G., & Sorenson, K. (1994). Helping in 36 U.S. cities. *Journal of Personality and Social Psychology, 67,* 69–82.

Levine, R. V., Norenzayan, A., & Philbrick, K. (2001). Cross-cultural differences in helping strangers. *Journal of Cross-Cultural Psychology, 32,* 543–560.

Levy, D. A., & Nail, P. R. (1993). Contagion: A theoretical and empirical review and reconceptualization. *Genetic, Social, and General Psychology Monographs, 119,* 233–284.

Levy, J. S., & Morgan, T. C. (1984). The frequency and seriousness of war: An inverse relationship? *Journal of Conflict Resolution, 28,* 731–749.

Lévy-Leboyer, C. (1988). Success and failure in applying psychology. *American Psychologist, 43,* 779–785.

Lewin, K. (1943). Defining the "field at a given time." *Psychological Review, 50,* 292–310.

Lewin, K. (1946). Action research and minority problems. *Journal of Social Issues, 2,* 34–46.

Lewin, K. (1947). Frontiers in group dynamics. *Human Relations, 1,* 5–41.

Lewin, K. (1948). *Resolving social conflicts: Selected papers in group dynamics.* New York: Harper.

Lewin, K. (1951). Problems of research in social psychology. In D. Cartwright (Ed.), *Field theory in social science* (pp. 155–169). New York: Harper.

Lewis, C. C. (1995). *Educating hearts and minds: Reflections on Japanese preschool and elementary education.* Cambridge: Cambridge University Press.

Lewis, K., Belliveau, M., Herndon, B., & Keller, J. (2007). Group cognition, membership change, and performance: Investigating the benefits and detriments of collective knowledge. *Organizational Behavior and Human Decision Processes, 103,* 159–178.

Lewis, M., & Ramsay, D. (2004). Development of self-recognition, personal pronoun use, and pretend play during the 2nd year. *Child Development, 75,* 1821–1831.

Leyens, J. P., Camino, L., Parke, R. D., & Berkowitz, L. (1975). Effects of movie violence on aggression in a field setting as a function of group dominance and cohesion. *Journal of Personality and Social Psychology, 32,* 346–360.

Liberman, A., & Chaiken, S. (1992). Defensive processing of personally relevant health messages. *Personality and Social Psychology Bulletin, 18,* 669–679.

Liberman, V., Samuels, S. M., & Ross, L. D. (2004). The name of the game: Predictive power of reputations versus situational labels in determining Prisoner's Dilemma Game moves. *Personality and Social Psychology Bulletin, 30,* 1175–1185.

Lieberman, M. (2007). Social cognitive neuroscience: A review of core processes. *Annual Review of Psychology, 58,* 259–289.

Lieberman, M. D., Jarcho, J. M., & Obayashi, J. (2005). Attributional inference across cultures: Similar automatic attributions and different controlled corrections. *Personality and Social Psychology Bulletin, 31*(7), 889–901.

Lieberman, M. D., & Rosenthal, R. (2001). Why introverts can't always tell who likes them: Multitasking and nonverbal decoding. *Journal of Personality and Social Psychology, 80,* 294–310.

Liebert, R. M., & Baron, R. A. (1972). Some immediate effects of televised violence on children's behavior. *Developmental Psychology, 6,* 469–475.

Liebert, R. M., & Sprafkin, J. (1988). *The early window* (3rd ed.). New York: Pergamon Press.

Lim, T.-S., & Choi, H.-S. (1996). Interpersonal relationships in Korea. In W. B. Gudykunst, S. Ting-Toomey, & T. Nishida (Eds.), *Communication in personal relationships across cultures* (pp. 122–136). Thousand Oaks, CA: Sage.

Lin, Y. H. W., & Rusbult, C. E. (1995). Commitment to dating relationships and cross-sex friendships in America and China. *Journal of Social and Personal Relationships, 12,* 7–26.

Lindsay, R. C. L., & Wells, G. L. (1985). Improving eyewitness identifications from lineups: Simultaneous versus sequential lineup presentation. *Journal of Applied Psychology, 70,* 556–564.

Lindsay, R. C. L., Wells, G. L., & Rumpel, C. M. (1981). Can people detect eyewitness-identification accuracy within and across situations? *Journal of Applied Psychology, 66,* 79–89.

Linville, P. W., Fischer, G. W., & Salovey, P. (1989). Perceived distributions of characteristics of in-group and out-group members: Empirical evidence and a computer simulation. *Journal of Personality and Social Psychology, 57,* 165–188.

Linz, D. G., Donnerstein, E., & Penrod, S. (1984). The effects of multiple exposures to filmed violence against women. *Journal of Communication, 34,* 130–147.

Lipkus, I. M., Dalbert, C., & Siegler, I. C. (1996). The importance of distinguishing the belief in a just world for self versus for others: Implications for psychological well-being. *Personality and Social Psychology Bulletin, 22,* 666–677.

Lippmann, W. (1922). *Public opinion*. New York: Free Press.

Lipsey, M. W., Wilson, D. B., Cohen, M. A., & Derzon, J. H. (1997). Is there a causal relationship between alcohol use and violence? A synthesis of evidence. In M. Galanter (Ed.), *Recent developments in alcoholism: Vol. 13. Alcohol and violence: Epidemiology, neurobiology, psychology, and family issues* (pp. 245–282). New York: Plenum.

Litt, M. D. (1988). Self-efficacy and perceived control: Cognitive mediators of pain tolerance. *Journal of Personality and Social Psychology, 54,* 149–160.

Little, A. C., & Perrett, D. I. (2002). Putting beauty back in the eye of the beholder. *Psychologist, 15,* 28–32.

Livesley, W. J., & Bromley, D. B. (1973). *Person perception in childhood and adolescence*. New York: Wiley.

Lloyd, S. A., & Cate, R. M. (1985). The developmental course of conflict in dissolution of premarital relationships. *Journal of Social and Personal Relationships, 2,* 179–194.

Locken, B., & Peck, J. (2005). The effects of instructional frame on female adolescents' evaluations of larger-sized models in print advertising. *Journal of Applied Social Psychology, 35,* 850–868.

Lockwood, P. (2002). Could it happen to you? Predicting the impact of downward comparisons on the self. *Journal of Personality and Social Psychology, 82,* 343–358.

Lodish, L. M., Abraham, M., Kalmenson, S., Lievelsberger, J., Lubetkin, B., Richardson, B., & Stevens, M. E. (1995). How TV advertising works: A meta-analysis of 389 real-world split-cable TV advertising experiments. *Journal of Marketing Research, 32,* 125–139.

Loftus, E. F. (1979). *Eyewitness testimony*. Cambridge, MA: Harvard University Press.

Loftus, E. F. (1993). The reality of repressed memories. *American Psychologist, 48,* 518–537.

Loftus, E. F. (2005). Planting misinformation in the human mind: A 30-year investigation of the malleability of memory. *Learning and Memory, 12,* 361–366.

Loftus, E. F., Garry, M., & Hayne, H. (2008). Repressed and recovered memory. In E. Borgida and S. T. Fiske (Eds.), *Beyond common sense: Psychological science in the courtroom* (pp. 177–194). Malden, MA: Blackwell.

Loftus, E. F., Loftus, G. R., & Messo, J. (1987). Some facts about "weapons focus." *Law and Human Behavior, 11,* 55–62.

Loftus, E. F., Miller, D. G., & Burns, H. J. (1978). Semantic integration of verbal information into a visual memory. *Journal of Experimental Psychology: Human Learning and Memory, 4,* 19–31.

Loftus, G. R., & Harley, E. M. (2005). Why is it easier to identify someone close than far away? *Psychonomic Bulletin and Review, 12,* 43–65.

Lonner, W., & Berry, J. (Eds.). (1986). *Field methods in cross-cultural research*. Beverly Hills, CA: Sage.

Lord, C. G., Lepper, M. R., & Preston, E. (1984). Considering the opposite: A corrective strategy for social judgment. *Journal of Personality and Social Psychology, 47,* 1231–1243.

Lord, C. G., Scott, K. O., Pugh, M. A., & Desforges, D. M. (1997). Leakage beliefs and the correspondence bias. *Personality and Social Psychology Bulletin, 23,* 824–836.

Lore, R. K., & Schultz, L. A. (1993). Control of human aggression. *American Psychologist, 48,* 16–25.

Lorenz, K. (1966). *On aggression* (M. Wilson, Trans.). New York: Harcourt Brace.

Lott, A. J., & Lott, B. E. (1961). Group cohesiveness, communication level, and conformity. *Journal of Abnormal and Social Psychology, 62,* 408–412.

Lott, A. J., & Lott, B. E. (1974). The role of reward in the formation of positive interpersonal attitudes. In T. L. Huston (Ed.), *Foundations of interpersonal attraction* (pp. 171–189). New York: Academic Press.

Lucas, J. W., & Lovaglia, M. J. (2005). Self-handicapping: Gender, race, and status. *Current Research in Social Psychology, 10,* 234–249.

Ludwig, T. D., Gray, T. W., & Rowell, A. (1998). Increasing recycling in academic buildings: A systematic replication. *Journal of Applied Behavior Analysis, 31,* 683–686.

Lumsdaine, A. A., & Janis, I. L. (1953). Resistance to "counterpropaganda" produced by one-sided and two-sided "propaganda" presentations. *Public Opinion Quarterly, 17,* 311–318.

Lundqvist, D., & Öhman, A. (2005). Caught by the evil eye: Nonconscious information processing, emotion, and attention to facial stimuli. In L. Barrett Feldman, P. Niedenthal, & P. Winkielman (Eds.), *Emotion and consciousness* (pp. 97–122). New York, Guilford Press.

Lun, J., Sinclair, S., Whitchurch, E., & Glenn, C. (2007). (Why) do I think what you think? Epistemic social tuning and implicit prejudice. *Journal of Personality and Social Psychology, 93,* 957–972.

Lykken, D., & Tellegen, A. (1996). Happiness is a stochastic phenomenon. *Psychological Science, 7,* 186–189.

Lynn, M., & Shurgot, B. A. (1984). Responses to lonely hearts advertisements: Effects of reported physical attractiveness, physique, and coloration. *Personality and Social Psychology Bulletin, 10,* 349–357.

Lynn, S. J., Lock, T., Loftus, E., Krackow, E., & Lilienfeld, S. O. (2003). The remembrance of things past: Problematic memory recovery techniques in psychotherapy. In S. O. Lilienfeld & S. J. Lynn (Eds.), *Science and pseudoscience in clinical psychology* (pp. 205–239). New York: Guilford Press.

Lysak, H., Rule, B. G., & Dobbs, A. R. (1989). Conceptions of aggression: Prototype or defining features? *Personality and Social Psychology Bulletin, 15,* 233–243.

Lyubomirsky, S., Caldwell, N. D., & Nolen-Hoeksema, S. (1993). Effects of ruminative and distracting responses to depressed mood on retrieval of autobiographical memories. *Journal of Personality and Social Psychology, 75,* 166–177.

Lyubomirsky, S., Sheldon, K. M., & Schkade, D. (2005). Pursuing happiness: The architecture of sustainable change. *Review of General Psychology, 9,* 111–131.

Maass, A., & Clark, R. D., III. (1984). Hidden impact of minorities: Fifteen years of research. *Psychological Bulletin, 95,* 428–450.

Maccoby, E. E., & Jacklin, C. N. (1974). *The psychology of sex differences.* Stanford, CA: Stanford University Press.

MacCoun, R. J. (1989). Experimental research on jury decision-making. *Science, 244,* 1046–1050.

MacDonald, T. K., Zanna, M. P., & Fong, G. T. (1996). Why common sense goes out the window: Effects of alcohol on intentions to use condoms. *Personality and Social Psychology Bulletin, 22,* 763–775.

Mackie, D. M. (1987). Systematic and nonsystematic processing of majority and minority persuasive communications. *Journal of Personality and Social Psychology, 53,* 41–52.

MacKinnon, C. (1993, July-August). Turning rape into pornography: Postmodern genocide. *Ms.,* pp. 24–30.

Maclean, N. (1983). *A river runs through it.* Chicago: University of Chicago Press.

MacNeil, M. K., & Sherif, M. (1976). Norm change over subject generations as a function of arbitrariness of prescribed norms. *Journal of Personality and Social Psychology, 34,* 762–773.

Maddon, S., Guyll, M., Spoth, R., & Willard, J. (2004). The synergistic accumulative effect of parents' beliefs on childrens' drinking behavior. *Psychological Science, 15,* 837–845.

Maddux, J. E. (1995). *Self-efficacy, adaptation, and adjustment: Theory, research, and application.* New York: Plenum.

Madon, S., Guyll, M., Buller, A. A., Scherr, K., Willard, J., & Spoth, R. (in press). The mediation of mothers' self-fulfilling effects on their children's alcohol use: Self-verification, informational conformity, and modeling processes. *Journal of Personality and Social Psychology.*

Madon, S., Smith, A., Jussim, L., Russell, D. W., Eccles, J. S., Palumbo, P., & Walkiewicz, M. (2001). Am I as you see me or do you see me as I am? Self-fulfilling prophecies and self-verification. *Personality and Social Psychology Bulletin, 27,* 1214–1224.

Madon, S., Willard, J., Buller, A. A., & Scherr, K. (in press). Self-fulfilling prophecies. *International encyclopedia of the social sciences* (2nd Ed.). Farmington Hills, MI: Thomson/Gale.

Madon, S., Willard, J., Guyll, M., Trudeau, L., & Spoth, R. (2006). Self-fulfilling prophecy effects of mothers' beliefs on children's alcohol use: Accumulation, dissipation, and stability over time. *Journal of Personality and Social Psychology, 90,* 911–926

Magaro, P. A., & Ashbrook, R. M. (1985). The personality of societal groups. *Journal of Personality and Social Psychology, 48,* 1479–1489.

Magoo, G., & Khanna, R. (1991). Altruism and willingness to donate blood. *Journal of Personality and Clinical Studies, 7,* 21–24.

Maier, N. R. F., & Solem, A. R. (1952). The contribution of a discussion leader to the quality of group thinking: The effective use of minority opinions. *Human Relations, 5,* 277–288.

Main, M., Kaplan, N., & Cassidy, J. (1985). Security in infancy, childhood, and adulthood: A move to the level of representation. In T. Bretherton & E. Waters (Eds.), *Growing points of attachment theory and research. Monographs of the Society for Research on Child Development, 50,* 66–104.

Maio, G. R., & Olson, J. M. (1995). Relations between values, attitudes, and behavioral intentions: The moderating role of attitude function. *Journal of Experimental Social Psychology, 31,* 266–285.

Major, B., & Gramzow, R. H. (1999). Abortion as stigma: Cognitive and emotional implications of concealment. *Journal of Personality and Social Psychology, 77,* 735–745.

Malamuth, N. M. (1981). Rape fantasies as a function of exposure to violent sexual stimuli. *Archives of Sexual Behavior, 10,* 33–47.

Malamuth, N. M., Addison, T., & Koss, M. (2000). Pornography and sexual aggression: Are there reliable effects and can we understand them? *Annual Review of Sex Research 11,* 26–91.

Malamuth, N. M., Linz, D. G., Heavey, C. L., Barnes, G., & Acker, M. (1995). Using the confluence model of sexual aggression to predict men's conflict with women: A 10-year follow-up study. *Journal of Personality and Social Psychology, 69,* 353–369.

Malle, B. F., & Knobe, J. (1997). Which behaviors do people explain? A basic actor-observer asymmetry. *Journal of Personality and Social Psychology, 72,* 288–304.

Malloy, T. E. (2001). Difference to inference: Teaching logical and statistical reasoning through on-line interactivity. *Behavior Research Methods, Instruments, and Computers, 33,* 270–273.

Malpass, R. S., & Devine, P. G. (1981). Eyewitness identification: Lineup instructions and the absence of the offender. *Journal of Applied Psychology, 66,* 482–489.

Malpass, R. S., Tredoux, C. G., & McQuiston-Surrett, D. (2007). Lineup construction and lineup fairness. *The handbook of eyewitness psychology,* Vol II: *Memory for people* (pp. 155–178). Mahwah, NJ: Lawrence Erlbaum.

Maner, J. K., Luce, C. L., Neuberg, S. L., Cialdini, R. B., Brown, S., & Sagarin, B. J. (2002). The effects of perspective taking on motivations for helping: Still no evidence for altruism. *Personality and Social Psychology Bulletin, 28,* 1601–1610.

Manning, R., Levine, M., & Collins, A. (2007). The Kitty Genovese murder and the social psychology of helping: The parable of the 38 witnesses. *American Psychologist, 62,* 555–562

Manstead, A. S. R. (1997). Situations, belongingness, attitudes, and culture: Four lessons learned from social psychology. In G. McGarty & H. S. Haslam (Eds.), *The message of social psychology: Perspectives on mind and society* (pp. 238–251). Oxford, England: Blackwell.

Marion, R. (1995, August). The girl who mewed. *Discover,* pp. 38–40.

Markey, P. M. (2000). Bystander intervention in computer-mediated communication. *Computers in Human Behavior, 16,* 183–188.

Markman, K., McMullen, M., & Elizaga, R. (2008). Counterfactual thinking, persistence, and performance: A test of the reflection and evaluation model. *Journal of Experimental Social Psychology, 44,* 421–428.

Markoff, J. (1996, December 21). Steven Jobs making move back to Apple. *New York Times,* p. 37.

Markus, H. R. (1977). Self-schemata and processing information about the self. *Journal of Personality and Social Psychology, 35,* 63–78.

Markus, H. R., & Kitayama, S. (1991). Culture and the self: Implications for cognition, emotion, and motivation. *Psychological Review, 98,* 224–253.

Markus, H. R., & Kitayama, S. (2001). The cultural construction of self and emotion: Implications for social behavior. In W. G. Parrott (Ed.), *Emotions in social psychology: Essential readings* (pp. 119–137). Philadelphia: Psychology Press.

Markus, H. R., Kitayama, S., & Heiman, R. J. (1996). Culture and "basic" psychological principles. In E. T. Higgins & A. W. Kruglanski (Eds.), *Social psychology: Handbook of basic principles* (pp. 857–913). New York: Guilford Press.

Markus, H. R., & Zajonc, R. B. (1985). The cognitive perspective in social psychology. In G. Lindzey & E. Aronson (Eds.), *Handbook of social psychology* (3rd ed., Vol. 1, pp. 137–230). New York: McGraw-Hill.

Marlowe, D., & Gergen, K. J. (1970). Personality and social behavior. In K. J. Gergen & D. Marlowe (Eds.), *Personality and social behavior* (pp. 1–75). Reading, MA: Addison-Wesley.

Marques, J., Abrams, D., & Serodio, R. (2001). Being better by being right: Subjective group dynamics and derogation of in-group deviants when generic norms are undermined. *Journal of Personality and Social Psychology, 81,* 436–447.

Martin, A. J., Berenson, K. R., Griffing, S., Sage, R. E., Madry, L., Bingham, L. E., & Primm, B. J. (2000). The process of leaving an abusive relationship: The role of risk assessments and decision certainty. *Journal of Family Violence, 15,* 109–122.

Martin, L. L., & Tesser, A. (1996). Some ruminative thoughts. In R. S. Wyer, Jr. (Ed.), *Advances in social cognition* (Vol. 9, pp. 1–47). Hillsdale, NJ: Erlbaum.

Martin, N. G., Eaves, L. J., Heath, A. R., Jardine, R., Feingold, L. M., & Eysenck, H. J. (1986). Transmission of social attitudes. *Proceedings of the National Academy of Science, 83,* 4364–4368.

Martinie, M. A., & Fointiat, V. (2006). Self-esteem, trivialization, and attitude change. *Swiss Journal of Psychology, 65,* 221–225.

Marx, D. M. & Roman, J. S. (2002). Female role models: Protecting women's math test performance. *Personality and Social Psychology Bulletin, 28,* 1183–1193.

Masicampo, E., & Baumeister, R. (2008). Toward a physiology of dual-process reasoning and judgment: Lemonade, willpower, and expensive rule-based analysis. *Psychological Science, 19,* 255–260.

Masuda, T., Ellsworth, P. C., & Mesquita, B. (2008). Placing the face in context: Cultural differences in the perception of facial emotion. *Journal of Personality and Social Psychology, 94,* 365-381.

Masuda, T., & Kitayama, S. (1996). *Correspondence bias in Japan.* Unpublished manuscript, Kyoto University.

Masuda, T., & Kitayama, S. (2003). Perceiver-induced constraint and attitude attribution in Japan and the US: A case for the cultural dependence of the correspondence bias. *Journal of Experimental Social Psychology, 40,* 409–416.

Masuda, T., & Nisbett, R. E. (2006). Culture and change blindness. *Cognitive Science: A Multidisciplinary Journal, 30,* 381–399.

Matsumoto, D., & Ekman, P. (1989). American-Japanese differences in intensity ratings of facial expressions of emotion. *Motivation and Emotion, 13,* 143–157.

Matsumoto, D., & Ekman, P. (2004). The relationship among expressions, labels, and descriptions of contempt. *Journal of Personality and Social Psychology, 87*(4), 529–540.

Matsumoto, D., & Kudoh, T. (1993). American-Japanese cultural differences in attributions of personality based on smiles. *Journal of Nonverbal Behavior, 17,* 231–243.

Mazur, A., Booth, A., & Dabbs, J. M. (1992). Testosterone and chess competition. *Social Psychology Quarterly, 55,* 70–77.

Mazzoni, G., & Lynn, S. J. (2007). Using hypnosis in eyewitness memory: Past and current issues. In M. P. Toglia, J. D. Read, D. F. Ross, & R. C. L. Lindsay (Eds.) *The handbook of eyewitness psychology,* Vol I: *Memory for events* (pp. 321–338). Mahwah, NJ: Erlbaum.

McAlister, A., Perry, C., Killen, J. D., Slinkard, L. A., & Maccoby, N. (1980). Pilot study of smoking, alcohol, and drug abuse prevention. *American Journal of Public Health, 70,* 719–721.

McAllister, H. A. (1996). Self-serving bias in the classroom: Who shows it? Who knows it? *Journal of Educational Psychology, 88,* 123–131.

McAndrew, F. T. (2002). New evolutionary perspectives on altruism: Multilevel-selection and costly-signaling theories. *Current Directions in Psychological Science, 11,* 79–82.

McArthur, L. Z. (1972). The how and what of why: Some determinants and consequences of causal attribution. *Journal of Personality and Social Psychology, 22,* 171–193.

McArthur, L. Z., & Baron, R. M. (1983). Toward an ecological theory of social perception. *Psychological Review, 90,* 215–238.

McArthur, L. Z., & Berry, D. S. (1987). Cross cultural agreement in perceptions of babyfaced adults. *Journal of Cross-Cultural Psychology, 18,* 165–192.

McArthur, L. Z., & Resko, G. B. (1975). The portrayal of men and women in American television commercials. *Journal of Social Psychology, 97,* 209–220.

McCabe, M. P., & Ricciardelli, L. A. (2003a). Sociocultural influences on body image and body changes among adolescent boys and girls. *Journal of Social Psychology, 143,* 5–26.

McCabe, M. P., & Ricciardelli, L. A. (2003b). A longitudinal study of body change strategies among adolescent males. *Journal of Youth and Adolescence, 32,* 105–113.

McCarthy, J. F., & Kelly, B. R. (1978). Aggressive behavior and its effect on performance over time in ice hockey athletes: An archival study. *International Journal of Sport Psychology, 9,* 90–96.

McCauley, C. (1989). The nature of social influence in groupthink: Compliance and internalization. *Journal of Personality and Social Psychology, 57,* 250–260.

McClellan, S. (2008). *What happened: Inside the Bush White House and Washington's culture of deception.* New York: Public Affairs.

McConahay, J. B. (1981). Reducing racial prejudice in desegregated schools. In W. D. Hawley (Ed.), *Effective school desegregation.* Beverly Hills, CA: Sage.

McConahay, J. B. (1986). Modern racism, ambivalence, and the Modern Racism Scale. In J. F. Dovidio & S. L. Gaertner (Eds.), *Prejudice, discrimination, and racism: Theory and research* (pp. 91–125). New York: Academic Press.

McCrea, S., Hirt, E., & Milner, B. (2008). She works hard for the money: Valuing effort underlies gender differences in behavioral self-handicapping. *Journal of Experimental Social Psychology, 44,* 292–311.

McCrea, S. M. (2008). Self-handicapping, excuse making, and counterfactual thinking: Consequences for self-esteem and future motivation. *Journal of Personality and Social Psychology, 95,* 274–292.

McCullough, M., Kimeldorf, M., & Cohen, A. (2008). An adaptation for altruism? The social causes, social effects, and social evolution of gratitude. *Current Directions in Psychological Science, 17,* 281–285.

McDonald, H. E., & Hirt, E. R. (1997). When expectancy meets desire: Motivational effects in reconstructive memory. *Journal of Personality and Social Psychology, 72,* 5–23.

McFadyen-Ketchum, S. A., Bates, J. E., Dodge, K. A., & Pettit, G. S. (1996). Patterns of change in early childhood aggressive-disruptive behavior: Gender differences in predictions from early coercive and affectionate mother-child interactions. *Child Development, 67,* 2417–2433.

McGlone, M., & Aronson, J. (2006). Social identity salience and stereotype threat. *Journal of Applied Developmental Psychology, 27,* 486–493.

McGraw, A. P., Mellers, B. A., & Tetlock, P. E. (2005). Expectations and emotions of Olympic athletes. *Journal of Experimental Social Psychology, 41,* 438–446.

McGregor, B., Antoni, M., Boyers, A., Alferi, S., Cruess, D., Kilbourn, K., et al (2004). Cognitive behavioral stress management increases benefit finding and immune function among women with early stage breast cancer. *Journal of Psychosomatic Research, 54,* 1–8.

McGuire, A. M. (1994). Helping behaviors in the natural environment: Dimensions and correlates of helping. *Personality and Social Psychology Bulletin, 20,* 45–56.

McGuire, W. J. (1964). Inducing resistance to persuasion. In L. Berkowitz (Ed.), *Advances in experimental social psychology* (Vol. 1, pp. 192–229). New York: Academic Press.

McGuire, W. J. (1968). Personality and susceptibility to social influence. In E. F. Borgatta & W. W. Lambert (Eds.), *Handbook of personality theory and research* (pp. 1130–1187). Chicago: Rand McNally.

McHugo, G. J., & Smith, C. A. (1996). The power of faces: A review of John T. Lanzetta's research on facial expression and emotion. *Motivation and Emotion, 21,* 85–120.

McIntyre, R. B., Paulson, R. M., & Lord, C. G. (2003). Alleviating women's mathematics stereotype threat through salience of group achievements. *Journal of Experimental Social Psychology, 39,* 83–90.

McNally, R. J. (2003). *Remembering trauma.* Cambridge, MA: Harvard University Press.

McNally, R. J., Bryant, R. A., & Ehlers, A. (2003). Does early psychological intervention promote recovery from posttraumatic stress? *Psychological Science in the Public Interest, 4,* 45–79.

McNally, R. J., Clancy, S. A., & Barrett, H. M. (2005). Reality monitoring in adults reporting repressed, recovered, or continuous memories of childhood sexual abuse. *Journal of Abnormal Psychology, 114*, 147–152.

McNamara, R. S. (1995). *In retrospect: The tragedy and lessons of Vietnam.* New York: Times Books.

McNally, R., & Breslau, N. (2008). Does virtual trauma cause posttraumatic stress disorder?. *American Psychologist, 63*, 282–283.

McPherson, J. M. (1983). The size of voluntary associations. *American Sociological Review, 61*, 1044–1064.

McPherson, M., Smith-Lovin, L., & Cook, J. M. (2001). Birds of a feather: Homophily in social networks. *Annual Review of Sociology, 27*, 415–444.

Medvec, V. H., Madey, S. F., & Gilovich, T. (1995). When less is more: Counterfactual thinking and satisfaction among Olympic medalists. *Journal of Personality and Social Psychology, 69*, 603–610.

Meertens, R. W., & Pettigrew, T. F. (1997). Is subtle prejudice really prejudice? *Public Opinion Quarterly, 61*, 54–71.

Meeus, W. H. J., & Raaijmakers, Q. A. W. (1995). Obedience in modern society: The Utrecht studies. *Journal of Social Issues, 51*, 155–175.

Mehta, M. D. (2001). Pornography in Usenet: A study of 9,800 randomly selected images. *Cyberpsychology and Behavior, 4*, 695–703.

Meissner, C. A., & Brigham, J. C. (2001). Thirty years of investigating the own-race bias in memory for faces: A meta-analytic review. *Psychology, Public Policy, and Law, 7*, 3–35.

Meissner, C. A., Tredoux, C. G., & Parker, J. F. (2005). Eyewitness decisions in simultaneous and sequential lineups: A dual-process signal detection theory analysis. *Memory and Cognition, 33*, 783–792.

Melara, R. D., De Witt–Rickards, T. S., & O'Brien, T. P. (1989). Enhancing lineup identification accuracy: Two codes are better than one. *Journal of Applied Psychology, 74*, 706–713.

Mellers B. A. (2001) Current Directions in Psychological Science, Volume 10, Number 6, December 2001, pp. 210–214(5). Blackwell Publishing

Mendez, L., Mihalas, S., & Hardesty, R. (2006). Gender differences in academic development and performance. *Children's needs III: Development, prevention, and intervention* (pp. 553–565). Washington, DC: National Association of School Psychologists.

Menec, V. H., Perry, R. P., Struthers, C. W., Schonwetter, D. J., Hechter, F. J., & Eichholz, B. L. (1994). Assisting at-risk college students with attributional retraining and effective teaching. *Journal of Applied Social Psychology, 24*, 675–701.

Menninger, W. (1948). Recreation and mental health. *Recreation, 42*, 340–346.

Menon, T., Morris, M. W., Chiu, C., & Hong, Y. (1999). Culture and the construal of agency: Attribution to individual versus group dispositions. *Journal of Personality and Social Psychology, 76*, 701–717.

Merton, R. K. (1948). The self-fulfilling prophecy. *Antioch Review, 8*, 193–210.

Messick, D., & Liebrand, W. B. G. (1995). Individual heuristics and the dynamics of cooperation in large groups. *Psychological Review, 102*, 131–145.

Meston, C. M., & Frohlich, P. F. (2003). Love at first fright: Partner salience moderates roller-coaster-induced excitation transfer. *Archives of Sexual Behavior, 32*(6), 537–544.

Metcalfe, J. (1998). Cognitive optimism: Self-deception or memory-based processing heuristics? *Personality and Social Psychology Review, 2*, 100–110.

Meyer, P. (1999). The sociobiology of human cooperation: The interplay of ultimate and proximate causes. In J. M. G. van der Dennen & D. Smillie (Eds.), *The Darwinian heritage and sociobiology: Human evolution, behavior, and intelligence* (pp. 49–65). Westport, CT: Praeger.

Meyerowitz, B. E., & Chaiken, S. (1987). The effect of message framing on breast self-examination attitudes, intentions, and behavior. *Journal of Personality and Social Psychology, 52*, 500–510.

Mezulis, A. H., Abramson, L. Y., Hyde, J. S., & Hankin, B. L. (2004). Is there a universal positivity bias in attributions? A meta-analytic review of individual, developmental, and cultural differences in the self-serving attributional bias. *Psychological Bulletin, 130*(5), 711–747.

Migration and geographic mobility in metropolitan and nonmetropolitan America, 1995–2000 (2003). United States Census Bureau. Accessed on April 16, 2006, at *www.census.gov/prod/2003pubs/censr-9.pdf.*

Mikulincer, M., Shaver, P. R., Gillath, O., & Nitzberg, R. A. (2005). Attachment, caregiving, and altruism: Boosting attachment security increases compassion and helping. *Journal of Personality and Social Psychology, 89*, 817–839.

Mikulincer, M., & Shaver, P. R. (2003). The attachment behavioral system in adulthood: Activation, psychodynamics, and interpersonal processes. In M. P. Zanna (Ed.), *Advances in experimental social psychology* (Vol. 35; pp. 53–152). San Diego, CA: Academic Press.

Mikulincer, M., & Shaver, P. (2005). Attachment security, compassion, and altruism. *Current Directions in Psychological Science, 14*, 34–38.

Milgram, S. (1961). Nationality and conformity. *Scientific American, 205*, 45–51.

Milgram, S. (1963). Behavioral study of obedience. *Journal of Abnormal and Social Psychology, 67*, 371–378.

Milgram, S. (1969, March). The lost letter technique. *Psychology Today*, pp. 30–33, 67–68.

Milgram, S. (1974). *Obedience to authority: An experimental view.* New York: Harper & Row.

Milgram, S. (1976). Obedience to criminal orders: The compulsion to do evil. In T. Blass (Ed.), *Contemporary social psychology: Representative readings* (pp. 175–184). Itasca, IL: Peacock.

Milgram, S. (1977). *The individual in a social world.* Reading, MA: Addison-Wesley.

Milgram, S., & Sabini, J. (1978). On maintaining urban norms: A field experiment in the subway. In A. Baum, J. E. Singer, & S. Valins (Eds.), *Advances in environmental psychology* (Vol. 1, pp. 9–40). Hillsdale, NJ: Erlbaum.

Mill, J. S. (1843). *A system of logic ratiocinative and inductive.* London.

Miller, A. G. (1986). *The obedience experiments: A case study of controversy in social science.* New York: Praeger.

Miller, A. G. (1995). Constructions of the obedience experiments: A focus upon domains of relevance. *Journal of Social Issues, 51*, 33–53.

Miller, A. G. (1998). Some thoughts prompted by "Speeding with Ned." In J. M. Darley & J. Cooper (Eds.), *Attribution and social interaction* (pp. 37–51). Washington, DC: American Psychological Association.

Miller, A. G., Ashton, W., & Mishal, M. (1990). Beliefs concerning the features of constrained behavior: A basis for the fundamental attribution error. *Journal of Personality and Social Psychology, 59*, 635–650.

Miller, A. G., Collins, B. E., & Brief, D. E. (1995). Perspectives on obedience to authority: The legacy of the Milgram experiments. *Journal of Social Issues, 51*, 1–19.

Miller, A. G., Jones, E. E., & Hinkle, S. (1981). A robust attribution error in the personality domain. *Journal of Experimental Social Psychology, 17*, 587–600.

Miller, C. E., & Anderson, P. D. (1979). Group decision rules and the rejection of deviates. *Social Psychology Quarterly, 42*, 354–363.

Miller, C. T. (1982). The role of performance-related similarity in social comparison of abilities: A test of the related attributes hypothesis. *Journal of Experimental Social Psychology, 18*, 513–523.

Miller, D. T., & Prentice, D. A. (1996). The construction of social norms and standards. In E. T. Higgins & A. W. Kruglanski (Eds.), *Social psychology: Handbook of basic principles* (pp. 799–829). New York: Guilford Press.

Miller, D. T., & Ross, M. (1975). Self-serving biases in the attribution of causality: Fact or fiction? *Psychological Bulletin, 82*, 213–225.

Miller, D., & Taylor, B. (2002). Counterfactual thought, regret, and superstition: How to avoid kicking yourself. In T. Gilovich, D. Griffiin, & D. Kahneman (Eds.), *Heuristics and biases: The psychology of intuitive judgement* (pp. 367–378). New York: Cambridge University Press.

Miller, J. G. (1984). Culture and the development of everyday social explanation. *Journal of Personality and Social Psychology, 46*, 961–978.

Miller, J. G., Bersoff, D. M., & Harwood, R. L. (1990). Perceptions of social responsibilities in India and the United States: Moral imperatives or personal decisions? *Journal of Personality and Social Psychology, 58*, 33–47.

Miller, N., & Bugelski, R. (1948). Minor studies in aggression: The influence of frustrations imposed by the in-group on attitudes expressed by the out-group. *Journal of Psychology, 25*, 437–442.

Miller, N., & Campbell, D. T. (1959). Recency and primacy in persuasion as a function of the timing of speeches and measurements. *Journal of Abnormal and Social Psychology, 59*, 1–9.

Miller, P. V. (2002). The authority and limitation of polls. In J. Manza, F. L. Cook, & B. I. Page (Eds.), *Navigating public opinion* (pp. 221–231). New York: Oxford University Press.

Mills, J. (1958). Changes in moral attitudes following temptation. *Journal of Personality, 26*, 517–531.

Mills, J., Clark, M., Ford, T., & Johnson, M. (2004). Measurement of communal strength. *Personal Relationships, 11*, 213–230.

Mills, J., & Clark, M. S. (1982). Communal and exchange relationships. In L. Wheeler (Ed.), *Review of personality and social psychology* (Vol. 2, pp. 121–144). Beverly Hills, CA: Sage.

Mills, J., & Clark, M. S. (1994). Communal and exchange relationships: Controversies and research. In R. Erber & R. Gilmour (Eds.), *Theoretical frameworks for personal relationships* (pp. 29–42). Hillsdale, NJ: Erlbaum.

Mills, J., & Clark, M. S. (2001). Viewing close romantic relationships as communal relationships: Implications for maintenance and enhancement. In J. Harvey & A. Wenzel (Eds.), *Close romantic relationships: Maintenance and enhancement.* (pp. 13–25). Mahwah, NJ: Erlbaum.

Milton, K. (1971). *Women in policing.* New York: Police Foundation Press.

Minard, R. D. (1952). Race relations in the Pocahontas coal field. *Journal of Social Issues, 8*, 29–44.

Mischel, W. (1968). *Personality and assessment.* New York: Wiley.

Misconceptions about why people obey laws and accept judicial decisions. (1997). *American Psychological Society Observer, 5*, 12–13, 46.

Mitchell, J., Heatherton, T., Kelley, W., Wyland, C., Wegner, D., & Macrae, C. (2007). Separating sustained from transient aspects of cognitive control during thought suppression. *Psychological Science, 18*, 292–297.

Miyamoto, Y., & Kitayama, S. (2002). Cultural variation in correspondence bias: The critical role of attitude diagnosticity of socially constrained behavior. *Journal of Personality and Social Psychology, 83*, 1239–1248.

Miyamoto, Y., Nisbett, R. E., & Masuda, T. (2006). Culture and the physical environment: Holistic versus analytic perceptual affordances. *Psychological Science, 17*, 113–119

Modigliani, A., & Rochat, F. (1995). The role of interaction sequences and the timing of resistance in shaping obedience and defiance to authority. *Journal of Social Issues, 51*, 107–123.

Moghaddam, F. M., Taylor, D. M., & Wright, S. C. (1993). *Social psychology in cross-cultural perspective.* New York: Freeman.

Mokdad, A. H., Marks, J. S., Stroup, D. F., & Gerberding, J. L. (2004). Actual causes of death in the United States. *Journal of the American Medical Association, 291*, 1238–1245.

Monin, J., Clark, M., & Lemay, E. (2008). Communal responsiveness in relationships with female versus male family members. *Sex Roles, 59*, 176–188.

Monson, C. M.; Langhinrichsen-Rohling, J. (2002). Sexual and Nonsexual Dating Violence Perpetration: Testing an Integrated Perpetrator Typology Violence and Victims, Volume 17, Number 4, 2002 , pp. 403–428(26). Springer Publishing Company

Montemayor, R., & Eisen, M. (1977). The development of self-conceptions from childhood to adolescence. *Developmental Psychology, 13*, 314–319.

Moore, J. S., Graziano, W. G., & Millar, M. C. (1987). Physical attractiveness, sex role orientation, and the evaluation of adults and children. *Personality and Social Psychology Bulletin, 13*, 95–102.

Moore, R. L. (1998). Love and limerance with Chinese characteristics: Student romance in the PRC. In V. C. de Munck (Ed.), *Romantic love and sexual behavior* (pp. 251–283). Westport, CT: Praeger.

Moore, T. E. (1982). Subliminal advertising: What you see is what you get. *Journal of Marketing, 46*, 38–47.

Moors, A., & De Houwer, J. (2006). Automaticity: A theoretical and conceptual analysis. *Psychological Bulletin, 132*, 297–326

Moos, R. H., & Holahan, C. J. (2003). Dispositional and contextual perspectives on coping: Toward an integrative framework. *Journal of Clinical Psychology, 59*, 1387–1403.

Moran, S., & Ritov, I. (2007). Experience in integrative negotiations: What needs to be learned? *Journal of Experimental Social Psychology, 43*, 77–90.

Moray, N. (1959). Attention in dichotic listening: Affective cues and the influence of instructions. *Quarterly Journal of Experimental Psychology, 11*, 56–60.

Moreland, R. L. (1987). The formation of small groups. In C. Hendrick (Ed.), *Review of personality and social psychology* (Vol. 8, pp. 80–110). Newbury Park, CA: Sage.

Moreland, R. L. (1999). Transactive memory: Learning who knows what in work groups and organizations. In L. L. Thompson & J. M. Levine (Eds.), *Shared cognition in organizations: The management of knowledge* (pp. 3–31). Mahwah, NJ: Erlbaum.

Moreland, R. L., & Beach, S. R. (1992). Exposure effects in the classroom: The development of affinity among students. *Journal of Experimental Social Psychology, 28*, 255–276.

Morgan, H. J., & Shaver, P. R. (1999). Attachment processes and committment to romantic relationships. In J. M. Adams & W. H. Jones, *Handbook of interpersonal commitment and relationship stability* (pp. 109–124). New York: Kluwer.

Morin, R. (2002, March 3). Bias and babies. *Washington Post*, p. B5.

Morling, B., & Evered, S. (2006). Secondary control reviewed and defined. *Psychological Bulletin, 132*, 269–296.

Morris, E. (Director). (1988). *The thin blue line* [Film]. New York: HBO Videos.

Morris, M. W., & Peng, K. (1994). Culture and cause: American and Chinese attributions for social and physical events. *Journal of Personality and Social Psychology, 67*, 949–971.

Morris, W. N., & Miller, R. S. (1975). The effects of consensus-breaking and consensus-preempting partners on reduction of conformity. *Journal of Experimental Social Psychology, 11*, 215–223.

Morry, M. M., & Staska, S. L. (2001). Magazine exposure: Internalization, self-objectification, eating attitudes, and body satisfaction in male and female university students. *Canadian Journal of Behavioural Science, 33*, 269–279.

Morse, D. R., Martin, J., & Moshonov, J. (1991). Psychosomatically induced death relative to stress, hypnosis, mind control, and voodoo: Review and possible mechanisms. *Stress Medicine, 7*, 213–232.

Moscovici, S. (1985). Social influence and conformity. In G. Lindzey & E. Aronson (Eds.), *Handbook of social psychology* (3rd ed., Vol. 2, pp. 347–412). New York: McGraw-Hill.

Moscovici, S. (1994). Three concepts: Minority, conflict, and behavioral style. In S. Moscovici, A. Mucchi-Faina, & A. Maass (Eds.), *Minority influence* (pp. 233–251). Chicago: Nelson-Hall.

Moscovici, S., Mucchi-Faina, A., & Maass, A. (Eds.). (1994). *Minority influence*. Chicago: Nelson-Hall.

Moscovici, S., & Nemeth, C. (1974). Minority influence. In C. Nemeth (Ed.), *Social psychology: Classic and contemporary integrations* (pp. 217–249). Chicago: Rand McNally.

Moyer, K. E. (1976). *The psychobiology of aggression*. New York: Harper & Row.

Moyer, K. E. (1983). The physiology of motivation: Aggression as a model. In C. J. Scheier & A. M. Rogers (Eds.), *G. Stanley Hall lecture series* (Vol.3). Washington, DC: American Psychological Association.

Mukai, T. (1996). Mothers, peers, and perceived pressure to diet among Japanese adolescent girls. *Journal of Research in Adolescence, 6*, 309–324.

Mukai, T., Kambara, A., & Sasaki, Y. (1998). Body dissatisfaction, need for social approval, and eating disturbances among Japanese and American college women. *Sex Roles, 39*, 751–771.

Mullen, B. (1986). Atrocity as a function of lynch mob composition: A self-attention perspective. *Personality and Social Psychology Bulletin, 12*, 187–197.

Mullen, B., Anthony, T., Salas, E., & Driskell, J. E. (1994). Group cohesiveness and quality of decision making: An integration of tests of the groupthink hypothesis. *Small Group Research, 25*, 189–204.

Mullen, B., Brown, R., & Smith, C. (1992). Ingroup bias as a function of salience, relevance, and status: An integration. *European Journal of Social Psychology, 22*, 103–122.

Mullen, B., & Cooper, C. (1994). The relation between group cohesiveness and performance: An integration. *Psychological Bulletin, 115*, 210–227.

Mullen, B., & Johnson, C. (1988). *Distinctiveness-based illusory correlation and stereotyping: A meta-analytic integration*. Unpublished manuscript, Syracuse University.

Mullen, B., Rozell, D., & Johnson, C. (2001). Ethnophaulisms for ethnic immigrant groups: The contributions of group size and familiarity. *European Journal of Social Psychology, 31*, 231–246.

Muller, D., & Butera, F. (2007). The focusing effect of self-evaluation threat in coaction and social comparison. *Journal of Personality and Social Psychology, 93*, 194–211.

Muller, D., Atzeni, T., & Fabrizio, B. (2004). Coaction and upward social comparison reduce the illusory conjunction effect: Support for distraction-conflict theory. *Journal of Experimental Social Psychology, 40*, 659–665.

Muraven, M., Tice, D. M., & Baumeister, R. F. (1998). Self-control as limited resource: Regulatory depletion patterns. *Journal of Personality and Social Psychology, 74*, 774–789.

Murphy, N. (2007). Appearing smart: The impression management of intelligence, person perception accuracy, and behavior in social interaction. *Personality and Social Psychology Bulletin, 33*, 325–339.

Murr, A., & Smalley, S. (2003, March 17). White power, minus the power. *Newsweek*, pp. 42–45.

Murstein, B. I. (1970). Stimulus value role: A theory of marital choice. *Journal of Marriage and the Family, 32*, 465–481.

Mussweiler, T. (2003). Comparison processes in social judgment: Mechanisms and consequences. *Psychological Review, 110*(3), 472–489.

Mussweiler, T., & Förster, J. (2000). The sex-aggression link: A perception-behavior dissociation. *Journal of Personality and Social Psychology, 79*, 507–520.

Mussweiler, T., Rüter, K., & Epstude, K. (2004). The man who wasn't there: Subliminal social comparison standards influence self-evaluation. *Journal of Experimental Social Psychology, 40*(5), 689–696.

Mussweiler, T., & Strack, F. (1999). Comparing is believing: A selective accessibility model of judgmental anchoring. In W. Stroebe & M. Hewstone (Eds.), *European review of social psychology* (Vol. 10, pp. 135–167). Chichester, England: Wiley.

Mussweiler, T., Strack, F., & Pfeiffer, T. (2000). Overcoming the inevitable anchoring effect: Considering the opposite compensates for selective accessibility. *Personality and Social Psychology Bulletin, 260*, 1142–1150.

Myers, D. G., & Scanzoni, L. D. (2006). *What god has joined together: The Christian case for gay marriage*. Harper Collins: San Francisco.

Nadler, A. (2002). Inter-group helping relations as power relations: Maintaining or challenging social dominance between groups through helping. *Journal of Social Issues, 58*, 487–502.

Nadler, A., Ellis, S., & Bar, I. (2003). To seek or not to seek: The relationship between help seeking and job performance evaluations as moderated by task-relevant expertise. *Journal of Applied Social Psychology, 33*, 91–109.

Nail, P. R. (1986). Toward an integration of some models and theories of social response. *Psychological Bulletin, 100*, 190–206.

Nail, P. R., McDonald, G., & Levy, D. A. (2000). Proposal of a four-dimensional model of social response. *Psychological Bulletin, 126*, 454–470.

Nail, P. R., Misak, J. E., & Davis, R. M. (2004). Self-affirmation versus self-consistency: A comparison of two competing self-theories of dissonance phenomena. *Personality and Individual Differences, 36*, 1893–1905.

Naimi, T., Brewer, B., Mokdad, A., Serdula, M., Denny, C., & Marks, J. (2003). Binge drinking among U.S. adults. *Journal of the American Medical Association, 289*, 70–75.

Napier, J., & Tyler, T. (2008). Does moral conviction really override concerns about procedural justice? A reexamination of the value protection model. *Social Justice Research, 21*, 509–528.

Nasco, S. A., & Marsh, K. L. (1999). Gaining control through counterfactual thinking. *Personality and Social Psychology Bulletin, 25*, 556–568.

Nathanson, S. (1987). *An eye for an eye? The morality of punishing by death*. Totowa, NJ: Rowman & Littlefield.

National Center for Health Statistics. (2005). Marriage and divorce. Retrieved on September 19, 2006, from www.cdc.gov/nchs/fastats/divorce.html

National Center for Vital Statistics. (2001). *Crime facts at a glance*. Retrieved from Bureau of Justice Statistics: www.ojp.usdoj.gov/bjs/glance/hmrt.htm

National Research Council (2003). *The polygraph and lie detection*. Washington, DC: National Academies Press.

National Trends in Risk Behaviors (2008). Youth Risk Behavior Surveillance System, Center for Disease Control and Prevention. Retrieved on December 30, 2008, from www.cdc.gov/HealthyYouth/yrbs/trends.htm

Neil v. Biggers, 409 U. S. 188 (1972).

Nel, E., Helmreich, R., & Aronson, E. (1969). Opinion change in the advocate as a function of the persuasibility of his audience: A clarification of the meaning of dissonance. *Journal of Personality and Social Psychology, 12*, 117–124.

Nelson, D. E., Bland, S., Powell-Griner, E., Klein, R., Wells, H. E., Hogelin, G., & Marks, J. S. (2002). State trends in health risk factors and receipt of clinical preventive services among US adults during the 1990s. *Journal of the American Medical Association, 287*, 2659–2667.

Nemeth, C. J., & Chiles, C. (1988). Modeling courage: The role of dissent in fostering independence. *European Journal of Social Psychology, 18*, 275–280.

Nes, L., & Segerstrom, S. (2006). Dispositional optimism and coping: A meta-analytic review. *Personality and Social Psychology Review, 10*, 235–251.

Neuberg, S. L. (1988). Behavioral implications of information presented outside of awareness: The effect of subliminal presentation of trait information on behavior in the prisoner's dilemma game. *Social Cognition, 6*, 207–230.

Newcomb, T. M. (1961). *The acquaintance process*. New York: Holt, Rinehart and Winston.

Newman, L. S. (1996). Trait impressions as heuristics for predicting future behavior. *Personality and Social Psychology Bulletin, 22*, 395–411.

Nichols, J. G. (1975). Casual attributions and other achievement-related cognitions: Effects of task outcome, attainment value, and sex. *Journal of Personality and Social Psychology, 31*, 379–389.

Nicholson, N., Cole, S. G., & Rocklin, T. (1985). Conformity in the Asch situation: A comparison between contemporary British and U.S. university students. *British Journal of Social Psychology, 24*, 59–63.

Nickerson, C., Schwarz, N., Diener, E., & Kahneman, D. (2003). Zeroing in on the dark side of the American Dream: A closer look at the negative consequences of the goal for financial success. *Psychological Science, 14*, 531–536.

Niedenthal, P. M., & Kitayama, S. (1994). (Eds.). *The heart's eye: Emotional influences in perception and attention*. San Diego, CA: Academic Press.

Niedenthal, P. M., Tangney, J. P., & Gavanski, I. (1994). "If only I weren't" versus "If only I hadn't": Distinguishing shame and guilt in counterfactual thinking. *Journal of Personality and Social Psychology, 67*, 585–595.

NIMH Multisite HIV Prevention Trial Group (1998, June 19). The NIMH Multisite HIV Prevention Trial: Reducing sexual HIV risk behavior. *Science, 280*, 1889–1894.

NIMH Multisite HIV Prevention Trial Group (2001). Social-cognitive theory mediators of behavior change in the National Institute of Mental Health Multisite HIV Prevention Trial. *Health Psychology, 20*, 369–376.

Nisbett, R. E. (1993). Violence and U.S. regional culture. *American Psychologist, 48*, 441–449.

Nisbett, R. E. (2003). *The geography of thought: How Asians and Westerners think differently . . . and why*. New York: Free Press.

Nisbett, R. E., Caputo, C., Legant, P., & Marecek, J. (1973). Behavior as seen by the actor and by the observer. *Journal of Personality and Social Psychology, 27*, 154–164.

Nisbett, R. E., Peng, K., Choi, I., & Norenzayan, A. (2001). Culture and systems of thought: Holistic vs. analytic cognition. *Psychological Review, 108*, 291–310.

Nisbett, R. E., & Cohen, D. (1996). *Culture of honor: The psychology of violence in the South*. Boulder, CO: Westview Press.

Nisbett, R. E., Fong, G. T., Lehman, D. R., & Cheng, P. W. (1987). Teaching reasoning. *Science, 238*, 625–631.

Nisbett, R. E., & Ross, L. (1980). *Human inference: Strategies and shortcomings of human judgment*. Englewood Cliffs, NJ: Prentice Hall.

Nisbett, R. E., & Wilson, T. D. (1977). Telling more than we can know: Verbal reports on mental processes. *Psychological Review, 84*, 231–259.

Nixon, R. M. (1990). *In the arena: A memoir of victory, defeat, and renewal*. New York: Simon & Schuster.

Noar, S. M., Benac, C. N., Harris, M. S. (2007). Does tailoring matter? Meta-analytic review of tailored print health behavior change interventions. *Psychological Bulletin, 133*, 673–693.

Noguchi, K., Albarracín, D., Durantini, M., & Glasman, L. (2007). Who participates in which health promotion programs? A meta-analysis of motivations underlying enrollment and retention in HIV-prevention interventions. *Psychological Bulletin, 133*, 955–975.

Nolan, J., Schultz, P., Cialdini, R., Goldstein, N., & Griskevicius, V. (2008). Normative social influence is underdetected. *Personality and Social Psychology Bulletin, 34*, 913–923.

Nolen-Hoeksema, S., Girgus, J. S., & Seligman, M. E. P. (1986). Learned helplessness in children: A longitudinal study of depression, achievement, and explanatory style. *Journal of Personality and Social Psychology, 51*, 435–442.

Norenzayan, A., Choi, I., & Nisbett, R. E. (1999). Eastern and Western perceptions of causality for social behavior: Lay theories about personalities and situations. In D. A. Prentice & D. T. Miller (Eds.), *Cultural divides: Understanding and overcoming group conflict* (pp. 239–272). New York: Russell Sage Foundation.

Norenzayan, A., Choi, I., & Peng, K. (2007). Perception and cognition. In S. Kitayama & D. Cohen (Eds.), *Handbook of cultural psychology* (pp. 569–594). New York: Guilford.

Norenzayan, A., & Heine, S. J. (2005). Psychological universals: What are they and how can we know? *Psychological Bulletin, 131*, 763–784.

Norenzayan, A., & Nisbett, R. E. (2000). Culture and causal cognition. *Current Direction in Psychological Science, 9*, 132–135.

Norenzayan, A., & Shariff, A. F. (2008). The origin and evolution of religious prosociality. *Science, 322*, 58–62.

North, A. C., Tarrant, M., & Hargreaves, D. J. (2004). The effects of music on helping behavior: A field study. *Environment and Behavior, 36*, 266–275.

Nosek, B. A., Greenwald, A. G., & Banaji, M. R. (2005). Understanding and using the implicit association test: II. Method variables and construct validity. *Personality and Social Psychology Bulletin, 31*, 166–180.

Nowak, A., Szamrej, J., & Latané, B. (1990). From private attitude to public opinion: A dynamic theory of social impact. *Psychological Review, 97*, 362–376.

O'Brien, S. (2004, May 21). Researcher: It's not bad apples, it's the barrel. Retrieved on January 20, 2005, from CNN.com *www.cnn.com/2004/US/05/21/zimbarbo.access/*

Ochsner, K. (2007). Social cognitive neuroscience: Historical development, core principles, and future promise. In A. W. Kruglanski & E. T. Higgins (Eds.), *Social psychology: Handbook of basic principles* (2nd ed., pp. 39–66). New York: Guilford.

O'Connor, K. M., & Carnevale, P. J. (1997). A nasty but effective negotiation strategy: Misrepresentation of a common-value issue. *Personality and Social Psychology Bulletin, 23*, 504–515.

O'Leary, A. (1990). Stress, emotion, and human immune function. *Psychological Bulletin, 108*, 363–382.

O'Sullivan, C. S., & Durso, F. T. (1984). Effects of schema-incongruent information on memory for stereotypical attributes. *Journal of Personality and Social Psychology, 47*, 55–70.

Ofshe, R., & Watters, E. (1994). *Making monsters: False memories, psychotherapy, and sexual hysteria*. New York: Scribner.

Oglesby, C. (2004, April 6). Survey: Adults still skip condom use. CNN.com. Retrieved on December 30, 2008, from www.cnn.com/2004/HEALTH/04/06/std.awareness/

Ogloff, J. R. P., & Vidmar, N. (1994). The impact of pretrial publicity on jurors: A study to compare the relative effects of television and print media in a child sex abuse case. *Law and Human Behavior, 18*, 507–525.

Ohbuchi, K., & Baba, R. (1988). Selection of influence strategies in interpersonal conflicts: Effects of sex, interpersonal relations, and goals. *Tohoku Psychologica Folia, 47*, 63–73.

Ohbuchi, K., Ohno, T., & Mukai, H. (1993). Empathy and aggression: Effects of self-disclosure and fearful appeal. *Journal of Social Psychology, 133*, 243–253.

Ohbuchi, K., & Sato, K. (1994). Children's reactions to mitigating accounts: Apologies, excuses, and intentionality of harm. *Journal of Social Psychology, 134*, 5–17.

Oishi, S., Rothman, A. J., Snyder, M., Su, J., Zehm, K., Hertel, A. W., et al. (2007). The socioecological model of procommunity action: The benefits of residential stability. *Journal of Personality and Social Psychology, 93*, 831–844.

Oishi, S., Schimmack, U., & Colcombe, S. J. (2003). The contextual and systematic nature of life satisfaction judgments. *Journal of Experimental Social Psychology, 39*, 232–247.

Oishi, S., Wyer, R. S., & Colcombe, S. J. (2000). Cultural variation in the use of current life satisfaction to predict the future. *Journal of Personality and Social Psychology, 78,* 434–445.

Olson, J., & Stone, J. (2005). The influence of behavior on attitudes. In D. Albarracín, B. T. Johnson, & M. P. Zanna (Eds.), *The handbook of attitudes* (pp. 223–271). Mahwah, NJ: Erlbaum.

Olson, J. M., Vernon, P. A., Harris, J. A., & Jang, K. L. (2001). The heritability of attitudes: A study of twins. *Journal of Personality and Social Psychology, 80*(6), 845–860.

Olson, M. A., & Fazio, R. H. (2001). Implicit attitude formation through classical conditioning. *Psychological Science, 12,* 413–417.

Olsson, N. (2000). A comparison of correlation, calibration, and diagnosticity as measures of the confidence-accuracy relationship. *Journal of Applied Psychology, 85,* 504–511.

Olweus, D. (1991). Bully/victim problems among schoolchildren: Basic facts and effects of a school-based intervention program. In D. Pepler & K. Rubin (Eds.), *The development and treatment of childhood aggression* (pp. 411–448). Hillsdale, NJ: Erlbaum.

Olweus, D. (1995a). Bullying or peer abuse at school: Facts and interventions. *Current Directions in Psychological Science, 4,* 196–200.

Olweus, D. (1995b). Bullying or peer abuse in school: Intervention and prevention. In G. Davies, S. Lloyd-Bostock, M. McMurran, & C. Wilson (Eds.), *Psychology, law, and criminal justice: International developments in research and practice* (pp. 248–263). Berlin: de Gruyter.

Olweus, D. (1996). Bullying at school: Knowledge base and an effective intervention program. In C. Ferris & T. Grisso (Eds.), *Understanding aggressive behavior in children* (pp. 265–276). New York: New York Academy of Sciences.

Olweus, D. (1997). Tackling peer victimization with a school-based intervention program. In D. Fry & K. Bjorkqvist (Eds.), *Cultural variation in conflict resolution: Alternatives to violence* (pp. 215–231). Mahwah, NJ: Erlbaum.

Olweus D. (2003). Prevalence estimation of school bullying. *Aggressive Behavior 29,* 239–268.

Omoto, A. M. (Ed.). (2005) *Processes of community change and social action.* Mahwah, NJ: Erlbaum.

Oppenheimer, D. M. (2004). spontaneous discounting of availability in frequency judgment tasks. *Psychological Science, 15,* 100–105.

Orbell, J. M., van de Kragt, A. J. C., & Dawes, R. M. (1988). Explaining discussion-induced comparison. *Journal of Personality and Social Psychology, 54,* 811–819.

Ortony, A., Clore, G., & Collins, A. (1988). The cognitive structure of emotions. Cambridge: Cambridge University Press.

Orvis, B. R., Cunningham, J. D., & Kelley, H. H. (1975). A closer examination of causal inference: The role of consensus, distinctiveness, and consistency information. *Journal of Personality and Social Psychology, 32,* 605–616.

Oskamp, S. (1995). Applying social psychology to avoid ecological disaster. *Journal of Social Issues, 51,* 217–238.

Oskamp, S. (2000). A sustainable future for humanity? How can psychology help? *American Psychologist, 55,* 496–508.

Oskamp, S., Burkhardt, R. I., Schultz, P. W., Hurin, S., & Zelezny, L. (1998). Predicting three dimensions of residential curbside recycling: An observational study. *Journal of Environmental Education, 29,* 37–42.

Osofsky, M. J., Bandura, A., & Zimbardo, P. G. (2005). The role of moral disengagement in the execution process. *Law and Human Behavior, 29,* 371–393.

Ostrom, T., & Sedikides, C. (1992). Out-group homogeneity effects in natural and minimal groups. *Psychological Bulletin, 112,* 536–552.

Oyserman, D., & Lee, S. (2008). Does culture influence what and how we think? Effects of priming individualism and collectivism. *Psychological Bulletin, 134,* 311–342.

Paik, H., & Comstock, G. (1994). The effects of television violence on antisocial behavior: A meta-analysis. *Communication Research, 21,* 516–546.

Palmer, J., & Loveland, J. (2008). The influence of group discussion on performance judgments: Rating accuracy, contrast effects, and halo. *Journal of Psychology: Interdisciplinary and Applied, 142,* 117–130.

Parish, A. R., de Waal, F. B. M., and Haig, D. (2000). The other "closest living relative": How bonobos (*Pan paniscus*) challenge traditional assumptions about females, dominance, intra- and intersexual interactions, and hominid evolution. *Annals of the New York Academy of Sciences, 907,* 97–113.

Park, B., & Rothbart, M. (1982). Perception of out-group homogeneity and levels of social categorization: Memory for the subordinate attributes of in-group and out-group members. *Journal of Personality and Social Psychology, 42,* 1051–1068.

Parke, R. D., Berkowitz, L., Leyens, J. P., West, S. G., & Sebastian, R. J. (1977). Some effects of violent and nonviolent movies on the behavior of juvenile delinquents. In L. Berkowitz (Ed.), *Advances in experimental social psychology* (Vol. 10, pp. 135–172). New York: Academic Press.

Parks, C. D., & Rumble, A. C. (2001). Elements of reciprocity and social value orientation. *Personality and Social Psychology Bulletin, 27,* 1301–1309.

Patel, R., & Parmentier, M. J. C. (2005). The persistence of traditional gender roles in the information technology sector: A study of female engineers in India. *Information Technologies and International Development, 2,* 29–46.

Patrick, C. J., & Iacono, W. G. (1989). Psychopathy, threat, and polygraph test accuracy. *Journal of Applied Psychology, 74,* 347–355.

Patterson, A. (1974, September). *Hostility catharsis: A naturalistic quasi-experiment.* Paper presented at the annual meeting of the American Psychological Association, New Orleans.

Patton, P. (1989, August 6). Steve Jobs out for revenge. *New York Times Magazine,* pp. 23, 52, 56, 58.

Paulus, P. B. (1998). Developing consensus about groupthink after all these years. *Organizational Behavior and Human Decision Processes, 73,* 362–374.

Paulus, P. B., McCain, G., & Cox, V. (1981). Prison standards: Some pertinent data on crowding. *Federal Probation, 15,* 48–54.

Pavlidis, I., Eberhardt, N. L., & Levine, J. A. (2002). Seeing through the face of deception: Thermal imaging offers a promising hands-off approach to mass security screening. *Nature, 415,* 35.

Payne, B. (2006). Weapon bias: Split-second decisions and unintended stereotyping. *Current Directions in Psychological Science, 15,* 287-291.

Payne, B. K. (2001). Prejudice and perception: The role of automatic and controlled processes in misperceiving a weapon. *Journal of Personality and Social Psychology, 81,* 181–192.

Peace in the Middle East may be impossible: Lee D. Ross on naive realism and conflict resolution. *American Psychological Society Observer, 17,* 9–11.

Pechmann, C., & Knight, S. J. (2002). An experimental investigation of the joint effects of advertising and peers on adolescents' beliefs and intentions about cigarette consumption. *Journal of Consumer Research, 29,* 5–19.

Pennebaker, J. W. (1990). *Opening up: The healing powers of confiding in others.* New York: Morrow.

Pennebaker, J. W. (1997). Writing about emotional experiences as a therapeutic process. *Psychological Science, 8,* 162–166.

Pennebaker, J. W. (2001). Dealing with a traumatic experience immediately after it occurs. *Advances in Mind-Body Medicine, 17,* 160–162.

Pennebaker, J. W. (2004). Theories, therapies, and taxpayers: On the complexities of the expressive writing paradigm. *Clinical Psychology: Science and Practice, 11,* 138–142.

Pennebaker, J. W., Barger, S. D., & Tiebout, J. (1989). Disclosure of traumas and health among Holocaust survivors. *Psychosomatic Medicine, 51,* 577–589.

Pennebaker, J. W., & Beale, S. K. (1986). Confronting a traumatic event: Toward an understanding of inhibition and disease. *Journal of Abnormal Psychology, 95,* 274–281.

Pennebaker, J. W., Colder, M., & Sharp, L. K. (1990). Accelerating the coping process. *Journal of Personality and Social Psychology, 58,* 528–537.

Pennebaker, J. W., & Francis, M. E. (1996). Cognitive, emotional, and language processes in disclosure. *Cognition and Emotion, 10,* 601–626.

Pennebaker, J. W., & Sanders, D. Y. (1976). American graffiti: Effects of authority and reactance arousal. *Personality and Social Psychology Bulletin, 2,* 264–267.

Penner, L. (2002). Dispositional and organizational influences on sustained volunteerism: An interactionist perspective. *Journal of Social Issues, 58,* 447–467.

Penner, L. A. (2000). The causes of sustained volunteerism: An interactionist perspective. *Journal of Social Issues, 58,* 447–467.

Penner, L. A. (2004). Volunteerism and social problems: Making things better or worse? *Journal of Social Issues, 60*(3), 645–666.

Penner, L. A., Dovidio, J. F., Piliavin, J. A., & Schroeder, D. A. (2005). Prosocial behavior: Multilevel perspectives. *Annual Review of Psychology, 56,* 365–392.

Pennington, J., & Schlenker, B. R. (1999). Accountability for consequential decisions: Justifying ethical judgments to audiences. *Personality and Social Psychology Bulletin, 25,* 1067–1081.

Pennington, N., & Hastie, R. (1988). Explanation-based decision making: Effects of memory structure on judgment. *Journal of Experimental Psychology: Learning, Memory, and Cognition, 14,* 521–533.

Pennington, N., & Hastie, R. (1990). Practical implications of psychological research on juror and jury decision making. *Personality and Social Psychology Bulletin, 16,* 90–105.

Penrod, S. D., & Cutler, B. (1999). Preventing mistaken convictions in eyewitness identification trials: The case against traditional safeguards. In R. Roesch, S. D. Hart, & J. R. P. Ogloff (Eds.), *Psychology and law: The state of the discipline* (pp. 89–118). New York: Kluwer.

Peplau, L. A., & Perlman, D. (1982). Perspectives on loneliness. In L. A. Peplau & D. Perlman (Eds.), *Loneliness: A sourcebook of current theory, research, and therapy* (pp. 1–18). New York: Wiley.

Perlstein, L. (1999, November 14). The sweet rewards of learning: Teachers motivate students with tokens for fries and candy. *Washington Post,* pp. A1, A14.

Perrett, D. I., May, K. A., & Yoshikawa, S. (1994). Facial shape and judgments of female attractivenesss. *Nature, 368,* 239–242.

Perrin, S., & Spencer, C. (1981). Independence or conformity in the Asch experiment as a reflection of cultural or situational factors. *British Journal of Social Psychology, 20,* 205–209.

Peters J. M., Avol, E., Gauderman, W. J., Linn, W. S., Navidi, W., London, S. J., Margolis, H., Rappaport, E., Vora, H., Gong, H. Jr., & Thomas, D. C. (1999). A study of twelve Southern California communities with differing levels and types of air pollution: II. Effects on pulmonary function. *American Journal of Respiratory and Critical Care Medicine, 159,* 768–775.

Peters, L. H., Hartke, D. D., & Pohlmann, J. T. (1985). Fiedler's contingency theory of leadership: An application of the meta-analysis procedures of Schmidt and Hunter. *Psychological Bulletin, 97,* 274–285.

Peterson, A. A., Haynes, G. A., & Olson, J. M. (2008). Self-esteem differences in the effects of hypocrisy induction on behavioral intentions in the health domain. *Journal of Personality, 76,* 305–322.

Peterson, C., & Park, N. (2007). Explanatory style and emotion regulation. In J. J. Gross (Ed.), *Handbook of emotion regulation* (pp. 159–179). New York: Guilford Press.

Peterson, C., & Seligman, M. E. P. (1984). Causal explanations as a risk factor for depression: Theory and evidence. *Psychological Review, 91,* 347–374.

Peterson, R. D., & Bailey, W. C. (1988). Murder and capital punishment in the evolving context of the post-Furman era. *Social Forces, 66,* 774–807.

Petrie, K. J., Booth, R. J., & Pennebaker, J. W. (1998). The immunological effects of thought suppression. *Journal of Personality and Social Psychology, 75,* 1264–1272.

Petroselli, D. M., & Knobler, P. (1998). *Triumph of justice: Closing the book on the Simpson saga.* New York: Crown.

Pettigrew, T., & Tropp, L. (2006). A meta-analytic test of intergroup contact theory. *Journal of Personality and Social Psychology, 90,* 751–783.

Pettigrew, T. (in press). Final reflections. In U. Wagner, L. Tropp, G. Finchilescu, & C. Tredoux (Eds.), *Emerging research directions for improving intergroup relations: Building on the legacy of Thomas F. Pettigrew.* Oxford, England: Blackwell.

Pettigrew, T. F. (1958). Personality and sociocultural factors and intergroup attitudes: A cross-national comparison. *Journal of Conflict Resolution, 2,* 29–42.

Pettigrew, T. F. (1969). Racially separate or together? *Journal of Social Issues, 25,* 43–69.

Pettigrew, T. F. (1979). The ultimate attribution error: Extending Allport's cognitive analysis of prejudice. *Personality and Social Psychology Bulletin, 5,* 461–476.

Pettigrew, T. F. (1985). New black-white patterns: How best to conceptualize them? *Annual Review of Sociology, 11,* 329–346.

Pettigrew, T. F. (1989). The nature of modern racism in the United States. *Revue Internationale de Psychologie Sociale, 2,* 291–303.

Pettigrew, T. F. (1991). Normative theory in intergroup relations: Explaining both harmony and conflict. *Psychology and Developing Societies, 3,* 3–16.

Pettigrew, T. F. (1998). Reactions toward the new minorities of Western Europe. *Annual Review of Sociology, 24,* 77–103.

Pettigrew, T. F., Jackson, J. S., Brika, J. B., Lemaine, G., Meertens, R. W., Wagner, U., & Zick, A. (1998). Outgroup prejudice in western Europe. *European Review of Social Psychology, 8,* 241–273.

Pettigrew, T. F., & Meertens, R. W. (1995). Subtle and blatant prejudice in western Europe. *European Journal of Social Psychology, 25,* 57–75.

Pettigrew, T. F., & Tropp, L. (2003). *A meta-analytic test and reformulation of intergroup contact theory.* Unpublished manuscript.

Pettigrew, T. F., & Tropp, L. R. (2006). A meta-analytic test of intergroup contact theory. *Journal of Personality and Social Psychology, 90,* 751–783.

Petty, R. E. (1995). Attitude change. In A. Tesser (Ed.), *Advanced social psychology* (pp. 195–255). New York: McGraw-Hill.

Petty, R. E., & Brock, T. C. (1981). Thought disruption and persuasion: Assessing the validity of attitude change experiments. In R. E. Petty, T. M. Ostrom, & T. C. Brock (Eds.), *Cognitive responses in persuasion* (pp. 55–79). Hillsdale, NJ: Erlbaum.

Petty, R. E., & Cacioppo, J. T. (1986). *Communication and persuasion: Central and peripheral routes to attitude change.* New York: Springer-Verlag.

Petty, R. E., Cacioppo, J. T., & Goldman, R. (1981). Personal involvement as a determinant of argument-based persuasion. *Journal of Personality and Social Psychology, 41,* 847–855.

Petty, R. E., Cacioppo, J. T., Strathman, A. J., & Priester, J. R. (2005). To think or not to think: Exploring two routes to persuasion. In T. C. Brock & M. C. Green (Eds.), *Persuasion: Psychological insights and perspectives.* Thousand Oaks, CA: Sage Publications, Inc.

Petty, R. E., Haugtvedt, C. P., & Smith, S. M. (1995). Elaboration as a determinant of attitude strength. In R. E. Petty & J. A. Krosnick (Eds.), *Attitude strength: Antecedents and consequences* (pp. 93–130). Hillsdale, NJ: Erlbaum.

Petty, R. E., & Wegener, D. T. (1999). The elaboration likelihood model: Current status and controversies. In S. Chaiken & Y. Trope (Eds.), *Dual-process theories in social psychology* (pp. 41–72). New York: Guilford Press.

Petty, R. E., & Wegener, D. T. (1999). The elaboration likelihood model: Current status and controversies. In S. Chaiken & Y. Trope (Eds.), *Dual-process theories in social psychology* (pp. 37–72). New York: Guilford Press.

Petty, R. E., Wells, G. L., & Brock, T. C. (1976). Distraction can enhance or reduce yielding to propaganda: Thought disruption versus effort justification. *Journal of Personality and Social Psychology, 34,* 874–884.

Pezdek, K., & Banks, W. P. (Eds.). (1996). *The recovered memory/false memory debate.* San Diego, CA: Academic Press.

Phillips, A. G., & Silva, P. J. (2005). Self-awareness and the emotional consequences of self-discrepancies. *Personality & Social Psychology Bulletin, 31,* 703–713.

Phillips, D. P. (1983). The impact of mass media violence on U.S. homicides. *American Sociological Review, 48,* 560–568.

Phillips, D. P. (1986). Natural experiments on the effects of mass media violence on fatal aggression: Strengths and weaknesses of a new approach. In L. Berkowitz (Ed.), *Advances in experimental social psychology* (Vol. 19, pp. 207–250). Orlando, FL: Academic Press.

Pickel, K. (2007). Remembering and identifying menacing perpetrators: Exposure to violence and the weapon focus effect. In R. C. L. Lindsay, D. F. Ross, J. D. Read, & M. P. Toglia (Eds.), *The handbook of eyewitness psychology,* Vol II: *Memory for people* (pp. 339–360). Mahwah, NJ: Erlbaum.

Pickett, C. L., & Gardner, W. L. (2005). The social monitoring system: Enhanced sensitivity to social cues as an adaptive response to social exclusion. In K. D. Williams, J. P. Forgas, J. P., & W. von Hippel (Eds.), *The social outcast: Ostracism, social exclusion, rejection, and bullying* (pp. 213–226). New York: Psychology Press.

Pickett, C. L., Silver, M. D., & Brewer, M. B. (2002). The impact of assimilation and differentiation needs on perceived group importance and judgments of ingroup size. *Personality and Social Psychology Bulletin, 28,* 546–558.

Piliavin, I. M., Piliavin, J. A., & Rodin, J. (1975). Costs, diffusion, and the stigmatized victim. *Journal of Personality and Social Psychology, 32,* 429–438.

Piliavin, J. A. (2008). Long-term benefits of habitual helping: Doing well by doing good. In B. A. Sullivan, M. Snyder, & J. L. Sullivan (Eds.), *Cooperation: The political psychology of effective human interaction* (pp. 241–258). Malden, MA: Blackwell.

Piliavin, J. A., & Charng, H. (1990). Altruism: A review of recent theory and research. *Annual Review of Sociology, 16,* 27–65.

Piliavin, J. A., Dovidio, J. F., Gaertner, S. L., & Clark, R. D., III. (1981). *Emergency intervention.* New York: Academic Press.

Piliavin, J. A., & Piliavin, I. M. (1972). The effect of blood on reactions to a victim. *Journal of Personality and Social Psychology, 23,* 253–261.

Pincus, W. (2006, February 10). Ex-CIA official faults use of data on Iraq. *Washington Post* (p. A01).

Pinker, S. (2002). *The blank slate: The modern denial of human nature.* New York: Viking.

Plant, E. A., & Peruche, B. M. (2005). The consequences of race for police officers' responses to criminal suspects. *Psychological Science, 16,* 180–183.

Plant, E. A., Devine, P. G., Cox, W. T. L., Coumb, C., Miller, S. L., Goplen, J., & Peruche, B. M. (2009). The Obama effect: Decreasing implicit prejudice and stereotyping

"Plastic oceans." (2008, November 13). Spencer Michels, reporter. *The Newshour with Jim Lehrer,* Public Broadcasting System.

Pleban, R., & Tesser, A. (1981). The effects of relevance and quality of another's performance on interpersonal closeness. *Social Psychology Quarterly, 44,* 278–285.

PollingReport.com. (2003, July 31). President Bush: Job ratings. Retrieved from *www.pollingreport.com/BushJob.htm*

Pomfret, J. (2005, November 20). Student turns body into billboard as the Shirtless Guy. *Washington Post,* p. A2.

Pope, H. G., Jr., Gruber, A. J., Mangweth, B., Bureau, B., de Col, C., Jouvent, R., & Hudson, J. I. (2000). Body image perception among men in three countries. *American Journal of Psychiatry, 157,* 1297–1301.

Pope, H. G., Jr., Olivardia, R., Gruber, A. J., & Borowiecki, J. (1999). Evolving ideals of male body image as seen through action toys. *International Journal of Eating Disorders, 26,* 65–72.

Pope, H. G., Jr., Phillips, K. A., & Olivardia, R. (2000). *The Adonis complex: The secret crisis of male body obsession.* New York: Freeman.

Poppe, E, (2001). Effects of Changes in GNP and Perceived Group Characteristics on National and Ethnic Stereotypes in Central and Eastern Europe. *J. Applied Social Psychology 31, 1689–1708.*

Porn in the USA. (2004, September 5). CBS News 60 Minutes. Retrieved on July 14, 2005, from *www.cbsnews.com/stories/2003/11/21/60minutes/main585049.shtml*

Porter, J. R. (1971). *Black child, white child: The development of racial attitudes.* Cambridge, MA: Harvard University Press.

Porter, J. R., & Washington, R. E. (1979). Black identity and self-esteem, 1968–1978. *Annual Review of Sociology, 5,* 53–74.

Porter, J. R., & Washington, R. E. (1989). Developments in research on black identity and self-esteem, 1979–1988. *Revue Internationale de Psychologie Sociale, 2,* 339–353.

Posada, S., & Colell, M. (2007). Another gorilla (Gorilla gorilla gorilla) recognizes himself in a mirror. *American Journal of Primatology, 69*(5), 576–583.

Postmes, T., & Spears, R. (1998). Deindividuation and antinormative behavior: A meta-analysis. *Psychological Bulletin, 123,* 238–259.

Postmes, T., Spears, R., & Cihangir, S. (2001). Quality of decision making and group norms. *Journal of Personality and Social Psychology, 80,* 918–930.

Powledge, F. (1991). *Free at last? The civil rights movement and the people who made it.* Boston: Little, Brown.

Pratkanis, A. R. (1992). The cargo-cult science of subliminal persuasion. *Skeptical Inquirer, 16,* 260–272.

Pratt, T. C., Cullen, F. T., Blevins, K. R., Daigle, L. E., & Madensen, T. D. (Eds.). (2006). *The empirical status of deterrence theory.* New Brunswick, NJ: Transaction.

Preston, S. D., & De Waal, F. B. M. (2002). Empathy: Its ultimate and proximate bases. *Behavioral and Brain Sciences, 25,* 1–72.

Preston, J., & Wegner, D. (2007). The eureka error: Inadvertent plagiarism by misattributions of effort. *Journal of Personality and Social Psychology, 92,* 575–584.

Prevalence of overweight and obesity among adults: United States, 2003–2004. National Center for Health Statistics. Retrieved on December 30, 2008, from www.cdc.gov/nchs/products/pubs/pubd/hestats/overweight/overwght_adult_03.htm

Pronin, E., Gilovich, T., & Ross, L. (2004). Objectivity in the eye of the beholder: Divergent perceptions of bias in self versus others. *Psychological Review, 111,* 781–799.

Pronin, E., Lin, D. Y., & Ross, L. (2002). The bias blind spot: Perceptions of bias in self versus others. *Personality and Social Psychology Bulletin, 28,* 369–381.

Pruitt, D. G. (1998). Social conflict. In D. T. Gilbert, S. T. Fiske, & G. Lindzey (Eds.), *The handbook of social psychology* (4th ed., Vol. 2, pp. 470–503). New York: McGraw-Hill.

Puente, M. (2005, March 2). Rent this space: Bodies double as billboards. USToday.com. Retrieved on December 23, 2005, from *www.usatoday.com/life/lifestyle/2005-03-02-body-ads_x.htm*

Purdham, T. S. (1997, March 28). Tapes left by cult suggest comet was the sign to die. *New York Times,* p. A2.

Putnam, R. D. (2000). *Bowling alone: The collapse and revival of American community*. New York: Simon & Schuster.

Qin, J., Ogle, C., & Goodman, G. (2008). Adults' memories of childhood: True and false reports. *Journal of Experimental Psychology: Applied, 14*, 373–391.

Quattrone, G. A. (1982). Behavioral consequences of attributional bias. *Social Cognition, 1*, 358–378.

Quattrone, G. A. (1986). On the perception of a group's variability. In S. Worchel & W. G. Austin (Eds.), *Psychology of intergroup relations* (2nd ed.). Chicago: Nelson-Hall.

Quattrone, G. A., & Jones, E. E. (1980). The perception of variability within ingroups and outgroups: Implications for the law of small numbers. *Journal of Personality and Social Psychology, 38*, 141–152.

Quick stats binge drinking (2008). Department of Health and Human Services, Center for Disease Control and Prevention. Retrieved on December 30, 2008, from www.cdc.gov/alcohol/quickstats/binge_drinking.htm

Quinn, A., & Schlenker, B. R. (2002). Can accountability produce independence? Goals as determinants of the impact of accountability on conformity. *Personality and Social Psychology Bulletin, 28*, 472–483.

Rajecki, D. W., Kidd, R. F., & Ivins, B. (1976). Social facilitation in chickens: A different level of analysis. *Journal of Experimental Social Psychology, 12*, 233–246.

Ramirez, A. (2005, December 2). New Yorkers take a stand standing up. *New York Times*, p. B1.

Ramsey, S. J. (1981). The kinesics of femininity in Japanese women. *Language Sciences, 3*, 104–123.

Rapoport, A., & Chammah, A. M. (1965). *Prisoner's dilemma: A study in conflict and cooperation*. Ann Arbor: University of Michigan Press.

Raps, C. S., Peterson, C., Jonas, M., & Seligman, M. E. P. (1982). Patient behavior in hospitals: Helplessness, reactance, or both? *Journal of Personality and Social Psychology, 42*, 1036–1041.

Reagan, R. (1990). *An American life*. New York: Simon & Schuster.

Rector, M., & Neiva, E. (1996). Communication and personal relations in Brazil. In W. B. Gudykunst, S. Ting-Toomey, & T. Nishida (Eds.), *Communication in personal relationships across cultures* (pp. 156–173). Thousand Oaks, CA: Sage.

Redlawsk, D. P. (2002). Hot cognition or cool consideration? Testing the effects of motivated reasoning on political decision making. *Journal of Politics, 64*, 1021–1044.

Regan, P. C., & Berscheid, E. (1997). Gender differences in characteristics desired in a potential sexual and marriage partner. *Journal of Psychology and Human Sexuality, 9*, 25–37.

Regan, P. C., & Berscheid, E. (1999). *Lust: What we know about human sexual desire*. Thousand Oaks, CA: Sage.

Reid, P. T., & Cooper, S. M., & Banks, K. H. (2008). Girls to women: Developmental theory, research, and issues. In F. L. Denmark & M. A. Paludi (Eds.), *Psychology of women: A handbook of issues and theories* (pp. 237–270). Westport, CT: Praeger.

Reifman, A. S., Larrick, R. P., Crandall, C. S., & Fein, S. (1996). *Predicting sporting events: Accuracy as a function of reasons analysis, expertise, and task difficulty*. Unpublished manuscript, Research Institute on Addictions, Buffalo, NY.

Reifman, A. S., Larrick, R. P., & Fein, S. (1988). *The heat-aggression relationship in major league baseball*. Paper presented at the annual meeting of the American Psychological Association, San Francisco.

Reis, H. T., & Judd, C. M. (Eds.). (2000). *Handbook of research methods in social and personality pschology*. New York: Cambridge University Press.

Reis, H. T., & Patrick, B. C. (1996). Attachment and intimacy: Component processes. In E. T. Higgins & A. W. Kruglanski (Eds.), *Social psychology: Handbook of basic principles* (pp. 523–563). New York: Guilford Press.

Reis, H. T., Wheeler, L., Speigel, N., Kernis, M. H., Nezlek, J., & Perri, M. (1982). Physical attractiveness in social interaction: 2. Why does appearance affect social experience? *Journal of Personality and Social Psychology, 43*, 979–996.

Reis, S. M., & Park, S. (2001). Gender differences in high-achieving students in math and science. *Journal for the Education of the Gifted, 25*, 52–73.

Reisman, J. M. (1990). Intimacy in same-sex friendships. *Sex Roles, 23*, 65–82.

Reiss, D., & Marino, L. (2001). Mirror self-recognition in the bottlenose dophin: A case of cognitive convergence. *Proceedings of the National Academy of Sciences, 98*, 5937–5942.

Reiter, S. M., & Samuel, W. (1980). Littering as a function of prior litter and the presence or absence of prohibitive signs. *Journal of Applied Social Psychology, 10*, 45–55.

Reitzes, D. C. (1952). The role of organizational structures: Union versus neighborhood in a tension situation. *Journal of Social Issues, 9*, 37–44.

Renaud, J. M., & McConnell, A. R. (2002). Organization of the self-concept and the suppression of self-relevant thoughts. *Journal of Experimental Social Psychology, 38*, 79–86.

Renner, M. J., & Mackin, R. S. (1998). A life stress instrument for classroom use. *Teaching of Psychology, 25*, 46–48.

Reno, R. R., Cialdini, R. B., & Kallgren, C. A. (1993). The transsituational influence of social norms. *Journal of Personality and Social Psychology, 64*, 104–112.

Rensink, R. A. (2002). Change detection. *Annual Review of Psychology, 53*, 245–277.

Rentfrow, P. J., & Gosling, S. D. (2006). Message in a ballad: The role of music preferences in interpersonal perception. *Psychological Science, 17*, 236–242.

Report on the global AIDS epidemic: Executive summary (2008). Joint United Nations Programme on HIV/AIDS (UNAIDS). Retrieved on December 30, 2008, from www.unaids.org/en/KnowledgeCentre/HIVData/GlobalReport/2008/2008_Global_report.asp

Rhodes, G., Yoshikawa, S., Clark, A., Lee, K., McKay, R., & Akamatsu, S. (2001). Attractiveness of facial averageness and symmetry in non-Western cultures: In search of biologically based standards of beauty. *Perception, 30*, 611–625.

Rhodes, N., & Wood, W. (1992). Self-esteem and intelligence affect influenceability: The mediating role of message reception. *Psychological Bulletin, 111*, 156–171.

Rhodewalt, F., Sanbonmatsu, D. M., Tschanz, B., Feick, D. L., & Waller, A. (1995). Self-handicapping and interpersonal trade-offs: The effects of claimed self-handicaps on observers' performance evaluations and feedback. *Personality and Social Psychology Bulletin, 21*, 1042–1050.

Rhodewalt, F., & Vohs, K. D. (2005). Defensive strategies, motivation, and the self: A self-regulatory process view. In A. J. Elliot & C. S. Dweck (Eds.), *Handbook of competence and motivation* (pp. 548–565). New York: Guilford.

Rholes, W. S., Newman, L. S., & Ruble, D. N. (1990). Understanding self and other: Developmental and motivational aspects of perceiving persons in terms of invariant dispositions. In E. T. Higgins & R. M. Sorrentino (Eds.), *Handbook of motivation and cognition: Foundations of social behavior* (Vol. 2, pp. 369–407). New York: Guilford Press.

Rholes, W. S., Simpson, J. A., & Friedman, M. (2006). Avoidant attachment and the experience of parenting. *Personality and Social Psychology Bulletin, 32*, 275–285.

Ricciardelli, L. A., & McCabe, M. P. (2003). A longitudinal analysis of the role of psychosocial factors in predicting body change strategies among adolescent boys. *Sex Roles, 48*, 349–360.

Richard, F. D., Bond, C. F. Jr., & Stokes-Zoota, J. J. (2001). 'That's completely obvious... and important": Lay judgments of social psychological findings. *Personality and Social Psychology Bulletin, 27,* 497-505.

Richardson, D., Hammock, G., Smith, S., & Gardner, W. (1994). Empathy as a cognitive inhibitor of interpersonal aggression. *Aggressive Behavior, 20,* 275–289.

Richeson, J. A., & Ambady, N. (2003). Effects of situation power on automatic racial prejudice. *Journal of Experimental Social Psychology, 39,* 177–183.

Richmond, V. P., & McCroskey, J. C. (1995). *Nonverbal behavior in interpersonal relations.* Needham Heights, MA: Allyn & Bacon.

Richter, C. P. (1957). On the phenomenon of sudden death in animals and man. *Psychosomatic Medicine, 19,* 191–198.

Riggs, J. Morgan, & Gumbrecht, L. B. (2005). Correspondence bias and American sentiment in the wake of September 11, 2001. *Journal of Applied Social Psychology, 35*(1), 15–28.

Ringelmann, M. (1913). Recherches sur les moteurs animés: Travail de l'homme [Research on driving forces: Human work]. *Annales de l'Institut National Agronomique,* series 2, *12,* 1–40.

Riordan, C. A. (1978). Equal-status interracial contact: A review and revision of a concept. *International Journal of Intercultural Relations, 2,* 161–185.

Robins, R. W., & Beer, J. S. (2001). Positive illusions about the self: Short-term benefits and long-term costs. *Journal of Personality and Social Psychology, 80,* 340–352.

Robins, R. W., Spranca, M. D., & Mendelson, G. A. (1996). The actor-observer effect revisited: Effects of individual differences and repeated social interactions on actor and observer attributions. *Journal of Personality and Social Psychology, 71,* 375–389.

Rodin, J., & Langer, E. J. (1977). Long-term effects of a control-relevant intervention with the institutional aged. *Journal of Personality and Social Psychology, 35,* 897–902.

Rodrigo, M. F., & Ato, M. (2002). Testing the group polarization hypothesis by using logit models. *European Journal of Social Psychology, 32,* 3–18.

Roesch, S. C., & Amirkhan, J. H. (1997). Boundary conditions for self-serving attributions: Another look at the sports pages. *Journal of Applied Social Psychology, 27,* 245–261.

Roese, N. J. (1997). Counterfactual thinking. *Psychological Bulletin, 121,* 133–148.

Roese, N. J., & Jamieson, D. W. (1993), Twenty years of bogus pipeline research: A critical review and meta-analysis. *Psychological Bulletin, 114,* 363–375.

Roese, N. J., & Olson, J. M. (1997). Counterfactual thinking: The intersection of affect and function. In M. P. Zanna (Ed.), *Advances in experimental social psychology* (Vol. 29, pp. 1–59). San Diego, CA: Academic Press.

Rogers, R. (1983). Cognitive and physiological processes in fear appeals and attitude change: A revised theory of protection motivation. In J. T. Cacioppo & R. E. Petty (Eds.), *Social psychophysiology: A sourcebook* (pp. 153–176). New York: Guilford Press.

Rogers, R., & Prentice-Dunn, S. (1981). Deindividuation and anger-mediated interracial aggression: Unmasking regressive racism. *Journal of Personality and Social Psychology, 41,* 63–73.

Rogers, T. B., Kuiper, N. A., & Kirker, W. S. (1977). Self-reference and the encoding of personal information. *Journal of Personality and Social Psychology, 35,* 677–688.

Rohan, M., & Zanna, M. P. (1996). Value transmission in families. In C. Seligman, J. M. Olson, & M. P. Zanna (Eds.), *The psychology of values: The Ontario Symposium on personality and social psychology* (Vol. 8, pp. 253–276). Mahwah, NJ: Erlbaum.

Rohrer, J. H., Baron, S. H., Hoffman, E. L., & Swander, D. V. (1954). The stability of autokinetic judgments. *Journal of Abnormal and Social Psychology, 49,* 595–597.

Roiphe, K. (1994). *The morning after: Sex, fear, and feminism.* New York: Little, Brown.

Rosch, E., & Lloyd, B. (Eds.). (1978). *Cognition and categorization.* Hillsdale, NJ: Erlbaum.

Roseman, I., & Smith, C. (2001). Appraisal theory: Overview, assumptions, varieties, controversies. In K. R. Scherer, A. Schorr, & T. Johnstone (Eds.), *Appraisal processes in emotion: Theory, methods, research* (pp. 3–19). New York: Oxford University Press.

Rosenberg, L. A. (1961). Group size, prior experience, and conformity. *Journal of Abnormal and Social Psychology, 63,* 436–437.

Rosenberg, M. (2006). Population growth rates and doubling time. Retrieved on June 21, 2006, from: *geography.about.com/od/populationgeography/a/populationgrow.htm*

Rosenberg, M. J., Davidson, A. J., Chen, J., Judson, F. N., & Douglas, J. M. (1992). Barrier contraceptives and sexually transmitted diseases in women: A comparison of female-dependent methods and condoms. *American Journal of Public Health, 82,* 669–674.

Rosenberg, S., Nelson, S., & Vivekananthan, P. S. (1968). A multidimensional approach to the structure of personality impressions. *Journal of Personality and Social Psychology, 9,* 283–294.

Rosenblatt, P. C. (1974). Cross-cultural perspectives on attraction. In T. L. Huston (Ed.), *Foundations of interpersonal attraction* (pp. 79–99). New York: Academic Press.

Rosenthal, A. M. (1964). *Thirty-eight witnesses.* New York: McGraw-Hill.

Rosenthal, R. (1994). Interpersonal expectancy effects: A 30-year perspective. *Current Directions in Psychological Science, 3,* 176–179.

Rosenthal, R., Hall, J. A., Di Matteo, M. R., Rogers, P. L., & Archer, D. (1979). *Sensitivity to nonverbal communication: The PONS test.* Baltimore: Johns Hopkins University Press.

Rosenthal, R., & Jacobson, L. (1968). *Pygmalion in the classroom: Teacher expectations and student intellectual development.* New York: Holt, Rinehart and Winston.

Ross, L. (1977). The intuitive psychologist and his shortcomings: Distortions in the attribution process. In L. Berkowitz (Ed.), *Advances in experimental social psychology* (Vol. 10, pp. 173–220). Orlando, FL: Academic Press.

Ross, L. (1998). Comment on Gilbert. In J. M. Darley & J. Cooper (Eds.), *Attribution and social interaction* (pp. 53–66). Washington, DC: American Psychological Association.

Ross, L., Amabile, T. M., & Steinmetz, J. L. (1977). Social roles, social control, and biases in social perception. *Journal of Personality and Social Psychology, 35,* 485–494.

Ross, L., & Nisbett, R. E. (1991). *The person and the situation: Perspectives of social psychology.* New York: McGraw-Hill.

Ross, L., & Ward, A. (1995). Psychological barriers to dispute resolution. In M. P. Zanna (Ed.), *Advances in experimental social psychology* (Vol. 27, pp. 255–304). San Diego, CA: Academic Press.

Ross, L., & Ward, A. (1996). Naive realism: Implications for social conflict and misunderstanding. In T. Brown, E. Reed, & E. Turiel (Eds.), *Values and knowledge* (pp. 103–135). Hillsdale, NJ: Erlbaum.

Ross, M., & Olson, J. M. (1981). An expectancy-attribution model of the effects of placebos. *Psychological Review, 88,* 408–437.

Ross, M., & Wilson, A. E. (2003). Autobiographical memory and conceptions of self: Getting better all the time. *Current Directions in Psychological Science, 12,* 66–69.

Ross, W., & La Croix, J. (1996). Multiple meanings of trust in negotiation theory and research: A literature review and integrative model. *International Journal of Conflict Management, 7,* 314–360.

Rosser, B. S. (1991). The effects of using fear in public AIDS education on the behaviour of homosexually active men. *Journal of Psychology and Human Sexuality, 4,* 123–134.

Rothbaum, F., & Tsang, B. Y.-P. (1998). Lovesongs in the United States and China: On the nature of romantic love. *Journal of Cross-Cultural Psychology, 29*, 306–319.

Rothman, A., Wlaschin, J., Bartels, R., Latimer, A., & Salovey, P. (2008). How persons and situations regulate message framing effects: The study of health behavior. In A. J. Elliot (Ed.), *Handbook of approach and avoidance motivation* (pp. 475–486). New York: Psychology Press.

Rothman, A. J. (2000). Toward a theory-based analysis of behavioral maintenance. *Health Psychology, 19*, 64–69.

Rothman, A. J., & Salovey, P. (1997). Shaping perceptions to motivate healthy behavior: The role of message framing. *Psychological Bulletin, 121*, 3–19.

Rothman, A. J., Salovey, P., Antone, C., Keough, K., & Martin, C. D. (1993). The influence of message framing on intentions to perform health behaviors. *Journal of Experimental Social Psychology, 29*, 408–432.

Rotter, J. B. (1966). Generalized expectancies for internal versus external control of reinforcement. *Psychological Monographs, 80*, 1–28 (Whole No. 609).

Rubin, Z. (1970). Measurement of romantic love. *Journal of Personality and Social Psychology, 16*, 265–273.

Rubin, Z., Peplau, L. A., & Hill, C. T. (1981). Loving and leaving: Sex differences in romantic attachments. *Sex Roles, 7*, 821–835.

Rudman, L., Phelan, J., & Heppen, J. (2007). Developmental sources of implicit attitudes. *Personality and Social Psychology Bulletin, 33*, 1700–1713.

Rudman, L. A. (1998). Self-promotion as a risk factor for women: The costs and benefits of counterstereotypical impression management. *Journal of Personality and Social Psychology, 74*, 629–645.

Rudman, L. A., & Borgida, E. (1995). The afterglow of construct accessibility: The behavioral consequences of priming men to view women as sexual objects. *Journal of Experimental Social Psychology, 31*, 493–517.

Ruiter, R. A. C., Abraham, C., & Kok, G. (2001). Scary warnings and rational precautions: A review of the psychology of fear appeals. *Psychology and Health, 16*, 613–630.

Rule, B. G., Taylor, B. R., & Dobbs, A. R. (1987). Priming effects of heat on aggressive thoughts. *Social Cognition, 5*, 131–143.

Rusbult, C. E. (1983). A longitudinal test of the investment model: The development (and deterioration) of satisfaction and commitment in heterosexual involvements. *Journal of Personality and Social Psychology, 45*, 101–117.

Rusbult, C. E. (1987). Responses to dissatisfaction in close relationships: The exit-voice-loyalty-neglect model. In D. Perlman & S. W. Duck (Eds.), *Intimate relationships: Development, dynamics, and deterioration* (pp. 209–237). Newbury Park, CA: Sage.

Rusbult, C. E. (1991). *Commitment processes in close relationships: The investment model*. Paper presented at the annual meeting of the American Psychological Association, San Francisco.

Rusbult, C. E., & Buunk, B. P. (1993). Commitment processes in close relationships: An interdependence analysis. *Journal of Social and Personal Relationships, 10*, 175–204.

Rusbult, C. E., Johnson, D. J., & Morrow, G. D. (1986). Impact of couple patterns of problem solving on distress and nondistress in dating relationships. *Journal of Personal and Social Psychology, 50*, 744–753.

Rusbult, C. E., & Martz, J. M. (1995). Remaining in an abusive relationship: An investment model analysis of nonvoluntary dependence. *Personality and Social Psychology Bulletin, 21*, 558–571.

Rusbult, C. E., Martz, J. M., & Agnew, C. R. (1998). The investment model scale: Measuring commitment level, satisfaction level, quality of alternatives, and investment size. *Personal Relationships, 5*, 357–391.

Rusbult, C. E., Olsen, N., Davis, N. L., & Hannon, P. (2001). Committment and relationship maintenance mechanisms. In J. H. Harvey & A. Wenzel (Eds.), *Close romantic relationships: Maintenance and enhancement* (pp. 87–113). Mahwah, NJ: Erlbaum.

Rusbult, C. E., & Van Lange, P. A. M. (1996). Interdependence processes. In E. T. Higgins & A. W. Kruglanski (Eds.), *Social psychology: Handbook of basic principles* (pp. 564–596). New York: Guilford Press.

Rusbult, C. E., Yovetich, N. A., & Verette, J. (1996). An interdependence analysis of accommodation processes. In G. J. O. Fletcher & J. Fitness (Eds.), *Knowledge structures in close relationships: A social psychological approach* (pp. 63–90). Mahwah, NJ: Erlbaum.

Rusbult, C. E., & Zembrodt, I. M. (1983). Responses to dissatisfaction in romantic involvements: A multidimensional scaling analysis. *Journal of Experimental Social Psychology, 19*, 274–293.

Rushton, J. P. (1989). Genetic similarity, human altruism, and group selection. *Behavioral and Brain Sciences, 12*, 503–559.

Russell, J., & Barrett, L. (1999). Core affect, prototypical emotional episodes, and other things called emotion: Dissecting the elephant. *Journal of Personality and Social Psychology, 76*, 805–819.

Russell, G. W. (1983). Psychological issues in sports aggression. In J. H. Goldstein (Ed.), *Sports violence* (pp. 157–181). New York: Springer-Verlag.

Rusting, Cheryl L., & Nolen-Hoeksema, Susan (1998). Regulating responses of anger: Effects of rumination and distraction on angry mood. *Journal of Personality and Social Psychology, 74*, 790–803.

Ryan, B., Jr. (1991). *It works! How investment spending in advertising pays off.* New York: American Association of Advertising Agencies.

Ryan, M. K., Haslam, S. A., Hersby, M. D., Kulich, C., & Atkins, C. (2008). Opting out or pushed off the edge? The glass cliff and the precariousness of women's leadership positions. *Social and Personality Psychology Compass, 2* www.blackwell-compass.com/subject/socialpsychology/.

Ryan, R. M., & Deci, E. L. (2000). Intrinsic and extrinsic rewards: Classic definitions and new directions. *Current Educational Psychology, 25*, 54–67.

Sacks, O. (1987). *The man who mistook his wife for a hat and other clinical tales.* New York: Harper & Row.

Sadker, M., & Sadker, D. (1994). *Failing at fairness: How America's schools cheat girls.* New York: Scribner.

Saffer, H. (2002). Alcohol advertising and youth. *Journal of Studies on Alcohol, 14*, 173–181.

Sagarin, B. J., Cialdini, R. B., Rice, W. E., & Serna, S. B. (2002). Dispelling the illusion of invulnerability: The motivations and mechanisms of resistance to persuasion. *Journal of Personality and Social Psychology, 83*, 526–541.

Sakai, H. (1999). A multiplicative power-function model of cognitive dissonance: Toward an integrated theory of cognition, emotion, and behavior after Leon Festinger. In E. Harmon-Jones & J. S. Mills (Eds.), *Cognitive dissonance: Progress on a pivotal theory in social psychology* (pp. 120–138). Washington, DC: American Psychological Association.

Sakamoto, A., Sekiguchi, K., & Shinkyu, A. (2003). Does media coverage of capital punishment have a deterrent effect on the occurrence of brutal crimes? An analysis of Japanese time-series data from 1959 to 1990. In K. Yang, K. Hwang, P. B. Pedersen, & I. Daibo (Eds.), *Progress in Asian social psychology: Conceptual and empirical contributions* (pp. 277–290). Westport, CT: Praeger.

Sakurai, M. M. (1975). Small group cohesiveness and detrimental conformity. *Sociometry, 38*, 340–357.

Salganik, M. J., Dodds, P. S., & Watts, D. J. (2006). Experimental study of inequality and unpredictability in an artificial cultural market. *Science, 311*, 854–856.

Salili, F. (1996). Learning and motivation: An Asian perspective. *Psychology and Developing Societies, 8*, 55–81.

Salovey, P., Mayer, J. D., & Rosenhan, D. L. (1991). Mood and helping: Mood as a motivator of helping and helping as a regulator of mood.

In M. S. Clark (Ed.), *Prosocial behavior: Review of personality and social psychology* (Vol. 12, pp. 215–237). Newbury Park, CA: Sage.

Salovey, P., & Rodin, J. (1985). Cognitions about the self: Connecting feeling states and social behavior. In P. Shaver (Ed.), *Self, situations, and social behavior: Review of personality and social psychology* (Vol. 6, pp. 143–166). Beverly Hills, CA: Sage.

Salovey, P., & Rothman, A. J. (2003). *Social psychology of health*. New York: Psychology Press.

Sampson, R. J. (1988). Local friendship ties and community attachment in mass society: A multilevel systemic model. *American Sociological Review, 53*, 766–779.

Sands, E. R., & Wardle, J. (2003). Internalization of ideal body shapes in 9- to 12-year-old girls. *International Journal of Eating Disorders, 33*, 193–204.

Sanger, D. E. (1993, May 30). The career and the kimono. *New York Times Magazine*, pp. 18–19.

Sangrigoli, S., Pallier, C., Argenti, A. M., Ventureyra, V. A. G., & de Schonen, S. (2005). Reversibility of the other-race effect in face recognition during childhood. *Psychological Science, 16*, 440–444.

Sanna, L. J. (1992). Self-efficacy theory: Implications for social facilitation and social loafing. *Journal of Personality and Social Psychology, 62*, 774–786.

Sanna, L. J., Meier, S., & Wegner, E. A. (2001). Counterfactuals and motivation: Mood as input to affective enjoyment and preparation. *British Journal of Social Psychology, 40*, 235–256.

Sanna, L. J., & Schwarz, N. (2004). Integrating temporal biases: The interplay of focal thoughts and accessibility experiences. *Psychological Science, 15*, 474–481.

Sanna, L. J., & Schwarz, N. (2007). Metacognitive experiences and hindsight bias: It's not just the thought (content) that counts! *Social Cognition, 25*, 185–202.

Sansone, C., & Harackiewicz, J. M. (1996). "I don't feel like it": The function of interest in self-regulation. In L. L. Martin & A. Tesser (Eds.), *Striving and feeling: Interactions among goals, affect, and self-regulation* (pp. 203–228). Mahwah, NJ: Erlbaum.

Sansone, C., & Harackiewicz, J. M. (1997). *"Reality" is complicated: Comment on Eisenberger and Cameron*. Unpublished manuscript, University of Utah.

Sarche, J. (2003, June 22). For new female cadets, an Air Force Academy in turmoil. *Boston Globe*, p. A12.

Sargent, J. D., Dalton, M. A., Beach, M. L., Mott, L. A., Tickle, J. J., Ahrens, M. B., & Heatherton, T. F. (2002). Viewing tobacco use in movies: Does it shape attitudes that mediate adolescent smoking? *American Journal of Preventive Medicine, 22*, 137–145.

Sastry, J., & Ross, C. E. (1998). Asian ethnicity and the sense of personal control. *Social Psychology Quarterly, 61*, 101–120.

Savitsky, K. (1998). Embarrassment study [E-mails]. Society for Personal and Social Psychology e-mail list archive. Retrieved from www.stolaf.edu/cgi-bin/mailarchivesearch.pl?directory=/home/www/people/huff/SPSP&listname=archive98

Schachter, S. (1951). Deviation, rejection, and communication. *Journal of Abnormal and Social Psychology, 46*, 190–207.

Schachter, S. (1959). *The psychology of affiliation*. Stanford, CA: Stanford University Press.

Schachter, S. (1964). The interaction of cognitive and physiological determinants of emotional state. In L. Berkowitz (Ed.), *Advances in experimental social psychology* (Vol. 1, pp. 49–80). New York: Academic Press.

Schachter, S., & Singer, J. E. (1962). Cognitive, social, and physiological determinants of emotional states. *Psychological Review, 69*, 379–399.

Schachter, S., & Singer, J. E. (1979). Comments on the Maslach and Marshall-Zimbardo experiments. *Journal of Personality and Social Psychology, 37*, 989–995.

Schafer, M., & Crichlow, S. (1996). Antecedents of groupthink: A quantitative study. *Journal of Conflict Resolution, 40*, 415–435.

Schaller, M., Asp, C. H., Rosell, M. C., & Heim, S. J. (1996). Training in statistical reasoning inhibits formation of erroneous group stereotypes. *Personality and Social Psychology Bulletin, 22*, 829–844.

Schaller, M., Simpson, J., & Kenrick, D. (Eds.) (2006). *Evolution and social psychology*. Madison, CT: Psychosocial Press.

Schama, S. (2003, March 10). The unloved American. *New Yorker*, pp. 34–39.

Scheier, M. F., Carver, C. S., & Bridges, M. W. (1994). Distinguishing optimism from neuroticism (and trait anxiety, self-mastery, and self-esteem): A revision of the Life Orientation Test. *Journal of Personality and Social Psychology, 67*, 1063–1078.

Schemo, D. J. (2003a, July 12). Ex-superintendent of Air Force Academy is demoted in wake of rape scandal. *New York Times*, p. A7.

Schemo, D. J. (2003b, July 24). Study of campus faults some antidrinking drives. *New York Times*, p. A17.

Scherer, K. R., Dan, E. S., & Flykt, A. (2006). What determines a feeling's position in affective space? A case for appraisal. *Cognition and Emotion, 20*, 92–113.

Schlegel, S. (1998). *Wisdom from a rainforest: The spiritual journey of an anthropologist*. Athens: University of Georgia Press.

Schlener, B. R. (2003). Self-presentation. In M. R. Leary & J. P. Tangney (Eds.), *Handbook of self and identity* (pp. 492–518). New York: Guilford.

Schlenger, W. E., Caddell, J. M., Ebert, L., Jordan, B. K., Rourke, K. M., Wilson, D., et al. (2002). Psychological reactions to terrorist attacks: Findings from the National Study of Americans' Reactions to September 11. *Journal of the American Medical Association, 288*, 581–588.

Schlenker, B. R., & Weingold, M. F. (1989). Self-identification and accountability. In R. A. Giacalone & P. Rosenfeld (Eds.), *Impression management in the organization* (pp. 21–43). Hillsdale, NJ: Erlbaum.

Schmeichel, B. J., & Baumeister, R. F. (2004). Self-regulatory strength. In R. F. Baumeister & K D. Vohs (Eds.), *Handbook of self-regulation: Research, theory, and applications* (pp. 84–98). New York: Guilford.

Schmitt, B. H., Gilovich, T., Goore, N., & Joseph, L. (1986). Mere presence and social facilitation: One more time. *Journal of Experimental Social Psychology, 22*, 228–241.

Schneider, D. J. (1973). Implicit personality theory: A review. *Psychological Bulletin, 79*, 294–309.

Schneider, D. J., Hastorf, A. H., & Ellsworth, P. C. (1979). *Person perception* (2nd ed.). Reading, MA: Addison-Wesley.

Schneider, M. E., Major, B., Luhtanen, R., & Crocker, J. (1996). Social stigma and the potential costs of assumptive help. *Personality and Social Psychology Bulletin, 22*, 201–209.

Schoeneman, T. J., & Rubanowitz, D. E. (1985). Attributions in the advice columns: Actors and observers, causes and reasons. *Personality and Social Psychology Bulletin, 11*, 315–325.

Schofield, J. W. (1986). Causes and consequences of the color-blind perspective. In J. F. Dovidio & S. L. Gaertner (Eds.), *Prejudice, discrimination, and racism* (pp. 231–253). Orlando, FL: Academic Press.

Scholten, L., van Knippenberg, D., Nijstad, B. A., & De Dreu, C. K. W. (2007) Motivated information processing and group decision-making: Effects of process accountability on information processing and decision quality. *Journal of Experimental Social Psychology, 43*, 539–552.

Schooler, J. W. (1999). Seeking the core: The issues and evidence surrounding recovered accounts of sexual trauma. In L. M. Williams & V. L. Banyard (Eds.), *Trauma and memory* (pp. 203–216). Thousand Oaks, CA: Sage.

Schooler, J. W., & Eich, E. (2000). Memory for emotional events. In E. Tulving & F. I. M. Craik (Eds.), *The Oxford handbook of memory* (pp. 379–392). Oxford: Oxford University Press.

Schooler, J. W., & Engstler-Schooler, T. Y. (1990). Verbal overshadowing of visual memories: Some things are better left unsaid. *Cognitive Psychology, 22*, 36–71.

Schopler, J., & Insko, C. A. (1999). The reduction of the interindividual-intergroup discontinuity effect: The role of future consequences. In M. Foddy & M. Smithson (Eds.), *Resolving social dilemmas: Dynamic, structural, and intergroup aspects* (pp. 281–293). Bristol, PA: Taylor & Francis.

Schriesheim, C. A., Tepper, B. J., & Tetrault, L. A. (1994). Least preferred co-worker score, situational control, and leadership effectiveness: A meta-analysis of contingency model performance predictions. *Journal of Applied Psychology, 79*, 561–573.

Schroeder, D. H., & Costa, P. T., Jr. (1984). Influence of life event stress on physical illness: Substantive effects or methodological flaws? *Journal of Personality and Social Psychology, 46*, 853–863.

Schultz, P. W., Oskamp, S., & Mainieri, T. (1995). Who recycles and when? A review of personal and situational factors. *Journal of Environmental Psychology, 15*, 105–121.

Schulz, R. (1976). Effects of control and predictability on the physical and psychological well-being of the institutionalized aged. *Journal of Personality and Social Psychology, 33*, 563–573.

Schulz, R., & Hanusa, B. H. (1978). Long-term effects of control and predictability-enhancing interventions: Findings and ethical issues. *Journal of Personality and Social Psychology, 36*, 1202–1212.

Schuman, H., & Kalton, G. (1985). Survey methods. In G. Lindzey & E. Aronson (Eds.), *Handbook of social psychology* (3rd ed., Vol. 1, pp. 635–697). New York: McGraw-Hill.

Schützwohl, A. (2004). Which infidelity type makes you more jealous? Decision strategies in a forced-choice between sexual and emotional infidelity. *Evolutionary Psychology, 2*, 121–2:128.

Schützwohl, A. & Koc S. (2004). Sex differences in jealousy. The recall of cues to sexual and emotional infidelity in personally more and less threatening context conditions. *Evolution and Human Behavior*, Volume 25, Issue 4, Pages 249–257.

Schwartz, J. (2003, June 7). Shuttle tests seem to back foam theory in accident. *New York Times*, p. A1.

Schwartz, J., & Wald, M. L. (2003, June 7). NASA's failings go beyond foam hitting shuttle, panel says. *New York Times*, p. A1.

Schwartz, S. H. (1992). Universals in the content and structure of values: Theoretical advances and empirical tests in 20 countries. In M. P. Zanna (Ed.), *Advances in experimental social psychology* (Vol. 25, pp. 1–65). San Diego, CA: Academic Press.

Schwarz, N., Bless, H., Strack, F., Klumpp, G., Rittenauer-Schatka, H., & Simmons, A. (1991). Ease of retrieval as information: Another look at the availability heuristic. *Journal of Personality and Social Psychology, 61*, 195–202.

Schwarz, N., & Clore, G. L. (1988). How do I feel about it? Informative functions of affective states. In K. Fiedler & J. Forgas (Eds.), *Affect, cognition, and social behavior* (pp. 44–62). Toronto, Ontario, Canada: Hogrefe.

Schwarz, N., Groves, R. M., & Schuman, H. (1998). Survey methods. In D. T. Gilbert, S. T. Fiske, & G. Lindzey (Eds.), *The handbook of social psychology* (4th ed., Vol. 1, pp. 143–179). New York: McGraw-Hill.

Schwarz, N., & Vaughn, L. A. (2002). The availability heuristic revisited: Ease of recall and content of recall as distinct sources of information. In T. Gilovich, D. W. Griffin, & D. Kahneman (Eds). *Heuristics and biases: The psychology of intuitive judgment* (pp. 103–119). New York: Cambridge University Press.

Schwarzer, R., & Leppin, A. (1991). Social support and health: A theoretical and empirical overview. *Journal of Social and Personal Relationships, 8*, 99–127.

Scott, J. E., & Cuvelier, S. J. (1993). Violence and sexual violence in pornography: Is it increasing? *Archives of Sexual Behavior, 22*, 357–371.

Scott, J. P. (1958). *Aggression*. Chicago: University of Chicago Press.

Secord, P. F., & Backman, C. W. (1964). *Social psychology*. New York: McGraw-Hill.

Sedikides, C., & Anderson, C. A. (1994). Causal perceptions of intertrait relations: The glue that holds person types together. *Personality and Social Psychology Bulletin, 21*, 294–302.

Sedikides, C., Gaertner, L., & Yoshiyasu, T. (2003). Pancultural self-enhancement. *Journal of Personality and Social Psychology, 84*, 60–79.

Seery, M., Silver, R., Holman, E., Ence, W., & Chu, T. (2008). Expressing thoughts and feelings following a collective trauma: Immediate responses to 9/11 predict negative outcomes in a national sample. *Journal of Consulting and Clinical Psychology, 76*, 657–667.

Seligman, M. E. P. (1975). *Helplessness: On depression, development, and death*. San Francisco: Freeman.

Seligman, M. E. P. (2002). Positive psychology, positive prevention, and positive therapy. In C. R. Snyder & S. J. Lopez (Eds.), *Handbook of positive psychology* (pp. 3–9). New York: Oxford University Press.

Seligman, M. E. P., Steen, T. A., & Park, N. (2005). Positive psychology progress: Empirical validation of interventions. *American Psychologist, 60*, 410–421.

Selye, H. (1956). *The stress of life*. New York: McGraw-Hill.

Selye, H. (1976). *Stress in health and disease*. Woburn, MA: Butterworth.

Senchak, M., & Leonard, K. E. (1992). Attachment styles and marital adjustment among newlywed couples. *Journal of Social and Personal Relationships, 9*, 51–64.

Sengupta, J., & Fitzsimons, G. J. (2004). The effect of analyzing reasons on the stability of brand attitudes: A reconciliation of opposing predictions. *Journal of Consumer Research, 31*, 705–711.

Senko, C., Durik, A., & Harackiewicz, J. (2008). Historical perspectives and new directions in achievement goal theory: Understanding the effects of mastery and performance–approach goals. In J. Y. Shah & W. L. Gardner (Eds.), *Handbook of motivation science* (pp. 100–113). New York: Guilford.

Seppa, N. (1997). Children's TV remains steeped in violence. *APA Monitor, 28*, 36.

Sergios, P. A., & Cody, J. (1985). Physical attractiveness and social assertiveness skills in male homosexual dating behavior and partner selection. *Journal of Social Psychology, 125*, 505–514.

Seta, C. E., & Seta, J. J. (1995). When audience presence is enjoyable: The influences of audience awareness of prior success on performance and task interest. *Basic and Applied Social Psychology, 16*, 95–108.

Seta, J. J., Seta, C. E., & Wang, M. A. (1990). Feelings of negativity and stress: An averaging-summation analysis of impressions of negative life experiences. *Personality and Social Psychology Bulletin, 17*, 376–384.

Shackleford, T. K. (2005). An evolutionary psychological perspective on cultures of honor. *Evolutionary Psychology, 3*, 381–391.

Shackleford, T. K., & Buss, D. M. (1996). Betrayal in mateships, friendships, and coalitions. *Personality and Social Psychology Bulletin, 22*, 1151–1164.

Shah, A. K., & Oppenheimer, D M.. (2008). Heuristics made easy: An effort-reduction framework. *Psychological Bulletin, 134*, 207–232.

Shah, J. (2003). Automatic for the people: How representations of significant others implicitly affect goal pursuit. *Journal of Personality and Social Psychology, 84*, 661–681.

Sharan, S. (1980). Cooperative learning in small groups. *Review of Educational Research, 50*, 241–271.

Shariff, A., & Norenzayan, A. (2007). God is watching you: Priming god concepts increases prosocial behavior in an anonymous economic game. *Psychological Science, 18*, 803–809.

Sharp, F. C. (1928). *Ethics*. New York: Century.

Sharpe, D., Adair, J. G., & Roese, N. J. (1992). Twenty years of deception research: A decline in subjects' trust? *Personality and Social Psychology Bulletin, 18*, 585–590.

Shaver, P. R., Wu, S., & Schwartz, J. C. (1992). Cross-cultural similarities and differences in emotion and its representation. In M. S. Clark (Ed.), *Review of personality and social psychology*: Vol. 13, *Emotion* (pp. 175–212). Newbury Park, CA: Sage.

Shavitt, S. (1989). Operationalizing functional theories of attitude. In A. R. Pratkanis, S. J. Breckler, & A. G. Greenwald (Eds.), *Attitude structure and function* (pp. 311–337). Hillsdale, NJ: Erlbaum.

Shavitt, S. (1990). The role of attitude objects in attitude function. *Journal of Experimental Social Psychology, 26*, 124–148.

Shavitt, S., Sanbonmatsu, D. M., Smittipatana, S., & Posavac, S. S. (1999). Broadening the conditions for illusory correlation formation: Implications for judging minority groups. *Basic and Applied Social Psychology, 21*, 263–279.

Shaw, J. I., & Skolnick, P. (1995). Effects of prohibitive and informative judicial instructions on jury decision making. *Social Behavior and Personality, 23*, 319–325.

Sheldon, K. M. (1999). Learning the lessons of tit-for-tat: Even competitors can get the message. *Journal of Personality and Social Psychology, 77*, 1245–1253.

Shepperd, J. A., & Taylor, K. M. (1999). Social loafing and expectancy-value theory. *Personality and Social Psychology Bulletin, 25*, 1147–1158.

Sherif, M. (1936). *The psychology of social norms*. New York: Harper.

Sherif, M. (1966). *In common predicament: Social psychology of intergroup conflict and cooperation*. Boston: Houghton Mifflin.

Sherif, M., Harvey, O. J., White, J., Hood, W., & Sherif, C. W. (1961). *Intergroup conflict and cooperation: The robber's cave experiment*. Norman: Institute of Intergroup Relations, University of Oklahoma.

Sherrod, D. R., & Cohen, S. (1979). Density, personal control, and design. In A. Baum & J. R. Aiello (Eds.), *Residential crowding and design* (pp. 217–227). New York: Plenum.

Shipp, E. R. (2005, October 25). Rosa Parks, 92, Intrepid pioneer of civil rights movement, is dead. *New York Times*, pp. A1, C18.

Shotland, R. L., & Straw, M. K. (1976). Bystander response to an assault: When a man attacks a woman. *Journal of Personality and Social Psychology, 34*, 990–999.

Shupe, L. M. (1954). Alcohol and crimes: A study of the urine alcohol concentration found in 882 persons arrested during or immediately after the commission of a felony. *Journal of Criminal Law and Criminology, 33*, 661–665.

Siero, F. W., Bakker, A. B., Dekker, G. B., & Van Den Burg, M. T. C. (1996). Changing organizational energy consumption behavior through comparative feedback. *Journal of Environmental Psychology, 16*, 235–246.

Sigall, H., & Page, R. (1971). Current stereotypes: A little fading, a little faking. *Journal of Personality and Social Psychology, 18*, 247–255.

Sigelman, J. D., & Johnson, P. (2008). Left frontal cortical activation and spreading of alternatives: Tests of the action-based model of dissonance. *Journal of Personality and Social Psychology, 94*, 1–15.

Signorielli, N., Gerbner, G., & Morgan, M. (1995). Violence on television: The Cultural Indicators Project. *Journal of Broadcasting and Electronic Media, 39*, 278–283.

Silver, L. B., Dublin, C. C., & Lourie, R. S. (1969). Does violence breed violence? Contributions from a study of the child abuse syndrome. *American Journal of Psychiatry, 126*, 404–407.

Silver, R., Holman, E. A., McIntosh, D. N., Poulin, M., & Gil-Rivas, V. (2002). Nationwide longitudinal study of psychological responses to September 11. *Journal of the American Medical Association, 2882*, 1235–1244.

Silverstein, B., Perdue, L., Peterson, B., & Kelly, E. (1986). The role of the mass media in promoting a thin standard of bodily attractiveness for women. *Sex Roles, 14*, 519–532.

Silverstein, B., Peterson, B., & Perdue, L. (1986). Some correlates of the thin standard of bodily attractiveness for women. *International Journal of Eating Disorders, 5*, 895–906.

Silvia, P. J., & Abele, A. E. (2002). Can positive affect induce self-focused attention? Methodological and measurement issues. *Cognition and Emotion, 16*, 845–853.

Sime, J. D. (1983). Affiliative behavior during escape to building exits. *Journal of Environmental Psychology, 3*, 21–41.

Simms, L. J. (2002). The application of attachment theory to individual behavior and functioning in close relationships: Theory, research, and practical applications. In J. H. Harvey & A. Wenzel (Eds.), *A clinician's guide to maintaining and enhancing close relationships* (pp. 63–80). Mahwah, NJ: Erlbaum.

Simmons, R. E., & Scheepers, L. (1996). Winning by a neck: Sexual selection in the evolution of giraffe. *The American Naturalist, 148*, 771–786.

Simon, H. A. (1990). A mechanism for social selection and successful altruism. *Science, 250*, 1665–1668.

Simons, D., & Ambinder. M. (2005). Change Blindness: Theory and Consequences. *Current Directions in Psychological Science, 14*, 44–48.

Simons, D. J., & Chabris, C. F. (1999). Gorillas in our midst: Sustained inattentional blindness for dynamic events. *Perception, 28*, 1059–1074.

Simons, D. J., & Levin, D. T. (2005). Change blindness: Theory and consequences. *Current Directions in Psychological Science, 14*, 44–48.

Simonton, D. K. (1984). *Genius, creativity, and leadership: Historiometric inquiries*. Cambridge, MA: Harvard University Press.

Simonton, D. K. (1985). Intelligence and personal influence in groups: Four nonlinear models. *Psychological Review, 92*, 532–547.

Simonton, D. K. (1987). *Why presidents succeed: A political psychology of leadership*. New Haven, CT: Yale University Press.

Simonton, D. K. (1998). Historiometric methods in social psychology. *European Review of Social Psychology, 9*, 267–293.

Simonton, D. K. (2001). Predicting presidential performance in the United States: Equation replication on recent survey results. *Journal of Social Psychology, 141*, 293–307.

Simpson, J. A. (1987). The dissolution of romantic relationships: Factors involved in relationship stability and emotional distress. *Journal of Personality and Social Psychology, 53*, 683–692.

Simpson, J. A., & Gangestad, S. W. (1992). Sociosexuality and romantic partner choice. *Journal of Personality, 60*, 31–51.

Simpson, J. A., & Rholes, W. S. (1994). Stress and secure base relationships in adulthood. In K. Bartholomew & D. Perlman (Eds.), *Advances in personal relationships*: Vol. 5. *Attachment processes in adulthood* (pp. 181–204). Bristol, PA: Kingsley.

Simpson, J. A., Rholes, W. S., Campbell, L., & Wilson, C. L. (2003). Changes in attachment orientations across the transition to parenthood. *Journal of Experimental Social Psychology, 39*, 317–331.

Simpson, J. A., Rholes, W. S., & Nelligan, J. S. (1992). Support seeking and support giving within couples in an anxiety-provoking situation: The role of attachment styles. *Journal of Personality and Social Psychology, 62*, 434–446.

Sinclair, R. C., Hoffman, C., Mark, M. M., Martin, L. L., & Pickering, T. L. (1994). Construct accessibility and the misattribution of arousal: Schachter and Singer revisited. *Psychological Science, 5*, 15–19.

Sinclair, S., Huntsinger, J., Skorinko, J., & Hardin, C. D. (2005). Social tuning of the self: Consequences for the self-evaluations of stereotype targets. *Journal of Personality and Social Psychology, 89*(2), 160–175.

Sinclair, S., Lowery, B. S., Hardin, C. D., & Colangelo, A. (2005). Social tuning of automatic racial attitudes: The role of affiliative motivation. *Journal of Personality and Social Psychology, 89*(4), 583–592.

Singelis, T. M. (1994). The measurement of independent and interdependent self-construals. *Personality and Social Psychology Bulletin, 20,* 580–591.

Singer, J. E., Baum, C. S., Baum, A., & Thew, B. D. (1982). Mass psychogenic illness: The case for social comparison. In M. J. Colligan, J. W. Pennebaker, & L. R. Murphy (Eds.), *Mass psychogenic illness: A social psychological analysis* (pp. 155–169). Hillsdale, NJ: Erlbaum.

Singer, M. (1990, January 29). Talk of the town. *New Yorker,* pp. 25–26.

Singer, M. (2002, May 20). A year of trouble. *New Yorker,* pp. 42–46.

Sip, K., Roepstorff, A., McGregor, W., & Frith, C. (2008). Detecting deception: The scope and limits. *Trends in Cognitive Sciences, 12,* 48–53.

Sirois, F. (1982). Perspectives on epidemic hysteria. In M. J. Colligan, J. W. Pennebaker, & L. R. Murphy (Eds.), *Mass psychogenic illness: A social psychological analysis* (pp. 217–236). Hillsdale, NJ: Erlbaum.

Skinner, B. F. (1938). *The behavior of organisms: An experimental analysis.* New York: Appleton-Century-Crofts.

Skinner, E. A. (1996). A guide to constructs of control. *Journal of Personality and Social Psychology, 71,* 549–570.

Skitka, L. J. (2002). Do the means always justify the ends, or do the ends sometimes justify the means? A value protection model of justice reasoning. *Personality and Social Psychology Bulletin, 28,* 588–597.

Slavin, R. E. (1996). Cooperative learning in middle and secondary schools. (Special section: Young adolescents at risk.) *Clearing House, 69,* 200–205.

Slavin, R. E., & Cooper, R. (1999). Improving intergroup relations: Lessons learned from cooperative learning programs. *Journal of Social Issues, 55,* 647–663.

Sloan, D., Marx, B., Epstein, E., & Dobbs, J. (2008). Expressive writing buffers against maladaptive rumination. *Emotion, 8,* 302–306.

Sloan, J. H., Kellerman, A. L., Reay, D. T., Ferris, J. A., Koepsell, T., Rivara, F. P., et al. (1988). Handgun regulations, crime, assaults, and homicide: A tale of two cities. *New England Journal of Medicine, 319,* 1256–1261.

Slovic, P., Fischhoff, B., & Lichtenstein, S. (1976). Cognitive processes and societal risk taking. In J. S. Carroll & J. Payne (Eds.), *Cognition and social behavior* (pp. 165–184). Hillsdale, NJ: Erlbaum.

Slusher, M. P., & Anderson, C. A. (1989). Belief perseverance and self-defeating behavior. In R. Curtis (Ed.), *Self-defeating behaviors: Experimental research, clinical impressions, and practical implications* (pp. 11–40). New York: Plenum.

Smith, D. D. (1976). The social content of pornography. *Journal of Communication, 26,* 16–24.

Smyth, J., & Pennebaker, J. (2008). Exploring the boundary conditions of expressive writing: In search of the right recipe. *British Journal of Health Psychology, 13,* 1–7.

Smith, M. B., Bruner, J., & White, R. W. (1956). *Opinions and personality.* New York: Wiley.

Smith, P. B., & Bond, M. H. (1999). *Social psychology across cultures* (2nd ed.). Needham Heights, MA: Allyn & Bacon.

Smith, S. S., & Richardson, D. (1983). Amelioration of deception and harm in psychological research: The important role of debriefing. *Journal of Personality and Social Psychology, 44,* 1075–1082.

Smith, T. (2006). Personality as risk and resilience in physical health. *Current Directions in Psychological Science, 15,* 227–231.

Smith, V. L. (1991). Prototypes in the courtroom: Lay representation of legal concepts. *Journal of Personality and Social Psychology, 61,* 857–872.

Snyder, C., & Lopez, S. (2007). *Positive psychology: The scientific and practical explorations of human strengths.* Thousand Oaks, CA: Sage.

Snyder, C. R., & Higgins, R. L. (1988). Excuses: Their effective role in the negotiation of reality. *Psychological Bulletin, 104,* 23–35.

Snyder, C. R., Irving, L. M., & Anderson, J. R. (1991). Hope and health. In C. R. Snyder & D. R. Forsyth (Eds.), *Handbook of clinical and social psychology* (pp. 285–305). New York: Pergamon.

Snyder, M. (1984). When belief creates reality. In L. Berkowitz (Ed.), *Advances in experimental social psychology* (Vol. 18, pp. 247–305). Orlando, FL: Academic Press.

Snyder, M. (1993). Basic research and practical problems: The promise of a "functional" personality and social psychology. *Personality and Social Psychology Bulletin, 19,* 251–264.

Snyder, M., & De Bono, K. G. (1989). Understanding the functions of attitudes: Lessons for personality and social behavior. In A. R. Pratkanis, S. J. Breckler, & A. G. Greenwald (Eds.), *Attitude structure and function* (pp. 339–359). Hillsdale, NJ: Erlbaum.

Snyder, M., Omoto, A. M., & Lindsay, J. J. (2004). In A. G. Miller (Ed.), *The social psychology of good and evil* (pp. 444–468). New York: Guilford.

Snyder, M., Tanke, E. D., & Berscheid, E. (1977). Social perception and interpersonal behavior: On the self-fulfilling nature of social stereotypes. *Journal of Personality and Social Psychology, 35,* 656–666.

Sloan, D., Marx, B., Epstein, E., & Dobbs, J. (2008). Expressive writing buffers against maladaptive rumination. *Emotion, 8,* 302–306.

Solomon, L. Z., Solomon, H., & Stone, R. (1978). Helping as a function of number of bystanders and ambiguity of emergency. *Personality and Social Psychology Bulletin, 4,* 318–321.

Sommers, S., & Kassin, S. (2001). On the many impacts of inadmissible testimony: Selective compliance, need for cognition, and the overcorrection bias. *Personality and Social Psychology Bulletin, 27,* 1368–1377.

Son Hing, L. S., Li, W., & Zanna, M. P. (2002). Inducing hypocrisy to reduce prejudicial responses among aversive racists. *Journal of Experimental Social Psychology, 38,* 71–78.

Sontag, S. (1978). *Illness as metaphor.* New York: Farrar, Straus & Giroux.

Sontag, S. (1988). *AIDS and its metaphors.* New York: Farrar, Straus & Giroux.

Sorenson, T. C. (1966). *Kennedy.* New York: Bantam Books.

Sorkin, R. D., Hays, C. J., & West, R. (2001). Signal-detection analysis of group decision making. *Psychological Review, 108,* 183–203.

Spalding, L. R., & Hardin, C. D. (1999). Unconscious unease and self-handicapping: Behavioral consequences of individual differences in implicit and explicit self-esteem. *Psychological Science, 10,* 535–539.

Spanier, G. B. (1992). Divorce: A comment about the future. In T. L. Orbuch (Ed.), *Close relationship loss: Theoretical approaches* (pp. 207–212). New York: Springer-Verlag.

Spears, T. (2008). Newspaper readers 'rational' thinkers. *Vancouver Sun,* p. A16.

Spelke, E. S. (2005). Sex differences in intrinsic aptitude for mathematics and science? *American Psychologist, 60,* 950–958.

Spelke, E., & Grace, A. (2007). Sex, math, and science. In S. J. Ceci & W. M. Williams (Eds.), *Why aren't more women in science: Top researchers debate the evidence* (pp. 57–67). Washington, DC: American Psychological Association

Spencer, S. J., Fein, S., Zanna, M. P., & Olson, J. M. (Eds.). (2003). *Motivated social perception: The Ontario Symposium* (Vol. 9). Mahwah, NJ: Erlbaum.

Spencer, S. J., Steele, C. M., & Quinn, D. M. (1999). Stereotype threat and women's math performance. *Journal of Experimental Social Psychology, 35,* 4–28.

Spiegel, D., Bloom, J. R., Kraemer, H. C., & Gottheil, E. (1989). Psychological support for cancer patients. *Lancet, 2,* 1447.

Sporer, S. L., Koehnken, G., & Malpass, R. S. (1996). Introduction: 200 years of mistaken identification. In S. L. Sporer, R. S. Malpass, & G.

Koehnken (Eds.), *Psychological issues in eyewitness identification* (pp. 1–6). Mahwah, NJ: Erlbaum.

Sprecher, S., Aron, A., Hatfield, E., Cortese, A., Potapova, E., & Levitskaya, A. (1994). Love: American style, Russian style, and Japanese style. *Personal Relationships, 1,* 349–369.

Sprecher, S., & Schwartz, P. (1994). Equity and balance in the exchange of contributions in close relationships. In M. J. Lerner & G. Mikula (Eds.), *Entitlement and the affectional bond: Justice in close relationships* (pp. 11–42). New York: Plenum.

Sprecher, S., Sullivan, Q., & Hatfield, E. (1994). Mate selection preference: Gender differences examined in a national sample. *Journal of Personality and Social Psychology, 66,* 1074–1080.

Sprink, K. S., & Carron, A. V. (1994). Group cohesion effects in exercise classes. *Small Group Research, 25,* 26–42.

Staats, H., Harland, P., & Wilke, H. A. M. (2004). Effecting durable change: a team approach to improve environmental behavior in the household. *Environment and Behavior, 36,* 341–367.

Stapel, D., & Koomen, W. (2006). The flexible unconscious: Investigating the judgmental impact of varieties of unaware perception. *Journal of Experimental Social Psychology, 42*(1), 112–119.

Stapel, D. A., & Koomen, W. (2000). How far do we go beyond the information given? The impact of knowledge activation on interpretation and inference. *Journal of Personality and Social Psychology, 78,* 19–37.

Stasser, G. (2000). Information distribution, participation, and group decision: Explorations with the DISCUSS and SPEAK models. In D. R. Ilgen & C. L. Hulin (Eds.), *Computational modeling of behavior in organizations: The third scientific discipline* (pp. 135–161). Washington, DC: American Psychological Association.

Stasser, G., & Birchmeier, Z. (2003). Group creativity and collective choice. In P. B. Paulus & B. A. Nijstad (Eds.), *Group creativity: Innovation through collaboration* (pp. 85–109). New York: Oxford University Press.

Stasser, G., Stewart, D. D., & Wittenbaum, G. M. (1995). Expert roles and information exchange during discussion: The importance of knowing who knows what. *Journal of Experimental and Social Psychology, 31,* 244–265.

Stasser, G., & Titus, W. (1985). Pooling of unshared information in group decision making: Biased information sampling during discussion. *Journal of Personality and Social Psychology, 48,* 1467–1478.

Staub, E. (1974). Helping a distressed person: Social, personality, and stimulus determinants. In L. Berkowitz (Ed.), *Advances in experimental social psychology* (Vol. 7, pp. 293–341). New York: Academic Press.

Staub, E. (1989). *The roots of evil: The origins of genocide and other group violence.* Cambridge: Cambridge University Press.

Steblay, N. M. (1987). Helping behavior in rural and urban environments: A meta-analysis. *Psychological Bulletin, 102,* 346–356.

Steblay, N. M. (1997). Social influence in eyewitness recall: A meta-analytic review of lineup instruction effects. *Law and Human Behavior, 21,* 283–297.

Steblay, N. M., Besirevic, J., Fulero, S. M., & Jimenez-Lorente, B. (1999). The effects of pretrial publicity on juror verdicts: A meta-analytic review. *Law and Human Behavior, 23,* 219–235.

Steblay, N. M., Dysart, J., Fulero, S. M., & Lindsay, R. C. L. (2001). Eyewitness accuracy rates in sequential and simultaneous lineup presentations: A meta-analytic comparison. *Law and Human Behavior, 25,* 459–473.

Steel, P. (2007). The nature of procrastination: A meta-analytic and theoretical review of quintessential self-regulatory failure. *Psychological Bulletin, 133*(1), 65–94.

Steele, C. M. (1988). The psychology of self-affirmation: Sustaining the integrity of the self. In L. Berkowitz (Ed.), *Advances in experimental social psychology* (Vol. 21, pp. 261–302). New York: Academic Press.

Steele, C. M. (1992, April). Race and the schooling of black Americans. *Atlantic,* pp. 68–78.

Steele, C. M. (1997). A threat in the air: How stereotypes shape intellectual ability and performance. *American Psychologist, 52,* 613–629.

Steele, C. M., & Aronson, J. M. (1995a). Stereotype threat and the intellectual test performance of African-Americans. *Journal of Personality and Social Psychology, 69,* 797–811.

Steele, C. M., & Aronson, J. M. (1995b). Stereotype vulnerability and intellectual performance. In E. Aronson, (Ed.), *Readings about the social animal* (7th ed.). New York: Freeman.

Steele, C. M., Hoppe, H., & Gonzales, J. (1986). *Dissonance and the lab coat: Self-affirmation and the free-choice paradigm.* Unpublished manuscript, University of Washington.

Steele, C. M., Spencer, S. J., & Aronson, J. M. (2002). Contending with group image: The psychology of stereotype and social identity threat. In M. P. Zanna (Ed.), *Advances in experimental social psychology* (Vol. 34, pp. 379–440). San Diego, CA: Academic Press.

Steele, C. M., Spencer, S. J., & Josephs, R. A. (1992). *Seeking self-relevant information: The effects of self-esteem and stability of the information.* Unpublished manuscript, University of Michigan.

Steiner, I. D. (1972). *Group process and productivity.* New York: Academic Press.

Stephan, W. G. (1978). School desegregation: An evaluation of predictions made in *Brown v. Board of Education. Psychological Bulletin, 85,* 217–238.

Stephan, W. G. (1985). Intergroup relations. In G. Lindzey & E. Aronson (Eds.), *Handbook of social psychology* (3rd ed., Vol. 2, pp. 599–658). New York: McGraw-Hill.

Sternberg, R. J. (1986). A triangular theory of love. *Psychological Review, 93,* 119–135.

Sternberg, R. J. (1988). *The triangle of love.* New York: Basic Books.

Sternberg, R. J. (1997). Construct validation of a triangular love scale. *European Journal of Social Psychology, 27,* 313–335.

Sternberg, R. J., & Vroom, V. (2002). The person versus the situation in leadership. *Leadership Quarterly, 13,* 301–323.

Stewart, D. D., & Stasser, G. (1995). Expert role assignment and information sampling during collective recall and decision making. *Journal of Personality and Social Psychology, 69,* 619–628.

Stewart, J. B. (2002). *Heart of a soldier.* New York: Simon & Schuster.

Stipek, D., & Gralinski, J. H. (1991). Gender differences in children's achievement-related beliefs and emotional responses to success and failure in mathematics. *Journal of Educational Psychology, 83,* 361–371.

Stoff, D. M., & Cairns, R. B. (Eds.). (1997). *Aggression and violence: Genetic, neurobiological, and biosocial perspectives.* Mahwah, NJ: Erlbaum.

Stone, A. A., Bovbjerg, D. H., Neale, J. M., Napoli, A., Valdimarsdottir, H., Cox, D., et al. (1993). Development of common cold symptoms following experimental rhinovirus infection is related to prior stressful life events. *Behavioral Medicine, 8,* 115–120.

Stone, J., Aronson, E., Crain, A. L., Winslow, M. P., & Fried, C. (1994). Inducing hypocrisy as a means of encouraging young adults to use condoms. *Personality and Social Psychology Bulletin, 20,* 116–128.

Stone, J., Lynch, C. I., Sjomeling, M., & Darley, J. M. (1999). Stereotype threat effects on Black and White athletic performance. *Journal of Personality and Social Psychology, 77,* 1213–1227.

Stone, J., Perry, Z., & Darley, J. (1997). "White men can't jump": Evidence for perceptual confirmation of racial stereotypes following a basketball game. *Basic and Applied Social Psychology, 19,* 291–306.

Stormo, K. J., Lang, A. R., & Stritzke, W. G. K. (1997). Attributions about acquaintance rape: The role of alcohol and individual differences. *Journal of Applied Social Psychology, 27,* 279–305.

Storms, M. D. (1973). Videotape and the attribution process: Reversing actors' and observers' points of view. *Journal of Personality and Social Psychology, 27,* 165–175.

Stouffer, S. A., Suchman, E. A., De Vinney, L. C., Star, S. A., & Williams, R. M., Jr. (1949). *The American soldier: Adjustment during army life* (Vol. 1). Princeton, NJ: Princeton University Press.

Strack, F., & Mussweiler, T. (2003). Heuristic strategies for judgment under uncertainty: The enigmatic case of anchoring. In G. V. Bodenhausen (Ed.), *Foundations of social cogntion: A Festschrift in honor of Robert S. Wyer Jr.* (pp. 79–95). Mahwah, NJ: Erlbaum.

Strahan, E. J., Spencer, S. J., & Zanna, M. P. (2002). Subliminal priming and persuasion: Striking while the iron is hot. *Journal of Experimental Social Psychology, 38,* 556–568.

Strauss, M. A., & Gelles, R. J. (1980). *Behind closed doors: Violence in the American family.* Garden City, NY: Anchor/Doubleday.

Stringfellow, T. (1841). A brief examination of scripture testimony on the institution of slavery. *Religious Herald.* Available on Internet.

Stroebe, W., & Stroebe, M. (1996). The social psychology of social support. In E. T. Higgins & A. W. Kruglanski (Eds.), *Social psychology: Handbook of basic principles* (pp. 597–621). New York: Guilford Press.

Studer, J. (1996). Understanding and preventing aggressive responses in youth. *Elementary School Guidance and Counseling, 30,* 194–203.

Stuhlmacher, A. F., & Citera, M. (2005). Hostile behavior and profit in virtual negotiation: A meta-analysis. *Journal of Business and Psychology, 20,* 69–93.

Stukas, A. A., Snyder, M., & Clary, E. G. (1999). The effects of "mandatory volunteerism" on intentions to volunteer. *Psychological Science, 10,* 59–64.

Stumpf, H., & Stanley, J. C. (1998). Stability and change in gender-related differences on the college board advanced placement and achievement tests. *Current Directions in Psychological Science, 7,* 192–196.

Stürmer, S., Synder, M., & Omoto, A. M. (2005). Prosocial emotions and helping: The moderating role of group membership. *Journal of Personality and Social Psychology, 88,* 532–546.

Sullivan, B., O'Connor, K., & Burris, E. (2006). Negotiator confidence: The impact of self-efficacy on tactics and outcomes. *Journal of Experimental Social Psychology, 42,* 567-581

Suls, J. M., & Fletcher, B. (1983). Social comparison in the social and physical sciences: An archival study. *Journal of Personality and Social Psychology, 44,* 575–580.

Suls, J. M., & Miller, R. L. (Eds.). (1977). *Social comparison processes: Theoretical and empirical perspectives.* Washington, DC: Hemisphere/Halstead.

Suls, J. M., & Wheeler, L. (Eds.). (2000). *Handbook of social comparison: Theory and research.* New York: Kluwer/Plenum.

Summers, G., & Feldman, N. S. (1984). Blaming the victim versus blaming the perpetrator: An attributional analysis of spouse abuse. *Journal of Social and Clinical Psychology, 2,* 339–347.

Swann, W. B., Jr. (1990). To be adored or to be known? The interplay of self-enhancement and self-verification. In E. T. Higgins & R. M. Sorrentino (Eds.), *Handbook of motivation and cognition* (Vol. 2, pp. 404–448). New York: Guilford Press.

Swann, W. B., Jr. (1996). *Self-traps: The elusive quest for higher self-esteem.* New York: Freeman.

Swann, W. B., Jr., & Pelham, B. W. (1988). *The social construction of identity: Self-verification through friend and intimate selection.* Unpublished manuscript, University of Texas, Austin.

Sweeney, P. D., Anderson, K., & Bailey, S. (1986). Attributional style in depression: A meta-analytic review. *Journal of Personality and Social Psychology, 50,* 974–991.

Sweeny, K., Carroll, P., & Shepperd, J. (2006). Is optimism always best?: Future outlooks and preparedness. *Current Directions in Psychological Science, 15,* 302–306.

Swim, J. K. (1994). Perceived versus meta-analytic effect sizes: An assessment of the accuracy of gender stereotypes. *Journal of Personality and Social Psychology, 66,* 21–36.

Swim, J. K., Borgida, E., Maruyama, G., & Myers, D. G. (1989). Joan McKay vs. John McKay: Do gender stereotypes bias evaluations? *Psychological Bulletin, 105,* 409–429.

Swim, J. K., & Sanna, L. (1996). He's skilled, she's lucky: A meta-analysis of observers' attributions for women's and men's successes and failures. *Personality and Social Psychology Bulletin, 22,* 507–519.

Symons, D. (1979). *The evolution of human sexuality.* New York: Oxford University Press.

Tajfel, H. (1982a). *Social identity and intergroup relations.* Cambridge: Cambridge University Press.

Tajfel, H. (1982b). Social psychology of intergroup relations. *Annual Review of Psychology, 33,* 1–39.

Tajfel, H., & Billig, M. (1974). Familiarity and categorization in intergroup behavior. *Journal of Experimental Social Psychology, 10,* 159–170.

Tajfel, H., & Turner, J. C. (1979). An integrative theory of social contact. In W. Austin & S. Worchel (Eds.), *The social psychology of intergroup relations* (pp. 162–173). Monterey, CA: Brooks/Cole.

Takaku, S. (2006). Reducing road rage: An application of the dissonance-attribution model of interpersonal forgiveness. *Journal of Applied Social Psychology, 36,* 2362–2378.

Tamres, L. K., Janicki, D., & Helgeson, V. S. (2002). Sex differences in coping behavior: A meta-analytic review. *Personality and Social Psychology Review, 6,* 2–30.

Tanford, S., & Penrod, S. D. (1984). Social influence model: A formal integration of research on majority and minority influence processes. *Psychological Bulletin, 95,* 189–225.

Tang, S., & Hall, V. C. (1995). The overjustification effect: A meta-analysis. *Applied Cognitive Psychology, 9,* 365–404.

Tavris, C. & Aronson, E. (2007). *Mistakes were made (but not by me)* New York: Harcourt.

Tavris, C. & Aronson, E. (2008) *Mistakes Were Made (but not by me).* New York: Harcourt.

Taylor, S. (2006). Tend and befriend: Biobehavioral bases of affiliation under stress. *Current Directions in Psychological Science, 15,* 273–277.

Taylor, S. E. (1981). A categorization approach to stereotyping. In D. L. Hamilton (Ed.), *Cognitive processes in stereotyping and intergroup relations* (pp. 418–429). Hillsdale, NJ: Erlbaum.

Taylor, S. E. (1989). *Positive illusions: Creative self-deception and the healthy mind.* New York: Basic Books.

Taylor, S. E. (2007). Social support. In H. S. Friedman & R. C. Silver (Eds.), *Foundations of health psychology* (pp. 145–171). New York: Oxford University Press.

Taylor, S. E., & Armor, D. (1996). Positive illusions and coping with adversity. *Journal of Personality, 64,* 873–898.

Taylor, S. E., & Aspinwall, L. G. (1993). Coping with chronic illness. In L. Goldberger & S. Breznitz (Eds.), *Handbook of stress: Theoretical and clinical aspects* (2nd ed., pp. 511–531). New York: Free Press.

Taylor, S. E., & Brown, J. D. (1988). Illusion and well-being: A social psychological perspective on mental health. *Psychological Bulletin, 103,* 193–210.

Taylor, S. E., & Brown, J. D. (1994). Positive illusions and well-being revisited: Separating fact from fiction. *Psychological Bulletin, 116,* 21–27.

Taylor, S. E., & Fiske, S. T. (1975). Point of view and perceptions of causality. *Journal of Personality and Social Psychology, 32,* 439–445.

Taylor, S. E., & Gollwitzer, P. (1995). Effects of mindset on positive illusions. *Journal of Personality and Social Psychology, 69,* 213–226.

Taylor, S. E., Klein, L. C., Lewis, B. P., Gruenewald, T. L., Gurung, R. A. R., & Updegraff, J. A. (2000). Biobehavioral responses to stress in females: Tend-and-befriend, not fight-or-flight. *Psychological Review, 107,* 411–429.

Taylor, S. E., Lichtman, R. R., & Wood, J. V. (1984). Attributions, beliefs about control, and adjustment to breast cancer. *Journal of Personality and Social Psychology, 46,* 489–502.

Taylor, S. E., Repetti, R. L., & Seeman, T. (1997). Health psychology: What is an unhealthy environment and how does it get under the skin? *Annual Review of Psychology, 48,* 411–447.

Taylor, S. E., Sherman, D. K., Kim, H. S., Jarcho, J., Takagi, K., & Dunagan, M. S. (2004). Culture and social support: Who seeks it and why? *Journal of Personality and Social Psychology, 87,* 354–362.

Taylor, S. E., Welch, W., Kim, H. S., Sherman, D. K. (2007). Cultural differences in the impact of social support on psychological and biological stress responses. *Psychological Science, 18,* 831–837.

Taylor, S. P., & Leonard, K. E. (1983). Alcohol and human physical aggression. In R. G. Geen & E. Donnerstein (Eds.), *Aggression: Theoretical and empirical reviews* (pp. 77–101). New York: Academic Press.

Teger, A. L., & Pruitt, D. G. (1967). Components of group risk taking. *Journal of Experimental Social Psychology, 3,* 189–205.

Tenenbaum, H., & Leaper, C. (2003). Parent-child conversations about science: The socialization of gender inequities? *Developmental Psychology, 39,* 34–47.

Tesser, A. (1988). Toward a self-evaluation maintenance model of social behavior. In L. Berkowitz (Ed.), *Advances in experimental social psychology* (Vol. 21, pp. 181–227). Orlando, FL: Academic Press.

Tesser, A. (1991). Emotion in social comparison and reflection processes. In J. M. Suls & T. A. Wills (Eds.), *Social comparison: Contemporary theory and research* (pp. 117–148). Hillsdale, NJ: Erlbaum.

Tesser, A. (1993). The importance of heritability in psychological research: The case of attitudes. *Psychological Review, 100,* 129–142.

Tesser, A. (2003). Self-evaluation. In M. R. Leary & J. P. Tangney (Eds.), *Handbook of self and identity* (pp. 275–290). New York: Guilford Press.

Tesser, A., Campbell, J. D., & Mickler, S. (1983). The role of social pressure, attention to the stimulus, and self-doubt in conformity. *European Journal of Social Psychology, 13,* 217–233.

Tesser, A., & Paulus, D. (1983). The definition of self: Private and public self-evaluation management strategies. *Journal of Personality and Social Psychology, 44,* 672–682.

Tesser, A., & Smith, J. (1980). Some effects of friendship and task relevance on helping: You don't always help the one you like. *Journal of Experimental Social Psychology, 16,* 582–590.

Tetlock, P. E. (1981). The influence of self-presentational goals on attributional reports. *Social Psychology Quarterly, 44,* 300–311.

Tetlock, P. E. (2002). Theory-driven reasoning about plausible pasts and probable futures in world politics. In T. Gilovich, D. W. Griffin, & D. Kahneman (Eds.), *Heuristics and biases: The psychology of intuitive judgment* (pp. 749–762). New York: Cambridge University Press.

Tetlock, P. E., Peterson, R. S., McGuire, C., Chang, S., & Field, P. (1992). Assessing political group dynamics: A test of the groupthink model. *Journal of Personality and Social Psychology, 63,* 403–425.

Teves, O. (2002, May 28). WHO warns Asia 25% of youth will die from smoking without curbed advertising. Associated Press.

The American freshman: National norms for 2005. (2006). Higher Education Research Institute, UCLA. Retrieved on June 22, 2006. from: *www.gseis.ucla.edu/heri/PDFs/ResearchBrief05.PDF*

The College Board. (2007). 2007 College-bound seniors total group profile report. Retrieved March 24, 2008, from www.collegeboard.com/ prod_downloads/about/news_info/cbsenior/yr2007/national-report.pdf

The NIMH Multisite HIV Prevention Trial Group (1998, June 19). The NIMH Multisite HIV Prevention Trial: Reducing sexual HIV risk behavior. *Science, 280,* 1889–1894.

The NIMH Multisite HIV Prevention Trial Group (2001). Social-cognitive theory mediators of behavior change in the National Institute of Mental Health Multisite HIV Prevention Trial. *Health Psychology, 20,* 369–376.

The number of people who say they have no one to confide in has risen. *Washington Post,* p. A3.

The Ontario Symposium (Vol. 5, pp. 3–39). Hillsdale, NJ: Erlbaum.

Thernstrom, M. (2003, August 24). Untying the knot. *New York Times Magazine,* p. 38.

Theus, K. T. (1994). Subliminal advertising and the psychology of processing unconscious stimuli: A review. *Psychology and Marketing, 11,* 271–290.

Thibaut, J. W., & Kelley, H. H. (1959). *The social psychology of groups.* New York: Wiley.

Thomas, J. (1997, January 30). Suspect's sketch in Oklahoma case called an error. *New York Times,* pp. 1–2.

Thomas, M. H. (1982). Physiological arousal, exposure to a relatively lengthy aggressive film, and aggressive behavior. *Journal of Research in Personality, 16,* 72–81.

Thomas, M. H., Horton, R., Lippincott, E., & Drabman, R. (1977). Desensitization to portrayals of real-life aggression as a function of exposure to television violence. *Journal of Personality and Social Psychology, 35,* 450–458.

Thomas, S. L., Skitka, L. J., Christen, S., & Jurgena, M. (2002). Social facilitation and impression formation. *Basic and Applied Social Psychology, 242,* 67–70.

Thomas, W. I. (1928). *The child in America.* New York: Knopf.

Thompson, J. (2000, June 18). "I was certain, but I was wrong." *New York Times,* p. D15.

Thompson, L. (1995). They saw a negotiation: Partisanship and involvement. *Journal of Personality and Social Psychology, 68,* 839–853.

Thompson, L. (1997). *The mind and heart of the negotiator.* Upper Saddle River, NJ: Prentice Hall.

Thompson, L. L. (2005). *The heart and mind of the negotiator* (3rd ed.). Upper Saddle River, NJ: Prentice-Hall.

Thompson, S. A., Gold, J. A., & Ryckman, R. M. (2003). The simulated video interaction technique: A new method for inducing infatuation in the laboratory. *Representative Research in Social Psychology, 27,* 32–37.

Thompson, S. C. (1999). Illusions of control: How we overestimate our personal influence. *Current Directions in Psychological Science, 8,* 187–190.

Thompson, S. C. (2002). The role of personal control in adaptive functioning. In C. R. Snyder & S. J. Lopez (Eds.), *Handbook of positive psychology* (pp. 202–213). London: Oxford University Press.

Thompson, W. M., Dabbs, J. M., Jr., & Frady, R. L. (1990). Changes in saliva testosterone levels during a 90-day shock incarceration program. *Criminal Justice and Behavior, 17,* 246–252.

Thornton, D., & Arrowood, A. J. (1966). Self-evaluation, self-enhancement, and the locus of social comparison. *Journal of Experimental Social Psychology, 1*(Suppl.), 40–48.

Timaeus, E. (1968). Untersuchungen zum sogenannten konformen Verhalten [Research into so-called conforming behavior]. *Zeitschrift für Experimentelle und Angewandte Psychologie, 15,* 176–194.

Tindale, R. S. (1993). Decision errors made by individuals and groups. In N. J. Castellan Jr. (Ed.), *Individual and group decision making* (pp. 109–124). Hillsdale, NJ: Erlbaum.

Tindale, R. S., Munier, C., Wasserman, M., & Smith, C. M. (2002). Group processes and the Holocaust. In L. S. Newman & R. Erber (Eds.), *Understanding genocide: The social psychology of the Holocaust* (pp. 143–161). New York: Oxford University Press.

Ting, J., & Piliavin, J. A. (2000). Altruism in comparative international perspective. In J. Phillips, B. Chapman, & D. Stevens (Eds.), *Between state and market: Essays on charities law and policy in Canada* (pp. 51–105). Montreal and Kingston, Ontario, Canada: McGill-Queens University Press.

Ting-Toomey, S., & Chung, L. (1996). Cross-cultural interpersonal communication: Theoretical trends and research directions. In W. B. Gudykunst, S. Ting-Toomey, & T. Nishida (Eds.), *Communication in personal relationships across cultures* (pp. 237–261). Thousand Oaks, CA: Sage.

Tippetts, A. S., Voas, R. B., & Fell, J. C. (2005). A meta-analysis of .08 BAC laws in 19 jurisdictions in the United States. *Accident Analysis & Prevention, 37*, 149–161.

Toch, H. (1980). *Violent men* (Rev. ed.). Cambridge, MA: Schenkman.

Toi, M., & Batson, C. D. (1982). More evidence that empathy is a source of altruistic motivation. *Journal of Personality and Social Psychology, 43*, 281–292.

Toobin, J. (1995, October 23). A horrible human event. *New Yorker*, pp. 40–49.

Tooby, J., & Cosmides, L. (2005). Conceptual foundations of evolutionary psychology. In D. M. Buss (Ed.), *The handbook of evolutionary psychology* (pp. 5–67). Hoboken, NJ: Wiley.

Tourangeau, R., Smith, T., & Rasinski, K. (1997). Motivation to report sensitive behaviors on surveys: Evidence from a bogus pipeline experiment. *Journal of Applied Social Psychology, 27*, 209–222.

Trafimow, D., & Finlay, K. A. (1996). The importance of subjective norms for a minority of people: Between-subjects and within-subjects analyses. *Personality and Social Psychology Bulletin, 22*, 820–828.

Trappey, C. (1996). A meta-analysis of consumer choice and subliminal advertising. *Psychology and Marketing, 13*, 517–530.

Trends in cigarette smoking among high school students: United States, 1991–2002. (2002). *Centers for Disease Control, Morbidity and Mortality Weekly Report, 51*, 409–412.

Triandis, H. C. (1989). The self and social behavior in differing cultural contexts. *Psychological Review, 96*, 506–520.

Triandis, H. C. (1990). Cross-cultural studies of individualism and collectivism. In J. J. Berman (Ed.), *Nebraska Symposium on Motivation, 1989* (pp. 41–133). Lincoln: University of Nebraska Press.

Triandis, H. C. (1994). *Culture and social behavior*. New York: McGraw-Hill.

Triandis, H. C. (1995). *Individualism and collectivism*. Boulder, CO: Westview Press.

Triandis, H. C. (2001). Individualism-collectivism and personality. *Journal of Personality, 69*, 907–924.

Triplett, N. (1898). The dynamogenic factors in pace making and competition. *American Journal of Psychology, 9*, 507–533.

Trivers, R. L. (1971). The evolution of reciprocal altruism. *Quarterly Review of Biology, 46*, 35–57.

Trivers, R. L. (1985). *Social evolution*. Menlo Park, CA: Benjamin-Cummings.

Trope, Y., & Gaunt, R. (2000). Processing alternative explanations of behavior: Correction of integration? *Journal of Personality and Social Psychology, 79*(3), 344–354.

Tseëlon, E. (1995). *The presentation of woman in everyday life*. Thousand Oaks, CA: Sage.

Tucker, P., Pfefferbaum, B., Doughty, D. B., Jones, D. E., Jordan, F. B., & Nixon, S. J. (2002). Body handlers after terrorism in Oklahoma City: Predictors of posttraumatic stress and other symptoms. *American Journal of Orthopsychiatry, 72*, 469–C475.

Turner, C., & Leyens, J. (1992). The weapons effect revisited: The effects of firearms on aggressive behavior. In P. Suedfeld & P. E. Tetlock (Eds.), *Psychology and social policy* (pp. 201–221). New York: Hemisphere.

Turner, C., Simons, L., Berkowitz, L., & Frodi, A. (1977). The stimulating and inhibiting effects of weapons on aggressive behavior. *Aggressive Behavior, 3*, 355–378.

Turner, F. J. (1932). *The significance of sections in American history*. New York: Henry Holt.

Turner, M. E., & Horvitz, T. (2001). The dilemma of threat: Group effectiveness and ineffectiveness under adversity. In M. E. Turner (Ed.), *Groups at work: Theory and research* (pp. 445–470). Mahwah, NJ: Erlbaum.

Turner, M., Pratkanis, A., Probasco, P., & Leve, C. (2006). Threat, cohesion, and group effectiveness: Testing a social identity maintenance perspective on groupthink. *Small Groups* (pp. 241–264). New York: Psychology Press.

Turner, M., Pratkanis, A., & Struckman, C. (2007). Groupthink as social identity maintenance. *The science of social influence: Advances and future progress* (pp. 223–246). New York: Psychology Press.

Tversky, A., & Kahneman, D. (1973). Availability: A heuristic for judging frequency and probability. *Cognitive Psychology, 5*, 207–232.

Tversky, A., & Kahneman, D. (1974). Judgment under uncertainty: Heuristics and biases. *Science, 185*, 1124–1131.

Twenge, J. M. (1997). Attitudes toward women, 1970–1995: A meta-analysis. *Psychology of Women Quarterly, 21*, 35–51.

Twenge, J. M. (2001). Changes in women's assertiveness in response to status and roles: A cross-temporal meta-analysis, 1931–1993. *Journal of Personality and Social Psychology, 81*, 133–145.

Twenge, J. M. (2008). Social exclusion, motivation, and self-defeating behavior: Why breakups lead to drunkenness and ice cream.. In J. Y. Shah & W. L. Gardner (Eds.), *Handbook of motivation science* (pp. 508–517). New York: Guilford.

Twenge, J. M., Baumeister, R., F. DeWall, C. N., Ciarocco, N. J., & Bartels, J. M. (2007). Social exclusion decreases prosocial behavior. *Journal of Personality and Social Psychology, 92*, 56–66.

Twenge, J. M., Zhang, L., & Im, C. (2004). It's beyond my control: A cross-temporal meta-analysis of increasing externality in locus of control, 1960–2002. *Personality and Social Psychology Review, 8*, 308–319.

Tyler, T. R. (1990). *Why people obey the law*. New Haven, CT: Yale University Press.

Tyre, P. (2006, Jan. 30). The trouble with boys. *Newsweek*, p. 44.

U.S. Department of Justice. (2000). *Violence by intimates*. Washington, DC: Bureau of Justice Statistics.

Uchino, B. N., Cacioppo, J. T., & Keicolt-Glaser, J. K. (1996). The relationship between social support and physiological processes: A review with emphasis on underlying mechanisms and implications for health. *Psychological Bulletin, 119*, 488–531.

Updegraff, J., Silver, R., & Holman, E. (2008). Searching for and finding meaning in collective trauma: Results from a national longitudinal study of the 9/11 terrorist attacks. *Journal of Personality and Social Psychology, 95*, 709–722.

Uzzell, D. (2000). Ethnographic and action research. In G. M. Breakwell, S. Hammond, & C. Fife-Schaw (Eds.), *Research methods in psychology* (2nd ed., pp. 326–337). Thousand Oaks, CA: Sage.

Vaananen, A., Buunk, B. P., Kivimaki, M., Pentti, J., & Vahteva, J. (2005). When is it better to give than to receive: Long-term health effects of perceived reciprocity in support exchange. *Journal of Personality and Social Psychology, 89*, 176–193.

Vala Jorge, P., Cicero, C.-L., Rui C. (2009) Is the attribution of cultural differences to minorities an expression of racial prejudice? *International Journal of Psychology, 44* (1), 20–28.

Valle, P. O. D., Rebelo, E., & Reis, E. (2005). Combining behavioral theories to predict recycling involvement. *environment and behavior, 37*, 364–396.

Vallone, R. P., Griffin, D. W., Lin, S., & Ross, L. (1990). The overconfident prediction of future actions and outcomes by self and others. *Journal of Personality and Social Psychology, 58*, 582–592.

van de Vijver, F., & Leung, K. (1997). *Methods and data analyses for cross-cultural research*. Thousand Oaks, CA: Sage.

Van Goozen, S. H. M., Cohen-Kettenis, P. T., Gooren, L. J. G., & Frijda, N. H. (1995). Gender differences in behavior: Activating effects of cross-sex hormones. *Psychoneuroendocrinology, 20*, 343–363.

Van Laar, C., Sidanius, J., & Levin, S. (2008). Ethnic related curricula and intergroup attitudes in college: Movement towards and away from the ingroup. *Journal of Applied Social Psychology, 38* (6), 1601–1638

Van Lange, P. A. M., Ouwerkerk, J. W., & Tazelaar, M. J. A. (2002). How to overcome the detrimental effects of noise in social interaction: The benefits of generosity. *Journal of Personality and Social Psychology, 82*, 768–780.

Van Lange, P. A. M., Rusbult, C. E., Drigotas, S. M., Arriaga, X. B., Witcher, B. S., & Cox, C. L. (1997). Willingness to sacrifice in close relationships. *Journal of Personality and Social Psychology, 72*, 1373–1395.

Van Overwalle, F., & De Metsenaere, M. (1990). The effects of attribution-based intervention and study strategy training on academic achievement in college freshmen. *British Journal of Educational Psychology, 60*, 299–311.

Van Vugt, M., & De Cremer, D. C. (1999). Leadership in social dilemmas: The effects of group identification on collective actions to provide public goods. *Journal of Personality and Social Psychology, 76*, 587–599.

Van Vugt, M., & Samuelson, C. (1999). The impact of personal metering in the management of a natural resource crisis: A social dilemma analysis. *Personality and Social Psychology Bulletin, 25*, 731–745.

Van Vugt, M. (2006). Evolutionary Origins of Leadership and Followership. *Personality and Social Psychology Review, 10*(4), 354–371.

Van Yperen, N. W., & Buunk, B. P. (1990). A longitudinal study of equity in intimate relationships. *European Journal of Social Psychology, 20*, 287–309.

Vedantam, S. (2006, June 23). Social isolation growing in U.S.

Vidyasagar, P., & Mishra, H. (1993). Effect of modelling on aggression. *Indian Journal of Clinical Psychology, 20*, 50–52.

Visscher, T. L. S., & Seidell, J. C. (2001). The public health impact of obesity. *Annual Review of Public Health, 22*, 355–375.

Visser, P. S., Krosnick, J. A., & Lavrakas, P. J. (2000). Survey research. In H. T. Reis & C. M. Judd (Eds.), *Handbook of research methods in social and personality psychology* (pp. 223–252). New York: Cambridge University Press.

Vissing, Y., Straus, M., Gelles, R., & Harrop, J. (1991). Verbal aggression by parents and psychosocial problems of children. *Child Abuse and Neglect, 15*, 223–238.

Viswesvaran, C., & Deshpande, S. P. (1996). Ethics, success, and job satisfaction: A test of dissonance theory in India. *Journal of Business Ethics, 10*, 487–501.

Voas, R. B., Holder, H. D., & Gruenewald, P. J. (1999). The effect of drinking and driving interventions on alcohol-related traffic crashes within a comprehensive community trial. *Addiction, 92*, S221–S236.

Vohs, K. D., & Baumeister, R. F. (2004). Sexual passion, intimacy and gender. In D. J. Mashek & A. Aron (Eds.), *Handbook of closeness and intimacy* (pp. 189–200). Mahwah, NJ: Erlbaum.

Vonk, R. (1995). Effects of inconsistent behaviors on person perception: A multidimensional study. *Personality and Social Psychology Bulletin, 21*, 674–685.

Vonk, R. (1999). Effects of outcome dependency on correspondence bias. *Personality and Social Psychology Bulletin, 25*, 382–389.

Vonk, R. (2002). Self-serving interpretations of flattery: Why ingratiation works. *Journal of Personality and Social Psychology, 82*, 515–526.

Vonnegut, K., Jr. (1963). *Cat's cradle*. New York: Delacorte Press.

Vrijheid, M., Dolk, H., Armstrong, B., Abramsky, L., Bianchi, F., Fazarinc, I., et al. (2002). Chromosomal congenital anomalies and residence near hazardous waste landfill sites. *Lancet, 359*, 320–322.

Wagenaar, A., & Maldonado-Molina, M. (2007). Effects of drivers' license suspension policies on alcohol-related crash involvement: Long-term follow-up in forty-six states. *Alcoholism: Clinical and Experimental Research, 31*, 1399–1406.

Wagenaar, A., Maldonado-Molina, M., Erickson, D., Ma, L., Tobler, A., & Komro, K. (2007). General deterrence effects of U.S. statutory DUI fine and jail penalties: Long-term follow-up in 32 states. *Accident Analysis & Prevention, 39*, 982–994

Wagner, M., & Armstrong, N. (2003). *Field guide to gestures*. Philadelphia: Quirk Books.

Wagstaff, G. (1982). Attitudes to rape: The "just world" strikes again? *Bulletin of the British Psychological Society, 35*, 277–279.

Wakefield, M., Flay, B., & Nichter, M. (2003). Role of the media in influencing trajectories of youth smoking. *Addiction, 98* (Suppl1), Special issue: Contexts and adolescent tobacco use trajectories, 79–103.

Walker, I., & Crogan, M. (1998). Academic performance, prejudice, and the jigsaw classroom: New pieces to the puzzle. *Journal of Community and Applied Social Psychology, 8*, 381–393.

Wallach, M. A., Kogan, N., & Bem, D. J. (1962). Group influences on individual risk taking. *Journal of Abnormal and Social Psychology, 65*, 75–86.

Walster, E. (1966). Assignment of responsibility for an accident. *Journal of Personality and Social Psychology, 3*, 73–79.

Walster, E., Aronson, V., Abrahams, D., & Rottman, L. (1966). Importance of physical attractiveness in dating behavior. *Journal of Personality and Social Psychology, 5*, 508–516.

Walster, E., & Festinger, L. (1962). The effectiveness of "overheard" persuasive communication. *Journal of Abnormal and Social Psychology, 65*, 395–402.

Walster, E., Walster, G. W., & Berscheid, E. (1978). *Equity: Theory and research*. Needham Heights, MA: Allyn & Bacon.

Walther, E. (2002). Guilty by mere association: Evaluative conditioning and the spreading attitude effect. *Journal of Personality and Social Psychology, 82*, 919–934.

Walther, E., Bless, H., Strack, F., Rackstraw, P., Wagner, D., & Werth, L. (2002). Conformity effects in memory as a function of group size, dissenters and uncertainty. *Applied Cognitive Psychology, 16*, 793–810.

Walton, G. M., & Cohen, G. L. (2003). Stereotype lift. *Journal of Experimental Social Psychology, 39*(5), 456–467.

Wang, O., & Ross, M. (2007). Culture and memory. In S. Kitayama & D. Cohen (Eds.), *Handbook of cultural psychology* (pp. 645–667). New York: Guilford.

Wann, D. L., & Schrader, M. P. (2000). Controllability and stability in the self-serving attributions of sport specators. *Journal of Social Psychology, 140*, 160–168.

Ware, L., Lassiter, G., Patterson, S., & Ransom, M. (2008). Camera perspective bias in videotaped confessions: Evidence that visual attention is a mediator. *Journal of Experimental Psychology: Applied, 14*, 192–200.

Ward, A., Lyubomirsky, S., Sousa, L., & Nolen-Hoeksema, S. (2003). Can't quite commit: Rumination and uncertainty. *Personality and Social Psychology Bulletin, 29*, 96–107.

Waston, J. B. (1925). *Behaviorism*. New York: Norton.

Watson, D. (1982). The actor and the observer: How are their perceptions of causality divergent? *Psychological Bulletin, 92*, 682–700.

Watson, D., & Pennebaker, J. W. (1989). Health complaints, stress, and distress: Exploring the central role of negative affectivity. *Psychological Review, 96*, 234–254.

Watson, J. (1950). Some social and psychological situations related to change in attitude. *Human Relations, 3*, 15–56.

Watson, R. I. (1973). Investigation into deindividuation using a cross-cultural survey technique. *Journal of Personality and Social Psychology, 25*, 342–345.

Watson, W. E., Johnson, L., Kumar, K., & Critelli, J. (1998). Process gain and process loss: Comparing interpersonal processes and performance of culturally diverse and non-diverse teams across time. *International Journal of Intercultural Relations, 22*, 409–430.

Wattenberg, M. P. (1987). The hollow realignment: Partisan change in a candidate-centered era. *Public Opinion Quarterly, 51,* 58–74.

Watts, D. P., Muller, M., Amsler, S. J., Mbabazi, G., and Mitani, J. C. (2006, February). Lethal intergroup aggression by chimpanzees in Kibale National Park, Uganda. *American Journal of Primatology, 68,* (2), 161–180.

Wax, E. (2008). In India, new opportunities for women draw anger and abuse from men. *Washington Post,* p. A11.

Weart, S. R. (2003). *The discovery of global warming.* Cambridge, MA: Harvard University Press.

Weary, G., & Arkin, R. C. (1981). Attributional self-presentation. In J. H. Harvey, W. J. Ickes, & R. F. Kidd (Eds.), *New directions in attribution research* (Vol. 3, pp. 223–246). Hillsdale, NJ: Erlbaum.

Webber, R., & Crocker, J. (1983). Cognitive processes in the revision of stereotypic beliefs. *Journal of Personality and Social Psychology, 45,* 961–977.

Weber, E. U., Bockenholt, U., Hilton, D. J., & Wallace, B. (1993). Determinants of diagnostic hypothesis generation: Effects of information, base rates, and experience. *Journal of Experimental Psychology: Learning, Memory, and Cognition, 19,* 1151–1164.

Weber, J. M., Kopelman, S., & Messick, D. M. (2004). A conceptual review of decision making in social dilemmas: Applying a logic of appropriateness. *Personality and Social Psychology Review, 8,* 281–307.

Weber, J. M., & Murnighan, J. K. (2008). Suckers or saviors? Consistent contributors in social dilemmas. *Journal of Personality and Social Psychology, 95,* 1340–1353.

Weber, N., Brewer, N., Wells, G., Semmler, C., & Keast, A. (2004). Eyewitness Identification Accuracy and Response Latency: The Unruly 10-12-Second Rule. *Journal of Experimental Psychology: Applied, 10,* 139–147.

Webster, D. M. (1993). Motivated augmentation and reduction of the overattributional bias. *Journal of Personality and Social Psychology, 65,* 261–271.

Wechsler, H., & Austin, S. B. (1998). Binge drinking: The five/four measure. *Journal of Studies of Alcohol, 59,* 122–124.

Wechsler, H., Lee, J. E., Kuo, M., Siebring, M., Nelson, T. F., & Lee, H. (2002). Trends in college binge drinking during a period of increased prevention efforts: Findings from 4 Harvard School of Public Health college alcohol study surveys, 1993–2001. *Journal of American College Health, 50,* 203–217.

Weeden, J., & Sabini, J. (2005). Physical attractiveness and health in Western societies: A review. *Psychological Bulletin, 131,* 635–653.

Wegener, D. T., & Petty, R. E. (1994). Mood management across affective states: The hedonic contingency hypothesis. *Journal of Personality and Social Psychology, 66,* 1034–1048.

Wegener, D. T., & Petty, R. E. (1995). Flexible correction processes in social judgment: The role of naive theories in corrections for perceived bias. *Journal of Personality and Social Psychology, 68,* 36–51.

Wegner, D. M. (1986). Transactive memory: A contemporary analysis of the group mind. In B. Mullen & G. R. Goethals (Eds.), *Theories of group behavior* (pp. 185–208). New York: Springer-Verlag.

Wegner, D. M. (1989). *White bears and other unwanted thoughts: Suppression, obsession, and the psychology of mental control.* New York: Viking.

Wegner, D. M. (1992). You can't always think what you want: Problems in the suppression of unwanted thoughts. In M. P. Zanna (Ed.), *Advances in experimental social psychology* (Vol. 25, pp. 193–225). San Diego, CA: Academic Press.

Wegner, D. M. (1994). Ironic processes of mental control. *Psychological Review, 101,* 34–52.

Wegner, D. M. (1995). A computer network model of human transactive memory. *Social Cognition, 13,* 319–339.

Wegner, D. M. (2002). *The illusion of conscious will.* Cambridge, MA: MIT Press.

Wegner, D. M. (2004). Precis of *The illusion of conscious will. Behavioral & Brain Sciences, 27,* 649–659.

Wegner, D. M., Ansfield, M., & Pilloff, D. (1998). The putt and the pendulum: Ironic effects of the mental control of action. *Psychological Science, 9,* 196–199.

Wegner, D. M., & Bargh, J. A. (1998). Control and automaticity in social life. In D. T. Gilbert, S. T. Fiske, & G. Lindzey (Eds.), *The handbook of social psychology* (4th ed., Vol. 1, pp. 446–498). New York: McGraw-Hill.

Wegner, D. M., Erber, R., & Raymond, P. (1991). Transactive memory in close relationships. *Journal of Personality and Social Psychology, 61,* 923–929.

Wegner, D. M., Fuller, V. A., & Sparrow, B. (2003). Clever hands: Uncontrolled intelligence in facilitated communication. *Journal of Personality and Social Psychology, 85,* 5–19.

Wegner, D. M., Quillian, F., & Houston, C. E. (1996). Memories out of order: Thought suppression and the disturbance of sequence memory. *Journal of Personality and Social Psychology, 71,* 680–691.

Wegner, D. M., Sparrow, B., & Winerman, L. (2004). Vicarious agency: Experiencing control over the movements of others. *Journal of Personality and Social Psychology, 86,* 838–848.

Wegner, D. M., Wenzlaff, R., Kerker, M., & Beattie, A. E. (1981). Incrimination through innuendo: Can media questions become public answers? *Journal of Personality and Social Psychology, 40,* 822–832.

Wegner, D. M., Wenzlaff, R. M., & Kozak, M. (2004). Dream rebound: The return of suppressed thoughts in dreams. *Psychological Science, 15,* 232–236.

Wehrle, T., Kaiser, S., Schmidt, S., & Scherer, K. R. (2000). Studying the dynamics of emotional expression using synthesized facial muscle movements. *Journal of Personality and Social Psychology, 78,* 105–119.

Weiner, B. (1985). "Spontaneous" causal thinking. *Psychological Bulletin, 97,* 74–84.

Weiner, B., Amirkhan, J., Folkes, V. S., & Verette, J. A. (1987). An attributional analysis of excuse giving: Studies of a naive theory of emotion. *Journal of Personality and Social Psychology, 52,* 316–324.

Weinstein, N. D. (1980). Unrealistic optimism about future life events. *Journal of Personality and Social Psychology, 39,* 806–820.

Weir, W. (1984, October 15). Another look at subliminal "facts." *Advertising Age,* p. 46.

Wells, G. (2008). Theory, logic and data: Paths to a more coherent eyewitness science. *Applied Cognitive Psychology, 22,* 853–859.

Wells, G., & Hasel, L. (2007). Facial composite production by eyewitnesses. *Current Directions in Psychological Science, 16,* 6–10.

Wells, G., & Hasel, L. (2008). Eyewitness identification: Issues in common knowledge and generalization. In E. Borgida & S. T. Fiske (Eds.), *Beyond common sense: Psychological science in the courtroom* (pp. 159–176). Malden : Blackwell.

Wells, G., Memon, A., & Penrod, S. (2006). Eyewitness evidence: Improving its probative value. *Psychological Science in the Public Interest, 7,* 45–75.

Wells, G. L. (1984). The psychology of lineup identifications. *Journal of Applied Social Psychology, 14,* 89–103.

Wells, G. L. (1993). What do we know about eyewitness identification? *American Psychologist, 48,* 553–571.

Wells, G. L., & Bradfield, A. L. (1998). "Good, you identified the suspect": Feedback to eyewitness reports distorts their reports of the witnessing experience. *Journal of Applied Social Psychology, 83,* 360–376.

Wells, G. L., Charman, S. D., & Olson, E. A. (2005). Building face composites can harm lineup identification performance. *Journal of Experimental Psychology: Applied, 11,* 147–156.

Wells, G. L., & Luus, C. A. E. (1990). Police lineups as experiments: Social methodology as a framework for properly conducted lineups. *Personality and Social Psychology Bulletin, 16,* 106–117.

Wells, G. L., Malpass, R. S., Lindsay, R. C. L., Fisher, R. P., Turtle, J. W., & Fulero, S. M. (2000). From the lab to the police station. *American Psychologist, 55,* 581–598.

Wells, G. L., Olson, E. A., & Charman, S. D. (2002). The confidence of eyewitnesses in their identifications from lineups. *Current Directions in Psychological Science, 11,* 151–154.

Wells, W. D. (Ed.). (1997). *Measuring advertising effectiveness.* Mahwah, NJ: Erlbaum.

Wenzlaff, R. M., & Bates, D. E. (2000). The relative efficacy of concentration and suppression strategies of mental control. *Personality and Social Psychology Bulletin, 26,* 1200–1212.

Werth, L., & Foerster, J. (2002). Implicit person theories influence memory judgments: The circumstances under which metacognitive knowledge is used. *European Journal of Social Psychology, 32,* 353-362.

Westen, D,. Blagov, P. S., Harenski, K., Kilts, C., and Hamann, S. (2006) Neural Bases of Motivated Reasoning: An fMRI Study of Emotional Constraints on Partisan Political Judgment in the 2004 U.S. Presidential Election. November, Vol. 18, No. 11, Pages 1947–1958. Posted Online October 27, 2006.

Weyant, J. M. (1996). Application of compliance techniques to direct-mail requests for charitable donations. *Psychology and Marketing, 13,* 157–170.

Wheeler, D. L., Jacobson, J. W., Paglieri, R. A., & Schwartz, A. A. (1993). An experimental assessment of facilitated communication. *Mental Retardation, 31,* 49–59.

Wheeler, L., & Kim, Y. (1997). What is beautiful is culturally good: The physical attractiveness stereotype has different content in collectivistic cultures. *Personality and Social Psychology Bulletin, 23,* 795–800.

Wheeler, L., Koestner, R., & Driver, R. (1982). Related attributes in the choice of comparison others: It's there, but it isn't all there is. *Journal of Experimental Social Psychology, 18,* 489–500.

"Where is our oil coming from?" (2008, May 21). Center for American Progress. Retrieved on October 16, 2008, from www.americanprogress.org/issues/2008/05/oil_imports.html.

White, H. (1997). Longitudinal perspective on alcohol and aggression during adolescence. In M. Galanter (Ed.), *Recent developments in alcoholism*: Vol. 13. *Alcohol and violence: Epidemiology, neurobiology, psychology, and family issues* (pp. 81–103). New York: Plenum.

White, J. (2007). Abu Ghraib officer cleared of detainee abuse; verdict means no one in army's upper ranks will be imprisoned for the 2003 mistreatment in Iraq. *Washington Post,* p. A05.

White, J. W., Donat, P. L. N., & Humphrey, J. A. (1995). An examination of the attitudes underlying sexual coercion among acquaintances. *Journal of Psychology and Human Sexuality, 8,* 27–47.

White, P. A. (2002). Causal attribution from covariation information: The evidential evaluation model. *European Journal of Social Psychology, 32,* 667–684.

White, R. K. (1977). Misperception in the Arab-Israeli conflict. *Journal of Social Issues, 33,* 190–221.

Whitehouse, W. G., Orne, E. C., & Dinges, D. F. (2005). The cognitive interview: Does it successfully avoid the dangers of forensic hypnosis? *American Journal of Psychology, 118,* 213–234.

Whittaker, J. O., & Meade, R. D. (1967). Social pressure in the modification and distortion of judgment: A cross-cultural study. *International Journal of Psychology, 2,* 109–113.

Whorf, B. L. (1956). *Language, thought, and reality.* New York: Wiley.

Wicker, A. W. (1969). Attitudes versus actions: The relationship between verbal and overt behavioral responses to attitude objects. *Journal of Social Issues, 25,* 41–78.

Wicker, B., Keysers, C., Plailly, J., Royet, J. P., Gallese, V., & Rizzolatti, G. (2003). Both us disgusted in my insula: The common neural basis of seeing and feeling disgust. *Neuron, 40*(3), 655–664.

Wicklund, R. A., & Brehm, J. W. (1998). Resistance to change: The cornerstone of cognitive dissonance theory. In E. Harmon-Jones & J. S. Mills (Eds.), *Cognitive dissonance theory: Revival with revisions and controversies* (pp. 310–322). Washington, DC: American Psychological Association.

Wiedenfeld, S. A., O'Leary, A., Bandura, A., Brown, S., Levine, S., & Raska, K. (1990). Impact of perceived self-efficacy in coping with stressors on components of the immune system. *Journal of Personality and Social Psychology, 59,* 1082–1094.

Wiekens, C. J., & Stapel, D. A. (2008). The mirror and I: When private opinions are in conflict with public norms. *Journal of Experimental Social Psychology, 44,* 1160–1166.

Wilder, D. A. (1981). Perceiving persons as a group: Categorization and intergroup relations. In D. L. Hamilton (Ed.), *Cognitive processes in stereotyping and intergroup behavior* (pp. 213–257). Hillsdale, NJ: Erlbaum.

Wilder, D. A. (1984). Intergroup contact: The typical member and the exception to the rule. *Journal of Experimental Psychology, 20,* 177–194.

Wilder, D. A. (1986). Social categorization: Implications for creation and reduction of intergroup bias. In L. Berkowitz (Ed.), *Advances in experimental social psychology* (Vol. 19, pp. 291–355). New York: Academic Press.

Wilder, D. A., & Shapiro, P. N. (1989). Role of competition-induced anxiety in limiting the beneficial impact of positive behavior by an out-group member. *Journal of Personality and Social Psychology, 56,* 60–69.

Willard, J., Madon, S., Guyll, M., & Spoth, R. (in press). Self-efficacy as a moderator of positive and negative self-fulfilling prophecy effects: Mothers' beliefs and children's alcohol use. *European Journal of Social Psychology.*

Williams, J. (1998). *Thurgood Marshall: American revolutionary.* New York: Times Books.

Williams, K. D. (2001). *Ostracism: The power of silence.* New York: Guilford Press.

Williams, K. R. (2005). Arrest and intimate partner violence: Toward a more complete application of deterrence theory. *Aggression and Violent Behavior, 10,* 660–679.

Williams, K. R., & Hawkins, R. (1986). Perceptual research on general deterrence: A critical review. *Law and Society Review, 20,* 545–572.

Williams, P. (2001). *How to be like Mike: Life lessons about basketball's best.* Deerfield Beach, FL: Health Communications.

Williams, T. P., & Sogon, S. (1984). Group composition and conforming behavior in Japanese students. *Japanese Psychological Research, 26,* 231–234.

Williamson, G. M., Clark, M. S., Pegalis, L. J., & Behan, A. (1996). Affective consequences of refusing to help in communal and exchange relationships. *Personality and Social Psychology Bulletin, 22,* 34–47.

Wilson, A. E., & Ross, M. (2000). The frequency of temporal-self and social comparisons in people's personal appraisals. *Journal of Personality and Social Psychology, 78,* 928–942.

Wilson, D. K., Purdon, S. E., & Wallston, K. A. (1988). Compliance in health recommendations: A theoretical overview of message framing. *Health Education Research, 3,* 161–171.

Wilson, D. S. (1997). Atruism and organism: Disentangling the themes of multilevel selection theory. *American Naturalist, 150,* S122–S134.

Wilson, D. S., & Wilson E. O. (2007, Nov. 3). Survival of the selfless. *New Scientist,* 42–46.

Wilson, D. S., Van Vugt, M., & O'Gorman, R. (2008). Multilevel selection theory and major evolutionary transitions: Implications for psychological science. *Current Directions in Psychological Science, 17,* 6-9.

Wilson, E. O. (1975). *Sociobiology: The new synthesis.* Cambridge, MA: Belknap Press.

Wilson, J. Q., & Hernstein, R. J. (1985). *Crime and human nature.* New York: Simon & Schuster.

Wilson, M., & Daly, M. (1985). Competitiveness, risk taking, and violence: The young male syndrome. *Ethology and Sociobiology, 6,* 59–73.

Wilson, M., Daly, M., & Weghorst, S. J. (1982). Male sexual jealousy. *Ethology and Sociobiology, 3,* 11–27.

Wilson, T. D. (2002). *Strangers to ourselves: Discovering the adaptive unconscious.* Cambridge, MA: Harvard University Press.

Wilson, T. D. (2005). The message is the method: Celebrating and exporting the experimental approach. *Psychological Inquiry, 16,* 185–193.

Wilson, T. D., Aronson, E., & Carlsmith, K. (in press). Data (Laboratory Experimentation). In S. T. Fiske, D. T. Gilbert, & G. Lindzey (Eds.), *Handbook of social psychology* (5th ed.). New York: Wiley.

Wilson, T. D., & Bar-Anan, Y. (2008). The unseen mind. *Science, 321,* 1046–1047.

Wilson, T. D., Damiani, M., & Shelton, N. (2002). Improving the academic performance of college students with brief attributional interventions. In J. Aronson (Ed.), *Improving academic achievement: Impact of psychological factors on education* (pp. 88–108). San Diego, CA: Academic Press.

Wilson, T. D., Dunn, D. S., Bybee, J. A., Hyman, D. B., & Rotondo, J. A. (1984). Effects of analyzing reasons on attitude-behavior consistency. *Journal of Personality and Social Psychology, 47,* 5–16.

Wilson, T. D., Dunn, D. S., Kraft, D., & Lisle, D. J. (1989). Introspection, attitude change, and attitude-behavior consistency: The disruptive effects of explaining why we feel the way we do. In L. Berkowitz (Ed.), *Advances in experimental social psychology* (Vol. 19, pp. 123–205). Orlando, FL: Academic Press.

Wilson, T. D., & Dunn, E. W. (2004). Self-knowledge: Its limits, value and potential for improvement. *Annual Review of Psychology, 55,* 493–518.

Wilson, T. D., Gilbert, D. T., & Wheatley, T. (1998). Protecting our minds: The role of lay beliefs. In V. Yzerbyt, G. Lories, & B. Dardenne (Eds.), *Metacognition: Cognitive and social dimensions* (pp. 171–201). New York: Russell Sage Foundation.

Wilson, T. D., & Gilbert, D. T. (2003). Affective forecasting. In M. P. Zanna (Ed.), *Advances in experimental social psychology* (Vol. 35, pp. 345–411). San Diego, CA: Academic Press.

Wilson, T. D., Hodges, S. D., & La Fleur, S. J. (1995). Effects of introspecting about reasons: Inferring attitudes from accessible thoughts. *Journal of Personality and Social Psychology, 69,* 16–28.

Wilson, T. D., Houston, C. E., Etling, K. M., & Brekke, N. C. (1996). A new look at anchoring effects: Basic anchoring and its antecedents. *Journal of Experimental Psychology: General, 125,* 387–402.

Wilson, T. D., Houston, C. E., & Meyers, J. M. (1998). Choose your poison: Effects of lay beliefs about mental processes on attitude change. *Social Cognition, 16,* 114–132.

Wilson, T. D., & Kraft, D. (1993). Why do I love thee? Effects of repeated introspections about a dating relationship on attitudes toward the relationship. *Personality and Social Psychology Bulletin, 19,* 409–418.

Wilson, T. D., Laser, P. S., & Stone, J. I. (1982). Judging the predictors of one's own mood: Accuracy and the use of shared theories. *Journal of Experimental Social Psychology, 18,* 537–556.

Wilson, T. D., Lindsey, S., & Schooler, T. Y. (2000). A model of dual attitudes. *Psychological Review, 107,* 101–126.

Wilson, T. D., & Linville, P. W. (1982). Improving the academic performance of college freshmen: Attribution therapy revisited. *Journal of Personality and Social Psychology, 42,* 367–376.

Wilson, T. D., & Linville, P. W. (1985). Improving the performance of college freshmen using attributional techniques. *Journal of Personality and Social Psychology, 49,* 287–293.

Wilson, T. D., Lisle, D., Schooler, J. W., Hodges, S. D., Klaaren, K. J., & La Fleur, S. J. (1993). Introspecting about reasons can reduce post-choice satisfaction. *Personality and Social Psychology Bulletin, 19,* 331–339.

Wilson, Timothy D.[1]; Gilbert, Daniel T. (2005). Current Directions in Psychological Science, Volume 14, Number 3, June 2005, pp. 131–134(4) Blackwell Publishing

Winerman, L. (2005). The mind's mirror. *Monitor on Psychology, 36*(9), 48–50.

Winslow, R. W., Franzini, L. R., & Hwang, J. (1992). Perceived peer norms, casual sex, and AIDS risk prevention. *Journal of Applied Social Psychology, 22,* 1809–1827.

Winter, R., & Greene, E. (2007). Juror decision-making. In F. T. Durso, R. S. Nickerson, S. T. Dumais, S. Lewandowsky, & T. J. Perfect (Eds.), *Handbook of applied cognition* (2nd ed., pp. 739–761). Hoboken, NJ: John Wiley.

Wiseman, C. V., Gray, J. J., Mosimann, J. E., & Ahrens, A. H. (1992). Cultural expectations of thinness in women: An update. *International Journal of Eating Disorders, 11,* 85–89.

Wittenbaum, G. M., & Moreland, R. L. (2008). Small-group research in social psychology: Topics and trends over time. *Social and Personality Psychology Compass, 2* (www.blackwell-compass.com/subject/socialpsychology/).

Wittenbaum, G. M., & Park, E. S. (2001). The collective preference for shared information. *Current Directions in Psychological Science, 10,* 72–75.

Wolf, S. (1985). Manifest and latent influence of majorities and minorities. *Journal of Personality and Social Psychology, 48,* 899–908.

Wolfe, C., & Spencer, S. (1996). Stereotypes and prejudice: Their overt and subtle influence in the classroom. *American Behavioral Scientist, 40,* 176–185.

Wolfson, A. (2005). "A hoax most cruel." The Courier-Journal, October 9. Retrieved on June 5, 2006, from *www.courier-journal.com/apps/pbcs.d11/article?Date=20051009&category=NEWS01*

Woll, S. (1986). So many to choose from: Decision strategies in videodating. *Journal of Social and Personal Relationships, 3,* 43–52.

Wong, R. Y., & Hong, Y. (2005). Dynamic influences of culture on cooperation in a Prisoner's Dilemma game. *Psychological Science, 16,* 429–434.

Wood, J. V., Taylor, S. E., & Lichtman, R. R. (1985). Social comparison in adjustment to breast cancer. *Journal of Personality and Social Psychology, 49,* 1169–1183.

Wood, W. (1982). Retrieval of attitude-relevant information from memory: Effects on susceptibility to persuasion and on intrinsic motivation. *Journal of Personality and Social Psychology, 42,* 798–810.

Wood, W. (1987). Meta-analytic review of sex differences in group performance. *Psychological Bulletin, 102,* 53–71.

Wood, W., & Eagly, A. H. (2002). A cross-cultural analysis of the behavior of women and men: Implications for the origins of sex differences. *Psychological Bulletin, 128,* 699–727.

Wood, W., Lundgren, S., Ouellette, J. A., Busceme, S., & Blackstone, T. (1994). Minority influence: A meta-analytic review of social influence processes. *Psychological Bulletin, 115,* 323–345.

Wood, W., Pool, G. J., Leck, K., & Purvis, D. (1996). Self-definition, defensive processing, and influence: The normative impact of majority and minority groups. *Journal of Personality and Social Psychology, 71,* 1181–1193.

Wood, W., & Quinn, J. M. (2003). Forewarned and forearmed? Two meta-analytic syntheses of forewarnings of influence appeals. *Psychological Bulletin, 129,* 119–138.

Wood, W., Wong, F. Y., & Chachere, J. G. (1991). Effects of media violence on viewers' aggression in unconstrained social interaction. *Psychological Bulletin, 109,* 371–383.

Woodward, B. (2004). *Plan of attack.* New York: Simon & Schuster.

Woodward, B. (2006). *State of denial.* New York: Simon & Schuster.

Woodward, B. (2008). *The war within: A secret White House history (2006–2008)*. New York: Simon & Schuster.

Word, C. O., Zanna, M. P., & Cooper, J. (1974). The nonverbal mediation of self-fulfilling prophecies in interracial interaction. *Journal of Experimental Social Psychology, 10*, 109–120.

Wortman, C. B. & Silver, R. C. (1989). The myths of coping with loss. *Journal of Consulting and Clinical Psychology, 57*, 349–357.

Wrangham, R. W., Wilson, M. L., & Muller, M. N. (2006, January). Comparative rates of violence in chimpanzees and humans. *Primates, 47*(1), 14–26.

Wright, D. B., & Stroud, J. N. (2002). Age differences in lineup identification accuracy: People are better with their own age. *Law and Human Behavior, 26*, 641–654.

Wright, E. F., Luus, C. A. E., & Christie, S. D. (1990). Does group discussion facilitate the use of consensus information in making causal attributions? *Journal of Personality and Social Psychology, 59*, 261–269.

Wright, L. (1994). *Remembering Satan*. New York: Knopf.

Wyer, R. S., Jr. (1988). Social memory and social judgment. In P. R. Solomon, G. R. Goethals, C. M. Kelley, & B. R. Stephens (Eds.), *Perspectives on memory research*. New York: Springer-Verlag.

Wyer, R. S., Jr., & Srull, T. K. (1989). *Memory and cognition in its social context*. Hillsdale, NJ: Erlbaum.

Wylie, L. W. (1977). *Beaux gestes: A guide to French body talk*. New York: Cambridge University Press.

Yamaguchi, K., & Kandel, D. B. (1984). Patterns of drug use from adolescence to young adulthood: III. Predictors of progression. *American Journal of Public Health, 74*, 673–681.

Yang, A. S. (1997). Poll trends: Attitudes toward homosexuality. *Public Opinion Quarterly, 61*, 477–507.

Yee, D., & Eccles, J. S. (1988). Parent perceptions and attributions for children's math achievement. *Sex Roles, 19*, 317–333.

York, A. (2001, April 26). The product placement monster that E.T. spawned. Salon [Online journal.] Retrieved from *archive.salon.com/tech/feature/2001/04/26/product_placement/print.html*

Yudko, E., Blanchard, D., Henne, J., & Blanchard, R. (1997). Emerging themes in preclinical research on alcohol and aggression. In M. Galanter (Ed.), *Recent developments in alcoholism*: Vol. 13. *Alcohol and violence: Epidemiology, neurobiology, psychology, and family issues* (pp. 123–138). New York: Plenum.

Zajonc, R. B. (1965). Social facilitation. *Science, 149*, 269–274.

Zajonc, R. B. (1968). Attitudinal effects of mere exposure. *Journal of Personality and Social Psychology, 9* (Monograph Suppl. 2, pt. 2).

Zajonc, R. B. (1980). Compresence. In P. B. Paulus (Ed.), *Psychology of group influence* (pp. 35–60). Hillsdale, NJ: Erlbaum.

Zajonc, R. B., Heingartner, A., & Herman, E. M. (1969). Social enhancement and impairment of performance in the cockroach. *Journal of Personality and Social Psychology, 13*, 83–92.

Zanna, M. P., & Fazio, R. H. (1982). The attitude-behavior relation: Moving toward a third generation of research. In M. P. Zanna, E. T. Higgins, & C. P. Herman (Eds.), *Consistency in social behavior: The Ontario Symposium* (Vol. 2, pp. 283–301). Hillsdale, NJ: Erlbaum.

Zanna, M. P., Goethals, G. R., & Hill, J. (1975). Evaluating a sex-related ability: Social comparison with similar others and standard setters. *Journal of Experimental Social Psychology, 11*, 86–93.

Zanna, M. P., & Rempel, J. K. (1988). Attitudes: A new look at an old concept. In D. Bar-Tal & A. W. Kruglanski (Eds.), *The social psychology of attitudes* (pp. 315–334). New York: Cambridge University Press.

Zanot, E. J., Pincus, J. D., & Lamp, E. J. (1983). Public perceptions of subliminal advertising. *Journal of Advertising, 12*, 39–45.

Zebrowitz, L. A. (1997). *Reading faces: Window to the soul?* Boulder, CO: Westview Press.

Zebrowitz, L. A., & Montepare, J. M. (1992). Impressions of baby-faced individuals across the life-span. *Developmental Psychology, 28*, 1143–1152.

Zeman, Z. A. B. (1995). The state and propaganda. In R. Jackall (Ed.), *Propaganda* (pp. 174–189). New York: New York University Press.

Zhong, C., & Leonardelli, G. J., (in press). Cold and lonely: Does social exclusion literally feel cold? *Psychology Science*.

Zillmann, D. (1978). Attribution and misattribution of excitatory reactions. In J. H. Harvey, W. J. Ickes, & R. F. Kidd (Eds.), *New directions in attribution research* (Vol. 2, pp. 335–370). Hillsdale, NJ: Erlbaum.

Zimbardo, P. (2007). *The Lucifer effect: Understanding how good people turn evil*. New York: Random House.

Zimbardo, P. G. (1970). The human choice: Individuation, reason, and order versus deindividuation, impulse, and chaos. In W. J. Arnold & D. Levine (Eds.), *Nebraska Symposium on Motivation, 1969* (Vol. 17, pp. 237–307). Lincoln: University of Nebraska Press.

Zimbardo, P. G., & Andersen, S. (1993). Understanding mind control: Exotic and mundane mental manipulations. In M. D. Langone (Ed.), *Recovery from cults* (pp. 104–125). New York: Norton.

Zimbardo, P. G., Weisenberg, M., Firestone, I., & Levy, B. (1965). Communicator effectiveness in producing public conformity and private attitude change. *Journal of Personality, 33*, 233–255.

Zubek, J. P. (Ed.). (1969). *Sensory deprivation: Fifteen years of research*. New York: Appleton-Century-Crofts.

Zuber, J. A., Crott, H. W., & Werner, J. (1992). Choice shift and group polarization: An analysis of the status of arguments and social decision schemes. *Journal of Personality and Social Psychology, 62*, 50–61.

Zuwerink, J., Monteith, M., Devine, P. G., & Cook, D. (1996). Prejudice toward blacks: With and without compunction? *Basic and Applied Social Psychology, 18*, 131–150.

Zwolinski, J. (2008). Biopsychosocial responses to social rejection in targets of relational aggression. *Biological Psychology, 79*, 260–267.

Credits 鸣谢

COVER Page xxx: Paul Turner/Paul Robert Turner, ?Don?t Panic?, 60? × 48?, Oil on Canvas, 2005.

Chapter 1 Page xxxii: Jochen Tack/DAS FOTOARCHIV/Peter Arnold, Inc.; Page 4: © Michael J. Doolittle/The Image Works; Page 5: © Rick Friedman/CORBIS All Rights Reserved; Page 6: Jewel Samad/Getty Images; Page 7: AP Wide World Photos; Page 10: Paul Chesley/National Geographic Image Collection; Page 13: Getty Images, Inc.; Page 14: Archives of the History of American Psychology, The University of Akron; Page 15 (top): Archives of the History of American Psychology, The University of Akron; Page 15 (bottom): Photograph courtesy of Trudy Festinger. Reprinted by permission.; Page 16: © Chuck Savage/CORBIS All Rights Reserved; Page 19: Bob Daemmrich/The Image Works.

Chapter 2 Page 22: AP Wide World Photos; Page 26: Henry Groskinsky/Getty Images/Time Life Pictures; Page 28: Michael Newman/PhotoEdit Inc.; Page 31: Courtesy of the Library of Congress; Page 32: Michael Newman/PhotoEdit Inc.; Page 37: Lewis J. Merrim/Photo Researchers, Inc.; Page 41 (left): REUTERS/Corbis/ Bettmann; Page 41 (right): David Austen/Stock Boston; Page 43 (top): Mark Harmel/Photo Researchers, Inc.; Page 43 (bottom): The Far Side® by Gary Larson © 1993 FarWorks, Inc. All Rights Reserved. Used with Permission.

Chapter 3 Page 50: Jack Haley/Daily Messenger/AP Wide World Photos; Page 52: Gala/SuperStock, Inc.; Page 53: Joshua Correll/Courtesy Charles Judd, University of Colorado; Page 55: National Archives and Records Administration; Page 56: Mark Lyons/AP Wide World Photos; Page 60: Mary Kate Denny/PhotoEdit Inc.; Page 64: © Jose Luis Pelaez/CORBIS All Rights Reserved; Page 68: © Joel Stettenheim/CORBIS All Rights Reserved; Page 69: Courtesy of Drs. Masuda & Nisbett; Page 71: Yuri Miyamoto, Ph.D.; Page 73: W. Lynn Seldon Jr./Omni-Photo Communications, Inc.; Page 74: Julian Finney/Getty Images.

Chapter 4 Page 82: M. Becker/ American Idol 2009/Getty Images; Page 87 (top left): Toby Maudsley/Getty Images, Inc.; Page 87 (top middle): Alan S. Weiner; Page 87 (top right): Lynn McLaren/Photolibrary.com; Page 87 (bottom left): © Guido Alberto Rossi/TIPS Images; Page 87 (bottom middle): Richard Pan/StockPhotos Inc./Globe Photos, Inc.; Page 87 (bottom right): Costa Manos/Magnum Photos, Inc.; Page 88: Paul Ekman Group, LLC.; Page 89: Paul Ekman Group, LLC/Human Interaction Laboratory; Page 90: Michel Setboun/© SETBOUN/CORBIS; Page 90: © Carol Beckwith & Angela Fisher/HAGA/The Image Works; Page 90: Sundberg, Dag/Getty Images Inc. - Image Bank; Page 90: Bill Bachmann/Photo Researchers, Inc.; Page 90: Sisse Brimberg/National Geographic Image Collection; Page 91: Elliot Aronson; Page 93 (top): Darlene Hammond/Getty Images Inc. - Hulton Archive Photos; Page 93 (bottom): John Slater/Getty Images, Inc.; Page 96: Hartmut Schwarzbach/Peter Arnold, Inc.; Page 99 (top): © Bettmann/CORBIS All Rights Reserved; Page 99 (bottom): Richard Perry/The New York Times; Page 106: SuperStock, Inc.; Page 108: Dear Ann Landers. © Creators Syndicate, Inc. Used with permission; Page 109: SEBASTIEN STARR/Getty Images, Inc.–Taxi.

Chapter 5 Page 116: Ezra Shaw/Getty Images; Page 118: PT Santana/Stone/Getty Images; Page 119 AP Wide World Photos; Page 125: ©The New Yorker Collection 1977 Edward Frascino from cartoonbank.com. All Rights Reserved.; Page 128: Gary Null/Picture Desk, Inc./Kobal Collection; Page 130 (top): David Mager/Pearson Learning Photo Studio; Page 130 (bottom): PEANUTS Reprinted by permission of United Features Syndicate, Inc.; Page 134: © Buddy Mays/CORBIS All Rights Reserved; Page 137: King Features Syndicate; Page 138: © The New Yorker Collection 1991 William Hamilton from cartoonbank.com. All Rights Reserved.; Page 142 (left): Michael Smith/Courtesy of the Library of Congress; Page 142 (right): Micheal Smith/Courtesy of the Library of Congress; Page 143 (left): © Robert Knudsen/John F. Kennedy Library/CORBIS All Rights Reserved; Page 143 (right): Corbis/Bettmann.

Chapter 6 Page 148: © Aaron Horowitz/CORBIS All Rights Reserved; Page 150: Charles Schultz/United Media/United Feature Syndicate, Inc.; Page 152: Donna Day/Getty Images Inc. - Stone Allstock; Page 153: © Norbert Schwerin/The Image Works; Page 154: Value RF/©Alan Levenson/CORBIS; Page 156: Yellow Dog Productions/Getty Images, Inc.; Page 158: Ewing Galloway,/Photolibrary.com; Page 161: David Young-Wolff/PhotoEdit Inc.; Page 164: Shannon Fagan/Getty Images, Inc.; Page 165: Value RM/© Gaetano/CORBIS All Rights Reserved; Page 166: Courtesy of The Historical Society of Pennsylvania Collection, Atwater Kent Museum of Philadelpha; Page 169: AP Wide World Photos; Page 171: Dylan Martinez/Corbis/Bettmann; Page 172: Sean Gallup/Getty Images, Inc.

Chapter 7 Page 176: Gaslight Advertising Archives, Inc. N.Y.; Page 177: ©The New Yorker Collection 2002 Alex Gregory from cartoonbank.com. All Rights Reserved.; Page 178: Richard Rowe/Universal Speres Inc./Goldenpalace.com; Page 179: Robert Kusel Photography Inc.; Page 182: ©Moodboard/Corbis; Page 183: Alex Brandon/AP Wide World Photos; Page 186: © David Young-Wolff; Page 190: Pierre Roussel/Newsmakers/Getty Images, Inc.; Page 191 (top): ©The New Yorker Collection 1989 Henry Martin from cartoonbank.com. All Rights Reserved.; Page 191 (bottom): Courtesy of CJFoundation for SIDS; Don Imus Pediatric Center; Hackensack University Medical Center, NJ; Page 193: Bill Aron/PhotoEdit Inc.; Page 195: Fox-TV/Picture Desk, Inc./Kobal Collection; Page 196: California Department of Health Services/AP Wide World Photos; Page 200: ©The New Yorker Collection Mick Stevens from cartoonbank.com. All Rights Reserved.; Page 201: Pierre Roussel/Newsmakers/Getty Images, Inc.; Page 202 (top): The Advertising Archives; Page 202 (bottom): AP Wide World Photos; Page 203: American Association of Advertising Agencies.

Chapter 8 Page 210: Ulli Michel/Corbis/Reuters America LLC; Page 211: Bill Horsman/Stock Boston; Page 214: © Ronald S. Haeberle/Life Magazine 1968, Time Warner, Inc.; Page 217: Jeremy Bembaron/Corbis/Sygma; Page 218: AP Wide World Photos; Page 219: The Southern Standard; Page 221: © Miguel Fairbanks; Page 223: Photo William Vandivert and Scientific American. From "Opinions and Social Pressure" by Solomon E. Asch, November 1955.; Page 227: © Henry Diltz/CORBIS All Rights Reserved; Page 229: © Sunset Boulevard/Sygma/CORBIS All Rights Reserved; Page 231: New York Times - Maps and Graphics; Page 234: © Staffan Wildstrand/zefa/CORBIS All Rights Reserved; Page 237: Getty Images Inc. - Hulton Archive Photos; Page 238: Liam Nicholls/Getty Images, Inc.; Page 241: Photo by John Florea/Time Life Pictures/Getty Images, Inc.; Page 242: © 1965 by Stanley Milgram. From "Obedience" (film) distributed by the Pennsylvania State University PCR. Courtesy of Alexandra Milgram.

Chapter 9 Page 252: Kevin Lamarque/Reuters Limited; Page 254: Marc Rochon/Getty Images, Inc.; Page 255: Philip G. Zimbardo Inc.; Page 256: Courtesy of Washington Post/Getty Images, Inc.; Page 260: Robert Harbison; Page 263: Danny Johnston/AP Wide World Photos; Page 268: ©The New Yorker Collection 1979 Henry Martin from cartoonbank.com. All Rights Reserved.; Page 270: Bruce Weaver/AP Wide World Photos; Page 274: AP Wide World Photos; Page 275: Steve Helber/AP Wide World Photos; Page 277: Zigy Kaluzny/Getty Images, Inc.; Page 282: © Patric Robert/CORBIS All Rights Reserved.

Chapter 10 Page 286: Jonathan Player/The New York Times; Page 289: Getty Images - Stockbyte, Royalty Free; Page 291 (top): © The New Yorker Collection 1998 Sam Gross from cartoonbank.com. All Rights Reserved.; Page 291 (bottom): Willie J. Allen Jr./The New York Times; Page 295 (top left/middle): Evan Agostini/Evan Agostini/Getty Images, Inc.; Page 295 (top right): Elisabetta Villa/Getty Images, Inc.; Page 295 (middle left): Evan Agostini/Getty Images, Inc.; Page 295 (middle center): AP Wide World Photos; Page 295 (middle right): ©

Frank Trapper/CORBIS All Rights Reserved; Page 295 (bottom): © Frank Trapper/CORBIS All Rights Reserved; Page 296: Courtesy of Judith H. Langlois/Dept. of Psychology/University of Texas; Page 297: Bill Brennan/PacificStock.com; Page 301: Picture Desk/The Kobal Collection; Page 303: Bill Bachmann/ Creative Eye/MIRA.com; Page 308: Ian Hooton © Dorling Kindersley; Page 309: ©2006 Harry Bliss. Used with permission of Pippin Properties, Inc.; Page 314 (left): David Hanover/Getty Images Inc. - Stone Allstock; Page 314 (right): GARY BUSS/Getty Images, Inc.–Taxi; Page 317: © The New Yorker Collection 2003 Steve Duenes from cartoonbank.com. All Rights Reserved.; Page 318: © Jeff Greenberg/The Image Works.

Chapter 11 Page 322: Suzanne Plunket/AP Wide World Photos; Page 324: © Ariel Skelley/CORBIS All Rights Reserved; Page 326: CALVIN AND HOBBES © 1995 Watterson. Reprinted with permission of UNIVERSAL PRESS SYNDICATE. All rights·reserved.; Page 330: UPI; Page 331: Robert Allison/Contact Press Images Inc.; Page 332: Themba Hadebe/AP Wide World Photos; Page 333: © Roy Morsch/CORBIS All Rights Reserved; Page 336 (left): © Bob Sacha/CORBIS All Rights Reserved; Page 336 (right): Grant Feint/Getty Images, Inc.; Page 337: Copyright © NM DNR Reprinted with Permission; Page 341: Steve McCurry/Magnum Photos, Inc.; Page 343: Value RF/© Floresco Productions/CORBIS; Page 345: Sergei Teterin/Corbis/Reuters America LLC. Page 346: Courtesy University of Pittsburgh/CIDDE. ©2006 All Rights Reserved. Photograph: Joseph Kapelewski.

Chapter 12 Page 350: © Robert Trippett/SIPA Press; Page 353: Catherine Ursillo/Photo Researchers, Inc.; Page 355: Karl Ammann/Nature Picture Library; Page 356: National General Pictures/ Picture Desk, Inc./Kobal Collection; Page 358: Mark Burnett/Stock Boston; Page 359: © The New Yorker Collection 1975 Dana Fradon from cartoonbank.com. All Rights Reserved.; Page 361: Yellow Dog Productions/Getty Images Inc. - Image Bank; Page 365: Bob Daemmrich/PhotoEdit Inc.; Page 366: Albert Bandura, D. Ross & S.A. Ross, Imitation of film-mediated aggressive models. "Journal of Abnormal and Social Psychology", 1963, 66. P. 8; Page 367: OLIPHANT © 1973. Reprinted with permission of Universal Press Syndicate. All rights reserved.; Page 368: Sean Murphy/Getty Images Inc. - Stone Allstock; Page 369: 20th Century Fox/the Kobal Collection/Bridges; Page 374: David Moore/Getty Images, Inc.; Page 375: Photo Researchers, Inc.; Page 376 (top): U. S. Army Photograph; Page 376 (bottom): © Bettmann/CORBIS All Rights Reserved; Page 380: Charles Moore/Stock Photo/Black Star; Page 381: © Michael Pole/CORBIS All Rights Reserved.

Chapter 13 Page 386: Lon C. Diehl/PhotoEdit Inc.; Page 388: 2009 Owen DB/Black Star/Newscom; Page 389: Laura Dwight/PhotoEdit Inc.; Page 390: Christoph Wilhelm/Getty Images, Inc.; Page 391: The New York Times Co. Reprinted by permission; Page 393 (top): CATHY ©1986 Cathy Guisewite. Reprinted with permission of UNIVERSAL PRESS SYNDICATE. All rights reserved.; Page 393 (bottom): www.CartoonStock.com; Page 396: AP Wide World Photos; Page 398: Gratn Haverson/Getty Images, Inc.; Page 401: © The New Yorker Collection 1995 Jack Ziegler from cartoonbank.com. All Rights Reserved.; Page 404: © Mika/Zefa/CORBIS. All Rights Reserved.; Page 405 (left): © Bettmann/CORBIS All Rights Reserved; Page 405 (right): The White House/Getty Images; Page 407: © Horacio Villalobos/epa/ CORBIS. All Rights Reserved; Page 409: David Young-Wolff/ PhotoEdit Inc.; Page 412: © Richard Melloul/Sygma/CORBIS All Rights Reserved; Page 413: ©The New Yorker Collection 1994 Bernard Schoenbaum from cartoonbank.com. All Rights Reserved.; Page 415 (left): Corbis/Bettmann; Page 415 (right): Courtesy of W.S. Hoole Special Collections Library, University of Alabama; Page 417: OLIPHANT ©. Reprinted with permission of UNIVERSAL PRESS SYNDICATE. All rights reserved.; Page 419: Jonathan Nourok/PhotoEdit Inc.; Page 421: Tom Watson/Merrill Education.

SPA-1 Page 426: Chico Batata/CORBIS All Rights Reserved; Page 428 (top): Reproduced with permission from Edward W. Lempinan, AAAS. Alaska. Copyright 2006 American Association for the Advancement of Science.; Page 428 (bottom): AP Wide World Photos; Page 429: ©The New Yorker Collection 1999 Mick Stevens from cartoonbank.com. All Rights Reserved.; Page 431: Thomas Nilsson/Getty Images, Inc.; Page 433: Aaron Haupt/Photo Researchers, Inc.; Page 434 (top): © The New Yorker Collection 1991 Mike Stevens from cartoonbank.com. All Rights Reserved.; Page 434 (bottom): Pearson Education/PH College; Page 438 (top): © Pedrick/The Image Works; Page 438 (bottom): © Philip James Corwin/CORBIS All Rights Reserved; Page 440: © A. Inden/zefa/CORBIS All Rights Reserved; Page 442: © Schultheiss Productions/zefa/CORBIS All Rights Reserved.

SPA-2 Page 446: Courtesy of Joanne K. Hill, author Rainbow Remedies for Life's Stormy Times, Moorhill Communications. Doris Holik Kelly; Page 449 (top): Doug Kanter/SIPA Press; Page 449 (bottom top right): Robert Brenner/PhotoEdit Inc.; Page 449 (bottom top left): Ryan McVay/Getty Images Inc. - PhotoDisc; Page 449 (bottom right): Thomas Hoepker/Magnum Photos, Inc.; Page 449 (bottom left): Elena Rooraid/PhotoEdit Inc.; Page 455: Telegraph Colour Library/ Getty Images, Inc.; Page 459: John Giustina/Getty Images, Inc.; Page 460: DILBERT reprinted by permission of United Media Feature Syndicate, Inc.; Page 462: SuperStock, Inc.; Page 465: David Young-Wolff/PhotoEdit Inc.; Page 466: © Vahan Shirvanian/ www.CartoonStock.com; Page 468: Markus Matzel/Das Fotoarchiv./ Peter Arnold, Inc.

SPA-3 Page 472: Miramax/Photofest; Page 474: Dallas Morning News; Page 477: Arnald Magnani/Getty Images, Inc.; Page 478: From: Simons, D.J. & Chabris, C.F., "Gorillas in Our Midst: Sustained inattentional blindness for dynamic events". Perception 1999, 28, p. 1070. Figure provided by Daniel Simons; Page 479: Loftus EF, Miller DG, Burns HJ, (1978). Semantic integration of verbal information into a visual memory. "Journal of Experimental Psychology"; Human Learning and Memory, 4, 19-31.; Page 480: Getty Images, Inc.; Page 481: CLOSE TO HOME © 2002 John McPherson. Reprinted with permission of UNIVERSAL PRESS SYNDICATE. All rights reserved.; Page 485: Michael L. Abramson/Woodfin Camp & Associates, Inc.; Page 487: Steve Bloom; Page 489: © The New Yorker Collection 1997 Mike Twohy from cartoonbank.com. All Rights Reserved.; Page 490: ©The New Yorker Collection 2002 Frank Cotham from cartoonbank.com. All Rights Reserved.; Page 491 (top): A/T MEDIA SERVICES/Pearson Education/PH College; Page 491 (botom): Photofest; Page 492: Thomas Dallal/DALLAL/SIPA Press; Page 493: Spencer Grant/ PhotoEdit Inc.

Name Index 人名索引

A

Aarts, H., 48, 203, 204, 214
Abdallah, B., 297
Abele, A. E., 124
Abelson, R. P., 180
Abraham, C., 191
Abraham, M. M., 48, 200
Abrahams, D., 293
Abrahamse, W., 432
Abrams, D., 111, 226, 233, 235, 255, 398
Abramson, L. Y., 111
Acker, M., 371
Adair, J. G., 45
Adams, G., 304
Adler, J., 49
Adler, N. E., 230
Adolphs, R., 87
Adonu, J. K., 304
Agnew, C. R., 300, 312
Ahmad, N., 277, 329, 345
Ahrens, A. H., 205, 228, 229
Aiello, J. R., 259
Ainsworth, M. D. S., 307
Ajzen, I., 179, 198
Akert, R. M., 48, 86, 89, 91, 317, 318
Albarracin, D., 129, 185, 200, 467
Alicke, M. D., 224
Allard, L. M., 310
Allen, B. P., 40, 266
Allen, M., 196, 372
Allen, V. L., 219, 233
Allison, P. D., 220
Allport, G. W., 3, 391, 405, 413, 418, 420
Altman, L. K., 219
Alvarez, L., 288
Alwin, D. F., 185
Amabile, T. M., 100
Amato, P. R., 336
Ambady, N., 52, 84, 87
Amir, I., 419
Amirkhan, J., 379
Amirkhan, J. H., 109, 110
Amodio, D. M., 292, 402
Amsler, S. J., 355
Andersen, S., 270
Andersen, S. M., 56, 129, 299
Anderson, B., 360
Anderson, C. A., 40, 75, 78, 92, 93, 111, 112, 360, 367, 369
Anderson, D. C., 360
Anderson, J. R., 118, 460
Anderson, K., 458
Anderson, N. B., 450
Anderson, S. L., 304
Anthony, T., 269
Antone, C., 467

Archer, D., 86, 89, 91, 358, 364, 373, 377, 493, 495
Arendt, H., 241
Argenti, A. M., 478
Argyle, M., 89
Arias, I., 96
Arkes, H. R., 488
Arkin, R. C., 109
Arkin, R. M., 142, 143
Armitage, C. J., 200
Armor, D., 152
Armor, D. A., 48, 461
Arms, R. L., 375
Armstrong, L., 459
Armstrong, N., 379
Arnett, J., 220, 221
Aron, A., 288, 304, 309
Aron, A. P., 135
Aron, E. N., 288
Aron, R., 377
Aronson, E., 7, 15, 16, 19, 38, 39, 45, 150, 152, 158, 161, 162, 164, 165, 171, 352, 372, 382, 383, 410, 418, 419, 420, 423, 437, 438
Aronson, J., 19, 409
Aronson, J. M., 390, 408
Aronson, V., 293
Arrowood, A. J., 138
Arthur, K., 84
Asch, S. E., 92, 222, 224, 232, 233
Ashbrook, R. M., 255
Ashmore, R. D., 93, 297, 298
Ashton, W., 99
Aspinwall, L. G., 138, 461
Associated Press, 217
Ato, M., 273
Atoum, A. O., 261
Atzeni, T., 261
Augoustinos, M., 399
Aune, K. S. 89
Aune, R. K., 89
Austin, S. B., 466
Averill, J. R., 454
Axelrod, R., 278
Azrin, N. H., 359

B

Baba, R., 381
Babad, E., 60
Back, K., 289
Back, K. W., 219
Backman, C. W., 299
Bacon, P. L., 121, 122, 147
Badr, L. K., 297
Bailey, S., 458
Bailey, W. C., 373, 495
Baker, P., 270
Bakker, A. B., 436, 437

Baldwin, M. W., 129, 311
Banaji, M. R., 182, 402
Bancroft, L., 359
Bandura, A., 247, 355, 365, 456, 457
Banks, C., 256
Banks, T., 357
Banks, W. P., 487
Barbee, A. P., 294, 296
Barber, N., 228
Barger, S. D., 464
Bargh, J. A., 52, 56, 57, 60, 67, 96, 203
Bar-Haim, Y., 478
Barker, R., 361
Barley, S. R., 255
Barnes, G., 371
Barnes, M. L., 293, 305
Barnes, P. J., 344
Baron, R. A., 353, 355, 363, 366, 379, 380
Baron, R. M., 86, 100
Baron, R. S., 216, 226, 269
Baron, S. H., 216
Baron, S. J., 448
Barrett, H. M., 487
Barron, K. E., 130
Barrouquere, B., 212, 213
Bartels, B., 234
Bartholomew, R. E., 218
Bartlett, F. C., 53, 68
Barton, W. H., 264
Bass, B. M., 273, 274
Bass, E., 487
Basset, R., 155
Bassin, E., 316
Bates, D. E., 75
Bates, J. E., 357
Batson, C. D., 40, 277, 326, 328, 329, 330, 332, 339, 340, 345, 346
Battle for your brain, 200
Baum, A., 219, 367
Baum, C. S., 219
Baumeister, R. F., 119, 121, 123, 124, 140, 141, 221, 254, 288, 301, 335, 337, 440
Baumgardner, A. H., 143
Baweyens, F., 180
Baxter, L. A., 316
Beach, S. R., 290
Beale, S. K., 464
Beals, K. P., 312
Beaman, A. L., 124, 344
Beauvois, J., 170
Bechky, B. A., 255
Bedau, H. A., 493, 497
Beer, J. S., 109
Behan, A., 168, 343
Bell, J., 302
Bell, S. T., 111

Bem, D. J., 129, 181, 272
Bem, S. L., 129, 299
Benet-Martinez, V., 105
Benight, C. C., 456
Benson, S. M., 335
Benthin, A. C., 151
Bergeron, N., 355
Berglas, S., 142
Berke, R. L., 202
Berkman, L. F., 463
Berkow, J. H., 305
Berkowitz, L., 335, 352, 353, 355, 359, 362, 363, 364, 367, 371, 373, 378, 413
Bernard, M. M., 194
Berns, G. S., 224, 225
Berry, D. S., 294
Berry, J., 41
Berry, J. W., 235
Berscheid, E., 93, 169, 288, 289, 291, 293, 295, 296, 297, 298, 300, 301, 302, 305, 307
Bersoff, D. M., 333
Bettencourt, B. A., 255, 358
Bhanot, R., 59
Biehl, M., 87
Biek, M., 153
Biers, D. W., 107
Biesanz, J. C., 61
Bigazzi, J., 395
Billig, M., 398
Birchmeier, Z., 266
Bjork, J. M., 357
Blackstone, T., 236
Blanchard, D., 359
Blanchard, R., 359
Blank, P. D., 60
Blanton, H., 138
Blascovich, J., 261
Blass, T., 240, 244
Blatt, S. J., 235
Blau, P. M., 299, 312
Blehar, M. C., 307
Blittner, M., 457
Bloom, J. R., 463
Blumstein, P., 293, 315
Bochner, S., 119
Bodenhausen, G. V., 182, 400, 407
Boechler, M., 357
Bohner, G., 111
Boldry, J., 310
Bonacci, A. M., 370
Bonanno, G., 448
Bonanno, G. A., 432, 448, 449
Bond, C., 395
Bond, C. F., Jr., 260, 261, 483, 485
Bond, M. H., 41, 111, 235, 333
Bond, R., 232, 235
Bono, J. E., 273
Bonta, B. D., 278
Booth, R. J., 75

569

Borgida, E., 56, 390
Boris, H. I., 144
Bornstein, B. H., 477
Bornstein, R. F., 204, 290
Borowiecki, J., 231
Borsari, B., 436
Borsch, F., 423
Bowdle, B. F., 356
Bower, G. H., 372
Bowes, J. M., 332
Bowlby, J., 307
Bown, N., 226
Boyden, T., 291
Boye, D., 169
Bradbury, T. N., 96
Bradfield, A., 24
Bradfield, A. L., 482
Braly, K. W., 400
Brandon, R., 474
Brannon, L. A., 203
Branscombe, N. R., 73, 375
Brase, G., 337
Breckler, S. J., 179
Brehm, J. W., 150, 154, 157, 196
Brendl, C. M., 56
Brewer, M. B., 38, 121, 254, 258, 326, 333, 397, 398, 419
Brewer, N., 482
Brezgel, K., 372
Bridgeman, D., 419
Bridgeman, D. L., 422
Bridges, F. S., 343
Bridges, M. W., 460
Brief, D. E., 244, 245
Brigham, J. C., 481
Brinson, L., 392
Brislin, R., 257
Brock, T. C., 189, 203
Brodsky, S. L., 142
Bromley, D. B., 119
Bromley, S., 416
Brophy, J. E., 61
Brouillard, M. E., 457
Brown, J. D., 152, 461
Brown, R., 273, 362, 398
Brown, R. J., 333, 397
Brown, R. P., 408
Brown, S. L., 331, 344, 463
Brown, T., 180
Bruner, J., 180, 181
Brunsman, B., 216
Bryant, R. A., 431
Buckhout, R., 481
Buehler, R., 75
Bugelski, R., 413
Bui, K.-V. T., 300, 317
Bull, V., 96
Buller, D. J., 326
Bunch, S., 428
Burger, J. M., 111
Burggraf, K., 205, 230
Burkhardt, R. I., 438
Burleson, B. R., 291, 292
Burns, H. J., 479
Burns, J. M., 274
Burnstein, E., 273, 325, 362
Busath, G. L., 364
Busby, L. J., 406

Busceme, S., 236
Busey, T. A., 482
Bush sought 'way' to invade Iraq, 271
Bushman, B. J., 40, 359, 360, 364, 369, 370
Buss, A. H., 126, 147
Buss, D. M., 42, 293, 305, 324, 353, 355, 393
Buston, P. M., 307
Buunk, B. P., 138, 300, 314, 315
Bybee, J. A., 128
Byrne, C. A., 96
Byrne, D., 291
Byrne, S., 29

C

Cacioppo, J. T., 155, 179, 185, 186, 187, 188, 200, 202, 218, 452, 462
Cafri, G., 230, 232
Cairns, R. B., 359
Calder, B. J., 131
Caldwell, M., 121
Calvert, J. D., 297
Camille, N., 73
Camino, L., 367
Campbell, A., 307
Campbell, D. T., 37
Campbell, E. Q., 414
Campbell, J. D., 219, 232
Campbell, L., 310, 311
Canary, D. J., 315
Cannon, W. B., 448, 461
Cantor, J., 336
Cantril, H., 218, 220
Caporael, L. R., 326
Caputo, C., 107
Carey, K. B., 436, 456
Carey, M. P., 456
Carli, L. L., 275, 410
Carlier, I. V. E., 431
Carlsmith, J. M., 39, 45, 164, 165, 360, 372
Carlsmith, K. M., 493
Carlson, M., 335, 336
Carnevale, P. J., 282
Carpenter, S., 121, 478
Carr, J. L., 32
Carr, T. S., 357
Carroll, J. R., 190
Carroll, J. S., 291
Carron, A. V., 258
Cartwright, D., 13, 253, 254
Carvallo, M., 75
Carver, C. S., 109, 123, 124, 139, 460
Caselman, T., 380
Caspi, A., 291
Cate, R. M., 317
Cervone, D., 457
Chabris, C. F., 478
Chachere, J. G., 366

Chaiken, S., 48, 129, 153, 179, 185, 186, 188, 189, 191, 198, 200, 202, 467
Chammah, A. M., 277
Chan, D. K.-S., 290
Chang, C., 263
Chang, S., 269
Charlin, V., 335
Charman, S. D., 481, 482
Charng, H., 332
Chassin, L., 196
Check, J. V., 370
Chemers, M. M., 273, 275
Chen, J., 32, 48, 263
Chen, M., 60
Chen, N. Y., 297
Chen, S., 48, 56, 188
Cheng, G. H.-L., 290
Cheng, P. W., 76, 77
Cherek, D. R., 357
Cheung, F. M., 93
Chiles, C., 233
Chiu, C., 92, 93, 104, 105, 107
Choi, H.-S., 216, 303
Choi, I., 103, 106, 107
Choi, S., 236
Choi, S. C., 235
Christen, S., 260
Christensen, L., 45
Christensen, P. N., 434
Christie, S. D., 97
Chung, L., 301
Cialdini, R. B., 155, 195, 215, 220, 222, 237, 238, 239, 331, 336, 398, 434, 435
Cihangir, S., 266
Cioffi, D., 457
Citera, M., 282
Clancy, S. A., 487
Clark, K., 389
Clark, M., 389
Clark, M. S., 168, 315, 335, 343
Clark, R., 450
Clark, R. D., III., 327, 341
Clark, S. E., 481
Clark, V. R., 450
Clary, E. G., 344, 346
Clayton, L. D., 491
Clayton, N. S., 118
Clayton, S., 495
Cleveland, M. J., 450
Cline, V. B., 368
Clore, G. L., 191
Coady, N. P., 343
Coats, E., 344
Cochrane, S., 233
Cody, J., 294
Coffman, T. L., 400
Cohen, A. R., 150
Cohen, D., 356
Cohen, G. L., 138
Cohen, J., 152
Cohen, M. A., 359
Cohen, R., 217
Cohen, S., 452, 462, 463
Cohen-Ketteinis, P. T., 357
Cohn, L. D., 230
Coie, J. D., 357

Coke, J. S., 346
Colangelo, A., 139
Colbert, A. E., 274
Colcombe, S. J., 56, 112
Colder, M., 464
Cole, S. G., 235
Coleman, J., 73
Colligan, M. J., 218, 219
Collins, B. E., 244, 245
Collins, M. E., 418, 419
Collins, N. L., 308, 310, 311
Comstock, G., 368
Conner, M., 200
Conolley, E. S., 232
Conway, L. G., III, 246
Cook, D., 402
Cook, J. M., 291
Cook, S. W., 316, 418, 419, 423
Cooke, R., 200
Cooley, C. H., 139
Cooper, C., 258
Cooper, H. M., 359
Cooper, J., 159, 410
Cooper, R., 423
Cope, J. G., 434
Corcoran, D. M., 343
Corpus, J. H., 130
Correll, J., 53, 54
Cosmides, L., 324, 325
Costa, P. T., Jr., 450
Cottrell, N. B., 261
Courage, M. L., 118
Courrier, S., 368
Cousins, S. D., 93
Crain, A. L., 162
Crandall, C. S., 76, 128, 230, 232, 325, 404, 410
Crocker, J., 344, 390, 406
Croft, R. G., 368
Crogan, M., 420
Cropper, C. M., 177
Crosby, F., 416
Cross, S. E., 121, 122, 147
Crott, H. W., 273
Crowley, A. E., 185
Crowley, M., 332
Croyle, R. T., 152
Crutchfield, R. A., 224
Csapo, B., 332
Csikszentmihalyi, M., 123
Cunningham, J. D., 97
Cunningham, M. R., 294, 296
Curtis, R. C., 293
Cusumano, D. L., 230
Cutler, B., 482
Cutler, B. L., 488

D

D'Alessio, D., 372
Dabbs, J. M., 40
Dabbs, J. M., Jr., 357
Dalal, R., 106, 107
Dalbert, C., 110, 113
Dallek, R., 142
Daly, M., 353, 354

NAME INDEX

Damiani, M., 459
Damon, W., 119
Dan, E. S., 136
Danielsen, E. M., 488
Darley, J., 254, 392
Darley, J. M., 26, 34, 39, 40, 41, 45, 138, 246, 338, 339, 340, 341, 342, 344, 493
Darwin, C. R., 42, 86
Das, E., 364
Davidson, A. J., 32
Davidson, A. R., 199
Davidson, L., 121
Davidson, R., 357
Davidson, R. J., 88
Davies, C., 474
Davis, C. G., 73, 461
Davis, D. D., 265
Davis, K. E., 96, 169, 311, 376
Davis, L., 487
Davis, N. L., 312
Davitz, J., 380
Dawes, R. M., 433
Dawkins, R., 324
De Bono, K. G., 180, 192
De Cremer, D. C., 275
De Dreu, C. K. W., 138, 236
De Gregorio, E., 109
de Groot, D., 263
De Hart, T., 75
De Houwer, J., 180
De Longis, A., 461
De Marco, P., 83
De Metsenaere, M., 459
de Schonen, S., 478
De Vinney, L. C., 184
De Vries, N. K., 236
De Waal, F. B. M., 325, 331, 355
de Wit, J. B. F., 191
De Witt–Rickards, T. S., 481
Dean, K. E., 371
Deaux, K., 122, 357, 393, 406
Deci, E. L., 130, 131
Deffenbacher, K. A., 477
Dekker, G. B., 436, 437
Dembo, T., 361
Dennett, D. C., 7
DePaulo, B., 486
DePaulo, B. M., 95, 483, 485
Deppe, R. K., 142, 143
Depret, E., 392
Derzon, J. H., 201, 359
Desforges, D. M., 100
Deshpande, S. P., 157
Desmond, E. W., 359
Desportes, J. P., 254
Deuser, W., 360
Deutsch, M., 215, 221, 222, 276, 278, 279, 281, 418, 419, 423
Devine, D. J., 258, 491
Devine, P. G., 182, 402, 403, 481
Di Candia, C., 395
Di Matteo, M. R., 89
Dickerson, C., 19, 437, 439
Diekman, A. B., 257
Diener, E., 124, 264, 440, 441, 442
Dietz, P. D., 29
Dietz, T., 438

Dijksterhuis, A., 48, 56, 67, 203, 204, 214
Dill, K. E., 367
Dinges, D. F., 487
Dion, K., 93, 297
Dion, K. L., 258, 288, 303, 304, 310
Dion, K. K., 288, 303, 304, 310
Dix, T., 105
Dobbs, A. R., 355, 360
Dodge, K. A., 357
Doi, T., 303
Dollard, J., 361, 374, 412
Domina, T., 438
Donat, P. L. N., 370
Donnerstein, E., 371, 379
Donnerstein, M., 379
Donohue, W. A., 196
Doob, L., 361, 374
Dougherty, D. M., 357
Douglas, J. M., 32
Douthitt, E. A., 259
Dovidio, J., 395
Dovidio, J. F., 182, 324, 327, 400, 414, 421
Downing, R. L., 264
Drabman, R., 369
Draper, R., 15
Drigotas, S. M., 317
Driskell, J. E., 269
Driver, R., 138
Driving while black, 72
Druen, P. B., 294
Drummond, T., 73
Duberman, L., 121
Dublin, C. C., 365
Duck, J., 399
Duck, S. W., 292, 293, 316
Duncan, B., 375
Dunford, B. B., 491
Dunn, D. S., 128
Dunn, E. W., 123
Dunning, D., 483
Durantini, M. R., 467
Durik, A. M., 130
Dutton, D. G., 135
Duval, T. S., 109, 123
Dweck, C. S., 92, 93, 136, 460
Dysart, J., 481

E

Eagly, A. H., 48, 93, 179, 185, 186, 198, 257, 263, 275, 276, 297, 298, 299, 326, 332, 358, 393
Eargle, A., 380
Earl, A. N., 467
Ebbesen, E., 375
Eberhardt, N. L., 485
Eccles, J., 394
Eccles, J. S., 59
Edison, S. C., 118
Educators for Social Responsibility, 380
Edwards, K., 153
Eggleston, T. J., 151

Ehlers, A., 431
Ehrlinger, J., 5
Eibl-Eibesfeldt, I., 87, 354
Eich, E., 487
Eisen, M., 118, 119
Eisenberg, N., 327, 332
Eisenstadt, D., 161, 421
Eisenstat, S. A., 359
Ekman, P., 86, 87, 88, 89
Elfenbein, H. A., 87
Ellin, A., 230
Elliot, A. J., 130
Elliot, J., 396
Ellsworth, P. C., 45, 95, 475, 481, 491, 493
Elsbach, K. D., 27
Emery, N. J., 118
Emlem, S. T., 307
Emsweiler, T., 393
Engstler-Schooler, T. Y., 483
Epley, E., 45
Epley, N., 92
Epstude, K., 138
Erber, R., 267
Erikson, G. A., 479
Eron, L. D., 19, 32, 366
Eshleman, A., 404
Eskenazi, J., 203
Esser, J. K., 269
Estrada-Hollenbeck, M., 335
Evans, B. E., 29
Evans, N., 400

F

Fabes, R. A., 327
Fabrigar, L. R., 188, 192
Fabrizio, B., 261
Fadiga, L., 84
Fairey, P. J., 232
False confessions, 490
Farhi, P., 265
Fazio, R. H., 180, 182, 197, 198
Feeney, B. C., 308, 310, 311
Feeney, J. A., 309, 310, 311
Feeney, M., 98
Fehr, B., 301, 311
Feick, D. L., 144
Fein, S., 102, 128, 142, 360
Feingold, A., 293, 297, 298, 299, 305
Feinstein, J., 188
Feld, S. L., 255
Feldman, N. S., 111
Feldman-Summers, S., 393
Fell, J. C., 493
Femlee, D. H., 316, 317
Fenigstein, A., 126, 147
Ferguson, M. J., 52
Fernald, J. L., 395
Ferris, T., 149
Feshbach, N. D., 380, 381
Feshbach, S., 191, 380
Festinger, L., 137, 150
Festinger, L., 27, 185, 226, 289
Fiedler, F., 97, 273, 274, 405

Field, P., 269
Figurski, T. J., 123
Finch, J. F., 119
Fincham, F. D., 96
Fine, G. A., 27
Finlay, K. A., 200
Finney, P. D., 45
Firestone, I., 166
Fischer, E. F., 302, 304
Fischer, G. W., 398
Fischhoff, B., 81
Fishbein, M., 179, 198, 200, 232
Fisher, R. P., 486
Fiske, S., 416
Fiske, S. T., 17, 92, 99, 101, 180, 392
Fitzsimons, G. J., 128
Flanagan, C. A., 332
Flanary, R., 316
Flaton, R., 489
Flay, B., 195
Fletcher, B., 137
Fletcher, G. J. O., 96, 105, 311
Flowers, M. L., 270
Flykt, A., 136
Foerster, J., 92
Fogassi, L., 84
Folkes, V. S., 379
Folkman, S., 449, 452, 454, 461
Fong, G. T., 76, 77, 359
Ford, M. B., 310
Forer, B. R., 65
Forgas, J. P., 191
Förster, J., 37, 56
Forsterling, F., 97
Forsyth, D. R., 253
Foster, J., 395
Fountain, J. W., 388
Fouts, G., 205, 230
Frady, R. L., 357
Frager, R., 234
Fraley, R. C., 308, 311
Frank, R. H., 442
Franzini, L. R., 232
Frazier, P. A., 316
Frederick, S., 66
Fredrickson, B. L., 230, 478
Freedman, J. L., 165, 372, 434
Freeman, J., 493
Freud, S., 276, 353, 374
Fried, C., 19, 162, 438
Fried, C. B., 409
Friedman, L., 406
Friedman, M., 308
Friedman, T., 170
Friesen, W. V., 86, 88, 89
Fritz, H. L., 454
Frodi, A., 364
Frohlich, P. F., 135
Fukuyama, F., 453
Fulero, S. M., 481
Fuller, V. A., 72
Fultz, J., 336
Furnham, A., 112, 113, 205, 410

G

Gabriel, S., 121
Gaertner, S. L., 182, 327, 414, 421
Galati, D., 87
Gallese, V., 84
Galley, D. J., 204
Gallup, G. G., Jr., 118
Gangestad, S. W., 305, 307
Gao, G., 302, 303, 304
Garcia, S. M., 342
Garcia-Marques, L., 405
Gardner, W., 381
Gardner, W. L., 121, 254
Garfinkle, H., 226
Garstka, T. A., 73
Gartner, R., 364, 373, 377, 493, 495
Gaunt, R., 95, 107
Gavanski, I., 73, 128
Gawronski, B., 99, 182
Geen, R. G., 258, 260, 353, 359, 366, 375
Geiselman, R. E., 486
Geller, E. S., 432
Gelles, R., 372
Gelles, R. J., 365
Gemmill, G., 413
Gentile, D. A. 367, 369
Gentile, J. R., 367
George, J. M., 255
Gerard, H. B., 16, 159, 232
Gerard, H. G., 215, 221, 222
Gerbner, G., 367, 369
Gerdes, E. P., 45
Gergen, K. J., 264
Gergen, M. M., 264
Gerhardt, M. W., 273
Gerin, W., 448
Gerrard, M., 450
Gersons, B. P. R., 431
Gervey, B. M., 93
Geyer, A. L., 235
Ghiselin, M. T., 59
Gibbons, F. X., 124, 138, 151, 450
Gibbs, N., 382
Giesen, H., 423
Giesler, R. B., 138
Gifford, R., 84
Gifford, R. K., 405
Gilbert, D., 6
Gilbert, D. T., 7, 96, 97, 99, 100, 101, 102, 138, 140, 204, 209
Gilbert, G. M., 400
Gilbert, M., 84
Gilbert, S. J., 246
Gilligan, J., 382
Gillis, R., 109
Gilovich, T., 5, 19, 48, 63, 66, 73, 78, 150, 260, 405
Gil-Rivas, V., 448
Gingras, I., 130
Girgus, J. S., 460
Gladue, B. A., 357
Gladwell, M., 392
Glass, D. C., 376
Glick, P., 416

Goethals, G. R., 138
Goffman, E., 109, 142
Gold, J. A., 135, 293
Goldberg, J., 457
Goldberg, P., 105, 390
Goldman, R., 187
Goldstein, J. H., 375
Goldstein, N. J., 215
Goleman, D., 152
Gollwitzer, P., 152
Gonzalez, A., 418, 420
Gonzalez, M. H., 45
Good, C., 409
Goode, E., 287, 288, 358
Goodheart, F. W., 216
Goodwin, R., 303
Goore, N., 260
Gopaul-McNicol, S. A. A., 390
Gordon, L. J., 143
Gossett, J. L., 29
Gottheil, E., 463
Gralinski, J. H., 394
Gramzow, R. H., 75
Granberg, D., 180, 234
Grant, P. R., 410
Gray, J. J., 205, 228, 229
Gray, S., 212
Gray, T. W., 438
Graziano, W. G., 119, 294, 297
Greenberg, J., 109, 124, 143, 401
Greene, D., 48, 131
Greenfield, B. S., 76
Greenfield, L. A. 359
Greenholtz, J., 41
Greenwald, A. G., 150, 180, 182, 203, 402
Griffin, A., 196
Griffin, D., 63
Griffin, D. W., 13, 75, 392, 452
Griffin, E., 290
Groom, R. W., 360
Gross, L., 369
Grossnickle, W. F., 434
Grote, N. K., 343
Groves, R. M., 31
Gruber, A. J., 231
Gruenewald, P. J., 493
Guagnano, G. A., 438
Gudykunst, W. B., 42, 89, 304
Guerin, B., 258
Guerra, N., 380
Guichard, A. C., 310
Guimond, S., 233
Guisinger, S., 235
Gully, S. M., 258
Gunter, B., 410
Gustafson, R., 362
Gyekye, S. A., 111

H

Hafer, C. L., 110
Hagestad, G. O., 317
Haidt, J., 87, 88, 440
Halberstadt, J. B., 128, 296
Hall, C., 335

Hall, E. T., 89
Hall, J. A., 84, 85, 89
Hall, V. C., 131
Hallinan, M. T., 292, 293
Ham, J. J., 108
Hamilton, D. L., 93, 405, 406
Hamilton, V. L., 244
Hamilton, W. D., 324
Hammock, G., 381
Hammond, J. R., 311
Hampton, M. C., 230
Han, S., 193
Haney, C., 256
Hankin, B. L., 111
Hannon, P., 312
Hansen, C. H., 86
Hansen, E. M., 107
Hansen, R. D., 86
Hanson, M., 346
Hansson, R. O., 343
Hanusa, B. H., 455
Harackiewicz, J. M., 130, 131, 142
Harbener, E. S., 291
Harber, K., 60, 61
Harder, J., 409
Hardin, C. D., 139, 143, 279, 433
Hare, A. P., 255
Hare, B., 84
Hargreaves, D. J., 335
Hargrove, M. F., 357
Haritos-Fatouros, M., 246
Harland, P., 437
Harless, D. W., 265
Harley, E., 476, 477
Harmon-Jones, E., 402
Harries, K. D., 360
Harrigan, J. A., 87
Harris, C. R., 67
Harris, J. A., 179
Harris, M. B., 61, 335, 362
Harris, V. A., 100, 102
Harrison, J. A., 40
Harrop, J., 372
Hart, A. J., 489
Hart, D., 119
Harter, S., 119
Hartke, D. D., 275
Hartstone, M., 399
Hartup, W. W., 288, 308, 315
Harvey, J. H., 316
Harwood, R. L., 333
Hashimoto, T., 288
Hashtroudi, S., 480
Hassin, R. R., 67
Hastie, R., 325, 488, 489, 490, 491, 492
Hastorf, A. H., 95
Hatfield, E., 84, 218, 288, 301, 302, 304, 305, 307, 314
Haugen, J. A., 344
Haugtvedt, C. P., 189
Hawkins, R., 493
Hays, C. J., 266
Hazan, C., 308, 310, 311
Heatherton, T. F., 335
Heavey, C. L., 371
Hebl, M., 395
Hecht, M. A., 89

Heckhausen, J., 456
Hedge, A., 336
Hedges, L. V., 58
Heider, F., 84, 95, 96, 99, 100, 101
Heiman, R. J., 213, 287
Heine, S. J., 41
Heingartner, A., 259.260
Helgeson, V. S., 138, 316, 317, 454, 462
Helgeson, V. S., 462
Helmreich, R., 161
Henderlong, J., 130, 131
Henderson-King, E., 402
Henley, N. M., 84, 89
Henne, J., 359
Henneberg, M. A., 359
Henry, R. A., 266
Henson, M., 226
Herman, E. M., 259, 260
Hernstein, R. J., 358
Hersch, S. M., 256
Hetherington, T. F., 140
Heunemann, R. L., 230
Heusel, C., 357
Hewstone, M., 97
Higgins, E. T., 56, 57, 139, 140, 216, 467
Higgins, R. L., 109
Hilgard, E. R., 372
Hill, C. T., 300, 317
Hill, J., 138
Hill, K., 294
Hilton, D. J., 97
Hilton, J. L., 102
Hinkle, S., 99
Hirt, E. R., 75, 130, 142, 143, 144, 479
Hixon, J. G., 102
Hoberman, H., 463
Hochstadt, S., 337
Hodes, R. M., 478
Hodge, C. N., 93
Hodges, B. H., 235
Hodges, S. D., 128
Hodson, R., 27
Hoffman, C., 93, 128
Hoffman, E. L., 216
Hoffman, M. L., 325
Hofstede, G., 213, 287
Hogg, M., 399
Hogg, M. A., 226, 233, 258, 398
Holahan, C. J., 461
Holden, G., 456
Holder, H. D., 493
Hollander, E. P., 233, 273
Hollingshead, A. B., 267
Holman, E. A., 448
Holmes, T. H., 450
Holtz, R., 258
Homans, G. C., 237, 299, 300, 312
Hong, G. Y., 170
Hong, Y., 92, 93, 104, 105, 107, 278
Hoog, N., 191
Hoose, P. M., 392
Hopper, C. H., 357
Hornsey, M. J., 226
Horton, R., 369

NAME INDEX

Horvitz, T., 279
House, J., 31
House, J. S., 463
Houston, C. E., 48, 200, 209, 487
Hovland, C. I., 184
Howard, J. A., 293
Howe, M. L., 118
Hoyer, W. D., 185
Hsu, S. S., 338
Huesmann, L. R., 366
Huff, C., 45
Huffman, K. P., 434
Huffman, K. T., 434
Hull, J. G., 123
Humphrey, J. A., 370
Hunt, G. T., 356
Hunter, J. E., 93
Hunter, S. B., 261
Huntsinger, J., 139
Hurin, S., 438
Hurley, D., 40, 266
Hutchinson, R. R., 359
Hwang, J., 232
Hyde, J. S., 111, 122
Hyman, D. B., 128
Hyman, J. J., 414

I

Ilies, R., 273, 274
Im, C., 453
Impett, E. A., 312
Inglehart, M. R., 448, 40, 452
Inglehart, R., 440
Inkster, J., 154
Insko, C. A., 224, 277, 279
Inzlicht, M., 409
Irving, L. M., 460
Isen, A. M., 334, 335
Isenberg, D. J., 272
Ivins, B., 260
Iyengar, S. S., 130
Izard, C. E., 86, 87

J

Jaccard, J. J., 199
Jacklin, C. N., 357
Jackson, J. M., 263
Jackson, J. S., 450, 452
Jackson, J. W., 411
Jackson, L. A., 93, 227
Jacobs, J., 394
Jacobs, P., 412
Jacobson, J. W., 72
Jacobson, L., 60, 61
Jain, S. P., 185
James, C., 84
James, L. M., 221
Jamieson, D. W., 416
Jang, K. L., 179
Janicki, D., 462
Janis, I. L., 184, 185, 191, 267, 268, 269
Jankowiak, W. R., 302, 304

Janoff-Bulman, R., 333, 419
Jarcho, J. M., 107
Jarvis, B., 188
Jasnoski, M. L., 346
Jaspars, J., 97
Jecker, J., 48, 168
Jemmott, J. B., III., 152
Jensen-Campbell, L. A., 119, 294
Jetten, J., 226
Johannesen-Schmidt, M. C., 257, 275
Johns, M., 409
Johnson, B. T., 200
Johnson, C., 27, 406
Johnson, D. J., 317
Johnson, D. R., 93
Johnson, D. W., 423
Johnson, K. J., 478
Johnson, L. B., 171
Johnson, M. K., 480, 487
Johnson, R. D., 264
Johnson, R. T., 423
Johnson, T. E., 363
Jonas, M., 454
Jones, C., 410
Jones, C. R., 57
Jones, D., 294
Jones, E. E., 96, 99, 100, 102, 107, 108, 142, 169, 376, 392, 398, 416
Jones, G., 428
Jones, M., 221
Jonsson, B., 332
Jordan, M., 144, 221
Joseph, L., 260
Josephson, W. D., 367
Joule, R., 170
Jouriles, E., 123
Jovanovic, J., 59
Jowett, G. S., 236, 237
Judd, C. M., 24
Judge, T. A., 273, 274
Judson, F. N., 32
Jurgena, M., 260
Jürgen-Lohmann, J., 423
Jussim, L., 59, 60, 61

K

Kagitcibasi, C., 235
Kahn, M., 376
Kahneman, D., 63, 66, 73, 78, 441, 442
Kaiser, S., 86
Kallgren, C. A., 198, 222, 237, 238, 239, 434, 435
Kalton, G., 31
Kalven, H., Jr., 488, 491
Kamarack, T., 463
Kambara, A., 228
Kameda, T., 325
Kandel, D. B., 196
Kappas, A., 86
Karau, S. J., 262, 263, 275, 276
Kardes, F. R., 75
Karlins, M., 400, 401

Karney, B. R., 96
Kashima, E. S., 106
Kashima, Y., 106
Kashy, D. A., 310
Kassarjian, H., 152
Katz, D., 180, 400
Kauffman, D. R., 142
Kawakami, K., 182
Keating, J. P., 180
Keefe, R. C., 305
Keelan, J. P. R., 310
Keicolt-Glaser, J. K., 462
Kelley, H. H., 55, 84, 96, 97, 108, 184, 215, 221, 276, 277, 299, 300, 327, 495
Kelly, B. R., 365
Kelly, E., 228
Keltner, D., 87, 88
Kenny, D. A., 293
Kenrick, D. T., 305, 360, 361, 393
Kent, M. V., 259
Keough, K., 467
Kerckhoff, A. C., 219
Kerr, N. L., 253, 265
Key, C. W., 364
Key, W. B., 203
Khanna, R., 332
Kidd, R. F., 260
Kiesler, C. A., 214
Kiesler, S. B., 214, 393
Kihlstrom, J. F., 487
Killen, J. D., 196, 230
Killian, L. M., 218
Kim, H., 213, 287
Kim, M. P., 92
Kim, S. H., 97
Kim, U., 235
Kim, Y., 297, 298
Kimble, C. E., 107, 142
Kimel, E., 130
Kim-Prieto, C., 106, 107
Kinder, D. R., 180
Kirkpatrick, L. A., 311
Kitayama, S., 104, 105, 106, 107, 112, 119, 121, 127, 213, 234, 278, 287, 325
Kivimaki, M., 315
Klenke, K., 273
Klentz, B., 124, 344
Klingemann, H., 440
Kloner, R. A., 448
Kluger, R., 178
Knapp, M., 84, 85
Knight, J., 485
Knight, S. J., 201
Knobe, J., 107, 108
Knopke, H., 414
Knowles, E. D., 107
Knowles, E. S., 142
Knox, R., 154
Knussen, C., 438
Koch, K., 438
Koehler, J. J., 66
Koehnken, G., 474
Koenig, A. M., 257
Koestner, R., 130, 138
Kogan, N., 272
Kok, G., 191

Kolbert, E., 427
Kollack, P., 315
Konecni, V., 375
Koomen, W., 56, 67, 93
Kopelman, S., 277, 433
Korda, M., 279
Kovera, M. B., 488
Kozak, M., 74
Krackow, E., 491
Kraemer, H. C., 463
Kraft, D., 128
Krakow, A., 244
Krauss, R. M., 279, 281, 434
Kremer, J. F., 363
Kressel, K., 282
Krosnick, J. A., 185
Krueger, J., 108
Kruger, A. B., 441
Kruger, K., 92
Krull, D. S., 102, 106, 107
Kubitschek, W. N., 292, 293
Kudoh, T., 88
Kuhl, J., 56
Kuhn, D., 489
Kulik, J. A., 362
Kunda, Z., 346, 392, 406
Kuo, Z. Y., 354
Kurdek, L. A., 314
Kuriloff, P. J., 111
Kuykendall, D., 180
Kuyper, H., 138

L

La Croix, J., 282
La Fleur, S. J., 128
La France, M., 89, 122, 357, 393, 406
La Voie, L., 293
Laitman, L., 216
Lake, E. A., 143
Lalancette, M. F., 235
Lamp, E. J., 203
Lampert, R., 448
Lamy, D., 478
Landau, S., 412
Landy, D., 48, 168
Lang, A. R., 111
Langer, E. J., 18, 71, 454, 455
Langlois, J. H., 295, 296, 298, 299
Larrick, R. P., 128, 360
Larsen, K. S., 235
Larsen, R. J., 305
Larson, C., 357
Laser, P. S., 126
Lassiter, D., 486
Lassiter, G. D., 95
Latané, B., 26, 34, 39, 40, 41, 45, 233, 338, 340, 341, 344
Lau, I., 93
Lau, R. R., 109
Laughlin, P. R., 266
Laursen, B., 308, 315
Lawler, E. J., 327
Lazarsfeld, P., 417
Lazarus, R. S., 452, 461

Le Bon, G., 218
Le Page, A., 363
Le, B., 300, 312
Lea, M., 263
Leary, M. R., 119, 140, 142, 221, 254, 288, 440
Leck, K., 236
Lederman, L. C., 216
Lee, A. Y., 290, 323
Lee, E., 265
Lee, F. A., 448
Lee, Y., 111
Lefkowitz, M. M., 366
Legant, P., 107
Leggatt, H. K., 333
Lehman, D. R., 41, 73, 76, 77, 461
Leippe, M. R., 161, 421
Leishman, K., 152
Lemaine, J. M., 254
Lempert, R. O., 76
Leonard, K. E., 359
Leone, D. R., 204
Leor, J., 448
Lepper, M. R., 48, 75, 130, 131
Leppin, A., 463
Lerner, M. J., 110, 111, 410
Leung, K., 41, 111, 333
Leventhal, H., 190
Levett, L. M., 488
Levin, D. T., 478
Levin, P. A., 334
Levin, S., 417
Levine, G. L., 128
Levine, J. A., 485
Levine, J. M., 216, 221, 226, 233, 236, 253, 254, 258, 276, 433
Levine, R., 288, 304
Levine, R. V., 333, 334, 337
Levy, B., 166
Levy, D. A., 218, 222
Levy, J. S., 276
Lévy-Leboyer, C., 19
Lewin, K., 4, 40, 41, 254, 361, 429, 430, 438
Lewis, B. P., 331
Lewis, C. C., 132
Lewis, L., 393
Lewis, M., 118
Leyens, J., 364
Leyens, J. P., 367
Liberman, A., 191
Liberman, N., 56
Liberman, V., 12, 278
Lichtenstein, S., 81
Lichtman, R. R., 138, 453, 453
Lieberman, M. D., 107
Liebert, R. M., 48, 200, 366
Liebrand, W. B. G., 278
Lilienfeld, S. O., 491
Lim, T.-S., 303
Lin, D. Y., 109
Lin, S., 75
Lin, Y. H. W., 312, 314
Linder, D., 7
Lindoerfer, J. S., 269
Lindsay, D. S., 480
Lindsay, J. J., 346
Lindsay, R. C. L., 475, 481, 482

Lindsey, S., 128, 182
Linford, K., 108
Linville, P. W., 398, 459, 460
Linz, D. G., 371
Lipkus, I. M., 110
Lippincott, E., 369
Lippmann, W., 391
Lipsey, M. W., 201, 359
Lishner, D. A., 345
Lisle, D. J., 128
Litt, M. D.
Little, A. C., 297
Livesley, W. J., 119
Lloyd, B., 397
Lloyd, S. A., 317
Lock, T., 491
Locken, B., 230
Lockwood, P., 138
Lodish, L. M., 48, 200
Loftus, E., 491
Loftus, E. F., 475, 477, 479, 482
Loftus, G. R., 477, 482
Longo, L. C., 93, 297, 298
Lonner, W., 41
Lord, C. G., 75, 77, 100, 409
Lore, R. K., 355
Lott, A. J., 299
Lott, B. E., 299
Lottes, I., 111
Lourie, R. S., 365
Lovaglia, M. J., 142
Lowery, B. S., 139
Lucas, J. W., 142
Luce, C., 331
Ludwig, T. D., 438
Luhtanen, R., 344
Lumsdaine, A. A., 185
Lundgren, S., 236
Lundgren, S. R., 294
Luus, C. A. E., 97, 481
Lykken, D., 440
Lynn, M., 293
Lynn, S. J., 491
Lysak, H., 355
Lyubomirsky, S., 335, 441

M

Maass, A., 235
Maccoby, E. E., 357
Maccoby, N., 185, 196
MacCoun, R. J., 491
MacDonald, T. K., 359
MacFarlane, S. W., 360, 361
MacKenzie, J., 438
Mackie, D. M., 189, 405
Mackin, R. S., 450
Maddux, J. E., 457
Madey, S. F., 73
Madon, S., 61
Madson, L., 121
Magaro, P. A., 255
Magoo, G., 332
Maier, N. R. F., 266
Maier, R. A., 291
Mainieri, T., 438

Maio, G. R., 180, 194
Majkut, L., 226
Major, B., 75, 344, 390
Mak, T., 205
Makhijani, M. G., 93, 275, 297, 298
Malamuth, N., M., 33, 370, 371
Malle, B. F., 107, 108
Malloy, T. E., 76
Malone, P. S., 99, 100, 101
Malpass, R. S., 474, 481
Manderlink, G., 131
Maner, J. K., 331
Mann, J. A., 421
Mannix, L., 395
Marecek, J., 107
Marino, L., 118
Marion, R., 64
Markey, P. M., 342
Markman, K. D., 75
Markoff, J., 274
Markus, H. R., 17, 53, 64, 92, 104, 105, 112, 119, 121, 213, 234, 235, 278, 287, 298
Marques, J., 255
Marques, J. M., 226
Marsh, K. L., 74
Martens, A., 409
Martin, C. D., 467
Martin, J., 448
Martin, L. L., 56
Martin, N. G., 179
Martinez, T. S., 337
Martz, J. M., 300, 314
Maruyama, G., 390
Marx, D. M. 409
Mashek, D. J., 288
Masser, B., 111
Masuda, T., 106, 107
Mathewson, G. C., 16, 159
Matsumoto, D., 87, 88
Matsumoto, H., 112
Matz, D. C., 434
Mauro, R., 475, 485, 491, 493
May, K. A., 296
May, S. T., 273
Mayer, J. D., 335
Mbabazi, G., 355
McAlister, A., 196
McAllister, H. A., 109
McAndrew, F. T., 324
McArthur, L. Z., 86, 97, 294, 406
McAuliffe, B. J., 226
McCabe, M. P., 231, 232
McCarthy, J. F., 365
McCaul, K. D., 357
McCauley, C., 270
McClellan, S., 15
McConahay, J. B., 414, 416, 423
McConnell, A. R., 75
McCrea, S. M., 144
McCroskey, J. C., 89
McDaniel, P., 358, 364
McDonald, H. E., 130, 479
McFadyen-Ketchum, S. A., 357
McGhee, D. E., 182
McGlone, M., 409
McGraw, A. P., 73

McGuire, A. M., 332
McGuire, C., 269
McGuire, W. J., 194
McHugo, G. J., 86
McIntosh, D. N., 448
McIntyre, R. B., 409
McKearney, S. J., 244
McKimmie, B. M., 226
McKinnon, J. R., 395
McNally, R. J., 431, 487
McNamara, R. S., 14, 171
McPherson, C. A., 448
McPherson, J. M., 254
McPherson, M., 291
McQuirk, B., 344
Meade, R. D., 234
Medvec, V. H., 48, 73
Meertens, R. W., 416
Meeus, W. H. J., 244
Mehta, M. D., 29
Meissner, C. A., 481
Melara, R. D., 481
Mellers, B. A., 73, 488
Melton, J. R., 130
Mendelson, G. A., 107
Mendes, W. B., 261
Menec, V. H., 459
Menninger, W., 374
Menon, T., 93, 104
Merbaum, M., 457
Mermelstein, R., 463
Messick, D., 278
Messick, D. M., 277, 433
Messo, J., 477
Meston, C. M., 135
Metcalfe, J., 75
Metzner, H. L., 463
Meyer, P., 324
Meyerowitz, B. E., 467
Meyers, J. M., 48, 200, 209
Meyers, S. A., 301
Mezulis, A. H., 111
Miceli, R., 87
Mickelson, K. D., 138
Mickler, S., 219
Miene, P. K., 344
Migration and Geographic Mobility, 337
Mikulincer, M., 308, 32
Milgram, S., 48, 226, 234, 241, 242, 243, 246, 343
Mill, J. S., 66
Millar, M. C., 297
Miller, A. G., 96, 99, 241, 244, 246
Miller, C. T., 138
Miller, D., 19, 73, 437
Miller, D. T., 73, 102, 109, 110, 11, 221, 479
Miller, J., 155
Miller, J. G., 105, 106, 333
Miller, K., 293
Miller, L. S., 366
Miller, N., 335, 336, 358, 361, 374, 375, 413, 419
Miller, R. L., 138
Miller, R. S., 233
Mills, J., 157, 315, 343
Mills, J. S., 16, 158

Milton, K., 419
Minard, R. D., 414
Misconceptions, 495
Mishal, M., 99
Mishra, H., 379
Misovich, S. J., 100
Mitani, J. C., 355
Mitchell, B. W., 230
Miyamoto, Y., 106
Modigliani, A., 246
Moeller, F. G., 357
Moghaddam, F. M., 235, 333
Monteith, M., 402
Montemayor, R., 118, 119
Montepare, J. M., 294
Moore, J. S., 297
Moore, R. L., 304
Moore, T. E., 48
Moos, R. H., 461
Moray, N., 67
Moreland, R. L., 236, 253, 254, 255, 258, 267, 290, 433
Morgan, H. J., 311
Morgan, M., 316, 367, 369
Morgan, T. C., 276
Morris, E., 473
Morris, K. A., 138
Morris, M. L., 121, 122, 147
Morris, M. W., 93, 104, 105, 106, 107
Morris, W. N., 233
Morrow, G. D., 317
Morry, M. M., 230
Morse, D. R., 448
Moscovici, S., 224, 235, 236
Moshonov, J., 448
Mosimann, J. E., 205, 228, 229
Moskowitz, G. B., 342
Moskowitz, J. T., 449, 454
Mosley, N. R., 293
Mowrer, O. H., 361, 374
Moyer, K. E., 356, 357
Mucchi-Faina, A., 235
Muellerleile, P. A., 200
Mukai, H., 381
Mukai, T., 228, 229
Mullen, B., 27, 258, 264, 269, 398, 406
Muller, D., 261
Muller, M., 355
Muller, M. N., 355
Munier, C., 237
Muraven, M., 141
Murphy, L. R., 218
Murr, A., 141
Murrell, A. J., 421
Musham, C., 124
Musselman, L., 295
Mussweiler, T., 37, 75, 137, 138
Myers, D. G., 390, 404

N

Nail, P. R., 218, 222
Naimi, T., 466
Nasco, S. A., 74

Nathanson, S., 373
National Center for Health Statistics, 178, 316
National Center for Vital Statistics, 373
National Research Council, 485
National trends in risk behaviors, 466
Neiva, E., 299
Nel, E., 161
Nelligan, J. S., 310
Nelson, D., 291
Nelson, S., 93
Nemeth, C., 235, 236
Nemeth, C. J., 233
Nesse, R. M., 344, 463
Neuberg, S. L., 204, 331
Newcomb, T. M., 139, 291
Newman, L. S., 100, 105
Ng, Z., 92
Nichols, J. G., 394
Nicholson, N., 235
Nichter, M., 195
Nickel, S., 97
Nickerson, C., 442
Nida, S., 40
Niedenthal, P. M., 73, 127
NIMH Multisite HIV Prevention Trial Group, 467
Nisbett, R. E., 6, 13, 17, 41, 48, 63, 66, 69, 76, 77, 78, 99, 100, 103, 104, 106, 107, 108, 119, 126, 356, 402, 438, 481
Nishida, T., 89
Nixon, R. M., 171
Nolen-Hoeksema, S., 378, 460
Noll, S. M., 230
Noller, P., 309, 310, 311
Norasakkunkit, V., 112
Nordgren, L. F., 69
Norenzayan, A., 103, 106, 333, 334
Norman, C., 288
Norrell, R., 414
North, A. C., 335
Nosek, B. A., 182, 402
Nowak, A., 233
Nowell, A., 58

O

Obayashi, J., 107
O'Brien, T. P., 481
O'Connell, D. M., 87
O'Connor, K. M., 282
O'Donnell, V., 236, 237
Ofshe, R., 487
Ohbuchi, K., 379, 381
Ohno, T., 381
Oishi, S., 56, 112, 440
Oldersma, F. L., 138
O'Leary, A., 452
Oleson, K. C., 142, 406
Olivardia, R., 231
Olsen, N., 312
Olson, E. A., 481, 482

Olson, J. M., 74, 135, 142, 179, 180, 194, 221
Olson, M. A., 180, 182
Olsson, N., 482
Olweus, D., 373
Omoto, A. M., 346
Opotow, S., 495
Oppenheimer, D. M., 63
Orbell, J. M., 433
Orbuch, T. L., 316
Orne, F. C., 487
Orvis, B. R., 97
Osborne, R. E., 102
Oskamp, S., 432, 438
Osofsky, M. J., 247
Ostrom, T., 399
O'Sullivan, M., 87
Ouellette, J. A., 236
Ouwerkerk, J. W., 278
Owen, S., 73

P

Packer, J., 92
Pagano, F., 190
Page, R., 416
Paglieri, R. A., 72
Paik, H., 368
Paisley, C., 143
Pallier, C., 478
Paluck, E. L., 89
Panter, A. T., 48, 91
Papa, A., 449
Park, B., 399
Park, H., 106, 107
Park, N., 345
Park, S., 58
Parke, R. D., 367
Parker, J. F., 481
Parks, C. D., 278
Pashler, H., 67
Patnoe, S., 19, 420
Patterson, A., 374
Patton, P., 274
Paulson, R. M., 409
Paulus, P. B., 269
Pavlidis, I., 485
Payne, B. K., 53
Peake, P., 457
Pechmann, C., 201
Peck, J., 230
Pegalis, L. J., 168, 343
Pelham, B. W., 75, 102
Peng, K., 41, 106
Pennebaker, J. W., 75, 197, 218, 378, 432, 450, 464, 465
Penner, L. A., 324, 346
Pennington, N., 488, 489, 490, 491, 492
Penrod, S., 371
Penrod, S. D., 224, 477, 482, 491, 492
Pentti, J., 315
Peplau, L. A., 121, 288, 300, 312, 317
Perdue, L., 228, 230

Perkins, R., 61
Perlman, D., 288
Perlstein, L., 129
Perrett, D. I., 296, 297
Perretta, S., 483
Perrin, S., 235
Perry, C., 196
Perry, Z., 392
Peters, J. M., 452
Peters, L. H., 275
Peters, M. D., 180
Peterson, B., 228, 230
Peterson, C., 454, 458
Peterson, R. D., 373, 495
Peterson, R. S., 269
Petrie, K. J., 75
Pettigrew, T. F., 390, 407, 414, 415, 416, 417, 419
Pettit, G. S., 357
Petty, R. E., 179, 185, 186, 187, 188, 189, 190, 192, 200, 202, 336
Pezdek, K., 487
Pfeiffer, T., 75
Philbrick, K., 333, 334
Phillips, A. G., 123
Phillips, D. P., 368
Phillips, K. A., 231
Piccolo, R. F., 274
Pickett, C. L., 254, 258
Pietromonaco, P., 57, 203
Pike, C. L., 294, 296
Piliavin, I. M., 40, 327
Piliavin, J. A., 40, 324, 327, 332, 333, 346
Pincus, J. D., 203
Pincus, W., 271
Pinel, E. C., 408
Pinker, S., 324
Pittman, G., 292
Pittman, T. S., 142
Plant, E., 388
Plant, E. A., 402
Pohlmann, J. T., 275
Pool, G. J., 236
Poole, W. K., 448
Pope, H. G., Jr., 231
Porn in the USA, 23
Porter, J. R., 390
Posavac, S. S., 185, 405
Postmes, T., 264, 266
Poulin, M., 448
Powell, A. A., 329
Powledge, F., 214
Pratkanis, A. R., 203
Prentice, D. A., 221
Prentice-Dunn, S., 402
Presson, C. G., 196
Preston, E., 75
Preston, S. D., 331
Priester, J. R., 179, 188
Procter, E., 113
Pronin, E., 19, 109
Pruitt, D. G., 273, 276, 277, 281, 282
Pryce, J., 488
Puente, M., 177, 183
Pugh, M. A., 100

Purdham, T. S., 6
Purdon, S. E., 19
Purvis, D., 236
Putnam, K., 357
Putnam, R. D., 442, 453
Pyszczynski, T., 109, 143, 401

Q

Quanty, M., 375
Quattrone, G. A., 102, 398
Quillian, F., 487
Quinn, D., 390
Quinn, D. M., 48, 230, 408
Quinn, J. M., 195

R

Raaijmakers, Q. A. W., 244
Rahe, R. H., 450
Rajecki, D. W., 260
Ramirez, A., 99
Ramsay, D., 118
Ramsey, S. J., 89
Rapoport, A., 277
Raps, C. S., 454
Rapson, R. L., 218, 288, 301, 304, 307, 314
Rasinski, K., 416
Raye, C. L., 48
Raymond, P., 267
Reagan, R., 171
Rebelo, E., 438
Rector, M., 299
Redlawsk, D. P., 180
Reeder, G. D., 96
Regan, P. C., 293, 302, 305, 307
Reifman, A. S., 128, 360
Reis, E., 438
Reis, H. T., 24, 288, 289, 291, 295, 296, 297, 298
Reis, S. M., 58
Reiss, D., 118
Reiter, S. M., 434
Reitzes, D. C., 414
Rempel, J. K., 179
Renaud, J. M., 75
Renner, M. J., 450
Reno, R. R., 222, 237, 238, 239, 434, 435
Rensink, R. A., 478
Repetti, R. L., 452
Resko, G. B., 406
Revenson, T. A., 467
Rhodes, G., 294, 296
Rhodes, N., 185
Rhodewalt, F., 142, 144
Rholes, W. S., 57, 105, 308, 10, 311
Riad, J. K., 357
Ricciardelli, L. A., 231, 232
Rice, W. E., 195
Richardson, D., 45, 381
Richardson, D. R., 353, 355
Richeson, J. A., 52
Richmond, V. P., 89
Richter, C. P., 40
Ridge, R. D., 344, 364
Riecken, H. W., 27
Rieser-Danner, L. A., 295
Ringelmann, M., 262
Riordan, C. A., 419
Ritter, J. M., 295
Rittle, R., 261
Rizzolatti, G., 84
Robbins, C., 463
Roberts, A. R., 294
Roberts, N., 309
Roberts, T., 230
Robins, R. W., 107, 109
Robinson, E., 392
Robinson, P. H., 493
Rochat, F., 246
Roche, T., 382
Rocklin, T., 235
Rodin, J., 40, 327, 336, 454, 455
Rodrigo, M. F., 273
Roesch, S. C., 109, 110
Roese, N. J., 45, 73, 74, 416
Rogers, P. L., 89
Rogers, R., 190, 402, 414
Roggman, L. A., 196, 295, 296
Rohan, M., 396
Rohrer, J. H., 216
Roiphe, K., 371
Roman, J. S., 409
Ronis, D. L., 150
Rosch, E., 397
Rosenberg, M., 428
Rosenberg, M. J., 32
Rosenberg, S., 92, 93
Rosenblatt, P. C., 307
Rosenhan, D. L., 335
Rosenthal, A. M., 24, 341
Rosenthal, R., 60, 61, 84, 89
Ross, C. E., 456
Ross, D., 365
Ross, L., 5, 12, 13, 17, 19, 63, 66, 75, 78, 99, 100, 108, 109, 110, 126, 278, 282, 438, 452
Ross, M., 75, 109, 110, 135, 138, 365
Ross, W., 282
Rosser, B. S., 468
Rothbart, M., 399
Rothbaum, F., 303
Rothgerber, H., 434
Rothman, A. J., 467, 468
Rotondo, J. A., 128
Rotter, J. B., 453
Rottman, L., 293
Rowell, A., 438
Rozell, D., 27
Ruback, R. B., 357
Rubanowitz, D. E., 108
Rubin, Z., 301, 317
Ruble, D. N., 105
Rudman, L. A., 56, 257
Ruiter, R. A. C., 191
Rule, B. G., 355, 360, 363
Rumble, A. C., 278
Rumpel, C. M., 475
Rusbult, C. E., 300, 312, 314, 316, 317
Russell, D., 109
Russell, G. W., 374, 375
Russell, J. A., 301
Rusting, C. L., 378
Rüter, K., 138
Ryan, B., Jr., 200
Ryan, R. M., 130, 131
Ryckman, R. M., 135, 293

S

Sabini, J., 226, 227, 305
Sacks, O., 54
Sadker, D., 59
Sadker, M., 59
Sadovsky, A., 332
Saffer, H., 201
Sagarin, B. J., 195
Sakai, H., 170
Sakamoto, A., 495
Salas, E., 269
Salili, F., 132
Salminen, S., 111
Salomon, K., 261
Salovey, P., 335, 336, 398, 467, 468
Samter, W., 291
Samuel, W., 434
Samuels, S. M., 12, 278
Samuelson, C., 436
Sanbonmatsu, D. M., 144, 405
Sanders, D. Y., 197
Sanders, J., 244
Sandilands, M. L., 375
Sands, E. R., 230
Sanger, D. E., 121
Sangrigoli, S., 478
Sanna, L., 394
Sanna, L. J., 24, 56, 259
Sansone, C., 131
Sargent, J. D., 195
Sasaki, Y., 228
Sastry, J., 456
Sato, K., 379
Sato, S., 288
Savitsky, K., 66, 344
Saxe, L., 416
Scanzoni, L. D., 404
Schachter, S., 27, 131, 133, 134, 221, 226, 255, 289
Schaller, M., 246
Schama, S., 389
Schaufeli, W. B., 300
Scheier, M., 139, 460
Scheier, M. F., 124, 126, 147, 460
Schemo, D. J., 216
Scherer, K. R., 86, 136
Schimmack, U., 56
Schkade, D., 335, 441
Schlegel, S., 356
Schlenger, W. E., 448
Schmader, T., 409
Schmeichel, B. J., 141
Schmidt, S., 86
Schmitt, B. H., 260
Schmitt, D. P., 305
Schneider, B. H., 355
Schneider, D. J., 92, 95
Schneider, M. E., 344
Schoeneman, T. J., 108
Schooler, J. W., 418, 483, 487, 488
Schooler, T. Y., 128, 182
Schopler, J., 277, 279
Schrader, M. P., 109
Schriesheim, C. A., 275
Schroeder, D. A., 324
Schroeder, D. H., 450
Schultz, L. A., 355
Schultz, P. W., 438
Schulz, R., 46, 455, 456
Schuman, H., 31
Schwartz, A. A., 72
Schwartz, D., 357
Schwartz, J. C., 303
Schwartz, J. L. K., 182
Schwartz, P., 293, 300, 315
Schwartz, S. H., 180, 346
Schwarz, N., 24, 31, 56, 63, 64, 65, 191, 356, 441, 442
Schwarzer, R., 463
Scott, K. O., 100
Sears, R. R., 361, 374
Sebastian, R. J., 367
Secord, P. F., 299
Sedikides, C., 92, 399
Seeman, T., 452
Sekerak, G. J., 261
Sekiguchi, K., 495
Seligman, M. E. P., 40, 111, 345, 440, 441, 454, 457, 458, 460
Selye, H., 449
Semmelroth, J., 305
Sengupta, J., 128
Sentis, K., 273
Seppa, N., 336
Sergios, P. A., 294
Serna, S. B., 195
Serodio, R., 255
Seta, C. E., 261, 450
Seta, J. J., 261, 450
Seying, R., 488
Sgoutas, D. S., 357
Shaffer, D. R., 297
Shah, J., 52
Shanahan, J., 369
Shapiro, L. R., 230
Shapiro, P. N., 420
Sharp, F. C., 329
Sharp, L. K., 464
Sharpe, D., 45
Shaver, P., 308, 310
Shaver, P. R., 303, 308, 311, 332
Shavitt, S., 192, 193, 405
Sheatsley, P. B., 414
Sheblanova, E., 332
Sheeran, P., 200
Sheldon, K., 255
Sheldon, K. M., 278, 335, 441
Shelton, N., 459
Shepperd, J. A., 262
Sherif, M., 215, 411, 418, 419, 420
Sherman, S. J., 196, 406

Shillito, D. J., 118
Shinkyu, A., 495
Shiota, M. N., 87
Shipp, E. R., 98
Shope, G., 375
Shotland, R. L., 40
Showers, C. J., 292
Shurgot, B. A., 293
Sibicky, M. E., 142
Sidanius, J., 417
Siegel, M., 106
Siegler, I. C., 110
Siero, F. W., 436, 437, 439
Sigall, H., 416
Signorielli, N., 367, 369
Silva, P. J., 123
Silver, L. B., 365
Silver, M. D., 258
Silver, R., 448
Silver, R. C., 73, 449
Silverstein, B., 228, 230
Silvia, P. J., 109, 123, 124
Sime, J. D., 325
Simms, L. J., 311
Simon, H. A., 325
Simons, D. J., 478
Simons, L., 364
Simonton, D. K., 273
Simpson, J. A., 307, 308, 310, 311, 316
Sinclair, L., 392
Sinclair, S., 139
Singelis, T. M., 119, 120, 147
Singer, J. E., 133, 134, 219, 467
Singer, M., 51, 413
Sini, B., 87
Sirois, F., 219
Skitka, L. J., 260
Skorinko, J., 139
Slade, K. M., 343
Slavin, R. E., 423
Slinkard, L. A., 196
Sloan, J. H., 364
Slovic, P., 81
Slusher, M. P., 78
Smalley, S., 141
Smith, A. P., 452
Smith, C., 398
Smith, C. A., 86
Smith, C. M., 237
Smith, D. D., 29
Smith, E., 153
Smith, J., 343
Smith, M. B., 180, 181
Smith, P. B., 41, 235
Smith, P. K., 203
Smith, R. H., 97, 224
Smith, S., 381
Smith, S. M., 189
Smith, S. S., 45
Smith, T., 416
Smith, V. L., 489
Smith-Lovin, L., 291
Smittipatana, S., 405
Smyer, M. A., 317
Snyder, C. R., 109, 460
Snyder, M., 61, 180, 192, 298, 344, 346

Sogon, S., 235
Solem, A. R., 266
Solomon, H., 341
Solomon, L. Z., 341
Solomon, S., 109
Sommer, K. L., 121
Sontag, S., 456
Sorenson, K., 337
Sorenson, T. C., 268
Sorkin, R. D., 266
Spalding, L. R., 143
Spangenberg, E. R., 203
Sparks, G. G., 290
Sparrow, B., 72
Spears, R., 263, 264, 266
Spelke, E. S., 59
Spencer, C., 235
Spencer, S. J., 48, 142, 204, 390, 408, 420
Spiegel, D., 463
Spinrad, T. L., 332
Sporer, S. L., 474
Sprafkin, J., 48, 200
Spranca, M. D., 107
Sprecher, S., 84, 300, 302, 304, 305, 316
Sprink, K. S., 258
Srull, T. K., 56
Staats, H., 437
Stadler, S. J., 360
Stafford, L., 315
Standing, L., 235
Stanley, J. C., 37, 58
Stapel, D. A., 56, 67, 93
Star, S. A., 184
Staska, S. L., 230
Stasser, G., 266, 267
Staub, E., 40, 236, 237, 240, 246
Staw, B. M., 131
Steblay, N. M., 336, 337, 481
Steele, C. M., 48, 390, 408
Steen, T. A., 345
Steffen, V. J., 257, 358
Steg, L., 432
Steiner, I. D., 142, 266
Steinmetz, J. L., 100
Stephan, W. G., 418, 420
Stephens, L., 363
Stern, L. B., 483
Stern, P. C., 438
Sternberg, B., 131
Stevens, N., 288
Stewart, D. D., 267
Stewart, J. B., 323
Stewart, L. P., 216
Stillwell, A. M., 335
Stipek, D., 394
Stocks, E. L., 329
Stoff, D. M., 359
Stone, A. A., 441, 452
Stone, J., 19, 162, 392, 408, 486
Stone, J. I., 126
Stone, J. L., 95
Stone, R., 341
Stonner, D., 375
Stormo, K. J., 111
Storms, M. D., 108
Stouffer, S. A., 184

Strack, F., 75
Strahan, E. J., 204, 230
Strathman, A. J., 179
Straus, M., 372
Strauss, M. A., 365
Straw, M. K., 40
Stritzke, W. G. K., 111
Stroebe, M., 288, 462, 463
Stroebe, W., 191, 288, 462, 463
Stroessner, S., 405
Stroud, J. N., 478
Studer, J., 380
Stuhlmacher, A. F., 282
Stukas, A. A., 346
Stumpf, H., 58
Suchman, E. A., 184
Sullivan, K., 144
Sullivan, Q., 305
Suls, J. M., 137, 138
Summers, G., 111
Svanum, S., 124
Swander, D. V., 216
Swann, A. C., 357
Sweeney, P. D., 458
Swim, J. K., 390, 393, 394
Syme, S. L., 463
Symons, D., 305
Szamrej, J., 233

T

Tajfel, H., 398
Takaku, S., 163, 380
Takezawa, M., 325
Tamres, L. K., 462
Tanaka, K., 106
Tanford, S., 224
Tang, S., 131
Tangney, J. P., 73, 119
Tanke, E. D., 298
Tarrant, M., 335
Tavris, C., 15, 150, 171
Taylor, B., 73
Taylor, B. R., 360
Taylor, C. B., 457
Taylor, D. M., 235, 333
Taylor, K. M., 262
Taylor, S., 224
Taylor, S. E., 17, 18, 48, 92, 99, 101, 138, 152, 392, 397, 452, 453, 454, 461, 462
Taylor, S. P., 359
Tazelaar, M. J. A., 278
Teger, A. L., 273
Tellegen, A., 440
Tepper, B. J., 275
Terry, D., 399
Terry, D. J., 226
Tesser, A., 56, 136, 179, 213, 343
Tetlock, P. E., 73, 109, 269
Tetrault, L. A., 275
Teves, O., 178
The American freshman, 442
Thernstrom, M., 316
Theus, K. T., 203
Thew, B. D., 219

Thibaut, J., 226, 277, 299, 495
Thibaut, J. W., 276, 299, 300, 327
Thibodeau, R., 19, 418, 437
Thomas, J., 480
Thomas, M. H., 215, 369
Thomas, S., 180
Thomas, S. L., 260
Thompson, J., 482
Thompson, J. K., 230
Thompson, L., 276, 282
Thompson, S. A., 135
Thompson, S. C., 73, 454, 456
Thompson, W. M., 357
Thornton, D., 138
Thye, S. R., 327
Tice, D. M., 141
Tiebout, J., 464
Timaeus, E., 235
Timko, C., 410
Tindale, R. S., 237, 253, 265
Ting, J., 333, 346
Ting-Toomey, S., 89, 301
Tippetts, A. S., 493
Titus, L. J., 260
Titus, W., 266, 267
Toch, H., 379
Toi, M., 329, 330
Tolan, P., 380
Tomasello, M., 84
Toobin, J., 388
Tooby, J., 324, 325
Tourangeau, R., 416
Trafimow, D., 200
Trappey, C., 203
Tredoux, C. G., 481
Triandis, H. C., 42, 105, 119, 170, 235, 287, 298, 333
Triplett, N., 260
Trivers, R. L., 325
Troccoli, B., 378
Trope, Y., 95, 107
Tropp, L. R., 417, 423
Trost, M. R., 220
Tsang, B. Y.-P., 303
Tsang, J., 345
Tschanz, B., 144
Tunnicliff, J., 482
Turner, C., 364
Turner, F. J., 213
Turner, J. C., 233, 398
Turner, M. E., 279
Tversky, A., 63, 66, 78
Twenge, J. M., 230, 257, 276, 453
Tyler, R. B., 400
Tyler, T. R., 495
Tyre, P., 58
Tyrrell, D. A. J., 452

U

Uchida, Y., 112, 119
Uchino, B. N., 462
Uleman, J. S., 67
Uzzell, D., 27

V

Vaananen, A., 315
Vahteva, J., 315
Vala, J., 390
Valle, P. O. D., 438
Vallone, R. P., 75
van de Kragt, A. J. C., 433
van de Vijver, F., 41
Van Den Burg, M. T. C., 436, 437
van Engen, M. L., 275
Van Goozen, S. H. M., 357
van Knippenberg, A., 56
Van Laar, C., 417
Van Lange, P. A. M., 278, 312
Van Leeuwen, M. D., 261
Van Overwalle, F., 459
Van Vugt, M., 275, 436
Van Yperen, N. W., 300
Vance, S. L., 402
Vandello, J. A., 216
VanDeusen, K. M., 32
Vaughn, L. A., 63
Vaughn, L. S., 295
Vedantam, S., 442
Ventureyra, V. A. G., 478
Verette, J., 317
Verette, J. A., 379
Verma, J., 288
Vernon, P. A., 179
Vidyasagar, P., 379
Viki, G. T., 111
Vinokur, A., 273
Vinokur, A. D., 344, 463
Vissing, Y., 372
Viswesvaran, C., 157
Vivekananthan, P. S., 93
Vlek, C., 432
Voas, R. B., 493
Voerman, A. E., 431
Vohs, K. D., 142, 301
Vonk, R., 93, 99, 142

W

Wack, K. L., 261
Wade, J., 224
Wagner, M., 379
Wagstaff, G., 410
Wakefield, M., 195
Walder, L. O., 366
Walker, I., 420
Wall, S., 307
Wallach, M. A., 272
Wallbom, M., 124
Waller, A., 144
Wallston, K. A., 19
Walster, E., 93, 111, 169, 185, 293, 297, 300, 315
Walster, G. W., 300, 301
Walters, G., 400
Walther, E., 97, 180, 219
Walton, G. M., 138
Wang, M. A., 450
Wann, D. L., 109, 375
Ward, A., 12, 282
Ward, C., 105
Wardle, J., 230
Washington, R. E., 390
Wasserman, M., 237
Waters, E., 307
Watson, B., 493
Watson, C. B., 273
Watson, D., 107, 450
Watson, J., 414
Watson, R. I., 264
Wattenberg, M. P., 180
Watters, E., 487
Watts, D. P., 355
Watts, J. C., 190
Weary, G., 109
Weaver, K., 342
Webber, R., 406
Weber, A. L., 316
Weber, E. U., 64
Weber, J. M., 277, 433
Webster, D. M., 102
Wechsler, H., 466
Weeden, J., 227, 305
Wegener, D. T., 188, 189, 336
Weghorst, S. J., 354
Wegner, D. M., 52, 70, 71, 72, 74, 127, 267, 465, 487
Wehrle, T., 86
Weiner, B., 83, 379
Weinstein, N. D., 461
Weinstock, M., 489
Weir, W., 48, 203
Weisenberg, M., 166
Wells, G. L., 24, 189, 475, 481, 482
Wells, R. B., 40
Wells, W. D., 200
Wenzlaff, R. M., 74, 75
Werner, J., 273
Werth, L., 92
Wessely, S., 218
West, R., 266
West, S. G., 367
Westen, D., 305

Wetherell, M., 233
Weyant, J. M., 155
Wheatley, T., 204, 209
Wheeler, D. L., 72
Wheeler, L., 138, 297, 298
Whitcup, M., 434
White, H., 359
White, J. W., 370
White, P. A., 97
White, R. K., 411
White, R. W., 180, 181
Whitehouse, W. G., 487
Whitney, D. J., 258
Whittaker, J. O., 234
Whorf, B. L., 94
Wicker, A. W., 197
Wicklund, R. A., 123, 150
Wiedenfeld, S. A., 457
Wiggins, E. C., 179
Wilder, D. A., 397, 398, 419, 420
Wilhelmy, R. A., 232
Wilke, H. A. M., 437
Williams, D. R., 450
Williams, J., 387
Williams, K. D., 132, 221, 262, 263
Williams, K. R., 493
Williams, R. M., Jr., 184
Williams, T. P., 235
Williamson, G. M., 168, 343
Wilson, A. E., 138
Wilson, C. L., 311
Wilson, D. B., 359
Wilson, D. K., 19
Wilson, E. O., 324
Wilson, J. Q., 358
Wilson, M., 353, 354
Wilson, M. L., 355
Wilson, T. D., 6, 38, 48, 49, 52, 67, 122, 123, 126, 127, 128, 129, 182, 200, 204, 209, 432, 459, 460, 481
Winerman, L., 72, 85
Winslow, M. P., 162
Winslow, R. W., 232
Wiseman, C. V., 205, 228, 229
Wittenbaum, G. M., 267
Wolf, S., 233
Wolfe, C., 420
Wolfson, A., 211, 212, 213
Woll, S., 293
Wong, F. Y., 366
Wong, R. Y., 278
Wood, J. V., 138, 453, 454

Wood, W., 48, 129, 153, 185, 186, 195, 198, 236, 263, 326, 366, 393, 434
Woodward, B., 15, 253
Worchel, P., 362
Word, C. O., 410
Word, L. E., 341
Wortman, C. B., 73, 142, 461, 449
Wrangham, R. W., 355
Wright, D. B., 478
Wright, E. F., 97
Wright, L., 487
Wright, S. C., 235, 333
Wu, C., 294
Wu, C. H., 297
Wu, S., 303
Wyer, R. S., 112
Wyer, R. S., Jr., 56, 129, 185, 400, 407
Wylie, L. W., 91

Y

Yamaguchi, K., 196
Yamauchi, L. A., 113
Yee, D., 59
Yoon, G., 235
Yoshikawa, S., 296
Young, R. D., 123
Yousif, Y. H., 336
Yovetich, N. A., 317
Yudko, E., 359
Yule, F., 438

Z

Zajonc, R. B. 17, 48, 92, 259, 260, 261
Zander, A., 253, 254
Zanna, M. P., 138, 142, 179, 197, 204, 359, 396, 410
Zanot, E. J., 203
Zebrowitz, L. A., 294
Zeisel, H., 488, 491
Zelezny, L., 438
Zembrodt, I. M., 316, 317
Zhang, L., 453
Zillmann, D., 135
Zimbardo, P., 256
Zimbardo, P. G., 166, 247, 256, 270
Ziv, T., 478
Zuber, J. A., 273
Zuwerink, J., 402

Subject Index 主题索引

A

Abortion, 75, 179, 180, 232
Abu Ghraib, prison abuse at, 256–257
Academic performance:
  gender differences in, 58–59
  learned helplessness, 459–460
  self-esteem and, 421
Acceptance, private, 215
Accessibility:
  hyperaccessibility, 75
  of schemas, 56, 57
Accountability, and deindividuation, 264
Accuracy:
  of attributions, 112
  of eyewitness testimony, 474–481, 482–483, 484
  normative social influence and, 225–226
  of response in surveys, 31
Acquisition, 476–478
  defined, 475
  sources of error, 476
Actor/observer difference, 107–108
  defined, 107
  perceptual salience, 107–108
  role of information availability in, 108
Acute intermittent porphyria (AIP), 64
Adair, Virginia Hamilton, 129
Adams, Randall, 473, 478–479, 480, 483, 484, 485, 488, 491, 494, 495
Adolescents:
  aggression in, 354, 365, 368
  bullying, 382
  media violence and, 368
  religion and, 33
  risky behavior in, 221, 232
  sexual scripts of, 370–371
  smoking and, 195, 196
  talents/gifts of, 59
  violent crime and, 492
  volunteer work, 332
Adventures of Huckleberry Finn, The, 232
Advertising, *See also* Subliminal advertising
  culture stereotypes and, 204–206
  gender stereotypes and, 205
  how it works, 200, 202
  influence of, 200
  mind control and, 204
  power of, 200–206
  reduced drug use and, 201
  social behavior and, 204–206
  subliminal, 202–204
Advocacy and hypocrisy applied to social problems, 161–166
  hypocrisy induction and road rage, 163
  hypocrisy paradigm, 162–163
  insufficient punishment, 164
  mild punishment, power of, 163–165
  self-persuasion, 165
  tangible rewards and punishments, 166

Affect blends, 88
Affective forecasting, 442
Affectively based attitude, 179
Africa, self-serving bias, 111
African Americans, *See also* Discrimination; Prejudice
  activation of stereotypes and, 401–402
  aggressive stereotypes, 407
  blaming victims for their victimization, 409
  lynching of, 264
  normative conformity and, 415
  segregation and the self-esteem of children, 389–390
  self-esteem, 389–390, 418
  stereotypes about, 53–54, 400, 403, 404, 407
Agentic behavior, 275, 276
Aggression, 351–383
  aggressive games, 374–375
  aggressive stimulus, 363–364
  alcohol and, 359
  among the lower animals, 354–355
  amygdala, 356–357
  anger management, 377–380, *See also* Anger
  blaming the victim for, 375–377
  catharsis and, 374–377
  changes in, across time, 356
  in children, 27
  Columbine massacre, 351–352, 381–383
  culture and, 355–356, 358
  defined, 352
  dehumanization of victims, 169–170, 380–381
  effect of war on, 377
  Eros, 353
  evolutionary agreement, 353–354
  fighting, 354
  frustration and, 361–362
  gender and, 357–359
  heat/humidity and, 361
  hostile, 352
  imitation and, 364–365
  inborn versus learned, 353
  instrumental, 352
  insults and, 364
  neutral and chemical influences on, 356–361
  pain/discomfort and, 359–360
  provocation and reciprocation, 363
  punishing, 372–373
  reducing, 372–381
  regionalism and, 356
  serotonin, 357
  social situations and, 361–372
  stereotypes and, 392
  subsequent, effects of aggressive acts on, 374–375
  testosterone, 357, 358
  Thanatos, 353
  violence among intimate partners, 358–359
  violence in the media, 365–372
    advertising and, 370

    effect on our view of the world, 369
    effects on adults, 368
    effects on children, 366–367
    numbering effect of TV violence, 368–369
    viewer's aggression and, 369–370
    violence against women, 370–372
    violence pornography, 370–372
  violent adults, using punishment on, 372–373
  against women, 370–372
Aggressive stimulus, 363–364
AIDS:
  death rate, 465
  denial and, 19
  perceived control and, 456
  prevention, 162
  safer sex, targeting, 467–468
AIP (acute intermittent porphyria), 64
Akert, Robert, 89, 220, 317–318
Alcohol:
  abuse and self-focus, 123
  aggression and, 359
  consumption, 466
Alfred P. Murrah Federal Building bombing, 480
Allport, Gordon, 391, 399, 418, 420, 477
al-Sadat, Anwar, 282
Alternatives, comparison level for, 300
Altruism, 328–331
  defined, 324
  empathy-altruism hypothesis, 328, 330
  motivated by self-interest, 329
  self-interest versus, 329–330
Altruistic personality, 331, 332
Amae, 303
Ambiguity and informational social influence, 219
American Anorexia Bulimia Association, 230
American civil rights movement, and conformity to the ideal nonviolent protest, 213–214
American mythology, 213
Amygdala, 356–357
Analytic thinking style:
  defined, 69
  versus holistic thinking style, 69–72
Anchoring and adjustment heuristic, 102
Anger, *See also* Aggression
  communication and problem-solving skills, training in, 379–380
  diffusing through apology, 379
  empathy, building, 380
  managing, 377–380
  nonaggressive behavior, modeling of, 379
  road rage, 379, 380
  venting versus self-awareness, 378
Annoyance:
  expression of, 379
  from frustration, 362
Anorexia nervosa, 230

579

Anti-Semitism:
  normative conformity and, 415
  stereotypes about Jews, 400, 407
Anxious/ambivalent attachment style, 308
Apology, anger management through, 379
Applewhite, Marshall Herff, 149, 172, 213
Applied research:
  basic research versus, 40–41, 430
  defined, 40
  in social psychology, 429–432
Appraisal theories of emotion, 136
Arapesh people (New Guinea), 355
Archer, Dane, 89
Archival analysis, 27–28
  observational research in the form of, 29
  women, men, and the media (sample), 28
Aristotle, 295
Armstrong, Lance, 458–459
Arousal:
  misattribution of, 134–135
  two-factor theory of emotion, 131–134
Arranged marriages, 287, 288
Asch line judgment studies, 222–225, 234, 235
Asian Americans, blaming victims for their victimization, 409
Asian cultures:
  aggression in, 358
  "beautiful" stereotype, 297, 298
  gender differences in social loafing, 263
  group autonomy, 104
  interdependence, 193
  self-critical attributions, 112
Assertiveness, 63, 64–65, 235, 257, 273
Atrocities, 169–170, 240–241
Attachment styles:
  anxious/ambivalent, 308
  avoidant, 308
  behavior in an experimental setting and, 310
  combinations, 311
  defined, 307
  genetic contribution to, 311–312
  in intimate relationships, 307–312
  measuring, 308
  secure, 307
Attachment theory, 308, 311
Attitude accessibility, 198
Attitude change, 183
  by changing behavior, 183–184
  confidence in one's thoughts and, 193–194
  emotion and, 189–193
  persuasive communications and, 184–189
Attitude inoculation, 194–195
Attitudes, See also Persuasive messages
  advertising, power of, 200–206
  change, See Attitude change
  defined, 178–179
  deliberative behaviors, predicting, 198–200
  explicit versus implicit, 182–183
  nature and origin of, 178–194
    affective component, 179–181
    behavioral component, 179, 181–182
    classical conditioning, 180
    cognitive component, 179
    operant conditioning, 180
    source of, 179–182
  perceived behavioral control, 199–200
  persuasive messages, resisting, 194–197

  predicting behaviors with, 197–200
  relationship between behavior and, 197
  specific, 198–199
  spontaneous behavior, predicting, 197–198
  subjective norms, 199
Attraction, 287–318, See also Interpersonal attraction; Physical attractiveness
  causes of, 288–300
  close relationships, 301–304
  comparison level, 300
  comparison level for alternatives, 300
  equity theory, 300
  intimate relationships, ending, 316–319
  love and relationships, 304–315
  physical attractiveness and liking, 293–299
  propinquity effect, 289–291
  reciprocal liking, 292–293
  similarity, 291–292
  social exchange theory, 299–300
  theories of, 299–300
Attractive people, assumptions about, 297–299
Attractiveness, See Physical attractiveness
Attribution process, See also Attributions
  consensus information, 96
  consistency information, 97
  correspondence bias, 98–102
  covariation model, 96–98
  distinctiveness information, 96–97
  fundamental attribution error, 99
  internal versus external attributions, 96–98
  nature of, 95–96
  steps in making attributions, 102
Attributional biases, 406–409
  dispositional versus situational explanations, 407–408
  stereotype threat, 408–409
  ultimate attribution error, 407
Attributions:
  accuracy of, 112
  global, 458
  internal, 458
  listening to formation of, 97
  self-serving, 109–111
  stable, 457
  theory, 95
Australia:
  aggression in, 358
  just world belief scale scores, 113
  self-serving bias, 111
Authority, See Obedience to authority
Autokinetic effect, 215
Automatic thinking, 52–72
  defined, 52
  mental strategies and shortcuts, 62–67
  with schemas, 53–62
    accessibility and priming, 56–58
    function of, 54–56
    self-fulfilling prophecy, 58–62
Availability and assertiveness, 63
Availability heuristic, 63–64
Avoidant attachment style, 308

B

Babyface features, 294

Background noises, 127
Bailey, Gamaliel, 332
Baker, Russell, 434
Baldwin, James, 365
Bantu people, 68–69, 234
Bargaining, 281–282
Base rate information, 66
Basic dilemma of the social psychologist, 39
Basic research:
  applied research versus, 40–41
  defined, 40
Battered women, 111, 314
Bay of Pigs invasion, 268, 270
Beamer, Todd, 323
Beauty, standards of, 228, 230, 294–296
Beerbohm, Max, 231
Befriending, 462
Behavioral control, perceived, 199–200
Behaviorally based attitude, 181–182
Behaviorism, 12
Behavior(s):
  advertising and, 204–206
  deliberative, 198–200
  justifying past, 15
  planned, 198–199
  predicting, 29–33
  prosocial, 323–347
    altruism, 324
    bystander effect, 337–342
    bystander intervention, 338–339
    communal versus exchange relationships, 342–343
    cultural differences in, 332–333
    defined, 324
    effects of mood on, 334–336
    evolutionary psychology, 324–327
    gender differences in, 332
    religion and, 333
    situational determinants of, 336–343
  rational versus rationalizing, 152–153
  risky behavior in adolescents, 221, 232
  social situations and, 9
  spontaneous, 197–198
Belief in a just world, 110–111, 112–113
Ben Franklin effect, 166–168
Benevolent sexism, 416–417
Bentham, Jeremy, 372
Berns, Gregory, 224
Beyea, Ed, 323, 327
Bias(es):
  attributional, 111–113
  culture and, 103–107
  hindsight, 24
  impact, 152
  in-group, 397–398
  own-race, 478
  self-serving, 111
Binge drinking, 466
Binge eating, and self focus, 123
Biological drives, as motivators, 18
Birth control methods, and sexually transmitted diseases (STDs) study, 32
Blake, William, 293, 378
Blaming the victim, 111
  aggression and, 375–377
  defined, 409
  prejudice/discrimination and, 409–410
  self-fulfilling prophecies, 410–411

Blogs, and deindividuation, 265
"Bloomers" label, 18, 60–61, 62
Body image, 227–232
　of men, 230–232
　of women, 227–230
Bolt, Robert, 224
"Boomerang effect," 239–240
Bradbury, Malcolm, 312
Breaking up:
　experience of, 317–318
　process, 316–317
　remaining friends, 318
Breast cancer, 454, 463
Bronte, Charlotte, 375
Brown v. Board of Education, 387
Browning, Robert, 304
Bulimia, 230
Bullying, 373–374, 382, 383
Bunting, Todd, 480
Burnett, Thomas, 323
Burns, Robert, 353
Bush, George H. W., 89, 183
Bush, George W., 172, 183, 202, 204, 253, 270–271
Bystander effect, 337–342
　assuming responsibility, 341–342
　deciding to implement the help, 342
　defined, 339
　diffusion of responsibility, 341
　interpreting event as an emergency, 340–341
　knowing how to help, 342
　noticing an event, 339–340
　pluralistic ignorance, 340
Bystander intervention, 338–339

C

Calley, William, 169, 214, 241
Canada:
　"beautiful" stereotype, 298
　self-serving bias, 111
Cancer, and perceived control, 454, 456
Carson, Rachel, 437
Castro, Fidel, 100, 102, 268
Casual theories, 127–128
Catharsis, and aggression, 374–377
Cat's Cradle (Vonnegut), 397
Central route to persuasion, 185
Chat rooms, and deindividuation, 265
Cheating, 156–157
Children:
　aggression in, 27
　destructive behaviors in, 361
　praise of, by parents, 132
　self-esteem and segregation, 389–390
Chillingworth, William, 327
China:
　attributional biases, 111, 112
　categories of personality in, 93
　correspondence bias, 104
　gan qing, concept of, 303
　group autonomy, 104
Choice Dilemmas Questionnaire (CDQ), 271, 272
Churchill, Winston, 363, 377, 406

Cigarette smoking, 466, 468
Classical conditioning, 180
Classroom, jigsaw, 420–423
Clinton, Bill, 7
Close relationships, 301–304
　culture and love, 303–304
　love, defined, 301–302
Cognitive appraisals, 136
Cognitive dissonance, 150–152, 183–184, *See also* Counterattitudinal advocacy
　brain process and, 157–158
　culture and, 170–171
　decisions and, 153–156
　defined, 150
　discomfort produced by, reducing, 150–152
　evolution and, 157–158
　impact bias, 152
　justification of effort, 158–159
　pain of disappointment, overestimation of, 152
　personal values and, 156–157
　rational behavior versus rationalizing behavior, 152–153
Cognitive interview, 486
Cognitive load, 75
Cognitively based attitude, 179
Cohen, Arthur R., 160
Cohen, Richard, 187
Cohesiveness of groups, 258
Collective interdependence, 121
Collectivistic cultures:
　arranged marriages, 288
　"beautiful" stereotype, 297–298
　conformity in, 234, 235
　correspondence bias, 105, 106
　dispositional attributions, 106, 107
　passionate love in, 301–302
Columbine High School massacre, 351–352, 381–383
Columbine massacre, 423
Commitment, 155, 173, 292, 310, 313, 314
Commons dilemma, 279, 433
Communal relationships:
　defined, 315
　exchange relationships versus, 342–343
Communication(s), *See also* Nonverbal communication
　computer-mediated, 290–291
　conflict and, 280–281
　facilitated, 72
　fear-arousing, 190–191
　how it works, 433
　multichannel nonverbal, 89, 91
　persuasive, 184–189
Community Game, Wall Street Game compared to, 11–12
Companionate love, 301
Comparison level for alternatives, 300
Competition, prejudice from, 411–413
Complementarity, 291
Complex and dysfunctional social behavior, understanding/explaining, 19
Computer-mediated communication, 290–291
Condom usage, and safe sex, 465, 467–468
Confessions, 489–491
Confidence, and accuracy in testimony, 482–483

Confiding in others, 465
Conflicts:
　bargaining, 281–282
　communication and, 280–281
　cooperation and, 276–283
　Deutsch and Krauss trucking game, 279–280, 281
　integrative solution, 282
　negotiation, 281–282
　peaceful resolution of, 276
　social dilemmas, 277–279
　using threats to resolve, 279–280
Conformity:
　accuracy, importance of, 225–226
　Asch line judgment studies, 222–225
　defined, 214
　informational social influence, 214–220
　McDonald's case study, 211–213
　normative, 414–416
　normative social influence, 221–237
　obedience to authority, 240–249
　social approval and, 222–225
　social influence, using, 237–240
Confucian tradition, 104
Connolly, Cyril, 314
Consensus information, 96
Conservation of energy, and competitiveness, 436–437
Consistency information, 97
Construals, 5, 13–14, 18
　defined, 4
　human motives and, 14–18
　　additional motives, 18
　　self-esteem approach, 15–16
　　social cognition approach, 16–18
Consumption, keeping track of, 436
Contact hypothesis, 417–418, 432
　six conditions for reducing prejudice, 418–419
Contagion, 218
Contingency theory of leadership, 274
Control:
　illusions of, 71
　need for, 18
　perceived, 453–456
　　defined, 454
　　health and, 456
　　increasing, in nursing homes, 454–456
　　internal-external locus of control, 453
　　mortality and, 455
Controlled social cognition, 72–77
Controlled thinking, 52, 73
Cooperation, 11, 121
　in groups, 276–283
　increasing, in the prisoner's dilemma game, 278–279
　interdependence and, 420–421
Coping styles, 461
Correlation coefficient, 30
Correlation versus causation, 32–33
　knowing the difference, 33
Correlational method, 24, 26, 29–33
　correlational coefficient, 30
　defined, 29
　limitations of, 32–33
　surveys, 30–31

Correspondence bias, 98–102, *See also* Fundamental attribution error
  actor/observer difference, 107–108
  anchoring and adjustment heuristic, 102
  culture and, 103–107
  defined, 99
  police interrogations and, 102–103
  role of perceptual silence in, 100–102
Cosmopolitan, 231
Cotton, Ronald, 482–483, 495
Counterattitudinal advocacy, 160
Counterfactual thinking/reasoning, 73–74
  defined, 73
  "if only" thinking associated with, 74
  influence on emotional reactions, 73–74
  rumination and, 74
Covariation model, 96–98
Cover story, 38
Crime rates, 33, 364, 377
  decrease in, 76
Criminal justice, 372, 388
Crisis situations, and informational social influence, 220
Critical Incident Stress Debriefing (CISD), 430–432
Crocker, Charles, 412
Cross-cultural research, 41–42
Cross-cultural studies, on aggression, 355–356
Cuban missile crisis, 270
Cultural anthropology, 27
Cultural determinants, of schemas, 68–69
Cultural differences:
  in aggression, 355–356, 358
  in cognitive dissonance, 170–171
  in correspondence bias, 103–107
  in feelings about physical attractiveness, 297–298
  in impression management, 144
  in normative social influence, 234, 235
  in prosocial behavior, 332–333
  in social loafing, 263
  in types of attitudes, 193
Cultural stereotypes, 204–206
Cultural truisms, 194
Culture of honor, 356
Cureg, Edgardo, 72

D

Dalai Lama, 335
Dasrath, Michael, 72
Date rape, 370, 371
Dating, speed, 288
Death instinct (Thanatos), 353
Death penalty, 493–495
  U. S. homicide rate and, 372–373
Debriefing, 44, 45
Deception, 44
Deception experiment, 44
Decision making:
  decision to behave immorally, 156
  distorting likes/dislikes, 153–154
  finality, advantage of, 155
  in groups, 265–276
  irrevocability of decision, creating illusion of, 155–156
  lowballing, 155
  permanence of the decision, 154–155
  postdecision dissonance, 154
Decoding, 86, 88, 94
Defensive attributions, 110
Dehumanization of victims, 169–170, 380–381
Deindividuation, 263–265
  accountability and, 264
  in cyberspace, 265
  defined, 263
  obedience to group norms and, 264
Deliberations, juries, 491–492
Deliberative behaviors, prediction of, 198–200
Denial, and AIDS, 19
Dependent variables, 35
Descriptive norm condition, 238
Descriptive norms, 434
  defined, 238
  littering and, 434–435
  role of, 238–240
Destructive relationships, 107, 314, 317
Details, 231
Deterrence theory, 492, 493
Deutsch and Krauss trucking game, 279–280, 281
Diallo, Amadou, 51–52, 56, 67, 73, 77–78
Diaphragms, 32
Dickens, Charles, 141, 215, 407
Diffusion of responsibility, 26, 341
Dilemmas, social, *See* Social dilemmas
Discrimination, 394–396, *See also* Prejudice
  defined, 394
  formal, 395
  against homosexuals, 395–396
  interpersonal, 395, 396
  tracking changes in, over time, 414
Display rules, 88
Dispositional attributions, 105–107
Dispositional versus situational explanations, 407–408
Distinctiveness information, 96–97
Divorce rate, 276, 287, 316
DNA evidence, 474, 482, 490, 494
Douglas, George Norman, 200
Downward social comparison, 138
Drinking, binge, 466
Drives, biological, 18
Dryden, John, 265
Duke, David, 141, 142, 144
Duke, James Buchanan, 178
Dysfunctional social behavior, challenge of, 19

E

Earning by learning, 130
East Asian cultures:
  group autonomy in, 104
  self-awareness and, 124, 125
Eating, binge, 123
Eating disorders, and conformity pressures, 230
Eichmann, Adolf, 241, 249
Elaboration likelihood model of persuasion, 185
Eliot, George (Mary Ann Evan Cross), 58, 344

E-mail:
  communicating without nonverbal cues, 91–92
  emotions, 91
Embarrassment, 16, 34, 87, 144, 239, 261, 339
Emblems, 89
Emergencies. *See also* Bystander intervention
  defined, 220
  helping in, 26, 34, 35–36
  informational social influence, 220
Emerson, Ralph Waldo, 85, 86, 267, 273
Emoticons, 91
Emotions:
  arbitrariness and, 134
  appeals, 195–196
  appraisal theories of, 136
  attitude change and, 189–193
  counterfactual thinking/reasoning and, 73–74
  facial expressions of, 86–88
    affect blends, 88
    decoding, 88
    evolution and, 86–88
  as a heuristic, 191–192
  peer pressure and, 195–196
  two-factor theory of, 131–134
  types of attitudes and, 192
  universality of, 86–87
Empathy, 328–331
  building, 380
  defined, 328
  teaching in, 381
Empathy-altruism hypothesis, 328, 330
Encoding, 86
Environmental problems, 427–429
  conservation of energy, and competitiveness, 436–437
  consumption, keeping track of, 436
  energy loss, 435
  recycling, 438–439
  root cause of, 428–429
Environmentally damaging behaviors, changing, 439
Epinephrine, 133–134, 462
Equity in long-term relationships, 314–315
Equity theory, 300, 307
Erasmus, 376
Eros, 353
Esquire, 231
E.T. the Extra-Terrestrial (movie), 195
Ethical research:
  debriefing, 44
  guidelines for, 44–45
  institutional review board (IRB), 44
Ethnic cleansing, 416
Ethnography, 27
Evaluation apprehension, 261
Evolutionary approach to love, 304–305, 307
Evolutionary psychology, 42, 324–327
  defined, 304
  group selection, 325–327
  kin selection, 324–325
  reciprocity norm, 325
  social norms, learning, 325
Evolutionary theory, 42
Exams, cheating on, 156–157
Exchange relationships:
  communal relationships versus, 342–343
  defined, 315

Execution team guards, 246–247
Experimental method, 24, 26, 33–41
  basic versus applied research, 40–41
  casual questions, answering, 33–41
  cross-cultural research, 41–42
  defined, 33
  dependent variables, 35
  direct intervention on the part of the researcher, 34
  external validity, 37–40
  field experiments, 38–39
  independent variables, 35
  internal validity, 36–37
  Latané and Darley experiment, 34–35, 36
  probability level (p-value), 36
  random assignment to condition, 36
  social psychologist, basic dilemma of, 39
Experts, instant, 6–7
Explicit attitudes, 182
Explicit values, 3
External attribution, 95
External justification, 159, 183
External validity, 37–40
  defined, 37
  generalizability:
    across people, 38–39
    across situations, 37–38
  replications, 39–40
Extrinsic motivation:
  defined, 130
  versus intrinsic motivation, 129–131
Eye contact and gaze, 89, 90, 91
Eyewitness identification, 216–217, 225, 474–475, 483
Eyewitness testimony:
  accuracy of, 474–481, 482–483, 484
  acquisition, 475, 476–478
  cognitive interview, 486
  confidence, and accuracy, 482–483
  errors in, 480–481
  false memory syndrome, 487
  improving, 486–487
  lie detection, 486
  lying witnesses and, 484–485
  own-race bias, 478
  polygraphs, 485
  reconstructive memory, 479
  recovered memories, 487
  responding quickly in, 483
  retrieval, 475, 480–481
  source monitoring, 480
  storage, 475, 478–480
  verbalization, problem with, 484

F

Facial expressions of, 86–88
  affect blends, 88
  decoding, 88
  evolution and, 86–88
  universality of, 86–87
Facilitated communication, 72
Facilitation, social, 259–262
  arousal:
    dominant response and, 260
    presence of others and, 260–262
  defined, 260
  simple versus difficult tasks, 260
Fads, 227
Failure of logic, 399–400
Falling in love, 288, 302, 305, 309
False memory syndrome, 487
Familiarity, power of, 296–297
Fatal attractions, 317, 318
Favors, motivation of, 18
Fear, motivation of, 18
Fear-arousing communications, 190–191
"Feel good, do good" effect, 334–335
"Feel bad, do good" effect, 335–336
Festinger, Leon, 14, 15, 24, 25, 27
Festinger-Carlsmith paradigm, 160
Feynman, Richard, 381
Field experiments, 38–39
Fight-or-flight response, 461
Finding a mate, 287, 288
Fixed mindset, 136
Folk wisdom, 7
Fonda, Henry, 491
Fore people, 86–87
Formal discrimination, 395
Franklin, Benjamin, 166–167, 219
Fraternity, hazing, 2, 15–16
"Freedom Riders," 213
Friends (television show), 128
Fromm, Erich, 299
Frustration, and aggression, 361–362
Fulbright, William J., 280
Fuller, Thomas, 213
Functional distance, 289, 290
Functional magnetic resonance imaging (fMRI), 224
Fundamental attribution error, 11, 99
  actor/observer difference, 107–108
  perceptual salience, 100–102

G

Gan qing concept, 303
Gandhi, Mohandas, 213
Gaze, 86, 89, 90
Gender differences:
  in aggression, 357–359
  in coping with stress, 461–462
  in defining self, 121–122
  in leadership, 275–276
  in prosocial behavior, 332
  in social loafing, 263
  stereotypes and, 393–394
Gender roles, in groups, 257
Gender stereotypes, 393–394
Geneen, Harold, 276
Generalizability:
  across people, 38–39
  across situations, 37–38
Genes, 324–327
Genovese, Kitty, 23–24, 26, 37, 337, 338, 341, 344
German immigrants, 412
Gestalt psychology, 13
Gestures, 89, 90
GI Joe, male body image and, 231
Gibbs, Jack, 495
Gide, Andre, 395

Gilbert, Daniel, 152
Gilbert, W. S., 107
Gilman, Charlotte Perkins, 237
Glamour, 231
Glick, Jeremy, 323
Global attribution, 458
Global warming, 427–428
Goddard, Donald, 368
Goebbels, Joseph, 236, 237
Goldberg, Philip, 390
Good deeds, 167
Gorbachev, Mikhail, 279
Gore, Al, 202, 204
Graham, Gary, 494
Great person theory, 273, 274
Group cohesiveness, 258
Group conflict theory, 412
Group decision making, 265–276
  group polarization, 271–273
  groupthink, 267–271
  leadership, 273–276
  process loss, 265–271
Group polarization, 271–273
Group processes, 253–283
Groups:
  benefits of, 254
  cohesiveness of, 258
  composition and function of, 254–258
  conflict and cooperation, 276–283
  decision making in, 265–276
  defined, 254
  deindividuation, 263–265
  gender roles, 257
  homogeneity of, 255
  individual behavior and, 258–265
  prison abuse at Abu Ghraib, 256–257
  reasons for joining, 254
  social facilitation, 259–262
  social loafing, 262–263
  social norms, 255
  social roles, 255–256
Groupthink, 267–271
  antecedents of, 269, 270
  avoiding, 270
  defined, 267
  symptoms of, 268, 269, 270
Growth mindset, 136
Guns, as aggressive stimulus, 363–364

H

Hale-Bopp Comet, 6, 149
Hamm, Mia, 117
"Hand-purse" gesture, 90
Happiness, 440–443
  affective forecasting, 442
  flow, 440–441
  helping others, 441
  money/materialism and, 441–442
  satisfying relationships, 440
  understanding, 442–443
Harris, David, 473
Harris, Eric, 351, 382
Hattou shin beauty, 228
Hazing, 2, 15–16

Health:
  definition of stress, 452
  health habits, changing, 468
  learned helplessness, 457–460
  opening up about traumatic events, 464–465
  perceived control, 453–456
  perceived stress and, 452–453
  preventable health problems, 465–466
  prevention, 465–468
  resilience, 448–450
  safe sex, 466–468
  self-efficacy, 456–457
  social psychological interventions and, 466–468
  social psychology and, 447–468
  stress and, 448–461
Heaven's Gate Cult, 6, 11, 149, 172–173, 213
Helping behavior, *See also* Bystander intervention; Prosocial behavior
  by bystanders:
    assuming responsibility, 341–342
    deciding to implement the help, 342
    defined, 339
    diffusion of responsibility, 341
    interpreting event as an emergency, 340–341
    knowing how to help, 342
    noticing an event, 339–340
    pluralistic ignorance, 340
  costs and rewards, 327
  empathy and altruism, 328–331
  increasing, 344–347
  pure motive for, 328–331
Helplessness, defined, 457–460
Heuristics:
  anchoring and adjustment, 102
  availability, 63–64
  defined, 63
  emotions as, 191–192
  judgmental, 63
  representativeness, 66
Heuristic-systematic model of persuasion, 191
High-control work situations, 274
High-effort thinking, 72–77
Hinde, Robert, 305
Hindsight bias, 24
Hiroshima, Japan, 376
Hispanic Americans:
  aggressive stereotype, 407
  blaming victims for their victimization, 409
Hitchcock, Alfred, 366
Hitler, Adolf, 236, 237
Hobbes, Thomas, 353
Holiday, Billie, 299
Holistic thinking style:
  defined, 69
  versus analytic thinking style, 69–72
Holmes, Olive Wendell Jr., 400
Holocaust:
  complex and powerful social pressures in, 241
  propaganda, power of, 236–237
Homeless people, 83, 346, 410
Homer, 196
Homicide rates, 356, 364, 368, 373, 377
Homogeneity groups:
  groups, 255
  out-group, 398–399

Homosexuals:
  blaming victims for their victimization, 409
  discrimination against, 395–396
  justification-suppression model of prejudice and, 404
  scapegoating of, 413
  stereotypes about, 402
Hong Kong, just world belief scale scores, 113
Honor, culture of, 356
Hormones, 357, 461–462
Hostile aggression, 352
Hostile sexism, 416, 417
Human body as advertising venue, 177
Human motives, 19
  construals and, 14–18
Human thinking:
  improving, 75–77
  overconfidence barrier, 75
  reasoning, 76–77
Hurons, 356
Hussein, Saddam, 172, 377
Hydraulic theory of aggression, 353
Hyperaccessibility, 75
Hypocrisy, inducing, 437–438
Hypocrisy induction, 163
Hypocrisy paradigm, 162–163
Hypotheses, 8
  based on personal observations, 26
  formulating, 25–26

Idiosyncrasy credits, 233
Ignorance, pluralistic, 340
Illness, mass psychogenic, 218–219
Illusory correlation, 405–406
Imitation, and aggression, 364–365
Impact bias, 152
Implementation intentions, 439
Implicit Association Test (IAT), 182
Implicit attitudes, 182
Implicit personality theories, 92–94
  China, categories of personality in, 93
  cultural variation in, 93
  culture and, 93–94
  defined, 92
Implicit values, 3
Impression management, 141–144
  culture and, 144
  defined, 142
  ingratiation, 142
  self-handicapping, 142–144
Independence and interdependence, questionnaire on, 120
Independent variables, 35
Independent view of the self, 119
India, love relationships, 303, 304
Individual autonomy, 104
Individual differences, 8
Infant-mother relationship, 303
Infidelity:
  emotional, 305
  sexual, 305
Influence, *See* Social influence

Information:
  actor/observer difference and availability of, 108
  consensus, 96
  consistency, 97
  distinctiveness, 96–97
  jury processing of, 489
Informational social influence, 214–220
  accuracy, importance of, 216–217
  ambiguity and, 219
  conformity to, 219–220
  contagion, 218
  crisis situation and, 220
  defined, 215, 230
  dramatic form of, 218–219
  emergencies and, 220
  example of, 214–215
  experts as sources of information, 220
  mass psychogenic illness, 218–219
  power of, 216
  private acceptance, 215
  public compliance, 216
  role of, 244–245
  Sherif's study of, 215, 216
  War of the Worlds broadcast, 218, 220
Informed consent, 44
Ingram, Paul, 487
Ingratiation, 142
In-group, 333
In-group bias, 397–398
Injunctive norm condition, 238
Injunctive norms, 433–434
  defined, 238
  reducing littering with, 434
  role of, 238–240
Instant experts, 6–7
Instincts, 324–327
Institutional review board (IRB), 44
Institutionalized racism, 414
Institutionalized sexism, 414
Instrumental aggression, 352
Insufficient justification, psychology of, 159–161
  counterattitudinal advocacy, 159–161
  external justification, 159
  internal justification, 160
Insufficient punishment, 164
Integrative solution, 282
Interdependent view of the self, 119
Interjudge reliability, 27
Internal attribution, 95–96, 97, 100, 102, 107, 110, 458
Internal justification, 160, 184
Internal validity, 36–37
Internal versus external attributions, 96–98
Internal-external locus of control, 453
Internet, and deindividuation, 265
Interpersonal attraction, 287–319, *See also* Attraction; Physical attractiveness
  attachment styles:
    anxious/ambivalent, 308
    avoidant, 308
    behavior in an experimental setting, 310
    combinations, 311
    defined, 307
    genetic contribution to, 311–312
    in intimate relationships, 307–312

measuring, 308
secure, 307
fatal attractions, 317, 318
intimate relationships:
attachment styles in, 307–312
ending, 316–319
violence among intimate partners, 358–359
long-term relationships:
equity in, 314–315
social exchange in, 312–314
love:
brain and, 309
choosing a mate, 304–305, 307
companionate versus passionate, 301–302
culture and, 303–304
defined, 301
evolutionary approach to, 304–305, 307
theories of, 299–300
Interpersonal discrimination, 395, 396
Intimate relationships, *See also* Interpersonal attraction
attachment styles in, 307–312
ending, 316–319
violence among intimate partners, 358–359
Intrinsic interest, preserving, 131
Intrinsic motivation:
defined, 130
versus extrinsic motivation, 129–131
Introspection:
about reasons, 128–129
defined, 122
self-awareness theory, 123–125
telling more than we can know, 125–128
Inuit people, 235
Investment model of close relationships, 312
Invisible support, 464
Iraq War:
aggression in, and prolonged occupation, 377
groupthink and, 270–271
mistakes, learning from, 172
Ironic processing, 74–75
Iroquois, 356
Irrevocability of decision, creating the illusion of, 155–156
Israel, just world belief scale scores, 113

J

James, P. D., 138
James, William, 62, 118, 123, 399
Japan:
cognitive dissonance and, 170, 171
conformity and, 234, 235
convenience agency in, 144
cultural display rules for nonverbal communication, 89
group autonomy, 104
hattou shin beauty, 228
hikikomori, 221
interdependent versus independent view of, 119
self-critical attributions, 112
self-enhancing behaviors in, 144
Jefferson, Thomas, 378
Jews, and the Holocaust, 170, 237, 241

Jigsaw classroom, 420–423, 432
cooperative learning, gradual spread of, 423
defined, 421
how it works, 420–421
jigsaw-type group study, 422
why it works, 421–422
Jobs, Steve, 274
Johnson, Lyndon, 14–15, 171
Jones, Timothy, 219
Jones, Reverend Jim, 2, 6, 7, 172
Jonestown massacre, 6–7, 8, 11
Jordan, Michael, 117
Journalists, 6–7
Judgmental heuristics, 63
Jung, concept of, 303
Juries:
confessions, 489–491
deliberations, 491–492
information process during trial, 489
story order, 489, 490
witness order, 489, 490
Just world, belief in, 110–111, 112–113
Just world belief scale score, 113
Justification of effort, 158–159
counterattitudinal advocacy, 159–161
defined, 158
external justification, 159
insufficient justification, psychology of, 159–161
internal justification, 160
justifying actions, 159
Justification-suppression model of prejudice, 404–405

K

Kant, Immanuel, 127
Kennedy, John F., 142, 267, 268, 270
Kennedy, Robert, 268
Kessinger, Tom, 480
Kin selection, 324–325
King, Martin Luther Jr., 274, 379, 380
Kipling, Rudyard, 264
Klebold, Dylan, 351, 382
Koffka, Kurt, 13
Kohler, Wolfgang, 13
Korea:
aggression in, 358
"beautiful" stereotype, 298
group autonomy, 104
interdependence, 193
self-critical attributions, 112
Koresh, David, 6, 172
Korsakov's syndrome, 54
Ku Klux Klan, 141, 264, 398
Kundera, Milan, 150

L

Ladies' Home Journal, 228
Lambert, Gerald, 202
Landers, Ann, 97, 107
Landon, Alf, 31
Lasorda, Tommy, 109

Latin American cultures, prosocial behavior in, 333
Law:
eyewitness testimony, 474–488
accuracy of, 474–481, 482–483, 484
acquisition, 475, 476–478
cognitive interview, 486
confidence, and accuracy, 482–483
errors in, 480–481
false memory syndrome, 487
improving, 486–487
lie detection, 486
lying witnesses and, 484–485
own-race bias, 478
polygraphs, 485
reconstructive memory, 479
recovered memories, 487
responding quickly in, 483
retrieval, 475, 480–481
source monitoring, 480
storage, 475, 478–480
verbalization, problem with, 484
juries:
confessions, 489–491
deliberations, 491–492
information process during trial, 489
story order, 489, 490
witness order, 489, 490
obedience to, 492–495
Are You Aware of the Penalties for Federal Crimes? (exercise), 494
death penalty, 493–495
deterrence theory, 492, 493
procedural justice, 495
severe penalties and crime rates, 492–495
social psychology, 473–495
Lawrence, D. H., 310
Leadership:
contingency theory of, 274
gender and, 275–276
in groups, 273–276
personality and, 273–274
relationship-oriented leader, 274–275
styles of, 274
task-oriented, 274
transactional leaders, 274
transformational leaders, 274
Learned helplessness, 457–460
defined, 457
global attribution, 458
internal attribution, 458
stable attribution, 457
theory of, 458, 459
Lebensraum, 236
le Carré, John, 95
Lee, Harper, 489
Lepchas, 355
Letter from "Carlos," 423–424
Leviathan (Hobbes), 353
Lewin, Kurt, 13, 14, 41, 439
Lie detection, 486
Life instinct (Eros), 353
Life Orientation Test, 460
Lincoln, Abraham, 172, 329, 331
Line judgment studies (Asch), 222–225, 234, 235
Lineup identification, 476, 480–481

Littering, 434–435
Loafing, social, 262–263
Logic, failure of, 399–400
Long-term relationships:
  equity in, 314–315
  social exchange in, 312–314
"Looking glass self," 139
Lost letter technique, 343
Love, *See also* Attachment styles; Attraction; Intimate relationships; Long-term relationships
  brain and, 309
  choosing a mate, 304–305, 307
  companionate versus passionate, 301–302
  culture and, 303–304
  defined, 301
  evolutionary approach to, 304–305, 307
  falling in, 288, 302, 305, 309
  motivation of, 18
  passionate, 301–302, 309
  relationships and, 304–315
  romantic, 287, 288, 301, 302, 303–304, 309
Lowballing, 155
Low-control work situations, 274
Low-effort thinking, 52–72
  automatic thinking with schemas, 53–62
  mental strategies and shortcuts, 62–67
  social cognition, cultural differences in, 68–72
  unconscious thinking, power of, 67–68
Lynching of African Americans, 264

M

Machiavelli, Niccolò, 226, 273
Maclean, Norman, 134
Major emotional expressions:
  human development and, 87
  universality of, 86–87
Malthus, Thomas, 428
Marijuana, 161, 189, 201, 204
"Marlboro Man" advertising campaign, 205, 213
Marriage:
  arranged, 287, 288
  among South Asians, 288
Marshall, Thurgood, 387, 389–390
Martin, Billy, 109
Marx, Karl, 259
Masako Owada's marriage to crown prince, 119–120, 121
Mass psychogenic illness, 218–219
Mate selection, 305
Maxim, 231
McCarthy, Mary, 92
McNamara, Robert, 171
McVeigh, Timothy, 480
Mead, Margaret, 418
Media campaign to reduce drug usage, 201
Media violence:
  advertising and, 370
  aggression and, 369–370
  effect on our view of the world, 369
  effects on adults, 368
  effects on children, 366–367
  numbering effect of TV violence, 368–369
  viewer's aggression and, 369–370
  violence against women, 370–372
  violence pornography, 370–372
Men, *See also* Gender differences
  aggression and, 357–358
  collective interdependence, 121
  psychological differences between women and, 121, 122
Mencken, H. L., 318
Men's body image, and social influence, 230–232
Men's Fitness, 231
Men's Health, 231
Mental strategies and shortcuts, 62–67
Merchant of Venice, The (Shakespeare), 407
Mere exposure effect, 290
Meta-analysis, 40
Methodology, 23–45
Milgram experiments, 241–249
Mindset, 136–137
Minimal groups, 398
Minority influence, 236
Mirror neurons, 84, 85
Misattribution of arousal:
  defined, 134, 135
  Dutton and Aron experiment, 135
Mistakes, learning from, 171–172
Mobro4000 barge, 428
Moderate control work situations, 274
Modern racism, 415–416
Molson, Lord, 408
Mondale, Walter, 31
Monitoring process, 74–75
Monroe, Marilyn, 228, 229
Montaigne, 484
Moral dilemmas, resolving, 156
Morrison, Toni, 303, 389
Mortality, and perceived control, 455
Mother-infant relationship, 303
Motivation, extrinsic versus intrinsic, 129–131
  personal relevance of the topic, 187–188
Motives:
  biological drives, 18
  pure, 328–331
  underlying prosocial behavior, 324–331
Multichannel nonverbal communication, 89, 91
Münsterberg, Hugo, 482
Murder, 26, 34, 241, 473–474
  Genovese murder, 23–24, 26, 37, 337, 338, 341, 344
  mass, 106, 416
Mutual interdependence, 418, 419, 432
My Lai massacre (Vietnam), 214, 219, 220, 240–241, 263
Mythology, American, 213

N

Nabokov, Vladimir, 107
Nagasaki, Japan, 376
Naïve realism, 5
Naruhito, Prince of Japan, 119
Natural selection, 42
Nature of Prejudice, The (Allport), 399, 418
Nazi regime, 13, 236, 237, 241, 407
Need for cognition, 188–189
Need to feel good, 14, 15–16
Negative emotions, 88, 89
Negative events, explaining, 457–460
Negative life events, effects of, 449–450
Negative moods, effects on prosocial behavior, 335–336
Negotiation, 281–282
Neil v. Biggers, 482
Nepal, 287, 288
New Zealand:
  aggression in, 358
  self-serving bias, 111
Nietzsche, Friedrich, 123
Nisbett, Richard, 31, 126
Nixon, Richard M., 269
Nodding, 90
Nonverbal behavior, 84–92
  correspondence bias, 98–102
  decoding, 86, 88, 94
  facial expressions, 86–88
  hand gestures, 84
  mirror neurons, 84–85
  nonverbal communication, 84
  nonverbal cues, 84, 85
  sarcasm, communication of, 92
  voice and, 84, 85
Nonverbal communication:
  cultural differences in, 90
  culture and channels of, 88–89
  defined, 84
  display rules, 88
  eye contact and gaze, 89, 90
  gestures, 89
  "hand-purse" gesture, 90
  multichannel, 89, 91
  nodding, 90
  personal space, use of, 89
  touching, 90
Nonviolent protest, 213, 214
Norepinephrine, 462
Norm of reciprocity, 325
Normative conformity, 415–416
Normative social influence, 221–237
  accuracy, importance of, 225–226
  conformity to, 232–235
  consequences of resisting, 226
  cultural values and, 235
  defined, 222, 230
  eating disorders, 229, 230
  in everyday life, 227–232
  failure to conform, punishment of, 221
  fashion and, 234
  idiosyncrasy credits, 233
  men's body image and, 230–232
  minority influence, 235–236
  propaganda, power of, 236–237
  role of, 243–244
  social impact theory, 232
  social norms, 221
  unveiling by breaking the rules, 227
  women's body image and, 227–230
North Korea, 268–269
Norway:
  Asch line judgment studies in, 234
  schoolyard bullying in, 373–374, 383

O

Obedience to authority, 240–249
   aggression and, 248–249
   conforming to the wrong norm, 245–246
   Milgram experiments, 241–249
   personal responsibility, loss of, 246–247
   self-justification, 246
Observational method, 24, 26, 27–29
   archival analysis, 27–29
   defined, 27
   ethnography, 27
   forms of, 29
   limits of, 29
Observational research, in the form of archival analysis, 29
OK sign, cultural meaning of, 89, 90
Oklahoma City bombing, 480
Oliver Twist (Dickens), 407
Onwueme, Tess, 235
Operant conditioning, 180
Operating process, 74–75
Optimism, 417, 460–461
Orestes, 294
Out-group homogeneity, 398–399
Out-groups, 333
Overconfidence barrier, 75
Overeating/obesity, 466
Overjustification effect, 130, 346
Ovid, 406
Ovulation, and male attractiveness, 306
Owada, Masako, 119–120, 121
Own-race bias, 478

P

Pain of disappointment, overestimation of, 152
Pakistan, love relationships, 303, 304
Parents:
   bigoted, 396
   praise for children, 132
Parks, Rosa, 98, 99
Passionate love:
   defined, 301
   scale, 302, 309
Past behavior, justifying, 15
Patmore, Coventry, 188
Patricia, Linville, 459
Pearl Harbor, 268, 376
Peer pressure, 195–196
Peoples Temple, 2
Perceived behavior control, 199–200
Perceived control:
   defined, 454
   health and, 456
   increasing, in nursing homes, 454–456
   internal-external locus of control, 453
   mortality and, 455
Perception, 13, *See also* Social perception
Perceptual salience:
   defined, 101
   effects of, 101
   manipulating, 101
   role in correspondence bias, 100–102
Performance-contingent rewards, 131

Peripheral route to persuasion, 186
Personal relevance of the topic, and motivation, 187–88
Personal responsibility, loss, 246–247
Personal space, use, 89, 90
Personal values, and cognitive dissonance, 156–157
Personality, leadership and, 273
Personality psychology, social psychology compared with, 8–9
Personality tests, and representativeness heuristic, 65
Persuasion:
   central route to, 185
   elaboration likelihood model, 185
   peripheral route to, 186
Persuasive communication and attitude change:
   ability to pay attention to arguments, 189
   achieving long-lasting attitude change, 189
   central route to persuasion, 185–186
   defined, 184
   elaboration likelihood model, 185
   need for cognition, 188–189
   peripheral route to persuasion, 186, 187
   personal relevance of the topic, 187–188
   Yale Attitude Change approach, 184–185
Persuasive messages:
   attitude inoculation and, 194–195
   peer pressure, 195–196
   product placement, 195
   reactance theory, 196–197
   resisting, 194–197
Pessimism, 457, 459
Philosophy, 7–8
Physical attractiveness, *See also* Attraction
   attractive people, assumptions about, 297–299
   cultural differences in stereotypes about, 297–298
   cultural standards of beauty, 294–296
   defined, 293–294
   familiarity, power of, 296–297
   liking and, 293–299
   potential sexual partners, 307
Planned behavior, theory of, 198
Plant, The (King), 277
Pluralistic ignorance, 340
Polygraph, 485
Poole, Bobby, 482
Pope, Alexander, 488
Population growth, curbing, 428–429
Pornography:
   aggression and, 28–29, 32–33, 37
   violent, 370–372
Porteus, Beilby, 301
Positive moods, effects on prosocial behavior, 334–335
Positive psychology, and prosocial behavior, 345–347
Positive reinforcement, 12
Postdecision dissonance, 154
Postman, Leo, 477
posttraumatic Stress Disorder (PTSD), 431
Powell, Adam Clayton, 235

Powell, Colin, 271
Praise, of children, 132
Prediction:
   of deliberative behaviors, 198–200
   of spontaneous behaviors, 197–198
Prejudice, 387, 430, 432, *See also* Contact hypothesis; Discrimination; Sexism; Social cognition
   appearance or physical state, 389
   behavioral component, 394–396
   of bigoted parents, 396
   built-in, 396
   causes of, 396–417
   classroom example of, 396–397
   cognitive component, 391–394
   contact hypothesis, 417–418
   danger of, 388, 389
   defined, 390–396
   discrimination, 394–396
   early desegregation, failure of, 419–420
   economic competition and, 411–413
   institutionalized racism, 414
   institutionalized sexism, 414
   justification-suppression model of, 404–405
   modern racism, 415–416
   nationality, 389
   normative conformity, 414–416
   normative rules, 414–416
   racial and ethnic identity, 389
   reducing, 417–424
   religion and, 405
   self-esteem and, 389–390
   social cognition, 397–406
   stereotypes, 391–394
   tracking changes in, over time, 390, 414
   in Western Europe, 416
Presidential Commission on Obscenity and Pornography, 371
Priming, 56, 57–58, 367
Prison abuse, at Abu Ghraib, 256–257
Prison guards, loss of personal responsibility, 246–247
Prisoner's dilemma (game), 277–279
Private acceptance, 215
Probability level (*p*-value), 36
Procedural justice, 495
Process loss, 265–271
Product placement, 195
Propaganda, power of, 236–237
Propinquity effect, 289–291
   computer-mediated communication, 290–291
   defined, 289
   example of, 289
   mapping, 290
Prosocial behavior, 323–347
   altruism, defined, 324
   bystander effect, 337–342
   bystander intervention, 338–339
   communal versus exchange relationships, 342–343
   cultural differences in, 332–333
   defined, 324
   effects of mood on, 334–336
   evolutionary psychology, 324–327
   gender differences in, 332
   helping behavior, increasing, 344–347

Prosocial behavior (cont.)
  helping behavior costs and rewards of, 327
  motives underlying, 324–327
  personal qualities and, 332–336
  positive psychology, 345–347
  religion and, 333
  residential mobility, 337
  rural versus urban environment, 336–337
  situational determinants of, 336–343
  World Trade Center disaster, 323
Protest, nonviolent, 213–214
Psychological debriefing, 431
Psychological realism, 37–38
Public compliance, 216
Public goods dilemma, 279
Punishment:
  insufficient, 164
  mild, power of, 163–165
  for violent adults, 372–373
P-value (probability level), 36
Pygmies, 355

R

Race, *See also* African Americans
  stereotype threat and, 408
  stereotypes about, 53–54
Racial prejudice, and automatic/conscious, deliberative thinking, 73
Racial profiling, 72–73
Racial segregation, 389–390
  early desegregation, failure of, 419–420
Racism, *See also* Discrimination; Prejudice
  institutionalized, 414
  modern, 415–416
Rampage killings, 351, 382, 476, *See also* Columbine High School massacre
Randell, Michael, 473
Random assignment to condition, 36
Random selection:
  defined, 29
  in political polls, 31
Rape, blaming victims for their victimization, 410
Rational behavior versus rationalizing behavior, 152–153
RATS incident, 202–203
Reactance theory, 196–197
Reagan, Ronald, 31, 279
Realistic conflict theory, 411–413
  defined, 411
  economic and political competition, 412–413
  scapegoat role, 413
Reasoning Quiz, 67
Reasons, introspecting about, 128–129
Reasons-generated attitude change, 128
Reciprocal liking, 292–293
Reciprocity norm, 325
  exercise, 326
Reconstructive memory, 479
Recovered memories, 487
Recycling, 438–439
Reed, Walter, 66
Regionalism, and aggression, 356

Relational interdependence:
  defined, 121
  measure of, 122
Relationship-oriented leader, 274
Relationships, *See also* Interpersonal attraction
  attachment styles:
    anxious/ambivalent, 308
    avoidant, 308
    behavior in an experimental setting, 310
    combinations, 311
    defined, 307
    genetic contribution to, 311–312
    in intimate relationships, 307–312
    measuring, 308
    secure, 307
  breaking up:
    experience of, 317–318
    process, 316–317
    remaining friends, 318
  close, 301–304
  communal, 315, 342–343
  destructive, 107, 314
  equity in, 314–315
  exchange, 315, 342–343
  social exchange in, 312–314
Relative depravation, 362
Religion, and prosocial behavior, 333
Religious expression and spirituality, and self-focus, 124
Reno, Janet, 7
Replications, 39–40
Representative heuristic:
  base rate information, 66
  defined, 66
  personality tests and, 65
Reproductive success, 304, 305
Rescorla, Rick, 323, 332
Research, 24–25
Research methods, 26
  correlational method, 24, 26, 29–33
  ethical principles in psychological research, 44
  experimental method, 24, 26, 33–41
    casual questions, answering, 33–41
  observational method, 24, 26, 27–29
Resilience, 448–450
Retrieval:
  defined, 475
  sources of error, 476
Richter, John Paul, 336
Risky shift, 272
Road rage, 379, 380
Robinson, Smokey, 179
Rochefoucauld, Francois de La, 144, 180, 199, 300, 327, 397
Role-playing technique, 196
Roles, Social, 255–256
Romantic love, 287, 288, 301, 302, 303–304, 309
Roosevelt, Eleanor, 420–421
Roosevelt, Franklin Delano, 31
Roosevelt, Teddy, 279
Ross, Lee, 5
Rousseau, Jean-Jacques, 353
Rumination, 74
Rusk, Dean, 268
Ruskin, John, 262
Russell, Bill, 131

Russo, Richard, 140
Ryan, George, 494
Ryan, Leo, 2

S

Sarcasm, 91, 92
"Saving face," 144
Scapegoat theory, 413
Schemas, 92
  accessibility, 56
  automatic thinking with, 53–62
  cultural determinants of, 68–69
  defined, 53
  function of, 54–56
  organization of the world into, 53
  priming, 56, 57–58
  and reduction in ambiguity, 55, 56
  self-fulfilling prophecy and, 58–62
    limits of, 61–62
Schematic processing, 400
Schlesinger, Arthur, 268
Schoolyard bullying, reducing, 373–374
Scripts, 370
Secure attachment style, 307
Segregation:
  early desegregation, life of, 389
  and self-esteem of children, 389–390
Self:
  attempting to escape, 123–124
  cultural differences in defining, 119–121
  functions of, 119
  gender differences in defining, 121–122
  independent view of, 119
  interdependent view of, 119
  nature of, 118
  in other species, 118
Self-awareness, 118
  venting versus, 378
Self-awareness theory:
  attempting to escape the self, 123–124
  defined, 123
Self-concept, 118, 137
  cultural differences in, 193
  social comparison theory, 137–139
  social tuning, 139
Self-consciousness, measuring, 126
Self-control, 119, 140–141
Self-efficacy:
  defined, 456
  smoking cessation and, 456–457
Self-enhancement and impression management, 144
Self-esteem, 19
  approach, 15–16
  defined, 15
  maintenance of, 343
  prejudice and, 389–390
Self-focus, 123–124
Self-fulfilling prophecy, 18
  avoiding, 62
  defined, 58, 410
  limits of, 61–62
  stereotyping/discrimination and, 410–411
Self-handicapping, 142–144

Self-help tapes, subliminal, 203
Self-image:
  self-justification and, *See* Self-justification
  threats to, *See* Cognitive dissonance
Self-justification:
  defined, 119
  Hiroshima/Nagasaki atomic bombs and, 376
  human tendency toward, 15–16, 171
Self-knowledge, 431
  cultural difference in defining the self, 119–121
  defined, 119
  gender difference in defining the self, 121–122
  mindsets, 136–137
  by observing our own behavior:
    appraisal theories of emotion, 136
    intrinsic versus extrinsic motivation, 129–131
    misattribution of arousal, 134–135
    self-perception theory, 129
    two-factor theory of emotion, 131–134
  through introspection, 122–129
    casual theories, 127
    consequences of introspecting about reasons, 128–129
    self-awareness theory, 123–125
  through other people, 137–140
    knowing ourselves by adopting other people's view, 139–140
    knowing ourselves by comparing ourselves to others, 137–139
Self-perception theory, 129
  appraisal theories of emotion, 136
  intrinsic versus extrinsic motivation, 129–131
  misattribution of arousal, 134–135
  two-factor theory of emotion, 131–134
Self-persuasion, 165
Self-presentation, 119
Self-recognition, development of, 118
Self-regulatory resource model, 141
Self-serving attributions, 109–111
  belief in a just world, 110–111, 112–113
  blaming the victim, 111
  defensive attributions, 110
  purpose of, 109
  self-esteem and, 109
  in sports pages, 109, 110
September 11, 2001 terrorist attacks, 170, 323, 324, 431, 448
Serotonin, 357
Sex differences, *See* Gender differences
Sexism:
  benevolent, 416–417
  hostile, 416, 417
  institutionalized, 414
  subtle, 416–417
Sexual behavior, AIDS and denial, 19
Sexual masochism, and self-focus, 123
Sexual stereotyping, 394
Sexually transmitted diseases (STDS), birth control methods and, 32
Shakespeare, William, 77, 121, 276, 301, 305, 407, 441
Shi gú personality type, 93, 94
Similarity, 291–292
  defined, 291
  interest and experiences, 292
  interpersonal style, 291–292
  opinions and personality, 291
Simpatía, 333
Simpson, O. J., 388
Simpson, Wallis, 228
Sitwell, Dame Edith, 125
Smoking, 162, 466
  in adolescents, 195, 196
  self-efficacy and quitting, 467
Snow, C. P., 245
Social approval, and conformity, 222–225
Social behavior, 24
  advertising and, 204–206
  describing, 27–29
  predicting, 29–33
Social cognition, 51–78, 397–406, *See also* Attributional biases
  Amadou Diallo case, 51–52, 77–78
  automatic thinking, 52–72
  controlled, 72–77
  controlled thinking, 51, 52
  cultural differences in, 68–72
  defined, 17
  failure of logic, 399–400
  high-effort thinking, 72–77
  illusory correlation, 405–406
  in-group bias, 397–398
  justification-suppression model of prejudice, 404–405
  low-effort thinking, 52–72
  out-group homogeneity, 398–399
  social categorization, 397
  stereotypes:
    activation of, 401–402
    automatic and controlled processing of, 402–404
    persistence of, 400–401
    stereotypical beliefs, changing, 406
Social cognition approach, 16–18
Social comparison theory, 137–139
  defined, 137
  downward social comparison, 138
  upward social comparison, 138–139
Social critics, 6–7
Social dilemmas, 277–279
  common dilemma, 279, 433
  defined, 277, 433
  prisoner's dilemma (game), 277–279
  public goods dilemma, 279
  resolving, 432–433
Social environment, 4
Social exchange:
  in long-term relationships, 312–314
  motivation of, 18
Social exchange theory, 299–300, 317, 327
Social facilitation, 259–262
  arousal:
    dominant response and, 260
    presence of others and, 260–262
  defined, 260
  simple versus difficult tasks, 260
Social groups, influence in, 253–283
Social impact theory, 232
  allies in group, 233–234
  collectivistic culture of group, 234, 235
  group size, 232
  group strength, 233
Social influence, 3, 6–8, 18, 24
  informational, 214–220
    accuracy, importance of, 216–217
    ambiguity and, 219
    conformity to, 219–220
    contagion, 218
    crisis situation and, 220
    defined, 215, 230
    dramatic form of, 218–219
    emergencies and, 220
    example of, 214–215
    experts as sources of information, 220
    mass psychogenic illness, 218–219
    power of, 216
    private acceptance, 215
    public compliance, 216
    role of, 244–245
    Sherif's study of, 215, 216
    War of the Worlds broadcast, 218, 220
  normative, 221–237
    accuracy, importance of, 225–226
    conformity to, 232–235
    consequences of resisting, 226
    cultural values and, 235
    defined, 222, 230
    eating disorders, 229, 230
    in everyday life, 227–232
    failure to conform, punishment of, 221
    fashion and, 234
    idiosyncrasy credits, 233
    men's body image and, 230–232
    minority influence, 235–236
    propaganda, power of, 236–237
    role of, 243–244
    social impact theory, 232
    social norms, 221
    unveiling by breaking the rules, 227
    women's body image and, 227–230
  power of, 11–14
    underestimating, 11–12
  using, 237–240
Social interpretation, power of, 4–5
Social Interpretation Task (SIT) videotape, 89, 91
Social learning theory, 365
Social loafing:
  cultural differences in, 263
  defined, 262
  gender differences in, 262
  in groups, 262–263
Social neuroscience, 42–43
Social norms:
  approach, 216
  conveying/changing, 433–436
  defined, 221
  in groups, 255
  learning, 325
Social perception, 83–113
  accuracy of attributions and impressions, 112
  attributional biases, 111–113
  casual attribution, 95–111
  defined, 84
  implicit personality theories, 92–94
  nonverbal behavior, 84–92

Social problems:
  advocacy and hypocrisy applied to, 161–166
    hypocrisy induction and road rage, 163
    hypocrisy paradigm, 162–163
    insufficient punishment, 164
    mild punishment, power of, 163–165
    self-persuasion, 165
    tangible rewards and punishments, 166
  and social psychology, 18–19
Social psychologist, basic dilemma, 39
Social psychology, 9–11, 39
  applied research in, 429–432
  compared with personality psychology, 8–9
  compared with sociology, 9–11
  culture and, 41–42
  defined, 3, 19, 24
  as an empirical science, 24–25
  ethical issues in, 43–45
  experimental method, capitalizing on, 430–432
  as experimentally based science, 5
  finding solutions to applied problems, 432
  focus on social behavior, 9
  goal of, 10
  happiness and sustainable life style, 440–443
  health and, 447–468
  law and, 473–495
  level of analysis, 9–10
  making a difference with, 427–443
  for rescue, 432
  research methods, 24, 26
  social interventions:
    assessing the effectiveness of, 430–431
    potential risks of, 431–432
  social problems and, 18–19
  subjective situations and, 13
  using to achieve a sustainable future, 432–439
  what's your prediction? (quiz), 24–25
Social Readjustment Rating Scale, 450
Social roles, 255–256
Social situation:
  behavior and, 9
  subjectivity of, 12–14
Social support, 462–464
Social tuning, 139
Social world, expectations about, 17–18
Sociology, compared with social psychology, 9–11
Source monitoring, 480
Specific attitudes, as predictors of behavior, 198–199
Speed dating, 288
Spencer, Herbert, 408
Spinoza, Benedict, 7
Spontaneous behaviors, prediction of, 197–198
Sports, stereotyping and, 392
Stable attribution, 457
Statistical and methodological reasoning, graduate training's influence on, 76–77
Steely, Mel, 130
Stereotype threat, 408–409
Stereotypes, 53
  about physical attractiveness, 297–298
  activation of, 401–402
  aggression and, 392
  automatic and controlled processing of, 402–404
  defined, 391
  gender and, 393–394
  persistence of, 400–401
  prejudice and, 391–394
  sports, race, and attribution, 392
  stereotyping as cognitive process, 391–392
Stereotypical beliefs, changing, 406
Stereotyping, 430
Stevenson, Adlai, 270
Stewart, Porter, 28
Storage, 478–480
  defined, 475
  sources of error, 476
Story order, 489, 490
Stress:
  coping styles, 461
  coping with, 461–465
    gender difference in, 461–462
  defined, 452
  fight-or flight response, 461
  health, 452–453
  social support and, 462–464
  tend-and-befriend response, 462
  traumatic events, making sense of, 464–465
Subjective norms, 199
Subliminal advertising, 202–204, See also Advertising
  auditory, 203
  debunking the claims about, 203
  laboratory evidence for, 203–204
Subliminal messages, 202
Subliminal self-help tapes, 203
Subtle sexism, 416–417
Suetonius, 332
Suicide, mass, 6–7, 11
"Surfing" on trains, 221
Surveys, 30–31
  accuracy of the responses, 31
  advantages of, 30
  defined, 30
  random selection, 30–31
  samples, 30
Survivor (reality program), 83–84
Sweden, aggression in, 358
Swift, Jonathan, 192

T

Taita people, 301, 302
Taliban, 41
Task-contingent rewards, 131
Telling more than we can know, use of term, 126
Tend-and-befriend response, 462
Terrorists, 72, 270, 323, 332, 431, 448
Testosterone, 357, 358
Texas police officer murder, 473–474
Thailand, love relationships, 304
Thanatos, 353
Theories, formulating, 25–26
Theory of planned behavior, 198
Thermal imaging, 485
Thin Blue Line, The (film), 473
Thinker, The (Rodin), 52
Thinking, *See also* Social cognition
  automatic, 52–72
    defined, 52
    mental strategies and shortcuts, 62–67
    with schemas, 53–62
  controlled, 52, 73
  counterfactual, 73–74
    defined, 73
    "if only" thinking associated with, 74
    influence on emotional reactions, 73–74
    rumination and, 74
  unconscious, 67–68
Thomas, Timothy, 51
Thompson, Jennifer, 482
Thoreau, Henry David, 13, 416
Thought suppression, 74–75
"Thumb up" gesture, 90
Tit-for-tat-strategy, 278, 315
To Kill a Mockingbird (Lee), 264, 489
Tobacco use, 466
Tocqueville, Alexis de, 332
Tolstoy, Leo, 166, 172
Touching, 90
Train surfing, 221
Transactional leaders, 274
Transactive memory, 267
Transformational leaders, 274
Traumatic events, making sense, 464–465
Trials, *See also* Juries; Law
  information processed during, 489
Trucking game studies, 279–280, 281
Truisms, cultural, 194
Truman, Harry S., 268–269
TV violence, 368–369
Twain, Mark, 180, 213, 225, 232
Twelve Angry Men (film), 491
Twiggy, 228
Twin studies of attitude, 179
Two-factor theory of emotion, 131–134
  Schachter and Singer experiment (Suproxin study), 133
Two-step process of attribution, 102

U

Ultimate attribution error, 407
Unconscious thinking, power of, 67–68
Unconscious thought thinking, example of, 67
United Airlines Flight, 323, 332
United Kingdom:
  individual rights, 104
  just world belief scale scores, 113
United States:
  "beautiful" stereotype, 298
  correspondence bias, 106
  gender differences in defining self, 122
  independence, 193
  just world belief scale scores, 113
  self-serving bias, 111
Unrealistic optimism, 461
Upward social comparison, 138–139
Urban overload hypothesis, 336
U. S. Supreme Court, 234, 387, 417, 482
Ustinov, Peter Sir, 288

SUBJECT INDEX

V

Validity:
  external, 37–40
  internal, 36–37
Venting of anger, 378
Vicary, James, 202–203
Victims:
  blaming, 111
    aggression and, 375–377
    prejudice/discrimination and, 409–410
  dehumanization of, 169–170, 380–381
  hating, 168–170
  of rape, 410
Vietnam War, 14
  dehumanization of victims, 380
  mistakes learning from, 171
  My Lai massacre, 214, 219, 220, 240–241, 263
Violence, *See also* Aggression
  in the media, *See* Media violence
    advertising and, 370
    effect on our view of the world, 369
    effects on adults, 368
    effects on children, 366–367
    numbering effect of TV violence, 368–369
    viewer's aggression and, 369–370
    violence against women, 370–372
    violence pornography, 370–372
  pornography and, 32–33, 37
Visible support, 464
Visual point of view, *See* Perceptual salience
Vogue, 228

Voice, as nonverbal cue, 84, 85
Volunteerism, 346

W

Wallace, George, 415
War of the Worlds broadcast, 218, 220
Warhol, Andy, 93
Warner, Charles Dudley, 195, 329
Warren, Earl, 390
Water conservation, 436, 437–438
Watergate coverup, 269
Weapons, stereotypes about, 53–54
Weapons of mass destruction (WMD), 172
Well-being, 187, 221, 346, 353, 456, *See also* Health
Welles, Orson, 218
Wertheimer, Max, 13
West African, love relationships, 303–304
Western cultures, gender differences in social loafing, 263
Western Europe, prejudice in, 416
"What is beautiful is good" stereotype, 93, 297–298
White Men Can't Jump (film), 392
Wik, William, 323, 332
Wilde, Oscar, 139, 293
Wilder, Thornton, 218
Wilkins, Richard, 72–73
Wilson, E. O., 325
Wilson, McLandburgh, 461
Wilson, Tim, 31, 126, 127, 152, 459
Witness order, 489, 490

Women, *See also* Gender differences
  aggression and, 357–358
  battered, 111, 314
  blaming victim for their victimization, 409
  Japanese, 89, 121, 228–229, 296
  psychological difference between men and, 121, 122
  relational interdependence, 121
  violence against, 370–372
Women's body image and social influence, 227–230
Wood, Robert, 473
World population growth, 428–429
World Trade Center disaster, 170
  Critical Incident Stress Debriefing (CISD), 431
  prolonged negative reactions, 448
World War I, scapegoating in, 413
World War II, 376
  Hiroshima/Nagasaki atomic bombs, 376
  propaganda, power of, 236, 376–377
Wozniak, Stephen, 274

Y

Yale Attitude Change approach, 184, 185
Yuan, 303

Z

Zelmanowitz, Abe, 323, 327, 332, 344
Zimbabwe, just world belief scale scores, 113

图书在版编目(CIP)数据

社会心理学=Social Psychology:英文 /(美)阿伦森(Aronson,E.)著. ——影印本. ——北京:世界图书出版公司北京公司,2012.11
(大学堂)
ISBN 978-7-5100-5327-6

Ⅰ.①社… Ⅱ.①阿… Ⅲ.①社会心理学—英文 Ⅳ.①C912.6

中国版本图书馆CIP数据核字(2012)第233206号

Original edition, entitled SOCIAL PSYCHOLOGY, 7E, 9780135074213 by ARONSON, ELLIOT; WILSON, TIMOTHY D.; AKERT, ROBIN M., published by Pearson Education, Inc, publishing as PEARSON EDUCATION ASIA LTD, Copyright © 2010, 2007, 2005 by Pearson Education, Inc.

All rights reserved. No part of this book may be reproduced or transmitted in any form or by any means, electronic or mechanical, including photocopying, recording or by any information storage retrieval system, without permission from Pearson Education, Inc.

China edition published by PEARSON EDUCATION ASIA LTD., and BEIJING WORLD PUBLISHING CORPORATION Copyright © 2012.

This edition is manufactured in the People's Republic of China, and is authorized for sale and distribution in the People's Republic of China exclusively (except Taiwan, Hong Kong SAR and Macau SAR).

本书封面贴有Pearson Education(培生教育出版集团)激光防伪标签。无标签者不得销售。

北京市版权局著作权合同登记号 图字01-2010-7740

社会心理学(影印第7版)

著者:(美)阿伦森 威尔逊 埃克特	丛书名:大学堂		策划出版:银杏树下
出版统筹:吴兴元	责任编辑:谢晗旸 张鹏	营销推广:ONEBOOK	装帧制造:墨白空间

出　　　版:世界图书出版公司北京公司
出　 版　人:张跃明
发　　　行:世界图书出版公司北京公司(北京朝内大街137号　邮编100010)
销　　　售:各地新华书店
印　　　刷:北京鹏润伟业印刷有限公司(北京市大兴长子营镇李家务村委会南200米　邮编102615)
(如存在文字不清、漏印、缺页、倒页、脱页等印装质量问题,请与承印厂联系调换。联系电话:010-80261198)

开　　　本:889×1194毫米　1/16
印　　　张:39　插页4
字　　　数:1148千
版　　　次:2012年12月第1版
印　　　次:2012年12月第1次印刷

读者服务:reader@hinabook.com 139-1140-1220
投稿服务:onebook@hinabook.com 133-6631-2326
购书服务:buy@hinabook.com 133-6657-3072
网上订购:www.hinabook.com (后浪官网)

ISBN 978-7-5100-5327-6　　　　定价:99.00元

后浪出版咨询(北京)有限公司法律顾问:北京市大成律师事务所　周天晖　copyright@hinabook.com

版权所有　翻印必究

性学观止
（插图第6版·上下册）

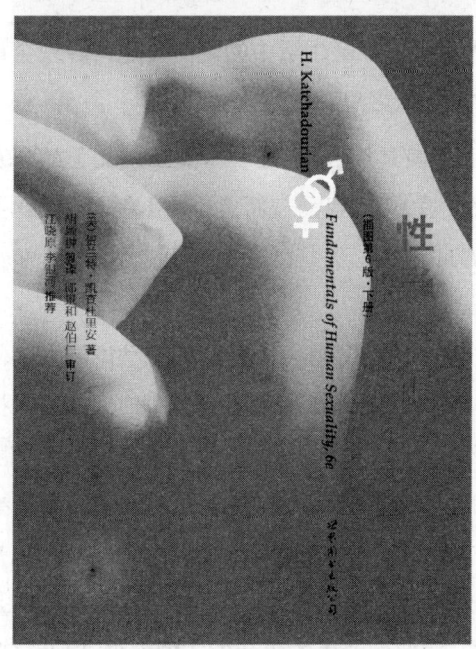

性学权威教科书最新第六版，
作者独家授权全球首发！
特为中国读者撰写全新章节，
讲述性与东方文化！

（美）贺兰特·A·凯查杜里安 著　胡颖翀等 译
郎景和　赵伯仁 审校　江晓原　李银河 推荐
ISBN 978-7-5062-8688-6
定价：88.00元　2009年12月出版

美国第一部成功的性教科书
风行全球高校三十余载的经典性学读本

1968年，凯查杜里安教授在斯坦福大学开设了世界上人类性学方面首批大学课程中的一门。从那时起，无数学子深受惠益。而这部从其课堂讲义脱胎而来的《性学观止》，多年来已被译成法语、西班牙语、葡萄牙语和汉语，风行全球。

在这部美国第一部成功的性学教科书中，作者不拘泥于生理学、解剖学、病理学等医学范畴，而是拓出一个更为开阔和纵深的角度，将性视为生物本能、生理驱动、精神意志、道德观念、法律习俗的多元辐射聚焦的焦点，在以科学客观的精神进行专业探索的同时，更倡导一种正视、理解、宽容、不滥用、不利用的性态度。在本书最令人称道的第六部分，作者以近二十万字的辉煌篇章，综合运用考古学、人类学跨文化比较手段，来探讨性与文化、历史、道德、法律之间千丝万缕的联系，揭示性的历史文化内涵和哲学美学意蕴，其用力之深、涵盖范围之广，举世罕见，令人叹为观止。这是一部公认的性学经典读本，被认为无论在清晰程度、说服力和材料的翔实可靠诸方面没有同类书可与之相媲美。"性不是游戏，它是快乐之源泉，也是至悲之出处。"

"中国文化中性的学问和智慧可以上溯几千年，是人类文化的一笔财富。"

——贺兰特·凯查杜里安

社会学与生活
（精要插图第 11 版）

(美) 理查德·谢弗 著　赵旭东等译
ISBN 978-7-5100-3163-2
定价：42.00 元　2011 年 3 月出版

★ 美国最经典的社会学教材《社会学与生活》精要版，全球超过 500 所院校采用。本书在美国、欧洲以及世界各地受到广泛欢迎，是社会学专业最受好评的基础教材，精要版更加适合社会科学相关学科的教学与学习。

★ 全方位的信息呈现，立体式、多层次的表现手法。剧照、漫画、图表生动地穿插于行文之中，尤其对非社会学专业读者来说，这是一部读起来毫不费力，却又能使人印象深刻的好书。

★ 内容编排与组织架构均简洁有力，便于教学。浓缩为 11 章，各章节内容自成一体，读者可以挑选其中任何一个自己感兴趣的话题轻松阅读。章节的设计和内容的编排上处处从教学情境出发，非常适合作为社会科学相关科系基础课的教材使用。

★ 取材广泛新颖，内容生动活泼。加入的最新资料和大量日常社会生活中的案例更能符合现今社会的需要，能激发读者对于社会学的兴趣，进而领悟社会学的迷人之思。

★ 以《社会学与生活》为蓝本，覆盖主要理论视角，全面且兼具综合性，是一本真正意义上的普及教材。为满足不同层次读者的阅读需求，我们在此奉上精要版，其内容涵盖面更广，相关社会议题更多；同时，简洁的编排方式为读者打开了快速进入社会学的方便之门。

本书简洁清晰地定义与分析社会学基本概念和研究方法，注重功能论、冲突论和互动论的平衡阐释，强调社会学家检验和质疑人们日常生活行为的独特方法，教导读者如何运用社会学的想象力来探讨自己生活情境中的社会议题。在全球化的视野下使用跨文化的实例说明性别、年龄、种族、族群和阶级等社会区隔及其影响，并提供近年来社会学重要议题的最新研究成果。同时，本书专辟"社会学要义"专栏，提出每章的重要概念及一系列相关问题，以启发并提供一种观察你身边事物的新视角，包括你自己的生活甚至更广阔的社会。这些问题正体现了本书的旨趣，即一种全球的文化关怀，而不只是站在文化观念的转变上。在此基础上，作者更关注文化差异、由此而产生的生活方式的差异，以及这些差异在真实生活中的体现。

总之，无论是内容还是形式，本书都更加适合社会学教学与学习。

社会科学导论
（插图第 12 版）

埃尔金·亨特　大卫·柯兰德　著

康敏　刘小蕾　彭雅琦　译

ISBN 978-7-5100-4458-8/C·210

定价：68.00 元　2012 年 8 月出版

美国大学最畅销的社会科学通识教材

　　本书是美国大学极为畅销的社会科学教科书，范围包括现代社会科学的全域，但又能以整体的观念来整合各学科于一炉，极具系统性，对社会科学的兼顾也很周全，不但可以使学生对各领域的重要概念和基本立场有所了解，也能帮助学生对现代社会的各面相，包括人与文化、社会阶层、社会制度、政治组织与社会问题、国际关系，以及经济制度等各方面，有一个整合性知识体系的吸收。

　　这本书的确不能告诉学生什么是对，什么是错，的确都是些猜想、假设、可能、或许……但是猜想、假设、可能、或许，这些正是属于大学里的东西，因为在学生们入学时，我们希望他们能够理解，知识不是别的，正是一些出色的猜想、合理的假设以及有逻辑的可能。

序言选摘

　　讲授社会科学的方式多种多样，有全球视角、人类学视角、心理学视角，还有社会学视角和历史视角，不一而足。在我看来，虽然每一种个别的社会科学视角都有益处，但是将社会科学课程与其他学科区别开来的，正是它从尽可能多的不同视角来看待问题，并依靠学者的常识针对某一特定问题选择一种最贴切的视角。常识的视角就是社会科学的视角。

　　社会科学是一门重要的课程。我们的教育体制往往在学生对学科有一个总体认识之前，在他们知道自己该朝什么方向发展之前，就仓促地要求他们进行专业划分。当学生有了总体认识之后，专业划分是必要的，但在拥有总体认识之前就划分专业，对学生们来说不公平。过早划分专业的学生还没有发展出常识的视角，他们对学科间的相互联系和共鸣还不敏感。最糟糕的情况是他们成了本学科的研究方法的奴隶，最好的情况是，他们有足够的智慧认识到解决问题可以有很多种方法，但缺乏训练使他们不得不重复劳动。如果他们掌握了其他学科的知识，就不必这么费事，而且效率会更高。

　　这就是我极力倡导社会科学这门课的原因，它是大学生在学期间最重要的课程之一。我认为，它也是进行专业课程学习的必要前提，因为它有助于我们正确认识其他课程。

社会心理学
（插图第7版）

（美）艾略特·阿伦森 提摩太·D·威尔逊 罗宾·M·埃克特 著

侯玉波 译

ISBN 978-7-5100-4863-0

定价：80.00元　2012年10月出版

《社会动物》学术教材版

哈佛大学、耶鲁大学等700多所大学使用的"畅销书式的教科书"

心理学大师不可错过的经典殿堂级力作

经典名著　本书主要作者阿伦森博士是美国心理学会（APA）120年历史上唯一一个包揽其三个主要奖项的人，即杰出写作奖（1975）、杰出教学奖（1980）和杰出研究奖（1999），许多其他的专业团体也对他的研究和教学作出嘉奖。他独立撰写的《社会动物》（The Social Animal）被誉为"美国社会心理学的《圣经》"。本书作为教材版，同样是美国高校广泛使用的社会心理学教材。

贴近生活　书中各章节不是从概念出发，而是以真实发生在社会中的典型事例为出发点，引出各章的核心概念和主要内容。在结构设置上，本书从个体行为的心理学讲起，然后进展到团体行为的心理学，进而讲解人际间关系的心理学以及在环境、健康、法律等领域中社会心理学的具体应用，可以让读者全面掌握生活中的社会心理学。

人文关怀　由于阿伦森博士自己特殊的生活经历，他一直致力于使用心理学改善社会环境，这种人文关怀贯穿在全书之中，成为本书的一大特色。

这是一本值得永远珍藏的好书。与其他《社会心理学》教材相比，作者阿伦森的语言和叙述风格使我们学习社会心理学成为一种享受。目前，这本书已经被美国哈佛大学、耶鲁大学等700多所高校所采用。相信，她将成为一本"畅销书式的教科书"。

——乐国安，中国心理学会副理事长、中国社会心理学会原理事长、南开大学社会心理学系主任

进入一门学科的最好办法是读好书。好书必是行家力作，非行家不能出好书；虽是行家，但不是力作，也很难是好书。以阿伦森为主的编写组在社会心理学方面是行家，他们的《社会心理学》出到第七版，则称得上是力作，故是好书。读一本好书，胜过读一批扰乱视听的混世著作。

——金盛华，北京师范大学心理学院教授、博士生导师